INSIGHT GUIDES

EastAfrican WILDLIFE

Edited and Produced by Geoffrey Eu
Editor in Nairobi: Deborah Appleton
Photography by Karl Ammann and Others

APA
PUBLICATIONS

EastAfricanWILDLIFE

First Edition
© 1989 APA PUBLICATIONS (HK) LTD
All Rights Reserved
Printed in Singapore by Höfer Press Pte Ltd

ABOUT THIS BOOK

Insight Guide: East African Wildlife is the second title in Apa Publications' Great Adventure series, following the highly successful guide to *Indian Wildlife*. It is also Apa's second venture into East Africa—*Kenya* was published in 1985. *East African Wildlife* represents Apa's continuing commitment to cover the world wildlife scene; Africa is one of the few remaining areas on earth where large concentrations of animals can still be seen in their natural habitats.

Into Africa

Editorial Director **Geoffrey Eu** arrived in Nairobi armed with a book outline, names of people to contact and, as a concession to technology, a fax machine. Although some unsympathetic customs officials relieved him of the latter item, Eu was eventually rescued by hotelier-turned-photographer **Karl Ammann**, a long-time Kenya resident and principal photographer for this guide. Together, they set their sights on tapping the talented pool of writers and wildlife experts to be found in East Africa.

The path to literary success turned out to be longer and more complicated than originally imagined, but led happily in the end to Project Editor **Deborah Appleton**. Since her arrival in Nairobi several years ago, Appleton has written numerous travel articles on Kenya. She is a consultant for the United Nations Environment Programme (UNEP) in Nairobi. She liaised with and briefed all the writers in this book.

A virtual art in East Africa, the safari comes in more permutations than one can imagine. *East African Wildlife* is aimed at the safari-seeking tourist, but in an effort to be timely, it also discusses some of the environmental and conservation issues which are all too often the subject of today's headlines.

The Dream Team

Dr. Harvey Croze acted as advisor on this project. His animal conservation and environmental expertise and his extensive knowledge of Kenyan game parks have added immeasurably to *East African Wildlife*. The Kenya-based Croze has been involved in many wildlife projects, and now acts as coordinator for the Global Resource Information Database at UNEP.

Another UN staffer, **Dr. Daniel Stiles** wrote the cultural and anthropological chapters for this guide. Stiles previously contributed several chapters to *Insight Guide: Kenya*.

Avid ornithologist **Peter Davey** works with illustrious Ker and Downey Safaris. He wrote the section on birdlife and also supplied numerous photos.

James Ashe is a Mombasa-based expert on all that slithers. He contributed the informative piece on reptiles.

Sir Michael Blundell, who wrote the piece on flora, is a renowned expert on the subject. He authored the extensive *Collin's Guide to the Wild Flowers of East Africa* in 1987.

Mary Anne Fitzgerald is a journalist and Apa contributor with a passion for the safari. A former Nairobi correspondent for London's *Financial Times*, Fitzgerald has spent a good deal of time out in the bush. She wrote the chapters on early hunting safaris, customised safaris and camel safaris.

Other important contributors to the safari section include angling expert **Peter Usher**, who gets us hooked on freshwater fishing

Eu and friend

Ammann

Appleton

H. Croze

Stiles

and **Dudley Chignall**, who extols the pleasures of hot air ballooning. Usher is an environmental meteorologist and long-time member of the Kenya Fly-Fishers' Club, while Chignall is a professional balloonist who has been lifting off from Kenyan game parks since 1976. **Leslie Duckworth** wrote the short feature on Rusinga Island and **Jackie MaConnell** penned the Tana Delta piece.

Iain Allan runs Tropical Ice Safaris in Nairobi. He is one of Kenya's finest climbers and wrote about East Africa's amazing snow-capped peaks. Allan also provided us with some sweeping shots from the summits.

Many years of living in Kenya laid the groundwork for **Cristina Boelcke** and **Anselm Croze** to write a book about the country's game parks. Boelcke is an agronomist at UNEP while Croze is a Nairobi-based artist/writer.

Jeanette Hanby and **David Bygott** have written a great deal on Tanzania. Having travelled throughout the country, they were able to impart valuable information on both the popular game parks and some of the lesser-known regions.

Fred de Vries journeyed through much of Uganda to give us the most up-to-date information on the country's game parks, some of which were only recently re-opened.

Dr. J. Chris Hillman is advisor to the Ethiopia Wildlife Conservation Organisation. He is a long-term resident of Ethiopia and readily admits to being bullish on what the country has to offer, despite recent economic and political setbacks. Hillman provides the written and pictorial account of the little-known game parks of Ethiopia.

David Keith Jones, a wildlife expert with many years of experience in East Africa, contributed valuable text and pictures. Jones, a former editor of *SWARA*, the East African Wildlife Society magazine, wrote the section on game parks in Rwanda and tackled the box on mountain gorillas. His splendid photography graces many pages of this book.

Current *SWARA* editor **Shereen Karmali** provided the Travel Tips information on wildlife and conservation organisations in East Africa.

Many of the superb photographs in *East African Wildlife* were taken by Karl Ammann. An award-winning photographer, Ammann has travelled throughout Africa in search of his sometimes elusive but always fascinating wildlife subjects. His work in this book, and his photo books *Cheetah* and *The Hunters and the Hunted* are fine examples of his patient, sensitive and rewarding style. Ammann also provides readers with some useful hints on wildlife photography.

Some historical photos came from the **Mary Evans Picture Library**, while the film stills for **Eva Ndavu's** entertaining article on Hollywood in Africa were from the London-based **The Kobal Collection**. Additional images came from the **Topham Picture Library, Tony Church, David Coulson, Alan Binks** and **Nicky Martin.**

East African Wildlife was completed with the assistance of a number of people. **Colin Church**, of Church Orr & Associates in Nairobi provided valuable help during the initial stages of the book and also contributed a lively piece on his grand passion: deep sea fishing. **Marti Colley**, a relative newcomer to East Africa, put her editorial skills to work and assisted throughout the project. **Cathy Beech** and **Cassie McIlvaine** provided technical assistance and devoted a great deal of time to fact checking.

—Apa Publications

Davey   *Fitzgerald*   *Boelcke*   *Jones*   *Colley*

CONTENTS

MAPS

TRAVEL TIPS

WELCOME TO EAST AFRICA

Visitors to East Africa are never short of superlatives when describing a trip there. It is a region of endless variety and stunning beauty. Africa's image of mystery and romance has long been fueled by tales of early explorers. Well-known adventurers from presidents and kings to writers and renegades have also been similarly awed.

In recent decades, mere mortals like ourselves have had the opportunity to sample some of East Africa's multifarious attractions. Chief among its delights is its wildlife, which still roam the open grasslands and mountain habitats in large numbers. Kenya, a long-established holiday destination, is a traditional starting point for people going on safari. Together with neighbouring Tanzania, Kenya shares one of the most spectacular backdrops in Africa, majestic Mount Kilimanjaro.The scenery and the large quantities of wildlife in these two countries, helped by a well-developed tourist infrastructure, make them the popular choice for travellers to East Africa.

Though lesser known, other countries in the region can boast of a number of impressive game parks and reserves. Uganda's enigmatic Mountains of the Moon, the mountain gorillas of Rwanda and eastern Zaire and the hot springs of Ethiopia's Awash National Park are just some of the attractions awaiting the initiated.

Where once the African safari was a romantic sojourn for the rich and famous, tours now feature experts who conduct safaris on geography, history, flora, birds, archaeology and other topics of special interest. Adventure safaris can take you up ice-clad peaks or down crocodile-infested rivers. A flight in a hot air balloon features fabulous views of migrating wildebeest while an overland trip across a barren landscape leads to a sea-green lake covered with thousands of pink flamingoes. *Insight Guide: East African Wildlife* provides information on safaris and the wildlife you are likely to encounter on the way. It is both a field guide and an armchair companion. Animals are categorised, game parks are discussed and there's even a look at Hollywood's place in Africa. With *East African Wildlife*, it's always likely to be a case of safari, so good.

Preceding pages: wildebeest make their annual journey across the Mara River; silverback mountain gorilla is a study in concentration; two of Africa's tallest—Mount Kilimanjaro and Maasai giraffe; elephants bathed in warm evening light, Tsavo West; rainy day in the Rift Valley. Left, shy young cheetah hides behind the high grass.

ORIGINS OF EARLY MAN

East Africa has provided more evidence of the physical and cultural evolution of Early Man than any other region on earth. But the story of the search for the "missing link" and the evolution of humankind is as much a question of differing opinions and personalities as it is of science.

The Great Rift Valley stretching from southern Turkey, through Israel and the Red Sea, and down the length of Ethiopia, Kenya and Tanzania into Mozambique contains a wealth of fossil remains. This huge, uneven

trough in the earth has acted as a geological museum to collect, preserve and display the remains of animals and plants which lived, evolved or became extinct over the past several million years.

A long series of lakes exists on the floor of the rift. These lakes fluctuate in size over time, sometimes disappearing completely. Bones of animals which died nearby were covered first by water, then by silts, a process that preserved them as fossils. After a lake dries up, or its shoreline recedes, soil erosion may expose the fossilized bones which can then be discovered by curious *Homo sapiens* —modern man.

The oldest history: The first curious *Homo sapiens* to look for human remains in East Africa was L.S.B. Leakey, sometimes called the father of East African archaeology. Louis Leakey was born in Kenya to an English missionary family. He intended to follow in his father's footsteps as a missionary, but after a rugby accident in 1926 he was sent to "rest" on a dinosaur fossil expedition to Tanganyika with the British Museum.

Over the next 45 years he conducted archaeological and palaeontological research into virtually every period between the Miocene, some 25 million years ago, up to the Later Stone Age only a few centuries past. Leakey's ideas about the evolution of early mankind influenced theories up to the present day. Since Leakey's death in 1972, his wife Mary, and their son Richard have continued to support his most controversial belief. He was convinced that the genus *Homo* had very ancient origins, contemporary with or even preceding the genus most experts accepted as the rightful ancestor, *Australopithecus*. Most debates during the 1960s and 1970s about early human evolution centred on this belief.

The most important site worked by the Leakeys was Olduvai Gorge in northern Tanzania. It was discovered in 1913 by a German, Hans Reck, who was chasing a butterfly across the Serengeti Plains. The Leakeys explored Olduvai from 1931 to 1959 without discovering a human fossil of any importance.

Then in 1959, Mary found the skull and jaws of a primitive hominid which was eventually *Australopithecus boisei*. This species became extinct about one million years ago.

At the time of discovery this large-toothed "Nutcracker Man" created a great sensation which led the National Geographic Society in the U.S. to fund the Leakeys' research. In subsequent years many other hominid fossils were discovered at Olduvai, ranging in age from 1.85 million years to only a few thousand years old. But rather than solving the evolutionary puzzle each new fossil created more confusion as researchers interpreted the size, shape and markings of the skull parts, teeth and limb bones in different ways.

The most controversial find was one identified as *Homo habilis* by Louis Leakey. He believed it to be the maker of the oldest stone tools. It lived some 1.8 to 1.6 million years ago at the same time as another small form called *Australopithecus africanus*, first discovered in limestone caves in South Africa. If his interpretation were correct, it meant there were two forms of *Australopithecus*, one large and one small, living alongside a genus *Homo*. This was difficult for many to accept. Leakey defended his *Homo* by claiming that it had a larger brain than *A. africanus*.

Controversial bones: Most scientists agree that a type of forest ape of the *dryopithecine* family was the ancestor of the first hominid. The first definite hominids begin to appear about four million years ago. A very early hominid can be recognised by bones which indicate that it stood erect and walked habitually on two legs. Further identifying traits are dental features such as small canines and a parabolic shaped jaw, and a bigger brain in relation to the face and body than shown by other apes.

The oldest evidence of upright walking, dating back almost four million years, was discovered at Maka in the Awash River Valley of Ethiopia, by J. Desmond Clark and Tim White of the University of California at Berkeley (UCB) in 1981.

The most exciting finds were made in 1974 and 1975 at Hadar in the Afar Triangle of Ethiopia by a team led by Donald Johanson, now director of the Institute for Human Origins in Berkeley. In 1974 the team found a three-million-year old fossil skeleton which was 40 percent complete: it was named "Lucy" after a *Beatles* song popular in the camp. In 1975 the remains of 13 individuals dating back three and a half million years were recovered. Johanson sparked a heated controversy with the

Left, *Homo Sapiens* ancestor? **Above**, petrified wood in Kenya's Sibiloi National Park dates back over 20 million years.

Leakey camp when he changed his mind about what these and other fossils from Hadar represented.

He had originally agreed with Mary and Richard Leakey that some of the fossil hominds were of the genus *Homo*. Later discoveries of hominds dating back 3.7 million years found by Mary Leakey at Laetoli near Olduvai showed similarities to Johanson's Hadar fossils and seemed to vindicate Louis Leakey's theory. Then in 1979 Johanson published a paper with Tim White which

announced an entirely new species of homind, *Australopithecus afarensis*, named after the Afar Triangle.

The race to find earliest man: In 1968 Richard Leakey began a research project on the east side of Lake Turkana, then Lake Rudolph, in collaboration with the late Glynn Isaac of UCB. Many significant fossils and stone tool sites were found around Koobi Fora, but in 1972 the most spectacular skull of all was discovered and named KNM-ER 1470 (Kenya National Museum-East Rudolf). A photograph of this skull made the cover pages of *Time, National Geographic* and the front pages of newspapers around the world. It caused a sensation because it was then thought to be 2.9 million years old and with its large brain it was undisputably a *Homo*.

Richard assigned KNM-ER 1470 to the species *habilis* created by his father. This seemed to settle the debate about an early *Homo*, and some distinguished opponents of the idea even conceded defeat.

But then questions began to appear about the accuracy of KNM-ER 1470's age. Some scientists condemned as faulty the dating methodology, called potassium/argon, practised by Richard Leakey's team.

The potassium/argon method was used to date fossils of ancient pigs and elephants

an early *Homo* at Hadar and Laetoli. To settle the matter, further rock samples from East Turkana were sent to be dated at UCB using a different technique from the potassium/ argon method. The UCB dates were a million years younger.

In 1980, after fighting the evidence for more than five years, Richard Leakey finally conceded that KNM-ER 1470 was not 2.9 million, but rather closer to 1.8 or 1.9 million years old. This fit well with the dates of *Homo habilis* at Olduvai, but now there were only the disputed Hadar and Laetoli fossils to support an early *Homo*.

The question remains: Experts quibbled endlessly about whether certain skull or

found in different layers of rock at East Turkana. Similar specimens had already been discovered and securely dated by a team working in the nearby Omo valley in southern Ethiopia. Although stages of animal evolution were contemporary in each sample, neither team could agree on the age of the rock deposits: the East Turkana dates were consistently found to be older than those at Omo.

This uncertainty over the accuracy of potassium/argon dating meant Leakey's theory of an early *Homo* was again in dispute. The argument was still raging when Johanson withdrew his support of the existence of

teeth features should be called *Australopithecus* or *Homo*. The remarkable thing about this long controversy is the absence of any real science being applied. The Leakey belief in the existence of an ancient *Homo* was really nothing more than a hunch, or intuition. First Louis, then Mary and Richard, devoted their efforts to trying to find fossils to support their predetermined belief.

The Leakey family spent their whole lives trying to solve the mysteries of evolution. Mary Leakey considers her greatest discovery to be a trail of hominid footprints found at Laetoli in 1978.

Their discovery was only overshadowed by Mary Leakey's find in the same area of preserved footprints of a man, woman and child who, 3.7 million years ago, walked across a field of soft, volcanic ash deposited by a recent eruption.

The hunt for fossils has overshadowed the study of humankind's cultural past which in real terms is more important for gaining an understanding of how we came to be as we are. Archaeological evidence is made up of cultural artifacts—stone, bone and wooden tools, structures, camp fires, the remains of meals, and the spatial distribution of it all. These ancient garbage heaps provide clues to our ancestors' behaviour and society.

Oldowan (pebble tools) and Acheulean (hand axe culture) dating to several hundred thousand years ago. This site is located in the Awash valley a few kilometres south of Addis Ababa. It is not practicable to try to visit Hadar or Omo.

In Kenya at Koobi Fora there is an interesting museum and simple *bandas* (huts) and a campsite where one can stay on the edge of Lake Turkana.

There are several ruins of Swahili stone towns, mosques and tombs between Mombasa and the border with Somalia in the north. Some of the more notable are the abandoned 14th-century towns of Gedi, on the turn-off to Watamu 14 kilometres (eight

Popular excavation sites: East Africa has an impressive wealth of archaeological sites from the oldest in the world, at Hadar, Omo, and west Lake Turkana in Kenya, all dating to more than two million years ago, up to Swahili coastal ruins of towns only a few centuries old.

Tourists can visit some of the more interesting sites, including Melka Konture in Ethiopia where there are several sites of

miles) south of Malindi, and Takwa, on Manda island across from Lamu.

The National Museum in Nairobi has a very interesting display on human evolution and archaeology.

In Tanzania visitors can explore a small museum and several of the sites at Olduvai Gorge excavated by Mary and Louis Leakey. Unfortunately, the site at Laetoli is not open to the public.

There are no excavation site museums in Uganda, Rwanda, Burundi or eastern Zaire, but archaeological research is going on in these countries. Interested travellers can ask for information at the local museums.

Left, prehistoric turtle fossil at Koobi Fora.
Above, the Leakeys inspect another dig.

27

THE SAFARI EXPERIENCE

"There are no words that can tell the hidden spirit of the wilderness, that can reveal its mystery, its melancholy and its charm," penned a ponderous but enchanted Theodore Roosevelt in his book *African Game Trails*. That nostalgic passage refers to one of the first commercial hunting safaris.

In 1909 Mr Roosevelt came to Kenya on an expedition to collect natural history specimens for museums in the United States. Accompanied by two legendary professional hunters, Frederick Selous and Philip Percival, as well as some 600 porters, the former U.S. president spent several months in the bush satisfying scientific curiosity and outraging some of the earliest conservation consciences by bagging over 500 animals and sending their skins back home.

Celebrity safaris: Roosevelt's caravan set off from the Norfolk Hotel, which today stands in downtown Nairobi and still is probably the finest lodging the city has to offer. Otherwise, safaris and Kenyan tourism have changed a lot since those turn-of-the-century years when setting off on foot across the African plains meant taking your life into your hands.

Edward, Prince of Wales, went on a shooting safari about the same time as Roosevelt and helped to popularise the concept of paying to go hunting in Africa by fascinating his friends with tales of shooting rhinos, elephants and lions at close range.

Farmers and ranchers were quick to see the potential and many did seasonal work, as some still do today, taking wealthy sportsmen and women from the United States and Britain big game hunting. In the 1950s, the dilettante aspect of the sport faded and hunting blossomed into a commercial enterprise, the forerunner of today's tourist industry.

Then in 1977, hunting was banned by the late President Jomo Kenyatta, who stated that a ban would help to stop poaching. Some hunters went to Tanzania where they still hunt today; others tried their hand, with less

success, in Sudan and the Central African Republic. Many more reluctantly packed their guns away, sent their trackers home to their farms in the bush and looked for other jobs.

The late 1970s marked the end of a golden era of hunting that spanned well over a century. The men who took clients out in search of trophies were risking their lives as much for pleasure as for profit.

An art: Hunting symbolised the gentleman's code by which European explorers,

farmers and settlers lived. For them, the safari experience embodied all the attractions that had brought them to Africa in the first place.

The sport was conducted along lines as carefully marked out as the rules of a gentleman's club off Picadilly. Apart from the exhilaration of testing vitality under dangerous conditions, there was the mystical communion with nature that culminated in the chase. Often an intimacy developed between hunter and hunted that, in the hunter's mind at least, was endowed with unspoken feelings of respect and friendship.

On the safaris that predated the elephant

Left, turn-of-the-century drawing satirizes "The Great White Hunter." **Above**, hunting plains game.

crisis, when out of work hunters turned a profit on their elephant licence by selling the ivory at a pound a pound in Mombasa or Dar es Salaam, the bulls were felled in a buisnesslike manner. But some clients who hunted regularly would walk for weeks and hundreds of miles without firing a single shot. For them the sport was in the chase and the trophy told all. When the wily old bull whose tusks weighed 45 kilograms (100 pounds) each evaded them, they chose to walk away empty handed.

Similar respect was sometimes shown for the rest of the "Big Five", as the dangerous game were called. The stealth and beauty of the leopard inspired visiting sportsmen as

catch the snap of a broken twig as the hunter approaches. Then they erupt from the shadows in an explosion of fury, bent head and very little else exposed to the poised gun.

It is hardly surprising that many hunters and, on rare occasions, clients too, have been gored and mauled not only by elephant, leopard and buffalo but also by lion and rhino. Most survived their misadventures but there were those who did not.

Vivienne de Watteville, then 24, and her father Bernard set out from Nairobi in 1923 on a prolonged expedition to collect specimens for the Berne museum. While shooting his 19th lion, Bernard de Watteville was mauled. He managed to thrust the muzzle of

they crawled through the bushes in a hopelessly clumsy fashion in the predawn dark. Leopards are so evasive that they are customarily shot from a hide overlooking the bait—usually a zebra strung in a tree.

For many hunters, buffalos were the most awesome animals. The thick boss of horn that curls over their head, a three-inch thick hide and overlapping rib cage makes them the Sherman tank of the animal world. Every professional hunter knows that buffalos are possibly the most difficult animals to down with one clean shot. If wounded, the tables are turned, for buffalos ambush their prey, lying up in the thick grass, ears twitching to

his rifle under its jaw and kill it. But the claws contracted in his body as *rigor mortis* set in. He had to tear them painfully out one by one before he could push the huge body off him. The elder de Watteville walked two hours back to camp, bleeding profusely from his wounds. His daughter washed and dressed the deep cuts, but his stoic performance was in vain. He died later that night.

The redoubtable Vivienne de Watteville continued the safari, using the bushlore she had learned from her father to complete the collection for the Berne museum. Like her peers, she had fallen under the sway of Africa's breathtaking beauty. The sight of untrammelled plains rimmed with volcanoes and carpetted with thousands of antelope and wildebeest moved the hearts of rogues as well as romantics.

Freedom: But above all, the attraction of the safari life was the unparallelled freedom it allowed. "England is too small. Much too small. I shall go to Africa. I need space," declared Denys Finch Hatton before sailing to Mombasa in 1911.

Until World War II, the writ of the government did not reliably extend very far beyond the towns. Once in the bush, a professional hunter could dispense justice, advice and medicine by virtue of the fact that he simply happened to be there. Neither was it likely, as

with supplies from the nearest market town just as today a Kenyan marketing manager making his rounds of the company's branches will say that he is going on safari.

There was little to differentiate a commercial safari from any other except for the extra larding of gunbearers, trackers and skinners. Clients slept in tents just as they do today and wallowed in hot water poured into collapsible canvas baths. Their trips sometimes took months and necessitated a long, snaking line of porters.

Everything that was needed was carried on a man's head. The baggage would be considered excessive by today's standards. On a hunting trip in 1891 to what is now Zim-

hunters roamed from country to country, that anyone would question their own actions— as long as they adhered to an unwritten gentleman's code born in cold schoolrooms and embodied in an ill-defined notion of honour.

In the early days hunters travelled with their clients, as everyone did, on foot. The *Swahili* word *safari* is rooted in the Arabic *safariya*, which means a "voyage". Colonial settlers went on safari when they stocked up

babwe, Lord Randolph Churchill took with him a piano as well as a red and gold wheelchair for the gout-afflicted Lobengula, King of Mashonaland.

The commercialisation of the sport was sired partially by the British imperative to empire build and partially by the Kenyan settlers' desire to pad out their bank accounts. By the time Teddy Roosevelt arrived in Nairobi in 1909, it was a libidinous frontier town that squatted on a swamp. Spear-carrying *Maasai* warriors mingled in the dusty streets with the restless younger generation of the British aristocacy. Ten years earlier, Nairobi had been the railhead for the Uganda

Left, loading tusks at Mombasa, circa 1920. Above, 1930s safari scene.

Railway while workers rested before tackling the inhospitable Kikuyu Escarpment.

The hunters of these years had either won their spurs hunting for ivory, as Frederick Selous had done, or they were farmers who moonlighted when the crops failed, or they simply wanted to earn more money and have some fun while doing it. There were the Cole brothers, Galbraith and Berkeley, brothers-in-law to Lord Delamare; Karen Blixen's husband Baron Bror von Blixen, and her lover, Denys Finch Hatton.

The tortured relationship between the two lovers was aggravated further by Denys Finch Hatton's habit of disappearing into the bush for months at a time. Karen Blixen was

It took eight weeks for a letter to reach England so safaris were arranged at least a year in advance.

Hunting safaris gained their élitist reputation as a pastime for the rich and famous thanks to clients such as the Duke and Duchess of Connaught. He was attended by an equerry; she was looked after by a lady-in-waiting. Seven-course dinners ended with savouries such as giraffe marrow on toast.

"White hunters": The term "white hunter" was coined by Lord Delamare. He employed two men to control the wildlife on his ranch, an Ethiopian and a professional hunter called Alan Black. To avoid confusion, he referred to Black as "the white

particularly peeved when both her husband and her lover took the Prince of Wales shooting, leaving her behind to mind the coffee farm.

Lord Cranworth's entrepreneurial spirit extended even further. He was a founding figure in Newland & Tarlton, the first safari outfitter. By 1914 it was the largest employer in Kenya, a point which angered colonial bureaucrats. They blamed Lord Cranworth and his partners for the labour shortage. The porters were paid the equivalent of US$4.50 a month.

Poor communications meant that publicity hardly existed except by word of mouth.

hunter". The term remained in use until well after Kenya and Tanzania gained independence from Britain.

The introduction of vehicles in the 1920s changed both the pace and the ethics of hunting. Clients travelled to campsites in wooden box body *Fords* that rolled through mud and sand on spoked wheels. There were no windows but canvas blinds could be rolled down when it rained.

Motorised transport encouraged some to shoot from the car, a practise that outraged the hunters. Denys Finch Hatton and others lobbied against instances such as the slaughter of 323 lion by two Americans. Eventually, the game department in Kenya ruled that no one could shoot within 200 yards of a vehicle.

Philip Percival, considered the finest sportsman of that period, traced the rise and decline of hunting with his own career. He came to Kenya in 1905 to join his brother Blainey, who later headed a fledgling game department. He took Teddy Roosevelt on safari and after the World War I went into partnership with Bror von Blixen.

Old photos show him in the hunting outfit that was *de rigueur* for both sexes—a terai hat with a double thickness of felt against sunstroke, breeches, puttees and boots. He chased lion on horseback over the stony

he made up for this in the lyrical passages of his novels set in Africa and at the mess table in the evenings. Philip Percival kept his ego under control by appealing to his wife Pauline to "throw a drink into the beast and he'll quiet down."

After World War II, Hollywood finally discovered Africa. America exported its fiery emotions and inflatable budgets into the bush to dramatise the literature of Hemingway, Haggard and others. In the vanguard was *The Macomber Affair*, filmed in Kenya in 1946.

The film's production company became the first clients of Donald Ker and Syd Downey, who celebrated the defeat of the

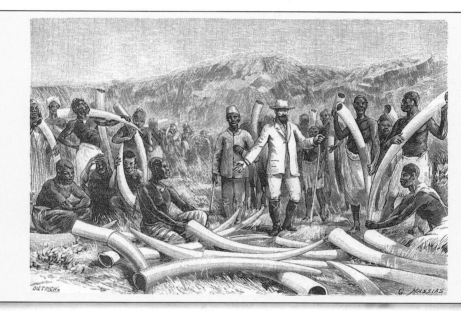

ground of his ranch near Machakos and charged £10 to shoot a lion while on the train going to Nairobi. Wanting a proper education for his children, he chose a Bristol boarding school because it was so near a zoo the lions could be heard roaring at night.

Philip Percival taught Ernest Hemingway his bushlore over two decades that spanned World War II. The author was not always as fine a shot as he would have liked to be but

Germans by creating Ker & Downey. It was to become the largest and most successful safari company in East Africa. Their theatrical tradition lives on. In 1985 Ker & Downey mounted a gigantic field operation that put 340 people under canvas for the making of *Out of Africa*.

While hunting continues in Tanzania, its heyday has long since vanished. The ban in Kenya marked the end of an era that represented an expansive lifestyle lived to the full. Those who were part of it mourn its passing and the rising incidence of poaching. They loved not only the life they led but also the animals.

Left, "I gave it the second bullet in the neck." **Above**, this type of scene was all too familiar in the late 1800s.

W.C.Harris.

BECHUANA

NG THE LION.

WILDLIFE AND AFRICAN CULTURE

Wildlife and the peoples of East Africa have had an intimate relationship since time immemorial. Wild animals and birds of the plains and mountains have always played an integral part in African culture and, more recently, in African economies. There is no other place on earth where humans still live in such close proximity to large numbers of free-roaming animals, which is both a curse and blessing for the governments and people concerned.

African attitudes towards wildlife vary in that order, were the basis of all life. Humankind was one small cog in the ecological nature machine, operating in small bands and graduating from the technology of wood and stone to metal only a few centuries ago. Controlled fire was the most influential factor affecting wildlife and environment, though the extent of its effect is still being debated. Some say that the great grass plains of Kenya and Tanzania, which today provide the necessary habitat for masses of wildlife, are a result of burning, first by hunters and

depending on tribal history and current local situations. These cultural dispositions are important as they will ultimately determine the future survival of wildlife. But vast areas of East Africa encompass a great number of different cultural groups which results in many predilections.

Hunter-gatherer: To simplify things, present day African attitudes can be classified according to profession. The oldest profession is hunter-gatherer, followed by agriculturalist and livestock pastoralist and finally, modern urban man. Between two million and 5,000 years ago all East Africans were hunter-gatherers. Wild plants and animals,

then by pastoralists.

Not surprisingly, hunter-gatherers have a very positive attitude towards wildlife since their lives depend upon it. No solely hunter-gathering peoples survive in East Africa, though groups still exist who, until recently, were hunter-gatherers and who still retain many of the cultural aspects, including occasional illegal hunts. Wildlife is not, and never was, threatened by these people. Animals were never killed indiscriminately en masse as they are by poachers today. Traditional hunters killed for a reason, whether it was for food, ritual, or something to sell. Each species represented a unique value in a cosmology interlinking natural and spiritual worlds. To kill an animal without reason was to violate all that was held sacred, and would surely result in later retribution for the killer from the spirits.

Hunter-gatherer society was originally classless and life was simple and mobile. Then 5,000 years ago domestic livestock and cultivated crops were brought south from Ethiopia and the Nile Valley by new groups of people. Experts speculate that hunter-gatherers at this time spoke *Khoisan*, the

guages with ancient Semitic language-speakers still widespread in Ethiopia.

The true hunters: Hunter-gatherers now became subservient to the better organised immigrants. Over time a caste relationship evolved in many parts of East Africa, with hunters occupying the lowest rung along with potters, iron smiths and tanners. In Ethiopia today the hunting caste is called *Wata* and similar peoples in the south are the *Manjo* and *Funa*. With the changing political situation in Ethiopia and diminishing

click language still used by southern African bushmen. The first immigrants spoke Southern *Cushite* languages from Ethiopia and Southern *Nilotic* languages from the Nile. Over the centuries many different groups came from the north speaking Eastern *Cushitic* and Southern and Eastern *Nilotic* languages and about 1,500 years ago *Bantu* speakers appeared from the west. The result today is a complex mixture of many lan-

wildlife, these people are being slowly absorbed by the dominant groups with whom they live.

Wata also exist in north and east Kenya where they traditionally lived in symbiosis with the *Oromo* and *Somali* pastoralist groups. They traded wildlife products and labour for protection, milk and use of land. In Kenya they are called variously *Sanye* or *Ariangulo*, often with the *Bantu* prefix *Wa*, which refers to a people. Two former hunting groups live in the Lamu District of Kenya, the *Aweer (Boni)* and the *Dhalo*. These groups, especially the *Wata*, were, until the 1960s, infamous long-bow elephant

Preceding pages: hunters and the hunted. <u>Left</u>, framed with ostrich feathers. <u>Above</u>, headress of bird carcasses, worn after circumcision ceremony.

hunters. Some of the *Wata* aces had bows which exceeded the famous English long-bows in drawing power.

Other hunting groups in Kenya are the *Okiek* and *Dorobo*, associated with *Kalenjin* and *Maasai*. They are culturally a very mixed bag: the same people switch cultural identities to suit the situation. They are generally highland people who trap and spear animals rather than use bows and arrows. Honey gathering is also important. The *Dorobo* and *Maasai* extend into Tanzania, though Kenya is their main home. In Tanzania there are also three small remnant hunting groups who today have taken up farming. These are Southern *Cushitic Iraqw*, and the

meat for the *Batwa*, and for some of the surrounding *Bantu* agriculturalists. But in the mid 1900s gorillas became more important for the money paid by foreign zoos and stuffed animal collectors for specimens, dead or alive. In spite of laws passed to protect mountain gorillas they were in danger of extinction by the early 1980s. Conservation organizations, local government support and the pioneering work of the late Dian Fossey have all contributed to reduce gorilla poaching dramatically in Rwanda, eastern Zaire and Uganda. The main strategy is to familiarize gorillas with humans: when these animals can be used as a tourist attraction the resulting income earned and daily

Sandawe and *Hazda*, whose language contains elements of the bushmen clicks. The *Hazda* live around Lake Eyasi and some of them still hunt and gather, against government wishes.

Uganda, Rwanda and Burundi still have low caste hunting groups called *Twa* or *Batwa*, the Bantu equivalent of the *Cushitic Wata* and *Nilotic Okiek/Dorobo*. Hunting is no longer practiced in Rwanda and Burundi, due to the high density population which is eliminating wildlife. A notable exception is in Rwanda's volcanic mountains, home to the mountain gorilla. Gorillas and monkeys were traditionally an important source of

human presence helps to discourage poachers.

The last hunting group in East Africa is the famous *Mbuti* pygmies of the Ituri Forest in eastern Zaire. The *Mbuti* hunt with both nets and bows and arrows and are proficient trappers. Nowadays, they still hunt for forest elephant as much for its meat as for the small tusks, but their infrequent kills are not a threat to elephant survival.

All these hunting groups have, or had until recently, strong cultural beliefs and practices involving wildlife. Wild animals and birds were important in ceremonies such as initiation, marriage and prayer. They were used in divination and prophecy, for medicine, clothing and, of course, food. Without wildlife these cultures would have no meaning and could not exist.

Herders: The herding peoples of East Africa also tend to have a benign attitude towards most wildlife species. Unlike their European or American counterparts, African livestock herders accept the right of animals other than cattle, sheep and goats to share land and water resources. Many pastoralist peoples even recognise the cape buffalo, eland and some antelope and gazelle species as honorary cattle. Most other animals, and especially birds and fish, are not regarded as fit for human consumption.

tion. Similarly, *Maasai moran* (warriors) organise formal lion hunts in which one *morani* tries to spear to death a cornered lion. Success means great prestige for the killer. Other wild, hoofed animals occupy a middle caste position: they are not fit to eat, but neither are they despised.

In normal times pastoralists did little hunting, since livestock were expected to satisfy all needs. It was a loss of prestige to have to resort to wild animals for subsistence. Associated hunter-gatherers were supposed to be the only ones to defile themselves in hunting activities, which were regarded in most cases as ritually impure. In abnormal times however, following

Just as many pastoralist groups created a caste system for people, so they have also established a hierarchy for animals. The *Borana* of southern Ethiopia and Kenya, for example, have their own "Big Four"—the lion, elephant, rhinoceros and buffalo. To kill one animal single-handedly for the first time is cause for celebration in the community and the person becomes a "man". Each subsequent kill increases the man's reputa-

Pastoral scenes: <u>Left</u>, tending camels in Turkana. <u>Above</u>, crossing the dusty plains of Amboseli.

drought, animal epidemics or raids, which resulted in greatly reduced numbers of livestock, pastoralists had to revert to hunting and gathering for survival. Some speculate that elephant and rhino were practically wiped out in Ethiopia and northern Kenya following a series of natural disasters in the late 1880s, as pastoralists sold tusks and rhino horn to traders coming from the coast. Herds were rebuilt with the resulting income, and even today *Boran* and *Gabra* can point to cattle which are descendants of those bought with ivory.

Wildlife is important to pastoralists both culturally and economically. Birds and feathers are particularly significant in ritual and dress. *Maasai* and *Samburu* boys, for example, make stuffed bird crowns to wear after circumsion, and ostrich feathers are worn in ceremonial headdresses by many different peoples.

The camel pastoralists: Three-quarters of Kenya is inhabited by pastoralists. The *Somali* are in the north-east and east, as are the *Borana*, who also extend down the Kenya coast and hinterland as the *Orma* group. In the north, to the east of Lake Turkana, one finds the *Gabra* and *Rendille* camel pastoralists, and to the south are the *Maasai*-related *Samburu*. West of Lake Turkana are the *Turkana* people and south of them live the *Pokot*; the semi-sedentary *Njemps* live south of Lake Baringo. Raiding and cattle rustling still occur, and the introduction of modern firearms at some raids has created serious problems for governments trying to control poaching.

The major pastoralist groups in Uganda are the *Karamajong* in the north-east who are related to the *Turkana*, and the *Bantu Ankole* in the south. The latter are famous for their long horn cattle. Burundi and Rwanda are occupied by the *Rundi* and the *Banyarwanda* respectively. In Burundi, the *Tutsi* (or *Watutsi*) and *Hima* are upper caste groups associated with livestock. The *Tutsi* also are present as a minority in Rwanda. The *Hutu* are a majority caste in Rwanda and a minority in Burundi. They are higher caste than the *Batwa* but fall below the *Tutsi* and *Hima*. This has caused considerable social strife since independence as the *Hutu* try to throw off *Tutsi* domination.

There are two main theories to explain the social and physical differences between the three main caste groups of Rwanda, Burundi and southern Uganda. The first suggests that *Batwa* hunters, generally short and dark, are descendants of the original inhabitants; *Hutu* are descendants of *Bantu* agriculturalist immigrants; and the tall *Tutsi* and *Hima* are the descendants of later immigrant pastoralists of *Cushitic* or *Nilotic* stock who, because of their warlike nature, came to dominate the hunters and farmers.

The second theory hypothesizes that castes developed long ago among a homogenous people and that selective marriage resulted in the breeding of three different physical types.

In Tanzania the main pastoral peoples are the *Maasai* in the north, with most other groups practising mixed agro-pastoralism and living sedentary lives.

The farmers: If hunter-gatherering and pastoralism were the only economies practised in East Africa, wildlife would be sure of a secure future. But farmers have very different attitudes to the sympathetic depiction of animals and birds in folk tales. An all out war has been raging for centuries over control of the land. The farmer is winning. Animals and birds which attack crops are his greatest enemy.

The first agricultural peoples to reduce wildlife populations to controllable limits were the *Amharic* and *Tigrinya* speakers living in highly structured states in highland Ethiopia. Over a period of 2,000 years, high density population, deforestation and use of weapons by formal armies from the 19th century onwards, resulted in the annihilation of wildlife. Internal and overseas trade stimulated localized extinction of desired species. The rise of state systems in Uganda among the *Baganda*, *Banyore*, *Batoro* and other *Bantu* peoples had a similar effect, though with lower population densities wildlife survived in large numbers in various parts of the country. But in the 1970s, social strife and the breakdown of effective government resulted in the slaughter of thousands of elephants and other animals.

Without habitats, wildlife cannot survive. Only a few small mountain areas still containing wildlife exist in Rwanda and Burundi, which are the most densely settled areas in Africa. Burundi's animal population, in particular, is sadly non-existent.

Fortunately, there are now encouraging attempts being made by indigenous wildlife clubs and conservation organizations to create awareness and respect for wildlife. But without traditional cultural values and with the increase in population and poverty, the future for wildlife in East Africa is in a precarious state. Tourism is one of the strongest forces working towards conserving the magnificent natural heritage of this part of the world.

Right, beaded and braided member of the Samburu tribe. Note his traditional ivory earplugs.

A VAST AND VARIED LAND

Visitors to East Africa should realise at the outset that the environment is not fragile, an adjective frequently used to beguile people into supporting environment and conservation related activities. Better adjectives would be harsh, unpredictable, fundamentally impoverished, or resilient. In fact, most evolution and species development in the region has occurred under harsh conditions which have been the rule since the Pleistocene era, some two million years ago. If the environment were truly fragile, as in the

delicate chemical balance of a coastal marine ecosystem or a conservative climax forest, then it would hardly have survived in more or less the same form for such a long time. Most African plants and animals are remarkably hardy, adaptable and able to survive despite what we persist in doing to them.

The ecosystem: The African environment is governed by a handful of ecological laws which appear at first glance almost simple in their concept. There is a finite amount of minerals and elements on the earth, just as there is a more or less finite, but of course smaller amount in an ecosystem.

An ecosystem is the collection of plants and animals, together with the soil storehouse of materials which create the building blocks of plants and animals, which occur in a particular region. The energy which brings such otherwise inert materials into life is provided by the sun, which is essential for the first food production—*photosynthesis.* Plants mobilize the nutrients in the soil together with the constituents of water to produce simple sugars which form the beginning of all terrestrial food chains. Herbivores eat plants, carnivores eat herbivores, and at one stage or another, decomposers, from bacteria to vultures, eat them all. So the basic materials are returned to the soil to be picked up by plants and sent through the ecosystem again in this sun-driven, water-lubricated carousel of life.

Limited jungles: Current popular attention to the Africa described by authors such as Karen Blixen, Elspeth Huxley, Beryl Markham or Doris Lessing has finally dispelled the Edgar Rice Burroughs image of Tarzan's equatorial jungle stretching from the Atlantic to the Indian Ocean. In fact, evergreen forest is the minority of vegetation cover in the continent, confined in East Africa to belts around major mountains such as the Virunga volcanoes in Rwanda, the Ruwenzoris in Uganda, Mount Kilimanjaro in Tanzania and Mount Kenya. Ground water forests occur where there is enough water seeping out of springs, such as at the base of the escarpment above Lake Manyara; riverine forests exist along major perennial water courses; along with remnant patches of low-lying coastal forest. Although tree species differ, the physiognomy is more or less the same: dense, layered canopies, trees up to 70 metres (230 feet) and a relatively thin undergrowth due to the shade of the dominant trees. To enter a forest from the surrounding grassland is like escaping inside on a hot summer day. The light dims, the temperature drops, the wind drops. One can almost feel the additional moisture in the soil and the air which the forest, by its very presence, retains.

The sweeping plains: The vast majority of East Africa is covered by vegetation which is essentially variations on the grassland theme. They are most commonly described by ecologists in terms of their physiognomy. Open grassland is the backdrop, such as the long grass plains of the Serengeti covered with red oat grass (*Setaria and Themeda*). Add scattered shrubs, such as the patches of "toothbrush" bush (*Salvadora*) in Queen Elizabeth National Park in Uganda, and one has bushed-grassland. Replace the bushes with widely-spaced, flat-topped acacias and spiny desert dates (*Balanites*), and the scene

touching, it is woodland, such as the vast *Brachystegia* woodlands in southern Tanzania and beyond. Dwarf shrub grasslands are found on desert fringes, hill thickets, coastal thickets, swamps, and the like.

The "seasons": The climate, comprised of average and actual precipitation and temperature, is a critical factor limiting the form and abundance of life in any ecosystem. The difference between an annual average rainfall and the actual pattern of delivery is important to consider. The Serengeti in Tanza-

is wooded grassland, most typical of *Out of Africa*.

If trees and shrubs are about equal in number, one has, not surprisingly, wooded and bushed grassland, like the *Acacia-Commiphora* region of Tsavo East in Kenya, which stretches to the north and east in what cynical old African hands call "MMBA"— miles and miles of bloody Africa! If trees are more numerous, with their canopies almost

nia, and Ireland have roughly the same amount of water falling on their territories each year. In Ireland, it rains almost constantly. In the Serengeti it rains in two peaks—April and November—when powerful storms bucket down more rain than the soil can possibly absorb at a time. Water runs down the slopes, boils down the watercourses, swells the great rivers and plunges eventually into one of the Rift Valley lakes or the Indian Ocean.

In the long rains, usually April to May, there may be some constantly rainy days. But more characteristically, rainfall is discontinuous. Both plants and animals have to

Left, forest stream in Kilimanjaro. Above, the Virunga volcanoes mark the border between Rwanda and Zaire.

43

be adaptive, mobile or both. "Adaptive" means, roughly, the ability to breed quickly when there is sufficient moisture. "Mobile" means having the ability to be carried, such as a seed clinging to a paw, or to migrate, demonstrated by the wildebeest in their 1,000-kilometre (600-mile) trek around the Serengeti, to places where the chance of reproduction and survival are better. Only trees and tortoises in East Africa stay in one place, and both do their best to make sure their progeny have the chance to get out of the neighbourhood if necessary.

The other important atmosphere-related characteristic, generally only the concern of those who visit East Africa's splendid

the Red Sea to Zimbabwe has rugged step faults which drop, for example, from the Ngong Hills 2,100 metres (6,888 feet) outside Nairobi, to the steaming soda of Lake Magadi at 610 metres (2,000 feet). There are active or recently extinct volcanoes— Virunga in Rwanda, Ol-Doinyo Lengai in Tanzania, Shetani and Teleki's in Kenya. Whole hill ranges are remnants of volcanic activities over the most recent geological eras, such as the Ruwenzoris in Uganda and the Chyulu Hills in Kenya.

All of these are associated with the restless state of the earth's crust at the edge of the two tectonic plates which make up either edge of the Rift. In East Africa the two plates are

beaches, is the intensity of the sunlight. Incoming solar radiation is particularly strong at the equator and when combined with the relatively high altitudes of much of East Africa (Nairobi is 1,500 metres/4,920 feet) above sea level) the light is intense indeed. In fact, it has led to the evolution of a chlorophyll type slightly different to that of temperate latitudes. The sun, which provides the power to generate the ecosystems, takes its toll: nearly 80 percent of rainfall is evaporated back into the atmosphere.

East Africa's geology: Much of East Africa looks unfinished: the gash of the Great Rift Valley which cuts through the country from

slowly pulling apart, unlike southern California where two others are pushing together. The relatively recent activity means that many of the soils of East Africa have a high content of ash delivered from nearby volcanoes: for example, the southern Serengeti from the Ngorongoro highlands; the Nairobi National Park and adjacent Athi-Kapiti plains from the Aberdares and Mount Kenya, and others.

Recent lava flows are common and look like black treacle poured over the landscape. Older lava flows boulders are exposed as escarpments and great granitic boulders as picturesque *kopyes* (or *Inselbergs*) from the age-old and continual erosion of the land surface.

Much of the variety of plant and animal life in East Africa is due to the variation in elevation, from sea-level to 6,000 metres (19,680 feet). This produces a range of temperature and humidity with extremes similar to both southern Florida and the Alps. Altitude produces impenetrable barriers to some species: baobabs are never found above 1,000 metres (3,280 feet), rock hyraxes rarely below 500 metres (1,640 feet).

Periodic drought: For thousands of years Africa has been subjected to short term fluctuations in the rains. Annual failures of the rains happen at least once every 10 years and the perennials.

Animal populations, too, respond to such fluctuations. In dry periods, reproductive success is suppressed by a failure to ovulate or for the foetus to implant. This is related to the mother's nutritional state which is lowered because of the lower plane of nutrition offered by plants in drier periods. The impact is relatively greater on herbivores than carnivores since lions can live quite well off skinny wildebeest, but wildebeest cannot survive on dust. When the rains come back and the vegetation is verdant, then herbivore populations, even elephants, are able to rebuild their numbers remarkably quickly.

Bush fires: Long before modern man, who

some decades are drier than others. The effect is to change temporarily the relative numbers of species and the reproductive success of those less tolerant to dry periods. For example, in certain areas of Kenya, during the dry mid-1970s, perennial grasses all but disappeared in favour of the more opportunistic annuals that re-seed each year. When the rains improved at the end of the decade, the balance shifted back in favour of

Left, scenic lake in Uganda. **Above**, spectacular soil erosion in Ethiopia.

loves lighting fires, African ecosystems were subjected to sporadic burning from natural causes such as lightning strikes. This is evidenced by the fact that many trees and shrubs are "fire-adapted", that is, not only able to withstand burning, but actually flourish or use the fire signal to put out flowers and seed. Fire keeps many of the grasslands of East Africa in an early stage of succession: if they were not burned periodically, by whatever means, they would start to develop towards bushland.

Modern herders and park wardens take advantage of this fact and deliberately set the grass alight each year. This both clears the regenerating shrubs and ensures that new grass can catch the next available rainfall unencumbered by stands of rank hay. Burning is best done early, before the standing crop of dry grass accumulates into a fuel dump that will destroy trees and soils alike when burnt.

In the annual burning, some animals win and some lose. Tortoises are often caught short and roasted in their shells; snakes and small mammals usually cannot outrun a fire fanned by a strong wind. Birds of prey and egrets have a feast at the leading edge of the fire.and later, the local herbivores, both wild and domestic, will have an unencumbered sward of fresh green grass.

Wildlife makes its mark: Animal signs are

giraffes hedge the smaller acacia trees and create a browsing table which is more dense than if the shrub were not browsed. By their feeding actions giraffes stimulate the plants to produce more foliage.

Most large herbivores, such as buffalos and elephants, are fond of taking mud and dust baths, to cool themselves and help rid the skin of parasites. This habit creates pits of activity, "animal furniture", around the ecosystem, spots which are temporarily clear of vegetation, but rich in the nutrients of the animals which visit them. When the wallow falls out of favour, the vegetation which recolonizes the spot is particularly lush.

Man's role: In modern times the greatest

everywhere. Some are subtle and fleeting, like the nests of birds and insects; others are etched into the very face of the ecosystem, such as the animal trails which criss-cross major wildlife areas. Some elephant trails have been followed by human engineers when executing a road cut up a difficult escarpment, and others have been recorded by cartographers who mistook the trails for all-terrain vehicle roads on aerial photographs.

In general, the major herbivores make their mark on the vegetation, and therefore the look of an area, more than the carnivores. Grass along large rivers is kept to croquet lawn height by hippos grazing at night. Feeding

modifier of natural systems is undeniably man. His activities have effects at varying levels of intensity: He can remove materials and put them more or less back, as in subsistence agriculture; he can remove materials and export them to other ecosystems, as in commercial agriculture or mining; or he can just make use of the space for dwelling or commerce and manufacturing, as in villages, urban complexes or industrial parks. Each of these have different levels of energy requirements and differing degrees of physical impact on the look of the land.

There is little point in placing value judgements on these varied levels of use—the

Noble Savage versus the Land Baron versus the Urban Slave—they are all here to stay.

Man continues to cut down forests, plough up the soil and kill or displace wild animals, just as he has always done over the last few millennia. Some modification is beneficial and non-destructive, such as early burning of grasslands, replacing some—not all—of the forest with tea or coffee plantations, or shifting cultivation with a cycle long enough to allow the cleared land to recover in an undisturbed fallow. Other forms of modification leave a lasting and denatured mark: forest clearing on steep slopes, the dumping of industrial wastes into the nearest waterway or the overexploitation of a vulnerable species, as in the poaching of elephants for their ivory tusks.

Feeling the heat: The current portent of change is, as they say in B-grade movies, likely to change life on earth as we know it today. There is now little doubt that the effect of increasing, largely man-produced gases in the upper atmosphere, the so-called "green house gases" (carbon dioxide, methane, ozone and others), will over the next three or four decades alter all major temperature and moisture regimes around the world.

First indications are that the centre of continents in the region of the equator will get hotter and drier. East Africa, however, may become on average wetter and warmer. Most of the models suggest that the sea level will almost certainly rise a metre or two, although history and better data may well prove these models wrong. Such changes will alter the shape of natural ecosystems both in terms of plant and animal species as well as physiognomy.

The loss of soil from the land under the indigenous farmer's plough or the hooves of the pastoralist's cattle is a favourite bugbear of well-meaning conservationists. The solution most usually put forward is to teach the natives how to farm properly or to demand that the herds be reduced in number. But a layer of silt at the bottom of the Indian Ocean off the East African coast proves that soil erosion has been occurring at varying rates over the last 25 millennia. The real reason for

soil loss today is that over this last, relatively dry, geological period in the region, soil has not been made.

Erosion tends to be cyclical. Vegetation thins out over a couple of very dry years; soils are sluiced away in the following excessively "good" rains; vegetation re-establishes itself during the rains, and the rate of soil loss slows down.

Conservation consciousness: Land management strategies must be practicable in the African setting, useful to African people and linked to their society and economy. Wise conservation schemes must involve local people, not just by informing them what is going on, but by making them a direct part of

the conservation process. At the simplest level this means getting some of the wildlife-generated revenue, such as game park takings, back to the landowners who bear the cost of having wildlife graze on their land.

We are only just beginning to learn that conservation attempts work best when they are woven into the desires and aspirations of those they purport to help. But now that we accept that the environment, in all its manifestations, is not the exclusive trophy of the West, perhaps developing countries will become more involved in helping to conserve the world which is, after all, the home of all mankind.

Left, lion lounging on a *kopje.* **Above,** volcanic rock formations in northern Kenya.

WILDLIFE: A WONDERFUL WORLD

Few experiences can replace the visceral excitement of standing amidst a herd of resting elephants, floating in a hot-air balloon over thousands of migrating wildebeest, being in on 'the kill' with a pride of hungry lions, or making eye contact with an imposing mountain gorilla.

Wildlife lovers will admire everything from the awesome majesty of the Big Five—elephant, rhino, lion, buffalo and leopard—to the astonishing variety of beautiful birdlife. They will also marvel in the knowledge that they are following in the footsteps of their *Homo habilis* ancestors who lived here over three million years ago.

Today, about 30 species of herbivores, two dozen carnivores, a dozen primates, over 1,000 species of birds, numerous reptiles, hundreds of coral reef fish and many more invertebrates offer an opportunity to discover the wonders of the East African ecosystem. This section of the guide discusses the larger mammals and some of the more common smaller species, including their normally observed behaviour and habitats. Separate chapters are also devoted to birds and flora.

Preceding pages: taking a real licking—big cats in a joint cleaning exercise; happiness is a wet wallow; migration spearhead: crossing a lake in Serengeti. **Left**, mother and cubs survey the Mara plains.

THE AFRICAN ELEPHANT

The African elephant (*Loxodonta africana*) is the largest living land animal. Most of its special characteristics are a consequence of unique body size of three- plus metres (10 feet) at the shoulder and up to five tonnes in weight. They have a disproportionately large head; toe nails instead of hooves; two breasts between the forelegs; testes carried in the body cavity, next to the kidneys; specialised grinding teeth; tusks nearly worth their weight in gold; a unique trunk; enormous ears and a 60-year life span.

Elephants once roamed throughout Africa. Now they occupy only one-fifth of the continent. Although they now number between 700,000 and one million, their range and numbers are dwindling rapidly. Poaching for ivory has over the past 20 years reduced most East African populations by 90 percent. Despite international concern for their threatened status, even conservative figures suggest that elephants will be virtually eliminated within the next 20 years.

Elephants occupy all African habitats from near desert to closed canopy forest. The inherent mobility of the animal allows it to select foods from a variety of habitats over a home range which may be thousands of square kilometres. The availability of grass for a good part of the year is important; the presence of perennial water within their range is essential. Elephants move daily and seasonally between different parts of the habitat: from woodland to grassland, from bushland to swamp, and back again.

Elephants are active both night and day, since their 16- to 20-hour waking period must necessarily spill into the dark hours. The bulk of time is spent feeding. A midday siesta in shade is common, and a period of deep sleep, with most of the group even lying down, will occur at night if the group feels secure.

Mud baths: Elephants bathe, wallow or dust whenever possible, at least once a day, for cooling to help get rid of parasites. Trunkfuls of liquid or dust are blown be-

A dust-covered herd heads for some liquid refreshment.

tween the legs, on top of the head or along the flanks. The habit of frequent mud bathing and dusting leaves elephants more the colour of local soil types than the natural grey of their skins. Adopted colours range from light grey, red, to dark brown, allowing the observer to guess from where a group of elephants has recently come.

The only serious threat to an adult elephant is humankind, who will eventually either displace all wild elephant populations as he spreads into marginal lands, or kill them directly in poaching for ivory. Elephants do, rarely, get their own back. An unarmed human has little chance at close range against an angry elephant. The frequently

observed head shake, accompanied often with an audible ear snap, is a warning to keep away. A serious charge is strangely quiet: the elephant runs at some 35 kph (22 mph), ears out, head lowered, trunk curled under.

Elephants are as sociable as primates. Greeting elephants will either put their trunks in each others' mouths, or touch and therefore smell each others' temporal glands. Such greeting gestures probably reveal subtle states of mood as well as identity. Like many other African herbivores, elephants may urinate or defecate to mark territory and for recognition. When two family units reunite after several days or weeks of separation, there is much squealing and trumpeting, pirouetting, backing up, greeting and excreting.

The family: The basic social group is the family unit, comprising several related adult females and their immature offspring. The family unit is led by the eldest cow, the matriarch. The herd bull does not exist, except in the preconceptions of observers. Adult males tag along with family units for short periods to inspect females for their readiness to mate. Females are "tasted" by putting the trunk to their vulvas, collecting a residue of urine, and inserting the sample into the mouth. There is a special organ in the palate sensitive to the hormonal content of the urine, and hence the female's reproductive state. These visiting bulls have no leadership role in the group, although they will assist in defence.

Bulls drift from family unit to family unit, and from time to time into loosely knit bull groups: two to 20 males who move together for a day, a week or a season. Bull group composition changes continually. Larger bulls go off to test females and mate: young bulls, newly ousted from their family unit, quickly find companionship, teachers and safety in numbers in bull groups.

A family unit of 15 is large. Beyond that size the group is likely to split into two, each new group going its own way, one led by the old matriarch, the other by one of her sisters or cousins. Family units may show strong associations with certain other units in a particular area. Such associations are the likely result of a blood relation between the matriarchs: they were probably sisters or cousins in a family unit which grew and split in the past.

With the rains and abundant grass growth, however, family groups are likely to join together in larger assemblages which, in places like the Serengeti, Selous, Luangwa and Tsavo, have numbered more than 1,000 elephants in sight from the same hilltop. Bull groups satellite such assemblages, and many bulls are within them testing females. The frequency of mating is high. Seasonal gathering of the clans may facilitate breeding in a wide-ranging and mobile beast.

Old elephants provide the family unit with a historical memory of watering holes, the location of seasonally available fruits, and other dispersed features of the elephant's world. Even a menopausal cow can retain her role as matriarch, suggesting that wisdom, and not just sex appeal, is a predominant quality for an elephant decision maker.

Recent research has shown that elephants are highly vocal animals. Low frequency sounds, well below or at the very edge of human perception, allow contact to be maintained for up to 10 kilometres (six miles). The deep rumble heard from time to time is a contact vocalisation ("here I am; where are you?") which just enters the range of human hearing. Low frequency sound is efficient for transmission where there is interference from vegetation. Elephants also roar and scream audibly through the trunk to produce

vulva and then puts the trunk tip in his mouth to confirm the test.

It was once thought that only Asian elephant males came into sexual season, a period of ill temper called musth. Recent studies show that African elephant males also show seasonal fluctuations in their temper and sexual motivation and display conspicuous physiological indicators, known to elephant watchers as the "green penis syndrome". The annual two to three months of irascibility is accompanied by the penis dangling, dribbling, and taking on a characteristic greenish hue and strong smell. The odour is detectable to human observers, so it must be nearly overwhelming to other ele-

classical trumpeting, either in anger or exultation, depending on the situation.

Check mate: Females may come into season every two or three months, if not pregnant or lactating. This, and the generally wide dispersal of an elephant population makes it necessary for males to move among family units, constantly testing for female readiness to mate. A testing male walks past a female's rear end, surreptitiously sniffs her

Left, this baby gets its back scrubbed during a mud bath. **Above**, a gathering at Samburu.

phants. The signs of musth, usually attributed only to irritable males, are now known to be inherent in both sexes. A liquid oozes from the temporal gland, a modified tear gland halfway between the ear and the eye, leaving a conspicuous dark stain along the side of the face. The secretion, called temporin, accompanies states of excitement, such as when there is a frightening disturbance or if close relatives reunite after a period of separation. A bull in musth is more likely to displace his peers when it comes to winning the favours of a female.

Occasionally, a female in oestrous and a large courting bull will consort for a time:

they stay close together, pay attention to one another, and exclude others from any intimacy. Consorting may be very subtle, or actually take the pair some distance away from the family unit and other bulls. This may account for the old tale of elephant "marriages".

Consorting may not always be so tender, and the male may have to catch her first. If the consorting female breaks into a run, the male takes after her. Females in general can outrun males if they wish, and getting caught is probably the female's way of choosing who catches her. Females mate most with bulls in musth.

The female usually stops when the male

tween mother and young. Calves suckle from the side, reaching for the teat just behind the mother's front leg. A young elephant that can walk under its mother's belly is probably less than a year old. A calf may suckle for up to five years. Young bulls stay with their family units until puberty, perhaps 10 to 15 years, after which they are encouraged to seek their fortunes. Young females in contrast may stay with the group for life. Young elephants in a relaxed, undisturbed and healthy population are a pleasure to watch playing with each other: chasing, play fighting, tug-o-wars and mounting. Their long childhood is only matched by higher primates, including man.

touches her, particularly if he is able to lay his trunk along her back or across her shoulders. He then rests his head and tusks on her rump and heaves himself up on his hind legs. By squatting slightly and hooking upward his highly mobile erect penis, he is able to enter her. Copulation lasts less than a minute. The rest of the family unit is either indifferent to the copulation, or capable of reacting with great excitement—vocalizing, earflapping, head shaking, turning, backing and excreting.

Habits: Elephant calves spend several years dependent on and learning from the adults. There is nearly constant contact be-

Group defence is common. If simply moving away does not work, the next line of defence is to draw up a formidable wall of adult females to face the intrusion with heads high, ears out, looking to and fro as if trying to make out the exact source of the annoyance. Young members of the group are pushed towards the rear. In full retreat, the group runs off in a tight bunch with the young in the middle.

A wounded or sick elephant causes great concern and excitement in the group. Faltering animals will be kept upright between two or more adults. Fallen animals will be fussed over with trunks and feet, and tusk- breaking attempts to lift a downed elephant have often been observed. The strange habit of burying a dead or immobilised fellow is also well-documented. Trunkfuls of dirt are tossed over the animal; branches are broken off and laid tenderly over the body, until it is completely covered. Human victims of elephant attacks have been treated in a similar manner. The reason is not known.

Elephants feed up to 16 hours a day, using their trunks from ground level to nearly five metres (16 feet). Feeding techniques are varied; nearly all vegetative material is eaten, from staples such as grass, trees and shrubs, to delicacies like fruits, seeds, herbs and creepers. Tree bark is stripped off *Acacia* trees in certain seasons. Elephants are attracted to over-ripe fruit trees and often gorge themselves to the point of intoxication on fermenting fruit.

The trunk is the principal feeding tool. Its main function is to reach downwards to harvest grass, the bulk of the elephant diet. The trunk evolved from a combining of nose and upper lip. It is an astonishingly mobile and dexterous collection of muscles. It has a "two-fingered" tip, used for smelling and for picking and plucking.

Tusks are also important tools, and are modified front biting teeth, not eyeteeth (canines), as might be expected. Tusks are used for chiselling, digging, prizing, levering and stabbing. Elephant ivory grows some 10 centimetres (four inches) per year, so the frequently broken tips are continually replaced by new growth. This has inspired suggestions of "live harvesting" of ivory to save elephant lives: complicated and costly, but feasible. No more than one or two percent of elephants are naturally tuskless.

Even while feeding on grassland, elephants detect the occasional herb or creeper by smell, and pluck them out. In this way, odd individuals break the feeding pattern as they come across an interesting "side dish" or a new bulk food. The entire group may then shift to the new delicacy.

The remaining elephant teeth, the molars, are also unique. An elephant has in its lifetime only six teeth on each side of each jaw,

24 in all. The teeth are large, 20 to 30 centimetres (eight to 12 inches) long, so only one, or two halves, end to end, are exposed on each jaw side at a time. Molars grow progressively forward, which provides scientists with a means of telling elephants' ages. Chewing is forward and backward: the lower jaw grinds against the upper in the forward stroke. Since elephants spend most of the day eating, they are almost continuously chewing.

An adult elephant can eat 150 to 200 kilograms (68 to 90 pounds) of vegetation a day. Water is essential—70 to 90 litres (123 to 158 pints) per day— both for helping digestion and for cooling. Water is sucked into

the trunk and then tipped and released into the mouth. Animals less than about six months old have generally not learned the trick; they drink from their knees, sucking water directly into the mouth. If water is not within a half day's march, elephants may use their trunks and tusks to dig for it, for example, in the bed of a sand river. Elephant wells, as much as a metre (three feet) deep, provide numerous other animals with access to water during dry periods. At such wells, or at a normal watering hole, elephants easily displace all other animals, including buffalos and rhinos, and have been known to kill them if it comes to a fight.

Left, family makes a river crossing. Above, playfighting on the banks of the Ewaso Ngiro River.

RHINO

In our lifetimes, black and white rhinoceros (*Diceros bicornis* and *Ceratotherium simum*) are doomed to virtual extinction in the wild, outside small protected areas. Rhinos' horns are leading the beast to the brink of extinction. The alleged pharmaceutical qualities of rhino horn, as a nerve tonic and general restorative rather than an aphrodisiac, have supported relatively modest ancient markets in the Far East. Most of the recent poaching in East Africa, however, has been to fulfill the demand for dagger handles, a male status symbol in South Yemen. One well-wrought *Jambia* made from one life-long grown horn can fetch up to US $15,000 in Sana'a.

Horns are not bone, but tightly packed bundles of hair-like structures, similar to hooves and toe nails, mounted on roughened areas of the skull. Apart from this, rhinos are virtually hairless. The unabated and apparently uncontrollable problem of poaching is more than the rhino's naturally very low population density and slow reproductive rate can support.

Rhinos are odd-toed ungulates, like horses. Their footprints are unmistakable with three large toes. There are two distinct species of rhinos, the black rhino and the so-called white rhino. Both are in fact grey. The latter's name is a corruption of the Afrikaans word for "wide", referring to its broad upper lip, which is designed for grazing. Black rhinos have longer necks than whites which helps them to reach up into vegetation for browsing. The white rhino's relatively longer head enables it to reach the ground to graze.

African rhinos have two long horns, one set behind the other. They are distinct from their cousins, the Indian rhinos (*Rhinoceros unicornis*), which only have a single horn.

The rhinos' keen senses of smell and hearing compensate for their weak eyesight. They can turn their ears to locate the source

Face-to-face with *Diceros bicornis*.

of any disturbance. Like other large bodied animals, rhinos have potentially long lifespans of up to 50 years.

There are two distinct population ranges of white rhinos. The northern range (*C. s. cottoni*) extends from southern Sudan west through Zaire towards Lake Chad. The southern species of (*C. s. simum*) occurs south of the Zambezi. There are marked differences between the two subspecies in the concavity of the forehead. Populations have not been contiguous in recent historical times.

Some populations of black rhino developed characteristic traits. "Gertie" and "Pixie" of Amboseli were famous for their remarkably long, straight horns. The gene for such horns has now been poached out of existence.

Habitat: Black rhinos range from moist, montane forest to semi-arid bushland. The white rhino prefers the drier habitat of grassland and wooded grassland. Both species characteristically seek shelter and shade in dense undergrowth and thickets. The white rhino is partly nocturnal; the black rhino more strictly diurnal. Black rhino may become partially or totally nocturnal in regions of persecution.

Rhinos are never found far from a source of water. During drought, however, they have been known to go for up to five days without drinking. Rhinos are fond of rolling on their sides in mud or dust wallows. They cannot roll on their backs because of the elongated, blade-like protrusions on their spines. They frequently rub their belly, flanks or face on rocks or stumps and "polished" rubbing sites are dotted throughout rhino country.

Man is the rhino's main predator although lions and hyaenas may try to attack very young calves. Rhinos are able to rout or dispatch most disturbances after a short 50 kph (30 mph) charge. Disturbed rhinos are prone to attack, often before they have properly located the source of disturbance so the initial charge may not be directly towards the intended target. Other charges may stop short of target, as though the real purpose is to get close for enough to identify and intimidate the disturbance. In such a case the rhino is more likely to wheel about and run off than follow through with the attack.

Rhinos are not very sociable, especially

black rhinos. White rhinos may form small, family groups including several females and immatures, but the most commmonly seen group is a female with her calf.

The territories of mature males vary from three square kilometres (just over one square mile) in forested areas to 90 square kilometres (35 square miles) in open grasslands. Old territorial males will only rarely stray from their familiar area. Territory is marked both around the edges and throughout the middle with large, conspicuous dung piles, or *middens*.

Middens may be a couple of square metres in extent. They are approached and sniffed by most passing rhinos, but only the domi-

nant male defecates and scatters his latest addition on to the pile with his hind feet. Horn rubbing in the pile is common. A white rhino territory may have 20 to 30 middens around the boundaries. Scientists think that middens might be a sort of range "mailbox", allowing all rhinos in an area to keep track of who is in the neighbourhood and their reproductive state.

White rhino females often engage in friendly nose to nose greetings when they meet. Males however, especially black rhino males, tend to be less amiable. On encountering each other, serious fighting can result if one rhino does not give way. Sometimes gaping wounds are inflicted by the upward sweep of an opponent's horn.

White rhinos appear to be more phlegmatic than black: two males may spend an hour staring at each other from a short distance, sometimes nose to nose, as if greeting, occasionally wiping their horns on the ground. They then turn around suddenly and trot back to the centre of their respective territories.

Mating: Their territories ensure that white rhino males have access to receptive females. Once a female is found, she is continuously, but gently, herded within the boundaries of the territory for up to two weeks, often accompanied by her most re-

for several days. Mating may last as long as an hour, during which the male ejaculates several times. This does little to dispel the popular perception of the qualities of rhino horn.

Single calves are born after a gestation of some 16 months. Newborn animals are very small at birth, only one-twentieth of the female's weight. Females seclude themselves at the time of birth and female white rhinos, after calving, may isolate themselves from other animals for a month. It is said that white rhino calves run in front of their mothers; black rhino calves run behind.

Births are most common during the rains. Calves stay with their mothers from two to

cent calf. This may in part explain the length of time the male spends manoeuvring and tagging her— as much to get away from the "teenager" as to get close to her. Once close, the male prods the female gently with his horn, rests his chin on her back, rubs his face on her flank, and generally softens her up for the final approach.

A courting male and female may consort

Left, pondering his fate? **Above**, taking a sugar cane break.

four years, depending on the birth of the next offspring.

The shape of the mouths of the two rhino species indicates the differences in their feeding habits. Black rhinos are browsers and have pointed, nearly prehensile upper lips, which allow them to choose and pluck small twigs, leaves, fruit and vines. Most plants, except grasses, are eaten by black rhino, nearly 800 species in some areas. White rhino are grazers with broad mouths and upper lips and teeth suitable for grinding grass. Both have lost the front biting teeth altogether and rely on their lips to gather vegetation.

BUFFALO

The African buffalo (*Syncerus caffer*) is traditionally known as the meanest beast in the bush, prone to launch a killing charge at the drop of a hat. It is an understandable reaction if one is being shot at, and solitary males are loath to be disturbed. But the majority of buffalos in cow-calf herds are nearly as docile as cattle.

There is the one main species, a very large blackpelted, grassland dweller, weighing up to 800 kilograms (1,764 pounds); one subspecies, the forest buffalo (*S. c. nanus*) which is smaller, reddish, with less robust horns; and at least two intermediate forms, *S. c. aequinoctialis* and *S. c. brachyceros,* found in grassland areas where large forests merge with grasslands. In East Africa, however, animals seen in forest clearings, or along grassy road verges, will certainly be African buffalos.

Buffalos in general favour open grassland, wooded grassland and bushed grassland. They are most active in evening, night and early morning, both for feeding and moving from place to place. The rest of their time is spent lying down and ruminating, in shade, if available, rather like cows in a field. Buffalos must drink daily, so are never found more than 15 kilometres (nine miles) from water. As with domestic cattle buffalo probably sleep not more than an hour a day.

The massive, bossed horns and exceptional size of the animal afford considerable protection. This has allowed blind, lame, even three-legged individuals to survive longer than could have been expected. Solitary bulls, without the redoubtable protection of numbers, commonly fall prey to prides of lions. It is not uncommon, though, for lions to be fatally injured during a prolonged battle with a wounded buffalo. A buffalo herd, when in danger of attack by lions, will form a defensive semi-circle, protected by bulls on the other flank, with the cows and calves grouped in the centre of the formation.

Delicate morning mist makes for a peaceful setting in the Maasai Mara.

An explosive snort heralds alarm. This is followed by a nose up posture orientated at the intruder, who should begin looking for the nearest tree if the buffalo is a lone male. An alarm in a cow-calf herd will bring the others to attention, and those close to the intruder may even move forward in a short-sighted manner, as if to have a better look. If the intruder stands his ground or even advances a few paces, the buffalos will invariably turn tail with high head tosses and the entire herd will run off.

Herd mentality: Buffalos live in herds which have a relatively stable composition, changed only by births and deaths. Herds may be as large as 2,000 for the African suckling calf and her two year old from last season's breeding. When any one of the three is incapacitated, the other two will stick together. Vocalizations play only a small role in social encounters: calves bleat; cows grunt to call calves. Otherwise buffalos are rather silent without the typical bovine lowing sounds.

Cow-calf groups do not appear to have obvious leaders. Decisions about which way a resting group should move next seem to be taken by a form of voting. During the period of resting and ruminating, individual females ocasionally stand up, face a particular direction for a few moments, and then lie down again to carry on chewing the cud.

buffalo but rarely larger than 20 for the forest sub-species. A figure of 350 was estimated as an average in Serengeti National Park between the wet and dry seasons. Large herds tend to fragment during the dry season and regroup in the wet. This spreads the grazing load when grass is in short supply. In the dry season, there is a tendency to concentrate along the rivers. In the wet season, spacing over the habitat is quite regular. Each herd has a particular, fairly constant range, and there is little overlap between adjacent herds.

Despite their herding instincts, the basic social unit appears to be an adult female, her After a couple of hours, the whole herd moves off in the direction most buffalos faced when standing. Voting seems to pay off, since it appears to take the herd in the direction of the greatest amount of grass in the neighbourhood.

A lot of bull: Bachelor groups of 10 to 15 are common, and may consist either of old, retired bulls who no longer bother to keep competing for females, or younger bulls nearing their prime during the off season for matings, usually when it is dry. Solitary old males or small bull groups are the ones likely to charge intruders.

Fighting males circle each other for long

periods, head tossing and pawing the ground. The major threat is a lateral display with the head lifted and nose pointed to the ground. Presented side-on, the thickness and power of the neck and shoulder muscles are shown to full advantage. Seen from the front, the posture emphasizes the size and raised surface edge of the horns. Two males squaring off will accentuate their horns with tossing, hooking movements, and by thrashing nearby bushes. Such displays usually end with one animal giving up by simply walking away. Fights are therefore rare which saves everyone potentially serious damage. When fights do occur, they consist of terrific head-on clashes.

Males test for females in heat by sniffing their urine and genitals. Male competition for females does not entail much fierce fighting. Posturing and mock fights serve as substitutes for conflict, which helps keep these large, powerful animals from injuring one another. Courtship entails a temporary male-female bond which lasts only until soon after mating.

The principal calving period is between December and February. Calves are carried for eleven and a half months, and are dropped in the midst of the herd, usually in the rains. The afterbirth is eaten, the calf is licked clean, stimulated to defecate and suckled. On completion of this procedure the

Wallowing in mud holes appears to have a social function as well as keeping animals cool and discouraging skin parasites. A particular wallow, apart from being foul-smelling in its own right, may take on the scent of the bull which lays claim to it. The wallow thus serves as a passive territory marker. Cattle egrets can often be found in the company of wallowing buffalos. These birds give away the presence of buffalo concealed within a swamp.

Left, making a pit stop at the aptly-named Buffalo Springs. **Above**, oxpecker and friend.

calf goes back to join the grazing herd.

Buffalos are strictly grazers. Different species of grass and even their parts— leaves, stems, inflorescences— are selected on a basis of smell, taste and protein content. The amount of protein is related to the tenderness of the grass so grazers weed out the nutritious from the coarse on the basis of the effort taken to pull the plant apart.

Seasonal changes in grass availability and nutritional value dictate the local movements of buffalo in semi arid areas. In the rains they will feed on open plains; in the dry season, they retreat to woodlands, hillslopes and river fringes.

KING OF BEASTS

Lions *(Panthera leo)* are the largest of the big cats, two to four times the weight of their cousins, the leopard and cheetah. Lions are far more social and also show greater differences between the sexes than other cats. Males have manes which are fully developed by four years old, and they are up to 50 percent heavier than females.

Young lions have a spotted coat which gradually, over the first two years, becomes a nearly uniform lion tawny. Like many of their prey, lions have a slighty counter-shaded colouration: a pelage darker on top grading to lighter underneath. This tends to neutralize the three-dimensional shadowing created by overhead lighting from the sun, as the shadow is lightened by the whitish belly fur. The overall effect is to enhance camouflage by flattening form.

Lions are widespread in wooded and bushed habitats. Although they are often seen in completely open grasslands, they prefer areas which have cover for hunting and hiding young. They appear to succeed in maintaining healthy populations in most game parks and reserves.

Lions are predominantly active in the evening, early morning, and intermittently through the night. They tend to spend nearly all daylight hours resting or asleep in the shade.

Roaring success: Both lions and lionesses roar, the males louder and deeper. Roaring typically consists of long moaning grunts followed by a series of shorter ones, the whole lasting 30 to 40 seconds. Roaring is most common at dawn and dusk or during the night. Its purpose appears to be definition and maintenance of territories, although it may well also be used to keep in contact on dark nights: a roar can be heard over two or three kilometres. Individual lions can recognise one another's roars. Cubs may make noises while older lions are roaring nearby. Lionesses often encourage their cubs by making soft moaning roars to them.

The high grasses help to hide lions from their intended prey.

Cool cats: Lions are the only really social cats. Prides are built around two to 15 related lionesses. These are accompanied by a coalition of males, many of whom are probably brothers unrelated to the females. The pride also contains dependent offspring. Young females mature and join their mothers and aunts as breeding pride members; young males emigrate and seek unrelated prides to attempt to take-over.

Lion prides are ever changing: males only hold sway over a group of females for an average of 18 months, before they are ousted, sometimes even killed, by stronger or more numerous newcomers. Only large male coalitions can aspire to control a pride

male initiates with the so-called mating snarl, which has been described as a sneeze-like grimace. The mating snarl may or may not convince the female to stop and crouch. The female, if she initiates, keeps unusually near the male and may rub her head on his shoulders and sides, emitting a deep, sensuous rumble, walking sinuously around him and flicking her tail. She may even back into the male and crouch to stimulate his interest.

Copulation is unmistakable, if perfunctory. The female yowls and the male often bites her neck in a similar manner to the subduing neck bite of domestic cats. After ejaculating, the male leaps off, often to avoid a blow from the female who may spin around

over a period of relative stability, measured in months rather than years.

Females may produce as many as six litters during a lifetime. Lionesses come into season sporadically; the periods between heats vary from a couple of weeks to months. Oestrus lasts about a week during which time males compete over receptive females. Male coalition partners however, who test females as they wander over the pride's range, are rarely aggressive towards each other in competition over potential mates. They seem to operate an agreed first-come-first-served system.

Either partner may initiate mating. The

when his weight is removed. Both animals then lie down. During one consorting week, the pair may copulate over 300 times, an average of once every 15 minutes during the waking hours. A successful pride male may mate 20,000 times in his lifetime: the King of Beasts indeed!

Gestation is relatively short: three and a half months. In a secluded, well hidden spot, often among rocks or dense riverside vegetation, the lioness gives birth to two or three cubs on average. She suckles and remains with them for long periods, only occasionally returning to the pride to hunt and feed. Litters are sometimes lost at this stage. After a month the cubs are led to the pride.

Lionesses appear to synchronise breeding activity; it is not unusual for several females in a pride to have litters at the same time. Unlike other mammals, lion mothers will commonly tolerate suckling by cubs of others in the pride, because they are generally all related. By providing milk to cubs belonging to her sisters and half sisters, a female feeds young lions that carry some of her own genes. Females do however more readily nurse their own offspring, who tend to approach boldly, mewing, purring, and pushing their mothers' faces before proceeding to suckle noisily. Cousins are more prone to sneak in from behind.

Nomadic males regularly kill cubs, presumably to eliminate from the population the genetic material of rivals. Cubs are also at risk from other predators such as spotted hyaenas and leopards. Lionesses keep their brood well hidden and move the hiding places if disturbed.

Getting a good grip: Lions' predatory habits have enhanced the evolution of a large head and powerful jaws equipped with long canines. Feet are large and retractable claws unsheath to present a catching tool as wide as a squash racket. Lions are the biggest African carnivores and routinely tackle prey, such as buffalos, that are beyond the ability of other predators. They stalk and ambush rather like cheetahs and leopards, but like hyaenas and hunting dogs, they also hunt collectively.

The majority of their prey are medium to large ungulates, such as wildebeest and zebra. There is, however, considerable seasonal and locational variation. In the Serengeti, for example, lions often hunt warthogs in the dry season when more favoured wildebeest and zebra have migrated north towards Kenya. At all times lions are opportunistic and take rodents, fledgling birds, ostrich eggs, etc. Males need to eat approximately seven kilograms (20 pounds) of meat a day; females five kilograms (11 pounds).

Females in the pride do most of the hunting but males, with their superior strength and weight, gain first access to a kill once the dirty work is done. There is a reason beyond sheer laziness: males have a distinct disadvantage in stalking with their manes, which appear like small hay stacks moving though the grass. Hunting tactics depend on prey and habitat. In open habitats lions tend to hunt at night, though they can be active during the day when there is enough vegetation to hide their approaches. River crossings and watering places are favourite sites for ambushes.

Stalking and rushing prey demands that lions get as close as possible. When several lions hunt together they tend to try to encircle prey to cut off lines of escape. Experts disagree on whether or not lions pay attention to wind direction, though hunts made upwind are usually more successful. Although lions can eventually reach nearly 60 kmh (37 mph), most of their prey can sprint faster. So lions must get within 30 metres (100 feet) before charging, overtaking, slapping down and grabbing the victim.

Once grabbed, the victim is subdued and suffocated with a relatively quick neck bite or a sustained bite over the muzzle. Larger prey may be overcome by several lions together and members of the pride may begin to open the victim while one lion is still suffocating it.

Left, the mating game. **Above**, the intense gaze of an alert lioness.

LEOPARD

Leopards *(Panthera pardus)* are the largest of the spotted cats. Their heavy build, pug-mark spots and thick, white-tipped tail distinguish them from the more slender cheetah. They are the most elusive of the large cats, principally because of their nocturnal and secretive habits. Leopards have been little studied so not much is known of their behaviour in the wild. They are active day and night, but veer strongly towards nocturnalism, due to harassment.

Leopards are found in all except the driest African habitats—woodland, bushland, wooded grassland and forest. They are the most widespread member of the cat family, even commonly occurring in suburban areas. Large rocks and *kopjes* and large trees along rivers are favourite resting sites. As long as there is an adequate food supply and a minimum of persecution, the leopard is at home. Despite their adaptability, persecution by those involved in the fur trade and competetion with man for living space, have reduced leopard numbers drastically.

Their characteristic call is a deep, rough cough, repeated 10 to 15 times, sounding like a saw cutting wood. Males have distinctly deeper voices than females. The sawing call serves to advertise presence and to discourage other leopards from trespassing into defended territory, thereby avoiding destructive territorial fights.

Greetings are often accompanied by a short growl. The beginning of an agressive charge may be heralded by two or three short coughs, and those foolish enough to corner a leopard never forget the beast rearing up on its hind legs and uttering a blood-curdling scream.

Blending in: Leopards have few natural enemies and their skill in climbing trees assures them protection from all but the most aggressive lions. Anyone who has scanned the branches and canopy of a tree for a leopard knows just how well they blend into the blotched light and shade. Even the cer-

This proud female displays a magnificent coat of fur.

tain knowledge that a leopard is in a particular tree is no guarantee that it will be discovered. The switch of a hanging tail is sometimes a giveaway.

Leopards are solitary animals. They occupy and defend home ranges which vary from one to 30 square kilometres (one to 12 square miles) depending on the availability of food. Males and females defend their own, often overlapping, territories from members of their own sex. Female territories tend to be smaller and several may be encompassed within one male territory. Males often fight over their space and mark trees and logs throughout their area by clawing bark and spraying urine.

Good breeding: Breeding can occur at any time of year. Leopards, like all other cats except lions, are solitary breeders. The only long term social bond is between a leopardess and her cubs. Females come on heat for about a week every 20 to 50 days. They advertise their receptiveness with the sawing call which soon attracts the nearest territory holding male. A pair will then consort during the week of heat when matings are frequent. Males court, consort and mate, but there the honeymoon ends: they leave and take no part in cub rearing.

Gestation lasts around 100 days. Between one and six (average three) young are dropped in solitary retreats such as rock crevices and caves. At birth the cubs are blind and do not emerge from their birthplace to follow the female until they are six to eight weeks old. Young are weaned after three months and independent after two years.

Most small to medium herbivores, large birds, rodents and primates, as well as smaller carnivores, such as servals and jackals are fair game to leopards.

Leopards use mainly stealth and surprise to capture their prey. Like cheetahs and lions, they are stalkers, but their tree climbing habit adds a third dimension to their hunts: it is a common tactic to leap out of trees onto prey. If the prey is not secured after a rush of a few metres, it invariably gets away. Long chases are avoided.

Out on a limb: leopard and its kill are far away from unwelcome intruders.

LARGE AND MEDIUM MAMMALS

CHEETAH

Cheetahs (*Acinonyx jubatus*) are lean, muscular cats, approximately 40 to 60 kilograms (90 to 130 pounds) in weight. They have spotted coats and a "tear stripe" running from eye to cheek. Their silhouette is long and lanky. Unlike the rest of the cat family, cheetahs do not have retractable claws.

You have a reasonable chance of observing cheetahs in Tanzania's Serengeti and Kenya's Amboseli, Maasai Mara and Nairobi National Parks. They are most common

females with dependent offspring. Young animals which have just left their mother tend to stay together for a time and males sometimes band together temporarily to defend a territory.

Males and females only socialize whilst the female is on heat. They select breeding areas that have a reasonable number of gazelles, with good hiding places for cubs, perennial water and relatively low densities of possible cub predators. Males congregate in these areas which allows them to mate

in savannah parks and wherever there are sufficient stocks of their preferred prey — species such as Thomson's gazelles. They are the most endangered of the three large cats perhaps because, unlike leopards, they are unable to adapt easily to the changes wrought to their habitat by man, who is gradually forcing them into marginal areas.

Cheetahs are diurnal animals with activity peaks at dawn. In game parks where they are hassled by tourist cars, they have taken to hunting during the heat of the day, at noon when tourists return to the lodges for lunch.

Cheetahs are generally silent, solitary animals except for consorting pairs and

with local females.

Born to run: After a gestation period of three months cheetah cubs are born blind, naked and helpless. Litter size varies from one to eight (usually three) cubs. Females hide them away for two to three weeks in dens, often in dense vegetation or among rocks on kopjes. Mothers hunt for food leaving the cubs in hiding, periodically returning to suckle them. Every few days she moves her litter between dens. Although adults are not very vulnerable to predators, cheetah cubs are preyed on by hyaenas and other big cats, including lions and leopards.

Cubs may be born at any time of year, but

there is a peak which coincides with the appearance of gazelle fawns, which are easy prey for females. In the Serengeti most litters are born between January and April, coinciding with the long rains.

At five to six weeks cubs venture out after their mother to join her at kills. This in an important period for cubs since, unlike all other cats, young cheetahs do not know instinctively how to stalk, chase, catch and kill their prey. A cheetah cub, presented with, say, a mouse for the first time, will stare stupidly at it, or perhaps even run away. A young leopard or serval cat, in contrast, will pounce on the mouse without hesistation. So cheetah mothers must bring dazed or half-

wildebeest, especially calves which are often taken during the mass calving on the Serengeti plains.

They select the least vigilant animal on the edge of the group as victim. Although cheetahs are the fastest land mammal, they cannot maintain their top speed of 95 kph (56 mph) for more than 200 to 300 metres (200 to 300 yards) so unless they can get undetected to within about 30 metres of the prey, before starting their chase, they are rarely successful.

In a typical kill cheetahs use their forefeet to knock the running animal off balance then clamp tightly on to its neck to strangle it. The dead prey is invariably dragged into cover

dead young gazelles or hares to their offspring and take them patiently through the process of being a hunter. Not surprisingly, many young cheetahs that have recently left their mothers do not have much chance of survival.

Cheetahs prey on relatively small animals such as Thomson's gazelles, relying on sight to locate, stalk and initiate pursuits. Groups of males can take on larger animals such as

**Left, the epitome of speed, power and grace.
Above, youngsters at rest.**

where the cheetahs will feed. Females will call their cubs to the kill with a soft, bird-like chirrup. Adults will only hunt about four days after a successful kill.

GIRAFFES

Giraffes (genus *Artiodactyla*) have three subspecies: Maasai (*Giraffa camelopardalis tippelskirchi*), reticulated (*Giraffa reticulata*), and Rothschild's giraffe (*Giraffa camelopardalis rothschildi*). These subspecies differ only in their blotch pattern, and their distribution. All other characteristics are the same. The pattern of their coats is fixed for life, making it possible for human observers to distinguish one animal from another. Animals tend to get darker with age. It is not easy to distinguish males from females although males tend to be a little bigger and seem to spend more time feeding from tree canopies than females, which prefer to feed on low-lying vegetation.

Giraffes have very long necks which curiously have only seven bones, no more than the necks of any other animals although giraffe vertebrae are elongated. Both sexes are born with horns which are covered by skin and topped with black hair.

Giraffes weigh up to 1,000 kilograms (2,200 pounds). They have a high centre of gravity and this together with their weight, may account for their strange gait. Walking is almost a "pace": both legs on one side appear to move at the same time making it look as if the giraffe is rolling. When galloping, the hindlegs swing forward together to plant in front of the forefeet. Giraffes can reach a maximum speed of 60 kph (37 mph).

They inhabit open woodland and wooded grassland. They may also be seen in bushed grassland and occasionally at a forest edge. Giraffes often frequent drainage line vegetation in the dry season. Riparian thickets are the only place you are likely to see them in dense vegetation.

Giraffes are diurnal, but also move about at night. They sometimes utter snorts and grunts, but are normally silent animals. Often the only noise to be heard when giraffes move by is the click of their hooves when the foot is lifted clear of the ground as weight is removed from them.

These long-legged animals have few enemies. They are most vulnerable when drinking when they splay their front legs and lower their heads often in the vicinity of thick, waterside vegetation. Animals will only drink after carefully looking around. Young animals may be taken by lions if the adults are not around. Females will defend their young against any attacker by kicking with their front legs. The mortality rate up to the age of three is about 8 percent—which is not so different from the 3 percent adult average.

Giraffes are not much hunted by man. They only rarely raid local maize farms and their feeding habits make them almost impervious to drought. This might be the reason why, as other wildlife species continue to disappear, the giraffe seems to have become the only remnant of a formerly impressive wildlife array.

The social group: The individual is the basic social unit in giraffe society. Animals are loosely gregarious, with a usual group size of between two and 12 (usually six or less). The composition of herds changes constantly as adults come and go. The home range of a female may be 120 square kilometres (48 square miles) but they spend most of their time in the central part of this range where they feed. Dominant males wander in and out of female home ranges.

Fights between dominant males are rarely seen. When they approach each other, they

frequently adopt a threat posture—"standing tall". This is normally enough to persuade the less dominant male to leave. Serious fighting occurs only when the fixed dominance hierarchy breaks down, for example, when a new nomadic male comes into the neighbourhood.

A ritualized form of fighting, known as "necking", is carried out by young males, normally between three and four years old. The animals intertwine necks, often accompanied by light blows with the head. The "winner" of the bout often climbs on the back of the "loser". This frequently leads the observer to the erroneous conclusion that necking is a courtship ritual.

Giraffes breed all year round. Females reach maturity at five years, males only at eight. Dominant males patrol the home range looking for females that come into heat. Males test females by smelling their vulvas or sampling their urine to see if they are receptive. If a dominant male finds a female in oestrus he will displace lesser males and consort with her until mating.

During their lifespan, females may have up to 12 calves weighing approximately 100 kilograms (220 pounds) each at birth. Calves are usually two metres (six feet) high. Twins are very rare. Births normally occur in a calving ground. This might lead to the for-

cias. All parts are taken—leaves, buds, shoots, fruits. Very infrequently, grass, forbs and creepers are eaten. Acacia fodder is harvested in a couple of different ways depending on the strength of the thorns: young, flexible thorns are flattened and the leaves stripped off with a sideways sweep: older, more robust thorns may also be flattened, engulfed in mucous and swallowed along with the branch. Very woody branches may simply be nibbled at selectively. The lips are used as agilely as the tongue.

The black tongue is long, 45 centimetres (18 inches), and mobile enough to curl around branch tips. Giraffe saliva is especially thick and viscous which undoubtedly

mation of "creches" in which the unweaned calves spend most of the day together on their own.

Feeding occurs generally between six and nine in the morning and three to six in the afternoon. Giraffes are ruminants and spend a good portion of the day resting and chewing the cud. They are exclusively browsers, with 95 percent of their feeding confined to the foliage of bushes and trees, mainly aca-

helps in dealing with thorny branches.

Normally, giraffes drink once a week, taking up 30 to 50 litres (63 to 105 pints) at a go. If vegetation is particularly dry, they may need to drink every two days.

ZEBRA

Zebra in *Swahili* means "striped donkeys". There is quite a controversy about the functions of the stripes but the general opinion is that they serve as a form of visual antipredator device, either as a camouflage or to break up form when seen from a distance.

Two species are found in Kenya: Grevy's (*Equus grevyi*) and Burchell's zebra (*Equus*

Left, **Maasai giraffe necking in the woods.**
Above, **reticulated giraffe amongst the acacias in Samburu.**

Burchelli) Grevy's zebras are only found in northern Kenya. There are still about 10,000 left, but their numbers are rapidly disappearing due to hunting by man for their skins. They have narrower stripes and larger ears than Burchell's zebra. Burchell's or common zebras are found throughout East and Central Africa. There are more than 100,000 in the Serengeti alone.

Zebras are animals of open and wooded grasslands and are never far from perennial water. Grevy's inhabit more arid areas and are much more drought-resistant than Burchell's, which is rarely found far from a source.

They are active round the clock but will males wander off with bachelor groups.

Burchell's zebra live in groups with permanent membership: there is a lead stallion and a number of females with their offspring. The Serengeti groups get together and participate in the great migrations of East and Central Africa when the range begins to deteriorate in the dry season.

Grevy's zebra have temporary associations that rarely last more than a few months. Territorial males defend large territories during the breeding season and attempt to keep female groups within their boundaries. Outside the breeding season, they mix with other male groups.

Breeding in both species is linked to the

look for shade at midday, resting periodically at night. Zebras make a typical horse-like neighing sound.

Among their enemies are lions, hunting dogs, spotted hyaenas, and, of course, man. A common response to alarm is bunching. Zebra stallions are fierce fighters and kick back with great ferocity. Mares are as brave as stallions when their foals are involved.

The basic zebra social unit is a more or less permanent group of females with young looked after by a dominant stallion. The tightest social bond is naturally between mare and foal. Young females stay with the family group: as they approach maturity

rains. Sexual maturity in males occurs at about one to two years but social maturity—the ability to take and defend a territory or female herd—does not come until about six years. Courtship is followed by repeat matings at one or two hour intervals over two days. Gestation takes around a year.

Young independence: Young foals are surprisingly independent, even at one month old. They may be left alone whilst the mare grazes hundreds of metres away or walks several kilometres to water. Animals up to about the age of six months are reddish-brown rather than black.

Zebras have evolved stomachs which allow them to feed on coarse, stemmy grass largely passed over by other members of the grazing community. This enables them to survive when other grazers cannot.

HIPPOPOTAMUS

Hippos (*Hippopotamus amphibius*) are the second largest terrestrial mammals, weighing up to 2,000 kilograms (4,400 pounds), with barrel shaped bodies and short legs. Their heads are adapted for life in water with eyes, ears and nose all on the upper side. Hippo jaws can open up to 150 degrees wide, which makes a very impressive sight when this is all that can be seen of the semi-submerged animal.

totally or partially submerged, floating beneath the surface and bouncing from the bottom to come up to breath every few minutes. Dives generally last less than five minutes but can be as long as 15. Hippos come out of the water only at night to feed on the shore.

They have a variety of vocalizations, among them the dominant male's: "MUH-Muh-muh"; bellows and roars when fighting; a high-pitched "neighing" when attacked and a sort of snort when submerged.

Man is the hippo's only real threat although a pride of lions will attack a solitary hippo on land, and crocodiles undoubtedly take the occasional baby hippo in the water.

Hippos live in still or slow-running water with frequent bends in the shoreline and deep pools with shallow sided banks, in the midst of open wooded or bushed grassland. The preferred water temperature is 18 C to 35 C (64 F to 95 F) and they have been seen along the sea coast. In the rainy season, males may take up temporary residence in seasonal water holes.

Hippos spend the whole day in water,

Left, Grevy's zebra have slimmer stripes and larger ears. **Above**, the more commonly seen Burchell's zebra.

Females defend their young by making use of their long tusks (canines).

Despite their benign look, hippos account annually for more wildlife-induced human deaths than any other animal, including lions and snakes. They specialize in capsizing boats which get too near, either drowning or biting the people inside. Hippos are also dangerous on land since they will run over anybody standing in their way to the water.

Gregarious groups: Hippos are gregarious and territorial. Group size averages 10 to 15 females with young, led by one dominant male. When water resources become scarce during droughts, groups of 150 have been observed. Dominant males space themselves out along the lake shore or river course advertising their dominance with the familiar "MUH-Muh-muh" call. Sexually mature males are kept on the edges of the group with threats and fights until, at eight to 10 years old, they feel strong enough to take on a territory holder. As the flow of river changes with seasons, territories may break down. In more stable lakes, territories may persist for years.

Hippos have a curious habit of spraying their dung around a two metre radius by rapidly whirling their stubby tails as they defecate. Defecation spots are communal and it is thought that there are used as a

season they may walk up to 10 kilometres (six miles) inland in search of food. Their half-metre wide lips allow them to eat very short grass. Fallen fruits, like water plants, are rarely taken.

The total amount of food taken by an adult hippo is less then that ingested by other cloven hoofed animals (only 1 to 1.5 percent compared with 2.5 percent of body weight). This is only possible because of the hippo's undemanding life-style: floating around the pool all day does not take much effort.

PIGS

African pigs (*Suidae*) are medium-sized herbivores with compact bodies, large heads

display to other hippos.

Courtship and mating occurs in the water. In theory, territorial males have exclusive mating rights, but they are continuously challenged by other males. Fights are common, leaving animals visibly scarred along their back and flanks.

Females give birth in shallow water, suckling occurs on land or in ankle-deep water and lasts for eight months.

Hippos are grazers and feed at night, coming out of the water along well-worn trails. They do not feed on aquatic vegetation. During the rainy season when grass is abundant they feed near the shore. In the dry

and short necks. They have coarse, bristly coats, small eyes, long ears, prominent snouts and tusks (elongated lower canines). The flattened face and broad snout, ending in the characteristic, naked pig nose, are related to both the search for food and fighting style. Despite their heavy bodies, pigs can swim and they are agile and quick. All male pigs are larger than females and have larger tusks and warts. Sight is, in general, the poorest of the pig senses.

A number of pigs can be found in East Africa, among them: giant forest hog (*Hylochoerus meinertzhageni*) covered with shaggy, dark, coarse hair; bushpig (*Potamo-*

choerus porcus) and red river hog members of the same species, varying in coat colour from reddish-brown in the forests to blackish-brown in the drier bushland, and warthogs (*Phacochoerus aethiopicus*) which are less hairy, but covered with sparse bristles with hairs along the neck and back that can be raised like a crest and serve as a signal during social interactions.

Pigs can be found in a series of different habitats ranging from grassland to bushed grassland (warthog), bushland to dry forest (bushpig), to moist evergreen forest (giant forest hog).

The warthog is an accomplished and compulsive digger and may dig its own

pressed with porcine squeals.

The most important pig predators are lions and cheetahs. The largely nocturnal forest hog is susceptible to leopards. Pigs will defend themselves from predators by using their lower tusks (canines) which are pointed and very sharp. Nevertheless, their main line of defence is retreat at speed, usually towards the nearest hole.

Bushpigs are often very destructive to local agriculture. Warthogs live in a more pastoral setting and therefore do not cause much damage to agriculture.

Pig society: The main social group consists of temporary female-young bonds and more lasting female-female associations.

burrow using its forefeet. Most other pigs seem to modify existing holes for their burrows. Bushpigs do not live in burrows.

All pigs are diurnal, except the forest hog which is mainly nocturnal.

Continuous, soft grunting serves as a contact sound to keep members of a foraging family group together. Tooth-grinding may be heard when the animal is aroused, presumably angry. Alarm and distress are ex-

Such associations account for the joining up of litters. There is no herd boar in a functional sense, although an adult male is usually attendant. Although not very territorial, males mark their 10- to 20-square-kilometre (four- to eight-square-mile) home ranges with secretions from lip glands, pre-orbital glands (warthog) or foot glands (bushpig) by rubbing them against tree trunks and stumps. Pigs are frequently seen rubbing their necks and spreading their saliva with their faces.

Greetings are mostly a matter of sniffing: nose to nose, to mouth, to pre-orbital region or rear end. They sniff the ground in places where another animal has stepped, presuma-

Left, hippos spend all day in the water. **Above**, amorous warthogs.

bly to taste the gland secretion. This may lead to a friendly greeting.

Pigs are rapid breeders. Females are able to conceive at the age of 18 months, and the size of their litter can be as many as a dozen young either born in a grass "nest" constructed by the sow or, more commonly, in a borrowed aardvark hole. Males, meanwhile, mature at nearly three years. This may explain why breeding males usually ignore fully grown yearlings.

As there is no marked male dominance among the pigs, conflicts between males are fierce when associated with a female in season. The strongest pig is the one that will mate. Fighting between male bushpigs may

come too close together. As farrowing approaches, pregnant sows may become more solitary and quick-tempered, engaging in male-like head-on encounters.

Females farrow in burrows. The piglets develop rapidly and can leave the burrow and begin to eat grass after only one week. However, they suckle for as long as four months. Suckling is generally done while the sow is standing, although she has to lie down in the burrow.

The previous young may try to rejoin their newly-farrowed mother but will be roundly chased off. This is a vulnerable time for yearling males since they have problems finding burrows to share with adults of either

involve upraised snouts and tusks slapped from side to side, accompanied by whirling around. Side blows may be followed up by biting. It seems that hierarchy is based on tusk length; if a tusks breaks, as frequently happens, then the pig loses status.

The male warthog's threat display is characterized by stiff-legged strutting, an erect mane and tail and head and shoulders raised with the snout pointed downwards and towards the opponent to present the tusks to full advantage.

Female fights are seen less commonly than male encounters and consist of rushes and display if two family groups happen to

sex: mortality from predation is correspondingly high. If, however, the female fails to conceive, then the young will stay with her until she conceives the next time.

Shared burrows are uncommon, especially for farrowing and only occasionally occurs with first-time breeders. Males and females take up companionship again after farrowing, to culminate in mating the next season.

African wild pigs are basically vegetarians. They eat a wide range of plants, grasses, forbs, ferns, fungi and consume almost any part of the plant. Small vertebrates and invertebrates are also eaten when found. All pigs are dependent on water and will always be found near a source.

The manner in which different species search for food is largely dictated by habitat. Warthogs are the most specialized feeders and eat mainly grass. While feeding, they walk from tuft to tuft, or move slowly forward in a characteristic "kneeling" or "bowing" posture, by lowering their short-necked front end and settling on their fore carpals. Tusks are used only occasionally to root out food: most digging is done with the rough upper and leading edge of the nose.

Bushpigs spend more time rooting by digging with the nose. It can dig several centimetres deeper than warthogs by taking

There are four distinct families or sub-families of smaller plains predators: hyaenas; the dog family (*Canidae*), broken down into African wild dogs and others such as jackals and foxes; and small cats.

HYAENAS

There are two distinct species of hyaena in East Africa: spotted hyaena (*Crocuta crocuta*) and striped hyaena (*Hyaena hyaena*).

Spotted hyaenas have powerful forelegs and shoulders, long necks and heavily built skulls with formidable teeth. Ears are round and the coat is spotted. Young hyaenas have darker spots then adults which appear almost

full advantage of its more flexible snout. Giant forest hogs feed mainly in grassy forest clearings where they eat mainly grass. In the forest, however, they like to eat a variety of herbs and plant parts. They rarely root with their snouts like other pigs. The combined length of their head and neck allows them to reach the grass sward usually without kneeling.

Left, sinister grin of the spotted hyaena. **Above**, one hyaena pack feeds while another waits its turn.

spotless.

Striped hyaenas share the powerfully-built shoulders and head, but they have longer legs and the forefeet are much larger than the hindfeet. They have a crest of hair running down the back to a very bushy tail. Their ears are more pointed. The body is light coloured, with the outer surface of the legs striped boldly. Senses are very well developed in both species.

Spotted hyaenas are more widespread than striped hyaenas. They are found in dry acacia bushland, open plains and rocky country where there is abundant wildlife. They are not common in heavily wooded country or in forests. They can live at high altitudes, up to 4,000 metres (13,200 feet).

Striped hyaenas inhabit the drier parts of East Africa. They have been found in deserts in areas where water is not available. for many miles.

Both species are very vocal. The characteristic "whoop whoop" howl can be heard throughout the African night. When fighting, they issue a hoarse "ahh ahh" sound. When excited, the hyaenas' uneven-pitched howl is eerily reminiscent of the laughetr of a demented soul. Man and lions are the hyaenas' prime enemies.

Spotted hyaenas are usually seen alone or in pairs, but in areas of concentration of number of males, of which one eventually mates with her. Young are born in dens shared by several females. After a gestation period of three to four months, one to three (usually two) cubs are born. Food is not carried to the den, so the young hyaenas depend entirely on their mother's milk for approximately eight months and are only weaned at 12 to 16 months when they can feed by themselves.

Striped hyaena females form a temporary bond with the male with which they have most recently mated. Gestation is three months and one to six (normally two to four) cubs are born in dens. Both parents will bring food to the cubs.

available prey they may form temporary or even permanent groups which share, patrol and defend a hunting territory against other clans.

Spotted hyaenas are not individually territorial. They make and break bonds with other hyaenas very easily. Once a group has been formed hyaenas become territorial.

The family: Striped hyaenas are basically solitary, forming a pair during the breeding season. Both parents help to rear the young and a family unit may be formed once young are mobile. Striped hyaenas occasionally congregate at a kill but do not form groups.

When in season spotted hyaenas attract a

Both species are opportunistic hunters and scavengers, taking advantage of wastes left by other animals or man. Hyaenas in general will take weaker or sick animals in preference to healthy ones. Spotted hyaenas show a primitive form of cooperative hunting which is generally more successful and is better able to resist the consequences of a counter attack by another wildebeest, for example. Both species will eat the dead of almost any mammal, bird, reptile, fish, irrespective of size or species. Striped hyaenas are more omnivorous than spotted hyaenas. Insects, birds, reptiles and fruit seem to be their main diet.

CANIDAE: AFRICAN WILD DOG

African wild dogs (*Lycaon pictus*), also called hunting dogs, are medium-sized carnivores. Adults are approximately the size of a labrador dog but are slimmer and light for their size, weighing an average of 25 kilograms (55 pounds).

Wild dogs have brindled coats of brown, black, yellow and white. They all have similar black face masks and white-tipped tails. The rest of the pattern is distinct for each dog. Large, rounded ears allow dogs to hear over long distances. They have very sharp shearing teeth.

Wild dogs are typically found in savannah grassland and woodland. They have also

Lions generally ignore wild dogs but will feed on the dog's kills after chasing them off.

Packs consist of a dominant breeding pair, five to six other adults and dependent young. With litters averaging 10, and bitches capable of producing 16 puppies, packs can build up to number as many as 50. Young females emigrate at between 18 months and three years of age: young males normally remain in their natal pack.

Like their hunting behaviour, the breeding system of wild dogs is an example of remarkable cooperation. In each pack only the dominant pair breeds: the other dogs help to rear their offspring. This is for the good of the pack since all dogs are related but only the

been seen at altitudes of 5,600 metres (18,480 feet) in the snow of Kilimanjaro or in the heat of deserts. They are most active in the early morning and evening and lie in shade during the day.

Wild dogs are surprisingly vocal. A bird-like yittering is often heard when the dogs greet one another. Alarmed dogs will bark: distressed puppies occasionally give a squeaky hoo-call.

Left, wild dogs crowd round a kill. **Above**, grooming time for these silver-backed jackals.

strongest genes are passed on. Breeding coincides with the rains.

Gestation lasts approximately 10 weeks and the dominant female whelps in a den. For the first fortnight the female suckles the litter, spending long periods underground with them. After two weeks in the den, puppies make their first unsteady forays outside and begin to feed on meat regurgitated to them by all the pack members. Within a month or so, they are feeding on meat alone.

Wild dogs kill a wide range of animals but specialize on small to medium-sized antelopes such as Thomson's gazelles and wildebeest. In bushed and wooded habitats their preferred prey are impalas. Such ungulates represent the vast majority of their kills, although they opportunistically snap up gazelle fawns, hares, hatchlings and other small prey they chance across. Antelopes as large as eland are only rarely taken.

Packs normally hunt once a day—more often if the group is large or there are puppies to be fed. Prey size also influences the number of hunts: a wildebeest will obviously satisfy more dogs than a gazelle.

CANIDAE: JACKALS AND FOXES

This group comprises smaller, dog-like carnivores: *jackals*—side-striped *(Canus*

from grasslands to semi deserts.

Small *Canidae* are active 24 hours a day; their tendency to be active at night is reinforced by human persecution.

All are vocal to a degree: black-backed jackals yapping is a familiar sound on the plains.

They are prey to larger carnivores and to rock python and large birds of prey, such as martial eagles. Alertness and quickness are their main defences.

They are very sociable animals. The basic social unit is a pair—either permanent or for a few seasons. Occasionally they pair up with the young of that year or with some of the previous year's offspring. Several breed-

adustus), golden *(C. aureus)* and black-backed or silver-backed *(C. mesomelas)*—and the relatively common bat-eared fox *(Otocyon megalotis).*

All of them have a striking similarity with domestic dogs in the way they move, lift their legs, raise their hackles, scratch, bury food and roll in something rotten. The senses of *Canidae* are all very well developed.

Small *Canidae* are fairly common and may occur in densities of around 10 per square kilometre (a third of a square mile).

Jackals frequent open wooded and bushed grassland. Golden jackal and the bat-eared foxes prefer more open and arid habitats,

ing and non-breeding adults form more or less permanent social groups within a home range, but essentially a pair marks and may defend a small territory which includes one or more subterranean dens.

Pair formation begins with consorting and mutual grooming some months before actual mating. Behavioural observations indicate that pairs tend to persist beyond one season, at least six years in the black backed jackal, and probably longer. Bat-eared foxes, for example, pair for life.

The young are born helpless, just like dog puppies, and will stay in the safety of the burrow, suckled by the mother. When they emerge from the den, they are still suckled and begin to be fed on regurgitated food by adults.

"Nannies": Black-backed jackals, golden jackals and probably the other species, have non-breeding "helpers", usually the young of previous seasons, which assist in care of the current young. This ensures a higher rate of survival of the pups.

Although perhaps not as sophisticated as with lions, hyaenas and wild dogs, cooperative hunting is important in jackals. In general, jackals and foxes are opportunistic carnivores. They will feed on almost anything they can catch or unearth—small vertebrates, invertebrates of any size, young animals, eggs, carrion, even some fruits. Only bat-eared foxes show a tendency to some specialization: 80 percent of their diet is insects, mainly *Hodotermes* termites.

Scavenging is one of the main elements of the jackals' search for food. As many as 30 jackals can be seen, often along with vultures, at the fringes of a lion or hyaena kill, waiting for a chance to dash in and grab a piece of meat from the carcass.

SMALL CATS

This group of the cat family *(Felidae)* includes a number of small cats which are relatively common but infrequently seen. These include: wild cat *(F. s. lybica)*, sand cat *(F. margarita)*, caracal *(Caracal caracal)* and serval *(Leptailurus serval)*.

Their sizes vary from the two- to three-kilogram (four- to six-pound) sand cat to the 15-plus kilogram (over 33 pounds) serval and caracal. In general, cats do not have a very good sense of smell, but their hearing is excellent and keenly directional; eyesight is acute in dim light. All species have retractable claws.

Small cats are generally found in all habitats with perennial water. Only caracal range in semi arid country to the edge of deserts. All species are active during the night or early hours of the evening and morning.

As with domestic cats, small wild cats communicate with a number of variations on the "meow" theme. They snarl and spit when

warning and purr when content. Servals have a characteristic little bark when calling to conspecifics.

Their main enemies are large raptors and other big predators. Their basic defence is alertness and avoiding open areas in which large birds of prey can fly.

All small cats are solitary except for short periods of consorting with a mate and during suckling and weaning of young. Individuals have a hunting range of 1.5 to three square kilometres. Males are territorial to other males within their range but permit females to wander in the territories unhindered.

Small cats are overwhelmingly carnivorous. Small living prey is stalked, pounced

upon, hooked with extended claws, and then killed. Killing techniques depend on the size of the prey: very small animals—insects, lizards, mice—are simply bitten to death or squeezed in the jaws until suffocated. Larger animals—rats, hyraxes, large birds—are characteristically killed with a prolonged bite to the nape of the neck, which effectively breaks it and eventually severs the spinal cord.

Caracal, serval and other large cats are able to bring down large birds, such as bustards, and the kids of gazelles and other small antelopes.

In some cases wild cats take domestic

Left, the hard-to-spot serval cat. **Above**, Ethiopia's equally elusive Simien fox.

stock. It rarely becomes a habit, however, and such small depredations are more than offset by their importance in controlling rodent pests.

PLAINS GRAZERS

The open and wooded grasslands and bushlands of East and Central Africa support the most splendid variety of small, medium and large herbivores in the world. All are members of the family *Bovidae* to which our domestic livestock also belong. "Small" in this context means about the size of a large dog, "medium" means about the size of a pony; "large" means like a small horse; "very large herbivores" are the really big

whitish underneath, and a white rump. Males are larger than females, have better developed S-shaped horns, a black-white blaze on their flanks, and a black-tipped, constantly wagging tail. The main species are Grant's gazelle (*Gazella granti*), Soemmering's gazelle (*G. soemmerringi*), Thomson's gazelle (*G. thomsoni*), Dorcas gazelle (*G. dorcas*), gerenuk (*Litocranius walleri*), dibatag or Clarke's gazelle, (*Ammodorcas clarkei*), and the springbok (*Antidorcas marsupialis*). Dibatag and gerenuk differ from the rest in having conspicuously long, slender necks.

Hippotraginae include the medium to large, thick necked, "horse-like" antelopes

ones, like elephants, buffalos and giraffe.

Alcelaphines are long-faced, rather foolish looking, medium sized antelopes with S-shaped, ridged horns and sloping backs. They include the spectacular Serengeti migrating wildebeest or gnu (*Connochaetes taurinus*), hartebeest or kongoni (*Alcelaphus buselaphus*), topi or tiang (*Damaliscus lunatus*), hirole or Hunter's hartebeest (*Beatragus hunterii*) and impala or swara (*Aepyceros melampus*).

There are some 20 species and subspecies of gazelles in the *Antilopini* family. All have the same general appearance with slender bodies, long legs, fawn-colouration on top,

that sport impressively long, swept-back or straight horns. They include: roan (*Hippotragus equinus*), sable (*H. niger*), oryx (*Oryx gazella*) and the virtually extinct addax (*Addax nasomaculatus*). The broad chested *Hippotraginae* run with powerful, sure-footed strides, hence the name "Horse-like antelopes". Roan's Latin name belabours the point: "horse-like horned horse".

Reduncinae are medium-sized antelopes whose males have somewhat lyre-shaped horns. Their coats are usually coarse, brown to reddish-brown to beige, usually with a white chevron at the throat. This group includes the waterbuck (*Kobus ellip-*

siprymnus), kob (*K. kob*) and reedbucks (*Redunca spp.*) . They range in bulk from heavy set waterbucks to spritely reedbucks. Waterbuck horns have a smooth, open sweep; those of reedbucks are shorter, forward pointing at the tips; and those of kobs have the classical impala-like lyre shape.

Tragelaphinae are medium to large, slender, round-backed, longish-necked antelopes, russet to grey-brown in colour, often with vertical white stripes or a line of dots on their sides and flanks. Males in particular have well-developed spiralling horns, and are larger and often darker or greyer than the females. The only real plains grazer is the eland (*Taurotragus oryx*). Sitatungas (*T.*

(*Neotraginae*), including dikdiks (genus *Madoqua*), steinbok, oribi (*Ourebia ourebi*) and klipspringer (*Oreotragus oreotragus*). They look more or less similar and are all less than 80 centimetres (31 inches) high; they inhabit areas of dense cover, are territorial and live in very small groups centred around life-long pairs; all mark their territories with secretions from conspicuous glands in front of their eyes. Their short-necked, arched back body frame assists in rapid movement through thick bush. Steinbok and oribis which inhabit open grasslands have a more upright posture, as do klipspringer which must balance upright as they spring from rock to rock. Males have horns; females are

spekei) live in a very restricted habitat in the swamps and have evolved long, splayed hooves to assist in walking over mud and boggy vegetation. All *Tragelaphinae* have a delicate, high-stepping gait, even the two-metre- (six-foot-) high eland.

The relatively smaller, round-backed, dainty antelopes are members of *Bovidae* in the subfamily *Antelopinae*. Among them are duikers (*Cephalophinae*); dwarf antelopes

Left, chaotic annual migration scene. **Above**, distinctive facial markings and straight horns of the oryx.

either hornless or have weak and poorly formed horns.

Habitats: Antelopes live in nearly all East African habitats. Where man has not extensively broken the soil wild herbivores can be seen. Wildebeest and their *Alcelaphine* relatives favour open and wooded grassland; bushland and thickets are generally avoided where grass growth is relatively weak and there is more cover for predators. Impalas, however, prefer woodlands, riverine strips and zones between vegetation types (transition zones). Gazelles have adapted to a wide range of habitats, from arid to semi arid country in the case of gerenuk and some

Grant's subspecies, to Thomson's gazelles which prefer better watered grassland. Roan and sable inhabit grasslands with good bush and tree cover and they both frequent well-watered grasslands and wooded valleys. In contrast, oryx prefer very arid habitat and can live in near-desert conditions.

All species of *Redundinae* antelopes prefer wetlands or tall, tussocky, marshy grasslands. Even hillside-living reedbuck are also associated with wet grasslands and hill marshes. Lechwes are almost semi-aquatic, and spend most of their time in marshes, swamps and inundated grasslands.

In general, *Tragelaphinae* live at low densities in arid to sub-humid areas, in re-

the cooler mornings and evening for feeding. Except for impala and some of the very small antelopes, most breed in a very narrow period, usually dropping the calves just before the rains.

They rely on alertness and flight to escape their enemies—big predators such as lions, leopards, cheetah, hunting dogs, hyaenas.

An eland group is usually made up of a few females and young with an adult male in attendance. This male is the one that will eventually mate with the group's females. Females reach sexual maturity at three years. Males are loosely territorial. During conception peaks, small groups aggregate into big groups of hundreds of elands which can

gions of thick cover, such as forest (bushbuck, bongo), bushland (bushbuck, lesser kudu, nyala) and hill thickets (greater kudu, mountain nyala). The two notable exceptions are elands which frequent open grasslands often roaming as high as 4,500 metres (14,850 feet), and the long-hoofed sitatunga, which splashes around in swamps and marshy lakesides.

Very small antelopes exploit a wide range of habitats: forests (duikers, suni) to thickets (dikdik), on kopjes or rock outcrops (klipspringers) to open grasslands (steinbok, grysbok, oribi).

All species are diurnal, with preference for

move over great distances and can be considered to a certain extent migratory.

Steinbok and oribi are strongly territorial and pair for life. Their territories are small, about 50 to 500 metres (165 to 1,650 feet) in diameter. This small size allows territory holders to explore every bit of their turf so that they come to know of all the best bolt holes and special food plants. Sexual maturity is reached in less than a year and gestation is about six months, allowing two births per year.

Waterbuck, kob and reedbucks have small, loose associations of adult females and young, moving through a world of male dominated territories. Groups are rarely bigger then 10 to 15 animals.

Kobs exhibit a variation on the territorial theme. They establish a *lek* or territorial breeding ground, where a group of dominant males display and mate. Gestation is about nine months and a single calf is dropped.

Breeding season: Some male *Antelopinae* (gazelles) and *Alcelaphinae* (wildebeest, hartebeest, topis) are territorial during the breeding season. Males that have set up their territory try to prevent females from leaving. Females tend to move on when the grass supply is diminishing.

These herbivores are rarely seen alone, except for the occasional territorial male

nised, particularly in wildebeest, into a calving peak which lasts only a few weeks. This floods the predators' market and, even though they eat their fill, the percentage of calves that they can take is much smaller than if calving were spread throughout the year.

Hippostraginae (roan, sable and oryx) have a system of matriarchal hierarchy, resulting in small herds of five to 20 animals with varying degrees of male participation. In sables, female herds range over adjacent male territories: in roan, a single male accompanies the females; in oryx, male groups satellite female ones for most of the year. Only the dominant male in a group of oryx

wildebeest forlornly standing his ground outside the breeding season. Most herds are usually made up of less than 100 animals, with the exception of large, migratory populations of topi and wildebeest which may be seen during the migrations in tens of thousands. Their herds spread over the landscape, often without any apparent structure. Breeding is polygamous with one male fertilizing many females. Births are synchro-

mates.

Herbivores are of four basic types: those which mainly graze (wildebeest, hartebeest); those which graze very selectively, allowing the animal to take a higher plane of nutrition (steinbok, oribi, waterbuck, reedbuck, roan, sable and oryx); those which both graze and browse (topi, impala, eland, gazelles); and those which predominantly browse (gerenuk). The relative shapes of their mouths makes the distinction clear. All are ruminants, that is, they have several stomachs for fodder in varying stages of digestion and they reprocess already swallowed fodder by chewing the cud, like

Left, long-faced Coke's hartebeest in Tsavo West. **Above**, the "horse-like" roan antelope.

domestic cattle.

BUSHLAND AND FOREST ANTELOPES

These antelopes can best be divided into two separate groups, the medium to larger ones, known as *Tragelaphinae* (eland also belong to this group) and the dwarf and small antelopes.

Tragelaphinae are slender, round-backed, longish-necked antelopes, russet to grey-brown in colour, often with vertical white stripes or line of dots on their sides and flanks. They have short-cropped pelage and a delicate, high-stepping gait. An erectable crest occurs on the back of the bushbuck. Males have horns and their colour is often also vulnerable to smaller cats, such as servals, caracals, golden cats and other predators such as rock python and crocodile. When threatened, animals emit a sharp bark as an alarm. Most rely on flight for protection.

The basic groups are made up of females and immature animals, with an adult male in attendance. Group numbers vary from two to three in bushbucks reaching a maximum of about 10 to 15 in lesser kudus.

The onset of female sexual maturity is around 18 months. Males continue to grow beyond sexual maturity, so that the differences in body size between the sexes becomes gradually more striking.

darker or more grey.

Members of this group are: eland (*Taurotragus oryx*), bushbuck (*Tragelaphus scriptus*), lesser kudu (*T. imberbis*), nyalas (*Tragelaphus buxtoni*), greater kudu (*T. T. strepsiceros*), and bongo (*T. T. euryceros*).

They live at low densities in sub-humid areas, in regions of thick cover, such as forest (bongo), bushland (bushbuck, lesser kudu, nyala) and hill thickets (greater kudu, mountain nyala). They are all diurnal, although bushbucks will become nocturnal in areas of persecution.

All species are preyed upon by the obvious large carnivores and the smaller species are

A single calf is born after a gestation of about six months. Calves are weaned at about three to four months.

Tragelaphinae are very selective browsers and pluckers. This allows them to have a highly nutritious diet. Fruits, seeds, pods, flowers, bark and tubers are taken as well as leaves. All species take grasses, but not as a bulk food.

DWARF AND SMALL ANTELOPES

This group is made up of small, round-backed antelopes with short necks and conspicuously large ears—except dikdiks (genus *Madoqua*). It includes duikers (genus

Cephalophinae), dwarf antelopes (*genus Neotraginae*), beira (*Dorcotragus melanotis*) and klipspringers (*Oreotragus oreotragus*). The males have horns; females are either hornless or with very weak and variable horns. The smallest is a *Neotragine*, the royal antelope at a height of some 25 centimetres (10 inches); the largest is a *Cephalophine*, the yellow-backed duiker which may approach a height of 80 centimetres (31 inches). The rest, however, are 40 to 60 centimetres (15 to 23 inches) at the shoulder.

Females can be larger than their males by as much as 20 percent in height and weight. The relatively large size of the females may arise from the fact that these antelopes form

day with peaks in early morning and evening. Their voices, used principally as an alarm, are high-pitched "zick-zick" sounds (hence the name dikdik) or a tiny snort. Most other species have an alarm whistle.

Their enemies are all large predators, plus an array of medium and small predators, including cats, snakes, birds of prey, ratels and baboons. Their only defence is to take to flight.

All these animals pair for life and are very territorial. Territory sizes may vary from 50 to 500 metres (165 to 1,650 feet) in diameter, depending on season and local conditions. Such relatively small territories allows the animals to know precisely both the location

a permanent pair bond, meaning the male does not have to fight continually with others for a mate. Females also share in the defence of territory and greater size in territorial conflicts is an advantage.

They are found in forests (duikers, suni), in thickets (dikdik) or on *kopjes* or rock outcrops (dikdik together with klipspringers and rare beira).

Small antelopes are generally active all

and season of food plants, the best escape routes and the most effective hiding places.

Sexual maturity may be reached in less than a year: gestation is about six months. Two births a year are therefore possible, given a relatively constant food supply.

At less than two years old, the young animal will leave its parents' territory.

Dwarf and small antelopes are almost exclusively browsers and nibblers on fine-structured vegetation. They take the most nutritious plants and parts which provide a high plane of nutrition. They are not normally seen drinking: moisture comes mainly from food plants.

There are many groups of small mammals in a number of families, ranging from small carnivores, such as genets, to herbivores such as hyraxes, to monkeys. They can be grouped into classes according to similar characteristics.

WEASELS, ZORILLAS, RATELS AND OTTERS

These small, carnivorous mammals belong to the family *Mustelidae*, which includes African weasels, such as the African striped or white-naped weasel (*Poecilogale albinucha*), zorilla or African striped polecat (*Ictonyx striatus*), ratel or honey badger (*Mellivora capensis*), spotted-necked otter (*Lutra maculicollis*) and the cape clawless otter (*Aonyx capensis*). They have elongated, flattened bodies, powerful jaws and relatively large brains. Except for otters, all these mammals have a striking horizontal black and white pattern.

They inhabit woodland, bushland and grasslands and tend to use one or more dens (holes in the ground) as bases. Otters are rarely far from river banks. Weasels and zorilla are mainly nocturnal; ratels are active most times except noon; otters are diurnal.

In general *Mustelids* are quite vocal, especially when annoyed. Otters are very vocal and have a range of twitters and chirps which serve as contact calls.

Few other animals will attack them due to their repulsive anal gland secretion and, in the case of ratel, its ferociousness. Weasels may be at risk from large owls. Otters are taken by crocodiles and rock pythons; zorillas are often run over by cars.

Otters live in small family groups of less than 10. Not much is known about their breeding behaviour except that a pair may consort temporarily for several months during the breeding season. Gestation is presumed to be two months.

Mustelids take almost any living prey smaller than or equal to their own body size. The zorilla's diet has been measured to consist of nearly 50 percent insects, 25 percent small mammals and the rest made up of birds, amphibians, spiders and plant material. Rodents are the main item in the ratel's diet although it may catch small antelopes.

Otters feed mainly on aquatic food such as crabs, fish, frogs, molluscs and insects which they catch during dives of about one and a half minutes each.

GENETS, CIVETS AND MONGOOSES

These small mammals are low slung, long tailed, largely nocturnal carnivores, with a variety of striking spottings, stripings or conspicuous tails. All members of the group have large eyes, facing front, and outstanding night vision.

The family *Viverridae* contains three sub-families: mongooses (*Herpestinae*), the true civets and genets (*Viverrinae*), and the palm civet (*Paradoxurinae*). There are some dozen species of more or less solitary mongooses, a dozen genets, one African civet (*Civettictis civetta*), and one two-spotted or African palm civet (*Nandinia binotata*).

Their habitat stretches from forest edge to semi-desert. Genets and palm civet are semi

Left, a large-spotted genet in the Aberdares. **Above**, eyeing the greater galago.

arboreal; true civets and mongooses, with the exception of the slender mongoose, are more likely to seek refuge in crevasses, holes in the ground tree trunks and tree roots.

Genets, civets, and most mongooses are nocturnal, occasionally crepuscular. Both Egyptian and slender mongooses are active by day, in the evening and on moonlit nights. The marsh mongoose is largely diurnal.

Vocalisations are used for contact (genets: "uff-uff-uff"; civets: "tsa-tsa-tsa"), as well as for alarm, excitement or threat, when they growl, spit and hiss.

Their enemies include medium sized predators such as African wildcats and large owls. When threatened they rely on stealth

tree holes. They are weaned after two to three months and become independent after nine.

Viverrids are carnivorous, almost omnivorous. They are generally opportunistic feeders but also function as quick and efficient predators. Their diet includes all vertebrates and invertebrates up to the size of antelope calves and domestic cats (in the case of the African civet).

Social mongooses: This is the second major division of the *Viverridae* and includes two main social mongoose species: dwarf mongoose (*Helogale parvula*) and banded mongoose (*Mungos mungo*). They are grouped together because they share ecological characteristics and are highly social, unlike the

and early warning. Genets have very good eyesight, especially at dusk. If disturbed, they will take to the nearest tree.

Viverridae are generally solitary and only occasionally seen in pairs. (The exception is social mongooses). Their striking black and white markings on faces, body and tail are undoubtedly used in sexual and social signalling.

Breeding occurs throughout the year with some indication of seasonal peaks. Courtship and mating has been described as catlike. Genet matings last three to five minutes; gestation is some three and a half months and two or three young are born in

rest of the family *Viverridae*.

They are small, lively mammals, often seen moving in through the bush with weasel-like gait, pausing from time to time to stand upright and look around.

Both the dwarf mongoose and banded mongoose frequent wooded and bushed grassland; the latter prefer a somewhat more open habitat. The pack's home range includes a number of burrow sites, such as termite mounds or loosely aggregated rock piles which are used for night-time dens, as breeding sites and as lookouts.

Social mongooses are very vocal, and much communication significance is attached to their squeaks and twitters. Their main enemies are larger carnivores and birds of prey. Alertness, speed and the propensity to dive into nearby holes are their main defences.

Social mongooses occur in packs averaging around a dozen animals, but up to as many as 30 in the dwarf mongoose. Dwarf mongoose packs are led by a dominant female which is the oldest adult female of the group. She is normally the only one that conceives in a pack.

Both dwarf mongooses and banded mongooses synchronize their breeding within the pack which ensures that the season's brood can be fed and protected together. In

ing hoard.

Social mongooses eat virtually any small terrestrial living creature, both vertebrate and invertebrate, as well as eggs and occasionally fruits. Poisonous snakes are frequently killed by the pack.

AARDVARK

The aardvark (*Orycteropus afer*) or ant bear is a peculiar looking, nocturnal animal with a humped back and a long snout and tail. An adult's body may be 1.3 metres (4.6 feet) from snout to rump, with the tail adding another 60 centimetres (two feet). They can weigh up to 65 kilograms (143 pounds). Males and females are the same size but can

sub-humid regions, such as western Uganda, social mongooses are capable of producing four litters a year. Mongoose young are born underground.

Mongoose packs tend to change dens every few days. This has a dual function: it ensures that a particular predator cannot focus its attention on restricted areas and it allows the neighbourhood food supply to recover from the depredations of the ravenous hoard.

Left, the African civet out looking for a meal.
Above, dwarf mongooses are playful characters.

be distinguished by the female's slightly lighter colour. Local soil colour often masks their true yellowish grey. Since they are entirely nocturnal aardvarks are very difficult to see except when caught in the glare of car headlights. Then, they appear to be a light grey colour.

Aardvarks are accomplished diggers, and can completely bury themselves in less than 10 minutes. Their eyesight is poor, but their scent and hearing are very good. They inhabit open grassland, woodland and bushland but are rare in forests. When moving, they make a snorting grunt sound.

Aardvarks are relatively vulnerable to

predation from all large mammalian predators and rock pythons. They invariably escape by running into a hole.

Breeding appears to be timed so that young are born at the onset of the short rains in East Africa. One or two naked young are born in burrows which consist of several metre-long runs with living chambers at the end. Although aardvarks are basically solitary, only coming together to mate, several animals may sleep in one burrow. Most likely these are related: a female and nearly grown young or a courting pair.

Their staple diet is termites, either looped up from the ground with their long, sticky tongues, or dug out of the ground.

gland which is active during states of arousal. Hyrax feet are shod with rubbery pads which sweat when running. The tacky surface allows them to climb up near vertical rock faces or tree trunks. Hyraxes have rudimentary tails and numerous long, tactile hairs over their bodies.

They inhabit *kopjes* in bushed and wooded grassland, although cliffs and rock faces form the centre of the rock hyrax's home range, from where they graze on the grassland surrounding the *kopje*. Tree hyraxes live in evergreen forests.

Hyraxes are diurnal with the exception of a forest species of tree hyrax. At night they sleep together for safety and mutual warmth.

HYRAXES

Rock hyraxes (*Heterohyrax brucei*) are found in most of East Africa.

Unbelievable as it may seem at first glance, these rather dull looking, medium-small, brownish-grey mammals are the closest living relatives to elephants and dugongs (sea-cows).

Many hyrax characteristics are elephantine: toenail-like claws which are really hoofs; two teats between the forelegs and another four in a more anterior position; internal testicles, a long gestation period of seven months which is remarkable for such a small beast; and a somewhat mysterious

Territorial males may call on moonlit nights.

Their most dangerous predator is Verreaux's eagle, which feeds almost exclusively on hyraxes. Other large birds of prey, rock pythons, civet cats, and baboons are also a threat. At an alarm call—an unmistakable, high-pitched shriek emitted by any member of the group—all hyraxes of both species, dive for cover in rock clefts.

Society: Hyraxes are extremely social and gregarious. Social organisation seems to be dictated by the size of kopjes. On small kopjes, both species live in family groups rather like harems, with one adult male overseeing three to seven (up to 17 in the bush hyrax) adult females and a number of juveniles of both sexes. The male is usually old and large, intolerant of immigrating adult males, and prone to frequent, raucous territorial display calls. Dominant males chase subordinant ones away.

On larger kopjes groups of females move within overlapping circles around core areas, which are dominated by a territorial male and younger, peripheral males. The numbers of hyraxes on a kopje is determined by the number of sleeping holes and retreats from predators as well as the quality of the local food supply.

Breeding is year-round, with a slight preference for the rainy season. Females are

newly-matured males wander off.

Rock hyraxes eat mainly grass and other vegetation. Bush hyraxes are predominantly browsers. All species can eat, without apparent harm, many poisonous plants distasteful to other herbivores . They are rarely seen drinking and it is thought that most water is taken from leaf surfaces during feeding.

BABOONS

Baboons are the largest and most terrestrial of the *Cercopithecidae* family. They are heavy shouldered with rounded heads and protruding muzzles. Their arm bones are relatively longer than other *Cercopithecidae*. Their coat is shaggy and the colour

receptive once or twice a year and have a gestation period of seven or eight months. All females in a family group usually give birth within three weeks. Up to six (usually two to three) open-eyed young are born which are fully praecocial (capable of feeding themselves immediately) and able to run about as soon as they are dry. Sexual maturity in both sexes is around 18 months. Like elephants, females stay with the group:

Left, rabbit-sized rock hyraxes are related to elephants. **Above**, playtime for this baboon and its young.

varies from the yellow baboon's (*Papio cynocephalus*) light sandy yellow to the almost olive green of the olive baboon (*Papio anubis*). They have short tails.

There are five main species of baboon but only common baboons—*Cynocephalus*—are found in East Africa. Yellow baboons live in lowland areas of East and Central Africa: olive baboons prefer highland regions of East Africa.

Baboons can be seen virtually anywhere in grassland and wooded grassland where perennial water and adequate forage can be found. They are strictly diurnal and will sleep in trees at night.

They exhibit a wide vocal repertoire, from sharp barks in alarm or warning, to squeals and titterings when siblings play together, to screams as subordinate animals are chased off by superiors, to murmuring between mother and young.

They are sometimes preyed upon by large carnivores but their main enemy is man, with whom they compete for space and agricultural produce—baboons tend to depredate crops. They are also susceptible to human diseases, such as tuberculosis and yellow fever.

The family: They are very gregarious and live in family troops from 10 to 150 strong, with a mixture of all ages and sexes. At the centre of the groups are females and daughters who stay with the family group as long as they live. Males leave the family group on reaching sexual maturity.

There are generally several reproductive males in an average troop but one is dominant until killed by an outside agent or displaced in a fight by a younger, stronger male. Certainly the largest male gets most, but not all, opportunities to mate.

Baboon society is based on enduring bonds between individuals, especially core friendships which are probably formed between females as they grow up. However, young baboons and even males exhibit close ties to one another. Although males are generally promiscuous, adult females in a troop will have close ties to just two or three males, normally mating with the most dominant. These males will defend her offspring against predators.

Baboons breed the whole year round. New-born infants have short, nearly black soft fur which changes to adult colour at three months of age.

Baboons are omnivorous. The hand is their main foraging tool, and with its highly manipulative, opposable thumb and fingers, it is used to pluck, pull, strip and tear edible bits from the environment.

Predation on small animals is common in order to add protein to the diet. Baboons sometimes catch and eat larger prey such as hares or young gazelles and impalas.

VERVETS

These archetypal monkeys belong to the sub-family *Cercopithecinae*. Vervets (*Cercopithecus aethiops*)—also known as green

monkeys, grivets, guenons, tantalus monkeys—are slight of build, agile and long tailed, and are always seen in noisy, bickering, family troops with lots of young animals. Both sexes are generally alike, although males are about 40 percent heavier, with conspicuous red, white and blue genital colouration.

They generally inhabit well-wooded and well-watered grasslands but can also be found from semi arid regions (generally near rivers or swamps) to evergreen forest edges at altitudes from sea-level to 4,000 metres (13,200). They are strictly diurnal animals although some feeding may occur on moonlit nights.

These monkeys are much less vocal then baboons. They are generally silent, except when defending their territory or when warning one another against any danger.

Vervets are prey to large raptors, snakes and cats ranging from servids to leopards. Their basic form of defence is alertness and flight.

Vervets are very gregarious and live in troops of between six and 60 animals, sometimes reaching as many as 100. Troops are comprised of one or more adult males, adult females and young of all ages and sizes. Troops are territorial and defend their range against neighbouring troops with noisy group displays at the territory boundary.

Breeding occurs all year round, although local peaks may be apparent depending on local nutrition conditions. Gestation is relatively long—180 to 200 days. A young vervet starts eating solid food at a very early age by reaching up and taking morsels from its mother's mouth whilst she is feeding. It will ride on her back and suckle until six months or until the arrival of the next sibling, often a year later.

Infant mortality from disease or predation is relatively high which keeps populations reasonably stable, although they get larger in periods of good rainfall and diminish during droughts.

with thick brownish or silver grey fur. They measure around 65 cm (25 inches) and their tails add about 30 cm (12 inches) to their length. Their large eyes are surrounded by a ring of darker fur and stare out from a pointed muzzle: their ears are cupped and rounded and their senses of hearing, sight and smell are excellent. They have small "hands" with long, thin fingers with flat nails and an extended claw on the second toe. Greater galagos are sometimes mistaken for bushbabies (*Galago senegalensis*) which are much smaller—only 40 cm (15 inches) long—and have comparatively longer, slimmer tails.

Greater galagos are arboreal and live in a range of habitats including rain-forested

Vervets are omnivorous with a predilection for vegetable matter. Their preferred tastes include fruits, flowers, grass seeds, shoots and bark, both wild and cultivated, as well as insects, reptiles, small mammals, young birds and eggs.

GREATER GALAGOS

Greater galagos (*Galago crassicaudatus*) are long, woolly-tailed, nocturnal primates

Left, primate portrait: a contemplative vervet monkey. Above, young vervet checks out the view.

mountain slopes up to a height of 4,000 metres (13,200 feet), bamboo thickets, wooded savannah grasslands and eucalyptus, mango and coffee plantations. They can sometimes be seen in suburban gardens. They establish territories which vary in size according to season with between 70 and 130 animals per square kilometre. Territories are marked out with excretions from breast, anal and foot glands which are rubbed on the ground, trunks and stems of trees and bushes. Neighbouring territories may overlap and family groups often share the same sleeping hole with as many as 12 sleeping holes in each territory, located in dense foliage.

BIRDLAND

The enormous variety and concentration of birdlife in East Africa has been sadly neglected. So far 1,293 bird species have been recorded and scientists believe that many unrecognised birds are yet to be discovered, especially in remote areas. Compare this figure with the 250 or so recorded bird species in Great Britain or the 850 in Canada, Mexico and United States and you will understand why Kenya, with over 1,100 different birds, is an ornithologist's delight.

Nature has provided East Africa with a

the annual journey, with some birds flying as far as the southern tip of the continent. Those that survive make the return journey each spring to breed in their chosen latitudes.

In East Africa there are only wet and dry seasons and even these vary dramatically from place to place and year to year. Driven by some age-old instinct birds know when to leave their breeding areas to go to find a better place to live.

Migration: This is instinctive, not learned behaviour. Many species that breed

tropical environment with every conceivable type of habitat. Snow on the equator from volcanic mountain ranges, cool lush forests on their slopes, vast open temperate plains, harsh dry deserts and lowland equatorial forests, sea shores and mangrove swamps providing perpetual food supplies, all contribute to this unique region. The vast majority of birds live and breed here year round, but several hundred species come from northern latitudes, when harsh winters destroy their food sources.

From as far east as the Bering Straits and as far west as northern Scandinavia it is estimated that up to 6,000 million birds make

in the northern latitudes and migrate to Africa each year, actually leave their young to find their own way south, or perish in the attempt. A perfect example of this is the Eurasian cuckoo (*Cuculus canorus*) which lays its eggs in the nests of foster parents. The young cuckoo, even when totally blind, instinctively and forcibly ejects any other egg or even young chick from its nest. Foster parents spend the next 20 or so days feeding this voracious monster until it can fly and feed itself. By now its parents have long since left for Africa, often weeks before the European weather turns miserable. The young cuckoo starts the long journey south with no guidance, following its instinct to go or die.

Many ducks and geese exhibit similar behaviour. Once breeding is over adult birds go into *eclipse* when they moult their flight feathers and cannot fly until new feathers have grown. In the meantime their new brood has learned to fly very well and they disappear south, well ahead of their parents.

Those that survive the long journey over harsh deserts, flying mostly at night, find rest and feeding grounds in the amenable climate of East Africa. There is a sudden influx of birds almost overnight as huge numbers appear in the bush country, forests and even surburban gardens.

Bird migration has fascinated man for centuries. Their ability to navigate over thousands of miles with none of man's sophisticated technology, and to return repeatedly to the same nest site to breed is a remarkable achievement.

Bird enthusiasts throughout the world have cooperated to study this extrordinary phenomenon. They set up mist nets mainly at night to trap birds which are then weighed, identified, and have their wing length and other data recorded. Then a small numbered ring is attached to one leg and the bird is released. In this way, if ever a bird is recovered or seen again, its route, flight pattern and time taken to cover the distance can be roughly estimated.

Numbers of birds recovered are very small but these studies add to the sum of man's knowledge and some startling data has come to light. A ringed shore bird was picked up dead in Kenya's Rift Valley. Investigations showed that it had been ringed just west of the Bering Straits in the Soviet Union by Russian enthusiasts, only 18 days before.

The sophistication of the migratory phenomenon is just beginning to be understood. We know why birds migrate but much work needs to be done before we understand the complexities of birds' highly-tuned navigation systems.

Preceding pages: close-up of a bateleur eagle. Left, black-headed weaver bird and nests. Right, the distinctive saddle-bill stork.

Conservation: Birds play an important role in the lives of man, not least for their aesthetic value. We all know how much pleasure can be derived from watching them in our gardens, but birds also perform an essential function in keeping the number of insects under control. Perhaps most important though is the way birds serve as an indication of man's destructive activities on the environment.

The classic example is the effect of DDT (dichlorodiphenyltrichloroethane) on the

eggs of birds of prey. This phenomenon was widely published and alerted governments throughout the world to the perils of using long term insecticides. Birds of prey are at the end of a food-chain. Their prey, be it mice, rats, lizards or other birds, all feed on grains or insects which, in this case, had been treated with DDT. The compound built up in their bodies, without serious effect, to very high levels. But the effect on the birds of prey was to weaken their egg shells, effectively destroying their ability to reproduce. Once this was realised and conclusively proven DDT was banned.

The East African climate is controlled by

two major factors: a meteorological phenomenon known as the *intertropical convergence zone,* which produces the two main rainy seasons with specific wind directions, and the various ranges and altitudes of mountains in relation to these winds, at different times of the year.

The water birds: On the coast the climate is tropical year round, and the beaches with wide tide differentials (up to four metres or 13 feet) provide massive food supplies for migrating waders or shore birds. At low tide from September to March, thousands of these birds can be seen feeding along the beaches, coral pools and mud flats.

Sanderlings (*Calidris alba*), Whimbrels

off-shore islands, and there is a confusing variety and large numbers of egrets, with all their oddities.

In shallow water without coral cliffs, mangrove swamps develop. Here, the mud attracts mangrove kingfishers (*Halcyon senegaloides*), night herons (*Nycticorax nycticorax*), and other species of heron, including the strange black heron (*Ardea melanocephala*), with its unique feeding behaviour. It paddles with bright yellow feet and then brings its wings up over its head in umbrella fashion to shade the water underneath.

There are also crab plovers (*Dronius ardeola*), and yellow billed storks, (*Ibis ibis*)

(*Numenius phaeopus*), Ringed Plovers (*Charadrius hiaticula*), Turnstones (*Arenaria interpres*), Oyster-catchers (*Haemantopus ostralegus*), Greenshanks (*Tringa nebularia*), and other migrants live and feed here storing up energy for the long flight back to their northern breeding grounds in the spring.

Resident birds are also much in evidence. Grey herons (*Ardea cinerea*) feed in the shallow pools, gulls of several species are ever present, and in the evening large flocks of terns come to roost on the coral cliffs. Breeding colonies of the roseate terns (*Sterna dougallii*) establish themselves on

which feed by sticking their partly opened, long bills into shallow water and, with sweeping action, snap them shut when they touch something edible.

Along the rivers: The great rivers flowing from the mountains hundreds of miles away, across semi-desert country down to the sea, create a third environment, known as riverine forests. Birds take advantage of this narrow strip of permanent water where food supplies are always available. Weavers of all kinds nest in the overhanging trees.

Tawny eagles (*Aquila rapax*), martial eagles (*Polemaetus bellicosus*), Wahlberg's eagles (*Aquila wahlbergi*) and others nest in the tree tops and feed off small mammals, dry country game and birds such as guinea fowl and francolin which come to the water to drink.

Blacksmith plovers (*Vanellus armatus*) nest on the sand-bars and huge flocks of sand grouse come to quench their thirst and bathe.

On each side of these rivers stretch vast areas of semi-desert and scrub. This is harsh land at relatively low altitude, with scarce and erratic rainfall. For most of the year it is extremely dry. When rain does fall, however, the land blooms: every living thing from plants to elephants takes advantage of the vast increase in food supply. Insects flourish, plants flower and seed madly, and

trees: black-crested snake eagles (*Circaetus gallicus pectoralis*) wait to snatch lizards or snakes.

Arid regions: In Kenya, particularly the north, lie vast areas of almost true desert, most of it uninhabited by man. Here are the true dry country birds which have evolved to take advantage of their enivronment: large Heuglin's bustard (*Neotis henglinii*), sand grouse which fly 30 to 50 kilometres (18 to 30 miles) each day to scarce water holes, and the tiny, short-crested lark (*Galerida cristrata*).

Vast areas of East Africa are covered by savannah—great open grass covered plains with varying degrees of tree and scrub exist

the bird life erupts to match.

Every tree is suddenly full of nesting birds: buffalo weavers (*Bubalornis niger* and *albirostris*), white-headed weavers, (*Dinemellia dinemelli*), thousands of queleas (*Quelea cardinalis*), hornbills of many types, yellow-necked francolin (*Francolinus leucoscepus*), and those that prey on this new abundance. Secretary birds (*Sagittarius serpentarius*) nest on the top of flat

Left, the bateleur is identified by its short tail. **Above**, enterprising Egyptian vulture uses pebble to crack an ostrich egg.

mostly at middle altitudes (1,000 to 2,000 metres or 3,300 to 6,600 feet). Rainfall is erratic, but usually good when it does fall. Water-courses, some permanent, others only seasonal, create bush and tree lined valleys which slice through the plains where larks (*Alaudidae*), and pipits (*Motacillidae*) of all types, plovers (*Charadriidae*), longclaws (*Macronyx*), and a vast variety of so-called grass warblers (*Cistocola*) breed and live. The ugly scavenging marabou stork (*Leptoptilos crumeniferus*) is often seen. Overhead soar almost every species of vulture. They nest in tree tops or on rocky cliffs many miles from the open plains that supply their food. Vultures can always be seen at the scene of a kill.

Along the valleys cutting through this region, heavier growth of trees and scrub provide shelter and nest sites for other birds, who feed on the plains: barbets (*Captonidae*) fruit and seed eating birds, bush shrikes (*Malaconotus*), francolins (*Francolinus*), guinea fowl and doves of all kinds.

Birds of prey, notably the chanting goshawks (*Melierax poliopterus, Melierax metabates*), find this environment much to their liking and bateleur eagles *(Terathopius ecaudatus)* effortlessly soar for hours at a time.

Rain forest birds: High altitude tropical rain *dropadus*) and greenbuls. From the forest floor to the treetops turacos with their brilliant scarlet wings and raucous calls feed on the abundant seeds and fruit.

On the forest floor, scaly francolins (*Francolinus squamatus*) scratch and worry the earth, while overhead the great crowned eagle (*Stephanoaetus coronatus*), possibly Africa's most powerful bird of prey, soars in display, sometimes only a speck in the sky, his piercing call drawing attention long before he is seen.

This is a place to sit quietly and watch. If the wild fig trees are fruiting, sit under one because the ripe fruit attracts green pigeons (*Treon australis*), more turacos (*Musoph-*

forest covers all the mountain ranges. Winds are predominantly easterly, blowing from the Indian Ocean so eastern facing slopes tend to have a higher rainfall and more morning mist. Forests grow all year round so they are always green, lush and cool, and provide a permanent home for bird life.

In the tree tops, insect-loving shrikes (*Laniidae and Prionopidae*) feed in noisy family parties, often accompanied by starlings (*Strunidae*) of several species.

At lower levels, nearer the moist, cool earth, plant and insect life are abundant. Robin chats (*Pycnonotidae*) of several species find this perfect. So do bulbuls (*An-* *agidae*), olive thrushes (*Turdus olivaceus*), starlings (*Sturnidae*) and barbets (*Capitonidae*) of many kinds. Over-ripe fruit attracts insects, which are followed by a huge influx of insect-eating birds.

Mountain regions: The group of East Africa's mountain ranges on or near the equator, lies in an environment that is described by scientists as afro-alpine, or equatorial alpine. High altitudes of up to 6,000 metres (19,680 feet), coupled with latitude, create a peculiar habitat.

Permanent glaciers predominate above 4,700 metres (15,416 feet) but snowfalls, which are regular and heavy, usually melt fairly rapidly in the tropical sun making it seem like winter every night and summer every day!

From one of Africa's great birds of prey, Mackinder's eagle owl (*Bubo capensis*), down to the tiny scarlet-tufted malachite sunbird (*Nectarinia johnstoni*), or the hill chat (*Pinarochroa sordida*), birds confined to this alpine zone could probably not survive elsewhere. There are many other species of birds but the environment tends to keep numbers and variety down. Of great interest, however, is the way birds have evolved to survive in any environment: vultures have been recorded on the snowline of several East African mountains although

tions of rainfall. Situated five kilometres (three miles) inland from the sea, this forest evolved to take advantage of the fertile coral-based soils, an erratic but heavy annual rainfall, and zero altitude. Much of this forest has now been destroyed by man, but in the Arabuku-Sokoke Forest, near Malindi, there are at least three species of birds that exist nowhere else in the world. The Sokoke Scops Owl (*Otus irenae*), the Sokoke Pipit (*Anthus sokokensis*) and Clarke's Weaver (*Ploceus golandi*) can all be seen with a bit of effort.

Swamps appear in deserts in years of unusual rainfall and immediately attract the attention of birds not generally found there.

there is no good explanation for their choice in habitat.

Low forest: True African jungle does not really exist in East Africa. Though there are remnants in Western Kenya's Kakamega Forest. But as this is at an altitude of over 1,500 metres (4,920 feet), it cannot properly be called lowland forest.

Along the Kenya coastline little remains of a once vast forest, created by local condi-

Since the swamp holds water long after the surrounding country has returned to normal, the birds will stay. Other swamps are more permanent. Water-loving birds always appear where there is food and disappear when the water dries up.

The rainy season in East Africa is the equivalent of spring elsewhere. Rain triggers food which in turn triggers breeding. So if you want to see bird-nesting sequences and behaviour you should plan your stay between April and May or in November and December. If you are more interested in seeing local birds rather than migrants then come between March and September.

Left, this early bird (superb starling) catches its worms. **Above**, the striking red and yellow barbet.

BIG BIRD

Ostriches (*Struthio camelus*) are the largest birds in the world, measuring up to 2.5 metres (eight feet) in height and weighing up to 135 kilograms (297 pounds). Males have attractive black and white plumage and are bigger than females which have the same dull, grey-brown feathers as their young.

There are two subspecies of ostrich in East Africa: Maasai ostrich (*S. c. massaicus*) can be distinguished by the male's flesh-coloured head, neck and legs which turn bright red during the mating season: Somali ostrich (*S. c. molybdophanes*) males have greyish-blue flesh.

Ostriches can be found throughout Africa although they prefer the lush, open grasslands of the savannah plains, dry thorn bush country and semi-desert. They are generally silent birds although during courtship rituals males sometimes make distinct reverberating calls.

Getting their kicks: Although ostriches still have flight feathers in their wings they cannot fly and have evolved long, powerful legs as their main form of defence. They have two toes on each foot and one kick is enough to kill a man. They can run up to 70 kph (45 mph) and can maintain speeds of 50 kph (30 mph) for up to 30 minutes. Their long necks enable them to sight enemies from a great distance and ostriches often serve as early warning systems for other plains animals. True to myth, they sometimes flatten their heads to the ground when approached.

The only real enemy of ostriches is man, who hunts males for their feathers and has decimated populations in certain areas. Ostrich eggs, however, are very vulnerable to predators, especially hyaenas and lions which may brave an attack by adults in search of this delicacy.

Ostriches live in family troups, small groups (up to 50 have been recorded in arid areas) or couples. They feed mostly off grass, bushes, leaves, succulent plants and berries. Their diet also includes small lizards and insects.

Birds of a feather: these long-limbed ostriches are easy to spot as they head across the wide open grasslands.

REPTILES

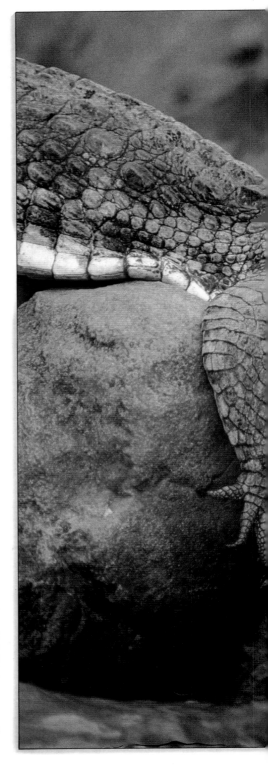

The richness of reptile fauna in East Africa compares favourably with any other part of the world. The region is a meeting ground for a number of zoogeographical zones, each with its own selection of species. Yet much of East Africa, including the whole of eastern Ethiopia, is largely *terra incognita* to the student of reptiles.

Fortunately, reptiles have no significant commercial value in East Africa. A few are killed for skins and smuggled out individually but, at least with snakes and lizards, the trade does not flourish. However, many reptiles are killed on sight by local people as a matter of principle. Sadly, the numbers of individual animals and even species are being rapidly reduced by habitat devastation and by the expanding population.

Lizards: Over 180 different species of lizard exist in East Africa, significantly more than the 150 to be found in the North American subcontinent. The variety of lizards is enormous, from the two-metre monitors (*Varanus niloticus* and *Varanus exanthamaticus*), to the tiny cat-eyed coral-rag skink (*Ablepharus boutonii*) which lives on outcrops of coral-rag and maintains an osmotic balance by having very saline blood.

There are many kinds of agama lizard (*Agama agama*), some with bright red or orange heads, others with steely purplish blue or shiny green heads.

About 40 forms of gecko are to be found here, including two transplants from Madagascar which probably arrived many generations ago with the dhow trade. These geckos are the brilliant emerald green common to the genus Phelsuma Gray. Native geckos are neither very large nor strikingly coloured. Giant plated lizards (*Gerrhosaurus major*) are handsome with skin that looks like chain mail, reddish brown in colour. Males are orange tinted on head and neck during the courting season. They are largely fructivorous but will eat insects and mice if opportunity allows. These lizards can be-

Green-eyed monster: the formidable Nile crocodile.

116

come very tame and sometimes will hang around campsites begging for scraps.

Chameleons are lizards, of course, but quite special ones. They come in many sizes and shapes, from the cat-sized Meller's chameleon (*Chamaeleo melleri*) which sometimes catches birds, to the tiny pygmy chameleon (*Rhampholeon kerstenii*), which is the size of a small mouse and lives on insects the size of a fruit fly. There are chameleons with three horns on the nose such as the dinosaur Triceratops, Jackson's and Johnston's chameleons (*Chamaeleo jacksonii* and *Chamaeleo johnstoni*). Others have two side by side protuberances looking like pineapples, such as Fischer's chameleon

they have little sense of humour and bite like weasels. The first of the pair is the widely distributed Nile soft-shelled turtle (*Trionyx triunguis*). This occurs in the northerly end of East Africa and grows to a very large size. The other is the Zambezi soft-shelled turtle (*Cycloderma frenatum*) which comes from the southern regions.

Only three species of land tortoise can be found here. The leopard tortoise (*Geochelone pardalis*) is the largest and can grow to well over 45 centimetres (18 inches). This rotund animal of kindly disposition is a dull yellow colour with black flecks and lives in the savannah.

The forest, or hinge backed tortoise (*Ki-*

(*Chamaeleo fischeri*). Still others have a single little spike on the nose and some even have plain, unadorned noses.

Of the standard lizard-shaped lizards there are too many to begin to describe individually but one deserves special mention: the serrated toed lizard (*Holaspis*). These are small lizards of the high primary forest, conspicuously marked with bright yellow longitudinal bars. They can glide from tree to tree like the Asiatic Dracos.

Turtles and tortoises: There are two freshwater varieties of turtles which have flattish rubbery shells and narrow pointed heads. Be careful when handling them as

nixys belliana) is quite carnivorous and can close up the back opening in its shell by a hinge more than halfway to the rear of its carapace. The back end closes down upon the plastron (under side of the shell) protecting the tucked in hind, limbs and tail. Other tortoises which can close their rear ends do so by having a hinge on the plastron which closes upwards. The forest tortoise's hinge is easy to see and looks a little as though the shell has been run over.

From the rocky areas comes the strangest of the three tortoises. Pancake tortoise (*Malachochersus torneiri*), so called because they are quite flat, have a flexible papery shell. Unlike most tortoises which when threatened retire into their shells, these fellows gallop off at a good speed and hide among the rocks like a lizard. Even when you find their hiding place they usually wedge themselves in so tightly that they are difficult to extricate.

Crocodilians: Where there was enough water the Nile crocodile (*Crocodylus niloticus*) used to be fairly ubiquitous at middle and lower altitudes. Although its range has been substantially reduced it is still far from uncommon in many areas. It grows to five metres (16.5 feet) and more. It has a very voracious appetite and, in spite of its reduced numbers, it accounts for many human lives

ters. The other is the dwarf crocodile (*Osteolaemus tetraspis*), which comes from Uganda and points west. It seldom reaches two metres in length. Neither of the two smaller crocodiles are considered hazardous to man.

Snakes and adders: East African snakes are very varied with representatives from many families. The giant snakes of the area are rock pythons (*Python sebae*) which can reach a length of six metres (20 feet) and more. As they are heavy bodied, even one of medium length is quite massive. While they prefer to be near water, they can be found anywhere except at very high altitudes. A large python can be a dangerous adversary

every year.

Two other smaller species of crocodile occur in East Africa but both are from the western limits. One is the long nosed crocodile (*Crocodylus cataphractus*) which grows to a little more than two metres (6.6 feet) in length. It is reminiscent of the Asiatic gavial with its narrow nose and quite large teeth. It feeds almost entirely on fish and lives in Lake Tanganyika and associated waters.

for man if disturbed but will not attack unless provoked.

The other members of the giant snakes are the boas. The family is represented in East Africa by a small relative, the sand boa (*Eryx colubrinus*), which rarely exceeds 45 centimetres (18 inches) and lives buried in the sand. Only the tip of its nose and eyes show and it ambushes any unwary, lunch-sized passing animal which it grabs and constricts before eating.

Some of the most venomous snakes in the world are to be found here. There are three species of mamba, the largest being the black mamba (*Dendroaspis polylepis*) which can

Left, the leopard tortoise is easy to spot. **Above**, monitor lizard lurks in the tall grass.

grow to more than five metres and is not black but a silvery olive colour. They have a nasty reputation for aggressive attack but experience shows that unless pursued or otherwise aggravated, they behave with the utmost discretion, which is just as well—black mambas can inflict a lightning bite, injecting immense quantities of exceedingly powerful venom.

The other two mambas rarely reach over two metres in length. One is the common green mamba (*Dendroaspis angusticeps*) seen along the coast; the other is Jameson's mamba (*Dendroaspis jamesoni*) from the west. Both are brilliant green but the Jameson's mamba has a velvet black tail.

ting cobra (*Naja mossambica*) and a subspecies, the red spitting cobra (*Naja mossambica pallida*).

Closely related to the true cobras is Storm's water cobra (*Boulangerina annulata*) from Lake Tanganyika and points west. Although it has adequate fangs and very toxic venom, it swims freely among fishermen waist deep in water, neither fishermen or snake giving each other much attention. The other large near-cobra comes from the forest canopy of the western primary forests of Uganda and western Kenya. It is Gold's cobra (*Pseudohaje goldii*) which is hoodless and only comes down to the forest floor to prey on toads.

They are quite deadly but their venom is only about one fifth as toxic as that of the black mamba.

Asia is often considered the home of cobras but Africa has many more and in more varied forms. In East Africa there are five types of true cobra and two closely related genera. Three of the true cobras can spit their venom quite a distance, aiming it accurately at the eyes of their antagonist. If the eyes are washed out quickly the effect is only temporary but acutely painful; if neglected, permanent damage to the eyesight can result. The three spitting cobras are the common spitting cobra (*Naja nigricollis*), Mozambique spit-

Three of the four giant vipers of the world can be found in this area. They are the Gaboon viper (*Bitis gabonica*); rhino viper (*Bitis nasicornis*), and puff adder (*Bitis arietans*). These are all large bodied snakes with wide heads. In exceptional cases all three can reach a length of two and a half metres (eight feet) and the Gaboon viper can grow up to two metres. The colouring of Gaboon and rhino vipers is striking and beautiful. They can all inflict multiple doses of lethal poison in just one bite.

There are a number of small vipers but three merit special mention. They are all endemic to a small area of Africa around

Mount Kenya. The small Worthington's viper (*Bitis worthingtoni*) is related to the three giants. It is an attractive little snake with black, brown, lilac and white markings, horns over its eyes, a saturnine face and an irascible disposition. It comes only from the hills around Lake Naivasha. The mountain, or Hind's viper (*Vipera hindii*) is a diminutive snake resembling a tiny melanotic European viper. It can be found only well above the treeline in moorland on top of the Aberdare mountains where there is a deep frost almost every night.

The last of the trio is the Mount Kenya bush viper (*Atheris desaixi*) which was only discovered in 1967. This snake belongs to a

West African genus and nobody suspected that a species existed this side of the Great Rift Valley.

Other snakes: There are only two back fanged snakes in the world known to be deadly; the boomslang (*Dispholidus typus*) and the twig, bird, or vine snake (*Thelotornis kirtlandii*). The former is a medium sized snake with large eyes. Typically, males are green and females grey or brown. The latter

is very slender with a large pointed head. The body looks exactly like a lichen covered twig and the head is white or off-white below and green, red or brown on top.

A third snake is suspect: Blanding's tree snake (*Boiga blandingii*) comes from the western forests. It is a long soggy-looking snake with a huge head which, when threatened, suddenly becomes very unsoggy indeed, expanding its neck and flattening its head into a very intimidating display.

There are too many harmless snakes to mention in detail, including specialist feeders such as centipede eaters, slug eaters, egg eaters and even a little shovel-nosed snake which lives off gecko eggs. Others are more general feeders, such as the sand snakes (*Psammophis*) which, amusingly enough, never live in sand. For some inexplicable reason Isis von Oken Boie named them this: *Psammos* is Greek for sand, *ophis* is Greek for snake. But that is not the only misnomer. The largest in the genus, the hissing sand snake (*Psammophis sibilans*)—*sibilans* is Latin for hissing—does not even hiss!

Where to find reptiles: Reptiles are difficult to find unless you know where to look. Fortunately each area in East Africa has its resident *Bwana Nyoka* (snake man) most of whom are excellent and well worth their hire. Reptiles can be found almost anywhere but places to hunt are by river or lake sides, forest verges, especially around weaver bird colonies and where one type of habitat merges into another.

Unfortunately there are few places to go to ask questions in Kenya. The National Museum in Nairobi (P.O. Box 40658, Nairobi) runs a long-established snake park opposite the main building with two additional satellites in Kisumu and Kitale. Kenya Crocodiles (Mamba Village, P.O. Box 85723, Mombasa) has an excellent display of reptiles and successfully combines an educational programme and sound conservation with commerce. Bio-Ken (P.O. Box 3, Watamu, Kenya) have a reptile farm and run a technical and advisory service for universities and museums.

The University of Dar es Salaam in Tanzania (P.O. Box 35091, Dar es Salaam) has a good herpetological section and Makerere University (P.O. Box 7062, Kampala) may be consulted by people wishing to visit Uganda.

Left, skeleton of a black mamba, one of the world's most poisonous snakes. **Above**, spitting cobra is ready to strike.

MARINE MAMMALS

All continents are edged by waters not more than 200 metres (660 feet) deep, covering the so called continental shelves. In East Africa, this shelf is very narrow, not more than 75 kilometres (46.5 miles) at its widest at Zanzibar, and often not more than two to 3.5 kilometres (one to two miles). The East African coast has a series of continental islands, which are part of the continent, separated only by sinking of the intermediate land. Zanzibar is one of these islands.

Pemba and Latham islands are oceanic ety of species commonly found in the East.

The distribution of plants and fish is affected by the currents impinging upon the continent. The South Equatorial Current which flows westwards towards the East African coast turns right once it reaches a point on the Somalia coast north of the equator. The effect of the current changes with the season of the year and the winds. Between April and October, the south-east monsoon (*Kusi*, in *Swahili*) blows in the same direction as the current, strengthening the flow

islands, rising straight out of the ocean. The flora and fauna of these oceanic islands is quite different from that of continental islands. On Pemba, for example, the fruit bat found is a genus found in Asia and Madagascar, but not on the African mainland.

Africa at one time is thought to have been part of a much larger continent, called Gondwanaland, which split into what is today known as India, Australia, Antarctica and South America. The existence of this larger continent helps to explain the presence of so many species common in East Africa which are also found on the Great Barrier Reef in Australia. Madagascar also has a great vari-

westwards and turning the current to push great water masses as far as Malindi. This effect is reversed between October and March when the north-east monsoon (*Kaskazi*) blows against the flow of the current. The temperature of the water is correlated to this water flow, being relatively lower in September—24 C to 25 C (75 F to 77 F)—compared with about 28 C (82 F) in March when the water is hottest.

Fish list: Open sea fish are the ones most affected by the currents. These fishes, among them marlin, sailfish, kingfish, tunny, runners, bonito, dorado, etc, are called pelagic fishes because they continually swim around the open water. They are most abundant during the fishing season from September to March off the north coast of Kenya as well as off Shimoni on the south coast. The narrow Pemba Channel is an excellent place for fishing during this time of the year.

Pelagic fishes are generally streamlined, with smooth bodies, slim tails, strong caudal fins and with dorsal and pectoral fins reduced in size. They swim mainly by rapid lateral movements of their tails and not with

whale shark are two of the largest fishes. The ray may measure up to six metres (20 feet) across and weigh two tons. Sharks are several metres in length and can weigh a ton. Both are quite harmless if left alone. Despite their formidable size and appearances, they both feed on small floating or swimming organisms, known as plankton.

Reef life: All reefs off the East African coast are fringing reefs. These reefs grow in warm, clear, shallow water on platforms of the continental shelf. They follow the out-

the movement of their fins as is common in fishes that live in sheltered waters. They are generally dull coloured, blue and silver with darker bars or markings.

Sharks also occur off the East African coast. They present little danger to humans with the exception of those present in places like Kilindi or Dar es Salaam harbours where they live largely by scavenging.

Manta ray or devil fish and the basking or

Left, coral fish off Malindi. **Above,** manta ray skims the ocean floor.

lines of the land and enclose lagoons.

The reefs are corals which are colonies of animals (polyps) of the same species as anemones and jellyfish. Polyps resemble small sea anemones and belong to the same phylum *Coelenterata*. They extract calcium carbonate from the sea to form a skeleton of lime on which they perch. When the polyps open to feed, they cover the skeleton with a filmy mass of tentacles. Corals grow continually, adding to their skeleton as long as they are covered with water, even at low tide. Coral reefs are the richest ecological environment in the world.

A typical coral garden can support some

15 families of fish containing up to 60 species which, if added to those fish in the surrounding water and those in rock caves and those in the seagrass beds, would come to more than 200.

Odd fins: In an easy morning's snorkeling around an undisturbed coral head you can expect to find globe fishes and puffers (*Diodontids* and *Canthigasterids*), which inflate themselves with water when disturbed and are poisonous to eat unless prepared by an elite Japanese cook. Keep an eye out for the queer-looking file and trigger fishes (*Monacanthids* and *Balistids*) which anchor themselves into the coral with their dorsal spines to keep from floating away whilst

trid) may partially roll over to allow the wrasse to pick skin parasites off its belly. In a classic example of aggressive mimicry, sabre-toothed blenny have evolved an almost perfect imitation of the cleaner wrasse's colouration and invitation dance. This combination allows the mimic to get close to otherwise wary fish. Unfortunately for them, blenny eat fish flesh, not skin parasites, and before they know what has happened, the impostor has taken a bite out of the proffered flank and made good his escape.

Red, black and white soldier or squirrel fish (*Holocentrids*), jewel fish (*Anthiid*) and yellow and black butterfly fish (*Chaetodon-*

asleep. Then there are parrot fishes, which graze on the living coral and help to convert the coral into sand. Further on, you might swim past shoals of snappers, and gaterins. Single, territorial damsel-fish (*Pomacentrids*) in a variety of colours and sizes, defend tiny parcels of the coral head. One genus, the *Abudefdufs*, are particularly belligerent and all 10 centimetres (four inches) of indignant fish will dash out to threaten a passing snorkeler.

Larger fish are kept parasite-free by cleaner wrasse (*Labroides*) which have conspicuous black and silver lateral stripes and approach potential customers with an undulating "invitation dance". A large angel fish (*pomacen-*

tid) can also be seen. Surgeon fish (*Acanthuridae*) are oval and laterally flattened. They have a razor-sharp "scalpel" protruding from either side of the base of the tail and if handled or touched, they can flick it to make a nasty incision.

Serranids are generally duller but very tasty. The largest of the group, sea bass or groupers, may grow to 300 kilograms (660 pounds) with a mouth that one would feel nervous about swimming too near. Groupers wait quietly camouflaged in rock crevasses and when something edible swims past, they open their enormous mouths so rapidly that anything in the immediate neighbourhood gets sucked into the temporary vacuum.

The ocean floor: The bottom of the lagoon is white sand often covered with a dense growth of weeds, spotted with dead coral that is being eroded away. *Cymodocea ciliata* is the most common weed growing on sandy or coral rubble. The weed is actually not an algae but a marine Angiosperm. The bright green wrasse (*Cheilio inermis*) and a small olive green fish (*Leptoscarpus vaigiensis*), are some of the few that live here.

Where there is more sand and some coral rubble, a greater number of fish are found, among them the rabbit fish (*Siganus oramini*) and snappers (*Lutjanus fulviflamma*)

(*Synanceja verrucosa*) which is found on the edges of lagoons and in pools. This brown, ugly and perfectly camouflaged fish lies at the bottom, often among rocks where it is very difficult to spot. If you should be so unfortunate as to step on one, its sharp dorsal spines that have poisonous sacs connected to them will penetrate any beach shoe and cause the most excruciating pain. Medical help has to be sought immediately as the sting can be fatal if not treated. Luckily, the fish will usually move out of the way of the unsuspecting walker.

Two marine mammals, dugongs and dolphins, live in the Indian Ocean off the East African coast. Dugongs (*Dugong dugon*) are

with yellowish fins and a big black spot on their sides. The sandy bottoms are favoured by species like red mullet (*Pseudopeneus macronema*) and sting ray (*Taeniura lymna*). The ray is brown, with blue spots and a long tail with a sting which has serrated spines and is very painful. The ray will take to flight when you approach it, so it is not very common to be stung by one.

Far more dangerous is the stonefish

heavy bodied, vaguely seal-like animals with almost atrophied hind limbs and a body that ends in a single flat flipper. Dugongs cannot move well out of water as their front flippers are weak and they must raise their bodies by the strength of their breathing muscles alone. They hide in mangrove swamps by day, coming up only to breathe. They feed on marine plants that grow on the bottom, normally some distance offshore. It takes some imagination and perhaps several months at sea to understand how dugongs could have given rise to the mermaid myth. Nowadays, dugongs and dolphins are threatened throughout their habitat.

Left, prolific coral growth in the warm waters of the Indian Ocean. **Above**, busy reef fish.

125

FLORA

The diversity of flora in East Africa is a result of the wide range of ecological and climatic conditions. Rainfall and altitude are the two major factors affecting the distribution and growth of different species of flora. The region rises from sea level to nearly 6,000 metres (19,600 feet), and varies in rainfall from 125 mm (five inches) to 2,500 mm (100 inches) per annum.

Geographical zones: Recognition of these geographical zones helps in identifying plant species. The coastal zone running along the Indian Ocean from north to south, extends approximately 16 to 24 kilometres (10 to 15 miles) inland, with a moisture index rarely below 10.

In semi-desert, often covered with arid bushland or dwarf shrub grasslands, rainfall is generally below 250 mm (10 inches) per annum. There are no true deserts in East Africa.

Bushland (*nyika* in *Swahili*) is generally found below 1,650 metres (5,445 feet) and is sometimes interspersed with grasslands. Rainfall varies between 250 mm and 400 mm (10 inches and 16 inches) per annum.

Grasslands are medium to dry rainfall areas with 400 to 600 mm (16 to 25 inches) per annum. They are found at altitudes of between 760 and 1,800 metres (2,492 and 5,904 feet).

Areas with medium to higher rainfall—625 to 1,000 mm (25 to 40 inches)—at altitudes of 1,100 to 2,000 metres (3,600 to 6,560 feet) are usually covered with wooded grasslands with *Acacia, Albizzia* and *Combretum* trees.

Highland areas between 1,800 and 3,650 metres (5,904 and 11,972 feet) contain moorland, upland grassy plains and higher rainfall forest which can be divided into two regions: on the main high altitude massifs, including mounts Kilimanjaro, Kenya, Elgon and the Ruwenzoris where there is considerable cloud cover and rainfalls exceed 1,000 mm (40 inches) per annum; and

dry forests which, although evergreen, have an average rainfall of less than 750 mm (30 inches) per annum. Examples can be seen around Nyeri district, the Chyulu Hills and Langata near Nairobi in Kenya. There is no true rainforest in East Africa, except possibly a small area on the Usumbara Mountains in Tanzania.

Above 3,650 metres lies the alpine zone with its own species of flora adapted to the extreme conditions.

Altitude has a great influence on the distri-

bution of flora throughout the region. Plants tend to extend their altitude range upwards as one moves westwards where the climate is influenced by both the mellowing effect of the great bodies of water in Lake Victoria and Lake Tanzania and their attendant satellite lakes, and by a reduction in the effect of glaciers on mounts Kenya and Kilimanjaro.

In the southern and extensive northern latitudes of the region, plants extend their range to lower altitudes due to the movement of the sun and its effect on mean temperatures. It must always be remembered that as altitude increases, the effect of rain is proportionately enhanced, and that on the high-

Left, tussock grass, high up in the Aberdares.
Above, rhino grazes by a giant cactus.

est mountains the rainfall is often less near the summit than on the slopes.

Plant families: The 22 main families of flowering plants in the East African region—excluding the *Gramineae* (grasses) and the *Cyperaceae* (hedges)—are represented in the following families: *Acanthaceae, Amaranthaceae, Asclepiadaceae, Capparaceae, Combretaceae, Commelinaceae, Compositae, Convolvulaceae, Cucurbitaceae, Euphorbiaceae, Labiatae, Leguminosae, Caesalpinioideae, Papilionoideae, Mimosoideae, Liliaceae, Malvaceae, Orchidaceae, Rubiaceae, Scrophularaceae,* and *Tiliaceae.*

Many of these families such as the *Malva-*

characteristics flora has adapted itself to meet them. In grassland areas often extending over a hundred miles or more, the genus *Acacia* has evolved to cope with fire and drought. In many species the seed germinates more easily after fire and leaves are thin, often turning their narrower margins towards the sun to limit transpiration.

In all the dryer areas the *Gramineae* (grasses) have an unusually plentiful supply of seed to enable them to survive long periods when no rain falls and seed germination is doubtful or impossible. Similarly, the flowers of many plants have a higher than average nectar content to attract bees to stimulate fertilization. Others such as *Loran-*

ceae, Compositae and *Orchidaceae* have a wide tolerance of changing ecological conditions and can be found throughout the region. Others such as the genus *Caralluma* are generally found in semi-desert and bushland where rainfall is limited and temperatures are distinctly high. *Orchidaceae,* both terrestrial and epiphytic (growing upon another plant), can be found from sea level to altitudes around 3,600 metres (11,808 feet) in conditions ranging from high humidity and warm temperature ranges, to dry conditions at high altitudes with wide variations in the nocturnal and diurnal temperatures.

Where ecological zones have marked

thaceae and *Aloes* have bright orange or red flowers to attract birds which can distinguish these colours since the dry conditions inhibit much insect life which normally performs the function of pollination. Many plants in semi-desert and bushland regions have grey and aromatic foliage: the colour limits transpiration and the scents attract moths and insects for pollination.

Higher ground: In high montane and alpine areas three curious evolutions can be noted: giant lobelia, tree groundsel (*Dendrosenecio*) and heaths (*Erica*). Both lobelia and tree groundsels grow to unusual heights, the former to four metres (13 feet) or more with an inflorescence of three metres (10 feet); and tree groundsels up to 10 metres (33 feet) with a flower panicle one metre long. Lobelia have evolved an exaggerated deep calyx in which the blue flower is almost hidden, a device which withstands the wide variation in temperatures which may range from 60 C (140 F) at midday to several degrees of frost at night.

Tree groundsels are selective in their altitude: none of them grow below 2,550 metres (8,364 feet) and most of them are found at 3,200 metres (10,496 feet) or more. They are also selective in their habitat and each mountain area, such as mounts Kenya, Kilimanjaro, Elgon and the Ruwenzoris, has

and 137 species of *Malvaceae*. Notable among them are *Hibiscus*, *Abutilon* and *Pavonia* which can be found mainly in grassy plains and, strangely enough, in rocky terrain and lava flows.

Papilionoideae, the pea family, is also prominent in grasslands, wooded grasslands and highlands. Represented strongly by the genus *Crotalaria*, of which there are probably more than 200 species in the region, they are widely distributed and can often be seen in considerable drifts of colour, mainly with yellow or yellow and orange flowers though there are one or two species which are predominantly blue.

No one knows how many species exist in

evolved its own subspecies.

In these high altitudes giant heather (*Erica arborea*) can be found. This many-branched tree grows up to eight metres (26 feet) in height with white flowers clustered at the end of the branches. Giant heath (*Philippea keniensis keniensis*), is found up to 4,250 metres (13,940 feet) on Mount Kenya.

In the medium altitude zones of grassland and wooded grassland there are 14 genera

Left, giant lobelia and tree groundsel in the Ruwenzoris. **Above**, golden showers of the *Cassia didimobotrya* plant.

this vast region but when botanists complete their international survey into flora of tropical East Africa, it is probable that more than 11,000 species will have been described.

Lilies in the field: Among the *Liliaceae* (lily family) are three outstanding species. *Gloriosa superba*, sometimes known as "the flame lily", is a particularly beautiful plant with a red, red and yellow or red and green striped flower whose outside petals bend abruptly backwards (reflexed perianth segments). It is widespread in the area below an altitude of 2,500 metres (8,200 feet). There is a singularly fine variant at lower altitudes with lemon coloured segments and a deeper violet meridian stripe. The plant grows from a V-shaped tuber and can reach five metres (16.5 feet).

Albuca wakefieldii or *abyssinica* is the most common lily in East Africa. This robust plant up to one metre tall has bell-shaped flowers rather widely spaced on the stalk (peduncle). Though they never open fully, these flowers are yellowish green in colour with a darkish stripe down the middle of each petal (perianth segment) with off-yellow on the margins.

Aloes are among the *Liliaceae* most widespread in the middle and lower altitudes. Red, orange or yellow with green spotted or striped leaves, they form dense groups of

jama lily after the pink stripes marking the long tubular flowers which curve at the end of a thick peduncle surrounded by heavy, dull green leaves. It grows throughout East Africa and is often seen at the sides of roads and in ditches.

The carpet flowers: A notable feature from sea-level to more than 3,350 metres (11,000 feet) is the *Convolvulaceae* family which have no less than 22 genera and 170 species in the region. Prominent everywhere is the genus *Ipomoea* whose myriad flowers scramble over coral at the coast, in semi-desert scrub, in wooded grasslands, forest glades and even on the moorlands.

Cycnium tubulosum tubulosum, with

beautiful colour especially in grassland areas where grazing has reduced competition. Elephants are particularly fond of the *aloe*.

In the family *Amaryllidaceae* are two beautiful species. *Scadoxus multiflorus*, the fireball lily, is an arresting sight. Growing from a deep rooted bulb in rocky places, riverine forest and open grassland, often in the shade of trees or on the side of antheaps, the flower spike arises before the leaves and is crowned with up to 150 small flowers making a single magnificent red to pink head, looking like a gigantic shaving brush. *Crinums* often flower at the same time, notably *C. macowanii*, named the py-

white "pocket handkerchief" flowers, a member of *Scrophuliaraceae,* is dotted all over the grassland plains, especially on black cotton soils. *C. tubulosum montanum* often grows alongside its near relative. It has large pink flowers and extends to slightly higher altitudes. Both are parasitic on the roots of grasses and speckle the countryside for mile after mile where grasses have been burnt or grazed heavily.

In dry open bushland is another parasitic plant from the *Orobanchaceae* or broom-rape family—*Cistanche tubulosa.* An erect, unbranched spike of yellow flowers like a large hyacinth springs out of a bare patch of

130

soil drawing its nourishment from the roots of neighbouring shrubs or trees.

In the family *Iridaceae* the genus *Gladiolus* has three beautiful species: *G. natalensis* grows up to 3,050 metres (10,000 feet) throughout the region and south to South Africa. It has yellowish-brown to orange flowers and is a relative of the garden varieties derived from *G. primulinus*. Above that altitude, the finest species of them all, *G. watsonioides* with bright red flowers, grows in stony soils only in alpine and subalpine regions on mounts Kenya, Kilimanjaro and Meru. *G. ukambanensis* is a delightful species with white, delicately scented flowers, produced copiously but capriciously in wet

years. It is restricted to stony soils in the Machakos district of Kenya and in the Maasai Mara and coast areas of Tanzania.

Throughout shady and damp places in higher rainfall regions, nestling in banks or decorating the sides of streams will be found members of the family *Balsaminaceae*, allied to "Busy Lizzies" of temperate gardens. There are more than 70 species in the region, ranging from near the coast, inland through

Left, bright flowers attract birds, which help in pollination. **Above**, this orchid plant is found in the higher altitudes.

the Ruwenzoris to Zaire and Cameroons in West Africa, and from the Red Sea Hills to the Drakensburg.

The desert rose (*Adenium obesum*), is found in semi-arid areas, often among inhospitable rocks. From the family *Apocynaceae,* this plant has magnificent long red to pink tubular flowers and fat fleshy branches: it appears a glowing mass of colour in a semi-lunar landscape.

Flowering trees: East Africa also boasts beautiful flowering trees. The Nandi flame *Spathodea campanulata* (family *Bignoniaceae*) is a magnificent sight when in flower, with large open chalice-like orange flowers growing up to 18 metres (60 feet) in height. Originating in areas from western Kenya to Zaire, it is now widely planted as an ornamental tree.

Calodendrum capense, the Cape chestnut (family *Rutaceae*) is another beautiful tree, recorded throughout East Africa and as far south as the Cape. It grows in heavy stands which set the whole area alight with its cyclamen coloured flowers.

In dryer bushland areas *Cassia singueana* and *C. abbreviata* (family *Caesalpinioideae*) both flower in front of their leaves and look as if golden sheets have been thrown over their branches. In contrast, in the wetter forest areas in the middle altitude range *Cordia africana* (family *Boraginaceae*) is a resplendent tree growing sometimes to 24 metres (80 feet), with stalkless white flowers massed in panicles inside a strongly ribbed, soft, brown calyx.

When flowering, the *Acacia*, sometimes called the "umbrella thorn", is covered with a mass of highly scented globular to elongate flowers. There are more than 50 species in East Africa: in particular, *A. senegal* and *A. mellifera*, which grow in meduim to low rainfall areas and decorate the bush for miles. *A. Seyal*, a species found in colonies on stony ground or black cotton soils, has lovely spherical flowers which appear in great profusion before the leaves.

Those who delight in the grotesque must not miss the Euphorbia tree. Numbering more than 20 species and ranging up to 30 metres (100 feet) in height, these trees have twisted triangular, quadrangular or hexangular fleshy branches. They exude copious amounts of latex and their flowers look like blobs of squashed plasticine.

AFRICA AT THE MOVIES

Those who travel to East Africa immediately fall in love with the dramatic scenery, herds of wildlife and various ethnic groups. Each new visitor relives the exciting moments of explorers of old who first glimpsed snow-capped Mount Kilimanjaro or descended into the Great Rift Valley to see plains' zebra and *Maasai* herdsmen with their ochred hair and coloured beads.

To the traveller these images are forever imprinted on the mind, like stills from an old movie. So it is surprising that the romantic appeal of Africa went pretty much unnoticed until Sydney Pollack's award-winning *Out of Africa* in the 1980s. But filmmaking is a complex business involving audience tastes, timing and perhaps most of all, production costs. That very terrain which is so appealing to the eye is not always so conducive to the rigours of locational filming. Hence many old full-length feature films about Africa were studio creations.

Mention Africa to the average movie buff and the response might be *Casablanca*, that 1942 Humphery Bogart/Ingrid Bergman classic, or the *Tarzan* series (most of which was filmed in up-state New York) or even Elizabeth Taylor's *Cleopatra* (1962)—but that's a bit north on the Nile.

African mystique: The allure of East Africa lies in its mountains, rain forests, jungles and deserts. There is the call of the wild. It is where the Big Five game animals dwell in simple, natural and beautiful environs and people likewise live in what might be described as rustic, even primitive, styles. Sunsets under the whispering palms of an Indian Ocean island or nights spent under a canopy of stars blanketing a campsite on a Nubian desert reiterate the mysteries of the universe. East Africa was the birthplace of mankind: now it is an Eden revisited.

Little wonder then that the Hollywood moguls ventured out to magnify the munificence of this continent, so dark in its ancient imagination and romance.

Adventure films tell of the lone hunter on a new frontier. And in the case of Robert Ruark's *Something of Value* (starring Sidney Poitier and Rock Hudson) or the more recent *Kitchen Toto*, the tale of human rights and freedoms is depicted in the pre-independence era of Kenyan history.

But at first it was the strange, exotic and unusual which drew the cinematographers to East Africa. Later, partition offered historic ethnographical subject matter for the creative filmmaker. When the Wild West was

won in American movies, cowboy heros gave way to new adventurers such as the Great White Hunter in the image of Ernest Hemingway, who added the *Swahili* words *safari* (journey) and *hatari* (danger) to the English language. These hunters were rugged he-men, not the playboys or sweltering, smouldering lovers in the vein of Rudolf Valentino's sheik.

In the 1930s Africa was still little known to filmmakers. In that star-studded era Marlene Dietrich came closest to the African theme with two films, *Morocco* and Richard Boleslawski's *The Garden of Allah*. Here she features with Charles Boyer setting out

Preceding pages: Grace Kelly fans the flame in *Mogambo*. **Left**, Sigourney Weaver in *Gorillas in the Mist*. **Above**, scene from the **1949 film**, *Sheena, Queen of the Jungle*. Note the tiger!

on a honeymoon in a sandstorm, portraying the fantasy and fatalism of love in the African desert. In *Morocco,* director Josef von Sternberg clothed her in mystery, portraying her as a shadowy café singer in a Foreign Legion town.

Perhaps the most memorable film to come out of Africa in the 1950s was John Huston's *The African Queen,* based on C.S. Forester's classic novel, and starring Humphrey Bogart and Katherine Hepburn. As with many of Huston's films, the story lived in him for a long time before he directed it.

Filmed in what was then the Congo (now Zaire), and on both the Congo and Kagera rivers, *The African Queen* combines a love

The African Queen is one of those rare films about an intelligent woman in love. The story was originally bought by Warner Brothers in 1938 and was to star Bette Davis and David Niven. Niven once revealed to Bogie that he had spent four weeks polishing up his Cockney accent and growing a beard which made him feel like a diseased yak before the whole thing was cancelled when Davis refused to be filmed out of doors. Hence the story was sold to Twentieth Century Fox.

The love stories: Lesser known films from the decade when television was beginning to rob cinemas of their big-screen-addicted audiences include *Mogambo* and a series by

story with both comedy and adventure. The two unlikely lovers are Rose (a prudish missionary) and Allnut (a gin-swigging riverboat captain). This is a love-under-the-mosquito-net plot that sees them commandeering the boat, *African Queen,* over dangerous rapids to torpedo a German battleship. Says Rose: "I never dreamed that any experience could be so stimulating!"

The script by Huston, John Agee and John Collier developed into comedy not readily apparent in the original novel. On location, Peter Viertel assisted with dialogue. He later wrote of the experience in his novel, *White Hunter, Black Heart.*

Warwick Films which produced *North of Mombassa, West of Zanzibar* and *Where No Vultures Fly,* most of which were filmed in Kenya and included such stars as Robert Taylor and Donna Reed.

Mogambo starred Grace Kelly, Ava Gardner and Clarke Gable. This 1953 film tells the story of a white hunter, whose world is invaded by an American showgirl. Together with an archaeologist and his wife, they all wander off on a gorilla hunt. The film also featured Kenya actor—David Makio.

Much of it was filmed in Amboseli National Park bordering Tanzania and at Lake Chala and Lake Jipe in Taita Taveta district.

The famed Grogan Castle, built by the Cape-to-Cairo explorer Captain Ewart Grogan at the turn of the century, was also used as a site. Director John Ford admitted that he had made the film because he didn't want to deprive himself of a trip to Africa.

His holiday mood was apparently in evidence on film, as one reviewer bemoaned the lack of direction, concluding that the cast was out-acted by the gorillas.

Leni Riefenstahl, famed for her German propaganda films of the 1930s, first fell in love with Africa in 1956 while touring Kenya and Tanzania (then Tanganyika). Since cinema had become a forbidden domain to her, she turned to photography. But

Further financial and world crises hindered her progress but not before she completed some documentary footage in 16mm and several ethnographic photograph collections, one of which resulted in *The Last of the Nuba*.

The Hemingway mystique lives on in many corners of the globe and Africa is no exception. In East Africa he played the big game hunter himself. One hotel, the *Blue Marlin*, in the Kenyan coastal town of Malindi, boasts a plaque—"Hemingway stayed here". The Indian Ocean satisfied his desire to go deep sea fishing. In both *The Snows of Kilimanjaro* and *The Green Hills of Africa* (Susan Hayward and Gregory Peck) Hem-

during that first visit she started a fictional documentary, *Black Cargo*, about contemporary slave traffic, which she planned to submit to the London Anti-Slavery Society. However, her plans were drastically altered after an accident with her landrover in northern Kenya. She spent several weeks in Nairobi Hospital suffering from a skull fracture and several broken ribs. In 1961 she returned to the Congo, Uganda, Sudan and Kenya.

Left, *Born Free* told a lion's tale. Above, *Out of Africa* brought mass recognition.

ingway's personal introspection and his quest for adventure are revealed on screen.

Animals as actors: African animals have been cast as hundreds of thousands of unpaid extras in a number of films, mainly shot in a *cinema verité* style. With no union or guild to plead their cause this runs nothing short of exploitation! But films have played a part in conservation efforts. Many a big producer has left substantial sums to the World Wildlife Fund or the East African Wildlife Society in gratitude for the participation of this silent majority.

Some producers have chosen to transport their own trained animals to location although many animals become surprisingly stubborn and wilful in the climate of their original roots. Others used stand-ins in films such as *Sheena, Queen of the Jungle* where ponies were painted as zebras. Still others have relied on the real thing in its natural habitat. *Sheena*, a female Tarzan-type adventure, also included the zebroid stallion Mariko, Chango the elephant and chimpanzees Tiki and M'Bongo of *Animal Actors*, Los Angeles.

Films such as *Jumbo, The African Lion* (an early Walt Disney True-Life Adventure), *The Lion* and *The Last Safari* continued the tribute to wildlife. Most of these were filmed in Kenya in the 1960s. *The Lion* featured told the poignant story of Elsa the lioness and the Adamsons' decision to release her from their camp at Kora in northern Kenya into the bush.

Virginia McKenna and William Travers brought the story of Joy and George Adamson to the screen. Local actor Peter Lukoye played the assistant to Joy. The theme song was used by *Kenya Airways* when planes approached the then Embakasi Airport. And the film itself developed into a television series, *Living Free*, which later led to the popular Ivan Tors *Daktari* series for the BBC.

In *Born Free* Joy is characterised as an angular British woman with a strange pen-

William Holden (a long way from *Sunset Boulevard*), Capucine (an equally long distance from *Walk on the Wild Side*) and Trevor Howard. Holden went on to become a household name in Kenya as one of the founder members of the original, exclusive Mount Kenya Safari Club. The club was visited regularly by Hollywood Types and later went on to gain fare as a wildlife sanctuary.

Born Free: Perhaps the one film that did as much, if not more than *Out of Africa*, to put Kenya on the map, especially for American audiences, was *Born Free*. This was based on Joy Adamson's book of the same title and chant for lionesses. Husband George is a bit leonine himself (remember Bert Lahr's *Cowardly Lion*?) but seems to understand his wife's motives. In real life Joy actually became known much earlier for her painting. Over 600 ethnographic portraits of the peoples of Kenya and an equally impressive collection of meticulously rendered watercolours of plant life are her legacy to the National Museum in Nairobi. The world was shocked by her untimely and mysterious death at Kora Camp in the early 1980s. George tells his own story in his autobiography, *My Pride and Joy*.

Documentaries: *Born Free* is probably

also responsible for a rash of documentary films made in the last 20 years. Alan Root's work is the most widely known, having appeared on numerous television networks and is still a favourite evening's entertainment in the up-country lodges and hotels of Kenya. Root's vivid photography has captured lions, elephants, hippos, wildebeest, hornbills, termites and almost every imaginable ecological subject. Anyone familiar with Albert Lamorisse's classic *The Red Balloon* will have heart palpitations and flights of fancy when they view Root's balloon safari which gracefully records the annual July migration of hundreds of thousands of wildebeest from Tanzania's Ser-

both films is the close proximity to those magnificent apes.

Kenyan poet, painter and filmmaker, Sao Gamba, won international awards with his study of the *Maasai* tribe, *Men of Ochre*.

In 1984 Hughes Fontaine, a young visiting French teacher at Pangani Girls School in Nairobi, finished his documentary film, *The Singing Wells*, for French television. This told of how the nomadic *Gabra* managed to find water during periods of drought. Tracing their wanderings from Maikona to Kalacha to Balesa, Fontaine's final shot features himself emerging from a Paris underground station, above which is a poster of Souleyman Cisse's *Vinye*.

engeti to Kenya's Maasai Mara Game Reserve.

Further afield there have been Jane Goodall's studies of chimpanzees at Gombe in Tanzania and Dian Fossey's gorilla work at Karisoke, Rwanda (*Gorillas in the Mist*, filmed in Kenya and Rwanda). Equally as impressive is Romain Baertsoen's *Ibirunga* about the volcanoes and gorillas of Akagera National Park in Rwanda. The fascination in

Apart from strictly informative documentaries about the beauties of African wildlife or the strange and exotic habits of birds and people, other films have been made to publicise a just cause or plea. *Serengeti Shall Not Die* made by Bernhard Grzimek (director of the Frankurt zoo) and his son Michael, set out to prove that vast herds of zebra and wildebeest, as well as other game, were in grave danger from hunters and poachers, especially if government plans were finalised to limit the park's boundaries. Michael Grzimek lost his life while making the film when a vulture struck the small plane he was piloting.

Left, **Clarke Gable plays a white hunter in** *Mogambo*. **Above**, **Susan Hayward and Gregory Peck in** *The Snows of Kilimanjaro*.

Serengeti Shall Not Die was not a highly organised or expensive film. The message is simple and clear: it deals with animal extinction as a loss to all mankind, with destruction blamed on both black and white man. Africans are shown with their wire snares and poisoned arrows: in another sequence a warehouse of what looks like tree stumps turns out to be elephants' feet made into souvenir wastebaskets and footstools.

More recently, the camera work of Kenya's own award-winning Mohamed Amin has opened the world's eyes to the devastating famine in Ethiopia. Prior to that Amin filmed countless coups and other news events in Kenya, Zanzibar, Central African

Republic and Uganda.

Kenya's archaeologists have also got in on the act. Richard Leakey's seven-part series, *The Making of Mankind*, begins and ends in East Africa, the palaeontologists' favourite hunting grounds for early man. Most notable are the scenes in Olduvai Gorge and Koobi Fora.

Making history: In recent years Kenya's colonial history has provided the storyline for scriptwriters. Danish baroness Karen Blixen's unsuccessful attempts at coffee farming in the 1930s coupled with her disastrous love life were woven into *Out of Africa*, based on her own enigmatic diaries. Meryl Streep and Robert Redford (playing Blixen's lover Denys Finch-Hatton) were filmed in Karen (the Nairobi suburb named after her), the Ngong Hills and the Karen Blixen Museum (formerly Blixen's home).

Woody Allen's *Annie Hall* brought Diane Keaton's "Kenyan basket" out of the bush and into the front windows of Bloomingdales, just as *Out of Africa* pushed rumpled khaki into everyone's closet.

Similar pages from the same chapter of Kenyan history resulted in *The Flame Trees of Thika* with Hayley Mills, a series based on Elspeth Huxley's childhood memories in Njoro and Thika, then a fast-growing agro-industrial town (pineapples, sisal, motor vehicles) to north of Nairobi.

Kenya's own flying ace, Beryl Markham, is brought to the big screen in *Shadow on the Sun* with Stephanie Powers, Clair Bloom and a host of other big names. Granada's *After the War* series has an episode filmed in Mombasa: *The Winds of Change* with Clair Higgins and Art Malik.

The unsolved murder in 1941 of playboy Josslyn Hay, the 22nd Earl of Erroll, was the subject of *White Mischief* by journalist James Fox. Produced by Michael White, Simon Perry and Michael Radford, the film version emphasises the hazy reality of the Happy Valley (*Wanjohi*) residents. The BBC continued this saga in *Happy Valley*.

Jumping back a century, *Mountains of the Moon* tells the story of explorers Richard Burton and John Speke. The title refers to the Ruwenzori Mountains shared by Uganda and Zaire and the *Unyamwezi* (people of the moon) of Tanzania. The story is loosely based on Burton's own accounts, *First Footsteps in East Africa* and *Lake Regions of Equatorial Africa,* and Speke's *Journal of the Discovery of the Source of the Nile.*

For filmmakers with panoramic vision, East Africa will provide a cinematic setting for a long time to come. Multicultural peoples, history, big game, adventure and mystery abound. And for subject matter, modern novels and short stories offer dozens of scripts the big producers haven't even considered yet.

Left, Rock Hudson and Sidney Poitier on location in *Something of Value*. **Right**, Hepburn and Bogart aboard *The African Queen*.

CUSTOMISED SAFARIS

When Robert Redford was filming *Out of Africa* he flew over Kenya's Maasai Mara Game Reserve in a small plane. Redford peered out of the window and saw a solitary male lion encircled by vehicles filled with camera-toting tourists. "I know just how he feels," Redford sighed.

As tourism became increasingly important to the Kenyan economy, so the old-style safaris under canvas beat a retreat, leaving in their wake conveyor-belt tours of the "today Naivasha, tomorrow the coast" variety.

Hauntingly beautiful wildlife areas have become so congested that the authorities are deeply concerned about the rapid deterioration of the environment. The game-drive rush hours—early morning and late afternoon—are turning grasslands into cauldrons of dust.

Zoologists report that some predators have developed neuroses because they can no longer stalk their prey without being trailed by a horde of onlookers. The cheetah, which normally hunts in daylight, is adapting to the crowds by hunting under the cover of darkness instead.

This is not what safaris are supposed to be like. There is a different type of trip to be had that is in tune with the slow, quirky tempo of life in the bush. On this voyage the true face of Africa—both majestic and intriguing— will unfold before you at a leisurely pace.

Customised safaris that take you off the beaten track and into the wild come in many different wrappings. Some cosset their clients with champagne and comfortable Range Rovers. Others are arduous and travel to the edge of reality. Deluxe or demanding, they both offer skilled guides who do what you want to do and take you where you want to go, ensuring that every moment is savoured before being thoroughly digested.

The guides are today's pioneers of Africa. The spirit of exploration prevails as they share a landscape close to their hearts. The alchemy of limitless horizons, hard physical

Preceding pages: floating above the Maasai Mara; going on camel safari. **Right,** Mount Kilimanjaro in your back yard.

146

exertion and encounters with lion, elephant and buffalo outside the confines of a car conjures up a heady and irresistible brew.

Tony Church, a third-generation Kenyan, runs trips on horseback through the virgin forests and undulating grasslands that are home to the nomadic *Maasai*. The sceptics predicted Church's horses would succumb to tsetse flies and lions, but they were proved wrong. He injected his ponies against sleeping sickness and employed *Maasai* warriors to guard the picket lines at night. Now a well-established holiday in equestrian circles, his safaris are always fully booked.

Those who sign up have the option of riding hundreds of miles for two weeks,

typify the trail-blazing spirit that is quintessential to out-of-the-ordinary trips. They lead safaris on foot and by boat through the dark heart of Tanzania's Selous Game Reserve. The Selous has been likened to a Disneyland without people. With the exception of Arab slavers and ivory hunters, it has been virtually ignored by humankind. Its miombo thickets and palm-lined rivers are rarely visited except by the occasional poacher.

Bonham's two-week safaris, partly by boat, and mostly on foot, emulate those of the 19th-century explorers. Bonham likes to live off the land, just as they did, and "shoots for the pot". His limit of eight visitors at a

moving camp each day, or splitting their time equally between game lodges visited by car, followed by a week of riding through the countryside that was so stunningly portrayed in the funeral scene from *Out of Africa*.

Whichever you choose, you will get plenty of close quarter game viewing from the saddle. The horses are accustomed to cantering alongside topi, giraffe, zebra and even rhino and buffalo but have learned to keep elephant, who are notoriously inquisitive, at a respectful distance.

Richard Bonham, the Kenya-born son of a British game warden, and Conrad Hirsch, a former mathematics teacher from Texas,

time endows trips with a feeling of truly personalised service. The meandering route varies, depending on whim. Walking time is kept down to a manageable three or four hours a day. Trekkers are followed by a snaking line of 30 porters, each of whom balances 18 kilograms (40 pounds) of equipment on his head.

What can rival the thrill of hearing an elephant trumpeting a few yards ahead as you walk along a river bank? Visitors who stalk these awe-inspiring creatures are rewarded with a front row view of cows and calves indulging in an impromptu shower as they suck up water in their trunks and spray their backs.

Bonham and others who take out foot safaris have a well-honed knowledge of bush lore that keeps their charges safe from harm. The secret of successful game viewing on foot is to approach downwind so that the animals do not catch the scent of approaching humans.

Conrad Hirsch prefers the tranquility of paddling down the Rufiji, East Africa's greatest river, in inflatable rubber boats. To reach his camp at the foot of the Shuguri Falls' precipitous red cliffs, visitors take the train from Dar es Salaam, then embark on a five-hour odyssey in Land Rovers. There are no roads and the tracks made by the four or

boats should flip, but visitors soon learn another danger lurks in the muddy depths. Thousands of hippos lie submerged, seeking protection from the sun's rays. Sometimes they surface as a boat passes overhead, lifting it out of the water. On very rare occasions, enraged by the intrusion, they bite a boat as it floats by.

Despite the adventure of rubbing shoulders with nature, open-air safaris are comfortable and well catered for. In fact, there is so much good food on offer that any resolutions to become as lean and lithe as your guide are hard to keep.

The magic of these safaris is that they give you the time to become properly acquainted

so vehicles that pass through each year are quickly outgrown. Hirsch admits to quite a bit of "searching around and getting lost".

By day you shoot white water rapids and paddle along sandy flats rimmed by doum palms. In the evening you put up tents on the river bank and eat Hirsch's personal gourmet specialities—Chinese stir fries, Ethiopian *wat* and Indonesian kebabs.

Hirsch's chief concern is if the rubber

Left, geared up for a 1930s safari. **Above**, these photo fiends have two willing subjects.

with East Africa's stunning visage and its intimate secrets: a porcupine quill half hidden in the sand; a valley stretching for 115 kilometres (70 miles) to a horizon of crystal clarity.

You will also get the chance to talk to local people such as the ochre-painted warriors who wear beaded bracelets in the shape of a watch, an irreverent comment on our preoccupation with timekeeping. All nomads can tell the time of day to within half an hour by the position of the sun, which is as close as you need to get when you have no appointments to keep. Safari-goers would do well to take a leaf out of their book.

HORSEBACK SAFARI

Horses are not indigenous to East Africa south of the Abyssinian Highlands and the Horn of Africa. In the past, any horse which ventured southwards from Kenya's arid northern region was soon an unfortunate victim of the fatal African horse or sleeping sickness (*Trypanosomiasis*).

Early riders: When European missionaries, pioneers and hunting parties penetrated the interior, they travelled mostly on foot or by oxwagon. One of these early adventurers

horses to be brought to East Africa.

Subsequent Europeans who ventured to East Africa to take up land brought their thoroughbred horses from the British Isles, only to have most of them succumb to a host of African diseases. So settlers soon cross-bred imported horses with hardy sure-footed Somali ponies and started what was to become a substantial herd of resilient country bred horses, adapted to conditions prevailing in East Africa.

was Lord Delamere, sometimes known as the Red Baron from stately Vale Royal in Cheshire. He later became the flamboyant leader of the British settler community. Delamere first visited what is today the highlands of Kenya in 1897 by way of Berbera in Somaliland and south across the baking hot Chalbi Desert. His main purpose was to hunt big game. His caravan of bearers, trackers and *askaris* (guards) were supported by tough little Somali ponies indigenous to the Horn of Africa and the highlands of Ethiopia. Ponies that survived the long journey and reached the crisp, clean, disease-free air of the Kenya highlands were among the first

At the outset of World War I in 1914 the British found themselves facing German settlers on their southern border with German East Africa (now Tanzania). When the colonial authorities realised the declaration of war in Europe was a serious matter they hurriedly sent despatches to the South African government for horses. These were shipped to the port of Mombasa to help the war effort. Settlers formed the East African Mounted Rifles, a Cavalry regiment, to patrol the border and pursue General von Lettow Vorbeck, the elusive and cunning German pioneer of guerilla warfare. Thousands of horses perished in this campaign as described in Charles Miller's *Battle for the Bundu*. But horses were obviously the most reliable source of transport during the Great War. Some early pioneers thought they could capture and harness wild zebras but this was a failure since zebras have weak hearts.

After the Treaty of Versailles in 1918, another wave of settlers under the Soldier Settler Scheme emigrated to the young colony. By now horses were firmly established horse as transport gave way to these machines. Horses were bred more and more for the race track, polo and as hunters. Cross-country journeys on horseback were seldom undertaken except during the long rains (April and May) when roads became a quagmire, or when following up a gang of cattle rustlers. Nomadic warrior tribes, particularly the *Maasai* and *Samburu* relish cattle raids on a moonlit night as all cattle are considered a god-given right of the tribe. Euro-

on colonial farms for pulling pony traps, checking long fence lines and scaring away lion and other predators which in those days were regarded as vermin. Theodore Roosevelt enjoyed big game hunting from horseback during his visit to East Africa in 1913 despite the fact that horse flesh was known to be a favoured delicacy for a pride of hungry lions.

As motor cars became more popular the pean farmers who were the target of most of these raids used their farm horses to follow up the marauders.

Short circuits: Mass tourism got under way in the mid-1960s with the advent of jet passenger aircraft. Fashionable safaris for the rich now came within the reach of anyone with a love of the wilds. No longer were expensive mobile deluxe hunting camps the only accommodation available in the game lands of Kenya. Shooting safaris with cameras rather than rifles became one of the most talked about experiences. Safari lodges and tented hotels were established at intervals along various tourist circuits.

Left, hunting on horseback. Above, still chasing giraffes, but only to shoot pictures.

Horseback trips were organised in the mid-1960s using Somali ponies and zebroids (a hybrid cross between wild zebra and a horse) as pack horses for parties climbing Mount Kenya. But long-distance riding safaris set up on a commercial basis were only started in earnest in 1972.

To outfit and escort safaris into the heart of game country for visitors from America or Europe was not easy. Horseback riding was regarded as a dangerous sport and carried with it real responsibilities and grave consequences should anything go wrong. Limited rides began on a daily and overnight basis across the Kitengela Plains and up on to the

dictable situations and most important be confident on horseback at all paces.

Longer trips: As these safaris gained popularity longer and more ambitious routes were pioneered. In 1972 a five-day trail was forged from the Athi Plains, over the southern shoulder of the Ngong Hills and into the Great Rift Valley, dropping into the Lookariak lugga (dry stream bed) and beyond to the Kedong River. Then across the great Akira plain between extinct volcanoes mounts Suswa and Longonot, finishing with a spectacular day through Hell's Gate Gorge to the shores of Lake Naivasha.

Tentage, camp gear, groceries, horse grain

Ngong Hills on the eastern edge of the Great Rift Valley. These wooded hills contain bushbuck, mountain reedbuck, eland, kongoni, Cape buffalo, colobus monkey, waterbuck and the occasional lion and rhino.

With picnic lunches carried in saddle bags, these early rides proved a great success. Riders returned to their Nairobi hotels after an exciting day in the saddle away from other tourists in minibuses. Horseback safaris endow an amazing sense of being on even terms with wild animals—no other sounds or smells except those of the bush. Of course, to enjoy such a riding experiences clients must be fit, mentally tuned in, able to face unpre-

and safari staff are carried by truck along bush tracks while riders go cross country covering between 25 and 40 kilometres (15 and 25 miles) a day. Picnic lunch and waterbottles together with a few personal effects are carried in saddle bags strapped to cavalry saddles.

Another spectacular riding safari leads from the wooded Nguruman escarpment, over the rolling Loita Hills down to Narosura spring before branching north west across the Loita plains always teeming with game to the Mara River. This ride finishes on the beautiful Esoit Oloolol escarpment which forms the western boundary of the Maasai

Mara Game Reserve.

Safaris Unlimited (Africa) Ltd are the outfitters and organisers of these horseback adventures, with stables and safari depot 16 kilometres (10 miles) outside Nairobi. Those wishing to undertake a horseback safari should book in good time since these safaris are organised by special arrangement or by joining a group put together by an overseas agent.

Riding today: On arrival in Nairobi you will be taken to one of the capital city's leading hotels for the night. The next day you will be driven to a very comfortable and picturesque camp set up in a glade of Podo

among huge herds of plains game, sometimes canter with giraffe or wade across muddy rivers, closely observed by families of hippo. You are always led by a highly experienced English-speaking guide.

Each day you head into the wild blue yonder while staff pull down the tents, drive round on bush tracks and then re-erect the whole camp at the next waterhole. After six or seven hours in the saddle (broken by a lunch stop) the party ride into the camp at about 4 p.m. for tea or cold drinks and hot showers before dinner.

The 10-day route leads from the swamps of Morijo, over the Subugo ridge to Naro-

and African Olive trees.

After a restful evening followed by a substantial English breakfast you head out in the African wilds with your own horse on a cross country trek that will take you through mountains, forests, grassy plains, rivers and escarpments filled with a variety of wildlife. There are no fences, telegraph poles or tarmac roads and the sense of space and freedom is quite overwhelming. You walk

Left, riding on the dusty plains. **Above**, a popular trail leads through Hell's Gate Gorge, near Lake Naivasha.

sura, Maji Moto (hot springs), Olare Lamun, and Olare Orok near the Maasai Mara where you rest for a day before the long ride across to Musiara, the Mara River and up on to the Esoit Oloolol escarpment to the site where Denys Finch-Hatton was buried in the famous scene from *Out of Africa*.

Finally, it's back to the Mara River for your last night under canvas in the riverine forest near Hippo Pool. Four-wheel drive station wagons are always nearby, enabling anyone to take a break from the horses and head into the game reserve to photograph animals at close quarters from the safety of a vehicle.

UP, UP AND AWAY!

The *Swahili* word *safari* conjures up images of dust-stained travellers winding their way across the savannah followed by lines of African porters. But imagine floating gracefully through the air above the dirt and insects of the plains and you'll have some idea of what balloon safaris are all about.

Jules Verne's novel *Five Weeks in a Balloon*, published in 1862, was the first to mention ballooning in Africa and was the inspiration for English gas balloonist Anthony Smith's visit 100 years later. Using a balloon lifted by hydrogen he successfully crossed from Zanzibar to Tanzania. He also completed flights over the Serengeti and the Great Rift Valley.

Accompanying Smith as camerman during these early flights was Alan Root, now a world-renowned wildlife film maker. He realised that if problems of expense and manoeuvrability could be overcome a balloon basket was the perfect place from which the majesty of the African landscape could be fully appreciated.

Alan Root had a hot air balloon delivered to Kenya and with the aid of a trained pilot set about learning to fly it. Early flights were hazardous until European flying techniques were adapted to African conditions. The result of Root's efforts was one of his most popular films, *Safari by Balloon*.

While on location Root was asked on several occasions by passing travellers for rides over the savannah. It was these visitors to Kenya, who wanted to see the game from a different perspective who prompted him to set up Kenya's first balloon company, appropriately named Balloon Safaris. Based at Keekorok Lodge in the Maasai Mara Game Reserve the company has flown 30,000 passengers since its inaugural flight in 1976. The original five passenger balloons with their cramped baskets have now been superseded by balloons three times bigger with baskets containing seats for 12 passengers.

Much hot air: Since those first flights balloon safaris have now become a major attraction for many visitors in Kenya. Other balloon companies have sprung up in the Mara based at Governor's Camp, Sarova Camp and Fig Tree Camp. Visitor's staying at any lodge or camp in the Mara are close to a balloon base if they wish to fly. Although open year round the optimum time to balloon in the Mara is from July to October during the annual wildebeest migration, when over one million animals cross the plains.

The once-daily flights lift off with the rising sun for an hour long journey over an average distance of eight miles. Being highly manoeuvrable the balloons can skim tree tops or rise to over 300 metres (984 feet) for panoramic views of the rolling Mara plains.

The basket is an ideal platform for photography. Binoculars are a bonus for spotting game from higher altitudes. Passengers often forget it is a hot air balloon and wear unnecessary extra clothing. However, a hat is recommended for any tall passengers who find that their place in the basket is located under the burner!

The vast plains are ideal places for landing balloons four times bigger than their counterparts in other countries. All balloon companies serve a champagne breakfast wherever they land in the park, something as memorable as the flight itself.

Because balloons are moved by the prevailing winds they cannot return to their take-off point. After breakfast passengers are driven slowly back to the lodge by retriever vehicles. All companies return passengers to their respective lodges by mid-morning after presenting them with a certificate to mark the occasion.

In 1988, balloon companies started flying in two other game parks. In Samburu Game Reserve ballooners have the chance to enjoy the magnificent scenery with Mount Kenya in the distance. Ballooning in the privately-owned Taita Hills Game Sanctuary near Tsavo West Game Reserve offers views of Kilimanjaro as well as a variety of game.

A balloon ride cost US$250 per person in early 1989. Visitors are advised to book before arrival.

Right, great care is taken to prepare a balloon for a flight, which invariably becomes the highlight of any East African safari.

GOING BY CAMEL

Camel safaris offer a leisurely face-to-face encounter with the real Africa. Those who have the vision and energy to travel this way, emulating the Samburu and Rendille nomads of northern Kenya, will be rewarded with a memorable adventure.

It can be an unsettling experience to enter a world where there is no sign of a building for hundreds of miles and where waterholes can be 50 kilometres (30 miles) or more apart. But this unparalleled solitude is the attraction for those who travel with camels.

lightful days becoming acquainted with at least some of this spectacular scenery.

By 6 a.m. trekkers will be awake and enjoying their first mug of tea around the campfire. In another hour trekkers will be perched atop the camels' humps or striding alongside the train, enjoying the brief cool that comes before the sun soars towards its zenith. By 9 a.m. they will be bathed in sweat and, for the first day at least, preoccupied with brushing off swarms of flies.

Trekkers should be reasonably fit and, of

You meander along dry watercourses known as *luggas* and have the option of either walking or, when you get tired, riding. You cover up to 24 kilometres (15 miles) each day and rest a few hours during the midday heat.

Camel safaris wander through a vast and varied landscape in northern Kenya: the sacred slopes of Mount Nyiru, where the Samburu sacrifice bulls on an altar of giant rock outcrops; the arid plains of El Barta, stippled with mauve grasses; the Leroghi plateau, rimmed with cedar forests; the Suguta Valley, an alien moonscape of laval scarps moulded by erupting volcanoes. Take a camel safari here and you will spend de-

course, accustomed to walking long distances. The average daily distance is 24 kilometres (15 miles), even though camels can cover 40 kilometres (25 miles) with ease. On the first day, every joint and muscle in your body complains. After that you should become attuned to the pace.

You are on the move for four hours in the morning, before the heat becomes intolerable, and two hours in the evening when the sun is sliding towards the horizon. The midday break is essential for camels and people alike to browse and rest.

Clothes are a matter of individual taste. They should be cool and comfortable and should not constrict your legs when striding. Bring a bathing suit for plunging into rivers, and a sweater or light jacket for chilly evenings. All this should be packed into a kit bag tough enough to survive the wear and tear of being strapped to a camel.

Trekkers spend the evenings sprawled in exhausted abandon around the campfire. Sleep comes easily on camp beds beneath an indigo sky. Camps are set up beside water holes that herdsmen have dug for their cattle. Each water hole is protected from wild animals and is reasonably clean.

kneecaps of their herders with one swift snap of their teeth.

By comparison, safari camels are well trained and usually obedient. To watch these silken-lashed beauties gliding eagerly over the sand is to be reminded of sailing ships coming into harbour on a stiff breeze. The impression, however, is erroneous. Once mounted, it feels more like being adrift in an Atlantic gale until you acquire your sea legs.

At first sight, mounting a camel appears a daunting task. However, once tried, it can be

Often the evenings are punctuated by the chilling laugh of hyaenas. And sometimes dawn reveals the spoor of a herd of elephants or a solitary lion.

The camel caravans are tended by local herders, who handle the mercurial moods of their charges with good humour. Camels can be cantankerous and wilful as well as beguiling. They have been known to crush the

executed with ease.

Some safari-goers make the daily journey almost entirely atop their mount. Others prefer to walk. To be perched on these beasts is less precarious than it seems though. Riders are never dislodged—perhaps because they realise it is too far to fall.

Mounted or not, you are hostage to the slow, quirky pace of African travel. And to the panoramas and pitfalls that unfold along the way.

Therein lies the magic of camel safaris. Africa's intimate secrets, hidden to those who travel by car, are revealed to passersby with more time to spare.

Left, loaded up and ready to roll. Above, resting by the warm glow of the campfire.

157

FRESHWATER FISHING

If you consider your angling to be a contemplative and sedentary pastime, fishing in East Africa is not for you. The variety of indigenous and exotic fish and the range of wild and unexploited locations turn a casual day out into an angling adventure.

East Africa, with its wealth of animals, has long been geared to the needs of the game safari traveller. Fishing safaris, on the other hand, are still relatively unstructured and consequently you need a sense of initiative, and adventure in your soul, if this is to be the holiday for you.

Head for the hills: Just an hour's drive from Nairobi, detouring off Kenya's main North road, you can climb into the foothills of the rolling Aberdare mountains, a series of steep ridges separated by narrow valleys, each with a dashing mountain stream. The precipitous slopes are heavily cultivated by Kikuyu whose tribal customs, ironically enough, revile cold-blooded creatures, including fish. So fishing here is reserved exclusively for visitors.

The nearest river, the Thiririka, is reached via Gatundu, the country home of Jomo Kenyatta. Trout can be found in the river just short of the forest to between 2,000 and 2,300 metres (6,560 to 7,545 feet), and deep within the forest itself to about 2,750 metres (9,020 feet). However, the rugged conditions will limit access to only a few kilometres from the river banks. This is quite sufficient, given the allowable limit for the river of six fish per day. The hardy angler, after bagging his limit, can traverse the ridge for a second bag on the adjacent river. But for most people the heavy going demands retreat until another day.

There are numerous rivers and trout holding streams on this side of the Aberdares including the Gatamayu, Ndurugu, Karimeno, Chania, Thika and Mathioya. There are also late opportunities for big fish on the plateau of the Aberdare National Park. Streams on the south-eastern slopes are narrow, little more than two metres (six feet) wide and consisting of a series of pools connected by narrow rapids overhung by bushes. A rising fish is a rare sight since, in the absence of a significant insect hatch, trout feed on underwater aquatic insects and crustaceans. Casting is not easy on the forested banks but the narrow streams do not need a long cast. Use a sunken fly, of the attractor rather than the imitative variety—a *coachman*, *invicta*, *Watson's fancy* and *butcher* are successful patterns as are "local" specials known as a *Mrs Simpson* or the *Kenyan bug*.

One delightful surprise in Kenya is the availability of high quality trout flies at very low cost. Produced for the overseas market, they are also made to order for local fishermen by the expert fly tyers of Kenya Trout and Salmon Flies at Kikuyu, just outside Nairobi, who pride themselves on reproducing any pattern you care to name.

On the Thiririka, as on most Kenyan rivers, trout are of the short, fat rainbow variety. Neither rainbow or brown trout are native to Kenya but were introduced in ova brought from Britain by Major Ewart Grogan in 1905. These, and later fish from South Africa were introduced to the Gura, Amboni and Nairobi rivers near Nyeri. (Do not confuse the Nairobi River with Nairobi City: the two are a hundred miles apart.)

By turning left into the Aberdares at Thika about 45 kilometres (30 miles) from Nairobi, and then driving the same distance again, you will arrive at the government fishing camp at Kamakia. Sleeping huts and firewood are available at little cost. The camp is ideally located on a ridge with the Chania and Kamakia rivers on either side of it. These rivers are cleaner, faster and shallower than the streams a few miles to the south and they provide a large population of rainbow trout.

The forest area is largely unfished and the more intrepid angler can descend close to 300 metres (1,000 feet) on the almost vertical elephant tracks that join the valley to the ridge. Elephants are rarely seen but evidence of their presence is all around you. The wise angler talks loudly to his companions as he descends the track, thereby avoiding any

Left, the one that didn't get away: giant Golden Nile perch.

159

possible confrontation with ascending elephant, rhino or buffalo. The simple rule is that East African anglers do not dispute possession of path or pool with the local big game!

Back at Thika, the Blue Post Hotel offers both accommodation and scenic beauty. It lies at the confluence of the Thika and Chania rivers which descend through the hotel gardens in two mighty waterfalls. Both rivers are stocked with trout in their upper reaches but at Thika the warm foaming waters contain barbus (*Barbus Thikensis*). These silver fish, streamlined and strong from a life in the fast flowing water, can be angled for, African-style, with some ledg-

also possible to exchange larger specimens for pineapples sold by the local roadside traders. This is a more refreshing reward for a successful day's fishing.

Gone fishing: As you continue to Nyeri and Nanyuki you will pass about 30 more trout streams flowing from the Aberdares and Mount Kenya. Two in particular merit special attention—the southern and northern Mathioya rivers belonging to the Kenya Flyfishers Club. These beautiful, crystal clear streams with manicured banks and paths provide the very best of fly fishing. Both brown and rainbow trout abound and the clubhouse walls are decorated with plaster-casts of specimen fish weighing up to

ered maize paste.

In the rivers fish barely reach 500 grams (one pound) but in the pools below the waterfalls at the Blue Post, fish weighing up to 4.5 kilograms (10 pounds) are caught. The idea is to clamber down to the tail of the pool and then carefully work your way to the falls. On a ledge beneath the waterfall itself, the bait can be cast into the white water and allowed to swing through the pool. The strike is hard and fish fight without showing themselves until they reach the landing net. Unfortunately they have too many bones so are not good to eat. Pickling in vinegar to dissolve the bones has been recommended, but it is

four kilograms (nine pounds).

On the banks of both rivers are elegant timber buildings, each with sleeping accommodation for eight. Cooks and other staff meet weary anglers on their return from the river and clean and prepare their fish for dinner. Unfortunately such comfort doesn't come cheap and no day tickets for visitors are sold. However, the determined angler may perhaps be able to wangle an invitation from a bona fide member.

The moorland streams of the Aberdare National Park are, however, open to the public and the Nyeri, Chania and Gura contain long lean trout. The open banks allow full reign to the elegant caster but on these rivers you should keep an eye open for wildlife. Elephant and buffalo are very common and usually resent your company. On at least one occasion the hunter has become the hunted! There are camping facilities for visitors although you will have to cook your own catch.

Nyeri and Nanyuki both boast first class hotels and the Ark Mountain Lodge game lodges allow visitors to combine fly fishing with a game safari.

As you descend from the Aberdare National Park on its west side you will reach the incredibly beautiful Lake Naivasha. Lying in the crater of a collapsed volcano, it is

lapia nigra average about 500 grams and can be caught with a float, fished worm or bread paste. Bass, however, are wary of predators and fall most easily to the variety of plugs, spinners and plastic worms designed by the United Nations specifically for catching this very fish.

An early start from Safariland will take you right across Lake Naivasha to Hippo Point in about 20 minutes. At this early hour the sky and lake blend together in a single pewter hue. Other fishers are already about their work: pied and iridescent malachite kingfishers patrol the shallows; African fish eagles prey on tilapia, and pink and white pelicans drive shoals of fish inshore before

surrounded by the extinct caldera of Longonot with its hot springs and exciting walks.

Several fine hotels and camping grounds flank the lake and from the Safariland Hotel on the south shore boats can be hired by the hour. This very beautiful lake, roughly circular and about 10 kilometres (six miles) in diameter, holds both tilapia, Kenya's favourite table fish and large mouth black bass first introduced in 1928 from America. *Ti-*

dipping together at some silent signal to scoop up beakfuls of the tiny fish.

At Hippo Point, so aptly named, casting and spinning will reap a rich harvest of bass of one kilogram each with a bigger catch coming often enough to confirm Naivasha as a high quality fishery.

Naivasha lies on the road to Uganda. On the way north there are more trout at Gilgil and at Kericho and in the tea dams above 2,600 metres (8,600 feet), Kenya's largest trout are found.

The great lake: Africa's great Lake Victoria is vast and barely explored. Although for generations it was the home of vast quanti-

Left, fishing for river trout. **Above**, Ethiopia's Lake Chamo is well stocked.

ties of the ubiquitous tilapia, stocks in recent years have been severely depleted by the introduction of Nile perch. The latter may be good to eat but they run a poor second to the sweet-tasting tilapia. The angler however is presented with a bonanza because a perch of under 14 kilograms (31 pounds) is considered a baby: specimen fish begin at a 45 kilograms (100 pounds) and double or triple that weight is possible.

Heavy tackle now comes into play and boat and shore fishing will provide you with anglers tales to beat them all. Great silver fish with bulging, orange eyes and cavernous mouths fall easy victim to a trolled plug or the long cast dead bait. The cheeks of Nile

Loyangalani Oasis on the east provide accommodation, boats and tackle for visitors.

Giant Nile perch is the favourite quarry but there are a whole host of other fishing delights available in the lake, to be caught with fly rod or light spinning rod. In a day you can expect to catch innumerable tiger fish, tilapia and a strange but delightful small-headed humpbacked fish, *citharinus gibbosus*, more popularly known by its *Swahili* name, *sahani*, which means "plate". This bream-like creature is attractive because it is never caught by its mouth. The spinner invariably lodges in the dorsal fin, possibly because it attempts to stun its prey before eating by striking it with its flat (plate-

perch are a delicacy without parallel and the great slabs of fillet, somewhat tasteless on their own, are delightful when curried or combined with more flavoursome ingredients in a pie.

Big fish : Twenty thousand crocodiles live in Lake Turkana but the quality of the fishing is so great that you'll forget your fear and wade waist deep in the lake in order to lengthen your cast. This lake, whose northern shore shares a border with Ethiopia, is fed by the Omo river. A fine highway runs parallel to its western shore or you can fly there by light aircraft. Fishing lodges at Ferguson's Gulf on the western side and

like) sides. Whatever the reason, the unconventionally hooked fish, weighing up to 4.5 kilograms, will not be constrained by a lure in its mouth. Only the greatest skill will keep the light tackle intact and eventually beach the fish.

The tiger fish is well named: each armour-plated jaw is fringed with needle sharp fangs. Their fight is as spectacular as any trout but wear gloves or hire an assistant to help remove hooks or you risk the loss of a fingertip or worse.

There are other fish less frequently caught, some of which are sufficiently unusual to require a visit to Kenya's National Museum to identify the specimen.

Uganda's lakes: From Kisumu and Lake Victoria a short drive will take you through the Uganda border at Busia and on the road to Kampala. At Jinja, the pools under Owen Falls have always offered the best sport for barbus. Similar to the Thika fish, possibly the same variety, they nevertheless grow considerably bigger and fish to nine kilograms (20 pounds) have been recorded, although an average fish is nearer three kilograms (6.6 pounds). A long cast into the boiling water under the falls yields generous rewards but hidden rocks and debris tend to snarl up tackle.

The Nile at Murchison Falls yields tiger nevertheless 20-kilogram (44-pound) fish are common and 50-kilogram (110-pound) fish do exist.

A dead bait tiger fish can attract big catfish. Tiger fish are easily caught for this purpose by using a small spoon. Alternatively you can follow the local example and knock down with your landing net some of the thousands of dragon flies on the river bank. Then catch your tiger fish on a number eight hook.

Nile perch, locally known as *mbuta*, can be found in the whole Nile system below Murchison Falls and can be fished for as far as the Sudan border. Security and access will prevent you from venturing too far off the

fish, catfish and Nile perch. At his most spectacular of scenes the full weight of the Nile roars over the narrowest of precipices. As with barbus, an accurate cast into the foaming waters beneath the falls is the way to take perch from the river. Use a wooden plug or large siver spoon as the lure. As it sweeps down the current the waiting perch grab and can be fought to the bank. Although generally smaller than fish in Lake Victoria,

Left, casting a fly in Lake Turkana. Above, flamingo-filled Lake Bogoria.

beaten track.

Lakes Albert and Kioga contain perch and a large variety of other fish including several species of barbus, tilapia, catfish and lung fish. The latter are reputed to grow to two metres (6.6 feet) long and feed on frogs, crabs, snails and small fish, though they prefer carrion and are particularly susceptible to dead bait. They are also reputed to bite fiercely and should be treated with caution if encountered.

The deeper waters of Lake Albert hold larger tiger fish up to 10 times the weight of its smaller cousin of Lake Turkana and the Nile at Murchison. Inshore, small tiger fish give wonderful sport but no evening feast since their armour plating conceals a host of small bones.

Trout were introduced to Uganda in 1932 and the Mabuku, Dwimi, Namwamba and Namusagani rivers were all stocked. However, there has been no stocking programme since 1970 although breeding conditions are good and it is possible that there are large wild fish waiting for the more adventurous angler.

Other parts: Rwanda's Lake Kivu is home to several species of tilapia and other *chichlidae*. There are about 300 members of this fish family in Africa and it is more than possible that you will not be able to identify

and *Bathybates fasciatus* have slim bodies, powerful tails and a long dorsal fin. Bluish-green on their backs and with yellow-tipped fins, they are respected as fierce fighters.

Trout can be found in the rivers of the West Usambara Mountains, particularly the Mkusu River. As you head north again towards Kenya, snowcapped Kilimanjaro offers an exciting diversion and the lower slopes host splendid fishing for rainbow trout. Arusha is an appropiate base and the Usa River offers the best prospects. A good tarmac road returns you to Kenya via Namanga.

East of Amboseli National Park you can explore the Athi and Bushwackers camp at

some of your catch without the aid of the larger reference books.

Burundi shares the northern part of Lake Tanganyika with Zaire and Tanzania. Nile perch are absent from these lakes divorced from the Nile, but many new species of cat fish can be encountered. Barbus of the type found at Jinja, in Uganda, are common and the streamlined *labes victoricinus* is often mistaken for a heavy tiger fish when first hooked. Its non-acrobatic fight and absence of teeth soon confirm otherwise. Two other fish, locally referred to as tiger fish because of their exceptionally fierce fangs, are actually of a different species. *Bathybates ferox*

Kibwesi for tilapia and catfish. The natural lakes at Hunters Lodge, 150 kilometres (93 miles) east of Nairobi contain barbus, small but obliging tilapia and giant eels, weighing up to three kilograms.

Ideally a fishing safari in one of the world's last wild places should take in lakes Naivasha, Victoria and Turkana, a trout stream or two on Mount Kenya or the Aberdares and a few hours on the rivers at Thika in search of barbus. Whatever the catch, it should be enough to guarantee a lasting reminder of an angling adventure in Africa.

Fishing Ethiopia: A fishing safari to East Africa would not be complete without a visit

TANA DELTA SAFARI

Kenya's Tana Delta is flat and low, criss-crossed with tidal channels, savannah grass-lands, stands of doum palms, swamp and thick forest. Some of the numerous and divergent tidal waterways are navigable for as far as 15 kilometres (nine miles) inland, either by small canoes through narrow channels or more slowly by larger dhow on the main waterway.

Guests are collected from Malindi and driven a couple of hours north along a rutted dirt track to a village on the river. From here

cattle down to drink. Elsewhere, Pokomo women wash cooking pots or clothes as their children wade in the shallows—in spite of the crocodiles which claim at least one victim per week.

Hippos wallow in deep pools on the river bends, snorting and blowing bubbles before submerging again. In grass clearings reed-buck, topi, buffalo and sometimes the rare bushbuck or a lone bull elephant roam.

The Tana River is most famous for its prolific birdlife, featuring the exotic, the

the dhow *African Queen* travels at a leisurely seven knots down the Tana River on a four hour journey to the camp.

Sitting on a deckchair on the 11-metre-(36-foot-) long, high-decked, diesel-powered boat, one travels through channels the colour of café au lait with dense jungle on either side. Where the banks slope gently to the water's edge, herdsboys of the *Orma* tribe, akin to the more famous *Maasai*, bring

spectacular and the merely odd. There are huge flocks of egrets, pelicans, ibis and storks on every sandbank. Beautifully coloured bee-eaters, hornbills, kingfishers and many other birds are a constant delight.

By sunset, the *African Queen* arrives at the small tented camp, which lies at the foot of a giant, white sand dune. There are no roads or other camps in this remote area. The tents are roomy, insect proof and secure with a large attached verandah in front of each and a private shower and toilet near by.

The ideal safari lasts four days. This gives you time to explore and birdwatch in the vast floodplain, either by boat or on foot.

Left, sailing to Rusinga. **Above**, taking a leisurely trip along the Tana.

167

Deep Sea Fishing

The abundance and variety of game fish, together with well-equipped boats and professional crews make the coast of East Africa a paradise for sports fisherman.

From Pemba Channel on the Kenya-Tanzania sea border all the way north to Diani, Mombasa, Mtwapa, Kilifi, Watamu, Malindi, Lamu and Kiwayu, there are efficient charter operators available during the recognised eight-month fishing season (August to March). The high winds of the rain-bearing *Kusi* (south-east monsoon) make waters (marlin and sailfish), Kenya offers many possibilities. Pemba Channel Fishing Club owned by the Hemphill family is located at Shimoni on the southern border with Tanzania; at Watamu big black and blue marlin are caught every year; and Malindi is one of the world's most prolific venues for Pacific sailfish.

Kenya's sport fishing grounds rank in the world's top five areas for high annual average catches of billfish. But billfish are not the only attraction. Kenyan and Tanzanian wa-

unfishable between late March and late July.

In Tanzania there are exhilarating fishing locations off Tanga in the north. From Dar es Salaam to Mafia Island and other spots along the extreme southern coast of the country there are numerous fishing opportunities.

The most challenging sport fish of the ocean—black, blue and striped marlin (*Makiara inoica, Makiara nigricans* and *Tetrapturus audax*) and Pacific sailfish (*Istiophorus platypterus*) all abound in these waters, as do the powerful yellowfin tuna (*Thunnus albacares*).

For both the enthusiastic beginner and those experts seeking the exciting billfish ters are teeming with a wide variety of game fish including barracuda (*Sphyraena barracuda*), dolphinfish (*Coryphaena hippurus*), kingfish (*Scomberomorus commerson*), pacific bonito (*Sarda spp*), mako shark (*Isurus spp*), tiger shark (*Galeocerdo cavieri*), and hammerhead (*Sphvrna spp*). There are strong seasonal runs of yellowfin tuna and some dogtooth (*Gymnosarda unicolor*), especially from August to December.

The broadbill swordfish (*Xiphias gladius*), one of the most elusive of the ocean game fish, is found in the indigo waters off the East African coast.

Fishing tackle and boats run by Kenya's

dedicated professional operators—about 20 in all—are based at points along the 402-kilometre (250-mile) coastline.

Boats up to 15 metres (50 feet) in length include such popular "fishing platforms" as *White Otter* (13.5 metres/44 feet), the catamaran *Pingusi* (nine metres/30 feet), and *Broadbill* (14 metres/46 feet) at Hemphill's Pemba Channel Club. James Adcock owns a fleet at Mtwapa; *Ol Jogi*, a 10-metre (33-foot) Bertram and *White Bear*, an 11.5-metre (38-foot) Sport Fisherman, are both

Kenya's extreme north coastal waters bordering Somalia. Though not as accessible as areas further south, there are charter boats available both from the Peponi Hotel at Lamu and from the exclusive and remote Kiwayu Lodge. Several very large marlin have been caught in these waters.

Prices are reasonable by world standards with rates for the large boats averaging around Ksh 5,000 to Ksh 6,000 (US$270 to US$335) per day, with up to six rods and a maximum of three fishermen for marlin or

based at Kenya's newly-opened deep sea fishing, diving and sports venue—Hemingway's in Watamu. This 100-bed luxury resort is fully geared to cater for sport fishing. Boats are available for charter all year round—subject to weather conditions.

At Malindi—the sailfish "Mecca"—there are charter operators who have become especially skilled at light tackle and fly casting for sailfish and dolphin.

Fish are plentiful off Lamu and Kiwayu on

four fishermen for smaller fish.

The Kenya Association of Sea Angling Clubs (KASAC) is the recognised body that oversees the organisation of deep sea fishing on the Kenya Coast. It arranges a full programme of deep sea fishing competitions and events are attracting an ever growing number of competitors from overseas. For further information write to: Kenya Association of Sea Angling Clubs, P. O. Box 84133, Mombasa, Kenya.

Deep sea fishing enthusiasts going to Tanzania should contact the Dar es Salaam Yacht Club, which can arrange a trip to your liking.

Left, heading for fishing grounds off Kenya's coral coast. **Above**, ready to reel 'em in.

PEAK EXPERIENCES

The great snowcapped peaks of Africa rise on the eastern side of the continent. Kilimanjaro at 5,895 metres (19,340 feet) straddles the border of Kenya and Tanzania; Mount Kenya at 5,199 metres (17,058 feet), stands in central Kenya. The Ruwenzori Mountains at 5,106 metres (16,763 feet) dominate the border of Uganda and Zaire.

Few mountains in the world are as steeped in legend and mystery as these giants of Africa, and for over 100 years they have drawn the curious traveller to their slopes. Their very discovery proved controversial: the sightings of Kilimanjaro and Mount Kenya in 1848 and 1849 respectively by Church Missionary Society preachers Johann Rebmann and Johann Krapf, was disbelieved by the Royal Geographical Society in London. Snow, they said, could not exist so close to the equator, and what the missionaries had seen could only be "calcareous earth". Rebmann and Krapf would not be vindicated until the Scottish explorer Joseph Thomson witnessed the snows of both peaks in 1883. Henry Morton Stanley met no resistance from Europe's Geographical Societies when he sent word back of his discovery of the Ruwenzoris in 1889.

Kilimanjaro: Kilimanjaro is East Africa's loftiest landmark. It is the highest mountain in Africa and one of the highest extinct volcanoes in the world. Its name is synonymous with Africa itself and few mountains anywhere on earth have been so immersed in romance and folklore. Even the names of towns that grace the base of the peak have a dream-like quality to them—Oloitokitok, Rongai, Moshi and Marangu.

Great writers with no interest in mountains have written about Kilimanjaro. Songs have been sung about it. Empires fought for it. Many stories and myths have grown, some true, some false. The partially preserved skeleton of a leopard does exist on the icy crater rim at 5,666 metres (18,600 feet); but Queen Victoria did not give the mountain to the Kaiser as a birthday present.

However one looks at it, Kilimanjaro possesses an atmosphere, a personality, the type from which legends are easily born.

The base of the mountain is approximately 80 kilometres (50 miles) long by 40 kilometres (25 miles) wide, and boasts three definite peaks. Shira to the west is the least obvious and reaches a height of 4,002 metres (13,140 feet). Its long, gentle, whale-back appearance can barely be distinguished from the general downward roll of the mountain slopes.

Mawenzi to the east attains an altitude of 5,145 metres (16,890 feet) and is a beautifully sculptured masterpiece of a peak.

Kibo rises to the highest point of the mountain and is young, resplendent, a giant upturned bowl of a summit with an almost perfect circular crater 2.5 kilometres (1.5 miles) wide. It is covered by three large icefields from which hang 15 extremely steep glaciers. When viewed from either the north or the south the great sweep of The Saddle captures the eye as one of the dominant features of the massif. This vast plain at 4,569 metres (15,000 feet) is about seven kilometres (4.3 miles) across and separates Mawenzi from Kibo.

Shira, Mawenzi and Kibo were all individual volcanoes. Research during the last 50 years would suggest that Shira was the site of the first eruption, followed later by Mawenzi. Kibo, geologically speaking, is recent and most of its activity occurred during the Pleistocene period. It is possible, however, that the last major episode of activity took place within the last few centuries.

Green belts: As with other mountains of eastern and central Africa, there are definite vegetational zones on Kilimanjaro. A thick belt of montane forest encircles the entire mountain between 1,888 metres (6,200 feet) and 2,985 metres (9,800 feet) and is dominated by podos trees which are of giant proportions with buttressed roots. Cedar also grows in profusion on the lower northern slopes and the majority of these trees are festooned with thick, woody lianes. An array of large ferns and nettles makes passage in the forest difficult but, unlike other African

Preceding pages: breathtaking view of Kilimajaro's Mawenzi peak at dawn. **Left,** rock climbing in Kenya.

mountains, virtually no bamboo grows on Kilimanjaro.

Kilimanjaro forest is a silent place and although it is inhabited by mammals they are not in the numbers which can be seen on Mount Kenya. Elephant and cape buffalo are the most common larger animals of the forest; bushbuck and duiker can also be seen. But the chances of the visitor seeing or hearing them, or even noticing so much as a sign of them, is remote. Spotting a Colobus monkey is probably your best chance of seeing any wildlife on Kilimanjaro.

In the higher regions of the mountain there are a few deep sheltered valleys and the slopes consist of very porous lavas, so the

climbed on October 5, 1889 by the German mountaineers Hans Meyer and Ludwig Purtscheller. This ascent to the summit of Kibo involved no great technical skills. Today thousands of visitors annually reach the lowest point of the crater rim, Gillman's Point, at 5,681 metres (18,650 feet). Some people continue clockwise round the crater for an extra 90 minutes to Uhuru Peak at 5,895 metres (19,340 feet), the highest point of Africa.

There are seven tracks up Kilimanjaro from both Kenya and Tanzania but at the time of writing all Kenyan routes had been closed. Ninety-five percent of visitors will ascend the peak by way of the tourist route

little water that falls as rain or descends as melt-water from the glaciers does so underground for long distances and is virtually unavailable to plants. Compared with other East African mountains, Kilimanjaro is floristically poor.

The spoor of leopard can often be seen on the trails of the upper moorlands and alpine zone though sightings of the animal itself is rare. For many years The Saddle has boasted a large herd of eland; they are interesting because their fur appears to be longer than that of the lowland species and the animals are larger.

Reaching the top: Kilimanjaro was first

from the little Tanzanian town of Marangu near Moshi. Moshi can be reached by rail or bus, but perhaps the most efficient way is by air to Kilimanjaro Airport, some 34 kilometres (21 miles) west of Moshi on the main road to Arusha. This modern airport is served by daily flights from Dar es Salaam, as well as international flights from Kenya and Europe. In Moshi there are two or three hotels and provision shops, but these shops should not be relied upon to stock sophisticated mountain food.

Marangu is 27 kilometres (17 miles) east of Moshi, and located here are two hotels which arrange for fully packaged mountain safaris up Kilimanjaro: Kibo Hotel, P. O. Box 102, Marangu, Kilimanjaro, and Marangu Hotel, P. O. Box 40, Moshi, Tanzania. These hotels will arrange porters, vehicles to the park gate and all food. Some trekking equipment can be hired. Hotel managers will also steer visitors through the tedious officialdom which most people encounter at the national park entrance.

Technically speaking, the ascent is no more than a stiff walk for those who arrive at the base in a state of reasonable fitness. The trick to climbing any large mountain is to go slowly. Mountain sickness tends to affect everyone to some degree and this can come in the form of headaches, loss of appetite,

is at 1,800 metres (5,909 feet), the path works its way up through the lower forests to Mandara Hut at 2,700 metres (8,864 feet). Although this walk can be done easily in about five hours, spend the entire day over it and keep your body fluid level up.

On the following day the trail traverses the southern slopes of the peak, leading out of the forest and on to the stark moorlands. Horombo Hut at 3,807 metres (12,500 feet) is reached late in the afternoon. If it is possible for you to arrange a two-night stay at Horombo Hut it is a very worthwhile plan. This hut is located at a fairly critical altitude and acclimatising well at this point will ensure stronger chances of success in the two

nausea and lack of energy. By walking slowly one can go a long way towards alleviating some of these ailments.

To make things easier the Kilimanjaro National Park has constructed an excellent series of huts at convenient intervals up the side of the mountain, and visitors are strongly recommended to spend four nights and five days for the ascent and descent of the peak. After leaving the park gate, which

Left, the southern glaciers of Kibo. **Above**, the summit of Africa—Uhuru Peak.

days to come.

After Horombo Hut the path climbs gradually to The Saddle at 4,264 metres (14,000 feet). This vast alpine desert is easily crossed towards the peak of Kibo, until the track begins to rise to Kibo Hut at 4,721 metres (15,500 feet). Not a great deal can be said for the location of this final hut on the way to the summit of Kilimanjaro. It is desolate and cold and the majority of walkers are in no mood to enjoy any small pleasures which the district may offer. Headaches and nausea are being nursed by many of the hut's occupants and most people are thoroughly intimidated by the prospect of the final 944 metres

(3,100 feet) of scree, the ascent of which will begin at 1 a.m.

There are good reasons for starting at this early hour. The scree which is composed of small pebble-like ash cinders is frozen then and is easier to climb; when the sun rises it does so from behind Mawenzi, beautifully illuminating the serrated silhouette of this peak. The higher you are up the Kibo scree by the time the sun rises, the grander the view. But for many, the third reason for beginning so early is the one which makes greatest sense: it is dark and therefore one cannot see the apparently endless distances ahead, which in daylight never seem to come any closer!

Gillman's Point will be quite enough! Descent is then made to Horombo Hut for another night, before returning to the park gate on the fifth day.

For succeeding on Kilimanjaro, the best advice is to hedge your bets by following these rules. Insist on a good guide from the hotels; wear good, warm equipment (do not be fooled by the mountain's proximity to the equator for Kilimanjaro is as cold as any other 5,800-metre (19,000-foot) peak in the world, and the temperature at the top will be well below freezing), take the ascent easily—do not walk fast, and remember to drink plenty of liquids.

"The Ostrich hill": Mount Kenya is 5,199

There is little genuine pleasure in the ascent of the final few hundred metres of Kibo and it is only when you reach the edge of the crater that you will appreciate why you chose to suffer all the pain. The path zigzags up the side of the mountain. The average walker begins by climbing perhaps 100 steps before resting, and this number of paces becomes for a few hours the focal point of your existence. By the time 5,483 metres (18,000 feet) is reached you'll have reduced the distance covered between rests to a few stumbling steps. The aim of the exercise is to reach Gillman's Point although some people will continue to the main summit. But for most,

metres (17,068 feet) high and a little over 100 kilometres (62 miles) in diameter. It is the second highest mountain in Africa and is in many ways more interesting than its larger neighbour Kilimanjaro. It is an ancient extinct volcano whose period of activity was between 3.1 milion and 2.6 million years ago, when it probably rose to over 7,615 metres (25,000 feet) with a shape resembling that of Kilimanjaro.

Today the shape of Mount Kenya belies the fact that it was ever a volcano at all. There is little trace of a crater left, so beaten has the mountain become through time and countless eruptions, but its majestically battered peaks, draped by 11 glaciers, radiate an air of supreme elegance. From the plains, the peaks of Mount Kenya seem to float like a distant fortress in the sky. Or as the Wakamba people who dwell some 200 kilometres (125 miles) away used to say: like a "cock ostrich". The contrast between its white glaciers and the dark rocks do indeed look like the black and white plumage of the male ostrich. This could well be the origin of the word "Kenya" for in the Wakamba language *Kiinya* means "The hill of the cock ostrich". For the Kikuyu people who dwell and farm around the foothills of Mount Kenya the mountain has special meaning. Since the earliest of times their lives have

early risers.

Forests, moors and glaciers: The heart of Mount Kenya lies in the thick, semitropical rain forests which grace its lower slopes up to an altitude of 3,350 metres (11,000 feet). These forests begin between 2,132 and 2,437 metres (7,000 and 8,000 feet) above the uppermost point of the Kikuyu's fertile farms or *shambas*. Giant trees of camphor wood, pencil cedar, podocarpus and East African olive, draped with vine-like lianes, rise above a tangled profusion of dripping ferns, nettles and bamboo. It is an area difficult for humans to penetrate and because of this, it is home to herds of cape buffalo and elephant, as well as bush-

been inextricably linked to this often uncompromising peak. It brings them their rain and therefore their livelihood, and during frequent periods of drought they would pray to it, and make sacrifices of lambs and goats. Even today, elder members of the Kikuyu rise early in the morning to offer prayer to *Ngai*—their god who lives among the summit peaks. It is said that by sunrise *Ngai* will have dispensed all of his blessings upon the

buck and the occasional black rhino.

With dramatic suddenness the forests end at 3,350 metres and the moorlands begin. This region which extends upwards to 4,264 metres (14,000 feet) is more compromising, with its stark beauty akin to the Scottish highlands. Tussock grasses, with intermittent heather growing occasionally over three metres (10 feet) in height, gradually transforms into the drier world of the exotic treelike giant groundsels and lobelia.

The area is studded with rock islands of porous volcanic ashes and agglomerates standing out like dark, incongruous sentinels. Big game is rarely seen here but its

Left, resting on the crater rim on the way to the top. **Above**, view of Mount Kenya's Point Lenana.

177

presence is always felt. The spoor of eland, cape buffalo, and leopard is always evident, and every now and again giant groundsel patches lie like withered carcasses, smashed to pieces by elephant.

There is a deceptive flatness about this area which at first appearance would seem to extend as high as the base of the summit peaks. But centuries of glacial activity have slowly eaten away the surface to the extent that the entire region surrounding the peaks has been carved into numerous valleys and gorges—some as deep as 609 metres (2,000 feet).

A vast carpet of lobelia and giant groundsels extend over these valleys, clustering

thickly along the edges of rivers which flow down them. But for the sounds of the rivers there is a profound silence in these valleys.

The valleys and gorges of Mount Kenya rise to a point at 4,417 metres (14,500 feet) where plants and vegetation can no longer survive. The green landscape becomes grey: rocks and boulders are suddenly of gigantic proportions, steep scree chutes of pebbles and cinders lead up to the snouts of glaciers and the final 609 metres of vertical rock and ice.

Climbing Mount Kenya: The summit of Batian, the highest peak on Mount Kenya, was first stood upon by Halford Mackinder,

Cesar Ollier and Joseph Brocherel on September 13, 1899. It was the culmination of a four-month expedition and the successful outcome was an outstanding achievement. The easiest route to the top of the mountain had involved scaling a 457-metre (1,500-foot) vertical rock and ice face, and it would be 30 years before it saw a second ascent.

Today few people attempt to reach the highest point of Mount Kenya, but many trek to the summit of the third highest peak— Point Lenana at 4,982 metres (16,355 feet). It is worth the effort as it gives a good idea of the atmosphere of this beautiful mountain.

The base for climbing Mount Kenya is at Naro Moru, which is located 171 kilometres (106 miles) from Nairobi on the main road to Nanyuki. The Naro Moru track is the shortest way to the peaks, and can be undertaken in three days. Because of this the bulk of tourists ascend the mountain this way, neglecting the more involved routes, of which there are seven. Naro Moru can be reached from Nairobi by bus or by a number of local taxi services, and most of these are centred around: East African Road Services, Racecourse Road, P.O. Box 30475, Nairobi. Tel: 23476.

The journey to Naro Moru will take between two and three hours and visitors are recommended to make their way to the hotel which is the undisputed starting point for the majority of Mount Kenya attempts: The Naro Moru River Lodge, P.O. Box 18, Naro Moru. Tel: Naro Moru 23. This lodge will arrange fully packaged ascents of Point Lenana.

The recommended way of ascending the Naro Moru track is as follows:

Day One: Begin at the National Park gate which is 17 kilometres (10 miles) from Naro Moru township. Hike to the Meteorological Clearing at 3,046 metres (10,000 feet). Camp here or stay in the bunkhouses which can be booked through the Naro Moru River Lodge.

Day Two: Walk up through the forest which soon becomes boggy moorlands. These are crossed to the edge of the Teleki Valley. Descend round into the valley and climb it to its head. At this point is the Mackinder's Lodge at 4,143 metres (13,600 feet), which is a good place to stay. Good campsites also exist in this area. The distance to the lodge can be covered from the Meteorological

Station in about five hours, but the entire day should be spent slowly working your way up to the head of the valley.

Day Three: A day spent resting and acclimatising in the Teleki Valley.

Day Four: Begin the trek to the summit of Point Lenana at 3 a.m. The path contours up the west side of the Teleki Valley, then strikes up the screes on the south side of the obvious Lewis Glacier to the Austrian Hut at 4,788 metres (15,720 feet). Point Lenana is ascended by way of the ridge above the hut and takes approximately one hour more. The descent to the Teleki Valley can be made in two hours and many parties go all the way to the Meteorological Station in the afternoon.

ria. Tel: Chogoria 26.

The Chogoria track is a very beautiful way up Mount Kenya and three days should be allowed to reach Point Lenana. A good trek is to ascend the Chogoria track to Lenana then descend the Naro Moru track so completing a full traverse of the mountain.

The main summit peaks of Batian at 5,199 metres (17,068 feet) and Nelion at 5,188 metres (17,032 feet) should only be undertaken by experienced mountaineers who understand the intricacies of climbing steep ice and rock at altitude.

If approached in the correct way Mount Kenya can give the trekker a more rewarding experience than Kilimanjaro. It offers far

Point Lenana is often ascended by way of the Chogoria Track on the eastern side of Mount Kenya. The town of Chogoria is located on the main road linking Nairobi to Meru and is 228 kilometres (141 miles) from Nairobi.

There are no hotels in Chogoria which offer fully equipped safaris up the mountain, but porters can be arranged through: Mr. Livingstone Barine, P.O. Box 5007, Chogo-

richer flora and fauna than the latter and the scenery is more spectacular. It should be noted that although the equator runs through Mount Kenya, visitors should not underestimate the weather conditions.

Mountains of the Moon: No other mountain range in Africa, perhaps in the world, is as steeped in legend as the Ruwenzoris—Ptolemy's fabled Mountains of the Moon. A trek to the icefields of this range is no ordinary climb—it is a journey to the pulse of the African continent.

The Ruwenzoris lie along the western border of Uganda and rise approximately 3,960 metres (13,000 feet) above the western

Left, looking towards the main peaks of Mount Kenya. **Above**, camping on the "Ostrich hill".

179

Rift Valley. The range is some 112 kilometres (70 miles) long by 50 kilometres (30 miles) wide and was formed from a block which was tilted and thrust up during the development of the rift. Unlike Kilimanjaro and Mount Kenya it is not of volcanic origin.

In the centre of the range there are six major peaks all draped with permanent snow and glaciers. Mount Stanley at 5,106 metres (16,763 feet) is the summit of the Ruwenzoris and it is surrounded by a complex system of other mountains such as Speke (4,886 metres/16,042 feet), Baker (4,840 metres/15,889 feet), Gessi (4,712 metres/ 15,470 feet), Emin (4,788 metres/15,720 feet) and Luigi di Savoia (4,624 metres/

range is arguably one of the wettest in the world but it has its worthy compensations in that it is a botanist's paradise. Giant groundsels and lobelia grow in thick forests above 3,046 metres (10,000 feet) and attain heights of up to 15 metres (50 feet). Heather can be found in clumps nine metres (30 feet) high.

For the traveller the Ruwenzori Mountains offer problems that other East African peaks do not. Merely reaching their base can be a mini expedition in its own right. Ascents to the peaks can be made from both Zaire and Uganda, but the former does not compare in either beauty or ambience. The approach from Uganda is the traditional way up to the icefields.

15,179 feet). On each of these mountains there are several peaks and glaciers.

Early travellers acknowledged the Ruwenzoris as the source of the Nile and the first information to be brought back from the interior was by Henry Morton Stanley after his 1888-89 expedition. The first expediton to explore the mountains thoroughly was led by the Duke of the Abruzzi in 1906.

Unlike the other great mountains of East Africa, the Ruwenzoris rarely dazzle the surrounding countryside with their shimmering snowfields. In fact they are hardly ever seen from the plains, being almost continually wrapped in thick cloud. The

Climbing from Uganda: All expeditions begin from the small town of Kasese, which is located on the south-eastern side of the range. To reach Kasese, the easiest way is by train from Kampala and there is, at the time of writing, a daily service connecting them. One should always allow a few "buffer" days for any trip to these mountains for in Uganda there can always be delays. Driving between Kampala and Kasese is currently inadvisable. The road is long and badly in need of repair. Charter flights between Entebbe and Kasese can be arranged.

In Kasese there are two hotels, the Saad and the Margherita. The latter is government-run and expensive. At the Saad, on the other hand, the management was friendly and able to provide transport to the roadhead at Ibanda. They will also assist with porters although it is advisable to book these through: John Matte, Shop and Club Agent, Ibanda, P.O. Box 88, Kasese.

The porters are very friendly and eager for work, but they do expect blankets to be purchased for them in advance. Allow two days around Kasese and Ibanda for finalising porter arrangements.

It should be stressed that the Ruwenzoris are alpine in character and the warmest mountain clothing should be carried to the peaks. It is a very wet range and good rain-

proof equipment is essential. Knee-high gumboots are very useful on the approach to the peaks. There are currently no national park services of any kind and all visiting parties should be totally self-sufficient.

The majority of climbers will start from Ibanda, which is approximately 32 kilometres (20 miles) from Kasese. The trek to the peaks can be done as a "horseshoe" so that the same ground is not covered twice.

The recommended route is as follows:

Day One: Camp at Ibanda at 2,437 metres (8,000 feet).

Day Two: Hike through the lower rainforests where you might be lucky enough to spot the Ruwenzori turaco flying amongst the branches. The walk today is about six hours long and in the late afternoon Nyabitaba Hut is reached at 3,046 metres (10,000 feet).

Day Three: The path continues up a narrowing ridge and after some three hours reaches the infamous Bigo Bog (3,350 metres (11,000 feet).

Day Four: The path steepens as the forests are left behind and the beautiful Bujuku Valley is reached. At the end of this valley is Bujuku Hut at 3,960 metres (13,000 feet).

Day Five: The path climbs into the relatively inhospitable alpine zone leaving all vegetation behind. At the edge of the Elena Glacier the Elena Huts are reached at 4,843 metres (15,900 feet).

Day Six: A climber's day, when the Elena Glacier is ascended to reach the Stanley Plateau. From here the summit peak of Margherita at 5,106 metres (16,763 feet) can be climbed in several hours.

Day Seven: In the morning a descent is made to the entrancing Kitandara lakes where Kitandara Hut is located at 3,960 metres (13,000 feet).

Day Eight: A trek is made across Freshfield Pass to descend into the Mobuku Valley. The Mobuku Caves are reached in the late afternoon. The altitude is 3,655 metres (12,000 feet).

Day Nine: The path traverses out of the Mobuku Valley and rejoins the ridge above Nyabitaba Hut, thus completing the "horseshoe" circuit.

Day Ten: The final descent into Ibanda.

To reach the highest point of the Ruwenzoris, Margherita Peak, requires some experience of snow and ice climbing. The majority of strong hikers wearing crampons and carrying ice-axes will be able to reach the Stanley Plateau, which in many ways is the most spectacular area of the entire range. This plateau, which is the largest single ice mass on the African continent, is the watershed of Uganda and Zaire and most hikers would be very satisfied to reach it. Margherita, which rises above the Stanley Plateau is ascended by its obvious East Ridge.

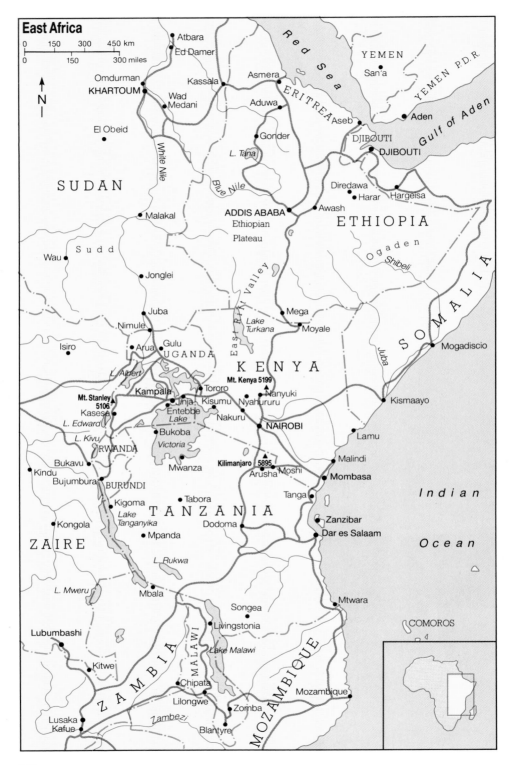

East Africa

GAME PARKS AND RESERVES

There is nothing quite like the drama of wildlife, and the game parks and reserves of East Africa provide the best and biggest stage from which to watch. A herd of elephants trudging across a grassy plain, hippos happily wallowing in a mud pool, vultures riding the air currents over a group of grazing gazelles—all are a part of the animal kingdom's daily routine. East Africa's game parks give a fascinating glimpse of animal life in a series of pristine habitats. This can't-miss combination of birds, animals and scenery brings thousands of visitors each year to some of the most famous reserves in the world.

Kenya and Tanzania are at the heart of the safari experience, and the vast majority of safari goers will be heading for destinations within these two countries. They possess the tourist infrastructure, the facilities and the variety of wildlife to pamper those who like to temper their adventure with the trappings of luxury, although arrangements can also be made for anyone who prefers to rough it out in the less-explored regions.

Political and economic uncertainties in recent years, coupled with the problems of poaching, have complicated the wildlife picture in Uganda and Ethiopia. However, their respective governments recognise the value of tourism and have embarked on recovery programmes to protect the game parks there.

The tiny nation of Rwanda is best known for its population of mountain gorillas, whose habitat extends across the border to eastern Zaire. Neighbouring Burundi is only mentioned in passing in this guide as its wildlife has, sadly, been almost completely poached out of existence. The struggle for conservation continues in each of the other countries.

Despite these inherent problems, East African game parks well deserve their reputation as destinations that exceed expectations. This section discusses all the major game parks in East Africa, and some of the lesser ones as well. Whether it's a day trip to a nearby reserve or an extended journey through the bush, a visit to the land that spawned the word *safari* is one that few are likely to forget.

Preceding pages: tree groundsel near the top of Kilimanjaro; volcanic hills near Lake Turkana; the Mara River winds its way past a tented camp; room with a view: Mount Kenya as seen from the lounge of the Safari Club.

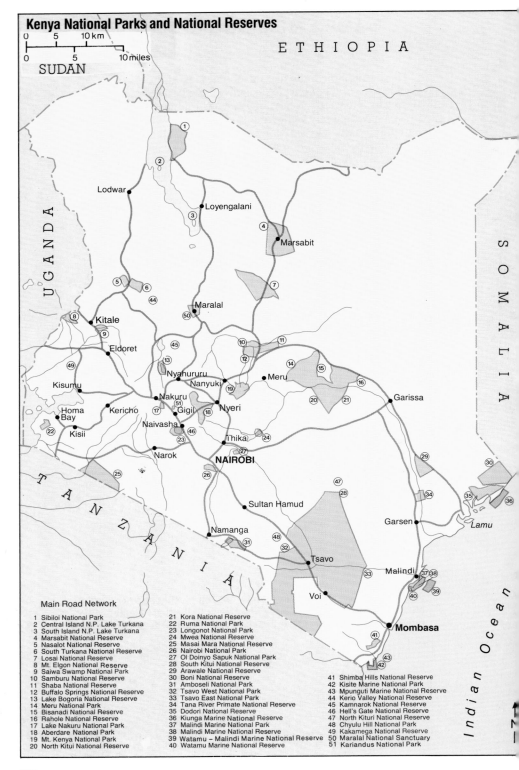

Kenya National Parks and National Reserves

0   5   10 km
0   5   10 miles

ETHIOPIA

SUDAN

UGANDA

SOMALIA

TANZANIA

Indian Ocean

Lodwar
Loyengalani
Marsabit
Maralal
Kitale
Eldoret
Nyahururu
Nanyuki
Meru
Garissa
Kisumu
Nakuru
Gigil
Nyeri
Homa Bay
Kericho
Naivasha
Kisii
Narok
Thika
NAIROBI
Sultan Hamud
Garsen
Lamu
Namanga
Tsavo
Malindi
Voi
Mombasa

Main Road Network

1 Sibiloi National Park
2 Central Island N.P. Lake Turkana
3 South Island N.P. Lake Turkana
4 Marsabit National Reserve
5 Nasalot National Reserve
6 South Turkana National Reserve
7 Losai National Reserve
8 Mt. Elgon National Reserve
9 Saiwa Swamp National Park
10 Samburu National Reserve
11 Shaba National Reserve
12 Buffalo Springs National Reserve
13 Lake Bogoria National Reserve
14 Meru National Park
15 Bisanadi National Reserve
16 Rahole National Reserve
17 Lake Nakuru National Park
18 Aberdare National Park
19 Mt. Kenya National Park
20 North Kitui National Reserve

21 Kora National Reserve
22 Ruma National Park
23 Longonot National Park
24 Mwea National Reserve
25 Masai Mara National Reserve
26 Nairobi National Park
27 Ol Doinyo Sapuk National Park
28 South Kitui National Reserve
29 Arawale National Reserve
30 Boni National Reserve
31 Amboseli National Park
32 Tsavo West National Park
33 Tsavo East National Park
34 Tana River Primate National Reserve
35 Dodori National Reserve
36 Kiunga Marine National Reserve
37 Malindi Marine National Park
38 Malindi Marine National Reserve
39 Watamu – Malindi Marine National Reserve
40 Watamu Marine National Reserve

41 Shimba Hills National Reserve
42 Kisite Marine National Park
43 Mpunguti Marine National Reserve
44 Kerio Valley National Reserve
45 Kamnarok National Reserve
46 Hell's Gate National Reserve
47 North Kituri National Reserve
48 Chyulu Hill National Park
49 Kakamega National Reserve
50 Maralal National Sanctuary
51 Kariandus National Park

192

KENYA

In 1985, the Academy-Award-winning film *Out of Africa* introduced a new generation of travellers to the beauty of Kenya. Cloudless, azure skies and golden savannah plains packed with animals fired the imagination of countless romantics and adventurers who wanted to experience this exotic Eden for themselves.

Long before that movie, though, a long line of writers, princes, poets and politicians had already enhanced Kenya's reputation as East Africa's leading safari destination, although cost and distance had hitherto prevented mass audiences of any sort.

The recent jump in visitor arrivals has been a welcome boost, and tourism is now Kenya's major earner of foreign exchange. Some of the increased revenue has been used to improve communications and tourist infrastructure. Nowadays, numerous highly organised companies offer scores of specialised safaris—horseback, walking, ballooning, mountaineering and bird-watching—to name just a few. Visitors may lodge at five-star hotels and dine on international-class cuisine, accompanied by views of unsurpassed beauty.

Ironically, as more people flock to Kenya, the once-vast animal stocks that draw them there have dwindled dramatically. In spite of international laws restricting imports of animal products, many animal species continue to be endangered. And animals are also at risk from Kenya's rapidly increasing human population—the fastest growing in the world.

Concerted government efforts to protect both wildlife and its habitats are showing slow, but mainly encouraging results and a wealth of conservation and wildlife organisations are contributing to the fights against ignorance and poaching. For the perceptive tourist, a visit to any of Kenya's magnificent parks and sanctuaries will be enough to convince him of the need to win the battle.

nal Parks (in alphabetical order)

Park	No.	Park	No.	Park	No.
Aberdare National Park	13	Lake Bogoria National Reserve	47	North Kituri National Reserve	
Amboseli National Park	17	Lake Nakuru National Park	27	Ol Doinyo Sapuk National Park	
Arawale National Reserve	23	Longonot National Park	16	Rahole National Reserve	
Bisanadi National Reserve	7	Losai National Reserve	22	Ruma National Park	
Boni National Reserve	37	Malindi Marine National Park	9	Saiwa Swamp National Park	
Buffalo Springs National Reserve	38	Malindi Marine National Reserve	10	Samburu National Reserve	
Central Island N.P. Lake Turkana	50	Maralal National Sanctuary	11	Shaba National Reserve	
Chyulu Hill National Park	4	Marsabit National Reserve	41	Shimba Hills National Reserve	
Dodori National Reserve	25	Maasai Mara National Reserve	1	Sibiloi National Park	
Hell's Gate National Reserve	14	Meru National Park	3	South Island N.P. Lake Turkana	
Kakamega National Reserve	43	Mpunguti Marine National Reserve	28	South Kitui National Reserve	
Kamnarok National Reserve	8	Mt. Elgon National Reserve	6	South Turkana National Reserve	
Kariandus National Park	19	Mt. Kenya National Park	34	Tana River Primate National Reserve	
Kerio Valley National Reserve	24	Mwea National Reserve	33	Tsavo East National Park	
Kisite Marine National Park	26	Nairobi National Park	32	Tsavo West National Park	
Kiunga Marine National Reserve	5	Nasalot National Reserve	40	Watamu Marine National Reserve	
Kora National Reserve	20	North Kitui National Reserve	39	Watamu—Malindi Marine National Reserve	

AMBOSELI

Amboseli is one of the oldest national parks in East Africa, having enjoyed more or less protected status for over 40 years. It was originally part of the Southern Maasai Reserve which also encompassed the **Kajiado** and **Narok** area where several clans of the nomadic, Nilo-hemitic Maasai people lived. The park became the Amboseli Reserve in 1948 when the right of the Maasai people to live there was recognised and a special area for wildlife was set aside. In 1961 the Amboseli Reserve was handed over to Maasai Tribal Control and became a Maasai Game Reserve together with the much larger Maasai Mara Reserve.

However, competition for grazing became such a problem that in 1970 a sanctuary around the swamp was preserved for game only and the *Maasai* were not allowed to enter. This ag-

grieved them so much that they killed many of the rhino population without even taking their horns. Consequently, a ring of bore holes around the park and a portion of the swamp was given back to the *Maasai* in exchange for an area to the north. Eventually, in 1977, Amboseli achieved full National Park status.

Elephant tales: Lying at the foot of Africa's highest mountain, Kilimanjaro, Amboseli National Park is famous for its tranquil beauty and easily approachable wildlife. The Amboseli elephant population, only some 600 strong, is one of the few in all of Africa which has not been ravaged by poachers. It is also one of the longest studied and best researched by Cynthia Moss and her colleagues who know every elephant by face and name and have written about them in the book, *Elephant Memories*.

Clouds of soda dust which blow up from the perennially dry bed of the pleistocene **Lake Amboseli** provide a stark contrast to the lush vegetation of the swamps which form the heart of the ecosystem. The swamps are fed by the melting snows of Kilimanjaro which percolate through porous volcanic soils, forming underground streams which rise close to the surface in the ancient lake basin.

Lake Amboseli, from which the park takes its name, is a dry lake, some 10 by 16 kilometres (six by 10 miles), and is only flooded during the rare occasions when there are heavy rains. The maximum depth in the wettest years is about half a metre (two feet) but the surface is more usually a dry, caked expanse of volcanic soil. The fine, alkaline dust has a habit of creeping into every crevice, so photographic equipment should be protected in plastic bags.

Forests of towering yellow-barked fever trees used to surround the swamps but their numbers were gradually reduced by the elephant population which stripped off and ate the bark and were initially blamed for all the damage. However, it was then discovered that the naturally rising water table, induced by a period of good rains, was bringing toxic salts to the surface which were

ft, this ture has great view Mount imanjaro.

Amboseli National Park

0   5   10 km

0   5   10 miles

Kajiado / Nairobi

To Emali

To Tsavo (Kilaguni Lodge)

Namanga Gate

Lake Amboseli (seasonal)

Lemeiboti Gate

Airstrip

Observation Hill

Amboseli New Lodge

Kilimanjaro Safari Lodge

Ol Tukai Self Service Lodge

Amboseli Serena Lodge

Kimana Gate

TANZANIA

Loitokitok

Mt. Kilimanjaro 5895m

"pickling" the tree roots. This caused physiological drought because the trees could not absorb enough water to compensate for that lost from the leaves through transpiration. Even today you can see moribund fever trees which appear to be dying from the top down. Overall however, the park has a varied habitat with open plains, umbrella acacia woodland and the swamps and surrounding marsh areas.

Park life: Due to the open nature of most of Amboseli, lions are easily found and can occasionally be watched stalking their prey. Buffalo numbers have increased and plains game such as zebra, giraffe and gazelle abound. Small groups of gerenuk can occasionally be found in the arid bush standing on their hind legs to browse upon more succulent leaves on the higher branches.

Hippos live in the open waters and swamp channels formed by seeping waters from Kilimanjaro. Buffalos feed in the shore line swamps and elephants penetrate deeper, often emerging with a high tide mark on their flanks.

For years ecological and behavioural studies of these beasts have been carried out in the park, so animals are accustomed to cars and visitors will be able to observe these large mammals in close proximity from inside their vehicles. However, historical as well as recent encounters with *Maasai* warriors have left the animals particularly wary of people on foot. An elephant feeding peacefully three metres (10 feet) from your car will run off in alarm—or attack in a rage—if someone suddenly gets out.

The density of visitors has had negative impacts on wildlife. Cheetahs, for example, have been so harassed by crowding vehicles, that they have abandoned their usual habit of hunting in the early morning and late afternoon, and have taken to hunting at midday, when most tourists are back at the lodge having lunch and a siesta. Since this is not the best time of day to hunt, the result has been a reduction in the cheetahs' reproductive success.

Elephants ambling across Amboseli.

The swamps and marshy areas support a wide variety of water fowl with no less than 12 species of heron. Over 400 different birds can be found since the park encompasses both dry and wet habitats. Taveta golden weavers are very common. Birds of prey are also represented with over 10 varieties of eagle, as well as kites, buzzards, goshawks and harriers.

Just the facts: Amboseli can be reached from Nairobi by two main routes, the most common one being along the main Kajiado-Namanga road, turning left at **Namanga**, entering the park through the main gate near Namanga and following the road to **Ol Tukai Lodge**. The distance from Nairobi to the lodge is 240 kilometres (150 miles). The second access point is along the main Mombasa road, turning right just beyond the railway bridge past **Emali** and then following the Oloitokitok road for approximately 65 kilometres (40 miles), taking another right turn near the flat-top **Lemeiboti hill** and following this road for 32 kilo-

metres (20 miles) before reaching the lodge. This route is shorter but the Namanga road is in better condition. Flights from Nairobi are also available.

The original camp at Ol Tukai was built as a film-set amenity in 1948 for *The Snows of Kilimanjaro*. These buildings remain as self-help *bandas* (grass-thatched, traditionally-styled houses), but nearby is **Amboseli Lodge** with international standards of accommodation and cuisine. Other lodges include: **Kilimanjaro Safari Lodge** with a seasonal swamp where game congregate, and **Amboseli Serena Lodge** which is built in the style of a *Maasai manyatta*, near the well-head of one of the springs feeding **Enkongo Narok** swamp.

Outside the park is **Kilimanjaro Buffalo Lodge**, about 15 kilometres (9 miles) from the **Kimana Gate** on the Emali road. Since this lodge is not restricted by game park regulations visitors are allowed to take game walks. **Kimana Lodge** is also outside the park, about 80 kilometres (50 miles) from Emali.

ebra and
ildebeest
e common
mpanions.

Tsavo

Tsavo is a vast arid region of roughly 21,000 square kilometres (8,400 square miles) comprising a series of habitats, ranging from open plains to savannah bushlands, semi-desert scrub, acacia woodlands, riverine forests, palm thickets, marshlands and even mountain forests on the Chyulu and Ngulia Hills. It is the largest park in Kenya. The park is divided by the Nairobi-Mombasa road and railway (the "Lunatic Express") into two sections: the north-east of the park is called **Tsavo East**, with headquarters near **Voi**; the part south-west of the road is called **Tsavo West**, with headquarters at **Kamboyo** near **Mtito Andei**.

Depleted herds: Tsavo was once world-renowned for its large elephant population. Only a few years ago, it was unthinkable to drive from Nairobi to Mombasa without seeing several herds.

Tsavo elephants have always been characteristically red, taking on the colour of the soil from dusting and mud bathing. However, the elephant herds which once roamed freely through Tsavo have now been devastated by rampant poaching for ivory. In 1987 conservationists counted less than 6,000 elephants, compared with 35,000 in a similar aerial survey in 1973. The animals that remain are wary of people and ready to run at the sight of a car. The same sad fate has befallen the once-large, now non-existent rhino population.

Both Tsavo parks have been the study sites for a number of significant wildlife research projects. They were also the arena for fierce controversy over the "elephant problem". One school held that there were too many elephants that were destroying the wooded and bushed habitats in times of drought, and that they should be scientifically culled. Such culling would provide valuable data on the population dynamics of the beasts, whose numbers would, of course, be altered by the culling itself.

Cloud-covered Kilimanjaro from Tsavo West.

Another school argued that, since most known animal populations have the ability to self-regulate their numbers through habitat-induced alterations in birth and death rates, there was no reason to believe that elephants do not have the same ability. As it transpired, when the rains returned, so did the grass and trees, but the elephants all but disappeared. A few died of starvation but most were killed by poachers. The results of the research were inconclusive, but favoured the school of *laissez-faire*.

Tsavo West: Much of Tsavo West is of recent volcanic origin and is therefore very hilly. Entering from the **Tsavo Gate**, one comes across the palm-fringed **Tsavo River** from where the country rises through dense shrub to the steep, rocky **Ngulia Hill** which dominates the area. Volcanic cones, rock outcrops and lava flows can be seen, the most famous being **Sheitani**, a black scar of lava looking as if it has only just cooled, near Kilaguni Lodge.

The famous **Mzima Springs** are found in this volcanic zone. The springs gush out 50 million gallons of water a day of which seven million gallons are piped down to provide Mombasa with water. The rest of the water flows into the Tsavo and Galana rivers. The water originates in the **Chyulu Hills** as rain which percolates rapidly through the porous volcanic soils.

Hippos followed by shoals of barbels and crocodiles can be watched from an underwater observation chamber. The best time for viewing is early in the morning; during the day hippos move to the shade of the papyrus stand and remain out of sight.

East of the springs (downstream) is a stand of wild date and raphia palms, the latter with fronds of up to nine metres (30 feet). North of the Mzima Springs are numerous extinct volcanoes, rising cone-shaped from the plains. Majestic Mount Kilimanjaro dominates the western horizon.

South of Mzima Springs is a beautiful picnic site at **Poacher's Lookout** on the top of a hill. The view across the plains to Kilimanjaro is worth the trip.

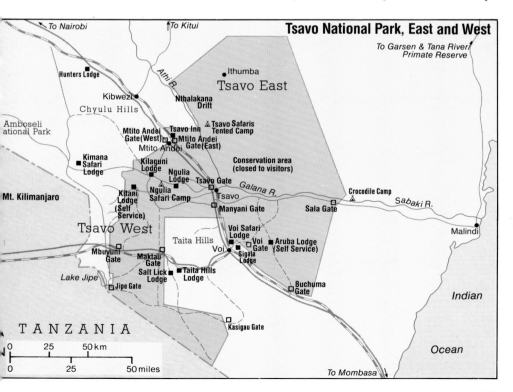

Tsavo National Park, East and West

Tsavo West stretches further south to the **Serengeti Plains** which, despite their name, have nothing to do with the Serengeti National Park, although the landscape is similar. This part of the park is crossed by the road and railway from Voi to **Taveta** and lies at the foothill of Kilimanjaro.

Birds and baobabs: Tsavo West has spectacular baobab trees, which used to be far more numerous. In the mid-1970s, there was an enormous and as yet unexplained attack by elephants on baobabs. Some claim it was because of the drought, others claim that there were "too many" elephants. Whatever the reason, the remaining baobabs are quite safe today.

The variety and sheer numbers of birds in Tsavo are incredible. **Lake Jipe**, at the southernmost tip of the park, is surrounded by tall reeds and is one of the most important wetlands in Kenya, providing a sanctuary for a number of water and marsh birds, including migrants from Europe. Some of the birds commonly seen at the lake are knob-billed geese, pied kingfishers, white-backed night herons, black herons, palm-nut vultures and the African skimmer. Lake Jipe can be reached by following the road to Taveta and then turning south after leaving the park through the old **Mbuyuni Gate** or following a murram road which begins near park headquarters across the Serengeti.

If you take an early morning game drive accompanied by a park ranger you might catch a glimpse of another endangered species. The few rhino left in Tsavo are protected in a fenced sanctuary at the foot of Ngulia Hill. Other wildlife in the park includes lion, cheetah, leopard, buffalo, spotted hyaena, warthog, Maasai giraffe, kongoni, duiker, waterbuck, klipspringer, impala, Grant's gazelle, oryx, eland and zebra. The lions of Tsavo are legendary but after the rains, when the grass grows very long, they are difficult to spot.

Staying: Accommodation is available at a series of lodges within the park. The floodlit waterhole at luxurious **Kilaguni Lodge** attracts an incredible

The victor reaps his spoils.

variety of animals, especially in the dry season. All the rooms have splendid views and the food is first class.

Ngulia Lodge, sited on the edge of a great escarpment, is frequently visited by leopards, some of which have been carefully studied by scientists who put radio collars on them to track their movements. Only five metres (16 feet) from the verandah there is a waterhole and salt lick where elephants converge to within touching distance and dig at the salt-bearing earth with their tusks.

Taita Hill and **Salt Lick lodges**, situated in a private reserve on the outskirts of Tsavo West on the Voi-Taiveta Road, offer excellent wildlife viewing with a luxury resort atmosphere. **Ngulia Safari Camp**, not far from Ngulia Lodge, has six *bandas* on the side of a hill overlooking a small dam visited by elephants and an incredible view over the valley where elephants gather. There is another self-catering camp at **Kitani**, not far from Mzima Springs. At minimal cost these self-help camps provide lamps, gas, bedrolls and mos-quito nets, although you may prefer to bring your own.

Tsavo East: The main physical feature in Tsavo East is the **Yatta Plateau** which runs almost parallel to, and is easily seen from, the Mombasa road. The plateau, which is between five and 10 kilometres (three to six miles) wide and about 305 metres (1,000 feet) high has its origins as a lava flow deriving from Ol Doinyo Sabuk east of Nairobi. Natural erosion over the millenia has exposed the flow to form the striking plateau seen today.

Around Voi, close to the road boundary, extends flat, dry, semi-desert thornbush country stretching as far as the eye can see. From Voi, running east, is the **Voi River**, which is partly swamp and does not flow all year round. It meanders slowly to **Aruba** where a large man-made dam, the remains of a defunct fish-farming scheme, makes an oasis for both animals and birds. Along the banks of the river is the dependent riverine woodland and numerous wildlife paths leading down to water holes.

Mom gets a grip on one of her cubs.

The road between Aruba dam and **Buchuma Gate** on the Mombasa road is heavily populated with weavers, starlings and lilac-breasted rollers with iridescent wings.

One of the most spectacular sights in the park is the **Lugard Falls** on the **Galana River**, 40 kilometres (25 miles) north of Voi. Here the river, which in its early reaches borders Nairobi National Park, rushes through water-worn coloured rock and at the narrowest point it is said one can step across the river. Perhaps the crocodiles downstream survive on those who try. A good spot to see them is **Crocodile Point** further along the river. Lesser kudu hide in the dry bushland along the river banks.

Mudanda Rock, a 1.5-kilometre-long rock between Voi and **Manyani Gate** is a water catchment area which supplies a natural dam at its base. It is a vital watering point during the dry season and therefore one of the best wildlife viewing areas in the park. Large numbers of elephants used to congregate there. Visitors can leave their cars at the rock and climb up to overlook the dam.

Feasting beasts: Tsavo lions were made famous by Colonel Patterson in his book, *The Maneaters Of Tsavo*, which records the havoc caused by marauding maneating lions to the imported Indian labour brought in to build the Mombasa-Nairobi railway during the early part of the century.

Grant's gazelles, zebra, impala, kongoni, giraffe and lion have replaced elephants as the most common animals in Tsavo East. Large herds of buffalo can also be found. Buffalo have enjoyed a well deserved reputation in the past as being extremely dangerous when wounded or hunted. But since the banning of hunting, buffalo no longer associate danger with man or vehicles so they are generally quite docile.

Some of the more rare and unusual animals include oryx, lesser kudu and klipspringers; the latter can be seen standing motionless on rocky outcrops. Rock hyraxes, the improbable first cousins of elephants, can be seen sun-

Salt Lick Lodge.

ning on rocks and chasing one another in and out of rocky crevices.

Conspicuous white-headed buffalo weavers (the most striking characteristic of which is arguably the red rump and not the white head) and red and yellow bishop birds are found everywhere. Some of the more unusual local birds include pale chanting goshawks, carmine bee-eaters, red and yellow barbets, palm-nut vultures, African skimmers, yellow throated longclaws and rosy-patched shrikes.

The roads north of the Galana River and east of the Yatta Plateau are closed to the public, except when special permits are granted by the park warden. The country is wild and woolly, and spotted with outcrops such as **Jimetunda** and seasonal rivers such as **Lag Tiva**.

Various accommodation is available. **Voi Safari Lodge** clings to the side of a hill overlooking the vast expanse of Tsavo and is literally built into the rock—many of the floors are natural rock. There are two water holes and even during the hottest times of day various wildlife, such as impala and warthog, come to drink.

Other accommodation can be found at the self-service **Aruba Lodge** near the Aruba dam and **Crocodile Tented Camp** on the road to Malindi, just outside the park beyond the **Sala Gate.** Every night, there is a ritual in which huge crocodiles are "called" out of the Galana River with chants and drums, up to the verandah to be fed on offal.

A dirt road from Mtito Andei runs to the west bank of the Athi River opposite **Tsavo Safari Camp** which is reached by boat. Don't miss the incredible view at sunset from Yatta Plateau. Plans are underway to re-open **Sheldrick Blind**, an overnight hideaway on the eastern wall of the plateau from where leopard and other nocturnal animals can be watched. It is named after David Sheldrick, the most famous of Tsavo park wardens.

Public camp sites with minimal facilities are available throughout both Tsavo East and West.

Looking out from Voi Safari Lodge.

THE MAASAI MARA

Although not the largest protected area, the **Maasai Mara** must be one of the best for game viewing. The Mara area is an extension of the famous Serengeti Plains (*serengeti* in *Maasai* means extended place) just over the border in Tanzania. Animals don't recognise international boundaries so every year, in July and August, over a million wildebeest and thousands of zebra migrate from the depleted grasslands of Tanzania to take advantage of the fresh grazing after the long rains in Kenya.

Migration madness: They follow an established, circular route which begins in February with calving on the Serengeti plains 150 kilometres (93 miles) to the south. The route is inherited by instinct and crosses the **Sand**, **Talek** and **Mara rivers** at exactly the same place each year. The instinct that drives the herds is so strong that in southern Serengeti they swim or wade across small **Lake Ndutu** when they could easily go around it. They are naturally reluctant to enter the thick riparian bush but the pressure of wildebeest pushing from behind builds up until the front animals are forced to take the plunge, in mad, lemming-like, suicidal leaps which Alan Root has so spectacularly captured on film. Many animals get swept away and drown. After the territorital encounters, courtship and rutting season they migrate back to Tanzania following the short rains in November and December.

The Mara Game Reserve was established in 1961 and covers an area of some 1,800 square kilometres (720 square miles). The southern boundary lies on the border with Tanzania's Serengeti National Park. The **Loita Hills** mark the eastern boundary; to the west lies the splendid **Siria Escarpment** and the north is bordered by the **Itong Hills**. The wide horizons are unforgettable and wildlife are clearly visible.

Herd of Burchell's zebra.

Plains Game: The lush grasslands interspersed with silver and russet leaved croton thickets, hillocks and forested river banks provides a good variety of habitats for wildlife. There is a small resident population of roan antelope, many buffalo as well as herds of Thomson's and Grant's gazelles, topi and impala. Predators include large prides of lions, a fair number of cheetahs and leopards, spotted hyaenas and the silver- or black-backed jackal. African wild dogs are also found and two bedraggled groups of females which had originally been marked with radio collars by researchers in the Serengeti, showed up in the Mara in the late 1980s.

There are over 450 recorded species of birds in this reserve, including the large orange-buff Pel's fishing owl which is a common sight along the Mara River but rare elsewhere. Other common birds include kori bustards and various birds of prey.

The best time of year to visit the reserve is from July to October when the migration is at its peak and as many as two million wildebeest and 500,000 zebra are grazing, fighting, courting and mating.

The Mara is the archetypical arena of conflicts between man and nature in modern Africa. Wheat-schemes and livestock improvement programmes to the north meet the greatest remaining wildlife migration to the south. At the interface, conservationists and ecologists strive to reconcile the needs and aspirations of the *Maasai* landowners. Although fraught with problems, many of the results have been encouraging— apart from elephant and rhino poaching which is a blight thoughout Africa. Many tourism-based enterprises, such as tented camps, are run by local landowners who recognize that wildlife can be a resource worth husbanding.

The route to the Maasai Mara is via the Nairobi-Naivasha road, turning left after 56 kilometres (35 miles) towards **Narok**, 103 kilometres (64 miles) further away. The road continues through Narok then forks: four-wheel drive vehicles are usually necessary on the

ting off
m the
vannah.

northern track leading to the west of the reserve. The road south leads to **Keekorok Lodge**, 106 kilometres (65 miles) away. Travelling from Nairobi can take anywhere between five and 10 hours depending on the season, but the travel time will get shorter as the roads improve nearer the reserve boundary.

Keekorok Lodge in the east was a traditional resting place on the long safari from the Serengeti to Nairobi. These days it is well laid out with cottages and good facilities including car mechanics—sometimes essential after the rough and bumpy roads!

Mara Serena Lodge in the west is set high on a saddle overlooking rolling grasslands and the far off Esoit Oloololo escarpment. Bedrooms are stylised mud *manyattas* grouped in outward-looking rings.

The Mara area has numerous tented camps including **Governor's Camp** on the Mara River where old colonial governors used to pitch their tents. It is now a very up-market retreat. **Kichwa Tembo** (in *Swahili*, "elephant's head")

Camp and **Fig Tree Camp** offer romantic settings where you can lose yourself in the true safari atmosphere. **Cottar's Camp** specializes in night drives and game walks. **Mara Buffalo Camp**, with thatched *bandas* is situated near the (supposedly) best stocked hippo pool in Kenya. A number of camp sites are also available, many of which are good examples of local entrepreneurship where *Maasai* landowners have recognised the potential gains to be made from wildlife. For all accommodation it is recommended to book in advance.

Taking flight: Balloon safaris can be taken every morning from Keekorok, Mara Serena and Governor's Camp. For an hour or so, up to 12 passengers float silently across the plains watching the game from barely 100 metres (330 feet) above. Vehicles follow the balloon to serve a champagne breakfast in the bush and bring the passengers back. Early morning fishing trips to Lake Victoria out of Governor's Camp can also be arranged.

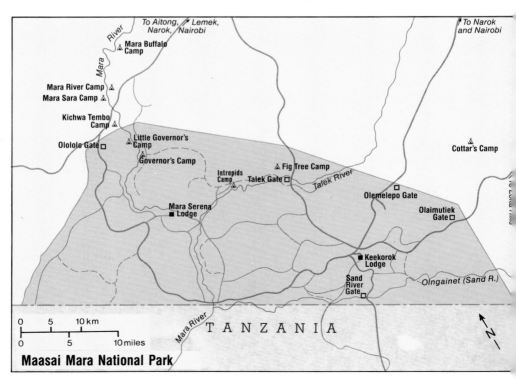

Maasai Mara National Park

ENDANGERED SPECIES

Three of the more endangered species in East Africa today are the black rhino, the elephant and the wild or hunting dog.

Rhino: At the start of the 20th century the myopic rhino was well represented in East Africa, but lucrative trade for various parts of its body has taken a devastating toll. Africa lost about 50 percent of its rhinos in the 1970s and the early 1980s. Since then there has been a further 40 percent decline in population. Kenya had 20,000 rhinos in 1970 but by 1987 only about 500 remained.

Lions and hyaenas are natural enemies of young rhinos, but man is the biggest predator of adult rhinos. For hundreds of years man has used rhino horn for medicinal purposes. Chinese, Japanese and Korean pharmacists throughout Asia continue to sell popular rhino products for colds and flu and to reduce fevers. In some countries the skin, dung, intestines and bone are also used. Horn, however, is the most widely used rhino product and the tip of a fresh, dark horn is most sought after.

In 1985 the President of Kenya launched a special "Save the Rhino" programme. Anti-poaching operations were stepped up and remnant rhino populations identified.

Elephant: In 1960 many of East Africa's elephants were shot in order to protect crops. Today, as the value of ivory increases on international markets, elephants continue to be slaughtered for their tusks.

East Africa has lost 145,000 elephants in the last 10 years and there are now only 109,000 left.

Wild dog: East Africa's wild dogs are endangered because they have lost a sizeable amount of their habitat to agriculture. They are also susceptible to epidemic disease and have been persecuted by man. They breed well in captivity, but now only about 10,000 remain in the wild.

rting out
ory
covered
m
achers.

NAIROBI NATIONAL PARK

Nairobi National Park is unique for its location, barely six kilometres (four miles) from the centre of a capital city. Created in 1946, it was the first park in Kenya and stretches a modest 120 square kilometres (48 square miles) south from Nairobi to the Mbagathi-Athi River system. Completely wild but tranquil animals can be seen grazing or hunting against the Nairobi skyline, while jet aircraft from all over Africa, Europe and the Far East make their final approach to Jomo Kenyatta International Airport. To the west, at the very edge of the Great Rift Valley, the gently saw-toothed Ngong Hills rise to an altitude of 2,458 metres (8,070 feet). On the northern horizon, beyond the city, one can see the Aberdares mountain range and to the east, on a clear morning, the peak of Mount Kenya. Being so close to the city, the park attracts many visitors on day trips and earns enough money to help subsidize some of the more remote protected areas.

City living: Almost 37 kilometres (23 miles) of fencing along the park's western boundary prevents wildlife from straying into human settlements and the rapidly-expanding and not very attractive industrial area. To the south, migratory wildebeest, zebras and Coke's hartebeest (kongoni) enter and leave the park more or less freely through the **Kitengela** portion of the of the northern **Athi-Kapiti plains**. Their movements depend on the availability of grazing and water: the animals are mostly out of the park during the short (November) and long (April) rains. As the pastures dry out, the animals pull back north into the park, until their density appears to rival that of the Serengeti herds. Absolute numbers are much less, however, and there are now fewer wildebeest and zebra than there used to be in the whole ecosystem which once stretched as far as Thika and the whale-shaped hill, **Ol Doinyo Sa-**

Male ostrich heads for the big city.

208

buk, which can be seen in the distance to the north-east.

Developments of farm buildings, rural residences and fences along the south-western edge of the park have raised fears that this free movement of animals could be affected which would make Nairobi's famous park no more then a big zoo. It is hoped that land use development policies will take into account the future of the park and its role in the annual movements of the migratory grazers, as well as its enormous potential as a money-earner for surrounding citizens.

Plant power: Though small, the park has a good variety of habitats. It slopes from about 1,740 metres (5,712 feet) in the western forest down to approximately 1,500 metres (4,925 feet) in the south-eastern plains. Forest in the west occupies almost 6 percent of the land and receives a rainfall of 700 mm to 1,100 mm (27 inches to 43 inches) a year, compared to the much drier south-eastern tip. Tree species in the forest include crotons, Kenya olive, yellow-flowered, long-seeded markhaemia, and Cape chestnut, with its lavender bunches of blossoms. Forested areas are home to at least a dozen black rhinos, some of which have been transported from less friendly neighbourhoods, buffalos and giraffe. Smaller wildlife such as dikdik, suni, duiker and bushbuck can also be seen here.

Bisected by valleys, the plains have less rainfall—about 500 mm to 700 mm (19 inches to 27 inches). They are covered with one of the most characteristic grassland types of the region, composed of *Themeda* (red oat grass) and *Setaria*, spotted with acacias, desert dates (*Balanites*) and the occasional arrow-poison tree (*Akocantha*) which are dark green and often stunted looking from years of harvesting branches for rendering the bark into poison. Visitors are allowed out of their cars at **Observation Hill**, a spectacular spot on the forest edge overlooking the central plain. From here herds of wildebeest, gazelle and zebra can be easily observed.

eetah
its in the
h grass.

In the open grassland just under the hill, a well-studied male ostrich, "Pointy-head", has held his territory for years, and he or his successor can usually be seen entertaining delighted onlookers by dancing to female ostriches or chasing off rival males.

The southern part of the park is criss-crossed by ridges, valleys and plains. Cliffs fall for about 100 metres (330 feet) to the valley floor. In the dry season, wildlife gather to drink at the isolated pools left in the gorges. The gorge cliffs, some of which are quite spectacular and attractive to rock-climbers, have vegetation ranging from cacti and bushes to grasses and moss. They are lined with acacia trees browsed by giraffe. Buffalo and rhino can be found here, together with lion and leopard. The latter feed on the numerous hyraxes which inhabit the cliff faces in, among other places, **Hyrax Gorge**.

The southern and eastern ends of the park consist of acacia wooded grassland bound by the Nairobi-Mombasa road and the **Mbagathi River**. This modest but perennial river becomes the Athi, which runs into the Galana, which becomes the Sabaki and eventually runs into the Indian Ocean just a little north of Malindi.

Trailing the animals: Visitors can park their cars and follow a 1.5-kilometre **nature trail** along the banks of the river which leads to a series of hippo- and crocodile-inhabited pools. Hippos usually give themselves away by their loud snorting. During the day animals stay submerged in the water and only come out at night to graze. Hippo trails can be seen etched into the bank. A few crocodiles can also be seen swimming about or sunning on banks, as well as impalas and hundreds of vervet monkeys. Another, slightly longer trail meanders through stands of yellow-barked fever acacias (*Acacia xanthophloea*) and their greenish-barked cousins, *Acacia kirkii*.

Birds are abundant at the edge of water, including kingfishers, darters, storks, herons, saddlebill storks and ibises. Hammerkops and beautiful

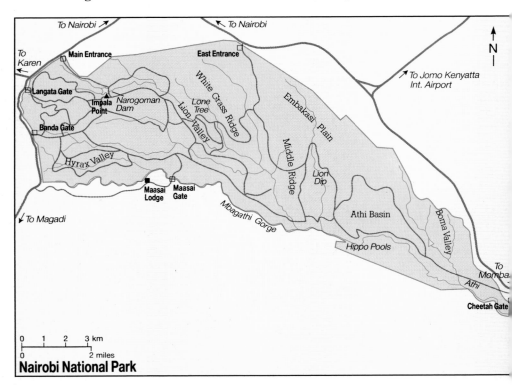

Nairobi National Park

crowned cranes are also common. The open plain features birds like ostriches, marabou storks, cattle egrets, secretary birds and vultures.

The best time of year to visit is during the dry seasons, in February-March and again in August-September, in order to catch the return of the antelope herds that disperse southwards towards the Athi plains during the rains and return to the park to gather around the permanent water holes. Big cats and impalas are permanent residents; wildebeest, kongoni, zebra and to a lesser extent giraffe are migratory. There is a strong chance of seeing lion, cheetah, buffalo and rhino.

Nairobi National Park is an excellent introduction to the art and sport of wildlife viewing. Tours lasting four or five hours are available from most tour companies and can be taken either in the morning or afternoon. They can be arranged through any of the big hotels in Nairobi. Roads in the park are murram, but are kept in very good condition, so even small rental vehicles can carry you to an away-from-it-all experience in the morning, and back to the more intense experience of bargaining for local handicrafts in the Nairobi market before lunch.

OL DOINYO SABUK

Ol Doinyo Sabuk is a minute reserve of only 18 square kilometres (seven square miles) which used to be the residence of the American, Sir Northrop MacMillan, who is buried on his reputedly haunted homesite at the foot of the hill. The park is located just 15 kilometres (nine miles) northeast of Nairobi, near **Thika**. The hill, also known as *Kilima Mbogo* ("Buffalo Hill" in *Swahili*), is a granitic kopje rising above the surrounding plain. It is almost entirely forested except for a small patch at the top. The area is inhabited by buffalo and bushbuck, but they are hard to see because of the dense undergrowth. Admission is free. There is no accommodation available, but it makes a very interesting and pleasant day trip from Nairobi.

gh plains
fter: lone
i.

THE ABERDARES

One of the three mountain parks, Aberdare covers 770 square kilometres (308 square miles) stretching from the 3,996-metre (13,120-foot) peak at **Ol Doinyo Lesatima** in the north to the nearly as high **Nyandarra Peaks** in the south. The eastern wall of the **Great Rift Valley** is the western boundary, and in the east there is an area known as the **Salient**. Two famous wildlife viewing lodges, **Treetops** and **The Ark**, are located in the eastern Salient. The park consists of high mountain rain forest, open moorland with hagenia woodlands and impenetrable bamboo forest.

Bamboo tunnels: Bamboo forests are found on some of the mountain slopes and extinct volcanoes and are criss-crossed by wildlife tracks that part the towering bamboo stalks. It is a fascinating experience to walk along these bamboo "tunnels". Extreme caution has to be exercised as they are regularly used by buffalo and elephant. Upon meeting wildlife, the only option is to clamber into the impenetrable bamboo and let the animals pass! Bamboo is a species of gigantic grass. Some stands of bamboo are apparently dead, as this particular type of bamboo to dies off after flowering every 30 years or so.

The moorland above the high treeline is covered in tussock grass with towering giant heather and typical alpine plants, some of which also occur in the Alps and Rocky Mountains. The view is phenomenal. **Karura** and **Guru waterfalls** are especially spectacular. Numerous rivers, such as the Chania, are faithfully restocked with brown and rainbow trout each year by the Kenya Fisheries Department—a most welcome relic of the colonial era. High fishing camps are operated on a self-help basis. The more exclusive camps are located outside the national park on the private reaches of fly fishing clubs. Fishing can also be arranged from some of the mountain lodges.

Far left, leopard ge his licks in

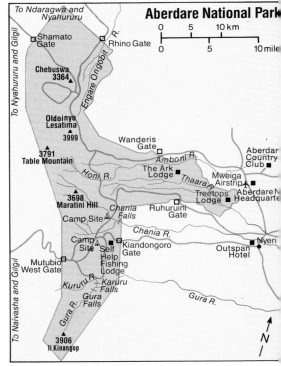

Not too tame: There were once a number of campsites within the park, but these had to be closed due to the lions that made themselves a nuisance. In this particular park larger wildlife is notorious for being aggressive, probably due to frequent unpleasant encounters with the high density human population in the surrounding area. Along a 37-kilometre (23-mile) stretch of park boundary above **Nyeri**, there is an experimental elephant proof ditch and electric fence to protect the maize shambas and people outside the park.

Some unusual and rare animals can be seen, such as bongo, a forest dwelling antelope that feeds at night and in the early morning. They are sleek and chestnut coloured, with about a dozen narrow, white, vertical stripes. Giant forest hogs can be recognised by their coarse, black hair and shy, retiring manner. *Asterix the Gaul* fans will be reminded of the boars beloved of *Obelisk*. Bushbuck are common—males are dark russet, with a white band across the chest—and hunchbacked red duiker oc-

casionally creep out of the undergrowth to graze in open forest lanes.

An unusual phenomenon of the high forest parks is the occurrence of melanistic (all black) cats. There are numerous and well-authenticated reports of sightings of black leopards and serval cats, although these are usually fleeting glimpses as the animal dashes across the road.

The bronze-naped pigeon, dusky turtle and tambourine doves and the iridescent turaco are a marvellous sight as they clamber around in the upper branches of forest trees. Trumpeter and crowned hornbills can be vociferous in the early mornings and their heavy undulating flight styles across forest clearings is unmistakable. There are numerous forest dwelling barbets and at least 12 species of sunbird.

Both Treetops (where Elizabeth II learned she had become Queen of England) and The Ark lodges are famous for their rewarding wildlife viewing, especially by night when their water holes and salt-licks are floodlit.

MOUNT KENYA

The 3,350 metre (11,000 feet) contour line around Mount Kenya is the boundary of **Mount Kenya National Park**. Nowhere else on earth is there perpetual snow actually on the equator. Mount Kenya National Park offers glaciers, 30 small mountain lakes and some of the world's greatest ice climbing, all within a day's drive of Nairobi and the hot upland plains.

Large troops of black and white colobus monkeys are common. Sykes monkeys are also found in abundance. Melanistic leopards and serval cats exist here although they are rarely seen. Comical giant forest hogs are common and the more elusive bongo can sometimes be seen emerging from the forests in the evenings.

There are about 150 species of birds. Green ibis and crowned and silvery-cheeked hornbills are found by streams. Mountain chats and white-starred bush robins live in the bamboo forests. There are many varieties of mountain warbler and Jackson's francolin call loudly in the evening before nesting in the bamboo clumps. The almost totally green parrot you might see is actually called the "red-fronted" parrot! It has a small patch of red on the forehead and a patch on the shoulders and wing edges. There are also many iridescent sunbirds, the main species being emerald coloured malachite sunbirds and tufted malachite sunbirds, which are duller, with tufts on their shoulders.

The **Mountain Lodge** at 2,193 metres (7,200 feet) boasts the most consistent record of wildlife seen nightly. There is a bunker by the floodlit waterhole, so that the drinking animals can be viewed virtually eye to eye. The light is sufficient for satisfactory photographs. Safaris can be arranged deeper into the mountain forest, and fishing enthusiasts can try their luck at trout fishing up the valley, with rods hired from the lodge.

Far left, national fl flies on Mount Kenya.

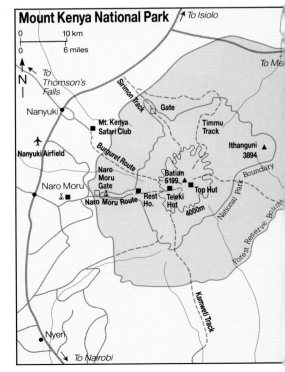

Mount Kenya National Park

To Isiolo

0   10 km
0   6 miles

N

To Thomson's Falls

Nanyuki

Sirmon Track

Gate

Mt. Kenya Safari Club

Timmu Track

Nanyuki Airfield

Burguret Route

Ithanguni ▲ 3894

Naro Moru Gate

Batian 5199 ▲

Boundary

Naro Moru

Naro Moru Route

Rest Ho.

Teleki Hut

Top Hut

4000m

National Park

Forest Reserve Bound

Kamweti Track

Nyeri

To Nairobi

To Me

WILDLIFE PHOTOGRAPHY

East Africa must be one of the destinations serious outdoor photographers have on their shortlist of places to visit. Nowhere else in the world is it possible to find such variety and concentrations of free-roaming creatures, not to mention the scenery.

Wildlife photography lagged behind wildlife painting as a form of illustration mainly because early cameras were too big to carry in the field. A turn-of-the-century picture shows an earnest photographer pursuing a rhino with a camera the size of a microwave oven. It weighed 7,168 grams (16 pounds). Exposure took minutes—too long to capture an unrestrained creature on film.

By the middle of this century wildlife photography had changed dramatically. Faster film, telephoto lenses and motordrives gave photographers additional flexibility.

Safari-goers will find that the most suitable cameras are 35 mm SLR (single lens reflex) models with interchangeable lenses.

Lenses are a wildlife photographer's most important accessories. A 600 mm telephoto lens is the practical, upper size limit for work in the field. But it cannot be handheld and tripods are very cumbersome when used in vehicles. Zoom lenses—in the 80 mm to 200 mm range—are more versatile and offer better value for money.

Telephoto lenses are prone to camera shake since they magnify image movement. Accurate focusing is also essential with long focal lenses. Shoulder supports help to reduce camera shake; so do sand or bean bags. These look like small pillows filled with dried beans or sand. Lay the bag down on the roof of your open safari vehicle and mould the lens on to it. Many safari companies provide these bags.

Recent years have seen the introduction of very fast colour film. The sharpness and grain of these films are perfectly acceptable even if pictures are blown up to A4 size. Films in Africa, when available, are expensive so visitors should bring more film than they expect to shoot.

On the equator, the best time to take pictures is before 10 a.m. and after 3.30 p.m. When it is overcast, midday hours can be acceptable.

During dry times of the year dust can be a serious hazard to your equipment. It is particularly important to protect the camera from wind-driven dust when loading and unloading film.

The majority of safari pictures are taken from the roofhatch of a vehicle, but taking all your pictures from there creates stereotyped images. Shooting from a lower angle out of a side window often results in more dramatic shots.

Timing, as they say, is everything. Most experienced wildlife photographers will tell you that when it comes to taking memorable pictures it all boils down to being in the right place at the right time. For that reason even old hands can be surpassed by a relative newcomer to the wildlife game.

w angle:
note-
ntrol
nera and
oject.

MERU, KORA
AND RAHOLE

Meru National Park achieved world recognition with Joy Adamson's *Born Free*, the story of Elsa the lioness that was rehabilitated to the wild. The similar tale of Pippa, her cheetah, was told in *The Spotted Sphinx*. After her release, Pippa eventually gave birth to two litters of fine cubs. Despite being one of the major national parks in Kenya and a very beautiful one, it is off the mainstream circuit for the majority of visitors. Still, it is strongly recommended you make an effort to visit this park.

The park covers an area of 800 square kilometres (320 square miles), lying to the west of Mount Kenya in the semiarid area of the country. It straddles the equator and ranges from an altitude of 1,000 metres (3,300 feet) in the foothills of the **Nyambeni Range** (the northern boundary) to less than 300 metres (990 feet) on the Tana River in the south.

The main tourist roads are in the western part with a few roads in the remote east. The eastern park boundary is bordered by the Bisanadi National Reserve and the Kora National Reserve. To the north of Kora is the Rahole National Reserve, which means that altogether there is an area of 4,670 square kilometres (1,868 square miles) of wildlife sanctuary.

Vegetation is mainly bushland with combretum bush prevailing in the north and commiphora in the south. The north-east is dominated by grassland with borassus palms and acacia woodland. There is plenty of water, the main perennial river being the Tana, which is the longest in Kenya. Many other small streams occur in the park. Most are bordered by riverine forest. Some valleys are partially flooded during the rainy season, providing a swampy grassland habitat favoured by buffalo and waterbuck.

Reviving stock: Animal life is now plentiful, but game had virtually vanished by 1959, when the local council of

Pale chanting goshawk stops for directions.

RHINO DRIFT
MUGHWANGO

the *Wameru* tribe seized the initiative from the colonial government and designated the area for conservation. Large numbers of buffalo can usually be found around the swamps and river. Big herds of elephant used to be seen quite often in the swamp area near the **Meru Mulika Lodge**. The Tana River provides a sanctuary for hippopotamus and crocodile. Black rhinos used to be abundant in the park, but sadly they too have been heavily poached, as was the small protected herd of white rhinos. In 1988 the five remaining animals were killed by poachers, aided, it is alleged, by a disgruntled park ranger who used to protect them. The white rhinos had been introduced from South Africa in the hope that they would breed to establish a viable herd. The name "white" does not refer to the colour of the animals but is a misinterpretation of the Africaans word *weit* which means "wide" and refers to their broad mouths. White rhinos are mainly grazers whereas black rhinos are browsers.

Leopards have also been the focus of a re-population bid. Over the years, many have been brought in from other parts of Kenya.

Meru supports a range of species more usually found in northern protected areas, such as Grevy's zebra (with narrower stripes than the more common Burchell's zebra), beisa oryx and reticulated giraffe (rust-red coloured with distinctive thin white lines creating a "crazy paving" effect). Dikdik, gerenuk (which supposedly do not need water and survive on dew) and the big cats are abundant, but sometimes difficult to see because of the tall grass cover and thick bush. Eland and kongoni prefer the wetter grassland areas. Lesser kudu—either alone or in pairs—can be found in thickets or in valley bottoms in the evening.

Birdwatchers should look out for the relatively uncommon palm-nut vulture, which feeds on a mixture of palm nuts and carrion. In addition, the palm swift can be seen building its nest on the underside of palm fronds. Pel's fishing owl and the rare Peter's finfoot live near

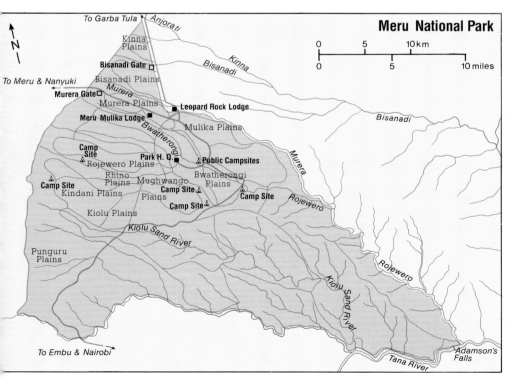

the Tana River. Peter's finfoot resemble long-necked slender ducks or small cormorants. They are very secretive and are usually seen swimming under overhanging trees close to the bank. Helmeted and vulturine (with slender, striped necks) guinea fowl are common.

Wilderness area: One section of the park has been designated a wilderness area, in which there are no roads. This area can only be reached by four-wheel drive vehicles, accompanied by an experienced ranger. Similarly, the 600 square kilometres (240 square miles) of the **Bisanadi National Reserve**, which adjoins Meru National Park, is undeveloped for tourism. Access is difficult even with four-wheel drive vehicles. The habitat, flora and fauna are similar to Meru, with more spectacular elongated rocky outcrops.

Two routes lead from Nairobi to Meru National Park: one around Mount Kenya, through **Nanyuki** and the other one through **Embu**. Both roads go to **Meru** town from where it is 78 kilometres (48 miles) to the park. If you go via Nanyuki, you can enter the park from the west using the **Murera Gate**.

Accommodation at Meru is available at the well-appointed Meru Mulika Lodge which has numerous thatched huts in an attractive setting. Below the lodge, large herds of elephant wander across **Mulika Swamp**. Some visitors prefer to fly in to avoid the slow and winding road.

Not far away, on the banks of **Murera River**, is **Leopard Rock Self-help Lodge** which has 10 *bandas* (rustic cabins with bathroom). You should bring your own food. There are also several other campsites which are marked on most maps.

KORA NATIONAL RESERVE

Bordering on the middle reaches of the Tana River, the 1,790 square kilometres (700 square miles) of the **Kora National Reserve** were made famous by George Adamson and Tony Fitzjohn who engaged for years in the dangerous business of re-introducing captive lions and leopards to the wild. Tragically,

Despite protection, these white rhinos were poached in 1988.

218

Adamson was ambushed and killed by bandits in August 1988. The remote Kora region is adjoined to Rahole National Reserve, and is composed of riverine woodland along the Tana River and miles of bushland in the interior. It is also renowned for rocky outcrops with their own unique habitats and fauna. Wildlife will not be seen in great numbers, but there are occasional sightings of lion, lesser kudu, elephant and waterbuck. The river is beautiful in this section and is well stocked with hippos and crocodiles.

Kora was the site of a major ecological survey in 1983 carried out by the National Museums of Kenya and the Royal Geographical Society with support from the US National Aeronautic and Space Administration and the United Nations Environment Programme. The results gave valuable insights and management information for a wild part of Africa increasingly encroached by Somali pastoralists.

Kora is about 130 kilometres (80 miles) from the township of **Garissa**.

There are no tourist facilities in what is essentially an area set aside for scientific research. Visits can, on occasion, be arranged to **Adamson's Camp** or the riverside research station which is now a ranger post.

RAHOLE NATIONAL RESERVE

North across the Tana River from Kora is the **Rahole National Reserve**. This reserve of 1,270 square kilometres (508 square miles) was developed to illustrate the potential for local wildlife to co-exist with tribes that live in the area. However, the experiment seems to have failed as poaching is rife and settlements abound. Until it can be developed to ensure a tourism industry with revenues for local pastoralists, the area will remain undistinguished and unremarkable, although there is plenty of splendid scenery.

There are no tourist facilities except at Meru, 40 kilometres (25 miles) upstream. However, in the dry season Rahole is really only accessible from the east, via the Garsen-Garissa road.

e late
eorge
damson
king a walk
remote
ora.

SAMBURU AND BUFFALO SPRINGS

Samburu and Buffalo Springs reserves lie in what used to be called the Northern Frontier District, a vast area of semi-desert and desert that stretches north from Mount Kenya to Sudan and Ethiopia. It is a stark, rugged landscape where nomads, who have changed little over centuries, still move their herds across the ecosystem chasing the ephemeral growth of grass. It is the emptiness and wildness that makes a visit to these reserves such an unforgettable experience.

Two into one: The two reserves, Samburu to the north of the **Ewaso Ngiro** (brown water) **River** and Buffalo Springs to the south are usually treated as one unit, by tour companies as well as wildlife. A bridge across the Ewaso Ngiro River a little way upstream of **Samburu Lodge** connects the reserves.

The major, central part of both reserves is dry, open, thorn bush country, which only becomes green during the rains. The river which originates on the **Laikipia Plateau**, fed by the runoff from the Aberdares and Mount Kenya, is a permanent source of water for animals and is lined by acacias, tamarind and doum palms.

A variety of animals can be found, including diminishing numbers of elephant and numerous buffalo and waterbuck that feed on the vegetation around the river and in the adjourning swamps. Impala herds, with one male guarding up to 50 females and young, graze along the riverine vegetation. Grevy's zebra, beisa oryx, reticulated giraffe and gerenuk are only found in this sort of dry semi-arid country. Grevy's zebra used to be poached for its fine, narrow striped skin by local poachers or exported to European zoos by expatriate entrepreneurs, and they are only slowly re-establishing a viable population. Oryx are very shy, relatively scarce animals with beautifully marked heads and long, straight horns. Dikdik are far more

Termite mounds and weaver nests are common Samburu sights.

common and particularly like the rocky hills and dry, acacia woodland to be found here.

Dinner guests: Crocodiles sun themselves on the banks of rivers. Lion, cheetah and leopard are also fairly easy to see, thanks to the sparse grass cover. If you fail to see a leopard on one of your game drives, you can always watch them in the evening from the verandah of your lodge as they come to eat the bait hung from nearby trees.

Smaller mammals include ground squirrels which are common around the lodges and dwarf mongooses are frequently seen scampering across the open ground looking for food.

Birds are abundant, including the blue-legged, northern Somali race of ostrich, which is particularly prominent during the breeding season. Numerous flocks of helmeted and vulturine guinea fowls can be seen especially in the afternoon as they go to the river to drink. Martial eagles, one of the largest of the eagles, are often seen perching on a vantage point scanning for movements in the grass indicating potential prey. Other birds of prey, such as bateleur and pygmy falcon are also common. Along the banks of the rivers, kingfishers and Layard's black weavers are found. The rare bright green and red chested Narina's trogan, a bird related to the parrot, is also found in the riverine woodland.

From Nairobi to the reserves, it is approximately 300 kilometres (186 miles) on tarmac up to **Isiolo**, then on dirt road for another 53 kilometres (33 miles). The most convenient entrance to the reserves is the **Gare Mara Gate**, 20 kilometres (12.5 miles) north of Isiolo, through the Buffalo Spring Reserve. Another entrance, three kilometres before reaching **Archer's Post**, is called **Buffalo Springs Gate**. The road directly into Samburu Reserve, reached from the township of Archer's Post, is in bad condition, but the journey is made more interesting by the several Samburu *manyattas* (enclosed villages) passed on the way.

The luxurious Samburu Lodge is on the north side of the river by the western

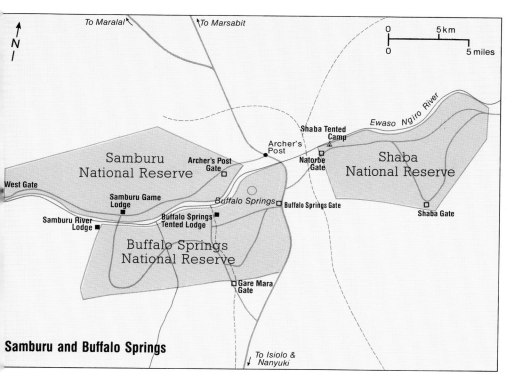

Samburu and Buffalo Springs

boundary. You can watch crocodiles being fed on leftovers, and there is a platform where goat carcasses are hung from trees to attract the big cats, especially leopards. A tarmac airstrip is located nearby for tourists who do not wish to endure the long drive.

The equally well-appointed **Buffalo Springs Tent Lodge** is on the south bank, not far from the eastern gate. A short distance away are the clear pools of Buffalo Springs. The story goes that during World War II an Italian bomb, dropped by a plane from occupied Somalia, missed Isiolo township and formed the pool.

SHABA NATIONAL RESERVE

Shaba National Reserve lies in the northern district to the south of the Uaso Nyiro River, covering 240 square kilometres (96 square miles). It takes its name from **Mount Shaba**, a copper-coloured sandstone hill which lies partially in the reserve which is famous for its lava flows that oozed down from the **Nyambeni Hills** only 5,000 years ago.

The western side of the reserve is bushed grassland savannah, dotted with thorn bushes, gradually becoming acacia woodland nearer Mount Shaba. Beyond the mountain the vegetation becomes grassland plains. A series of springs bubble up in the river in the north-eastern side of the reserve. One spring, **Penny's Drop**, was named after Joy Adamson's leopard Penny, which she released back to the wild in Shaba Reserve. It was in her Shaba camp that Joy Adamson died in 1980.

Although heavy poaching in Shaba has made animals very shy, you might be lucky enough to see elephant, lion, cheetah, leopard, waterbuck, as well as all the animals specially adapted to the dry region: beisa oryx, gerenuk, Grevy's zebra, reticulated giraffe and Somali ostrich.

The reserve is about 300 kilometres (186 miles) from Nairobi. Access is by a turn-off two kilometres (just under one mile) short of Archer's Post through the **Natorbe Gate**, seven kilometres (4.3 miles) from the main road.

Shy dikdik move in pairs.

MARSABIT

Marsabit National Park and Reserve is situated in what used to be known as Kenya's "Northern Frontier District". Marsabit itself is an improbable forested volcanic mountain which rises like an oasis out of the dry black lava-strewn surrounding semi-desert.

Climatic oddity: The park encompasses the mountain and is only some 20 square kilometres (eight square miles) in extent. The much older surrounding reserve covers approximately 2,100 square kilometres (840 square miles). The eastern slopes of **Mount Marsabit** are dry and barren, whereas the western slope is covered in perpetual mist and enjoys heavy rainfall which has given rise to dense rainforest. The reason for this climatic oddity is that when hot air blown off the surrounding desert rises and cools over the mountain, clouds are formed and rain occurs.

The mountain microclimate allows for the growth of lush, tropical, evergreen forest in which elephant and greater kudu can be found. Herds of buffalo—some claim a smaller "mountain" variety—are also common.

Ahmed the elephant: Lake Paradise, at the bottom of one of the mountain's craters, hosts a variety of waterbirds. Some of the biggest elephant tuskers have lived here, including the famous Ahmed, now sadly dead. Ahmed was renowned for his splendid downsweeping tusks and was protected by presidential decree. In the late 1970s, just a couple of years before his death, he was assigned a ranger to watch over him and to keep his location known for visitors. From his teeth, it was clear that he was about 65 (old for an elephant), had an abscess on one side of his jaw, and was obliged to chew on the other side. He was on his last set of molars, and their diminishing and smoothing surfaces were clearly incapable of processing the necessary amount of vegetation. So he had the added distinction of

being one of the last great tuskers to die a natural death: debilitation caused by undernourishment. His position has been filled by another big tusker known as Mohammed II, who can be seen in the crater swamp in front of the **Marsabit Lodge**.

Marsabit National Park is 560 kilometres (347 miles) north of Nairobi. The asphalt road finishes at Isiolo which means that 270 kilometres (167 miles) has to be driven on corrugated dirt road. In order to drive to Marsabit one must obtain permits from Provincial Headquarters at Isiolo. From here, it is recommended to drive in convoy and to carry petrol, water and supplies for the journey. Various charter companies at Wilson Airport in Nairobi will arrange flights to the reserve.

Accommodation in the park is provided by the Marsabit Lodge at the edge of the forest, overlooking the swamp and lake in the **Sokortre Dika** crater. The lodge is comfortable and food is provided as well as lunch boxes for game drives. Nights are cold so a sweater is needed for when you are not sitting around the lodge fireplace. Rooms face the crater lake where greater kudu, reticulated giraffe and, if you are lucky, the elusive Lammergeyer can be seen. Campsites are available—the most beautiful is the one located at Lake Paradise.

LOSAI NATIONAL RESERVE

Located to the south-west of Marsabit, across the **Kaisut Desert**, the 1,735-square-kilometre (694-square-mile) **Losai National Reserve** is an area of impenetrable mountain forest on the north-eastern edge of the central highlands. The Great North road runs through the eastern section, but it is a wild area and is generally inaccessible, except by four-wheel drive vehicle in the dry season. For the more intrepid visitor, a walk up the seasonally-dry bed of the **Milgis** is an incomparable experience. It is like a broad avenue, bordered by some of the most magnificent umbrella acacias (*Acacia tortilis*) in Kenya.

Sand dune north of Marsabit.

RIFT VALLEY LAKES

LAKE NAKURU

Lake Nakuru National Park was created in 1961 as a bird sanctuary. Originally, it comprised only the lake and its immediate surroundings, including the escarpment at its western side known as **Baboon Cliffs**. It was expanded in 1974 with help from the World Wildlife Fund, and now includes an extensive area of savannah to the south. Today the total area of the park is about 200 square kilometres (80 square miles). The name Nakuru is derived from the *Maasai* word *en-akuro*, meaning "swirling dust".

Pretty in pink: The park is famous for its concentrations of both greater and lesser flamingoes, which cover the lake in a layer of shocking pink. The numbers of flamingoes fluctuates in accordance with the availability of blue-green algae known as *Spirulinga*. The algae is sensitive to the salt concentration of the water so its "blooming" is related to the amount of rainfall which in turn determines the amount of water available to dilute or concentrate the salt solution. The lake level varies considerably. In the late 1950s, for example, it dried out completely and the resulting dustbowl made life unbearable in the busy farming town of **Nakuru** on the lakeside. When conditions are right, there can be around two million flamingoes milling about the shallows—the spectacle is truly awe-inspiring. When disturbed, the pink clouds reeling through the sky are an amazing sight.

For many years it was a mystery where flamingoes went to nest in reliable numbers since they do not nest on the lake. The well-known ornithologist, Leslie Brown, spent many years trying to establish their nesting grounds. He even took flying lessons, and eventually found their regular nesting site on another Rift Valley water body, **Lake Natron**, just over the border in Tanza-

ssed
mingoes
Lake
goria.

225

nia. His fascinating book *The Mystery of the Flamingoes* is essential reading for any birdwatcher visiting Kenya.

Birds of paradise: The park is considered an ornithological paradise. Over 400 varieties of birds can be seen altogether, although not at the same time since many are migrant visitors from the northern hemisphere. During the European and East Asian winters the park becomes an important feeding ground for migrant waders. Among them are little stints, curlew sandpipers, marsh sandpipers and greenshanks. Great numbers of pelicans can be seen at the southern and eastern shores. The numbers of these birds has increased considerably since the alkaline and high temperature-tolerant *Tilapia grahami* fish were introduced to the lake in the early 1960s. Pelicans feed by working as a team, herding the fish towards each other, and then dipping into the water in unison to increase their catch.

Verreaux's eagles can be seen using the updrafts around Baboon Cliffs to search for prey along the cliffs. Other birds of prey commonly seen are long crested eagles, Augur buzzards, harrier eagles, fish eagles, gabar goshawks and harrier hawks. The acacia woodlands harbour a number of birds, including red-chested cuckoos (the bird which chants: "it-will-rain, it-will-rain" before the rains), African hoopoes and grey-headed kingfishers.

The park has now been fenced in to make a rhino sanctuary. Rhinos have been moved here from elsewhere in Kenya and they seem to be thriving in this environment. Other species of mammal include lion, leopard and hyaena. It is the best place in Kenya to see Bohor reedbuck and Defassa waterbuck. A herd of Rothschild giraffe was introduced in 1977.

Lake Nakuru is 150 kilometres (93 miles) from Nairobi on a good tarmac road. Part of the way is along the edge of the **Rift Valley Escarpment** and the views are spectacular.

Lion Hill Camp is perched on higher ground by the eastern boundary overlooking the lake. It is also adjacent to

Flamingoes perform a courtship dance.

Kenya's finest euphorbia forest with grotesque, giant cactus-like trees. On cold evenings a fire is lit by the bar. **Lake Nakuru Lodge** used to be part of Lord Delamare's estate and, apart from the main manor house, there are new *bandas*. Safari vehicles are available for hire and an airstrip is close by. There are also two well-maintained campsites with good water supplies.

LAKE NAIVASHA

Lake Naivasha is one of the Rift Valley's cleanest freshwater lakes, renowned equally for its great variety of birdlife, its scenic beauty, and its role as a retreat for the zany white settlers of "Happy Valley" fame. The infamous, pink painted **Gin Palace** still perches preposterously overlooking the southeastern shoreline, fringed with papyrus and secluded lagoons with splendid blue water lilies. The lake is little more than an hour's drive from Nairobi, using the Trans-Africa Highway.

At present the lake covers about 150 square kilometres (60 square miles) since recent rains have been good. The water level has varied markedly from year to year, having almost dried out in the 1890s. The hectarage and the fortunes of the lakeside vegetable farmers flutuate widely.

The ecology of the lake has been changed considerably by human intervention. Sport fishing was introduced in the 1920s and later, species like the American red swamp crayfish and black bass were introduced both for commercial and sport fishing. Various aquatic plants were also introduced, the most prominent being water hyacynth, which forms thick carpets of vegetation and can become a serious problem to waterways. The South American coypu, an aquatic rodent, is also present in the park, having escaped from a fur farm. The area surrounding the lake is extensively irrigated to grow fruits and vegetables. Controversy about the detrimental effects of these introductions and the irrigation schemes has been going on for years. No final conclusion has been reached.

hite
licans on
ishing
pedition.

Crescent Island: A little crater lake at the bottom of a small volcano at the western side of Lake Naivasha and the wildlife sanctuary on **Crescent Island** can be visited. Crescent Island is a peninsula or island, depending on the lake level, joined to the mainland by a causeway. In 1988, the lake level dropped sufficiently to allow Crescent Island to become part of the mainland.

On the eastern end of the island sailing is possible at a private boating club. Sunday regattas are an incongruous sight on the bottom of the Rift Valley and the view of the Rift Valley walls from the lake is an altogether exhilarating experience.

Among the resident birds are fish eagles, ospreys, lily-trotters, black crakes and a variety of herons. Hippo also live in the lake. A number of mammals can be seen grazing in the surrounding lake environs, such as zebra, impala, buffalo, giraffe, Kongoni and, at night, hippos.

Lake Naivasha is 80 kilometres (50 miles) from Nairobi on the main Nairobi-Kisumu road. The old road, tracking an ancient elephant trail, snakes down the eastern Rift Valley Wall Escarpment and is to be avoided except by the bravest: it has been relegated to the lorry transport category. The newer road skirts along the top of the escarpment from **Limuru**, only dropping down into the Rift just south of Naivasha. From either, there is a magnificent view of Lake Naivasha and the extinct volcanoes, Suswa and Longonot, in the valley bottom.

Accommodation is available at **Lake Naivasha Hotel** or **Safariland Lodge**. The resplendent traditional Kenya Sunday Lunch at Lake Naivasha Hotel is recommended, even if you are not staying there. The view over the lake, from the well-manicured lawn, in the shade of yellow-barked fever trees, will not be soon forgotten.

There are a series of campsites on the southern side of the lake, probably the best known being **Fisherman's Camp**, where *bandas* can be rented or you can pitch your own tent. *Bandas* are also

Mount Longonot overlooks Lake Naivasha.

available at **YMCA Camp** and at **Top Camp**. If you have camping gear, Safariland Lodge also has a campsite.

Going to Hell: Hell's Gate National Park, a dramatically beautiful slice through the volcanic ridge south of Lake Naivasha, has only been recently created. It lies some 13 kilometres (eight miles) south-east of Naivasha and is about 68 square kilometres (27 square miles) in area.

The park is an impressive gorge with towering cliffs. Close to the entrance is **Fisher's Tower**, a lone 25-metre- (82-foot-) high rock. Powerful geysers, which gave the park its name, have been harnessed with foreign aid to generate electricity. The geothermal electricity project has been carefully executed so that it does not affect the beauty of the park.

Among the birds to be seen are a colony of Ruppell's vulture and a pair of resident lammergeyers that breed on the cliffs. The lammergeyers have developed the habit of scavenging bones, flying them to considerable heights and dropping them onto rocks to crack open and reveal the bone marrow. There are several "dropping points" in Hell's Gate. There are also Verreaux's eagles, the largest of the East African eagles, invariably seen soaring in pairs, and many other notable birds of prey. Secretary birds have taken up residence in a low acacia tree near the track which cuts up through the gorge. Mammals found in the park include Thomson's gazelle, antelope, zebra, hyrax, cheetah and leopard.

Camping is the only available accommodation. It might be wise to enter into a private arrangement with a local Maasai warrior to guard your vehicle for the night.

LONGONOT NATIONAL RESERVE

Longonot National Reserve encompasses an extinct volcanic crater, protruding from the floor of the Great Rift Valley and towering impressively over the southern side of Lake Naivasha. It is very visible from the Nairobi-Naivasha road. In all, Longonot Reserve covers

ppos ound in ke waters.

152 square kilometres (61 square miles). **Mount Longonot** can be climbed on foot from various access points.

Plains wildlife can be seen on the lower slopes, and various other animals, including leopards, are occasionally found in the crater. As might be expected from its variable altitude and vegetation, it is a haven for birds. On the middle-to-lower slopes, stands of leleshwa grow like weeds and are relatively impervious to the frequent grass fires which rage up from the plains in the dry season. The wood of leleshwa is extremely hard and good for carving in the manner of briar: the fragrant, light green and slightly hairy leaves are used for personal hygiene by trekking *Maasai* who tuck a bunch of them under each arm.

LAKE BOGORIA
Lake Bogoria National Reserve was gazetted to protect the herds of greater kudu which live mainly on the western slopes of the **Laikipia Escarp-**ment, which towers over the lake to the east. The reserve covers approximately 110 square kilometres (44 square kilometres) and includes the shallow soda lake which attracts huge flocks of flamingoes. Bogoria was formerly known as Lake Hannington during the colonial era. It was named after the missionary bishop who was murdered in Uganda.

Hot rocks: Hot springs and spectacular spluttering steam jets are one of the main attractions and are located approximately three-quarters of the way down the western lake shore heading south. The water in the springs is boiling hot and spouts up from subterranean aquifers surrounded by magma heated rock. Extreme caution should be exercised in walking around the springs. Some of the apparently solid ground is merely a crust on top of extremely hot mud. The sides of the larger springs are treacherously slippery, and more than one unfortunate soul has died after complications from scalding. If you get a bit hungry there is often a helpful fellow who, for a few shillings, will arrange to

Secretary Birds live on a diet of snakes and other reptiles.

230

have fresh maize boiled to a turn on the end of a pole in the springs.

The entire lake is fed by hot, sulphur rich springs which make swimming impossible but have created an environment of particular interest for the geomorphologist, ornithologist, or those interested in the special adaptations of fish. Even the layman will marvel at the primaeval scenery.

Lake Bogoria (formerly Lake Hannington) is 64 kilometres (40 miles) north of Nakuru and can be reached either from the south by taking a turning to the right about 38 kilometres (24 miles) from Nakuru or by continuing along the tarmac road until near to **Marigat** and then turning right at the sign post for **Loboi Gate**. The approach from the south gives a spectacular view of the lake which can suddenly be seen after a bend in the road. However, only four-wheel drive vehicles should be taken and even then progress is very slow, particularly along the lava flows near the entrance to the reserve. The northern road is good and can be negotiated by any saloon car up to the hot springs.

The only accommodation is **Acacia**, **Fig Tree** and **Riverside campsites** at the southern end of the lake. No facilities are available. All necessary water has to be brought along since the water in the lake is not drinkable. There is also a campsite just outside the northern entrance to the reserve, where water is available.

LAKE BARINGO

Lake Baringo lies 15 kilometres (nine miles) north of the little town of Marigat. It is a freshwater lake, twice the size of Lake Naivasha. It is home to great numbers of birds and hippos, which can be seen in the evenings grazing at the shoreside. Lake Baringo does not enjoy any particular protected status, except for the respect of the surrounding population for the value of its fish and the employment generated by tourism.

The lake has noticeably more sediment than other rift valley lakes, which

een roundings Lake ivasha.

can be seen from its brownish colour viewed from the shoreline or detected in the light it reflects to earth resources satellites. It has probably always been like this although much development aid is currently being spent to forestall erosion. The lake level fluctuates from year to year, sometimes by several metres, depending on rainfall in the surrounding hills.

The colony of nesting goliath herons on **Gibraltar Island** attracts many ornithologists. It is also possible to see Verreaux's eagles, bristle-crowned starlings and Hemprich's hornbill on the escarpment on the western side of the lake. Many other species of birds live in the acacia woodland bordering the lake, including west Nile red bishops and silverbirds.

First class accommodation is available either at the **Lake Baringo Club** or at **Island Camp**, on **Ol Kokwa Island**. The Lake Baringo Club offers a number of local excursions, including guided birdwatch walks, boat trips, water-skiing, and, in contrast, camel rides. Island Camp is a luxury tented lodge with swimming pool and water sport facilities. Camping facilities, as well as *bandas* are available at **Robert's Camp** on the lakeshore. Showers and toilets are provided.

LAKE MAGADI

Soda lake: The shallow, highly alkaline **Lake Magadi** is the southernmost of the Rift Valley lakes in Kenya. It lies in a semi-desert region where temperatures soar to over 40 C (104 F) during midday. A vigorous commercial enterprise which extracts sodium and calcium salts is supported by evaporation pans excavated into the lake, which is almost poisonously rich in salts because it has no external drainage. All of the rainfall runoff from the surrounding countryside brings with it dissolved minerals and ends up in Magadi (which, not surprizingly, means "soda" in *Maa*, the Maasai language). Since there is no outlet to the lake, the searing heat and fierce sun evaporates much of the water, leaving a concentrated salt solution. This is spread out over some 100 square

kilometres (40 square miles) and the lake bed appears to be one enormous sheet of white.

A number of hot springs can be found around the periphery of lake, the most accessible being to the south. Water birds are abundant, most notably the chestnut-banded sand plover which, in Kenya, can be found only at this lake. Flamingoes are usually very prominent. The southern shore is one of the sites in Kenya of annual gatherings of ornithologists who, during the northern hemisphere winter, set up skeins of fine "mist nets" to capture and ring-band some of the hundreds of thousands of birds which have migrated from the southern reaches of Europe to spend winter in East Africa. As you watch birds being extracted by expert hands from the tangles of a mist net, it is astounding to realise that their last port of call was quite likely near the southern steppes of Russia.

The trip to Lake Magadi is stark, beautiful and, thanks to the Magadi Soda Company, tarmacked all the way from the northern edge of the Ngong Hills. The road drops through a series of spectacular step faults down the eastern wall of the Rift Valley, from 2,100 metres (6,894 feet) at the Ngong Hills to 609 metres (2,000 feet) at the lake. Wildlife such as gerenuk and giraffe and fringe-eared oryx can be seen on the way.

Site for sore eyes: On the way to Magadi, it is worth stopping off for a look at **Olookisaili**, one of Kenya's most important archaeological excavation sites, on the shores of an ancient Pleistocene lake. There, *Homo habilis* hunted a fauna much richer than today's, and *Homo sapiens* may spend a rustic night in the self-help *bandas*. Arrangements must be made beforehand at the National Museums of Kenya office in Nairobi.

At Magadi itself, there is no accommodation available, unless you are fortunate enough to be invited to the Soda Company's Club. However, camping is allowed although no facilities are provided. It is essential to bring your own water and other provisions.

Right, soda shores of Lake Magadi.

LAKE TURKANA

Lake Turkana, known from Count Teleiki's first exclamation as the Jade Sea, is so far off the beaten track that it gives the impression that time has stood still. The surrounding scrub desert enhances the colour of the lake which looks even more impressive because there is no contrasting greenery. It is set in the midst of volcanic formations and dry rivers known as "luggas" and is the northern-most lake in the Kenyan part of the Great Rift Valley, where temperatures can reach up to 50 C (122 F). From here, our earliest ancestors probably started organised hunting, harvesting and society. Today, the ethnic peoples inhabiting this region are nomadic pastoralists who seem hardly affected by modern life.

The largest population of Nile crocodiles in Kenya lives on the shores of the lake and a population of the largest freshwater fish in East Africa, the Nile perch, inhabits the lake and can grow to over 100 kilograms (220 pounds), much to the joy of sport fishermen.

The area is rich in birdlife. In (northern hemisphere) spring, black-tailed godwits and spotted redshanks can be seen in full breeding plumage. European migrants use this area as a stopover on their way north. Birds of prey are also abundant.

Ferguson's Gulf is 64 kilometres (40 miles) north of **Lodwar**. It presents some of the best fishing opportunities in the country. Accommodation can be found at **Lake Turkana Fishing Lodge**, which is reached by taking a boat from the lake shore across Ferguson's Gulf. The lodge is comfortable, with basic facilities. It even has a swimming pool filled with lakewater, which has an unmistakably soapy feel. Nothing harmful, except crocodiles, could survive in that! The food is good and the menu consists mainly of lake fish.

The gulf itself was quite dry during 1989 but it will certainly fill again as the

Central Island and its crater lakes.

234

lake level rises with the next good period of rains. As you drive to the jetty from the airstrip or the end of the tarmac road from Nairobi, the hulk of a beached Norwegian fishing boat can be seen, a monument to a development aid scheme gone wrong. The *Turkana* are adaptable people and are able to survive in such a harsh environment by embracing fishing as well as herding. They also enjoy a deserved reputation as fearless watchmen.

The **Cherangani Hills** to the south and west of Ferguson's Gulf are one of the great unknown trekking areas in the world. The view from the ridge tops is magnificent yet has only been seen by a handful of hearty walkers.

Central Island, in the middle of Lake Turkana, can be reached by boat from Ferguson's Gulf. The island's main crater lake is a nesting point for an extremely large number of crocodiles and many water birds. Once on the island, the rest of the trip has to be undertaken on foot, which can be very strenuous in the heat of the day. Until recently, the island was populated more by immigrant *Luo* fishermen from Lake Victoria than by crocodiles.

South Island is the birdwatcher's and Nile perch fisherman's paradise of Lake Turkana. Care must be exercised if you are camping rough since the ever-present large population of crocodiles can be dangerous. The airstrip on the island is a twisted, rock-strewn horror and a challenge for every bush pilot in Kenya!

Adjacent to the eastern shores of Lake Turkana, **Sibiloi National Park** covers 2,500 square kilometres (1,000 square miles) of barren, semi-arid bushland. Richard Leakey has found many important fossils of early man and animals in this ancient location and a fascinating archaeological museum has been opened at **Koobi Fora**. Grevy's zebra and beisa oryx can be seen. There is no water here so come prepared if venturing into this area by car. Access is mostly by plane, unless you have at least a week and access to a sturdy four-wheel drive vehicle.

235

To the West

Mount Elgon National Park is famous for its forest which has gigantic podocarpus trees and impressive stands of juniper and elgon olive. The mountain, like most in Kenya, is a long-extinct volcano. The park covers approximately 170 square kilometres (68 square miles). It lies between 2,500 and 4,300 metres (8,200 and 14,100 feet) up the side of the mountain, the summit of which is in Uganda. Despite its small size, the park has a variety of habitats, from savannah to woodlands and mountain forest to alpine moorlands.

Salt caves: In the side of the mountain are vast caves, the most famous of which is **Kitum**, into which elephants have walked for thousands of years. There is good reason to believe that elephants dug the caves themselves since they enter them every two or three days to get salt. There, in complete darkness, nearly 200 metres (660 feet) into the side of the mountain, they use their tusks to gouge mineral salts out of the cave walls. This remarkable population has learned to move about in the dark *en masse*, with mothers guiding their young past dangerous holes and crevasses using their trunks. Like nearly all other elephants in East Africa, they have been heavily poached in the last few years and they are now under serious threat of complete extinction, despite the valiant efforts of Kenya's Wildlife Conservation and Management Department and the Anti-Poaching Unit.

Colobus monkey, leopard, golden cat, black-fronted duiker, elephant and buffalo live in the rain forest and on the moorland. The park also has a wealth of afro-alpine flowers.

The entrance to the park is 27 kilometres (17 miles) from **Kitale** along the Endebess road. Although there is no accommodation in the park, one can stay at **Mount Elgon Lodge** near the entrance. The lodge is a converted farm

Comfortab
Mount Elg
Lodge.

house with a beautiful view. Alternatively, one can stay at **Kitale Hotel** or at **Lokitela Guest House**, run by the Mills family on their farm (19 kilometres/12 miles) west of Kitale.

It is also possible to climb Mount Elgon. For more information contact the Mountain Club of Kenya.

KAKAMEGA FOREST

Kakamega Forest National Reserve was gazetted in 1985, but the status of the park which was scheduled for gazetting two years earlier is still unclear. The 97 square kilometres (39 square miles) comprise the most eastern area of the Congo Central African rain forest, to the east of Kakamega, and is known for its birdlife, mammals and vegetation. Many of the birds and mammals that occur here cannot be found anywhere else in Kenya. Characteristic species include grey parrots, great blue turacos, Ross's turacos, red-chested owlets and African broadbills, wattle-eyes and many others. The Angolan black and white colobus may also be found, although in smaller numbers.

LAMBWE VALLEY

Lambwe Valley National Park covers 120 square kilometres (48 square miles) of tall grasslands mixed with woodlands and acacia thickets in **South Nyanza** near **Homa Bay**, Lake Victoria. The reserve was created to preserve the lovely roan antelope, a small population of which are resident. Other mammals include oribi and Jackson's hartebeest. Giraffes, zebra and ostrich have been introduced from Samburu to help reduce the dense vegetation. Birds are abundant in this area and can be easily observed.

Lambwe is in one of the most highly populated areas of Kenya, and has long been a centre of controversy. Tsetse flies abound and it is considered a reservoir for human and animal sleeping sickness. The park was subjected to large amounts of DDT spraying until the practice was stopped by conservationist movements. Nonetheless, the will of the people prevailed and the park was de-gazetted in 1989.

SAIWA SWAMP

Saiwa Swamp National Park is the smallest in Kenya, covering an area of only 1.9 square kilometres (0.76 square miles). It encloses the fringing belt of rain forest and the swamps fed by the **Saiwa River**.

Saving sitatungas: Saiwa was created specially to protect the sitatunga antelopes (about 80 to 100 in number) which live there. They spend most of the day half-submerged and hidden amid the floating vegetation. The hooves of this antelope are enormously elongated to about 18 centimetres (seven inches) which enable the animal to support its weight on the marshy ground. Camouflaged platforms have been built to allow visitors to see these rare animals. Another rare species is the Brazza's monkey, of which some 30 of the 200 left in Kenya live in the park. Other animals include spotted-necked otter, nocturnal potto and giant forest squirrel. The park lies 15 kilometres (nine miles) north of Kitale to the east of the main road to Lake Turkana.

k marks
salt
e.

COASTAL PARKS

Shimba Hills National Park is situated 56 kilometres (35 miles) south of **Mombasa** and consists of an area of 310 square kilometres (124 square miles), encompassing a line of gently rolling hills (rising up to 450 metres/ 1,500 feet) which run more or less parallel to the Kenya coastline. For sheer tranquility and lovely coastal views it is unbeatable. There are areas of open glades alternating with impressive stands of coastal rain forest. Herds of roan and spectacular sable antelope (occurring nowhere else in the country) can be found grazing here.

Fowl town: Lone bull buffalo can be seen and there is a resident herd which spends most of midday sheltering under the shade of one or two trees, normally in the area of the landing strip. There are signs of elephant everywhere and they can be seen going to drink in the mornings and evenings. They sometimes even wander into the outskirts of **Kwale** town. However, most of the time the herd are deep in the seemingly impenetrable forest in the middle of the park. Forest loving red duiker, bushbuck, waterbuck and grey duiker are also found. Lions and leopards are also present, although not in abundance. Birdlife, however, is profuse. Keep an eye out for the spur fowl—*kwale* in *Swahili*—from which the town takes its name.

An easy drive from any of the beach resorts south of Mombasa, the Shimba Hills offer a cool change from the humidity of the coastal strip. There are stunning views of the ocean and Tanzania's Usambara and Pare mountains.

There is a new lodge just outside the park gate and self-help thatched *bandas* are located on the edge of an escarpment. Bring food and bedding for these. Otherwise, there's plenty of beachfront accommodation between the townships of **Tiwi** and **Diani**, a 21-kilometre (13-mile) stretch south of Mombasa.

This sable antelope h perfectly proportion horns.

238

MALINDI-WATAMU

These parks are situated on the coast by **Malindi**, and cover an area of beaches from the high tide line and coral reefs out to the edge of the continental shelf. The coral gardens abound with mostly unspoilt underwater wildlife. Snorkeling and scuba diving are the best way to see the myriad aquatic flora and fauna. The fish are habituated to people and will eat out of your hand.

There is perennial concern that the Malindi reefs are under threat from siltation from the effluent of the **Sabalki River** just north of Malindi town. The coral polyps are unable to feed and breath under the layer of accumulated silt. There are numerous luxury hotels at Malindi and **Watamu**, and these give easy access on a daily basis.

MIDA CREEK

Mida Creek is located on the north coast of Kenya, a few kilometres south of **Gedi**, an early Islamic coastal city that was abandoned in the 17th century for no apparent reason. The ruins are well kept and worth visiting.

Mudflats and mangroves: The creek is a series of tidal mudflats surrounded by mangrove trees. It is known for the numbers of waders that stop there between March and May on their way north during the annual migration. Birds seen include sanderlings, turnstones, curlew sandpipers, greenshanks, little stints, wimbrels, Terek sandpipers and grey plovers. Ospreys, several species of terns and the rare, nonmigrant crab plover also inhabit the creek. In the mangroves flocks of the brilliant carmine bee-eaters flash in the sunlight.

Snorkeling is possible for the more daring. When the tide is right you can enter the creek at park headquarters and float down and back up the dark, murky water with the current. Look out for the sea carp weighing up to to 182 kilograms (400 pounds) that lurk in the caves.

The creek is reached via the Mombasa-Malindi road. Turn right 35 kilometres (22 miles) after the Kilifi ferry.

slow day
Shimba.

KISITE-MPUNGE

Established in 1978 as Kenya's second marine reserve, this park encompasses the outer and inner **Mpunguti Islands**, and the sand bar of **Kisite**, south of **Wasini** at **Shimoni**. The water is crystal clear and ideal for snorkeling. The only access is by boat from Shimoni which takes 90 minutes. *Shimo* in *Swahili* means hole—named after the large cave that was used as a holding tank for slaves before shipment. There is excellent deep sea fishing here.

ARABUKU-SOKOKE

The **Arabuku-Sokoke Forest Reserve** runs parallel to the coastline between **Kilifi** and Gedi for a stretch of about 360 square kilometres (144 square miles). Tightly surrounded by farmland, it is the last remaining extensive patch of brachestygia woodland and lowland coastal rain forest of azeleas left in Kenya.

Rare mammals: The forest is home to a number of interesting and rare mammals including Zanzibar duiker, Ad-der's duiker, the bristle-tailed and the yellow-rumped elephant shrew. All are difficult to see because of their shy nature and small size. Elephant shrews, with their elephantine snouts, are the largest members of this peculiar African family, measuring 50 centimetres (20 inches) long.

A number of rare and common local birds are also found in this forest. These include the Sokoke scops owl, thick-billed cuckoo, Retz helmet shrike, Amani sunbird, African pitta (rare), Fisher's turaco, Sokoke pipit and southern-banded harrier eagles. Clarke's weavers occur in flocks of 100 or more but their nests have never been found. Another memorable sight are the thousands of butterflies that drink along the pools near the forest tracks.

Take the Mombasa-Malindi road to reach the forest. Some 20 kilometres (12 miles) after crossing the gorge with the Kilifi ferry, the forest can be seen on the left. There are several access routes, most of which require four-wheel drive vehicles.

The popula
coastal tov
of Malindi

TO THE EAST

Remote and undeveloped, **Arawale National Reserve** consists of a 533-square-kilometre (213-square-mile) triangle adjacent to the eastern banks of the **Tana River** in the north-eastern part of Kenya. It was created in 1974 specifically for the protection of Hunter's hartebeest or hirole, a rarely-seen antelope with lyre-shaped horns similar to the impala's and a white stripe across the forehead between the eyes. Small herds comprising a territorial males accompanied by his females, tend to favour the open grassland patches between the more dense bushland. Grevy's zebra and lesser kudu are also found, as are herds of buffalo and rapidly diminishing numbers of elephants.

Hunter's hartebeest is only found in this part of Kenya and although potentially threatened because of range restriction and small numbers, they seem to be holding their own. They are under little threat, since there is not much competetion with man for living space in this remote part of the world and there has been no official hunting allowed in Kenya since the blanket ban on hunting wildlife imposed in 1977. Although the range of Hunter's hartebeest probably extends eastward into southern Somalia, the species has never been reliably recorded on the western banks of the Tana. There are no accommodation or camping facilities in Arawale.

TANA RIVER PRIMATE RESERVE

Halfway between the Arawale Reserve and the mouth of the Tana River at the Indian Ocean, some 130 kilometers (81 miles) north of Malindi, lies the **Tana River Primate Reserve**. This is a small protected area of riverine forest covering 169 square kilometres (68 square miles) which was gazetted in 1976 specifically to protect the world's only population of one of the four subspecies of crested mangabey monkey, the endangered Tana mangabey (*Cer-*

ch colours
Ross's
aco.

241

cocebus galeritus galeritus). There are two subspecies which live in the high forests of Zaire, about which almost nothing is known, and another endangered subspecies in the Uzungwa mountains of Tanzania, the Sanje crested mangabey, which was only discovered by scientists in 1981.

The Tana mangabey is at serious risk and, despite protection in the reserve, its population has dropped from around 2,000 in the early 1970s to between 800 and 1,000 today. The major threats to its narrow belt of riverine habitat include clearing for agriculture, felling of large trees for making traditional dugout canoes, annual burning of the flood plain grasses which is inexorably eroding away the forest edge, and natural changes to the river course in this relatively flat, flood plain area. The Tana mangabey is therefore included in the most threatened category of the 1973 International Convention on Trade in Endangered Species of Wild Fauna and Flora (CITES), which makes it difficult, but not impossible to export this rare beast. However, habitat changes due to the inevitable expansion of human populations rather than trade are likely to bring about its demise in the near future.

There is also a small group of threatened red colobus monkey as well as red river hog and numerous hippos, crocodiles and other riverine animals. Birdlife is prolific.

Visitors must either camp or attempt to book at **Baomo Lodge** (often closed) to the north of the reserve.

BONI, DODORI AND KIUNGA

Boni National Reserve is situated on Kenya's eastern border with Somalia, with one corner just touching the Indian Ocean, in 1,339 square kilometres (535 square miles) of undeveloped wilderness. It is the only area in Kenya with coastal lowland groundwater forest. It was set aside partly as a buffer, and partly as a refuge for large populations of coastal topi and elephants so that the latter would journey down through neighbouring **Dodori National Reserve** to the seashore, often wading out at low tide to "Elephant Island".

Dodori National Reserve is 877 square kilometres (350 square miles) in area, and is situated just north of **Lamu**. It almost joins on to Boni National Reserve to the north and **Kiunga Marine National Reserve** adjacent to the coast. Dodori was established in 1976 to provide protection of major breeding grounds for the local topi population.

Elephants are still found in small numbers as are lesser kudu. Birdlife is rich, with many waterbirds, birds of prey and nothern migrants. Dugongs, or seacows—the original mermaids of seafaring lore—used to breed along the coast, but their numbers are rapidly declining due to encounters with local fishermen.

With 250 square kilometres (100 square miles) of islands, beaches and coral reefs in north-east Kenya by the Somali border, the Kiunga Marine National Reserve is a prime sea-bird breeding ground, most notably for Hemprich's gull which nests between July and October.

Right, deserted beach on t north coas

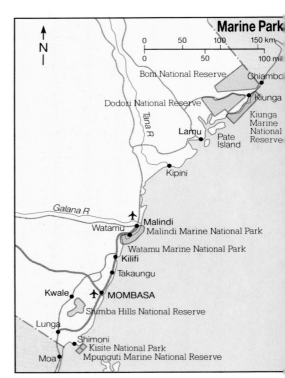

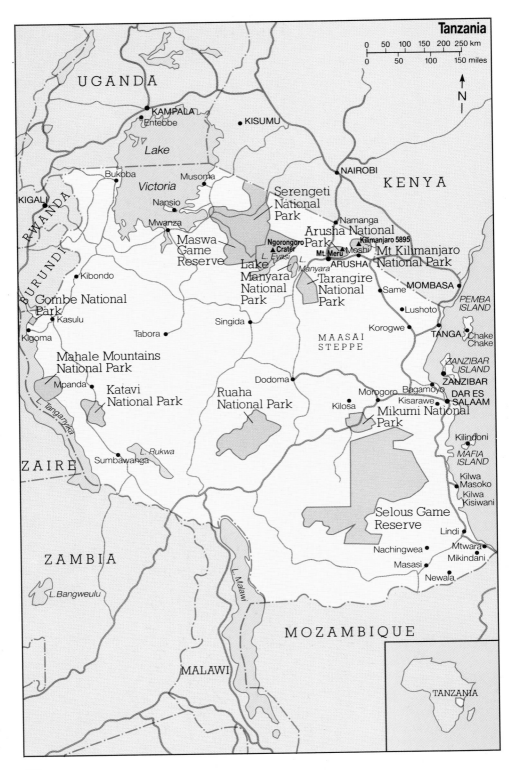

TANZANIA

Situated just south of the equator, Tanzania stretches from the Indian Ocean westward across more than 1,000 kilometres (620 miles) to Lake Tanganyika, which marks the boundary with Zaire and the Congo forests. Lake Victoria indents Tanzania's northern frontier and Lake Malawi the southern. Some 800 kilometres (496 miles) of unspoiled coastline strewn with islands contrast with the vast interior where Africa's highest mountain, Kilimanjaro, stands along with many other spectacular mountains amid enormous stretches of woodland, bush, savannah and marsh. Cleaving much of the country is the Great Rift Valley. The combination of scenery, magnificent wildlife and luxurious lodges makes the safari experience in Tanzania an exquisite one.

Tanzania is a republic made up of Tanganyika, the mainland, and Zanzibar Island. The total area of the nation is about 380,000 square kilometres (147,820 square miles) and the population in 1988 was about 22 million. People are concentrated in the coastal areas, around Lake Victoria and on the fertile slopes of the volcanoes in the north. There are over one million people in the capital city, Dar es Salaam ("Peaceful Harbour"), but only a few hundred thousand in any of the secondary towns: the majority live in rural areas.

Tanzania's history as a nation started in 1961 when Tanganyika, the mainland, became the first colony in East Africa to receive independence from Britain. Zanzibar became independent in 1963 and the two nations joined to become the United Republic of Tanzania in 1964. Julius Nyerere, from the Lake Victoria area, was the first president until he retired in 1985 to become the chairman of the political party, Chama cha Mapinduzi. His successor is Ali Hassan Mwinyi, from Zanzibar.

Tanzania's unrecorded history covers a span of millions of years. Some visible traces remain at prehistoric and stone age sites all over the country. At Laetoli, are the ancient footprints of human ancestors preserved in ash on the slopes of volcanoes making up the Ngorongoro Highlands. The stones and bones of our ancestors have been left at Olduvai Gorge and fascinating rock paintings at Kondoa and other sites testify to the artistic skills and abilities of ancient hunters and gatherers.

Preceding pages: baobab trees can have trunks of up to 10 metres (33 feet) in diameter. These fill up the landscape in Tarangire National Park.

SERENGETI

With its wide open spaces, bright blue skies and creature-filled landscape, the fabled **Serengeti** typifies everyone's version of "dream Africa". It is one of the last places in the world where vast numbers of large animals can be seen in their natural habitat.

Serengeti was established in 1951. It is Tanzania's largest and oldest national park. Its rolling plains, bordered with ranges of hills and sprinkled with rocky outcrops, spread out over almost 14,500 square kilometres (5,790 square miles). Reflecting the varied terrain is the park's annual rainfall, which ranges from about 500 mm (19.5 inches) in the south-west to about 1,200 mm (46.8 inches) in the north and west.

In spite of its fame, Serengeti has not been ruined by tourism. Roads into the park can be rough going and local tracks are not much smoother. Accommoda-tion is comfortable but not luxurious, there are no balloon rides, night safaris, foot safaris or fashionable camps. Visi-tors and staff are expected to adapt to the environment, instead of changing the environment to cater to human whim. It is this lack of human influence which gives the park its charm.

Serengeti can be visited in either dry or wet season. During the rains from November to May, the annual wilde-beest migration takes place. When it is wettest and food is plentiful wildebeest spread far out on the plains, only retreat-ing to the bush and woodland when the savannah dries out. When all the green grass is eaten they gather along the western edge of the plains then trickle north and west searching for food until they reach the Maasai Mara in the north where there is more pasture and perma-nent water. When the rains begin again in November, they stream back south-wards to seek the fresh, nutritious grass that grows on the volcanic soils in the lee of the **Ngorongoro Highlands**.

During the dry months, from June to

Far left, thi cheetah cu resembles fur ball.

Serengeti National Park

September, the wildebeest along with several hundred thousand zebra are massed on the short grass plains in the south of the park.

In February, most female wildebeest calve, so visitors may see a birth and the period of imprinting immediately after. This is the short time when mother and calf get to know one another intimately enough to survive most separations. The calf can run as fast as its mother within half an hour of being born, even before it has its first drink of milk. Some of the other ungulates giving birth at this time include zebras, gazelles and eland, although their birth season is somewhat more extended.

But life and death are inseparable: vulnerable new-born calves attract predators, which in turn are accompanied by scavengers that clean up the carcasses left scattered on the plains. Only the strong survive.

Gazelles, particularly Thomson's, are the first to take advantage of the new grass. Zebras, elands, topi and hartebeest move from the woodland edge out to the plains.

Some buffalo are tempted out along the watercourses. It is a myth that predators come out to follow their prey. Most predators are resident in a well-defined range and those that move out on to the plains most likely live adjacent all year round. So you won't find vast numbers of lions, hyaenas, jackals, cheetahs or wild dogs congregating with the vast herds. Hyaena, jackal or wild dog dens on the plains are special attractions and well worth a look; you might find these predators hunting or tending their young.

The rain in the plains: The plains are incredibly beautiful during the rains, with dramatic skies full of storm clouds. Birds arrive from Asia and Europe to take advantage of the many insects that are present then. The bird migration can be even more impressive than the wildebeests'. Thousands of European storks cover the plains, kestrels and harriers hover or swoop after rodents and dung beetles, caspian plovers from the Russian steppe fly in tight forma-

tion, European swallows, swifts and terns pursue flying insects and yellow wagtails catch grasshoppers.

When the plains dry up, their character changes completely. The unending green becomes a vast expanse of short, brown grass. The lack of trees becomes more obvious. *Kopjes* stick out more and seem more interesting because much life still clings to their water-filled crevices. Most of the large animals depart, leaving only a few hardy warthogs, Grant's gazelles, topi and hartebeest. Small creatures go underground; the plains look bare but lizards, mice and beetles are still hidden under rocks, in holes and grass clumps.

During the dry season animals retreat to places where there is permanent water. If you follow the many tracks around the rivers in the centre of the park at **Seronera**, or northwards to **Lobo**, or westwards to **Kirawira**, you will always find many animals along the rivers, in open grasslands and woodlands. The main residents are impalas, topis, buffalos, giraffes, waterbucks,

reedbucks, bushbucks, dikdiks, warthogs, baboons and vervet monkeys. The smaller or shyer animals include mongooses, civets, genets, servals, caracals, leopards, bat-eared foxes, bushbabies, oribi, duikers, pangolins, aardvarks, aardwolves and many birds.

Serengeti has a few oddities. In the western corridor, which follows the **Grumeti River** to **Lake Victoria**, there are black and white colobus monkeys, more like those of Uganda and eastern Kenya than those found at Mount Kilimanjaro and Meru. On the open grasslands by the Grumeti are wide-ranging groups of orange-haired patas monkeys. There might still be a remnant group of roan antelope around **Banagi Hill**. Their presence here so far out of their normal range gives credence to the idea that in former times the vegetation of Serengeti was like that of southern Tanzania, which is composed of miombo woodland.

Near the end of the Grumeti River where it begins to enter the ancient

Seronera Lodge is designed to complemen its surrounding

floodplains of Lake Victoria there are Nile crocodiles up to four metres (13 feet) long. Small and medium crocodiles travel as far upstream as Seronera where they inhabit some of the pools in the **Seronera River**.

Studying Serengeti: Father and son Bernard and Michael Grzimek, were the first to make systematic studies of the Serengeti ecosystem. They flew their famous zebra striped airplane from Frankfurt to Tanzania in the 1950s and pioneered aerial census methods over the plains and woodlands. Thanks to their research there are records of the low numbers of wildebeest at that time. The Grzimeks also studied the grasslands and produced a best-selling book and subsequent movie, *Serengeti Shall Not Die*, which did much to make people aware that Serengeti existed. The book was later translated into 24 languages.

By the early 1960s Serengeti was well known enough to attract funding and cooperation in setting up a complete and well-equipped research facility near Seronera. In the mid-1960s, scientists at the Serengeti Research Institute (SRI) started work in earnest. An ecological monitoring programme began which systematically counted animals, measured rainfall and studied burning. Studies were started on lions, hyaenas, wildebeest, zebras, giraffes, impalas, buffalos, elephants, gazelles, topis, birds, vegetation and soils.

Most of this first generation of scientists left by the mid-1970s and were followed by others who continued certain species studies or tackled new subjects such as mongooses. Much of what we now know about East African wildlife comes from this research on Serengeti animals. Scientific vigour, which declined in the 1970s, has now revived and SRI is again producing much important information on wildlife ecology. One of their most important findings was to recognise the crucial need to monitor rainfall, fire, vegetation and animal numbers. We are learning that the balance of nature only works like a see-saw in motion, always changing, never static. But the complexities of the ecosystem have only been glimpsed. We cannot hope to "manage" any wildlife area successfully without understanding how life there manages itself without human interference.

Serengeti is a unique living laboratory that continues to play a vital role in promoting understanding of wild animals and their environment.

The Musoma road leading from Arusha across the Rift Valley and over the shoulder of Ngorongoro carries on across the Serengeti plain through the park's centre at Seronera and leaves the park to the west by **Ikoma Gate**. This is the major route to and through Serengeti but there are two other gates: **Bologonja Gate** in the north at the border between Kenya and Tanzania and **Ndabaka Gate** in the west which almost touches on the main road between Musoma and Mwanza around the shore of Lake Victoria. The main road is passable all year round but other roads in the park are not maintained regularly and their condition should be checked before setting out.

artial
gle is
ised for
ke-off.

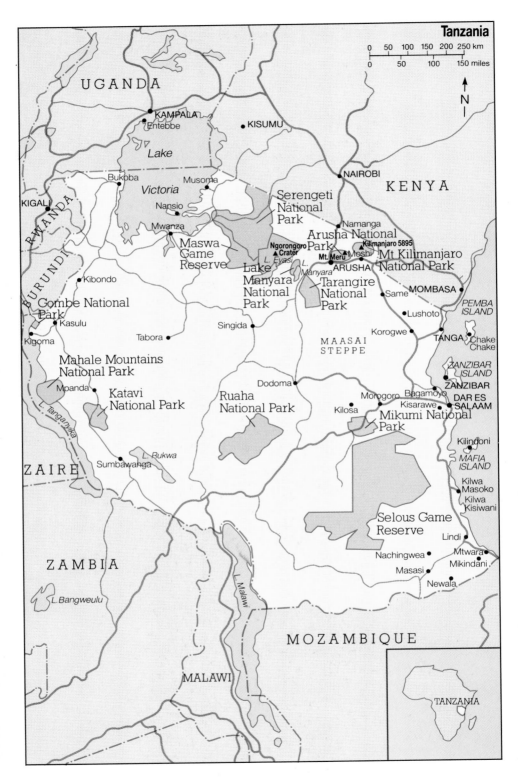

Tanzania

0 50 100 150 200 250 km
0   50   100   150 miles

N

UGANDA

KAMPALA
Entebbe

KISUMU

Lake

Bukoba

Musoma

Victoria

Nansio

NAIROBI

KENYA

Mwanza

KIGALI

RWANDA

BURUNDI

Kibondo

Serengeti National Park

Arusha National Park

Maswa Game Reserve

Ngorongoro Crater

L. Eyasi

Mt. Meru

Namanga

Kilimanjaro 5895

Moshi

Mt Kilimanjaro National Park

ARUSHA

Lake Manyara National Park

L. Manyara

Tarangire National Park

Same

MOMBASA

PEMBA ISLAND

Lushoto

Gombe National Park

Kasulu

Kigoma

Korogwe

TANGA

Chake Chake

MAASAI STEPPE

Tabora

Singida

Mahale Mountains National Park

Mpanda

L. Tanganyika

Katavi National Park

ZANZIBAR ISLAND

ZANZIBAR

Dodoma

Ruaha National Park

Kilosa

Morogoro

Bagamoyo

Kisarawe

DAR ES SALAAM

Mikumi National Park

Kilindoni

MAFIA ISLAND

L. Rukwa

Sumbawanga

ZAIRE

Kilwa Masoko

Kilwa Kisiwani

Selous Game Reserve

Lindi

ZAMBIA

Nachingwea

Mtwara

Mikindani

Masasi

L. Bangweulu

L. Malawi

Newala

MOZAMBIQUE

MALAWI

TANZANIA

NGORONGORO CONSERVATION AREA

Ngorongoro Crater has been called the eighth wonder of the natural world. It has been designated a World Heritage Site and a Biosphere Reserve and the crater deserves every bit of its fame— yet it represents only about 3 percent of the entire **Ngorongoro Conservation Area** (NCA), which covers 8,280 square kilometres (3,196 square miles), stretching from **Lake Eyasi** in the Rift Valley north to the Serengeti Plains. The region contains at least seven extinct volcanoes and is probably one of the most varied terrains in East Africa. Altitude in the park varies from Lake Eyasi at 1,000 metres (3,280 feet) to the peak of **Lolmalasin** mountain at 3,640 metres (11,940 feet).

The Ngorongoro Highlands on their southern and eastern slopes are clothed in forest which captures water for all the farmland to the south and also supports Manyara's special ground water forest at the base of the rift. The massif of old volcanoes surrounding the Ngorongoro **caldera** includes several craters and mountains of beauty and importance.

The plains to the north are critical to the migration of wildebeest. Note that at least half of the Serengeti Plains are in Ngorongoro Conservation Area and another plain, the **Salei**, is protected only by the NCA. Annual rainfall ranges from around 300 mm (11.7 inches) in the dry regions such as Lake Eyasi to over 1,000 mm (39 inches) up in the highlands.

Archaeological sites: The NCA was set up in the late 1950s in response to complaints by the *Maasai* that they were being pushed out of their traditional grazing areas by the formation of Serengeti National Park, which at that time included Ngorongoro. The conservation area was set up as a unique test of the idea that humans who lead a pastoral life-style, utilizing livestock only for sustenance, should be able to co-exist with wildlife. The area was also to cater to tourists, protect the forest to the south

and guard unique archaeological sites such as **Olduvai Gorge** and **Laetoli**. The Laetoli site has footprints of our hominid ancestors that are dated firmly at over 3.5 million years old.

At Olduvai many fossils and artifacts dating from the last two million years have been found embedded in rich deposits containing remains of contemporary animals and plants. A visit to the small and excellent museum at Olduvai gives one a chance to fathom the beginnings of mankind, within an area where the first humans are believed to have evolved.

There are other archaeological sites round the conservation area, some even in the crater itself. Humans have been living here for millions of years so it is fitting that the conservation area enables local tribes to live with the wildlife that has also evolved here.

Wildlife in the crater: Ngorongoro is not only a fascinating lesson in land use and the modern problems of how to reconcile human desires with nature, it is also one of the most picturesque set-

tings for viewing wildlife. All animals are so used to cars that you can get close enough both to study their behaviour and to take excellent photographs.

All the usual grassland dwelling animals live in the crater: wildebeest, zebras, Thomson's gazelles, Grant's gazelles, elands, hartebeest, buffalos, warthogs, ostriches, kori bustards, crowned cranes, and predators such as bat-eared foxes, jackals, hyaenas, lions and, rarely seen, cheetahs.

In the forest and swamps are some elephants, all males, perhaps because there is not enough food for the normally much larger female and calf groups. Also near the forests are a few waterbuck and bushbuck. Around the marshes and streams are reedbuck and serval cat, and birds—masses of ducks, geese, herons, ibis, plovers, widow and whydah birds. Flamingoes often provide a pink fringe to the little soda lake in the crater's centre, and you can drive close enough to see and photograph them well. Hippos can be seen at two exceptionally pretty sites: the pool at

Mandusi swamp and the lake at **Ngoitokitok springs** where visitors can eat their picnic lunch in the shade of fig trees where starlings, weavers and fish eagles perch. You should, however, beware of the African kites which swoop with incredible accuracy to steal food.

There is another picnic site in the **Lerai Forest** (a *Maasai* word for yellow-barked acacia trees) where there is running water and vervet monkeys and large numbers of baboons. Leopards live along the **Munge River** and forested slopes all round, yet they are seldom seen. Rhinos also take refuge in the forest but are often in the open on the soda flats or along watercourses. Some mountain reedbuck live in the brush on the inner crater wall. Impala and giraffe can be seen only on the outer slopes, never in the crater, because there is not enough of their food to support a breeding population. Male elephants are only temporary feeders in the crater and leave from time to time to join the female groups which range the forest

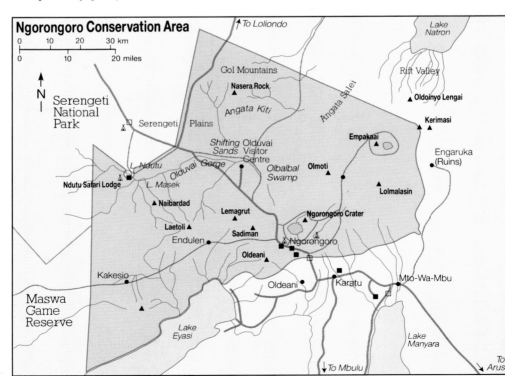

outside.

It is impossible to visit the crater without noticing all the wildflowers and the beautiful mantle of forest along the south. Even the dry, thorny northern side has picturesque plants. If you can reach it the remoteness and pristine beauty of **Empaakai Crater** and the lovely walk from **Olmoti's bowl** to climb down among mountain wildflowers is worth the effort. From here you can see the stark cone of the still active volcano **Oldoinyo Lengai** at the northeast corner of the conservation area.

Granite cliffs: The granite outcrops and the ancient crystalline **Gol Mountains** with their great gorges are reached by crossing bumpy plains strewn with windswept sand dunes. Here, sparkling pink granite cliffs provide ancient nesting sites for griffon vultures. Right at the northern bases of the great volcanoes lie the archaeological sites of Olduvai and Laetoli. In the western end of Olduvai Gorge, thick acacia woodland surrounds **Ndutu**, with its precious lakes providing water for the animals

there and also those from the surrounding savannah.

The Serengeti and the Salei plains are the location of the annual migrations of wildebeest, zebras, gazelles, elands, ostriches, and other birds. The vast green sward dotted with kopjes is a fitting scene for the births and deaths of great numbers of animals.

So Ngorongoro means more than just the famous crater. With its streams and lakes, forests, open grasslands, bushy slopes and wildlife, NCA is a microcosm of East Africa and its historical significance for humankind makes it unique among game parks.

The main road between Arusha and Lake Victoria cuts right through the conservation area, running around the west rim of Ngorongoro Crater. It is gravel surfaced and seldom muddy enough to make the crater inaccessible; however, all roads in the conservation area vary greatly in their condition, especially during the heavy rains of March to May. Go with a good driver and check first at park headquarters.

-eared
es play
k-a-boo.

KILIMANJARO

Kilimanjaro is a huge mountain but the park that protects its upper reaches is really quite small, only 756 square kilometres (292 square miles). It was established in 1973 and ranges in altitude from 1,000 metres (3,280 feet) to 5,895 metres (19,340 feet) at Kibo peak, the highest point in Africa. The lower slopes are protected by being both a forest and game reserve. The park may be expanded in the future but now has several corridors or rights of way through the forest. The alternative routes to the peaks follow these lush forest corridors.

The peaks: Kilimanjaro is composed of three extinct volcanoes: **Kibo**, **Mawenzi** (5,145 metres/16,890 feet) and **Shira** (4,002 metres/13,140 feet). Kibo, being highest, is the peak that most visitors wish to climb. The top is breathtaking, not only because it is a long, steep climb at very high altitude but also because the views from Kibo are stunning. From the rim you can survey (weather permitting!) a vast surround of plains and other Rift Valley mountains (most notably Mount Meru to the west). Looking inward one sees the ash cone and, around the interior, sparkling glacier ice carved by wind and rain and melted by the sun into fantastic shapes. The exhilaration of having successfully reached the top adds to the sense of being on Africa's highest point.

Most people reach Kibo by way of a well-planned route along the eastern slopes. There are chalets and huts along the way, providing food and rest at each night's stop. From the park gate at **Marangu** there are two trails; one directly up a fairly open ridge; the other through forest with monkeys and birds—Hartlaub's turaco is especially easy to see. The trails join well before reaching the first huts at **Mandara** at 2,700 metres (8,856 feet).

On the second day one can visit

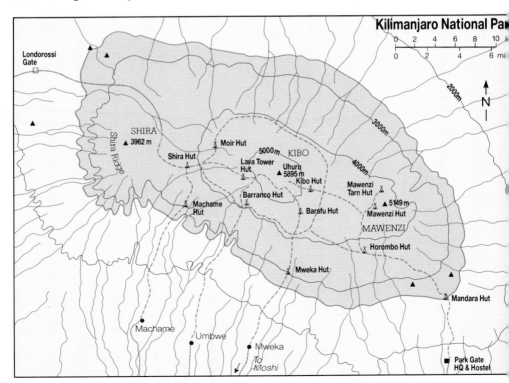

Maundi Crater, one of the many little "parasitic cones" that deck the flanks of the mountain. Here you can see the huge creamy protea flower in its native habitat. Also along the way are great hagenia trees with clusters of dark red flowers, bright green hypericum bushes with large yellow flowers, and the dramatic red or yellow spikes of poker flowers. A common bushy tree that might look familiar to visitors from northern climes is the giant heather with delicate little white flowers.

The trail continues across valleys and streams and emerges finally on to the upper moorlands where one is greeted by the strange forms of Senecio and lobelia trees. The high moor and grassland is decked with beautiful grasses, flowers and birds. The air is crisp, the views splendid; the altitude here is not yet high enough to spoil your enjoyment of this delightful walk.

The second set of huts at **Horombo** 3,807 metres (12,500 feet) are located on the slope above a particularly pretty and interesting valley. From here there are trails to less-visited areas of Kilimanjaro, such as the circuit route, Mawenzi and **Mawenzi Tarn**. Since the number of bunks is double that of the other hut complexes it is worth staying an extra day to explore this striking and beautiful area lying just below the "altitude sickness" zone.

Once above the heath and moorland, the climb ceases to be a major wildlife experience. Even so, there are still many fascinating sites: compact everlasting plants with pretty, hardy blooms, intrepid spiders hunting among rocks that bear lichens perhaps hundreds of years old. And there are the transients across **The Saddle**: tracks of eland, leopard or African hunting dogs and lovely butterflies blown high on the wind, or croaking white-naped ravens soaring above your head.

After crossing the rocky, bare Saddle between the flattened peak of Kibo and the jagged peak of Mawenzi, there is a rise that leads to **Kibo Hut** at 4,721 metres (15,500 feet). Here climbers usually spend the third night—short

efield
mnants on
ount
limanjaro.

though it is! Ordinarily, you are roused just after midnight in order to get to the top of Kibo at dawn while the scree is still frozen and there is time to get all the way back down to Horombo Hut.

The long hike, usually in the dark, means one foot ahead of the other up numerous switchbacks to Kibo's summit—there are really two: **Gillman's Point** at 5,681 metres (18,650 feet) is a few hundred metres lower and a couple of kilometres closer than **Uhuru Peak**, Kibo's highest point at 5,895 metres (19,340 feet). There's not much wildlife up here, but early explorers found a leopard frozen on the rim and others were pursued by a pack of hunting dogs. Most people reach either of the two peaks of Kibo then head back down, stopping at Horombo overnight, bypassing Mandara and reaching the Marangu Gate by afternoon. Thus the total hike takes about five days.

Mawenzi, a ragged cone of hard but crumbling lava can be seen across The Saddle from Kibo. It tempts only the hard-core rock climbers and some have met their death there. There are several climbing routes up Mawenzi and four major alternative routes to the top of Kibo: **Mweka, Umbwe, Machame** and Shira. Each route has its own distinctive character.

Shira peak, on the west side of Kibo, is hidden by the bulk of the mountain. It is much eroded, hardly more than a shallow crater with some higher edges and forms a broad plateau. Shira is by far the most beautiful side of Kilimanjaro and has the advantage of being accessible by four-wheel drive vehicle, along a track which climbs from wheat farms and plantation forest through natural forest to moorland. From the plateau formed by the old Shira volcano one can climb further on to the flanks of Kibo from the west and join the circuit trails, or continue on up to the peak by way of the **Great Western Breach** or **Barranco**.

Shira plateau has wonderful and plentiful plant life and some large mammals as well; common duikers, small herds of eland and even the odd

Left and far left, Helichrysum flowers are a familiar sight.

stray lion or leopard. The scenery is magnificent and currently unspoiled by the clutter of accommodation or the litter of myriad climbers.

Plant life: Kilimanjaro is one of the best places in the world to see how plant life changes with altitude. Lush rain forest gives way to highland desert further up the mountain. Besides freezing and desiccation caused by the increase in altitude, daily fluctuations in temperature and intense radiation mean that some days plants have ice crystals instead of water at their roots with hot sun on the leaves. As the soil unfreezes, the roots can be disturbed by soil movements and the leaves can dry out.

Only about 50 kinds of hardy plants survive above 4,000 metres (13,120 feet) on Kilimanjaro. Besides the lichens and mosses that cling to rocks and soil there are several flowering plants. Tussock grasses survive by growing in a clump, the old leaves forming a cushion that insulates the roots and retains moisture. Leaves are long and thin to reduce evaporation.

Giant senecios and lobelias survive by insulating their trunks with their dead leaves. They also produce a sort of "anti-freeze" fluid in their leaves and have tiny, protected flowers.

Easy access: Kilimanjaro National Park is one of the most accessible parks in Tanzania. It has a good tarmac road from **Moshi**, the town at the mountain's foot, to Marangu, the main entry gate. Moshi itself lies on the main road and railway from Dar es Salaam to Arusha and is 56 kilometres (34.7 miles) east of Kilimanjaro International Airport. Roads go to all points except the northern side (which borders on Kenya and is currently closed to climbers).

Climbing the mountain by routes other than the main Marangu route requires prior clearance from the park headquarters at Marangu.

The best weather for climbing is January, February or September and the mountain is best avoided in April and May. Rainfall varies between 1,500 mm (58.5 inches) at the park boundary to 100 mm (3.9 inches) at the top.

rekkers
ake a break
t the base
f Kibo.

LAKE MANYARA

Lake Manyara National Park is spectacularly set on a narrow band of lakeshore along the western wall of the Great Rift Valley. The park covers just 330 square kilometres (132 square miles), two thirds of which is taken up by the lake. Altitude varies between 960 metres (3,149 feet) at the lake to 2,000 metres (6,560 feet) at the top of the escarpment. Rainfall is variable, ranging from 250 mm to 1200 mm (9.75 inches to 46.8 inches) yearly, but the springs and streams emerging from the base of the rift wall water a forest that could not otherwise grow in such a dry area.

The approach to Manyara is dramatic because the rift wall is so clearly defined and can be seen running north and south into the hazy distances. The road to Lake Victoria passes the north gate and park headquarters of Manyara. If permission is gained beforehand one can enter and exit by the southern gate which is on a seasonal track that roughly follows the base of the rift, joining the main Arusha-Dodoma road at **Magagu**. This track should be avoided during the wet season.

Driving across the valley, one can see giraffes and often a variety of other plains dwellers such as wildebeest, zebra and ostrich, even before reaching the park.

Mto-wa-Mbu village (the name means "mosquito river") spreads out below the **Simba River**, just a couple of kilometres from the Manyara park gate. The village has a thriving local market with a colourful mix of peoples—it was claimed that over 100 different languages could be heard here.

Bubbling brooks: At the park entrance the water that has travelled so far from the Ngorongoro Highlands, underground through lava rock, emerges in abundance. The bubbling brooks and clear streams water a mature forest composed largely of mahogany trees,

Lovely Lake Manyara.

fig trees, fat sausage trees, crotons with heart-shaped leaves, and many others typical of riversides and upland forests.

The cool, shady forest is a welcome and beautiful respite from the normally hot dry glare of the Rift Valley floor. Other primates find the forest a good place too; there are many troops of baboons and vervets in the more open patches of trees. Blue monkeys are a special treat here because they are habituated to cars and people, and the trees are not too thick or tall. Elephants occasionally loom out of the forest where they shelter and feed. More abundant but more rarely seen are the shy, solitary or nocturnal animals such as bushbuck, rhinos, aardvarks, pangolins, civets, leopards, and wild cats. Waterbucks in Manyara are the common type with a white "bull's eye" ring on their rumps.

Big termite mounds dot the forest floor and above, silvery-cheeked hornbill and crowned hornbill call. At the forest edge and in more open areas, ground hornbills are often seen feeding in family groups. Grasslands stretch long the lake flats, providing food for wildebeest, zebra, gazelle, ostrich, buffalo and warthogs. Giraffe browse among the thorn bushes and on the lake perimeters. Sometimes young bulls neck fight. The older, almost black giraffe with huge knobs on their heads are the breeding bulls.

The Mosquito River cuts through forest and across the grassy plain to enter the lake at the north end. It emerges from a thick stand of yellow-barked acacias which are well browsed by giraffes and it offers a place for hippos and birds to rest and bathe.

Life at the lake: The birdlife at Mto-wa-Mbu is stunning in its abundance and diversity. Most of the birds have been feeding in the lake and they come to the freshwater river to drink and to wash the sticky soda from their feathers. Pelicans, storks and cormorants are the main bathers along with crowds of Egyptian geese, spur-winged geese, strange sounding whistling ducks, plus terns, gulls, thickknees and others.

ar right, ellow-illed stork oes fishing.

Lake Manyara National Park

The entry of the river into the lake is hidden by sedges and rushes but this upper end of the lake is often fringed pink by flamingoes in their thousands. Flamingoes are forever on the move, searching for the right food in lakes up and down the Rift Valley. Unless the lake is particularly wet or dry, flamingoes gather there in vast numbers, turning the lake pink all along its length. Although it is difficult to get close, the sight, sound and smell of a million flamingoes is unforgettable.

A large herd of buffalo lives on the flats, where they become prey for the local lions. The lions can sometimes be seen feeding on a kill by the swamp where the river enters the lake.

The rest of this park lies to the south. Look out for the "wild mango" tree which grows on the fringe of the forest. It is a bushy tree with long, shiny green leaves and masses of white waxy flowers that look like gardenia and fill the air with a magical fragrance of jasmine.

Leaving the forest and lakeshore you enter a more shrubby habitat and eventually emerge into acacia woodland. The dominant trees are the familiar flat-topped *Acacia tortilis*. In places there are thick stands of bushes that hide animals from view but in the many open areas are long views out to the lake shore where ostriches parade, elephants bathe in the river or lake shores and impala wander with baboons through the low trees.

Packs of banded mongooses and dwarf mongooses gather around termite mounds and dikdik pairs hide in bushes. Lions sometimes rest on the broad limbs of acacia trees, and you might spot the occasional leopard. Most abundant of all are the tsetse flies which keep out livestock and protect the area from human encroachment.

Birds are plentiful, especially during the migrations of Eurasian species from October to April. Then large numbers of European bee-eaters and rollers join the local species, as well as various cuckoos, buzzards, hawks, falcons and eagles.

Where the cliffs get more rocky and

Family of cormorants

you can see the white streaks of the rock hyrax "toilets", you might see the Verreaux's eagle. It is the largest East African eagle, mostly black with white scapulars and rump. They often soar in pairs, patrolling the cliffs in search of hyraxes, their main prey. Although Verreaux's eagles travel the length of Manyara, their main haunts are around the **Endabash** area in the south.

The Endabash River: Wander along some of the tracks towards the escarpment or down along the **Endabash River**. Where the river enters the lake, there is a broad pasture with many grazing animals spread across it. Along the river the mix of trees and bush forms an unusually rich composite of riverine forest. The Endabash cascades down a steep granite cliff behind the ranger post. Sometimes the river crossing that leads across Endabash to the south is difficult because of high water so a ranger must take you there. But if you can cross, the visit to **Maji Moto** ("hot springs") less than five kilometres (three miles) further on is well worth the trip. These springs come out from the base of a granite cliff on which grow Terminalia trees with reddish pods that look like flowers, and some Euphorbias, lots of mixed brush and big gardenia bushes. A stunted old baobab marks the lower side of the point where you walk down to the pool to test the water. Be careful of slippery stones: the water is definitely HOT, about 60 C (140 F).

If you head further south, there is another large grassy plain just past Maji Moto. A long waterfall falls from the rift wall at the edge of the plain, then you enter a strange forest made up almost entirely of *Acacia robusta*. This southern extension to the park was farmed until the 1960s and you may still find signs of human settlement, although the area has reverted to native vegetation.

After the ranger post and jacaranda trees, you know you have left the park because suddenly there are coffee bushes and tractors and barns—a reminder that Manyara is only a tiny strip of the wild, between human habitation, the lake and rift wall.

SELOUS

Selous Game Reserve is the largest in Africa, covering some 51,200 square kilometres (19,763 square miles). Its immense size and remoteness from populated areas make it particularly attractive both to wildlife and adventurers who can explore on foot or in a boat.

The varied terrain is undulating with rocky outcrops cut by many, usually dry, watercourses. Altitude varies between 110 metres (361 feet) and 1,250 metres (4,100 feet).

It is best to visit Selous between July and March, out of the rainy season. An average of 600 mm to 1,000 mm (24 inches to 39 inches) of rain falls yearly, most of it from March to June.

The pristine landscape is dominated by the great **Rufiji River** system, the largest in East Africa. Three huge sand rivers, the **Great Ruaha**, **Kilombero** and **Luwegu** flow through the reserve and meet before being channelled through the spectacular **Stiegler's Gorge**. Named after a German explorer who was killed by an elephant there in 1907, the gorge can be traversed by a swaying footbridge over the raging waters.

Selous was originally established as a hunting preserve by the Germans just after the turn of the 20th century. It is still visited by occasional hunters who pay dearly for the privilege.

Selous was named in 1922 after the naturalist, elephant-hunter and explorer, Frederick Courtney Selous who, as captain of a British unit, was killed in action during the advance against the Germans at the end of the First World War I. His grave is north along a tributary of the **Behobeho River.**

Over 1,700 species of plants have been identified in Selous, along with hundreds of bird species. Since the area is relatively well watered, there is an abundance of trees and bush, providing excellent shelter for the wildlife.

Large and lesser game: Selous is

Cooling down in the Ruaha River.

most famous for its huge herds of elephants, although their numbers have been reduced by poachers. Huge buffalo herds come to drink at the river in dry season. A boat trip on the Rufiji will reveal hippos and crocodiles in abundance, and you may also see waterbuck, the southern reedbuck and bushbuck. The beautiful sable antelope with its long curved horns and the slightly larger roan antelope and greater kudu like to hide in the tall grass while lesser kudu are more often seen among the rocky hills and dry bush. Impalas and Lichtenstein's hartebeest are common as are zebras and the southern race of wildebeest, which is marked with a distinctive white chevron on its long face. Rhinos have been almost exterminated by poachers but small numbers may still exist.

Selous is of great scientific importance because it has a history of research and a wildlife station in the reserve. At **Kingupira** in the east, a Miombo Research Centre was established in 1966. Monitoring has shown, sadly, that the estimated 100,000 elephant population in 1977 dropped to about 50,000 in 1987.

The easiest way to reach Selous is by air to one of the airstrips (each of the four major camps/lodges has its own strip). The Tanzam railway from Dar es Salaam runs along the northern boundary of the reserve. The views are superb. There are several stations four to six hours from Dar es Salaam where you can disembark and enter Selous, provided transport or a foot safari has been organized in advance. The major station is at **Fuga**.

Getting to Selous by road takes about eight hours or more from Dar es Salaam. If arriving from the east, you need to plan to come in the dry season and with a four-wheel drive vehicle. The main, and much better but longer road goes west, although access to the reserve is only via tracks leading off south from **Morogoro** or **Mikumi**. Once inside Selous you can travel about only by four-wheel drive, on foot, with an armed escort or in a boat along the river.

Starting off on a foot safari.

RUAHA

Ruaha is Tanzania's second largest national park, covering 10,200 square kilometres (3,937 square miles) of undulating plateau with some mountains, rocky hills and two extensive river valleys on the east and western borders. Together with two important game reserves, **Rungwa** and **Kizigio**, that buffer Ruaha's northern boundary, the total protected area of some 25,600 square kilometres (9,886 square miles) makes for a very impressive wildlife area indeed. Ruaha was originally created in 1964 from half of Rungwa.

The park lies on a combination of ancient granite and more recent sediments brought about by the extensive rifting through Tanzania. On average only 600 mm (24 inches) of rain per year falls on poor soils on the plateau and richer valley soils. In the east, where rainfall is least, this amount just barely supports a bushland and trees that are adapted to dry conditions, including spiny commiphora and acacia species, and the splendid baobabs.

The mountains in the far west of the park catch more rain and so are covered by an evergreen upland forest that is yet to be fully explored and appreciated. Rainfall increases up to 800 mm (31 inches) towards the west and south, supporting a miombo woodland that covers half of Ruaha.

Miombo is composed predominantly of *Brachystegia* trees of which there are about 15 different species in Tanzania. Together with many other plants these trees create a rather special woodland. Some trees such as "mninga" (*Pterocarpus angolensis*) are valuable for timber. Miombo trees are all about 10 metres (33 feet) in height and there is a sparse understory. The woodland has a gentle, rather pretty but monotonous appearance during most the year. But just before the start of the rainy season, after the tall grass catches fire, the forest is transformed into a breathtaking,

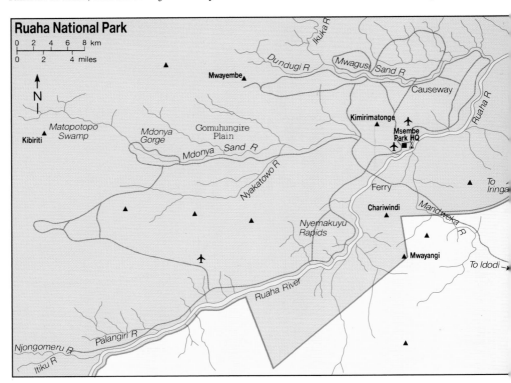

Ruaha National Park

0 2 4 6 8 km
0   2   4 miles

N

multi-hued tapestry of pale green, yellow, russet, purple, red, crimson and copper.

The Ruaha River: The park is bound by two long rivers but the **Ruaha River** in the south is the major attraction. Here, water flows over a broad sandy bed, roaring and wide in wet season, a trickle in dry season. The river itself and its fringing vegetation provide water, food and homes for many creatures, including human visitors. Most of the passable tracks and accommodation are along the river banks or in the drier areas. Visitors should persevere and be adventurous enough to explore the more remote and wilder miombo and western mountains. You will be rewarded with some of the country's most spectacular scenery.

More than 1,600 plant species and approximately 400 bird species have been recorded here. The vegetation, especially the distinctive flowers found in the miombo during the rainy season, attracts many insects and birds. The tsetse fly, with its irritating bite, is so abundant that it has dissuaded both people and livestock from coming into the area.

Some larger mammals are spread over a wide area of the park, but only in very small concentrations. These include both greater and lesser kudu, the reddish Lichtenstein's hartebeest and sable and roan antelopes. Elephants were once so abundant that there was fear of them destroying the huge *Acacia albida* trees so characteristic of the river banks. Now, as in most other parks in East Africa, elephant numbers have been drastically reduced by poaching for ivory.

Crocodiles basking on the sandbanks and bathing hippos enliven the river and you might even see a clawless otter catching fish. Reedbuck, waterbuck and buffalo frequent the river edges along with yellow baboons and vervet monkeys.

In grassland and bushland there are giraffes, eland, impala, zebra, warthog, Grant's gazelle, dikdik, mongoose, ostrich, the elusive ratel civet, wild cat,

porcupines and other small creatures. Predators one is likely to see include lion, cheetah, leopard, jackal and the African hunting dog.

From October to November and March to April thousands of birds flock to Ruaha on their annual migration from Europe and Asia. Together with resident hornbills, green wood-hoopoes, kingfishers, plovers, bee-eaters, sunbirds and water birds, skimmers can be seen dragging their specialized lower bills along the water in search of a meal. Nearby, hammerkops can be seen making repairs to their gigantic nests or swooping down on unsuspecting frogs.

Research difficulties: Scientists have sporadically studied some of the vegetation, baboons and elephants in Ruaha but, although there is scope to study the rarer large animals such as sable, roan, lesser and greater kudu, it is unlikely that extensive wildlife research will occur here. The logistical difficulties, especially the park's remoteness and seasonal isolation make such work difficult. This means that interested visitors can still contribute substantially to information about Ruaha.

Road access to Ruaha is via the historic highland town of **Iringa**, which is 112 kilometres (70 miles) from the park. From the park boundary it is a further eight kilometres (five miles) to the Ruaha River. Here you check in at a guard post before driving to a wooden ferry which is pulled by hand across the river. This is an exciting way to enter the park when the river is low but during the rainy season access is difficult or impossible.

Other roads and entry points do exist but they should be carefully checked up on before a visit to determine feasibility. The best time to visit the park is during the dry season, from June to November.

There is an airstrip for light aircraft at park headquarters at **Msembe** beside the Ruaha River. Flying time from Nairobi is about three and a half hours. Contact Tanzania National Parks (TANAPA) on arrival in Tanzania for more details.

Impalas on the move.

MIKUMI

Mikumi National Park, established in 1964, is Tanzania's third largest park and the one most popular with residents because of its accessibility and proximity to populated areas. The grassy flood plain surrounded by tiers of hills and misty mountains rising to 2,000 metres (5,660 feet) in the east gives Mikumi a particularly attractive landscape covering 3,230 square kilometres (1,274 square miles). Rainfall varies between 600 mm and 800 mm (24 inches to 31 inches): the wettest season is between November and May with a drier period between January and March.

Many distinctive trees grow here, including the tall Sterculia (*Sterculia appendiculata*) with long, smooth, pale yellow trunks, the well-shaped afzelias (*Afzelia quanzensis*), chunky sausage trees (*Kigelia aethiopum*), fat baobabs (*Adansonia digitata*) and the tree which gives the park its name, the Borassus palm (*Borassus flabellifer*) with a swelling high on the trunk.

Wonderful views: The **Mkata River** area and flood plain at an altitude of 500 metres (1,640 feet) is an open area well covered by roads. Animals in the tourist area are mostly habituated to cars and thus easy to watch and photograph. Further afield in the hills, animals are shyer and the heavier vegetation makes glimpses of them more exciting. The southern hills are covered with *Brachystegia* woodland and cut by watercourses. There are hot springs and wonderful views.

North of the main road is the area most frequented by visitors and one can find a large variety of animals in a relatively short time. There are herds of elephants, pools crowded with hippos, wallowing buffalos, swamps with reedbucks and waterbirds, and plains dotted with yellow baboons, warthogs, wildebeest, zebras, elands and Lichtenstein's hartebeest. In bushier spots you may see greater kudu. Lions and leopards are

th time for
ese
ffalos.

often seen but packs of African hunting dogs in open areas provide a special treat as they are often very tame.

In the hills impala are widespread and elephants are often encountered. To the south of the park sable antelope are sometimes seen. Bush and woodland birds are abundant and include many species of hornbills, sunbirds, cuckoos, shrikes and birds of prey.

Animal research: Mikumi is a very important educational park with a large hostel for university students and visiting school groups who are shown how to do animal counts, measure tree growth, gauge the extent of fires and study the distribution of grasses, among other tasks. Mikumi also has an Animal Behaviour Research Unit whose scientists have been studying the behaviour of yellow baboons since 1974.

One finding in particular illustrates the importance of ecology on social behaviour. The optimal time for giving birth for baboons in Mikumi is March to July at the end of the rainy season. For some months afterwards there is

enough food to keep a certain number of nursing mothers and their babies healthy. But during the critical weaning period at six months of age, food is not so plentiful. Baboons have developed a way to decide which females will bear babies so that only the "right" number of young are born.

Adult females in the troop form coalitions. Two or more females threaten and attack other females, some of whom become disturbed at not having babies that season, although they always have another chance later on. In this way the more dominant females have fewer competitors for the food that their own children will need during weaning.

Mikumi is 300 kilometres (186 miles) from Dar es Salaam along the road from the coast to Zambia via Morogoro and Iringa. This road cuts through the park for about 50 kilometres (31 miles). There is a railway station at **Mikumi village**, about 22 kilometres (13 miles) from the park entrance. Light aircraft can land on the airstrip at park headquarters.

Thorny perc for this red- billed hornbill.

TARANGIRE

Tarangire National Park was established in 1970 and covers 2,600 square kilometres (1,000 square miles) of gently undulating plains with two large *Mbunga* (flat pans) that are seasonal swamps in the south. A river cuts through numerous rocky hills rising from 1,000 metres (3,280 feet) to 1,675 metres (5,495 feet) at the top of **Kirogwa**.

Tarangire is best seen during the dry season when there are great concentrations of animals. Rainfall averages 800 mm (31.2 inches) per year and falls mostly between November and May, when the southern roads and unbridged river crossings become impassable.

However, during the dry season, Tarangire is the main refuge for wildlife from the surrounding areas on the floor of the Rift Valley. These animals move about an ecosystem ranging across 20,000 square kilometres (8,000 square miles) from Lake Natron in the north to Maasai Steppe in the south, including Lake Manyara.

River of life: The importance of the Tarangire River to the animals in this ecosystem cannot be over-estimated: wildebeest—the rift valley race with lighter coloured, wider horns—zebras, elands, elephants, Coke's hartebeest, buffalos and the elegant fringe-eared oryx flock to its waters and valleys in their thousands. These migrants join the resident waterbuck, impalas, warthogs, dikdiks, giraffes, lesser kudus and there are even a few rhinos, plus predators such as lions, leopards and cheetahs.

There are pools and open water in the river all year round, but during dry season much of the water travels underneath the sandy riverbed. To get at the water, elephants dig holes which other animals also use for drinking.

The high bluff at the end of a row of tents at **Tarangire Lodge** is a particularly good spot for game viewing. At dusk local baboons gather at a bend in

Plants adapt to the dry landscape.

the river to groom and fight. Near dark they climb into the tall doum palms to be safe from leopards. This scene also occurs at the large grove of palms just after crossing the **Engelhard Bridge**, opposite the campsites.

From your camp or lodge you can hear the barks of baboons, especially strident when a leopard is near (recognisable by its deep sawing roar). Listen too for lion roars and for elephants trumpeting.

At the permanent water spots in the river are numerous birds, such as kingfishers, herons—especially goliath heron—ducks, geese, hammerkops and more. Tarangire has a wealth of birdlife at all times and it is one of the very best spots to see flocks of green wood hoopoes, African hoopoes, green and yellow "brown" parrots, Fischer's and yellow-collared lovebirds, bare-faced and white-bellied go-away birds, Tanzanian endemic ashy starling, a large number of different kinds of doves, pigeons, mousebirds, cuckoos, swifts, swallows, hornbills, and many others.

Swamps and baobabs: The large swamps in the south which dry up gradually after the rains stop form huge pastures for elephants with seepages that provide water for many birds. Many pythons gather here. These huge, very beautifully patterned, non-poisonous snakes—they kill their prey by squeezing it to death—leave the marshes when dry and take refuge from predators by going up into the crowns of the flat-topped acacia. They wind themselves into a coil that looks like a nest from the ground. During the long dry season, pythons "aestivate", not eating but conserving their resources until rats, birds and small animals are plentiful in the swamps again. Sometimes they congregate, either for habitat or to seek mates.

In north Tarangire, the **Lemiyon** and **Matete** areas have rolling landscapes with monumental baobabs. These giant "upside down" trees are often hollow or punctured with holes where elephants have ripped off the bark or poked through the fibrous trunk. Poachers

Far left, a huge baobab.

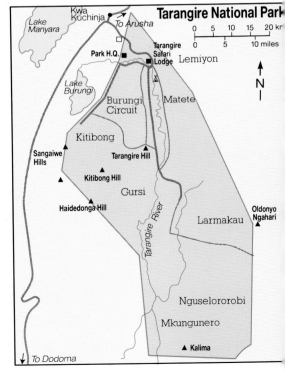

sometimes use these ready-made caves as hideouts. More usually, barn owls as well as any number of bats (there are at least 10 species in Tarangire) nest inside the baobabs.

Many birds use baobabs as nest sites during the rainy season. The large communal nests of the red-billed buffalo weavers are especially conspicuous. If you see a hornbill visiting a certain site on a baobab look for its nest-hole too; the male walls up his mate inside, feeding her through a narrow slit, until the eggs hatch. Then she emerges to help feed the nestlings, who remain sealed in until big enough to fly. Baobab flowers are pollinated by bats and the pithy pods are deliciously astringent. Fruits fall off in dry season and are eagerly snapped up by a variety of animals.

Other trees include stout sausage trees along the river. Huge fruits dangle down from thick ropey stems and are eaten by baboons, rhinos and elephants. When sausage trees bloom the nectar-filled blossoms open only at night, intended solely for the fertilizing touch of certain fruit bats. In the early morning the trees are literally attacked by groups of vervet monkeys and baboons who dash up to suck any remaining nectar. In the very early morning hordes of insects rush to feed on the maroon blooms.

Common flat-topped acacia can be found in most areas, along with multi-branched *Commiphora* and many short, leafy *Combretum* and bushy *Dalbergia* trees—better known as African blackwood or ebony—whose very dense, hard wood is used for carvings. These trees are usually damaged or stunted from elephant attacks. Except for *combretums*, all these and most other trees have spines or poisonous latex to deter animals.

Tarangire is a good park to see how plants adapt to an arid area with meagre seasonal rain.

Tarangire is easy to reach: a tarmac road heads south-west from Arusha, and in about two hours (112 kilometres or 70 miles) you will reach the park entrance at **Minjingu**.

ARUSHA

Arusha National Park (ANP) is close to major human cultivation and settlements. It is small—only 137 square kilometres (53 square miles)—yet has varied terrain with a distinct feeling of wildness. There are fresh to alkaline lakes separated by hummocks in the **Momela** area; a small crater, **Ngurdoto**, with steep inner walls: and the extinct volcano, **Mount Meru**, with a breached crater and many valleys on its flanks leading down to farm land on the lower slopes.

Altitude ranges from 1,500 metres (4,920 feet) at Momela to 4,566 metres (14,990 feet) at the top of Mount Meru. Most rain falls between November and May, although there is often a less rainy period from December to February when skies clear to offer magnificent views of Mount Meru and Kilimanjaro. In the dry season views tend to be a little more hazy.

Ngurdoto, Momela and Mount Meru are easily accessible. Since there are no lions in the park, a number of observation points have been prepared where you can get out of your vehicle. This feeling of freedom, with time to look about on foot, greatly contributes to the enchantment of a visit here.

There are two main entrances: **Ngurdoto Gate** lies at the base of Ngurdoto Crater: **Momela Gate** is situated where the main Ngare-Nanyuki track crosses a high ridge connecting Mount Meru with the rest of the park. **Ngurdoto Crater** is always a good entry point to the park. There is a small museum at the gate surrounded by forest trees. Here you can get out of your vehicle and scan the treetops with your binoculars. Look into the ascending branches of the open-crowned African olive, one of the most valuable timber trees in Africa. The deep, staccato roars you might hear are made by the local troop of black and white colobus monkeys. The population in ANP is particularly striking,

The extinct crater of Mount Mer

being a breed which lives only in highland areas such as here and on Mount Kilimanjaro. The hair of their cape and tail is exceptionally long and white and streams behind them as they leap amongst the trees. There are troops of colobus throughout the park's forests. You may also meet the blue monkey, mostly grey and black with a long slender tail.

The huge silvery-cheeked hornbill is usually seen in pairs, has an ivory coloured casque above its beak and a call sounding like maniacal laughter.

The crater: Surrounding Ngurdoto Crater are very beautiful forests containing huge strangler figtrees with long roots descending from on high. Wild mangos, medium sized trees with shiny, dark green leaves and clusters of white waxy flowers and inedible fruit, are also common.

The crater itself is about 2.4 kilometres (1.5 miles) across. The inside has been designated a private sanctuary for wildlife, and no humans are allowed onto the crater floor.

From any viewpoint on the rim of Ngurdoto you look out over a wide bowl; the bottom is usually marshy and grades into grassy swards around the edges before disappearing into lush forest on the inner slopes. Palm trees lean out of places where water seeps on the walls and stand out among the lacy-leafed *Albizia*, dark *Bersama,* gnarled *Nuxia* and tall *Olea* trees on the rim.

At **Leitong**, the highest point at 1,853 metres (6,077 feet) on the north side of the crater, you can see unusual lobelia plants as well as a splendid view across the crater. In the sky eagles, ravens, buzzards and hawks ride the updraughts. If it is clear you can see to Kilimanjaro.

Returning through lower forest on the outside slopes of Ngurdoto look for the shy red duiker. This rust-red antelope is larger than a dikdik but might be confused with a female bushbuck, which is also reddish with white spots on its throat and sides.

In the lower forest, trees grow in decorative groves and clumps, with a

mping
side the
ater.

very short green sward spreading below to catch the dappled light. The most common trees are crotons, recognizable by the silvery undersides of their pale green leaves. *Croton macrostachyus* has heart-shaped leaves that turn orange when old. It is very widespread in open areas all over the park; *Croton megalocarpus* is taller, with narrower leaves and is even more abundant.

The road between Ngurdoto Crater and the Momela lakes passes by several side-roads leading to viewpoints. They all offer different perspectives of the ponds, marshes, valleys and lakes. Hides and observation points near the Momela lakes look out on the surrounding terrain which was formed when Mount Meru blew its top and muddy, rocky avalanches spread debris all the way to the foot of neighbouring Kilimanjaro. From a high point, such as **Boma la Megi**, you can see the widespread array of hills and lakes in and beyond the park.

The Momela lakes: In this area lakes range from fresh to alkaline water, most of it coming from underground streams. They sometimes appear to be different colours, as a result of algal growths. Each lake attracts a distinctive clientele: the pinker, lesser flamingo chooses lakes rich in blue-green algae, its only food. The paler, greater flamingo mainly eats crustacea which feed on algae and, because it is less numerous and taller, can exploit different and deeper lakes. Pelicans visit from time to time. Large varieties of ducks, geese and waders, both residents and migrants, can also be seen.

Leaving the lakes there is a broad undulating area of grass and bush. In patches of trees and thick bush embellishing the hills, look carefully for herds of elephants or buffalo, solitary bushbuck or eland and the tiny dikdik—if you see one you know its mate is somewhere near. The most commonly seen animals throughout this area between Momela lakes and Mount Meru are giraffes, which are very tame.

To explore Mount Meru, one must cross the **Ngare Nanyuki River** and

Typical forest foliage.

ascend the steep mountain track in a four-wheel drive vehicle. This extinct volcano is covered with treasures: the lower slopes have marshy, flower-filled glades, hidden waterfalls, clear streams, butterfly- and bushbuck-flecked clearings and a blossoming, bushy forest with leaping colobus monkeys.

Beyond the drive-through fig tree arch, the upper forest has enormous junipers and podos with olive pigeons, red-fronted parrots or Hartlaub's turacos in the uppermost branches. Above the **Kitoto** viewpoint this forest gives way to giant heather. In the flat floor of Meru's crater is a heath dotted with lilies, red hot pokers and other flowers. There is also a dead forest covered in pale green lichen. Many high altitude plants grow in this vast amphitheatre with slopes of bare scree, steep cliffs of crumbling rock and a jagged summit.

There are mountain huts and guides for those who want to make the steep climb up the ridge of Meru's cone to the peak at 4,566 metres (14,990 feet). The walk up the mountain from its base is not only relatively easy but thoroughly rewarding.

Conservation and conflict: Arusha National Park, established in 1960, is named after the large town spread over its south-west flank, about 35 kilometres (22 miles) away. The town in turn is named after the *Warusha* people who live mostly on the west and driest side of the mountain. They are said to be *Maasai* people who settled around Mount Meru in order to grow crops instead of leading a totally pastoral way of life, dependent on livestock. Another large group of people, called the *Meru* who are relatives to the *Wachagga*, live on Mount Kilimanjaro.

Wildlife enthusiasts use Arusha as the gateway to game parks in the region, including Serengeti, Mount Kilimanjaro, Tarangire and Ngorongoro Conservation Area.

From many places in the park one can see evidence of the squeeze along the boundaries by people and farms. In addition to cultivated plots, a broad band of mostly pine forest stretches over many kilometres of the southern and western flanks. The trees were planted many years ago to provide timber for the area. Along the borders the native vegetation abruptly changes where humans have modified the area for their own uses.

In the pristine forest on Mount Meru people secretly cut down trees to provide wood for homes and tourist lodges and even to make carvings for tourists to buy. Trophy poachers prowl the slopes in search of the last rhinos and elephants. In Ngurdoto Crater, meat poachers have cleared out most of the larger wildlife, and around the Momela lakes people illegally fish, reducing food for birds and scaring away wildlife. Although they suffer from a lack of funds, staff and equipment, the park authorities continue to fight the endless battle to protect wildlife.

Arusha demonstrates the considerable dangers of a relatively self-contained ecological unit being pressed on all sides by the demands and self-interests of humanity.

GOMBE, MAHALE AND OTHER PARKS

Gombe and Mahale national parks are both located on the eastern shore of Lake Tanganyika. The primary purpose of both is to protect endangered populations of chimpanzees (*Pan troglodytes*). The two parks are, however, very different in ease of access, size, terrain and ecology.

Gombe National Park was established in 1968 and covers an area of 52 square kilometres (20 square miles). From the lake shore to the ridge tops ranges between 770 and 1,440 metres (2,525 and 4,723 feet) with an average annual rainfall of 1,000 mm (39 inches). This park can be reached in 40 minutes by speedboat from Kigoma. Alternative transport by water taxi takes between four and six hours.

Even so, Gombe National Park is relatively easier to get to than Mahale and has numerous other primates in addition to chimps: olive baboons, red colobus, red-tailed monkeys, blue monkeys and vervet monkeys. Another common primate has very important effects on this little park: *Homo sapiens*.

Human beings live on all sides of Gombe except for the lake. Even here, many fishermen come to spread out their catch of small *dagaa* fish (a bit like white bait) to dry on the shore. Poaching and encroaching are major problems.

A boat ride along the impressively big Lake Tanganyika is a memorable part of a visit to Gombe. But there is so much more: lush vegetation, beautiful birds, butterflies and other insects, wildlife, helpful rangers and researchers and, above all, the thrill of meeting chimpanzees face to face in their natural habitat. You can swim in the lake and go snorkeling to look for the many aquarium fish that come from this lake.

Mahale: Mahale Mountains National Park is much larger and more remote than Gombe, with a more complex landscape, many more animals and better potential for long-term survival

Wizened youngster at Gombe.

as an ecosystem.

It was established in 1986 and covers an area of 1,200 square kilometres (480 square miles). Altitude ranges from 770 metres (2,525 feet) along the lake shore to 2,460 metres (8,070 feet) on the mountain tops. There are many steep valleys with miombo woodland plains in the south. Average rainfall is 1,000 mm (39 inches) per year. Access to Mahale is by boat from Kigoma which can take any time from 10 to 24 hours. It may be wise to check the state of the airstrip first.

The Mahale Mountains rise from the lakeshore to misty heights, their steep slopes swathed in thick jungle-like vegetation. The mountains provide both a habitat for many kinds of animal life and also help to protect the park from human encroachment. The lake shore confines the western side of the park and the tsetse fly-infested miombo woodland to the south helps buffer inroads from that side.

People live and farm along Mahale's northern boundary (there is a village where you can stop to get supplies of fresh food), but it is somewhat isolated here due to the **Malagarasi River.** It enters Lake Tanganyika to the north of Mahale and has a vast swamp behind its wide mouth, across which no road has yet been built. Local people use the lake as their road, with a variety of different size boats. Transport inside Mahale is strictly by foot!

Mahale is a remnant of the forests that once stretched across all of equatorial Africa and harbours a wide variety of animals: bushbucks, waterbucks, bushpigs, buffalos, elephants, leopards, the same wide variety of primates as at Gombe and many different kinds of forest birds. In the south are giraffes, roan and sable antelopes, kudus, elands, lions and a host of miombo birds. Clawless otters feed off the fish in the lake.

Championing chimps: Dr Jane Goodall and her team in Gombe, together with Drs Itani, Nishida and their colleagues in Mahale, have been studying chimpanzee behaviour since the

d elephant es.

early 1960s. These normally shy apes have become completely habituated to human observers. The studies have revolutionised our understanding of our closest animal relative.

The chimps live in large, loosely-knit communities where family bonds are very important throughout life. The community's range is defended by a coalition of related males.

Mostly vegetarian, chimps also eat substantial amounts of ants and termites, using stems and grasses as simple tools to extract the insects from their nests. They also frequently cooperate to hunt and eat larger prey such as monkeys and bushpigs.

Chimps are excitable and emotional; between the males of a community there is often a vigorous struggle for status, and between communities gang warfare has been seen, sometimes resulting in death. They are capable of infanticide, and of dying of grief at the loss of a mother. Yet on the whole they are peaceful, likeable, more handsome than their threadbare cousins in zoos, and more like ourselves than we may care to admit.

OTHER NOTABLE AREAS

Eastern Arc mountains: These are three mountain ranges in Eastern Tanzania, close enough to the Indian Ocean to receive high rainfall. Lush forests have clothed these ancient crystalline mountains ever since jungle vegetation million years ago, by climatic change and by the formation of the Great Rift Valley. And like isolated islands, each has developed its own endemic flora and fauna. Out of 2,000 species of plants so far identified in these mountains, some 25 to 30 percent are found nowhere else in the world. There are also many rare and unique reptiles, amphibians and insects.

The **Usambara Mountains** in the north have patches of protected forest where one can walk in virgin areas and see wild African violets (*Saintpaulia ionantha*), as well as orchids, wild coffee bushes and buttressed trees. Though mammals are rare, there are many small

Giraffes on moonlit stroll.

creatures such as millipedes, frogs and chameleons that are unique to the Usambaras. It has been said that these forests constitute the richest biological community in Africa.

The **Uluguru Mountains**, inland from the central coast, are particularly beautiful. Rising from the **Morogoro Plain** in a compact and rugged bunch, their steep slopes are covered with forest and full of interesting plants and birds.

The **Uzungwa Mountains** are the source of the Kilombero River which flows through the Selous Game Reserve. There is a proposal to make about 1,200 square kilometres (480 square miles) of the mountains into a national park which would protect the forested habitat of much unique wildlife, including an unusual red colobus monkey (*Colobus badius gordonorum*). In the Uzungwa-Kilombero area a new species of weaver bird, a new cisticola, and the rufous-winged sunbird were only discovered in the 1980s. Even a new subspecies of monkey, the Sanje crested mangabey was only described in 1981.

Around Lake Rukwa: **Rukwa Valley**, **Katavi National Park** and **Uwanda Game Reserve**, located in south-west Tanzania, comprise a large area surrounding **Lake Rukwa**. Seasonal flooding and drying up of the lake creates a wide shore of grass that attracts large numbers of grazing animals, most notably topi, buffalos, elands and zebras. Elephants, hippos, Defassa waterbuck, Lichtenstein's hartebeest, southern reedbuck, impala, roan, greater kudu and giraffe are also evident. Perhaps the least common species is the puku (*Kobus vardoni*), whose closest relative is the Uganda kob (*Adenota kob*). The puku is a reddish brown colour, rather stocky and shaggy with thick lyrate horns. Around the lake and in the valley over 400 species of birds have been identified.

Occasionally Lake Rukwa dries up to the point where hippos, crocodiles and fish are confined to the few remaining muddy bogs. The coming of the first

rare roan antelope.

rain storms, usually in November, causes the grasses and sedges on the perimeter of the flood plain to sprout and fill many ponds and pools that lure waterfowl. A great British biologist, Vesey Fitzgerald, wrote: "there can be no more fascinating scene in the whole of Africa than the lawns of new grass in the (Rukwa) valley at this season".

Northern Tanzania: Mkomazi and **Umba Game Reserves** along the northern border of Tanzania to the east of Kilimanjaro, cover 2,500 square kilometres (1,000 square miles) of varied habitats, including dry plains with many valleys, part of the Pare Mountains, and steppe stretching eastward towards the Indian Ocean. This stretch of land is an important buffer zone for animals in the vast Tsavo National Park across the invisible border between Tanzania and Kenya.

There is encroachment on all sides of the reserves by pastoralists and cultivators; sometimes livestock seems more common than wildlife. Increased use of the reserves by non-hunting visitors will lead to improvements in facilities and protection but meanwhile, the landscape remains incredibly beautiful. There is a fascinating variety of semi-arid plants, including many euphorbia with their poisonous latex and the knobbly-spined *Erythrina burtii* with striking red flowers. Numerous birds including thousands of migrating European swallows (*Hirundo rustica*) and golden-breasted starlings (*Cosmopsarus regius*) live or visit this area.

Rubondo Island: Rubondo Island National Park is a large island in Lake Victoria. The whole area covers 457 square kilometres (182 square miles), half of which is water. A flight over the southern part of this largest lake in Africa will show Rubondo as the only island still extensively covered with forest. The trees and bush are set off most attractively by a fringe of shore with beaches and papyrus swamps. Professor Bernard Grzimek of the Frankfurt Zoo, who did so much to encourage the protection of homes for wild animals, took a special interest in

Bristle-like mop of the crowned crane.

Rubondo and helped to get it gazetted as a park in 1977.

Because Rubondo is offshore and the human population is restricted, some of the more endangered species such as rhinos, elephants, roan antelopes, suni, black and white colobus and chimpanzees were introduced. They are now thriving and it is hoped that their descendants will repopulate areas where numbers are currently depleted.

Hippos, bushbuck, sitatunga, vervet monkeys, mongooses, and crocodiles are among the indigenous species. There are no large predators on the island (though poachers come in canoes to kill rhinos), so it will be of interest to see how the populations of native and introduced species will regulate themselves. Besides the mammals, Rubondo has a good variety of reptiles, amphibians and insects and there are numerous lake, swamp, plains and forest birds—you can probably see 100 different kinds of birds during a walk around part of the island.

Zanzibar: Zanzibar and its **Jozani**

Forest Reserve is an off-the-beaten-track delight. Zanzibar Island, with its old Arab town and narrow streets, palaces, dank caves, churches and groves of coconuts, cinnamon, cloves, cocoa and pepper, all testify to Zanzibar's history as an important centre for trade, including the infamous slave trade. The beaches of Zanzibar are lovely and there are some good areas for snorkeling among the wonderful fishes and corals on the reef.

Jozani, on the southern part of the island, is a small reserve with pandanus palms and other remnants of a once-flourishing indigenous vegetation plus introduced plots of non-native trees. While the reserve is of interest botanically, the presence of duiker, such as the Zanzibar blue duiker (*Cephalophus monticola sundervalli*) and the dwarf red duiker (*Cephalophus callipygus adersi*) and the brightly coloured and very rare Zanzibar red colobus (*Colobus badius kirkii*) make Jozani especially interesting. Be sure to bring binoculars for watching the monkeys and birds.

minescent lours of e green-aded nbird.

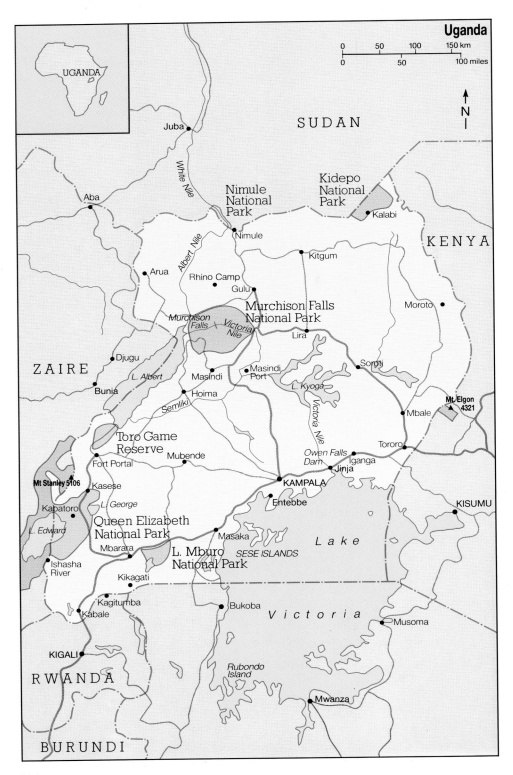

UGANDA

Uganda's position in East Africa is unique. It is at the centre of migratory routes for animals travelling between the north, south, east and west of the continent. It combines the best of these worlds, and enjoys a greater diversity of animal and plant species. Tropical forest, lakes, snow-capped mountains and endless plains are host to wildlife usually associated with West and Central Africa and Tanzania, Kenya and Somalia.

Unfortunately, almost two decades of instability and civil war have left deep scars in Uganda's once-spectacular national parks and game reserves, and the tourist flow has been reduced to a trickle. The regimes of Idi Amin (1971-79), Milton Obote (1980-85) and Tito Okello (August 1985 to January 1986) paved the way for rampant poaching, large-scale encroachment of land and the local population's negative, or at best indifferent attitude towards wildlife. At the same time the infrastructure suffered tremendously and efforts by well-meaning government officials, game wardens and rangers were futile.

However, since President Yoweri Kaguta Museveni took power in 1986 things have gradually improved. Serious efforts are being made to restore Uganda's old glory as a tourist resort. The Ministry of Tourism has been whipping tourist organisations into shape and the export of animals such as parrots and monkeys is now strictly controlled.

Uganda today has four national parks, 12 game reserves, 14 controlled hunting areas (hunting has been banned since 1980) and eight animal sanctuaries. Park names were changed under Amin's rule, but are now known by their original names. Maps still bear Amin's changes and visitors need to take note of the "double names" of each region. Under Amin, Murchison Falls became Kabalega Falls, Queen Elizabeth National Park became Ruwenzori National Park, Lake Albert was Lake Mobutu Sese Seko and Lake Edward changed to Lake Idi Amin Dada. As conditions gradually improve, some of the hitherto neglected wildlife areas, especialy the mountains and forests, will again become accessible to nature lovers.

Preceding pages: spectacular Murchison Falls plunges some 350 metres into the Nile River.

QUEEN ELIZABETH NATIONAL PARK

Situated on the edge of the majestic Ruwenzori mountains on the border with Zaire, **Queen Elizabeth National Park** (QEP) is the jewel in Uganda's crown. The park, with its exceptional mixture of plains, lakes, mountains, craters and tropical forest spread over 1,980 square kilometres (792 square miles), is one of the most beautiful and versatile spots in Africa.

The park is surrounded by other conservation areas: the Ruwenzori mountains in the west, Virunga National Park of Zaire in the south, Kigezi Game Reserve in the south-west, the Rift Valley and Lake George in the west, and Kibale Forest Corridor and Game Reserve in the north.

The varied natural land features have endowed QEP with a rich variety of fauna. Elephants, hippo, waterbuck, bohor's reedbuck, bushbuck, Uganda kob, warthog, sitatunga, baboon, chimpanzee, lion, leopard and topi are just a few of the mammals that can be found.

Four hundred and ninety-two species of birds have already been identified, mainly along the 32-kilometre (20-mile) **Kazinga Channel**, which connects **Lake George** with **Lake Edward**. The same channel is the abode of hundreds of hippos. The **Mweya Lodge**, built on a bluff overlooking Lake Edward, has been recently restored.

Poaching problems: Tragically, heavy poaching during the 1970s turned QEP into something of a nightmare for conservationists. Elephant, buffalo and hippo were the main victims. The number of elephants dwindled from 3,884 in 1966 to an paltry 153 in 1980. These days, however, the numbers are slowly increasing and have almost reached the magic 1,000 mark. This is mainly due to improved security, more efficient anti-poaching units, and better cooperation with the local population.

The position of hippo and buffalo, which also suffered from mass butcher-ing, is somewhat less alarming. Many young animals survived and both species are capable of making a quick recovery, provided sufficient protection continues to be given.

The second problem facing QEP is encroachment of land, which indirectly gives rise to poaching. A large number of fishing villages have appeared over the last 20 years, resulting in overfishing of the lakes and overgrazing, with park land illegally taken over for agricultural use.

Natural beauty: Nevertheless, QEP's natural beauty will always remain. To drive along the **Kikorondo craters** route with the mountain massif of the Ruwenzori ons one side, and on the other the bright green plains, will be forever a blissful experience. The craters, numbering over 80, including seven lake craters, are mainly found in the north and east. They were formed approximately 20 million years ago during the mid-Pleistocene era. One of the biggest, **Lake Katwe**, is currently used for salt mining.

Just as spectacular is a trip on the Kazinga Channel, which is more like a lake and is fed by numerous streams. Here, spotting a hippo is as easy as spotting a star on a cloudless night. Bird lovers will have a field day watching the largest concentration of birds in Uganda. Large white- and pink-backed pelicans (*Pelecanus onocrotalus* and *P. rufescens*) are worth looking out for.

Vegetation in the park is dominated by bush thickets mixed with short grass and grassland. But savannah, swamps and semi-deciduous forest can also be found.

Nature has divided the area into three sections: north and south of the channel, with the south side split by the thick, nearly impenetrable **Maramagambo Forest**. Despite its relative proximity, it is no longer possible to reach the **Ishasha** side (south of the forest) from the Mweya side.

Although difficult to reach Ishasha in the south, this section of the park should definitely be included in a safari since it is widely described as the most unspoilt game area south of the Nile. Apart from

, unique
-
nbing
s.

one small village, there are few signs of human habitation.

The main attractions within these 70 square kilometres (28 square miles), which can only be reached by four-wheel drive vehicle from **Kabale** or by aircraft, include tree-climbing lions, the highest density of Ugandan kob in the world, the only place in QEP where topi roam, two pools literally jam-packed with hippos, and a gallery forest along the rivers. This is the habitat for monkeys, chimpanzees and giant forest hogs and numerous forest birds such as turacos and hornbills.

Branching out: Lions have chosen the fig tree for their uncommon behaviour. No good explanation for this curious habit has yet been given, although some zoologists claim that it may have something to do with avoiding flies that carry diseases. Others think that the lions climb to relax after feeding because it is cooler in the trees. Whatever the reason, it is indeed bizarre to see a huge, lazy lion resting on a tree branch with his belly bulging over. The only other place

in the world where tree climbing lions can be found is Lake Manyara National Park in Tanzania.

Topi, which feature only on the Ishasha side of QEP, have been heavily poached by Tanzanian troops after they ousted Idi Amin in 1979. Conservationists claim that one year of Tanzanian soldiers on the rampage did more damage to the topi population than eight years of Amin.

At certain times of the year, when cloud cover is scarce, it is possible to see from Ishasha both the Ruwenzori mountains and the Virunga volcanoes in Rwanda.

At present, QEP—especially the northern side—is Uganda's main tourist attraction. It is virtually the only place in Uganda that needs advance booking during Christmas and Easter.

Both sides of the park have enormous potential for tourism, if only the roads to Mweya and Ishasha and between the various sectors can be improved. There is an airstrip for light aircraft at Mweya, while larger planes can land at Kasese.

Far left, inquisitive ground squirrel.

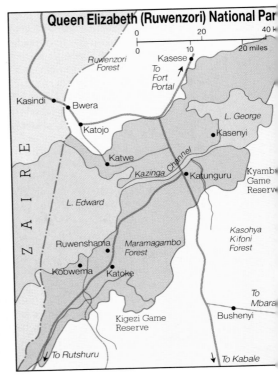

Queen Elizabeth (Ruwenzori) National Park

MURCHISON FALLS

Before the tragic effects of the Amin regime in the late 1970s, **Murchison Falls National Park** (MFNP) was the pride of the country and the main attraction for tourists. Its abundant game and dazzling scenery, together with a spectacular waterfall and the excellent fishing possibilities (especially for huge nile perch) had made it into a very appealing holiday resort. Two luxurious lodges, at **Chobe** and **Paraa**, offered all possible comforts to visitors.

The 3,900-square-kilometre (1,560-square-mile) park, the biggest in Uganda, is split into two sections by the **River Nile**, and is situated in the northwest of the country, close to where the Nile enters Lake Albert. The southern sector in **Masindi district** is bigger than in the north, but has fewer animals.

The park was gazetted in 1952 after sleeping sickness earlier this century made the area unsuitable for the grazing of livestock. It derived its name from the glorious **Murchison Falls** near the park headquarters at Paraa, where the Nile narrows to a mere two metres (6.6 feet) before it plunges 350 metres (1,150 feet) into the calmer waters below. Here is a completely different world where hippos, crocodiles and water birds quietly roam and elephant and buffalo gather to quench their thirst. This is a beautiful stretch of the river.

Loss of wildlife: The present state of the game in MFNP recounts the sad history of wildlife in Uganda from the mid-1970s onwards. The days when elephant were the biggest threat to vegetation were abruptly curtailed. The devastating extent of poaching in MFNP has been unequalled elsewhere.

In the early 1980s carcasses outnumbered living elephants by a shocking three to one. Numbers of elephants were reduced from 15,000 in the early 1970s to only 1,200 in 1980. Continuing conflicts, especially in the northern sector, have made recent countings impossible,

orm
uds
proach the
rk.

although game wardens are of the opinion—perhaps somewhat optimistically—that herds are once again on the increase.

Meanwhile, white and black rhinoceros are now completely extinct, and herds of buffalo, hippo and crocodile have been decimated in a similarly dramatic manner.

Other animals have fared somewhat better and Uganda kob, Jackson's hartebeest, oribi, bohor's reedbuck, duiker, warthog, Rothschild's giraffe, lion, leopard, hyaena and numerous birds can still be found in the park.

Like most parks in the country, MFNP offers a wide variation in vegetation, ranging from semi-deciduous closed forest with *Cynometra alexandri* in the northern sector, to swamp vegetation along the valley floors. Savannah and shrubby acacia woodland cover large sections of the park.

In the 1960s and early 1970s woodlands suffered much damage from burning and being trampled by large herds of elephants. The lack of mid-term growth of trees has also led to the vast expansion of grasslands.

The future for MFNP still looks relatively grim. The northern sector remains insecure because of pockets of anti-government rebels, making work or visits to this remote section of the park virtually impossible, or at least very risky. Only the more adventurous will travel here.

Meanwhile, access to the southern part is hindered by badly maintained roads. **Paraa Lodge** was restocked in 1987 but looted again later that same year. Moreover, the ferry which connects the two sections of the park has been out of order for many years.

On the brighter side, construction of the main road to Murchison Falls, built with the assistance of the European Economic Community, was finished in early 1989, and has opened up the southern section to the public once again. The first visitors to the northern section were reported in January 1989. There are also airstrips for light aircraft near the lodges.

Far left, feeding tin for this youngster.

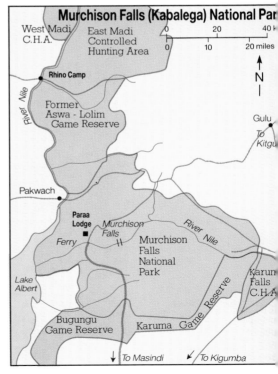

Murchison Falls (Kabalega) National Par

West Madi C.H.A.

East Madi Controlled Hunting Area

20   40 k
0   10   20 miles

N

Rhino Camp

River Nile

Former Aswa - Lolim Game Reserve

Gulu
To Kitgu

Pakwach

Paraa Lodge

Ferry

Murchison Falls

Murchison Falls National Park

River Nile

Karun Falls C.H.A

Lake Albert

Karuma Game Reserve

Bugungu Game Reserve

↓ To Masindi   ↙ To Kigumba

KIDEPO VALLEY

Situated in an almost inaccessible part of Uganda—the north-east corner of **Karamoja** that borders **Sudan** and is close to the semi-desert **Turkana district** of Kenya—**Kidepo Valley National Park** (KVNP) may well be the most unspoilt park in the world.

The 1,400 square kilometres (560 square miles) of KVNP deserve more attention than they currently receive. Persistent insecurity in the east between 1987 and 1989 practically cut off the area from the rest of Uganda. Anyone interested in visiting Kidepo had to rely on aircraft, provided that clearance could be obtained, and even then, lack of transport facilities within the park, and a lodge without food or diesel for electricity, made a visit here one of the least likely options for tourists in Uganda.

Years of civil war turned KVNP into a temporary free-for-all where cattle rustlers and poachers from Uganda and Sudan gladly participated. The presence now of an army detachment and some 70 armed game rangers has greatly improved security in the park and poaching is controlled to a considerable extent. This should make the park safe for tourists.

This area was made into a game reserve in 1958; four years later it was gazetted as a national park. In 1967 conservationists welcomed an extension to the southern region with the addition of the **Narus River**, used by wild animals during dry season grazing. Kidepo means *to pick* in the local dialect and refers to the coconuts left to pick at a spot near the Narus River.

Wild Africa: High, freakish mountainscapes in the west, south and east and two seasonal rivers, the Narus and the **Kidepo**, offer an impression of how wild Africa must have looked. **Mount Morongole** is the eastern peak and the 2,700-metre (8,856-foot) top of **Lotuke** marks the border with Sudan.

A flight from **Entebbe** airport reveals the almost surrealist mountain ridges.

The intricate interplay of clouds, rain and sun adds to their uniqueness. Sporadic *manyattas* of the nomadic Karamajong tribesmen can be spotted from the air and clouds of smoke mark the areas being burnt when the rainy season has finished.

Unlike other Ugandan parks KVNP resembles the physical lay-out of game parks in the drier neighbouring countries of Kenya and Tanzania. But unlike Kenya, what makes Kidepo so attractive is the lack of noisy convoys of tourist buses: a drive through Kidepo will be a very lonesome and isolated experience.

The park is characterised by four main types of vegetation which are closely bound up with the seasonal flow of the two rivers. The **Valley of the Narus**, which is well watered, has savannah woodland, later gradually merging into fire-climax grassland in the south. Trees include several species of acacia. Apart from the savannah woodland, large areas are covered with a mixture of shrub steppe, bushland and

dry thicket.

Naturally, the animal population is closely associated with the various types of vegetation. Giraffe, elephant, buffalo and rare (in Uganda) Burchell's zebra favour the savannah woodland around the two rivers. Oryx, greater and lesser kudu, Grant's and Bright's gazelle and mountain reedbuck, klipspringer and ostrich can be found in the slightly drier areas.

Like everywhere else animal populations have decreased considerably since the 1970s and recent counts have not been available. KVNP used to be a stronghold for elephant and rhino but this is no longer the park's claim to fame.

During the Amin era, however, KVNP was saved some of the torment that befell other parks, both because of its remoteness and isolation and thanks to the excellent work of game warden Paul Ssali. The laudable efforts of this "warrior for wildlife" have been imaginatively described in John Hemingway's book, *No Man's Land*.

The Kidepo Valley even blossomed during the days of Amin: it seems the former dictator visited the park and took a keen interest in animals. From the lodge's balconies looking out over the yellow and green Narus Valley, the view is spectacular. Elephant, giraffe, zebra, antelope and waterbuck are easy to spot, especially during the dry season (December to April).

During the 1960s and 1970s KVNP was often fully booked. It had a shop selling frozen and canned foods and a lorry frequently brought new supplies. Although those days are over, the lodge has benefitted from a very dedicated and honest workforce, and has not been looted like the lodges in Murchison Falls. The white linen tablecloths, cutlery and wine glasses have survived the years of civil strife, and the 16 double rooms can be used at any time, provided visitors bring their own food and drink.

The future for KVNP looks somewhat brighter, although work still needs to be done to bring the area and facilities up to standard.

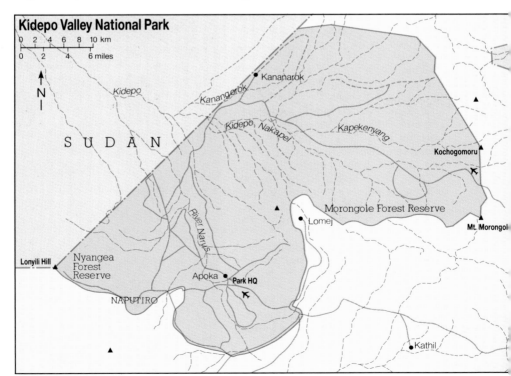

Kidepo Valley National Park

LAKE MBURO

Lake Mburo National Park (LMNP) is the latest Ugandan national park—it was officially gazetted in 1982. However, the original 642 square kilometres (256 square miles) have turned into a political hotbed which has overshadowed its great potential as a holiday resort both for the local urban population and foreign tourists.

Earlier this century, the area was such an attractive place for wild animals that in 1936 the government was forced to declare it a controlled hunting area. The Kenyan born writer Brian Herne vividly describes those days—when the park boasted many lions—in his book, *Ugandan Safaris*. In 1964 the area was turned into a game reserve, having been cleared of tsetse fly in preceding years.

Conflicting interests: The clash of human and wildlife interests started in the mid-1970s. Cattle ranches blos- somed at the edge of the reserve, and during the Amin years, ranch owners were able to claim huge tracts of land for themselves. At the same time the prevailing lawlessness opened up the reserve to *Bahima* herdsmen who immediately took over the good grassland and watering holes, and even poisoned the game which were competing for grazing pasture. When the reserve was declared a national park, no less than 6,000 people and 40,000 head of cattle had to be evicted. Lack of compensation and subsequent unrest in the country worsened the situation.

Tight negotiations between the ranchers, herdsmen, government, park authorities and conservationists finally resulted in an agreement to divide the park into two: 386 square kilometres (154 square miles) for the people evicted in 1982, and 256 square kilometres (102 square miles) for the wildlife. A task force is currently working to establish the exact boundaries.

Worth the effort: Despite its problems, LMNP remains worth visiting, if

awny eagle
reads its
ings.

only for those animals that cannot be found elsewhere south of the Nile—impala, klipspringer, eland, roan antelope and oribi. Other species of game include numerous topi, waterbuck, bohor reedbuck, sitatunga, bushpig, bushbuck, porcupine, baboon, vervet monkey, greater galago, leopard, hyaena, hippo and buffalo. This is one of the few places in the country where numbers of animals increased between 1982 and 1985.

Already 258 species of birds have been identified. Future discoveries are likely to bring the actual number closer to 400.

Six bird species cannot be found in any other park. These include rufous bellied heron, black-throated barbet, red-faced barbet, tabora cisticola, green-capped eremomela and southern red bishop.

The slowly rolling hills and bright green plains have become dominated by *Acacia gerrardii* and *Acacia hockii* at the expense of grass. This alarming trend has been attributed to overgrazing by cattle. Grass becomes too short for regular burning, resulting in the unimpeded spread of acacia trees. Park authorities are considering reintroducing giraffe, which feed on acacia, in the hope of halting any further advance.

One advantage of LMNP is that the absence of lions makes it reasonably safe for visitors to walk through the park, although they should be cautious of the occasional lone buffalo.

Depending on the outcome of negotiations with the herdsmen, LMNP has the potential to become a short trip holiday resort, especially for the urban populations of **Kampala** and nearby **Masaka** and **Mbarara**. It is only a short drive to the park from all these towns. Roads and tracks have been badly damaged by the weather and lack of maintenance, but the current park staff are doing a commendable job in making the main circuits manageable again. Although facilities are somewhat lacking, this should not discourage anyone from visiting. There are excellent natural camping sites near the lake.

Helmeted guinea fowl—one the many bird specie found here.

FORESTS AND MOUNTAINS

The ridges of the Ruwenzoris, Mount Elgon and the Virunga volcanoes display an unrivalled scenic splendour. But even more important will be Uganda's rich and unexplored forests which have the potential to revive the country's tourist industry. These include the Bwindi Impenetrable Forest, Kigezi Game Reserve and Kibale Forest Corridor Game Reserve.

The Ruwenzoris in the west, on the border with Zaire and the volcanoes in the south-west on the border with Rwanda, and Mount Elgon in the east next to Kenya offer excellent opportunities for mountain climbing, with long walks through unique flora where numerous animal species roam.

Plans are being discussed to turn part of the Ruwenzoris into a national park. The mountain ridge with the snow-capped peak of Margherita on Mount

Stanley harbours elephant, buffalo, leopard, red forest duiker, giant forest hog, chimpanzee, blue monkey, Stuhlman's monkey and the Ruwenzori hyrax. It is the only place in Uganda where the extremely rare Ruwenzori colobus can be found.

Unfortunately, if the area is not soon gazetted into a game reserve or park, it may be damaged by the slow encroachment that is already taking place. Similarly, at Mount Elgon, there is great potential for tourism although cattle raiders have made this area relatively insecure.

The third mountain corridor is the **Kigezi Mountain Gorilla Reserve** in the south-west, dominated by the Virunga volcanoes. The 43-square-kilometre (17-square-mile) reserve lies between the towering peaks of mounts Muhabura and Gahinga.

The **Travellers' Rest Hotel** at **Kisoro** is the starting point for a trek to see the famous mountain gorillas (*Gorilla gorilla beringei*). Visitors need to check with the game warden in Kabale before

enic walk the wenzoris.

proceeding to Kisoro to register at the hotel, which will provide them with a guide. He only takes visitors up twice a week, preferably on Saturdays and Wednesdays.

A three- to four-hour climb takes you to the habitat of the mountain gorilla, though chances of actually seeing this huge primate are less than 100 percent. (A generous tip for the guide improves your chances!) But, the reserve offers other spectacular sights, including thick bamboo forest and the rare golden monkey (*Ceropithecus mitis kandti*), which make the climb worthwhile. Other animals to be seen include buffalo, bushbuck and giant forest hog.

The drive from Kabale to Kisoro is simply spectacular. This area is rightly referred to as the "Switzerland of Uganda", and is made up of green mountains, dangerous hair-pin bends, misty valleys, terraced fields, and idyllic lakes, such as the romantic **Lake Bunyonyi**, just a few kilometres from Kabale off the Kisoro road.

Jungle walks: In the south-west lies the 560-square-kilometre (224-square-mile) **Impenetrable Bwindi Forest/ GameSanctuary** which has one of the richest forest mammal faunas in Africa with 97 species. Most special is the mountain gorilla; other mammals include chimpanzee, elephant, and several species of duiker.

This well-watered area was gazetted as a game sanctuary in 1961, mainly because of the mountain gorilla whose numbers are currently estimated at 115. This figure has dwindled since the early 1960s and the government and conservationists are therefore extremely cautious about letting visitors into this area.

Much better suited for tourists is the **Kibale Forest Reserve**. Together with the adjacent **Kibale Forest Corridor and Game Reserve** (KFCGR) the area covers 900 square kilometres (360 square miles) close to the western town of **Fort Portal**, where accommodation is readily available.

The Kibale Forest Corridor and Game Reserve is quite well protected, especially around the research centre of the New York Zoological Society, only

16 kilometres (10 miles) from Fort Portal, which has been turned into a paradise for everybody who likes to walk in thick tropical rain forest. The reserve harbours the largest concentration of primates anywhere in the world: no less than 11 species can be found here in large numbers. Among them are: red colobus, black and white colobus, chimpanzee (the focus of American research), blue monkey, red-tailed monkey, L'Hoest monkey, mangabey, and olive baboon.

They can be spotted quite easily during a daytime walk through the dark pines and bright green jungle. The trek on foot has been facilitated by the 300 kilometres (186 miles) of paths and tracks which have been laid out by American researchers. A map and all the necessary information can be obtained from the research headquarters.

Other animals to be found in the forest reserve include two species of duikers, bushpig, bushbuck, warthog, giant forest hog, waterbuck, sitatunga, serval, golden, palm and civet cat.

However, KFCGR no longer harbours many large animals. The main purpose of gazetting the area was the now quite unbelievable fact that it provided a migratory route for elephants moving along a south-north axis, all the way from Zaire to Sudan, via Queen Elizabeth National Park, the Kibale Corridor, Katonga Game Reserve and Murchison Falls!

Today, massive encroachment in the KFCGR and elsewhere clearly prohibits this type of movement. Without doubt, forests are Uganda's most latent tourist attraction. The national parks, although spectacular, have to compete with neighbouring countries where facilities are much better.

The forests, however, are unique to Uganda, which is the only English-speaking country where mountain gorillas can be seen. The population of 600 to 800 chimpanzees in KFCGR cannot easily be found elsewhere. The animals are quite easy to spot because they have become used to human beings, although this does not detract from their natural behaviour.

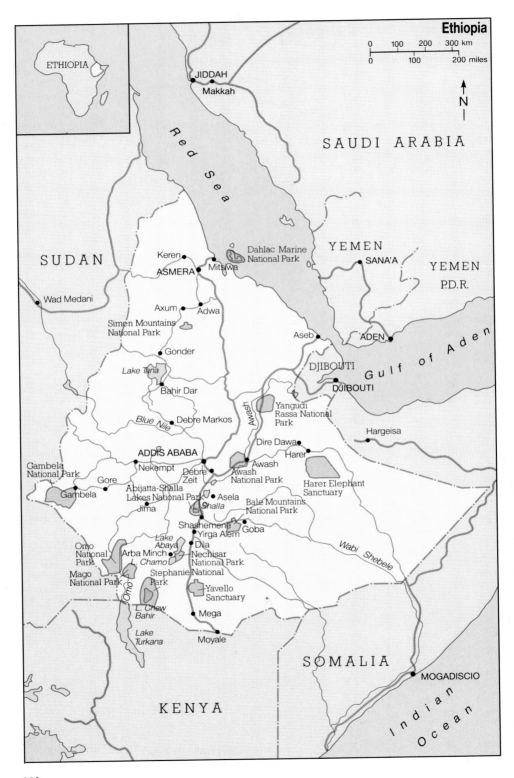

Ethiopia

0 100 200 300 km
0 100 200 miles

N

ETHIOPIA

SAUDI ARABIA

Red Sea

JIDDAH
Makkah

YEMEN

SANA'A

YEMEN
P.D.R.

SUDAN

Dahlac Marine
National Park

Keren
ASMERA   Mitsiwa

Wad Medani

Axum   Adwa

Simen Mountains
National Park

Aseb   ADEN

Gonder

DJIBOUTI

Gulf of Aden

Lake Tana

DJIBOUTI

Bahir Dar

Awash

Blue Nile   Debre Markos

Yangudi
Rassa National
Park

Dire Dawa

ADDIS ABABA   Harer

Gambela
National Park   Nekempt   Debre
Zeit   Awash
Awash
National Park

Gore   Abijatta-Shalla
Lakes National Park

Harer Elephant
Sanctuary

Gambela

Jima   Asela
Shalla

Bale Mountains
National Park

Shashemene   Goba
Yirga Alem

Wabi Shebele

*Lake
Abaya*   Dila

Omo
National
Park   Arba Minch
L. Chamo   Nechisar
National Park

Mago
National Park   Stephanie National
Park

Yavello
Sanctuary

*L. Chew
Bahir*   Mega

*Lake
Turkana*   Moyale

SOMALIA

MOGADISCIO

KENYA

*Indian
Ocean*

302

ETHIOPIA

Ethiopia is a vast wrinkled tableland, divided by two blocks of highlands with numerous peaks and valleys. The Ethiopian highlands were first formed 40 million years ago, when lava flowed over a huge area, both from volcanoes and from a gradual and insidious outpouring of molten rock. The Great Rift Valley subsided, splitting the highland block in two, to form the more extensive western highlands—on which the capital city of Addis Ababa is located—and the horseshoe-shaped eastern highland chain.

The country varies in altitude from some 100 metres (328 feet) below sea level in the Dalol Depression, to over 4,500 metres (14,760 feet) at the highest peak of Ras Dedjen in the Semien Mountains. In between these two extremes, 40 percent of Ethiopia is formed by the highland blocks lying 2,000 metres (6,560 feet) and more above sea level. The highlands have been cut off from similar high country in other parts of Africa for 20 million years by the arid lowlands surrounding them. Their size and isolation have ensured that many of the less mobile animal and plant species have evolved to cope with the unique conditions into forms not found elsewhere. Hence the very high numbers of endemic species found only in Ethiopia.

While wildlife conservation is not a priority for the government, given the more pressing problems facing the country, tourists are welcome and facilities will continue to develop. Four of the national parks are already well developed and accessible to tourists. Most of the others can be visited, although it requires considerable organisation and expense on the part of the vistor, and a willingness to cope with the logistical problems involved in getting to little known areas.

Although this guide deals specifically with its wildlife parks, visitors should not confine themselves to an appreciation of Ethiopia's wildlife. Many elements have influenced the country over time, making Ethiopia a land of mystery and a land apart.

Preceding pages: the eastern edge of Ethiopia's Sanetti Plateau.

ABIJATTA-SHALLA LAKES

Situated in the Great Rift Valley, only 200 kilometres (124 miles) south of Addis Ababa, and in the **Lake Langano** recreational area, the **Abijatta-Shalla Lakes National Park** attracts numerous visitors. It was created primarily for its aquatic bird life, particularly those that feed and breed on lakes Abijatta and Shalla in large numbers.

The park comprises the two lakes, the isthmus between them and a thin strip of land along the shorelines of each. Developments have been limited to a number of tracks on land, and the construction of seven outposts. While attention is focused on the water birds, the land area does contain a reasonable amount of other wildlife.

Two different lakes: The two lakes are very different in character. Abijatta is shallow at about 14 metres (46 feet): Shalla has a depth of 260 metres (853 feet) and is calculated to hold a greater volume of water than all of the Ethiopian Rift Valley lakes put together. Abijatta is surrounded by gentle, grass-covered slopes and swathed in acacia woodlands. Shalla exudes a sense of mystery and foreboding, surrounded as it is by steep, black cliffs and peaks that reflect in its deep waters, which are liable to be whipped up by sudden storms and flurries of wind. It contains nine small, isolated islands, rarely visited since there are no boats on the lake. These islands provide an excellent breeding ground for many bird species.

The network of tracks in this park is always developing. At present you can enter at four different points, three of which are inter-connected. Approaching from Addis you first reach the **Horakello** entrance, where the small Horakello stream flows between lakes Langano and Abijatta. The stream mouth is a source of relatively fresh water, much frequented by water birds for drinking and bathing.

Abijatta itself is very alkaline but shallow, so flamingoes can be seen scattered over most of its surface, and especially along the windward edge where their algal food source concentrates. You can approach quite closely, but beware of treacherous deep mud if the lake is low. Large numbers of both greater and lesser flamingoes gather here, together with great white pelicans and a host of other water birds.

A track which runs for 20 kilometres (12 miles) along the treeline of the eastern shore of Lake Abijatta connects Horakello with the park headquarters further south at **Dole.** From here you can see other parts of Lake Abijatta and some mammal species, especially Grant's gazelle, warthog and occasionally the oribi.

Hot springs: The headquarters houses a small museum, currently being upgraded, which gives an excellent idea of the wealth of birdlife in the park. There are over 400 species recorded here, almost half the number recorded for the whole country. A further track leads on from Dole to the shores of Lake Shalla where hot steam, mud and water

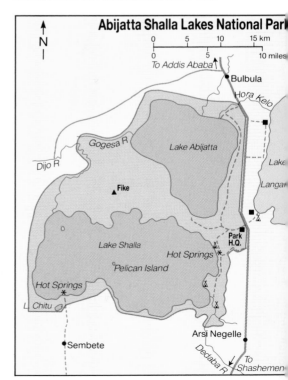

304

bubble to the earth's surface. Revered locally for their medicinal properties, the hot springs (*Filwoha*) have a sense of primaeval mystery about them, especially in the cooler early mornings. They are relics of the massive volcanic activity that has formed this amazing country and landscape.

A further entrance to this park exists in the south, where a rough track leads to another small hot spring area at **Ghike**. Here you can stay in a wooden self-help guest house, perched high on a cliff above the lake, with a view across the islands. There are plans to install a boat at the lake which will ferry small groups of people to the islands to observe the breeding colonies of thousands of great white pelicans and greater flamingoes. The great white pelican colony is estimated to be visited by up to 13,000 pairs annually, and is the most important breeding site for the species in the world.

There is no accommodation in the park but Lake Langano, which lies just over the main road marking the park boundary, has two reasonable hotels on its shores, the **Wabe Shebelle** and the **Bekelle Mola**, from which all parts of the park are easily reached. It is possible to camp at the hot springs and further south on the track east of Shalla, leading to the **Dedaba River** and outpost.

In association with the Abijatta-Shalla Lakes National Park is **Senkello Swayne's Hartebeest Sanctuary**, some 70 kilometres (43 miles) from the town of **Shashemene**, and close to the **Chike** entrance of the park. The sanctuary was established for this endemic subspecies of the hartebeest (*Alcelaphus buselaphus swaynei*) which once roamed the plains of Somalia and Ethiopia in thousands, but is now restricted to four small localities in Ethiopia. The sanctuary is small but well worth a visit. Set beneath a small rounded hill, over 2,000 of these rich, chocolate-coloured hartebeest are packed into this area of wooded grassland, along with bohor reedbuck (*Redunca redunca*), oribi and many different species of birds.

spoilt ke Shalla.

AWASH

Situated only 225 kilometres (140 miles) south east of Addis, down in the Rift Valley, **Awash National Park** was created for its concentrations of arid grassland and acacia woodland fauna. Dominated by the volcano **Mount Fantale**, the valleys, plains and gorges contain an abundance of mammals and birds which are easily seen from the excellent network of tracks. A good tarmac road connects Awash with Addis, and there is accommodation at the **Kereyou Lodge**, which comprises large caravans set in a beautiful location overlooking the junction of the Arba and Awash river gorges. The nearby park headquarters, beside the **Awash River**, has a small informative museum and campsite, and is close to the **Awash Falls.**

Various circuits exist south of the main road, enabling you to travel through the **Illala Sala plains** where large numbers of beisa oryx, Soemmering's gazelle, ostrich and kori bustard (*Ardeatis kori*) can be seen. Look at these animals carefully, for besides the usual red-billed oxpeckers (*Buphogus erythorhynchus*) on their backs you will also see jewelled carmine bee-eaters (*Merops nubicus*) hitching rides, and using their mobile perches as lookout points to watch for the insects disturbed by the animals' feet. To see one of these birds nestled down between the wings of an ostrich, or riding a stern kori bustard is an unforgettable sight.

A small group of Swayne's hartebeest lives in the park where thousands used to roam in the past. They were re-introduced about 20 years ago, and their numbers are slowly increasing.

Simply gorgeous: Other circuits lead you along the edge of the spectacular **Awash River gorge** and through areas of dense wait-a-bit thorn scrub where careful observation will reveal both greater and lesser kudu, as well as scores of Salt's dikdik

Beisa oryx and passenger

(*Madogua Saltiana*) at the cooler times of day. A journey along the upper reaches of the river above the falls will give you sightings of defassa waterbuck, warthog, vervet monkey and olive baboon. Observe these baboons carefully: Awash is the site of a cross-breeding exercise between the olive and the hamadryas baboon (*Papio hamadryas*) and several of the troops in this southern area exhibit hybrids and individuals of both species.

Travel north of the main road into the bulk of the park with a wildlife scout, and take the circuit that leads to the **hot springs.** There you will see the hamadryas baboon in its pure form, the males with their spectacular silvery capes blowing in the wind as they come to drink from the warm streams. This species is absent from the rest of East Africa, but its presence in the mountains of Yemen across the Red Sea indicates that there were ancient links between these two areas.

The hot springs gush from the ground at over 35 C (95 F), collecting in deep,

clear, blue pools—inviting but enervating for those who dare to take the plunge.

This circuit continues around Mount Fantale through attractive rolling country with faults, ridges, lava flows and eroded features. This needs a full morning or afternoon and takes you from the main gate back to the main road at the **Sabober gate.** Greater kudu are common here, as are herds of oryx at different times of the year. Don't expect giraffe and zebra since both species are curiously absent, although Grevy's zebra are present nearby and can sometimes be seen wandering within the park boundary.

An interesting track leads you up the steep slopes of Fantale, through the changing vegetation, to a spectacular view from the crater's rim. Early in the morning, steam can be seen rising from the vents in the centre; vultures glide lazily beneath you, and you may be able to catch the occasional glimpse of the bushy-tailed Chanler's mountain reedbuck (*Redunca fulvorufula chanleri*).

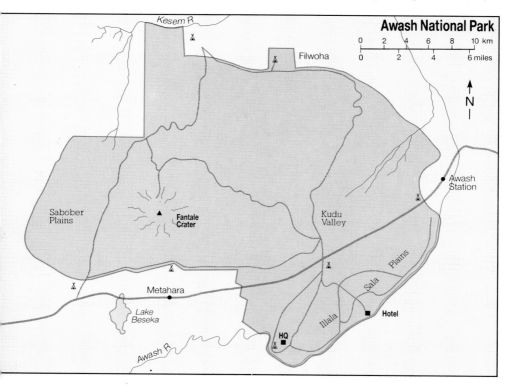

THE BALE MOUNTAINS

The road to the **Bale Mountains National Park** takes you 250 kilometres (155 miles) on tarmac south down the Rift Valley to Shashamene, and then 150 kilometres (93 miles) due east on a good gravel road across the high wheat-growing plateau and up into the mountain massif. Alternatively you can take the Nazareth road towards Awash, turn south to **Asella**, then take the gravel road south to the mountains. It is worth doing a circuit, going one way, returning the other, and taking in Awash and Abijatta-Shalla Lakes national parks in the process.

You first encounter the park as you ascend the mountains, travelling along part of its northern boundary. A steep juniper-filled valley, rising through giant heather (*Erica arborea*) moorlands and topped by volcanic plugs and dykes, forms the gateway to the mountains. After climbing to 3,600 metres (11,800 feet), visitors drop into the **Gaysay valley** and cross the small area of montane grasslands that form the northern extension of the park. The village of **Dinsho** nestles against the mountains here, and houses the park's headquarters, campsite, self-help lodge and museum.

Dinsho is located right in the north of the park with the bulk of the mountains lying to the south. To reach these, you can either go by vehicle 20 kilometres (12 miles) south into the **Web valley** along the **Simbirro** track, and continue by foot or on horseback to the central peaks area, or you can continue east by vehicle to **Goba**, the capital of the Bale region. Here the excellent **Goba Ras Hotel** provides a good base for exploration of the main part of the park.

Mountain high, valley low: A good gravel road climbs into the mountains south of Dinsho, rising through juniper, hagenia and hypericum and forest zones to heather moorlands, and eventually on to the flat expanse of the

A dip in the hot springs.

Sanetti Plateau. This is the highest all-weather road in Africa, at over 4,000 metres (13,120 feet) above sea level. The road travels for 30 kilometres (18 miles) along the plateau to the southern edge, and then performs a spectacular zigzag descent of the **Harenna Escarpment**. In 10 kilometres (six miles) it falls over 1,000 metres (3,280 feet) into the top of the **Harenna Forest**, and then descends gradually over the next 60 kilometres (37 miles) to the southern edge of the forest and park boundary.

The park is spread over 2,200 square kilometres (880 square miles). Approximately half of this comprises the high plateau and mountain area; the other half is the dense Harenna Forest. Altitude varies from 1,500 metres (4,920 feet) at the southern edge of the Harenna Forest, to 4,377 metres (14,357 feet) at the top of **Tullu Deemtu**, the highest peak in southern Ethiopia and outside the Semien Mountains.

The Gaysay Valley is the best place to see larger wildlife, either by vehicle or on horseback. Large numbers of the endemic mountain nyala (*Tragelaphus buxtoni*) occur here, forming the best concentration of the species in the world. In the wet season the flower-filled valley is popular grazing land for nyala, bohor reedbuck, grey duiker (*Cephalophus grimmia*), warthog, and Menelik's bushbuck (*Tragelaphus scriptus meneliki*). Serval and Egyptian mongoose (*Herpestes ichneumon*) are particularly common, and caracal are occasionally seen.

The mountain block comprises the Sanetti Plateau to the east, separated from the wide **Upper Web valley** by lava flows and skirted by steep heather moorlands. When allowed to grow unmolested the tree-like heather reaches heights of five metres (17 feet) and is difficult to penetrate, either on foot or on horseback.

High-altitude desert: The open Afro-alpine moorlands above the treeline are home to the simien fox (*Canis simensis*), a long-legged, long-snouted endemic member of the dog family, whose

ar right, e tractive ale ountains.

Bale Mountains National Park

overall population of less than 1,000, mainly here in Bale, gives cause for concern.

Other animals include low numbers of mountain nyala and at least seven rodent species, most endemic to Ethiopia. These occur in large numbers, scurrying away as you pass through and squeaking in indignation at the intrusion. Although not normally considered wildlife by most people, it is worth taking the time to watch these rodents as they try to detect the numerous predators which gather to feast on them.

Perhaps the most interesting animal is the giant molerat which is endemic to the Bale mountains. It has modified the habitat considerably since glaciation over 10,000 years ago. The molerats' constant burrowing, collection of surface vegetation and heaps of discarded rubbish near their nests have created a ploughed landscape dotted with mounds covered in different vegetation. Giant molerats weigh almost one kilogram (2.2 pounds) and are preyed upon by the simien fox which will wait patiently for hours over an open burrow.

In the high altitude desert there are no trees but several interesting plant species have adapted to the extreme conditions. Look in particular for a plant that has opted for gigantism—the endemic giant lobelia which is over five metres (17 feet) tall when it flowers.

Temperatures on the plateau in the dry season (November to February) can fall as low as -20 C (-4 F), but within 24 hours will rise to 26 C (79 F) at noon. This amazing change explains many of the adaptations and behaviour of the animals and plants in this area as they seek to avoid being alternatively baked, frozen and desiccated.

The best way to see the mountains is to hire horses from the park office in Dinsho. There are a number of routes starting there which can be designed to suit the time you have available. Simple circular routes returning to Dinsho can take one to three days; longer routes go through the Web valley, lava flows and across the plateau where your vehicle can meet you. Take a wildlife scout or

Mountain nyala in the Gaysay Valley.

guide from Dinsho to help you find your way and to lead you to the mineral springs, alpine tarns and cave shelters you would otherwise probably miss.

The Harenna Forest is well worth a visit, if only to add to a day trip from Goba. The escarpment is cloud-covered in the wet season but the forest below is often sunny and bright. It is worth diverging to the natural grass clearing of **Katcha**, 10 kilometres (six miles) below the village of **Rira**, and even camping there, to experience the forest with its rich, abundant bird and mammal life. Leopard, black serval (*Leptailurus serval*), lion, all three of Africa's pig species, Menelik's bushbuck, grey duiker, black and white colobus—better known in Ethiopia as "Guereza"—olive baboon, grivet (*Cercopithecus aethiops*) and Sykes monkey are commonly seen. Mountain nyala also occur here in low numbers.

Bale is a bird haven with many habitats at different altitudes which attract a broad variety of species. Over 200 different birds have been recorded and once the forest is properly studied, considerably more will probably be discovered. Fifteen of Ethiopia's 27 endemic bird species have been recorded there and a week spent bird watching in the various habitats should enable you to see a wide variety.

Bale is Ethiopia's flagship conservation area, containing so many different habitats and species typical of the Ethiopian Highlands that no visit to the country is complete without spending a reasonable amount of time there.

A day trip from Goba will take you to the **Sof Omar limestone caves**, 110 kilometres (68 miles) east of the town of **Robe**. The **Web River** flows from the mountains through a total of 15 kilometres (nine miles) of tunnel eroded over aeons by the water and its organic acid content. The journey there and back takes you through very different country to that of the mountains, and well illustrates the extremes of this fascinating nation: from frost and simien fox down to the lowlands and camel in a mere 150 kilometres (93 miles).

NECHISAR AND OTHER LAKES

Set on the isthmus between two more of Ethiopia's Rift Valley Lakes—**Chamo** and **Abbaya**—**Nechisar National Park** is a jewel of magnificent scenery and plentiful wildlife. Park headquarters is located near the town of **Arba Minch** (Forty Springs), 500 kilometres (310 miles) south of Addis, passing through the town of Shashemene after 250 kilometres (155 miles) of tarmac. A good gravel road leads along the western edge of the rift to Arba Minch.

Good roads in the park lead through the **Kulfo River ground water forest** in the floor of the rift below Arba Minch. Across the river, the main route into the park passes across the isthmus between the lakes via a series of spectacular and rugged climbs across faults in the rift floor, and up an escarpment to the **Nechisar** (white grass) **Plains** for which the park is named. Four-wheel drive vehicles are essential.

Greater kudu are commonly seen crossing the isthmus, and this area is said to be one of the best locations for the species in Africa. Guenther's dikdik abound at every turn and a short track leads you to the **Crocodile Market** at the northern edge of Lake Chamo where monster crocodiles lie out on the lake shore at close quarters.

Once up on the plains, several different circuits take you through a mass of Burchell's zebra, Grant's gazelle, large troops of olive baboons and some Swayne's hartebeest, all against the backdrop of the highlands to the east, the jewelled lakes far below and the soaring mountains of the western highlands above Arba Minch.

It is well worth spending time in Kulfo River ground water forest if birds are your main interest. There is an excellent campsite set beneath giant fig trees beside the river in the forest. You may also camp at the hot springs on the far side of the Nechisar Plains, a good starting point for early morning obser-

Looking out on Lake Chamo.

vation of the plains' animals.

Yangudi Rassa: North of the Awash and still in the Rift Valley, **Yangudi Rassa National Park** was established for its population of wild ass (*Asinus africanus*). It is possible to stay in the little hotel in **Gewane** and follow park staff on regular trips for fleeting glimpses of these interesting animals in their semi-desert habitat.

Harer Elephant Sanctuary: This is worth a trip as an extension of a visit to the historic walled city of **Harer**. The elephants here are an endemic subspecies, but difficult to see because of limited viewing tracks.

Far south: At the southern end of Ethiopia, the **Omo and Mago national parks** are situated close together on each side of the **Omo River**. Good dry season roads exist, or you can fly with charter aircraft, having arranged with the official travel agency, National Tour Organisation (NTO) for ground transport to meet you. Good campsites have been made but with no facilities. Fuel is also difficult to procure in this area and you are advised to take all you need with you. Large numbers of larger wildlife species such as elephant, buffalo, eland and Lelwel hartebeest (*Alcelaphus buselaphus lelwel*) occur, but there are few usable tracks.

Yavello Sanctuary: This sanctuary is close to the main tarmac road south from Addis to the Kenya border. There are small hotels in **Yavello** town, and a few tracks from which to explore the area. Reasonable numbers of both lesser and greater kudu and gerenuk, Grevy's zebra, beisa oryx and dikdik can be seen, as well as ostrich and giraffe. The area is most significant, however, as a centre for a group of endemic birds: Stresemann's bush crow (*Zavattariornis stresemanni*), the degodi and Sidamo lark, the white-tailed swallow (*Hirundo megaensis*) and—further east—Prince Ruspoli's turaco (*Tauraco ruspoli*).

Other Areas: Developments are limited in most cases. Some, such as **Dahiak**, **Semien**, and **Cambella** are inaccessible to visitors.

r right, the Ifo River ound water rest.

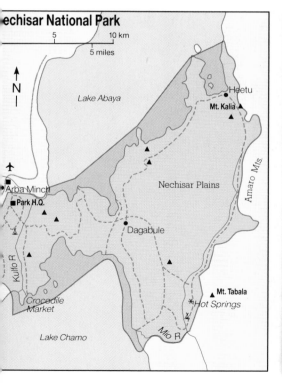

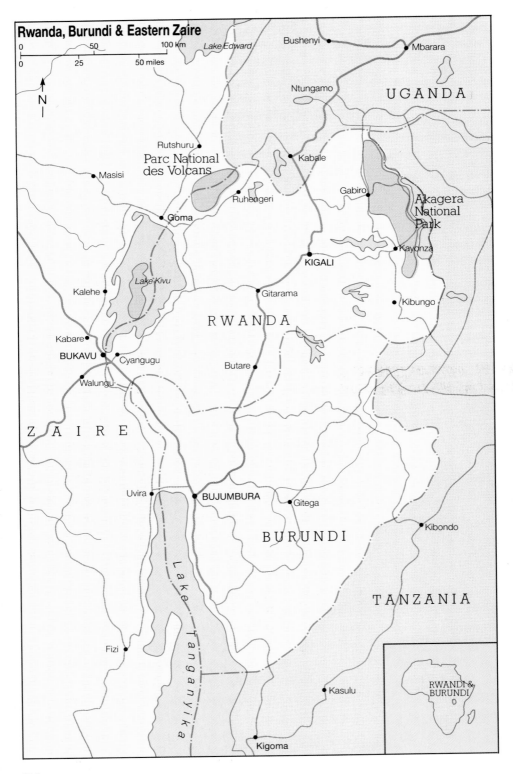

Rwanda, Burundi & Eastern Zaire

Lake Edward

Bushenyi

Mbarara

Ntungamo

UGANDA

Rutshuru

Parc National
des Volcans

Kabale

Masisi

Ruhengeri

Gabiro

Akagera
National
Park

Goma

Kayonza

KIGALI

Kalehe

Lake Kivu

Gitarama

Kibungo

Kabare

RWANDA

BUKAVU

Cyangugu

Butare

Walungu

Z A I R E

Uvira

BUJUMBURA

Gitega

Kibondo

BURUNDI

TANZANIA

Fizi

Lake Tanganyika

Kasulu

RWANDI &
BURUNDI

Kigoma

RWANDA

Rwanda is a tiny country in the mountains of east central Africa just south of the equator. It borders Tanzania on the east, Uganda on the north, Zaire and Lake Kivu on the west, and Burundi on the south. Rwanda's land area of 26,340 square kilometres (10,290 square miles) is only about the size of some of East Africa's larger national parks, but with over six million people it has the highest population density on the African continent.

The country is mountainous in the extreme, varying from 1,200 metres (3,960 feet) to over 4,500 metres (14,760 feet). Much of the land is spectacularly beautiful. Steep mountains are cleft by deep precipitous valleys, many of them jewelled by lakes. There is an excellent system of well engineered roads, two major national parks and some good hotels and lodges.

A German explorer, Lieutenant Von Goetzen, was the first European to reach what is now Rwanda when he crossed the Akagera River (one of the headwaters of the Nile) near Rusumo, in the south-east of the country, in 1884. Here he found a feudal hierarchy headed by Tutsi nobles, members of one of the country's three indigenous tribes.

In 1899, after many centuries as a feudal society with social classes similar to those of medieval Europe, Rwandans were made to recognise German sovereignty. This lasted until World War I, when Belgium took over Rwanda (and neighbouring Burundi). Colonial ties were severed on July 1, 1962, with the formation of the Republic of Rwanda.

A second (and present) Republic was formed in 1973. Since then, tourism and other industries have been developing. Tourism is an important source of foreign exchange and much has been done to improve facilities and promote the country in recent years. Rwanda's best known attraction is the gorilla tracking in the famous Parc National des Volcans; but this is by no means its only virtue. There is a variety of wildlife at Akagera National Park and the scenery alone makes any road journey through Rwanda a worthwhile endeavour.

Preceding pages: the deep green valleys on the way to Ruhengeri are partially obscured by cloud cover.

AKAGERA

First created in 1934, this is Rwanda's largest national park, with an area of 2,500 square kilometres (1,000 square miles). It is undulating, even hilly, country with a mixture of bush and grassland savanna studded by an extensive chain of lakes that drain into the **Akagera River**, which forms the park's eastern boundary, before eventually flowing into Lake Victoria and becoming one of the sources of the Nile.

The park is 120 kilometres (75 miles) east of **Kigali** and **Hotel Akagera**, near the southern end of the park, can easily be reached in a morning from the capital, most of the journey being on smooth tarmac roads. A similar 150-kilometre (90-mile) stretch of tarmac links Kigali with the **Gabiro Guest House** in the north of the park.

Birds and more birds: At a fishing village on the shores of **Lake Ihema**, one can take a boat out to the nearby islands, alive with cormorants, darters, herons, storks and other water birds. Up to 12 species can be seen nesting here. Birds are the main strength of Akagera and it is a wonderful place for ornithologists; not only is bird life prolific but the park is far enough west across the African continent to have different species from the major countries of East Africa. Bennett's woodpecker, the golden-backed weaver, the short-tailed pipit, Souza's shrike, and the violet-crested turaco can all be seen in Rwanda more easily than in Kenya or Tanzania. More than 520 species have been recorded in Akagera National Park and competent ornithologists can hope to see as many as 100 on a single day.

A strong metal boat with a sun canopy has been launched on **Lake Mahindi** in the northern part of the park by the World Wildlife Fund who are anxious to encourage Rwanda's conservation programmes. From this boat visitors can view water birds and ease along the channels connecting Lake Mahindi to the Akagera River and other lakes. Here it is possible to see some very unusual birds skulking in the papyrus. The forest gallery on either side of the water channels is unique.

Game drives: There are several circuits in the park for game viewing. From Hotel Akagera one can take a half-day drive along the rolling hills of the **Ridge Circuit** or spend a full day going north to Gabiro Guest House. This is a journey of about 130 kilometres (80 miles) on a road reminiscent of a farm track in England. The undulating, lush countryside, studded with lakes, resembles a deserted English Lake District in the summer, were it not for the wildlife. There are very large numbers of impala, plenty of topi, waterbuck and many African Cape buffalo. Some of the old male buffalo have spectacular horns; spans of 1.1 metres (44 inches) are not uncommon. There is a very small number of elephants which were reared as orphans and now run free. Lion, leopard, serval cat, African hunting dogs, hyaena and jackal also exist here though none of them will be

as easy to find as in the best of East Africa's parks.

Night driving is allowed in Akagera; aardvark, civet and genet are among the animals one might see after dark.

The road from Hotel Akagera to Gabiro passes, in turn, lakes Ihema, **Hago** and Mahindi. All these give lovely views and chances to observe hippos and other water animals. At Lake Mahindi there is a fine picnic site where hippos are much in evidence, often standing out of the water near clumps of papyrus.

Ten kilometres (six miles) further north, on the shores of **Lake Rwanyakizinga**, there is a wooden observation tower specially built to view sitatunga antelopes who live in the marsh. These animals are adapted to swamp life with long hooves that lie forwards and support them on soft ground. With binoculars it is often possible to enjoy good views of these comparatively rare creatures grazing in open glades.

Spending a full day over the drive from Hotel Akagera to Gabiro Guest House is an excellent way of touring the park and seeing its major attractions, and the guest house is a pleasant place to stay. Located on a large spread out site with many individual touches in its layout and design, Gabiro's individual stone cottages seem appropriate in a national park.

Though it is easy to return to Kigali from Gabiro many visitors will drive on to **Ruhengeri** and the Parc National des Volcans through scenery which becomes steadily more interesting. Deep, heavily cultivated valleys separate huge hills which march with increasing drama towards the Virunga volcanoes, Rwanda's frontier to the north-west. This is the home of the famous mountain gorillas, the country's most valuable wildlife asset. Before reaching Ruhengeri it is worth making a side trip to see beautiful **Lake Ruhondo** (about 10 kilometres before you reach Ruhengeri town). Nestled in a valley and studded with islands, this is one of the finest views in a country of memorable panoramas.

autiful
ke
hondo.

MOUNTAIN GORILLAS

Gentle giants: In the make-believe world of Hollywood the gorilla has been invested with all the aggression of *Homo sapiens* to create a parody which has no relation to the original, gentle creature whose form he takes.

Almost entirely vegetarians, mountain gorillas (*gorilla gorila beringei*) eat over 100 different plants (and some insects). They live in stable groups which vary in size between two and 30 individuals. Each group is dominated by a senior male, normally more than 15 years old (ages of up to 35 years are known in captivity but many workers think gorillas may live even longer). Such males stand about 1.75 metres (5 feet 9 inches) tall, weigh around 180 kilos (396 pounds) and are the undisputed leaders of their groups. Easily recognised by the saddle of silver hairs which form across their backs with increasing age, these 'silverbacks' weigh about twice as much as a mature female and are immensely strong without being aggressive. Such a silverback will normally have several sexual partners who will remain with him for life. There may be another, immature, male in the group between eight and 13 years old, along with other juveniles and infants. Because the gorillas have permanent relationships they form strong ties; but as in other species both males and females leave their natal groups when they reach sexual maturity so there is little or no inbreeding in normal populations. Males are driven out by the silverbacks and may spend several years alone before they can attract females to form a group of their own. Females usually leave their natal groups when two families meet at the overlapping edges of their territories.

Gorilla babies are born after a gestation period of nine months—give or take three weeks depending on the individual—and suckle until the age of 18 months, though they begin eating vege-

Looks fierc but this silverback only yawning.

tation at about 10 weeks. Once she has reached the age of eight and is sexually mature, a female will have a baby roughly every four years, but 30 percent will be lost through infant mortality. Because of their bulk and weight gorillas move and climb slowly being careful not to break branches. Strictly diurnal, at night they sleep in crude nests made of leaves and branches, usually on the ground but sometimes on platforms which they make a few feet up in trees. Typical behaviour involves waking at dawn, feeding for two hours, resting for a few hours and then feeding again. At night the whole group will sleep within 50 metres (165 feet) of each other. But they are continuously on the move, normally sleeping at a new site each night.

Gorillas communicate via a variety of grunts, screams and roars; they also beat their chests with their hands, producing an intimidating slapping sound which travels a long way in the forest.

Gorilla tracking: To go gorilla tracking in the Parc National des Volcans you must have a permit to visit one of the four groups which are habituated to humans. In 1989 these were known as Group 9, Group 11, Group 13 and the *Suza* Group. Permits for Group 9 are sometimes available for purchase at the park office at Kinigi, 11 kilometres (6.5 miles) from Ruhengeri, where you meet up with your guide. All other permits are sold in advance to travel companies specialising in African safaris, so it is much easier to work with one of these in order to avoid disappointment. In 1989 a permit cost US$172. Only six tourists per day are allowed with each gorilla group and this rule is strictly enforced. People with colds, flu or stomach problems are not allowed because of the danger of infecting the gorillas.

Each party of visitors is allotted a guide—usually English speaking—whose charges are included in the cost of the permit. Porters are available for hire at park headquarters and are highly recommended as gorilla tracking can be extremely strenuous. To locate your allotted group, the guide will lead you to where the gorillas were sighted on the previous day and then literally track them through the forest. The terrain is very rough, often over steep slopes covered with matted vegetation. Be prepared for rain, mud and giant stinging nettles. Long trousers, leather gloves and a waterproof jacket will help.

With any group you might be out in the forest for many hours; usually a trek of one to three hours will bring you to the gorillas. After reaching the animals each party spends one hour with them before returning to park headquarters. This is adequate time to enjoy very good, close-up sightings.

Appropriate behaviour is essential when gorilla watching and your guide will advise you on this. Hard-eyed stares are as aggressive to gorillas as they are to ourselves; and you should not stand higher up than the gorillas in an open space. No doubt because these rules are observed, accidents with tourists are unknown; however, silverback males often make a false charge at some point during the day, giving visitors the thrill of a lifetime.

Parc National des Volcans

Most visitors to the **Parc National des Volcans**—and indeed to the country of Rwanda—come to see gorillas. Thanks to a very successful conservation project it is now possible to virtually guarantee close-up sightings of these massive apes and many hundreds of people enjoy this privilege each year.

The Virunga Volcanoes: Rwanda, Uganda and Zaire come together at the summit of 4,127-metre (13,540-foot) **Muhabura**—one of an extensive range of volcanic peaks in central Africa which form the boundaries between these three countries. **Karisimbi** ("white shell"), at 4,507 metres (14,786 feet), is the highest in the chain—tall enough to create the frequent showers of snow which justify its name. The border between Rwanda and Zaire runs from Karisimbi over the crests of **Vịsoke**, **Musinde**, **Sabynyo** (at 500,000 years the oldest of the volcanoes) and **Gahinga** to Muhabura.

These mountains bring an incredible 10 percent of Rwanda's rain to the 0.5 percent of the country which is made up by the Parc National des Volcans. This high rainfall (183 cm/72 inches annually) sustains the vegetation typical of high mountains in east and central Africa; on the lower slopes there is mixed woodland—though much of the original woodland has been felled to make way for agriculture. Then comes a zone of dense bamboo which extends from about 2,286 metres (7,500 feet) up to between 2,591 metres (8,500 feet) and 2,988 metres (9,800 feet) depending on the local area. Above the bamboo is an ancient forest of gnarled *Hagenia abyssinica* trees, many of them draped with mosses and decorated with orchids and ferns. Among the dominant *hagenia*, St. John's Wort (*Hypericum lanceolatum*) is another common tree which often supports *Unsea* lichen or 'Old Man's Beard' with its long trailing strands so reminiscent of Spanish moss.

The volcanic peak of Muhabura.

Above the *hagenia* and *hypericum* forest, at about 3,354 metres (11,000 feet) is the so called sub-alpine zone, an open moor-like area with a fascinating array of plants found only at high altitude in the tropics. Here giant senecios and lobelias grow to five metres (15 feet) and fields of everlasting *helichrysum* flowers decorate the ground. But few visitors venture so far up these volcanoes.

Early roots: The oldest national park in Africa, the Parc National des Volcans was originally created as part of the Parc National Albert in 1925, largely due to the influence of an unusual American, Carl Ethan Akeley (1864-1926). The son of a farmer from upstate New York, Akeley became an expert at mounting museum specimens and he made several expeditions to Africa. Akeley's Hall of African Mammals remains one of the major exhibits at the American Museum.

In 1921 he visited the Belgian Congo, partially in order to collect gorilla specimens for the museum, and became fascinated by the great apes. Although he did take four gorillas for the museum Akeley became alarmed at the extent of hunting and persuaded the Belgian government to create the Parc National Albert—named after the then King of Belgium. (Akeley died on a subsequent visit to gorilla country and was buried at Kabara, on the Ugandan side of the Virunga volcanoes, in 1926.)

In those days both modern Rwanda and Zaire came under the aegis of the Belgium Government so the Parc of 1925 included most of the mountains of the Virunga Volcanoes in Rwanda and Zaire. In 1960 the Parc was divided into two new parks: in Zaire the Parc National des Virunga and in Rwanda the Parc National des Volcans.

Owing to the population pressure for new agricultural land the Parc National des Volcans has been reduced in size since 1960; it now has an area of 125 square kilometres (50 square miles). But Zaire's Parc National des Virunga and the Kigezi Gorilla Sanctuary in Uganda are both contiguous with the

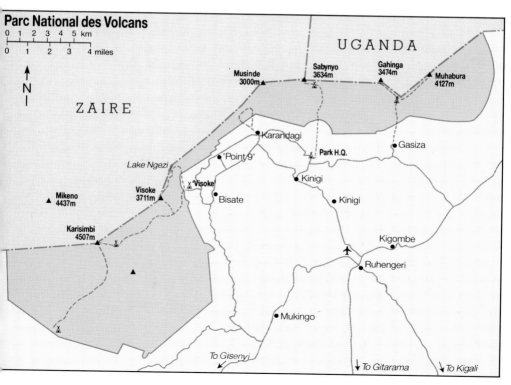

Rwandan park so the total area of this protected mountain habitat is still 375 square kilometres (150 square miles).

Gorilla Conservation: Many dedicated individuals have contributed to the conservation of the mountain gorillas of the Virunga volcanoes. After Akeley's influence in setting up the original Parc National Albert, the next notable conservationist was Walter Baumgartel, who established the Travellers' Rest Hotel in Kisoro, on the Ugandan side of the volcanoes, used for many years by tourists and research scientists working on gorillas. It was here that George Schaller, the eminent wildlife scientist, stayed in 1960 when he conducted a study involving over 450 hours of observing of wild gorillas.

Since then there has been enormous world-wide interest in gorilla research, much of it stimulated by the fact that gorillas are such near relatives to ourselves. Only four species of mammals—all primates—share the characteristics of being without tails, having two nipples and having five digits on both hands and feet, one of which is an opposable thumb. These are the three great apes—chimpanzees, orangutans, gorillas—and *Homo sapiens*. Many workers, notably Drs Louis and Mary Leakey (famous for their work on the fossils of early man in Africa) believed it was important to study gorillas in their natural habitat in order to find out more about how early man may have behaved in prehistoric times. Dr Leakey was among those who encouraged Dian Fossey to begin her research on the gorillas, which she started with Walter Baumgartel in 1963. By late 1967 she was establishing a new camp and the **Karisoke Research Centre.** Her book *Gorillas in the Mist* has done much to publicise the plight of these great apes. Dian Fossey was murdered in the park in 1985, probably by poachers, but her work, made famous through many documentary and feature films, still continues through the Mountain Gorilla Project.

Many dedicated scientists have worked here on gorilla research and on

Eyeball-to-eyeball with a mountain gorilla.

habituating them to humans so that it is possible for visitors to enjoy them. There are many encouraging signs that these aims are being fulfilled. The tourism side of conservation is making a substantial contribution to Rwanda's foreign exchange and there have been no poaching losses of gorillas in those groups which are visited by tourists. Indeed some scientists believe that in the 1980s the numbers of gorillas in the Parc National des Volcans may have increased slightly. In a 1986 census a total of 279 individuals were counted.

Nyungwe Forest: In south-west Rwanda, mid-way between the towns of **Cyangugu** (at the southern end of Lake Kivu) and **Butare**, is the **Foret Naturelle de Nyungwe**, an extensive area roughly 60 kilometres (37 miles) long and 30 kilometres (19 miles) wide.

This beautiful tropical forest is rich in plants, butterflies, birds and primates. There are nine different species of monkeys; notable are the Angolan black and white colobus (*Colobus angolensis*) which can sometimes be seen in troops of up to 300. Very different from the Abyssinian black and white colobus (*Colobus abyssinicus*), frequently seen in the mountain forests of East Africa, the Angolan has no white cape around the lower part of the body. Like all colobus they spend most of their time high in the trees, seldom coming down to the ground.

Another monkey found here is L'Hoest's monkey (*Cercopithecus l'hoesti*). This is a beautiful animal with a red back and a prominent ruff of white whiskers around its dark face; unique in its class of monkeys L'Hoest's has a prehensile tail with a hooked tip.

The area is also good for ornithologists: Ruwenzori and great blue turacos, Western green tinkerbirds, purple-breasted and regal sunbirds are some of the notable species to be found here. There are tracks through the forest which make it easy to walk; but it is wise to take a local guide from Cyangugu or one of the villages. The **Ibis Hotel** in Butare could also be used as a base when visiting Nyungwe.

ake Kivu nd the Hotel leridien at isenyi.

EASTERN ZAIRE

Parc National de Kahuzi Biega is named after the two volcanic peaks of **Kahuzi** (3,308 metres/10,850 feet) and **Biega** (2,790 metres/9,120 feet), the highest peaks in the western wall of the western branch of the Great Rift Valley. The park offers excellent gorilla tracking. Here one sees the Eastern Lowland gorilla (*Gorilla gorilla graueri*) which has minor differences from the *Gorilla gorilla berengei* of the Parc National des Volcans in Rwanda. The Kahuzi Biega gorillas have lower foreheads, shorter hair and longer arms, but they are every bit as impressive as their Rwandan cousins.

Unless your journey is planned by a travel company which is making arrangements for you, gorilla trackers should book in advance through the IZCN (Institut Zairois Pour la Conservation de la Nature) office, 185 Avenue President Mobutu, Bukavu.

Fees must be paid at the park entrance office at **Tshivanga**, 31 kilometres (20 miles) from Bukavu on the actual day of the excursion. In 1989 the fees were US$100 per person per day. Eight people are allowed in each party and gorilla tracking begins at 9 a.m. each day. In 1989 only three groups of gorillas were habituated to human visitors.

The Kahuzi Biega forest is very beautiful; the trees, plants, butterflies and birds all add great interest to a visit. Occasionally visitors are unable to reach the gorillas because of elephants and buffalo; but the guides and trackers are experts at avoiding problems.

Mount Kahuzi and Mount Bugulumiza can both be climbed and give fine views of Lake Kivu. Modest fees must be paid at the park office at Tshivanga.

Mount Kahuzi is a five-hour excursion for strong, well-clad mountain walkers. There is a good track and a guide can be found at the **Kahuzi Patrol Post** at the base of the mountain on the western boundary of the park, reached via the tarmac road which leads

Far left, sitting in a gorilla nes Below, the Virunga volcanoes.

326

from Tshivanga to Bunyakiri, Irangi and Walikale.

Mount Bugulumiza has a well-kept track which rises gently for six kilometres (four miles) to an open plateau with spacious views. Four-wheel drive vehicles can negotiate the track and there is a hut near the summit, a good spot for a picnic lunch.

A different world: Reached in 90 minutes from **Bukavu** (or an hour from Kahuzi Biega), the village of **Irangi** is in a world by itself. Here at only 800 metres (2,625 feet) the climate is warmer and more humid. The village is at the edge of a tropical rain forest on the banks of the fast flowing and beautiful **Lwana River**. More luxuriant than the montane forests of the gorillas, Irangi has fantastic bird life and incredible butterflies. King Leopold III's **hunting cottage**, built on the river bank in 1957, is still intact at modest charges. Not far from the cottage a wobbly but safe footbridge, woven from rattan and bamboo, gives access to the forest paths.

Parc National des Virunga: Originally part of the Parc National Albert, this huge park has an area of 8,000 square kilometres (3,200 square miles). The park contains the Zairean side of the Virunga volcanoes which form the watershed between the largest of the continent's rivers, the Nile and the Zaire (formerly the Congo). One of these, the **Nyiragongo**, at 3,170 metres (10,400 feet), is still active and can be climbed with a guide from the town of **Goma** at the northern end of Lake Kivu. From time to time there are obvious signs of volcanic activity with steam jets and even red-hot lava being visible inside the crater.

Some 160 kilometres (100 miles) north of Goma, gorilla safaris are available at **Djomba**. From a scenic spot in the shadow of Mount Sabynyo, guests at the comfortable log cabins of the **Djomba Intrepids Club** can make daily treks to visit two mountain gorilla families. Nearby Hutu villages also provide some colourful insight into tribal life.

TRAVEL TIPS

GETTING THERE

BY AIR

Visitors travelling to Kenya by air will arrive at either Jomo Kenyatta International Airport (JKA), Nairobi, or the slightly smaller Moi International Airport, Mombasa. Carriers from Europe, America, Asia and within Africa all offer scheduled services to Nairobi. Check with your travel agent for details. Standard amenities are available in JKA, including a 24-hour bank, a post office, shops, cafés, restaurants and bars. Porters and handcarts are provided to help with luggage. Taxis are the main form of transport from the airport to the city centre. Pay about Ksh 250. If you are part of a group tour, they should provide a minibus with driver; alternatively one can always hire a self drive vehicle from the major car hire companies at one of the desks in the arrival hall.

BY RAIL

Mombasa is mainly a cargo and military port and there is an outside possibility that one could obtain a berth on a cargo ship from a European port. Another option is a stop-over in Mombasa as part of a luxury liner trip (*Cunard/Ellerman*). These normally include short safaris around the country if desired by passengers. Recently the *Virgin Butterfly*, a hydrofoil speed boat, has started a service between Mombasa, Dar es Salaam and Zanzibar.

BY ROAD

Overland trips are usually arduous and time consuming, especially if one is undertaking it on an individual basis. Some tour companies offer exotic trips—check the advertisements in international newspapers. One company, *Siafu*, has offices in Nairobi and London. To do it yourself you would need four wheel drive vehicles equipped for extensive travelling across desert terrain. Also, consult with the embassies of countries through which you intend to travel. Minimum required documentation includes International Driving Licence, International Certificate of Insurance and International Touring documents—Carnet de Passage and Triptique.

The Automobile Association (AA) in London has up-to-date information on self-drive trips throughout Africa.

TRAVEL ESSENTIALS

VISAS & PASSPORTS

All visitors must have a valid passport. Visas are required by everyone, except for the citizens of most commonwealth countries, and some other countries with which Kenya has reciprocal waiver agreements. The commonwealth exceptions are Australia, Nigeria and Sri Lanka. Indian, Bangladeshi and Pakistani citizens also require visas. At present, visas can be obtained at the port of entry, for a fee of about US$10, or the equivalent in convertible currency. A "Visitors Pass" is stamped in your passport upon arrival. This is usually valid for one month, extendable to three months at Department of Immigration offices in Nairobi, Kisumu and Mombasa. Officials will want to see a return ticket.

MONEY MATTERS

On arrival, a currency declaration form is issued, upon which all imports of foreign cash or travellers' cheques should be recorded. All encashments should be recorded on this form by authorised dealers only (banks, bureaux de change and most major hotels). Exchange rates fluctuate. On departure, Kenyan shillings held by visitors must be converted back, or given away. No Kenyan money may be exported from the country. The Kenya shilling is not a convertible currency. Destruction of Kenyan money is an offence.

Kenyan currency is based on the decimal system, with 100 cents to 1 shilling. Copper coins are 5 and 10 cents; silver coins are 50 cents, 1 and 5 shillings. Notes are 10, 20, 50, 100, 200 and 500 shillings. Major credit cards (*American Express, Diners, Visa*) are accepted in some establishments throughout the country.

HEALTH

Malaria is endemic in Kenya below altitudes of 1,830 metres (6,000 feet). Start taking malaria prophylactics two weeks before you enter Kenya; continue taking them during your stay and for one month after you return home.

Inoculations against yellow fever and cholera are not mandatory unless you are arriving from the Far East, Central America, South, Central and West Africa.

AIDS is a problem in East Africa and the rule of thumb on prostitutes is look and dance, but don't touch. Blood is screened for AIDS at Nairobi Hospital. In an emergency where blood donations are needed, contact your embassy or high commission.

Swimming in slow-flowing or still rivers or lakes can result in bilharzia (*Schistosomiasis*)—an unpleasant disease that resides in river snails. In the sea, swimmers are protected from large marine predators by a barrier reef. There are the usual coastal hazards, however, including sea urchins, fire coral, and the occasional poisonous fish or ray. Wear tennis shoes if walking around rock pools.

The sun is directly overhead, and a silent danger to all unwary tourists. Tropical sunburn is painful and dangerous, so avoid it: exposure must be gradual, mornings and afternoons only until the skin tans. Use sunblock creams, and make children wear T-shirts.

Above 1,525 metres (5,000 feet) visitors may feel lightheaded or tired but one soon gets used to it. When climbing above 3,463 metres (13,000 feet) watch out for altitude sickness (*pulmonary oedema*) which can kill if the afflicted person is not taken down immediately.

In rural areas boil all water before drinking. Water in Nairobi is safe to drink but most hotels and restaurants now serve bottled water.

Medical insurance is available locally, there are plenty of doctors in town, and the *Flying Doctor* will rescue stomped or mauled tourists from the wildest areas.

WHAT TO WEAR

As a rule, clothing should be loose, comfortable and casual. In Nairobi and further upcountry it can get cold at night so a sweater or jacket is necessary. Safari clothing can be easily and economically bought in Nairobi. Drip dry clothes are convenient and dry fast. *Khangas* and *kikoys* (brightly coloured, patterned sarongs) are useful as beachwear, pyjamas or wraparound skirt. *Bata* safari boots are cheap and durable footwear.

If your visit falls in the rainy season, buy an umbrella in Nairobi.

CUSTOMS

A reasonable amount of personal effects, including cameras and film can be imported duty free. A deposit (foreign currency, refundable) may be required for radios, tape recorders, video or movie equipment and computers. Duty free allowances are 200 cigarettes or 50 cigars, one litre of spirits and a quarter of a litre of perfume. Banned imports include agricultural or horticultural produce, pets, game trophies, pornographic literature and illegal drugs.

ON DEPARTURE

Arrive at the airport two hours before your flight leaves. Upon checking in, an *Airport Passenger Service Charge* (departure tax) of US$20 (or other convertible currency) is levied. On domestic flights, Ksh 50 must be paid before boarding. After checking in, identify your bags for customs, and give them your currency form. Prior to boarding the aircraft there are normal passport, ticket and security checks.

GETTING ACQUAINTED

GOVERNMENT & ECONOMY

Executive power is held by the President, Daniel arap Moi, who is aided by his vice president and cabinet chosen from the National Assembly (parliament). This legislature consists of 158 publicly elected members, 12 presidential nominees, the Attorney General and the Speaker. There is one political party, the Kenya African National Union (KANU) but governmental processes are fundamentally democratic. Kenya obtained independence in 1963, and is part of the Organisation for African Unity (OAU), the Commonwealth and the United Nations.

Kenya is one of the more prosperous countries in black Africa, due to a good record of sound governing and stable politics. Kenya's primary exports are coffee and tea. Other exports include pineapples, string beans, pyrethrum and other cash crops.

Tourism is another primary source of foreign exchange. Kenya is also regarded as the regional (East Africa) centre for financial and commercial activities.

GEOGRAPHY AND POPULATION

One can find the entire spectrum of geographical features in Kenya, from sea level to 5,200 metres (17,000 feet). Beaches, desert, forest, savannah and snow are all present, with accompanying fauna.

The population is another cross section of cultures, including about 18 million Africans (of all tribes), 200,000 Asians, 65,000 Europeans and 42,000 Arabs.

TIME & CLIMATE

Three hours ahead of GMT.

Temperatures vary according to altitude and situation. The coastal and lake areas are humid; average annual high and low daytime temperatures range from 22C to 30C (72F to 87F). Usually a fresh breeze blows from the ocean. The plateau and Nairobi, at an altitude of 1,675 metres (5,500 feet) are cool in the mornings and evenings with constant winds in the dry seasons (January to March and June to October). Average annual high and low temperatures are 10C to 26C (50F to 79F).

CULTURE AND CUSTOMS

Common sense, tact and politeness, regardless of situation, should be applied across the board. A few guidelines: show respect for authority, primarily the president, members of parliament, judges, the police force and army. Do not take photos of military installations or government figures or indeed of any person without their consent. Usually a fee will be demanded, between Ksh 15 Ksh 20 is standard.

Never destroy or deface money, the flag or any picture of the president—offences punishable by jail.

Black market vultures lurk on street corners, approaching the innocent tourist with fantastic exchange rates. Dealings with these people may well lead to jail, or deportation, or both.

Prostitution is rife, and primary concern should be the risk of disease. AIDS is a growing problem in Kenya as in the rest of the world.

The authorities take a hard line with drugs, and can make life very uncomfortable for anybody caught taking them into or out of the country.

Nudity is illegal. Skimpy clothing may be frowned upon by the locals in rural and Muslim coastal areas. To call a waiter use the word *bwana* which means "mister".

WEIGHTS AND MEASURES

Metric is used throughout the country—weights are measured in kilograms (one kilogram = 2.205 pounds); distances are in kilometres (one kilometre = 0.6214 miles); and liquids are measured in litres (one litre = 1.76 pints).

ELECTRICITY

Kenya uses a 240 volts, 50 hertz supply. If you want to use appliances that run on 110 volts, bring a converter. Plugs are three pin, square peg (as in Britain).

BUSINESS HOURS

These vary, according to the store. Generally stores are open from 0900hrs to 1730hrs, with at break for lunch between 1300 hrs and 1400 hrs. Some stores are open till evening, and over the weekends. In Mombasa trade begins earlier, from 0700 hrs to 1230 hrs, and then a siesta till 1500 hrs or 1600 hrs to avoid the heat. They reopen until about 2000 hrs. Bargaining takes place in markets and small stores, especially in Mombasa.

Most banks offer a currency exchange facility, and they are open on weekdays from 0900 hrs to 1400 hrs. Some are open in the morning on the first and last Saturdays of each month. At JKA there are 24-hour branches for visitors. Banking can be a lengthy process, so be patient. Remember to have your currency declaration form stamped at each place where you cash travellers' cheques or change money.

RELIGIOUS SERVICES

Whatever your religious inclination, Kenya will probably have a representative church, chapel, mosque, synagogue or temple. Freedom of worship is taken seriously, and missionaries abound. For services check the daily papers.

TIPPING

Tips are usually ten percent of the bill, unless a service charge and training levy has already been added, in which case tip the waiter at your discretion. Porters expect Ksh 2 to Ksh 5 per bag. Pay tour drivers according to how helpful and courteous they are, up to Ksh 20 per passenger per day.

LANGUAGE

English is understood by many people in up-country Kenya, but not so much at the coast which is predominantly Muslim, speaking the Afro-Arab-Indian mix *Swahili*. It's not a difficult language and it's worth learning a few words.

English is taught in schools all over the country, so there is always someone who will understand what you're taking about, even in the remote bush. At the coast, more locals are responding to the European continental tourist invasion and speak German, French and Italian.

A few useful Swahili words and phrases are as follows:

Hello ....*Jambo*
How are you? ....*Habari?*
I am well (good, fine, etc.) ....*Mzuri*
Thank you (very much) ....*Asante (sana)*
Goodbye ....*Kwaheri*
Hotel ....*Hoteli*
Room ....*Chumba*
Bed ....*Kitanda*

Food ....*Chakula*
Coffee ....*Kahawa*
Beer ....*Tembo (or Pombe)*
Cold ....*Baridi*
Hot ....*Moto*
Tea ....*Chai*
Meat ....*Nyama*
Fish ....*Samaki*
Bread ....*Mkate*
Butter...*Siagi*
Sugar ....*Sukari*
Salt ....*Chumvi*
Bad ....*Mbaya*
Today..*Leo*
Tomorrow ....*Kesho*
Now ....*Sasa*
Quickly ....*Haraka*
Slowly
........*Pole-pole* (Pronounced pol-i…pol-i)
Hospital ....*Hospitali*
Police ....*Polici*
Where is the Hotel? ....*Hoteli iko wapi?*
Where does this road lead to?
.............................*Njia hii ina-enda wapi?*
Please help me push this car
.............*Tafadhali nisaidie kusukuma gari*
Please change this wheel
..........*Tafadhali badilisha gurudumu hili*
Good morning ....*Habari ya asubuhi*
Good afternoon ....*Habari ya mehana*
Good evening ....*Habari ya jioni*
Please come in ......*Karibu ndani tafadhali*
Please sit down ....*Keti tafadhali*
You're welcome ....*Una karibishwa*
Where do you come from?
.............................*Ume kuja kutoka wapi?*
I come from ....*Nime toka*
What is your name? ....*Jina lako nani?*
My name is ....*Jina langu ni…*
Can you speak Swahili?
.....................*Waweza kuongea kiswahili?*
Yes ....*Ndiyo*
No ....*Hapana*
Only a little ....*Kidogo tu*
I want to learn more
.............................*Nataka kujifunza zaidi*
How do you find Kenya?
....*Waonaje Kenya?*
I like it here ....*Hapa napenda*

Where are you going ..*Una kwenda wapi?*
I am going to ....*Nak wenda*
Turn right ....*Geuka kulia*
Turn left ....*Geuka kushoto*
Go straight.................*Enda moja kwa moja*
Please stop here ....*Simama hapa tafadhali*
How much?.................................*Ngapi?*
Wait a minute ....*Ngoja kidogo*
I have to get change
......................*Ni badilishe pesa kwanza*
Excuse me ....*Samahani*
Where is the toilet? ....*Wapi choo?*
In the back ....*Upande wa nyuma*
Where may I get something to drink?
.................*Naweza kupata wapi kinywaji?*
One cup of coffee
...................*Kikombe kimoja cha kahawa*
How much does this cost?
...........................*Inagharimu pesa ngapi?*
That's quite expensive
...................................*Waweza kupunguz?*
Fine ....*Sawa*
I will buy it ....*Nita nunua*

More Words

Mr ....*Bwana*
Mrs ....*Bibi*
Miss ....*Bi*
I ....*Mimi*
You ....*Wewe*
He, She ....*Yeye*
We ....*Sisi*
They ....*Wao*
What? ....*Nini?*
Who? ....*Nani?*
Where? (Place) ....*Mahali gani?*
Where? (Direction)
................................*Wapi (Upande gani?)*
When? ....*Hini?*
How ....*Vipi*
Why?...*Kwanini?*
Which? ....*Ipi? (gani)*
To eat ....*Kukula*
To drink ....*Kukunywa*
To sleep ....*Kulala*
To bathe ....*Kuoga*
To come ....*Ijayo*
To go..*Ku-enda*
To stop ....*Kusimama*
To buy ....*Kununua*

To sell	*Kuuza*
Street/road	*Barabara*
Airport	*Uwanja wa Ndege*
Shop	*Duka*
Money	*Fedha*
Cent	*Senti*
One	*Moja*
Two	*Mbili*
Three	*Tatu*
Four	*Ine*
Five	*Tano*
Six	*Sita*
Seven	*Saba*
Eight	*Nane*
Nine	*Tisa*
Ten	*Kumi*
Eleven	*Kumi na moja*
Twelve	*Kumi na mbili*
Thirteen	*Kumi na tatu*
Twenty	*Ishirini*
Twenty-one	*Ishirini na moja*
Twenty-two	*Ishirini na mbili*
Twenty-three	*Ishirini na tatu*
Thirty	*Thelathini*
Forty	*Arobaini*
Fifty	*Hamsini*
One hundred	*Mia moja*
One thousand	*Elfu moja*

COMMUNICATIONS

MEDIA

Radio and television are both operated by the government. There is one English radio station, maintained by the Voice of Kenya (VOK). The one television station is mixed Swahili/English, starts at 1700 hrs and ends at 2330 hrs, with news and shows in both languages.

There are three English newspapers; the *Standard*, the *Nation*, and the *Kenya Times*. Many foreign newspapers are also available, a day or so late including local and international weekly and monthly newsmagazines. The *Weekly Review*, printed on Fridays, is recommended.

POSTAL SERVICES

There is a post office in most major shopping centres in Nairobi, and the system is efficient. Mail can also be sent from major hotels. International and local speedpost and parcel services are offered by several independent operators.

Poste Restante is free: the main pick up point is the Central Post Office, Haile Selassie Avenue. Telegrams can be sent by phone; call the operator (900) to ask for help.

TELEPHONE AND TELEX

International and local calls can be made with ease (direct dial or operator assisted). Payphones are plentiful, and cardphones (for international calls) are starting to come into vogue.

Internal and external direct dial telex and fax facilities are also available. Check with your hotel on the nearest location.

EMERGENCIES

SECURITY AND CRIME

Kenya is quite a secure place, despite the numerous legends about tourists getting eaten (either by wildlife or locals), knifed or generally assaulted. Bag snatching and mugging occasionally take place, but shout "thief" (*mwizi*) and if there are any people around they will descend upon the hapless miscreant, and mete out swift and severe punishment—mob justice. Violent crime rarely involves tourists, but in a threatening situation do what you are told, and remain quiet and calm. Do not walk about at night through dark areas of town, or on deserted beaches. Always lock your car, and hide valuables in the boot, or better still, in the hotel safe. Dial 999 for police.

PHARMACIES

There are plenty of chemists in Kenya, with well stocked drug stores. If you cannot get your exact prescription filled, there is usually an alternative drug. The best policy is to bring enough special medication to cover the duration of your visit. Chemists are closed on Saturday afternoons, Sundays and public holidays. During these times the name of the duty chemist is usually posted on drug store doors, or can be found in the newspapers.

THINGS TO DO

GETTING AROUND

TRAVEL PACKAGES

There are many tour operators in Kenya that offer safaris ranging from day trips to two-week excursions. Some of the more extensive tours can be booked through travel agents abroad, and most (except for the extremely exclusive) can be booked in Nairobi. Minibus tours are most common, economical, and they cover most of Kenya. However, for more remote areas four wheel drive trucks are laid on and light aircraft can be chartered to anywhere. Tour information can be found at any travel agent or hotel, but shop around for a specific preference, because the selection is wide.

DOMESTIC TRAVEL

AIR

Kenya Airways, the international airline, provides domestic services to and from Nairobi, Mombasa, Malindi and Kisumu. There are also a number of smaller private companies (including Air Kenya) which are based at Wilson Airport, Nairobi. These offer regular charter services to the Maasai Mara, Samburu and Lamu. Ring *Africair* at 501210 for further information and to rent planes.

RAIL

Kenya Railways operate sleeper trains from Nairobi to Mombasa and Kisumu. (Tel: 21211 ext. 2700-2 for information)

PUBLIC TRANSPORT

Privately-owned *matatus*(the alternative to buses) can be anything from a Peugeot saloon to an Isuzu bus. Minibuses have become very popular. *Matatus* are usually more frequent, faster, fuller and dearer than the buses. The national bus company, Kenya Bus Service (KBS), is very cheap, and covers an extensive network. KBS headquarters are located around the junction between Accra and River roads. Their buses are always packed with commuters morning and evening. Private long haul bus companies serve most towns in Kenya.

PRIVATE TRANSPORT

One can rent self or chauffeur driven cars from a number of local and international car-hire firms. (Hertz, Avis etc.)

Drive on the left. Get your national drivers' licence endorsed at Nyayo House. Some rural roads are bad (muddy when wet), and one might meet the occasional reckless driver, but locals are willing to help lost tourists. When travelling out of town, always take a spare tyre, some tools, spare petrol and water. If one is going a long way into the bush, serious planning is required. A local guide (check tour companies), at least two vehicles and numerous extra supplies are strongly recommended.

WHERE TO STAY

HOTELS AND LODGINGS

Many internationally famous hotels and lodgings are located in Nairobi and Mombasa. Standards are world-class. Throughout Kenya all forms of good to excellent lodging are available. Consult a tour operator or *What's On*, a weekly guide available at newsstands, for listings.

Nairobi

Hilton International has high standards of accommodation and service. P.O. Box 30624, Nairobi.

Hotel Inter-Continental is located in the city centre and is large and brightly decorated. P.O. Box 30667, Nairobi.

Safari Park Hotel is situated out of town along the road to Thika and incorporates a Korean-run restaurant. P.O. Box 45038, Nairobi.

Norfolk Hotel is perhaps the most famous hotel in Nairobi and a favourite lunchtime spot for resident Kenyans. P.O. Box 31067, Nairobi.

New Stanley Hotel has the most popular meeting spot in Kenya at the Thorn Tree Café and is located in the heart of the city. P.O. Box 30687, Nairobi.

Mount Kenya Safari Club is very exclusive and is managed by Inter-Continental. Only suites are available. P.O. Box 43564, Nairobi.

Pan-Afric Hotel provides full amenties and services and is located slightly out of town, on the top of a hill. P.O. Box 30486, Nairobi.

Six-Eighty Hotel is located in the city centre. P.O. Box 43436, Nairobi.

Meridian Hotel is a family style hotel. P.O. Box 14175, Nairobi.

Boulevard Hotel is situated just beyond the Norfolk and is a smallish garden hotel. P.O. Box 42831, Nairobi.

Millimani Hotel is just outside the city centre and is modestly located in a garden setting. P.O. Box 30715, Nairobi.

Fairview Hotel is long-established and was renovated in 1989. P.O. Box 40482, Nairobi.

The coast

Sinbad Hotel. P.O. Box 30, Malindi.

Watuma Beach Hotel. P.O. Box 300, Malindi.

Suli Suli Inn. P.O. Box 648, Malindi.

Blue Marlin Hotel. P.O. Box 20, Malindi.

Eden Roc Hotel. P.O. Box 350, Malindi.

Lawfords Hotel. P.O. Box 20, Malindi.

Turtle Bay Beach Hotel. P.O. Box 457, Malindi.

Seafarers Hotel. P.O. Box 182, Malindi.

Peponi Hotel. P.O. Box 24, Lamu.

Oceanic Hotel. P.O. Box 90371, Mombasa.

Up-country

Mount Kenya Safari Club. P.O. Box 35, Nanyuki.

Siriwaka Hotel. P.O. Box 3361, Eldoret.

Sunset Hotel. P.O. Box , Kisumu.

Outspan Hotel. P.O. Box 24, Nyeri.

Aberdare Country Club. P.O. Box 449, Nyeri.

Golf Hotel. P.O. Box 118, Kakamega.

Tea Hotel. P.O. Box 75, Kericho.

Lake Naivasha Hotel. P.O. Box 15, Naivasha.

Safariland Club. P.O. Box 72, Naivasha.

Lake Baringo Club. P.O. Box 47557, Nairobi.

GAME LODGES

Amboseli National Park

Amboseli Serena Lodge. P.O. Box 48690, Nairobi.

Kilimanjaro Buffalo Lodge. P.O. Box 72630, Nairobi.

Amboseli New Lodge. P.O. Box 30139, Nairobi.

Kilimanjaro Safari Lodge. P.O. Box 30139, Nairobi.

Maasai Mara

Keekorok Lodge. P.O. Box 40075, Nairobi.

Mara Serena Lodge. P.O. Box 48690, Nairobi.

Tsavo West

Kilanguni Lodge. P.O. Box 30471, Nairobi.

Ngulia Safari Lodge. P.O. Box 30471, Nairobi.

Taita Hills Lodge. P.O. Box Durai via Voi.

Salt Lake Lodge. P.O. Box Durai via Voi.

Tsavo East

Voi Safari Lodge. P.O. Box Voi, Tsavo East.

Samburu Game Reserve

Samburu Game Lodge. P.O. Box 40075, Nairobi.

Mount Kenya Game Park

Mountain Lodge (Nyeri). P.O. Box 30471, Nairobi.

Aberdare National Park

Treetops (Nyeri). P.O. Box 40075, Nairobi.

The Ark. P.O. Box 449, Nyeri.

Meru National Park

Meru Mulika Lodge. P.O. Box 484, Meru.

Lake Nakuru

Lake Nakuru Lodge. P.O. Box 561, Nakuru.

Naro Moru River Lodge. Located between Nyeri and Nanyuki. P.O. Box 16, Nyeri.

Maralal

Maralal Safari Lodge. P.O. Box 70, Maralal.

TENTED CAMPS

Buffalo Springs

Buffalo Springs Lodge. P.O. Box 71, Isiolo.

Maasai Mara

Governor's Camp. P.O. Box 48217, Nairobi.

Kichwa Tembo. P.O. Box 59470, Nairobi.

Fig Tree Camp. P.O. Box 40414, Nairobi.

Mara Buffalo Camp. P.O. Box 45655, Nairobi.

Little Governor's Camp. P.O. Box 48217, Nairobi.

Tsavo East

Tsavo Safari Camp. P.O. Box 48059, Nairobi.

Crocodile Tented Camp. P.O. Box 510, Malindi.

Lake Baringo

Island Camp. P.O. Box 42475, Nairobi.

Lake Naivasha

Fisherman's Camp. P.O. Box 14982, Naivasha.

Lake Nakuru

Lion Hill Camp. P.O. Box 7094, Nakuru.

TOUR OPERATORS

Further information on accommodation and safaris throughout Kenya can be found at the following specialist travel companies.

Let's Go Travel. P.O. Box 60342, Nairobi. Tel: 29539.

Abercrombie and Kent Ltd. P.O. Box 59749, Nairobi. Tel: 334955.

Bunson Travel Service. P.O. Box 45456, Nairobi. Tel: 21992/337604/337605.

Ker and Downey Safaris Ltd. P.O. Box 41822, Nairobi. Tel: 556466/556164/553222.

Kenya Tourist Development Corporation. P.O. Box 42013, Nairobi. Tel: 29751.

FOOD DIGEST

CULTURE PLUS

WHERE TO EAT

Throughout Kenya restaurants of all nationalities are found. Dining out guides are available at bookstores. In general, food is of excellent quality and very reasonably priced.

Wines and spirits are imported and therefore cost their European equivalent in Kenya shillings.

MUSEUMS

Visit the National Museum of Kenya: it has some excellent displays of stuffed animals and tribal artifacts. Next to it is the snake park where the inhabitants are very much alive, from cobras to crocodiles.

ART GALLERIES

Indigenous art is flourishing in Kenya, and there is a different exhibition every week. Try Gallery Watatu, French Cultural Centre, African Heritage Ltd, and Paa-ya-Paa gallery for up and coming African art. There is also an art gallery at the National Museum which is reserved for East African artists only.

THEATRES

The National Theatre, Phoenix Players, Braeburn Theatre and French Cultural Centre all offer classical, traditional and contemporary stage productions of a high standard.

MOVIES

There are about 10 movie theatres in Nairobi: the Nairobi, Kenya and 20th Century offer the best facilities and newest movies. Check newspapers for listings.

MUSIC

Check the entertainments page of the daily newspapers. Otherwise the Carnivore offers live band entertainment, and the International Casino complex is a good place to eat, drink, dance and gamble.

DIARY OF EVENTS

Hotels generally provide traditional dancing and other activities. Otherwise, visit the Bomas of Kenya—an interesting experience close to Nairobi. Check the entertainment page of daily newspapers or the *What's On* guide for information.

SHOPPING

Most towns offer the tourist something in the way of curios. Mostly, these consist of baskets, bracelets and other jewellery, wood and stone carvings, batiks and other fabrics. Argue, haggle, beg for discounts, threaten to walk away and use every other trick in the book to beat prices down. Tourists will be approached with "elephant hair" or "ivory" curios—usually fake, and definitely illegal. Do not buy ivory: Kenya's elephant population is being decimated by poachers.

There are a number of clothing shops near the large hotels; other non-souvenir items from batteries to brandy are available.

SPORTS

Check clubs (Impala, Nairobi, Parklands, Muthaiga) for most field and court activities. Horse racing takes place most Sundays at the Ngong Road racecourse. Deep sea fishing and other watersports can all be arranged through hotels at the coast. The Safari Rally takes place every Easter, and is internationally acknowledged as the most gruelling race of its kind.

SPORTS CLUBS

Temporary memberships are offered to visitors in most sports clubs around Kenya. Listed below are some of these clubs and the sporting activities you may find there. To avoid a wasted trip it's advisable to telephone the clubs concenrned to confirm the availability of the squash or tennis courts, golf course, etc.

Impala Club: Ngong Road, P.O. Box 41516, Nairobi, Tel: 568573, (Tennis, Squash, Rugby, Football, Hockey, Cricket.)
Nairobi Club: Ngong Road, P.O. Box 30171, Nairobi, Tel: 336996. (Squash, Tennis, Cricket, Hockey, Bowls, Basketball.)
Parklands Sports Club: Ojijo Road, P.O. Box 40116, Nairobi, Tel: 742829. (Tennis, Squash, Rugby, Hockey, Cricket, Snooker.)

Golf Clubs
Karen Golf Club: Tel: 88405.
Muthaiga Golf Club: Tel: 27333.
Royal Nairobi Golf Club: Tel: 27332.
Sigona Golf: Tel: Kikuyu 2152.
All the clubs have 18-hole courses.

Sailing
Nairobi Sailing Club: Nairobi Dam, P.O. Box 49973, Tel: 501250.

Mountaineering/Caving
Mountain Club of Kenya: P.O. Box 45741, Nairobi. Tel: 501747.
Cave Exploration Group of East Africa: P.O. Box 47583, Nairobi. Members of both the clubs meet every Tuesday after 7.30 pm at the Mountain Club of Kenya clubhouse. Wilson Airport, Tel: 501747.

Horse Racing
Jockey Club of Kenya: P.O. Box 40373, Nairobi, Tel: 566109. Racing most Sundays (check with the newspapers). First race at 2.15 pm. Admission, Adults shs 30. Children shs 5. Silver ring free.

Chess
Nairobi Chess Club: P.O. Box 50443, Nairobi, Tel: 25007.

Lions Clubs
Mombasa (Central). P.O. Box 82569, Mombasa, Tel: See 25061.
Mombasa (Pwani). P.O. Box 81871, Mombasa, Tel: See 20731.
Nairobi (Host), P.O. Box 47447, Nairobi, Tel: See 742266.
Nairobi (Central), P.O. Box 44867, Nairobi, Tel 338901.
Nairobi (City), P.O. Box 30693, Nairobi, Tel: See 27354.
Nairobi (North), P.O. Box 42093, Nairobi, Tel: See 21251.
Nairobi (Westlands), P.O. Box 42539, Nairobi, Tel: See 556020.
Nairobi (Kikuyu), P.O. Box 47301, Nairobi, Tel: See 24023.
Lions International (District 411), P.O. Box 45652, Nairobi, Tel: See 331709.

Rotary Clubs
Eldoret, P.O. Box 220, Eldoret, Tel: See Eldoret 2936.
Kilindini, P.O. Box 99067, Mombasa, Tel: See 25157.

REEF HOTELS – KENYA

Relax around the sparkling freshwater pool. Learn to dive at the best equipped diving centre in Mombasa or windsurf in the dream waters of the beach. Other amenities include a well-equipped Fitness Centre with Sauna, Hair-dressing Salon, Masseur, Shops, two floodlit Tennis Courts and Conference Rooms for 30 to 120 people. Membership at a nearby Golf Course is also available. In the evenings, regular entertainment includes live tropical bands and traditional African Dance Shows. The Reef Hotel is also within 15 minutes of Mombasa Town, renowned for its bustling shopping centre and lively night life, casinos and cabaret shows.

THE REEF HOTEL Friendly service in a relaxed atmosphere.

Lagoon Reef's spectacular swimming pool has [been] especially designed to [cater] for all types of swimmers. [The] waters vary in level from [a few] inches to deep areas pe[rfect] for scuba-diving tuition [and] water polo. Other s[ports] activities on offer in[clude] windsurfing, aerobics, v[olley]ball, table-tennis and tw[o full] size tennis courts floo[dlit at] night.

Come to Lagoon Ree[f and] enter another world.

Shimoni Reef Lodge is the perfect place to unwind. Situated on an exotic and untamed headland – close to the Pemba Channel (famous for its rich variety of marine life) – and overlooking the Wassini Channel, Shimoni Reef Lodge is an ideal centre for diving, big game sea fishing, or relaxing in the sun.

Let Shimoni Reef cast its spell — you'll be enchanted forever.

REEF HOTEL: P.O.BOX 82234, MOMBASA TEL: (011) 471771 TLX: 21199 REEF KE FAX: (011) 471349
LAGOON REEF HOTEL: P.O.BOX 83058, MOMBASA TEL: (01261) 2627, 2213/6 TLX: 21316 LAGOON KE
SHIMONI REEF LODGE: P.O.BOX 82234, MOMBASA TEL: MSAMBWENI 5Y9 OR REEF HOTEL, MOMBASA
REEF HOTELS BOOKING OFFICE: P.O.BOX 61408, NAIROBI TEL: 728622 TLX: 25679 REHTLS KE FAX: (02) 332702

Mombasa, P.O. Box 90570, Mombasa, Tel: See 25924.

Nairobi, Tel: See 742269.

Nairobi North, c/o P.O. Box 30751, Nairobi, Tel: 21624

Nairobi South, c/o P.O. Box 46611, Tel: See 337041.

Rotary International (District 920), c/o P.O. Box 41910, Tel: D Gov 24128.

Others

Nairobi Photographic Society, P.O. Box 49879, Nairobi, Tel: 337129. Meetings are held at the St. John Ambulance Headquarters (behind Donovan Manle Theatre) at 8.30 pm on the first and third Thursdays of each month.

Mombasa Rowing Club: P.O. Box 82037, Mombasa, Club House at Ras Liwatoni next door to the Outrigger Hotel. Daily membership for tourists – Shs 10.

Kenya Divers Association, P.O. Box 95705, Mombasa, Tel: 471347.

The Aquarist Club of Kenya, P.O. Box 49931, Nairobi, Tel: (Nairobi) 25975 (day), 559281 or 746636 (evening). Meets at 10 am the second Sunday of every month in the Fairview Hotel. Visitors and prospective members welcome.

The Caledonian Society of Kenya. P.O. Box 40755, Nairobi, Tel: Sec 520400 (evenings).

American Women's Association: P.O. Box 47806, Nairobi, Tel: 65342 (Membership Chairman).

Nairobi Branch of the Royal Society of St. George, P.O. Box 48360, Nairobi, Tel: 891262.

Geological Club of Kenya, P.O. Box 44749, Nairobi.

Geographical Society of Kenya, P.O. Box 41887, Nairobi.

East African Wildlife Society, P.O. Box 20110, NBI, Hilton Hotel, Nairobi.

Wildlife Clubs of Kenya, National Museum, P.O. Box 40658, Nairobi.

African Cultural Society, P.O. Box 69484, Nairobi, Kenya, Tel: 335581 (Cultural Festivals Lectures and Theatre).

PHOTOGRAPHY

Film is easy to get, but expensive. Processing is fast, with good results. If there is no hurry, take your unprocessed films home, taking the usual precautions through airport X-ray security machines. Bring a telephoto lens for long distance wildlife shots. Panoramic views look best on wide angle lenses. 100/200 ASA film should cover most eventualities, but 1000 ASA is good for firelight or water hole scenes where a flash would not work. Mornings (until 1000 hrs) and afternoons (after 1500 hrs) are the best time to take pictures; the lack of shadows at midday flattens out pictures. Keep your camera protected against heat and dust, and do not leave it lying about or it will get stolen.

SPECIAL INFORMATION

East Africa has a number of non-governmental organisations which compliment official conservation efforts.

African Fund for Endangered Wildlife (AFEW)

Established in 1978 specifically to save the endangered Rothschild's giraffe, AFEW runs a Nature Education Centre on the property of the founders, Jock and Betty Leslie-Melville. Students feed giraffe, see wildlife films and take nature walks through the adjacent indigenous forest. It is a small family foundation that does much for Kenyan wildlife conservation. Address: P.O. Box 15004, Nairobi. Tel: 891658.

African Wildlife Foundation (AWF)

AWF was established in 1961 in Washington D.C., USA. It opened its African field office in Nairobi in 1963 to help develop and supervise worthy projects. The foundation supports a number of conservation and environmental education programmes and the development of protected area management, planning and operations. It helped launch, and continues to support, two wildlife colleges for African wildlife managers, in Tanzania and Cameroon.

Address: P.O. Box 48177, Nairobi. Tel: 23235.

Elsa Wild Animal Appeal (Elsa)

Formed by the late Joy Adamson. Elsa is funded by the generous donations of royalties from the films and works originating from Joy Adamson's books. The main policies of the trustees are conservation education, particularly among indigenous people in Africa, and assistance to the Kenya Government in retaining wildlife habitats. Elsa has developed a baby animal wildlife clinic at Nairobi National Park and a Conservation Centre at Elsamare on Lake Naivasha, where conservationists can stay at a reasonable cost. Address: P.O. Box 30092, Nairobi. Tel: 742121.

The David Sheldrick Memorial Appeal

This appeal was established in 1977 following the death of David Sheldrick, founder warden of Kenya's Tsavo National Park. David's closest friends form the advisory committee which governs policy and direction. The appeal has raised funds to support anti-poaching efforts, education and translocation of animals and has compiled a field manual, *The Wilderness Guardian*, which covers park development and wildlife management and conservation.

Address: P.O. Box 15555, Nairobi.

The East African Wild Life Society (EAWLS)

This is the oldest local organisation, founded in 1956 with a worldwide membership of 15,000. EAWLS publishes a popular bi-monthly magazine, *Swara*, and a scientific journal for its members.

Active in conservation education, research, anti-poaching, animal capture and relocation and wildlife policy formulation and facilitation. The society runs a shop and welcomes both members and donations.

Address: P.O. Box 20110, Nairobi. Tel: 27027, 337422/3, 331888.

Gallmann Memorial Foundation (GMF)

This foundation was set up by Kuki Gallmann in memory of her husband Paolo and son Emmanuel who were keen conservationists. It supports ecological, environmental and educational programmes on Ol Ari Nyiro Ranch in northern Kenya in addition to other projects in East Africa. Address: P.O. Box 45593, Nairobi.

Wildlife Conservation International

(WCI)

A division of the New York Zoological Society. Designs, funds and directs a wide range of projects.

Address: P.O. Box 48177, Nairobi. Tel: 21699.

Wildlife Clubs of Kenya

Founded in 1969 by a group of boys in a boarding school, WCK has since spread to schools countrywide and is the most grass-roots movement. Members organise trips, seminars, rallies and workshops. Its main objectives are to spread interest, awareness and knowledge about wildlife and the environment. Due to tremendous growth operations are now being decentralized. Address: P.O. Box 40658, Nairobi. Tel: 740811, 742564.

Worldwide Fund for Nature (WWF)

Founded in 1961, the regional office of WWF in Nairobi manages and develops projects throughout Africa. Address: P.O. Box 40075, Nairobi. Tel: 332963.

USEFUL ADDRESSES

TOURIST INFORMATION

Official Information Bureaux are situated in Kimathi Street (Tel: 23285) in Nairobi, and near the "tusks" on Moi Avenue in Mombasa. Otherwise, local tour companies are usually glad to help. Publications are plentiful—maps, guides and *What's On* pamphlets are available at most bookshops.

DIPLOMATIC MISSIONS

A complete list of all embassies, consulates and High Commissions in Kenya can be found in the complimentary monthly magazine *What's On*, available at hotels and tour companies throughout Nairobi.

every pocket. Public transport is cheap but normally very overcrowded. There are taxi services in most large towns but it is wise to agree upon a price before the trip. It is virtually impossible to hire a self-drive car, but chauffeur-driven vehicles are available.

If you bring your own car, you should note that driving is on the left, traffic signs are international but very sparse, and fuel is subject to occasional shortages so an ample reserve should be carried, especially if you are visiting remote areas.

GETTING THERE

BY AIR

The main international airports at Dar es Salaam, Kilimanjaro and Zanzibar are served by several international airlines. The national airline, *Air Tanzania*, covers domestic flights to all major cities and there are very few domestic air charter companies which can fly small groups to more remote locations.

BY RAIL

There are three main routes: the Central Line, from Dar es Salaam via Dodoma and Tabora to Kigoma, with a side branch from Tabora to Mwanza; the Tanga line, from Tanga to Moshi and Arusha; and the Tanzam or Uhuru line, from Dar to the Zambian border. Sleeping accommodation is available but should be booked well in advance. All services are generally slow and crowded.

BY ROAD

Very few roads are surfaced although a determined effort is being made to upgrade the major routes. You can expect to experience a wide range of conditions, even on a short journey.

Most visitors arrange their travel with one of the many tour operators based in Arusha or Dar es Salaam, who offer safaris to suit

TRAVEL ESSENTIALS

VISAS & PASSPORTS

Visas must be obtained in advance by all visitors except citizens of Britain and the Commonwealth and the Scandinavian countries. Entry is prohibited to residents and nationals of South Africa and to anyone with a South African stamp in their passport.

Visitors, particularly those entering Tanzania by air, are required to change US $50 per head into local currency on arrival. Although it is theoretically possible to change unspent Tanzania shillings back to your own currency on departure, in practice there is seldom the opportunity to do so. Unless entering the country at an airport with a bank on the premises, it is usually easier to change money at hotels with exchange facilities than at one of the crowded banks.

A departure tax is levied on all passengers embarking on any international or domestic flight at any airport in Tanzania.

HEALTH

Visit Tanzania in good health. Hospitals and doctors are few and far between. Check with your doctor for any vaccinations you might need. Yellow fever and cholera are officially required: many visitors also get vaccinated against tetanus, polio, and typhoid. A gamma-globulin shot gives some protection against infectious hepatitis. You should come with malarial prophylaxis and any medications that you need or habitually use.

Many travellers who come with a safari company will have taken out temporary memberships with the Flying Doctors. Check with your travel agent or write for your own membership: Flying Doctor Service, c/o Kilimanjaro Christian Medical Centre (KCMC), P.O. Box 3010, Moshi, Tanzania.

WHAT TO WEAR

Light cotton clothing is the best for all conditions; trousers and shorts, skirts and open necked shirts. A sweater or jacket is useful, particularly in the highlands and during the cold season from June to August. A waterproof jacket is good for protection from rain, wind and sun.

On the coast and in other Muslim areas "revealing" outfits such as swimsuits or short skirts and shorts should not be worn in public places. However, locally made cotton cloths are very useful to buy to wear as a wraparound, for a shawl, extra towel or seat cover etc: *Kangas* are patterned clothes with a rectangular border and are usually sold in pairs; continuously patterned cloth without a border is called *kitenge*: the heavier, tasselled *kikoi* is usually worn by men. Hats, sunglasses and sun block creams are essential. Insect repellents are necessary practically everywhere against mosquitoes, tsetse flies, nuisance flies, midges, fleas or ticks. Repellents with 100 percent "deet" (diethyltoluamide) are the most effective (*Jungle Formula*).

Bring a torch with spare batteries and a water bottle with a cup top. Water sterilization tablets are also useful but remember that food is more likely to have bacteria new to you in troublesome quantities: any new diet is likely to bother visitors in any country so be careful in choosing foods. It is often best to stick to light, non-greasy dishes.

GETTING ACQUAINTED

CLIMATE

The rainy season is generally from November to May. During these months the days are warm and it can be very humid, especially on the coast. The coming of the rains brings not only changes in vegetation and migratory patterns of wildlife, but can affect the roads too.

The short rains in November and December help to settle the dust. In many places facing the Indian Ocean, the rains slow or cease for a period during January and February. At this time the air is especially clear, views magnificent and it's a good time for climbing mountains. The longer heavier period of rains is usually from March to May when some lowlying or poorly maintained roads become impassable.

Most of Tanzania is high plateau country, above 1,000 metres (3,940 feet), which means cool nights and pleasant-to-warm days. The coastal strip is hot and humid, especially from December to March, while breezes and cooler weather make May to October rather more pleasant.

The higher mountains, such as Kilimanjaro and Ngorongoro, can be very cold in June and July, when rain ceases throughout the country and the grass is long. In August and September there is little rain but strong winds and fires make the air hazy.

At all times of the year, even during the rainy season, be prepared for dust. The fine dust around volcanoes is especially insidious and can affect binoculars, cameras and contact lenses in particular. Bring plenty of plastic bags and fluids for protection.

LANGUAGE

Swahili is spoken throughout Tanzania. It is basically a *Bantu* language with a large component of Arabic words. Nowadays many English words have been assimilated though the spelling has changed, such as *sharti* meaning "shirt" or *Kekei* which is "cake".

WHERE TO STAY

LODGES & HOTELS

Lodges and hotels offering services of a high standard or expressly for visitors are available in many wildlife areas. In addition there are many local hotels and inns that cater to residents and non-residents alike and are generally less expensive. Prices fluctuate greatly and there is often an extra charge for service (usually 5 percent), a government hotel levy (12 percent to 17 percent) and a sales tax on all bills.

Dar es Salaam
Kilimanjaro Hotel, is large with a swimming pool and overlooks the harbour. P.O. Box 9574, Dar es Salaam. Tel: 21281.

Motel Agip is located near the centre of town. P.O. Box 529, Dar es Salaam. Tel: 23511.

Oysterbay Hotel is located to the north of the city on the beach front. It has a pleasant, relaxed atmosphere. P.O. Box 2261, Dar es Salaam. Tel: 68631.

Beach hotels near Dar es Salaam
Bahari Beach Hotel is a large African-style village. P.O. Box 9313, Dar es Salaam. Tel: 47261.

Kunduchi Beach Hotel is in the style of an Arab palace. P.O. Box 9313, Dar es Salaam. Tel: 47101/2.

Arusha Town
Mount Meru Hotel is big, modern and has many facilities. P.O. Box 817, Arusha. Tel: 2712/13.

Mount Meru Game Lodge is small with a charming atmosphere and is adjacent to the game sanctuary. P.O. Box 427 Arusha. Tel: Usa River 43 or contact Abercrombie & Kent office: Arusha 7803.

Ngare Sero Lodge is small in exceptionally lovely grounds with natural forest and springs. P.O. Box 425 Arusha. Tel: Arusha 3629.

Momela Lodge has bungalows or rondavels and is just outside the park. P.O. Box 418, Arusha. Tel: Arusha 3038.

Gombe National Park
Campsites and a rest house; arrange through TANAPA.

Mahale National Park
Campsites can be arranged through TANAPA. Before or after visiting these parks you may have to stay in Kigoma.

Kigoma
New Kigoma Railway Hotel, Private Bag, Kigoma. Tel: Kigoma 64.

Kilimanjaro National Park
Kibo Hotel is located on the slopes below the park gate and is very spacious. Climbs can be arranged through reception. P.O. Box 102 Marangu. Tel: 4.

Marangu Hotel has lovely gardens and climbs can be arranged through reception. P.O. Box 40 Marangu. Tel: 11.

Climbing Kilimanjaro requires booking huts either through the hotels above (or in Moshi town), or directly through TANAPA which also has two comfortable hostels at the Marangu Entry Gate.

Lake Manyara
Lake Manyara Hotel is large and dramatically set on the edge of the rift. P.O. Box 1369 Arusha. Tel: 3300.

If you would like to rent *bandas* in a lovely forest setting before the park entrance, contact TANAPA.

There are several campsites and a hostel which can be arranged through TANAPA.

Gibbs Farm (Ngorongoro Safari Lodge) is less than an hour's drive from Manyara at the edge of the forest above Karatu town. It is charming with lovely grounds. P. O. Box 1501 Karatu. Tel: Karatu 25.

Mikumi National Park
Mikumi Wildlife Lodge is located in the centre of the park and is built around a water hole. P.O. Box 2485 Dar es Salaam. Tel: 23491.

Mikumi Wildlife Camp is informal but comfortable. P.O. Box 1097 Dar es Salaam. Tel: 68631.

Ngorongoro Conservation Area
Ngorongoro Crater Lodge is rustic, comfortable and perched on the crater rim. P.O. Box 751 Arusha. Tel: 3530.

Ngorongoro Wildlife Lodge is large, scenic and hangs over the edge of the crater. P.O. Box 1369 Arusha. Tel: 3300.

Ngorongoro Rhino Lodge is situated in the forest and is run by the Conservation Authority. It has an informal atmosphere. P.O. Box 1 Ngorongoro or NCAA.

Camping is permitted in the Conservation Area: contact NCAA.

Ndutu Safari Lodge is simple but comfortable located on the Serengeti plains at the western end of Olduvai Gorge. P.O. Box 1501 Karatu.

Gibbs Farm (Ngorongoro Safari Lodge) is outside the NCA but at the edge of the forest above Karatu town. It is charming with lovely grounds. P.O. Box 1501, Karatu. Tel: 25.

Selous Game Reserve
Mbuyu Safari Camp is located on the Rufiji River and provides luxurious tents. It was named after the giant baobabs all round. P.O. Box 5350, Dar es Salaam. Tel: 31597.

Stiegler's Gorge Camp overlooks the gorge, and has charming chalets. P.O. Box 9320, Dar es Salaam. Tel: 48221.

Behobeho Safari Camp has *bandas* to rent which are situated on hill slopes with lovely views. P.O. Box 2261, Dar es Salaam. Tel: 68631.

Rufiji River Camp, with tents perched above the river, has great views. P. O. Box 20058, Dar es Salaam. Tel: 63546.

Serengeti National Park
Seronera Wildlife Lodge is large and dramatically set in a rock outcrop in the centre of the park. P.O. Box 1369, Arusha. Tel: 3300.

Lobo Wildlife Lodge is built into a *kopje* with lovely views of northern Serengeti. P.O. Box 1369 Arusha. Tel: 3300.

Campsites and hostels can be arranged through TANAPA.

Tarangire National Park
Tarangire Safari Lodge is a tented camp on a river bend with good views all round. P.O. Box 1177, Arusha. Tel: 7182.

Campsites should be arranged through TANAPA.

CAMPGROUNDS

Camping is only permitted at authorized sites which you should try to book beforehand to avoid disappointment. Most campsites have minimal or no facilities despite the high price paid for their use, so you should be prepared to dig your own toilet and bury or burn litter and you should travel with sufficient water containers for your basic needs. Most campsites are unprotected, so camping is strictly at your own risk.

Direct questions concerning facilities, campsites, roads, etc. should be addressed to the appropriate park or reserve at its head office:

Tanzania National Parks TANAPA (all parks), P.O. Box 3134 Arusha, Tanzania. Tel: Arusha 3181 ext: 1386

Wildlife Division (all game reserves and controlled areas), P.O. Box 1994 Dar es Salaam, Tanzania. Tel: Dar es Salaam 27271.

Ngorongoro Conservation Area Authority (NCAA), P.O. Box 776 Arusha, Tanzania. Tel: 3339.

BOOKING & FEES

Bookings and fees will be handled by the tour operator, but if you organise your own safari you should note these points: an entry fee is payable for every 24 hour period spent in the park, measured from your time of entry. Non-residents must pay this in foreign exchange and it is advisable to carry sufficient cash or travellers' cheques for this purpose. If you are camping, you must also pay a camping fee per night.

SHOPPING

WHAT TO BUY

Tanzania is the home of Makonde art—carvings in African ebony of intertwined people or openwork "spirit" forms. Other types of carvings, masks, necklaces and beadwork, baskets and batiks, etc., can be found in all curio shops in the larger towns and at villages along the routes to the national parks.

Notable markets are at Mwanza, Morogoro and Dar es Salaam; the small market at Mto-wa-Mbu near Manyara has a wide variety of curios and a tradition of exchange and barter for clothing, hats, sunglasses, etc. Ask your driver or guide for help if you want to bargain. Locally made *kanga* and *kitenge* cloth also make excellent gifts.

Most hotels have gift shops with their own selection of goods.

Books of any kind are hard to find so bring field guides. However, Tanzania National Parks sells very useful guides to the parks, available at the park headquarters in Arusha in the Conference Centre.

GETTING THERE

BY AIR

Currently *Sabena* is the only European air company connecting Western Europe with Uganda, with two flights per week between Brussels and Uganda's Entebbe International Airport some 40 kilometres (25 miles) from Kampala. Planes leave Brussels on Tuesday and Wednesday, to return on Wednesday and Thursday. The Russian airline *Aeroflot* has a monthly flight from Moscow to Entebbe. *Uganda Airways* also has a weekly flight between London and Entebbe, departing both London and Entebbe on Saturdays.

Another possibility is to go through Kenya. *Kenya Airways* and *Uganda Airways* together have nine flights per week between Nairobi and Entebbe.

Frequency of flights to Entebbe may increase in the near future. *British Airways* intends to start a regular service between London and Entebbe.

On leaving the country by plane every passenger has to pay US$20 in airport tax. Only citizens and residents are allowed to pay this amount in local currency.

Sabena, Kibathi Avenue, P.O. Box 3966, Kampala. Tel: 234200/1/2 or 259880.

Aeroflot, Kimathi Avenue, P.O. Box 6302, Kampala. Tel: 231703.

Kenya Airways, Uganda Metropole House, Entebbe Road, P.O. Box 6969, Kampala. Tel: 233068.

Uganda Airways, Airways House, 6 Colville Street, P.O. Box 5740, Kampala. Tel: 232990.

British Airways, 23 Kampala Road, P.O. Box 3464, Kampala. Tel: 257414/5/6.

BY ROAD

Uganda can easily be reached by road from Kenya via Busia and Malaba. Access by road is also possible via Rwanda, Zaire and Tanzania. The road to Sudan is temporarily closed because of rebel activities both in northern Uganda and southern Sudan.

TRAVEL ESSENTIALS

VISAS & PASSPORTS

All passport holders from non-Common-wealth countries require a visa for Uganda which can be obtained from the various Ugandan High Commissions throughout the world. The maximum stay for a tourist visa is 90 days. For longer stays, one has to go to the Immigration Department on Jinja Road in Kampala.

MONEY MATTERS

The highest denomination is the 100 shilling note. Since prices are usually in the range of several thousand shillings, you often have to carry large wads of notes around. Visitors have to change US$150 at the airport and an additional US$30 per day. Full or partial exemption if you are staying with friends or relatives can be obtained from the Ministry of Finance.

Uganda has a thriving black market for dollars, but changing money unofficially remains unlawful and can result in a heavy prison sentence.

Only the most expensive hotels accept American Express.

It is prohibited to import or export Uganda shillings.

HEALTH

Certificates of inoculation against cholera and yellow fever are necessary. Immigration officials at Entebbe Airport check for these.

Malaria is widespread, so bring prophylactic tablets (chloroquine and paludrine).

Water should only be drunk in the best hotels, otherwise it should be boiled. Typhoid is still common.

Medical facilities in Uganda are under review. The main hospital in Kampala is Mulago Hospital, but Nsambya Hospital is generally considered as the best.

It is advised to bring along sterile needles as a precaution against AIDS.

WHAT TO WEAR

Casual wear is most appropriate, although shorts, miniskirts and very open blouses should be avoided in general.

The sun can be very hot so good sun-block cream is essential.

FOREIGN EXCHANGE

You are allowed to bring in any amount of foreign exchange as long as you declare it on your currency declaration form. Whenever money is changed the bank should make a note on the form which you should keep safely and submit to customs on leaving the country. You can bring in one bottle of spirits, 225 grams (half a pound) of tobacco, one bottle of perfume, and cats and dogs if you can prove they have had the necessary vaccinations.

Tax is payable on expensive personal items such as video cameras.

GETTING ACQUAINTED

GOVERNMENT AND ECONOMY

Uganda has had eight different presidents since the country gained independence in 1962 and has been plagued by tribal and religious differences. Economic and political decline really started with the takeover by Idi Amin in 1971. He was ousted by Tanzanian and liberation forces in 1979. A year later elections were held and officially won by former president Milton Obote. But according to many, they were rigged, and those dissatisfied with the results went into the bush and started a guerilla war. In January 1986 this resulted in a takeover by current President Yoweri Kaguta Museveni, who has been trying to bring about a process of democratisation. "Resistance Committees" play a very important role in this process. They are elected by the people and eventually are represented in the Ugandan parliament by the National Resistance Council. A special committee is currently drafting a new constitution, the third since Uganda gained independence.

Political instability remains a problem, especially in the north and east which have been hit by rebel activities since 1986, soon after Museveni took over. A peace agreement signed in June 1988 has brought some 35,000 rebels out of the bush, and since then security has dramatically improved.

The economic situation is closely related to the political turmoil, and now Uganda is trying to regain some of its former glory. A recovery programme supported by IMF and World Bank puts great emphasis on restoration of roads, diversification of exports and rehabilitation of the basic industrial sector. Inflation was successfully curbed in the financial year 1988-89, and GNP grew by 4.5 percent in 1987-88.

TIME AND CLIMATE

Uganda is three hours ahead of GMT.

The climate is extremely enjoyable throughout the year. The hottest months are January and February when temperatures can reach over 30 C (86 F). The relatively coolest months are July and August.

Higher areas in the southwest, west and east, are colder, so bringing a sweater to wear in the evenings is recommended. The highest town is Kabale. The forests and mountains experience a lot of rain so some kind of waterproof protection is advisable.

Most of the country has rain throughout the year, especially late in the afternoon and at night. The dry season starts in December and lasts until early March. The longer rains fall during March to May and early September. Only the northeast part of Karamoja has a comparatively dry climate.

CULTURE AND CUSTOMS

Ugandans are generally considered extremely generous, hospitable and polite. Following the British tradition, men are addressed as "Sir" and women as "Madam".

A handshake starts and ends almost every conversation. Women, especially in the southern and western rural areas, often kneel when greeting an elder person. Kissing is almost never done in public.

Food which is offered when visiting someone's house should be eaten. It is considered an insult if this is not done.

Ugandans are good talkers and love a friendly chat or argument. Don't be suprised therefore if people greet you on the streets or simply start talking to you.

A tip in a restaurant should usually be

between 5 percent and 10 percent. Given their very basic salary, waiters are usually very happy to accept a tip. Boys who help you with your shopping expect a 50- to 100-shilling tip. Taxi drivers usually calculate their tip in the bill. Bargaining is very common in Kampala, in markets, with streetsellers and in most of the informal shops. Actual prices to be paid will often be two-thirds of what is asked. Outside Kampala, and even outside the narrow city centre people usually ask the right prices.

ELECTRICITY

Most towns have an irregular power supply of 240 volts. The main hotels use a generator in case of powercuts. Protection for expensive equipment against power surges is advisable and a small flashlight is very useful.

BUSINESS HOURS

Most shops open at 0830 hrs and close at 1730 hrs. The small shops in the various suburbs remain open until about 2130 hrs. On Sundays only these shops are open.

Banks open at 0830 hrs and close at 1400 hrs from Monday to Friday. Main banks are Uganda Commercial Bank, Barclays Bank, Nile Bank and Grindlay's Bank.

Uganda Commercial Bank, Kampala Road, P.O. Box 973, Kampala. Tel: 234710/23.

Barclays Bank, Kampala Road, P.O. Box 2971, Kampala. Tel: 232597.

Nile Bank, 22 Jinja Road, P.O. Box 2834, Kampala. Tel: 231904.

Grindlay's Bank, Kampala Road, P.O. Box 7131, Kampala. Tel: 230811/2.

The Post Office opens at 0800hrs and closes at 1700 hrs from Monday to Friday. On Saturday it closes at 1200hrs.

HOLIDAYS

East African holidays other than Christmas and New Year:

January 26: The day that the National Resistance Army took Kampala.

October 9: Independence Day.

RELIGIOUS SERVICES

Most Ugandans are either Protestant, Catholic or Muslim. There are churches and mosques for all these beliefs. Kampala has the central *Bahai* temple for Africa.

LANGUAGE

English is the official language in Uganda and is understood by most people in urban areas. *Luganda* is the most common local language. *Swahili* is widely spoken in the northern part of the country.

COMMUNICATIONS

MEDIA

Uganda enjoys considerable freedom of press with a varying number of newspapers and magazines, both in English and the local *Luganda*. The government-owned *New Vision* is the best and most widely available daily newspaper: the highly critical *Weekly Topic* is the most entertaining weekly magazine. The latest issues of *Time, Newsweek* and African weeklies and monthlies are usually sold along Kampala's main roads.

There is one television channel and several radio stations, including one that broadcasts in English.

TELEPHONE AND TELEX

The Central Post Office in Kampala has counters for international phonecalls, fax and telex. The offices for overseas telegrams is in Entebbe Road in Kampala. It also has a fax machine and is open 24 hours daily.

Uganda's telephone communications have been upgraded, and it should now be possible to make direct calls outside East Africa. Otherwise, calls must be made through the operator by dialing 0900 or 0905

Other useful numbers:
990: Telegrams and telegram enquiries
901: Directory enquiries
902: Telephone call enquiries
903: Time announcement in English
It should be noted that many telephones are commonly out of order.

GETTING AROUND

FROM THE AIRPORT

There are "special taxis" from Entebbe Airport to Kampala which are quite expensive at around 10,000 shillings (negotiable). An irregular bus service to town is available and minibuses, also referred to as "taxis", take people to the capital.

DOMESTIC TRAVEL

AIR

Several local companies offer air services to various parts of the country. The most reliable include:

Uganda Airways, Airways House, 6 Colville Street, P.O. Box 5740, Kampala. Tel: 232990.

Blacklines Tours, Diamond Trust Building, Kampala Road, P.O. Box 6968, Kampala. Tel: 243984 or 235385.

Bel-Air, Jinja Road, Kampala. Tel: 257716.

TRAVEL PACKAGES

Katatumba Black Line Tours (Tel: Kampala 259175) is virtually the only company that organizes tourist trips to several parts of the country, either by road or by air.

PUBLIC TRANSPORT

Kampala has just re-established its bus services and has a "taxi park" where private mini-buses follow regular bus routes.

Services from Kampala to most other major towns exist and buses leave from the area close to the "taxi park".

"Special taxis" can be found in town, especially near the Nakasero Market and at the main hotels. There are no particular signs for these taxis and the price is negotiable.

Two army/police roadblocks will be encountered between Entebbe and Kampala, and invariably several others between Kampala and any other city. Soldiers are usually good humoured, but sometimes do not speak English. You may have to show your identity card and, if driving a foreign registered vehicle, possibly your registration and import documents. You are obliged to stop at the roadblocks. It is advisable to always carry some kind of identification with you.

PRIVATE TRANSPORT

Hertz car hire services operate at the airport. But it should be noted that hiring a car in Uganda is very expensive, never less than US$100 per day. To reach most parts of the country you will need a four-wheel drive vehicle. Please note that there are no breakdown services outside Kampala. If your car breaks down you will have to stop another passing car and go to the nearest village or town to get help. Petrol may be a problem on long trips. Always carry one or two spare jerrycans.

Hertz car hire services, Spear Touring Safaris Co. Ltd., Spear House, 22 Jinja Road, P.O. Box 5914, Kampala. Tel: 59950 or 32395 (Airport Tel: 26518).

WHERE TO STAY

HOTELS

Kampala has a number of good, albeit expensive, hotels. The best and most exclusive is Nile Mansions within the Conference Centre. The newly-renovated Sheraton Hotel has the largest number of self-contained rooms complete with video. Budget hotels are virtually non-existent.

Other hotels include: Hotel Diplomat, Silver Springs, Fairway Hotel, Speke Hotel and the slightly cheaper Lion Hotel and Summer Hotel. The best restaurants with continental food can be found in Nile Mansions and Sheraton Hotel. The down-town meeting place is the Nile Grill on Kampala Road, which has a busy terrace and offers reasonable food.

Nile Mansions, Siad Barre Avenue, P.O. Box 7057, Kampala. Tel: 258041.

Kampala Sheraton Hotel, P.O. Box 7041, Kampala. Tel: 244590.

Hotel Diplomate Tank Hill, P.O. Box 6968, Kampala. Tel: 268311/268314/268341/268343.

Silver Springs, Port Bell Road, Kampala. Tel: 221301.

Speke Hotel, Nile Avenue, P.O. Box 7036, Kampala. Tel: 233610.

Lion Hotel, Namirembe Road, P.O. Box 6751, Kampala. Tel: 243490.

Summer Hotel, Gaba Road, P.O. Box 8578, Kampala. Tel: 268416.

Katatumba Resort Hotel, P.O. Box 1177, Mbarara. Tel: 15290.

For lodge reservations for the following hotels:

Fairway Hotel, Kampala; Imperial Hotel, Kampala; Crested Crane Hotel, Jinja; Mount Elgon Hotel, Mbale; Lira Hotel, Lira; White Horse Inn, Kabale; Kisoro Travellers' Rest, Kisoro, Hotel Marguerita, Kasese, Mountains of the Moon Hotel, Fort Portal; Rippon Falls Hotel, Jinja; Rock Hotel, Tororo; Acholi Inn, Gulu; White Rhino Hotel, Arua; Mweya Safari Lodge, Queen Elizabeth National Park; write to Uganda Hotels Ltd, c/o Uganda Tourist Development Corporation, Metropolitan House, Entebbe Road, P.O. Box 7211, Kampala. Tel: 243822.

FOOD DIGEST

FOOD AND DRINK

The local food is *matoke* (mashed green banana) with ground nut sauce, or *luwumbo* (chicken boiled in banana leaf). The local alcoholic beverage is *Uganda waragi*, a distilled spirit not unlike gin. Several locally distilled, much stronger, variations exist in the rural areas. Uganda has three readily available beers that can be differentiated by blue, black or white caps. *Creps* is the locally produced soft drink, made out of pineapples.

The big hotels offer international food, mainly chips with fish or steak. To sample Ugandan food, go to the outdoor UNICEF restaurant, or to Campus View in Wandeguya, not too far from Makerere University.

Another restaurant well worth trying is Nile Grill, Kampala Road, P.O. Box 1295, Kampala. Tel: 233522.

Wild life Safari with Tropical Beach Holiday in Kenya

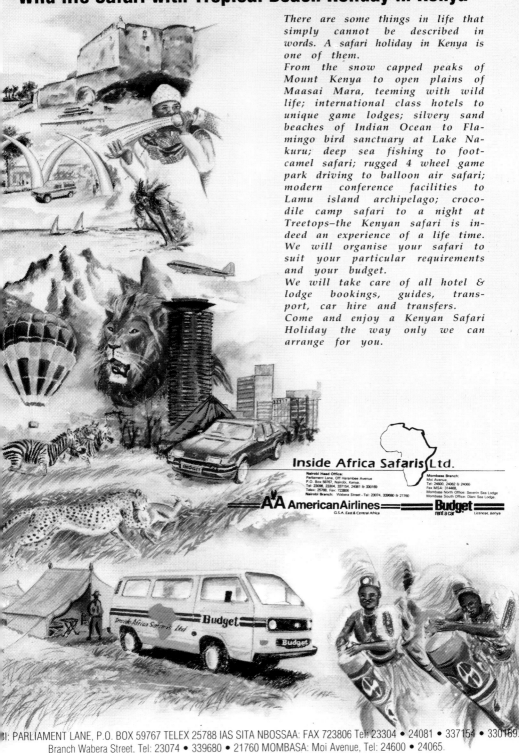

There are some things in life that simply cannot be described in words. A safari holiday in Kenya is one of them.

From the snow capped peaks of Mount Kenya to open plains of Maasai Mara, teeming with wild life; international class hotels to unique game lodges; silvery sand beaches of Indian Ocean to Flamingo bird sanctuary at Lake Nakuru; deep sea fishing to foot-camel safari; rugged 4 wheel game park driving to balloon air safari; modern conference facilities to Lamu island archipelago; crocodile camp safari to a night at Treetops—the Kenyan safari is indeed an experience of a life time. We will organise your safari to suit your particular requirements and your budget.

We will take care of all hotel & lodge bookings, guides, transport, car hire and transfers.

Come and enjoy a Kenyan Safari Holiday the way only we can arrange for you.

Inside Africa Safaris Ltd.

Nairobi Head Office:
Parliament Lane, Off Harambee Avenue
P.O. Box 58767, Nairobi, Kenya.
Tel: 23098, 23304, 337154, 24081 & 330169
Telex: 25788. Fax: 723806.
Nairobi Branch: Wabera Street - Tel: 23074, 339680 & 21760

Mombasa Branch:
Moi Avenue
Tel: 24600, 24062 & 24065
Fax MSA: 314468.
Mombasa North Office: Severin Sea Lodge
Mombasa South Office: Diani Sea Lodge.

American Airlines
G.S.A. East & Central Africa

Budget rent a car
Licencee, Kenya

PARLIAMENT LANE, P.O. BOX 59767 TELEX 25788 IAS SITA NBOSSAA: FAX 723806 Tel: 23304 • 24081 • 337154 • 330169,
Branch Wabera Street, Tel: 23074 • 339680 • 21760 MOMBASA: Moi Avenue, Tel: 24600 • 24065.

INSIGHT GUIDES

Indian WILDLIFE

CULTURE PLUS

Kampala has one National Museum on Kitante Road, with exhibits explaining the history and culture of the country. There is also a music gallery with a display of traditional instruments.

The capital has two art galleries: Nummo Gallery is just behind the Sheraton Hotel and exhibits contemporary art by Ugandan artists. At Makerere University there is a small art gallery near the Faculty of Fine Arts, which is certainly worth visiting.

The National Theatre in the city centre has regular plays, but usually in Luganda. It also has musical events and a cinema. Big banners in town announce the programmme.

National Theatre, Siad Barre Avenue, P.O. Box 3187, Kampala. Tel: 254567.

The Alliance Française housed in the National Theatre building offers French films with English sub-titles every Wednesday. Other cinemas no longer exist; they have been transformed into video parlours.

NIGHTLIFE

Kampala could once boast the best night-life in East Africa. However, during the 1980s night-life almost disappeared, but is now picking up again.

The most popular discos are Tropicana 110 and Club Cloud; the partly open-air Bat Valley on Bombo Road has an excellent live band on Saturdays.

During the early evenings most of Kampala's suburbs transform into colourful meeting places where blacks and whites mix effortlessly. Kabalagala on Tank Hill has many outdoor bars and eating places.

SHOPPING

SHOPPING AREAS

The UNICEF shop on Bombo Road, a few kilometres outside the city centre, has an excellent variety of Ugandan crafts. The country is famous for its batiks, mats and baskets.

A string of shops in the city centre close to the Imperial Hotel (currently under renovation) sells a similar range of souvenirs and crafts. Here prices are negotiable.

SPORTS

Soccer is the most popular sport, played every Saturday at 1600 hrs in the Nakivubo Stadium. Lugogo Stadium on Jinja Road has seven tennis courts, open to everybody. The American Club in Makindye has another two, but here you need an introduction from another member. The Club also has a clean swimming pool. Sheraton Hotel has a lovely swimming pool for hotel guests only. A well-kept golf course can be found along Natete Road, just outside the city centre.

GETTING THERE

ETHIOPIA

TRAVEL ESSENTIALS

BY AIR

Addis Ababa is sometimes known as the "diplomatic capital of Africa" due to the presence of both the Organisation of African Unity (OAU) and the UN Economic Commission for Africa (ECA). As a result, the city is well-served by international air routes, particularly by the national carrier *Ethiopian Airlines* (EAL), deservedly known as the best airline on the African continent. Bole International Airport is only six kilometres (four miles) from Addis city centre, and receives flights direct from Europe (including London, Frankfurt, Rome, Moscow, Berlin, Athens), Asia (including Jeddah, Abu Dhabi, Bombay, Peking) and many African cities (including Nairobi, Entebbe, Dar es Salaam, Djibouti, Lusaka, Harare, Khartoum, Cairo and many West African cities). Additional airlines serving Addis Ababa include *Kenya Airways, Lufthansa, Aeroflot, Alitalia, Air Djibouti, Yemenia.*

There is no airport tax at departure. Check in is two hours before for international flights. It is very important to confirm your onward flight at least three days before departure.

VISAS & PASSPORTS

All nationalities require a visa to enter Ethiopia, except Kenyan citizens. Tourist visas valid for up to 30 days can be obtained from Ethiopian embassies abroad. They can also be obtained on arrival at Bole airport, provided your airline allows you to fly without a visa. Tourist visas can be extended in Addis. Transit visas are also available for brief stopovers, your passport being held at the airport in exchange for a transit visa card.

Travel within Ethiopia requires a travel permit which can be obtained for the areas you require by the National Tour Organisation (NTO).

MONEY MATTERS

The official exchange rate is fixed to the US dollar. It is advisable to change your currency in Addis before proceeding on your travels within the country.

You are only allowed to take Et birr 10 out of the country. Amounts in excess of this, but less than Et birr 100 may be changed back at the airport before departure, provided you can prove from your currency form that you imported it as foreign currency when you arrived, and can show exchange receipts.

Amounts in excess of this must be changed back at the main bank in Addis. American Express cards are acceptable at a few large government hotels, and at the NTO.

HEALTH

A valid inoculation certificate against yellow fever is required upon entry to Ethiopia. A cholera inoculation certificate is needed if you have come within six days from an area where the disease is prevalent.

Diseases are no more common in Ethiopia than in other parts of Africa and provided simple precautions are taken, you should have no major problems. Some people will find the spicy local food strong for their digestions at first. Malaria occurs in some areas of the country and prophylactic medication should be taken. Medicines are readily available and well-stocked pharmacies are a feature of most towns. Addis has a good selection of hospitals which can cope with most situations and problems, but you are advised to bring your own stock of prescription medicines and sterile needles to avoid complications.

WHAT TO WEAR

Respectable western attire is perfectly acceptable. It is as well to be prepared for all climatic situations if you intend to travel widely in the country. Nights and days tend to be cool at high altitudes but at lower altitudes you may wish to wear shorts by day. However be prepared for cooler nights. If you intend to go into the high mountains (Bale and Semien) you will need warm, wind and waterproof clothing.

CUSTOMS

Electronic goods must be declared on arrival. Serial numbers will be recorded on your currency form to ensure that goods are re-exported at your departure. Duty free allowances include 200 cigarettes, 50 cigars or a pound of tobacco; one litre of alcoholic beverage; one litre or two bottles of perfume.

Special permission may be required to import and use video cameras and, occasionally, binoculars. Export permits are required for all wildlife products and for antiques.

GETTING ACQUAINTED

unique to the continent. Many books have been written on the subject. The monuments at Lalibela, Gondar, Harer, and Axum are some of the most famous. NTO can arrange trips by road or air to all these places, weather conditions allowing. Good hotels exist near most of these monuments.

TIME ZONES

Ethiopia is three hours ahead of GMT.

The popular advertisment for the country is "the land with 13 months of sunshine!" This follows from the continued use of the Julian calendar. There are 12 equal length months of 30 days each, and one month of five days—six in a Leap Year. New Year's Day is on September 11 (September 12 in a Leap Year).

ELECTRICITY

The mains supply is 220 volts and 50 cycles AC. Rural hotels and lodges may have their own generators, usually of the same voltage as the mains.

LANGUAGE

The official language in Ethiopia is *Amharic*, with its beautiful ancient script. English is widely understood, as is Italian.

CLIMATE

Ethiopia has a varying climate depending upon the altitude and orientation of any location. Generally speaking, there are two wet periods and two dry periods, but in many higher locations the wet periods run into each other, giving one long wet and one dry season. The months of October to March are usually dry and warm, but with very cold nights at high altitude. The period May to June may be dry. Wet periods are characterised by warmer nights and cooler days.

CULTURE & CUSTOMS

Ancient cultures that have evolved in isolation in the vastness of the Ethiopian highlands have left their stamp on the countryside, especially in the form of buildings

COMMUNICATIONS

International communications include a good postal system, telephone and telex. Internally there is a widespread postal system, a telephone system which is improving daily as micro-wave links are constructed, and some radio communication.

There is a daily newspaper in English, *The Ethiopian Herald* in addition to daily Amharic papers.

GETTING AROUND

DOMESTIC TRAVEL

Ethiopian Airlines domestic service reaches over 40 destinations within Ethiopia, served with Twin Otter, ATR 42, Boeing 737 and Boeing 727 aircraft. There is also a charter branch of the airline called *Admas* which goes to off-route destinations.

PUBLIC TRANSPORT

TAXIS AND HIRE CARS

The NTO locate their cream-coloured Mercedes taxis at all major hotels in the capital, and at Bole International Airport. Fares are fixed and receipts given. In addition, NTO is able to provide chauffeur driven cars for destinations away from Addis. These vary from saloon cars to comfortable Toyota Landcruisers, and 60 seater air-conditioned Mercedes buses, capable of reaching surprisingly remote and rugged parts of the country. NTO also has a few self-drive cars.

ON FOOT AND HORSEBACK

One of the joys of Ethiopia is to travel on foot or horseback in the mountainous areas along routes still rarely travelled and uncrowded, where you could not take a vehicle if you wanted to. Horses and mules are still an important form of transport in rural areas and can usually be hired by the day for an agreed price.

THINGS TO DO

The most efficient way to see the country is to make your arrangements through the NTO, which is the only official tourist travel agent in Ethiopia. They can do everything, from simply obtaining travel permits, to organising all aspects of your travel in Ethiopia, including camping and cooking equipment. They also arrange for hunting and fishing expeditions.

WILDLIFE VIEWING

There are many endemic species in Ethiopia. Most remaining wildlife now exists in national parks and sanctuaries. NTO can make arrangements to take you to most of these by vehicle and/or aircraft, and to supply your needs while you are there.

The tourist infrastrucure is still very basic: you may have to work hard to see these animals but it makes the experience all the more rewarding.

Bird trips are proving extremely popular as ornithologists seek to add Ethiopia's 27 endemic bird species to their life lists.

TREKKING

The mountainous areas of Ethiopia are what make the country so very different. The abysses dictate that roads pass along ridge tops for the most part, so to see the spectacular scenery you must walk, or use horses and mules. Organising such trips in the Bale

Mountains is relatively easy, but there are many other locations, where even a few hours walking or on horseback can prove very rewarding. Such places include the Kessem River gorge, the Chacha River gorge, the Arssi Mountains, Kuni Mountain, Mulu Valley, Debre Libanos and a host of others. Trekking on foot can also be very tough but rewarding in the arid lowlands. Whitewater rafting trips of two weeks' duration are regularly run on the lower reaches of the Omo River.

SHOPPING

WHAT TO BUY

The highlands of Ethiopia have influenced the art and clothing. Examples of both are readily available to purchase, and make excellent and, in many cases, practical presents. Choose from beautiful white cotton *shamma* ware, in the form of shawls, bags, stoles, and blankets; ancient (and more recent) silverware, as beads, famous Ethiopian crosses, bracelets and earrings; more expensive and usually modern gold articles; modern paintings on parchment; old church relics; parchment books; colourful Harer basketry; Ethiopian herbs and spices; delicious Ethiopian coffee or horse artifacts such as the colourful saddle cloths.

All these and much more are available, in formal tourist shops near the main Post Office on Churchill road, near the National Theatre, in hotel curio shops and, of course, at the famed *Mercato*—reputed to be Africa's biggest market. Country markets, often held on a Wednesday, also yield a host of "real" artifacts, practical and fascinating items of everyday use to their makers and purchasers alike.

WHERE TO STAY

FOOD DIGEST

HOTELS

You are obliged to stay in one of the excellent government hotels in Addis, which range from the luxurious Hilton and Ghion, to the less opulent, but perfectly adequate, Ethiopia, Ras, Wabe, Shebelle and several others spread through the capital. Larger towns also have good hotels belonging to the same chains, and a few private hotels such as the Bekelle Mola chain. In addition, even in the most remote village, there exist basic *buna beits* (coffee houses) which will offer a roof over your head and food and drink, to sustain you in your exploration of this varied country.

WHERE TO EAT

Where you eat depends upon your constitution and sense of adventure and discovery. Addis can offer many cuisines, including European, Italian, Chinese, Armenian and Indian, but you will do the country an injustice if you don't try its own dishes. There are infinite possibilites, but most hotels will offer national food of some variety. Special national food restaurants exist at the Ghion and National Hotel, and at the Filwoha Hotel, where you eat in an attractive old Ethiopian building. Further detailed information is available in the excellent guide to Addis, produced by the Ethiopian Tourist Trading Corporation.

WHAT TO EAT

Ethiopia offers a cuisine unlike any other in Africa and you either like it or you don't! Most do. An endemic grass (*tef*) provides the staple carbohydrate source for most of the country. From it a large thin circular pancake (*injera*) is made, which is the vehicle for all foods. A large variety of sauces and stews, generically known as *wat,* is available. These vary from mild (*alichas*) from the north to fiery red (*ky wat*) made with vegetables (*atkilt*), meat (*siga*), pulses (*shiro*), chicken (*doro*), eggs (*inkulal*), liver fillet and tripe (*dulet*), and so on. *Wat* is traditionally placed on the *injera*, which is laid out flat on a circular, colourful, woven basketware table tray and cover combined (*massob*). You then proceed to tear off pieces of the *injera* from the edges, wrap it around a morsel from the centre, and deftly pop it into your mouth with one hand. At the end of the meal, when you think you have finished, your hostess will, on occasion, scoop up tasty morsels of the remnants (*gursha*) and put them into your mouth to ensure you really are satisfied and her cuisine has been appreciated!

Fear not—even in remote areas western cuisine is available if the above description should worry you! So is Italian cuisine, especially various pastas, cooked with addition of Ethiopian herbs and spices.

DRINKING NOTES

Ethiopia produces a remarkable array of drinks, including standard western "fizzies", four varieties of bottled beer, a wonderful mineral water named after its source *Ambo*, over 10 varieties of wine, a local champagne, brandy, ouzo and gin, and local *arakis*—clear liqueurs that are not sweet and sticky, made from coffee, milk, honey, plum, orange, lemon, and even from the *kosso* tree (*Hagenia abyssinica*) which is prized as a cure for tapeworm for those who overindulge in raw meat! A favourite!

USEFUL ADDRESSES

(All are Government agencies: no private tourism is permitted.)

ETHIOPIAN TOURISIM COMMISSION (ETC)

P.O. Box 2183, Addis Ababa, Ethiopia. Tel: 15-98-79; 44-74-70; telex: 21067 ETC.
In overall charge of tourism, planning, promotion, and the production of most promotional material.

NATIONAL TOUR ORGANISATION (NTO)

P.O. Box 5709, Addis Ababa, Ethiopia. Tel: 15-29-55; 15-91-86; telex: 21370.
The national travel agent, concerned with the actual operation of tourism, vehicles, guides, itineraries, permits etc.

ETHIOPIAN TOURISM AND TRADING CORPORATION (ETTC)

P.O. Box 5640, Addis Ababa, Ethiopia. Tel: 18-06-41; telex: 21411.
Concerned with production of some brochures, booklets, postcards, and souvenir material and management of duty free shops.

ETHIOPIAN HOTELS CORPORATION (EHC)

P.O. Box 1263, Addis Ababa, Ethiopia.
Telephone: 15-27-00; telex: 21067.
Manage and operate all government ho-
tels in the country where tourists stay, in-
cluding Kerayu Lodge in Awash National
Park.

ETHIOPIAN WILDLIFE CONSERVATION ORGANISATION (EWCO)

P.O. Box 386, Addis Ababa, Ethiopia.
Tel: 44-59-70; 15-44-36; telegram:
WILDGAME.
Management of all Conservation Areas
(National Parks, Sanctuaries, Wildlife Re-
serves, Controlled Hunting Areas); control
of hunting; control of wildlife utilisation.

ETHIOPIAN AIRLINES (EAL)

P.O. Box 1755, Addis Ababa, Ethiopia.
Tel: 8-22-22; telex: 21012 ETHAIR.

Overseas offices:
85-87 Jermyn Street, London SW1Y 6JD,
England.
Tel: 01-839-1663.

Kaiserstrasse 33, D-6000 Frankfurt/
Main, West Germany.
Tel: 069-250077.

405 Lexington Avenue, New York NY
10174, USA.
Tel: 212-867-0095.

RWANDA AND EASTERN ZAIRE

GETTING THERE

RWANDA

BY AIR

Kigali, the small town capital, has a neat and tidy modern airport which can be reached via Kenya Airways from Nairobi, by Sabena direct from Brussels or by Air France from Paris.

BY ROAD

Kigali is accessible by paved road from Rusumo (on the border of Tanzania), Uganda (via Byumba) and to the Burundi border.

EASTERN ZAIRE

BY AIR

Bukavu, at the southern end of Lake Kivu, and Goma, at the northern end of the lake, are the gateways to eastern Zaire. From Rwanda though, most visitors cross the border between Cyangugu in Rwanda and Bukavu. Cyangugu (close to Kamembe airport) can be reached by Air Rwanda from both Kigali and Gisenyi.

TRAVEL ESSENTIALS

VISAS AND PASSPORTS

All travellers to Rwanda and Zaire must be in possession of a valid passport along with a Rwandan and/or Zairean visa which must be obtained before entering the country. If you intend to visit Zaire and then return to Rwanda you will need a multiple or double entry visa. Rwanda has embassies in Brussels, Nairobi, New York, Ottawa, Paris, Washington, and a number of other countries where such visas can be obtained.

MONEY MATTERS

Rwanda: The currency in Rwanda is the Rwanda *franc* (FRW). You can buy FRW on arrival at the airport, in banks and hotels but since it is difficult to turn them back into foreign exchange, obtain only what you think you will need — or keep carefully all Encashment Certificates and receipts. American Express and Access credit cards are accepted in most good accommodations.

Zaire: The official currency is the *zaire* (Z), which is divided into 100 makuta (K).

HEALTH

You are very strongly advised to make arrangements for documentation before setting off for Rwanda and Zaire. It is also necessary to have vaccination certificates for yellow fever and cholera. Allow plenty of time (at least two weeks) for visas.

Only the best hotels will have water which is safe to drink. If you intend to rough it take water sterilising tablets with you—or stick to beer and soda water. Good beer and soft drinks are manufactured in Rwanda. Other drinks are often in short supply. Bottled water is imported from Europe and is consequently very expensive.

GETTING ACQUAINTED

ON DEPARTURE

In Rwanda, there is an airport tax for all departing flights: 800 FRW for international flights and 250 FRW for domestic flights. In Zaire, the airport tax is US$10.

ECONOMY AND INDUSTRY

Agriculture is the main industry with many crops being grown successfully on the steep, terraced slopes of the valleys and mountains. Due to the varied altitudes cash crops such as tea, coffee, tobacco, rice, sugar and many others can be grown. Such is the pressure on land that there are few farm animals so a herd of cattle is a very rare sight in Rwanda. What does spring to the eye are the enormous numbers of bananas grown mainly for local consumption. There are many varieties; some are eaten raw, others must be cooked, yet others are used for brewing a local beer.

The country has few mineral resources; but hydro-electric power is generated in Rwanda on quite a large scale.

Because Rwanda is a land-locked country very far from the nearest ocean many goods are expensive and in short supply. Most imports are trucked in from Mombasa or Dar es Salaam on the Indian ocean, a distance of over 1,600 kilometre (1,000 miles).

TIME AND CLIMATE

Rwanda and eastern Zaire are two hours ahead of GMT.

Rwanda's climate is similar to other East African countries with four main seasons:-

A long rainy season, from mid-March to mid-May. The heaviest rains fall in this season, usually in the form of torrential storms alternating with lovely clear skies.

Even during this period a holiday in Rwanda can be very rewarding.

A long dry season, from mid-May to mid-September.

A short rainy season, from mid-September to mid-December. The rain normally comes in short scattered showers in this season.

A short dry season, from mid-December to mid-March.

Throughout the year it is warm during the day and cooler at night with Rwanda's generally high altitude ensuring that it is never excessively hot. The mean daily temperature is about 24C (76F) going up to a high of approximately 34C (94F). Minimum night temperatures are around 10C (50F).

ELECTRICITY

Electrical supplies throughout Rwanda are rated at 220 volts.

LANGUAGE

Throughout Rwanda the main African language is *Kinyarwanda* which is one of the two official languages, with French being the other. French is the most widely used European language; English is little known—even in the travel industry. *Kiswahili* is understood by many people. French is spoken countrywide in Zaire, while *Kiswahili* is spoken in the east.

GETTING THERE

DOMESTIC TRAVEL

Air Rwanda links Kigali with the towns of Gisenyi, Ruhengeri, Butare and Kamembe (for Cyangugu and Bukavu in Zaire) on most days of the week.

Rwanda's main roads are paved with tarmac and engineered to high standards. Many journeys are enjoyable because the scenery is so spectacular. Even off the tarmac most routes are good. Drivers must be careful as crowds often walk along the roads; but Rwandans are friendly—and most do not mind being photographed.

PUBLIC TRANSPORT

Taxis are available at both the airport and the major hotels.

WHERE TO STAY

HOTELS: RWANDA

In Kigali: Built in hilly country so that there are several good viewpoints Kigali has three comfortable modern hotels of international standard, all with spacious grounds. The Hotel des Milles Collines (Hotel of a Thousand Hills) has a swimming pool and the Hotel des Diplomates a tennis court, while the Hotel Meridien Umubano has both pool and courts.

Where to stay while gorilla tracking:

The Muhabura Hotel in Ruhengeri is the nearest accommodation to the Parc National des Volcans. It is a small local hotel, definitely not up to international standards, but it does have hot baths and the food is acceptable. From here it is a mere 11 kilometres (7 miles) to the Parc headquarters at Kinigi on the lower slopes of Sabynyo, but because of the excellent road system it is not necessary to stay in Ruhengeri. By leaving very early in the morning many visitors travel from Kigali or Gisenyi in time to go gorilla tracking. You should aim to reach the Parc by 0800 hrs, 0645 hrs for the Suza Group.

In Gisenyi: Gisenyi, on the shores of Lake Kivu, is 70 kilometres (43 miles) from the park and has the Palm Beach Hotel and Hotel Meridien Izuba (the more modern and luxurious of the two) which both overlook the beautiful lake. The drive is spectacular and the lake is a resort in its own right, at 100 kilometres (60 miles) long and 40 kilometres (25 miles) wide and set in a mountain landscape. Its sandy beaches are safe for bathing and the views are picturesque.

HOTELS: EASTERN ZAIRE

In Bukavu: The Hotel Residence on the main street, once fine but now run-down, is adequate but can be noisy. It has spacious rooms and an atmosphere redolent of Belgium colonies. Further out of town, quieter and overlooking the lake, is the Hotel Riviera. This family run hotel has good Italian style food.

In Djomba: For gorilla watching at Djomba Intrepids Camp, contact United Touring Company, P.O. Box 42196, Nairobi, Kenya. Tel: 331960, Telex: 25070.

CULTURE PLUS

The three main ethnic groups in Rwanda are the Bahutu (90 percent), Bututsi (9 percent) and Batwa (1 percent). The Bututsi (popularly known as the Tutsi) are exceptionally tall people; many of them are over seven feet. In contrast the Batwa are tiny pygmoids.

Although the town of Kigali cannot claim to be a sophisticated modern city there are an adequate number of shops and a colourful market where attractive locally made basket ware is on sale.

A few miles from Kigali at the Rutongo Mission, Flemish nuns supervise a well-run cottage industry where hundreds of young African women do embroidery, including table cloths in the best Belgian tradition. A large number of finished goods are normally on display and available for purchase.

Another attraction only 15 kilometres (10 miles) from Kigali is the pygmoid village of Shyrongi. Here members of the Batwa people make and sell pottery and entertain visitors with their incredibly vibrant tribal dancing. The village has splendid views of the Nyaborongo River.

EAST AFRICAN ANIMALS

Here are the scientific names of some of the animals you will see during your visit to East Africa:

COMMON NAME	SCIENTIFIC NAME
Aardvark	*Orycteropus afer*
Aardwolf	*Proteles cristatus*
African buffalo	*Syncerus caffer*
Bat-eared fox	*Otocyon megalotis*
Beisa oryx	*Oryx gazella beisa*
Black rhino	*Diceros bicornis*
Black-fronted duiker	*Cephalophus nigrifrons*
Bohor reedbuck	*Redunca redunca*
Bongo	*Boocercus eurycerus*
Burchell's zebra	*Hippotigris (Quagga) quagga*
Bush duiker	*Cephalophus grimmia*
Bush pig	*Potamochoerus porcus*
Bushbuck	*Tragelaphus scriptus*
Caracal	*Caracal caracal*
Chanler's mountain reedbuck	*Redunca fulvorufula*
Cheetah	*Acinonyx jubatus*
Chimpanzee	*Pan troglodytes*
Civet	*Viverra civetta*
Clawless otter	*Aonyx capensis*
Colobus monkey	*Colobus (Colobus) polykomos*
Common giraffe	*Giraffa camelopardalis*
Common waterbuck	*Kobus ellipsiprymnus*
Crocodile	*Crocdylus niloticus*
Defassa waterbuck	*Kobus defassa*
Dorcas gazelle	*Gazella dorcas*
Dwarf mongoose	*Helogale undulata*
Eland	*Taurotragus oryx*
Elephant	*Loxodonta africana*
Galago	*Galago crassicaudatus*
Genet cat	*Genetta genetta*
Gerenuk	*Litocranius walleri*
Giant forest hog	*Hylochoerus meinertzhageni*
Giant molerat	*Tachyoryctes rex*
Gnu/wildebees	*Connochaetes taurinus*
Golden cat	*Profelis aurata*
Grant's gazelle	*Gazella granti*
Greater kudu	*Tragelaphus strepsiceros*
Grevy's zebra	*Hippotigris (Dolichohippus) grevyi*
Grey duiker	*Cephalophus monticola*
Guenther's dikdik	*Madoqua (Rhynchotragus) guentheri*
Hippo	*Hippopotamus amphibuis*
Hunter's hartebeest	*Damaliscus hunteri*
Hunting dog	*Lycaon pictus*
Hyrax	*Heterohyrax brucei*
Impala	*Aepyceros melampus*
Jackson's hartebeest	*Alcelaphus buselaphus jacksoni*
Kirk's dikdik	*Madoqua (Rhynchotragus) kirkii*
Klipspringer	*Oreotragus oreotragus*
Kongoni	*Alcelaphus buselaphus cokii*
L'Hoest monkey	*Cercopithecus l'Hoesti*
Leopard	*Panthera pardus*
Lesser kudu	*Strepsiceros imberbis*
Lichtenstein's hartebeest	*Alcelaphus lichtensteinii*
Lion	*Panthera leo*
Maasai giraffe	*Giraffa camelopardalis tippelskirchi*
Mountain gorilla	*Gorilla gorilla beringei*
Mountain nyala	*Tragelaphus (Tragelaphus) buxtoni*
Nyala	*Tragelaphus (Tragelaphus) angasi*
Olive baboon	*Papio (papio) cynocephalus*
Oribi	*Ourebia ourebi*
Palm civet	*Nandinia binotata*
Patas monkey	*Erythrocebus patas*
Porcupine	*Hystrix galeata*
Puku	*Adenota vardonii*
Ratel/honey badger	*Mellivora capensis*
Red colobus monkey	*Colobus (Colobus) badius*
Red duiker	*Cephalophus harveyi*
Red tailed monkey	*Cercopithecus nictitans*
Reticulated giraffe	*Giraffa reticula*

Roan antelope	*Hippotragus equinus*
Rothschild giraffe	*Giraffa camelopardalis rothschildi*
Sable antelope	*Hippotragus niger*
Sanje crested mangabey	*Cercocebus galeritus*
Serval	*Felis serval*
Sharpe's grysbok	*Raphicerus sharpei*
Sitatunga	*Tragelaphus spekei*
Southern reedbuck	*Redunca arundinum*
Spotted hyaena	*Crocuta crocuta*
Springbok	*Antidorcas marsupialis*
Steinbok	*Raphicerus campestris*
Striped hyaena	*Hyaena hyaena*
Suni	*Nesotragus moschatus*
Sykes' monkey	*Cercopithecus mitis*
Thomson's gazelle	*Gazella thomsonii*
Topi	*Damaliscus lunatus*
Uganda kob	*Adenota kob*
Vervet monkey	*Cercopithecus aethiop*
Wart hog	*Phacochoeru aethiopicus*
White rhino	*Ceratotherium simum*
Yellow baboon	*Papio (papio) anubis*
Zanzibar duiker	*Cephalophus adersi*
Zorilla	*Ictonyx striatus*

EAST AFRICAN BIRDS

Here are the scientific names of some of the birds you will see during your East African trip:

COMMON NAME	SCIENTIFIC NAME
African darter	Anhinga rufer
African hoopoe	Upupa epops africana
African skimmer	Rhynchops flavirostris
Ashy starling	Cosmopsarus unicolor
Augur buzzard	Polyboroides radiatus
Barn owl	Tyto alba
Bateleur	Terathopius ecaudatus
Black-bellied bustard	Eupodotis melanogaster
Black crake	Limnocorax flavirostra
Black heron	Egretta ardesaica
Bristle-crowned starling	Galeopsar salvadorii
Bronzed-naped pigeon	Turturoena delegorguei
Brown parrot	Poicephalus meyeri
Carmine beeeater	Merops nubicus
Caspian plover	Charadrius asiaticus
Cattle egret	Bubulcusibis
Chestnut-banced sand plover	Charadrius pallidus
Common helmeted guinea fowl	Numida mitrata
Common hornbill	Tockus nasutus
Crowned crane	Balearica regulorum
Crowned hornbill	Tockus alboterminatus
Curlew sandpiper	Tringa stagnatilis
Egyptian goose	Alopochen aegyptiaca
European stork	Ciconia ciconia
European swallow	Hirundo rustica
Fantailed widow bird	Euplectes axillaris
Fischer's lovebird	Agapornis fischeri
Fish eagle	Haliaeetus vocifer
Gabar goshawk	Melierax gabar
Go-away-bird (barefaced)	Corythaixoides personata
Go-away-bird (whitebellied)	Corythaixoides leucogaster
Golden breasted starling	Cosmopsarus reguis
Goliath heron	Ardea Goliath
Great white pelican	Pelecanus onocrotalus
Greater flamingo	Phoenicopterus ruber
Green ibis	Lamppribis olivacea akleyorum
Green wood hoopoe	Phoeniculus purpureus
Greenshank	Tringa nebularia
Grey-hooded kingfisher	Halcyon leucocephala
Ground hornbill	Bucoruus leadbeateri
Hammerkop	Scopus umbretta
Harrier hawk	Polyboroides radiatus
Helmeted guinea fowl	Numida melagris
Hemprich's hornbill	Tockus hemprichii
Jackson's francolin	Francolinus jacksoni
knob-billed goose	Sarkidiornis melanota
Kori bustard	Ardeotis kori
Lammergeyer vulture	Gypaetus barbatus
Layard black weaver	Plocueus nigriceps
Lesser flamingo	Phoenicopterus minor
Lilac-breasted roller	Coracias caudata
Lily trotter	Actophilornis africanus
Little stint	Calidris minuta
Long-crested eagle	Lophaetus occipitalis
Longtailed cormorant	Phalacrocorax africanus
Malachite sunbird	Nectarina regia
Marabou stork	Leptoptilus crumeniferus
Martial eagle	Polemaetus bellicosus
Mountain chat	Pinarochroa sordida
Olive pigeon	Columba arquatrix
Osprey	Pandion haliaetus
Ostrich	Struthio camelus
Pale chanting goshawk	Melierax poliopterus
Palm swift	Cypsiurus parvus
Palm-nut vulture	Gypiohyerax angolensis
Pel's fishing owl	Scotopelia peli
Pel's fishing own	Scotopelia peli
Peter's (African) finfoot	Podica senegalensis
Pied kingfisher	Ceryle rudis
Pink backed pelican	Pelecanus rufescens

Prince Ruspoli's turaco	*Tauraco ruspoli*
Pygmy falcon	*Poliohierax Semitorquatus*
Red-and green-chested Narina's trogan	*Apaloderma narina*
Red and yellow barbet	*Trachyphonus erythrocephalus*
Red-fronted parrot	*Poicephalus gulielmi*
Red-billed buffalo weaver	*Bubalornis niger*
red-billed oxpecker	*Buphagus erythorhynchus*
red-chested cuckoo	*Cuculus solitarius*
Rosy patched shrike	*Rhodophoneus cruentus*
Ruppell's vulture	*Gyps rueppellii*
Rwenzori turaco	*Tauraco johnstoni*
Sacred ibis	*Threskiornis aethiopicus*
Saddlebill stork	*Ephippiorhynchus*
Secretary bird	*Sagittarius serpentarius*
Silverbird	*Empidornis semipartitus*
Silvery-cheeked hornbill	*Bycanistes brevis*
Spurwinged goose	*Plectropterus gambensis*
Stresemann's bushcrow	*Zavattariornis stresemanni*
Tambourine dove	*Tympanistria tympanistria*
Thicknee	*Burphinus capensis*
Trumpeter hornbill	*Bycanistes bucinator*
Turtle dove	*Streptopelia lugens*
Verreaux' eagle	*Aquila verreauxii*
Violet crested turaco	*Tauraco porphyreolophus*
Vulturine guinea fowl	*Acryllium rulturinum*
West Nile red bishop	*Euplectes oryx*
Whistling duck	*Dendrocygna viduata*
White-backed night heron	*Nyticorax leuconotus*
White-headed buffalo weaver	*Dinemellia dinemelli*
White-necked cormorant	*Phalacrocorax carbo*
White-starred bush robin (*Vieillot*)	*Pogonicichla stellata*
White tailed swallow	*Hirondo megaensis*
Whitewinged bishop	*Euplectes albonotatus*
Yellow bishop	*Euplectes capensis*
Yellow-mantled bishop	*Euplectes macrourus*
Yellow-throated longclaw	*Macronyx croceus'*
Yellow wagtail	*Motacilla flava*
Yellow-collared loverbird	*Agapornis personata*

ART/PHOTO CREDITS

INDEX

A

B

C

D

H

I

M

P

R

S

T - U

W9-AUE-789

Fodor's

PROVENCE & THE FRENCH RIVIERA

8th Edition

Where to Stay and Eat
for All Budgets

Must-See Sights
and Local Secrets

Ratings You Can Trust

Fodor's Travel Publications   New York, Toronto, London, Sydney, Auckland
www.fodors.com

FODOR'S PROVENCE & THE FRENCH RIVIERA

Editor: Robert I. C. Fisher

Editorial Contributors: Sarah Fraser, Rosa Jackson, Nancy Wilson

Production Editors: Evangelos Vasilakis, Carrie Parker
Maps & Illustrations: David Lindroth, *cartographer*; Bob Blake, Rebecca Baer, *map editors*; William Wu, *information graphics*
Design: Fabrizio La Rocca, *creative director*; Guido Caroti, Siobhan O'Hare, *art directors*; Tina Malaney, Chie Ushio, Ann McBride, Jessica Walsh, *designers*; Melanie Marin, *senior picture editor*
Cover Photo (Bicyclist walking through sunflower field, Provence): Bryan F. Peterson/ Corbis
Production Manager: Angela L. McLean

8th Edition

ISBN 978-1-4000-1913-7

ISSN 1944-2912

SPECIAL SALES

This book is available at special discounts for bulk purchases for sales promotions or premiums. Special editions, including personalized covers, excerpts of existing books, and corporate imprints, can be created in large quantities for special needs. For more information, write to Special Markets/Premium Sales, 1745 Broadway, MD 6-2, New York, New York 10019, or e-mail specialmarkets@randomhouse.com.

AN IMPORTANT TIP & AN INVITATION

Although all prices, opening times, and other details in this book are based on information supplied to us at press time, changes occur all the time in the travel world, and Fodor's cannot accept responsibility for facts that become outdated or for inadvertent errors or omissions. So **always confirm information when it matters**, especially if you're making a detour to visit a specific place. Your experiences—positive and negative—matter to us. If we have missed or misstated something, **please write to us.** We follow up on all suggestions. Contact the Provence & the French Riviera editor at editors@fodors. com or c/o Fodor's at 1745 Broadway, New York, NY 10019.

PRINTED IN THE UNITED STATES OF AMERICA

10 9 8 7 6 5 4 3 2 1

Be a Fodor's Correspondent

Your opinion matters. It matters to us. It matters to your fellow Fodor's travelers, too. And we'd like to hear it. In fact, we need to hear it.

When you share your experiences and opinions, you become an active member of the Fodor's community. That means we'll not only use your feedback to make our books better, but we'll publish your names and comments whenever possible. Throughout our guides, look for "Word of Mouth," excerpts of your unvarnished feedback.

Here's how you can help improve Fodor's for all of us.

Tell us when we're right. We rely on local writers to give you an insider's perspective. But our writers and staff editors—who are the best in the business—depend on you. Your positive feedback is a vote to renew our recommendations for the next edition.

Tell us when we're wrong. We're proud that we update most of our guides every year. But we're not perfect. Things change. Hotels cut services. Museums change hours. Charming cafés lose charm. If our writer didn't quite capture the essence of a place, tell us how you'd do it differently. If any of our descriptions are inaccurate or inadequate, we'll incorporate your changes in the next edition and will correct factual errors at fodors.com immediately.

Tell us what to include. You probably have had fantastic travel experiences that aren't yet in Fodor's. Why not share them with a community of like-minded travelers? Maybe you chanced upon a beach or bistro or B&B that you don't want to keep to yourself. Tell us why we should include it. And share your discoveries and experiences with everyone directly at fodors.com. Your input may lead us to add a new listing or highlight a place we cover with a "Highly Recommended" star or with our highest rating, "Fodor's Choice."

Give us your opinion instantly at our feedback center at www.fodors.com/feedback. You may also e-mail editors@fodors.com with the subject line "Provence & the French Riviera Editor." Or send your nominations, comments, and complaints by mail to Provence & the French Riviera Editor, Fodor's, 1745 Broadway, New York, NY 10019.

You and travelers like you are the heart of the Fodor's community. Make our community richer by sharing your experiences. Be a Fodor's correspondent.

Happy Traveling!

Tim Jarrell, Publisher

CONTENTS

MAPS

ABOUT
THIS BOOK

Our Ratings

Sometimes you find terrific travel experiences and sometimes they just find you. But usually the burden is on you to select the right combination of experiences. That's where our ratings come in.

As travelers we've all discovered a place so wonderful that its worthiness is obvious. And sometimes that place is so experiential that superlatives don't do it justice: you just have to be there to know. These sights, properties, and experiences get our highest rating, **Fodor's Choice**, indicated by orange stars throughout this book.

Black stars highlight sights and properties we deem **Highly Recommended,** places that our writers, editors, and readers praise again and again for consistency and excellence.

By default, there's another category: any place we include in this book is by definition worth your time, unless we say otherwise. And we will.

Disagree with any of our choices? Care to nominate a place or suggest that we rate one more highly? Visit our feedback center at www.fodors. com/feedback.

Budget Well

Hotel and restaurant price categories from ¢ to $$$$ are defined in the opening pages of each chapter. For attractions, we always give standard adult admission fees; reductions are usually available for children, students, and senior citizens. Want to pay with plastic? **AE, D, DC, MC, V** following restaurant and hotel listings indicate if American Express, Discover, Diners Club, MasterCard, and Visa are accepted.

Restaurants

Unless we state otherwise, restaurants are open for lunch and dinner daily. We mention dress only when there's a specific requirement and reservations only when they're essential or not accepted—it's always best to book ahead.

Hotels

Hotels have private bath, phone, TV, and air-conditioning and operate on the European Plan (aka EP, meaning without meals), unless we specify that they use the Breakfast Plan (BP, with a full breakfast), Modified American Plan (MAP, with breakfast and dinner), or Full American Plan (FAP, including all meals). We always list facilities but not whether you'll be charged an extra fee to use them, so when pricing accommodations, find out what's included.

Many Listings

★	Fodor's Choice
★	Highly recommended
⌧	Physical address
♁	Directions
⌂	Mailing address
☎	Telephone
🖷	Fax
⊕	On the Web
✉	E-mail
🎫	Admission fee
☉	Open/closed times
Ⓜ	Metro stations
▭	Credit cards

Hotels & Restaurants

🏠	Hotel
🛏	Number of rooms
♨	Facilities
⑂	Meal plans
✕	Restaurant
⌥	Reservations
⌕	Smoking
⑃	BYOB
✕🏠	Hotel with restaurant that warrants a visit

Outdoors

⛳	Golf
⛺	Camping

Other

☚	Family-friendly
⇨	See also
⌧	Branch address
☞	Take note

Experience Provence & the French Riviera

WORD OF MOUTH

"Avoid Provence if you don't want a slow pace, incredible light, and wonderful food. Watching a French couple spend 30 minutes waiting for their bottle of wine to open up opened my eyes that my go-go, don't-stop-to-smell-the-roses lifestyle was less than optimal for traveling here. Instead, open wine, wait, pour some in a glass, wait, swirl and sniff, wait, then drink. What a wonderful life! But if like my father-in-law, you answer 'how was your vacation' with 'drove 8,000 miles in five days,' don't go."

—travel_buoy

WHAT'S WHERE

The following numbers refer to chapters.

2 The Alpilles, Arles & the Camargue. Between the Rhone River delta and the hills of the Alpilles, this region has been a major crossroads since the Romans, as witness the ancient arenas at Arles and Nîmes and spectacular Pont du Gard aqueduct. Haunting natural beauty can be found in the Camargue but nearby are the cosmopolitan centers of feisty Latin Nîmes, chic St-Rémy, and Van Gogh's golden Arles.

3 The Vaucluse. Anchored by the medieval city stronghold of Avignon, the Vaucluse spreads luxuriantly north into the Rhône vineyards of Châteauneuf-du-Pape and east along the Lavender Route. Check out the Roman theater in Orange, then head to the Luberon—the quintessential Provençal landscape—set with magical hilltop towns like Gordes and Roussillon.

4 Aix, Marseille & the Central Coast. Famous for its tree-lined boulevards, sleek, smart Aix-en-Provence has a bevy of posh cafés where you can enjoy some perfect people-watching, just like homeboy Cézanne used to do. South lies Marseille—France's second largest city—a Mediterranean melting pot as tasty as its bouillabaisse. Studded with the rocky Calanques, the nearby coast has pockets of natural beauty that could pass for an Aegean island.

5 The Western Côte d'Azur. This is where the legend begins: palm trees, parasol pines, and sea improbably blue, all framed against the red-rock Massif de l'Estérel. There's St-Tropez, with its white-sand beaches and its port bars thick with off-duty celebs plus sportif resorts like St-Raphaël. Inland, the woolly backcountry of Haute Provence headlines the Gorges du Verdon.

6 Nice & the Eastern Côte d'Azur. A sunbelievable shangri-la, this is the heart of the glamorous Côte d'Azur. Cross the high rises of Hong Kong with the amusement-park feel of Disneyland, add a royal touch, and there you have Monte-Carlo—all 473 acres of it. Much nicer is Nice, thanks to its Old Town's bonbon-colored palaces. Eastward lies Cannes, famed for its May film festival, and the zillion-dollar hotels of Cap d'Antibes and St-Jean-Cap-Ferrat. Eastward hovers the sky-kissing *village perché* of Èze, while the rainbow ends in the famous art villages: Renoir's Haut-de-Cagnes, Picasso's Antibes, and Matisse's St-Paul and Vence.

TOP PROVENCE & FRENCH RIVIERA ATTRACTIONS

Arles

(A) Arles actually manages to live up to the beauty of Van Gogh's swirling renditions (and capitalizes on them with ubiquitous "Vince" T-shirts), but the town's biggest attractions are the Roman theater and amphitheater, built around 46 BC. Time seems to have stood still since 1888 in pockets of the vieille ville (Old Town).

Pont du Gard

(D) No other ancient Roman sight in Provence rivals this 2,000-year-old bridge, the highest the Romans ever built. Magnificent views can be had from the opposite bank and at night, when it is spectacularly illuminated.

The Camargue

(B) Provence's amazing nature park is set with plains of marsh grass stretching to the sea, interrupted only by explosions of flying flamingoes bursting into waves of color or modest stampedes of stocky bulls. Tour the region like a local: on horseback, led by one of the area's gardians, or "cowboys."

Avignon

(E) Once considered the "second Rome," the medieval walled city of Avignon is surprisingly youthful and vibrant—this art-filled spot allows you to spend the day at the famous 14th-century Pope's Palace, then attend a 21st-century avant-garde theatrical "happening" in the evening at the summer Festival d'Avignon.

The Lavender Route

(C) Like Holland's May tulips, the lavender of Haute-Provence is in its glory only once a year: the last two weeks of July, when for miles the landscape breaks out in saturated shades of purple in the region east of the Rhône and north of the Luberon. The views are scent-sational!

Aix-en-Provence

(F) Home-town of Cézanne and Zola, ritzy and charming Aix is epitomized by its Cours Mirabeau—"the Champs-Elysées of Provence"—a tree-lined boulevard with lovely cafés in which a lengthy roster of famous literati have lounged about.

St-Paul-de-Vence

(G) Have lunch at La Colombe D'Or in St-Paul and sit under a real Picasso, or wander into the gardens to have coffee and dessert next to the Rodin sculpture. It's not difficult to understand why some call this the most beautiful inn on the French Riviera, perhaps in all of France.

St-Tropez

(I) Make a summer pilgrimage to Brigitte Bardot and St-Tropez, the town she made famous, if only to sit along the port eating ice cream and watching the wildly wealthy file on by. And, darling, don't forget your Tod's espadrilles.

Marseille

(K) Visit the Vieux Port of Marseille and relish in the way the light and the cries of the fishmongers bounce off the anchored sailboats; then bring your wide-angle lens to capture the Cinemascopic views of the entire city from the crow's-nest church of Napoléon III's Notre-Dame-de-la-Garde.

St-Rémy-de-Provence

(J) This cosmopolitan town remains a haven for chic urbanites and a mellow retreat dappled with the shade of ancient plane trees and surrounded by fields of sunflowers immortalized by Van Gogh.

The Calanques

(H) Probing the tall white cliffs just west of picture-perfect Cassis are the rocky, pine-studded finger-coves called the Calanques—be sure to enjoy a plunge into the turquoise waters of these film-set lagoons.

PROVENCE & THE FRENCH RIVIERA PLANNER

How's the Weather?

Spring and fall are the best months to experience the dazzling light, rugged rocky countryside, and fruited vineyards of Provence. Though the lavender fields show peak color in mid-July, summertime here is beastly hot; worse, it's always crowded on the beaches and connecting roads. Avoid winter, when the razor-sharp mistral wind can cut to the bone. Surprisingly enough, it does rain (and has even snowed)—for about four weeks out of the year. Otherwise it's mostly hot and dry. It does get chilly at night, so it's wise to bring warm clothing for those evening strolls through the lavender fields.

As for the French Riviera, the sexy south of France may be reputed for many steamy things, but it's not at all humid. It is, in fact, hot and dry for most of the year. Recent high-season temperatures have gone up to 105°F, while spring and fall still see highs of 68°F. Summer wear usually boils down to a bikini and light wrap. Rainfall between March and October cools things off. According to the locals, winter (November–early March) is cold, rainy, miserable—which may be relative, as the area's famous for having more than 340 days of sunshine per year.

Making the Most of Your Time

The rugged, unpredictable charm of Provence catches the imagination and requires long, thoughtful savoring—like a fine wine over a delicious meal. Come here in any season except November or January, when most of the hotels close and all of Provence seems to be on holiday.

The best place to start your trip is in Avignon. It's on a fast train link from Paris, but even if you arrive in record time, it's at exactly this moment that you need to slow down. As you step off the train and are confronted with all that magnificent architecture and art, breathe deeply. Provence is about lazy afternoons and spending "just one more day," and Avignon is a good place to have a practice run: it's cosmopolitan enough to keep the most energetic visitor occupied, while old and wise enough to teach the value of time. From here you can access every part of Provence easily, either by train, by bus, or by car.

If you're settling into one town and making day trips, it's best to divide your time by visiting west and then east of Nice. Parallel roads along the Corniches allow for access into towns with different personalities. The A8 main *autoroute*, as well as the coastal train, makes zipping up and down from Monaco to Fréjus–St-Raphael a breeze. Visit different resort towns, but make sure you tear yourself away from the coastal *plages* (beaches) to visit the perched villages that the region is famed for.

Food plays a crucial role here, and some of the best restaurants aren't so easy to access; make sure to include taxi money in your budget to get to some of the more remote restaurants, or plan on renting a car. Try to come in truffle, lavender, or olive season.

Unless you enjoy jacked-up prices, traffic jams, and sardine-style beach crowds, avoid the French Riviera coast like the plague in July and August. Many of the better restaurants simply shut down to avoid the coconut-oil crowd, and the Estérel is closed to hikers during this flash-fire season. Cannes books up early for the film festival in May. Between Cannes and Menton, the Côte d'Azur's gentle microclimate usually provides moderate winters, so even November can be gentle and caressing.

Getting Around

Public transport in the South of France is very well organized, with most areas accessible by plane, train, bus, or boat. Flying in is a good option, as Nice and Marseille have two of the largest airports in France and regular flights come in from Paris and London. And although the Aéroport Toulon-Hyères is much smaller, it also has frequent flights in and out. If you prefer the more scenic route, note that the high-speed trains—the fabulous TGV's—go directly to Marseille, Aix-en-Provence, Toulon, and Nice in about the same time as a flight, and a big selection of local and regional trains will take you quick-as-a-wink to many towns along the Riviera coast. There is a moderately good network of buses run by a large number of independent bus companies—make sure that you check with the local tourism office for which one operates in the area you wish to travel, since the who's who in the bus world here is very confusing. A lovely way of transport is to float: boat services run from Nice, Cannes, Marseille, and Toulon out to most of the coast, to the Isles de Hyères, the Calanques, and the Chateau d'If. The freedom of driving is always advisable, but do try to relax in the summer when traffic is at its height and traffic-jams can cause frayed tempers. Try to stick to the National or District roads, which are far less scary to drive than the speeding highways, and depending on the season you could find yourself swathed in purple lavender or surrounded by silvery olive trees or driving along empty stretches of golden beaches. People are friendly if you get lost, and the long stretches of road are marvelously beautiful. Get a good map, as the road signs are often as clear as mud, especially off the main autoroute (toll highway).

Parlez-Vous English?

After struggling through weeks of searching through your English-French dictionary, let your brain slide into the peaceful lanes of full comprehension. Riviera Radio 106.5 is the Riviera's English–language radio station, with news, weather, traffic, and wisecracking DJs programmed to do just that. Many hotels and tabacs carry the *Herald,* which is the international English paper, and the *Riviera Times,* which is for local English Riviera news. You'll find other travelers at Heidi's Books in Antibes (24 rue Aubernon; 04–93–34–74–11) and the Irish pub called Morrison's in Cannes (10 rue Tesseire; 04–92–98–16–17), notorious for not speaking French at all.

Finding a Place to Stay

Space is at a premium in Provence.

The bigger cities will always have somewhere to stay, but the good and reputable hotels book up quickly at certain times of the year. June, July, and August are considered to be high season.

In the larger cities, be careful to note where your hotel is located because even if the hotel is deluxe, there are unsavory neighborhoods that can make for an unpleasant—if not downright scary—stay, especially at night.

In the smaller towns, make sure to always call ahead at least a month or two in advance as in the off-season many of the smaller hotels close and in the high season they are often full long in advance.

In the summer months it is particularly difficult to find a place to stay.

Book as far in advance as possible for some of the more popular spots—it's not uncommon to book up to six months to a year in advance.

Many return visitors book their next year's stay at the end of this year's visit.

If you are having trouble finding somewhere, check with the local tourism office. They will have a list of rooms and contact numbers.

QUINTESSENTIAL
PROVENCE & FRENCH RIVIERA

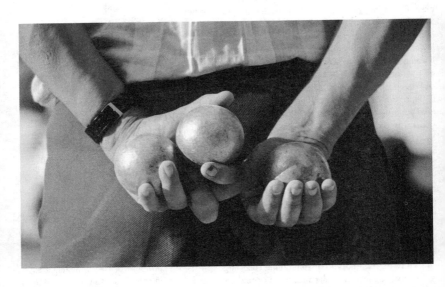

Pastis & Pétanque

In every village from the Rhône Valley to the Italian border, under every deep-shaded *allée* of plane trees, the theater of Provençal life plays itself out slowly, serenely, and sociably. The café is a way of life in Provence, a cool outdoor living room where friends gather like family and share the ritual of the long, slow drink, the discussion of the weather (hot), and an amble over to the *pétanque* (lawn-bowling) court. The players stand, somber and intense, hands folded behind backs, and watch the intricate play of heavy metal balls rolling and clicking. A knot of onlookers gathers, disperses, is reinforced. In this region of the animated debate, the waving gesture, the forefinger punching to chest, it is a surprisingly quiet pastime.

Just as refined a ritual is the drinking of the requisite pastis. The server arrives with a tray loaded with the appropriate props: a carafe of water emblazoned with "Ricard" or "51"; a bowl with an ice cube or two; a bowl of olives, black as jet; and a stubby glass cradling two fingers of amber liquid redolent of anise and licorice. Plop an ice cube into the liquor, then slowly pour a rope of cool water into the glass, watching for the magic moment when the amber transforms itself to milky white. Sip slowly, mop your forehead, and settle in.

Dining à la Midi

You'll eat late in the Midi (south of France), rarely before 1 for lunch, usually after 9 at night. In summer, shops and museums may shut down until 3 or 4, as much to accommodate lazy lunchers as for the crowds taking sun on the beach. But a late lunch works nicely with a late breakfast—and that's another southern luxury. As morning here is the

coolest part of the day and the light is at its sweetest, hotels of every class take pains to make breakfast memorable and whenever possible served outdoors. There may be tables in the garden with sunny-print cloths and a nosegay of flowers, or even a tray on your private balcony table. Accompanied by birdsong and cool morning sun, it's one of the three loveliest meals of the day.

Yours for the Basking

With their worldwide fame as the earth's most glamorous beaches, the real thing often comes as a shock to first-timers: much of the Côte d'Azur is lined with rock and pebble, and the beaches are narrow swaths backed by city streets or roaring highways. Some beaches are reviled for their famous *galets,* round white stones the size of a fist, heaped along the shoreline, just where the sand should be. Not surprisingly, some resorts ship

in truckfuls of sand or shovel in loads from deep water. There are some natural sand beaches on the southern French coast—especially between St-Tropez and Cannes—and some beaches like La Garoupe on Cap d'Antibes enjoy legendary status. Provence's coastline—between the Camargue and St-Tropez—alternates sandy pockets with rocky inlets called *criques* and *calanques,* where you perch on black rocks and ease yourself into turquoise water.

Many beaches are privately operated, renting parasols and mattresses to anyone who pays; if you're a guest at one of the local hotels, you'll get a discount. Fees for private beaches average €6–€15 for a dressing room and mattress, between €2 and €4 for a parasol, and between €10 and €25 for a cabana. Happily, the sun is free, even though it will make you feel like a millionaire.

IF YOU LIKE

Being Scott & Zelda

Married new money? Made a stock-market killing? Or just remember the old adage "if you don't travel first class, your heirs will"? Well, the Riviera has been a hard place to practice self-denial ever since F. Scott Fitzgerald arrived with the rest of his Jazz Age literati. So drain that glass of Dom. Enough lollygagging! It's time for a power decision: which luxurious pleasure palace will you treat yourself to? Hey, if you can't be self-indulgent on the French Riviera, where can you be?

Cap–Eden Roc, Cap d'Antibes. Where once Hemingway ordered another Pernod and Zelda wore her latest Poiret, this famous hotel is today the rendevous of the film stars. You may find Michael and Catherine in the bar, Harrison behind his *Herald-Tribune,* and Barbra keeping a low profile under her parasol by the cliff-edge pool. Try to be cool and focus on the menu.

Château de la Chevre d'Or, Èze. Seemingly set just below cloud level, this sky-high aerie occupies some of the choicest real estate in Èze, that magical island-in-the-sky perched 1,500 feet over the sea and St-Jean-Cap-Ferrat. Little wonder the views out your window rival those from a NASA space capsule.

La Colombe d'Or, St-Paul-de-Vence. Yes, those are real Picassos, Mirós, Braques, and Bonnards over your dinner table. This legendary hotel and restaurant was once the favored hangout of these artists when you could buy one of their daubs for $5. Today, it is super-stylish, utterly elegant, and you can't move without bumping into a Calder mobile—or an off-duty celebrity dining on the enchanting terrace.

Villages Perchés

Practically defying gravity, the sky-kissing, hilltop-perched villages of Provence and the Riviera are some of the most spectacular sights in France. In the Middle Ages, pirates and Saracens drove village life to put its wagons, as it were, in a circle—and well above the fray. Thus sprouted these villages from the hilltops, Babel-like towers of canted cubes and blunt cylinders seeming to grow out of the rock. Houses mount several levels; thus freed from obstructing neighbors, their windows take in light and wide-open views. The tiniest of streets weave between rakish building blocks, and the houses seem tied together by arching overpasses and rhythmic arcades. Wells spring up in miniature *placettes* (little squares), the trickling sound echoing loud in the stone enclosure. Succumb to their once-upon-a-timeliness and be sure to visit two or three.

Èze. As cute as a Fisher-Price toy village, Èze is so relentlessly picturesque it will practically click your camera for you.

Haut-de-Cagnes. Topped by a Grimaldi castle, once a forgetaway favored by the likes of Renoir, Soutine, and Simone de Beauvoir, this enchanting labyrinth of steep alleys and Renaissance stairways is a magical place where time seems to be holding its breath.

Oppède-le-Vieux. Isolated above the Luberon, this village stands alone in the mist, lovingly cared for by its residents but utterly uncommercial.

Peillon. This perfect example of the eagle's-nest village above the Riviera coast has been voted boutique-free forever by its citizens, and remains marvelously ancient, even primeval, in atmosphere.

Relishing the Riviera

The Côte d'Azur is home to top chefs who are redefining the "new Mediterranean cuisine" in all its costly splendor: "scrambled" sea urchins; herb sausages with chopped truffles and lobster; frogs' legs soup with fresh mint; and poached sea bass flan with crayfish sauce. Grand names like Alain Ducasse still present such delights at showplaces like Monaco's Le Louis XV, but there are any number of young stars on the make. But with access to some of the world's best ingredients, Provençal chefs face a dilemma—do they uphold tradition or go out on a limb? Here are four legends who balance both schools beautifully.

Le Louis XV, Monte Carlo. Crystal, gilt, and period pomp frame the extraordinary cuisine of Alain Ducasse—truffle-sprinkled artichokes, ember-grilled pigeon breast, and salt-seared foie gras, anyone?

Moulin des Mougins, Mougins. Culinary wizard Alain Llorca has given a radical face-lift to this Roger Vergé landmark, as you'll discover with one bite of the incredible Mediterranean sea bass steamed with seaweed and white coco beans.

Le Cagnard, Cagnes-sur-Mer. While feasting on Jean-Yves Johany's black-truffle lasagna, look up to see the medieval ceiling slide open to reveal the evening sky.

Mirazur, Menton. Argentinian-Italian Mauro Colagreco excels at "la jeune cuisine" thanks to studying with Bernard Loiseau and Alain Ducasse, then adding in those much-talked-about Spanish "techniques" such as spuma (foam).

Where Art Comes First

Artists have been drawn to the south of France for generations, awed by its luminous colors and crystal clear light. Monet, Renoir, Gauguin, and Van Gogh led the way, followed over the years by Léger, Matisse, Picasso, Chagall, and Cocteau. Cézanne had the good fortune to be born in Aix, and he returned to it, and to his beloved country home nearby, throughout his life. The artists left behind them a superb legacy of works, utterly individual but all consistently bathed in Mediterranean color and light. That's why a visit to this region can be as culturally rich as a month in Paris and just as intimately allied to the setting that inspired the work. Art museums abound—but don't forget to pay your respects to Cézanne's studio in Aix and Renoir's garden home in Cagnes.

Fondation Maeght, St-Paul-de-Vence. With its serene setting in a hilltop woods and its light-flooded displays of modern works, this gallery-museum is the best mixed-artist exhibition space in the south of France.

Musée de l'Annonciade, St-Tropez. St-Tropez was the Riviera's first "Greenwich Village" and artists—Signac, Derain, and Matisse, among them—flocked here in the early 20th century. Today, the collection has its share of masterworks.

Musée Matisse, Nice. In a superb Italianate villa above Nice, Matisse's family has amassed a wide-ranging collection of the artist's works.

Musée Picasso, Antibes. In view of the scenes of enchanting Antibes that inspired them, vast paintings by Picasso are mounted in the rooms where they were created.

GREAT ITINERARIES

In addition to the following two tours, check out our Lavender Route three-day itinerary in Chapter 3 and our overview of the Modern Art Road in Chapter 6.

FIRST-TIME TOUR
14 Days

First-time travellers to this belle region can make the most of a short visit by going straight to the highlights. You may only have a week, but try to take two. You need that much time to ease out of the fast-paced-telephone-ringing-crazy-car-driver madness of the big city and into the slow, luscious let's-stop-and-enjoy world of the South of France. The region, much like extraordinarily fine food, should be savored with lazy afternoon naps in-between meals.

Days 1–2: Avignon and the Luberon

Arriving at the western border of the South of France, take in the monuments and backstreets of Avignon, starting with the magnificent Popes' Palace, then consider a quick trip out to the majestic Roman aqueduct, the Pont du Gard. Then head eastward to the Luberon—this is chicest Provence, famous for its lavender fields and towns still firmly anchored in the past, such as the honey-tone village of Bonnieux—and end up amid the ruby red cliffs of Roussillon. ⇨ *Chapter 3*.

Days 3–4: Arles & the Camargue

Soak in Old Provence and revel the golden light that drove Van Gogh to distraction. It's easy to see why he was so prolific here; the finger itches to capture the vivid colors. Visit the Roman monuments, unparalleled in France, and trace history back thousands of years. Then head out to the wild, windswept, and achingly beautiful landscapes of the Camargue nature preserve; book into a country mas (farmhouse), luxuriate in the smells of the countryside, and settle into this world apart. ⇨ *Chapter 2*.

Days 5–6: Marseille

You can visit all the salient points of Marseille in a long day, but why would you? It's a vibrant port town that combines fashion with New York edginess and feisty Metropolitan determination with classical grace and it deserves the time you can give it. Start the day early and get to the Vieux Port's Marche aux Poissons (fish market), which is like going to a piece of theater but in real, daily life—hawkers yell, buyers negotiate, and the rows and rows of fresh fish get scooped up in no time. Don't miss the Centre de la Vielle Charité with its magnificent Baroque chapel, the Abbaye de St-Victor with its Romanesque design and its evocative nooks and crannies, the time-stained Le Panier neighborhood, or hilltop-cresting Notre-Dame-de-la-Garde. ⇨ *Chapter 4*.

Days 7–8: Aix-en-Provence

Gracious and wonderfully cultivated, with centuries of well-bred elegance evident in its fine art and noble architecture, Aix has a wellspring of sights to see. Start in the historic heart along the famous Cours Mirabeau and take note of all the fountains shadowed by giant plantain trees. Make sure you stop off at the Cathedrale de St-Sauveur and take a peek at the magnificent *Triptyque du Buisson Ardent* by Nicholas Froment. Day 8 should be consecrated to the prodigal son of Aix, Paul Cézanne. The Atelier Cézanne is right in the town center, and glory in the simple objects that featured so prominently in his still lifes. Then head south to the family estate, the Jas de Bouffon, with its

ITALY

Avignon
Roussillon
MONTAGNE DU LUBERON
Bonnieux
Arles
Aix-en-Provence
St-Jean-Cap-Ferrat
Vence   Èze
St-Paul   Villefranche-sur-Mer
Cagnes-sur-Mer   Nice
Antibes
Cap d'Antibes
RGUE
Etang de
Vaccarès
Etang de
Berre
Golfe
de Fos
Marseille
Mediterranean Sea

quintessentially beautiful manor house and park—nearby is the famed lookout point where the father of modern art so often immortalized Mont St-Victoire on canvas. ⇨ *Chapter 4.*

Days 9–10: Nice & Haut-de-Cagnes
Leapfrog eastward over to Nice, draped over the Baie des Anges and rich with local museums and cuisine. This large city harbors an Old Town studded with 18th-century palaces and adorable alleyways. Saunter down the Promenade des Anglais beachfront to end up at the oh-so-charming Cours Saleya marketplace, then head up to the city suburb of Cimiez to visit the noted museums devoted to Matisse and Chagall. For a complete change of pace, the next day take the coastal train for a quick ride to Cagnes-sur-Mer and bus it up the hill to the most gorgeous little village along the coast, Haut-de-Cagnes, crowned by a Grimaldi fortress, threaded with ageless streets lined with tiny hobbit houses, and once home to Renoir. ⇨ *Chapter 6.*

Day 11: St-Paul-de-Vence & Vence
Time to head up into the Côte d'Azur's arrière-pays, or backcountry, to discover two fabled art towns: St-Paul, home to the Riviera's most beautiful and historic inn, La Colombe d'Or—yes, you can dine under real Picassos here—and the masterpiece-studded Fondation Maeght, and then nearby Vence, where all make a beeline for Matisse's great Chapelle du Rosaire. ⇨ *Chapter 6.*

Day 12: Antibes & Cap d'Antibes
No wonder Picasso loved Antibes—it is picture-book pretty, lined with history-stained streets, and hosted a procession of visiting artists. The great Pablo set up shop in the waterfront château, now the Musée Picasso, to paint the most joyous works of his career. A 10-minute bus ride away is that favorite of billionaires and movie stars, Cap d'Antibes, but anyone can indulge in the Belle Epoque splendors of its Villa Eilenroc or its spectacular seaside path called the Sentier Tirepoil. ⇨ *Chapter 6.*

GREAT ITINERARIES

Days 13–14: Eze & St-Jean-Cap-Ferrat

This is the heart of the land of beaches, bathing beauties, and expensive clothing—a few train stops pass Villefranche-sur-Mer (residents include Bill Gates and Tina Turner) you'll hit the eagle's nest that is Eze, France's most fabulous village perché (perched village). It's cute as a Fisher-Price toy and has limitless views high over the bluer-than-blue Mediterranean. There below, curving around the bay, is fashionable St-Jean-Cap-Ferrat, where you can visit the treasure-filled Villa Ephrussi de Rothschild. Back home at your hotel toast the good life with a well-deserved glass of chilled rosé. Tomorrow, it's back to reality. ⇨ *Chapter 6.*

ANTIQUITIES TOUR
10 Days

If you want to make a pilgrimage to the ancient and mysterious world of Roman architecture, there is no other region in France with such a large selection of lovely and well-preserved ruins to choose from.

Days 1–2: Orange & Vaison-la-Romaine

Every year thousands are drawn to the heart of the Vaucluse region to see Orange's spectacular Theatre Antique, a colossal Roman structure built in the time of Caesar Augustus, and its equally beautiful Arc de Triomphe. From here, head off to Vaison-la-Romaine to see two broad fields of skeletal ruins of villas, museums, and landscaped gardens and the Cathedrale-Notre-Dame-de-Nazareth built from recycled fragments of a Gallo-Roman basilica. ⇨ *Chapter 3.*

Day 3: Pont du Gard

Erected some 2,000 years ago as part of a 48-km (30-mi) canal supplying water to Roman Nîmes, this magnificent three-tiered aqueduct is perhaps the greatest bridge the Romans ever built. Much of the canal passes through underground channels carved out of solid rock, but fragments of it and lost aqueduct arches still scatter the area approaching the bridge, and a trail to follow them is clearly marked and can take a full day to follow. ⇨ *Chapter 2.*

Day 4: Nîmes

Tracing back its feisty, noisy, and raucous ways back to its Roman incarnation when arrogant soldiers swelled the population, Nîmes is a detour from peaceful, lazy Provence. Even its Old Town has none of the gentrified grace of St-Rémy or Les Baux, and the city's lively café society creates a constant buzz. What Nîmes does better than any other Provence city, however, is seamlessly marry big city life with a wealth of architectural heritage. Without a doubt, it has some of the best-preserved antiquities in Continental Europe, including the famous Arena and the Maison Carrée. ⇨ *Chapter 2.*

Days 5–6: Arles

The medieval center of Arles was built over Roman ruins and still incorporates earlier vestiges into its more modern structure. The narrow and rather dark streets provide protection from the Mistral, and the cobbled streets provide wonderful glimpses of history. It is in this lovely city that you will find the sister arena to Nîmes, also called les Arenes—beside it lies the Theatre Antique, described once by Henry James as "the most touching ruins I had ever beheld." Today, it is a mess

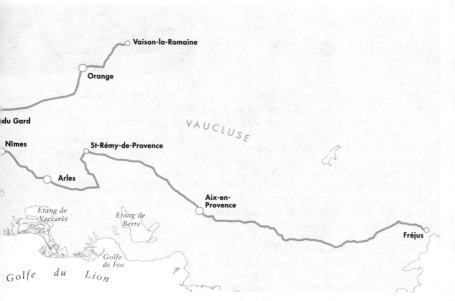

of broken columns and fragmented stone carvings, but it is a particularly romantic setting, as is the Thermes Constantin, the 4th-century Roman baths where you can still see the vaulted caldarium, warm bath, and underground heated floor, and the mysterious Crytoportiques, oddly-shaped arched Roman tunnels whose use is still in question today. ⇨ *Chapter 2.*

Days 7–8: St-Rémy-de-Provence

Host of the two most miraculously preserved classical monuments in the modern world, simply called Les Antiques, St-Remy offers up a diverse rendering of wonderful Roman ruins. Spend at least a day marvelling over the Mausolée, (dedicated to Julien—largely thought to be Julius Caesar) and the Arc Triomphal, dating from 20 AD and wander through Glanum, a maze of Greek and Roman stone walls, foundations, and towers at the base of a ragged cliff. Don't forget to tour St-Rémy itself, littered with ancient Roman baths and architecture. ⇨ *Chapter 2.*

Days 9–10: Aix-en-Provence & Fréjus

On the way back to the coast, stop off at Aix's Thermes Sextius, now a high-tech grand luxury spa built on the old ruins, for a well-deserved break. Take the time to visit some of the other ruins in the area before heading out to the coastal queen of Roman antiquities: Fréjus. Here you'll find a perfectly preserved Roman theater, grandiose Roman arena, and partially intact aqueduct, demanding at least a day's worth of time. ⇨ *Chapters 4 & 5.*

WHEN TO GO

July and August in Provence and the Côte d'Azur can be stifling, not only because of the intense heat but the crowds of tourists and vacationers. June and September are the best months to be in the region, as both are free of the midsummer crowds and the weather is summer-balmy. June offers the advantage of long daylight hours, although cheaper prices and many warm days, often lasting well into October, make September attractive. Try to avoid the second half of July and all of August, when almost all of France goes on vacation. Huge crowds jam the roads and beaches, and prices are jacked up in resorts. Don't travel on or around July 14 and August 1, 15, and 31, when every French family is either going on vacation or driving home. Watch out for May, riddled with church holidays—one a week—and the museum closings they entail. Anytime between March and November will offer you a good chance to soak up the sun on the Côte d'Azur. After All Saints (November 1) the whole region begins to shutter down for winter, and won't open its main resort hotels until Easter. Still, off-season has its charms— the pétanque games are truly just the town folks' game, the most touristy hill towns are virtually abandoned, and when it's nice out—more often than not—you can bask in direct sun in the cafés.

Climate

Provence has a basically Mediterranean climate, distinguished by winds like the mistral, or "master" wind, which blows down the Rhône up to 150 days a year. This and other winds make the soil here dry and the night sky bright and clear. Temperatures soar on the coast in July and August, and it rains less in summer than at other times of the year.

Forecasts **Weather Channel Connection** (☎900/932–8437), 95¢ per minute from a Touch-Tone phone.

Weather conditions in France can be checked on the Web, at ⊕*www.meteo.fr.*

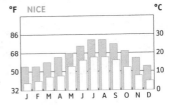

The Alpilles, Arles & the Camargue

THE PONT DU GARD, NÎMES, THE RHÔNE DELTA & THE LANGUEDOC FRONTIER

Roman amphitheater, Arles

WORD OF MOUTH

"I don't think you can go wrong by basing anywhere in the 'middle' of the areas you want to explore . . . my husband and I were pleasantly surprised at how close all these villages are to each other and how they can be grouped easily for day trips."

—carolits

WELCOME TO THE ALPILLES, ARLES & THE CAMARGUE

Wild horses of the Camargue

TOP REASONS TO GO

★ **Vincent van Gogh's Arles:** Ever since the fiery Dutchman immortalized Arles in all its chromatic drama, this town has had a starring role in museums around the world.

★ **A dip in the Middle Ages:** Wander the ghostly ruins of the Château des Baux in Les Baux-de-Provence: a tour de force of medieval ambience.

★ **Provence unplugged:** The famous lagoons of the Camargue will swamp you with their charms once you catch sight of their white horses, pink flamingos, and black bulls.

★ **St-Rémy's relentless charm:** Find inspired gourmet cooking, meditate quietly on Greco-Roman antiquity, or browse bustling markets, basket in hand, at this fashionable village enclave.

★ **The Pont du Gard:** This aqueduct of the ancient Roman era is also a spectacular work of art.

1 **Languedoc frontier.** The westernmost edge of Provence is highlighted by **Nîmes,** which competes with Arles and Orange as "the Rome of France" and is home to the Maison Carrée, the best-preserved ancient temple in Provence (Thomas Jefferson admired it so much he used it as a model for the Virginia state capitol). To the north is the **Pont du Gard,** most awe-inspiring in the early morning light.

2 **The Camargue.** A bus ride away from Arles and bracketed by the towns of Aigues-Mortes and Stes-Maries-de-la-Mer, the vast **Camargue nature park** is one of France's most fascinating areas. Horseback ride across its mysterious marshland, then enjoy home-style cooking at one of the exclusive *mas* (converted-farmhouse) hotels.

3 **The Alpilles.** These spiky mountains guard treasures like **Les Baux-de-Provence**—be bewitched by both its ville morte (dead town) and its luxurious L'Oustau de la Baumanière inn. Nearby is ritzy **St-Rémy-de-Provence,** Van Gogh's famous retreat.

Mediterranean Sea

0   10 mi
0   10 km

4 **Arles.** While little is left of the town that Van Gogh once painted, there are spots where you can still channel his spirit. Today, **Arles** remains fiercely Provençal and is famed for its folklore events.

Maison Carrée, Nîmes

GETTING ORIENTED

Rugged and beautiful, this is landscape that is different from everywhere else in the South. Nowhere else will you find the Camargue's hypnotic plane of marshland stretching out to the sea, or the rocky Alpilles that jut upward hiding medieval fortress towns. Yet city folk find joy here, too, in Van Gogh's colorful Arles or in feisty, fiercely independent Nîmes. And if it all gets just a bit too dusty, there is a plethora of options for some pampered R&R.

Hiking in the Alpilles, Bouches du Rhône

ont du Gard

ALPILLES, ARLES & CAMARGUE PLANNER

Main Regional Tourist Offices

Regional tourist offices prefer written queries only. Local tourist offices for major towns covered in this chapter can be phoned, faxed, or reached by mail.

The Comité Régional du Tourisme du Languedoc-Roussillon provides information on all towns west of the Rhône.

The remainder of towns covered in this chapter are handled by the Comité Regional du Tourisme de Provence-Alpes-Côte d'Azur.

For information on the area around Arles and St-Rémy, contact the Comité Départemental du Tourisme des Bouches-du-Rhône.

Addresses: **Comité Régional du Tourisme du Languedoc-Roussillon** (⊠*20 rue République34000Montpellier* ⊕*www.sunfrance.com*). (**Comité Regional du Tourisme de Provence-Alpes-Côte d'Azur** ⊠*12 pl. Joliette13002Marseille* ⊕*www.discover-southoffrance.com*). (**Comité Départemental du Tourisme des Bouches-du-Rhône** ⊠*13 rue Roux de Brignole Marseille* ⊕*www.visitprovence.com*).

Finding a Place to Stay

Although Arles, Les Baux, and St-Rémy have stylish, competitive hotels with all the requisite comforts and Provençal touches, from wrought iron to *folklorique* cottons, Nîmes doesn't attract—or much merit—the overnight crowds; thus its hotels, with rare exception, have little in the way of charm. But throughout the region and well outside the towns you'll find lovely converted *mas* (farmhouses), blending into the landscape as if they'd been there a thousand years—but offering modern pleasures: gardens, swimming pools, and sophisticated cooking. For information on *gîtes* (houses offered as a vacation rental) and *chambres d'hôtes* (bed-and-breakfasts in private homes), check out the Lodging section in the Travel Smart chapter.

The Provençal Market

In Provence, forget about the supermarket and head to the marketplace—an integral part of French culture anywhere in France, but even more so in Provence. Every town, small or large, worth its weight in salt will have a market brimming over with succulent produce, a rainbow of colorful vegetables, wide selection of cheeses, and meats. You can also find products typical to the region; lavender soap, olive oils, and regional snacks. Market days change depending on the town, but catch them when you can.

DINING & LODGING PRICES IN EUROS				
¢	$	$$	$$$	$$$$
Restaurants				
Under €13	€14–€19	€20–€24	€25–€31	Over €32
Hotels				
Under €55	€56–€85	€86–€135	€136–€200	Over €201

Restaurant prices are per person for a main course at dinner, including tax (19.6%) and service; note that if a restaurant offers only prix-fixe (set-price) meals, it has been given the price category that reflects the full prix-fixe price. Hotel prices are for a standard double room in high season, including tax (19.6%) and service charge.

Loosen Those Belts

If eating is the national pastime in France, it is a true vocation in Provence. And the pleasure of relaxing in a shady square over a pitcher of local rosé, a bowl of olives, and a regional *plat du jour* is only enhanced in western Provence by quirky local specialties. Consider nibbling tiny *tellines,* salty clams the size of your thumbnail, fresh from the Camargue coast. Or try a crockery bowl of steaming bull stew (*gardianne*), a sinewy daube of lean-and-mean beef from the harsh Camargue prairies, ladled over a scoop of chewy red Camargue rice. The mouth-watering oddity called *brandade* (salt cod pestled with olive oil and milk into a creamy spread) has a peculiar history; cod isn't even native to Nîmes, but was traded, in its leathery salt-dried form, by medieval Breton fishermen in exchange for south-coast salt. The Nîmois mixed in local olive oil and created a regional staple.

It's true that every meal is a culinary event here, but during the summer months the local cafés and hotels make a special effort to make breakfast memorable. In turn, breakfast is one of the loveliest meals of the day. It's coolest in the morning—the birds chirp, the air is crisp, and the smell of freshly baked croissants can tempt even the most faithful *avocat* (lawyer) out of his *grace matinée* (sleep-in). Stroll out to the nearest square to sit under shady plane trees and listen to the relaxing bustle of Provence waking up. Tables are adroitly nestled in gardens or sprawled across freshly swept cobblestones, wrapped in flowerprint tableclothes and sprinkled with nosegays made of local flowers. Waiters bustle to and fro calling out friendly greetings while the first cups of gilt-edged espressos are prepared. Of course, "early morning" can be misleading: it could very well be 10 or 11 AM, but another example of southern charm is the option of a late breakfast. Hey, it makes a great excuse for a long late lunch!

How's the Weather?

July and August are very much the high season, especially along the coast, and are best avoided if possible, both because of the crushing crowds and the grilling heat. In winter (from November through February, even into March) you'll find a lot of tourist services closed, including hotels and restaurants, and much of the terrace life driven indoors by rain and wind. Around Easter, the plane trees begin to leaf out and the café tables to sprout.

Making the Most of Your Time

The rugged, unpredictable charm of this area tickles the imagination but requires long, thoughtful savoring . . . like long-aged fine wine. Come here in any season except November or late January, when most of the hotels close. The region is best in late spring, summer, or fall when the temperatures are high enough to eat outdoors after sunset.

Summer months can be busy with tourists, and therefore require patience, but these are also the months when there are lively festivals, full markets, and a general excitement. The best place to start your trip is either in Arles or Nîmes, as they both have direct train links to most major cities in France. Here you can start the process of slowing down—Provence is all about spending lazy afternoons.

From either city you can easily plan trips into the countryside by bus or by car. July and August are very much the high season, especially along the coast, and are best avoided if possible. In winter you'll find a lot of tourist services closed, including hotels and restaurants, and much of the terrace life driven indoors by rain and wind. Around Easter, travelers begin to arrive. This easy midseason period maintains its lazy, pleasant pace from Easter through June and September to late October.

GETTING AROUND PLANNER

Transportation Basics

Public transport is well organized in the Alpilles, Arles, and the Camargue, with most towns accessible by train or bus. It's best to plan on combining the two—take a train to Nîmes or Arles and then bus to the smaller towns like Les Baux or St-Remy. Driving is also a good option, but try to stick to the National or District roads, which are far less scary to drive than the speeding highways, and depending on the season you could find yourself swathed in purple lavender or surrounded by silvery olive trees. People are friendly if you get lost, and the long stretches of empty road are marvellously beautiful.

By Horse

The best way to tour the Camargue park is on horseback, although the wild glamour of the ancient race of Camargue horses becomes downright pedestrian when the now-domesticated beauties are saddled en masse. Rent-a-horse stands proliferate along the marshland highways. Since much of this land is limited to walkers and riders, a trip on horseback lets you experience this unique landscape without getting your feet wet—literally.

By Bus

A moderately good network of private bus services links places not served, or badly served, by trains.

Arles is one of the largest hubs, serviced out of the *gare routière* (bus station) on Av. Paulin-Talabot, opposite the train station.

Within the city, bus stations are mainly on Blvd. G. Clémenceau.

You can travel from Arles to such stops as Nîmes (Ligne 26, €7, 1 hour, four daily) and Avignon (Ligne 18, €7.10, 45 minutes, 10 daily).

Four buses daily also head out to Aix-en-Provence and Marseille (only two run on weekends).

Out of Arles, Les Cars de Camargue and Ceyte Tourisme Mediterranée can take you on round-trip excursions to an array of interesting destinations.

Top spots include the Camargue's Stes-Marie-de-la-Mer (€5.10, one hour, three daily), Mas du Pont de Rousty, Pont de Gau.

There are also stops in the Alpilles area, including Les Baux-des-Provence and St-Rémy-de-Provence (neither have train stations).

You can also reach the latter's bus station at Place de la République by frequent buses from Avignon.

From Nîmes's bus station on Rue Ste-Félicité, you can connect to Avignon and Arles, while Cars Fort runs you into the deep country and offers tourist circuits as well.

As for Pont du Gard, this is a 40-minutes ride from Nîmes; you are dropped off 1 km (½ mi) from the bridge at Auberge Blanche.

Bus Information **Les Cars de Camargue** (⊠ *1 rue Jean-Mathieu Artaud, Arles* ☎ *04–90–96–36–25* ⊕ *www.carsdecamargue.com*). **Ceyte Tourisme Mediterranée** (⊠ *14 bd. Georges Clémenceau, Arles* ☎ *04–90–18–96–33* ⊕ *www.autocars-ctm.com*). **Cars Fort** (⊠ *27 av. Jean-Jaurès, Nîmes* ☎ *04–66–36–60–80*).

By Car

The A6/A7 toll expressway (*péage*) channels all traffic from Paris toward the south. It's called the Autoroute du Soleil (Highway of the Sun) and leads directly to Provence. From Orange, A9 (La Languedocienne) heads southwest to Nîmes. Arles is a quick jaunt from Nîmes via A54.

With its swift autoroute network, it's a breeze traveling from city to city by car in this region. But some of the best of Provence is experienced on back roads and byways, including the isolated Camargue and the Alpilles. Navigating the flatlands of the Camargue can feel unearthly, with roads sailing over terrain uninterrupted by hills or forests; despite this, roads don't always run as the crow flies and can wander wide of a clean trajectory, so don't expect to make time. Rocky outcrops and switchbacks keep you a captive audience to the arid scenery in the Alpilles; to hurry—impossible as it is—would be a waste.

By Train

There's regular rail service from all points north to Avignon and then to nearby towns, and the TGV (Trains à Grande Vitesse) *Méditerranée* connects Paris to Avignon in 3½ hours. This TGV train makes stops in two towns in this chapter: Nîmes (eight trains daily on the four-hour trip from Paris) and Arles (only one TGV train from Paris arrives daily)—first class, one-way tickets cost about €90. From these cities you must transfer to local trains to get to Tarascon or Arles, the only other cities served by rail lines. Arles's train station (gare centrale) is located on Av. Paulin Talabot; from here, you can connect to Nîmes (€7, 30 minutes), Marseille (€12, 1 hour), Avignon Centre (€6, 1 hour), and Aix-en-Provence (€24, 2 hours with connection). Nîmes's train station is on Blvd. Talabot and trains link Avignon Centre (€8, 45 minutes) and Arles (€7, 30 minutes). Overnight trains run daily to Avignon from Paris, Strasbourg, and other cloud-bound cities, allowing soggy travelers to stretch out on a couchette and wake up to indigo skies (⇨ *By Train in the Travel Smart chapter*) but no service beats the TGV for speed and ease.

Although good rail service connects Avignon to Nîmes, Tarascon, and Arles, trains don't penetrate the Alpilles; connections to St-Rémy and Les Baux must be made by bus.

Train Information SNCF (☏*08-36-35-35-35* ⊕*www. ter-sncf.com/uk/paca*). **TGV** (☏*877/284-8633* ⊕*www.tgv. com*).

By Air

Marseille (an hour's drive from Arles) is served by frequent flights from Paris and London.

Daily flights from Paris arrive at the smaller airport in Nîmes.

In summer, Air France flies direct from New York to Nice, 200 km (124 mi) from Arles.

Guided Tours

The Arles tourist office offers individual tours of the town, including visits to the Roman monuments, during the summer season.

Dates and times vary depending on demand; check with them regarding English-speaking guides.

To learn more about Nîmes's monuments and Old Town, contact the Service des Guides at the tourist office.

This office is also handy for arranging a guided tour in English

For about €23, you can tour the town in a taxi for an hour.

When you stop in front of a monument, the driver slips in a cassette with commentary in the language of your choice.

For €45, **Taxis T.R.A.N.** (☏*04-66-29-40-11*) can take you on a round-trip ride from Nîmes to the Pont du Gard (ask the taxi to wait while you explore for 30 minutes).

Updated by
Sarah Fraser

SCOURED BY THE MISTRAL AND leveled to prairie flatlands by aeons of earth deposits carried south by the Rhône, this region is Provence in its rawest form. At first glance it is endless space broken only by the occasional gully lined with wildflowers, yet after a few moments it starts to take form as one of the most beautiful and intriguing regions in France. It is big-sky country here: mysterious, romantic, and colored with a kaleidoscope of lavenders, wheat-yellows, vibrant greens, and burnt reds. Only the giant rock outcrops of the Alpilles interrupt the horizon, dusted with silvery olives and bristling with somber cypress spears. To the west, where the Provençal dialect gives way to Languedoc, the ancient language of the southwest, vineyards swathe the countryside in rows of green and black. Along the southern coast, the Camargue's savage landscape of reeds and cane secrets exotic wildlife—rich-plumed egrets, rare black storks, clownish flamingos—as well as domestic oddities: dappled white horses and lyre-horned bulls descended from ancient, indigenous species.

The scenery is surpassed only by the genuine warmth of the populace and the fiesty energy of the cities. In-your-face, tatty Nîmes has a raffish urban lifestyle that surges obliviously through a ramshackle, gritty-chic Old Town and a plethora of Roman architectural marvels. Graceful, artsy Arles, harmonious in Van Gogh hues, mixes culture with a healthy dose of late-night café street life. Chic, luxurious St-Rémy is a gracious retreat for cosmopolitan regulars. Often misleadingly dubbed the Hamptons of Provence, it's not all about luxe, for St-Rémy has an amazingly steady infusion of style, art, and street sass mixed with a love of all things Provençal.

Each of these cities would be fascinating to explore even without its trump card: classical antiquities, superbly preserved, unsurpassed in northern Europe. The Colosseum-like arenas in Nîmes and Arles are virtually intact, solid enough to serve their original purpose as stadiums; they date from the time of Christ. The mausoleum and *arc de triomphe* outside St-Rémy are still so richly detailed they look like reproductions, but they're signed by the children of Caesar Augustus. And across the street, the vivid high-relief ruins of Glanum trace back to the Hellenism of the 3rd century BC.

Rich in history and legends, the region is as varied as the people who inhabit it. There are precise and perfect miniature fortress towns, like Aigues Mortes and Les Baux-de-Provence—where it is sometimes difficult to distinguish between bedrock and building—or the wide open marshlands of the Camargue, dotted with hidden natural treasures. Add to these attractions Romanesque châteaux and abbeys, seaside fortresses that launched crusades, and sun-sharpened landscapes seen through the perceptive eyes of Van Gogh and Gauguin, and you have a region not only worth exploring in depth, but worth savoring every minute.

EXPLORING THE ALPILLES, ARLES & THE CAMARGUE

This is the kind of country that inspires a Latin latitude (if not lassitude), so with all the ruins and châteaux to visit, allow yourself time to wander through food markets and to sit on a shady terrace watching the painterly changes in light. Although Nîmes belongs in spirit to the Languedoc, its proximity to the Camargue and Arles makes it a logical travel package with them. With their rugged hills and rich olive groves, the Alpilles are a world apart, but easily accessible from Arles and environs. You can move from site to site, or choose a central base— say, Arles—and explore them all without driving more than an hour to any one attraction. A couple of days passing through the region allows you to see world-class antiquities; five days allows time to wander the Camargue; a week lets you see the principal sites, enjoy a nature tour, and take a break by the sea. And don't forget that the ravishing old city of Avignon (⇨ *Chapter 3*) is just an hour's easy run up from Arles.

Numbers in the text correspond to numbers in the margin and on the Alpilles, the Camargue, and the Languedoc Frontier, Nîmes, and Arles maps.

THE LANGUEDOC FRONTIER

Nîmes and its famous aqueduct hold forth in the département of Gard, considered more a part of the Languedoc culture than that of Provence. Yet because of its proximity to the heart of Provence and its similar climate, terrain, and architecture, it is included as a kindred southern spirit. Center of gaily printed *indienne* cottons, Camargue-style bullfights, and spectacular Roman ruins, it cannot be isolated from its Provençal neighbors. After all, the *langue d'oc* (language of oc) refers to the ancient southern language Occitane, which evolved from Latin; northern parts developed their own *langue d'oïl*. Their names derive from their manner of saying yes: *oc* in the south and *oïl* in the north. By an edict from Paris, the *oïls* had it in the 16th century, and *oui* and its northern dialect became standard French. Languedocien and Provençal merely went underground, however, and still crop up in gesticulating disputes at farmers' markets today.

PONT DU GARD

★ *24 km (15 mi) northeast of Nîmes, 25 km (16 mi) north of Arles, 25 km (16 mi) west of Avignon.*

GETTING HERE

The best way to get to Pont du Gard is via Nimes, which is on the direct TGV line from Paris, and takes about 3 hours (☎08-36-35-35-35 ⊕*www.voyages-sncf.com*). The Nîmes bus station is right behind the train station, and from here STD Gard (⊕*www.stdgard.fr* ☎04-66-29-27-29) runs several buses daily except Sunday (about one hr, €5 one way, €9 round-trip) between Nîmes and Pont du Gard. If you are coming by car, take the A9 to Nîmes, exit 50. Then take the

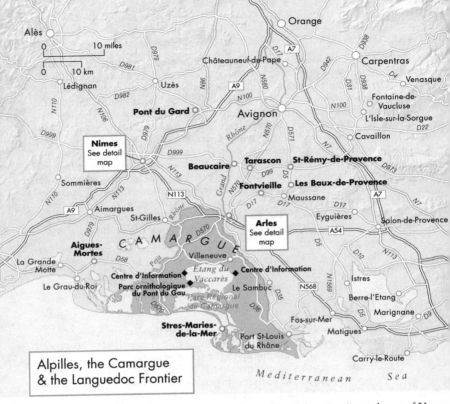

D979, direction Uzes. Pont du Gard is 14 km (9 mi) southeast of Uzes on the D981.

EXPLORING

No other ancient Roman sight in Provence rivals the Pont du Gard, a mighty, three-tiered aqueduct midway between Nîmes and Avignon and the highest bridge the Romans ever built. Erected some 2,000 years ago as part of a 48-km (30-mi) canal supplying water to Roman Nîmes, it is astonishingly well preserved. You can't walk across it anymore, but you can get close enough to it to see the amazing gigantic square blocks of stone (some weighing up to six tons) by traversing the 18th-century bridge built alongside it.

If you come to the Pont du Gard very early in the morning—before dawn is ideal—you can discover Provence in its purest blend of natural beauty and antiquity. Interestingly, the Pont du Gard was built with a slight bend in it to withstand flooding, and it has stood intact when other bridges—Roman and otherwise—collapsed in heavy rain years. As the silhouettes of olives emerge from the darkness and the diamond-sharp air wells up slowly with birdsong, you can see the ancient tiers as they were in the days when they carried water to Nîmes. The aqueduct is shockingly noble in its symmetry, the rhythmic repetition of arches resonant with strength, testimony to an engineering concept that was

2

relatively new in the 1st century AD, when the structure was built under Emperor Claudius. And, unsullied by tourists and by the vendors of postcards and Popsicles that dominate the site later in the day, the nature is just as resonant, with the river flowing through its rocky gorge unperturbed by the work of master engineering that straddles it.

In the afternoon, however, crowds become a problem. Even off-season, no one wants to miss this wonder of the world. You can approach the aqueduct from either side of the Gardon River. Whether you choose the Rive Gauche (north side), or the Rive Droite (south side), parking costs the same (€7). However, the Rive Gauche entry is closest to the **Public Information Center**, which contains an interesting multimedia exhibit on the life of Roman cities, their use of water, and the construction of the aqueduct and the Pont du Gard monument itself. There are also a "Ludo"—a space for kids to play—and a film on the history of the monument in English at 3 PM daily. Try to park as close to the attendant's booth as possible, as unfortunately break-ins are a problem. There's also a tourist office on the Rive Gauche with information and postcards. Note that this is also the side that tour buses prefer. ☎08–20–90–33–30 ⊕*www.pontdugard.fr* ☎*€12, including parking* ⊙ *Mar.–Apr. and Oct., daily 10–6; May–Sept., daily 9:30–7; Nov.–Feb., daily 9:30–5.*

WHERE TO EAT & STAY

$$$$ ⌕**Le Vieux Castillon.** Just up the road from the Rive Gauche of the Pont du Gard, this medieval hotel is made up of several restored houses and has sweeping views of the Ventoux valley, rooms tastefully styled in a variety of tasteful themes—from Egyptian to Provençal accents. All have spacious and modern bathrooms. The honey-color stone terraces and wonderful views further enhance chef Gilles Dauteuil's inventive and rich cooking, one of the highlights of which is local lamb roasted in garlic. The wine list is extensive, especially the Rhône Valley selection, and the cheeses are excellent. **Pros:** a wonderfully romantic getaway with discreet but warm welcome; the food is hearty and good. **Cons:** only one elevator in the main house, making access to some rooms farther away from reception a bit trying at the end of the day. ✉*10 Rue Turion SabatierCastillon-du-Gard* ☎*04–66–37–61–61* ⊕*www. relaischateaux.fr/vieuxcastillon* ⇲*29 rooms, 3 suites* ⌕*In-room: refrigerator. In-hotel: restaurant, bar, pool, Wi-Fi, some pets allowed* ☐*AE, DC, MC, V* ⊙*Closed Jan.–mid-Feb. Restaurant closed Mon., no lunch Tues.* ⎮⊙⎮*MAP.*

NÎMES

24 km (15 mi) southwest of Pont du Gard, 29 km (18 mi) northwest of Arles.

GETTING HERE & AROUND

On the Paris-Avignon-Montpellier train line, Nîmes has a direct rail link to and from Paris (about a three-hour ride). For TGV and train information go to: www.voyages-sncf.com, or call 08–36–35–35–35. The Nîmes gare routière (bus station) is just behind the train station.

Cars de Camargue (04–90–96–36–25) runs several buses to and from Arles (four daily Mon.–Sat., two Sun.). STD Gard (04–66–29–27–29) has several buses (daily except Sun.) between Avignon and Nîmes and Uzès and Nîmes. Some Uzès buses stop at Remoulins for the Pont du Gard and a few continue on to St-Quentin-la-Poterie. Note that although all the sites in Nîmes are walkable, the useful La Citadine bus (TNC 04–66–38–15–40) runs a good loop from the station and passes by many of the principal sites along the way €1.30.

VISITOR INFORMATION

Nîmes Tourist Office (⊠ *6 rue Auguste30000* ☎ *04–66–58–38–00* ⊕ *www. ot-nimes.fr/english_nimes/index.php*).

FROM NÎMES, WITH LOVE

Blue jeans were first created in Nîmes: The word "denim" is derived from the phrase "de Nîmes" ("from Nîmes"). Originally used by local farmers to make wagon covers and work clothes, denim soon made its way to San Francisco, thanks to Bavarian merchant Levi Strauss. Strauss's durable denim work pants, or jeans (which, incidentally, comes from the American misprounun-ciation of the Italian port Gênes, from which the fabric was origi-nally shipped) became an instant success with gold miners.

EXPLORING

If you have come to the south to seek out Roman treasures, you need look no further than Nîmes (pronounced *neem*), for the Arènes and Maison Carrée are among Continental Europe's best-preserved antiqui-ties. But if you have come to seek out a more modern mythology—of lazy, graceful Provence—give Nîmes a wide berth. It's a feisty, run-down rat race of a town, with jalopies and Vespas roaring irreverently around the ancient temple, and rock bands blasting sound tests into the Arena's wooden stands. Its medieval Old Town has none of the gentri-fied grace of those in Arles or St-Rémy. Yet its rumpled and rebellious ways trace directly back to its Roman incarnation, when its popula-tion swelled with soldiers, arrogant and newly victorious after their conquest of Egypt in 31 BC. Already anchoring a fiefdom of pre-Roman *oppida* (elevated fortresses) before ceding to the empire in the 1st cen-tury BC, this ancient city bloomed to formidable proportions under the Pax Romana. A 24,000-seat coliseum, a thriving forum with a mag-nificent temple patterned after Rome's temple of Apollo, and a public water network fed by the Pont du Gard attest to its classical prosperity. Its next golden age bloomed under the Protestants, who established an anti-Catholic stronghold here and violated iconic architectural trea-sures—not to mention the papist minority. Their massacre of some 200 Catholic citizens is remembered as the Michelade; many of the victims were priests sheltered in the *évêché* (Bishop's Palace), now the Musée du Vieux Nîmes (Museum of Old Nîmes). Chapels throughout the sur-rounding countryside were damaged by Calvin's righteous rebels.

Perhaps inspired by the influx of architects who studied its antique trea-sures, Nîmes has opted against becoming a lazy, atmospheric Proven-çal market town and has invested in progressive modern architecture. Smack-dab across from the Maison Carrée stands the city's contemporary answer, the modern-art museum dubbed the Carré d'Art (Art Square) after its ruthlessly modernist four-square form—a pillared, symmetrical glass reflection of its ancient twin. Other investments in contemporary art and architecture confirm Nîmes's commitment to modern ways.

If you want to see everything, or a lot of things in Nîmes, then the **Visite Ensemble** is good value for the money. The ticket costs a mere €10, is valid for three days, and can be purchased at most local monuments and sites.

❷ The **Arènes** *(Arena)* is considered the world's best-preserved Roman
★ amphitheater. A miniature of the Colosseum in Rome, it stands more than 520 feet long and 330 feet wide, with a seating capacity of 23,000. Bloody gladiator battles and theatrical wild-boar hunts drew crowds to its bleachers. As barbarian invasions closed in on Nîmes, the structure was transformed into a fortress by the Visigoths. Later, medieval residents found comfort and protection for tightly packed thatch-and-timber houses (as well as a small château and chapel). Nowadays the amphitheater has been restored almost to its original look, including exit signs marked VOMITORIUM. For the best views, climb to the top tier (in ancient days reserved for slaves and women) and sit in the original stone block seats. A high-tech steel and glass roof covers the arena in winter, allowing for various exhibits and shows to occupy the space, year-round; concerts and tennis tournaments are held here in summer. There are even two multimedia rooms to visit at the end of the tour. The arena's most colorful event is the *corrida,* the bullfight that transforms the Arena (and all of Nîmes) into a sangria-flushed homage to Spain. ✉*Bd. des Arenes* ☎*04–66–21–82–56* ⊕*www.arenes-nimes. com* 🎫*€7.70; joint ticket to Arènes and Tour Magne €9.80* ☯*Nov.– Feb., daily 9:30–5; Mar. and Oct., daily 9–6; Apr., May, and Sept., daily 9:30–6:30, June–Aug., daily 9–7.*

❸ At the **Musée des Beaux-Arts** *(Fine Arts Museum)*, a few blocks south of the Arènes, is a vast Roman mosaic with an imposing facade. The skylighted central atrium hosts the Roman mosaic, *The Marriage of Admetus,* and provides intriguing insights into the Roman aristocratic lifestyle. Old Master paintings (by Nicolas Poussin, Pieter Brueghel, Peter Paul Rubens) and sculpture (by Auguste Rodin) are among the highlights of the collection, along with seven paintings illustrating the saga of Anthony and Cleopatra by the home-grown 18th-centruy painter Natoire. ✉*Rue de la Cité-Foulc* ☎*04–66–67–38–21* ⊕*www. nimes.fr* 🎫*€5.10; Pass Musée (4 museums) €9.40* ☯*Tues.–Sun. 10–6, Thurs. 10–9.*

❹ The **Musée Archéologique et d'Histoire Naturelle** *(Museum of Archaeology and Natural History)*, a few blocks northeast of the Arènes, occupies a restored Jesuit college. Relics from local digs range from the Iron Age to the Roman period, with a plethora of artifacts from daily life over the ages: coins, dice, earrings, and crockery. There is also a rich array of Roman artworks, as well as a rare pre-Roman statue called the Warrior of Grezan and the Marbacum Torso (which goes back to the

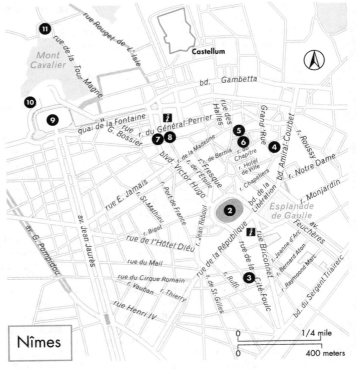

Nîmes

Celts, before the Roman period), dug up at the foot of the Tour Magne. ⊠ *13 bd. de l'Amiral-Courbet* ☎ *04–66–76–74–80* ⊕ *www.nimes.fr* 🎫 *€5.10; Pass Musée (4 museums) €9.40* ⊙ *Tues.–Sun. 10–6.*

❺ Destroyed and rebuilt in several stages, with particular damage caused by rampaging Protestants who slaughtered eight priests from the neighboring *évêché,* the **Cathédrale Notre-Dame et St-Castor** still shows traces of its construction in 1096. Is that fragment of classically symmetrical pediment an 11th-century reference to the Maison Carrée? Within its walls a miraculously preserved Romanesque frieze dates, for the most part, from the original construction. Its lively Old Testament scenes—reminiscent in style of its contemporary, the Bayeux Tapestry—portray Adam and Eve's cowering shame, the gory slaughter of Abel, and a flood-weary Noah. Inside, look for the 4th-century sarcophagus (third chapel on the right) and a magnificent 17th-century chapel (in the apse). ⊠ *Pl. aux Herbes* ☎ *04–66–36–33–50* 🎫 *Free* ⊙ *Daily 8:30–12, 3–6.*

❻ The **Musée du Vieux Nîmes** *(Museum of Old Nîmes),* opposite the cathedral in the 17th-century Bishop's Palace, has embroidered garments in exotic and vibrant displays, and an exhibit on the history on those blue jeans so popular around the world. Look for the 14th-century jeans jacket made of blue serge "de Nîmes." There are evocative interiors of 17th-century bourgeois homes, complete with painted wood paneling and local pottery. Don't miss the gift shop, where you might find a piece of pottery or fabric copied from period examples, depending on what is being shown. ⊠ *Pl. aux Herbes* ☎ *04–66–76–73–70* ⊕ *www.nimes. fr* ⊠ *Free* ⊙ *Tues.–Sun. 10–6.*

2

❼ Lovely and forlorn in the middle of a busy downtown square, the
★ exquisitely preserved **Maison Carrée** *(Square House)* strikes a timeless balance between symmetry and whimsy, purity of line and richness of decor. Built between AD 3 and 5 and dedicated to Emperor Augustus's grandsons, Caius and Lucius, it has survived subsequent use as a medieval meeting hall, an Augustinian church, a storehouse for Revolutionary archives, and a horse shed. It was modeled on temples to Apollo in Rome and Greece, and so inspired Thomas Jefferson that he had its chaste line of columns copied for the Virginia state capitol in Richmond. Today the building houses Roman statues from the 1st century AD, mosaics from the 1st century BC, and a good background display on the Maison Carrée and its history, including a fun 3-D projection of the heros of Nîmes. ⊠ *Bd. Victor-Hugo* ☎ *04–66–21–82–56* ⊕ *www.arenes-nimes.com* ⊠ *€5.40 (or Tour Magne and Maison Carrée, €9.80)* ⊙ *June–Aug., daily 10–7; Apr., May, Sept., daily 10–6:30; Mar., daily 10–6; Oct., daily 10–12:30, 2–6.*

❽ The glass-fronted **Carrée d'Art** (directly opposite the Maison Carrée) was designed by British architect Sir Norman Foster as its neighbor's stark contemporary mirror. It literally reflects the Maison Carrée's creamy symmetry and figuratively answers it with a featherlight deconstructed colonnade. Homages aside, it looks like an airport terminal. It contains a library, archives, and the **Musée d'Art Contemporain** (Contemporary Art Museum). The permanent collection falls into three categories: French painting and sculpture; English, American, and German works; and Mediterranean styles, all dating from 1960 onward. There are often temporary exhibits of new work, too. But as lovely as the museum is, the facade suffers traffic pollution and could do with a bit of a cleanup. ⊠ *Pl. de la Maison Carrée* ☎ *04–66–76–35–70* ⊠ *€5* ⊙ *Tues.–Sun. 10–6.*

❾ The **Jardin de la Fontaine** *(Fountain Garden)*, an elaborate formal garden, was landscaped on the site of the Roman baths in the 18th century, when the Source de Nemausus, a once-sacred spring, was channeled into pools and a canal. It's a shady haven of mature trees and graceful stonework, and a testimony to the taste of the Age of Reason. It makes for a lovely approach to the Temple of Diana and the Tour Magne. ⊠ *Corner of Quai de la Fontaine and Av. Jean-Jaurès* ☎ *04–66–58–38–00* ⊠ *Free* ⊙ *Mid-Sept.–Mar., daily 7:30–6:30; Apr.–mid-Sept., daily 7:30 AM–10 PM.*

❿ Just northwest of the Jardin de la Fontaine is the shattered Roman ruin known as the **Temple de Diane,** which dates from the 2nd century BC. The temple's original function is unknown, though it is thought to be part of a larger Roman complex that is still unexcavated. In the Middle

Ages, Benedictine nuns occupied the building before it was converted into a church. Destruction came during the Wars of Religion.

⑪ At the far end of the Jardin de la Fontaine is the octagonal **Tour Magne** (*Magne Tower*)—the remains of a tower that the emperor Augustus had built on Gallic foundations; it was probably used as a lookout post. Despite having lost 33 feet over time, it still provides fine views of Nîmes for anyone energetic enough to climb the 140 steps. ⊠*Quai de la Fontaine* ☎*04–66–21–82–56* ⊕*www.arenes-nimes.com* ✉ *€2.70; joint ticket with Arènes €9.80* ⊗*Nov.–Feb., daily 9:30–1, 2–4:30; Mar.–Oct., daily 9:30–1, 2–6; Apr.–May, daily 9:30–6:30; Sept., daily 9:30–1, 2–6:30; June–Aug., daily 9–7.*

WHERE TO EAT & STAY

$$ ✕**Le Bouchon et L'Assiette.** With its warmly decorated and elegant room, cheerful, friendly service, and innovative menu with modern Mediterranean leanings, this increasing well-known restaurant has firmly moved into the upper realms of the Nîmes gastronomic circles. Try the escargot ravioli with crushed parsley coulis, or the truly wonderful olive oil soup. Do save room for dessert—the chocolate fondant (hot chocolate cake) is worth every sinful calorie. ⊠*5 rue de la Sauve* ☎*04–66–62–02–93* ▭*AE, MC, V* ⊗*Closed Tues. and Wed.*

$$ ✕**Chez Jacotte.** Duck into an Old Town back alley and into this cross-
★ vaulted grotto that embodies Nîmes's Spanish-bohemian flair. Candlelight flickering on rich tones of oxblood, cobalt, and ocher enhance the warm welcome from the staff. Guests can choose to sit under the lovely vaulted ceilings or out on the flower-filled terrace. Mouthwatering goat-cheese-and-fig gratin, mullet crisped in olive oil and basil, herb-crusted lamb, and seasonal fruit crumbles show off a distinct flair with local ingredients. The homemade cakes and pastries are irresistible. ⊠*15 rue Fresque (Impasse)* ☎*04–66–21–65–59* ▭*MC, V* ⊗*Closed Sun. and Mon. No lunch Sat.*

$$ ✕**L'Enclos de la Fontaine.** Nîmes's most fashionable post-corrida gathering spot is in the Hotel Impérator, with warm-weather dining in an idyllic garden court. The food is hearty and delicious, with surprisingly Spanish touches. Chef Victor Santos carefully structures his menu, sprinkling in dishes such as almond duck, dried cod stuffed in red peppers, and roasted lamb cooked in wild mint. Have an after-dinner drink in the Bar Hemingway; after all, they named it for him because he loved to drink here. ⊠*15 rue Gaston-Boissier* ☎*04–66–21–90–30* ⊕*www. hotel-imperator.com* ▭*AE, MC, V.*

$$ ✕**Le Jardin d'Hadrien.** This chic enclave, with its quarried white stone, ancient plank-and-beam ceiling, and open fireplace, would be a culinary haven even without its lovely hidden garden, a shady retreat for summer meals. Generous portions of simple but sophisticated dishes seem like so much gravy when the setting's this nice. Mussel soup with saffron and cream, fresh cod fried with olive oil and lemon, or zucchini flowers filled with *brandade* (the creamy, light paste of salt cod and olive oil), and a frozen parfait perfumed with licorice all show Chef Alain Vinouze's subtle skills. ⊠*11 rue Enclos Rey* ☎*04–66–22–07–01* ▭*AE, MC, V* ⊗*Closed Wed. No dinner Tues. Closed Sun. and no lunch Mon. in July and Aug.*

$ ✕**Vintage Café.** This popular Old Town wine bar draws a loyal crowd of oenophiles for serious tastings and simple, compatible foods—cod stew, hot lentil salad with smoked haddock, beef stewed with capers and pickles, and a pressed-goat-cheese terrine. The bar still dominates— all the better for bellying up to a glass of *côstières de Nîmes*—but the dining room has expanded to embrace the neighboring building. Bright ceramics and warm lamplight enhance the warm-ocher Mediterranean interior. Summer nights on the terrace are idyllic. ✉*7 rue de Bernis* ☎*04–66–21–04–45* ▤*MC, V* ⊘*Closed Sun. and Mon. No lunch Sat.*

¢   ✕**Le Wine Bar/Chez Michel.** This classic mahogany-and-brass wine bar, owned and managed by a former sommelier, has more than 350 different wines to serve along with their good seafood—including *brandade de morue* (salt-cod paste)—and brasserie classics: foie gras salad, fried calamari, simple steaks. The more adventurous diner will enjoy the superb fried pigs' feet and traditional steak tartar (raw meat). You may opt to dine on the sidewalk terrace, adjacent to the square. Menus start at just €15. ✉*1 place des Arenese* ☎*04–66–76–19–59* ▤*AE, MC, V* ⊘*Closed Sun. No lunch Mon. and Sat.*

$$$$ ▥**La Maison de Sophie.** Far from the hustle of town and yet just five minutes from the Arenas, this luxurious *hôtel* particulier has all the charm that the city itself often lacks. Guest rooms are elegant and the drifting scents of jasmine lead you out to the garden, where colorful bougainvillea gently mixes with the deep blue of the pool. Wander back to the lovely sitting room in the early evening for a cup of tea or a glass of wine, and curl up with one of the many good books thoughtfully provided by your hosts. **Pros:** big-city elegance mixes nicely with country charm and quiet nights; the warm welcome of the owners makes guests feel right at home. **Cons:** often fully booked far in advance; pool is quite small. ✉*31 av. Carnot30000* ☎*04–66–70–96–10* ⊕*www. hotel-lamaisondesophie.com* ⬐*5 suites* ⌂*In room: Wi-Fi. In-hotel: pool, parking (fee), some pets allowed (fee)* ▤*MC, V.*

$$$ ▥**New Hôtel La Baume.** In the heart of scruffy Old Nîmes, this noble 17th-century *hôtel particulier* (mansion) has been reincarnated as a chic hotel with an architect's eye for mixing ancient detail with modern design. The balustraded stone staircase is a protected historic monument, and stenciled beam ceilings, cross vaults, and archways counterbalance hot ocher tones, swagged raw cotton, leather, and halogen lights. However, some of the hip interior shows signs of wear and tear. See if one of the wood-ceiling rooms (the largest and prettiest) is available. **Pros:** centrally located with old-world charm; hard-to-beat location. **Cons:** some of the rooms are small and stuffy; lobby needs overhaul. ✉*21 rue Nationale30000* ☎*04–66–76–28–42* ⊕*www.new-hotel. com* ⬐*34 rooms* ⌂*In-room: refrigerator. In-hotel: restaurant, parking (fee), some pets allowed (fee)* ▤*AE, DC, MC, V* ⍟*CP.*

$ ▥**Amphithéâtre.** Just behind the Arena, this big, solid old private home has fortunately fallen into the hands of a loving owner, who has stripped 18th-century double doors and fitted rooms with restored-wood details, white-tiled bathrooms, and antique bedroom sets. A generous breakfast buffet is served in the dining room. Ask for one of the three air-conditioned rooms overlooking the Place du Marché, where you can watch café life from your balcony. **Pros:** ideally located and good value for the price. **Cons:** rooms can be small and a bit stuffy; amenities are limited. ⊠4 rue des Arènes30000 ☎04–66–67–28–51 ⊕perso.wanadoo.fr/hotel-amphitheatre ➪17 rooms ⚘In-room: no a/c (some). In-hotel: some pets allowed ⊟MC, V ❄OⅠBP.

$ ⚏**Royal Hôtel.** Jazz, Art Deco ironwork, and caged birds set the Latin
★ tone at this bohemian, family-run, shabby-chic urban hotel. Whitewash and scrubbed concrete set off 1930s details and trendy flea-market finds. Bathrooms have new-ish tiles, and amenities are reasonably up-to-date. The house-proud owners are eager to please and its Spanish restaurant serves easy-to-eat tapas on the pedestrian Place d'Assas, but the lobby bar is where you'd expect to run across Picasso slumming over absinthe. **Pros:** the hotel is studiously casual; palm-filled lobby and club chairs are a nice touch. **Cons:** rooms can be quite small, and some are noisy. ⊠3 bd. Alphonse Daudet30000 ☎04–66–58–28–27 ⊕www.royalhotel-nimes.com ➪23 rooms ⚘In-hotel: restaurant, bar, Wi-Fi, parking (fee), some pets allowed ⊟AE, DC, MC, V.

SPORTS & THE OUTDOORS

The *corrida* (bullfight) is a quintessential Nîmes experience, taking place as it does in the ancient Roman Arena. There are usually three bullfighting times a year, always during the carnival-like citywide *férias* (festivals): in early spring (mid-February), at Pentecost (end of May), and during the wine harvest (end of September). These include parades, a running of the bulls, and gentle Camargue-style bullfights (where competitors pluck a ring from the bull's horns). But the focal point, unfortunately, is a twice-daily Spanish-style bullfight, complete with *l'estocade* (the final killing) and the traditional cutting of the ear. Those with delicate nerves will stay away. For tickets and advance information, contact the Arena's *bureau de location* (*ticket office* ⊠4 rue de la Violette, Nîmes ☎04–66–02–80–80 ⊕www.arenesdenimes.com).

Aquatropic (⊠39 chemin de la Hostellerie ☎04–66–38–31–00) is a swimming spot with a difference: an indoor and an outdoor pool, wave machines, slides, water cannons, and whirlpools add to the fun for kids and adults. It's open weekdays 10–8 and weekends 11–7 for €5.50 (€1.95 children under eight). Since it's south of the city, it's best to exit the autoroute at Nîmes Ouest.

SHOPPING

In Nîmes's Old Town you'll find the expected rash of chain stores mixed with fabulous interior-design boutiques and fabric shops selling the Provençal cottons that used to be produced here en masse (Les Indiennes de Nîmes, Les Olivades, Souleiado). Antiques and collectibles are found in tiny shops throughout the city's backstreets, but there is a concentration of them in the Old Town. Anywhere near the arena abounds with bullfighting memorabilia, but if you want to really get into the spirit, you can find your complete toreador outfit at **Maria Sara Création** (⊠40 bis rue de la Madeleine ☎04–66–21–18–40). She was famous in her day as a female bullfighter. Fashionable shoppers check out the celebrated Nîmes-founded house of **Cacharel** (⊠2 pl. de la Maison Carée ☎04–66–21–82–82).

The Monday-morning *marché* (*market;* ✉ *Bd. Jean-Jaurès*) stretches the length of the Boulevard Jean-Jaurès and highlights bright regional fabrics, linens, pottery, and *brocante* (collectibles). The permanent covered market called **Les Halles** is at the heart of the city and puts on a mouthwatering show of olives, fresh fish, cheeses, and produce. The colorful *marché aux fleurs* (flower market; parking in the Stades des Costières), though

> **NÎMES IN A JAR**
>
> The only authentic commercial maker of *brandade*, Nîmes's signature salt-cod-and-olive-oil paste, is **Raymond** (✉ *24 rue Nationale* ☎ *04–66–27–11–98*). It's paddled fresh into a plastic carton or sold in sealed jars so you can take it home. Brush toast points with olive oil, and spread it on.

far from the center, is worth seeking out by car. **FNadal** (✉ *7 rue St-Castor* ☎ *04–66–67–35–42*) is a tiny shop selling a wonderland of olive oil from vats, herbed soaps, honey, coffee, and spices. The long-time local favorite *boulangerie/patisserie* **Villaret** (✉ *13 rue de la Madeleine* ☎ *04–66–67–41–79*) is the best place to buy Nîmes's other specialty: jaw-breaking *croquants* (roasted almonds in caramelized sugar).

THE CAMARGUE

For 150,000 hectares, the vast alluvial delta of the Rhône River known as the Camargue stretches to the horizon, an austere marshland unrelievedly flat, scoured by the mistral, swarmed over by mosquitoes. Between the endless flow of sediment from the Rhône and the erosive force of the sea, its shape is constantly changing. Even the Provençal poet Frédéric Mistral described it in bleak terms: *"Ni arbre, ni ombre, ni âme"* ("Neither tree, nor shade, nor soul"). Yet its harsh landscape harbors a concentration of exotic wildlife unique in Europe, and its isolation has given birth to an ascetic and ancient way of life that transcends national stereotype. It is a strange region, one worth discovering slowly, either on foot or on horseback—especially as its wildest reaches are inaccessible by car. If people find the Camargue interesting, birds find it irresistible. Its protected marshes lure some 400 species, including more than 160 in migration—little egrets, gray herons, spoonbills, bitterns, cormorants, redshanks, and grebes, and the famous flamingos. All this nature surrounds a few far-flung villages, all good launching points for forays into the marshlands. *See* pages 46–51 for a special photo feature.

AIGUES-MORTES

★ *39 km (24 mi) south of Nîmes, 45 km (28 mi) southwest of Arles.*

VISITOR INFORMATION
Aigues-Mortes Tourist Office (✉ *Porte de la Gardette* ☎ *04–66–53–73–00* ⊕ *www.ot-aiguesmortes.fr*).

EXPLORING

Like a tiny illumination in a medieval manuscript, Aigues-Mortes (pronounced ay-guh-*mort*-uh) is a precise and perfect miniature fortress-town, contained within perfectly symmetrical castellated walls, with streets laid out in geometric grids. Now awash in a flat wasteland of sand, salt, and monotonous marsh, it once was a major port town from whence no less than St-Louis himself (Louis IX) set sail to conquer Jerusalem in

> **THINK PINK**
>
> In the Camargue, ivory-pink flamingos are as common as pigeons on a city square. Their gangly height, dodolike bill, and stilty legs give them a cartoonish air, and their flight style seems comic up close. But the sight of a few thousand of these creatures taking flight in unison is one you won't forget.

the 13th century. In 1248 some 35,000 zealous men launched 1,500 ships for Cyprus, engaging the infidel on his own turf and suffering swift defeat; Louis himself was briefly taken prisoner. A second launching in 1270 led to more crushing losses, and then Louis succumbed to typhus in Tunis.

Despite his lack of success in the crusades, Louis's **fortress-port** flourished and grew stronger still, its massive stone walls rising double-thick. Completed in 1300, they remain intact and astonishingly well preserved in salt sea winds. Within them now lies a small Provençal village milling with tourists, but the visit is more than justified by the impressive scale of the original structure.

If you're driving, park in one of the lots outside the formidable walls and enter by the main **Porte de la Gardette**; the tourist office is to the left of the entrance. The monumental ramparts, punctuated by massive towers, make for a great walk. To your right, you'll see the town's stronghold, called the **Tour de Constance**. Its 20-foot-thick walls date from 1241–44, when it was built to protect a larger building lost to history. Enter via the 17th-century **Logis du Gouverneur** (Governor's Lodging), itself a conglomerate of several centuries' construction. The tower still contains a small votive chapel dedicated to St-Louis and an upper hall that served as prison to generations of political outcasts. (One Protestant, the heroic Marie Durand, survived 38 years in the tower without relinquishing her faith; she carved the word *résister*—resist—on her cell wall. Her endurance and courage so impressed the Languedoc governor that he had her released along with a handful of her colleagues.) You can climb all the way to the top of the steepled tower, which once served as a lighthouse lantern. From here you can appreciate the rigorous geometry of the fortifications and imagine medieval fleets surging out to sea. ⊠ *Porte de la Gardette, Centre des Monuments Nationaux* ☎ *04–66–53–61–55* ⊕ *www.aigues-mortes. monuments-nationaux.fr* ⊠ *€6.50* ⏱ *Easter–late May, daily 10–6; late May–mid-Sept., daily 9:30–7; mid-Sept.–Easter, daily 10–5:30.*

It's not surprising that the town within the rampart walls has become tourist oriented, with the usual plethora of gift shops and postcard stands. But **Place St-Louis**, where a 19th-century statue of the father of the fleur-de-lis reigns under shady pollards, has a mellow village feel, and the pretty bare-bones **Église Notre-Dame des Sablons** that corners it has a timeless air (it dates from the 13th century, but the stained glass is ultramodern).

WHERE TO EAT & STAY

$$$$ ✕ **Chez Bob.** In a smoky, isolated stone farmhouse chockablock with
★ old posters, you'll taste Camargue cooking at its rustic best. There is just the daily menu which can include anything from *anchoïade* (whole crudités with hard-cooked egg—still in the shell—and anchovy vinaigrette), homemade duck pâté thick with peppercorns, and often the pièce de résistance: a thick, sizzling slab of bull steak grilled in the roaring fireplace. Sprinkle on hand-skimmed sea salt and dig in, while listening to the migrating birds pass by. ⊠ *At Villeneuve/Romieu intersection of D37 and D36 (watch for tiny sign)* ☎ *04–90–97–00–29* ⊕ *www. restaurantbob.fr* ▤ *MC, V* ⊘ *Closed Mon. and Tues.*

$$ 🏨 **Les Arcades.** This beautifully preserved 16th-century house offers
★ big, airy guest rooms, some with tall windows overlooking a green courtyard. Pristine white-stone walls, color-stained woodwork, and rubbed-ocher walls frame antiques and lush fabrics, and bathrooms are all new, in white tile. There's even a little courtyard terrace with a small pool where you can eat breakfast (included in the price) and the long successful restaurant offers classic cooking. Highlights include lotte (monkfish) in saffron and poached turbot in hollandaise, and the set menu at €34 is a steal. **Pros:** the lovely courtyard is a wonderful place to sit and contemplate, especially while nibbling on something yummy from the fragrant kitchen. **Cons:** some travelers have remarked on the cool reception; long wait for service. ⊠ *23 bd. Gambetta30220* ☎ *04–66–53–81–13* ⊕ *www.les-arcades.fr* ⤳ *9 rooms* ⚙ *In-hotel: restaurant, pool, Wi-Fi, some pets allowed* ▤ *AE, MC, V* ⊘ *Closed 1st 2 wks of Mar., 1st 2 wks of Oct.* ⓄⅠ*BP.*

$$ 🏨 **Les Templiers.** In a 17th-century residence within the ramparts, this delightful hotel sets the stage with stone, stucco, and terra-cotta floors. Furnishings are classically simple and softened with antiques. Try the quaint little restaurant in the hotel—they'll happily cook a whole side of beef in the fireplace, and serve up a perfectly grilled Mediterranean fish. On the ground floor are two small, cozy sitting areas; breakfast, weather permitting, is served in the small flower-filled courtyard. **Pros:** the welcome is wonderfully warm; space is charmingly intimate— you'll feel right at home in no time. **Cons:** some rooms are small; amenities are lacking (no minibars). ⊠ *23 rue de la République30220* ☎ *04–66–53–66–56* ⊕ *www.hotellestempliers.fr* ⤳ *14 rooms, 2 suites* ⚙ *In-hotel: pool, parking (fee), Wi-Fi, some pets allowed* ▤ *MC, V*

$ 🏨 **St-Louis.** Within the rampart walls, close to the Tour de Constance and just off Place St-Louis, this homey little hotel warms its medieval construction of cool stone with Provençal charm and comfort. Guest rooms, with strong floral accents and scattered antiques, are pleasantly decorated if not stylish. They look out on the flower-filled garden below the ramparts or onto the sunny street. In winter, dinner is served in the small white-washed and beamed restaurant, known for its fresh products and grilled bull steak, and in summer, in the shady garden. **Pros:**

situated in the center of the medieval village, this hotel offers up an authentic visit into Provençal past; the welcome is genuine; great value for money. **Cons:** some rooms are small and can be hot in the summer; no pool. ⊠ *10 rue Amiral Courbet30220* ☎*04–66–53–72–68* ⊕*www.lesaintlouis.fr* ⇝*22 rooms* ⋔*In-room: no a/c. In hotel: restaurant, some pets allowed* ⊟*AE, MC, V* ⊙*Closed late Nov.–mid-Mar.* ⫢*BP.*

FESTIVALS

In early October, the **Fêtes Votive d'Aigues-Mortes** *(town festival)* has bull races, parades, and dancing in the main square.

STES-MARIES-DE-LA-MER

31 km (19 mi) southeast of Aigues-Mortes, 40 km (25 mi) southwest of Arles.

GETTING HERE

The nearest train station is in Arles, and from here several buses a day run to Stes-Maries-de-la-Mer. The most frequent companies are Cevennes Cars (☎04–66–84–96–86) or Les Cars de Camargue (☎04–90–96–36–25) who run buses three times a day. The trip takes about 45 minutes and costs €5.20 one way, €9 return. By car, take the A54 and at exit 4 take the D570 directly to Stes-Maries-de-la-Mer.

VISITOR INFORMATION

Stes-Maries-de-la-Mer Tourist Office (⊠ *5 av. Van Gogh13732* ☎*04–90–97–82–55*).

EXPLORING

The principal town within the confines of the Parc Régional de Camargue, Stes-Maries is a beach resort with a fascinating history. Provençal legend has it that around AD 45 a band of the very first Christians was rounded up and set adrift at sea in a boat without a sail and without provisions. Their stellar ranks included Mary Magdalene, Martha, and Mary Salome, mother of apostles James and John; Mary Jacoby, sister of the Virgin; and Lazarus, risen from the dead (or another Lazarus, depending on whom you ask). Joining them in their fate: a dark-skinned servant girl named Sarah. Miraculously, their boat washed ashore at this ancient site, and the grateful Marys built a chapel in thanks. Martha moved on to Tarascon to tackle dragons, and Lazarus founded the church in Marseille. But Mary Jacoby and Mary Salome remained in their old age, and Sarah stayed with them, begging in the streets to support them in their ministry. The three women died at the same time and were buried together at the site of their chapel.

A cult grew up around this legendary spot, and a church was built around it. When in the 15th century a stone memorial and two female bodies were found under the original chapel, the miracle was for all practical purposes confirmed, and the Romanesque church expanded to receive a new influx of pilgrims. But the pilgrims attracted to Stes-Maries aren't all lighting candles to the two St. Marys: the servant girl

Sarah has been adopted as an honorary saint by the Gypsies of the world, who blacken the crypt's domed ceiling with the soot of their votive candles lighted in her honor. Two extraordinary festivals take place every year in Stes-Maries, one May 24–25 and the other on the Sunday nearest to October 22. On May 24 Gypsy pilgrims gather from across Europe and carry the wooden statue of Sarah from her crypt, through the streets of the village, and down to the sea to be washed. The next day they carry a wooden statue of the two St. Marys, kneeling in their wooden boat, to the sea for their own holy bath. The same ritual is repeated by a less colorful crowd of non-Gypsy pilgrims in October, who carry the two Marys back to the sea.

★ On entering the damp, dark, and forbidding fortress-church, **Église des Stes-Maries,** what is most striking is its novel character. Almost devoid of windows, its tall, barren single-aisle nave is cluttered with florid and sentimental ex-votos (tokens of blessings, prayers, and thanks) and primitive and sentimental artworks of the famous trio. On the wall to your left, you'll see the wooden statue of the Marys in their boat; in the crypt below, Sarah glows in the light of dozens of candles. Another oddity brings you back to this century: a sign on the door forbids visitors to come *torse nu* (topless). For outside its otherworldly role, Stes-Maries is first and foremost a beach resort, dead-flat, whitewashed, and more than a little tacky. Unless you've made a pilgrimage to the sun and sand, don't spend much time in the town center; if you've chosen Stes-Maries as a base for viewing the Camargue, stay in one of the discreet mas (country inns) outside its city limits.

ARLES

31 km (19 mi) southeast of Nîmes, 40 km (25 mi) northwest of Stes-Maries.

GETTING HERE & AROUND

If you're arriving by plane, note that Arles is roughly 20 km (12 mi) from the Nîmes-Arles-Camargue airport (☎04–66–70–49–49). The easiest way from the landing strip to Arles is by taxi (about €30). Buses run between Nîmes and Arles three times daily on weekdays and twice on Saturday (not at all on Sunday), and four buses weekdays between Arles and Stes-Maries-de-la-Mer, through Cars de Camargue (☎04–90–96–36–25). The SNCF (☎08–92–35–35–35) runs three buses Monday–Saturday from Avignon to Arles, and Cartreize (☎08–00–19–94–13 ⊕*www.lepilote.com*) runs a service between Marseille and Arles. Arles is along the main coastal train route, and you can take the TGV (Trains à Grands Vitesses) to Avignon from Paris and jump on the local connection to Arles. For all train information, check out www.voyages-sncf.com, or call.

VISITOR INFORMATION

Arles Tourist Office (✉ *43 bd. de Craponne13200* ☎*04–90–18–41–20* ⊕*www. ville-arles.fr).*

Continued on page 52

DON'T FENCE ME IN:
FRANCE'S "WILD WEST"

Time: 7:30 AM. Place: The Camargue reserve, Provence's extraordinary nature park. A flock of flamingos suddenly erupts from a stand of black-green parasol pines. To your left, a group of herons mince one-legged through rice paddies. Ahead, a bandanna-wrapped *gardian*—a kind of open-range cowboy—roams the field on a sturdy dappled-white horse, prodding a flock of prong-horned bulls whose bloodlines predate the cave paintings of Lascaux. Atop your pony, you turn your binoculars to watch the rising sun turn the sky rosy red over the endless savannas. This is why you got up so early: to see the Camargue at dawn, primeval and virgin-pure, the last gasp of the Rhône as it seeps over the delta into the Mediterranean sea. This Edenic preserve, where exotic fauna and flora live in splendor in lagoons and salt marshes, remains France's most distinctive nature wonderland.   By Sarah Fraser

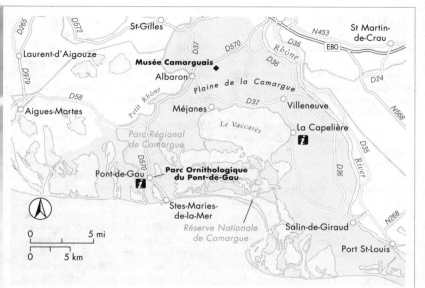

A land of haunting natural beauty, the Camargue was one of the *oubliettes* (forgotten areas) of France only a few decades ago. Today, it is *à la mode*. No matter that the mosquitoes are large and hungry in the summer, or that the mistral wind whistles furiously over sand and sea in the early spring, when thousands of tenderfeet begin to head here to discover a peculiar ecosystem all its own and a culture—wild, quirky, isolated—just as unique.

With its hypnotic plane of marsh grass stretching to the sea, the Camargue is what the French call a *désert d'eau*, a watery desert. Expanses of saltwort, canals, reedbeds, marshy plains, and *è'tangs* (saltwater lagoons) alternate with vast salt-marsh islands called *sansourire*. Little wonder you can appear to be standing in a body of water—beware: there are treacherous pits of quicksand in places—and sink on flat land. The Camargue is formed by the alluvial deposits of the two arms of the Rhône flowing south to the Mediterranean, and the sea does its best to fight back. So much so that an enormous system of dikes, known as the Digue à la Mer, has been built along a 15-mi stretch of the coast near Stes-Maries-de-la-Mer and is now one of France's most spectacular seaside promenades (and best biking routes).

At the Camargue's heart is the Réserve Nationale Zoologique et Botanique de Camargue, a 30,000-acre area set around the Étang de Vaccarès lagoon—a birdwatcher's paradise famed for its rich sightings of egrets, bee-eaters, avocets, cranes, sandpipers, flamingos, and hundreds of other species. Nature has been left blissfully untouched—almost. Man has only squatters' rights to these eternal tidal flats, yet here and there you'll find isolated *mas* (farmhouses, now sometimes converted to luxurious dude ranches); *manades,* the French style of ranches, where the famous bulls are often corralled; and *cabanes,* whitewashed houses with plaited straw roofs used as residences by the gardians. Horses are for rent everywhere, and a gallop across this wide, lonely prairie country will set you apart from the ordinary run of tourists.

A TOUR OF THE PARC RÉGIONAL DE CAMARGUE

As you drive the few roads that crisscross the Camargue, you'll usually be within the boundaries of the **Parc Régional de Camargue** (⊕www.parc-camargue.fr). Unlike state and national parks in the United States, this area is privately owned and utilized within rules imposed by the state. The principal owners, the famous *manadiers* (the Camargue equivalent of a small-scale ranchers), with the help of their gardians, keep it for grazing their wide-horned bulls and their broad-bellied, dappled-white horses. The strong, heavy-tailed Camargue horse has been traced to the Paleolithic period (though some claim the Moors imported an Arab strain) and is prized for its stolid endurance and tough hooves. The curved-horned bull, if not indigenous, may have been imported by Attila the Hun. When it's not participating in a bloodless bullfight, a bull may well end up in the wine-rich regional stew called *gardianne de taureau*, an acquired taste.

WHERE TO FIND THE BIRDS

Up north a few miles from Stes-Maries-de-la-Mer, the main town in the Camargue, is a private reserve called the ☾ **Parc Ornithologique du Pont-de-Gau** (Ornithological Park of the Pont-de-Gau). On some 150 acres of marsh and salt lands, birds are welcomed and protected (but in no way confined); injured birds are treated and kept in large pens, to be released if and when ready. Boardwalks (including a short, child-friendly inner loop past the easy-viewing stands) snake over the wetlands, the longest leading to a blind where a half hour of silence, binoculars in hand, can reveal unexpected treasures. Near the park entrance is the Hostellerie Pont-de-Gau, which offers hearty meals much favored by local ranchers. ✉*Pont-de-Gau, 5 km (3 mi) north of Stes-Maries-de-la-Mer on D570* ☎*04–90–97–82–62* ⊕ *www.parcornithologique.com* ⌨*guided tours, €9* ⊙*Oct.–Mar., daily 10–sunset; Apr.–Sept., daily 9–sunset.*

DEEP IN THE HEART OF . . . PROVENCE?

While the thought might give pause to some Texas residents, historians now tell us that the American cowboy is actually descended from the French gardian, the Provençal cowboy. "Go West," Horace Greeley once advised, and in the early 19th century, these Camargue ranchers did exactly that: shipping out to the French colony of New Orleans, they then fanned out across America as the first bronc-stompers and horse-wranglers. Although they traded in their iron *trident* pole for a lariat, they brought along their black felt hats, string ties, and—to the later gratification of Levi Strauss—*bleus de travail*, or "jeans" (invented in the Provence city of Nîmes). Their festival wear, including traditional velvet vests—seen in full glory during the Fête des Gardians in Arles in May—inspired a local homeboy, couturier Christian Lacroix. Today, les gardians are a unique breed, proud of their centuries-old traditions and disdainful of the Hollywood "cowboy" poseur. Insular, Byronic, and taciturn, they love to kid you when they first meet you. If you don't take offense, they'll warm up quickly; if you do, they'll kid you even more!

The unique Camargue saddle

Heading out on a *Ballade* tour

WHERE TO FIND THE NATURE TRAILS

If you're an even more committed nature lover, venture into the inner sanctum of the Camargue, the **Réserve Nationale de Camargue**. This intensely protected area contains the central pond called **Le Vaccarès**, mostly used for approved scientific research. The wildlife—birds, nutria, fish—is virtually undisturbed here, and you won't come across the cabins and herds of bulls and horses that most people expect from the Camargue. Pick up maps and information at the **Centre d'Information du Parc Naturel Régional du Camargue** (☎ 04–90–97–00–97 ⊕ www.reserve-camargue.org ⊗ Apr.–Sept., daily 10–6; Oct.–Mar., Sat.–Thurs. 9:30–5). It's just up the D570 from the Parc Ornithologique at Pont-de-Gau. To explore this area, you'll have to

ON THE HORNS OF A DILEMMA

Car, bus, boat, bike, or foot? When you're out to learn about the birds and the bulls of the Camargue, the best way to tour their territory is by horse. Some 30 places rent them for a *promenade équestre* (horseback tour). The **Association Camarguaise de Tourisme Équestre** publishes a list of names and numbers, available at the **Centre d'Information du Parc Naturel Régional du Camargue** at Pont-du-Gau or at the **Stes-Maries tourist office** (5 av. van Gogh). Stables line the roads throughout the Camargue, so they're easy to find; several are concentrated along D570 north of Stes-Maries as well as along the eastern loop D85. An hour's ride averages between €15 and €30, and a whole day €60 to €90 (with *pique-nique* thrown in).

While a *promenade à cheval* can last all day, most are two hours long; accompanied by commentary on such topics as folklore and ecology, these are called *ballades*. They are occasionally led by gardian cowboys, some—ironically—leading their horses on foot (have to give those legs a stretch). As you wend your way over cattle tracks and wooden footbridges, you'll realize this is the way to get out into those marshy fields yet avoid getting your feet wet. The gardian rides a typical short-stepping Camarguaise horse, small enough to be considered a pony. Most tourists, however, will wind up on an "Arab," a larger, dappled white horse. Tip for tenderfeet: If a horse knows you are afraid of him, he'll press his advantage—so don't let your steed get your goat.

Don't wear red.

strike out on foot, bicycle, or horseback paths. Note that you are not allowed to diverge from marked trails.

If you continue north past the village of Albaron, you'll come across the converted sheep-ranch-now-museum, the **Musée Camarguais** (⊠Mas du Pont de Rousty, D570 ☎04–90–97–10–82 📧€4.60 ⓈApr.–June, daily 9:15–5:45; July–Aug., 9:15–6:45; Sept., 9:15–5:45; Oct.–Mar., 10:15–4:45). Lying between Arles and Stes-Maries-de-la-Mer, it explains the region's history, produce, and people. It's also a good place to pick up information on nature trails.

WHERE TO FIND THE BULLS

Near the northern shore of the Étang de Vaccarès, one of the larger ranches in the Camargue has been turned into a showplace for all things taurine. Bullfights, ferrades, horse rides, and *spectacles taurine* (bull-baiting) are just some of the activities offered at the **Domaine de Méjanes Paul Ricard,** 4 km (2½ mi) north of Albaron on D37). You'll learn about the history of the unique regional species of bullfight, the *cours camarguaise,* in which bulls are not killed in the arena but simply taunted by *raseteurs* (runners) who try to pluck off a red cockade and two white tassels mounted on the bull's horns. Bulls live to enter the arena again and again, and some become such celebrities they have appeared on the covers of French magazines. At the Domaine, you can also ride a *petit train* for a fun 20-minute tour of the marshlands. ⊠*D37, on edge of Étang de Vaccarès* ☎*04–90–97–10–10* ⊕*www.mejanes. camargue.fr.*

At the easternmost point of the Étang du Vaccarès, another good visitor center is found at La Capelière. The **Centre d'Information de la Réserve Nationale de Camargue** has maps, exhibits on wildlife, and three *sentiers de découverte* (discovery trails). ⊠*5 km (3 mi) south of Villeneuve/Romieu, off D37* ☎*04–90–97–00–97.*

IN THE PINK

Les fleurs qui volent ("the flowers that fly"), flamingos are the most spectacular residents of the Camargue. Proving the preserve's success, the indigenous population of the *flamants roses* (pink flamingos) is now a healthy 50,000.

Flamingos, Camargue, ornithological park

HOME ON THE RANGE

When it comes to the Camargue, you can merely visit it or you can *live* it. A number of renovated *mas* (farmhouses) and *manades* (ranches) now offer a luxurious counterbalance to the region's hard gothic landscapes: fashionable dude ranches *à la provençale*, replete with firelit interiors, regional antiques, and creature comforts. You can spend the day roughing it on a *ballade* horseback tour. At dusk, however, silt-splashed and leather-stained, enjoy a spell in a canopy-draped bathub and then a candlelit dinner in a grand old ranch-house kitchen. Here are some hotels and restaurants with authentic bull-in-a-china-shop ambience.

★ **$$$$** ☷ **Le Mas de Peint.** This may be the ultimate mas experience, set as it is in a 17th-century farmhouse on some 1,250 acres of Camargue ranchland. Luxurious Provençal fabrics and antiques grace the old stone floors, and burnished beams warm the firelit salon and library. Rooms are lavished with brass beds, monogrammed linens, even canopied bathtubs. At dinnertime, guests gather in the kitchen to chat with the cook and settle in for sophisticated specialties using home-grown products (ratatouille and lamb dishes as well as Camargue rice and bull). Diners not staying in the hotel are welcome too, for lunch or dinner; the restaurant is closed Wednesday, and advance reservations are required. In summer (mid-June–mid-September) a light lunch is served by the pool. You're only 20 km (12 mi) south of Arles here, but you should plan on a relaxing immersion in the country rather than a heavy sightseeing itinerary. Owner Jacques Bon now conducts a *Manade* (traditional horseback ride), explaining the lifestyle of a Camargue cowboy, with lunch, for a mere €37.

✉ *Le Sambuc, 13200 Arles* ☎*04–90–97–20–62* ⊕*www.masdepeint. com* ⇌*8 rooms, 3 suites* ⚐*Restaurant, pool, horseback riding, some pets permitted (fee)* ▭*AE, DC, MC, V* ⊗*Closed mid-Nov.–mid-Dec. and mid-Jan.–mid-Mar.* ⦿|*MAP.*

★ **$$$$** ☷ **Mas de la Fouque.** With stylish rooms and luxurious balconies that look out over a beautiful lagoon, this upscale converted farmhouse is a perfect escape from the rigors of horseback riding and bird-watching. Outside are acres of sculpted land, inside is comfort personified—cool elegance, plush carpets, large baths, and prompt service. Every Saturday night Gypsy musicians play flamenco in the lovely bar area. Sprawl out in front of the large stone fireplace and drink in the splendid views over the Camargue. The food doesn't disappoint, either: dive into a mean leg of roasted lamb or savor the tender catch of the day after a refreshing dip in the large pool. ✉*Rte. du Petit Rhone, 13460* ☎*04–90–97–81–02* ⊕*www.masdelafouque.com* ⇌*3 rooms* ⚐*Restaurant, refrigerator, pool, some pets permitted (fee)* ▭*AE, DC, MC, V* ⊗*Closed 3 wks. Dec.–Jan.* ⦿|*MAP.*

Mas de la Fouque

EXPLORING

Seated in the shade of Arles's plane trees on the Place du Forum, sunning at the foot of the obelisk on the Place de la République, meditating in the cloister of St-Trophime, or strolling the rampart walkway along the sparkling Rhône, you'll see what enchanted Gauguin and drove Van Gogh mad with inspiration. It's the light: intense, vivid, crystalline, setting off planes of color and shadow with prismatic concentration. As a foil to this famous light, multihued Arles—with its red and gold ocher, cool gray stone, and blue-black shade—is unsurpassed.

Reigning over the bleak but evocative landscape of the marshlands of the Camargue, the small city of Arles is fiercely Provençal, nurturing its heritage and parading its culture at every colorful opportunity. Warming the wetlands with its atmosphere, animation, and culture, it is a patch of hot color in a sepia landscape—and an excellent home base for sorties into the raw natural beauty and eccentric villages of the Rhône delta.

If you were obliged to choose just one city to visit in Provence, lovely little Arles would give Avignon and Aix a run for their money. It's too chic to become museumlike yet has a wealth of classical antiquities and Romanesque stonework; quarried-stone edifices and shuttered town houses shading graceful Old Town streets and squares; and pageantry, festivals, and cutting-edge arts events. Its atmospheric restaurants and picturesque small hotels make it the ideal headquarters for forays into the Alpilles and the Camargue.

Yet compared to Avignon and Aix, it's a small town. You can zip into the center in five minutes without crossing a half hour's worth of urban sprawl. And its monuments and pretty old neighborhoods are conveniently concentrated between the main artery Boulevard des Lices and the broad, lazy Rhône.

It wasn't always such a mellow site. A Greek colony since the 6th century BC, little Arles took a giant step forward when Julius Caesar defeated Marseille in the 1st century BC. The emperor-to-be designated Arles a Roman colony and lavished funds and engineering know-how on it, transforming it into a formidable civilization—by some accounts, the Rome of the north. Fed by aqueducts, canals, and solid roads, it profited from all the Romans' modern conveniences: straight paved streets and sidewalks, sewers and latrines, thermal baths, a forum, a stadium, a theater, and an arena. It became an international crossroads by sea

THE DA VINCI CODE, PROVENÇAL-STYLE

Ever since Dan Brown's *The Da Vinci Code* popularized the notion that Mary Magdalene—one of the Marys who arrived in Stes-Maries by boat back when—was the consort of Jesus Christ (and mother of his child), buses of photo-snapping, Bermuda-shorts wearing visitors arrive daily here. True believers can check out the two-week expedition Magdalene Tours (⊕ *www.magdalenetours. com*) conducts from the shores of Marseille to the Basilica at St. Maximin-Ste. Baume, where her enshrined skull is purportedly held.

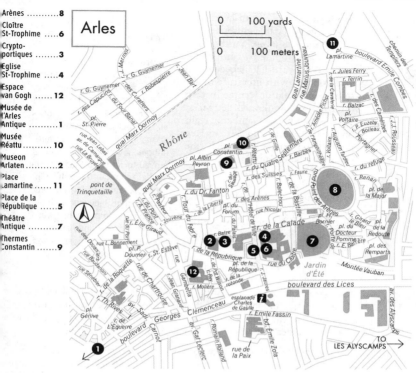

and land and a market to the world, with goods from Africa, Arabia, and the Far East. The emperor Constantine himself moved to Arles and brought with him Christianity.

The remains of this golden age are reason enough to visit Arles today. Yet its character nowadays is as gracious and low-key as it once was cutting-edge.

Remember: If you plan to visit many of the monuments and museums in Arles, you can purchase a *visite generale* ticket for €12 at most of the town sites and monuments. This covers the €5.50 entry fee to the Musée de l'Arles Antique and any and all of the other museums and monuments (except the independent Museon Arlaten, €1), which normally charge €4 each per visit. It's good for the length of your stay.

A GOOD WALK

The best of Arles is enclosed in the inner maze of streets and alleyways known as the Old Town, nestled along the Rhône, where you'll find noble 18th-century architecture cheek-by-jowl with antiquities. Only the museum of antiquities lies across the Rhône, easily accessed by shuttle bus.

★ Though it's a hike from the center, a good place to set the tone and context for your exploration of Arles is at the state-of-the-art **Musée** de l'**Arles Antique**. From here, take advantage of the free museum shuttle; there's an adjacent parking lot if you're day-tripping by car. Get off at the Boulevard Clémenceau and arm yourself with literature at the **tourist information center** just up the road, on Boulevard des Lices. Then walk up Rue Gambetta, right on Rue Molière, and left up Rue Rey to the **Espace Van Gogh**, the hospital where Van Gogh repaired for his decline into insanity. Continue up Rue du President Wilson to the Rue de la République and the intensely local **Museon Arlaten**. Just behind, on Rue Balze, explore the underground Roman galleries called the **Cryptoportiques**.

> ### WHISPERS ABOUT VAN GOGH'S EAR
>
> Ill-received and ostracized in Arles, Van Gogh was packed off to an asylum in nearby St-Rémy after he cut off the lobe of his left ear on December 23, 1888. Theories abound, but historians believe he made the desperate gesture in homage to Gauguin, who had arrived to set up a "Studio of the South." Following the fashion in Provençal bullrings for a matador to present his lady love with an ear from a dispatched bull, Vincent wielded the knife after arguing with Gauguin, whom he had come to idolize.

Follow Rue Balze to the broad **Place de la République**, where you'll study the extraordinary Romanesque facade of the **Église St-Trophime**. Next door, enter the hidden oasis of the **Cloître St-Trophime**. Continue up Rue du Cloître to the **Théâtre Antique**, now in Byronesque ruins. Just above rears the **Arènes**, site of gladiator battles and modern bullfights.

Now wander down evocative backstreets to the river and the **Thermes Constantin**, the ruins of Roman baths. On Rue du Grand Prieuré, stop into the **Musée Réattu**, which glorifies native-son painter Jacques Réattu and 20th-century peers. Not Van Gogh, alas. Pay homage to that painter by walking up Rue du Quatre Septembre and Rue Amédée Pichot to **Place Lamartine**, where the star-crossed artist lived in his famous Maison Jaune, destroyed in the second World War.

SIGHTS TO SEE

8 ★ **Arènes** *(Arena)*. Rivaled only by the even-better-preserved version in Nîmes, this amazingly functional Roman arena dominates Old Arles. Its four medieval towers are testimony to its transformation from classical sports arena to feudal fortification in the Middle Ages—at the sacrifice of a full row of arches and much of the original structure. Younger than Arles's theater, it dates from the 1st century AD and, unlike the theater, seats 21,000 to this day. Its primary function: as a venue for the traditional spectacle of the corridas, or bullfights, which take place annually starting with the Fête des Gardians ("cowboys") on May 1, when the Queen of Arles is crowned, and culminating in early July with the award of the Cocarde d'Or (Golden Rosette) to the most successful toreador. Tickets are usually available on site, but book ahead for the more popular fights. Climb to the top of the tallest medieval tower, by the entry, to see the arena as a whole and take in Old Arles. ✉*Rond Point des Arènes* ☎*04–90–49–59–05* ⊕*www.tourisme.ville-arles.fr*

€5.50 joint ticket Arènes and Thermes ⊗ *May–Sept., daily 9–6:30; Oct., daily 9–6; Nov.–Feb., daily 10–5; Mar. and Apr., daily 9–6.*

❻ Cloître St-Trophime *(St-Trophime Cloister).* Tucked discreetly behind St-
★ Trophime, this pillared enclosure is a peaceful haven, a Romanesque treasure worthy of the church and one of the loveliest cloisters in Provence. Next to the church portals, enter via broad wooden doors that open onto the Place de la République and cross a peaceful courtyard to the entrance. The slender elegance of its pillars contrasts gracefully with the florid decorations of the capitals, each carved with fine detail and a painterly hand. Even drapery and feathers pop into high relief. Beautiful Aubusson tapestries, Roman sarcophagi, and 17th-century Dutch paintings line the austere nave, and the clear dichotomy of Gothic and Romanesque styles—curving vaults versus delicate cross vaults—harmonizes beautifully, as does the cloister as a whole: you wouldn't be surprised to come upon Cyrano's Roxanne embroidering quietly in the light dappling through the oleander. ⊠ *Off Place de la République* ☎ *04–90–49–59–05* ⊕ *www.tourisme.ville-arles.fr* €3.50 ⊗ *May–Sept., daily 9–6:30; Oct., Mar., and Apr., daily 9–6; Nov.–Feb., daily 10–5.*

❸ Cryptoportiques. At the entrance to a 17th-century Jesuit college, these ancient and evocative underground galleries have long been a noted Arles sight but, at press time, visits were not permitted due to structural concerns. Dating from 30 to 20 BC, this horseshoe of vaults and pillars buttressed the ancient forum from underneath. Used as a refuge for Resistance members in World War II, these galleries still have a rather ominous atmosphere. Yet openings let in natural daylight, and artworks of considerable merit and worth were unearthed here, including the extraordinary bust long thought to be a portrait of the young Octavius wearing the whiskers of mourning for the murdered Julius Caesar. (Current research, alas, identifies it as his grandson Caius.) ⊠ *Rue Balze* ☎ *04–90–49–59–05* ⊕ *www.tourisme.ville-arles.fr.*

❹ Église St-Trophime. Classed as a world treasure by UNESCO, this extraor-
★ dinary Romanesque church alone would justify a visit to Arles, though it's continually upstaged by the antiquities around it. Its transepts date from the 11th century and its nave from the 12th; the church's austere symmetry and ancient artworks (including a stunningly Roman-style 4th-century sarcophagus) are fascinating in themselves. But it is the church's 12th-century **portal**—its entry facade—that earns it international respect. Superbly preserved and restored sculptures with high-relief modeling, complex layers of drapery, and a detail of expression that are nearly classical embellish every inch of the portal's surface. Indeed, it is that classicism that marks it as late Romanesque; Chartres Cathedral, of the same era, had long since ventured into fluid Gothicism. The **tympanum** (the half-moon over the door) tells the story of the Last Judgment, inherently symmetrical, with its separation of the blessed who surge toward Christ and the damned who skulk, naked and in chains, toward hell. Christ is flanked by his chroniclers, the evangelists: the eagle (John), the bull (Luke), the angel (Matthew), and the lion (Mark). ⊠ *Pl. de la République* ⊕ *www.tourisme.ville-arles.fr* Free.

⑫ The most strikingly resonant site, impeccably restored and landscaped to match one of Van Gogh's paintings, is the courtyard garden of what is now the **Espace van Gogh**, featured in *Le Jardin de l'Hôtel-Dieu*. This was the hospital to which the tortured artist repaired after cutting off his earlobe. Its cloistered grounds have become something of a shrine for visitors and there are photo plaques comparing the renovation to some of the master's paintings, including *Le Jardin de la Maison de Santé*. The exhibition hall here is open for temporary exhibitions; the garden is always on view, and in spring and summer blooming flowers decorate the live canvas. Check out shows of contemporary art inspired by "Vince" at the nearby Fondation Vincent van Gogh, located at 24 bis Rond-point des Arènes. For more information about Van Gogh, see the Close-Up Box, "Van Gogh in Arles and St-Rémy" and Place Lamartine, below. ⊠*Pl. Dr. Félix-Rey* ☎*04–90–49–39–39* ⊕*www. tourisme.ville-arles.fr* ⊠*Free.*

❶ **Musée de l'Arles Antiques** (*Museum of Ancient Arles*). This is the place
★ to steep yourself in Arles's spectacular classical history. The building was erected on the site of an enormous Roman *cirque* (chariot-racing stadium). It hides its prehistoric collections in a womblike interior but bathes displays of the Roman renaissance in wall-to-wall daylight. Natural materials and earth colors provide counterpoint to the high culture on display, and a preconceived viewing plan enhances the narrative flow of history (ask for the English-language guidebook). And there's more here than glass cases full of toga buckles. You'll learn about all aspects of Arles in its heyday, from the development of its monuments to details of daily life in Roman times. Perhaps the most instructive and fascinating aspect of this museum is its collection of tiny, precise models: a miniature cirque shows tiny chariots charging around its track, with an unfinished cross section that demonstrates building techniques; the amphitheater, forum, and theater as they were used; and a sophisticated 16-wheel water mill used to grind grain. The quantity of art treasures gives an idea of the extent of Arles's importance. Seven superb floor mosaics can be viewed from an elevated platform, and you exit via a hall packed tight with magnificently detailed paleo-Christian sarcophagi. As you leave you will see the belt of St-Césaire, the last bishop of Arles, who died in AD 542 as the countryside was overwhelmed by the Franks and the Roman era met its end. ⊠*Presqu'île du Cirque Romain (follow Bd. Clémenceau to N113 and cross over)* ☎*04–90–18–88–88* ⊕*www.arles-antique.cg13.fr* ⊠*€5.50, free the 1st Sun. of every month* ⊗*Apr.–Oct., daily 9–7; Nov.–Mar., daily 10–5.*

❿ **Musée Réattu.** Arles can't boast a single Van Gogh painting—excusable, given that his works sell for $20 million today—but did they have to name their art museum after Jacques Réattu, a local painter of dazzling mediocrity? Thankfully, the art museum only lavishes three rooms on his turn-of-the-19th-century ephemera. It also houses a collection of contemporary art (including paintings by the Belgian Alechinsky), photography, and a gathering of 57 drawings by Picasso, including a delightful tongue-in-cheek depiction of noted muse and writer Lee Miller in full Arles dress. They were donated to Arles by Picasso himself, to thank the town for amusing him with their bullfights. The best thing about the Réattu may be the building, a Knights of Malta priory dating from the 15th century, with its fortress-facade overlooking the Rhône. ✉10 *rue Grand Prieuré* ☎04–90–49–37–58 ⊕*www.tour isme.ville-arles.fr* 🎫€4 ⊘ *Mar.–June, mid-Sept.–Oct., daily 10–12:30 and 2–6:30; July–mid-Sept., daily 10–7; Nov.–Feb., daily 1–5.*

❷ Museon Arlaten *(Museum of Arles)*. Take the time to comb leisurely
★ through the quirky old collection of local paraphernalia housed in this grand 16th-century town house. Created by the father of the Provençal revival, turn-of-the-century poet Frédéric Mistral (he paid for it with his Nobel Prize winnings), it enshrines a seemingly bottomless collection of regional treasures. There are spindled-oak bread boxes (mounted high on the wall like bird cages); bizarre traditional talismans (a ring fashioned from the third nail of a horseshoe to ward off hemorrhoids); the signature Arlésienne costumes, with their pretty shoulder scarves crossed at the waist; dolls and miniatures; an entire Camargue gardian hut, with reconstructed interior; and dioramas with mannequins—tiny tableaux of Provençal life. Following Mistral's wishes, women in full Arlésienne costume oversee the labyrinth of lovely 16th-century halls. ✉*29 rue de la République* ☎*04–90–93–58–11* ⊕*www.museonarlaten. fr* 🎫*€14, free 1st Sun. of every month* ⊘*Apr., May, and Sept., Tues.– Sun. 9:30–noon and 2–5:30; June–Aug., daily 9:30–12:30 and 2–6; Oct.–Mar., Tues.–Sun. 9:30–12:30 and 2–6:30.*

⓫ You'll have to go to Amsterdam to view Van Goghs. But the city has provided helpful markers and a numbered itinerary to guide you from one landmark to another—many of them recognizable from his beloved canvases. Van Gogh resided in Arles from February 1888 to May 1889 and did about 300 drawings and paintings while here. You can stand on **Place Lamartine** (between the rail station and the ramparts), which is the site of his residence here, the now-famous Maison Jaune (Yellow House); it was destroyed by bombs in 1944. The artist may have set up his easel on the Quai du Rhône, just off Place Lamartine, to capture the view that he transformed into his legendary *Starry Night.*

Eight other sites are included on the city's "Promenade Vincent van Gogh" (⊕*int.tourisme.ville-arles.fr/uk/a4/a4.htm*), linking sight to canvas, including the Place du Forum; the Trinquetaille bridge; Rue Mireille; the Summer Garden on the Boulevard des Lices; and the road along the Arles à Bouc canal.

❺ Place de la République. The slender, expressive saints of St-Trophime overlook the wide steps that attract sunners and foot-weary travel-ers who enjoy the modern perspective over this broad urban square, flanked by the classical symmetry of the 17th-century **Hôtel de Ville.** This noble Italianate landmark is the work of the great 17th-century Parisian architect François Mansart (as in mansard roofs); a passage-way allows you to cut through its graceful vestibule from Rue Balze. The **obelisk**, of Turkish marble, used to stand in the Gallo-Roman cirque and was hauled here in the 18th century.

Van Gogh in Arles & St-Rémy

It was the light that drew Vincent van Gogh to Arles. For a man raised under the iron-gray skies of the Netherlands and the gaslight pall of Paris, Provence's clean, clear sun was a revelation. In his last years he turned his frenzied efforts to capture the resonance of " . . . golden tones of every hue: green gold, yellow gold, pink gold, bronze or copper colored gold, and even from the yellow of lemons to the matte, lusterless yellow of threshed grain."

Arles, however, was not drawn to Van Gogh. Though it makes every effort today to make up for its misjudgment, Arles treated the artist very badly during the time he passed here near the end of his life—a time when his creativity, productivity, and madness all reached a climax. It was 1888 when he settled in to work in Arles with an intensity and tempestuousness that first drew, then drove away his companion Paul Gauguin, with whom he had dreamed of founding an artists' colony.

Frenziedly productive—he applied a pigment-loaded palette knife to some 200 canvases in that year alone—he nonetheless lived within intense isolation, counting his sous, and writing his visions in lengthy letters to his long-suffering, infinitely patient brother Theo. Often heavy-drinking, occasionally whoring, Vincent alienated his neighbors, goading them to action. In 1889 the people of Arles circulated a petition to have him evicted, a shock that left him more and more at a loss to cope with life and led to his eventual self-commitment to an asylum in nearby St-Rémy. The houses he lived in are no longer standing, though many of his subjects remain as he saw them. The paintings he daubed

Vincent van Gogh, Self-Portrait, 1887, Musée d'Orsay, Paris, France.

and splashed with such passion have been auctioned elsewhere.

Thus you have to go to Amsterdam or Moscow to view Van Gogh's work. But with a little imagination, you can glean something of Van Gogh's Arles from a tour of the modern town. In fact, the city has provided helpful markers and a numbered itinerary to guide you between landmarks. You can stand on the Place Lamartine, where his famous Maison Jaune stood until it was destroyed by World War II bombs. *Starry Night* may have been painted from the Quai du Rhône just off Place Lamartine, though another was completed at St-Rémy.

The Café La Nuit on Place Forum is an exact match for the terrace platform, scattered with tables and bathed in gaslight under the stars, from the painting *Terrace de café le Soir*; Gauguin and Van Gogh used to drink here. (Current owners have determinedly maintained the Fauve color scheme to keep the atmosphere.) Both the Arènes and Les Alyscamps were fea-

2

Vincent van Gogh, Sunflowers, 1888, National Gallery, London, England.

tured in paintings, and the hospital where he broke down and cut off his ear is now a kind of shrine, its garden reconstructed exactly as it figured in *Le Jardin de l'Hôtel-Dieu*. The drawbridge in *Le pont de Langlois aux Lavandières* has been reconstructed outside of town, at Port-de-Bouc, 3 km (2 mi) south on D35.

About 25 km (15½ mi) away is St-Rémy-de-Provence, where Van Gogh retreated to the asylum St-Paul-de-Mausolée. Here he spent hours in silence, painting the cloisters. On his ventures into town, he painted the dappled lime trees at the intersection of Boulevard Mirabeau and Boulevard Gambetta. And en route between the towns, you'll see the orchards whose spring blooms ignited his joyous explosions of yellow, green, and pink.

⑦ Théâtre Antique (*Ancient Theater*). Between the Place de la République and the Arena, you'll come across the picturesque ruins of the amphitheater built by the Romans under Augustus in the 1st century BC. Now overgrown and a pleasant, park-like retreat, it once served as an entertainment venue to some 20,000 spectators. None of its stage walls and only one row of arches remains of its once high-curved back (it was not a natural amphitheater); its fine local stone was borrowed to build early Christian churches. Only a few vestiges of the original stone benches remain, along with the two great Corinthian columns. Nonetheless, it serves today as a concert stage for the Festival d'Arles (in July and August) and a venue for the Recontres Internationales de la Photographie (Photography Festival). ⊠*Rue du Cloître on angle with Rue de la Calade* ☎04–90–49–59–05 ⊕*www.tourisme.ville-arles.fr* ⊠€3 ⊗*May–Sept., daily 9–6:30; Oct., daily 9–noon and 2–6; Nov.–Feb., daily 10–noon and 2–6; Mar. and Apr., daily 9–noon and 2–6.*

> **YOU OUGHTA BE IN PICTURES**
>
> In July the famous **Rencontres Internationales de la Photographie** (*Photography Festival* ⊡*10 Rond-point des Arènes, BP 96, Arles Cedex 13632* ☎04–90–96–76–06) brings movers and shakers in international photography into the Théâtre Antique for five days of highly specialized colloquiums and homages. Ordinary folks can profit, too, by attending the photography exhibits displayed in some 17 venues in Arles, open to the public throughout July and August.

⑨ Thermes Constantin (*Constantine Baths*). Along the riverfront stand the remains of vast and sophisticated Roman baths, luxurious social centers that once included sports facilities and a library—the Barnes & Noble of the 4th century. You can still see the caldarium and bricks of the under-floor heating system, ⊠*Pl. Constantin at the corner of Rue de l'Hôtel de Ville* ☎04–90–49–59–05 ⊕*www.tourisme.ville-arles.fr* ⊠€5.50 (joint ticket Arenes and Thermes) ⊗*Apr.–Sept., daily 9–7; Oct.–Mar., daily 10–6:30.*

OFF THE BEATEN PATH

Though **Les Alyscamps,** the romantically melancholy Roman cemetery, lie away from the Old Town, it's worth the hike if you're in a reflective mood. Follow the Boulevard des Lices past the Jardin d'Été, the post office, and the *gendarmerie* (police station), then cut right. This long necropolis amassed the remains of the dead from antiquity to the Middle Ages; bodies were shipped up the Rhône to this prestigious resting place. Greek, Roman, and Christian tombs line the long shady road that was once the entry to Arles—the Aurelian Way—and the ruins of chapels and churches are scattered among the sarcophagi. The finest of these stone coffins were offered as gifts in feudal times, and tombstones were mined for building stone. Thus no one walk of surpassing beauty remains, but the ensemble has an aura of eternity. ☎04–90–49–59–05 ⊕*www.tourisme.ville-arles* ⊠€3.50 ⊗*May–Sept., daily 9–6:30; Oct., daily 9–noon and 2–6; Nov.–Feb., daily 10–noon and 2–6; Mar. and Apr., daily 9–noon and 2–6.*

WHERE TO EAT & STAY

$$$ ✕**La Chassagnette.** Set in a sophisticated farmhouse, this restaurant is the latest fashionable address and continues to garner rave reviews. With stone walls, burnt-sienna tiles, and comfortable settees brightened by colorful pillows, the setting is fetching; better yet, the dining area extends outdoors to include large family-style picnic tables under a wooden canopy overlooking extensive gardens. Innovative chef Luc Rabanel serves up melt-in-your-mouth open-rotisserie style menus that use ingredients grown right on the property and are certified organic. Try the braised sea bream served with mixed vegetables and a glass of eco-certified wine. ✉*Rte. du Sambuc, 13 km (8 mi) south of Arles on D36* ☎*04–90–97–26–96* ⊕*www.chassagnette.fr* ✍*Reservations essential* ▤*MC, V* ⊘*Closed Tues. and Nov.–mid-Dec. No lunch Wed.*

$$$ ✕**Lou Marquès.** Whether you dine indoors, surrounded by glowing woodwork and rich Provençal fabrics, or amid the greenery of this former Carmelite cloister, atmosphere figures large in your evening at this Arles institution in the Jules César Hotel. Chefs Pascal Renaud and Joseph Kriz mix classical grandeur with Provençal rusticity: lobster risotto, roast pigeon with cèpes, grilled bull steak, salsify with veal and tomato polenta, and strawberries in a pastry shell with fresh cream. The wine list is as ambitious as Caesar himself. ✉*Jules César Hotel, Bd. des Lices* ☎*04–90–52–52–52* ⊕*www.hotel-julescesar.com* ✍*Reservations essential* ▤*AE, DC, MC, V.*

$$ ✕**Brasserie Nord-Pinus.** With its tile-and-ironwork interior straight out
★ of a design magazine and its Place du Forum terrace packed with all the right people, this cozy-chic retro brasserie highlights light, simple, and purely Provençal cooking in dishes such as roast rack of lamb au jus and panfried fillet of beef in a morel and cream sauce. The fois gras cocotte is simply delicious. Discreet service and a nicely balanced wine list only add to its charm. And wasn't that Christian Lacroix (or Kate Moss or Juliette Binoche) under those Ray-Bans? ✉*Pl. du Forum* ☎*04–90–93–58–43* ✍*Reservations essential* ▤*AE, MC, V* ⊘*Closed Mon. in June–Sept. and Mon. and Tues. in Nov.–May.*

$$ ✕**L'Affenage.** A vast smorgasbord of Provençal hors d'oeuvres draws
★ loyal locals to this former fire-horse shed. They come here for heaping plates of fried eggplant, green tapenade, chickpeas in cumin, and a slab of ham carved off the bone—followed by roasted potatoes and lamb chops grilled in the great stone fireplace. In summer you can opt for just the first-course buffet and go back for thirds; reserve a terrace table out front if you can—in the summer, call at least a week in advance. ✉*4 rue Molière* ☎*04–90–96–07–67* ▤*AE, MC, V* ⊘*Closed Sun. and 3 wks in Aug. No lunch Mon.*

$$ ✕**La Gueule du Loup.** Serving as hosts, waiters, and chefs, the ambitious couple that owns this restaurant tackles serious cooking—Provençal specialties such as *rouget* (red mullet) with puréed potatoes, *caillette d'agneau* (lamb baked in herbs), and crème brûlée with anise—and maintains a supercool vibe. You have to get to your table through the kitchen, bustling with chopping, sizzling, and wafting scents of fresh spices, all mingling with the jazz music and vintage magic posters inside which bring the old Arles stone-and-beam interior up-to-date. ✉*39*

rue des Arènes ☎*04–90–96–96–69* ▭*DC, MC, V* ☉*Closed Sun. and Mon. in Oct.–Mar.; closed Sun. and no lunch Mon. in Apr.–Sept.*

$ ✕**Chez Gigi.** Casual, charming, and affordable, it's no wonder that Canadian owner Gigi has turned what was once a neighborhood secret into a must-stop restaurant in Arles. Vegetarians and seafood lovers are in heaven with hearty fish soup served with crusty bread and cheese, grilled sea bream with regional herbs served with whipped garlic potatoes, and a delicious vegetable terrine. Portions are as generous as your host but try to save room for dessert—the crème brûlée is a little piece of frothy delight. ⊠*49 rue des Arenes* ☎*04–90–96–68–59* ▭*AE, MC, V* ☉*Closed Sun. and Mon.*

$ ✕**Lou Caleu.** In a charming 16th-century building behind the Amphitheater, this popular, unpretentious place serves regional specialties cooked by the genial owner and chef Christian Gimenez—homemade salt-cod brandade, *jarret d'agneau* (lamb roasted with black olives), and bourride (Provençal soup)—at good prices. The puréed potatoes with truffled olives are a remarkable garnish, and make sure to order the excellent 1999 Domaine de la Solitude with the fish and to avail yourself of the terrific lunch deals. ⊠*27 rue Porte de Laure* ☎*04–90–49–71–77* ▭*AE, MC, V* ☉*Closed Sun. and Mon. and 15 days in Aug.*

$$$$ ▥**L'Hôtel Particulier.** Once owned by the Baron of Chartrouse, this extraordinary 18th-century hôtel particulier (mansion) is delightfully intimate and carefully discreet behind a wrought-iron gate. Decor is sophisticated yet charmingly simple: stunning gold-leaf mirrors, white-brocaded chairs, marble writing desks, artfully hung curtains, and hand-painted wallpaper. Rooms look out onto beautifully sculpted lawns; even if you take the five-minute walk to the center of town you can come back, stretch out in front of the pool, and listen to the birds chirp. **Pros:** off the beaten track, this hotel is a charming retreat into a modernized past—all the history with modern high-tech conveniences; restaurant is for guests only. **Cons:** pool is small, which can be difficult when you and every other guest want to be in the water. ⊠*4 rue de la Monnaie13200* ☎*04–90–52–51–40* ⊕*www.hotel-particulier.com* ⬅*10 rooms and 5 suites* ⌂*In-room: refrigerator. In-hotel: restaurant, pool, Wi-Fi, parking (fee), some pets allowed* ▭*AE, DC, MC, V.*

$$$$ ▥**Jules César.** This elegant landmark, once a Carmelite convent but styled like a Roman palace, anchors the lively Boulevard des Lices. Low-slung, with spacious guest rooms, it's an intimate, traditional hotel, conservatively decorated with richly printed fabrics and burnished woodwork. Rooms are pure Souleiado, from the flower-sprigged fabrics on the wall to the bathroom tiles; the antiques are classic, curvy Provençal. Some windows look over the pool and some over the pretty cloister, where breakfast is served under a vaulted stone arcade. The hotel also owns the beautiful *ancienne baroque* chapel next door, with its statue of St. Thérèse d'Avila. **Pros:** some rooms look over a lovely interior courtyard, and the ceilings inside are wonderfully high, with lovely carved arches. **Cons:** very large complex, easy to get lost in; some rooms are very small ⊠*Bd. des Lices* ☎*04–90–52–52–52* ⊕*www.hotel-julescesar.fr* ⬅*53 rooms, 5 suites* ⌂*In-room: refrigerator. In-hotel: 2 restaurants, pool, Wi-Fi, parking (fee), some pets allowed* ▭*AE, DC, MC, V* ⊚*BP, MAP.*

$$$$ **Nord-Pinus.** The adventurer and mail-order genius J. Peterman would ★ feel right at home in this quintessentially Mediterranean hotel on the Place du Forum; Picasso certainly did. Rooms are individually decorated: wood or tile floors, large bathrooms, and tasteful (if somewhat exotic) artwork are cleverly set off to stylish art-director chic advantage. All this works together to create a richly atmospheric stage-set for literati (or literary poseurs), decor-magazine shoots, and people who refer to themselves as "travelers." Its scruffy insider-chic is not for everyone—but this is where you might brush past a *Vogue* editor on the way to breakfast. **Pros:** the unique atmosphere in this hotel transports you to a time less complicated, when bullfighting was not part of the political arena, and people still dressed for dinner. **Cons:** rooms can be noisy at the front of the hotel, especially in summer, and the decor is not to everyone's taste. ⊠*Pl. du Forum* ☎*04–90–93–44–44* ⊕*www. nord-pinus.com* ➥*26 rooms* ⌂*In-room: some refrigerators. In-hotel: bar, parking (fee), some pets allowed* ⊟*AE, DC, MC, V.*

$$$ **Hôtel d'Arlatan.** Once home to the counts of Arlatan, this noble 15th-★ century stone house stands on the site of a 4th-century basilica, and a glass floor reveals the excavated vestiges under the lobby. Digging an excavation in your lobby is just another aristocratic pastime for the friendly owners of this jewel of a hotel, with rows of rooms that horseshoe around a lovely fountain courtyard. Rooms are decorated with a chic, light hand, with quarry tiles and Pierre Frey fabrics. The intimate lobby bar is a cool, quiet haven. Breakfast is served in pretty courtside salons. **Pros:** staying at this hotel is an experience in French hospitality: the pace is slow, the welcome warm and the food good. **Cons:** the pool is quite small; hotel seems crowded in high season. ⊠*26 rue du Sauvage13200* ☎*04–90–93–56–66* ⊕*www.hotel-arlatan.fr* ➥*41 rooms, 7 suites* ⌂*In-room: refrigerator. In-hotel: pool, Wi-Fi, parking (fee), some pets allowed* ⊟*AE, DC, MC, V* ⊘*Closed Jan.* Ⓞ*BP.*

$ **Le Cloître.** Built as the private home for the provost of the Cloisters, ★ this grand old medieval building has luckily fallen into the hands of a friendly, multilingual couple devoted to making the most of its historic details—with their own bare hands. They've chipped away plaster from pristine quarried stone walls, cleaned massive beams, restored tile stairs, and mixed natural chalk and ocher to plaster the walls, which are prettily decorated with stencils. Bargain hunters should opt for the sweet little top-floor rooms, with bath but sans WC, with views over the ancient rooftops. **Pros:** the lovely architecture is made apparent with clever use of color, and the proud owners are eager to talk about the history of their hotel. **Cons:** rooms can be sparse to the point of barreness; during the Feria season, it can be noisy. ⊠*16 rue du Cloître13200* ☎*04–90–96–29–50* ⊕*www.hotelcloitre.com* ➥*30 rooms* ⌂*In-room: no a/c (some), no TV (some). In-hotel: Wi-Fi, parking (fee), some pets allowed* ⊟*AE, MC, V* ⊘*Closed Nov.–Mar.*

$ **Muette.** With 12th-century exposed stone walls, a 15th-century spiral stair, weathered wood, and an Old Town location, a hotelier wouldn't have to try very hard to please. But the couple that owns this place does: hand-stripped doors, antiques, fresh white-and-blue–tiled baths, hair dryers, good mattresses, Provençal prints, and fresh sunflowers in every room show that they care. **Pros:** the authentic, enthusiastic welcome translates to a down-home country-kitchen feel, which can be a refreshing change for travelers. **Cons:** like many of the hotels near tourist attractions, the hotel has some rooms that can be noisy, especially in the summer. ⊠ *15 rue des Suisses13200* ☎*04–90–96–15–39* ⊕*perso.wanadoo.fr/hotel-muette* ✍*18 rooms* ⌂*In-hotel: parking (paid), some pets allowed* ⊟*AE, MC, V* ☾*Closed Jan.*

FESTIVALS

Arles is a true festival town, offering a stimulating mix of folklorique and contemporary arts events. The **férias,** with traditional corridas, or bullfights, vie with the **Fêtes du Riz** (with corrida) in September and the **Fêtes d'Arles** from the end of June to the beginning of July. All have traditional games and races in the Arena, parades, folk-dance events, and—their raison d'être—the beautiful traditional costumes of Arles.

NIGHTLIFE & THE ARTS

To find out what's happening in and around Arles (even as far away as Nîmes and Avignon), the free weekly *Le César* lists films, plays, cabaret, jazz, and rock events. It's distributed at the tourist office, in bars, clubs, and cinemas.

Though Arles seems to be one big sidewalk café in warm weather, the place to drink is the hip bar-restaurant **El Patio de Camargue** (⊠*Chemin de Barriol* ☎*04–90–49–51–76* ⊕*www.chico.fr*) on the banks of the Rhône. They serve great tapas and you can hear Gypsy guitar, song, and dance from Chico and Los Gypsies, led by a founding member of the Gypsy Kings. In high season the cafés stay lively until the wee hours; in winter the streets empty out by 11. **Le Cargo de Nuit** (⊠*7 av. Sadi-Carnot* ☎*04–90–49–55–99*) is the main venue for live jazz, reggae, and rock, with a dance floor next to the stage. There are three concerts per week (Thursday, Friday, and Saturday), and the restaurant serves food until 2 AM.

SHOPPING

Despite being chic and popular, Arles hasn't sprouted the rows of designer shops found in Aix-en-Provence and St-Rémy. Its stores remain small and eccentric and contain an overwhelming variety of Provençal goods. Regional fabric is available at every turn, including a boutique for **Les Olivades** (⊠*2 rue Jean-Jaurès* ☎*04–90–96–22–17*). Les Olivades' principal rival, **Souleiado** (⊠*18 bd. des Lices* ☎*04–90–96–37–55*), has a shop here as well. Though the charming terra-cotta folk miniatures called *santons* originate from around Marseille, the **Maison Chave** (⊠*14 Rond Point des Arènes* ☎*04–90–96–50–22*), across from the Arena, is a good place to find them. There's always someone painting impossibly tiny fingernails or Barbie-scale kerchiefs, and you're welcome to watch without buying. Best buys are local products such as perfumes, incense, soaps, and candles. There is a nice selection at **L'Occitane** (⊠*58 rue de la République* ☎*04–90–96–93–62*). If you want to get into the spirit of things before heading out to the Camargue, **L'Arlésienne** (⊠*12 rue de la République* ☎*04–90–93–28–05*) is the best place to buy Provençal fabrics, waistcoats, frilly skirts, and gardian (cowboy) shirts.

Arles's colorful **markets,** with produce, regional products, clothes, fabrics, wallets, frying pans, and other miscellaneous items, take place every Saturday morning along the Boulevard des Lices, which flows into the Boulevard Clemenceau. On the first Wednesday of the month there's a **brocante market,** where you can find antiques and collectibles, many of them regional.

ABBAYE DE MONTMAJOUR

★ *6 km (4 mi) north of Arles, direction Fontvieille.*

An extraordinary structure looming over the marshlands north of Arles, this magnificent Romanesque abbey stands in partial ruin, with shrieking rooks ducking in and out of its empty stone-framed windows. Begun in the 12th century by a handful of Benedictine monks, it grew according to an ambitious plan of church, crypt, and cloister. Under corrupt lay monks in the 17th century it grew more sumptuous; when those lay monks were ejected by the church, they sacked the place. After the Revolution it was sold to a junkman, who tried to pay the mortgage by stripping off and selling its goods. A 19th-century medieval revival spurred its partial restoration, but its 18th-century portions remain in ruins. Ironically, because of this mercenary history, what remains is a spare and beautiful piece of Romanesque architecture, bare of furniture and art—an abstraction of massive stone arches, vaults, and flowing curves that seem to be poured and molded instead of quarried and fitted in chunks. And its cloister rivals that of St-Trophime in Arles for its balance, elegance, and air of mystical peace. Van Gogh was drawn to the womblike isolation of Abbaye de Montmajour and came often to the abbey to paint and reflect. ⊠ *On D17 northeast of Arles, Rte. de Fontvielle, direction Fontvieille* ☎ *04–42–96–12–29* ⊕ *montmajour. monuments-nationaux.fr* ☜ *€6.50* ⊘ *May–Sept., daily 10–6:30; Oct.– Apr., Wed.–Mon. 10–5.*

TARASCON

18 km (11 mi) north of Arles, 16 km (10 mi) west of St-Rémy.

GETTING HERE
Cartreize (☎ *08–00–19–94–13* ⊕ *www.lepilote.com*) is an umbrella organization of buses that services Arles to Tarascon (three buses daily except Sun., €2.80 one way, ½ hr). **STD Gard** (☎ *04–66–29–27–29* ⊕ *www.stdgard.fr*) also runs buses from Nîmes, although this is a longer journey (1 hr 15 mins) and more expensive (€7). You can also drive. Take the D999 (which turns into the D99) from Nîmes or the N570 from Arles. Local trains also stop at Tarascon on the Avignon-Centre-Arles line (☎ *08–36–35–35–35* ⊕ *www.voyages-sncf.com*).

VISITOR INFORMATION
Tarascon Tourist Office (⊠ *59 rue Halles13151* ☎ *04–90–91–03–52.*

Those Ubiquitous Provençal Cottons

Vivid medallion prints, soft floral sprigs, assertive paisley borders—they've come to define the Provençal Experience, these bright-patterned fabrics, with their sunny colors, naive prints, and country themes redolent of sunflowers and olive groves. And the southern tourist industry is eager to fulfill that expectation, swagging hotel rooms and restaurant dining rooms with gay Provençal patterns in counterpoint to the cool yellow stucco and burnished terra-cotta tiles. Nowadays, both in Provence and on the coast, it's all about country—back to the land with a vengeance.

These ubiquitous cottons are actually Indian prints (indiennes), first shipped into the ports of Marseille from exotic trade routes in the 16th century. Ancient Chinese wax dyeing techniques—indigo dyes taking hold where the wax wasn't applied—evolved into wood-block stamps, their surfaces painted with mixed colors, then pressed carefully onto bare cotton. The colors were richer, the patterns more varied than any fabrics then available—and, what's more, they were easily reproduced.

They caught on like a wildfire in a mistral, and soon mills in Provence were creating local versions en masse. Too well, it seems. By the end of the 17th century, the popular cottons were competing with royal textile manufacturers. In 1686, under Louis XIV, the manufacture and marketing of Provençal cottons was banned.

All the ban did was contain the industry to Provence, where it developed in Marseille (franchised for local production despite the ban) and in Avignon, where the Papal possessions were above royal law. Their rarity and their prohibition made them all the sexier, and fashionable Parisians—even insiders in the Versailles court—flaunted the coveted contraband. By 1734, Louis XV cracked down on the hypocrisy, and the ban was sustained across France. The people protested. The cottons were affordable, practical, and brought a glimmer of color into the commoners' daily life. The king relented in 1758, and the peasants were free to swath their windows, tables, and hips with a limitless variety of color and print.

But because of the 72-year ban and that brief burgeoning of the southern countermarket, the tight-printed style and vivid colors remained allied in the public consciousness with the name "Provençal," and the region has embraced them as its own. If once they trimmed the windows of basic stone farmhouses and lined the quilted petticoats of peasants to keep off the chill, now the fabrics drape the beveled-glass French doors of the finest hôtel particuliers (private mansions) and grandest Riviera hotels.

Two franchises dominate the market and maintain high-visibility boutiques in all the best southern towns: Souleiado and Les Olivades. Fierce rivals, each claims exclusive authenticity—regional production, original techniques. Yet every tourist thoroughfare presents a hallucinatory array of goods, sewn into every salable form from lavender sachets to place mats to swirling skirts and bolero jackets. There are bread bags and bun warmers, undershorts and toilet kits, even olive-sprigged toilet-paper holders. For their fans around the world, these folklorique cotton fabric prints can't be beat.

EXPLORING

Tarascon's claim to fame is the mythical Tarasque, a monster said to emerge from the Rhône to gobble up children and cattle. Luckily, Saint Martha (Ste-Marthe), who washed up at Stes-Maries-de-la-Mer, tamed the beast with a sprinkle of holy water, after which the natives slashed it to pieces. This dramatic event is celebrated on the last weekend in June with a parade and was immortalized by Alphonse Daudet, who lived in nearby Font-vieille, in his tales of a folk hero known to all French schoolchildren as *Tartarin de Tarascon.* Unfortunately, a saint has not yet been born who can vanquish the fumes that emanate from Tarascon's enormous paper mill, and the hotel industry is suffering for it.

> **A STORE THING**
>
> Yes, that grand pooh-bah of Parisian chic **Christian Lacroix** (✉ *52 rue de la République* ☎ *04-90-96-11-16*) is actually an Arles homeboy and his exuberant style fills this, his original shop.

★ Despite the town's modern-day drawbacks, with the walls of its formidable **Château** plunging straight into the roaring Rhône, this ancient city on the river presents a daunting challenge to Beaucaire, its traditional enemy across the water. Begun in the 15th century by the noble Anjou family on the site of a Roman *castellum,* the castle grew through the generations into a splendid structure, crowned with both round and square towers and elegantly furnished. René the Good (1409–80) held court here, entertaining luminaries of the age. Nowadays the castle owes its superb preservation to its use, through the ensuing centuries, as a prison. It first served as such in the 17th century, and released its last prisoner in 1926. Complete with a moat, a drawbridge, and a lovely faceted spiral staircase, it retains its beautiful decorative Renaissance stonework and original cross-mullioned windows. ✉ *D970 at the riverfront, Blvd. du Roi René, direction Beaucaire* ☎ *04–90–91–01–93* ✆ *€6.50* ☉ *Mid-Mar.–mid-Oct., daily 9:30–6:30.*

THE ALPILLES

Whether approaching from the damp lowlands of Arles and the Camargue or the pebbled vineyards around Avignon, the countryside changes dramatically as you climb into the arid heights of the low mountain range called the Alpilles (pronounced ahl-*pee*-yuh). A rough-hewn, rocky landscape rises into nearly barren limestone hills, the fields silvered with ranks of twisted olive trees and alleys of gnarled *amandiers* (almond trees). It's the heart of Provence, and is appealing not only for the antiquities in St-Rémy and the feudal ruins in Les Baux, but also for its mellow pace when the day's touring is done. Here, as much as anywhere in the south, is the place to slip into espadrilles, nibble from a bowl of olives, and attempt nothing more taxing than a lazy game of *pétanque* (lawn bowling). Hence, the countryside around St-Rémy is peppered with gentrified *gîtes* and *mas,* and is one of the most sought-after sites for Parisians' (and Londoners') summer homes.

FONTVIEILLE

19 km (12 mi) northeast of Arles, 20 km (12½ mi) southeast of Tarascon.

The village of Fontvieille (pronounced fohn-*vyay*-uh), set among the limestone hills, is best known as the home of 19th-century writer Alphonse Daudet.

Summering in the Château de Montauban, Daudet frequently climbed the windswept, pine-studded hilltop to the rustic old windmill that ground the local grain from 1814 to 1915. There the sweeping views of the Rhône valley and the Alpilles inspired his famous, folkloric short stories called *Lettres de Mon Moulin.* Today you can visit the well-preserved **Moulin de Daudet** *(Daudet's Windmill)*, where there's a small museum devoted to his writings; you can walk upstairs to see the original milling system. ☎04–90–54–60–78 ✉€2.50 ☯Apr.–Sept., daily 9–7; Oct.–Mar., daily 10–noon and 2–5. Closed Jan.

LES BAUX-DE-PROVENCE

Fodor's Choice
★

9 km (5½ mi) east of Fontvieille, 19 km (12 mi) northeast of Arles.

GETTING HERE
The easiest way to get to Les Baux is by car. Take the A7 until you reach exit 25, then the D99 between Tarascon and Cavaillon. Les Baux is 8 km (5 mi) south of St-Rémy by the D5 and the D27. Otherwise, there is a bus run by Cartreize (☎08–00–19–94–13 ⊕www.lepilote. com) that runs a service (daily except Sun., €7) between Avignon and Les Baux via Chateaurenard and St-Rémy (€4.40) or Arles-St.-Rémy-Les Baux (daily except Sunday, €3.60). Local trains stop at Tarascon (☎08–36–35–35–35 ⊕www.voyages-sncf.com) and from here you can take a Cartrieze bus to St-Rémy and Les Baux (20 minutes, €1.60).

VISITOR INFORMATION
Les Baux-de-Provence Tourist Office (✉30 Grand-rue13520 ☎04–90–54–34–39 ⊕www.lesbauxdeprovence.com).

EXPLORING
When you first search the craggy hilltops for signs of Les Baux-de-Provence (pronounced *boh*), you may not quite be able to distinguish between bedrock and building, so naturally do its ragged skyline of towers and crenellation blend into the sawtooth jags of stone. As dramatic in its perched isolation as Mont-St-Michel and St-Paul-de-Vence, this tiny château-village ranks as one of the most visited tourist sites in France. Its car-free main street (almost its *only* street) is thus jammed with shops and galleries and, by day, overwhelmed with the smell of lavendar-scented souvenirs. But don't deprive yourself for fear of crowds. Stay late in the day, after the tour buses leave; spend the night in one of its modest hotels; or come off-season, and you'll experience its spectacular character—a tour-de-force blend of medieval color and astonishing natural beauty.

From this intimidating vantage point, the lords of Baux ruled throughout the 11th and 12th centuries over one of the largest fiefdoms in the south, commanding some 80 towns and villages. Mistral called them "a race of eagles, never vassals," and their virtually unchallenged power led to the flourishing of a rich medieval culture: courtly love, troubadour songs, and knightly gallantry. By the 13th century the lords of Baux had fallen from power, their stronghold destroyed. Though Les Baux experienced a brief renaissance and reconstruction in the 16th century, the final indignity followed hard upon that. Richelieu decided to eliminate the threatening eagle's nest once and for all and had the castle and walls demolished in 1632. Its citizens were required to pay the cost themselves. Only in the 19th century did Les Baux find new purpose. The mineral bauxite, valued as an alloy in aluminum production, was discovered in its hills and named for its source. A profitable industry sprang up that lasted into the 20th century before fading into history, like the lords of Baux themselves.

Today Les Baux offers two faces to the world: its beautifully preserved Renaissance village and the ghostly ruins of its fortress, once referred to as the *ville morte* (dead town). In the village, lovely 16th-century stone houses, even their window frames still intact, shelter the shops, cafés, and galleries that line the steep cobbled streets.

Vestiges of the Renaissance remain in Les Baux, including the pretty **Hôtel de Manville,** built at the end of the 16th century by a wealthy Protestant family. Step into its inner court to admire the mullioned windows, Renaissance-style stained glass, and vaulted arcades. Today it serves as the *mairie* (town hall). Up and across the street, the striking remains of the 16th-century Protestant temple still bear a quote from Jean Calvin: POST TENEBRAS LUX, or "after the shadows, light."

In the Hôtel des Porcelet, which dates from the 16th century, the **Musée Yves-Brayer** *(Yves Brayer Museum)* shelters this local 20th-century artist's works. Figurative and accessible to the point of naiveté, his paintings highlight Italy, Spain, even Asia, but demonstrate most of all his love of Provence. Brayer's grave lies in the château cemetery. The house at No. 4 on Place de l'Eglise is also decoratred with frescos by the artist. ✉ *Pl. F. de Herain* ☎ *04–90–54–36–99* ⊕ *www.yvesbrayer.com* 🎫 *€4* ☉ *Apr.–Sept., daily 10–12:30 and 2–6:30; Oct.–Mar., Wed.–Mon. 10–12:30 and 2–5:30.*

The main site to visit in town is the 17-acre cliff-top sprawl of ruins contained under the umbrella name **Château des Baux.** Climb the Rue Neuve and continue up Rue Trencat to the Tour du Brau, which contains the **Musée d'Histoire des Baux.** Entry to this small collection of relics and models gives access to the wide and varied grounds, where Romanesque chapels and towers mingle with skeletal ruins. A numbered audio program (available in English) guides you from site to site—the 16th-century hospital, the windmill, the 13th-century donjon—many of which are recognizable only by their names. Kids are especially fascinated by reconstructions of gigantic medieval siege machines. But be sure to stop into the cemetery; a more dramatic resting place would be hard to find.

And the tiny **Chapelle St-Blaise** shelters a permanent film, *Van Gogh, Gauguin, Cézanne au Pays de l'Olivier,* of artworks depicting olive orchards in their infinite variety. You can see painterly views over patchwork olive orchards, as well as vineyards, almond orchards, and low-slung farmhouses, from every angle of the château—reason enough alone to pay entry. ⊠ *Rue du Trencat* 🕾 *04–90–54–55–56* ⊕ *www.chateau-baux-provence. com* ⊠ *€7.60 with audioguide* ☉ *Mar.–May, Sept., and Oct., daily 9–6:30; June–Aug., daily 9–8; Nov.–Feb., daily 9–5.*

> **CAREFUL!**
>
> Readers should be warned that the *ville morte* (dead town) of Les Baux can be one dangerous place—the area is riddled with crevasses, sinkholes, and collapsed floors. Beware: your next step could be your last!

About half a mile north of Les Baux, off D27, you'll find the unusual **Cathédrale d'Images,** in the majestic setting of the old limestone quarries. Towering rock faces and stone pillars are transformed into a series of colossal screens for an evocative audiovisual program. The theme changes each year and you walk through the series of towering halls, following the 30-minute spectacle. Bring a sweater. ⊠ *Rte. de Maillane* 🕾 *04–90–54–38–65* ⊠ *€7* ☉ *Mid-Feb.–Sept., daily 10–7; Oct.–mid-Jan., daily 10–6.*

WHERE TO EAT & STAY

$ ✕ **Café Cinarca.** The tiny dining room is nice enough, but the garden courtyard of this small, unpretentious restaurant is a shady haven from the steady flow of tourists climbing the hill. A limited blackboard menu includes a simple fixed-price meal, including *tartes* and salads embellishing one or two hearty meat dishes: beef daube (stew), or *caillette aux herbes* (pork meat loaf) served hot or cold. It's also worth coming for afternoon tea, as the cakes and pastries are homemade and delicious. ⊠ *Rue Trencat* 🕾 *04–90–54–33–94* ⊟ *MC, V* ☉ *Closed Tues.*

$$$$ ⊡ **L'Oustau de la Baumanière.** Sheltered by rocky cliffs below the village

Fodor's Choice   of Les Baux, this long-famous hotel, with its formal landscaped ter-

★   race and broad swimming pool, has a guest book studded with names like Winston Churchill, Elizabeth Taylor, and Picasso. The interior is luxe-Provençal chic, thanks arched stone ceilings, and brocaded settees done up in Canovas and Halard fabrics. Guest rooms—breezy, private, and beautifully furnished with antiques—have a contemporary flair. As for the famed Baumanière restaurant (reservations essential), chef Jean-André Charial's hallowed reputation continues to attract culinary pilgrims who delight in the varied menu—lobster cooked in Châteauneuf-du-Pape and set on a bed of polenta is a typical dazzler. **Pros:** probably the most quietly glamorous country inn in France, this is the ultimate mas experience; service is excellent. **Cons:** restaurant is very crowded, especially in the summer; waiting list is long for both the restaurant and the hotel. ⊠ *Val d'Enfer13520* 🕾 *04–90–54–33–07* ⊕ *www.oustaudebaumaniere.com* ⬙ *16 rooms, 14 suites* ⬙ *In-room: refrigerator. In-hotel: restaurant, tennis courts, pool, Wi-Fi, parking (fee), some pets allowed* ⊟ *AE, DC, MC, V* ☉ *Hotel and restaurant* *closed Jan. and Feb.; restaurant closed Wed. and for lunch Thurs. in Nov.–Dec.* 🍽 *MAP*

$$$ **La Benvengudo.** With manicured grounds shaded by tall pines, this graceful shuttered mas feels centuries old but was built to look that way some 30 years ago. Its heavy old beams, stone fireplace, and terra-cotta tiles enhance the homey, old-fashioned interior. Guest rooms are simple and elegant, with homey touches (throws on the settees, comfy cushions on the bed, large bathrooms), and the views out over green lawns. The resident dogs greet you just before the friendly owners do. Dinner (prix fixe Provençal-Mediterranean menu is €28) is served by the olive-shaded pool, or you can have a drink on the stone-tabled terrace. **Pros:** quiet and secluded; affordable; friendly service. **Cons:** some rooms could do with a face-lift; some rooms do not have refrigerators ✉ *Below Les Baux, direction Fontvieille Vallon de l'Arcoule* ☎ *04–90–54–32–54* 🌐 *www.benvengudo.com* *25 rooms, 2 apartments* *In-room: refrigerator (some). In-hotel: restaurant, tennis court, pool, parking (free), some pets allowed* *AE, MC, V* *Closed mid-Nov.–Feb.* 🍽 *MAP.*

A BUDGET BAUMANIÈRE?

You can try a less expensive, though still stylish, Oustau experience a kilometer away at **La Cabro d'Or** (✉ *Mas Carita, Rte. D'Arles* ☎ *04–90–54–33–21* 🌐 *www.lacabrodor.com*). Run by the same owners, it's plush farmhouse chic (€180), but more rustic—don't be surprised to see a billy goat wander by your guest-room window. Exquisitely prepared food is served inside or on the serenely beautiful garden terrace. The inn is closed November through mid-December.

$$ ★ **Le Prince Noire.** Each of the three rooms of this unique bed-and-breakfast is carved right out of the stone face but the semi-troglodyte effect is softened by jute carpets, warm woods, and unbeatable views over the Val d'Enfer. It is the highest house in the city, nestled in the heart of the château. The owner's warm welcome leaves you feeling right at home and it is a truly remarkable experience to wake up in the morning and see the sun rise over the valley below. Book well in advance for this unforgettable place. **Pros:** stunning vistas from each window; unbeatable service. **Cons:** rooms are cold in the winter, and lacking amenities. ✉ *Rue de Lorme, Cité Haute* ☎ *04–90–54–39–57* 🌐 *www.leprincenoir.com* *1 room, 1 suite, 1 studio* *In-room: no TV. In-hotel: Wi-Fi, some pets allowed* *AE, MC, V* *Closed mid-Jan.–Feb.* 🍽 *BP.*

$ **La Reine Jeanne.** Sartre and de Beauvoir had separate rooms but a shared balcony—and what a balcony. Jacques Brel and Winston Churchill were also happy guests at this modest but majestically placed inn and stood looking over rugged views worthy of the châteaux up the street. The inn is located right at the entrance to the village and offers rooms that are small, simple, and—despite the white, vinyl-padded furniture—fondly decorated with terra-cotta tiles and stencil prints. Good home-style cooking (try *l'aïoli*—a garlic mayonaise fish dish) and a fine plat du jour are served in the restaurant, which offers views from both the panoramic dining room and a pretty terrace; it's one of the best settings for a meal in Les Baux. **Pros:** the familial atmosphere allows for a relaxed stay, and the warm welcome makes for instant appeal; views are lovely. **Cons:** some rooms are tiny; only two small balconies. ⊠ *Grande Rue* ☎ *04–90–54–32–06* ⊕ *www.la-reinejeanne. com* ➟ *10 rooms* ⚠ *In-hotel: restaurant, Wi-Fi, some pets allowed* ⊟ *AE, MC, V* ⊘ *Closed mid-Jan.–mid-Feb.*

SHOPPING

An extravagant choice of souvenirs ranging from kitsch (Provençal-print toilet-paper holders) to class (silk challis shawls from Les Olivades) virtually reach out and grab you as you climb the hill lined with tempting (and not-so) shops. But come with cash: only the post office is equipped to change money, and there's no bank.

ST-RÉMY-DE-PROVENCE

FodorsChoice
★ *11 km (7 mi) northeast of Les Baux, 25 km (15½ mi) northeast of Arles, 24 km (15 mi) south of Avignon.*

GETTING HERE

Like Les Baux-de-Provence, the easiest way to get to St-Rémy is by car. Take the A7 until you reach exit 25, then the D99 between Tarascon and Cavaillon, direction St-Rémy on the D5. Otherwise, there is a bus run by Cartreize (☎ *08–00–19–94–13* ⊕ *www.lepilote.com*) that runs a service (daily except Sunday) between Avignon and Les Baux via Chateaurenard and St-Rémy (€4.40) or Arles–St-Rémy–Les Baux (daily except Sun., €4.40). Local trains stop at Tarascon (☎ *08–36–35–35–35* ⊕ *www.voyages-sncf.com*) and from here you can take a Cartrieze bus to St- Rémy (20 minutes, €1.60).

VISITOR INFORMATION

St-Rémy Tourist Office (⊠ *Pl. Jean-Jaurès* ☎ *04-90-92-05-22* ⊕ *www.saintremy-de-provence.com*).

EXPLORING

There are other towns as pretty as St-Rémy-de-Provence, and others in more dramatic or picturesque settings. Ruins can be found throughout the south, and so can authentic village life. Yet something felicitous has happened in this market town in the heart of the Alpilles—a steady infusion of style, of art, of imagination—all brought by people with a respect for local traditions and a love of Provençal ways. Here, more than anywhere, you can meditate quietly on antiquity, browse redolent markets with basket in hand, peer down the very row of plane trees you remember from a Van Gogh, and also enjoy urbane galleries, cosmopolitan shops, and specialty food boutiques. An abundance of chic choices in restaurants, mas, and even châteaus awaits you; the almond and olive groves conceal dozens of stone-and-terra-cotta gîtes, many with pools. In short, St-Rémy has been gentrified through and through, and is now a sort of arid, southern Martha's Vineyard or, perhaps, the Hamptons of Provence. Important note: St-Rémy is one of the most popular Provençal destinations but has surprisingly few hotels. Book months in advance! St-Rémy has always attracted the right sort of people. First established by an indigenous Celtic-Ligurian people who worshiped the god Glan, the village Glanum was adopted and gentrified by the Greeks of Marseille in the 2nd and 3rd centuries before Christ. They brought in sophisticated building techniques—superbly cut stone, fitted without mortar, and classical colonnades. Rome moved in to help ward off Hannibal, and by the 1st century BC Caesar had taken full control. The Via Domitia, linking Italy to Spain, passed by its doors, and the main trans-Alpine pass emptied into its entrance gate. Under the Pax Romana there developed a veritable city, complete with temples and forum, luxurious villas, and baths.

The Romans eventually fell, but a town grew up next to their ruins, taking its name from their protectorate abbey St-Remi in Reims. It grew to be an important market town, and wealthy families built fine hôtels (mansions) in its center—among them the family De Sade (whose distant black-sheep relation held forth in the Lubéron at Lacoste). Another famous native son, the eccentric doctor, scholar, and astrologer Michel Nostradamus (1503–66), is credited by some as having predicted much of the modern age; Catherine de Medici consulted him on every life decision.

Perhaps the best known of St-Rémy's visitors was the ill-fated Vincent van Gogh. Shipped unceremoniously out of Arles at the height of his madness (and creativity), he had himself committed to the asylum St-Paul-de-Mausolée and wandered through the ruins of Glanum during the last year of his life. It is his eerily peaceful retreat as well as the ruins that draw visitors by the busload to the outskirts of modern St-Rémy, but the bulk of them snap their pictures and move on to Les Baux for the day, leaving St-Rémy to its serene, sophisticated ways.

To approach Glanum, you must park in a dusty roadside lot on D5 south of town (in the direction of Les Baux).

★ Before crossing, you'll be confronted with two of the most miraculously preserved classical monuments in France, simply called **Les Antiques.** Though dating from the era of the Caesars, they could be taken for Romanesque, so perfectly intact are their carvings and architectural details. The **Mausolée** (Mausoleum), a wedding-cake stack of arches and columns built about 30 BC, lacks nothing but its finial on top, yet it is dedicated to a Julian (as in Julius Caesar), probably Caesar Augustus. Allegorical scenes in bas-relief represent myths of Greek origin but most likely refer to Julius Caesar's military triumphs. Two sculptured figures, framed in its column-ringed crown, must surely be the honorees; the dedication reads SEX. L.M. IVLIEI C.F. PARENTIBUS SUEIS, or "Sextius, Lucius, Carcus son of Caius, of the family of Julii, to their parents." A few yards away stands another marvel: the **Arc Triomphal,** most likely dating from around AD 20. All who crossed the Alps entered Roman Glanum through this gate, decorated with reliefs of battle scenes depicting Caesar's defeat and the capture of the Gauls.

★ Across the street from Les Antiques, a slick visitor center, set back from D5, prepares you for entry into **Glanum** with scale models of the site in its various heydays. A good map and an English brochure guide you stone by stone through the maze of foundations, walls, towers, and columns that spreads across a broad field; Greek sites are helpfully noted by numbers, Roman ones by letters. At the base of rugged white cliffs and shaded with black-green pines, it is an extraordinarily evocative site and inspires contemplation in even the rowdiest busload of schoolchildren. ⊠*Rte. Des Baux de Provence, off the D5, direction Les Baux* ☎*04–90–92–64–04 info phone at Hôtel de Sade* ⊕*www.glanum.monuments-nationaux.fr* ⊠*€7; €7.50 includes entry to Hôtel de Sade* ☉*Apr.–Sept., daily 9–6:30; Oct.–Mar., daily 9–5. Closed Mon.*

You can cut across the fields from Glanum to **St-Paul-de-Mausolée,** the lovely, isolated asylum where Van Gogh spent the last year of his life (1889–90), but enter it quietly. It shelters psychiatric patients to this day—all of them women. You're free to walk up the beautifully manicured garden path to the church and its jewel-box Romanesque **cloister,** where the artist found womblike peace. A small boutique shows works of current patients—*art brut* reminiscent of Munch and Basquiat—for sale. You can climb a stairway to a memorial bust of Van Gogh (donated by the American sculptor Klapholz after the original was stolen) and a picture window that frames a garden view he loved and painted. ⊠*Next to Glanum, off D5 direction Les Baux* ☎*04–90–92–77–00* ⊕*www.cloitresaintpaul-valetudo.com* ⊠*€4* ☉*Apr.–Sept., daily 9:30–7; Oct.–Mar. 10:30–5; closed Jan.*

St-Rémy is wrapped by a lively commercial boulevard, lined with shops and cafés and anchored by its 19th-century church **Collégiale St-Martin.** Step inside to see the magnificent 5,000-pipe modern organ, one of the loveliest in Europe. Rebuilt to 18th-century specifications in the early 1980s, it has the flexibility to interpret new and old music with pure French panache; you can listen to it Saturday afternoon at 5:30 from July through September for free. ⊠*Pl. de la République.*

Within St-Rémy's fast-moving traffic loop, a labyrinth of narrow streets leads you away from the action and into the slow-moving inner sanctum of the **Vieille Ville.** Here high-end, trendy shops mingle pleasantly with local life, and the buildings, if gentrified, blend unobtrusively.

Make your way to the **Hôtel de Sade,** a 15th- and 16th-century private manor now housing the phenomenal abundance of treasure unearthed with the ruins of Glanum. There are a statue of Hercules and a graceful bas-relief of Hermes, funeral urns and crystal jewelry, and surprisingly sophisticated tools. There are also the remains of Gallo-Roman funeral obelisks and early Christian altars. The De Sade family built the house around remains of 4th-century baths and a 5th-century baptistery, now nestled in its courtyard. ⊠*Rue du Parage* ☎*04–90–92–64–04.*

The 18th-century Hôtel Estrine is now the **Centre d'Art Présence Van Gogh** and has many reproductions of the artist's work, along with letters to his brother Theo and exhibitions of contemporary art, much of it inspired by Vincent. It also houses temporary exhibitions and a permanent collection dedicated to the father of Cubism, Albert Gleize, who lived in St-Remy for the last 15 years of his life. ⊠*Hôtel Estrine,*

8 rue Estrine ☎*04–90–92–34–72* ⊕*www.ateliermuseal.net* ⊠€*3.20* ⊗*May–Sept., Tues.–Sun., 10–12:30 and 2–7, Wed. 10–7; Mar., Apr., and Oct.–Feb., Tues.–Sun. 10:30–12:30 and 2–6.*

WHERE TO EAT & STAY

$$$ ✕ **Bistrot d'Eygalières.** Belgian chef Wout Bru's understated restaurant in
★   nearby Eygalières is quickly gaining a reputation (and Michelin stars) for light and subtly balanced cuisine like sole with goat cheese, lobster salad with candied tomatoes, and foie gras carpaccio with summer truffles. Gastronomes who have indulged too much can stagger upstairs to the seven charming guest rooms, which are chic and comfortable. ⊠*Rue de la République (10 km [6 mi] southeast of St-Rémy on D99 and then on D24), Eygalières* ☎*04–90–90–60–34* ⊕*www.chezbru. com* ⊟*AE, MC, V* ⊗*Closed Mon. and Tues. lunch, closed two wks. in Nov. and two wks. in Feb.*

$$$ ✕ **La Maison Jaune.** This modern retreat in the Old Town draws crowds of summer people to its pretty roof terrace. The decor of sober stone and lively contemporary furniture, both indoors and out, reflects the cuisine. With vivid flavors and a cool, contained touch, chef François Perraud prepares grilled sardines with crunchy fennel and lemon confit, ham-cured duck on lentils with vinaigrette, and grilled lamb chops carmalized with honey. Prices are high but one bargain lunch menu offers a minimalist smorgasbord of tastes, and wine is included. ⊠*15 rue Carnot* ☎*04–90–92–56–14* ♨*Reservations essential* ⊟*AE, MC, V* ⊗*Closed Mon. No dinner Sun. No lunch Tues. Closed Jan. and Feb.*

$$ ✕ **L'Assiette de Marie.** Though life is lived outdoors in St-Rémy, there
★   are rainy days and winter winds, and this is the place to retreat. Marie Ricco is a collector, and she's turned her tiny restaurant into an art-directed bower of attic treasures—unscrubbed, unrestored, as is. Fringed lamp shades are artfully askew, ancient wallpaper curls from a door, the coat rack sags with woolen uniforms, and classic jazz and candlelight complete the scene. Seated at an old school desk, you choose from the day's specials, all made with Marie's Corsican-Italian touch—marinated vegetables with tapenade, a cast-iron casserole of superb pasta. There's a wide choice of St-Rémy wines as well. ⊠*1 rue Jaume Roux* ☎*04–90–92–32–14* ♨*Reservations essential* ⊟*MC, V* ⊗*Closed Thurs., and Nov.–Mar.*

$ ✕ **La Gousse d'Ail.** An intimate, indoor Old Town hideaway, this family-run bistro lives up to its name (The Garlic Clove), serving robust, highly flavored southern dishes in hearty portions: zucchini timbale, rich homemade pasta in powerful pesto with almonds, and homemade ice cream crepes with fresh fruit. A ceramic pitcher of ice water and a thick flask of house wine offer counterbalance, and the bill is delivered with much-needed mints. The cozy interior (dark timbers, niches full of puppets) matches the warm welcome. Aim for Thursday night when there is Gypsy music and jazz. ⊠*6 blvd. Marceau* ☎*04–90–92–16–87* ⊕*www.la-goussedail.com* ⊟*AE, MC, V* ⊗*Closed mid-Jan.–Feb.*

$ ✕ **Le Bistrot des Alpilles.** This popular institution has a broad sidewalk terrace, glassed in brasserie-style in winter, and a feel of easygoing professionalism. Cheap lunch menus and a reasonable evening menu make the good, traditional cooking a bargain. Service is quick, good, and friendly. There's a melt-in-your-mouth *agneau à la ficelle* (local roast lamb), a daily fish specialty, a good rum cake in an orange sauce, and a wine list that includes most of the best wines from the south. ⊠*15 bd. Mirabeau* ☎*04–90–92–09–17* ⊕*www.lebistrodesalpilles.com* ⌂*Reservations essential* ▤*AE, MC, V.*

$$$$ 🏨 **Château des Alpilles.** At the end of an alley of grand old plane trees, this early-19th-century manor house lords over a vast park. If public spaces are cool and spare to the point of sparseness, rooms are warm and fussy, with lush Provençal prints and polished antiques. Outer buildings offer jazzy modern apartments with kitchenettes, and the poolside grill gives you a noble perspective over the park. **Pros:** hotel's lush park is beautiful; nights are quiet. **Cons:** some rooms are small and can be stuffy. ⊠*Ancienne rte. du Grès* ☎*04–90–92–03–33* ⊕*www.chateaudesalpilles.com* ⇄*17 rooms, 4 suites* ⌂*In-hotel: restaurant, tennis court, pool, Wi-Fi, some pets allowed* ▤*AE, DC, MC, V* ⊙*Closed mid-Nov.–mid-Dec. and Jan.–mid-Feb.* ⅋❘*BP.*

$$$$ 🏨 **Domaine de Valmouriane.** This genteel mas-cum-resort, beautifully isolated on a broad park, offers you a panoply of entertainment, from billiards to a Jacuzzi. Inside, soft, overstuffed English-country furnishings mix cozily with cool Provençal stone and timber, and massive stone fireplaces warm public spaces. The restaurant is run by chef Pascal Volle, who is determined to please with game, seafood, local oils, and truffles; his ravioli foie gras is sheer decadence. The pool, surrounded by a slate walk and a delightful garden, is most inviting. **Pros:** warm welcome from the owners Philippe and Martin Capel makes you feel like an honored guest; service at restaurant is top-notch. **Cons:** some rooms are small; isolated location. ⊠*Petite rte. des Baux (D27)* ☎*04–90–92–44–62* ⊕*www.valmouriane.com* ⇄*12 rooms, 1 suite* ⌂*In-room: refrigerator. In-hotel: restaurant, tennis court, pool, Wi-Fi, parking (fee)* ▤*AE, DC, MC, V* ⊙*Closed mid-Dec.–mid-Jan.* ⅋❘*FAP, MAP.*

$$$$ 🏨 **Mas de Cornud.** An American mans the wine cellar and an Egyptian runs the professional kitchen (by request only), but the attitude is pure Provence. David and Nitockrees Carpita (a CCP, or "certified culinary professional") have turned their farmhouse, just outside St-Rémy, into a bed-and-breakfast filled with French country furniture and objects from around the world. Guests and hosts unwind with a nightly pastis and a pétanque match. Table d'hôte dinners, cooking classes (with or without staying in the hotel), and market tours can be arranged. Breakfast is included and rooms should be reserved in advance (using PayPal on-site). **Pros:** friendly welcome; lovely atmosphere, with a convivial meal at the end of the day. **Cons:** some rooms can be hot in the summer. ⊠*Rte. de Mas-Blanc* ☎*04–90–92–39–32* ⊕*www.mascornud.com* ⇄*5 rooms, 1 suite* ⌂*In-room: no a/c, no TV. In-hotel: restaurant, pool, parking (free), some pets allowed* ▤*No credit cards* ⊙*Closed Nov.–Mar.* ⅋❘*BP.*

$$$ 🏨 **Hotel les Ateliers de l'Image.** Young Lyonnais photographer Antoine Godard created this wonderfully eccentric hotel, the latest hot spot in St-Rémy. It harmonizes bits of several countries: the restaurant is run by Japanese chef Maseo Ikeda who serves dishes like leek soup with langoustine gyoza and soy-laquered lamb with Japanese aubergines;

2

the rooms mix Scandinavian simplicity with a Provençal touch; and the ever-changing artwork features photography from around the world. **Pros:** modern decor; fun and dynamic vibe; gorgeous estate; genuine welcome. **Cons:** public salons seems more photograph galleries than welcoming hotel. ✉36 bd. Victor Hugo13210 ☎04–90–92–51–50 ⊕*www.hotelinprovence.com* ⤢*26 rooms, 6 suites* ⚬*In-room: refrigerator. In-hotel: room service, pool, parking (free), some pets allowed* ⊟*AE, DC, MC, V* ⊗*Closed Jan. and Feb.*

$$ ⌂**Château de Roussan.** In a majestic park shaded by ancient plane trees
★ (themselves protected landmarks), its ponds and canals graced by swans and birdsong, this extraordinary 18th-century château is being valiantly preserved by managers who (without a rich owner to back them) are lovingly restoring it. Glorious period furnishings and details are buttressed by brocante and bric-a-brac, and the bathrooms, toggled into various corners, have an afterthought air. Cats outnumber the staff. Yet if you're the right sort for this place—backpackers, romantic couples on a budget, lovers of atmosphere over luxury—you'll blossom in this three-dimensional costume drama. **Pros:** eccentric and atmospheric stay requires a good sense of humor. **Cons:** the château still needs work; some rooms look a little worse for wear. ✉Rte. de Tarascon ☎04–90–92–11–63 ⊕*www.chateau-de-roussan.com* ⤢*22 rooms* ⚬*In-hotel: restaurant, some pets allowed* ⊟*AE, DC, MC, V* ⦿*MAP.*

$ ⌂**Auberge de la Reine Jeanne.** With all the luxurious mas and châteaus to choose from in St-Rémy, you don't have to be scared away if you're on a budget: This charming Logis-de-France property, in a 17th-century stone building that surrounds a green courtyard, offers more-conventional lodgings right in the heart of town. Its strong point is its restaurant, where modestly priced, mainstream French cooking is served in the courtyard in summer and in a firelit, dark-timber hall in winter. Room decor isn't up to St-Rémy style (blue carpeting, polyester quilts), but the best rooms overlook the court and are clean and comfortable. **Pros:** bargain charm; genuine welcome; sincere service. **Cons:** decor is lacking in style; no pool. ✉12 bd. Mirabeau13210 ☎04–90–92–15–33 ⤢*10 rooms, 1 apartment* ⚬*In-hotel: restaurant, Wi-Fi, some pets allowed* ⊟*AE, DC, MC, V* ⊗*Closed Jan.* ⦿*BP.*

FESTIVALS

St-Rémy is fond of festivals, borrowing traditions of bull races and ferias from its lowland neighbors and creating a few of its own. On Pentecost Monday (the end of May), the **Fête de la Transhumance** celebrates the passage of the sheep from Provence into the Alps, and costumed shepherds lead some 4,000 sheep, goats, and donkeys through the streets. The **Grande Feria,** in mid-August, brings the Camargue to the hills, with bull games, fireworks, and flamenco guitar. Three weekends a year (Ascension in May, late June, and mid-September) are devoted to the **Fête de la Route des Peintres de la Lumière en Provence** (Festival of the Route of Painters of Light in Provence), an enormous contemporary-art fair.

NIGHTLIFE & THE ARTS

La Forge des Trinitaires (⊠*Av. de la Libération* ☎*04–90–92–31–52*) draws the young, the restless, and the trendily dressed for African and Antillaise music every Friday and Saturday night 11 PM–4:30 AM. At **La Haute Galine** (⊠*Chemin Cante Perdrix et Galine* ☎*04–90–92–00–03*) a very young crowd gathers (on Friday and Saturday nights only) to eat by the pool and dance into the night. On the second Friday of the month in July and August, **Pégomas** (⊠*3 av. Jean-Moulin* ☎*04–32–60–01–90*) is the site of a live jazz concert.

At 5:30 every Saturday in July, August, and September, you can hear the magnificent **organ of St-Martin Collégiale** (⊠*Pl. de la République*) in a free recital, often featuring the boy wonder *organiste-titulaire* Jean-Pierre Lecaudey.

SHOPPING

Every Wednesday morning St-Rémy hosts one of the most popular and picturesque **markets** in Provence, during which the Place de la République and narrow Old Town streets overflow with fresh produce, herbs and spices, olive oil by the vat, and tapenade by the scoop, as well as fabrics and brocante (collectibles). There's a smaller version Saturday morning.

Interior design is a niche market in this region of summer homes, so **decor shops** abound, not only featuring Provençal pottery and fabrics but also a cosmopolitan blend of Asian fabrics, English garden furniture, and Italian high-design items. Individual artisans fill gallery-style boutiques with their photography, picture frames, and wrought-iron furniture. The common denominator is high here, so good taste has stonewalled tourist kitsch. **Souleiado** (⊠*Pl. de l'Église, 2 av. de la Résistance* ☎*04–90–92–45–90*) has high-end Provençal fabrics and linens. **Les Olivades** (⊠*28 rue Lafayette* ☎*04–90–92–00–80*) has beautiful displays of delightful Provençal fabrics. The design shops, fabric shops, and art gallery–cum–gift shops are scattered throughout the Vieille Ville and along the boulevards that surround it. At **La Boutique des Jardins** (⊠*1 bd. Mirabeau* ☎*04–90–92–11–60*), Françoise Gérin displays the booty she trolls on her Asian and African travels, from Egyptian cottons to Indian hanging lamps and tooled metal frames.

The Vaucluse

AVIGNON, THE LUBERON & MONT VENTOUX

Village of Gordes

WORD OF MOUTH

"Because the lavender fields are very important to you—and why not?—I strongly suggest that you locate yourselves anywhere north of the Montagne du Luberon. Saignon, Bonnieux, Gordes, and L'Isle-sur-la-Sorgue fit this criterion. Better yet, go further north, say around Vaison-la-Romaine—there are numerous fields near there."

—TuckH

WELCOME TO THE VAUCLUSE

TOP REASONS TO GO

★ **The walled city of Avignon:** While most exciting during the theater festival at the Palais des Popes in July, Avignon is surprisingly youthful and vibrant year-round.

★ **Châteauneuf-du-Pape:** Probably the most evocative Côtes du Rhône vineyard but just one of many villages in this area where you can sample exceptional wines.

★ **Lovely Lavender:** Get hip-deep in purple by touring the Lavender Route between the Abbaye de Senanque and the historic towns of Sault and Forcalquier.

★ **The Sky's No Limit!:** Experience the perched villages of the region, including Gordes and Bonnieux, in a patchwork landscape right out of a medieval Book of Hours.

★ **Seeing Red in Roussillon:** With its ochre cliffs that change tones—copper, pink, rust—depending on the time of day, this town is a gigantic ruby embedded in the Vaucluse bedrock.

1 Avignon. Avignon's most famous bridge—the subject of a French children's song—now stretches only halfway across the river, so don't make the mistake of trying to drive across it. Take the next bridge to L'Ile de la Barthelasse, an amazingly rural setting minutes from the city where you can ride a bike through vineyards and overnight in lovely auberges.

St-Saturnin-les-Apt

2 **Mont Ventoux.** Highest peak of Provence, Mont Ventoux is the most difficult stage of the Tour de France cycling race, but anyone with good leg muscles can rent a racing bike and attempt it (expect a two- to six-hour slog depending on your level of fitness). You can also ride up to the top in a van and cruise down—no one has to know the truth.

3 **The Luberon.** Like so many Luberon villages, Gordes might seem a touch too perfect at first sight. Persist and you will find real charm in its narrow, hilltop streets—and most of the boutiques are actually rather tasteful. To get off the beaten track, head instead to once-upon-a-timefied Oppède-le-Vieux, Bonnieux, and Lacoste.

4 **L'Isle-sur-la-Sorgue.** If you're fond of antiques, plan to join the festive hordes trawling for treasures at the famous Sunday flea-market in L'Isle-sur-la-Sorgue. After exploring the fancier *antiquaires* in town, enjoy an idyllic lunch by one of the town watermills, then track down the "source" of the River Sorgue in the famous spring of Fontaine de Vaucluse.

GETTING ORIENTED

The absence of the scantily clad Demoiselles from Picasso's famous early cubist painting may damper your image of beautifully preserved Avignon, but this city has plenty to compensate: with medieval streets, crenelated palaces, and sweet museums, it is an ideal gateway to explore the lower Rhône area. Just up the highway is the sun-scorched vineyards of the Côtes du Rhône and the Roman ruins of Vaison-la-Romaine and Orange; just east is the perfectly picturesque Luberon countryside; while 20 mi north lie the storybook hilltop villages of the Haut Vaucluse.

DRÔME

NTOUX

D974

D974

D164

D942

D950

D1

Sault

D30

UCLUSE

D943

Lagarde-d'Apt

DE   VAUCLUSE

D2   St-Saturnin-les-Apt   D51

ordes

Roussillon   D4   Apt

N100   Saignon   N100

D36   D943

erbes   Buoux

Lacoste   Bonnieux

ONTAGNE   DU LUBERON

D956   Courbières

D973   Cadenet

Pertuis   Mirabeau

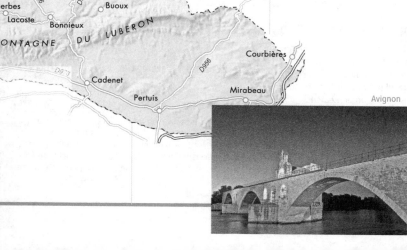

Avignon

THE VAUCLUSE PLANNER

Markets

Browsing through the *marché couvert* (covered food market) in Avignon is enough to make you renounce dining in the tempting local restaurants.

All the fantastique seafood, free-range poultry, olives, and produce cry out to be gathered in a basket and cooked in their purest form.

Village open-air markets are carefully scheduled to cover in turn all the days of the week, including boulevard Limbert on Saturdays and a flea market at Place des Carmes on Sundays.

But food plays second fiddle at one of the most famous markets in Provence.

L'Isle-sur-la-Sorgue draws crowds of bargain hunters and collectors to its Sunday antiques and *brocante* (collectibles) fair.

The event is strung in picturesque disarray along the town's water mills and canals.

The best pickings in linen sheets, silverware, engravings, pewter, oak furniture, and quirky collectibles can be had if you arrive early, *naturellement*.

However, the after-lunch stroll-and-browse bodes to become a fashionable tradition.

Finding a Place to Stay

One of the most popular vacation regions in France, after the seaside, the Vaucluse has a plethora of sleek and fashionable converted *mas* (farmhouses), landscaped in lavender, cypress, and oil jars full of vivid flowers. Given the crushing heat in high summer, the majority have swimming pools and, these days, air-conditioning (but it's wise to check ahead if you're counting on it). However, only a few provide *moustiquaires*, mosquito netting put over the bed or window screens to keep out troublesome flies. Reservations are essential most of the year, and many hotels close down altogether in winter.

Grape Expectations

The most serious wine center in the south of France is the southern portion of the Côtes du Rhône, home to the muscular reds of Gigondas, Vacqueyras, Rasteau, Cairanne, and of their more famous neighbor Châteauneuf-du-Pape. Nearby Beaumes-de-Venise is famous for its sweet, light muscat. Not to be overlooked are the wines of the Côtes du Ventoux and the Côtes du Luberon. You can visit most vineyards without an appointment. If you find that slightly intimidating or impractical, most wine-making towns have a shop where local wines are sold at the producer's price, with no markup.

DINING & LODGING PRICES IN EUROS

¢	$	$$	$$$	$$$$
Restaurants				
Under €13	€14–€19	€20–€24	€25–€31	Over €32
Hotels				
Under €55	€56–€85	€86–€135	€136–€200	Over €201

Restaurant prices are per person for a main course at dinner, including tax (19.6%) and service; note that if a restaurant offers only prix-fixe (set-price) meals, it has been given the price category that reflects the full prix-fixe price. Hotel prices are for a standard double room in high season, including tax (19.6%) and service charge.

Eating Well in the Vaucluse

As the cultural capital of the Vaucluse, Avignon might logically be considered the culinary capital, too. Visit during the July theater festival, however, and you'll have the opposite impression. Sunny sidewalk tables spill out temptingly onto the streets, but nearly all serve the kind of food designed for people on tight schedules: salads, pizzas, and charcuterie plates, often of indifferent quality. For more generous and imaginative Provençal food, you will have to seek out Avignon's few culinary gems or scour the countryside, where delightful meals can be had in roadside restaurants, renovated farmhouses, and restaurants with chefs whose talents are as stunning as hilltop settings they operate in. Be sure to indulge in the sun-drenched local wines from the Luberon, the Côtes du Ventoux, and the Côtes du Rhône (especially its lesser-known vineyards), and if a full bottle seems too much for two people, order one of the 50 cl bottles now popular here (the equivalent of two-thirds of a regular bottle). It pays to do research—too many restaurants, especially in summer, are cynically cashing in on the thriving tourist trade, and prices are generally high.

Making the Most of Your Time

The Vaucluse is more refined than its flashy counterpart, the Côte d'Azur, so take advantage of its gastronomic blessings and sign up for a wine tasting or cooking course. Hotel La Mirande in Avignon offers a cheese and wine course with no less than 20 cheeses and two wines to sample with each. Or at La Maison sur la Sorgue, they owners will arrange visits (and be the designated drivers) to several of the local vineyards for a dose of viticulture and tasting. While you're in L'Isle-sur-la-Sorgue, arrange to stay over on a Saturday and wake up to the chatter and clatter of the Sunday antique vendors. Avignon is almost a never-ending festival: Les Hivernales dance festival (February); Film Festival (June); Arts Festival (July); Le Off Festival (also July); and the Côtes de Rhone Wine Festival (November). On another musical note for July: Lacoste has a successful arts festival; Orange takes on opera; and noted dance troops take part in Vaison-la-Romaine's Dance Festival, held at the town's Roman theatre. But if you want to tip-toe through the best lavender, keep in mind that claims of bizarre weather patterns are now faulted for smaller, less superior crops, so you'll want to drive through the Luberon during July to take in endless rows of glorious lavender before it's too late.

How's the Weather?

High heat and high season hit in July and August with a wallop: this lovely region is anything but undiscovered, thanks in part to Peter Mayle's revelations (he took a break from Provence to avoid the crowds he inspired, then relocated to the quieter south face of the Luberon). June and September are still intense, but better. Low season falls between mid-November and mid-March, when many restaurants and hotels take two or three months off. That leaves spring and fall: if you arrive after Easter, the flowers are in full bloom, the air cool, and the sun warm, and you'll still be able to book a table on the terrace. The same goes for October and early November, when the hills of the Luberon turn rust and gold, and game choices figure on every menu.

Main Regional Tourist Office

The Comité Départemental de Tourisme du Vaucluse accepts written queries and calls; specify your needs by category (lodging, restaurants, etc.). ⊕ www.provenceguide.com is useful, too.

Comité Départemental de Tourisme en Vaucluse (⌂ 12 rue Collège de la Croix, B.P. 147, 84008 Avignon Cedex 1 ☎ 04–90–80–47–00 ⊕ www. tourisme-en-vaucluse.com).

GETTING AROUND PLANNER

Transportation Basics

If arriving in Avignon by plane (flights arrive from Paris and a few U.K. cities) or TGV train (Paris and Avignon 2 hrs 40 mins; Nice-Avignon 3 hrs 15 mins), arrange for a rental car prior to arrival. Driving is the best choice allowing you to control your schedule and not fall slave to a public system which isn't on par with that of the Alpes-Maritimes.

Even anxious drivers will find roads linking one village to the next rather easy (pleasant even!) to handle—the only downside is that the driver won't be able to take in all those breathtaking views, like when driving from Le Barroux down into the Luberon. The Web site www.asf.fr can give you road conditions, rates, and suggested itineraries.

Travelling by train in the region is limited mostly to Orange and Avignon while Vaucluse regional buses are few and far between with, as admitted by local tourist offices, infrequent schedules. Consult www.cars-lieutaud.fr or www.vaucluse.fr (look for "transport interurbain: lignes, horaires") for up-to-the-minute listings and fares of Avignon, Orange, Vaison, Carpentras, and other bus routes.

By Bus

Major bus transport companies carry travelers from surrounding cities into towns not accessible by rail; bus and rail services usually dovetail. Avignon's gare routière (bus station) has the heaviest interregional traffic.

A reasonable network of private bus services (called, confusingly enough, *cars*) links places not served or poorly served by trains. Ask for bus schedules at train stations and tourist offices. Avignon has a sizable station, with posted schedules.

Cars Lieutaud has a booth just outside the Avignon train station, offering daily bus excursions into different regions—for instance, the Luberon, Vaison, and the Alpilles. The main destinations serviced to/from the Avignon bus station (10 to 20 buses daily) are Orange (€5.90, 45 minutes) and Carpentras (€4.40, 45 minutes). Five or fewer buses daily connect with: Aix-en-Provence (€14, 1½ hrs); Apt (€8.20, 1 hr); Arles (€7.10, 1½ hrs); Cavaillon (€3.80, 1 hr); Vaison-la-Romaine (€8.10, 1 hr); Nîmes (€8.10, 1½ hrs); and Pont du Gard (€6.50, 1 hr).

As for the Luberon villages, a bewildering number of bus companies feature routes with (infrequent) buses; the bus station in Cavaillon has routes to L'Isle-sur-la-Sorge, Aix-en-Provence, and Avignon, and some of the hard-to-get hilltop villages. You can get to Gordes on the two-to-four buses daily run by Les Express de la Durance.

Autocars Sumian has routes that service Loumarin, Bonnieux, and Apt. Voyages Arnaud has routes that include L'Isle-sur-la-Sorgue, Fontaine-de-Vaucluse, and Bonnieux. Autocars Barlatier runs buses that stop in Bonnieux and rarely Oppède-le-Vieux. Rubans Bleu connects Avignon with Cavaillon and Lourmarin.

Bus Travel Information **Gare routière (bus station)** (✉ *Bd. St-Roch, 5 ave. Monclar* ☎ *04-90-82-07-35*). **Autocars Barlatier** (☎ *04-90-73-23-59*). **Autocars Sumian** (☎ *04-91-49-44-25*). **Cars Lieutaud** (☎ *04-90-86-36-75*, ⊕ *www.cars-lieutaud.fr*). **Les Express de la Durance** (☎ *04-90-71-03-00*). **Rubans Bleu** (☎ *04-90-79-19-25*. **Voyages Arnaud** (☎ *04-90-38-15-58*).

By Car

The A6/A7 toll (*péage*) expressway channels all traffic from Paris to the south. At Orange A7 splits to the southeast and leads directly to Avignon and N100 (in the direction of Apt), which dives straight east into the Luberon. To reach Vaison and the Mont Ventoux region from Avignon, head northeast toward Carpentras on D942. D36 jags south from N100 and leads you on a gorgeous chase over the backbone of the Luberon, via Bonnieux and Lourmarin; from there it's a straight shot to Aix and Marseille or to the Côte d'Azur. Or you can shoot back west up D973 to Cavaillon and Avignon.

With spokes shooting out in every direction from Avignon and A7, you'll have no problem accessing the Vaucluse. The main *routes nationales* (national routes, or secondary highways) offer fairly direct links via D942 toward Orange and Mont Ventoux and via N100 into the Luberon. Negotiating the roads to L'Isle-sur-la-Sorgue and Fontaine-de-Vaucluse requires a careful mix of map and sign reading, often at high speeds around suburban *giratoires* (rotaries). But by the time you strike out into the hills and the tiny roads—one of the best parts of the Vaucluse—give yourself over to road signs and pure faith. As is the case throughout France, directions are indicated by village name only, with route numbers given as a small-print afterthought. Of course, this means you have to recognize the minor villages en route.

By Train

Trains arrive in Marseille from the main northern cities, including Paris, Strasbourg, Nantes, and Bordeaux. Those from Paris and Strasbourg pass through Orange and Avignon. The quickest train connection remains the TGV *Méditerranée* line that arrives in Avignon after a 2 hour, 40-minute trip from Paris. These TGV trains then connect with Nîmes (€13.50, 15 mins), Marseille (€27, 35 mins), and Nice (€51.20, 3 hrs). From Avignon's main rail station, the Gare Avignon Centre, connections include Orange (€5.30, 20 mins), Arles (€9.10, 20 mins), and L'Isle-sur-la-Sorgue. Another big rail nexus is the city of Orange: note the center city is a 10-minute walk from the train station. But no trains go to the Luberon villages, although some bus routes do. Note that it costs 34¢ a minute for train information. After a recorded message, there is a pause. At this moment say the words Billet Loisir (pronounced Bee-yay Lwah-zeer) and this directs you to a service agent.

Train Information **SNCF** (☎*3635 France; 33–892–35–35–35 outside France* ⊕*www.sncf.com*). **TGV** (☎*3635* ⊕*www.tgv.com*).

By Air

Marseille's Marignane airport is served by frequent flights from Paris and London; it's about an hour's drive from Avignon.

The smaller Avignon Caumont airport has frequent daily flights from Paris and Clermont Ferrand.

Air Travel Information **Marignane airport** (☎*04–42–14–14–14* ⊕*www.marseille.aeroport.fr*). **Avignon Caumont airport** (⊠*141 allée de la Chartreuse Montfavet, southeast of Avignon* ☎*04–90–81–51–51* ⊕*www.avignon.aeroport.fr*).

By Boat

There are four boat tour companies operating out of Avignon (all of which have the same contact information) that offer various outings to such local sites as Arles and Châteauneuf-du-Pape.

Trips cost anywhere from €8 to €63, and can include lunch, dinner, and dancing.

New riverboats cruises for two to four people (champagne optional) depart from the Pont d'Avignon.

Boat Travel Information **Les Grand Bateaux de Provence** (⊠*Allées de L'Oulle, Avignon* ☎*04–90–85–62–25* ⊕*www.mireio.net*).

Updated by
Nancy Wilson

FOR MANY, THIS IS THE only true Provence: one vast Cézanne masterpiece where sun-bleached hills and fields are tapestries of green-and-black grapevines and silver-gray olives, and rolling rows of lavender harmonize with mountains that loom purple against an indigo sky. It is here, in his beloved Luberon, that British author Peter Mayle discovered and described the simple pleasures of breakfasting on melons still warm from the sun, buying fresh-dug truffles from furtive farmers in smoke-filled bars, and life without socks. The world shared his epiphany, and vacationers now flock here in search of the same sensual way of life, some retreating to lavishly renovated farmhouses with cypress-shaded pools, others heading for the luxurious inns that cater to people fleeing the city's smog. There are budget accommodations, too, in the form of cheerful *chambres d'hôtes* and modest but well-run hotels, which often have very good restaurants. Given the intense summer heat and the distance from the sea, swimming pools and air-conditioning are de rigueur, with a few exceptions higher up in the mountains where there is a refreshing breeze.

As if an invisible hand had drawn lines dividing this region into three, the Vaucluse changes character dramatically from north to south, west to east. East of Avignon, you'll find sun-scorched *villages perchés* (perched villages) that lord over the patchwork valleys—Gordes, Bonnieux, Ménerbes, and ocher-tinted Roussillon. Though mass tourism has given them something of a Disney feel, you need only wander off the main shopping drags to get a sense of medieval life in the labyrinthine back alleys and pollard-shaded squares resonant with the splashing of ancient fountains. The otherwise tranquil town of L'Isle-sur-la-Sorgue has become a magnet for international antiques fiends, reaching its peak of activity on Sundays when the entire town turns into a giant *brocante* (antiques fair).

Lying north of Avignon, the Côtes du Rhône produce some of the world's most muscular wines: Châteauneuf-du-Pape and Beaumes-de-Venise are two of the best-known villages, though the names Vacqueyras, Gigondas, and St-Joseph also give wine buffs goose bumps. Despite their renown, this area feels off the beaten track even in midsummer, when it's favored by French rather than foreign tourists. A brisk wind cools things off in summer, as do the broad-leaved plane trees that shade the sidewalk tables at village restaurants and cafés. East of here, the countryside grows increasingly dramatic, first with the jaw-droppingly jagged Dentelles de Montmirail, whose landscape is softened by olive groves and orchards, then the surprisingly lush Mont Ventoux, best known as the Tour de France's most difficult stage. Along the way, you'll find villages such as Séguret and Vaison-la-Romaine where you can sample the slow-paced local lifestyle over a game of pétanque or a lingering apéro. And all this lies a stone's throw from thriving Avignon, its feudal fortifications sheltering a lively arts scene and a culture determinedly young.

EXPLORING THE VAUCLUSE

Avignon as well as the Roman centers and papal vineyards to its north lie in arid lowlands, and getting from point to point through these flats can be uninspiring. It's to the east that the real Vaucluse rises up into the green-studded slopes of Mont Ventoux and the Luberon. Here, the back roads are beautiful—the temptation to abandon your rental car in favor of foot travel is often irresistible. Give in; the combination of the smells of wild thyme, lavender, wet stone, and dry pine can be as heady as a Châteauneuf-du-Pape. Anchored by the magnificent papal stronghold of Avignon, the glories of the Vaucluse region spread luxuriantly eastward of the Rhône. Its famous vineyards seduce connoisseurs, and its Roman ruins in Orange and Vaison-la-Romaine draw scholars and arts lovers. Plains dotted with orchards of olives, apricots, and cherries give way, around formidable Mont Ventoux, to a rich and wild mountainous terrain, then flow into the primeval Luberon, made a household name by Peter Mayle.

Avignon is a must, and if you're a wine lover, you'll enjoy exploring the vineyards north of it. If you're a fan of things Roman, you need to see Vaison-la-Romaine and Orange. The antiques market in L'Isle-sur-la-Sorgue makes for a terrific Sunday excursion, as does the nearby Fontaine-de-Vaucluse, a dramatic spring cascade (outside drought season). But the Luberon and its villages perched high up in the hills are a world of their own and worth allowing time for—perhaps even your whole vacation. Note that the Pont du Gard, the superbly preserved Gallo-Roman aqueduct, is just a 30-minute drive west of Avignon, and that Arles, Nîmes, and the windswept Camargue (⇨ *Chapter 1*) are only a stone's throw to the south and west.

Numbers in the text correspond to numbers in the margin and on the Vaucluse and Avignon maps.

AVIGNON

GETTING HERE & AROUND

Avignon is a major rail crossroads and springboard for the Vaucluse and has plenty of car-rental agencies located at the Gare Avignon TGV (best to reserve your car in advance). The quickest train link, of course, is the high-speed TGV (Trains à Grande Vitesse) Méditerranée line that connects Paris and Avignon (2 hrs 40 mins). Nice-Avignon on the TGV (3hrs 15 min) costs at least €45. Keep in mind that the Gare Avignon TGV is located on Chemin du Confluent, a few miles southwest of the city (a navette shuttle bus connects with the train station in town every 15 minutes from early morning to late at night). Other trains, such as the Avignon–Orange line (€5.30; 20 mins) use the Gare Avignon Centre station located at 42 bd. St-Roch; other lines go to Arles, Nîmes, Orange, Toulon, and Carcassonne. Just next door at 5 avenue Monteclar, you'll find the bus terminal (☎ 04–90–82–07–35); buses run to and from Avignon, Arles (45 mins, €6), Carpentras (€4; 45 mins), Cavaillon (€4; 1 hr), Nîmes (€9; 1½ hrs), or farther afield to Orange,

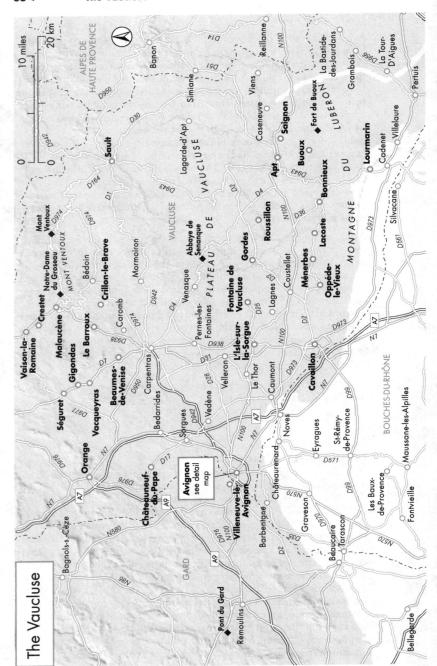

Isle/Sorgue, Marseille, Nice, and Cannes. The Avignon-Orange bus runs several times during the day and takes under an hour and is €3 one-way. In addition, there are 27 city buses to get you around Avignon itself, run by TCRA (⊕*www.tcra.fr*).

VISITOR INFORMATION
Avignon Tourist Office (✉ *41 cours Jean-Jaurès84000* ☎ *04-32-74-32-74* ⊕ *www.avignon-tourisme.com*).

EXPLORING
Of all the monuments in France—cathedrals, châteaux, fortresses—the ancient city of Avignon (pronounced ah-veen-*yonh*) is one

> ### TIRED TOOTSIES?
>
> Tired feet after too many rocky cobblestone paths? Head over to the Allées de l'Oulle and take a cruise along the river Rhône. For €8 (children under eight free), Le Mireio (⊕ *www.mireio.net*) runs a year-round 45-minute cruise from Avignon to the Isle of Bathelasse to Villeneuve-lez-Avignon. A lunch cruise around the Popes' Palace or the vineyards near Châteauneuf-du-Pape is also a more civilized way to take in the surrounding sights.

of the most dramatic. Wrapped in a crenellated wall punctuated by towers and Gothic slit windows, its old center stands distinct from modern extensions, crowned by the Palais des Papes (Popes' Palace), a 14th-century fortress-castle that's nothing short of spectacular. Standing on the Place du Palais under the gaze of the gigantic Virgin that reigns from the cathedral tower, with the palace sprawling to one side, the bishops' Petit Palais to the other, and the long, low bridge of childhood song fame stretching over the river ("Sur le pont d'Avignon on y danse tous en rond . . ."), you can beam yourself briefly into the 14th century, so complete is the context, so evocative the setting.

Yet you'll soon be brought back to the present with a jolt by the skateboarders leaping over the smooth-paved square. Avignon is anything but a museum; it surges with modern ideas and energy and thrives within its ramparts as it did in the heyday of the popes—like those radical church lords, sensual, cultivated, cosmopolitan, with a taste for lay pleasures. For the French, Avignon is almost synonymous with its theater festival in July—thousands pack the city's hotels to bursting for the official festival and le Festival OFF, the fringe festival with some 700 shows. If your French isn't up to a radical take on Molière, look for the English-language productions, or try the circus and mime—there are plenty of shows for children, and street performers abound.

Avignon was transformed into the Vatican of the north when political infighting in the Eternal City drove Pope Clement V to accept Philippe the Good's invitation to start afresh. In 1309 his entourage arrived, preferring digs in nearby priories and châteaux; in 1316 he was replaced by Pope John XXII, who moved into the bishop's palace (today the Petit Palais). It was his successor Pope Benedict XII who undertook construction of the magnificent palace that was to house a series of popes through the 14th century. During this holy reign Avignon evolved into a sophisticated, cosmopolitan capital, attracting artists and thinkers and stylish hangers-on. Founded in 1303, the university burgeoned, with thousands of the faithful from across Europe making the pilgrimage. As the popes' wealth and power expanded, so did their formidable palace. And its sumptuous decor was legendary, inspiring horror and disdain from the poet Petrarch, who wrote of "towers both useless and absurd that our pride may mount skyward, whence it is sure to fall in ruins." The abandoned Italians dubbed Avignon a "second Babylon."

After a dispute with the king, Pope Gregory XI packed up for Rome in 1376, but Avignon held its ground. On his death in 1378, the French elected their own pope, Clement VII, and the Great Schism divided the Christian world. Popes and antipopes abused, insulted, and excommunicated each other to no avail, though the real object of dispute was the vast power and wealth of the papacy. When the king himself turned on the last antipope, Avignon lost out to Rome and the extravagant court dispersed.

Though it is merely the capital of the Vaucluse these days, Avignon's lively street life, active university, and colorful markets present a year-round spectacle far beyond the 800-plus productions on view during the summer Avignon Theater Festival. To add to the allure, many of the landmark buildings and churches have been enhanced with new lighting fixtures that literally light up the nights. To take it all in, see the city's steep streets via the tourist train, a type of tram car that resembles a children's party ride (⊕ *www.petittrainavignon.com*). Two trains, each following the same circuit, leave from the Popes' Palace Square daily every 20 minutes and take you through the Rocher des Doms gardens, the historic city center, and the major monuments, for €7, March 15 through October 15.

THE HISTORIC CENTER

A GOOD WALK

Begin your walk at the train station (there's a good parking garage). Crossing the busy ring road, walk through the Porte de la République, an opening in **Les Remparts**, the magnificent ramparts surrounding the entire Old Town. Head straight north up Rue de la République. Past the post office on your left, duck left into a backstreet and peek into the **Espace St-Louis**, a 17th- and 18th-century retreat that retains its magnificent courtyard shaded by gigantic plane trees. Today it's home to the Centre National du Théâtre (National Theater Center) and the hotel-restaurant Cloître St-Louis.

At the corner of Rue Joseph-Vernet, stop in at the tourist office for maps and information. A block up from the tourist office, a lovely little 17th-century Jesuit chapel shelters a fascinating jumble of classical stonework in the **Musée Lapidaire**. Double back and turn right (west) onto Rue Joseph-Vernet; two blocks up, you can stop into the tiny, eccentric **Musée Requien**, with its very personal displays on natural history. Next door, don't miss the **Musée Calvet**, a Neoclassical stone mansion housing a collection of 17th- and 18th-century French art, much of it created in Avignon. Continue up Joseph-Vernet to Rue St-Agricol, and follow it right into the animated heart of the city, the **Place de**

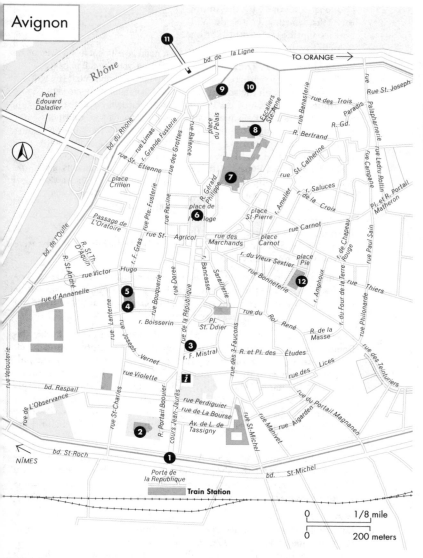

Avignon

Rhône

Pont Edouard Daladier

TO ORANGE →

bd. de la Ligne

Pont St-Bénézet — 11

Petit Palais — 9

Rocher des Doms — 10

Escaliers Ste-Anne

rue des Trois Paradis

Rue St. Joseph

Palabhanerie

rue Ledru Rollin

rue Campane

R. Gd.

R. Bertrand

Cathédrale Notre-Dame-des-Doms — 8

place du Palais

rue Banasterie

rue St. Catherine

bd. du Rhône

rue Limas

r. Grande Fusterie

rue des Grottes

rue Balance

rue St.-Étienne

place Crillon

R. Gérard Philippe

Palais des Papes — 7

r. Amelier

r. de la Croix

r. Saluces

Pl. et R. Portail Matheron

Passage de L'Oratoire

rue Pte. Fusterie

rue Racine

place de l'Horloge — 6

place St-Pierre

rue Carnot

place Carnot

R. St-Th. D'Aquin

r. F. Gras

rue St.- Agricol

rue des Marchands

r. du Vieux Sextier

place Pie

r. de Chapeau Rouge

r. du Four de la Terre

rue Paul Sain

bd. de l'Oulle

rue Victor -Hugo

r. Bancasse

Sabatterie

rue Bonneterie

Les Halles — 12

r. Amphoux

rue Thiers

Musée Calvet — 5

rue d'Annanelle

rue Bouquerie

rue Dorée

Pl. St. Didier

rue du Roi René

R. de la Masse

rue Philonarde

rue des Teinturiers

Musée Requien — 4

rue Lanterne

Pl. St. André

r. Boisserin

rue Joseph -Vernet

r. F. Mistral

Musée Lapidaire — 3

R. et Pl. des Études

rue des Lices

rue du Portail Magnanen

rue de l'Observance

rue Violette

cours Jean-Jaurès

R. Portail Boquier

rue St-Charles

bd. Raspail

rue Perdiguier

rue de La Bourse

Av. de L. de Tassigny

rue Aigarden

rue Manivet

rue St-Michel

Espace St-Louis — 2

Les Remparts — 1

bd. St-Roch

NÎMES

Porte de la République

Train Station

bd. St-Michel

0 ——— 1/8 mile

0 ——— 200 meters

l'Horloge, anchored by the imposing 19th-century Hôtel de Ville
and its Gothic Tour de l'Horloge
(Clock Tower).

Tear yourself away from the sidewalk cafés, merry-go-round, jugglers, and mimes on the square and
continue north to Place du Palais.
Walk straight up the square and
bear left until you're opposite the
entry gate, so you can take in the
full, wide-angle view of the magnificent **Palais des Papes**. After an
hour or two touring the awesome
interior, recross the square to study
the magnificent facade of the Hôtel
des Monnaies, a heavily sculpted
Baroque masterpiece from the
17th century. Then cut across to the relatively humble but evocative
Cathédrale Notre-Dame-des-Doms.

> ### THE AVIGNON PASSION PASS
>
> A good investment is the *Avignon Passion*: you pay full price for the first site/monument you visit and thereafter there are vari-ous reductions on all the other sites, depending on which of them you visit. The 15-day pass, available for free at the tourist office, as well as participat-ing sites and monuments, gives discounts of 20%–50% on visits to every site in Avignon and Villeneuve-lez-Avignon.

At the far end of Place du Palais, the **Petit Palais**—once home to Avignon's bishops and the first of its resident popes—houses a marvelous
collection of Italian paintings, much of it (coincidentally) from the era
of the popes and antipopes themselves.

Leave the square and climb up Montée du Moulin into the **Rocher des
Doms**, a serene hilltop garden park replete with sculptures and black
swans a-swimming. From here you can look out over the city, the palace, and the river to the ancient enemy of papal Avignon, the fortified
town of Villeneuve. Above all, you'll be able to take in the famous
Pont St-Bénézet in its stunted state and imagine dancers turning *tous en
rond* (round and round). From the park, you can climb down past the
Tour de Chiens in the ramparts to reach the bridge; or cut behind the
Petit Palais.

Follow the scenic Escaliers Ste-Anne down and head right on Rue Banasterie, but don't let the shops lining the winding backstreets around
Place Carnot keep you from stopping in to salivate over the delicious
goods in **Les Halles**, the indoor market on Place Pie (pronounced *pee*).

MAIN ATTRACTIONS

8 **Cathédrale Notre-Dame-des-Doms.** First built in a pure Provençal
Romanesque style in the 12th century, then dwarfed by the extravagant palace beside it, this relatively humble church rallied in the 14th
century with a cupola—which promptly collapsed. As rebuilt in 1425,
it's a marvel of stacked arches with a strong Byzantine flavor and is
now topped with a gargantuan Virgin Mary lantern—a 19th-century
afterthought—that glows for miles around. The Baroque styling in the
nave dates from 1670. That's the tomb of Pope John XXII in the cen-
ter-left chapel—but not his likeness, as his *gisant* (recumbent funeral
statue) was wrecked in the Revolution and replaced with the likeness of

a mere bishop, which he was before he rose to infamy. ✉*Pl. du Palais* ☎*04–90–86–81–01* ⊕*www.cathe drale-avignon.fr* ☉*May–Oct., daily 7:30–7; Nov.–Apr., daily 8–5.*

HOW TO PLAY THE PALACE

The Palais des Papas is one of those grand, must-see monuments that can be overwhelmed by shutter-popping groups of travelers at times. But it should be seen nonetheless; aim for visiting during opening time, lunchtime, or evenings if you are there in the middle of summer.

⑤ Musée Calvet. Worth a visit for the beauty and balance of its architecture alone, this fine old museum holds a rich collection of art, acquired and donated by an 18th-century Avignon doctor who had a hunger for antiquities and an eye for the classically inspired. Later acquisitions are Neoclassical and Romantic, and almost entirely French, including works by Manet, Daumier, and David, such as *La Mort du Jeune Bara* (*The Death of Young Bara*). The main building itself is a Palladian-style jewel in pale Gard stone dating from the 1740s; the garden is so lovely that it may distract you from the paintings. ✉*65 rue Joseph-Vernet* ☎*04–90–86–33–84* ⊕*www.musee-calvet.org* ⬚*€6* ☉*Wed.–Mon. 10–1 and 2–6.*

⑦ Palais des Papes. The Renaissance chronicler Jean Froissart called this

Fodor's Choice
★

palace "the loveliest and strongest house in the world," while Petrarch sneered, "The houses of the apostles crumble as (popes) raise up their palaces of massy gold." Within these magnificent Gothic walls, one of the heydays (or low points) in French history took place, a period of extraordinary sacred and secular power and, to skeptics, outrageous wealth. Once densely decorated in tapestries, frescoes, and sumptuous fabrics, it hosted feasts of Lucullan extravagance and witnessed intrigues of Gothic proportion. The pope ruled within as half god, half prince, eating alone at an elevated table in the crowded dining hall, sleeping in a lavishly decorated bedroom distinctly devoid of sacred reference. His chamberlain's bedroom had eight hiding holes, complete with trapdoors concealed under carpets; who knows to what use they were put?

But don't expect to see eye-boggling luxury today. Resentful revolutionaries hacked away most traces of excess in the 1780s, and, ironically, what remains has a monastic purity. Most of all you may be struck by the scale; either one of its two wings dwarfs the cathedral beside it, and between them they cover almost 50,000 feet of surface. The grand-scale interiors are evocative as well, with a massive wooden barrel vault arching over the dining hall like a boat belly and a kitchen with fireplaces big enough to house a family. The **Grande Audience** (Grand Audience Hall) and the **Grande Chapelle** are as vast as cathedrals.

From your first exterior view of them, note the difference between the two wings of the palace. The north end, toward the cathedral, is the Palais Vieux (Old Palace), a severe Cistercian bastion built by the sober Pope Benedict XII between 1335 and 1342; the south end was built over the next ten years with slightly airier fantasy by Pope Clement VI, who prized his creature comforts.

An enthusiastic patron of the arts, Clement VI brought in a team of artists from Italy to decorate his digs. It was led by no less than Simone Martini himself, imported from Siena and Assisi (where he had worked with Giotto). On his death, Mattheo Giovanetti took the lead, and the frescoes that covered every surface must have been one of the wonders of the world. Some of the finest traces remain in Clement's study, called the **Chambre du Cerf** (Stag's Room), where the walls still retain the lovely frescoes he commissioned in 1343. Unlike the Raphael masterpieces that decorate the Vatican chambers in Rome, which use lofty classical themes and powerful Christian images, these paintings depict simple hunting scenes: a stag hunt, bird snaring, and fishing. They're graceful, almost naive in style, and intimate in scale, but the attempts at perspective in the deep window frames remind you that this was an advanced center of culture and learning in the 14th century, and perspective was then downright avant-garde, fresh from the sketchbooks of Giotto. Among many fragments, one other example of Giovanetti's work can be viewed in its entirety in **Chapelle St-Jean** (St. John Chapel), a masterpiece of composition in which the interplay of hands and the implied lines of gazes create a silent dialogue.

Though you may be anxious to see the more famous spaces, take time on entering to read the displays about the evolution of this UNESCO splendor and to study the scale model of the palace in its medieval context. Only then can you take in its enormity, looming like Olympus over the tiny half-timber houses that crowded the Place du Palais—a palace worthy of a royal dynasty and a temple to holy hubris.

For wine lovers, there's a wine cellar devoted to Côtes du Rhônes at the **Bouteillerie** (☎04–90–27–50–85) of the Popes' Palace where you can sample and buy regional wines; the selection changes every year and the shop is open daily. Although it's in the Palais, you don't need to pay admission to go to the store. ⊠*Pl. du Palais* ☎*04–90–27–50–00* ⊕*www.palais-des-papes.com* ⊡*€10.50 (summer) and 8.50 (winter), entry includes individual audioguide; €13(summer) and 11 (winter) includes audioguided tour to Pont St-Bénézet* ⊙*Daily Nov. 2–Feb. 28, 9:30–5:45; Mar. 1–Mar. 14, 9–6:30; Mar. 15–June 30, 9–9; July, 9–8; Aug., 9–9; Sept. 1–Sept. 15, 9–8; Sept. 16–Nov. 1, 9–7.*

❾ ★ Petit Palais. This former residence of bishops and cardinals houses a large collection of Old Master paintings, the majority of them Italian works from the Renaissance schools of Siena, Florence, and Venice—styles with which the Avignon popes would have been familiar, but it's a coincidence. The paintings were acquired in the 19th century by the extravagant Italian marquis Campana and bought, on his bankruptcy, by Napoléon III. Divided among provincial museums throughout France, they remained scattered until after World War II; then the 300-some treasures were reunited under this historic roof. But even though the works weren't amassed by the popes, as you move through hall after hall of exquisite 14th-century imagery, you'll get a feel for the elevated tastes of the papal era. A key piece to seek out in the 15th-century rooms is Sandro Botticelli's *Virgin and Child,* a masterpiece of tenderness and lyric beauty created in his youth; 16th-century master-works include Venetian works by Carpaccio and Giovanni Bellini. ⊠ *Pl. du Palais* ☎ *04–90–86–44–58* ⊕ *www.petit-palais.org* ⊠ *€6* ⊘ *Wed.– Mon. 10–1 and 2–6.*

⑥ Place de l'Horloge *(Clock Square).* This square is the social nerve center of Avignon, where the concentration of bistros, brasseries, and restaurants draws swarms of locals and tourists to the shade of its plane trees. After a play, the doors of the **Théâtre Municipal** open onto the square and the audience spills into the nearest sidewalk café for a post-performance drink. The **Hôtel de Ville** (Town Hall) on the west side of the square was built in the 19th century around its dominating Gothic clock tower, from which the square gets its name.

⑪ Pont St-Bénezet *(St. Bénezet Bridge).* "Sur le pont d'Avignon on y danse,
★ on y danse . . ." Unlike London Bridge, this other fragment of childhood song (and UNESCO World Heritage site) still stretches its arches across the river, but only partway. After generations of war and flooding, only half remained by the 17th century. Its first stones allegedly laid with the miraculous strength granted St-Bénezet in the 12th century, it once reached all the way to Villeneuve. It's a bit narrow for dancing "tous en rond" (round and round) though the traditional place for dance and play was under the arches. For a fee, you can rent an audioguide and climb along its high platform for broad views of the Old Town ramparts. ⊠ *Port du Rhône* ☎ *04–90–27–51–16* ⊠ *€4.50; €13 for combination ticket with Palais des Papes and audioguide* ⊘ *Daily Apr.–June, 9–7; July, 9–8; Aug.–Sept. 14, 9–9; Sept. 15–Nov., 9–7; Dec. 1–Mar. 14, 9:30–5:45; Mar. 15–31, 9:30–6:30.*

❶ Les Remparts *(The Ramparts).* More than 4 km (2½ mi) long, these protective crenellated walls and towers were built by the popes in the 14th century to keep out rampaging brigands and mercenary armies attracted by legends of papal wealth. It's extraordinarily well preserved, thanks in part to the efforts of architect Viollet-le-Duc, who restored the southern portion in the 19th century. Modern-day Avignon roars around its impervious walls on a noisy ring road that replaced a former moat.

⑩ Rocher des Doms *(Rock of the Domes).* This ravishing hilltop garden, with statuary and swans under grand Mediterranean pines and subtropical greenery, would be a lovely retreat by itself, but its views make it extraordinary. From side to side you can look over the palace, the rooftops of Old Avignon, the St. Bénezet Bridge, and formidable Villeneuve across the Rhône. On the horizon loom Mont Ventoux, the Luberon, and Les Alpilles. ⊠ *Montée du Moulin, beside Pl. du Palais.*

ALSO WORTH SEEING

❷ Espace Saint Louis. This graceful old 17th-century Jesuit cloister has been converted for office use by the well-known Avignon Festival—a performing arts event which lasts most of the month of July. The cloister's symmetrical arches (now partly enclosed as the sleek Hôtel Cloître Saint Louis) are shaded by ancient plane trees. You can wander around the courtyard after you've picked up your festival information. Occasional exhibits are held inside as well. ⊠*20 rue du Portail Boquier* ☎*04–90–27–66–50* ⊕*www.festival-avignon.com.*

⑫ **Les Halles.** By seven every morning (except Monday) the merchants and artisans have stacked their herbed cheeses and arranged their vine-ripened tomatoes with surgical precision in pyramids and designs that please the eye before they tease the salivary glands. This permanent covered market is as far from a farmers' market as you can get, each booth a designer boutique of *haute de gamme* (top-quality) goods, from jewel-like olives to silvery mackerel to racks of hanging hares worthy of a Flemish still life. Even if you don't have a kitchen to stock, consider enjoying a cup of coffee or a glass of (breakfast) wine while you take in the sights and smells or watch Saturday's cooking demonstration from 11 to noon. ⊠*Pl. Pie* ☎*04–90–27–15–15* ⊕*www. avignon-leshalles.com* ☉*Tues.–Sun.* 6 AM–1 PM.

❸ **Musée Lapidaire.** Housed indefinitely in a pretty little Jesuit chapel on the main shopping street, this collection of classical sculpture and stonework highlights funeral stones and works from Gallo-Roman times (1st and 2nd centuries), as well as samples from the Musée Calvet's collection of Egyptian, Greek, and Etruscan works. They are haphazardly labeled and insouciantly scattered throughout the noble chapel, itself slightly crumbling but awash with light. ⊠*27 rue de la République* ☎*04–90–85–75–38* ⊕*www.musee-lapidaire.org* ⊠€2 ☉*Wed.–Mon. 10–1 and 2–6.*

❹ **Musée Requien.** Don't bother to rush to this eccentric little natural history museum, but since it's next door to the Calvet Museum, and free, you might want to stop in and check out the petrified palm trunks, the dinosaur skeleton, the handful of local beetles and mammals, and the careful and evocative texts (French only) accompanying them. The museum is named for a local naturalist and functions as an entrance to the massive **library** of natural history upstairs. ⊠*67 rue Joseph-Vernet* ☎*04–90–82–43–51* ⊕*www.museum-avignon.org* ⊠*Free* ☉*Tues.– Sat. 10–1 and 2–6.*

WHERE TO EAT & STAY

$$$$
Fodor'sChoice
★

✕**Christian Etienne.** Known as the pope of Avignon cooking, Christian Etienne is ensconced in a 12th-century building next to the Palais des Papes with a fabulous terrace overlooking the theatrical square. Eating here is tantamount to a religious experience, especially if you opt for the €65 tomato menu, available only from June to September, whose seven courses range from the apparently simple (tomato tartare) to the extravagant (cheese cake de chèvre, with crushed Marmande tomatoes and basil and pine nut vinaigrette). If you're seeking to satisfy sophisticated tastes on a budget, the prix-fixe lunch menu for €35 could be the answer to your prayers. ⊠*10 rue de Mons* ☎*04–90–86–16–50* ⊕*www.christian-etienne.fr* ⌕*Reservations essential* ⊟*AE, DC, MC, V* ☉*Closed Sun. and Mon. (open daily during the theater festival).*

$$$$ ✕**La Mirande.** Whether you dine under the 14th-century coffered ceil-
★ ings, surrounded by Renaissance tapestries, or in the intimate garden
under the Popes' Palace walls, the restaurant of the luxurious Hôtel
de la Mirande transports you to another time. Chef Julien Allano
rediscovers this establishment's roots with authentic organic menus:
pan-seared pike perch, crayfish, and artichokes in a ravioli with Nan-
tua-style sauce, and pork in four different ways with mashed potatoes. Foodies, take note: Tuesday and Wednesday dinners are table
d'hôtes, and one week every month the restaurant's cooking school,
Le Marmiton, invites guest chefs to teach casual, multilingual cooking classes for six to 12 people around the kitchen table, followed by
a feast—and there are classes for children, too. ⊠*4 pl. de la Mirande*
☎*04–90–85–93–93* ⊕*www.la-mirande.fr* ⌕*Reservations essential*
⊟*AE, DC, MC, V* ☉*Closed Tues., Wed., and Jan.*

$$$$ ✕**La Vieille Fontaine.** Summer-evening meals around the old fountain
Fodor'sChoice and boxwood-filled oil jars in the courtyard of the Hôtel d'Europe
★ would be wonderful with *filet de boeuf* alone, but combine this romantic backdrop with stellar southern French cuisine and you have a special event. Give yourself over to one of the most renowned restaurants
in the Vaucluse, complete with the best regional wines and an army of
urbane servers—and hope for moonlight. The €35 lunch menu, coffee
and parking included, quickly refuels before tackling the afternoon's
touring. ⊠*12 pl. Crillon* ☎*04–90–14–76–76* ⊕*www.heurope.com*
⌕*Reservations essential* ⊟*AE, MC, V* ☉*Closed Sun.–Mon.; first wk
in Jan.; first two wks in Feb.; last 2 wks in Aug.*

$$$ ✕**La Fourchette.** It doesn't have a terrace, but La Fourchette can be
forgiven this small flaw given the quality of the cooking—this is prob-
ably Avignon's best-value restaurant, and it's a short walk from the
Place de l'Horloge. Philippe Hiely doesn't get too complicated with
his €32 prix-fixe menu (or €26–€28 lunch menu), preferring to perfect
the classics of Provençal cooking, such as marinated sardines and a
daube *d'agneau* (lamb stew) made in the local style with white wine,
anchovies, capers, and gherkins. The high-backed wooden chairs and
white tablecloths give the dining room a charming old-fashioned feel
and, of course, the forky decor will give you something to talk about.
⊠*17 rue Racine* ☎*04–90–85–20–93* ⊟*MC, V* ☉*Closed weekends
and 3 wks in Aug.*

$$$ ✕**L'Essentiel** Opened in February 2008, this chic new hot spot is founded
★ on two concepts: a gastronomic restaurant with two set menus (€26
and €37) served in a white tableclothed, Zen-esque atmosphere and
a bar à tatines which serves lip-smacking, grilled open-faced sandwiches, pasta pistou, or salad (about €11) in a brighter, slightly less
formal room. Trained by Bardet and Senderens, chef-owner Laurent
Chouviat's experience is apparent with dishes like open ravioli with
asparagus and small peas in a creamed basil sauce with garlic or roast
cod with confit tomatoes, fresh coriander, and Arborio risotto. The
quaint terrace on this side street will allure passersby but the romantic
17th-century interior courtyard will keep them coming back. There's a
lunch menu for €17 and a glass of wine starts at €4.50. ⊠*2 rue Petite*

3

Fusterie, ☎04–90–85–87–12 ⊕*www.restaurantlessentiel.com* ▤*AE, MC, V* ⊘*Closed Sun.*

$$$ ✕**Le Moutardier.** The papal mustard used to be made here and while
★ some establishments would hide behind such a heavenlypedigree and offer mediocre fare, the Perrin family has successfully married their setting in the Palace Square with the simplicity of Provençal food. Appetizing dishes, such as a tuna fillet with carrot compote flavored with vanilla or steamed asparagus with Parmesan and pistou, are light and uncomplicated, not disguised in heavy sauces, and are presented as objets d'art. The shaded terrace with its white-clothed tables is spectacular yet unpretentious while the frescos and chandeliers dazzle alongside the crème and gold interior. More than 80 Vaucluse wines are listed and the €25 lunch menu is, in addition to €33 or €46 menus, available at both meals. ⊠*15 pl. du Palais des Papes* ☎04–90–85–34–76 ⊕*www.restaurant-moutardier.fr* ⌖*Reservations essential in summer* ▤*AE, MC, V* ⊘*Closed Dec. and Jan.*

$$ ✕**L'Epicerie.** L'Epicerie doesn't have great gastronomic pretensions, but the cheerful food, hip waiters, and perfect terrace in the quiet, cobbled Place St-Pierre make it a local favorite. Order a steak with *vraies frites* (real, chunky French fries) and soak up the atmosphere with the help of some well-chosen local wine. ⊠*10 pl. St-Pierre* ☎04–90–82–74–22 ⌖*Reservations essential* ▤*MC, V* ⊘ *Closed Nov.–Mar.*

$ ✕**La Compagnie des Comptoirs.** Glassed into the white-stone cloister, this chic brasserie sports a theatrical dell'arte decor with a long, narrow fountain down the center of the courtyard terrace, a young, laid-back waitstaff, and a cool bar. The cooking is French fusion with international influences created by twin chefs Laurent and Jacques Pourcel—this is a member of their worldwide chain of bistros dedicated to former French trading posts. Calamari à la planchais (octopus on a board) is one of their most lauded dishes. ⊠*83 rue Joseph-Vernet* ☎04–90–85–99–04 ▤*AE, MC, V* ⊘*Closed Mon. in Oct.–Apr.*

$ ✕**Le Grand Café.** Behind the Popes' Palace, in a massive former fac-
★ tory—a setting of carefully preserved industrial decay—this hip entertainment complex combines an international cinema, a bar, and this popular bistro. Gigantic 19th-century mirrors and dance festival posters hang on brick disguised with pleated mauve-y fabric, and votive candles half-light the raw metal framework—an inspiring environment for intense film talk and a late supper of foie gras, goat cheese in pastry, or dishes served in terra-cotta *tajines* (domed stew pots), depending on the season. Grilled fish, chicken, and beer are all on the menu, as is pasta for €16. Splash it down with a glass of Côte de Rhône starting from €2.50. ⊠*La Manutention, 4 rue des Escaliers Ste-Anne* ☎04–90–86–86–77 ⊕*www.legrandcafe-avignon.com* ▤*AE, MC, V* ⊘*Closed Mon. in winter.*

$ ✕**Simple Simon.** Since the 1970s, this quaint (there is no other word for it) English tearoom—dark wooden beams, teapots on shelves, a table laden with cakes and pies—has catered to homesick expats and locals, who are intrigued by the pieman's tempting wares and the properly brewed teas served in silver pots. Owned since the beginning by a Frenchwoman whose mother was English, it's a real ode to British tradition, with cornish salad, bacon, and eggs and hot dishes such as shepherd's pie, cheese-and-onion crumble tart, or turkey hotpot at lunch. During the theater festival, it's also open for dinner. ⊠*26 rue Petite Fusterie* ☎*04–90–86–62–70* ▭*AE, MC, V* ⊘*Closed Sun. and Mon. and Aug.*

\$\$\$\$

★

🍴**Hostellerie les Frênes.** Five minutes outside Avignon, this adorably charming 19th-century country house combines the refinement of Louis XV furnishings with modern touches and all-around elegance. The mansard-roofed main house—which looks like it could have stood in for the Germonts' Provence residence in *La Traviata*—has rooms adorned with antiques and heirlooms; those in the annex are done in bright, southern-Provençal style. There are whirlpool baths in every room and a small spa with sauna. Better yet, the manicured park is a total enchantment, studded with one of the prettiest pools in Provence. The restaurant serves innovative twists on regional dishes which can now be savored on its recently added terrace. **Pros:** quiet setting; walking distance to boulangerie in Montfavet. **Cons:** not a five-minute drive to Avignon as advertised on Web site—more like a 20-min drive to the Popes' palace. ⊠*645 av. des Vertes-Rives, Montfavet* ⊹*5 km [3 mi] outside Avignon* ☎*04–90–31–17–93* ⊕*www.lesfrenes.com* ⟲*12 rooms, 4 suites, 2 apartments* ⚙*In-room: refrigerator, Wi-Fi. In-hotel: restaurant, pool, gym, parking (fee), some pets allowed* ▭*AE, DC, MC, V* ⊘*Closed Nov. 2–Apr. 4.*

\$\$\$\$

Fodor's Choice

★

🍴**Hôtel de la Mirande.** Arguably Avignon's loveliest hotel, this famous landmark exults Provence in all its 18th-century charm and splendor. A former cardinal's palace (set, in fact, just below the Palais des Papes), it has been superbly restored, with interiors richly decorated with exquisite reproduction chintzes and toiles de Jouy and beeswax-buffed antiques—the Salon Rouge is a jewel lined with red-and-lime silk and warmed by chandeliers and comfy chairs covered with paisley shawls *à la anglaise.* The enclosed garden is a breakfast and dinner oasis, the central lounge a skylit and jazz-warmed haven. Heavily decorated guest rooms are comfortable with new sleek TVs built into antiquated mirrors and the luxurious marble bathrooms have deep soaking tubs and elegant touches. Half the rooms face the garden, the other half the palace facade; a few even have tiny balconies with rooftop views. Ask about the table d'hôtes or the cooking classes, both of which take place downstairs in the original medieval foundations. If you're driving, get detailed directions; the roads are very narrow and the entrance is tricky to find by car (hint: look for the back of the Palace). **Pros:** like walking into a different era; free Evian and Badoit bottled water in-room during duration of stay. **Cons:** stuffy—especially the elevator; très expensive breakfast. ⊠*4 pl. de la Mirande* ☎*04–90–85–93–93* ⊕*www.la-mirande.fr* ⟲*19 rooms, 1 suite* ⚙*In-room: refrigerator, Wi-Fi. In-hotel: restaurant, bar, parking (fee), some pets allowed elevator* ▭*AE, DC, MC, V.*

\$\$\$\$

★

🍴**Hôtel d'Europe.** Napoléon slept here, and so did Robert and Elizabeth Browning, Picasso, and Jacqueline Onassis, and any number of artists and writers, right up to the theater luminaries who stay here today. This 16th-century home, built by the Marquis of Graveson, was turned into a hotel in 1799 by Mme. Pierron, lady friend of Napoléon who himself used to say on various campaigns in Russia, "Now do not complain, men, we are not at Mme. Pierron's place." With historic vibes—along with modern amenities such as Wi-Fi Internet access—hyperclassic, uncluttered decor, and a seasoned staff, this place will attract festival goers for centuries to come. The pricier guest rooms are vast, with two suites overlooking the Popes' Palace, but there are also smaller options for those on tighter budgets. No two rooms are alike and recent renovations have renewed the ambience without compromising the whispers of centuries gone by. The restaurant, La Vieille Fontaine, allures with fine wood paneling and remains one of Avignon's finest. **Pros:** two free public-access computers; staff are welcoming with no ostentatious airs. **Cons:** room decor can verge on "18th-century-style generic"; pricey breakfast. ⊠*12 pl. Crillon* ☎*04–90–14–76–76* ⊕*www.hotel-d-europe.fr* ⇘*44 rooms* ⚭*In-room: refrigerator, Wi-Fi. In-hotel: restaurant, bar, parking (fee), some pets allowed* ▭*AE, DC, MC, V.*

$$$ ⬚**À l'Ombre du Palais.** You will not find a better, unobstructed panoramic rooftop view in such close proximity of the Palais du Papes than this and accessing it is half the fun. There's also a street-level terrace with a commanding view, equally divine for sipping cocktails. The B&B's interior is a homogeneous mix of orange, red, and yellow paints and fabrics with Thai furniture. Equally as vibrant, opera-loving Sabine pays attention to her guests' needs (lovely soap and shampoo; bottled water on arrival; and even scented sachets as a souvenir). Breakfast is included, dinner by request, and reserve in advance for the special New Year's Eve menu with champagne, wine, and digestifs. **Pros:** unique rooftop terrace and views; pedestrian exit of Palais des Papes parking is in front B&B's door. **Cons:** rooms are fitted only with fans, so things could get sticky; owner smokes in house. ⊠*6 rue de la Vieille Juiverie, Place du Palais du Papes* ☎*06–23–46–50–95* ⊕*www.alombredup alais.com* ⇘*5 rooms* ⚭*In-room: no a/c, no phone, no TV. In-hotel: Wi-Fi* ▭*MC, V* ☾*Closed Jan.* ⦿*BP*

$$$ ⬚**Cloître Saint-Louis.** Standing serene and noble within its sturdy 16th-★ century walls, this sleek hotel encloses a magnificently cloistered courtyard lined with grand old plane trees. In this cloister setting, you can enjoy meals served in summer, with a market-inspired menu during the week and a popular buffet lunch on Sundays. The early Baroque building, erected by the Jesuits in 1611, was first a theological school for novitiates and later a hospital, before it became a hotel. Now interiors are stripped and modernist (especially those in a wing newly designed by Jean Nouvel), playing up the cool old stone. A recent nip and tuck in some rooms and bathrooms has enhanced the style and level of comfort. There's a small roof-top pool, and the hotel is a block's walk from the main train station. **Pros:** exquisite building; heated pool. **Cons:** rooms lack character; some rooms with handheld showers. ⊠*20 rue du Portail-Boquier* ☎*04–90–27–55–55* ⊕*www.cloitre-saint-louis. com* ⇘*80 rooms* ⚭*In-room: Internet. In-hotel: restaurant, bar, pool, Wi-Fi* ▭*AE, DC, MC, V.*

$$$ ⬚**Le Limas.** Located two minutes from the famous Avignon bridge, this contemporarily decorated B&B offers a rooftop terrace view of

the Palace but also tranquillity away from the noisy Palace streets. Opaque glass metal doors open to clean and bright guest rooms, with white bedding, white paint, white furniture, and canvases and artwork coloring the walls. English- and German-speaking owner Marion Wagner provides all the amenities of a hotel like soaps, a welcome bottle of water, and a candy dish at the door and she also serves a mean breakfast (included) on the terrace or by the fireplace in off-season. **Pros:** rooftop terrace fridge stocked with rosé so you can enjoy evening cocktails with a fab view; computer available. **Cons:** no credit cards; only one room can accommodate more than two people. ⊠*51 rue de Limas 84000* ☎*04–90–14–67–19* ⊕*www.le-limas-avignon.com* ➾*4 rooms* ⚴*In-room: no phone, no TV. In-hotel: Wi-Fi* ⊟*No credit cards* ⓘⓄⓘBP.

$ ⛭**Du Palais des Papes.** This third-generation family-run institution is a notably solid and comfortable place—all the better for its location just off the Place du Palais. Renovated rooms pair exposed stone and beams, updated with ironwork furniture and rich fabrics, with modern tile baths. A film-set Louis XIII restaurant downstairs is more for honeymooners than gastronomes, although it has been serving local Provençal food for the past 100 years and has two terraces—*one palace-facing, and the other on the horlage (clock-facing) side*. **Pros:** 40% reduction on Palais des Papes parking with hotel stamp; some rooms with double-glazed windows. **Cons:** can be stifling in summer; aspects of decor appear touristy kitch. ⊠*3 pl. du Palais,* ☎*04–90–86–04–13* ⊕*www.hotel-avignon.com* ➾*23 rooms, 4 suites* ⚴*In-room: no a/c, Wi-Fi. In-hotel: restaurant, bar, some pets allowed* ⊟*AE, MC, V.*

$ ⛭**Hôtel du Blauvac.** Just off Rue de la République and Place de
★ l'Horloge, this 17th-century nobleman's home has been divided into 16 guest rooms, many with pristine exposed stonework, and lovely tall windows that look, alas, onto backstreet walls. Pretty fabrics and a warm, familial welcome more than compensate, however. It's a simple budget hotel (no elevator, no air-conditioning) and utterly charming. **Pros:** well-priced for location. **Cons:** smallish rooms; street noise but need to leave windows open as there's no air-conditioning. ⊠*11 rue de la Bancasse,* ☎*04–90–86–34–11* ⊕*www.hotel-blauvac.com* ➾*16 rooms* ⚴*In-room: no a/c, refrigerator (some), Wi-Fi. In-hotel: some pets allowed (fee)* ⊟*AE, MC, V.*

¢ ⛭**Hôtel Innova.** You may feel like a student boarder in this modest budget lodging, but guest rooms are big enough and clean, and have been completely renovated with new beds, tiles, showers, paint jobs . . . the works; all have a phone and most have a TV, plus free Wi-Fi. Friendly owners Jean Claude and Elise are on hand to welcome and look after you. It's just about 80 feet from the tourist office. **Pros:** new owners have upped the quality of this budget beauty; new mattresses. **Cons:** it ain't the Ritz; one room on each floor has a bathroom down the hall ⊠*100 rue Joseph-Vernet,* ☎*04–90–82–54–10* ✉*hotel.innova@ wanadoo.fr* ➾*11 rooms* ⚴*In-room: no a/c, no TV (some), Wi-Fi.* ⊟*MC, V* ⊘*Closed Christmas–New Year's Day.*

NIGHTLIFE & THE ARTS

Small though Avignon is, its inspiring art museums, strong university, and 60-some years of saturation in world-class theater have made the city an antenna for the arts south of Paris. Held annually in July, France's oldest festival, known officially as the **Festival d'Avignon** (☎04–90–27–66–50 ⊕*www.festival-avignon.com*), has been bringing the best of world theater to this ancient city since 1947. Some 800 productions—some official, others "off" and "off-off"—take place every year; the prestigious, big-budget showpiece every year is held in the *cour d'honneur*, the courtyard of the Palais des Papes. You can get information about the unofficial performances at the Web site for **le festival OFF** (⊕*www.avignonleoff.com*)—tickets go on sale in June (and don't delay in placing your order).

A winter festival, **Les Hivernales** (☎04–90–82–33–12 ⊕*www.hivernales-avignon.com*), celebrates French contemporary dance over one week every February at various cultural locations throughout Avignon. Its central venue is La Manutention (at 4 rue des Escaliers Ste-Anne).

For information on events and tickets, too, stop into the massive book-and-record chain **FNAC** (⊠*19 rue de la République* ☎08–92–68–36–22).

La Manutention (⊠ *4 rue des Escaliers Ste-Anne* ☎04–90–82–33–12) is a cultural complex on Rue des Escaliers Ste-Anne. It includes the cinema Utopia-La Manutention, La Grande Café, the contemporary dance association Les Hivernales, and the jazz club Ajmi. **Opéra-Théâtre d'Avignon** (⊠*1 rue Racine* ☎04–90–82–42–42) proves that culture and the arts are not limited to Festival season.

NIGHTLIFE Within its fusty old medieval walls, Avignon teems with modern nightlife well into the wee hours. The **Bistrot d'Utopia** (⊠*4 rue des Escaliers Ste-Anne* ☎*No phone*) serves drinks in a dark, intimate space just outside the cinema in La Manutention. **Pub Z** (⊠*58 rue Bonneterie* ☎04–90–85–42–84) is the hot spot for rock, sometimes live; the black-and-white interior incorporates a zebra theme. **Le Delirium** (⊠*23 rue de la République* ☎04–90–85–44–56), an über-cool hangout for live music and entertainment, covers its walls with ongoing exhibits to create a truly artsy atmosphere. **Le Bakao's** (⊠*9 bis Quai St Lazare* ☎04–90–82–47–95), a funky disco lounge for younger crowds open Wednesday through Saturday from 10 to 5, offers its own shuttle-bus navette to get you to and from the party. **Les Ambassadeurs** (⊠*27 rue Bancasse* ☎04–90–86–31–55) attracts a more mature crowd but don't let these well-dressed revelers fool you; drinks are decently priced and dancing ends around 2, Thursday through Saturday. **Palais Royale** (⊠*10 bis rue Peyrollerie* ☎04–90–14–02–54) presents a dinner show cabaret-style with singers and dancers every Friday and Saturday night, except during August. On other nights other musical groups perform.

THE ARTS Two cinema complexes show first-run, mainstream movies in *v.o.* (*version originale*, meaning in the original language with French subtitles). **Cinéma Utopia-La Manutention** (⊠*4 rue des Escaliers Ste-Anne* ☎04–90–82–65–36) shows hard-to-find international independent works. **Cinéma Utopia-République** (✉ *5 rue Figuière* ☏ *04–90–82–65–36*) is a popular cinema.

At **AJMI** (*Association Pour le Jazz et la Musique Improvisée* ✉ *4 rue des Escaliers Ste-Anne* ☏ *04–90–86–08–61*), in La Manutention entertainment complex, you can hear jazz performed by artists of some renown.

SHOPPING

Avignon is too big and too resident-oriented to be full of tourist-aimed boutiques; instead, it has a cosmopolitan mix of French chains, youthful clothing shops (it's a college town), and a few plummy dress shops. **Rue des Marchands,** off Place Carnot, is one shopping stretch, but **Rue de la République** is the main artery. Dominating the main drag is trendy, cheap-chic clothing store **Zara** (✉ *25 rue de la République* ☏ *04–90–80–64–40*). The more luxurious shops along rue Joseph-Vernet and St Agricole in the **Joseph Vernet quarter** merit some lèche-vitrine (window licking, as the French say). If you're into Louis Seize, the **Fusterie quarter** caters to antique hunters and interior decorators. If you're hungry for books in English, find **Shakespeare** (✉ *155 rue Carreterie* ☏ *04–90–27–38–50*); in addition to new and used books in English, it has a tearoom, café, and terrace.

If you're a fan of fine French cookware, head to **Jaffier-Parsi** (✉ *42 rue des Fourbisseurs* ☏ *04–90–86–08–85*), a professional cooking supply store that has been stocking heavy copper pots, stainless-steel ladles, mortar-and-pestle sets, and great knives since 1902. Among the myriad vendors of Provençal pottery throughout the region, **Terre et Provence** (✉ *26 rue République* ☏ *04–90–85–56–45*) maintains a high aesthetic standard, with lovely pitchers, platters, and tureens.

All those famous, gorgeous Provençal fabrics can be found at **Souleïado** (✉ *5 rue Joseph-Vernet* ☏ *04–90–86–47–67*). More goods made from the signature printed fabrics can be found at Souleïado's competitor **Les Olivades** (✉ *56 rue Joseph Vernet* ☏ *04–90–86–13–42*).

Mouret Chapelier (✉ *20 rue Marchands* ☏ *04–90–85–39–38*) has a cornucopia of old-fashioned, old-world, and marvelously eccentric hats in a jewel-box setting.

HAUT VAUCLUSE

Situated north and northeast of Avignon, this land of rolling orchards and vineyards spreads lazily at the foot of Mont Ventoux, redolent of truffles, lavender, and fine wine. Perhaps that's why the Romans so firmly established themselves here, erecting grand arenas and luxurious villas that still in part remain. From Avignon head north into the vineyards, making a brief tour of Châteauneuf-du-Pape, even if you don't stop to drink and buy wine. Orange is just up the highway; though the town isn't the most picturesque, its Roman theater is a must-see. Between Orange and Mont Ventoux are wine centers (Beaumes-de-

Venise, Gigondas, Vacqueyras) and picturesque villages such as Crestet, Séguret, Le Barroux, and Malaucène, which the first French pope preferred to Avignon. Visit Vaison-la-Romaine for a strong concentration of Roman ruins.

VILLENEUVE-LEZ-AVIGNON

★ *2 km (1 mi) west of Avignon.*

GETTING HERE
The No. 11 from the Avignon TGV train station runs every 20 minutes and costs €1.20 and for the 5-minute ride. To drive, it's only 2.5 mi (4 km) from Avignon so just follow the signs.

VISITOR INFORMATION
Villeneuve-lez-Avignon (✉ *1 pl. Charles-David 30400* ☎ *04–90–25–61–33* ⊕ *www.villeneuvelezavignon.fr*).

EXPLORING
Just across the Rhône from Avignon, this medieval town glowers at its powerful neighbor to the east. Its abbey, fortress, and quiet streets offer a pleasant contrast to Avignon's bustle.

In the 14th century Villeneuve benefited enormously from the migration of the popes into Avignon, as an accompanying flood of wealthy and influential cardinals poured over the river. No fewer than 15 of the status-seeking princes of the church built magnificent homes on this neighboring hilltop—in truth, some simply requisitioned mansions from other owners, giving these "freed" town palaces the unfortunate moniker *livrées cardinalices*. In addition, kings Philip the Fair and Louis VIII built up formidable defenses on the site to keep an eye on the papal territories.

However, it was the bounty and extravagant lifestyles of the cardinals that nourished the abbey here, known as **Chartreuse du Val-de-Bénédiction** or, literally, the Charterhouse of the Valley of Blessings. Inside the abbey are spare cells with panels illuminating monastic life, the vast 14th-century **cloître de cimetière** (cemetery cloister), a smaller Romanesque cloister, and, within the remains of the abbey church, the Gothic tomb of Pope Innocent VI. Theatrical events are staged here during Avignon's annual theater festival. ☎*04–90–15–24–24* ⊠*€6.50* ⊙*Apr.–Sept., daily 9:30–6; Oct.–Mar., daily 9:30–5.*

At the top of the village is the **Fort St-André**, which once ostensibly protected the town of St-André, now absorbed into Villeneuve. The fortress's true importance was as a show of power for the kingdom of France in the face of the all-too-close Avignon popes. You can explore the fortress grounds and the bare ruined walls of inner chambers (there's a good view from the Notre Dame de Belvézet church within the fort walls), and you can also climb into the twin towers for broad views over Avignon, the Luberon, and Mont Ventoux. Don't miss the fortress's formal Italianate **gardens** (☎*06–71–42–16–90*), littered with remains of the abbey that preceded the fortifications. Admis-

Du Bon Vaing pour Votre Sangté

As much as it is identified with olives and cypress trees, the Provençal landscape is defined by the retreating perspective of row on rocky row of gnarled grapevines, their green shoots growing heavy through the summer and by fall sagging under the weight of ripe fruit. Although Provence has a few fine wines—notably the lower Rhône greats such as Châteauneuf-du-Pape and Beaumes-de-Venise and a few excellent whites from Cassis, Bandol, and Palette—the majority of wine drunk here is unpretentious, sunny stuff, with the most by far being rosé. Red or rosé, it is usually drunk icy-cold, whether to quench arid thirsts or to hide a less than rounded finish.

There are several subregions of southern wines. In the eastern Languedoc, above the Camargue, spreads the region known as Costières-de-Nîmes, and a straightforward table wine from the Côtes-de-Luberon appears on every Vaucluse table, alongside the equally unpretentious Côtes-du-Ventoux. But generally from the Rhône eastward—most heavily focused in the Haut Var behind Saint-Tropez—the wines fall under the undemanding umbrella title of Côtes de Provence. Remember that in these parts the word *vin* (wine) twangs through the nose like a broken banjo string and sounds more like *vaing*. *Santé* (to your health)!

sion to the gardens, which are privately owned, is €5. They are open Tuesday through Sunday 10–12:30 and 2–6 (closes at 5 Oct.–Mar.). ☎04–90–25–45–35 ⊕*www.monum.fr* ☑*Towers: €5* ☉*Apr.–Sept., daily 10–1 and 2–6; Oct.–Mar., daily 10–1 and 2–5.*

★ Below the abbey, the **Musée Pierre de Luxembourg** gives you access to one of the luxurious, 14th-century cardinals' manors. Here you'll find a notable collection of art, including the spectacularly colorful and richly detailed *Couronnement de la Vierge* (*Coronation of the Virgin*), an altarpiece painted in 1453 by Enguerrand Quarton. One of the greatest paintings of the 15th century, it shows rows and rows of Avignonnais hieratically sitting around the figures of God the Father and God the Son. Depicted by Quarton—the leading painter of the Avignon School—as identical twins, they bless Mary and hover over a surreal landscape that places Montagne St-Victoire in between Heaven and Hell. ☎04–90–27–49–66 ⊕*www.gard-provencal.com/musees/ pdluxem.htm* ☑*€3* ☉*Apr.–Sept., Tues.–Sun. 10–12:30 and 2–6:30; Oct.–Mar., Tues.–Sun. 10–12 and 2–5; closed Feb.*

CHÂTEAUNEUF-DU-PAPE

18 km (11 mi) north of Avignon, 22 km (13½ mi) west of Carpentras.

GETTING HERE
The Avignon bus (€2) runs twice a day and takes 35 minutes. Going the other direction, however, from Châteauneuf-du-Pape to Avignon, only has one bus a day. Or to/from Orange, the 25 minute journey is €1.50 with several possibilities throughout the day both directions. Best to

drive: take the N7 direction Isle-sur-la-Sorgue and then follow signs to Châteauneuf (about 30 mins).

VISITOR INFORMATION
Châteauneuf-du-Pape Tourist Office (⊠ *Pl. du Portail* ☎ *04–90–83–71–08* ⊕ *www.paysprovence.fr*).

EXPLORING
The countryside around this famous wine center is a patchwork of rolling vineyards, of green and black furrows striping the landscape in endless, retreating perspective. Great gates and grand houses punctuate the scene, as symmetrical and finely detailed as the etching on a wine label, and signs—discreet but insistent—beckon you to follow the omnipresent smell of fermenting grapes to their source. Behind barn doors, under cellar traps, and in chilly caves beneath châteaux, colossal oak vats nurture this noble Rhône red to maturity. The pebbly soil here is particularly suited to the growth of vines: The small stones act like a wool sweater, retaining the heat of the sun's rays and keeping the vines warm and cozy during the night.

Once the source of the table wine of the Avignon popes, who kept a fortified summer house here (hence the name of the town, which means "new castle of the pope"), the vineyards of Châteauneuf-du-Pape had the good fortune to be wiped out by phylloxera in the 19th century. The wine's revival as a muscular and resilient mix of up to 13 varietals moved it to the forefront of French wines, with an almost portlike intensity (it can reach 15% alcohol content). The whites, though less significant, are also to be reckoned with.

To learn more about local wine production, stop in at the **Musée des Outils de Vignerons Père Anselme,** a private collection of tools and equipment displayed in the *caveau* (wine cellar) of the Brotte family. ⊠ *Ave. Pierre de Luxmebourg* ☎ *04–90–83–70–07* ⊕ *www.brotte.com* ☑ *Free* ☉ *Apr.–Sept., daily 9–1 and 2–7; Oct.–Mar., daily 9–noon and 2–6.*

There are *caves de dégustation* (wine-tasting cellars) on nearly every street; get a free map of the caves from the tourist office on Place du Portail. Also head to the discreet *vignobles* (vineyards) at the edge of town. Some of the top Châteauneufs (and the oldest) come from Domaine de la Nerthe, Château de Vaudieu, and Château Fortia, and are priced accordingly. If you're not armed with the names of a few great houses, look for *medaille d'or* (gold medal) ratings from prestigious wine fairs; these are usually indicated by a gold sticker on the bottle.

If you're disinclined to spend your holiday sniffing and sipping, climb the hill to the ruins of the **Château.** Though it was destroyed in the Wars of Religion and its remaining donjon (keep) blasted by the Germans in World War II, it still commands a magnificent position. From this rise in the rolling vineyards, you can enjoy wraparound views of Avignon, the Luberon, and Mont Ventoux.

WHERE TO EAT & STAY

$$ ✕**Le Verger des Papes.** It's well worth the slog up the hill to the château simply to linger on the terrace of this long-established restaurant and savor the view over Mont Ventoux, Avignon, the Luberon, and the Rhône. The Estenevins have lived in Châteauneuf-du-Pape for three generations, and Philippe and Jean-Pierre took over the restaurant from their parents a few years ago. Their specialty, tarte à la tomate confite with goat's cheese and iced white cheese reveals their love for the region's cuisine, and you can visit the restaurant's well-stocked wine cellar on your way to the top. ✉*Rue Montée du Château* ☎*04–90–83–50–40* ⊕*www.vergerdespapes.com* ▤*MC, V* ⊙*Closed Dec. 20–Mar. 1. No dinner Nov.–Apr. and Sun. May–Oct.*

> SWIRL. SIP. SAVOR.
>
> Storefront wineries invite tasters of every level of experience to sample their vintages. Feel free to enter and taste; most outlets are happy to let you try a few without pressure to purchase. (Although etiquette dictates that you leave a few euros tip if you've been slurping down glass after glass.)

$ ✕**Le Pistou.** Provençal specialties such as whole herb-roasted dorade (a small Mediterranean fish), lamb shank with Provençal herb sauce, or saffron crème brûlée will make your choice difficult. The welcome is warm, the interior has been recently dressed up with colorful tablecloths, fresh paint, and pictures, and the prix-fixe menus start cheap from €15 to €27. ✉*15 rue Joseph-Ducos* ☎*04–90–83–71–75* ▤*MC, V* ⊙*Closed Mon., no dinner Sun., and closed Jan.*

$$ ▦**La Garbure.** With four modest rooms decked in jewel tones upstairs and a tiny formal dining room downstairs, this intimate hotel offers a romantic, slightly old-fashioned stopover. Jean Louis has been preparing the meals for 28 years and aims for the haute rather than the hearty, with dishes like red mullet fillets with olives, joue de boeuf made with Châteauneuf-du-Pape for €11, and a heady sorbet of Marc de Châteauneuf-du-Pape, the eau-de-vie made of local grapes. You can dine here without staying over, but make sure to reserve in advance, since seating is limited. **Pros:** soundproof rooms; one of the best terraces in town. **Cons:** late check-in time; rooms have either shower or bath ✉*3 rue Joseph-Ducos,* ☎*04–90–83–75–08* ⊕*www.la-garbure.com* ⇥*8 rooms* ⌂*In-room: refrigerator, Wi-Fi (some). In-hotel: restaurant, parking (fee), some pets allowed* ▤*AE, MC, V* ⊙*Closed Nov.*

ORANGE

12 km (7 mi) north of Châteauneuf-du-Pape, 31 km (19 mi) north of Avignon.

GETTING HERE

The Paris TGV at 3 hrs 20 mins serves Orange twice daily, but from Nice to Orange by TGV is more complicated. Take Nice to Marseille and then change trains to Orange. Fare is about €47 but with the stopover, it takes about 5 hrs 30 mins. From Orange to Gare Avignon Centre it costs €5.30 for the 20-minute train. Orange's center city is a 10-minute walk from the train station (head from Avenue F. Mistral to Rue de la République, then follow signs). By bus to Avignon's gare routière (bus station) there are 10 to 20 buses daily at €3 one way (45 mins) departing from the train station. Sadly, there are very few regional buses from Orange.

VISITOR INFORMATION
Orange Tourist Office (✉ 5 cours A. Briand, ☎ 04–90–34–70–88 ⊕ www. otorange.fr).

EXPLORING

★ Even less touristy than Nîmes (⇨ Chapter 2) and just as eccentric, the city of Orange (pronounced oh-*rawnzh*) sprawls somewhat gracelessly over the Rhône flatlands. Its hotels and restaurants have a vaguely bohemian air—eclectic decors, patchwork menus—and its insular attitude offers little of the easy grace of the rest of the Vaucluse. The air of neglect may be due in part to efforts to boycott the city since the election of a far-right-leaning government. Nonetheless it draws thousands every year to its spectacular **Théâtre Antique,** a colossal Roman theater built in the time of Caesar Augustus. The vast stone stage facade, bouncing sound off the facing hillside, climbs four stories high—Louis XIV famously called it "the greatest wall in my kingdom"—and the niche at center stage contains the original statue of Augustus, just as it reigned over centuries of productions of classical plays. The theater has a seating capacity of 9,000; from its last row atop **Colline St-Eutrope** you can see the ruins of the château of Orange's princes, razed by Louis when he annexed the principality of Orange for France. Today this setting inspires and shelters world-class theater, as well as concerts of dance, classical music, poetry readings, and even rock concerts. Orange's summer opera festival is one of Europe's best, and one of its best-known. A newly inaugurated vast glass roof has been installed at a height of 105 feet, enabling human voices to carry better throughout the entire arena. ✉ *Rue Madeleine Roch* ☎ 04–90–51–17–60 ⊕ *www.theatre-antique. com* 🎟 €7.70 *with audioguide, includes entry to Espace Culturel* ⊙ *Nov.–Feb., daily 9:30–4:30; Apr., May, and Sept, daily 9–6; Mar. and Oct., daily 9:30–5:30; June–Aug., daily 9–7.*

Across the street from the theater, the small **Musée d'Orange** displays antiquities unearthed around Orange, including fragments of three detailed marble *cadastres* (land survey maps) dating from the 1st century. Upstairs a vivid series of 18th-century canvases shows local mills producing Provençal fabrics, each aspect illustrated in careful detail. There are also personal objects from local aristocrats and a collection of faience pharmacy jars. ✉ *Rue Madeleine Roch* ☎ 04–90–51–17–60 ⊕ *www.theatre-antique.com* 🎟 €7.70, *joint ticket with Théâtre Antique* ⊙ *Nov.–Feb., daily 9:30–4:30; Apr., May, and Sept., daily 9–6; Mar. and Oct., daily 9:30–5:30; June–Aug., daily 9–7.*

★ North of the city center and in the middle of modern-day traffic stands the magnificent **Arc de Triomphe** that once straddled the Via Agrippa between Lyon and Arles. Three arches support a heavy double attic (horizontal top) floridly decorated with battle scenes and marine symbols (notably a ship's prow, referring to Augustus's victories at Actium, where he defeated Mark Anthony). The arch commemorates Caesar's triumph over the Gauls, a fact of which the Romans were inordinately proud. The arch, which dates from about 20 BC, is superbly preserved, particularly the north side, but to view it on foot you'll have to cross a roundabout seething with traffic. ⊠*North of the center on Av. de l'Arc, direction Gap.*

Vieil Orange, the Old Town neighborhood you must cross to hike from one Roman monument to the other, carries on peacefully when there's not a blockbuster spectacle in the theater. Lining its broad squares, under heavy-leaved plane trees, are a handful of shops and a few sidewalk cafés.

WHERE TO EAT & STAY

$ ✕**La Yaka.** At this intimate, unpretentious bistro you are greeted by the beaming owner/host/waiter, then pampered with an embarrassment of riches in bargain menu choices (from €14 to €25 for a full meal). The regional home cooking draws local regulars. Specialties are emphatically *style grandmère*—slow cooked and heavily seasoned—it's all in a charming stone-and-beam interior, complete with a Gothic archway. ⊠*24 pl. Sylvian* ☎*04–90–34–70–03* ▤*AE, MC, V* ⊘*Closed Wed.; Nov and Dec. No dinner Tues.*

$$ ▥**Arène.** On a quiet square in the old center, this comfortable hotel is filled with a labyrinth of spacious guest rooms decorated in Provençal yellow and blue with Italian-styled bathrooms and LCD TVs. Go for the "Henri" junior suite with its king-size bed and Jacuzzi à deux with a view. As it's been constructed of several fine old houses cobbled together, there's no elevator, but a multitude of stairways instead. **Pros:** ecological rooms available; lots of in-room amenities. **Cons:** can't access rates by Internet. ⊠*Pl. de Langes,* ☎*04–90–11–40–40* ⊕*www.hotel-arene.fr* ⮑*33 rooms, 2 suites* ⚄ *In-room: refrigerator, Wi-Fi (some). In-hotel: restaurant, bar, Wi-Fi, parking (fee), some pets allowed,* ▤*AE, DC, MC, V.*

$$ ▥**Hôtel Lou Cigaloun.** After a short-lived stint as part of a chain, this central hotel has undergone a few transformations. The new owner, brightening each guest room with Provençal fabrics and replacing beds, has also added modern comforts such as air-conditioning and Wi-Fi. **Pros:** new beds. **Cons:** only two parking spots (and you have to pay); not the prettiest exterior. ⊠*4 rue Caristie,* ☎*04–90–34–10–07* ⊕*www.hotel-loucigaloun. com* ⮑*28 rooms* ⚄*In-room: Wi-Fi. In-hotel: parking (fee), some pets allowed* ▤*AE, DC, MC, V* ⊘*Closed Dec. 15–Jan. 15.*

UNDER THE STARS

To witness the torches of *Nabucco* or *Aïda* flickering against the 2,000-year-old Roman wall of the Théâtre Antique and to hear the extraordinary sound play around its semicircle of ancient seats is one of the great summer festival experiences in Europe. Every July and the first week in August, **Les Chorégies d'Orange** (☎*04-90-34-24-24* ⊕*www. choregies.com* ✉*Chorégies, B.P. 205, Orange Cedex 84107*) echo tradition and amass operatic and classical music spectacles under the summer stars in Orange. Be sure to book tickets well in advance; they go on sale the previous October.

$ **L'Orangerie.** Just 4 km (2½ mi) north of Orange, the new owners of this 18th-century auberge spared no corner during renovations. Light guest rooms are spacious and welcoming and the restaurant's menu reflects their Provençal roots. **Pros:** new beds and flat-screen TVs. **Cons:** Web site not informative. ⊠*4 rue de l'Ormeau, Piolenc* ☎*04–90–29–59–88* ⊕*www.orangerie.net* ⊅*5 rooms* ⚘*In-room: Wi-Fi. In-hotel: restaurant, parking, some pets allowed* ⊟*AE, MC, V* ⊗*Closed one wk at Christmas.*

> **TRIP TIP**
>
> If you have access to a computer while traveling, a good Web site to consult is ⊕*www.asf.fr*. It not only gives directions for highways and village roads in the South of France, but also indicates weather conditions and traffic problems.

BEAUMES-DE-VENISE

23 km (14 mi) east of Orange.

VISITOR INFORMATION
Beaumes-de-Venise Tourist Office ⊠ *Grand Rue,* ☎*04–90–66–11–66* ⊕*www.tourisme-venasque.com.*

Just west of the great mass of Mont Ventoux, surrounded by farmland and vineyards, is Beaumes-de-Venise, where streets of shuttered bourgeois homes slope steeply into a market center. This is the renowned source of a delicately sweet muscat wine, but if you're tasting, don't overlook the local red wine. Look for **Domaine des Bernardins** (⊠*Rte de Lafare* ☎*04–90–62–94–13*), a vineyard with a tasting cave (open Mon.–Sat., 8:30–12 and 2–6:30), for both.

In the town center you can also buy fruity, unfiltered olive oil produced in the area; it's made in such small quantities that you're unlikely to see it anywhere else.

Beaumes lies at the foot of the **Dentelles de Montmirail,** a small range of rocky chalk cliffs eroded to lacy pinnacles—whence their name *dentelles* (lace). From tiny D21, east of town, you'll find dramatic views north to the ragged peaks and south over lush orchards and vineyards interspersed with olive groves, pine and yew trees. It's a splendid drive, and if you love nature it would be well worth staying in this area—many of the stone houses have been converted into bed-and-breakfasts.

WHERE TO STAY
$$$ **Le Clos Saint Sourde.** Jérôme and Geraldine, both of whom speak English, have a winning way of meeting all your needs but remaining discreetly in the background. Within this converted farmhouse you'll find classic and chic decors set against stone walls—the results are spacious and totally unique. Country breakfast is included and table d'hôtes are offered Tuesday and Friday nights. Independent cabin rental by the week for a minimum group of eight includes a private pool, parking, and a gas grill. **Pros:** vineyard views from breakfast terrace and pool; picnic essentials available should you wish to prepare a basket yourself. **Cons:** toiletries not provided; the main terrace is in front of the parking

area. ✉*Rte. de St Véran,* ☎*04–90–37–35–20* ⊕*leclossaintsaourde. com* ⇔*2 rooms, 2 suites, cabin* ⚷*In-room: no a/c, Wi-Fi. In-hotel: pool, parking* ⊟*MC, V* ❄*BP*

VACQUEYRAS

5 km (3 mi) northwest of Beaumes-de-Venise.

Smaller and more picturesque than Beaumes, with stone houses scattered along its gentle slopes, Vacqueyras gives its name to a robust, tannic red wine worthy of its more famous neighbors around Châteauneuf-du-Pape or Gigondas. Wine domaines beckon from the outskirts of town, and the center strikes a mellow balance of plane trees and cascading wisteria, punctuated by discreet tasting shops. Thanks to its consistently rising quality, Vacqueyras was the latest of the Côtes du Rhônes to earn its own appellation—the right to put its village name on the bottle instead of the less prestigious, more generic Côtes-du-Rhône label.

GIGONDAS

★ *3 km (2 mi) north of Vacqueyras.*

The prettiest of all the Mont Ventoux Côtes-du-Rhône wine villages, Gigondas is little more than a cluster of stone houses stacked gracefully up a hillside overlooking the broad sweep of the valley below. At the top, a false-front Baroque church anchors a ring of medieval ramparts; from here you can take in views as far as the Cévennes.

Its few residents share one vocation: the production of the vigorous Grenache-based red that bears the village name. At the more than 60 *caveaux* (tasting caves) scattered through the village and the surrounding countryside, you're welcome to visit, taste, and buy without ceremony. Pick up a contact list from the tourist office at the village entrance beside the town hall.

WHERE TO EAT & STAY

$$ ⬚ **Les Florêts.** Winter or summer, Les Florêts makes a romantic hideaway with its full-on view of the Dentelles de Montmirail and a salon centered around a giant white fireplace and body-hugging red armchairs. Guest rooms are equally warm, dressed up with bright colors and antique furniture, and the restaurant is one of the best in the area—try the skewer of lamb fillet roasted flavored with liquorice or the crayfish and exotic fruits with guacamole. Lunch menus start at €24.50, dinner is pricier from €42.50. **Pros:** "Wine Uncovered" visits can be arranged; breathtaking scenery from charming rooms. **Cons:** mistrals could dampen outings. ✉*Rte. des Dentelles,* ☎*04–90–65–85–01* ⊕*www.hotel-lesflorets.com* ⇔*15 rooms* ⚷*In-room: no a/c. In-hotel: restaurant, Wi-Fi, parking, some pets allowed* ⊟*AE, MC, V* ❄*Hotel closed Jan. and two wks in Feb. during school holidays.*

SÉGURET

8 km (5 mi) northeast of Gigondas.

Nestled into the sharp rake of a rocky hillside and crowned with a ruined medieval castle, Séguret is a picture-book hill village that is only moderately commercialized. Its 14th-century clock tower, Romanesque St-Denis Church, and bubbling Renaissance fountain highlight steep little stone streets and lovely views of the Dentelles de Montmirail cliffs. Here, too, you'll find peppery Côtes du Rhône for the tasting.

WHERE TO EAT & STAY

$$$$ ☐**La Table du Comtat.** Clinging to the top of the village and enjoying breathtaking valley views, this 14th-century former hospice now functions as a simple hotel and serious restaurant. It wouldn't matter if you choose chef Josian Seisson's €25 or €48 menu because anything with a view this spectacular is going to wow. Upstairs, eight plain, stucco rooms (set to undergo a face-lift by new owners in 2009) look over the valley or the pretty garden. The kidney-shaped pool melts into a hillside terrace. **Pros:** glorious panoramas; daily menus online. **Cons:** ask about renovations (and consequent noise issues). ⊠*Just after Pl. de l'Église* ☎*04–90–46–91–49* ⊕*www.table-comtat.fr* ☞*8 rooms* ♿ *In-hotel: restaurant, pool, Wi-Fi, parking, some pets allowed* ⊟*AE, MC, V* ⊘*Hotel closed Nov. 15–Dec. 15 and Feb.; restaurant closed Tues. dinner and Wed.*

$ ☐**La Bastide Bleue.** An idyllic youth hostel until a few years ago, this old stone farmhouse is now an unpretentious but enchanting country inn. It's set in a pine-shaded garden court, and its blue-shuttered windows conceal pretty rooms done in stone, pine, and stucco, with bright, artisanal-tiled baths. Downstairs is a low-slung dining room with plank tables by a stone fireplace. Breakfast (included) can be enjoyed on a sweet terrace and the €26 dinner menu includes typical regional specialties garlic-roasted lamb, duck breast with honey and rosemary, and lavender-scented crème brûlée. **Pros:** garden-lined pool. **Cons:** proper and clean but not chichi. ⊠*La Bastide Bleue, 1 km (½ mi) south of Séguret on D23* ☎*04–90–46–83–43* ⊕*perso.wanadoo.fr/labastide-bleue* ☞*7 rooms* ♿*In-hotel: restaurant, pool, parking, some pets allowed.* ⊟*AE, MC, V* ⊘*Closed Jan. and Feb.; closed Christmas–New Year's* ⦿*BP.*

VAISON-LA-ROMAINE

Fodor'sChoice
★ *10 km (6 mi) northeast of Séguret, 27 km (17 mi) northeast of Orange.*

GETTING HERE

There's a 40-minute bus (€3) running through the day from Avignon TGV station which also stops at Avignon Gare and Orange before arriving at Vaison. There's also a 45-minute bus from Carpentras (€3). A taxi to Orange is €43 or to Avignon, count on at least €85 during the week (and weekend fares are 50 percent more).

VISITOR INFORMATION
Vaison-la-Romaine Tourist Office
(✉ *Pl. du Chanoine Sautel, B.P. 53*
☎ *04–90–36–02–11* ⊕ *www.vaison-la-romaine.com*).

EXPLORING

In a river valley green with orchards of almonds and apricots, this ancient town thrives as a modern market center. The Provençal market on Tuesdays is a major tourist draw (there is also a smaller organic farmers' market on Thursday mornings), as is the five-day food festival in early November. Yet it retains an irresistible Provençal charm, with medieval backstreets, lively squares lined with cafés and, as its name implies, remains of its Roman past. Vaison's well-established Celtic colony joined forces with Rome in the 2nd century BC and grew to powerful status in the empire's glory days. No gargantuan monuments were raised, yet the luxurious villas surpassed those of Pompeii.

> **FAST FORWARD TO THE 1300S**
>
> Take the time to climb up into Vaison's **Haute Ville**, a medieval neighborhood perched high above the river valley. Its 13th- and 14th-century houses owe some of their beauty to stone pillaged from the Roman ruins below, but their charm is from the Middle Ages: a trickling stone fountain, a bell tower with wrought-iron campanile, soft-color shutters, and blooming vines create the feel of a film set of an old town.

There are two broad fields of **Roman ruins**, both in the center of town: before you pay €8 entry at either of the ticket booths, pick up a map (with English explanations) at the **Office de Tourisme** (☎ *04–90–36–02–11*), which sits between them. It's open daily 10–12 and 2–5 from November through February and 10–12:30 and 2–5:30 from March through October.

★ Like a tiny Roman forum, the **Quartier de Puymin** spreads over the field and hillside in the heart of town, visible in passing from the city streets. Its skeletal ruins of villas, landscaped gardens, and museum lie below the ancient Theater, all of which are accessed by the booth across from the tourist office. Closest to the entrance, the foundations of the **Maison des Messii** (Messii House) retain the outlines of its sumptuous design, complete with a vast gentleman's library, reception rooms, an atrium with a rain-fed pool, a large kitchen (the enormous stone vats are still there), and baths with hot, cold, and warm water. It requires imagination to reconstruct the rooms in your mind (remember all those toga movies from the '50s), but a tiny detail is enough to trigger a vivid image—the thresholds still show the hinge holds and scrape marks of swinging doors. A formal garden echoes a similar landscape of the time; wander under its cypresses and flowering shrubs to the **Musée Archéologique Théo-Desplans**. In this streamlined venue, the accoutrements of Roman life have been amassed and displayed by theme: pottery, weapons, gods and goddesses, jewelry, and, of course, sculpture, including full portraits of the emperor Claudius (1st century) and a strikingly noble nude Hadrian (2nd century). Cross the park behind the museum to climb into the bleachers of the 1st-century **Theater,** which is smaller than Orange's but is still used today for concerts and plays. Across the parking lot is the **Quartier de la Villasse**, where the remains of a lively market town evoke images of main-street shops, public gardens, and grand private homes, complete with floor mosaics. The most evocative image of all is in the *thermes* (baths): a neat row of marble-seat toilets lined up over a raked trough that rinsed waste instantly away. ✉*Rue Burrus* ☎*04–90–36–02–11* 🏛*Ruins, museum, and cloister, €8* ⊙*Quartier de Puymin and museum: June–Sept., daily 9:30–6:30; Mar. and Oct., daily 10–12:30 and 2–5:30; Nov.–Feb., daily 10–noon and 2–5; Apr. and May, daily 9:30–6. Quartier de la Villasse: June–Sept., daily 10–noon and 2:30–6:30; Mar. and Oct., daily 10–12:30 and 2–5:30; Nov.–Feb., daily 10–noon and 2–5; Apr. and May, daily 10–noon and 2:30–6.*

In the medieval Haute Ville, stop into the sober Romanesque **Cathédrale Notre-Dame-de-Nazareth**, based on recycled fragments and foundations of a Gallo-Roman basilica. Its **cloister** is the key attraction. Created in the 12th and 13th centuries, it remains virtually unscarred, and its pairs of columns retain their deeply sculpted, richly varied capitals. ✉*Av. Jules-Ferry* ⊙*June–Sept., daily 10–12:30 and 2–6:30; Mar.–May and Oct., daily 10–noon and 2–5; Nov.–Feb., daily 2–5.*

The remarkable single-arch **Pont Romain** *(Roman Bridge)*, built in the 1st century, stands firm across the River Ouvèze; it was one of the few structures to survive the devastating flood that roared through Vaison in 1992, destroying 150 homes and killing 37 people. It's a living testimony to Roman engineering and provokes reflection: had it not been "quarried" for medieval projects, how much of Roman Vaison would still be standing today?

FodorśChoice ★ While Vaison has centuries-old attractions, the most popular for Americans may well now be **Patricia Wells's Cooking Classes** (⊕*www.patricia wells.com*). A living monument of Provence, the celebrated food critic first made her name known through posh food columns and *The Food Lover's Guide to France*. First-hand, she now introduces people to the splendors of French cooking in her lovely farmhouse near Vaison through week-long cooking seminars—luxe ($5,000 a student), 12 students only, and set over Madame Wells's own Chanteduc vineyards. The truffle workshop in January is usually sold out, so book early.

WHERE TO STAY

$$ ★ **Évêché.** If you want to base yourself in the medieval part of town, stay in one of the tranquil rooms in this turreted 17th-century former bishop's palace, owned by the friendly Verdiers. The warm welcome and rustic charm—delicate fabrics, exposed beams, wooden bedsteads—have garnered a loyal following among travelers who prefer B&B character to modern luxury. In summer, breakfast is served in a bower of greenery overlooking the Ouvèze Valley. Make sure to look into their groin-vaulted art gallery across the street. **Pros:** Aude and Jean-Loup speak some English and are congenial hosts; the collection of posters, prints, and books will fascinate. **Cons:** no parking, so drop your things off before finding a spot outside the medieval village; no

credit cards. ⊠*Rue de l'Évêché,* ☎*04–90–36–13–46* ⊕*www.eveche. com* ⇥*3 rooms, 2 suites* ⟁*In-room: no a/c, no phone (some), no TV, Wi-Fi* ▭*No credit cards* |◎|*BP.*

$$ ⬚ **Le Beffroi.** Perched on a cliff top in the Old Town, this gracious grouping of 16th-century mansions comes together as a fine hotel. The extravagant period salon leads to curving stone stairs and up to sizable rooms with beamed ceilings and antiques. The corner rooms have wonderful views. By day you can take a dip in the courtyard pool. In season, have dinner on the walled-in terrace, where the sweeping view takes precedence over the decent if unexciting food. The restaurant is a good spot for children thanks to the adjoining garden equipped with a swing set. **Pros:** free parking in front; light food available all day. **Cons:** village pool can fill up quickly with kids; very narrow street to reach the hotel. ⊠*Rue de l'Évêché,* ☎*04–90–36–04–71* ⊕*www.le-beffroi.com* ⇥*22 rooms* ⟁*In-room: no a/c, refrigerator, Wi-Fi (some). In-hotel: restaurant, pool, Wi-Fi, some pets allowed (fee)* ▭*AE, DC, MC, V* ⊙*Closed mid-Jan.–mid-Mar.*

CRESTET

7 km (4½ mi) south of Vaison-la-Romaine.

Another irresistible, souvenir-free aerie perched on a hilltop at the feet of the Dentelles de Montmirail cliffs and of Mont Ventoux, Crestet has it all—tinkling fountains, shuttered 15th-century houses, an arcaded *place* at the village's center, and a 12th-century castle crowning the lot. Views from its château terrace take in the concentric rings of tiled rooftops below, then the forest greenery and cultivated valleys below that.

MALAUCÈNE

9 km (5½ mi) southeast of Crestet, 10 km (6 mi) southeast of Vaison-la-Romaine.

Yet another attractive composition of plane trees, fountains, and *lavoirs* (public laundry fountains), crowned by a church tower with campanile, this sizeable market town began as a fortified church-village. Its 14th-century church follows classic Provence Romanesque form (a broad, vaulted nave, a semicircle apse) and houses an ornate carved-oak organ from the 18th century. The town's nerve center is the Cours des Isnards, where butchers, bakers, and cafés draw commerce from the tiny near-ghost-towns scattered through the countryside. Since Internet cafés are not exactly thick on the ground in these parts, it's good to know about **Net & Cie** (⊠*Av. de Verdun*), open Monday–Friday 9:30–12:30 and 2–6 and Saturday 9:30–12.

Just east of town, the **Chapelle Notre-Dame-du Groseau** is all that remains of the mighty 12th-century Benedictine abbey that Pope Clement V preferred as lodging before he settled into Avignon. The cliffs and woodlands are just as wild and wonderful today. This is also a good place to launch a scenic circle drive over the crest of Mont Ventoux (⇨*below*). ⊠*Off D974, direction Col des Tempêtes.*

¢ ▦**L'Origan.** Directly on the tree-lined main commercial street, this family-run hotel/restaurant offers simple, comfortable rooms and straightforward, homey cooking. As we print, new owners are modernizing rooms and installing new TVs and Wi-Fi. **Pros:** bargain price; new beds and decor. **Cons:** no Web site. ⊠ *9 cours des Isnards,* ☎ *04–90–65–27–08* ⊕ *aubergedela-poste@wanadoo.fr* ⟿ *23 rooms* ⚘ *In-room: no a/c, no phone, refrigerator, Wi-Fi. In-hotel: restaurant, some pets allowed* ▭ *AE, MC, V* ⊘ *Closed Dec. 15.–Jan. 15.*

LE BARROUX

Fodor'sChoice *6 km (4 mi) southwest of Malaucène, 16 km (10 mi) south of*
★   *Vaison-la-Romaine.*

Of all the marvelous hilltop villages stretching across the south of France, this tiny ziggurat of a town has a special charm. A labyrinth to the past, Le Barroux has more than a whiff of fairy tale in the air, lording over a patchwork landscape as finely drawn as a medieval illumination, luminous as an illustration in a children's book. This aerie has just one small church, one post office, and one tiny old *épicerie* (small grocery) selling canned goods, yellowed postcards, and today's *Le Provençal.* You are forced, therefore, to look around you and listen to the trickle of the ancient fountains at every labyrinthine turn. Houses, cereal-box slim, seem to grow out of the bedrock, closing in around your suddenly unwieldy car.

Its **château** is its main draw, though its Disney-perfect condition reflects a complete restoration after a World War II fire. Grand vaulted rooms and a chapel date from the 12th century; other halls serve as venues for contemporary art exhibits. Even if you don't go in, climb up to its terrace, where you can gaze across farmlands toward competing châteaus at Crillon and Caromb. ☎ *04–90–62–35–21* ▭ *€5* ⊘ *Apr.–June, daily 2–6; July–Aug., daily 10–7; Sept., daily 10–6; Oct., daily 2–6, weather permitting.*

$ ▦**Les Géraniums.** Set alone a lofty cliffside, this family-run auberge is hidden among leafy vineyards and orchards. Strongly encouraged and highly recommended is the demi-pension which includes a three-course dinner menu plus cheese plate. Spend the day sightseeing and come back to a modest, peaceful guest room, newly renovated, with panoramic valley views that seem nearly dreamlike. New rooms in the annex across the street take in panoramic views. **Pros:** price; endless valley views; scrumptious regional food. **Cons:** you need to specify room with a bath or shower; parking closed from 11 PM to 7 AM. ⊠ *Pl. de la Croix* ☎ *04–90–62–41–08* ⊕ *www.hotel-lesgeraniums.com* ⟿ *22 rooms* ⚘ *In-room: no a/c, no TV. In-hotel: restaurant, bar, Wi-Fi, some pets allowed* ▭ *MC, V* ⊘ *Closed mid-Nov.–mid-Mar., but open over Christmas.*

Perched Villages

The Haut Vaucluse has a bevy of *villages perchés* (perched villages). Each is often often wrapped in a wall and crowned with the two strongest assurances of protection, sacred and secular: a steeple and a watchtower. Nowadays many of the hill towns are nearly ghost towns, though more and more are tapping into the tourist boom. Those closest to the coast and to urban centers—in the Luberon and in Nice's backcountry, in par-

ticular—have become souvenir malls choked with galleries of dubious quality. Yet as the tourist packs rove on in search of authenticity, the other hill towns develop their commerce and find new life. In these, you can still wander aimlessly through the maze of tunnel-like *ruelles* (alleys) and feel the isolation—often idyllic, sometimes harsh—of these eagle's-nest enclaves, high above the world.

CRILLON-LE-BRAVE

12 km (7 mi) south of Malaucène (via Caromb), 21 km (13 mi) southeast of Vaison-la-Romaine.

The main reason to come to this minuscule hamlet, named after France's most notable soldier hero of the 16th century, is to stay or dine at its hotel, the Hostellerie de Crillon-le-Brave. But it's also pleasant—perched on a knoll in a valley shielded by Mont Ventoux, with the craggy hills of the Dentelles in one direction and the hills of the Luberon in another. Today the village still doesn't have even a *boulangerie* (bakery), let alone a souvenir boutique. The village makes a good base camp for exploring the region if you can afford to stay at the hotel; with no other commercial establishments in the village, and little more to visit than a tiny music-box museum and an ocher quarry, you're a captive audience.

WHERE TO EAT & STAY

$$$$ ★ 🏨 **Hostellerie de Crillon le Brave.** The views from these interconnected Relais & Châteaux hilltop houses are as elevated as their prices, but for this you get a rarefied atmosphere of medieval luxury. Set on a series of terraces *à l'italienne*, the stone facades—oh-so-prettily decked out with baby-blue shutters—look out over vineyards and Mont Ventoux. Inside, a cozy-chic southern decor runs throughout, from the book-filled salons to the brocante-trimmed guest rooms. Some guest rooms have terraces looking out over the surrounding hills and plains. The showpiece of the complex is the Maison Roche, a wonderfully vaulted stone two-story space (once the village school), where you can sample Philippe Monti's superstylish Mediterranean cooking—winners include the sea-perch cooked in wine à la ventoux, the rabbit with truffles, and gambas (huge shrimp) ragout with spring vegetables. **Pros:** Vi-Spring beds and Italian linens; cooking classes in English available in October. **Cons:** lots of climbing up and down cobblestones on property. ✉*Pl. de l'Église* ☎*04–90–65–61–61* ⊕*www.crillonlebrave.com* ⇱*35 rooms*

⚘ *In-room: refrigerator, Wi-Fi. In-hotel: restaurant, tennis court, pool, spa, some pets allowed,* ▭ *AE, DC, MC, V* ⊗ *Closed Jan.–mid-Mar.*

MONT VENTOUX

In addition to all the beautiful views *of* Mont Ventoux, there are equally spectacular views *from* Mont Ventoux. From Malaucène or any of the surrounding hill towns you can take an inspiring circle drive along the base and over the crest of the mountain, following the D974. This road winds through the extraordinarily lush south-facing greenery that Mont Ventoux protects from vicious mistral winds. Abundant orchards and olive groves peppered with stone farmhouses make this one of Provence's loveliest landscapes. Stop for a drink in busy **Bédoin,** with its 18th-century Jesuit church at the top of the Old Town maze.

Mont Ventoux was the site of the first recorded attempt at *l'escalade* (mountain climbing), when Italian poet-philosopher Petrarch grunted his way up in 1336. Although people had climbed mountains before, this was the first "do it because it's there" feat. Reaching the summit itself (at 6,263 feet) requires a bit of legwork. From either Chalet Reynard or the tiny ski center Mont Serein you can leave your car and hike up to the peak's tall observatory tower. The climb is not overly taxing, and when you reach the top you are rewarded with gorgeous panoramic views of the Alps. And to the south, barring the possibility of high-summer haze, you'll take in views of the Rhône Valley, the Luberon, and even Marseille. Hiking maps are available at maisons de la presse (newsstands) and tourist offices. Town-to-town treks are also a great way to explore the area; one of the most beautiful trails is from Malaucène to Séguret. In the off-season, lonely Mont Ventoux is plagued with an ungodly reputation due to destructive winds. Attempts at saving its soul are evidenced by the chapels lining its slopes. Whether it's possessed by the devil or not, don't attempt to climb it in inclement weather. From late fall to early spring, in fact, the summit is closed by snow.

WHERE TO EAT

$ ✕**Le Chalet Reynard.** Opened in 1927, this is the spot for lunch and a bask in the sun (or on the covered terrace) on your way up the eastern slope of Mont Ventoux. Bikers, hikers, and car-trekkers alike gather at plank tables on the wooden deck or warm themselves in the chalet-style dining area. The food is far beyond the merely acceptable, from simple dishes such as omelets (with truffles in season) to the traditional hearty tartiflette (baked dish of potatoes, cheese, and bacon from the Savoie region) or even spit-roasted pig for groups of 15 or more. ⊠ *At the easternmost elbow of D974* ☎ *04–90–61–84–55* ⊕ *www. chalet-reynard.fr* ▭ *MC, V* ⊗ *Lunch only; dinner for large groups by reservation.*

SAULT

★ *41 km (25½ mi) southeast of Malaucène, 41 km (25½ mi) northeast of Carpentras.*

VISITOR INFORMATION
Sault Tourist Office (✉ *Av. de la Promenade,* ☎ *04–90–64–01–21* ⊕ *www. saultenprovence.com*).

Though at the hub of no fewer than six *routes départementales,* Sault remains an utterly isolated market town floating on a stony hilltop in a valley of lavender. Accessed only by circuitous country roads, it remains virtually untouched by tourism. The landscape is traditional Provence at its best—oak-forested hills and long, deep valleys purpled with the curving arcs of lavender. In the town itself, old painted storefronts exude the scent of honey and lavender. The damp church, Église Notre Dame de la Tour, dates from the 12th century; the long, lovely barrel nave was doubled in 1450.

From Sault all routes are scenic. You may head eastward into Haute Provence, visiting (via D950) tiny **Banon,** source of the famed goat cheese. Wind up D942 to see pretty hilltop Aurel or down D30 to reach perched **Simiane-la-Rotonde.** Or head back toward Carpentras through the spectacular **Gorges de la Nesque,** snaking along narrow cliff-edge roads through dramatic canyons carpeted with wild boxwood and pine. If you're exploring the Lavender Route, head eastward some 48 km (27 mi) to discover the epicenter of Haute-Provence's fabled lavender in the sleepy, dusty town of **Forcalquier.**

WHERE TO EAT & STAY

$$$$ ⚏ **Hostellerie du Val de Sault.** A holiday feel infiltrates this quiet retreat, once a summer camp. Five modern buildings range over the casually landscaped grounds, separated by low drystone walls and shaded by pines. Rooms are small and modular, with pine plank floors and private decks looking over the valley. Suites offer tiny sitting rooms (which can double as children's bedrooms) and whirlpool baths, and four new Provence-Asie rooms depart from Provençal clichés. Head to the main lodge for the rich regional cooking of the affable owner-chef Yves Gattechaut, with dishes such as asparagus and mountain ham served in a foie gras sauce, Sault lamb roasted in cassis and lavender, and Carpentras strawberries in pastry with candied chestnuts. Work it all off in the fitness center, which is equipped with a sauna and a whirlpool perfumed with lavender essence. **Pros:** at 2,600 feet nights are cool for sleeping even after the hottest of days; six-day cycle tours offered. **Cons:** breakfast and dinner demi-pension plan required. ✉ *Route St-Trinit,* ☎ *04–90–64–01–41* ⊕ *www.valdesault.com* ⇆ *15 rooms, 5 suites* ⟡ *In-room: no a/c, refrigerator, no TV (some), Wi-Fi. In-hotel: restaurant, bar, tennis courts, pool, gym, bicycles, parking, some pets allowed* ▤ *AE, DC, MC, V* ⊘ *Closed Nov.–Mar.* ⍩ *BP.*

THE SORGUE VALLEY

This gentle, rolling valley east of Avignon follows the course of the River Sorgue, which wells up from caverns below the arid hills of the Vaucluse plateau, gushes to the surface at Fontaine de Vaucluse, and rolls down to turn the mossy waterwheels in picturesque L'Isle-sur-la-Sorgue. It is a region of transition between the urban outskirts of Avignon and the wilds of the Luberon to the east.

L'ISLE-SUR-LA-SORGUE

Fodor'sChoice ★   *30 km (19 mi) east of Avignon.*

GETTING HERE

There's a 40-minute bus from the Avignon train station that stops at Place Robert Vasse in Isle-sur-la-Sorgue (where the large Caisse d'Epargne bank is). It's €2 one-way or if you return on the same day, it's €1. You could also take a train from Avignon to Fontaine du Vaucluse (€4.20) and then take the €2 bus to Isle-sur-la-Sorgue (about 15 mins). By car the distance is only 3 mi (5 km), but it's worth noting that you can no longer rent cars here.

VISITOR INFORMATION

L'Isle-sur-la-Sorgue Tourist Office (⊠ *Pl. de la Liberté,* ☎ 04–90–38–04–78 ⊕ *www.oti-delasorgue.fr*).

EXPLORING

Crisscrossed with lazy canals and still alive with waterwheels that once drove its silk, wool, and paper mills, this charming valley town retains its gentle appeal . . . except on Sunday. Then this easygoing old town transforms itself into a Marrakech of marketeers, "the most charming flea market in the world," its streets crammed with antiques and brocante, its cafés swelling with crowds of chic bargain browsers making a day of it. Yves St-Laurent bigwig Pierre Bergé, Viscount Linley (the noted furniture designer and son of Princess Margaret), and interior decorator Jacques Grange all flock here. Even hard-core modernists inured to treasure hunts enjoy the show as urbane couples with sweaters over shoulders squint discerningly through half lenses at monogrammed linen sheets, zinc washstands, *barbotine* ware, china spice sets, Art Deco perfume bottles, tinted engravings, and the paintings of modern almost-masters. For high-style big purchases—furniture, $5,000 quilts, and the like—head to the town's noted antiques shops (⇨ *Shopping, below*). There are also street musicians, food stands groaning under rustic breads, vats of tapenade, cloth-lined baskets of spices, and miles of café tables offering ringside seats to the spectacle. After London's Portobello district and the flea market at St-Ouen outside Paris, L'Isle-sur-la-Sorgue is reputedly Europe's third-largest antiques market. L'Isle's antiques market ratchets up to high speed twice a year when the town hosts a big antiques show, usually four days around Easter and another in mid-August, nicknamed the *Grand Déballage*—the "Great Unpacking." Prices can be high but remember that in many cases, dealers expect to bargain.

Continued on page 129

Just exactly where does Provence's famous Lavender Route begin? Any number of towns have fields gloriously carpeted with the purple flower, but chances are this particular journey starts back home with your first sight of a travel poster showing hills corduroyed with rows of lilac, amethyst, and mauve. Or when that vial of essence of *Lavandula vera* is passed under your nose and

BLUE GOLD: THE LAVENDER ROUTE

you inhale the wild, pure-blood ancestor of the incense-intense aroma that characterizes all those little folkloric potpourris. Sated with the strong scent of gift-shop soaps and sachets, you develop a longing for the real thing: the fragrance of meadow-soft, mountain-fresh lavender. Well, let your nostrils flare, for your lavender lust is about to be requited.

By Sarah Fraser

OUR LAVENDER MAGICAL MYSTERY TOUR

If you want to have a peak lavender experience—literally—detour 18 km (10 mi) to the northwest and take a spectacular day's drive up the winding road to the **summit of Mont Ventoux** (follow signs from Sault to see the lavender-filled valleys below).

MONT VENTOUX

Carpentras

Monteux

Pernes-les-Fontaines

Villes-s-Auzon

GORGES

Col de Murs

PLATEAU

Abbaye Notre-Dame de Sénanque

L'Isle-a-la-Sorgue

Gordes

Roussillon

Musée de la Lavande

Coustellet

Cavaillon

Have your Nikon ready for the beautifully preserved Cistercian simplicity of the **Abbaye Notre-Dame de Sénanque**, a perfect foil for the famous waving fields of purple around it.

No shrinking violet, the hilltop village of **Gordes** is famous for its luxe hotels, restaurants, and lavender-stocked shops.

Get a fascinating A to Z tour—from harvesting to distilling to production—at the **Musée de la Lavande** near Coustellet.

KEY

🝙 *Distillery*

⬮ *Lavender field*

Provence is threaded by the "Routes de la Lavande" (the Lavender Routes), a wide blue-purple swath that connects over 2,000 producers across the Drôme, the plateau du Vaucluse, and the Alpes-de-Haute-Provence, but our itinerary is lined with some of the prettiest sights—and smells—of the region. Whether you're shopping for artisanal bottles of the stuff (as with wine, the finest lavender carries its own Appellation d'Origine Contrôlée), spending a session at a lavender spa, or simply wearing hip-deep purple as you walk the fields, the most essential aspect on this trip is savoring a magical world of blue, one we usually only encounter on picture postcards.

To join the lavender-happy crowds, you have to go in season, which runs from

Purple haze

Gordes

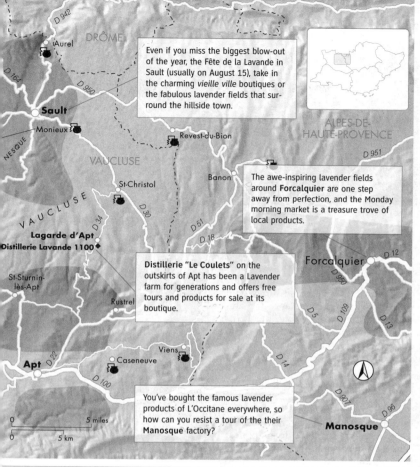

Even if you miss the biggest blow-out of the year, the Fête de la Lavande in Sault (usually on August 15), take in the charming *vieille ville* boutiques or the fabulous lavender fields that surround the hillside town.

The awe-inspiring lavender fields around **Forcalquier** are one step away from perfection, and the Monday morning market is a treasure trove of local products.

Distillerie "Le Coulets" on the outskirts of Apt has been a Lavender farm for generations and offers free tours and products for sale at its boutique.

You've bought the famous lavender products of L'Occitane everywhere, so how can you resist a tour of the their **Manosque** factory?

June to early September. Like Holland's May tulips, the lavender of Haute-Provence is in its true glory only once a year: the last two weeks of July, when the harvesting begins—but fields bloom throughout the summer months for the most part. Below, we wind through the most generous patches of lavender. Drive the colorful gambit southeastward (Coustellet, Gordes, Sault, Forcalquier,

and Manosque), which will give you good visiting (and shopping) time in a number of the villages that are *fou de la lavande* (crazy for lavender). And for the complete scoop on the hundreds of sights to see in lavender land, contact. **Les Routes de la Lavande** *through the association La Grande Traversée des Alpes in Grenoble* ☎*04–76–42–08–31* ⊕*www.grande-traversee-alpes.com.*

Lavender Harvest Festival, Sault

Monday Morning Market. Forcalquier

Abbaye Notre-Dame de Sénanque

DAY 1

SÉNANQUE:
A Picture-Perfect Abbey

An invisible Master of Ceremonies for the Lavender Route would surely send you first to the greatest spot for lavender worship in the world: the 12th-century Cistercian **Abbaye Notre-Dame de Sénanque**, which in July and August seems to float above a sea of lavender, a setting immortalized in a thousand travel posters. Happily, you'll find it via the D177 only 4 km (2½ mi) north of Gordes, among the most beautiful of Provence's celebrated perched villages. An architecture student's dream of neat cubes, cylinders, and pyramids, its pure Romanesque form alone is worth contemplating in any context. But in this arid, rocky setting the gray stone building seems to have special resonance—ancient, organic, with a bit of the borie about it. Along with the abbeys of Le Thornet and Silvacane, this is one of the trio of "Three Sisters" built by the Cistercian order in this area. Sénanque's **church** is a model of symmetry and balance. Begun in 1150, it has no decoration but still touches the soul with its chaste beauty. The adjoining **cloister,** from the 12th century, is almost as pure, with barrel-vaulted galleries framing double rows of discreet, abstract pillars (you'll find no child-devouring demons or lurid biblical tales here). Next door, the enormous vaulted **dormitory** and the **refectory** shelter a display on the history of Cistercian abbeys. The few remaining monks here now preside over a cultural center that presents concerts and exhibitions. The bookshop is one of the best in Provence, with a huge collection of Provençaliana (lots in English). ☎04–90–72–05–72 ✉€7 ⊘ *Guided tours of the abbey in French only by reservation. Bookshop open Mar.–Oct., Mon.–Sat. 10–noon, 2–6, Sun. 2–6; Nov.–Feb., daily 2–6:30.*

THE ESSENCE OF THE MATTER

Provence and lavender go hand in hand—but why? The flower is native to the Mediterranean, and grows so well because the pH balance in the soil is naturally perfect for it (pH 6–8). But lavender was really put on the map here when ancient Romans arrived to colonize Provence and used the flower to disinfect their baths and perfume their laundry (the word comes from Latin *lavare,* "to wash"). From a small grass-roots industry, lavender proliferated over the centuries until the first professional distillery opened in Provence in the 1880s to supply oils for southern French apothecaries. After World War I, production boomed to meet the demand of the perfumers of Grasse (the perfume center of the world). Once described as the "soul of Haute-Provence," lavender is now farmed in England, India, and the States, but the harvest in the South of France remains the world's largest.

After spending the morning getting acquainted with the little purple flower at Sénanque, drive south along the D2 (or D177) back to **Gordes**, through a dry, rocky region mixed with deep valleys and far-reaching plains. Wild lavender is already omnipresent, growing in large tracts as you reach the entrance of the small, unspoiled hilltop village, making for a patchwork landscape as finely drawn as a medieval illumination. A cluster of houses rises above the valley in painterly hues of honey gold, with cobbled streets winding up to the village's picturesque Renaissance château, making it one of the most beautiful towns in Provence. Gordes has a great selection of hotels, restaurants, and B&Bs to choose from (see our listings under Gordes, *above*). Spend the early afternoon among tasteful shops that sell lovely Provençal crafts and produce, much of it lavender-based, and then after lunch, head out to Coustellet.

COUSTELLET:
A Great Lavender Museum
Set 2 mi south of Gordes, Coustellet is noted for its **Musée de la Lavande** (take the D2 southeast to the outskirts of Coustellet). Owned by one of the original lavender families, who have cultivated and distilled the flower here for over five generations, this museum lies

on the outskirts of more than 80 acres of prime lavender-cultivated land.

Not only can you visit the well-organized and interesting museum (note the impressive collection of scythes and distilling apparatus), you can buy up a storm in the boutique, which offers a great selection of lavender-based products at very reasonable prices. ☎04–90–76–91–23 ⊕*www.museedela lavande.co* ✉€6 ⊙*Daily, Feb.–Mar., and Dec., 9–12:15 and 2–6; Apr. and Oct., 9–1 and 2–6; May–Sept., 9–7 9–7.*

There are four main species. True lavender (*Lavandula angustifolia*) produces the most subtle essential oil and is often used by perfume makers and laboratories. Spike lavender (*Lavandula latifolia*) has wide leaves and long floral stems with several flower spikes. Hybrid lavender (*lavandin*) is obtained from pollination of true lavender and spike lavender, making a hybrid that forms a highly developed large round cluster. French lavender (*Lavendula stoechas*) is wild lavender that grows throughout the region and is collected for the perfume industry. True lavender thrives in the chalky soils and hot, dry climate of higher altitudes of Provence. It was picked systematically until the end of the 19th century and used for most lavender-based products. But as the demand for this remarkable flower grew, so did the need for a larger production base. By the beginning of the 20th century, the demand for the flower was so great that producers planted fields of lavender at lower altitudes, creating the need for a tougher, more resistant plant: the hybrid *lavandin*.

Lavender Harvest Festival, Sault

DAY 2

LAGARDE D'APT:
A Top Distillerie

On the second day of your lavender adventure, begin by enjoying the winding drive 25 km (15 mi) east to the town of **Apt**. Aside from its Provençal market, busy with all the finest food products of the Luberon and Haute Provence, Apt itself is unremarkable (even actively ugly from a distance) but is a perfect place from which to organize your visits to the lavender fields of Caseneuve, Viens, and Lagarde d'Apt. Caseneuve (east exit from Apt onto the D900 and then northwest on the D35) and Viens (16 km/10 mi east from Apt on the D209) are small but charming places to stop for a quick bite along the magnificent drive through the rows upon rows of lavender, but if you have to choose between the three, go to the minuscule village of Lagarde d'Apt (12 km/7 mi east from Apt on the D209) and the miniscule village (population 35) of Lagaede d'Apt (24 km northeast from Apt on the D943) are small but charming places to stop for a quick

bite along the magnificent drive through the rows upon rows of lavender. Or for a closer look, take the D22 direction Rustrel a few kilometres outside of Apt to **Distillerie "Les Coulets"**. From June to September, you can take a free tour of the distillery, visit the farm and browse the gift shop. ☎04–90–74–07–55 ☉ July and Aug. 9–noon and 1:30–7.

SAULT:
The Biggest Festival

To enjoy a festive overnight, continue northwest from Lagarde d'Apt to the village of **Sault**, 15 km (9 mi) to the northeast. Beautifully perched on a rocky outcrop overlooking the valley that bears its name, Sault is one of the key stops along the Lavender Route. There are any number of individual distilleries, producers, and fields to visit—to make the most of your visit, ask the Office du Tourisme (☎04–90–64–01–21, ⊕www.tourism.fr/office-du-tourisme/sault.html) for a list of events. Make sure to pop into the **Centre de Découverte de la Nature et du Patrimoine Cynégétique** (⊠Av. de l'Oratoire ☎04–90–64–13–96 ☜€3) to see the exhibitions on the natural history of the region, including some on lavender. Aim to be in Sault for the not-to-be-missed **Fête de la Lavande** (⊠along the D950 at the Hippodrome le Defends ⊕www.saultenprovence. com), a day-long festival entirely dedicated to lavender, the best in the region, and usually held around August 15. Village folk dress in traditional Provençal garb and parade on bicycles, horses leap over barrels of fragrant bundles of hay, and local producers display their wares at the market—all of which culminates in a communal Provençal dinner (€20) served with lavender-based products.

DAY 3

FORCALQUIER:
The Liveliest Market

On your third day, the drive from Sault over 53 km (33 mi) east to Forcalquier is truly spectacular. As you approach the village in late July, you will see endless fields of *Lavandula vera* (true wild lavender) broken only by charming stone farmhouses or discreet distilleries. The epicenter of Haute-Provence's lavender cultivation, **Forcalquier** boasts a lively Monday morning market with a large emphasis on lavender-based products, and it is a great departure point for walks, bike rides, horse rides, or drives into the lavender world that surrounds the town. In the 12th century, Forcalquier was known as the capital city of Haute-Provence and was called the *Cité des Quatre Reines* (City of the Four Queens) because the four daughters (Eleanor of Aquitaine among them) of the ruler of this region, Raimond Béranger V, all married royals. Relics of this former glory can be glimpsed in the Vieille Ville of Forcalquier, notably its Cathédrale Notre-Dame and the Couvent des Cordeliers. However, everyone heads here to marvel at the lavender fields outside town. Contact Forcalquier's Office du Tourisme (⊠13 pl. Bourguet ☎04–92–75–10–02 ⊕www.

BLOOMING:

Lavender fields begin blooming in late June, depending on the area and the weather, with fields reaching their peak from the first of July to mid-October. The last two weeks in July are considered the best time to catch the fields in all their glory.

HARVESTING:

Lavender is harvested from July to September, when the hot summer sun brings the essence up into the flower. Harvesting is becoming more and more automated; make an effort to visit some of the older fields with narrow rows—these are still picked by hand. Lavender is then dried for two to three days before being transported to the distillery.

DISTILLING:

Distillation is done in a steam alembic, with the dry lavender steamed in a double boiler. Essential oils are extracted from the lavender by water vapor, which is then passed through the cooling coils of a retort.

forcalquier.com) for information on the lavender calendar, then get saddled up on a bicycle for a trip into the countryside at the town's Moulin de Sarret. Plan on enjoying a fine meal and an overnight stay (reserve way in advance) at the town's most historic establishment, the **Hostellerie des Deux Lions** (⊠11 pl. du Bourguet ☎04–92–75–25–30).

MANOSQUE:
Love That L'Occitane

Fifteen mi (25 km) south of Forcalquier is Manosque, home to the **L'Occitane** factory. You can get a glimpse of what the Luberon was like before it became so hip—Manosque is certainly not a tourist epicenter—but a trip here is worth it for a visit to the phenomenally successful cosmetics and skin care company that is now the town's main employer. Once you make a reservation through the Manosque Tourist Office, you can take a two-hour tour of the production site, view a documentary film, get a massage with oils, then rush into the shop where you can stock up on L'Occitane products for very reasonable prices. From Manosque you can head back to Apt and the Grand Luberon area or turn south about 52 km (30 mi) to Aix-en-Provence. ⊠*Z. I. St-Maurice* ☎*04–92–70–19–00* ⊕*www.loccitane. com* ☺*Mon.-Sat. 10–7.*

BRINGING IT HOME

Yes, you've already walked in the pungent-sweet fields, breathing in the ephemeral scent that is uniquely a part of Provence. Visually, there is nothing like the waving fields rising up in a haze of bees. But now it's time to shop! Here are some top places to head to stop and smell the lavender element in local wines, honey, vinegar, soaps, and creams. A fine place to start is the 8 km (5 mi) east of Sault at the **Ho! Bouquet de Lavande** (⊠ follow signs on the D189, Ferrassières ☎04–75–28–87–52). Take a free guided visit and cut your own lavender bouquet before buying up all the inventory available in the shop. In Gordes and Sault there are lovely Provençal markets that have a wide range of lavender-based products, from honey to vinegar to creams. A great selection of the finest essential oils is available at **Distillerie du Vallon** (⊠Rte. des Michouilles, Sault ☎04–90–64–14–83). **L'Occitane** (⊠Z.I. St-Maurice, Manosque ☎04–92–70–19–00) is the mother store. In nearby Volx you can hit the **Maison aux Huiles Essentiels** (⊠Z.I. La Carretière, Volx ☎04–92–78–46–77) for aromatherapy in all its glory.

SCENT-SATIONAL

On a non-market day, life returns to its mellow pace. There are plenty of antiques dealers doing business year-round, but also fabric and interior design shops, bookstores, and food stores to explore. People curl up with paperbacks on park benches by shaded fountains and read international papers in cafés. While the food stands and arts and crafts shops hold forth along the Avenue de la Libération, the antiquaires hold Sunday squatters' rights from the Place Gambetta up the length of Avenue des 4 Otages. Dealers and clients catch up on gossip at the Place Gambetta fountain and at the Café de France, opposite the church of Notre-Dame-des-Anges. Most of the clusters of antiques dealers, known as the Villages d'Antiquaires, lie just outside the ring formed by the canals of La Sorgue. Wander the maze inside the ring to admire a range of architectural styles, from Gothic to Renaissance, with the occasional burst of color where an owner has broken from local tradition to paint an archway indigo blue or a pair of shutters lemon yellow.

The Provençal Venice, L'Isle, is dotted with watermills and canals that once drove the wheels of silk, paper, oil, grain, and leather mills. Today, these wheels—12 of them—turn idly, adding to the charm of the winding streets. If you want to explore the vestiges of L'Isle's 18th-century heyday, stop in the tourist office and pick up a brochure called "Vagabondages L'Isle-sur-la-Sorgue." This map and commentary (available in English) will guide you to some of the town's grand old hôtels particuliers.

One of the finest of L'Isle's mansions, the **Hôtel de Campredon–Maison René Char,** has been restored and reinvented as a modern-art gallery, mounting temporary exhibitions of modern masters. ⌂*20 rue du Docteur Tallet* ☎*04–90–38–17–41* ⊕ *www.maison-renechar.fr* ⧆ *6.20* ☉*July–Aug., Tues.–Sun. 10–1 and 3–7; Sept.–June, Tues.–Sun. 10–12:30 and 2–5:30.*

L'Isle's 17th-century church, the **Collégiale Notre-Dame-des-Anges,** is extravagantly decorated with gilt, faux marble, and sentimental frescoes. Its double-colonnaded facade commands the center of the Old Town. ⌂*Pl. de l'Église.*

WHERE TO EAT & STAY

$$$$ ✕**Le Jardin du Quai.** Daniel Hébet made his name at La Mirande in Avi-
★ gnon and Le Domaine des Andéols in St-Saturnin-lès-Apt before opening this bistro in his own image—young, jovial, and uncompromising when it comes to quality. Off a noisy street near the train station is the gate to this garden haven, with metal tables under the trees and an airy interior with a vintage tile floor. Hébet offers a single set menu at lunch and another at dinner, and the food is so good that no one is complaining at the lack of choice (though he has been known to substitute meat for fish on request): poached egg with truffles, Saint Pierre with a hint of green onion, lobster in ever-so-delicate pastry, and cherry meringue are all yumptious. This is where the local antiques dealers come to eat, and the place feels so welcoming that it would be easy to linger for hours. ⌂*91 av. Julien-Guigue* ☎*04–90–20–14–98* ⊕*www.danielhebet. com* ▤*MC, V* ☉*Closed Tues. and Wed.*

$$$
Fodor's Choice
★

✕Le Vivier. Patrick and Céline Fischnaller returned from London only three years ago and have already received a Michelin star with this dazzler just outside L'Isle-sur-la-Sorgue's center. Start off with a glass of wine (from €3) on the orange sofa in the deco lounge before devouring some foie gras and smoked eel terrine, pigeon pie, or strawberry soup with basil and black olives from the €43 menu (or

opt to go à la carte). But be sure to leave room for the sublime roast beef with cherry marmalade or roasted cod with stuffed pequillos peppers. The couple's philosophy that wine is equally as important is reflected in an extensive list. Did we mention the Sorgue river runs underneath the terrace? ⊠*800 cours Ferande-Peyre* ☎*04-90-38-52-80* ⊕*www.levivier-restaurant.com* ⌖*Reservations essential* ☐*AE, MC, V* ⊘*Closed Mon.; May–Aug., no lunch Sun.–Wed., Sept.–Apr., no lunch Fri.–Sat., no Sun. dinner. Closed last wk Feb.–mid-Mar.*

$

✕Lou Nego Chin. In winter you'll sit shoulder to shoulder in the cramped but atmospheric dining room (chinoiserie linens, brightly hued tiles), but in summer tables with striped table cloths are strewn across the lively street, on a wooden deck along the river. Ask for a spot at the edge so you can watch the ducks play, and order the house wine and the inexpensive three-course (€18) menu du jour, often a hot salad and a steak or a good and garlicky stew. ⊠*12 quai Jean-Jaurès* ☎*04-90-20-88-03* ☐*MC, V* ⊘*Closed Nov.*

$$$$
Fodor's Choice
★

La Maison sur la Sorgue. Frédéric and Marid-Claude have done their architectural homework. This 17th-century home, deliciously renovated in 2004, will win you over as soon as you walk in the door with a composed elegance and authentic style that one rarely comes across in a hotel setting. Each of the four unique rooms, tasteful in tones and modern fixtures, is spacious and displays one of its original walls. Each makes its own mark, whether with a courtyard terrace, view of the Virgin Mary statue from the facing church, or even a sunset surprise. Obliging hosts, books everywhere, the disappearing pool, and a shop next door to purchase some last-minute antique indulgences . . . makes a return visit inevitable. **Pros:** five-star treatment plus amenities (shampoos and soaps); courtyard breakfast includes morning surprises beyond the basic croissant and jam fare. **Cons:** moquette carpet (while practical) is rough on the feet; some handheld showers. ⊠*6 rue Rose Goudard,* ☎*04-90-20-74-86* ⊕*www.lamaisonsurlasorgue.com* ⊃*2 rooms, 2 suites* ⌖*In-room: refrigerator. In-hotel: pool, Wi-Fi, parking (fee)* ☐*AE, MC, V* ⊘*Closed last wk of Jan.–mid-Feb.* ⏐⊙*BP.*

$$$
★

La Prévôté. With all the money you saved bargaining on that chipped Quimper vase, splurge on dinner at this discreet, pristine convent hidden off a backstreet courtyard. An indigo-blue archway (not belonging to the hotel) draws your eye down a quiet street to this place, which shares a wall with the neighboring church. The newly added guest rooms are decorated with the fine local materials; they are spacious and elegant in decor. In the restaurant, Jean-Marie Alloin works with local flavors—try his *tian d'agneau* (caramelized lamb) with tapenade and confit eggplant, or fillet of duck with courgette chutney. The wine list is succinct and favors reasonably priced local reds. But evening and à la carte meals are an investment best suited to buyers of antiques rather than brocante. **Pros:** romantic plus; look for special deals on their Web site. **Cons:** check-in from 5 PM; not easy to drive to. ⊠*4 rue Jean-Jacques-Rousseau84800* ☎*04–90–38–57–29* ⊕*www.la-prevote. fr* ⟿*5 rooms* ⸋ *In-room: a/c (some), Wi-Fi. In-hotel: restaurant, some pets allowed* ⊟*AE, MC, V* ⦿*BP.*

$$ ★   ⚏**Le Mas de Cure Bourse.** For a real taste of the countryside, base yourself at this graceful yet casual 18th-century postal-coach inn well outside the fray, snugly hedge-bound in the countryside amid fruit trees and fields southwest of the town. Here you can relax on six acres of green landscape, read by the large pool, and sleep in rooms freshly decked out in Provençal prints and painted country furniture. Meals are memorable, whether taken by the grand old fireplace or on the terrace. The sophisticated cooking keeps a local touch with dishes such as mousse of fois gras with brioche and caramelized cassis salad, and deliciously decadent chocolate cake with chocolate sauce. **Pros:** grounds are beautiful; rooms are nonsmoking. **Cons:** have to drive to town; little English spoken. ⊠*120 chem. de la Serre,* ☎*04–90–38–16–58* ⊕*www. masdecurebourse.com* ⟿*13 rooms* ⸋*In-room: Wi-Fi. In-hotel: restaurant, pool, parking, some pets allowed* ⊟*MC, V.*

$ ⚏**La Gueulardière.** After a Sunday glut of antiquing along the canals, you can dine and sleep amidst a cache of collectible finds, from the school posters in the restaurant to the oak armoires and brass beds that furnish the simple lodgings just up the street. Each room has French windows that open onto the enclosed garden courtyard, where you can enjoy a private breakfast in the shade. **Pros:** easy to find on main road; price is excellent for location. **Cons:** rooms with shower or bathtub; street noise on market days. ⊠*1 cours René-Char84800* ☎*04–90–38–10–52* ⊕*www.gueulardiere.com* ⟿*5 rooms* ⸋*In-room: no a/c, no TV (some). In-hotel: restaurant, Wi-Fi, parking, some pets allowed* ⊟*AE, MC, V* ⦿*Closed Dec. 15–Jan. 15.*

SHOPPING

Throughout the pretty backstreets of L'Isle's Old Town (especially between Place de l'Église and Avenue de la Libération), there are boutiques spilling baskets full of tempting goods onto the sidewalk to lure you inside; most concentrate on home design and Provençal goods. **Sous l'Olivier** (⊠*16 rue de la République* ☎*04–90–20–68–90*) is a food boutique crammed to the ceiling with bottles and jars of tapenade, fancy mustards, candies shaped like olives, and the house olive oil.

Of the dozens of antiques shops in L'Isle, one conglomerate concentrates some 40 dealers under the same roof: **L'Isle aux Brocantes** (⊠*7 av. des Quatre Otages* ☎*04–90–20–69–93*). It's open Friday through Monday. The high-style crowd adores the higher-end antiques concentrated at the shop of **Xavier Nicod** (⊠*9 av. des Quatre Otages* ☎*04–*

90–38–07–20), which is open weekends and by appointment. Many collectors make a weekend beeline for the treasures found at **La Maison Biehn** (⊠ *7 av. des Quatre Otages* ☎ *04–90–20–89–04*) which are crammed into a gorgeous ivy-covered town house. **Espace Béchard** (⊠ *1 av. Jean-Charmasson* ☎ *04–90–38–25–40*) throws a dozen different dealers of 20th-century contemporary design together, all with fabulously overscaled objects too big to carry home on the plane, every Saturday, Sunday, and festival day from 9:30 to 7. **Un Jour Ailleurs** (⊠ *Place Ferdinand Buisson* ☎ *04–90–38–50–19*) showcases Brun de Vian Tiran—they've been making wool blankets, quilts, and bed accessories for over 200 years—along with BVT's cashmere or mohair shawls and scarves.

FONTAINE DE VAUCLUSE

7 km (4½ mi) east of L'Isle sur la Sorgue, 30 km (19 mi) east of Avignon.

VISITOR INFORMATION
Fontaine de Vaucluse Tourist Office (⊠ *Chemin du Gouffre* ☎ *04–90–20–32–22* ⊕ *www.oti-delasorgue.fr*).

Like the natural attraction for which it is named, this village has welled up and spilled over as a Niagara Falls–type tourist center; the rustic, pretty, and slightly tacky riverside town is full of shops, cafés, and restaurants, all built to serve the pilgrims who flock to its namesake. And neither town nor fountain should be missed if you're either a connoisseur of rushing water or a fan of foreign kitsch.

★ There's no exaggerating the magnificence of the **Fontaine de Vaucluse**, a mysterious spring that gushes from a deep underground source that has been explored to a depth of 1,010 feet . . . so far. Framed by towering cliffs, a broad, pure pool wells up and spews dramatically over massive rocks down a gorge to the village, where its roar soothes and cools the visitors who crowd the riverfront cafés.

You must pay to park, then run a gauntlet of souvenir shops and tourist traps on your way to the top. But even if you plan to make a beeline past the kitsch, do stop in at the legitimate and informative **Moulin Vallis-Clausa**. A working paper mill, it demonstrates a reconstruction of a 15th-century waterwheel that drives timber crankshafts to mix rag pulp, while artisans roll and dry thick paper *à l'ancienne* (in the old manner). The process is fascinating and free to watch (the guided tour lasts half an hour and must be arranged in advance, minimum 10 people), though it's almost impossible to resist buying note cards, posters, even lamp shades fashioned from the pretty stuff. Fontaine was once a great industrial mill center, but its seven factories were closed by strikes in 1968 and never recovered. All the better for you today, since now you can enjoy this marvelous natural spot in peace. ⊠ *On the riverbank walk up to the spring* ☎ *04–90–20–34–14* ⊙ *Daily 10–6.*

Fontaine has its own ruined **château**, perched romantically on a forested hilltop over the town and illuminated at night. First built around

The Gîte Way

You come home from a hard day's sightseeing, slip off your shoes, pull a pitcher of cold water from the fridge, pour a pastis, and carry it out to the terrace. There's a basket heavy with goodies from the village market—a fresh rabbit, three different tubs of olives, a cup of fresh-scooped tapenade, apricots, and melons warm from the sun. After your drink, you'll sort it all out and fix supper, French pop music playing gently on the radio. You'll eat as long and as late as you like, and carry the children to their twin beds in the back room before you take a stroll through the almond grove or crunch through the wild thyme to look at the city lights strung far below. Even doing the dishes in the sink seems okay in this faraway, summer-cottage mode, far from the minibars, lobby lounges, and snooty waiters of the beaten tourist track.

This is the gîte way, the alternative to hotels and restaurants and even to the anonymous seaside vacation flats farmed out by agencies abroad. The national network known as Gîtes de France has organized and catalogued a vast assortment of rural houses, many of them restored farmhouses and old village bastides, most of them rich in regional character and set in the picturesque countryside. The participating houses are inspected and categorized by comfort level (for example, three stars includes a washing machine), with standardized lists of minimum furnishings (from corkscrews to salad spinners to vegetable peelers).

But the key to the charm is the personal touch: Gîtes de France owners greet their guests on arrival, and may pop by (discreetly, rarely) during the week with lettuce from their garden, a bottle from their vineyard, holiday candy for the kids. There's a cupboard full of maps and brochures on local museums, and often the name of a nearby restaurant if you're too sunburned to cook. And they'll come to collect the key a week later and wish you a bon voyage.

There are drawbacks, of course. You'll have to bring towels and linens, and make up the beds yourself (you can often rent linens from the host if you prefer), and you are requested to leave the house in the same condition in which you found it—which usually means impeccable, and requires some mopping and scrubbing.

But the privacy and independence counterbalance any drudgery, and you'll meet people far different from the tourists and supercilious concierges of standardized hotels: farmers, teachers, winemakers, artists, anyone with the time to care for a cottage, a neighboring farmhouse, a converted stone barn.

Contact the headquarters of the département you plan to visit and request a catalogue of properties, then make a reservation by phone or fax. You must give them a 25% down payment with your reservation, then the rest when you return the contract, one month before your visit. *For more information on the gîte way, ⇨ see Accomodations in the Travel Smart chapter.*

the year 1000 and embellished in the 14th century by the bishops of Cavaillon, it was destroyed in the 15th century and forms little more than a sawtooth silhouette against the sky.

The great Renaissance poet Petrarch, driven mad with unrequited love for a beautiful married woman named Laura, retreated to this valley to nurse his passion in a cabin with "one dog and only two servants." He had met her in the heady social scene at the papal court in Avignon, where she was to die years later of the plague. Sixteen years in this wild isolation didn't ease the pain, but the serene environment inspired him to poetry, and the lyrics of his *Canzoniere* were dedicated to Laura's memory. The small **Musée de Fontaine de Vaucluse Pétrarch,** built on the site of his residence, displays prints and engravings of the virtuous lovers, both in Avignon and Fontaine de Vaucluse. ⊠ *On the left bank, direction Gordes* ☎ *04–90–20–37–20* 🖅 *€3.50* ⊙ *Apr.–Nov., Tues.– Sun. 10–12 and 2–6. Closed Dec.–Mar.*

WHERE TO EAT & STAY

$ ✕**Philip-Jardin de Pétrarque.** If you want a truly regional experience, take
★ a seat on the shaded terrace of Restaurant Philip, opened in 1926 by Philip's uncle. Set apart from the other eateries, it's located just before the trail to the spring. Enjoy the river views and dig in to some cuisses de grenouille or trout from the Sorgue cooked in white butter sauce or pink trout marinated in olive oil. A three-course menu goes for only €24, and there's a decent regional wine list. Sandwiches, salads, and ice cream can be ordered next door at its Bar Glacier. ⊠ *Chem. de la Fontaine* ☎ *04–90–20–31–81* ⊟ *AE, V* ⊙ *Open Apr. 1–Sept. 30; lunch only Apr., May, June, and Sept.*

$$ 🏨**Hotel des Sources.** Situated near the park surrounding the Fontaine de Vaucluse (replete with benches, bi-century trees, and two natural springs), this three-star hotel just steps from town aims to please. Polyglot owners, the Gayards, renovated the 17th-century home and offer simple and proper accommodation with gracious hospitality. There's a common room where you can read or pay for a game of pool and a shady terrace to enjoy your included breakfast. **Pros:** lovely street entrance; window views of the Sorgue river. **Cons:** comfy rooms but not luxe; restaurant closed for lunch and dinner as of 2009. ⊠ *Quartier Châteauvieux84800* ☎ *04–90–20–31–84* ⊕ *www.hoteldessources.com* 🛏 *9 rooms* ⌂ *In-room: no a/c, Wi-Fi. In-hotel: parking, some pets allowed* ⊟ *MC, V* ⊙ *Closed Nov.–mid-Mar.* �🍽⧉*BP*

THE LUBERON

" 'Have you ever been to the Luberon? Between Avignon and Aix. It's getting a little chichi, specially in August, but it's beautiful—old villages, mountains, no crowds, fantastic light . . . . Leave the autoroute at Cavaillon, and go towards Apt.' . . . Murat poured the red wine and raised his glass. '*Bonnes vacances,* my friend. I'm serious about the Luberon; it's a little special. You should try it.'"

After Peter Mayle, no doubt barefoot by the pool, typed these words in his first novel *Hotel Pastis,* the world took a map in hand. They had already taken note when his chronicles *A Year in Provence* and *Toujours Provence* painted a delicious picture of backcountry sunshine, copious feasts, and cartoonishly droll local rustics; now they had directions to get there.

They came. They climbed over Mayle's hedges for autographs. They built pink and yellow houses, booked his favorite restaurant tables, traced his footsteps with the book in hand. And not only the English. *A Year in Provence* sold 5 million copies and was translated into 38 languages, including French (where its sequel corrected his grammar to *Provence Toujours*). His name is a household word here (Peet-aire May-eel) and doesn't always bring the oft-described grin and shrug from the locals. Perhaps that's why Mayle took a sabbatical from Provence, relinquishing the home with the famously immovable stone table. He has since returned, putting down roots on the south face of the Luberon, in Lourmarin.

The dust has settled a bit, and despite the occasional Mayle Country bus tour rattling through from Cavaillon, the Luberon has returned to its former way of life. There were always Lacoste shirts here, and converted mas with pools (after all, Mayle's mas was already gentrified when they installed central heating), and sophisticated restaurants catering to seekers of the Simple Life. They're all still here, but so are the extraordinarily beautiful countryside, the golden perched villages, the blue-black forests, and the sun-bleached rocks.

The broad mountain called the Luberon is protected nowadays by the Parc Naturel Régional du Luberon, but that doesn't mean you should expect rangers, campsites, and his-and-hers outhouses. It has always been and remains private land, though building and forestry are allowed in moderation and hiking trails have been cleared.

The N100, anchored to the west by the market town of Cavaillon and to the east by industrial Apt, parallels the long, looming north face of the Luberon, and from it you can explore the hill towns and valley villages on either side. To its north, the red-ocher terrain around Roussillon, the Romanesque symmetry of the Abbaye de Sénanque, and the fashionable charms of Gordes punctuate a rugged countryside peppered with ancient stone *bories* (dry-stone huts). To its south lie Oppède-le-Vieux, Ménerbes, Lacoste, and pretty perched Bonnieux. From Bonnieux you can drive over the rugged crest through Lourmarin and explore the less gentrified south flank of the mountain. Although the Luberon is made up of two distinct regions, only the more civilized Petit Luberon, up to Apt, is covered in this chapter. If you're a nature lover, you may want to venture into the wilder Grand Luberon, especially to the summit called Mourre Nègre.

GORDES

★ *10 km (6 mi) east of Fontaine de Vaucluse, 39 km (24 mi) east of Avignon.*

GETTING HERE
There is only one bus that stops at the Place du Château in Gordes and that's the Cavaillon-Roussillon. It runs twice a day, morning and night and costs €4.30. Otherwise you'll need a car or take a taxi: to Avignon it's about €75 or to Fontaine du Vaucluse €40.

VISITOR INFORMATION
Gordes Tourist Office (⊠ *Salle des Gardes du Château* 📞 *04–90–72–02–75* ⊕ *www.gordes-village.com*).

EXPLORING
The famous village perché of Gordes is only a short distance from Fontaine de Vaucluse, but you need to wind your way south, east, and then north on D100A, D100, D2, and D15 to skirt the impassable hillside. It's a lovely drive through dry, rocky country covered with wild lavender and scrub oak and may tempt you to a picnic or a walk. How surprising, then, to leave such wildness behind and enter resort country. Once a summer retreat favored by modern artists such as Andre Lhôte, Marc Chagall, and Victor Vasarely, Gordes used to be a famous, unspoiled hilltop village; it has now become a famous, unspoiled hilltop village surrounded by luxury vacation homes, modern hotels, restaurants, and B&Bs, much patronized by chic Parisians. No matter. The ancient stone village still rises above the valley in painterly hues of honey gold, and its mosaiclike cobbled streets—lined with boutiques, galleries, and real-estate offices—still wind steep and narrow to its Renaissance château.

The town **château** was built by the d'Agoult-Gordes family in the 13th century, then made over in Renaissance style by the Lords of Simiane. The only way to see its interior is to pay to see its collection of mind-stretching photo paintings by Pop artist Pol Mara, who spent his last years in Gordes. It's worth the price to look at the fabulously decorated stone fireplace, created in 1541; it covers an entire wall with Neoclassic designs and stretches to frame two doors. ⊠ *Pl. du Château* 📞 *04–90–72–02–75* 🎫 *€4* ⊘ *Daily 10–noon and 2–6.*

Head downhill from the château and follow signs to the **belvédère** overlooking the miniature fields and farms below. From this height all those modern vacation homes blend in with the ancient mas—except for the aqua blue pools.

Before leaving town be sure to pay a call on the village's church of **St-Fermin**, whose interior is overblown Rococo—all pink and gold.

★ Just outside Gordes, on a lane heading north from D2, follow signs to the **Village des Bories.** Found throughout this region of Provence, the bizarre and fascinating little stone hovels called *bories* are concentrated some 20 strong in an ancient community. Their origins are provocatively vague. Built as shepherds' shelters with tight-fitting, mortarless stone in a hivelike form, they may date back to the Celts, the Ligurians, even the Iron Age—and were inhabited or used for sheep through the 18th century. This village was reconstructed from remains. From Gordes, take D15, turning right to D2. ☎*04–90–72–03–48* 🎫*€6* ☯*Daily 9–sunset or 8, whichever comes earlier.*

Gordes is surrounded by beautiful lavender fields and one of the most beautiful is found at the celebrated 12th-century **Abbaye de Sénanque,** a great place to start off exploring the region's famous Lavender Route. *For complete information on the Abbaye and the "Routes de La Lavende" see the special feature "Blue Gold: The Lavender Route." in this chapter.* ☎*04–90–72–05–72* ⊕*www.senanque.fr* 🎫*€7* ☯*Bookshop open Mar.–Oct., Mon.–Sat. 10–noon and 2–6:30, Sun. 2–6:30; Nov.– Feb,. Sat. 2–6:30. Guided tours (in French only) must be arranged with Abbaye in advance.*

WHERE TO EAT & STAY

$ ✕**Le Jardin du Levant.** Formerly a popular Thai restaurant, the ever-welcoming owner now dishes up traditional, reasonably priced fare. Enjoy grillades and salads (no fish, though) on the bigger and better terrace, brightened with tropical plants and parasols and its vaulted stone dining room cheerfully furnished with Formica and wooden tables and mismatched chairs. ✉*Rte. de la Combe* ☎*04–90–72–12–43* 🖃*MC, V* ☯*Closed all day Fri. and Sat. morning.*

$ ✕**Les Cuisines du Château.** Directly across from the château, this tiny bistro serves an international clientele without a trace of condescension. At lunchtime, when tables spill out onto the square, the menu highlights a daily seasonal smorgasbord of asparagus omelets, whole sea bass, and tartare à la provençe. Lots of grilled meats to chose from plus a lunch menu at €22 or €30 dinner menu. Hit the sweet-tooth jackpot with crème brûlée à carambar to finish off your meal. Although the food may not be as refined as under the previous owner, reasonable prices along with the '30s-style bistro tables and architectural lines are a relief from Gordes's ubiquitous rustic-chic. ✉*Pl. du Château* ☎*04–90–72–01–31* ⚠*Reservations essential* 🖃*MC, V* ☯*Open daily July–Aug. Hours vary off-season. Closed Nov.–Feb.*

$$$$ ▦**La Bastide de Gordes.** There is no shortage of luxury accommodation in this region, but this hotel in the center of Gordes stands out for its vast, three-level spa by Daniel Jouvance and two swimming pools (indoor and outdoor). The rather old-fashioned rooms have all the comforts you could dream of and, to complement the restaurant with its panoramic view of the area, there is a wine shop and cellar. **Pros:** rooms with a village view are substanially cheaper; meditation room in spa. **Cons:** breakfast and minibar expensive; lots of levels. ✉*Le Village* ☎*04–90–72–12–12* ⊕*www.bastide-de-gordes.com* 🛏*40 rooms, 5 suites* ⚙*In-room: refrigerator, Wi-Fi. In-hotel: restaurant, bar, pools, spa* 🖃*AE, MC, V* ☯*Closed Jan. to first week of Feb.*

$$$ ▦**Domaine de l'Enclos.** Though this cluster of private stone cottages has had a major face-lift (eradicating much patina), antique tiles and faux patinas keep it looking fashionably old. There are panoramic views and a heated pool, babysitting services by arrangement, and a welcome that

is surprisingly warm and familial for an inn of this sophistication. **Pros:** look for last-minute online deals which include breakfast; ideal for families. **Cons:** no restaurant service until 2010. ⊠ *Rte. de Sénanque,* ☎ *04–90–72–71–00* ⤶ *11 rooms, 3 suites* ⚐ *In-room: refrigerator. In-hotel: pool, Wi-Fi, parking, some pets allowed* ▤ *AE, MC, V.*

$$$ ▦ **Le Mas des Romarins.** At this 18th-century farmhouse on a hilltop crossroads on the outskirts of town you can gaze across the valley at Gordes while you breakfast on a sheltered terrace. Guest rooms are clean, well lit, and feel spacious with mostly village or valley views. Warm rugs, antique furniture around the fireplace in the sitting room, and a pool surrounded by borie-like stone add to your contentment. There is no restaurant, but meals are available to guests on Monday, Wednesday, Friday, and Saturday. **Pros:** breakfast included; the table d'hôte menus are excellent value for this expensive village. **Cons:** bit of a walk to town; look at cancellation policy. ⊠ *Rte. de Sénanque,* ☎ *04–90–72–12–13* ⊕ *www.masromarins.com* ⤶ *13 rooms, 1 suite* ⚐ *In-room: refrigerator. In-hotel: pool, Wi-Fi, parking, some pets allowed* ▤ *MC, V* ⊗ *Closed first week of Jan. to mid-Mar.* ⑩ *BP*

SHOPPING

If you're shopping for a gift or souvenirs, you'll find tasteful Provençal tableware at **Le Jardin** (⊠ *Rte. des Murs* ☎ *04–90–72–12–34*) which also has a charming tearoom in its leafy courtyard garden. **Sud** (⊠ *Pl. du Château* ☎ *06–75–05–72–19*) has an unusually good selection of AOC (Appellation d'Origine Contrôlée) Provençal olive oils, most of which are difficult if not impossible to find outside France.

ROUSSILLON

★ *14 km (9 mi) southeast of Gordes, 43 km (27 mi) southeast of Avignon.*

GETTING HERE

The Cavaillon-Roussillon bus runs twice a day, morning and night, and costs €4.30. The only other way to arrive in Roussillon is by car from the D4. There's also a daily bus from Cavaillon to Bonnieux (€2), with stops at Lacoste and Menerbes (€1.50).

VISITOR INFORMATION

Roussilon Tourist Office (⊠ *Pl. de la Poste* ☎ *04–90–05–60–25* ⊕ *www.roussillon-provence.com*).

EXPLORING

A rich vein of ocher runs through the earth of Roussillon, occasionally breaking the surface in Technicolor displays of russet, deep rose, garnet, and flaming orange. Roussillon is a mineral showcase, perched above a pocket of red-rock canyonlands that are magically reflected in the stuccoes applied on every building in town, where the hilltop cluster of houses blends into the red-ocher cliffs from which their stones were first quarried. The ensemble of buildings and jagged, hand-cut slopes are equally dramatic, and views from the top look over a landscape of artfully eroded bluffs that Georgia O'Keeffe would have loved.

Old as the Hills

Since the cave paintings of Lascaux, man has extracted ocher from the earth, using its extraordinary palette of colors to make the most of nature's play between earth and light. Grounded in these earth-based pigments, the frescoes of Giotto and Michelangelo glow from within, and the houses of Tuscany and Provence seem to draw color from the land itself—and to drink light from the sky. Says Barbara Barrois of the Conservatoire des Ocres et Pigments Appliqués at Roussillon, "Ça vibre à l'oeil!" (literally, "It vibrates to your eyes").

The rusty hues of iron hydroxide are the source of all this luminosity, intimately allied with the purest of clays. Extracted from the ground in chunks and washed to separate it from its quartz-sand base, it is ground to fine powder and mixed as a binder with chalk and sand. Applied to the stone walls of Provençal houses, this ancient blend gives the region its quintessential repertoire of warm yellows and golds, brick, sienna, and umber.

In answer to the acrylic imitations slathered on new constructions in garish shades of hot pink and canary yellow (following a Côte d'Azur trend), there is an ocher revival under way, thank goodness.

Unlike neighboring hill villages, there's little of historic architectural detail here; the pleasure of a visit lies in the richly varied colors that change with the light of day, and in the views of the contrasting countryside, where dense-shadowed greenery sets off the red stone with Cézannesque severity. There are pleasant *placettes* (tiny squares) to linger in nonetheless, and a Renaissance fortress tower crowned with a clock from the 19th century; just past it, you can take in expansive panoramas of forest and ocher cliffs.

Choose from local flavors such as *calisson d'Aix* (almond candy), *pain d'épice,* and melon at the ice-cream shop and café of **L'Ocrier** (⊠*Les Ocres, av. Burlière* ☎04–90–05–79–53) before wandering through the village or taking the *sentier* (hiking path) to explore the cliffs.

This famous vein of natural ocher, which spreads some 25 km (15½ mi) along the foot of the Vaucluse plateau, has been mined for centuries. You can visit the old **Usine Mathieu de Roussillon** *(Roussillon's Mathieu Ochre Works)* to learn more about ocher's extraction and its modern uses; though it has long since been closed as a mine, it functions today as the Conservatoire des Ocres et Pigments Appliqués (Conservatory of Ochers and Applied Pigments). There are explanatory exhibits, ocher powders for sale, and guided tours in English with advance request. ⊠*On D104 southeast of town* ☎04–90–05–66–69 ☉*Daily 9–7.*

WHERE TO EAT & STAY

$$$ ⊞ **Le Clos de la Glycine.** This newish hotel combines modern comforts (an elevator, air-conditioning) with Provençal tradition, though the decor is still too fresh to have acquired the patina found in more established places. The most desirable rooms have terraces with views of the ocher cliffs, a panorama shared by the terrace of Restaurant David,

which plays to a full house in summer with dishes such as fish of the day in spider-crab juice with calamari pieces, and roasted rabbit with rosemary and ricotta gnocci. **Pros:** perfect for sunrise views; easy-walking distance to town. **Cons:** menus start at €33; not a great Web site. ⊠*Pl. de la Poste,* ☎*04–90–05–60–13* ⊕*www.luberon-hotel.com* ⌂*9 rooms* ⌂*In-room: refrigerator, Wi-Fi. In-hotel: restaurant, bar, parking, some pets allowed* ⊟*AE, MC, V.*

CAVAILLON

15 km (9½ mi) north of Salon de Provence, 16 km (10 mi) southeast of Avignon.

Geographically, Cavaillon is a great place to use as a base of operations—this is a good spot for bus and train connections. It's also known as one of the biggest agricultural market towns in France and is famous for its honey-scented melons. At one point in history, Cavaillon had the largest Jewish population in the papal enclave, but after the Revolution the majority of Cavaillon's Jews moved to the bigger cities of Provence.

What does remain of the Jewish legacy is a beautiful **synagogue** with its own museum on Rue Hébraïque. Tours can be booked through the Cavaillon tourist office. ⊠*6 rue Hébraïque* ☎*04–90–76–00–34* ☉*May–Oct., Wed.–Mon., 9:30–12:30 and 2:30–6:30; Nov.–Apr., Mon., Wed.–Sat. 9–12 and 2–5* ☑*€3.*

OPPÈDE-LE-VIEUX

25 km (15½ mi) southeast of Avignon, 15 km (9 mi) southwest of Gordes.

Heading toward Apt on D22 out of Avignon, follow signs right into the vineyards, toward Oppède. You'll occasionally be required to follow signs for Oppède-le-Village, but your goal will be marked with the symbol of *monuments historiques:* Oppède-le-Vieux. A Byronesque tumble of ruins arranged against an overgrown rocky hillside, Oppède's charm—or part of it—lies in its preservation. Taken over by writers and artists who choose to live here and restore but not develop it, the village offers a café or two but little more.

Cross the village square, pass through the old city gate, and climb up steep trails (beware hidden holes and precarious stairs) past restored houses to the church known as **Notre-Dame-d'Alydon.** First built in the 13th century, its blunt buttresses were framed into side chapels in the 16th century; you can still see the points of stoned-in Gothic windows above. The marvelous hexagonal bell tower sprouts a lean, mean gargoyle from each angle. It once served as part of the village's fortifications; the views from the plateau it dominates overlook the broad valley toward Ménerbes.

You can also clamber up to the ruins of the **château,** first built in the 13th century, then lorded over by Baron d'Oppède, who laid waste to the Waldensians, and then transformed in the 15th century. From the left side of its great square tower, look down into the dense fir forests of the Luberon's north face. Just outside town is the **Sentier Vigneron d'Oppède,** a long hiking trail through vineyards and olive groves and lined with descriptive plaques.

MÉNERBES

5 km (3 mi) east of Oppède-le-Vieux, 30 km (19 mi) southeast of Avignon.

As you drive along D188 between Oppède and Ménerbes, the rolling rows of grapevines are punctuated by stone farmhouses. But something is different. These farmhouses have electric gates, tall arborvitae hedges, and swimming pools. Peter Mayle isn't the only outsider to have vacationed here and contrived to stay.

The town of Ménerbes itself clings to a long, thin hilltop over this sought-after valley, looming over the surrounding forests like a great stone ship. Plenty to see but it's all from the outside; most of the homes and sites here are private and closed to the public.

At its prow juts the **Castellet,** a 15th-century fortress.

At its stern rears up the 13th-century **citadelle.** These redoubtable fortifications served the Protestants well during the War of Religions—until the Catholics wore them down with a 15-month siege.

A campanile tops the Hôtel de Ville (Town Hall) on pretty **Place de l'Horloge** *(Clock Square),* where you can admire the delicate stonework on the arched portal and mullioned windows of a Renaissance house. Just past the tower on the right you'll reach an overlook taking in views towards Gordes, Roussillon, and Mont Ventoux.

But what you really came to see is **Peter Mayle's house,** right? Do its current owners a favor and give it a wide berth. After years of tour buses spilling the curious into the private driveway to crane their necks and snap pictures, the heirs to the stone picnic table, the pool, and Faustin's grapevines wish the books had never been written. And besides, Peter Mayle has moved now, to the other side of the mountain.

WHERE TO EAT & STAY

$$$ ★ ⊞ **Hostellerie Le Roy Soleil.** In the imposing shadow of the Luberon and the hilltop village of Ménerbes, this luxurious country inn has pulled out all stops on comfort and furnishings. (Think wrought-iron beds and marble and granite bathrooms.) But the integrity of its 17th-century building, with thick stone walls and groin vaults and beams, redeems it just short of pretentiousness (unlike the much more expensive La Bastide de Marie across town) and makes it a wonderful place to escape to. Sophisticated meals are served in the vaulted dining room but, in summer, no one can resist dining on the picture-perfect roofed patio facing the trees. **Pros:** three tennis courts close by; free parking. **Cons:** location may over compensate service; Web site has long been under construction. ⊠*Rte. des Beaumettes* ☎*04–90–72–25–61*

⊕*www.roy-soleil.com* ⊃9 *rooms, 9 suites, 3 apartments* ⊖*In-room: refrigerator, Wi-Fi. In-hotel: restaurant, bar, pool, parking, some pets allowed* ☐*AE, MC, V* ⊘*Closed Jan.–Feb.*

LACOSTE

7 km (4½ mi) east of Ménerbes, 37 km (23 mi) southeast of Avignon.

Like Ménerbes, gentrified hilltop Lacoste owes its fame to an infamous literary resident.

Little but jagged ruins remain of the once magnificent **Château de Sade,** where the Marquis de Sade (1740–1814) spent some 30 years of his life, mostly hiding out. Exploits both literary and real, judged obscene by various European courts, kept him in and out of prison despite a series of escapes. His mother-in-law finally turned him in to authorities, and he was locked away in the Paris Bastille, where he passed the time writing stories and plays. Written during his time in the Bastille, *120 journées de Sodome (120 Days of Sodom)* featured a Black Forest château suspiciously similar in form and design to his Lacoste home. The once-sumptuous château was destroyed with particular relish in the Revolution but for some years, the wealthy Paris couturier Pierre Cardin has been restoring the castle wall by wall. Under his generous patronage the **Festival Lacoste** takes place here throughout the month of July. A lyric, musical, and theatrical extravaganza, events (and their dates) change yearly, ranging from outdoor poetry recitals to ballet to colorful operettas. Lacoste has a few lodging options, the oldest of which is Le Café de France. ⊠*Carrière du Château* ☎*04–90–75–93–12* ⊕*www. festivaldelacoste.com* ✉*Festival performances: €60–€150.*

BONNIEUX

★ *5 km (3 mi) southeast of Lacoste, 42 km (26 mi) southeast of Avignon.*

VISITOR INFORMATION
Bonnieux Tourist Office (⊠7 pl. Carnot84480 ☎04–90–75–91–90 ⊕www. bonnieux.com).

The most impressive of the Luberon's hilltop villages, Bonnieux (pronounced Bun-*yer*) rises out of the arid hills in a jumble of honey-color cubes that change color subtly as the day progresses. Strewn along D36, the village is wrapped in crumbling ramparts and dug into bedrock and cliff. Most of its sharply raked streets take in wide-angle valley views, though you'll get the best view from the pine-shaded grounds of the 12th-century **Église Vieille du Haut,** reached by stone steps that wind past tiny niche houses. Shops, galleries, cafés, and fashionable restaurants abound here, but they don't dominate. It's possible to lose yourself in a back *ruelle* (small street) most of the year. If you have a car, you're in luck—to every point of the compass, there are lovely drives from Bonnieux threading out through Le Petit Luberon. Of the four, the best is the eastward course, along the D943 and D113, which leads to the Romanesque ruins of the Prieuré de St-Symphorien.

WHERE TO EAT & STAY

$$$ ✕**Le Fournil.** In a natural grotto deep in stone, lighted by candles and arty torchères, this restaurant would be memorable even without its trendy decor touches (new red floors to contrast the contemporary white linens) and stylishly presented Provençal cuisine. There are enticing three-course lunch (€27) and dinner (€41) menus but add adventurous dishes such as tomato-crisped pigs'-feet *galette* (patty), subtle seafood, an informed wine list, and the option of sitting on the terrace by the fountain, and you have an experience to note in your travel diary. ⊠*5 pl. Carnot* ☎*04–90–75–83–62* ▤*MC, V* ☾*Closed Mon. and Tues. during off-season; Mon. and Tues. lunch during summer; mid-Nov.–mid-Dec. and mid-Jan.–mid-Feb.*

$$$$ ▨**Auberge de l'Aiguebrun.** An anti-perched village experience, this rustic former relais postale is set deep in the valley among walking paths and endless greenery. The soft and simple decor of the rooms, with private toilette and bath, equals the tranquillity offered by the location. The small cabins, equipped with showers, are less expensive and situated just beyond the garden with access by car. And although the village is only a 10-minute drive, you'll probably end up eating most of your meals here after a taste of owner-chef Francis Motta's exquisite dishes. **Pros:** dream for nature lovers; breakfast included for double rooms. **Cons:** toilets in cabins separated by shutters (not in a different room); small towels. ⊠*Domaine de la Tour, RD 943* ☎*04–90–04–47–00* ⊕*www.aubergedelaiguebrun.fr* ⊷*7 rooms, 4 cabins* ㅿ*In-room: no a/c (some), TV (some), no refrigerator. In-hotel: restaurant, bar, pool, Wi-Fi, parking, some pets allowed* ▤*AE, MC, V* ☾*Closed Jan.–mid-Mar.*

$$ ▨**Le Clos du Buis.** At this Gîtes de France B&B, whitewash and quarry
★ tiles, lovely tiled baths, and carefully juxtaposed antiques create a regional look in the guest rooms. Relaxed, homey public spaces, with scrubbed floorboards, a fireplace, and exposed stone, invite you to hang around barefoot, like lodgers or weekend guests. It even has a pool and a pretty garden, and it overlooks the valley from the village center. **Pros:** full access to kitchen to cook or keep stock in fridge; plenty of restaurants within easy walking distance. **Cons:** parking is difficult. ⊠*Rue Victor Hugo* ☎*04–90–75–88–48* ⊕*www.leclosdubuis. com* ⊷*8 rooms* ㅿ*In-room: no refrigerator, no TV, Wi-Fi. In-hotel: pool, parking* ▤*MC, V* ☾*Closed mid-Nov.–mid-Dec. and first wk of Jan.–Feb.*

BUOUX

8 km (5 mi) northeast of Bonnieux, 9 km (5½ mi) south of Apt.

To really get into backcountry Luberon, crawl along serpentine single-lane roads below Apt, past orchards and lavender fields studded with bories. Deeply ensconced in the countryside, the tiny hamlet of Buoux (pronounced Bu-*ooks*) offers little more than a hotel and a café, sheltered by white brush-carpeted cliffs. If you squint, you can just make out the dozens of rock-climbers dangling, spiderlike, from slender cables along the cliff face.

An even tinier road can take you to the **Fort de Buoux,** the ruins of an ancient village and a fortification that has defended the valley since Ligurian and Roman times. Several houses and an entire staircase were chiseled directly into the stone; it's uncertain whether they're prehistoric or medieval. Louis XIV dismantled the ancient fortifications in the 17th century, leaving Turneresque ruins to become overgrown with wild box and ivy. ☎ *04–90–74–25–75* *€3* *Daily sunrise–sunset, except when weather is bad.*

WHERE TO EAT & STAY

¢ ★ **Auberge des Seguins.** Delve deep into this romantic valley to find this fabulous hideaway, at the foot of an imposing white-rock cliff. The *dortoires* (shared public bunk rooms) and simple tile-and-stucco rooms make it a terrific retreat for families, hikers, and rock-climbers. Better yet, meals at the restaurant are several cuts above summer-camp chow. As the owner is passionately Provençal, he insists on fresh regional food. This is where the French come for reunions and weekends with friends, to lounge in lawn chairs or dip in the stream-fed swimming pool. In high season, make a dining reservation ahead of time. Half-board is mandatory for overnight stays. **Pros:** great location for hikers and bikers; French immersion program offered. **Cons:** no à la carte; children's rates are for ages seven and under. ✉ *3 km (2 mi) below downtown Buoux,* ☎ *04–90–74–16–37* *www.aubergedesseguins.com* *27 rooms, 20 bunks* *In-room: no a/c, no phone. In-hotel: restaurant, bar, pool, Wi-Fi, parking, some pets allowed* *MC, V* *Closed mid.-Nov.–Feb.* *BP.*

SAIGNON

15 km (9 mi) northeast of Buoux, 5 km (3 mi) southeast of Apt.

Set on the Plateau de Claparédes and draped just below the crest of an arid hillside covered with olive groves, lavender, and stone farms, Saignon is an appealing hill town anchored by a heavyset Romanesque church. Neat cobbled streets wind between flower-festooned stone houses and surround a central *placette* (small square) with a burbling fountain. Yes, it's been gentrified with a few boutiques and restaurants, but the escapist feel hasn't been erased.

WHERE TO EAT & STAY

$–$$ **Auberge du Presbytère.** Three stone houses on the village's central *place* join to make this graceful inn. Their country roots show in the exposed rafters, vaulted ceilings, weathered quarry tiles, and blue-shuttered windows. One bargain room has a bathroom down the hall; another offers spectacular valley views from a private terrace. Generally, the rooms are pretty, cool, and accented with lovely bursts of color. The restaurant (closed Wednesday) aims high with a pair of regional menus, including vegetarian dishes. **Pros:** delightful garden terrace; excellent bakery steps away for breakfast. **Cons:** menus start at €28—no à la carte; small windows in some of the rooms. ⊠*Pl. de la Fontaine,* ☎*04–90–74–11–50* ⊕*www.auberge-presbytere.com* ⇌*16 rooms* ⌂*In-room: no TV, Wi-Fi. In-hotel: restaurant, bar, some pets allowed* ⊟*MC, V* ☉*Closed Dec.–Jan.*

APT

40 km (25 mi) east of Avignon.

Actively ugly from a distance, with a rash of modern apartment blocks and industrial buildings, Apt doesn't attract the tourism it deserves. Its central Old Town, with tight, narrow stone streets shaded with noble stone houses and strings of fluttering laundry, seethes with activity. The best time to visit is Saturday, when the town buzzes with a vibrant Provençal market, selling crafts, clothing, carpets, jewelry, and—not incidentally—all the finest food products of the Luberon and Haut Provence.

EN ROUTE Between Apt and Lourmarin, the *départemental* road D943 winds dramatically through deep backcountry, offering the only passage over the spine of the Luberon. Bone-dry and bristling with scrub oak, pine, coarse broom, and wild lavender, it's a landscape reminiscent of Greece or Sicily. If you climb into the hills, you won't get views; this is landlocked, isolated terrain, but it's wildly beautiful.

WHERE TO EAT & STAY

$$$$ 🏨 **Le Domaine des Andéols.** In a complete departure from Provençal chic, this collection of cubic houses, which recently joined the Alain Ducasse group, immerses guests in a contemporary environment—each individually decorated house contains works by top designers and artists. Wildest is the Maison du Voyageur, with its stuffed tiger, zebra skin, and antler sculpture, while the Maison des Lointains has a barbed-wire chandelier, suggestive black-and-white photos, and a stone bath in each room. You can sip an aperitif accompanied by delicious house nibbles on your own terrace before venturing down to the restaurant, where a young Ducasse-trained chef concocts a set menu that changes daily. From the swimming pool and the dramatic stepped garden patios, admire dramatic views of the countryside; there is also an indoor pool should the mistral (fierce wind) strike. What really makes this place special, though, is the staff in their flowing white clothes, who seem to anticipate your every need. **Pros:** very trendy setting; stunning infinity pool. **Cons:** breakfast €22; rooms not available until 4 PM. ⊠*St-Saturnin-lès-Apt* ☎*04–90–75–50–63* ⊕*www.domainedesandeols.com* ⇌*10 houses* ⌂*In-room: kitchen, a/c (some). In-hotel: restaurant, bar, pools, spa, Wi-Fi, parking, some pets allowed* ⊟*AE, MC, V* ☉*Closed Dec.–Feb.*

LOURMARIN

12 km (7 mi) southeast of Bonnieux, 54 km (33 mi) southeast of Avignon.

VISITOR INFORMATION
Lourmarin Tourist Office (✉ *9 av. Philippe de Girard, 84160* ☎*04–90–68–10–77* ⊕ *www.lourmarin.com*).

The highly gentrified village of Lourmarin lies low-slung in the hollow of the Luberon's south face, a sprawl of manicured green. Albert Camus loved this place from the moment he discovered it in the 1930s. After he won his Nobel prize in 1957 he bought a house here and lived in it until his death in 1960 (he is buried in the village cemetery).

Loumarin's Renaissance-era **Château** is its main draw, privately restored in the 1920s to appealing near-perfection. Of the old wing (15th century) and the new (begun in 1526 and completed in 1540), the latter is prettiest, with a broad-ranging art collection, rare old furniture, and ornate stone fireplaces—including one with exotic *vases canopes* (ancient Egyptian figure vases). In summer, the château hosts concerts. ☎*04–90–68–15–23* ▭*€5.50* ⊘*May, June, and Sept., daily 10:30–11:30 and 2:30–5:30; July and Aug., daily 10–6; Mar., Apr., and Oct., daily 10:30–11:30 and 2:30–4:30; Nov., Dec., and Feb., daily 10:30–11:30 and 2:30–4; Jan. closed except 2:30–4 on weekends (may vary with daylight).*

WHERE TO STAY

$ ▦ **Villa Saint Louis.** In a town as gentrified as Lourmarin, it's surprising to find such a bargain as this B&B set in a 17th-century house replete with antiques and enclosed garden. Mme. Lassalette bought this former post house nearly 20 years ago, and her decorator husband made the interior look as though it hadn't changed in centuries—the house has been featured in decorating magazines worldwide. Rabbits run free in the grassy garden, where breakfast (included in the price) is sometimes served. There is no pool, but guests have been known to cool off their feet in the fountain. **Pros:** attractive price includes breakfast; shared fridge. **Cons:** no credit cards; if you're allergic, be warned—Madame's cat wanders around freely. ✉*35 rue Henri de Savornin* ☎*04–90–68–39–18* ⊕*www.villasaintlouis.com* ▭*5 rooms* ⌂*In-room: no a/c, Wi-Fi. In-hotel: parking, some pets allowed* ▭*No credit cards* ⦿*BP.*

Aix, Marseille & the Central Coast

AUBAGNE, CASSIS & THE ILES D'HYÈRES

Outdoor fish market, Old Port, Marseille

WORD OF MOUTH

"Ah, complicated Marseille—its reputation was already a bit fishy for me, and movies like the French Connection didn't exactly help. But what about the restoration of some seriously stunning architecture, the welcoming smiles of the people, and the TGV from Paris? Marseille is a study in contrasts. So maybe, then, it's best to be surprised—kind of like when you eat that first steaming spoonful of savory bouillabaisse."

—Cheyne

WELCOME TO AIX, MARSEILLE & THE CENTRAL COAST

Produce market, Aix-en-Provence

TOP REASONS TO GO

★ **Aix's extraordinary Cours Mirabeau:** The "Champs-Elysées" of posh Aix-en-Provence, this boulevard is lined with lovely cafés like Les Deux Garçons, where the espressos are as good as they were when it opened in 1792.

★ **Go fishing for Marseille's best bouillabaisse:** Order ahead at Chez Fon-Fon's and indulge in classic bouillabaisse—this version will practically make your tastebuds stand up and sing "La Marseillaise."

★ **Become a Calanques castaway:** Near Cassis, these picturesque coves make you feel like you've stumbled onto a set of The Blue Lagoon.

★ **Paul Cézanne, Superstar:** Tour Cézanne Country in the area around Montaigne Ste-Victoire, outside the artist's hometown of Aix-en-Provence.

★ **Iles d'Hyéres, nature's paradise:** In season the cell phone rings as tourists arrive en masse but the sense of pure escape can still be enjoyed on these islands covered with pine forests.

1 **Aix-en Provence.** Join all those fashionable folk for whom café-squatting, people-watching, and boutique shopping are a way of life in Aix-en-Provence for one day, then track the spirit of its most famous homeboy, Paul Cézanne. Head into the countryside to visit the Jas de Bouffon, his newly opened family estate, and **Montaigne Ste-Victoire,** the main "motif" of the founder of modern art.

2 **Marseille.** France's second largest city, Marseille is the place to head to enjoy the colorful sights and smells of a Mediterranean melting pot, where different people have mingled ever since the Greeks invaded about 600 BC. Tour its cathedrals and museums, visit its **Vieux Port,** famous haunt of Pagnol's Fanny, then head east to **Aubagne** to walk its Circuit Pagnol.

3 **Cassis & the Calanques.** From Cassis—a lovely harbor town that conjures up the St-Tropez of 1940—take an excursion boat to the famously beautiful Calanques coves: enjoy a picnic and a chilled bottle of Cassis white and clamber down the steep sides to the hidden golden beaches and fjord-like finger bays that probe the coastline.

Self portrait of Paul Cézanne

4 Iles d'Hyéres. Not far
from the big city lights of
Toulon are the idyllic Iles
d'Hyéres: the **Ile des Porquerolles, Ile du Levant,** and
Ile de Port-Cros. Porquerolles, the largest of the
islands, is almost the real-
ization of a film producer's
idea of the Garden of Eden,
but today's would-be Adam
and Eves can now enjoy
chic resorts.

GETTING ORIENTED

Rough-hewn and fiercely
beautiful, this is the
sculpted land of Cézanne
and Pagnol: from a coast-
line of lonely pine-studded
cliffs and enchanting
calanque coves to neat
rows of touristy striped
sun beds and seafood
platters served with a
saucy comment in the
local patois. Sophisticated
and posh Aix-en-Provence
stands carefully aloof
from Marseille, tough,
vibrant, and larger-than-
life. Yet the backcountry
between them ambles
along at a 19th-century
pace of boules, pastis,
and country markets.

AIX, MARSEILLE & CENTRAL COAST PLANNER

Transportation Basics

Public transport in Marseille, Aix, and the Central Coast is very well organized, with most areas accessible by plane, train, bus, or boat.

Flying in is a good option, as Marseille has on of the largest airports in France and regular flights come in from Paris and London.

The Toulon-Hyéres airport is much smaller but also has frequent flights.

If you prefer the more scenic route, note that the high-speed TGV trains go directly to Marseille, Aix-en-Provence, and Toulon in about the same time as a flight, and a big selection of local and regional trains will take you to the towns along the central coast.

There is a moderately good network of buses run by a large number of independent bus companies but check with the local tourism offices for the one you need since the "who's who" in the bus world here is confusing.

If driving, get a good map, as the road signs are often as clear as mud, especially off the main autoroute (toll highway).

Finding a Place to Stay

Accommodations in the area range from luxury villas to modest city-center hotels. This is no longer just converted *mas* (farmhouse) country. Nonetheless, hotels in this region favor Provençal flavor and aim to provide outdoor space at its loveliest, from gardens where breakfast is served to parasol pine-shaded pools. The bigger cities will always have somewhere to stay, but the good and reputable hotels book up quickly at certain times of the year. June, July, and August are considered to be high season, so reserve ahead of time. In the larger cities, particularly Marseille, be careful to note where your hotel is located because, even if the hotel is deluxe, there are unsavory neighborhoods that can make for an unpleasant, if not downright scary, stay (especially at night).

Yours for the Basking

Wherever there's water in France, *les plages* (beaches) of every shape and substance fill up with sun lovers from June to September. The most popular beach resort is Bandol, but for a quieter retreat, head for genteel Cassis, where you can perch on rocky promontories along the *calanques* (coves). The shipbuilding port town of La Ciotat has the most sandy beach surface at the Clos des Plages, situated just beyond the pleasure-boat port.

DINING & LODGING PRICES IN EUROS				
¢	$	$$	$$$	$$$$
Restaurants				
Under €13	€14–€19	€20–€24	€25–€31	Over €32
Hotels				
Under €55	€56–€85	€86–€135	€136–€200	Over €201

Restaurant prices are per person for a main course at dinner, including tax (19.6%) and service; note that if a restaurant offers only prix-fixe (set-price) meals, it has been given the price category that reflects the full prix-fixe price. Hotel prices are for a standard double room in high season, including tax (19.6%) and service charge.

Bon Appétit

One eats late in Provence: rarely before 1 PM for lunch (and you can happily find yourself still at the table at 4 PM) and 8 to 9 PM for dinner: Be prepared for somewhat disdainful looks—"tourists!"—and slow responses if you try to come any earlier.

Most restaurants close between lunch and dinner, even in the summer, and no matter how much you are willing to spend or how well dressed you are, you will be firmly turned away.

If you are craving an afternoon glass of rosé *bien frais* and a light snack, head to one of the smaller beach or roadside sandwich kiosks, and/or the local *boulangerie* (bakery), which usually has a selection of fresh treats.

The more intrepid sort can try a slice of Provençal life and brave one of the smoky, lottery playing, coffee-and-pastis drinking *tabacs* that line every main street in the South. You'll find they also often have basic fare for a reasonable price.

Making the Most of Your Time

This is an area that moves a little faster than traditional Provence, since the main hubs of Marseille, Aix-en-Provence, and Toulon are large cities, but the average day still includes a two-hour lunch.

Take care, the time to enjoy an afternoon stroll, a long lunch, a little siesta—because this is, fundamentally, what makes living in Provence so charmingly worthwhile. And even if the cities are, well, cities, you'll note that much of general life comes to a halt between midday and two, so plan accordingly.

Keep your sense of humor intact and learn the Gallic shrug (a typical shoulder movement that can mean anything from "I don't know" to "I really don't care") when you are politely refused service because you are late (or too early); it's a different mentality, one focused on the quality of life for everyone and emphasizing the value of taking the time to dwell on the important things.

To really take advantage of the area, start your trip in a large and vibrant city center like Marseille. From here you can spiral out to Aix, Aubagne, and the coast with ease via train, car, or bus. If you want a chic and delightful mix of urban chic and countrytown beauty, though, Aix-en-Provence can't be beat for a kick-off point.

How's the Weather?

High season falls between Easter and October, but if you come in the winter you may be pampered with warm sun and cool breezes. When the mistral attacks (and it can happen year-round), it channels all its forces down the Rhône Valley and blasts into Marseille like a one-way tornado. But, happily, the assault may last only one day. This is not the day, however, to opt for a boat ride from Cassis or Porquerolles; aim instead for the sheltered streets of Aix.

Main Regional Tourist Offices

The regional tourist office, the Comité Départemental du Tourisme du Var, has extensive documentation on lodging, restaurants, rentals, hikes, and attractions in Var. The same is true for the Comité Départemental du Tourisme des Bouches-du-Rhône.

Comité Régional du Tourisme de Provence-Alpes-Côte d'Azur (✉ *12 pl. Joliette, Marseille* ☎ *04–91–56–47–00* ⊕ *www. crt-paca.fr*). **Comité Départemental du Tourisme du Var** (✉ *1 bd. Maréchal Foch, Draguignan* ☎ *04–94–50–55–50*). **Comité Départemental du Tourisme des Bouches-du-Rhône** (✉ *13 rue Roux de Brignole, Marseille* ☎ *04–91–13–84–13* ⊕ *www. visitprovence.com*).

GETTING AROUND PLANNER

By Air

Marseille has one of the largest airports in France, the Aéroport de Marseille Provence in Marignane, about 20 km (12 mi) northwest of the city center. Regular flights come in daily from Paris and London. In summer Delta Airlines flies direct from New York to Nice (about 190 km [118 mi] from Marseille and about 150 km [93 mi] from Toulon). Airport shuttle buses to Marseille center leave every 20 minutes 4:30 AM–12:10 PM daily (€8.50). Shuttles to Aix leave hourly 8 AM–11:10 PM (€8). For schedules see ⊕ *www. navettemarseilleaeroport.com*.

Aéroport de Marseille Provence in Marignane (☎ *04–42– 14–14–14* ⊕ *www.marseille.aero port.fr*).

Sea for Yourself

If you find yourself without a yacht on this lovely coastline, it's easy to jump on a tourist cruiser, whether you putter from calanque to calanque between Marseille and Cassis or commute to the car-free Iles d'Hyères. Many boats are glass-bottomed for underwater viewing, and most allow you to climb onto the top deck and face the wind as the cruiser bucks the waves.

By Bus

A good network of private bus services (confusingly called *cars*) strikes out from Marseille's *gare routière* (bus station), adjacent to the Metro Gare St-Charles train station, and carries you to points not served by train. Tickets costs €1.60 and multiple ticket carnets are available.

From Marseille, buses link many destinations, including Aix-en-Provence (€5, 1 hour, leaving every half hour), Nice (€26.50, 3 hrs, serviced by Phocéens Cars, 5 buses daily), Cassis (€4.60 1½ hrs, every 20 minutes), Carpentras (€14, 2 hrs, 3 buses daily), Cavaillon (€10.50, 1 hr, 3 buses daily), and Avignon (€18.60, 2 hrs, 7 buses daily).

As for Aix-en-Provence, it has a dense network of bus excursions from its station.

To/from destinations include Marseille (€4.60, 1 hr, every 20 minutes), Arles (€10, 1½ hrs, two to five daily), and Avignon (€14, 1½ hrs, two to four daily).

C.A.P. (Compagnie Autocars de Provence) makes daily forays from 2 to 7 into Marseille, the Calanques of Cassis, Les Baux, the Luberon, and Arles, departing in front of the tourist office, at the foot of Cours Mirabeau. Two Web sites that provide in-depth info on bus travel are ⊕ *www.beyond.fr* and ⊕ *www.lepilote.com*.

Aix-en-Provence has a municipal bus that services the entire town and outlying suburbs (such as Jas de Bouffon). A ticket costs €1.10 and you can get a carnet of 10 or a one-day pass (€7.30).

There is a navette shuttlebus that connects La Rotonde/ Cours Mirabeau with the bus and train station, as well as one that heads out to the TGV station (departing from bus station), which is some 8 km (13 mi) west of town, and the Marseille-Provence airport.

Bus Information Aix-en-Bus (⊠ *Pl. du Général du Gaulle* ☎ *04–42–26–37–28* ⊕ *www.aixenbus.com*). **Aix-en-Provence's** *gare routière* (*bus station* ⊠ *Av. de la Europe* ☎ *04–42–91–26–80*). **Marseille's** *gare routière* (*bus station* ⊠ *3 pl. Victor Hugo* ☎ *04–91–08–16–40*). **C.A.P** (*Compagnie Autocars de Provence* ☎ *04–42–97–52–10* ⊕ *www.beyond.fr*). **Phocéens Cars** (☎ *04–93–89–41–45*).

By Train

The high-speed TGV *Méditerranée* line ushered in a new era in *Trains à Grande Vitesse* (or "Trains at Great Speed") travel in France; the route (lengthened last year from the old terminus, Valence, in Haute Provence) means that you can travel from Paris's Gare de Lyon to Marseille in a mere three hours. Not only is the idea of Provence as a day trip now possible (though, of course, not advisable), you can even whisk yourself there directly upon arrival at Paris's Charles de Gaulle airport.

After the main line of the TGV divides at Avignon, the southeast-bound link takes in Aix-en-Provence, Marseille, Toulon, and the Côte d'Azur city of Nice. There is also frequent service by daily local trains to other towns in the region from these main TGV stops. With high-speed service now connecting Aix, Nîmes, Avignon, and Marseille, travelers without cars will find a Provence itinerary much easier to pull off. For full information on the TGV *Méditerranée*, log onto the TGV Web site; you can purchase tickets on this Web site or through RailEurope, and you should always buy your TGV tickets in advance. It's also easy to take a night train from Paris and wake up in Marseille. From Marseille it's a brief jaunt up to Aix. The main rail line also continues from Marseille to Toulon.

Aix has train routes to Marseille (€6.70 30 minutes, 44 trains daily), Nice (€35, 5½ hrs, eight trains daily), and Cannes (€32, 5½ hrs, eight trains daily), along with other destinations. Marseille has train routes to Aix-en-Provence (€6.70, 30 minutes, 44 trains daily), Avignon (€17.60, 1 hour, hourly), Nîmes (€25, 1½ hours), Arles (€13, 1 hour), and Orange (€20.80, 1½ hour). Once in Marseille, you can link up with the coastal train route with links all the resort towns lining the coast eastward to Monaco and Menton. You can also catch trains to Cassis, Bandol, Aubagne, and Toulon. One Web site that provides in-depth info on train travel is ⊕ *www.beyond.fr*. Another is ⊕ *www.voyages-sncf.com*.

Marseille boasts a Metro system. Most of the two metro lines service the suburbs, but several stops in the center city can help you get around quickly, including the main stop at Gare St-Charles, Colbert, Vieux Port, and Notre-Dame. A ticket costs €1.60, with multiple carnet tickets available.

Train Information **Aix-en-Provence's** *Gare SNCF* (*train station* ⊠ *Av. Victor Hugo* ☎ *04-91-08-16-40*). **Marseille's** *Gare St-Charles* (*train station* ☎ *04-91-08-16-40*). **SNCF** (☎ *08-36-35-35-35* ⊕ *www.ter-sncf.com/uk/paca*). **TGV** (☎ *877/284-8633* ⊕ *www.tgv.com*).

By Car

The A6/A7 toll expressway (*péage*) channels all traffic from Paris toward the south. At Orange, A7 splits to the southeast and leads directly to Aix. From there A51 leads to Marseille. Also at Aix, you can take A52 south via Aubagne to Cassis and A50, the coastal autoroute tollway. The Aix-Marseille-Toulon triangle is well served by a network of autoroutes with a confusing profusion of segmented number-names (A50, A51, A52, A55). Hang on to your map and follow the direction signs. As with any major metropolis, it pays to think hard before driving into Marseille: if you want to visit only the port neighborhoods, it may be easier to make a day trip by train.

However, you'll need to drive to visit the smaller ports and bays outside the center. To approach downtown Marseille, try to aim for the A51 that dovetails down from Aix; it plops you conveniently near the Vieux Port, while A55 crawls through industrial dockside traffic. The autoroute system collapses inconveniently just at Toulon, forcing you to drive right through jammed downtown traffic. Beautiful backroads between Aix, Marseille, and Aubagne carry you through Cézanne and Pagnol country; the N96 between Aix and Aubagne is worth skipping the freeway for. The D559 follows the coast, more or less scenically, from Marseille through Cassis to Hyères.

4

Updated by
Sarah Fraser

WHEN YOU CROSS THE IMAGINARY border into Provence for the first time, you may experience a niggling sense of déjà vu. The sun-drenched angular red rooftops, the dagger-narrow cypresses, the picture-perfect port towns, and the brooding massifs fire the imagination in a deep, soul-stirring way. And it's no wonder: Some of the world's greatest artists were inspired by the unforgettable landscapes found here. Cézanne colored his canvases in daubs of russet and black-green, the rough-cut structure of bluff and twisted pine inspiring a building-block approach to painting that for others jelled into Cubism. Marcel Pagnol painted pictures with words: the smells of thyme and rosemary crunching underfoot, the sounds of thunder rumbling behind rain-starved hills, the quiet joy of opening shutters at dawn to a chorus of blackbirds in the olive grove. Both Cézanne and Pagnol were native sons of this region east of the Rhône who were inspired to eloquence by the primordial landscape and its echoes of antiquity. And yet, like most who visit the region, they were equally fascinated with the modern Provençal world and its complex melding of the ancient with the new.

For here you'll find that the stylish, charming, 200-year-old village hotel will more often than not have Internet access. In the midst of the prettiest lavender field, you'll hear the chirp of cell phones almost as often as of cicadas. And, increasingly, the influx of *bon chic, bon genre* crowds looking for the newest Michelin-starred restaurant will eclipse the pastis-drinking knot of *pépés* at the local bar. Yet it will still be possible to find the idyllic Provence of old mixed in with all this newness—the local Monday morning market where sheep bells tonk behind ancient stone walls and rosy-cheeked *paysannes* proffer homemade cheese; the narrow, cobblestone streets riddled with local cafés and tinkling fountains and historic monuments; and some of the finest Roman ruins in Europe. No wonder the world continues beat a path here to seek out its understated wonders.

A visit to this region encompasses the best of urban culture, seaside, and arid backcountry. Aix is a small, manageable city with a leisurely pace, studded with stunning architecture and a lively concentration of arts, due in part to its active university life. Marseille offers the yang to Aix's yin. Its brash style, bold monuments, and spectacular sun-washed waterfront center are reminiscent of those of Naples or modern Athens; it is much maligned for its crime rate and big-city energy, and often unfairly neglected by visitors. Up in the dry inland hills, Pagnol's hometown of Aubagne gives a glimpse of local life, with a big farmers' market in the plane tree-lined town center and makers of *santons* (terra-cotta figurines) at every turn. Both the lovely port-village of Cassis and the busy beach town of Bandol allow time to watch the tides come and go, though for the ultimate retreat, take the boat that leaves for the almost tropical Iles d'Hyères. Like most of this region, these islands are a true idyll, but even more so since they are car-free.

EXPLORING AIX, MARSEILLE & THE CENTRAL COAST

Aix lies at a major crossroads of autoroutes: one coming in from Bordeaux and Toulouse, then leading up into the Alps toward Grenoble; the other a direct line from Lyons and Paris. Aix is extremely well placed for trips to the Luberon, Avignon, and Arles, and it's a quick half hour from Marseille. All the coastal towns line up for easy access between Marseille and Toulon, so you can cruise along A50, which follows the coastline, and take in all the sights. Although Marseille is one of the biggest cities in France, it's a matter of minutes before you're lost in deep backcountry on winding, picturesque roads that lead to Cassis or Aubagne and beyond.

To make the most of your time in this region, plan to divide your days between big-city culture, backcountry tours, and waterfront leisure. You can "do" Marseille in an impressive day trip, but its backstreets and tiny ports reward a more leisurely approach. Aix is as much a way of life as a city charged with tourist must-sees; allow time to hang out in a cours Mirabeau café and shop the backstreets. Aubagne must be seen on a market day (Tuesday, Saturday, or Sunday) to make the most of its charms. Cassis merits a whole day if you want to explore the calanques and enjoy a seaside lunch; Bandol is less appealing unless you're committed to beach time. The complete seaside experience, with rocky shoreline, isolated beaches, a picturesque port, and luxurious near-tropical greenery, can be found on the island of Porquerolles, one of the Iles d'Hyères; if your budget and schedule allow, spend a night or two in one of its few hotels and have much of the island to yourself.

AIX-EN-PROVENCE: CITY OF CÉZANNE

GETTING HERE & AROUND

The Aix TGV station is 10 km (6 mi) west of the city and is served by regular shuttle buses. The old Aix train station is on the slow Marseille–Sisteron line, with trains arriving roughly every hour from Marseille St-Charles. The center of Aix is best explored by foot, but there is a municipal bus service that serves the entire town and the outlying suburbs. Most leave from La Rotonde in front of the tourism office (☎04–42–16–11–61 ⊕www.aixenprovencetourism.com), where you can also buy tickets (€1.30 one way) and ask for a bus route map.

VISITOR INFORMATION

Aix-en-Provence Tourist Office (✉2 pl. du Général de Gaulle, B.P. 160, Cedex 1 ☎04–42–16–11–61 ⊕www.aixenprovencetourism.com).

EXPLORING

Longtime rival of edgier, more exotic Marseille, the lovely town of Aix-en-Provence (pronounced *ex*) is gracious, cultivated, and made all the more cosmopolitan by the presence of some 40,000 university students. In keeping with its aristocratic heritage, Aix quietly exudes well-bred suavity and elegance—indeed, it is now one of the ten richest townships in France. The influence and power it once had as the old capital

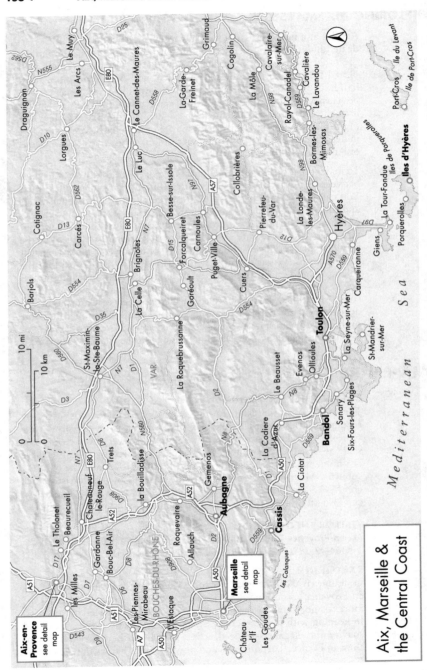

Aix, Marseille &
the Central Coast

of Provence—fine art, noble architecture, and graceful urban design—remain equally important to the city today. And, although it is true that Aix owns up to a few modern-day eyesores, the overall impression is one of beautifully preserved stone monuments, quietly sophisticated nightlife, leafy plane trees, and gently splashing fountains. With its thriving market, vibrant café life, spectacularly chic shops, and superlative music festival, it's one of the towns in Provence that really should not be missed.

The Romans were first drawn here by mild thermal baths, naming the town Aquae Sextiae (Waters of Sextius) in honor of Roman consul Sextius who defeated the Celto-Ligurians at Entremont in 122 BC; the remains of his camp lie just outside the city. In 142 BC the great Roman general Marius flanked and pinned 200,000 invading Germans against the mountain known ever since as Ste-Victoire. The name Marius is still popular in Provence today.

The fall of the Roman Empire saw a corresponding decline in Aix, although it remained significant enough to have its first cathedral built in the 5th century. Under the wise and generous guidance of Good King René in the 15th century, it became a center of Renaissance arts and letters. A poet himself and patron of the arts, the king encouraged a veritable army of artists to flourish here. The artists in turn gratefully left a handful of masterpieces, including Nicolas Froment's *Triptyque du Buisson Ardent* (*Burning Bush Triptych*) in the Cathédrale St-Sauveur. At the height of its political, judicial, and ecclesiastical power in the 17th and 18th centuries, Aix profited from a surge of private building, each *grand hôtel particulier* (mansion) meant to outdo its neighbor. The ring of boulevards, the *cours*, punctuated by great fountains and intriguing passageways, date from this time.

It was into this exalted elegance that artist Paul Cézanne (1839–1906) was born, though he drew much of his inspiration not from the city itself but from the raw countryside around it, often painting scenes of Montagne Ste-Victoire. A schoolmate of Cézanne's made equal inroads on modern society: the journalist and novelist Emile Zola (1840–1902) attended the Collège Bourbon with Cézanne and described their friendship as well as Aix itself in several of his works. You can sense something of the vibrancy that nurtured these two geniuses in the streets of modern Aix, not only charged by its large university population but continually injected with new blood from exchange programs: Vanderbilt, California State, Michigan, and Wisconsin all send students to this stimulating city. Aix is also home to a high-tech industry nexus that rivals Sophia Antipolis on the Côte d'Azur, with numerous research institutes and France's biggest appeals court outside Paris. There's also a British-American Institute and an American Center—in short, enough students and intellectuals to keep the crêperies and cafés crowded into the wee hours and to sustain a branch of The Gap.

It's not just the universities that keep Aix young: its famous Festival International d'Art Lyrique (International Opera Festival) has imported and created world-class opera productions as well as related concerts

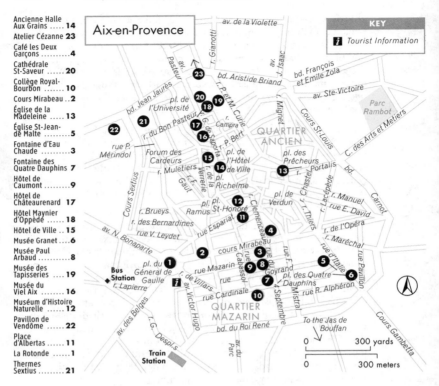

Aix-en-Provence

and recitals since 1948. Most of the performances take place in elegant, old Aix settings, and during this time the cafés, restaurants, and hotels spill over with the *beau monde* who've come to Aix especially for the July event.

THE HISTORIC HEART

The famous Cours Mirabeau, a broad, shady avenue that stretches from one grand fountain to another, bisects old Aix into two distinct neighborhoods. Below the Cours, the carefully planned Quartier Mazarin is lined with fine 17th- and 18th-century mansions. Above, the Old Town twists and turns from square to fountain square, each turn leading to another row of urban boutiques and another buzzing cluster of café tables. If you turn a blind eye to these enticing distractions, you can see the best of Aix in a day's tour—but you'll be missing the point. The music of the fountains, the theater of the café crowds, and the painterly shade of the plane trees are what Aix is all about.

A GOOD WALK

Begin at the tourist office, which anchors the Cours Mirabeau at Place du Général de Gaulle. The spiraling traffic, kiosks, newsstands, events posters, and crowds of students contrast sharply with **La Rotonde**, the monumental sculpture-fountain in black and white marble that towers above the swirl of modernity. Walk up the **Cours Mirabeau,** which is both the physical and social heart of the city. With vibrant café life to your left and grand old mansions to your right, you pass a series of fountains, including the magnificently mossy **Fontaine d'Eau Chaude** (which actually steams with thermal-spring water). At No. 55 are traces of the hat shop founded by Cézanne's father, now worn away by time: the sign still reads CHAPELLERIE DU COURS MIRABEAU, GROS ET DÉTAIL (Hat shop of the Cours Mirabeau, wholesale and retail). Cézanne himself hung out at the **Café les Deux Garçons,** the landmark café-restaurant that still serves gold-rimmed cups of espresso to artists and dreamers, all nowadays

> ### IT'S AN ILL WIND THAT BLOWS
>
> If you come to Provence in late autumn or early spring, bring your windbreaker. The infamous mistral is a bitterly cold, dry wind that comes sweeping down from the north whenever a low pressure weather system develops over the Mediterranean. The temperature can drop dramatically in just a matter of minutes. Many roads, fields, and towns have wind-breaks of closely planted trees or stone walls to give some shelter form these fierce winds, which, some say, often bring out irritable "mistral nerves" in the locals—one reason the Aixois have a reputation for being snappy.

armed with mobile phones. If you want to explore Cézanne sites in-depth, be sure to pick up the fabulous pamphlet, "In Cézanne's Footsteps" at the tourist office: it has all the details on the sites, linked together by the **Circuit Cézanne,** a series of brass plaques right on the sidewalks that mark the itinerary.

Now cut right down the lively market street Rue d'Italie and turn left at the **Église St-Jean-de-Malte,** once the chapel for a Knights of Malta priory and one of the earliest Gothic structures in France. Just across the way, the **Musée Granet,** to reopen in summer 2006 with a blockbuster show, "Cézanne in Provence," co-curated with the National Gallery of Art in Washington, D.C. Beyond its beautiful exterior, the museum houses a quite formidable collection of French art and archaeology. Follow Rue Cardinale to the heart of the elegant Quartier Mazarin, the city's 18th-century district: the **Fontaine des Quatre Dauphins,** a graceful obelisk framed by curving dolphins, which set off the patrician symmetry of the regal homes around it. Turn right up Rue du 4 Septembre (home to several spiffy antique shops) to the **Musée Paul Arbaud,** with its highly personal collection of faïence and regional books. Then continue west down Rue Goyrand to Rue Cabassol; No. 3 is the imposing **Hôtel de Caumont,** now home to the Conservatoire de Musique Darius-Milhaud. Head down Rue Cabassol (away from Cours Mirabeau) to Rue Cardinale, and you may see students of the Lycée Mignet crossing the courtyard of the former **Collège Royal-Bourbon,** just as alumni Cézanne and Zola once did.

Now head back up Rue Cabassol and cross Cours Mirabeau to enter the lovely labyrinth above it. Plunge straight in and veer left; on your right is the graceful **Place d'Albertas**, lined with fine old shuttered mansions. The **Muséum d'Histoire Naturelle**, with its collection of dinosaur fossils (including hundreds of eggs found on Ste-Victoire), is just behind you in the Hôtel Boyer d'Eguilles. Follow Rue Espariat to Place de Verdun, where the Palais de Justice looms over an antiques market held three times a week. Walk the length of the square and the adjoining Place des Prêcheurs to the **Église de la Madeleine**, where you'll find Barthélemy Van Eyck's *Annunciation*, a landmark in art history texts and one of the most famous paintings of the Franco-Netherlandish 15th-century school. Next wind your way back via Rue de Montigny to Place Richelme and the **Ancienne Halle aux Grains**, these days a post office. Walk around to the front and admire its allegorical frieze of the rivers Rhône and Durance. You're now on the gorgeous Place de l'Hôtel de Ville, often the setting for a flower market. Up and to the left stands the **Hôtel de Ville**, with its soaring, 15th-century clock tower.

Continue up Rue Gaston de Saporta to the **Musée du Vieil Aix**, which houses eclectic memorabilia from Aix's past, including a wonderfully fragile line of mechanical puppets that depict the Corpus Christi procession that was a staple of Aix's life every June until the 20th century. Just beyond it on the left is the **Hôtel de Châteaurenard**, where interesting trompe-l'oeil murals are concealed around a grand staircase; peek in, as it's a public building. Next door in the **Hôtel Maynier d'Oppède** is a French-language school; its courtyard is where concerts are held during the July opera festival. Across the street, the luxurious Palais de l'Archevêché (Bishop's Palace) houses the **Musée des Tapisseries**, containing a rich collection of Beauvais tapestries including a particularly lively series of scenes from *Don Quixote*; an open-air theater occupies its majestic courtyard during the summer. Next to it, the **Cathédrale St-Sauveur** provides a survey course in architectural history, from its 5th-century baptistery to its Gothic-Romanesque double nave, and shelters the magnificent *Triptyque du Buisson Ardent*.

You're not far now from the very last traces of the medieval ramparts that once surrounded this ancient city; they're just up from the cathedral and to the left. Continue past this old stone wall, and you'll reach an even older landmark: the **Thermes Sextius**, now a high-tech treatment center. Just behind, turn left along the busy Boulevard Jean-Jaurès and continue to the **Pavillon de Vendôme**, an extremely elegant 17th-century country house displaying regional furniture and art. From here, you may want to make a pilgrimage across the busy boulevard to the **Atelier Cézanne**, built by the artist when the beloved country house in which he worked was sold. Heading to the south of the city, the family estate of Cézanne, the **Jas de Bouffan**, recently opened to the public as part of the 2006 commemoration of the 100th anniversary of the painter's death. It is a quintessentially beautiful (and melancholy) Provençal house and park, immortalized in numerous canvases by Cézanne who spent his formative years here.

MAIN ATTRACTIONS

②③ Atelier Cézanne *(Cézanne Studio).*
Fodor'sChoice After the death of his mother forced
★ the sale of Paul Cézanne's beloved
country retreat known as Jas de
Bouffan, he had this studio built
just above the town center. In the
upstairs work space, the artist created some of his finest paintings,
including *Les Grandes Baigneuses
(The Large Bathers).* The latter was
so large, in fact, that the artist had
a special slot built into the studio
wall, as the canvas was too broad
to carry down the stairs. But what

GUIDED TOURS

Two-hour Aix walking tours are
organized by the tourist office;
tours of the Old Town (in French)
leave at 3 on Wednesday and
Saturday (€8). A tour of Cézanne
landmarks (with an optional finish at his Atelier) leaves from the
tourist office at 9:30 Saturday
morning (€8); it follows the bronze
plaques in the city sidewalks. You
can request the tour in English.

4

is most striking is the collection of simple objects that once featured
prominently in the still lifes he created: the tin milk can, the ginger
jar, the flowered crockery, bottles and glasses from *La Nature Morte
aux Oignons (Still Life with Onions),* and a tin coffee pot from *La
Femme à la Cafétière (The Woman with the Coffee Pot).* Also here
are Cézanne's redingote and bowler hat, hanging from pegs just as
he left them; brushes, paint tubes, and the engravings with which he
surrounded himself—works by Courbet, Delacroix, and Poussin. The
atelier is behind an obscure garden gate on the left as you climb the Avenue Paul-Cézanne. Be sure not to miss the after-dark "Nuit des Toiles"
shows that take place in July and August, or the literary/gastronomic
evenings also held in July. ⊠*9 av. Paul-Cézanne* ☎*04-42-21-06-53*
⊕*www.atelier-cezanne.com* ☒*€5.50* ☉*Apr.–Sept., daily 10–noon and
2–6; Oct.–Mar., daily 10–noon and 2–5.*

❹ Café-Brasserie les Deux Garçons. Cézanne enjoyed his coffee and papers
Fodor'sChoice here, as have generations of *beau monde,* intellectuals, and neighbor-
★ hood *habitués* since its founding in 1792. The gilt-and-muraled interior
is original, so be sure to take a look. The locals often prefer to take
a table on the boulevard terrace of the Cours Mirabeau, considering
it to be *the* place to sit to see and be seen. But if you want to travel
back in time to the *époque consulaire,* sit inside. ⊠*53 cours Mirabeau*
☎*04-42-26-00-51*

②⓪ Cathédrale St-Sauveur. Built, according to legend, on the site of an
★ ancient temple of Apollo, this marvelous cathedral was originally built
in the 5th century but had ongoing construction up until the 18th
century. The resulting architectural hodgepodge is quite spectacular,
and is immediately obvious as soon as you look at the facade. To the
south, a 12th-century Romanesque gate tucks into a Roman wall; to
the north a richly sculpted Gothic gate leads to a tower erected in
the 13th century. Although the interior may pale by first comparison,
closer inspection reveals a remarkable double nave, Romanesque and
Gothic side by side. The right-hand nave has an extraordinary Merov-
ingian (5th-century) **baptistery,** its colonnade mostly salvaged from old
Roman temples. Shutters hide the ornate **portals,** opened by a guide

Paul Cézanne, Superstar

Matisse called him "the father of us all." He helped catapult Picasso into Cubism. And nearly every artist working today owes a huge debt to the man who finally kicked over the traces of traditional art—Paul Cézanne (1839–1906), Aix-en-Provence's most famous native son. His images of Mont Ste-Victoire and his timeless still-lifes are the founding icons of 20th-century painting. With them, he not only invented a new pictorial language but immortalized his Provençal homeland.

Great Cézannes may hang in museums (or appear for sale—one brought $50,000,000 in 2003) but you can't really understand the artist without experiencing his Provence firsthand. As it turns out, he is everywhere: Aix even has a Cézanne trail (marked with "C" copper studs) to mark sites within town.

The two most moving locales, however, are set just outside the city. Cézanne's father bought the Jas de Bouffon estate in 1859 to celebrate his rise from hatmaker to banker. The budding artist lived here until 1899. Today, its salons are empty but the grounds are full of his spirit, especially the Allée de Marronniers out front. The Jas is a mile south of town and can only be visited on tour by booking a minibus seat through the

A Cézanne self-portrait seen on an Aix street

town's central tourist office ⊕ *www.aixenprovencetourism.com*, €5.50, Nov.–Feb., Wed., Sat., 10 AM; Oct.–Apr., Tues., Thurs., Sat., 10:30–5:30; June–Sept., daily 10:30–5:30). One mile north of Aix's center is "Les Lauves," the studio the artist built in 1901 *(see Atelier Cézanne in What to See)*, set in a magically overgrown olive grove. The high point here lies a mile along the Chemin de la Marguerite: the belvedere spot from which the artist painted his last views of Mont Ste-Victoire (indeed, he died shortly after being caught in a storm here).

The Mona Lisa of modern art, Cézanne painted self-portraits that were inscrutable and hiding many secrets. He was illegitimate; he wound up having an 17-year-long affair with Hortense Piquet; and he hid his own illegitimate son from his father to inherit the family fortune. Indeed, this "painter of peasants" never worked a day in his life. Unless, that is, you consider revolutionizing the art of painting "work."

The Allée des Marronniers, Jas de Bouffon.

Mont Ste-Victoire.

When he abandoned Aix's art academy for the dramatic landscapes of the surrounding hills, he became smitten with the stark, high-noon light of Provence, rejecting the sugar-almond hues of Impressionism. Instead of mixing colors to create shadows like Monet, he simply used black. Instead of using translucent haze to create an effect of distance, he focused on ruler-straight Provençal streets (laid out by ancient Romans) to hurtle the eye from foreground to background.

At the Les Lauves studio.

In the end, Cézanne wanted to impose himself on the landscape, not vice versa. So why not do the same? With brochures from the Aix tourist office, head out into Cézanne Country—the roads leading to Le Tholonet and Mont Ste-Victoire. Walk these shady trails and you'll learn just how Cézanne became the trailblazer of modern art.

on request, and the hole in the ground is a curious testament to the old days of baptism by total immersion.

At the very end of the left-hand nave is a 17th-century **Corpus Domini chapel** with a painting by Jean Daret. But by far the most remarkable element is the 15th-century altarpiece painted by Nicolas Froment, the *Triptyque du Buisson Ardent* (Mary and the Burning Bush Triptych). It depicts the generous art patrons King René and Queen Jeanne kneeling on either side of the Virgin, who is poised above a burning bush. An artist himself (his illuminated *Book of the Broken Heart* is one of the most beautiful works of art of the Late Gothic), René founded one of Europe's most refined courts in nearby Tarascon. The extraordinary details of Froment's painting are charged with biblical references—for example, the imperfect mirror in the Virgin's hand (St. Paul to the Corinthians: "For now we see through a glass, darkly") and Moses barefoot in the thorns and thistles (the burning bush to Moses: "Put off thy shoes from off thy feet, for the place whereon thou standest is holy ground"). There's even a complete trio of Adam, Eve, and a serpent in an angel's cameo. Froment was eager to show off his newly acquired perspective technique in the rippling planes of red drapery and the juxtaposition of the king and queen: if you imagine the side panels fitted together at a 45-degree angle, the background detail falls into one plane—and the king and queen kneel side by side before the Virgin. The painting owes its extraordinary condition to having been hidden away in a Carmelite convent for centuries and opened only once a year. It's just as delicate today, and there's the rub—now it's kept closed indefinitely to prevent its oil and tempera mix from being damaged. If you care passionately about seeing it (as you should), you can view it on Tuesday from 3 to 4, or make your wish known to the porters and administration and even the tourist office. An impassioned plea could open doors—or protective shutters. ⊠ *Pl. des Martyrs de la Resistance, Rue Gaston de Saporta* ☎ *04-42-23-45-65* ⊕ *www.cathedrale-aix.net.*

② ★ **Cours Mirabeau.** At the heart of the city, with its deep shade of tall plane trees interlacing their heavy leaves over the street, Cours Mirabeau is the social nerve center of Aix. One side of the street—the northern border of the Quartier Mazarin—is lined with dignified 18th-century mansions that house mostly banks or businesses; you can view them from a seat in one of the dozen or so cafés and restaurants that spill onto the sidewalk on the opposite, sunnier, side. The street is named after the radical, not to mention hypnotically ugly, Count of Mirabeau. A rake in his youth, he scandalized society by leaving his carriage—*all night*—outside the home of his fiancée before their wedding. He went on, despite this extraordinary lapse in judgment, to be elected to the quasi-noble Third Estate in Aix in 1789.

③ **Fontaine d'Eau Chaude** (*Hot Water Fountain*). Deliciously thick with dripping moss, this 18th-century fountain is fed by Sextius's own thermal source. It seems representative of Aix at its artfully negligent best. In sunny Provence, Aix was famous for its shade and its fountains; apropos, James Pope-Hennessy, in his *Aspects of Provence,* compares living in Aix to being at the bottom of an aquarium, thanks to all the fountains' bubbling water and the city's shady streets and boulevards. ⊠*Cours Mirabeau.*

❼ **Fontaine des Quatre Dauphins** *(Four Dolphins Fountain).* Within a tiny square at a symmetrical crossroads in the Quartier Mazarin, this lovely 17th-century fountain has four graceful dolphins at the foot of a pine cone–topped obelisk. Under the shade of a chestnut tree and framed by broad, shuttered mansions, it makes an elegant ensemble worth contemplating from the park bench. ⊠*Pl. des Quatre Dauphins.*

⓯ **Hôtel de Ville** *(City Hall).* Built between 1655 and 1678 by Pierre Pavillon, the City Hall is fronted by a pebble-encrusted courtyard set off by a wrought-iron gateway. At the back, a double stairway leads to the Salle des Etats de Provences, the old regional assembly room (where taxes were voted on) that is hung with interesting portraits and pictures of mythological characters. From the window, look for the unmistakable 16th-century clock tower with an open ironwork belfry. The tree-lined square in front—where cafés set up tables right into the center of the space—is a popular gathering place. ⊠*Pl. de Hotel-de-Ville* ☏*04–42–91–90–00.*

❻ **Musée Granet.** In the graceful Quartier Mazarin and set below the Cours Mirabeau, this museum was once the town's École de Dessin (Art School). Its entry in the history books is a bit inglorious, as it once granted Cézanne a *second* prize in 1856. The academic teacher in charge pooh-poohed the young Paul and, in fact, wouldn't allow any Cézannes to enter the museum collection while he was alive (surprisingly, this philistine attitude is still shared by a large number of Aixois). Once the priory of the Église St-Jean-de-Malte, the museum was beautifully renovated in 2006 and now has a complete selection showcasing over 600 paintings. Collection highlights include paintings by Rubens, Davis, and Giacometti, as well as a collection of works by the museum's founder, François Granet. There are also eight of Cézanne's paintings, with a nice collection of his watercolors and drawings (interesting enough, bestowed on the museum by the national government, since the locals still have mixed feelings about their resident master). ⊠*Pl. St-Jean-de-Malte* 04–42–26–88–32 ⊕*www.museegranet-aixenprovence.fr* ⊠€4 ◷ *June–Sept., Tues.–Sun. 11–7; Oct.–May, Tues.–Sun. 12–6.*

❽ **Musée Paul Arbaud.** A rich and varied collection of Provençal faïence is displayed in this grand mansion in the Mazarin quarter. It also contains a library full of books on Provençal culture. ⊠*2 rue du 4-Septembre* ☏*04–42–38–38–95* ⊠€3 ◷*Musée Mon.–Sat. 2–5; library Tues. and Thurs. 2–5.*

⓳ **Musée des Tapisseries.** Housed in the hyper-elegant 17th-century **Palais** ★ **de l'Archevêché** (Archbishop's Palace), this sumptuous collection of tapestries actually decorated the walls of the bishops' quarters. Their taste was excellent: there are 17 magnificent hangings from Beauvais, including a lush series on the life of Don Quixote from Compiègne. The main opera productions of the Festival International d'Art Lyrique are presented in the spacious courtyard. ⊠*Pl. de l'Ancien-Archevêché*

☎04–42–23–09–91 ☞€2.50 ⊙ Oct.–Dec. and Feb.–Apr., Wed.–Mon. 1:30–5; Apr.–Oct., Wed.–Mon. 10–6.

⑯ Musée du Vieil Aix *(Museum of Old Aix)*. An eclectic assortment of local treasures resides in this 17th-century mansion, from faïence to santons (terra-cotta figurines). There are 19th-century puppets displayed in historic tableaux, and ornately painted furniture. The building itself is lovely, too, from the dramatic stairwell to the painted beams and frescoes. The lovely boudoir is capped with a cupola decked with garlands of flowers, painted by artists who worked on the trompe l'oeil in the Châteaurenard. ⊠ *17 rue Gaston de Saporta* ☎04–42–21–43–55 ☞€4 ⊙ Apr.–Oct., Tues.–Sun. 10–noon and 2:30–6; Nov.–Mar., Tues.–Sun. 10–noon and 2–5.

⑫ Muséum d'Histoire Naturelle *(Natural History Museum)*. An unusual collection of dinosaur eggs discovered on Mont Ste-Victoire is this museum's claim to fame. Even if these don't interest you, the 17th-century Hôtel Boyer d'Eguilles's interiors are magnificent, with ornate woodwork and sculpture scattered among the fossilized bones. ⊠ *6 rue Espariat* ☎04–42–26–23–67 ☞€2.50 ⊙ June–Oct., daily 10–6; Nov.–May, daily 10–noon and 1–5.

㉒ Pavillon de Vendôme. This extravagant Baroque villa was first built in 1665 as a "country" house for the Duke of Vendome; its position just outside the city's inner circle allowed the duke to commute discreetly from his official home on the Cours Mirabeau to this love nest, where his mistress, La Belle du Canet, was comfortably installed. Though never officially inhabited, it was expanded and heightened in the 18th century to showcase the classical orders—Ionic, Doric, and Corinthian—in its parade of neo-Grecian columns. Inside its cool, broad chambers you'll find a charming collection of Provençal furniture and artwork. Note the curious two giant Atlantes that hold up the interior balcony. ⊠ *34 rue Celon* ☎04–42–21–05–78 ☞€2 ⊙ Mar.–mid-Sept., Wed.–Mon. 10–6; mid-Sept.–Dec. and Feb., Wed.–Mon. 1:30–5

FodorśChoice ★ (margin note for Pavillon de Vendôme)

⑪ Place d'Albertas. Of all the elegant squares in Aix, this one is the most evocative and otherworldly. Set back from the city's fashionable shopping streets, it forms a horseshoe of shuttered mansions, with cobbles radiating from a simple turn-of-the-20th-century fountain. No wonder chamber music concerts are held here in summer. ⊠ *Intersection of Rue Espariat and Rue Aude.*

➊ La Rotonde. If you've just arrived in Aix's center, this sculpture-fountain is a spectacular introduction to the town's rare mix of elegance and urban bustle. It's a towering mass of 19th-century attitude. That's Agriculture yearning toward Marseille, Art leaning toward Avignon, and Justice looking down on the Cours Mirabeau. But don't study it too intently—you'll likely be sideswiped by a speeding Vespa. ⊠ *Pl. de Gaulle.*

★ (margin note for La Rotonde)

㉑ Thermes Sextius *(Thermal Baths of Sextius)*. Warm natural springs first discovered under the leadership of Sextius, the Thermes now house the glass walls of an ultramodern health spa. The small fountain in the interior marks the warm spring of the original 18th-century establishment; today the facility's offerings include a great gym, pressure showers, mud treatments, and underwater massages. ⊠*55 cours Sextius* ☎*08–00–63–96–99* ⊕*www.thermes-sextius.com* ⊙*Weekdays 8:30–7:30, Sat. 8:30–1:30 and 2:30–6:30; gym also open Sun. 8:30–7:30.*

OFF THE BEATEN PATH

Jas de Bouffon. Cézanne's father bought this lovely estate—whose name translates as "the sheepfold"—in 1859 to celebrate his rise from hatmaker to banker. The budding artist lived here until 1899 and painted his first images of Mont Ste-Victoire—the founding seeds of 20th-century art—from here. Today its salons are empty but the grounds are full of his spirit, especially the Allée des Marronniers out front. The Jas is a mile south of the center of town and can only be visited on tour by booking a minibus seat through the town's central tourist office. ⊠*80 rte. de Valcros* ☎*04–42–16–10–91* ⊕*www.aixenprovencetourism. com* ⊠*€5.50* ⊙*Daily, 10–6 for reserved tours.*

ALSO WORTH SEEING

⑭ **Ancienne Halle aux Grains** *(Old Grain Market).* Built in 1761, this former grain market serves as a post office today—a rather spectacular building for a prosaic service. The frieze, portraying an allegory of the Rhône and Durance rivers, is the work of Aix sculptor Jean Chaste (1726–93); he also created the fountain out in front. That's a real Roman column at the fountain's top. ⊠*Pl. Richelme.*

⑩ **Collège Royal-Bourbon.** It's within these walls, which now belong to the Lycée Mignet, that Cézanne and his schoolmate Emile Zola discussed their ideas. Cézanne received his baccalauréat *cum laude* here in 1858 and went on to attend a year of law school to please his father. ⊠*Rue Cardinale at Rue Joseph-Cabassol.*

NEED A BREAK?

For an excellent cup of inexpensive, fresh-roast coffee, wander into **La Brûlerie Richelme** (⊠*Pl. Richelme*). Comfy chairs and lively student patronage add to the casual ambience and the light snacks are just the thing.

⑬ **Église de la Madeleine.** Though the facade now bears 19th-century touches, this small 17th-century church still contains the center panel of the fine 15th-century *Annunciation Triptych,* attributed to the father of Jan Van Eyck, the greatest painter of the Early Netherlandish school. Some say the massive painting on the left side of the transept is a Rubens. The church is used regularly for classical concerts. ⊠*Pl. des Prêcheurs* ☎*04–42–38–02–81* ⊙*Daily 8–11:30 and 3–5:30.*

❺ **Église St-Jean-de-Malte.** This 12th-century chapel of the Knights of Malta, a medieval order of friars devoted to hospital care, was Aix's first attempt at the Gothic style, and its delicate groin-vaulted ceilings and tall windows have a touching purity of line. It was here that the counts of Provence were buried throughout the 18th century; their tombs (in the upper left) were attacked during the Revolution and only partially repaired. ⊠*Intersection of Rue Cardinale and Rue d'Italie.*

⑨ Hôtel de Caumont. This elegant mansion built in 1720 contains the **Conservatoire de Musique Darius-Milhaud** (Darius Milhaud Music Conservatory). A native of Marseille, the composer Milhaud (1892–1974) spent several years of his childhood in Aix and returned here to die. He was a member of the group of French composers known as Les Six, and created fine-boned, transparent works influenced by jazz and Hebrew chant. Aix has yet to make a museum of his memorabilia. ⊠*3 rue Joseph-Cabassol* ☎*04–42–26–38–70* ⊠*Free.*

⑰ Hôtel de Châteaurenard. Across from a commercial gallery that calls itself the Petit Musée Cézanne (actually more of a tourist trap), this 17th-century mansion once hosted Louis XIV—and now houses government offices. This means that during business hours you can slip in and peek at the fabulous 18th-century stairwell, decorated in flamboyant trompe l'oeil. Pseudo-stone putti and caryatids pop into three dimensions—as does the false balustrade that mirrors the real one in stone. ⊠*19 rue Gaston de Saporta* ⊙ *Weekdays 9–4.*

⑱ Hôtel Maynier d'Oppède. This ornately decorated mansion houses the **Institut d'Etudes Françaises** (Institute of French Studies), where foreign students take French classes. During the July opera festival its courtyard is used for a series of classical concerts. ⊠*23 rue Gaston de Saporta* ☎*04–42–21–70–92.*

WHERE TO EAT

$$$$
★
✕**Le Clos de la Violette.** Whether you dine in the shade of the broad chestnut trees or in the airy, pastel dining room of this noble old house, you'll experience the Mediterranean cuisine of top chef Jean-Marc Banzo, whose Spanish father and Italian mother influenced his famously colorful cooking. Banzo spins tradition into gold, from panfried tuna with crushed basil, smoked bacon, and crystallized shallots to poached crab set atop a humble white-bean-and-shrimp salad to rack of herb-encrusted lamb served with roasted goat cheese and rosemary potatoes. The wine list is devoted to the best of the region, too. The restaurant is not far from the Atelier Cézanne, outside the Old Town ring; note that some feel that the service can be erratic, but the welcome is consistently warm. ⊠*10 av. de la Violette, 13100* ☎*04–42–23–30–71* ⊕*www.closdelaviolette.fr* ♠*Reservations essential. Jacket required* ⊟*AE, MC, V* ⊙*Closed Sun. No lunch Mon. and Wed.*

$$$
Fodor'sChoice
★
✕**L'Amphitryon.** For years now, this restaurant has led the pack of soigné and refined *cuisine moderne* spots in Aix. With chef Bruno Ungaro at the helm, elegant, seasonal menus triumph yet so does utter, utter deliciousness. You may have to go way back in your memory-book to remember such memorably raffiné and scrumptious creations: portobello mushrooms are given a newer-than-now nouvelle spin stuffed with king crab and clove cream, salmon is a dazzling fusion of Provence and Asia, and desserts are colorful confections that are pretty-as-a-picture. ⊠*2–4 rue Paul Doumer, 13100* ☎*04–42–26–54–10* ⊟*AE, MC, V* ⊙*Closed Sun.–Mon.*

$$ ✕**Brasserie Les Deux Garcons.** Cézanne and Émile Zola used to chow
FodorsChoice down here back when, so who cares if the food is rather ordinary. Eat-
★ ing isn't what you came for. Instead, revel in the exquisite gold-ivory
style Consulate decor, which dates from the restaurant's founding in
1792. It's not so hard to picture the greats—Mistinguett, Churchill,
Sartre, Picasso, Delon, Belmondo, and Cocteau—enjoying their demi-
tasse under these mirrors. Better, savor the linen-decked sidewalk tables
that look out to the Cours Mirabeau, the fresh flowers, and the white-
swathed waiters serving espressos in tiny gilt-edge cups. In winter at
night, the upstairs turns into a cozy, dimly lighted piano bar buzzing
with an interesting mix of local jazz lovers, tourists, and students. ⊠*53
cours Mirabeau, 13100* ☎*04–42–26–00–51* ⊟*AE, MC, V.*

$$ ✕**Café La Chimére.** Although the decor in this artists' hangout is an
★ somewhat kitschy mix of gilt, crimson, and relics—are those statues
of angels?—the food is excellent. Not only are the plates lovingly balanced creations but the presentation of each dish is distinctly impressive. There is a sense of playful whimsy in the vertically arranged
concoctions of fresh, local ingredients garnished with shaved fennel,
spun sugar, or drizzled sauces that makes eating each creation a pleasure. The prices are a fantastic bargain and the atmosphere lively, making this an altogether fun place to spend an evening. ⊠*15 rue Brueys*
☎*04–42–38–30–00* ⊟*V* ⊙*Closed Tues. No lunch.*

$$ ✕**Le Bistro Latin.** With soft tones of orange and yellow and wood-backed
chairs, this unpretentious and ultra-friendly little restaurant has only
two menus with lots of choice, each combining fresh ingredients and
equally fresh ideas. Doing honor to southern cooking, olive oil fig-
ures large, as do typical Provençal herbs and spices. Consider mussels
and spinach in a saffron sauce, roasted pork loin with honey and gar-
lic, lamb stew, or a subtle terrine of chickpeas and fresh goat cheese
with balsamic vinegar. ⊠*18 rue de la Couronne* ☎*04–42–38–22–88*
⊟*MC, V* ⊙*Closed Sun.; no lunch Sat. and Mon.*

$$ ✕**Le Passage.** An edgy, urban brasserie from chef Franck Dumond, this
★ is a wildly popular spot for good, affordable food. Located in a sleekly
converted former candy factory in the center of town, the three-story
complex also includes a bookstore, cooking workshop, and a small wine
and épicerie all arranged around a sunny atrium. Its New York appeal
runs from the Andy Warhol reproductions in the main dining room to
the menu: roasted beef fillet with thick-cut fries and a terrific raspberry
crème brûlée with fig chutney. ⊠*10 rue Villars* ☎*04–42–37–09–00*
⊕*www.le-passage.fr* ⚑*Reservations essential* ⊟*AE, MC, V.*

$$ ✕**La Rotonde.** Trendy, young, and cool, this hotter-than-hot spot is the
place to hit before heading out for a night on the town. Decor is funky,
service is fun, and the food is very good. Chef Philippe Sublet comes
up with easy-to-eat, fresh, and inexpensive cuisine while the house DJ
plays soft Buddha Bar–style music in the background: a combination
that is a sure recipe for a convivial evening. Try the dual salmon lasagna
with spinach and ricotta, or the risotto with marinated artichokes and
pancetta bacon. And don't forget the lemon tart with orange shavings—
it is exactly the right way to finish off the meal. ⊠*Pl. Jeanne D'Arc*
☎*04–42–91–61–41* ⊕*www.larotonde-aix.com* ⊟*MC, V.*

4

$$ ✕ **La Vieille Auberge.** A large fireplace reaching up to the wood-beamed ceiling, lightly painted pink walls hung with clusters of dried flowers and herbs, and sparkling white tablecloths only enhance the small-town country Provençal feel of this charming restaurant. Chef Jean-Marie Merly's refined cooking and creative cuisine is high in regional color and flavor, seen in dishes such as red mullet stuffed with eggplant and Parmesan on a red pepper *pain perdu,* and is nicely presented on delicate rose-rimmed tableware. ✉63 *rue Espariatt* ☎04–42–27–17–41 ☰MC, V ⊘Closed Mon. lunch and Jan.

$ ✕ **Antoine Coté Cour.** Trendy insiders and fashion-conscious Aixois fill this lively Italian restaurant. An ornate entrance off the Cours Mirabeau leads to a perfect hideaway withfloor-to-ceiling windows that give almost every table a view of the plant-filled courtyard. Delicious smells wafting out from the open kitchen make the patrons practically hum in hungry anticipation. Pastas are superb; try the mushroom and prosciutto fettuccine, veal Milanese, or the gnocchi à la Provençal. And—get your taste buds ready to bow—all hail the tiramisu. ✉19 *cours Mirabeau* ☎04–42–93–12–51 ☰DC, MC, V ⊘Closed Sun. No lunch Mon.

$ ✕ **Chez Maxime.** Delightfully eclectic and much sought-after, this buzzing and atmospheric restaurant specializes in meat. Maxime himself carves up great hunks of beef and lamb, slapping it on to a large charcoal grill and serving it out in big hungry-man portions. Ignore the rather lackluster vegetables—you're not here for fancy fixin's—what interests you is the most succulent, mouthwateringly good steak in Aix. ✉12 *pl. Ramus* ☎04–42–26–28–51 ☰DC, MC, V ⊘Closed Sun. No lunch Mon.

$ ✕ **Chez Thomé.** At a crossroads deep in Cézanne country east of Aix, near the Château Noir and in the shadow of Montagne de Ste-Victoire, this ramshackle, fashionably bohemian hunting lodge conceals a series of intimate dining rooms and a broad terrace shaded by massive chestnut trees. Service is young and laid-back, the set menu a steal at €26, and portions are more than generous: lamb roasted in tangy tapenade, zucchini carpaccio with market vegetables and goat-cheese terrine, and crème brûlée perfumed with lavender. ✉D12, 5 km (3 mi) east of Aix, La Plantation, Le Tholonet ☎04–42–66–90–43 ☰MC, V ⊘Closed Mon.

$ ✕ **Le Grillon.** Another contender for the mobile-phone set on the lively stretch of Cours Mirabeau, this brasserie terrace gives sun-baskers and hair-tossers a place to preen and be seen. Not just for tourists, many of the Aixois eat here, too. It has waiters in black and white, crisp linens, and a simple but proficient menu that's especially strong at lunch with a selection that includes fish dishes and roast lamb with herbs. Service is quick and friendly and the wine by the carafe is affordable. ✉49 *cours Mirabeau* ☎04–42–27–58–81 ☰MC, V.

¢ ✕ **La Pizza.** The perfect setting for a romantic rendezvous, this little pizzeria comes alive every night with candlelit tables spilling out onto the cobblestones overlooking the gorgeous Place Albertas. The pizzas are fresh from the wood-fired oven, and the pastas and risottos are served with genial Italian hospitality. Try the gnocchi—in any flavor combination—and save room for dessert. ⊠ *3 rue Aude* ☎ *04–42–26–22–17* ⊟ *AE, MC, V.*

WHERE TO STAY

$$$$

Fodor'sChoice

★

⚑ **Le Pigonnet.** Cézanne painted Ste-Victoire from what is now the large flower-filled garden terrace of this enchanting abode, and the likes of Princess Caroline, Iggy Pop, and Clint Eastwood have spent a few nights under the luxurious roof of the family-owned, old-world, country-style hotel. Spacious and filled with light, each guest room is a marvel of decoration: baby-soft plush rugs, beautifully preserved antique furniture, rich colors of burnt reds, autumn yellows, and delicate oranges. The restaurant's terrace spills out onto a sculpted green, but the inside dining salon is equally pleasant on a rainy day, thanks to its softly draped yellow curtains and large picture windows. Ablaze with flowers and ornamented with topiary obelisks, the garden has to be one of the most striking in France. For sheerest Provençal gloss, this place can't be beat. **Pros:** its unique garden setting in the center of Aix; the sweeping vista from garden-facing rooms out to the mountains. **Cons:** some rooms are small for the price; reception can be cool; some say this is getting too worn at the edges. ⊠ *5 av. du Pigonnet* ☎ *04–42–59–02–90* ⊕ *www.hotelpigonnet.com* ⚑ *49 rooms, 2 villas* ⚑ *In-room: refrigerator, Wi-Fi. In-hotel: restaurant, pool, parking (fee), some pets allowed* ⊟ *AE, MC, V.*

$$$$

★

⚑ **Villa Gallici.** Perched on a hill overlooking the pink roofs of Aix, this former archbishop's palace was transformed into a homage to *le style provençal* thanks to the wizardry of three designers, Gilles Dez, Charles de Montemarco, and Daniel Jouvre back in the high-style 1980s. Don't come here for sunbaked walls, white tiles, and urns with cactus—this is the gilded Provence that Parisian aristos enjoyed back in the 19th century. Hued in the lavenders and blues, ochers and oranges of Aix, guest rooms swim in the most gorgeous Souleiado and Rubelli fabrics and trim and some have private gardens. If a Louis Seize chair covered in gingham check gets to be a bit much, just step outside to the Florentine-style garden and beckoning pool. There is an excellent restaurant where chef Christophe Gavot specializes in fish, and the hotel stands serenely apart from the city center on the outskirts of town (offering great views), and that means the shops of Cours Mirabeau are a 15-minute walk away. **Pros:** picture-perfect decor; handsome welcome. **Cons:** restaurant can be hit or miss depending on the season; pool is quite small. ⊠ *Av. de la Violette* ☎ *04–42–23–29–23* ⊕ *www.villagallici.com* ⚑ *18 rooms, 4 suites, 3 duplexes* ⚑ *In-room: refrigerator, Wi-Fi. In-hotel: restaurant, pool, parking (free), some pets allowed* ⊟ *AE, DC, MC, V.*

$$$

★

⚑ **Hôtel Cézanne.** Three blocks from Cours Mirabeau and the train station, this smart, very spiffy, and cozily stylish hotel is a very handy option. Just a minute's stroll away is the Quartier Mazarin, the 18th-century district lined with some of Aix's most beautiful buildings and antiques shops. While the hotel is set on a busy avenue, all noise and distractions disappear with just one foot inside the glowing red lobby, mightily warmed by the friendliness of the staff. Upstairs, the guest rooms are classic Provençal—modern in comfort yet with old armoires, elegant chandeliers, patterned historic wallpapers, and very comfy beds. Out back is an Aix garden-courtyard with looming trees that would tempt Cézanne's own paintbrush, so try to book a room in the back. **Pros:** the breakfast buffet is one of the very best around; the honor bar is a treat. **Cons:** there's no pool; some rooms get street noise. ✉ *40 av. Victor-Hugo13100* ☎ *04–42–91–11–11* ⊕ *www.hotelaix.com/cezanne* ➥ *55 rooms, 12 suites* ♻ *In-room: refrigerator. In-hotel: bar some pets allowed* ☰ *AE, MC, V.*

$$$ 🏨 **Hôtel des Augustins.** The best aspect of this Old Town hotel, just a half block back from Cours Mirabeau, is its reception area. The groin-vaulted stone, stained glass, and ironwork banister date from the 15th century, when the house was an Augustinian convent (Martin Luther was once a guest). The guest rooms are perfectly nice but a bit of a letdown. Instead of monastic oak and pristine linens, you get heavy carpeting and fabric-covered walls. Bathrooms are all-white tile and marble, and a few rooms have private balcony-terraces with views of the steeple of St-Esprit. The staff is efficient and eager to please. **Pros:** you can't beat the location; sincere welcome is a pleasure. **Cons:** rooms are quite ordinary; some are quite small. ✉ *3 rue de la Masse* ☎ *04–42–27–28–59* ⊕ *www.hotel-augustins.com* ➥ *29 rooms* ♻ *In-room: refrigerator, Wi-Fi* ☰ *AE, DC, MC, V.*

$$ 🏨 **Nègre-Coste.** Legend says Louis XIV once stayed here, while the guest book proves such VIPs as 19th-century chanteuse Yvette Guilbert opted for this hotel. Its lavish public areas and great central location make this 18th-century town house still a popular hotel, especially with musicians during the summer festivals. If people-watching is your thing, you may cotton to the hotel's prominent perch on the very bustling Cours Mirabeau thoroughfare. If not, be sure to request a quieter room at the back of the hotel where the view extends to the cathedral. With period furniture, marble busts, and lots of old-fashioned style, guest rooms are bright with Provençal gold fabric, antique tables, and small chandeliers. **Pros:** unbeatable location; friendly service; big rooms. **Cons:** some rooms are noisy; some bathrooms are very small. ✉ *33 cours Mirabeau* ☎ *04–42–27–74–22* ⊕ *www.hotelnegrecoste.com* ➥ *36 rooms, 1 suite* ♻ *In-room: refrigerator. In-hotel: Wi-Fi, parking (fee)* ☰ *AE, MC, V.*

$$ 🏨 **St-Christophe.** With so few mid-price *hôtels de charme* in Aix, you might as well opt for this glossy art deco–style hotel, where the comfort and services are remarkable for the price. The Roaring Twenties look dates from 1994, but the Cézannesque murals, burled-wood curves, and Constructivist leather chairs carry you back to the Jazz Age. Rooms are slickly done in deep jewel tones, and the top-floor rooms have artisanal tiles in the bathrooms. For a pittance more, you can have a junior suite with a sleeping loft with views out over the central plaza. **Pros:** location; price-service ratio. **Cons:** hotel-chain feel; decor lacks charm. ✉ *2 av. Victor-Hugo* ☎ *04–42–26–01–24* ⊕ *www.hotel-saintchristophe.com* ➥ *50 rooms, 10 suites* ♻ *In-hotel: restaurant, Wi-Fi, parking (fee), some pets allowed* ☰ *AE, DC, MC, V* 🍽 *BP, MAP.*

$ **Cardinal.** In a lovely 18th-century house in the Quartier Mazarin,
Fodor'sChoice this eccentric and slightly threadbare inn is the antithesis of slick. Its
★ large rooms are furnished gracefully enough with secondhand finds,
and some rooms have original 18th-century painted door panels. If
you like charm, you'll notice the novel furniture, the elegance of the
structure, and the music of the bells of St-Jean-de-Malte. A favorite
among writers, artists, and musicians on hand for the festival, it also
has kitchenette suites; the two that are across from the Musée Granet
and the ground-floor one with a private garden are the best. **Pros:**
the price for the location is excellent; rooms are clean and bright.
Cons: rooms can be noisy and hot in summer. ⊠*24 rue Cardinale*
☎*04–42–38–32–30* ⊕*www.hotel-cardinal-aix.com* ⬦*2 rooms, 6*
suites ⚒*In-room: refrigerator (some), no TV. In-hotel: parking (fee),*
some pets allowed ⊟*MC, V.*

$ **Quatre Dauphins.** In the gorgeously elegant Mazarin neighborhood
★ south of the Cours Mirabeau, this modest but impeccable lodging
inhabits a noble *hôtel particulier.* Its pretty, comfortable little rooms
have been spruced up with *boutis* (Provençal quilts), les Olivades fabrics, quarry tiles, jute carpets, and hand-painted furniture. The tiny top-
floor rooms are even more charming. The house-proud but unassuming
owner-host bends over backward to please and the charming reception
area is a perfect place to curl up with a book and sip afternoon tea.
Pros: ideal center-of-town location; super-friendly staff. **Cons:** rooms
are small; in summer nearly impossible to book a room. ⊠*55 rue Roux*
Alphéran ☎*04–42–38–16–39* ⊕*www.lesquatredauphins.fr* ⬦*13*
rooms ⚒*In-hotel: Wi-Fi, some pets allowed* ⊟*MC, V.*

NIGHTLIFE & THE ARTS

To find out what's going on in town, pick up a copy of the events calendar *Le Mois à Aix* or the bilingual city guide *Aix la Vivante* at the
tourist office.

Every July during the **Festival International d'Art Lyrique** (*International*
Opera Festival ☎*04–42–17–34–00 for information* ⊕*www.operabase.*
com), you can see world-class opera productions in the courtyard of
the Palais de l'Archevêché. It is one of the most important opera festivals in Europe, and cutting-edge productions involve the best artists
available—guests in the past have included director Peter Brook, cho-
reographers Trisha Brown and Pina Bausch, and conductor Claudio
Abbado. The repertoire is varied and often offbeat, featuring works
like Britten's *Curlew River* and Bartók's *Bluebeard's Castle* as well as
the usual Mozart, Puccini, and Verdi. Most of the singers, however,
are not celebrities, but rather an elite group of students who spend
the summer with the Academie Européenne de Musique, training and
performing under the tutelage of stars like Robert Tear and Yo-Yo Ma.
Tickets can be purchased as early as November for the following summer, but it's usually possible to find seats a month in advance. After
that, seats are scarce.

As for nightspots, **Hot Brass** (⊠*Rte. d'Eguilles, Celony* 🕾*04–42–21–05–57*) draws an older, car-owning crowd to the suburbs for live concerts of funk, soul, rock, blues, and Latin bands, mainly local. **Le Scat Club** (⊠*11 rue de la Verrerie* 🕾*04–42–23–00–23*) is the place for live soul, funk, reggae, rock, blues, and jazz. **Le Mistral** (⊠*3 rue Frédéric-Mistral* 🕾*04–42–38–16–49*) is an established student club with big-name DJs and a strict door policy, so get dressed up and get there early. **Le Divino** (⊠*Mas des Auberes, Rte. de Venelles [5 km from town]* 🕾*04–42–99–37–08*) is New York–stylish and draws the hip, young, and beautiful people. **The Bistrot Aixois** (⊠*37 cours Sextius* 🕾*04–42–27–50–10*) is newly renovated and still the hottest student nightspot in town, with young BCBG's lining up to get in. **IPN** (⊠*23 cours Sexitus* 🕾*04–42–26–25–17*) has great ambience, good music, and reasonable prices. **The Red Clover** (⊠*30 rue de la Verrerie* 🕾*04–42–23–44–61*) is a friendly, boisterous Irish pub. Don't expect to speak any French here.

For a night of playing roulette and the slot machines, head for the **Casino Municipal** (⊠*2 bis av. N.-Bonaparte* 🕾*04–42–26–30–33*).

The **Cézanne** (⊠*Rue Marcel Guillaume* 🕾*08–36–68–72–70*) and **Renoir** (⊠*24 cours Mirabeau* 🕾*08–36–68–72–70*) cinemas both show some films in *v.o.* (*version originale, i.e., not dubbed*).

The stunningly inventive choreography of **Le Ballet Preljocaj** (⊠*Rue Allumettes* 🕾*04–42–93–48–00*) can be seen September to May in Aix, their home base.

THE OUTDOORS

Because it's there, in part, and because it looms in striking isolation above the plain east of Aix, its heights catching the sun long after the valley lies in shadow, Cézanne's beloved **Montagne Ste-Victoire** inspires climbers to conquest. The Grande Randonée stretches along its long, rocky crest from the village of Le Bouquet at its western end all the way east to Puyloubier. Its alternate route climbs the milder north slope from Les Cabassols. Along the way it peaks at 3,316 feet at Pic des Mouches, from where the view stretches around the compass. But the real draw lies to the east at the **Croix de Provence** (3,100 feet), a gargantuan cross rising 92 feet above the mountaintop. You'll have sweeping views over the whole of Provence from the Luberon to the Alps. From Les Cabassols to the Cross, allow 3½ hours round-trip for this fairly strenuous hike. A bus from Aix's *gare routière* (bus station) carries hikers toward Vauvenargues and Les Cabassols departure point. Pick up detailed maps at the tourist office.

SHOPPING

Aix is a very snazzy market town, and unlike the straightforward, country-fair atmosphere of nearby Aubagne, a trip to the market here is a foodie's delight, with rarefied, high-end delicacies shoulder to shoulder with garlic braids. You'll find fine olive oils from the Pays d'Aix (Aix region), barrels glistening with olives of every hue and blend, and vats of tapenade (crushed olive, caper, and anchovy paste). Melons, asparagus, and mesclun salad are piled high, and dried sausages bristling with Provençal herbs hang from stands. A **food and produce market** takes place every morning on Place Richelme; just up the street on Place Verdun is a good, high-end *brocante* (collectibles) market Tuesday, Thursday, and Saturday mornings.

In addition to its old-style markets and jewel-box candy shops, Aix is a dazzlingly sophisticated modern shopping town—perhaps the

> **TOUT SWEET**
>
> A great Aixois delicacy is *calissons*. A blend of almond paste and glazed melon, they are cut into geometric almond shapes and stacked high in *confiserie* windows. The most picturesque shop specializing in calisson candies is Bechard (✉ *12 cours Mirabeau* ☎ *04-42-26-06-78*). **Leonard Parli** (✉ *35 av. Victor Hugo* ☎ *04-42-26-05-71*), housed in a sugar-sweet, 19th-century emporium, also offers a lovely selection.

best in Provence. The winding streets of the Vieille Ville above Cours Mirabeau—focused around **Rue Clémenceau, Rue Marius Reinaud, Rue Espariat, Rue Aude, Rue Fabrot,** and **Rue Maréchal Foch**—have a plethora of goods, from high-end designer clothes such as Sonia Rykiel, Escada, and Yves Saint Laurent, to Max Mara, Laura Ashley, and The Gap. On the fashion front, particularly noteworthy is **Gago** (✉ *18–21 rue Fabrot* ☎ *04-42-27-60-19*), a fashion leader with stylish designer wear for men and women including Prada, Helmut Lang, and Gucci. You'll also find **Max Mara** and **Yohji Yamamoto** on the same street (no. 12 and no. 3). **Gérard Darel** (✉ *13 rue Fabrot* ☎ *04-42-26-38-45*) is the shop for classic French tailoring. **Tehen** (✉ *6 rue Cleéenceau* ☎ *04-42-26-85-50*) sells soft, draped knits. **Mephisto** (✉ *16 bis pl. Verdun* ☎ *04-42-38-23-23*) sells its signature walking shoes and boots to a mostly foreign clientele, as French women find them unaesthetic. **Catimini** (✉ *9 pl. Chapeliers* ☎ *04-42-27-51-14*) offers an imaginative, jazzy stock of kids' sweaters, jackets, and dresses. Toddlers will love the traditional wooden toys at **Le Nain Rouge** (✉ *47 rue Espariat* ☎ *04-42-93-50-05*). Fabrics, pottery, and decorative arts for the home also figure large. **Les Olivades** (✉ *15 rue Marius Reinaud* ☎ *04-42-38-33-66*) is one of the last *maisons* that print Provençal fabrics in the traditonal Marseille style. Sophisticated Provençal pottery can be found at **Scènes de Vie** (✉ *3 rue Granet* ☎ *04-42-21-13-90*). Splurge for your one-of-a-kind made-to-order embroidered chair cover at **Arts Vivendi** (✉ *2 av. Villemus* ☎ *04-42-21-22-83*). Aix's most celebrated santon, or miniature statue, maker is **Santon Fouque** (✉ *65 cours Gambetta* ☎ *04-42-26-33-38*). The **Book in Bar** (✉ *1 bis rue Joseph Cabassol* ☎ *04-42-26-60-07*) is a cozy English bookshop near the Cours Mirabeau and is not only a great place to buy and read Engish-language books, but also to meet other English speakers.

MARSEILLE

GETTING HERE

The main train station is the Gare St-Charles on the TGV line, with frequent trains from Paris, the main coast route (Nice/Italy), and Arles. For train and ticket information: ⊕*www.voyages-sncf.com* ☎ *08–36–35–35–35*). Handy to note that inside the train station, SOS Voyageurs (☎*04–91–62–12–80*, Mon.–Sat. 9–7) helps with children, the elderly, and lost luggage. The Gare Routière (bus station) is on Place Victor Hugo (☎*04–91–08–16–40*). Here you will find Cartrieze (☎*08–00–19–94–13* ⊕*www.lepilote.com*) controlling the routes into and from the Bouches du Rhone; Eurolines (☎*04–91–50–57–55* ⊕*www.eurolines.fr*) operating coaches between Marseille, Avignon, and Nice via Aix-en-Provence. Marseille also has a métro system, most of the lines service the suburbs, but several stop in the city center (including Gare St-Charles, Colbert, Vieux Port, and Notre Dame; tickets €1.60) and can help you get around quickly.

VISITOR INFORMATION

Marseille Tourist Office (⊠*4 La Canebière13001* ☎*04–91–13–89–00* ⊕*www. marseille-tourisme.com*).

EXPLORING

Popular myths and a fishy reputation have led Marseille to be unfairly maligned as a dirty urban sprawl plagued with impoverished immigrant neighborhoods and slightly louche politics. It is often given wide berth by travelers in search of a Provençal idyll. What a shame. As so often is the case here, there is no simple truth: Marseille, even its earliest history, has maintained its contradictions with a kind of fierce and independent pride. Yes, there are scary, even dangerous neighborhoods, some modern eyesores, even a high crime rate—but there is also tremendous beauty. Cubist jumbles of white stone rise up over a picture-book seaport, bathed in light of blinding clarity, crowned by larger-than-life neo-Byzantine churches, and framed by massive fortifications; neighborhoods teem with multiethnic life; souklike African markets reek deliciously of spices and coffees; and the labyrinthine Old Town radiates bright shades of saffron, cinnamon, and robin's-egg blue.

And now the TGV (fast train) phenomenon that makes Marseille a mere three hours from Paris has also brought in an influx of "weekend tourists" who are snapping up more and more pieds-à-terre and throwing themselves into renovation projects. The government is also in the spirit and is in the process of completing an ambitious project to clean up and revitalize the Vieux Port. The second largest city in France, Marseille remains a vibrant city. Fiesty and fond of broad gestures, it is also as complicated and as cosmopolitan now as it was when the Phoenicians first founded it as an international shipping port 2,600 years ago.

In 600 BC a band of Phoenician Greeks sailed into the well-placed natural harbor that is today's Vieux Port. Legend has it that on that same day a local chieftain's daughter, Gyptis, needed to choose a husband,

and her wandering eyes settled on the Greeks' handsome commander Protis. Her dowry brought land near the mouth of the Rhône, where the Greeks founded Massalia, the most important Continental shipping port in antiquity. The port flourished for some 500 years as a typical Greek city, enjoying the full flush of classical culture, its gods, its democratic political system, its sports and theater, and its naval prowess. Caesar changed all that, besieging the city in 49 BC and seizing most of its colonies. Massalia's Greeks were left only their famous university and their highly valued independence. They struggled until the 12th century when Marseille finally reactivated its port and started making money embarking and maintaining supply lines to the Crusaders. In 1214 Marseille was seized by Charles d'Anjou and was later annexed to France by Henri IV in 1481, but it was not until Louis XIV took the throne that the biggest transformations of the port began; he pulled down the city walls in 1666 and expanded the port to the *Rive Neuve* (New Riverbank). The city was devastated by plague in 1720, losing more than half its population. By the time of the Revolution, Marseille was on the rebound once again, with industries of soap manufacturing and oil processing flourishing, encouraging a wave of immigration from Provence and Italy.

With the opening of the Suez Canal in 1869, Marseille became the greatest boomtown in 19th-century Europe. With a large influx of immigrants from areas as exotic as Tangiers, the city quickly acquired the multicultural population it maintains to this day. By 1964 the population had outgrown available space, and housing shortages demanded rapid, and unfortunately somewhat careless, construction of new neighborhoods. By the mid-1970s these areas often had high unemployment and serious problems with drugs and crime. Thrown into the volatile mix was a series of political scandals centered around corruption and extortion, cementing Marseille's unsavory reputation. Since then, "reform" has become the new buzzword, with the conservative right-wing mayor introducing new plans that have both revitalized the economy and started the cleanup process for the badly tattered Marseillais image. And so, with the enthusiastic support of its very cosmopolitan population, it seems that one of France's oldest cities is finally rising up (again) from the proverbial ashes.

THE QUAI DU PORT AND LE PANIER

Though Marseille is the second-largest city in France, it functions as a conglomerate of distinct neighborhoods—almost little villages. One of these microcosms—the Neapolitan-style maze of laundry-lined lanes called Le Panier—merits intimate exploration and the will to wander. There are also myriad museums tied into Marseille's nautical history, and the striking museum complex of the Vieille Charité, all worth a browse.

A GOOD WALK

Begin at the tourist office at the base of the Vieux Port, known as the Quai des Belges. Be sure to start early because this is the stage for the first of a series of theatrical scenes that are part of Marseille's daily life:

Marseille

Rade
de
Marseille

Bassin
de la
Grande
Joliette

Avant-Port
de la
Joliette

Fort
St-Jean

LE PANIER

Vieux
Port

Jardin
du Pharo

Jardin
P. Puget

TO ANSES,
PLAGE DU PRADO
↓

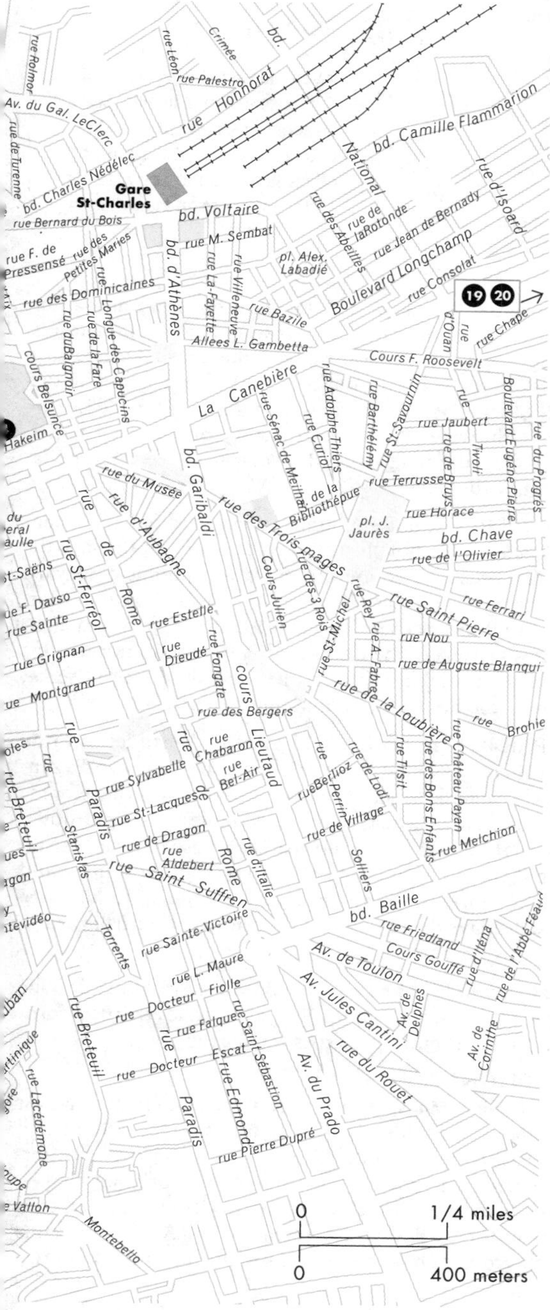

- Abbaye St-Victor **16**
- Les Arcenaulx **12**
- Bar de la Marine **13**
- Cathédrale de la Major **7**
- Centre de la Vieille Charité **6**
- Ferry Boat **10**
- Fort St-Nicolas and Fort St-Jean **17**
- Jardin des Vestiges **5**
- Jardin du Pharo **18**
- Marché aux Poissons **1**
- Musée des Docks Romains **9**
- Musée d'Histoire de Marseille **4**
- Musée de la Marine et l'Economie de Marseille **2**
- Musée de la Mode **3**
- Musée du Vieux Marseille **8**
- Musée Grobet-Labadie **20**
- Notre-Dame de la Garde **15**
- Palais de Longchamp **19**
- Place Thiars **11**
- Théâtre National de Marseille La Criée **14**

4

the **Marché aux Poissons.** The port behind them is a show in itself, with its colorful mix of gleaming white pleasure boats, scruffy blue and green fishing boats, and even a couple of restored schooners, all bobbing together in the vast horseshoe of water. Don't bother to come if the mistral has been roaring over the water; then the fishermen keep their boats safely tied in port.

> **TRIP TIP**
>
> If you plan on visiting many of the museums in Marseille, buy a museum *passport* (city pass) for €16 (2 days €23) at the tourism office. It covers the entry fee for all the museums in Marseille.

Walk up La Canebière to the **Musée de la Marine et de l'Economie de Marseille,** where you can learn about the port's history through miniatures, paintings, and engravings. Just past the port is the unusual **Musée de la Mode,** where high-fashion clothes from the 1930s to today are on display. Head a half block over into the mall to enter the **Musée d'Histoire de Marseille,** which illustrates the classical history of this ancient city. Then wander into the adjoining **Jardin des Vestiges** to see the foundations of Greek fortifications.

Next, head up broad Rue de la République, past grand old apartment buildings and Place Sadi Carnot. Just past the square, on the left, the elegant Passage de Lorette leads you into a claustrophobic courtyard with laundry fluttering like medieval banners overhead, typical of Marseille. From here, climb the steep stairs that lead into the famous neighborhood known as **Le Panier.** The anchor of the revitalization of this decaying but appealing neighborhood is the **Centre de la Vieille Charité,** once a hospice, now the home of two museums.

Follow Rue du Petit Puits to Place des 13 Cantons, head left on Rue Ste-Françoise, then cross Avenue Robert Schumann to the neo-Byzantine **Cathédrale de la Nouvelle Major.** Then wind back down the Montée des Accoules to Place Daviel, turn right and double back right down Rue du Lacydon to the **Musée du Vieux Marseille.** Housed in the Maison Diamantée, it highlights collections of pottery, furniture, costumes, and santons (terra-cotta figurines). Just a block up from the port, the **Musée des Docks Romains** displays the remains of 1st-century waterfront warehouses that lined this busy port.

Go down to the Quai du Port and past the Baroque-era Hôtel de Ville (City Hall). At the water's edge wait for the picturesque **Ferry Boat** (pronounced *fay*-ree *bow*-aht) and ride across the port in style.

MAJOR ATTRACTIONS

7 **Cathédrale de la Nouvelle Major.** A neo-Byzantine church, the largest built in France since the Middle Ages, that was started in 1852 and completed in 1893, it's remarkable for its marble and rich red porphyry inlay. Napoléon III ordered the 11th-century original chapel, the Ancienne Major (parts of which date back to Roman times), torn apart to make way for its flashy new replacement. All that remains of the old church are the choir and the transept: restoration continues, but it is in a bad state of disrepair. ⊠*Pl. de la Major, Le Panier* ☎*04–91–90–53–57.*

❻ Centre de la Vieille Charité *(Center of the Old Charity).* Built between
★ 1671 and 1749 and designed by Pierre and Jean Puget, this delightful complex, originally constructed as a shelter for the poor, has beautiful open balconies on three stories nestled around a courtyard. Dominated by a magnificent Baroque chapel with a novel oval-shaped dome, the inner court offers an interesting retreating perspective of the triple arcades. The *salon de thé* (tearoom) serves drinks and light meals alfresco under the lovely arches.

Renovated and reopened as a cultural center in 1986, the former chapel houses temporary exhibitions. Further along are two excellent museums. The larger is the **Musée d'Archéologie Méditerranéenne** (Museum of Mediterranean Archaeology), with a superb collection of archaeological finds from the Mediterranean and Provence, including a sizable collection of ceramics, bronzes, funeral stelae, statues from ancient Greece, and Roman glassware. It also has the most important Egyptian collection in France outside of Paris. Along with mummified people, cats, and flowers, there are plenty of hieroglyphics and gorgeous sarcophagi in evocative tomb-like surroundings. The **Musée d'Arts Africains, Océaniens et Amérindiens** (Museum of African, Oceanian, and American Indian Art) has artifacts from Africa, the Pacific, and the Americas. The spectacular masks and sculptures—including some rather tastefully engraved human skulls—are mounted along a black wall, eerie with indirect lighting. Labels and explanations are across the aisle. ⊠*2 rue de la Charité, Le Panier* ☎*04–91–14–58–80* 💶*€2 per museum* ☉*May–Sept., Tues.–Sun. 11–6; Oct.–Apr., Tues.– Sun. 10–5.*

❿ Ferry Boat. To hear the natives say *"fay-ree bow-aht"* (they've adopted the English) is one of the joys of a visit to Marseille. For a pittance (it's free but tipping the crew is appropriate) you can file onto this little wooden barge, which serves as handy mass transit just as it did in Marcel Pagnol's play *Marius.* It chugs between Place des Huiles on the Quai de Rive Neuve side and the Hôtel de Ville on the Quai du Port 8 AM to 6:30 PM daily. 💶*Free.*

❶ Marché aux Poissons *(Fish Market).* Up and going by 8 AM every day, this
★ market—immortalized in Marcel Pagnot's *Fanny* (and Joshua Logan's sublime 1961 film adaptation)— puts on a vivid and aromatic show of waving fists, jostling chefs, and heaps of fish from the night's catch still twitching. You'll hear the thick soup of the Marseillais accent as blue-clad fishermen and silk-clad matrons bicker over prices, and you'll wonder at the rainbow of Mediterranean creatures swimming in plastic vats before you, each uglier than the last: the spiny-headed *rascasse* (scorpion fish), dog-nosed *grondin* (red gurnet), the monstrous *baudroie* or *lotte de mer* (monkfish), and the eel-like *congre.* "Bouillabaisse" as sold here is a mix of fish too tiny to sell otherwise; the only problem with coming for the early morning show is that you have to

wait so long for your bouillabaisse lunch. ⊠ *Quai des Belges, Vieux Port* ⊙ *Daily 8–1.*

❹ **Musée d'Histoire de Marseille** *(Marseille History Museum).* With the Jar-
★ din des Vestiges in its backyard and its front door in a shopping mall, this modern, open-spaced exhibition illuminates Massalia's history by mounting its treasure of archeological finds in didactic displays. You can learn about ancient metallurgy, Gallo-Roman pottery making, and shipbuilding. There's a section on medieval Marseille, and some back-ground on the marks Louis XIV and Vauban left on the city. Best by far is the presentation of Marseille's Classical halcyon days. There's a recovered wreck of a Roman cargo boat, its 3rd-century wood amaz-ingly preserved, and the hull of a Greek boat dating from the 4th cen-tury BC. And that model of the Greek city should be authentic—it's based on the eyewitness description of Aristotle. ⊠ *Centre Bourse, entrance on Rue de Bir-Hakeim, Vieux Port* ☎ 04–91–90–42–22 ☞ €3 *includes entry into Jardin des Vestiges* ⊙ *June–Sept., Mon.–Sat. 10–7; Oct.–May, Tues.–Sun. 10–5.*

★ **Le Panier.** This louche, scruffy *quartier* is the oldest part of the city, slicing between Quai du Port and Rue de la République, and has been a traditional first stop for successive waves of immigrants. A maze of high-shuttered houses looming over narrow cobbled streets, Le Panier is the principal focus of the city's efforts at urban renewal, with plans for the restoration of over 1,500 houses. It's hard to resist the charm of steep stairways, narrow streets, and pastel-painted shops selling pottery and soap. And, with its population gradually changing to hip young artists and students, more and more chic boutiques and stylish restau-rants are opening up, changing the area from seedy to atmospheric. Locals warn that Le Panier can still be a bit dubious late at night; it's best to wander during daylight hours only, or in groups.

ALSO WORTH SEEING

❺ **Jardin des Vestiges** *(Garden of Remains).* Discovered in 1967 while the foundations for the Center Bourse shopping center were being dug, the remains of Marseille's Greek walls, a necropolis, 1st-century loading docks, and a corner of the Roman port are all well-preserved here. The gardens are now a part of the **Musée d'Histoire de Marseille** (Marseille History Museum), which also has a remarkably well-preserved 3rd-century ship recovered from the sea in 1974. ⊠ *Centre Bourse, Vieux Port* ☎ 04–91–90–42–22 ☞ €3 *includes entry to Museum of History* ⊙ *Mon.–Sat. noon–7.*

❾ **Musée des Docks Romains** *(Roman Docks Museum).* Nazis destroyed the neighborhood along the Quai du Port in 1943—a rather brutal act of urban renewal—ironically laying the groundwork for new dis-coveries. During postwar reconstruction, workers dug up remains of a 1st-century Roman shipping house. The museum created around the site preserves documents, equipment, and techniques used in maritime trade with exhibits of terra-cotta jars and coins. ⊠ *2 Pl. de Vivaux, Vieux Port* ☎ 04–91–91–24–62 ☞ €2 ⊙ *Oct.–May, Tues.–Sun. 10–5; June–mid-Sept., Tues.–Sun. 11–6.*

② **Musée de la Marine et de l'Economie de Marseille** *(Marine and Economy Museum).* Inaugurated by Napoléon III in 1860, this impressive building houses both the museum and the city's Chamber of Commerce. The front entrance and hallway to the museum are lined with medallions celebrating the ports of the world with which the city has traded, or trades still. The museum charts the maritime history of Marseille from the 17th century onward with paintings and engravings. It is a model-lover's dream, with hundreds of steamboats and schooners, all in miniature. ⊠*Palais de la Bourse, 7 La Canebière, La Canebière* ☎*04–91–39–33–33* ⊠*€3* ⊗*Daily 10–6.*

③ **Musée de la Mode** *(Fashion Museum).* Adding a bit of panache and style to the normal museum rounds are these galleries filled with clothes. More than 3,000 dresses and accessories, dating mainly from 1945 onward, form a permanent collection, while temporary exhibits highlight anything from a star designer's collection to the contents of a fashion diva's wardrobe. ⊠*11 La Canebière, La Canebière* ☎*04–96–17–06–00* ⊕*www.espacemodemediterranee.com* ⊠*€3* ⊗*Tues.–Sun. 10–6.*

⑧ **Musée du Vieux Marseille** *(Museum of Old Marseille).* The 16th-century **Maison Diamantée** (Diamond House), named for its diamond-faceted Renaissance facade, was built in 1570 by a rich merchant and was one of the few buildings in this quarter spared by Hitler. Focusing on the history of Marseille, the painstakingly renovated museum presents santons, crèches, and furniture, offering a glimpse into 18th-century Marseille life. ⊠*Rue de la Prison, Vieux Port* ☎*04–91–55–28–69* ⊠*€3.*

GUIDED TOURS

Marseille walking tours are organized by the tourist office; these cover various neighborhoods and take place three times a week. In July and August they leave the tourist office on Monday, Wednesday, and Friday at 2 PM. The tours cost €8 per person and you can request them in English. If you're feeling flush or footsore, splurge on a Marseille taxi tour with cassette commentary in English, offered by the tourist office (€32)—you'll be whisked up to the hard-to-reach Notre-Dame-de-la-Garde and Palais du Pharo; on the two-hour trip (€54) you'll also cruise the seaside cliff called the Corniche and duck into the picturesque fishing port Vallon des Auffes.

THE QUAI DE RIVE NEUVE

If in your exploration of Le Panier and the Quai du Port you examined Marseille's history in miniature via myriad museums, this walk will give you the "big picture." From either the crow's-nest perspective of Notre-Dame-de-la-Garde or the vast green Jardin du Pharo, you'll take in spectacular Cinemascope views of this great city and its ports and monuments. Wear good walking shoes and bring your wide-angle lens.

MAJOR ATTRACTIONS

⑯ ★ Abbaye St-Victor. Founded in the 4th century by St-Cassien, who sailed into Marseille's port full of fresh ideas on monasticism acquired in Palestine and Egypt, this abbey grew to formidable proportions. A spectacular fortified medieval church built on the remains of an ancient necropolis, its severe exterior of crenellated stone and the spare geometry of its Romanesque church would be as much at home in Middle East as its founder. The earlier church, destroyed by invading Saracens, was the city's first basilica and, with its formidable proportions, an impressive seat of religious power. It was rebuilt in the 11th century, then fortified against further attack in the 14th century. Its crudely peaked windows demonstrate the dawning transition from Romanesque arches to Gothic points; in the nave the early attempts at groin vaulting were among the first in Provence.

Chunks of the earlier church remain in what is by far the best reason to come: **the crypt,** St-Cassien's original, which is buried under the new church's medieval structure. In evocative nooks and crannies you'll find early medieval sarcophagi, including a 5th-century one that allegedly holds the martyr's remains. Upstairs look for the tomb of St-Victor, who was ground to death between two millstones, probably by the Romans. There's also a passage into tiny **catacombs** where early Christians worshipped St-Lazarus and Mary Magdalene, said to have washed ashore at Stes-Maries-de-la-Mer. The boat in which they landed is reproduced in canoe-shaped cookies called *navettes,* which are sold during the annual procession for Candelmas in February as well as year-round. ⊠*3 rue de l'Abbaye, Rive Neuve* ☎*04–96–11–22–60* ⊕*www.saint victor.net* ☒*Crypt entry €2* ⊘*Daily 8:30–6:30.*

⑬ Bar de la Marine. Even if you've never read or seen Marcel Pagnol's trilogy of plays and films *Marius, Fanny,* and *César* (think of it as a three-part French *Casablanca*), you can get a feel for its earthy, Old Marseille feeling by stopping into the bar it was set in. The walls are blanketed with murals and comfortable café chairs fill the place, all in an effort to faithfully reproduce the bar as it was in the days when the bartender César, his son Marius, and Fanny, the shellfish girl, lived out their salty drama of love, honor, and the call of the sea. ⊠*15 quai Rive Neuve, Vieux Port* ☎*04–91–54–95–42.*

⑮ ★ Notre-Dame-de-la-Garde. With its hilltop perch, gargantuan gilt statue of Madonna and child (almost 30 feet high), and a Technicolor interior of red-and-beige stripes and glittering mosaics, this neo-Byzantine church, erected in 1853 by Napoléon III, is one of the emblems of Marseille. Deeply loved by locals and visitors alike, the Virgin attracts thousands who give thanks for having spared them from disease, car crashes, and other modern-day plagues. The walls are filled with *ex-votos,* stilted but passionate art offered in genuine gratitude (mostly by fishermen, who recognize Notre-Dame as their patron saint) for each eleventh-hour divine intervention. Venetian floor tiles and marble pillars add charm to the surprisingly intimate chapel, and the esplanade around the basilica offers spectacular views of the city. ⊠*On foot climb up Cours Pierre-Puget, cross the Jardin Pierre-Puget, cross a bridge to*

Rue Vauvenargues, and hike up to Pl. Edon. Or catch Bus 60 from Cours Jean-Ballard ☎04–91–13–40–80 ☼*May–Sept., daily 7* AM–*8* PM*; Oct.–Apr., daily 7–7.*

ALSO WORTH SEEING

⑫ Les Arcenaulx *(The Arsenal).* In this broad, elegant stone armory, first built for Louis XIV, a complex of upscale shops and restaurants has given the building—and neighborhood—new life. Its bookstore has a large collection of publications on Marseille, all in French (as well as art, photography, history, and rare books); a boutique sells high-end cooking (and serving) goods with a southern accent; and a book-lined restaurant serves sophisticated cuisine. It's worth a peek to remind yourself that Marseille is not the squalid backwater people continue to expect. ⊠*25 cours d'Estienne d'Orves, Vieux Port* ☎04–91–59–80–30 ☼*Bookstore Mon.–Sat. 10* AM*–midnight; boutique Mon.–Sat., 10:30–6:30; restaurant Mon.–Sat., noon–2:30* PM*, 8–10* PM.

⑰ Fort St-Nicolas and Fort St-Jean. This complex of brawny fortresses encloses the Vieux Port's entry from both sides. In order to keep the feisty, rebellious Marseillais under his thumb, Louis XIV had the fortresses built with the guns pointing *toward the city.* The Marseillais, whose local identity has always been mixed with a healthy dose of irony, are quite proud of this display of the king's (justified) doubts about their allegiance. They're best viewed from the Jardin du Pharo. To view them, climb up to the Jardin du Pharo. Sometime in early 2009, the Fort St-Jean will open under the banner of the Musée National des Civilisations de LEurope et de la Mediterranée, exhibiting the folk arts collection of the former Musée des Arts et Traditions Populaires in Paris. ⊠*Quai du Port, Vieux Port* ☎04–96–13–80–90 ⊕*www.musee-europe mediterranee.org* ☞€2 ☼*Mon., Wed., Sun., 10–noon, 2–7.*

⑱ Jardin du Pharo *(Pharo Garden).* The Pharo, another larger-than-life edifice built to Napoléon III's epic tastes, was a gift to his wife, Eugénie. It's a conference center now, but its green park has become a magnet for city strollers who want to take in panoramic views of the ports and fortifications. ⊠*Above Bd. Charles-Livon.*

⑪ Place Thiars. An ensemble of Italianate 18th-century buildings frames this popular center of activity, where one sidewalk café spills into another, and every kind of bouillabaisse is yours for the asking. At night the neighborhood is a fashionable hangout for young professionals on their way to and from the theaters and clubs on Quai de Rive Neuve. ⊠*Framed by Quai Neuve, Rue Fortia, Rue de la Paix Marcel-Paul, and Cours d'Estienne d'Orves.*

⑭ Théâtre National de Marseille La Criée *(National Theater of Marseille at "The Fish Auction").* Behind the floridly decorated facade of this grand old fish-auction house, a prestigious state theater company performs. Innovative director Jean-Louis Benoit brings an edgy streetwise energy to the season's productions. ⊠*30 quai Rive Neuve, Vieux Port* ☎04–91–54–70–54 *for reservations* ☼*Box office Tues.–Sat. 11–6* ☞€10–€25.

OFF THE BEATEN PATH

Château d'If. This wildly romantic island fortress, its thick towers and crenellated walls looming in the sea spray just off Marseille's coast, is the stuff of history—and legend. François I, in the 16th century, recognized the strategic advantage of an island fortress surveying the mouth of Marseille's vast harbor, so he had one built. Its effect as deterrent was so successful, it never saw combat and was eventually converted to a prison. It was here that Alexandre Dumas locked up his most famous character, the Count of Monte Cristo. Though he was fictional, the hole Dumas had him escape through is real enough, and it's visible in the cell today. (By contrast, the real-life Man in the Iron Mask, whose cell is still being shown, was not actually imprisoned here.) As you walk from cell to cell, each labeled for the noble (or ignoble) prisoner it held, video monitors replay scenes from film versions of the Dumas tale, including the Count's Houdini-like underwater escape from a body bag thrown from the tower. Even the jaded and castle-weary will find themselves playing nightwatch from the ramparts. The GACM boat ride (from the Quai des Belges, €10; for information call ☎04–91–55–50–09) and the views from the broad terrace alone are worth the trip. ☎04–91–59–02–30 ▧ *Château €4.60 (no credit cards)* ☉ *Apr.–Sept., daily 9:30–6:30; Oct.–Mar., Tues.–Sun. 9:30–5:30.*

LA CANEBIÈRE

In a direct line east from the Vieux Port, this famous avenue used to serve as the dividing line between those Marseillais who had money and those who did not. In the last hundred years it has lost much of its former glory, and is now dominated by shopping malls and fast-food restaurants. It's architecture and 19th-century wedding-cake facades still make for an interesting walk, and it's a great place from which to make forays through the North African neighborhood along Rue Longue-des-Capucins, to the bohemian Cours Julien via Rue d'Aubagne, and on to the Palais Longchamp and its fine-arts and natural-history museums.

WHAT TO SEE

La Canebière. This wide avenue leading from the port, known affectionately as the "Can o' Beer" by American sailors, was once crammed with cafés, theaters, bars, and tempting stores full of zoot suits and swell hats, and figured in popular songs and operettas. It's noisy but dull today, yet you may take pleasure in studying the grand old 19th-century mansions lining it.

Cours Julien. A center of bohemian *flânerie* (hanging out), this is a lovely place to relax by the fountain, in the shade of plane trees, or under a café umbrella. Its low-key and painterly tableau is framed by graceful 18th-century buildings.

⑲ Palais de Longchamp. This recently renovated extravagant and grandiose 19th-century palace, inaugurated in 1869, was built to celebrate the completion of an 84-km (52-mi) aqueduct bringing the water of the Durance river to the open sea. The massive, classical-style building crowns a hill, and is splayed with impressive symmetrical grace around a series of fountains with a triumphal arch at its center and museums in either wing. In the **Musée des Beaux-Arts** (Fine Arts Museum) are 16th- and 17th-century paintings, including several by Rubens, as well as fine marble sculptures and drawings by the Marseille architect Pierre Puget. There's a delightful group of sculptures by caricaturist Honoré Daumier, and a collection of French 19th-century paintings, including Courbet, Ingres, and David, is strong. In the right wing of the palace is the **Musée d'Histoire Naturelle** (Natural History Museum) with a collection of prehistoric and zoological artifacts, plus a large aquarium with fish from around the world. ⊠*End of Bd. Longchamp, La Canebière* ☎*04–91–14–59–30 or 04–91–14–59–50* ⊠*€2, Musée des Beaux-Arts; €3, Musée d'Histoire Naturelle* ☉*May–Sept., Tues.–Sun. 11–6; Oct.–Apr., Tues.–Sun. 10–5.*

Musée Grobet-Labadié. This lovely and intimate museum houses the private art collection of the wealthy 19th-century couple of the same name. Their 1873 mansion, beautifully renovated, offers an intriguing glimpse into the cultivated art tastes of the time, ranging from 15th- and 16th-century Italian and Flemish paintings to Fragonard and Millet. ⊠*140 bd. Longchamp, La Canebière* ☎*04–91–62–21–82* ⊠*€2* ☉*May–Sept., Tues.–Sun. 10–6; Oct.–Apr., Tues.–Sun. 10–5.*

Rue Longue-des-Capucins/Rue d'Aubagne. Stepping into this atmospheric neighborhood, you may feel you have suddenly been transported to a Moroccan souk. Shops with open bins of olives and coffee beans and tea and spices and dried beans and chickpeas and couscous and peppers and salted sardines serve the needs of Marseille's large and vibrant North African community. Tiny shoebox cafés proffer exotic sweets.

ANSES: EAST OF TOWN

Along the coastline east of Marseille's center, a series of pretty little *anses* (ports) leads to the more famous and far-flung Calanques. These miniature inlets are really tiny villages, with pretty, balconied, boxy houses (called *cabanons*) clustered around bright-painted fishing boats. Don't even think about buying a cabanon of your own, however; they are part of the fishing community's heritage and are protected from gentrification by the outside world.

A GOOD DRIVE

Drive up the Quai de Rive Neuve to the Corniche J.-F. Kennedy, which roars along the dramatic cliff top above the Mediterranean. The Art Deco **Monument aux Héros de l'Armée d'Orient et des Terres Lointaines** (Monument to the Heroes of the Army of the East and Faraway Lands) marks your turning point. Head left into the picture-perfect little fishing port called the **Vallon des Auffes.** You could paddle across it in two strokes, but this miniature inlet concentrates all the color (blue, red, and green fishing boats, azure water) of a Rossellini film set.

Continue past the wealthy **Roucas-Blanc** neighborhood and the full-scale 19th-century reproduction of Michelangelo's *David,* standing incongruously at the center of Avenue du Prado. When the Marseillais do

Continued on page 194

CUISINE OF THE SUN

By
Rosa Jackson

Why do colors seem more intense in Provence, flavors more vivid? It could be the hot, dry climate, which concentrates the essence of fruit and vegetables, or the sun beaming down on the market stalls. Or perhaps you are just seeing the world through rosé-tinted (wine) glasses. Whatever the reason, the real story of Provençal food is one of triumph over the elements. Here's how to savor its *incroyable* flavor.

FROM HOT TO HAUTE

As you bite into a honey-ripe Cavaillon melon or a snow-white, fennel-perfumed sea bass fillet, you might think that nature has always been kind to Provence. Not so. On the wind-battered coast of Marseille, fishermen salvaged the boniest rock fish to create a restorative soup—bouillabaisse—that would become legendary worldwide. In the sun-blasted mountains north of Nice, impoverished farmers developed a repertoire of dishes found no-where else in France, using hardy Swiss chard, chickpea flour, and salt cod (shipped in from Scandinavia to compensate for a scarcity of fresh fish). Camargue cowboys tamed the wild bull to create their own version of *daube*, a long-simmered stew that transforms tough cuts of meat into a gourmet marvel. Olive oil, the very symbol of Provençal food, is only now overcoming a 1950s frost that entirely wiped out France's olive groves—the local production is tiny compared to that of Spain or Italy but of exceptionally high quality. Even the tomato has a relatively short history here, having been introduced in the 1820s and at first used only in cooked dishes.

FISH TALES

If Provençal cooking is united by a common struggle against the very conditions that give its ingredients their intensity—brilliant sunshine, arid soil, fierce wind, infrequent, pounding rain—it is divided by the area's dramatically changing landscapes. In the Vaucluse alone, scorched plains punctuated by ocher cliffs give way to remarkably lush, orchard-lined mountains and gently sloped vineyards. The wild Calanques of Marseille—source of spiky sea urchins and slithering octopuses—ease into the more tranquil waters of St-Tropez, home

AIL DE PROVENCE

An indispensable ingredient in Provençal cooking, these garlic bulbs can be white, pink, or purplish; the darker the color, the stronger the flavor.

OLIVES DE NICE

True Niçois olives are not uniformly black but come in delicate shades of green and deep violet.

to gleaming bream and sea bass. Everywhere you will find sun-ripened fruit dripping provocatively with nectar and vegetables so flavor-packed that meat might seem a mere accessory. The joy of visiting this region lies in discovering these differences, which might be subtle (as in a local version of boullabaisse or fish soup) or unmistakable (as in the powerful scent that signals truffle season in Carpentras).

POTS, PANS & PICKS
The best Provençal chefs remain fiercely proud of the dishes that define their region or their village, even while injecting their own identities and ideas into the food. Thanks to its ports, Provence has always been open to outside influences, yet the wealth of readily available ingredients prevents chefs from straying too far from their roots—when the local basil is so headily perfumed, why use lemongrass? If menus at first seem repetitive, go beyond the words *(tapenade, ratatouille, pistou)* to notice how each chef interprets the dish: this is not a land of printed recipes but of spontaneity inspired by the seasons and the markets. Don't expect perfect food every time, but with the help of this book, seek out those who love what they do enough to make *la cuisine de soleil* even more dazzling than the sunshine.

LA VIE EN ROSE

One sip and you'll agree: rosé wine tastes wonderful in the south of France, particularly along the coast. Some experts claim that the sea air enhances the aroma, which might explain why a bottle of Côtes de Provence rosé loses some of its holiday magic at home. French rosés are generally dry, thirst-quenching, and best served chilled. They are considered easy-drinking holiday wines, and quality is constantly improving. Be sure to try a Bandol at least once; the rest of the time, you can't go wrong with a good local rosé.

THE TOP TEN DISHES

AÏOLI

The name for both a dragon's-breath mayonnaise made with helpings of garlic and also a complete recipe of salt cod, potatoes, hard-boiled eggs, and vegetables, aïoli pops up all over Provence, but seems most beloved of the Marseillais. Not an indigenous food, salt cod arrived on the French coast in the Middle Ages from Scandinavia. In keeping with Catholic practice, some restaurants serve it only on Fridays. And it's a good sign if they ask that you place your order at least a day in advance. A grand aïoli is a traditional component of the Niçois Christmas feast.

BOUILLABAISSE

Originally a humble fisherman's soup made with the part of the catch that nobody else wanted, bouillabaisse—the famous fish stew—consists of four or five kinds of fish: the villainous-looking rascasse (red scorpion fish), grondin (sea robin), baudroie (monkfish), congre (conger eel), and rouget (mullet). Snobs add lobster. The whole lot is simmered in a stock of onions, tomatoes, garlic, olive oil, and saffron, which gives the dish its golden color. When presented properly, the broth is served first, with croutons and rouille, a creamy garlic sauce that you spoon in to suit your taste. The fish comes separately, and the ritual is to put pieces into the broth after having a go at the soup on its own.

Bourride

BOURRIDE

This poached fish dish owes its anise kick to pastis and its garlic punch to aïoli. The name comes from the Provençal bourrido, which translates less poetically as "boiled." Monkfish—known as baudroie in Provence and lotte in the rest of France—is a must, but chefs occasionally dress up their bourride with other species and shellfish.

DAUBE DE BOEUF

To distinguish their prized beef stew from boeuf bourguignon, Provençal chefs make a point of not marinating the meat, instead cooking it very slowly in tannic red wine that is often flavored with orange zest. In the Camargue, daube is made with the local taureau (bull's meat), while the Avignon variation uses lamb. In Nice, try ravioli à la daube.

FOUGASSE

The Provençal answer to Italian focaccia, this soft flatbread is distinguished by holes that give it the appearance of a lacy leaf. It can be made savory—flavored with olives, anchovy, bacon, cheese, or anything else the baker has on hand—or sweet, enriched with olive oil and dusted with icing sugar. When in Menton, don't miss the sugary fougasse mentonnaise.

LES PETITS FARCIS

The Niçois specialty called les petits farcis are prepared with tiny summer vegetables (usually zucchini, tomatoes, peppers, and onions) that are traditionally stuffed with veal or leftover daube (beef stew). Enjoy them warm (not hot); this is the best temperature to appreciate their flavors. Like so many Niçois dishes, they make great picnic food.

Fougasse, the Provençal answer to Italian focacia

RATATOUILLE

At its best, ratatouille is a glorious thing—a riot of eggplant, zucchini, bell peppers, and onions, each sautéed separately in olive oil and then gently combined with sweet summer tomatoes. A well-made ratatouille, to which a pinch of saffron has been added to heighten its flavor, is also delicious served chilled.

SOCCA

You'll find socca vendors from Nice to Menton, but this chickpea pancake cooked on a giant iron platter in a wood-fired oven is really a Niçois phenomenon, born of sheer poverty at a time when wheat flour was scarce. After cooking, it is sliced into finger-lickin' portions with an oyster knife. Enjoy it with a glass of pointu, chilled rosé.

SOUPE AU PISTOU

Provençal's answer to pesto, pistou consists of the simplest ingredients—garlic, olive oil, fresh basil, and Parmesan—ideally pounded together by hand in a stone mortar with an olivewood pestle. Most traditionally it brings a potent kick to soupe au pistou, a kind of French minestrone made with green beans, white beans, potatoes, and zucchini.

TIAN DE LÉGUMES

A tian is both a beautiful earthenware dish and one of many vegetable gratins that might be cooked in it. Again showing the thrifty use of ingredients in Provençal cooking, the tian makes a complete meal of seasonal vegetables, eggs, and a little cheese. Swiss chard is a favorite ingredient in winter, while eggplant and tomato are best bets in summer.

THE ITALIAN CONNECTION

The most distinctive food on the Riviera comes from Nice. It's a curious mixture of Parisian, Provençal, and Italian cuisine, pungent with garlic, olives, anchovies, and steaming shellfish. Among the specialties here: pissaladière, an onion tart laced with black olive puree and anchovies; pan bagnat, a French loaf—a baguette—split down the middle, soaked in olive oil, and garnished with tomatoes, radishes, peppers, onions, hard-boiled eggs, black olives, and a sprig of basil; and l'estocaficada, a ragout of stockfish (air-dried unsalted fish, often cod), soaked in water before being cooked and served with potatoes, tomatoes, and zucchini.

THE TASTEMAKERS

It is not entirely surprising that some of France's best chefs now work in Provence and on the Riviera. It was here—in Villeneuve-Loubet, outside Cannes—that **Auguste Escoffier**, the legendary founding father of haute cuisine, was born (his villa is now a museum). Today, Escoffier's heirs are forging new paths in the "new Mediterranean cuisine" in all its costly splendor. Everybody knows the name of Alain Ducasse, whose luxurious cuisine moderne is on show at Monaco's Le Louis XV. Here are the newer stars that are making gastronomes genuflect today.

Alain Llorca

Former Negresco chef **Alain Llorca**—whose name reveals his Basque roots—has found the perfect setting for his Spanish-influenced style in the freshly renovated, plum-and-white dining room of the Moulin de Mougins, the famous culinary temple put on the map years ago by Roger Vergé. No matter how simple or complex the dish, Llorca makes each ingredient sing—a crisp-skinned farmer's chicken breast proves tender enough to cut with a fork, its accompanying spring vegetables straight from his own potager (vegetable garden). Llorca's sense of humor comes through in his ronde des tapas—look for such whimsical nibbles as foie gras bonbons, goat cheese croque-monsieur, and bouillabaisse-style octopus.

Antique dealers feel at home at Le Jardin du Quai in L'Isle-sur-la-Sorgue, which jovial young chef **Daniel Hébet** runs like an open house. In summer, regulars linger on the garden patio reading the paper and chatting, while in winter the high-ceiling bistro-style dining room exudes the same welcoming vibe. Shrugging off the constraints of haute cuisine with a no-choice set menu at lunch and dinner, Hébet still makes clever use of techniques, serving vivid green, individually skinned broad beans in a frothy sauce with barely cooked chanterelles and artfully peeled fat white asparagus. Don't miss his quinoa-crusted cod.

After over 20 years of superstar chefdom, **Jacques Maximin** has left his widely acclaimed restaurant in Vence, La Table d'Amis, and will become a top consultant for the Alain Ducasse Formation school. He has been asked to join the École Supérieure de la Patisserie (Superior School of Pastries and Desserts) and to create a reference base of French cuisine of the 20th century. If you want to participate in a course, contact the school (✉ 41 rue de l'Abbé Ruelan, Argenteuil, ☎ 01-34-34-19-10). A mere €1,500 later (for a 4-day course), you will be an expert in "cuisine de bien être et bon goût" (cuisine of well-being and good taste).

The summer tomato menu has become a much-anticipated annual tradition at **Christian Etienne**'s restaurant next to the Palais des Papes in Avignon, where each year he celebrates the versatility of this vegetable with a tasting extravaganza that might include tartare of three varieties with oil from the Bleu Argent olive mill in Provence, foie gras with Roma tomato petals, and tomato macaroon with lime sorbet. Etienne is one of the long-established masters of Provençal cooking, and if his cooking sometimes makes generous use of butter (rather than uniquely olive oil), his customers aren't complaining.

Christian Etienne

TO MARKET, TO MARKET

Marché aux poissons, Marseille

Markets define Provençal living, from the see-and-be-seen Cours Saleya in Nice to villages that spring to life once or twice a week as the trucks bearing goat cheese or sunny-yolked farmers' eggs pull up to the main square. Below are a few of the best; all are open Tuesday through Sunday except Cotignac.

Cours Saleya, Nice – The coast's most colorful market, as much for the people as for the goods on display (it's liveliest on weekends). Local producers cluster in Place Pierre Gauthier.

Marché Forville, Cannes – Though not the best-known market on the Côte d'Azur, Forville has an extraordinary selection, from the small producers who line the center aisle to the small fish market, which is usually sold out by late morning.

Marché Richelme, Aix-en-Provence – This market is legendary, and rightly so, for its lovely setting in the Old Town and its eye-popping range of goods. No wonder Cézanne immortalized such apples and pears.

Marché aux poissons, Marseille – You'll understand the wonder of bouillabaisse once you've visited this market on the Vieux Port: colorful fishing boats pull up to the quay and fill blue plastic tubs with still-leaping fish and lively octopuses.

Cotignac market (Tuesday) – One of dozens of small markets in Provence, Cotignac has retained a real village atmosphere and provides the perfect excuse to visit this seductive town.

TRUFFES DE CARPENTRAS

This town in the Vaucluse is the center of the "black diamond" trade, thanks to its Saturday truffle market, held from November to March.

something, they do it big. The city's main beaches lie at David's feet in the **Parc Balnéaire** du Prado, including the Plage de David. From the sands, you'll have breathtaking views of the Iles de Frioul (Frioul Islands), which you can visit by boat from Marseille's port.

★ After David and the beaches, continue up the road to **Port de Plaisance de la Pointe Rouge** and then **La Madrague,** both postcard-pretty anses wedged with bobbing boats and toy-block cabanons in saturated tints. Pursue the road to its dead end at **Les Goudes** and climb over boulders and tidal pools to the extraordinary **Anse Croisette,** a rough inlet paradise of crashing waves and rock. It was near here, known to the Marseillais as the Bout du Monde (End of the World), where the *Grand St-Antoine*—the ship that brought the plague to Marseille in 1720—was sunk, but too late to save the 100,000 who died from its deadly cargo.

OFF THE BEATEN PATH

L'Estaque. At this famous village north of Marseille, Cézanne led an influx of artists eager to capture its cliff-top views over the harbor. Braque, Derain, and Renoir all put its red rooftops, rugged cliffs, and factory smokestacks on canvas. Pick up the English-language itinerary "L'Estaque and the Painters" from the Marseille tourist office and hunt down the sites and views they immortalized. It's a little seedy these days, but there are cafés and a few fish shops making the most of the nearby Criée (fisherman's auction). This is where the real wholesale auction moved from Marseille's Quai de Rive Neuve. A novel way to see Cézanne's famous scenery is to take a standard SNCF train trip from the Gare St-Charles to Martigue; it follows the L'Estaque waterfront and (with the exception of a few tunnels) offers magnificent views.

WHERE TO EAT

$$$$ ✕**Chez Fonfon.** For the perfect bouillabaisse, take a taxi to the Vallon
★ des Auffes, one of Marseille's myriad charming fishing ports—here, Chez Fonfon serves the specialty against a nearly film-set backdrop. Once presided over by cult chef "Fonfon," this fabled Marseillais landmark used to be a favorite movie-star hangout. Plain, fresh seafood impeccably grilled, steamed, or roasted in salt crust is still served in two pretty pink dining rooms with picture windows that overlook the fishing boats that supply your dinner. The crowds come to indulge in classic bouillabaisse served with all the bells and whistles—decadently rich broth, hot-chili rouille, and flamboyant table-side filleting. Incidentally, when bouillabasse is presented properly, the broth is served croutons and rouille, a creamy garlic sauce that you spoon in to suit your taste. The fish comes separately, and the ritual is to put pieces into the broth after having a go at the soup on its own. ⊠*140 rue du Vallon des Auffes, Vallon des Auffes* ☎*04–91–52–14–38* ⊕*www.chez-fonfon. com* ⚑*Reservations essential* ⊟*AE, DC, MC, V* ☉*Closed Sun. and 1st 2 wks in Jan. No lunch Mon.*

$$$$ ✕**L'Epuisette.** Artfully placed on a rocky, fingerlike cliff surrounded by the sea, this seafood restaurant offers gorgeous views of crashing surf on one side and the port of Vallon des Auffes on the other. Chef Guil-

How to Eat a Sea Urchin

". . . But answer came there none—/ And this was scarcely odd, because/ They'd eaten every one," wrote Lewis Carroll in *Through the Looking Glass.*

Urchins, those spiny little balls, are cracked open and served belly up on a platter of seaweed, usually six or a dozen at a time. To the uninitiated, they're not a pretty sight: each black demi-globe comes with quills still . . . well, waving, but only slightly. Within this macabre natural bowl floats a dense puddle of (it must be said) muddy brown grit and bile-green slime. Supporting the rim with your left thumb and index finger (taking

care not to impale yourself), scrape said slime to the sides with the point of your spoon. Here lies what the fuss is all about: there are six coral-pink strips of sea-perfumed stuff inside, more foam than flesh (you may have experienced a more substantial version in sushi). Scrape these gently up and spread them on a slice of baguette. Or just slide them into a spoon and bite. An ocean of milky-sweet flavor is concentrated in this rosy streak. Granted, a dozen won't make a meal, but keep the little guys company with oysters, mussels, clams, sea snails, a crock of butter, a basket of bread, and an icy bottle of Cassis.

laume Sourrieu has acquired a big reputation (and Michelin stars) for sophisticated cooking—shellfish risotto with violet and coriander fritter, or sea bass baked in a salt crust, are some top delights, all matched with a superb wine list. Save room for dessert. ⊠ *Anse du Vallon des Auffes, Vallon des Auffes* ☎ *04–91–52–17–82* ⊟ *AE, DC, MC, V* ⊘ *Closed Sun. and Mon.*

$$$$ ✕ **Mets de Provence.** Climb the oddly slanted wharf-side stairs and enter a cosseted Provençal world. With boats bobbing outside the window and a landlubbing country decor, this romantic restaurant makes the most of Marseille's split personality. Classic Provençal hors d'oeuvres—tapenade, brandade (salt-cod dip), aioli—lead into seafood (dorado roasted with fennel and licorice) and meats (rack of lamb in herb pastry). The four-course lunch (€40 including wine) is marvelous. ⊠ *18 quai de Rive Neuve, Vieux Port* ☎ *04–91–33–35–38* ⊟ *MC, V* ⊘ *Closed Sun. No lunch Sat. No dinner Mon.*

$$$$ ✕ **Restaurant Peron.** Chic and stylishly modern with a dark-wood interior and large windows overlooking the sea to some of the best views in the city, this restaurant is a magnet for hip, young professionals—you'll need to book ahead. Surprisingly service-oriented and very friendly, the staff are efficient and quietly accommodating. You can have delicious bouillabaisse (€48 per person), the catch of the day (price by the weight), or a bargain prix-fixe price of €58 which include three courses. Highly recommended is the fois gras with Kumquat marmalade and the fresh scallops pan-fried with lime confit polenta. ⊠ *56 corniche J.-F. Kennedy, Endoume* ☎ *04–91–52–15–22* ⊕ *www.restaurant-peron. com* ⊟ *AE, DC, MC, V.*

$$$ ✕ **Baie des Singes.** On a tiny rock-ringed lagoon as isolated from the
★ nearby city as if it were a desert island, this beautiful cinematic spot was once a customs house under Napoléon III. You can rent a mat-

tress and lounge chair (€10), dive into the turquoise water, and shower off for the only kind of meal worthy of such a location: fresh fish. There's bouillabaisse, of course, but also fresh-grilled sardines, mullet, and baudroie; and crabs, lobster, and local *cigales de mer* (shrimplike "sea locusts"). It's all served at terrace tables overlooking the water. The expansive owner, son of a fishmonger and grandson of a fisherman, knows his craft, and boasts—literally—Jacques Chirac and Catherine Deneuve among his loyal clientele. ⊠*Anse des Croisettes, Marseille* ☎*04–91–73–68–87* ⊟*MC, V* ⊘*Closed Oct.–Mar.*

$$$ ✕**Miramar.** A Marseille institution, this restaurant is justifiably famous
★ for its bouillabaisse, and is one of the best places to sample the city's fabled dish. It maintains a '60s style of red-velvet-and-wood-paneling elegance (you almost expect to spot Jackie O in a pillbox hat at the next table) but the portside terrace tables cut through the stuffiness. Unlike many seafood restaurants in town, it always has bouillabaisse on the menu, so you don't have to order in advance. Desserts are spectacular, thanks to an innovative pastry chef, and with a chilled bottle of Cassis it is truly a dining event. ⊠*12 quai du Port, Vieux Port* ☎*04–91–91–10–40* ⊟*AE, MC, V* ⊘*Closed Sun., Mon., and 2 wks in Jan.*

$$$ ✕**Une Table au Sud.** After learning as much as he could from super-chef Alain Ducasse in Paris, Lionel Lévy quickly won his own reputation for modern French cooking when he opened this stylish and contemporary restaurant. The rather stark interior is softened by draping yellow curtains, warm red-toned carpets, and lots of sunlight. Rich desserts like *croquant au chocolate fondant* (chocolate ganache layered inside almond pastry) add a nice finish to an already delightful meal—try the zucchini flowers stuffed with feta cheese followed by grilled tuna steak with teriyaki gelée—and friendly service encourages you to linger over a last glass of wine while gazing out at the port. ⊠*2 quai du Port, Vieux Port* ☎*04–91–90–63–53* ⊟*MC, V* ⊘*Closed Sun. and Mon.*

$$ ✕**L'Escale.** In the sleepy little village of Les Goudes, 20 minutes outside of the center of Marseille, this seaside dining room and terrace has become a village landmark. The catch of the day couldn't be much fresher, and former fisherman and fishmonger Serge Zarokian brings years of experience to a hearty, earthy bouillabaisse (order in advance) or delicately sautéed baby squid. It's very popular, especially for Sunday lunch, so book ahead. ⊠*2 bd. Alexandre Delabre, Les Goudes* ☎*04–91–73–16–78* ⌲*Reservations essential* ⊟*AE, DC, MC, V* ⊘*Closed Jan. No lunch Mon. and Tues. in May–Sept. Closed Mon. and Tues. in Oct.–Apr.*

$$ ✕**Les Arcenaulx.** At this book-lined, red-walled haven in the stylish print-and-boutique complex of the renovated arsenal, you can have a delicious and refined Provençal lunch—and read while you're waiting. Seafood figures large on the menu—try the fresh sea bream from the market two blocks away or the garlic-perfumed octopus stew. The fact that diners enter by passing rows of burnished leather-bound antique tomes appeals to Marseille's finer side, and you'll find an interesting mix of politicians, actors, and professors inside. ⊠*25 cours d'Estienne*

d'Orves, Vieux Port ☎04–91–59–80–30 ⊟AE, DC, MC, V ⊘Closed Sun. and 1 wk in Aug.

$ ✕**Caffè Milano.** With its old mirrors and pictures of famous (mostly French) stars who have stopped by for a meal, this popular spot serves Italian and Provençal dishes in an upscale, busy space. Photographers, models, and fashion wannabes mix and mingle downstairs while the rather imposing mezzanine is a good place to people-watch. Quick service and simple fare make this spot ideal to have lunch or dinner. The daily pasta special is usually worth a try, and the salad with chicken and ginger makes a nice light snack. ⊠43 rue Sainte, Vieux Port ☎04–91–33–14–33 ⊟MC, V ⊘Closed Sun. No lunch Sat.

$ ✕**Chez Jeannot.** This is the poor man's Chez Fonfon, around the port from the prestigious restaurant and run by a member of the same family. It's so popular that it's become something of a theme-restaurant version of itself (plastic menus, wedding-banquet-style dining rooms), but it's a wonderful place to get away from town and enjoy a casual meal in an lovely spot. The pizzas are heavy, and there are towering platters of shellfish still twitching—but you're here for the film-set scenery as much as for the food. Terrace tables overlooking the fishing boats justify taxi fare from the center, but reserve in advance or you'll end up in the dark interior. ⊠129 Vallon des Auffes, Vallon des Auffes ☎04–91–52–11–28 ⊟AE, V ⊘Closed Mon. No lunch Tues.–Fri.

$ ✕**Chez Vincent.** Although it's in the mini-red-light district of the Vieux Port, this little Italian restaurant is all it's cracked up to be. The decor is pure Italian bistro with pristine white table cloths and copper pots, bunches of dried spices, and flowers on the wall. The spaghetti with tiny clams is excellent, as is the lasagna and the tiramisu. It is jammed with lively night-owl regulars, including singers from the Opéra around the corner, and the happy buzz moves down to a satisfied murmur at the end of the meal. Often full, this spot requires reservations in advance. ⊠25 rue Glandèves, Vieux Port ☎04–91–33–96–78 ⊟No credit cards ⊘Closed Mon. No lunch Sun.

¢ ✕**Au Petit Naples.** With huge portions, a convivial vibe, and a small, busy beachfront location in the Estaque suburb, this restaurant is jammed with locals and savvy tourists from every walk of life. Some connoisseurs say that the pizza here is even better than at Etienne's, and if you are looking for a real Marseille experience, eating here is a perfect opportuntiy; the chef knows everyone, as do the servers, and happy banter livens up the atmosphere. Seafood, especially fried calamari, is another specialty but come hungry or share a plate as servings are truly enormous. ⊠14 plage de l'Estaque ☎04–91–46–05–11 ⊟No credit cards ⊘Closed Sun. No lunch Sat.

¢ ✕**Pizzeria Etienne.** A historic Le Panier hole-in-the-wall, this small piz-
★ zeria is filled daily with politicos and young professionals who enjoy the personality of the chef Stéphane Cassero, who was famous at one time for having no printed menu and announcing the price of the meal only after he'd had the chance to look you over. Remarkably little has changed over the years, except now there is a posted menu (with prices). Brace yourself for an epic meal, starting with a large anchovy pizza from the wood-burning oven, then dig into fried squid, eggplant

gratin, and a slab of rare grilled beef all served with the background of laughter, rich patois, and abuse from the chef. ✉ *43 rue de la Lorette, Le Panier* ☎*No phone* ⊟*No credit cards* ☙*Closed Sun.*

¢ ✕**Toinou Dégustation.** You can join the crowd at the outdoor stand and split a few oysters on the hoof. But it's more comfortable settling into a brasserie booth at this landmark shellfish joint where you can get heaps of Cassis urchins, cream-filled *violets* (a kind of monstrous sea slug), clams, mussels, and, of course, oysters. Try the North African hot sauce or opt for the powerful aïoli. ✉ *3 Cours St-Louis, Vieux Port* ☎*04–91–54–08–79* ⊕*www.toinou.com* ⊟*No credit cards* ☙*Closed Sun. and Aug.; no lunch Mon.*

WHERE TO STAY

$$$$ 🏨 **Le Petit Nice.** Despite its name, this glamorous hideaway out-Rivieras
★ anything in Nice. On a rocky promontory overlooking the harbor and the Iles de Frioul, this turn-of-the-20th-century Greek-style villa was bought from a countess in 1917 and converted to a hotel/restaurant in anticipation of the Jazz Age rush to the Côte d'Azur. The Passédat family has been getting it right ever since. Most of the modern designer rooms are sleek and minimalist and open onto balconies overlooking the sea. For a more time-burnished ambience, opt for a room in the Marina Wing. In summer, fresh meals (try the succulent laurel, pear, and cucumber langoustine) from the excellent restaurant (reservations essential) are served by the heated saltwater pool overlooking the crashing surf. All in all, some might consider this a Hollywood set for the South of France of their dreams. **Pros:** sea-front location; glorious restaurant; intimate charm. **Cons:** reception can be cool. ✉ *Anse de Maldormé, Corniche J.-F. Kennedy, Endoume* ☎*04–91–59–25–92* ⊕*www.passedat.com* ⇔*13 rooms, 3 suites* ♿*In-room: refrigerator. In-hotel: restaurant, pool, Wi-Fi, parking (free), some pets allowed* ⊟*AE, DC, MC, V* ⦿*MAP.*

$$$$ 🏨 **Pullman Palm Beach.** Sleek with stunning 260-degree views of the bay and the islands, this white-on-white modern hotel offers designs by Starck, Zanotta, and Emu. Service is prompt and unobtrusive, and the huge windows make for a light-filled reception area. The saltwater pool is fed by a natural spring and the rooms are up-to-the-minute in decor. Specialties of the good modern restaurant include rack of lamb basted with olive tapenade and black grain mustard and sea bass baked with Provençal vegetables. **Pros:** the view out to sea is truly remarkable, and the rooms are large, most with balconies. **Cons:** service lacks warmth and there are too many rooms for a personalized welcome. ✉*200 corniche J.-F. Kennedy, Endoume* ☎*04–91–16–19–00* ⊕*www. sofitel.com* ⇔*150 rooms, 10 suites* ♿*In-room: refrigerator. In-hotel: restaurant, pool, Wi-Fi, parking (fee), some pets allowed* ⊟*AE, DC, MC, V* ⦿*BP.*

$$$ 🏨 **Mercure Beauvau Vieux Port.** Chopin spent the night and George Sand
★ kept a suite in this historic hotel overlooking the Vieux Port. It recently underwent a complete overhaul—even closing for more than a year— but its loyal clientele were not disappointed when the doors finally reopened. Public rooms still have real antiques, burnished woodwork,

Provençal-style decor, and plush carpets, all comprising a convincing part of this intimate urban hotel's genuine old-world charm. Guest rooms are in the same style but have been updated to include all the modern comforts. Harbor-view rooms, with balconies high over the fish market, more than justify the splurge. **Pros:** recent renovations keep all the charm and take away all the inconveniences (noise, etc.); service is excellent. **Cons:** some rooms are small and a bit dark. ⊠4 *rue Beauvau, Vieux Port* ☎*04–91–54–91–00, 800/637–2873 for U.S. reservations* ⊕*www.mercure.com* ⇗*70 rooms, 2 suites* ⌂*In-room: refrigerator. In-hotel: restaurant, parking (fee), some pets allowed* ⊟*AE, DC, MC, V* ⏃*BP*

$$$ ▦ **New Hotel Vieux Port.** In the heart of things, at the crossroads of the Quai du Port and the Quai des Belges, this old, urban hotel is being slicked up a little bit more every month with its ongoing, yet amazingly quiet, renovations. The cage elevator and the weathered marble stairs lead up to spare, modern rooms with tile baths. Ask for a corner room overlooking the ports. **Pros:** prompt service and great location. **Cons:** some rooms are small, and some are a bit noisy. ⊠*3 bis rue Reine-Elisabeth, Vieux Port* ☎*04–91–99–23–23* ⊕*www.new-hotel.com* ⇗*42 rooms* ⌂*In-room: refrigerator. In-hotel: Wi-Fi* ⊟*AE, DC, MC, V.*

$$$ ▦ **Residence du Vieux Port.** The flat glass-and-concrete facade of this postwar structure grants all the rooms here broad picture-window views all the way to Notre-Dame-de-la-Garde. Lower rooms are classic and pastel-modern, but be aware that unless you have a discerning eye for the subtleties of heavy floral design, the pricier Provençal rooms are not much different. There is a generous breakfast buffet, worth the small supplement. Note that at press time, the hotel was closed for renovations; date of completion is projected to be in June 2009. **Pros:** with so few good value hotels in Marseille, this is a great option with its ideal location and great views. **Cons:** decor is bland. ⊠*18 quai du Port, Vieux Port* ☎*04–91–91–91–22* ⊕*www.hotelmarseille.com* ⇗*40 rooms, 6 suites* ⌂*In-room: refrigerator. In-hotel: Wi-Fi, some pets allowed* ⊟*AE, DC, MC, V* ⏃*BP.*

$$ ★ ▦ **Hotel Peron.** A family-run jewel, this eclectic, rather eccentric hotel features rooms with different decorative themes, from delicate, rather austere Japanese to playful Dutch to colorful Moroccan. It was the first hotel in Marseille to install baths in the 1960s, and, yes, the originals are still here—charming but very small. Almost every room has a stunning sea view. The nights are very quiet, and the service is excellent. **Pros:** price is excellent value, especially for sea views; very friendly service. **Cons:** some rooms need freshening up (new paint) and some rooms are quite small. ⊠*119 corniche J.-F. Kennedy, Endoume* ☎*04–91–31–01–41* ⊕*www.hotel-peron.com* ⇗*26 rooms* ⌂*In-room: no a/c. In-hotel: public Wi-Fi, some pets allowed* ⊟*AE, MC, V* ⏃*BP.*

$$ ▦ **Le Rhul.** This is the Hôtel Le Petit Nice for ordinary people: a broad, '60s-style roadside inn to the *left* of the corniche but still taking in spectacular sea views. Okay, so the stark architecture is cozied up with doilies and overstuffed chairs, and the rooms have beige laminate built-ins. But its restaurant is renowned for its bouillabaisse, and all but three rooms

overlook the sea; three others have little balconies from which you can thumb your nose at the more famous inn below. **Pros:** jaw-dropping sea views from the restaurant terraces; friendly service. **Cons:** rooms need freshing up, and some are quite small. ⊠*269 corniche J.-F. Kennedy, Endoume* ☎*04–91–52–54–54* ⊕*www.bouillabaissemarseille. com* ⇆*14 rooms* ⚘*In-room: refrigerator. In-hotel: restaurant, parking (fee), some pets allowed* ⊟*AE, MC, V* ❏|*MAP.*

$$ 🏨 **Saint Ferréol.** Set back from the port in the heart of the shopping district, this cozy, charming little hotel offers a warm reception and a homey breakfast room–cum–bar. Guest rooms are beautifully decked out in homage to various artists—Picasso in red, black, and gilt, for example, with jazzy Cubist curtains or Matisse in grey-backed walls with colorful prints. **Pros:** cheerful and helpful service; center-of-town location is ideal. **Cons:** some rooms are small and the street-facing ones can be noisy. ⊠*19 rue Pisançon (at Rue St-Ferréol), Vieux Port* ☎*04–91–33–12–21* ⊕*www.hotel-stferreol.com* ⇆*17 rooms* ⚘*In-hotel: public Wi-Fi* ⊟*MC, V* ❏|*BP.*

$ 🏨 **Alizé.** On the Vieux Port, its front rooms taking in postcard views, this straightforward lodging has been modernized to include tight double windows, slick modular baths, and a laminate-and-all-weather-carpet look. Public spaces have exposed stone and preserved details, and a glass elevator whisks you to your floor. It's an excellent value and location for the price range. **Pros:** ideal location in the center of the Vieux port; cozy lobby. **Cons:** rooms can be noisy; decor is uninspired. ⊠*35 quai des Belges, Vieux Port* ☎*04–91–33–66–97* ⊕*www.alize-hotel. com* ⇆*39 rooms* ⚘*In-hotel: public Wi-Fi, some pets allowed* ⊟*AE, DC, MC, V.*

$ 🏨 **Hermès.** Although the rooms are rather snug, this modest city hotel is right around the corner from the Quai du Port and is good value. Decor is simple and sufficient, and even the street-facing rooms are quiet, and the service is prompt and friendly. Ask for one of the fifth-floor rooms with tiny balconies overlooking the port—or the crow's nest "nuptiale" double with private rooftop terrace. **Pros:** location and price are excellent value in Marseille. **Cons:** rooms are small and the bathrooms even smaller. ⊠*2 rue Bonneterie, Vieux Port* ☎*04–96–11–63–63* ⊕*www. hotelmarseille.com* ⇆*28 rooms* ⚘*In-hotel: public Wi-Fi, some pets allowed* ⊟*AE, DC, MC, V.*

NIGHTLIFE & THE ARTS

With a population of more than 800,000, Marseille is a big city by French standards, with all the nightlife that entails. Arm yourself with *Marseille Poche*, a glossy monthly events minimagazine; the monthly *In Situ*, a free guide to music, theater, and galleries; *Sortir*, a weekly about film, art, and concerts in southern Provence; or *TakTik*, a hip weekly on theater and new art. They're all in French.

Le Trolleybus (⊠*24 quai de Rive Neuve, Bompard* ☎*04–91–54–30–45*) is still the hottest disco in town, and the starting—and ending—point of Marseille nightlife. Different dance "grottos" offer techno, salsa, and funk, and a young, hip crowd ranging from bankers to rappers in Nike track suits and gold jewelry. **The New Cancan** (⊠*3 rue Senac-de-Meilhan, Vieux Port* ☎*04–91–48–59–76*) is Marseille's largest gay club, with stage shows and great music, as well as a friendly, mixed crowd that livens up a rather dark space. **Dôme-Zénith** (⊠*48 av. St-Just, St-Just* ☎*04–91–47–01–25*) is Marseille's big modern venue for international rock acts and various French celebrities.

The Red Lion (⊠*231 av. Pierre Mendès France, Vieux Port* ☎*04–91–25–17–17*) is a mecca for English speakers, who pour onto the sidewalk, pints in hand, pub-style. There's happy hour daily (5 to 8) and live music Wednesday.

At **La Part des Anges** (⊠*33 rue Saint, Vieux Port* ☎*04–91–33–55–70*), good wines are brought in from all over France and served by the glass or by the bottle. Open until 2 AM daily, it attracts an eclectic crowd, from hip, arty, and trendy to overdressed women and men in bad suits.

Watch out for the local group Gachempega; they play on occasion at **L'Intermediaire** (⊠*63 pl. Jean-Jaurès, La Canebière* ☎*04–91–47–01–25*), which is the hippest venue in town for jazz, blues, and rock concerts. For rap and techno, try **L'Affranchi** (⊠*212 bd. de St-Marcel, La Canebière* ☎*04–91–35–09–19*). The long-standing and very active **Espace Julien** (⊠*39 cours Julien, Notre Dame du Mont* ☎*04–91–24–34–14*) has international blues, pop, and local techno. At the vast **Docks des Suds** (⊠*Bd. de Paris, Vieux Port* ☎*04–91–99–00–00* ⊕*www.dock-des-suds. org*), host to the Fiesta des Suds each autumn, you'll now find world and Latin music year-round. **Le Moulin** (⊠*47 bd. Perrin, St-Just* ☎*04–91–06–33–94*) is a converted cinema that has become one of Marseille's best live-music venues for visiting French and international music stars.

Marseille's vibrant multicultural mix has evolved a genre of music that fuses all the sounds of Arabic music with rhythms of Provence, Corsica, and Southern Italy, and douses it with reggae and rap.

In a beautifully restored 1901 building, **Le Café Parisien** (⊠*1 pl. Sadi Carnot, up Rue de la République, Le Panier* ☎*04–91–90–05–77*) is a dynamic melting pot where workers take their breakfast and the club crowds come when the clubs close. At night, intellectuals and the BCBG's mingle at night over drinks and Latin music, digging into first-rate tapas (€10 for a large plate) on Thursday and Friday. **La Caravelle** (⊠*34 quai du Port, Vieux Port* ☎*04–91–90–36–64*) has a cocktail bar, great live jazz, and a narrow balcony that has a picture-perfect view over the port.

Classical-music concerts are held in the **Abbaye St-Victor** (☎*04–96–11–20–60 for information*). Operas and orchestral concerts take place at the **Opéra Municipal** (⊠*2 rue Molière, Pl. Ernest Reyer, Notre Dame du Mont* ☎*04–91–55–00–70*).

At the **Théâtre National de Marseille La Criée** (⊠*Quai de Rive Neuve, Vieux Port* ☎*04–91–54–74–54*), a strong and solid repertoire of classical and contemporary works is performed. **Théâtre Off** (⊠*Quai de*

Rive Neuve, Vieux Port ☎04–91–33–12–92) presents alternative productions of classics. Celebrity-cast road shows and operettas are performed in the Théâtre Municipal's **Espace Odéon** (⊠*163 La Canebière, La Canebière* ☎04–91–92–79–44).

At **Badaboum** (⊠*Quai de Rive Neuve, Vieux Port* ☎04–91–54–40–71), adventurous, accessible productions for children are performed. The **Théâtre des Marionettes** (⊠*Theatre Massalia, 41 rue Jobin, La Canebière* ☎04–91–11–45–65) entertains a young audience with puppets, dance, and music—occasionally in English. It's by the Gare St-Charles.

SPORTS & THE OUTDOORS

Marseille's waterfront position makes it easy to swim and sunbathe within the city sprawl. From the Vieux Port, Bus 83 or Bus 19 takes you to the vast green spread of reclaimed land called the **Parc Balnéaire du Prado**. Its waterfront is divided into beaches, all of them public and well equipped with showers, toilets, and first-aid stations. The beach surface varies between sand and gravel. You can also find your own little beach on the tiny, rocky **Iles de Frioul**; boats leave from the Vieux Port and cost €10.

If you want to venture into wilder coastal country, and have a car, drive it to the end of the world. Head out the coastal road to Les Goudes, then penetrate even farther (up the road marked SANS ISSUE, or dead end) until you reach Callelongue. From here you can strike out on foot, following the GR 98 to the idyllic **Calanque de Marseilleveyvre**, a rocky finger-inlet perfect for an isolated swim. From this point, the famous Calanques continue all the way to Cassis; though most of them lie on Marseille's official turf, they are most often accessed from Cassis. You can visit them by boat from Marseille, too, on a four-hour minicruise with the **Groupement des Armateurs Cotiers Marseillais** (*G.A.C.M.* ⊠*1 quai des Belges, Vieux Port* ☎04–91–55–50–09). Tours leave at 2 on Wednesday, Saturday, and Sunday (except in stormy mistrals).

Marseille is a major center for diving (*plongée*), with several organizations offering "baptêmes" ("baptisms," or first dives) to beginners. The coast is lined with rocky inlets, grottos, and ancient shipwrecks, not to mention thronging with aquatic life. For general information contact **Plongée Marseille** (☎04–91–25–23–64 ⊕*www.plongee-marseille.com*). **Océan 4** (⊠*83 av. de la Pointe-Rouge, Vieux Port* ☎04–91–73–91–16) is an English-speaking company that offers initiations and day trips, and has equipment, showers, and storage. There are initiations, day trips, equipment rental, and showers and storage at the English-speaking **Palm Beach Plongée** (⊠*2 promenade de la Plage, Vieux Port* ☎04–91–22–10–38).

SHOPPING

The locally famous bakery **Four des Navettes** (⊠*136 rue Sainte, Notre Dame* ☎04–91–33–32–12), up the street from Notre-Dame-de-la-Garde, makes orange-spice, shuttle-shaped navettes. These cookies are modeled on the little boat in which Mary Magdalene and Lazarus washed onto Continental shores (⇨ *Stes-Maries-de-la-Mer in Chapter 1*), before Lazarus worked his way over to Aix and Marseille.

Savon de Marseille (Marseille Soap) is a household expression in France, often sold as a satisfyingly crude and hefty block in odorless olive-oil green. There's a world market, though, for the chichi offspring of this earth mother: dainty pastel guest soaps in almond, lemon,

> **QUEL PASTIS!**
>
> Specializing in pastis, anisette, and absinthe, the smart little shop of **La Maison du Pastis** (⊠ *108 quai du Port, Vieux Port* ☎ *04–91–90–86–77*) offers a dizzying range, but to really savor these unique delights, just head next door to L'Heure Vert, an "absinthe café."

vanilla, and other scents. If you're not one for lingering in the odoriferous boutiques that sell these in gilt gift boxes, consider the no-nonsense outlet of **La Compagnie de Provence** (⊠ *1 rue Caisserie, Vieux Port* ☎ *04–91–56–20–97*), at the foot of Le Panier. Here blocks of soap are sold in plain brown boxes, but you can have them gift wrapped on request. For every kind of nautical doodad, from brass fittings for your yacht's bathroom to sturdy pea coats and oilskins, head down the quai to **Castaldi** (⊠ *25 quai de Rive Neuve, Vieux Port* ☎ *04–91–33–30–49*). For exotic food products shipped into this international port, browse in the **Arax** (⊠ *24–27 rue d'Aubagne, La Canebière* ☎ *04–91–54–11–50*), crammed floor to ceiling with Armenian specialties and aromatic goodies from North Africa, China, and the Middle East. For good old-fashioned big-city shopping, the Rue St-Ferréol (four blocks back from the Vieux Port) is flanked with major department stores: **Nouvelles Galeries** (⊠ *Centre Bourse/Bir Hakeim, Vieux Port* ☎ *04–91–56–82–12*), a mid-price department store, anchors the corner one block back from the port and the tourist office. Check out the hip boutique **La Thuberie** (⊠ *14–16 rue Thubaneau, Belsunce* ☎ *04–91–90–84–55*), run by designer Linda Cohen. It's a showcase for local talent, and has some beautiful cutting-edge designs plus furniture and housewares. Offbeat designer clothing created in Marseille can be found on Cours Julien, including the home-base for the trendy, high-texture clothes and jewelry made by **Madame Zaza of Marseille** (⊠ *73 cours Julien, Notre Dame* ☎ *04–91–48–05–57*). At **Diable Noir** (⊠ *69 cours Julien, Belsunce* ☎ *04–91–42–86–73*), next door to Zaza on the Cours Julien, you'll find glamorous, slightly retro evening gowns in extravagant tulles and taffeta. Diable Noir's "downtown" shop anchors the edgy shopping district along **Rue de la Tour,** across from the Centre Bourse off Place du Général de Gaulle; dubbed "Rue de la Mode," it parades the earthy creativity of Marseille's fusion-fashion culture.

THE CENTRAL COAST

With the floods of vacationers pouring onto the beaches from St-Tropez to Menton every summer, it's surprising that the coast between Marseille and Hyères is often dismissed. Although there are a few indus-

The S is (Hardly Ever) Silent

(Or, how to brag to your friends about staying in a beautiful mas outside Cassis without mispronouncing a thing.)

The rule of thumb in Provence is to pronounce everything, even to the point of pronouncing letters that aren't there. *Pain,* in the north pronounced through the nose without a final consonant, becomes "peng" in the south. *Vin* becomes "veng," *enfin* "on feng," etc.

But there are words in constant dispute, especially among a people toilet-trained on the Academie Française, that holy arbiter of the French language. One of the words caught in the crossfire: *mas.* This old Provençal word for farmhouse is a "mahss" in

the south, but Parisians hold out for a more refined Frenchification: "ma."

Cassis, on the other hand, is a booby trap. For one thing, there are two drinks named Cassis, one a black-currant liqueur made in Burgundy to be blended in white wine *kirs,* the other the famous wine from the coastal country east of Marseille. The liqueur is always called "cass-*eess,*" and Northerners (who consume the most kirs) insist on pronouncing the wine "Cass-*eess*" but the village "Cass*ee.*" But ask the locals, and they'll snort in disdain. "C'est 'Cass-*EESS,*'" they'll explain, as if all the words in the French language followed the pattern.

There you have it: In Paris, it's cass-ee and mah; in Provence, it's cass-eess and mahss.

trial pockets around La Ciotat and Toulon, there are just as many sections of magnificent coastline—white cliffs peppered with ragged, wind-twisted pines.

Just inland, in the dry white hills, lies the peaceful market town of **Aubagne**; climb to the top of its outlying hills, and you can see the ocean sparkling below. **Cassis** is the jewel of this region, a harbor protected by the formidable Cap Canaille, 1,300 feet high. Between Cassis and Marseille stretch the extraordinary **Calanques,** a series of rocky fjords that probe deep into the coastline. Following the coastal highway, you come to La Ciotat, a gargantuan (but oddly picturesque) naval shipyard, and reach the popular beach resort of **Bandol**—incidentally the source of one of Provence's most famous wines. A popular rainy-day excursion from Bandol leads to the hilltop medieval village of Le Castellet; you may want to stop at some of the wineries along the way. **Toulon** is an enormous naval base and a tough big city with an interesting Old Town for the intrepid; just east of the city is where you catch the ferry to Porquerolles, the best of the wild and beautiful **Iles d'Hyères.**

AUBAGNE

15 km (9 mi) east of Marseille, 10 km (6 mi) north of Cassis.

VISITOR INFORMATION
Aubagne Tourist Office (⊠ *6 Av. Antide Boyer* ☎ *04–42–03–49–98* ⊕ *www. aubagne.com*).

EXPLORING

This easygoing, plane-tree-shaded market town (pronounced oh-*bahn*-yuh) is proud of its native son, the dramatist, filmmaker, and chronicler of all things Provençal, Marcel Pagnol, best known to Anglophones as author of *Jean de Florette, Fanny,* and *Manon des Sources* (*Manon of the Springs*). Here you can spend the morning exploring the animated market or digging through used Pagnol books and collectibles in the Old Town.

GUIDED TOURS

Even if you don't choose to hike the 12-km (7-mi) or 20-km (12-mi) loop through the garrigues above Aubagne, there's a bus tour of Marcel Pagnol landmarks that leaves from the tourist office. It takes place in July and August on Wednesday and Saturday at 4; the cost is €7. Request an English-speaking guide in advance.

Make sure you visit Aubagne on a market day (Tuesday, Saturday, or Sunday), when the sleepy center is transformed into a tableau of Provençal life. The Tuesday market is the biggest.

You can study miniature dioramas of scenes from Pagnol stories at **Le Petit Monde de Marcel Pagnol** *(The Small World of Marcel Pagnol)*. The characters are all santons, and there are superb portraits of a humpback Gerard Départieu and Yves Montand, resplendent in mustache, fedora, and velvet vest, just as they were featured in *Jean de Florette.* ✉ *Esplanade de Gaulle* 🖼 €2 🕙 *Daily 9–noon and 2–6.*

Aubagne claims the title of santon capital of Provence. The craft, originally from Marseille, was focused here at the turn of the 20th century, when artisans moved inland to make the most of local clay. The more than a dozen studios in town are set up for you to observe the production process.

Daniel Scaturro is one of the best. He specializes in portraits, mostly of Pagnol's film characters—but you can have one made of yourself for €8. His main display studio, simply called **Daniel Scaturro** (✉ *20a av. de Verdun* 🖼 *04–42–84–33–29*), is on the edge of town in an industrial quarter. Scaturro's sons demonstrate the family craft on a smaller scale in a shop in the central **Old Town** (✉ *Bd. Jean-Jaurès/Rue Martinot*).

The history of the craft of santon-making and other uses to which the local clay was put—faience and hand-painted tiles—can be studied at the **Ateliers Thérèse Neveu,** named for Aubagne's first master *santonière* (santon maker). Also on display are excellent temporary exhibitions about pottery. ✉ *Chemin Entrecasteaux, at the top of the Old Town hill* 🖼 *04–42–03–43–10* 🖼 *Free* 🕙 *Tues.–Sun. 10–noon and 2–6.*

Even if you haven't read Pagnol's works or seen his films, you can enjoy the **Circuit Pagnol,** a hike in the raw-hewn, arid *garrigues* (scrublands) behind Marseille and Aubagne. Here Pagnol spent his idyllic summers, described in his *Souvenirs d'un Enfance* (*Memories of a Childhood*), crunching through the rosemary, thyme, and scrub oak at the foot of his beloved Garlaban. When he grew up to be a famous playwright and filmmaker, he shot some of his best work in these hills, casting his wife, Jacqueline, as the first Manon of the Springs. After Pagnol's

CLOSE UP

Little Saints with Feet of Clay

They beckon from shop windows in every hill town, these miniatures called *santons*, from the dialect *santouns* for "little saints." But whatever commercial role they may play today, their roots run deep in Provence.

The Christmas crèche has been a part of Provençal tradition since the Middle Ages, when people reenacted the tableau of the birth of Christ, wise men, shepherds, and all. When the Revolution cracked down on these pastoral plays, a crafty Marseillais decided to substitute clay actors. The terra-cotta figures caught on and soon upstaged their human counterparts for good.

A Marseille tradition that eventually migrated to Aubagne in the hills above (the clay was better), the delicate doll-like figurines spread throughout Provence, and are displayed every Christmas in church crèches that resemble a rustic back-country hill village as much as they do Bethlehem. Against a miniature background of model stone houses, dried-moss olive groves, and glass creeks, quaint, familiar characters go about their daily tasks—the lumberjack hauling matchstick kindling, the fisherman toting a basket of waxy fish, the red-cheeked town drunk leering drolly at the pretty lavender-cutter whose basket hangs heavy with real dried sprigs. The original cast from Bethlehem gets second billing to a charming crowd of Gypsies, goatherds, and provincial passersby. And

wait—isn't that Gérard Depardieu? And Raimu? And Yves Montand? Even beloved film actors have worked their way into the scene.

It's a highly competitive craft, and while artisans vie for the souvenir trade, some have raised it to an art form: Daniel Scaturro, of Aubagne, was named a Meilleur Ouvrier de France in 1997, one of the highest national honors granted to craftsmen.

Molded, dried, then scraped with sharp tools down to the finest detail—wrinkled foreheads and fingernails—the santons are baked at 1,000°C (1,832°F). Once cool, they are painted with a watchmaker's precision: eyelashes, nostrils, and gnarled knuckles. The larger ones have articulated limbs to allow for dressing; their hand-sewn costumes, Barbie-scaled, are lavished with as much fine detail as the painted features.

Many artisans maintain highly public studios, so you can shop direct. Little ones (about an inch high), without articulated limbs, run about €4; big ones (8 to 10 inches), dressed and painted by the best artists, cost around €40. Or you can splurge and commission a portrait of yourself for the mantel—€8 at Scaturro's.

But the preferred format is the crèche tableau, and it's easy to get hooked on building a collection of Provençal rustics to be lovingly unwrapped and displayed every Christmas season.

death, Claude Berri came back to the Garlaban to find a location for his remake of *Manon des Sources*, but found it so altered by brush fires and power cables that he chose to shoot farther east instead, around Cuges-les-Pine and Riboux. (The lovely village and Manon's well were filmed in Mirabeau, in the Luberon.) Although the trail may no longer shelter the pine-shaded olive orchards of its past, it still gives you the chance to walk through primeval Provençal countryside and rewards you with spectacular views of Marseille and the sea. To access the marked trail by yourself, drive to La Treille northeast of Aubagne and follow the signs. For an accompanied tour with literary commentary, contact the **Office du Tourisme** (☎ *04–42–03–49–98*).

Aubagne on a **market** day is a feast, in more ways than one. For sale are fresh local asparagus, plant-ripened tomatoes and melons, and mesclun scooped by the gnarled fingers of blue-aproned ladies in from the farm. The Tuesday market is the biggest, with clothing, purses, tools, and pots and pans spilling onto the esplanade, but the Saturday and Sunday markets make more of regional products; those labeled Pays d'Aubagne must be organically raised. You won't find the social scene you'll see in Aix, but this is a more authentic farmers' market.

Another claim to fame for Aubagne: it's the headquarters for the French Foreign Legion. The legion was created in 1831, and accepts recruits from all nations, no questions asked. The discipline and camaraderie instilled among its motley team of adventurers, criminals, and mercenaries have helped the legion forge a reputation for exceptional valor—a reputation romanticized by songs and films in which sweaty deeds of heroism are performed under the desert sun. The **Musée de la Légion Étrangère** *(Museum of the Foreign Legion)* does its best to polish the image by way of medals, uniforms, weapons, and photographs. ✉ *Caserne Viénot (to get there, take a left off D2 onto D44A just before Aubagne)* ☎ *04–42–18–82–41* 🎟 *Free* ⊙ *June–Sept., Tues.– Thurs. and weekends 10–noon and 3–7, Fri. 10–noon; Oct.–May, Wed. and weekends 10–noon and 2–6.*

WHERE TO EAT & STAY

$$ ✕ **La Farandole.** Cosseted here by rustic Provençal lemon-print cloths, lace curtains, and the region's typical bow-legged chairs, you can enjoy good home cooking specializing in seafood and dishes with a Morrocan slant with the local regulars who claim the same table every day. They are drawn to the flower-filled terrace with a small fountain, friendly waitresses, and home-baked cakes, all of which enhance the small-town feel. The inexpensive daily menu may contain crisp green salad with foie gras in a raspberry vinaigrette or baked goat cheese; wine is included. ✉ *6 rue Martino (off Cours Maréchal, on a narrow street leading into the Old Town)* ☎ *04–42–03–26–36* ⊕ *www.kelrestaurant. com* ▭ *MC, V* ⊙ *No dinner Sun. or Mon.*

$ ✕ **Le Triskel.** This miniature shoebox of an Old Town restaurant has a
★ living santon for a chef—mustache, toque, and broad gestures worthy of Pagnol. While gesticulating and bantering with the loyal locals who crowd in elbow to elbow, he hauls heavy daubes from the wood-fire oven and ladles pot-au-feu over duck-leg confit. There are kidneys grilled with thyme, homemade gnocchi, eggplant gratiné, and, almost incidentally, yummy pizzas loaded with toppings and dripping with gooey cheese. ✉ *12 rue Jean-Jacques Rousseau* ☎ *04–42–03–59–86* ▭ *No credit cards* ⊙ *Closed Wed.*

$$ ▥ **Hostellerie de la Source.** Despite its suburban location 4 km (2 mi) outside of Aubagne, this good value hotel is a nice option for travelers with a car. The 17th-century country house stands in vast boxwood

gardens surrounding tennis courts and an indoor-outdoor pool. Inside there's a slick hotel feel well suited to banquets and conferences. Guest rooms are bright and tidy, if a trifle sparse, and were entirely rebuilt in the late 1980s. **Pros:** quiet and secluded; nice pool; decent restaurant. **Cons:** they cater to conferences and large groups, so if you are unlucky, you have to share the space with multitudes. ⊠ *St-Pierre-des-Aubagne* ☎ *04–42–04–09–19* ⊕ *www.hdelasource.com* ⋑ *24 rooms, 1 suite* ⌕ *In-room: refrigerator. In-hotel: restaurant, pool, Wi-Fi, parking (free), some pets allowed* ▤ *MC, V* ⦿ *MAP.*

CASSIS

★ *22 km (14 mi) southeast of Marseille, 10 km (6 mi) north of Aubagne.*

GETTING HERE
Hourly trains between Marseille and Toulon stop at Cassis, but the station is about 3km (1.5 mi) from the centre (☎ *08–36–35–35–35* ⊕ *www.voyages-sncf.com*). From the station, there is a local shuttle to the town centre that runs every 20 minutes and costs €1. Cartrieze (☎ *08–00–19–94–13* ⊕ *www.lepilote.com*) runs buses between Aix-en-Provence and Cassis (€9.20, 45 minutes) four times daily, except Sundays. By car, leave the A50 from Marseille and Toulon and take exit 8 for Cassis. The D559 from Marseille to Cassis is dramatically beautiful, continuing along the coast to Toulon, but is very curvy for motion-sickness sufferers.

VISITOR INFORMATION
Cassis Tourist Office (⊠ *Pl. Baragnon* ☎ *04–42–01–71–17* ⊕ *www.cassis.fr*).

EXPLORING
Surrounded by vineyards, flanked by monumental cliffs, guarded by the ruins of a medieval castle, and nestled around a picture-perfect fishing port, Cassis is the prettiest coastal town in Provence. Best known for its delicate white wines and wild Calanques, it is a quiet fishing village out of season and inundated with sun-worshippers in the summer. The pastel houses at rakish angles framing the port and harbor attracted early-20th-century artists including Dufy and Matisse. Even the mild rash of parking-garage architecture in the outer neighborhoods can't spoil the effect of unadulterated charm. Stylish without being too recherché, Cassis provides shelter to numerous pleasure-boaters, who restock their galleys at its market, replenish their Saint James nautical duds in its boutiques, and relax with a bottle of local wine and a platter of urchins in one of its numerous waterfront cafés.

The imposing **Château de Cassis** has loomed over the harbor since the invasions of the Saracens in the 7th century, evolving over time into a walled enclosure crowned with stout watchtowers. It's private property today and best viewed from a sunny port-side terrace.

Touring the **Calanques,** whose fjord-like finger bays probe the rocky coastline, is a must. Either take a sightseeing cruise in a glass-bottom boat that dips into each Calanque in turn (tickets, sold at the eastern end of the port, are €10–€18 depending on how many Calanques you see) or hike across the cliff tops, clambering down the steep sides to these barely accessible retreats. Or do both, going in by boat and hiking back; make arrangements at the port (⇨ *see the Close-Up box, "Touring the Calanques")*. Of the Calanques closest to Cassis, **Port Miou** is the least attractive. It is also the only one fully accessible by car. It was a *pierre de Cassis* (Cassis stone) quarry until 1982 when the Calanques became protected sites, and now has an active leisure and fishing port. **Calanque Port Pin** is prettier, with wind-twisted pines growing at angles from white-rock cliffs. But with its tiny beach and jagged cliffs looming overhead, covered with gnarled pine and scrub and its rock spur known to climbers as the "finger of God," it's **Calanque En Vau** that's a small piece of paradise.

> **CLOS ENCOUNTERS**
>
> If you're a wine lover, pick up the brochure "Through the Vineyards" from the tourist office. There are 12 domaines open for tasting and buying, but the most spectacularly sited is the **Clos Sainte Magdeleine** (⊠ *Chemin du Revestel* ☎ *04–42–01–70–28*), set on the slopes of towering Cap Canaille.

WHERE TO EAT & STAY

$$ ✕ **Chez Nino.** This is the best of the many restaurants lining Cassis's harbor, with top-notch Provençal food and wine and a spectacular terrace view. The owners, Claudie and Bruno, are extremely hospitable as long as you stick to the menu—don't ask for sauce on the side—and you are as passionate about fish and seafood as they are. The sardines in *escabeche* are textbook perfect, as are the grilled fish and the bouillabaisse. And if you want to indulge, there are now two suites (€700) and one room (€300) available for the night, beautifully decorated with views of the sea. ⊠ *1 Quai Barthélémy* ☎ *04–42–01–74–32* ⊕ *www.nino-cassis.com* ⊟ *AE, DC, MC, V* ⊘ *Closed Mon. and mid-Dec.–mid-Feb. No dinner Sun. off-season.*

$$$ ▥ **Les Roches Blanches.** Perched above the sea facing Cap Canaille, this cliff-side villa takes in superb views of Cassis's port. There's a beautifully landscaped terrace shaded by massive pines and an infinity pool that seems to spill into the sea. Rooms, in traditional Provençal style, are airy and light-filled; the bland '60s-style annex just behind the main building compensates for its looks with full-length balconies. The aura is far from snooty or deluxe; it's friendly, low-key, and pleasantly mainstream and the panoramic restaurant is a good sunset-watching spot. **Pros:** excellent views; friendly service. **Cons:** the restaurant is uninspired even if the views are. ⊠ *Rte. des Calanques* ☎ *04–42–01–09–30* ⊕ *www.roches-blanches-cassis.com* ⇆ *19 rooms, 5 suites* ⌂ *In-room: refrigerators. In-hotel: 2 restaurants, bar, pool, parking (free), some pets allowed (fee)* ⊟ *AE, MC, V.*

$$ ▥ **Jardin d'Émile.** Just off the waterfront, tucked under massive cliffs
★   and parasol pines, this stylish but homey rose-colored inn stands in a tropical garden and has views of the cape from the restaurant and some rooms. View or not, the rooms are intimate and welcom-

Touring the Calanques

To go on a **boat ride** to Les Calanques, get to the port around 10 AM or 2 PM and look for a boat that's loading passengers. Two of the best choices are the *Moby Dick III* and the *Ville de Cassis*—they have glass-bottom views and full commentary (in French only). But a slew of alternative boats won't leave you stranded. Round-trips should include at least three calanques and average €11. In July and August there is a "Spectacle Son et Lumiere" boat trip that leaves nightly at 10:30 PM (€10). For specific daytime departure times, contact **La Visite des Calanques** (☎04–42–01–90–83).

You can also visit the Calanques from Marseille's Vieux Port on a four-hour minicruise with the *Groupement des Armateurs Cotiers Marseillais (G.A.C.M)*. Tours leave at 2 every Wednesday, Saturday, and Sunday (except in stormy mistrals). ✉*1 quai des Belges* ☎04–91–55–50–09

To really get up close and personal, remember that the Calanques offer some of the best diving in France.

Weather permitting, there are spectacular cave daily dives to view brightly colored coral and abundant fish. Maestro diver Henri Cosquer (famous for discovering one of the oldest caves in the area) runs **Cassis Services Plongée** (☎04–42–01–89–16 ⊕*www. cassis-services-plongee.fr* ☉*Closed mid-Nov.–mid-Mar.*).

To hike the Calanques, gauge your skills: the GR98 (marked with red-and-white bands) is the most scenic route, but requires ambitious scrambling to get down the sheer walls of En Vau. The alternative is to follow the green markers and approach En Vau from behind. The faded markers could use revision nonetheless. If you're ambitious, you can hike the length of the GR98 between Marseille and Cassis, following the coastline, a distance of roughly 30 km (18 mi). Arrange in advance for a boat pickup or drop-off at En Vau. For guided nature walks, diving, kayaking, or sailing along the Calanques, contact **Marseille Tourisme** (☎04–91–13–89–00 ⊕*www. marseille-tourisme.com*).

ing, with rubbed-chalk walls, scrubbed pine, weathered stone, and soft lighting to enhance the romantic surroundings. The restaurant (closed Monday), encircled by a garden terrace and, by night, illuminated cliffs, offers regional specialties with a cosmopolitan twist, such as fresh tuna with zucchini, almonds, and Spanish peppers or sardines with eggplant and cumin. **Pros:** an intimate feel with lots of charm and comfort. **Cons:** often booked in the summer months; reception in high season can be cool. ✉*Av. Admiral Ganteaume, Plage du Bestouan* ☎*04–42–01–80–55* ⊕*www.lejardindemile.fr* ↩*7 rooms* &*In-room: refrigerators. In-hotel: Wi-Fi, parking (no fee), some pets allowed* ▭*AE, DC, MC, V* ☉*Closed mid-Nov.–mid-Dec., and last wk of Jan.*

BANDOL

25 km (15½ mi) southeast of Cassis, 15 km (9 mi) west of Toulon.

VISITOR INFORMATION

Bandol Tourist Office (✉ *Pavillon du Tourisme, on the waterfront* ☎ 04–94–29–41–35 ⊕ *www.bandol.fr*).

EXPLORING

Although its name means wine to most of the world, Bandol is also a popular and highly developed seaside resort town. In the 1920s, the glamorous social life of the Riviera stretched this far west, and grand seaside mansions rivaled Cap d'Antibes and Juan-les-Pins for high society and literati. Today its old port is a massive gray parking lot and the Old Town that fronts the quays is lined with seafood snack shops, generic brassieres, and palm trees. Yet westward, toward the Baie de Renecros, are some of the Belle Epoque houses that once made Bandol famous. In high season the harbor is filled with yachts, and the waterfront promenade is packed with summer tourist crowds. A port-side stroll up the palm-lined Allée Jean Moulin feels downright Côte d'Azur. If you're not a beach lover, pick up an itinerary from the tourist office and visit a few Bandol vineyards just outside of town.

Several sights around Bandol are worth pursuing. Three kilometers ℧ (2 mi) north on the D559 is the **Jardin Exotique et Zoo de Sanary Bandol** *(Sanary Bandol's Exotic Garden and Zoo)*, where cacti and hundreds of exotic tropical plants grow to remarkable sizes. In a small zoo setting, animals such as flamingos, gibbons, and gazelles frolic in shady gardens. ⊹ *Exit Bandol from A8, take first right (direction Route de Beausset) and follow the signs to the Zoo, being careful not to miss the very first right after the autoroute exit* ☎ 04–94–29–40–38 ◫ €8.50 ⊙ *June–Aug., Mon.–Sat. 8–noon and 2–7, Sun. 2–7; Sept.–May, Mon.–Sat. 8–noon and 2–6, Sun. 2–6.*

Continuing north on the same D559 is the village of **Le Castellet,** perched high above the Bandol vineyards. Its narrow streets, 17th-century stone houses, and (alas!) touristy shops are designed for beach lovers on a rainy day.

Paul Ricard Boats (☎ 06–11–05–91–52 ◫ €6) make the 2-km (1.2-mi) sail from the Embarcadéro to the **Ile de Bendor** hourly. The Ile de Bendor was only a large rock until pastis magnate Paul Ricard bought it in the 1950s and turned it into a tourist center with fine beaches, crafts shops, and an *espace culturel* (cultural space) showing Paul Ricard's lifetime works. Although local restaurants offer a surprisingly wide selection, sunny days and scenic views make for a lovely picnic.

Just east of Bandol, still on the D559, past the smaller resort of Sanary, as you turn left onto the D63 you'll see signs pointing to the small stone chapel of **Notre-Dame de Pépiole.** It's hemmed in by pines and cypresses and is one of the oldest Christian buildings in France, dating from the 6th century and modeled on early churches in the Middle East. The simple interior has survived the years in remarkably good shape, although the colorful stained glass that fills the tiny windows is modern—composed mainly of broken bottles. ☉*Most afternoons 3–5.*

From Notre-Dame de Pépiole, retrace your route toward Sanary and head south on D616 around the **Cap Sicié** for a tremendous view across the Bay of Toulon.

Or head north on D11 to Ollioules; just past the village, follow N8 (in the direction of Le Beausset) through a 5-km (3-mi) route that twists its scenic way beneath the awesome chalky rock faces of the **Gorge d'Ollioules.**

Even more spectacular: take a left at Ollioules on D20 and follow the winding road along the crest of **Le Gros Cerveau.** You'll be rewarded first with inland mountain views, then an expansive panorama of the coastline.

OFF THE BEATEN PATH

La Cadiere d'Azur (6 km/4 mi north of Bandol). This is one of Provence's secrets, a beautiful, sleepy medieval town perched on a limestone hill overlooking the majestic vineyards of Bandol. Van Gogh and French painter Favory passed through here, as did several writers and poets. Small, generations-old shops selling local pottery and produce line the main street today. An added attraction is the special trip–worthy Hostellerie Bérard.

WHERE TO EAT & STAY

$$$
★

☒**Hostellerie Bérard.** Master Chef René Bérard is as celebrated for his haute cuisine as he is for his elegant country inn. The rooms, decorated in suavely handsome Provençal style, are scattered throughout a cluster of beautifully restored old buildings, including an 11th-century monastery. In the airy and window-filled restaurant, delicious Mediterranean-inspired Provençal meals emphasizing local seafood and fresh produce grace the tables. Try the ravioli stuffed with goat cheese, sorrel, and Parmesan in a lemon chicken broth, then proceed to lightly grilled red mullet wrapped in seaweed and topped with peas and fresh rosemary. If you want to attempt similar gastronomic heights at home, Chef Bérard, cheerfully sympathetic to all cooking woes, has weeklong culinary getaways. **Pros:** sumptuous weekend getaway with lovely rooms and great food. **Cons:** service can be abrupt; some rooms are small. ☒*83740, La Cadiere d'Azur* ☎*04–94–90–11–43* ⊕*www.hotel-berard.com* ⬐*37 rooms, 4 suites* ⭗*In-room: refrigerator. In-hotel: restaurant, pool, Wi-Fi, parking, some pets allowed* ▤*AE, DC, MC, V.*

TOULON

67 km (41½ mi) east of Marseille, 29 km (18 mi) northwest of La Tour Fondue (departure point for the Iles d'Hyères).

GETTING HERE

Toulon is on the main TGV line from Paris, and is served by regional and local trains from Marseille and Nice, so it is easy to navigate your way on the system (☎*08–36–35–35–35* ⊕ *www.voyages-sncf.com*). Once in Toulon, there is a great network of inner-city buses run by the

RMTT (☎*04–94–03–87–03* ⊕*www.reseaumistral.com*). No. 23 goes to the beaches at Mourillon, No. 40 to the cable car. By car take the A50 from Marseille in the west and if you are coming from the east, the A57. The coastal D559 goes between Marseille and Toulon via Bandol.

VISITOR INFORMATION
Toulon Tourist Office (✉ *Sq. William et Catherine Booth* ☎*04–94–18–53–00* ⊕*www.toulontourisme.com*).

EXPLORING
Toulon is a city of big contrasts: ugly with crowded postwar high-rises, yet surprisingly beautiful with its tree-lined littoral; a place with some frankly unappealing nightlife and yet by day, charming and colorful with its restaurant scene. Best known for the day in World War II when 75 French ships sunk themselves rather than fall into the hands of attacking Germans, Toulon has kept its place as France's leading naval port with a kind of dogged determination. Though you may see nothing but endless traffic and graffiti-covered block-style apartments crossing the city, the Vieille Ville (Old Town) and port area have well-kept cafés and a sunny waterfront where yachts and pleasure boats—some available for trips to the Iles D'Hyères or around the bay—add bright splashes of color. Back from the port lies the gritty red-light district Le Petit Chicago, currently undergoing restoration. Once in the heart of the Old Town, the maze of streets is packed with designer shops and quirkily appealing stretches of ruined medieval houses mixed with lurid neon.

Park your car under Place de la Liberté and take Boulevard de Strasbourg, turning right onto Rue Berthelot, which leads into the heart of the pedestrians-only streets of the **Vieille Ville.** Wander through **Place des Trois Dauphins,** with its mossy and fern-lined fountain, or stop in the café-filled **Place Puget**; Victor Hugo lived in No. 5 when he was researching *Les Misérables*. One block east, the **Cours Lafayette** becomes a wonderfully animated, authentic Provençal morning market (daily except Monday), and the **Hôtel de Ville** has evocative Baroque figures, carved by the Marseillais sculptor Pierre Puget.

Behind the port and the Vieille Ville lies the new town.

At Place Victor Hugo, the **Opera de Toulon** (✉*Pl. Victor Hugo* ☎*04–94–92–70–78* ☉*Box office: weekdays 10–12:30 and 2:30–5:30*) hosts theater, opera, and dance productions.

Farther west is the **Musée des Beaux Arts** showing paintings by Vernet and Fragonard as well as postwar abstract art and the cartoon-influenced Di Rosa brothers. ✉*113 bd. Maréchal Leclerc* ☎*04–94–36–81–00* 💲*Free* ☉*Daily 1–6.*

Avenue de la République, an ugly arrangement of concrete apartment blocks, runs parallel to the waterfront. At the western edge of the gray is the **Musée National de la Marine** *(Naval Museum)*, with large models of ships, figureheads, paintings, and other items related to Toulon's maritime history. Photographs of the World

War II sinking bring the sickening story to life. ✉ *Pl. Monsenergue* ☎ *04–94–02–02–01* 🎟 *€5* ☉ *Apr.–Sept., daily 10–6:30; Oct.–Mar., Wed.–Mon. 10–noon and 2–6.*

Mount Faron rises above the town and can be reached by taking the circular Route du Faron in either direction or in six minutes by cable car from Boulevard Admiral Jean-Vence. ☎ *04–94–92–68–25* 🎟 *€8 round-trip* ☉ *July–Aug., Tues.–Sun. 9:30–7:45; Mon. 2:15–7:45; Sept.–June, Tues.–Sun. 9:30–noon and 2:15–6. Closed on windy days.*

At Mt-Faron's summit are a zoo, a great view, and the **Musée du Débarquement** commemorating the 1944 liberation of Provence. ☎ *04–94–88–08–09* 🎟 *€4* ☉ *July–Aug., daily 9:45–11:45 and 1:45–5:30; Sept.–June, daily 9:45–11:45 and 1:45–4:30.*

OFF THE
BEATEN
PATH

Brignoles. (45 km/28 mi north of Toulon) Although known as the market center for the wines of the Var, the largest attraction is still the Abbaye de la Celle, a 12th-century Benedictine abbey that served as a convent until the 17th century. The abbey was abandoned until Maria Fournier, owner of the Iles of Porquerolles, decided to open it as a hotel in 1945. In spite of its suddenly becoming more upscale with the likes of Charles de Gaulle vacationing here, the town continued to firmly resist change. In fact, the simple Romanesque chapel housing a 14th-century Christ figure largely acclaimed as an anonymous masterpiece still serves today as the parish church. It's here in this historic spot that celebrated chef Alain Ducasse has his culinary hideaway Hostellerie de l'Abbaye de La Celle (⇨ *below*).

WHERE TO EAT & STAY

$$$
★

✕ **Le Gros Ventre.** In a cozy and romantic space enhanced by soft lighting, tasteful decorations, and tables set at discreet distances from each other, you can enjoy some of the best Provençal cooking in Toulon. Specializing in seafood and beef, self-taught Chef Audibert brings to the table delights like fillet of beef served with grapes and foie gras, or fish, caught daily by the restaurant's personal fisherman, steamed with fresh Mediterranean garden-grown vegetables. An enormous wine list of more than 5,000 bottles can be a little intimidating, but friendly servers help guide you through it. ✉ *297 Littoral F. Mistral le Mourillon* ☎ *04–94–42–15–42* ⊕ *www.legrosventre.net* ▤ *AE, MC, V* ☉ *Mid-Sept.–Apr., no lunch Tues.–Thurs.; May–mid-Sept., closed Tues. and no lunch.*

$$$$
Fodor'sChoice
★

🏨 **Hostellerie de l'Abbaye de La Celle.** Superchef Alain Ducasse put this country inn—buried in the unspoiled backcountry north of Toulon and just south of Brignoles—back on the map a decade ago. Up the road from the town's royal abbey, this beautifully restored 18th-century *bastide* (country house)—a dream in ocher-yellow walls, Arles green shutters, and white stone trim—was once part of the convent where future queens of Provence were raised. Guest rooms mix Louis XVI and regional accents; half are split-level with their own gardens, some with views of vineyards, others of a park thick with chestnut and mulberry tress. Wherever you bed down, the scent of fresh thyme and lemon basil waft through the windows from the gardens. Today, the formidable kitchen is headed up by Chef Benoît Witz, whose seemingly magical creations find a superb balance between taste and texture: velouté of crawfish gently covering a bruschetta topped with tomatoes and garden herbs, or duck breast with polenta and cherries. **Pros:** an ideal country escape with charming service and lots of comfort. **Cons:** restaurant can be noisy; some bathrooms are small. ⊠*Pl. du Général de Gaulle La Celle* ☎*04–98–05–14–14* ⊕*www.abbaye-celle.com* ➡*9 rooms, 1 suite, 3 duplexes* ⚹*In-room: refrigerator. In-hotel: restaurant, pool, public Wi-Fi, parking (free)* ⊟*AE, DC, MC, V.*

$$ ⛨**Résidence du Cap Brun.** Tucked away down a side road leading to the sea, this charming hotel has smallish rooms in pastel shades. With acres of strollable garden around it, not to mention the sweet scent of a newly planted orange grove, weddings are a serious summertime business here, and Saturday mornings can be noisy. This picturesque spot is a delightful surprise after the hustle and bustle of Toulon; be sure to ask for a room with a terrace and a view. **Pros:** with so few charming hotels in Toulon, this is an excellent value choice. **Cons:** rooms can be noisy, especially in wedding season; hot in the summer. ⊠*192 chemin de l'Aviateur Gayraud, Cap Brun* ☎*04–94–41–29–46* ➡*15 rooms* ⚹*In-room: no a/c. In-hotel: pool, parking* ⊟*V* ⊘*Closed Nov.–Mar.* ⛨*BP.*

ILES D'HYÈRES

32 km (20 mi) off the coast south of Hyères.

VISITOR INFORMATION
Iles d'Hyères Tourist Office (⊠ *Carré du Port* ☎*04-94-58-33-76* ⊕*www. porquerolles.com*).

EXPLORING
Strung across the Bay of Hyères and spanning some 32 km (20 mi) is an archipelago of islands reminiscent of a set for a pirate movie. In fact, they have been featured in several, thanks not only to their wild and rocky coastline but also their real pirate history. In the 16th century the islands were seeded with convicts meant to work the land; they promptly ran amok, ambushing and sacking passing ships heading for Toulon.

★ Today the pirates are long gone, replaced by a thriving local population and tourists. The islands consist of three main bodies: Levant, Port-Cros, and Porquerolles. Eight percent of **Levant** is military property, and is kept strictly guarded with barbed-wire fences. The remaining area, Héliopolis, is a nudist colony, where you're welcome if you want to participate, as opposed to simply being curious. **Port-Cros** is a magnificent national park with no cars, no smoking, and no dogs. You can hike on pine-scented trails with astonishingly spectacular views, or follow the underwater path, snorkeling or diving with fish and aquatic life representative of the Mediterranean. **Porquerolles** (pronounced pork-uh-*rohl*) is the largest and most popular escape from the modern world. The village of Porquerolles was originally used as a retirement colony for Napoleonic officers (the Fort du Petit-Langoustier and the Fort

Ste-Agathe, although no longer active, still loom imposingly over the marina), which explains its remarkable resemblance to a military outpost. At the turn of the 20th century a Belgian engineer named François-Joseph Fournier made a killing in the Panama Canal, then bought Porquerolles at auction as a gift for his new bride. It was only in 1970 that France nationalized the island, leaving Fournier's widow with a quarter of her original inheritance; her granddaughter now helps run the luxurious Mas du Langoustier. Off-season it's a castaway idyll of pine forests, sandy beaches, and plunging cliffs over a rocky coastline. Inland, its preserved pine forests and orchards of olives and figs are crisscrossed with dirt roads to be explored on foot or, if you prefer, on bikes rented from one of the numerous rental outfits in both port and village. In high season (April to October), day-trippers pour off the ferries, running for the beaches and soap boutiques, and T-shirt shops appear out of the woodwork to cater to vacationers' whims.

Ferries run from La Tour Fondu in Giens (every 30 minutes in summer and every 60 to 90 minutes in winter for €15 round-trip) for the 20-minute trip to Porquerolles, and from Hyères at Hyères Plages to Port-Cros and Levant (€19–€24 round-trip). You can also get to all three islands from Port-de-Miramar or Le Lavandou (35- to 60-minute crossing, €21 round-trip).

WHERE TO EAT & STAY

$$$$ 🏠**Le Manoir.** A mix of southern-coast bourgeois and Provençal touches adds a splash of color to the sunlit, airy rooms of this family-owned colonial-style hotel. Private patios look over a large secluded park bordered by eucalyptus, pink oleanders, and palm trees. Thoughtful service and absolute calm firmly encourage relaxation. After a day of hiking through forests, swimming in the pool, or simply sitting on the flower-filled terrace, you can sample Chef Vincent Cordier's delicious, hearty Provençal fare, such as smoked duck salad garnished with grilled tomatoes, or rack of lamb with island herbs and ratatouille. Diners stop in from all over the island to immerse themselves in the intimate charm of the simply decorated restaurant, murmuring comfortably over a final warmed brandy. **Pros:** with a price that can include both your meals and your accommodation, this is a gentle touch of civilization in the isolated wilderness and much in demand. **Cons:** some south-facing rooms are hot in the summer. ⊠*Isle de Port-Cros* 🕾*04–94–05–90–52* 🛏*23 rooms* ⚷*In-room: no a/c, no TV. In-hotel: restaurant, bar, pool* ⊟*MC, V* ⊘*Closed end-Oct.–mid-Apr.* �†○*MAP.*

$$$$ ★   🏠**Mas du Langoustier.** Amid stunningly lush terrain at the westernmost point of the Ile de Porquerolles, 3 km (2 mi) from the harbor, this luxurious hideout is a popular getaway for the yacht-and-helicopter set and a standard day trip from high-season St-Tropez. Madame Richard, the granddaughter of the lucky woman who was given this island as a wedding gift, picks you up at the port. Choose between big California-modern or old-style Provençal rooms. Chef Joël Guillet creates inspired southern French cuisine. Try the tuna tartare with oysters and wasabi vinaigrette, the open ravioli with sautéed artichokes and pesto, or the roasted lobster tail with green apple puree and vanilla.

Wash it all down with a rare island rosé. **Pros:** prices include breakfast and dinner; setting is magnificent. **Cons:** service can be a trifle cold; some rooms are small. ⊠*Pointe du LangoustierIsle de Porquerolles* ☎*04–94–58–30–09* ⊕*www.langoustier.com* ⇆*45 rooms, 4 suites, 1 apartment* ⌂*In-room: refrigerator. In-hotel: restaurant, pool, tennis court, beachfront, Wi-Fi* ⊟*AE, DC, MC, V* ⊘*Closed Oct.–Apr.* ⏏*MAP.*

$$$ ⚏ **Les Glycines.** In soft shades of yellow-ocher and sky-blue, this sleekly modernized little *bastide* (country house) has an idyllic enclosed courtyard, verdant with lemon trees, ivy, and an ancient *figuier* (fig tree). Back rooms look over a jungle of mimosa and eucalyptus. Public salons have Provençal chairs and fabrics. The restaurant, with seating on the terrace or in the garden, has port-fresh tuna and sardines. In the summer season (April through September) children stay (and eat) for free. The inn is just back from the port in the village center. **Pros:** familial atmosphere that comes at a great price and includes breakfast and dinner. **Cons:** rooms can be noisy and hot in high season. ⊠*Pl. d'ArmesIle de Porquerolles* ☎*04–94–58–30–36* ⊕*www.auberge-glycines.com* ⇆*8 rooms, 3 suites* ⌂*In-room: no a/c. In-hotel: restaurant, bar, Wi-Fi* ⊟*AE, MC, V* ⏏*MAP.*

THE OUTDOORS

You can rent a mountain bike (*velo tout-terrain,* or VTT) for a day to pedal the paths and cliff-top trails of Porquerolles at **Cycle Porquerol** (⊠*Rue de la Ferme* ☎*04–94–58–30–32*) or **L'Indien** (⊠*Pl. d'Armes* ☎*04–94–58–30–39*).

If you prefer to explore on foot, pick up a map at the tourist kiosk on the landing docks, or simply follow the arrows. The main road back from the village leads over the island's forested crest to the Cap d'Arme, with dramatic views of the lighthouse. To its right you can strike out toward the Gorges du Loup; the precarious trail breaks out in the open over a spectacular rocky cove with crashing surf. If you head right of town you'll pass through a series of botanical-study orchards, full of hybrid figs and olives, with a series of inlets and rocky coves for picnics and reflection. If you head left you'll follow the broad stretch of beaches, first the popular Courtade, then the isolated, pine-shadowed Notre-Dame. Roads and trails are marked for difficulty, but only a few are narrower than Jeep-width.

Locamarine 75 (⊠*At the port* ☎*04–94–58–35–84*) rents motorboats to anyone interested, whether or not you have a license. At the **Club de Plongée du Langoustier** (⊠*7 carré du Port* ☎*04–94–58–34–94*) you can take a diving class, hire a guide, rent diving equipment, and refill scuba tanks.

The Western Côte d'Azur

ST-TROPEZ TO THE ESTÉREL, THE HAUT VAR & THE GORGES DU VERDON

Moustiers-Ste-Marie, Alpes de Haute-Provence

WORD OF MOUTH

"St-Tropez really is a spectacle. Great window shopping, friendly people, great market days. Yachts the size of the Queen Mary, or just about! And I'm not talking about a few boats; I'm talking hundreds. I was fascinated with the sheer beauty of most of them, with the.people who came and went on them, with the free live entertainment of watching them have dinner on the deck. The people driving around the harbor in Ferraris were just as amazing. I became a gawker."

—susanna2

WELCOME TO THE WESTERN CÔTE D'AZUR

TOP REASONS TO GO

★ **St-Tropez à go-go:** Brave the world's most outlandish fishing port in high summer and soak up the scene. Just don't forget the fake-tan lotion.

★ **Les Gorges du Verdon:** Peer down into its vertiginous green depths and you'll understand why this is one of the most dramatic natural sites in France.

★ **Picture-perfect Moustiers-Ste-Marie:** Best known for its faïence, this town is also worth visiting for the sight of houses clinging to the cliffs—often with entrances on different levels.

★ **A gothic château extravaganza:** In Mandelieu-La Napoule, discover the most bizarrely extravagant house of the coast—the Château de la Napoule, festooned with tapestries, peacocks, and art students.

★ **Beguiling Cotignac:** With almost no boutiques but a lively weekly market, this is a place to experience Provençal life in the slow lane.

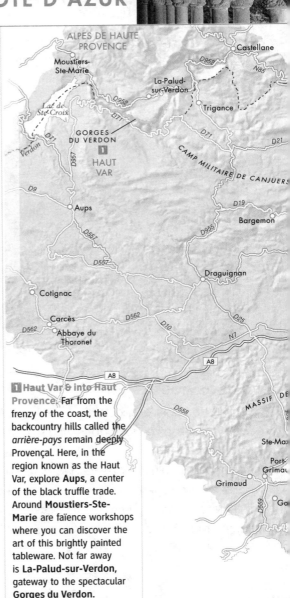

1 Haut Var & into Haut Provence. Far from the frenzy of the coast, the backcountry hills called the *arrière-pays* remain deeply Provençal. Here, in the region known as the Haut Var, explore **Aups**, a center of the black truffle trade. Around **Moustiers-Ste-Marie** are faïence workshops where you can discover the art of this brightly painted tableware. Not far away is **La-Palud-sur-Verdon**, gateway to the spectacular **Gorges du Verdon**.

St-Tropez at sunset

2 The Estérel Resorts.
To the east of the twin
waterfront resorts of **Fréjus**
and **St-Raphaël,** the Massif
de l'Estérel is pure hiking
heaven. Made up of red
volcanic rocks and softened
by patches of lavender and
gorse, its shore is lined with
calanque coves and the
Corniche de l'Estérel, one
of the coast's most spec-
tacular drives.

Estérel

5

GETTING ORIENTED

If it's most often associated with celeb-heavy
coastal resorts, par-
ticularly St-Tropez, the
Western Côte d'Azur
is also a nature-lover's
paradise. North of the
coast, the Massif des
Maures and the Mas-
sif de l'Estérel remain
remarkably wild and
unspoiled, while farther
up, the Gorges du Verdon
draws hard-core hikers
willing to forego the
local rosé to keep their
wits about them as they
tackle France's answer
to the Grand Canyon.

3 St-Tropez. St-Tropez is
really quite low-key in the
off-season, when the giant
yachts moored in the port
serve as the only reminder of
its glamour. In high-season,
dodge the paparazzi by going
to the nearby hilltop villages
of **Gassin** and **Ramatuelle,**
where some streets are so
steep even goats have difficulty with them.

WESTERN CÔTE D'AZUR PLANNER

Main Regional Tourist Offices

For information on travel within the Var region—St-Tropez to La Napoule—write to the Comité Départemental du Tourisme du Var.

For Cannes and environs, write to the Comité Regional du Tourisme Riviera Côte d'Azur.

For the Haute-Provence region between Moustiers and Manosque, contact the Agence Développement Touristique des Alpes de Haute Provence.

For the Verdon, contact Verdon Office du Tourisme.

Addresses Comité Départemental du Tourisme du Var (⌂ 1 bd. Maréchal Foch, Draguignan ☎ 04–94–50–55–50 ⊕ www.tourismevar.com). **Agence de Développement Touristique des Alpes de Haute Provence** (⌂ Immeuble François Mitterand, B.P. 170, Digne-les-Bains Cedex ☎ 04–92–31–57–29 ⊕ www. alpes-haute-provence.com). **Comité Regional du Tourisme Riviera Côte d'Azur** (⌂ 400 promenade des Anglais, B.P. 3126, Nice Cedex 3 ☎ 04–93–37–78–78 ⊕ www. guideriveria.com).

Sun, Sand, and Sex

Following upon their worldwide fame as the earth's most glamorous beaches, the real things often come as a shock to first-time visitors. Much of the Côte d'Azur is lined with rock and pebble, and the beaches are narrow swaths backed by city streets or roaring highways. Only St-Tropez, on this stretch of the Mediterranean, has the curving bands of sandy waterfront you've come to expect from all those '50s photographs—and even there, the 3-mi stretch of Pampelonne Beach supports no fewer than 35 restaurants and private businesses. Note that there's a range of acceptable behaviors on these beaches: some are topless, some feature nudity, some are favored by gays. You won't need a diagram to tell you which is which.

Finding a Place to Stay

If you've come to this area from other regions in France you'll notice a sudden sharp hike in hotel prices skyrocketing to dizzying heights in summer. St-Tropez's rates vie with those in Monaco. You'll also notice a difference in decor: the look leans toward "le style Côte d'Azur," a slick, neo-Deco pastiche that smacks of Jazz-Age glamour. Up in the hills you'll find the charm you'd expect, both in sophisticated inns and in mom-and-pop auberges; the farther north you drive, the lower the prices.

DINING & LODGING PRICES IN EUROS				
¢	$	$$	$$$	$$$$
Restaurants				
Under €13	€14–€19	€20–€24	€25–€31	Over €32
Hotels				
Under €55	€56–€85	€86–€135	€136–€200	Over €201

Restaurant prices are per person for a main course at dinner, including tax (19.6%) and service; note that if a restaurant offers only prix-fixe (set-price) meals, it has been given the price category that reflects the full prix-fixe price. Hotel prices are for a standard double room in high season, including tax (19.6%) and service charge.

How's the Weather?

Summer days are like the film Groundhog Day—everyday seems exactly the same as the day before with the piercing azure blue sky and sticky sunshine heat. July and August are hot, people move slower and, yes, sweat. By rule of folklore thumb, locals cite August 15th as the beginning of changing weather: clouds tend to roll in frequently and temps become noticeably cooler in the mornings and evenings. April and October tend to be the rainier months and of course, the Mistral can come at any time bringing terrible gusts and nippy drafts. To see the Gorges du Verdon in full fall color, aim for early October, though the odds of rainy days increase as autumn advances.

Making the Most of Your Time

Unless you enjoy jacked-up prices, traffic jams, and sardine-style beach crowds, avoid the coast like the plague in July and August, especially the last week of July and first three weeks of August. Many of the better restaurants simply shut down to avoid the coconut-oil crowd. Another negative about July and August: the Estérel is closed to hikers during this flash-fire season. From Easter through October the café life is in full swing; May is mild and often lovely, but the best restaurants and hotels may be crowded with spillover from the Cannes film festival. Planet St-Tropez is really only open for business April through October. During the warmer months, people-watching in the port and lunching at Pampelonne Beach's Club 55 is a must but even at the end of season, there's lots of stuff going on: Regatta races, an Australian Film Festival and the annual sale "La Grande Braderie"—held during the last weekend of October when even you can afford to shop in St-Tropez (okay, so it's last season's stuff, but hey . . .). Moustiers-Ste-Marie celebrates the Fête de la Cité de la Faïence (earthenware) over three days in late spring every other (even numbered) year. In February, La Napoule hosts its annual Mamosa festival, complete with competing floats parades. Southwest, in Bormes-les-Mimosas, you can visit the President's summer home during the Heritage Day Weekend ("Les Journées du Patrimoine") over the third weekend in September when many closed-to-the-public establishments open their doors . . . and for free! Also in September, Fréjus celebrates the Giant Omelette Festival. You can work off all that eggcess during a week of guided walks around hilltop villages near St-Raphaël during the Var Rambling Week in October.

Taster's Choice

Restaurants in the coastal resorts are expensive and often a risky investment, as they cater mostly to crowds *en passage*. St-Tropez prices can be higher than prices in Paris. It's a fine town for a (staggeringly expensive) fish feast; however, it is home to one of the country's finest fish markets, just off the port. Inland, you'll tap into a culture of cozy auberges (inns) in hilltop villages and have a better chance of finding good home cooking for your money. You can also judge how hard a restaurant is trying to please by the children's menu, which in the better restaurants goes beyond the standard *steak-haché* (bunless hamburger) and frites, sometimes offering gourmet grub such as roast lamb with scalloped potatoes.

In St-Tropez don't forget to try the *tropézienne*, a rich, pastry cream-filled brioche topped with grainy sugar that provides yet another example of the French Paradox when you see the flawless bodies sprawled on the beach.

Around the Gorges du Verdon, a magnet for hikers and climbers, food becomes less of a priority—expect to find mostly pizzas, salads, and simple hikers' fare.

As a general rule, the curlier the printing on a menu the more pretensions a country auberge has; some of the best post only handwritten chalkboard menus.

5

GETTING AROUND PLANNER

Transportation Basics

Public transportation is not as good here as in other regions of the Riviera and Provence, and some itineraries may require cars. To calculate highway tolls from the Côte d'Azur, see www.escota.fr and www.prix-carburants.gouv.fr for the lowest prices at the pump. Driving is the best way to village-hop in the Haut Var and take in the spectacular Gorges du Verdon, but be prepared for some challenging bends along the way like the Route des Crêtes (D23) from La-Palud-sur-Verdon (if white knuckles are not for you, opt for the nearby D952).

If traveling by bus, remember that just because you actually found a local bus that stops at the village of choice, don't bet that it's going to drop you in the heart of town. During the summer season, there is no way to avoid the bumper-to-bumper traffic along the N98 Coast route, the Corniche de l'Estérel. Taking a train or bus (for schedules, go to w *www.sodetrav.fr*) is much easier than the Haut Var where there are few options. From roughly April to September, ferries to St-Tropez depart from Nice (2 hrs 30 mins), Cannes (1 hr 15 mins) and St-Raphaël (1 hr) and offer a scenic, hassle-free coastal route.

By Bus

Local buses cover a network of routes along the coast and stop at many out-of-the-way places that can't be reached by train.

Timetables are available from tourist offices, train stations, and local bus stations (*gares routières*).

Ask for information on commercial bus excursions, too; there are several day-trip tours out of Fréjus and St-Raphaël into the more popular backcountry towns.

St-Tropez's Gare Routière (bus station) is located on Ave. du Général de Gaulle and has bus routes run by Sodetrav. These include a popular run to/from St-Raphaël (€10.30, 1½ hours, 10 daily), the town with the nearest railway station, with stops in Grimaud and Port Grimaud, Ste-Maxime, and Fréjus (€10.30, 1 hour).

Note that in high season, the traffic jam to St-Tropez can lead to two-plus-hour bus rides, so if you arrive in St-Raphaël, it may be best to hop on the shuttle boats that connect the two ports (see By Boat).

Buses also link up with Ramatuelle and Gassin (€3.50 and €3.40, respectively, 25 minutes, three daily in peak season).

Buses also route over to Toulon (€19.70, 2½ hrs).

St-Raphaël's bus station is on Avenue Victor Hugo next to the train station and has buses linking up with St-Tropez (via Grimaud and Ste-Maxime, €10.30, 2 hours), some towns in the Haut Var, and selected stops along the coastal Corniche de l'Estérel, which is also covered by RafaelBus.

Fréjus's bus station is on Place Paul-Vernet and Estérel buses have routes to St-Tropez.

Some Haut Var towns are serviced by Les Rapides Varois, departing from the train stations at Les Arcs and Draguignan.

Bus Travel Information Estérel-Forum Autocars (☎04–94–53–78–46). **RafaelBus** (☎04–94–83–87–63). **Les Rapides Varois** (☎04–94–47–05–05). **Sodetrav** (☎04–94–95–24–82 ⊕ *www.sodetrav.fr*).

By Train

The main rail crossroads from points north and west are at Fréjus's main station on Rue Martin-Bidoure and St-Raphaël's Gare de St-Raphaël on Rue Waldeck-Rousseau, where the rail route begins its scenic crawl along the coast to Italy, stopping in La Napoule and Cannes. St-Raphaël is the main train hub, on the coastal rail line between Menton and Marseille (it's about one hour and 20 minutes from the latter by rail, with hourly trains costing between €16 and €21, depending on when you travel). The resort port of Mandelieu–La Napoule is on the main rail line between St-Raphaël and Cannes. There is no rail access to St-Tropez; St-Raphaël and Fréjus are the nearest stops. The train station nearest the Haut Var and the Gorges du Verdon is at Les Arcs, below Draguignan. From there you have to rent a car or take local buses offered by Les Rapides Varois into the hills. The scenic little Chemins de Fer de Provence leads from Nice to Digne and makes a local stop at St-André-les-Alpes, about 20 km (12 mi) north of Castellane, the eastern gateway to the Gorges du Verdon.

The private (it's owned by Vivendi) Provence Railroad network follows the coast from St-Raphaël to Mandelieu, stopping at the coastal resorts. For further sightseeing you have to resort to renting a car or taking a bus excursion.

Train Information **SNCF** (🕿 3635 ⊕ www.ter-sncf.com/uk/paca). **TGV** (🕿 3635 ⊕ www.tgv.com). **Chemins de Fer de Provence (Provence Railroad)** (✉ 4 bis rue Alfred Binet, Nice 🕿 04–97–03–80–80 ⊕ www.trainprovence.com).

By Boat

Considering the congestion buses and cars confront on the road to St-Tropez, the best way to get to that resort is to train to St-Raphaël, then hop on one of the four boats each day (between April and October) that leave from the Gare Maritime de St-Raphaël on Rue Pierre-Auble. The trip takes about an hour and costs €13. Transports Maritimes MMG also offers a shuttle-boat linking St-Tropez and Ste-Maxime April to October; tickets are €6.60 and the ride is a half-hour. Once in St-Tropez, stay on the water for a one-hour boat ride tour offered by MMG of the Baie des Cannebiers (nicknamed the "Bay of Stars") to see some celebrity villas.

Boat Travel Information **Transports Maritimes MMG** (✉ Quai L.-Condroyer, Ste-Maxime 🕿 04–94–96–51–00). **Transports Maritimes Raphaelois** (✉ St-Raphaël 🕿 04–94–95–17–46).

By Car

A8 provides swift, easy access to Fréjus and other towns along the coast. To reach resorts along the Estérel, you must follow the coastal highway N98 east. To get to St-Tropez and the resorts at the foot of the Massif des Maures, follow N98 southwest from Fréjus. To explore the hill towns and the Gorges du Verdon, slow and scenic roads lead north and west from Fréjus and Cannes, including the famous Route Napoléon (D85). Sailing from Fréjus and St-Raphaël toward Cannes is a breeze on A8, but N98, which connects you to coastal resorts in between, can be extremely slow, though scenic. To the north and east of this region, you break into the country, and the roads are small, pokey, and pretty. If you want to explore any hill towns in depth and at will, a car is indispensable.

By Foot

Contact local tourist offices for information on hikes in the rugged backcountry of the Massif de l'Estérel. While several *sentiers du littoral* (waterfront trails) route around the St-Tropez Peninsula, *grande randonnées* (national hiking trails) GR51 and GR49 ascend the Estérel heights. The GR49 intersects with France's most spectacular grande randonnée, the GR4, which threads the Gorges du Verdon.

Updated by
Nancy Wilson

THE SERIES OF PICTURE-BOOK GULFS that scoop into this part of the French Mediterranean coastline is less famous and less exotic than its other half to the east. Above the coastline of the Var *département* (county), the horizon is dominated from all directions by the rugged red-rock heights of the Massif de l'Estérel and the green-black bulk of the Massif des Maures. Blue-green waters lap at the foot of thriving resort towns—St-Tropez, of course, but also Fréjus, St-Raphaël, Mandelieu, and La Napoule. Like France's perennially popular rock star Johnny Hallyday, St-Tropez never fades—it just gets another face-lift and keeps going, brasher than ever. The difficulty reaching this portion of the coast—the train only goes as far as Ste-Maxime—naturally separates the wheat (who swan in by helicopter) from the chaff (who crawl along in midsummer traffic jams, sweaty and miserable). You need to be a little masochistic to visit St-Tropez in August, but the town does have a fair number of budget hotels and sheds most of its pretension in the off-season, becoming simply a small fishing port with very big yachts. Neighboring resorts can't help but feel lower-key, providing stretches of sandy beach and guaranteed balmy temperatures to sun-starved northerners. In high summer, masses flood the beaches, feast on the fish, fill up the marinas, luxuriate in the spa treatments, and crowd the hotels and cafés. Bored, sunburned, or regarding each other in mutual *snobbisme,* they then take to the hills—the glorious vineyard-lined, village-crowned hills that back the coast as the continent climbs gently toward the Alps.

They are a virtual subculture, these *villages perchés* (perched villages) and historic towns, which live in touristic symbiosis with the coast. To the east lie the famous, gentrified tourist towns of Grasse, St-Paul, and Vence; to the north rises Fayence, a definitive 18th-century Provençal town that now lives as much off the renown of its souvenirs as its spectacular views.

These towns make great day trips from the coast, though they're often dominated in high season by busloads of excursion-takers out of Cannes or St-Raphaël. But if you have a car and the time to explore, you can plunge even deeper into the backcountry, past the coastal plateau into the Haut Var. Here the harsh and beautiful countryside—raw rock, pine, and scrub oak—is lightly peppered with little hill villages that are almost boutique-free. You can hear the *pétanque* (lawn bowling) balls thunk, the fountains trickle, and the bells tolling within their wrought-iron campaniles. If you like what you see and press on, you'll be rewarded with one of France's most spectacular natural wonders: the Gorges du Verdon, a Grand Canyon–style chasm roaring with milky-green water and edged by one of Europe's most hair-raising drives. Backpacks, hiking boots, and picnics (or quick café meals) are de rigueur around the Gorges, until you reach lovely Moustiers-Ste-Marie, an atmospheric center for *faïence* where you can treat yourself to a leisurely meal and take in breathtaking views.

EXPLORING THE WESTERN CÔTE D'AZUR

You can visit any spot between St-Tropez and Cannes in an easy day trip, and the hilltop villages and towns on the coastal plateau are just as accessible. Thanks to the efficient raceway A8, you can whisk at high speeds to the exit nearest your destination up or down the coast; thus even if you like leisurely exploration, you can zoom back to your home base at day's end. Above the autoroute things slow down considerably, and you'll find the winding roads and overlooks between villages an experience in themselves. Venturing farther north, either by the Route Napoléon or D995, is a bigger commitment and, to be fully enjoyed, should include at least one overnight stop.

Situated between the watercolor port of St-Tropez and the rugged red rock of the Estérel, this captivating stretch of the Riviera has drawn sun lovers and socialites since the days of the Grand Tour. Here the coastal highway hugs the spectacular waterfront, snaking past sophisticated getaway towns as well as a staggering concentration of restaurants, high-rise resorts, gas stations, tourist traps, and beach discos. Proceed just a few miles inland to find picturesque Provençal villages perched above the fray; penetrate farther still and you'll be rewarded with mountain scenery and serene little towns.

Numbers in the text correspond to numbers in the margin and on the Western Côte d'Azur, St-Tropez, and The Haut Var and into Haute Provence maps.

ST-TROPEZ & THE MASSIF DES MAURES

Shielded from the mistral by the broad, forested mass of the Massif des Maures, this small expanse of pampered coastline is crowned by the sparkling lights of St-Tropez, itself doubly protected by the hills of the Paillas. A pretty pastel port in winter, in season it becomes glamorous "*St-Trop.*" For day trips you can escape to the simple life in the hill towns of Ramatuelle and Gassin or delve deep into the Maures in La Garde-Freinet. Ordinary mortals, especially vacationing families on a budget, usually aim for Ste-Maxime, across the bay, where the hyperdevelopment typical of the Riviera begins.

ST-TROPEZ

35 km (22 mi) southwest of Fréjus, 66 km (41 mi) northeast of Toulon.

GETTING HERE

Keep in mind that while St-Tropez can be heaven, getting there can be hellish. Out on a limb, scorned by any train route, you can only get to St-Trop by car, bus, or boat (from nearby ports like St-Raphaël). Driving a car can test anyone's mettle, thanks to the crowds, the narrow roads, and the Parking du Port parking lot (opposite the bus station on Avenue du Général de Gaulle, with shuttle bus into town mid-March to October) or the new Parc des Lices (beneath the Place des Lices) in the

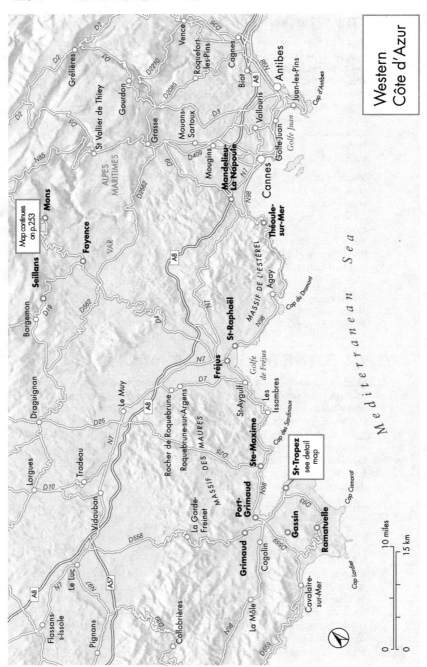

Western
Côte d'Azur

center of town and their fees: a staggering €5 an hour in peak season. A train-bus connection can be made if you're leaving from Nice center: take the train (direction St-Raphaël) from the center city Gare SNCF station (✉ *Av. Thiers* ☎ *04–92–14–80–80* ⊕ *www.voyages-sncf.com*), which costs €9.20 one way; from St-Raphael, there's daily bus service with Sodetrav (☎ *08–25–00–06–50* ⊕ *www.sodetrav.fr*), with one-way costing €10.10. Make sure you get to St-Raphaël's bus station early or you'll be elbowed out of a seat by aggressive bronzed ladies and forced to stand the whole way. Travel time from St-Raphael to St-Tropez is 1½ hours. The other option is to take a boat from the Nice harbor with Trans Côte d'Azur (☎ *04–92–00–42–30* ⊕ *www.trans-cote-azur.com*), which has daily trips from June to September. If you decide to rent a car, take the N98 coast road (the longest route but also the prettiest, with great picnic stops along the way).

VISITOR INFORMATION
St-Tropez Tourist Office (✉ *Quai Jean-Jaurès, B.P. 183, St-Tropez* ☎ *08–92–68–48–28* ⊕ *www.ot-saint-tropez.com*).

EXPLORING
At first glance, it really doesn't look all that lovely. There's a pretty port, but it's crammed with overscale yachts, double parking, and cafés charging €5 for a coffee. There's a picturesque old town in sugared-almond hues, but there are many prettier in the hills nearby. There are sandy beaches, rare enough on the Riviera, and old-fashioned squares with plane trees and pétanque players, but these are a dime a dozen throughout Provence. So what made St-Tropez an internationally known locale? Two words: Brigitte Bardot. When this *pulpeuse* (voluptuous) teenager showed up in St-Tropez on the arm of Roger Vadim in 1956 to film *And God Created Woman,* the heads of the world snapped around. Neither the gentle descriptions of writer Guy de Maupassant (1850–93) nor the watercolor tones of Impressionist Paul Signac (1863–1935), nor the stream of painters who followed (including Matisse and Bonnard) could focus the world's attention on this seaside hamlet as did this one voluptuous woman in a head-scarf, Ray-Bans, and capris.

With the film world following in Bardot's footsteps, St-Tropez became the hot spot it to some extent remains. Celebrity-spotting remains the foremost local sport, and largely free (unless Sir Elton John can only be found deep inside an expensive restaurant). In 2004, *Vanity Fair* ran a big article, "Saint Tropez Babylon," detailing the over-the-top petrodollar parties, mega-yachts, and Beyoncé–d paparazzi. But don't be turned off: the next year, Stewart, Tabori & Chang released an elegant coffee-table book, *Houses of St-Tropez,* packed with photos of supremely tasteful and pretty residences, many occupied by fashion designers, artists, and writers. Once a hangout for Colette, Anaïs Nin, and Françoise Sagan, the town yet earns its old moniker, the "Montparnasse of the Mediterranean".

St-Trop ("Saint Too Much," as the French call it) has become such a byword for wealth, sun, and glitter that you might be surprised to find

that it's so small and insulated. The lack of train service, casinos, and chain hotels keeps it that way. Yet fame, in a sense, came too fast for St-Trop. Unlike the chic resorts farther east, it didn't have the decades-old reputation of the sort that would attract visitors all year around. For a good reason: its location on the south side of the gulf puts it at the mercy of the terrible mistral winter winds. So, in summer the crowds descend and the prices rise into the stratosphere.

In July and August, you must be carefree about the sordid matter of cash. After all, at the most Dionysian nightclub in town, a glass of tap water goes for $35 and when the mojo really gets going, billionaires think nothing of "champagne-spraying" the partying crowds—think World Series celebrations but with $1,000 bottles of Roederer Cristal instead of Gatorade. Complaining about summer crowds, overpricing, and lack of customer service has become a tourist sport and yet this is what makes St-Tropez—described by the French daily newspaper Le Figaro as the place you'll see "the greatest number of faces per square meter"—as intriguing as it is seductive. It is, after all, the hajj for hedonists.

Anything associated with the distant past seems almost absurd in St-Tropez. Still, the place has a history that predates the invention of the string bikini, and people have been finding reasons to come here since AD 68, when a Roman soldier from Pisa named Torpes was beheaded for professing his Christian faith in front of Emperor Nero, transforming this spot into a place of pilgrimage. Today, a different sort of celeb is worshipped: Ever since St-Tropez became "hot" again, there have been, David & Victoria, Paris, Bono, Jack, and Bruce sightings. Most stars, however, stay hidden in villas, so the people you'll see are mere mortals, lots of them, many intent on displaying the best (or at least the most) of their youth, beauty, and wealth. In the heat of summer days tourist crowds are thick, gawking at the golden boys swabbing yacht decks and perusing the art daubed and painted along the port. By night, when the crowds thin and the air softens, stylish couples make for the cafés, where they subtly preen among others who share their creed.

Still, if you take an early-morning stroll (before the 11 AM breakfast rush at Le Gorille Café) along the harbor or down the narrow medieval streets—the rest of the town will still be sleeping off the Night Before— you'll see just how charming St-Tropez is. There's a weekend's worth of boutiques to explore and many cute cafés where you can sit under colored awnings and watch the spectacle that is St-Trop saunter by. Along medieval streets lined with walled gardens and little squares set with dripping fountains you'll be able to discover historic delights like the Chapelle de la Misericorde, topped by its wrought-iron campanile, and Rue Allard, lined with picturesque houses such as the Maison du Maure. In the evening, everyone moves from the cafés on the quais to the cafés on the squares, particularly Place des Lices, where a seat at the Le Café allows you to watch the boules players under the glow of hundreds of electric bulbs (paging Deborah Kerr and David Niven in *Bonjour Tristesse*). In the end, it's not too hard to experience what the artists first found to love and what remain the village's real charms: its soft light, its warm pastels, and the scent of the sea wafting in from the waterfront.

Start your St-Trop tour at the *nouveau bassin* (new harbor) for private pleasure boats. There's a large parking lot and the bus station here. With the sea on your left, walk around to the Vieux Port (old harbor), enjoying the life of the quays and the views around the bay as you go.

❶ The **Vieux Port**, bordered by the Quai de l'Epi, the Quai Bouchard, the Quai Peri, the Quai Suffren, and the Quai Jean-Jaurès, is the nerve center of this famous yachting spot, a place for strolling and looking over the shoulders of artists daubing their versions of the view on easels set up along the water's edge, surreptitiously looking out for any off-duty celebs. For it is here, from folding director's chairs at the famous port-side cafés Le Gorille (named for its late exceptionally hirsute manager), Café de Paris, and Sénéquier's—which line Quai Suffren and Quai Jean-Jaurès—that the cast of St-Tropez's living theater plays out its colorful roles. **Sénéquier** provides a fine front-row seat from which to observe the multicolored scene. Arrive at breakfast time and you'll find those who danced all night mingling with those who just got up; arrive at sunset, and the glory of the view may distract you from people-watching.

2 ★ Just inland from the southwest corner of the Vieux Port stands the extraordinary **Musée de l'Annonciade,** where the legacy of the artists who loved St-Tropez has been lovingly preserved. The Annunciation Museum, housed in a 16th-century chapel, traces the evolution of painting from neo-Impressionism to the Fauves—many of whom painted in and around St-Tropez. It was Paul Signac who "discovered" the seductive light of this fishing village, using fine sprays of confetti dots to explore the vacillations of light and color on its pale-ocher houses and rippling water. A rich man, he had been sailing the coast in his yacht (*L'Olympia*, named after Manet's infamous nude), when bad weather forced him to make port. Smitten, he built La Hune (on Rue Paul-Signac) and his house parties transplanted the best from Paris's St-Germain-des-Pres. Before long, fellow artists Bonnard, Matisse, Marquet, Dufy, Derain, Vlaminck, and Van Dongen fell in love with the town. Several of Signac's port views may be on display at any given time, buttressed by those of lesser-known followers. A handful of bold Fauvist paintings includes the moody *L'Estaque* by Braque, painted north of Marseilles. Although there are only 50 or so paintings and a handful of sculptures, few small museums achieve such a balance of theme and concentration of quality. ⊠ *Quai de l'Épi / Pl. Georges Grammont* 🕾 *04–94–17–84–10* 🗺 *€6.00* ⊙ *June–Sept., daily 10–1 and 2–9; Oct. and Dec.–May, Wed.–Mon. 10–noon and 2–6.*

Head back past the Quai Suffern—a statue of the Bailli de Suffren, an 18th-century customs official, stands guard—past the famous cafés. If the wind isn't too strong, walk out along the Mole Jean Réveille, the harbor wall, for a good view of Ste-Maxime across the sparkling bay, the hills of Estérel and, on a clear day, the distant Alps. Retrace your

3 4 steps along the mole and quayside to the 15th-century **Tour du Portalet** and head past it to the old fisherman's quarter, the **Quartier de la Ponche,** just east of the Quai Jean-Jaurès. Here you'll find the **Port des Pécheurs** (Fishermen's Port), on whose beach Bardot did a star-turn in *And God Created Woman*. Twisting, narrow streets, designed to break the impact of the mistral, open to tiny squares with fountains. Complete with gulf-side harbor, St-Tropez's Old Town maze of backstreets and old ramparts is daubed in shades of gold, pink, ocher, and sky-blue. Trellised jasmine and wrought-iron birdcages hang from the shuttered windows, and many of the tiny streets dead-end at the sea.The main drag here, Rue de la Ponche, leads into Place l'Hôtel de Ville, landmarked by a **mairie** (town hall) marked out in typical Tropezienne

5 hues of pink and green. Head up Rue Guichard to the Baroque **Église de St-Tropez,** to pay your respects to the bust and barque of St. Torpes, every day but May 17th, when they are carried aloft in the Bravade parade honoring the town's namesake saint.

6 Continue northward over a few blocks to Rue de la Citadelle, which leads away from the port up to the looming Citadel, set on a hill to the west of town. St-Tropez's 16th-century **Citadelle** stands in a lovely hilltop park. The views from its terrace take in the whole of the gulf and the hills behind and are the sort to tempt any artist to set up an easel in a jiffy. ⊠*Rue de la Cita-delle* ☎*04–94–97–06–53* 💶*€2.50* 🕓*Daily 10–6.*

⑦ Leaving the Citadelle, make your way down to the Montée Ringrave, past the 17th-century **Chapelle de la Miséricorde** (on Rue de la Misé-ricorde) to the social center of the old town, the **Place des Lices** (also called the Place Carnot). Here, you'll hear pétanque balls—a south-ern version of boules—clicking in the sand square. Lying two blocks inland, straight back from the Quai Suffren, the square's symmetrical forest of plane trees (what's left of

them) provides shade to rows of cafés and restaurants, skateboarders, children, and the grandfatherly pétanque players. Enjoy a time-out in the town "living room," Le Café (not be be confused with the nearby Café des Arts). The square becomes a moveable feast (for both eyes and palate) on market days—Tuesday and Saturday. Heading back to the Vieux Port area, take in the boutiques lining rues Sibilli, Clmenceau, or Gambetta to help accessorize your evening look—you never know when that photographer from *Elle* will snapping away at the trendies.

⑧ A block west of Rue Clémenceau is the **Musée du Papillon.** In a pretty house at the end of a typically Tropezien lane, the Museum of But-terflies is a delight for children (and their parents). Sweetly aflutter, the 35,000 specimens can be toured by appointment with the collec-tor, Dany Lartigue. ⊠*9 rue Etienne Berny* ☎*04–94–97–63–45* 💶*€3* 🕓*Apr. 1–Nov. 1, Mon.–Sat. 2:30–6.*

To experience St-Tropez's natural beauty up close, consider walking parts of the *sentier du littoral (coastal path)* around the peninsula. Try the 12 km (7 mi) long route that takes an average of four hours, with longish stretches on sand beach. Leave from the Tour du Portalet or the Tour Vieille at the edge of the Quartier de la Ponche. Follow the foot-path from Plage des Graniers along the beaches and cliffs overlooking the water, often with views toward the Estérel or out to the open sea. From Cavalaire, at the southwest root of the peninsula, you can catch one of the few buses back to St-Tropez if you plan ahead.

WHERE TO EAT & STAY

$$$$ ✗ **L'Escale Joseph.** Ivana Trump put this hot spot on the map when she hosted a white tie and tiara party here a few years back and now all the big kids come out to play: Beyoncé, Madonna, Tom Cruise. Must be the appeal of eating on the beach . . . in the port. White sand scat-tered across the floor, Brigitte Bardot gracing the walls—this could only work in St Trop. Set menu at €39. Specialties include les encornets comme on les aime à L'Escale and le tartare de bœuf coupé au couteau à l'italienne, or really bust your budget with L'Escale's famous Loup

C'est Délicieux!

Typical throughout Provence is a garlicky mayonnaise called *aïoli*, a staple condiment that's especially at home with a cold serving of fresh coastal fish. In the words of poet Frédéric Mistral, "Aïoli sums up the heat, the strength, and the joy of the Provençal sun. Its other virtue: It drives off flies." Made of mortar-crushed raw garlic whipped with egg yolk and olive oil, aïoli can bring tears to your eyes—and later, to those of your fellow travelers. Never mind: heap it on hard-boiled eggs, poached salt cod, or raw vegetables. And watch for it as a Friday lunch special, when all of the above appear in a Provençal smorgasbord.

Even more pungent than aïoli is the powerful paste called *anchoïade*. Whether spread on tiny toasts or used as a dip for raw vegetables, its base of Mediterranean anchovies provides an emphatic kick of concentrated salt and fish.

Another staple of the region is *pistou*, the Provençal pesto (which originates from the Italian port of Genoa, nearby). Made of a savory blend of basil, garlic, Parmesan, and olive oil, minus the pine nuts found in Italian pesto, it shows up in *soupe au pistou* (reminiscent of minestrone), *pâtes* (pasta) *au pistou*, and as a sauce for almost anything.

en croûte de sel for two. ⊠*9 quai Jean-Jaurès* ☎*04–94–97–00–63* ▱*AE, DC, MC, V.*

$$$ ✕**Le Bistrot.** Think roast chicken with truffled potato mash or open-faced club sandwiches. This "brasserie-lounge bar" serves comfort cooking until 5 PM but switches to a more refined dinner menu—*fois gras pressé* or *carré agneau frotté au thym*—as reflected in the price. Separate menu for *les sushis* and, as of 2008, Japanese specialties (from €23). Sample liquids in the *cave à vin* or *cave à thé* or, for designated drivers, the *cave des eaux* offers water from around the world—you can even sip and go online at no extra charge in *l'espace lecteur*. Prices are more than acceptable considering the über-chic setting and amazing people-watching potential of the terrace on the leafy Place des Lices. Watch out for dangling chandeliers! ⊠*3 pl. Carnot* ☎*04–94–97–11–33* ⊕*www. bistrot-saint-tropez.com* ▱*AE, MC, V.*

$$$ ✕**Le Café.** A landmark once famed as a hangout for literati and artists, this big, convivial brasserie on the Place des Lices draws regulars for the generous *plats du jour* of classic bistro fare: *gigot* (leg of lamb), *loup du pays grillé*, fresh ravioli au basilic, local seafood, and homemade desserts. Except for chicken lovers, the menu should please all palates and the tables set up on the square provide courtside seats for the pétanque games. Open 365 days a year from 7 AM—the later it gets the more reservations come in handy. ⊠*Pl. des Lices* ☎*04–94–97–44–69* ⊕*www. lecafe.fr* ⚐*Reservations essential* ▱*AE, MC, V.*

$$$ ✕**Le Girelier.** Fish, fish, and more fish—sea bass, salmon, sole, sardines, monkfish, lobster, crayfish, fish eggs spread on a thin slice of toast—they're trying to jump for their lives as the boats come into the Old Port. Will they make it? Not if new chef Fernand Vaz gets to them first. The renovated bateau rive (shore boat)–style back dining area nicely contrasts the buffed and bronzed clientele who enjoy the casual sea-

shanty space and the highly visible Vieux Port terrace tables. Grilling is the order of the day, with most fish sold by weight, but this is also a stronghold for bouillabaisse. The €39 lunch and dinner menus won't disappoint. ⊠ *Quai Jean-Jaurès* ☎*04–94–97–03–87* ⊕*www.legirelier.fr* ☐*AE, MC, V* ⊘*Closed Nov.–Mar.*

$$$ ✕**La Table du Marché.** With an afternoon tearoom and a summer sushi
★ bar, this charming bistro, masterminded by celebrity chef Christophe Leroy, offers up a mouthwatering spread of regional specialties. For something light, sink into one of the overstuffed armchairs in the upstairs dining room, cozy with warm colors, chic Provençal accents, and antique bookshelves or if you're feeling moody, the piano bar on the main floor serenades daily from 7 PM. Try the tomato pistou tart or dive into the €19.50 (lunch) or €29 (dinner) set menu. Open every day from 7 AM to midnight. ⊠ *38 rue Georges-Clémenceau* ☎*04–94–97–85–20* ⊕*www.christophe-leroy.com* ☐*AE, MC, V.*

$$$ ✕**Villa Romana.** George Clooney, Penelope Cruz, and other lotharios seek asylum from the paparazzi in the privacy of this away-from-the-port eatery. The decor is "Tropezienne"—an over-the-top orgy of neo-Pompeian murals, leopard-skin banquettes, overstuffed chairs, and red-velvet tassels, providing a slinky backdrop for the nightly fashion show and DJ festivities. Along with the usual tuna and veal numbers, the kitchen's new head Thierry Deveaux prepares everything from caviar to pizzas to a chocolate blow-out called "Hallicarnasse." Open in the evenings only, this place-to-be-seen closes on certain weeknights in low season. Dress code and reservations a must. ⊠ *Chemin des Conquettes* ☎*04–94–97–15–50* ⊕*www.villa-romana.com* ⚑*Reservations essential* ☐*AE, MC, V* ⊘*Closed Oct.–Mar.*

$–$$ ✕**Le Canastel.** Reputed to be the best pizza in town, Le Canastel is equally as charming as it is delicious. Pastas—penne, tagliatelli, or spaghetti—with your choice of sauce for around €15. Pizzas range from €11.50 to €16 (try their specialties jambon cru or truffle pizza) with traditional veal and beef dishes starting at €22.50. All served to intimate side-by-side tables under covered vines along a tiny cobblestone street down from the Citadel. ⊠ *1 rue des Féniers,* ☎*04–94–97–26–60* ☐*MC, V* ⊘*Closed Nov.–Feb.*

¢–$ ✕**Restaurant de la Citadelle.** Just up from the port, this family restaurant is fantastic for both food and price. Salmon tagiatelli or marinated mussels for only €10; aioli Provencal for €14.50 (lunch). Stews, grilled fish, or beef are also available for slightly more and there's a €25 menu. Cozy interior with yellow walls, beamed ceiling, and local oil paintings but the outside street lined tables are much more fun. You won't miss any people-watching from here while you enjoy a glass of wine (€4). No reservations needed and dinner services start from 6. ⊠ *24 rue de la Citadelle,* ☎*04–94–54–81–19* ☐*MC, V* ⊘*Closed Oct.–Mar.*

$$$$ ⌂**Le Byblos.** Arranged like a toy Mediterranean village, fronted with
★ stunning red, rust, and yellow facades, and complete with ocher-stucco cottage-like suites grouped around courtyards landscaped with palms, olive trees, and lavender, this longtime fave of the glitterati began life as a "Phoenician-style" resort (the name means Bible) and was dreamed up by a Lebanese millionaire. Forty years later, it has seen the jet set *jet,*

jet, jet. This is where "les beautiful people" come to shine in all their gold-and-white Frenchness. Lavishly bored, many wind up lounging in *the* place to dine: Le Byblos's Spoon, über-chef Alain Ducasse's concept restaurant, which attains the height of hip multiethnic Mediterranean cuisine (richly infused with spicy North Africa). Chef Vincent Maillard fixes light and healthy soups, salads, steamed dishes, grilled fish, and *tajines.* If you can't drag yourself away from the pool, share plates at the revamped loungy poolside restaurant B: salads and burgers for lunch or goat cheese samosa and nems (Vietnamese egg rolls) with langoustine and fennel in the evening. You won't need to leave the hotel to hit one of the hottest nightspots in town either—les Caves du Roy is on-site (expect the old St-Tropez narrow-eyed once-over before they let you in). Recovering from it all is easy at the exclusive Byblos Spa by Sisley Cosmetics, opened 2007. Maybe the Essential Awakening Deep Scrub for the morning after (if you can get up) or the Saint-Tropez Sunset massage before starting all over again. **Pros:** attention to detail; automatic access to Les Caves du Roy. **Cons:** not near the beach; few chairs poolside. ⊠ *Av. Paul-Signac,* ☎ *04–94–56–68–00* ⊕ *www.byblos .com* ⇆ *52 rooms, 43 suites* ⇩ *In-room: refrigerator. In-hotel: 2 restaurants, bar, pool, gym, spa, Wi-Fi, parking (free), some pets allowed* ▭ *AE, DC, MC, V* ⊗ *Closed mid-Nov.–Easter.*

$$$$ **La Résidence de la Pinède.** Perhaps the most opulent of St-Tropez's luxe hangouts, this balustraded white villa and its broad annex sprawl elegantly along a private waterfront, wrapped around an isolated courtyard and a pool shaded by parasol pines. The freshly renovated rooms are Mediterranean decor at its best: simple and light with splashes of hue-intense blues, greens, and reds. Spend a day lounging with a book underneath a parasol by the heated swimming pool and manicured lawns, or take to the sea where you can scuba dive, sail, windsurf, and jet ski. Pay extra for a seaside room, where you can lean over the balcony and take in broad coastal views over the private sand beach (and the distant range of grey-blue mountains) and the large seafront restaurant; the chef has a celebrated reputation—the famous red book that bestowed chef Donckele one star is the same book that named La Pinede St-Tropez's best restaurant, and you'll understand why after one taste of his red mullet and lobster tart. Rates including half-board are available. **Pros:** private, quiet sand beach; great food; stellar service. **Cons:** overpriced food; €5 charge each way for shuttle bus to and from St-Tropez; one of the higher rack room rates in the world (€915 in peak season). ⊠ *Plage de la Bouillabaisse,* ☎ *04–94–55–91–00* ⊕ *www.residence pinede.com* ⇆ *33 rooms, 6 suites* ⇩ *In-room: refrigerator, Wi-Fi. In-hotel: restaurant, bar, pool, parking (fee), some pets allowed* ▭ *AE, DC, MC, V* ⊗ *Closed mid-Oct.–mid-Apr.*

$$$ **Hôtel B. Lodge.** All the small, delicately contemporary rooms of this four-story charmer overlook the Citadelle's green park, some from tiny balconies. If you're more than two, ask for the pretty loft suite, with its private spiral-stair entrance. Continental breakfast (€10/person) is served in the cozy "Barock" bar or at the petite terrasse outside. **Pros:** no smoking in any of the rooms or bar; good deal for location. **Cons:** with only two available parking spots, street parking is a sticky propo-

sition; small rooms. ⊠*23 rue de l'Aïoli,* ☎*04–94–97–06–57* ⊕*www. hotel-b-lodge.com* ➪*13 rooms, 2 suites* ⚐*In-room: no a/c (some), Internet (some). In-hotel: bar, Wi-Fi, some pets allowed* ▤*MC, V* ⊘*Closed mid-Nov.–mid-Dec.*

$$
Fodor'sChoice
★

🏨 **Lou Cagnard.** Inside a lovely enclosed garden courtyard is this pretty little villa hotel owned by an enthusiastic young couple, who have fixed it up room by room, and recent renovations include satellite TV and Wi-Fi (no extra charge) in each room. Seven ground-floor rooms open onto the flowered and manicured garden, where breakfast (€10/ person) is served in the shade of a fig tree. Most rooms have regional-tile baths, quarry-tile floors, and Provençal fabrics. If you're willing to share a toilet down the hall, four of the rooms are real bargains. **Pros:** fantastic value for your money (try room No. 17); walking distance to everything. **Cons:** few of the older rooms share a bathroom. ⊠*18 av. Paul-Roussel,* ☎*04–94–97–04–24* ⊕*www.hotel-lou-cagnard.com* ➪*19 rooms* ⚐*In-room: Wi-Fi. In-hotel: parking* ▤*MC, V* ⊘*Closed Nov. 1–Dec. 28.*

$

🏨 **La Belle Isnarde.** The Robert family has been offering rooms in this villa just minutes from the Parking des Lices since 1965. Small rooms are as basic as you can get but clean with hand held showers, towels, and shampoo. It's ideal if you want a place to lay your economical head in St-Tropez and have a car (it's just outside walking distance to town and there are no buses) but you can't really enjoy a chill-out: walls are thin and beds weigh in on the soft side. Christine has a loyal international clientele so you need to book in advance. For €60, two rooms with shared bathrooms are also available. **Pros:** lots of free parking; cheap rates for St-Tropez. **Cons:** a 3-minute taxi to town costs €20; zero amenities. ⊠*Début Route de la Plage Tahiti, B.P. 3983992* ☎*04–94–97–13–64* ➪*11 rooms* ⚐ *In-room: no a/c, no television, no telephone. In-hotel: closed parking, some pets (no fee)* ▤*No credit cards* ⊘*Closed Oct. 15–Easter.*

NIGHTLIFE & THE ARTS

Entrance is free to many of *les boîtes* (nightclubs) in St-Trop but the joy stops there. Costing the devil and often jammed to the scuppers, **Les Caves du Roy** (⊠*Av. Paul-Signac* ☎*04–94–97–16–02*), a glorious disco in the Byblos Hotel, is *the* place to see and be seen—even the VIP are separated from the BIP (Byblos Important People); it's filled with svelte model types and their wealthy, silver-haired fans. There's a horrific door policy during high season; don't worry, it's *not* you. It's so worth trying, though, and, once inside, wait to hear the theme from *Star Wars* to know another €35,000 Methuselah of Champagne has just been ordered. Seeking light, action, and music with giddy determination, teens, twentysomethings, and Hollywood Venuses and Tarzans cram into the vast **Le Papagayo** (⊠*Résidence du Port* ☎*04–94–97–95–95*), which anchors the end of a commercial and residential building called the Résidence du Port. The **VIP Room** (⊠*Résidence du Port, just off the main parking lot* ☎*04–94–97–14–70*) symbolizes *le saint-tropez atti-tude.* If you are young, fun, tanned, rich, and love to dance, you have just found paradise. The scene peaks only after 2 AM, winding down around 6, and the club is closed off-season (Oct.–Easter) like Les Caves

5

and Le Papagayo. Set in the picturesque La Ponche neighborhood, **Le Pigeonnier** (⊠*13 rue de la Ponche* ☎*04–94–97–36–85*) is the leading gay-friendly disco. You, too, may be doused with Moët during one of those champagne-spraying midnight parties—so many bottles are set off, waiters are given football helmets.

Every July 15 to August 15, **classical music** (and some) **jazz concerts** take place in the sultry, palm-studded gardens of the private manor house called the **Château de la Moutte** (⊠*Rte. des Salins* ⊕*www.festival-chateau delamoutte.com*). For ticket information about Le Festival des Nuits du Château de La Moutte, inquire at the tourist office.

SHOPPING

There is something about St-Tropez that makes shopping simply irresistible. **Rue Sibilli**, behind the Quai Suffren, is lined with all kinds of trendy boutiques, many carrying those all-important sunglasses. **Zadig & Voltaire** (⊠*Rue François-Sibilli* ☎*04–94–79–12–06*), open year-round, sells beautifully cut clothes by this popular Parisian designer. To dress like a local, visit the St-Tropez institution **Blabla** (⊠*Pl. de la Garonne* ☎*04–94–97–45–09*), which sells head-turning clothes by designers scoped out around the world—just don't forget you'll need the tan to match. Prefer more traditional luxe? Don't miss **Le Dépot** (⊠*Bd. Louis-Blanc* ☎*04–94–97–80–10*), which stocks castoffs by Chanel, Prada, Gucci, et al. The **Place des Lices** overflows with produce and regional foods, as well as clothing and *brocantes* (secondhand items), every Tuesday and Saturday morning. The picturesque little **fish market** occupies the Place aux Herbes every morning.

RAMATUELLE

12 km (7 mi) southwest of St-Tropez.

A typical hilltop whorl of red-clay roofs and dense inner streets topped with arches and lined with arcades, this ancient market town was destroyed in the Wars of Religions and rebuilt as a harmonious whole in 1620. Now its souvenir shops and galleries attract day-trippers out of St-Tropez, who enjoy the pretty drive through the vineyards as much as the village itself. After a morning at the beach, cool off with a pain bagnat and pression at one of the cafés in the town's center. During high season, traffic jams can be spectacular between Ramatuelle and St-Tropez inflating what should be a short drive into a three-hour crawl. During July and August, a courtesy bus will take you from the car parks to the top of the village on Thursday and Sunday for Market days. At the top of the village you can visit the Moulin de Paillas, on Route du Moulin de Paillas, a windmill recently restored in the old style with a mechanism made entirely of wood; the site offers a panoramic view of the coastline. Free guided tours of the windmill are held every Tuesday 5–7. The town cemetery is the final resting place of Gérard Phillipe, an aristocratic heartthrob who died in 1959 after making his mark in such films as *Le Diable au Corps*.

Life's A Beach

Despite the hip-to-hip commerce and piped-in pop music, the *plages* (beaches) around St-Tropez are the most isolated on the Côte d'Azur, providing one of the rare stretches where your back doesn't lean up against the coastal highway. The closest to town, just at the base of the Citadelle, is the **Plage des Graniers,** easily accessible on foot and the most family-friendly. To the southwest of the port (and the vast expanse of parking lot that precedes it) stretch the beaches of **La Bouillabaisse**. But the best beaches lie on a long ribbon of white sand that wraps around the peninsula east of the center, reached by the Route des Plages and its parallel fork, the Route de Tahiti. From here you'll find signs pointing to the two principal beaches: the relatively unexploited **Les Salins** and the famous, highly commercialized **Plage de Pampelonne.** The 5-km-long (3-mi-long) sweep of the white Pampelonne is home to some 50 private beachside restaurants, including the dignified, chic **Moorea,** the clothing-optional **Tahiti,** and the classic **Club 55**—the latter, with a moneyed and Bel Air crowd, is the place to lunch. Most notorious of all—famous for A-list debauches and a regular clientele of mega-movie stars and nymphet wannabes—are **La Voile Rouge** and **Nikki Beach** (visualize March break on stilettos). All these beaches are divided into private turf right up to the waves, and you must pay an average of €10 to €25 per day to access their restaurants, colorful lounge chairs, hot showers, and mattress-side bar service. Be sure to get there early to get a good spot; everybody wants to lounge in the sun on a mattress comfortable enough to take a nap on. You may want to avoid poolside at Nikki Beach where the 5 PM mayhem of champagne showers spares no one. There are, however, a few public-access beaches between the private ones, many equipped with showers and less-than-perfect toilets with a long line of frazzled tourists waiting impatiently. There are cane-shaded parking lots near most of these beaches, though you might consider renting a bike for an easy getaway at sundown. There is a beach for every lifestyle, for families, for gays (**Coco**), and for those who don't mind a parade of exposed aureolae (**Tahiti**). Note that when you head to the beach bars and restaurants, you are expected to cover up a bit.

Bicycles are an ideal way to get to the beaches. **Rolling Bikes** (⊠ *14 av. Général-Leclerc* ☏ *04–94–97–09–39*) rents mountain bikes at €15 for a full 24 hours and you can reserve in advance at ⊕ *www.rolling-bikes. com.* There are also minibuses linking St-Tropez's central Place des Lices and the beaches at Salins and Pampelonne, as well as a bus from the gare *routière* (bus station).

EN ROUTE   From Ramatuelle, the lovely ride through vineyards and woods full of twisted cork oaks to the hilltop village of Gassin takes you over the highest point of the peninsula (1,070 feet).

WHERE TO EAT & STAY

$$$$ **Les Moulins de Ramatuelle.** A satellite of planet St-Tropez, this outpost of showbiz chef Christophe Leroy lures off-duty celebrities and the swank to its lovely perch 5 minutes from Pampelonne beach. Rat-

tan chairs and blond-wood accents heighten the pleasure of the scrumptious dishes served here—don't miss out on the vichyssoise with truffles. Upstairs are five cozy, rustic guest rooms. **Pros:** perfect romantic getaway. **Cons:** narrow stairwell; noise from rooms and staff. ⊠ *Rte. des Plages,* ☎ *04–94–97–17–22* ⊕ *www.christophe-leroy.com* ➪ *5 rooms* ⟁ *In-room: refrigerator, Wi-Fi. In-hotel: restaurant, parking, some pets allowed* ☐ *AE, MC, V* ⊘ *Closed Oct. 10–Apr. 27.*

$$$$ ⚏ **Villa Marie.** It's not quite your own private paradise, but it might feel ★ like it as you are whisked off in a golf cart up the hill, having left your car at the bottom. Jocelyne and Jean-Louis Sibuet, best known for their luxury ski retreats in Megève (notably Les Fermes de Marie), infuse each of their hotels with inimitable French style. Here, they play up the location facing the Bay of Pampelonne with pastel colors, four-poster beds, embroidered curtains, baroque bathtubs, and a stunning estate garden. Each of the rooms is individually decorated, and the bar and restaurant focus on fish with seashell motifs and a simple, fresh southern French cuisine accompanied by Luberon wines from their vineyard Domaine de Marie. To complete the experience, treat yourself to an outdoor spa treatment using the products developed for Les Fermes de Marie. **Pros:** everything is as exactly what you expect from looking at the Web site. **Cons:** not always the friendliest of service; few bathroom amenities. ⊠ *Rte. des Plages, Chemin Val de Rian,* ☎ *04–94–97–40–22* ⊕ *www.villamarie.fr* ➪ *42 rooms* ⟁ *In-room: refrigerator, Wi-Fi. In-hotel: restaurant, pool, spa, Wi-Fi, parking, some pets allowed* ☐ *AE, DC, MC, V* ⊘ *Closed mid-Oct.–Apr.*

$$ ⚏ **Ferme Ladouceur.** Not far from the talcum-powder beach of Pampelonne and surrounded by vineyards is this naïf farmhouse, domain of Constance Ladouceur, whose paintings adorn the recently renovated hallways and whose restaurant is a draw for budget-minded locals. Quirky, simple, affordable, with breakfast included in the price—little wonder you need to book here far in advance. **Pros:** fixed menus include wine; country-home feel. **Cons:** little last-minute availability. ⊠ *Quartier la Rouillère,* ☎ *04–94–79–24–95* ⊕ *www.fermeladouceur. com* ➪ *7 rooms* ⟁ *In-room: no a/c, no phone, no TV, Wi-Fi. In-hotel: restaurant, parking, some pets allowed* ☐ *AE, MC, V* ⊘ *Closed Nov.– Mar., open 2 wks at Christmas* ⏀ *BP.*

GASSIN

7 km (4 mi) northwest of Ramatuelle.

Though not as picturesque as Ramatuelle, this hilltop village gives you spectacular views over the surrounding vineyards and St-Tropez's bay. In winter, before the summer haze drifts in and after the mistral has given the sky a good scrub, you may be able to make out a brilliant-white chain of Alps looming on the horizon. There's less commerce here to distract you; for shops, head to Ramatuelle.

EN ROUTE The dramatic forest scenery of D558 winding west and northwest of St-Tropez merits a drive even if you're not heading up to A8. This is the **Massif des Maures**, named for the Moors who retreated here from the Battle of Poitiers in 732 and profited from its strong position over the sea. The forest is dark with thick cork oaks, their ancient trunks girdled for cork only every 10 years or so, leaving exposed a broad band of sienna brown. Looming even darker and thicker above are the chestnut trees cultivated for their thick, sweet nuts, which you are not allowed to gather from the forest floor, as signs from the growers' cooperative warn. Between wine domaines' vineyards, mushroom-shaped parasol pines, unique to the Mediterranean, crowd the highway.

WHERE TO EAT & STAY

$$$$ **Villa Belrose.** Perched on the highest point of the peninsula, this Hollywoodesque palace has unrivaled views of the Gulf of St-Tropez and the kind of decadently rich élan that would make Scott and Zelda feel right at home. Public salons have Louis XVI and Florentine accents, while guest rooms are spacious yet cozy, with Italian marble bathrooms and romantic balconies. Besides the 180-degree views, the Michelin star restaurant, run by Alain Ducasse disciple Thierry Thiercelin, supplies first-rate Mediterranean cuisine, pleasant service, and a top-drawer wine list. Rates including half-board are available. **Pros:** very clean; complimentary bottle of water nightly. **Cons:** some rooms are small; Trump-y decor touches. ⊠ Bd. des Crètes, ☎ 04–94–55–97–97 ⊕ www.villabelrose.com ⇆ 38 rooms, 2 suites, 2 apartments ⧄ In-room: refrigerator, Wi-Fi. In-hotel: restaurant, bar, pool, spa, parking, some pets allowed ☰ AE, DC, MC, V ⊗ Closed Nov.–early Mar.

GRIMAUD

10 km (6 mi) west of St-Tropez.

Once a formidable Grimaldi fiefdom and home to a massive Romanesque château, the hill-village of Grimaud is merely charming today, though the romantic castle ruins that crown its steep streets still command lordly views over the forests and the coast. The labyrinth of cobbled streets is punctuated by pretty fountains, carved doorways, and artisans' gallery-boutiques. Wander along the Gothic arcades of the Rue des Templiers to see the beautifully proportioned Romanesque **Église St-Michel**, built in the 11th century.

WHERE TO EAT

$$$ ✕ **La Ferme du Magnan.** Just 10 km (6 mi) west of St-Tropez and 4 km (2½ mi) south of Grimaud and the village of Cogolin, this bucolic old farmhouse looms on a hillside over forests dense with cork oak and chestnuts. Whether you eat on the terrace or in the rustic dining room, the food tastes and smells of the surrounding country: snails with sharp, garlicky aïoli, mussels grilled on grape leaves, duck sim-

mered with olives, and guinea fowl stewed in Bandol. ⊠*Rte. de la Mole, RN 98, Cogolin* ☎*04–94–49–57–54* ⊟*AE, MC, V* ⊘*Closed mid-Oct.–mid-May.*

PORT-GRIMAUD

5 km (3 mi) east of Grimaud, 7 km (4½ mi) west of St-Tropez.

Although much of the coast has been targeted with new construction of extraordinary ugliness, this modern architect's version of a Provençal fishing village works. A true operetta set and only begun in 1966, it has grown gracefully over the years, and offers hope for the pink concrete-scarred coastal landscape. It's worth parking and wandering up the village's Venice-like canals to admire its Old Mediterranean canal-tile roofs and pastel facades, already patinated with age. Even the church, though resolutely modern, feels Romanesque. There is, however, one modern touch some might appreciate: small electric tour boats (get them at Place du Marché) that carry you for a small charge from bar to shop to restaurant throughout the complex of pretty squares and bridges.

WHERE TO EAT

$$$$ ✕**La Table du Mareyeur.** For Ewan and Caroline Scutcher, the honey-
Fodor'sChoice moon's definitely not over. The couple hasn't left Port Grimaud since
★ they married here 20 years ago and set up this waterside gem, now reputed as one of the Riviera's finest. In a fun and relaxed atmosphere, they make no apologies for finding the freshest fish and seafood on the Coast and certainly the politicians, royalty, and film stars (think Leonardo diCaprio) who dine portside here amongst the locals don't complain. Selection is simple, uncomplicated, and the €25 lunch menu, wine and coffee included, is a deal. Avoid traffic and ask Le Table to arrange for a water taxi upon reservation. ⊠*10/11 place des Artisans,* ☎*04–94–56–06–77* ⊕*www.mareyeur.com* ⊟*AE, D, MC, V* ⊘*Closed Nov.–late Dec.*

STE-MAXIME

8 km (5 mi) northeast of Port-Grimaud, 33 km (20 mi) northeast of St-Tropez.

You may be put off by its heavily built-up waterfront, bristling with parking garage–style apartments and hotels, and its position directly on the waterfront highway, but Ste-Maxime is an affordable family resort with fine, easily accessible, sandy beaches. It even has a sliver of car-free Old Town and a stand of majestic plane trees sheltering the central Place Victor-Hugo. Its main beach, north of town, is the wide and sandy **La Nartelle.**

WHERE TO EAT

$$ ✕**La Maison Bleue.** Cheerful blue-and-white-checked tablecloths, massive colorful throw-cushions, and a polished wood facade give this "blue house" on the main pedestrian street a welcoming air that matches the straightforward fresh pasta (tagliatelle pistou, ravioli, or gnocchi)

and simple grilled fish dishes, accompanied by well-chosen local wines. *✉48 rue Paul Bert ☎04–94–96–51–92 ▭AE, D, MC, V ⊗Closed Nov.–Dec.; Mon. and Tues. Jan.–Mar.; Tues. in Apr., May, and Oct.*

EN ROUTE

As you cling to the coastline on dramatic N98 between Ste-Maxime and Fréjus, you'll see a peculiar mix: pretty beaches and fjordlike *calanques* (rocky coves) dipping in and out of view between luxury villas (and their burglar-wired hedges), trailer-park campsites, and the fast-food stands and beach discos that define much of the Riviera. The **Calanque des Louvans** and the **Calanque du Four à Chaux** are especially scenic, with sand beaches and rocks shaded by windblown pines; watch for signs.

FRÉJUS, ST-RAPHAËL & THE ESTÉREL RESORTS

5

Though the twin resorts of Fréjus and St-Raphaël have become somewhat overwhelmed by waterfront resort culture, Fréjus still harbors a small but charming enclave that evokes both the Roman and medieval periods. As you then follow the coast east, a massive red-rock wasteland, known as the Massif de l'Estérel, rears up high above the sparkling water. Formed of red volcanic rocks (porphyry) carved by the sea into dreamlike shapes, the harsh landscape is softened by patches of lavender, mimosa, scrub pine, and gorse. At the rocks' base churn azure waters, seething in and out of castaway coves, where a series of gentle resort bays punctuates the coastline. N98 leads to one of the coast's most spectacular drives, the Corniche de l'Estérel. And if you take N7, the mountain route to the north, you can lose yourself in the Estérel's desert landscape, far from the sea. The resorts that cluster at the foot of the Estérel are densely populated pleasure ports, with an agreeable combination of cool sea breezes and escapes into the near-desert behind.

FRÉJUS

19 km (12 mi) northeast of Ste-Maxime, 37 km (23 mi) northeast of St-Tropez.

GETTING HERE

The direct bus from the Nice-Côte d'Azur airport (Terminals 1 & 2) to Fréjus takes just over an hour and costs €21.

Arriving by train, you'll have to stop at St-Raphaël and take one of the five daily buses (€1.10 to €1.50) that heads to Fréjus. A taxi for the same distance runs around €15. There's also a 45-minute bus to St-Tropez (€10), which also runs daily. Fréjus's bus station is on Place Paul-Vernet and Estérel buses have routes to St-Tropez. By car, you are only 35 minutes from the airport on the A8 highway (take the No. 38 exit FRÉJUS/ST-RAPHAËL). You can take the N7 or N38 for a more scenic drive but it takes a lot more time, particularly with summer traffic.

VISITOR INFORMATION
Fréjus Tourist Office (✉ *249 rue Jean-Jaurès, Fréjus* ☎ *04-94-51-83-83* ⊕ *www.frejus.fr*).

EXPLORING

Confronted with the gargantuan pink holiday high-rises that crowd the Fréjus–St-Raphaël waterfront, you may be tempted to forge onward. But after a stroll on the sandy curve in tacky, overcommercialized Fréjus-Plage (Fréjus Beach), turn your back on modern times and head uphill to Fréjus-Centre. Here you'll enter a maze of narrow streets lined with butcher shops, patisseries, and neighborhood stores barely touched by the cult of the lavender sachet. The farmers' market at the foot of the cathedral (Monday, Wednesday, and Saturday mornings) is as real and lively as any in Provence, and the cafés encircling the fountains and squares nourish an easygoing social scene.

Fréjus (pronounced fray-*zhooss*) also has the honor of having some of the most important historic monuments on the coast. Founded in 49 BC by Julius Caesar himself and named Forum Julii, this quiet town was once a thriving Roman shipbuilding port of 40,000 citizens. In its heyday, Roman Fréjus had a theater, baths, and an enormous aqueduct that brought water all the way from Mons in the mountains, 45 km (28 mi) north of town. Today you can see the remains: a series of detached arches that follow the main Avenue du Quinzième Corps (leading up to the Old Town).

Just up northbound D37 from the Old Town is the Roman **theater**; its remaining rows of arches are mostly intact and much of its stage works are still visible at its center. The town's more impressive remains, however, are the **Arènes** (often called the *Amphithéâtre*), still used today for concerts and bullfights. To reach the Arènes, follow Avenue du Verdun west of the Old Town toward Puget.

NEED A BREAK?

To drink in the atmosphere of Old Fréjus, settle under the shade of the great plane trees and listen to the sound of the fern-heavy fountain at the **Bar du Marché** (✉ *5 pl. Liberté* ☎ *04-94-51-29-09*). Here a *croque monsieur* (grilled ham and cheese toast), sundae, or apéritif will buy you time to watch the neighborhood putter through its daily rituals.

Set 6 km (2½ mi) north of Fréjus on the RN7 is the eccentric **La Chapelle Notre Dame de Jérusalem.** Designed by Jean Cocteau as part of an artists' colony that never happened, it is unusual not only for its octagonal shape, stained glass, and frescos depicting the mythology of the first Crusades, but also because the tongue-in-cheek painting of the apostles above the front door boasts the famous faces of Coco Chanel, Jean Marais, and poet Max Jacob. ✉ *Av. Nicolaï, la Tour de la Mare* ☎ *04-94-53-27-06* 💶 *€2* ⊙ *Nov.–Mar., Tues.–Sun. 9:30–12:30 and 2–6; Apr.–Oct., Tues.–Sun. 9:30-12:30 and 2–5.*

★ Fréjus is graced with one of the most impressive religious monuments in Provence: the **Groupe Épiscopal,** an enclosed ensemble of cathedral, cloisters, and baptistery. The early Gothic **cathedral** consists of two parallel naves, the narrower one from the 12th century (with barrel vaults) and the broader from the 13th century, with groin vaults supported by heavy pillars. The ensemble is spare and somber, with modern windows. Through the heavy arches of the 15th-century narthex you reach the entrance to the **baptistery,** which dates from the 5th century. This extraordinary structure retains the style of arches and columns that shows just how Roman these early Christians were. The bishop himself baptized them, washing their feet in the small pool to the side, then immersing them in the deep font at the room's center. Outside the baptistery, stairs lead up to the early Gothic **cloister,** redolent of boxwood and framing a stone well. There are two stories of pillared arcades, the lower ones pointed, the upper ones round (an odd effect, yet all were executed during one architectural period). The capitals on the lower pillars are graceful and abstract; the grotesques and caricatures you'd expect appear instead in the unusual and striking wooden roof covering the lower gallery, painted in the 15th century in sepia and earth tones with a phantasmagorical assortment of animals and biblical characters. Off the entrance and gift shop, you can peruse a small museum of archaeological findings from Roman Fréjus, including a complete mosaic and a sculpture of a two-headed Hermes. ⊠ *58 rue de Fleury* ☎*04–94–51–26–30* ✉*Cathedral free; cloister, museum, and baptistery €5* ☉*Cathedral daily 8:30–noon and 2:30–6:30. Cloister, museum, and baptistery Apr.–Sept., daily 9–6:30; Oct.–Mar., Tues.– Sun. 9–noon and 2–5.*

SPORTS & THE OUTDOORS

Diving off the calanques between Fréjus and Ste-Maxime gives you interesting underwater insight into the marine life lurking in the rocks. Contact the **Centre International de Plongée** (*International Diving Center* ⊠*Port Fréjus* ☎*04–94–52–34–99* ⊕*www.cip-frejus.com*) for instruction, equipment rental, and guided outings.

The urban **beaches** draped at the foot of Fréjus are backed by a commercial sprawl of brasseries, beach-gear shops, and realtors (for sun-struck visitors who dream of buying a flat on the waterfront). The beaches outside the city, however, are public and wide open, with deep sandy stretches toward St-Aygulf. The calanques just south are particularly wild and pretty, with only tiny sand surfaces.

ST-RAPHAËL

3 km (2 mi) east of Fréjus, 30 km (19 mi) southwest of Cannes.

GETTING HERE

To take the Nice airport bus from either terminal, it's €21.20 for the 75-minute journey. If you take a taxi, it'll be around €100. The TGV Paris–St-Raphaël (4 hrs 45 mins) runs throughout the year and there are numerous trains arriving from Nice and Cannes. St-Raphaël is the western terminus of the TER line that runs along the Riviera. To get to towns farther west, you have to take a bus from just behind the train station. If you want a day trip to St-Tropez, from April through October, there's a 1-hour ferry ride (€13 one-way or €22 return) or a taxi for at least €100. St-Raphaël's bus station is on Avenue Victor-Hugo next to the train station and has buses linking up with St-Tropez (via Grimaud and Ste-Maxime, €10.30, 2 hrs), some towns in the Haut Var, and selected stops along the coastal Corniche de l'Estérel, which is also covered by Rafaël Bus. There are about five daily buses to Fréjus (€1.10 to €1.50), or take a taxi for about €15. Popular ferries leave from St-Raphaël's Vieux Port from St-Tropez, the Iles-de-Léerins, and the Calanques de l'Estérel.

VISITOR INFORMATION

St-Raphaël Tourist Office (⊠ *Quai Albert 1er, BP 210, St-Raphaël Cedex* ☎ *04–94–19–52–52* ⊕ *www.saint-raphael.com*).

EXPLORING

Right next door to Fréjus, with almost no division between, spreads St-Raphaël, a sprawling resort city with a busy downtown anchored by a casino. It's also a major sailing center, has five golf courses nearby, and draws the weary and indulgent to its seawater-based thalassotherapy. Along with Fréjus, it serves as a rail crossroads, the two being the closest stops to St-Tropez. The port has a rich history: Napoléon landed at St-Raphaël on his triumphant return from Egypt in 1799; it was also from here in 1814 that he cast off in disgrace for Elba. And it was here, too, that the Allied forces landed in their August 1944 offensive against the Germans.

Augmenting the Atlantic City vibe of this modern pleasure port is the gingerbread-and-gilt dome of the neo-Byzantine **Église Notre-Dame-de-la-Victoire** (⊠ *Bd. Félix-Martin*), which watches over the yachts and cruise boats sliding into the port.

If you wish to gamble, head to **Casino Barrière** (⊠ *Square de Grand* ☎ *04–98–11–17–77*), open daily 10 AM–4 AM, 5 AM on Saturday, which looks out over the waterfront, catering to the city's many conventioneers.

The reward is worth the bother of penetrating dense city traffic and cutting inland past the train station and into the Vieille Ville (Old Town), a tiny enclave of charm crowned by the 12th-century **Église St-Pierre-des-Templiers** (⊠ *Rue des Templiers*), a miniature-scale Romanesque church.

On the same quiet square as St-Pierre, shaded by an old olive tree, the intimate little **Musée Archéologique Marin** *(Marine Archaeology Museum)* offers a quirky diversion. Its few rooms contain a concise and fascinating collection of ancient amphorae gleaned from the shoals offshore, where centuries' worth of shipwrecks have accumulated; by studying this chronological progression of jars and the accompanying sketches, you can visualize the coast as it was in its heyday as a Greek and Roman shipping center. The science of exploring these shipwrecks was relatively new when French divers began probing the depths; the underwater Leicas from the 1930s and the early scuba gear from the '50s on display are as fascinating as the spoils they helped to unearth. Upstairs, a few objects—jewelry, spearheads, pottery shards, and skulls—illustrate the Neolithic and Paleolithic eras and remind you of the dense population of Celto-Ligurians who claimed this region long before the

Greeks and Phoenicians. A few of their dolmens and menhirs are still visible on the Estérel. ⊠*Rue des Templiers* ☎*04–94–19–25–75* ⌑*Free* ⊙*Tues.–Sat. 9–noon and 2–6 (also open Thurs. until 9 in July and Aug.).*

WHERE TO EAT & STAY

$$$–$$$$ ✕**Restaurant L'Arbousier.** Chef Philippe Troncy has created an FodorsChoice authentic varois restaurant with ★ a reputation as the best in and around town, complete with a wine list of more than 200 choices to accompany your gastronomic journey. Whether you are seated under the magnolias on the summer terrace or in the more intimate, newly decorated interior, this affordable fine dining will dazzle your palate: poached cod and lobster, zucchini flower with goat cheese and artichoke oil, special pork ragout, cheeses from Robert Bedot. À la carte and changing menus with the freshest of local ingredients include Le Repas du Marché (€30; lunch only) or San Rafeu (€44) or go for Le Repas du Rocher (€59; €79 with 4 glasses of wine). ⊠ *6 ave. de Valescure (intersection with rue Marius Allongue)* ☎*04–94–95–25–00* ⊕ *www.arbousier.net* ⌑*Reservations essential* ⊟*AE, MC, V* ⊙*Closed Mon. and Tues. Nov.–Mar.; two weeks in late Dec.*

$$$ ⌂**Excelsior.** This urban hotel has been under the careful management of one family for three generations. Its combination of straightforward comforts and a waterfront position in the center of town attracts a regular clientele. Guest rooms have nearly all been renovated and pastels replaced by more trendy earth tones and reds; be sure to request a room with a view of the sea. The café and restaurant attract nonguests for dependable fare and sea views. **Pros:** minutes from the sea, train, and bus station; buffet breakfast included. **Cons:** smallish rooms; €8 a day for public parking. ⊠*Next to Le Grand Casino on the Promenade Coty,* ☎*04–94–95–02–42* ⊕*www.excelsior-hotel.com* ⌑*36 rooms* ⌑*In-room: refrigerator. In-hotel: restaurant, bar, Wi-Fi, some pets allowed* ⊟*AE, DC, MC, V* ⌑*BP.*

$ ⌂**Le Thimothée.** Philippe and Jean-Claude, the charming owners of this ★ bargain lodging, have thrown themselves wholeheartedly into improving what was an already attractive 19th-century villa, including recent bathroom renovations. They're incredibly helpful, too: they will rent you a bike, book an excursion, and give you seconds on coffee at the traditional French breakfast (fee) usually served in the garden, where grand palms and pines shade the walkway to a pretty little swimming pool. Be sure to request one of the top-floor rooms with a balcony and spectacular view of the sea. **Pros:** boulangerie and mini-mart within a few minutes walk; secluded spot. **Cons:** some may find town too far to walk. ⊠*375 bd. Christian-Lafon83700* ☎*04–94–40–49–49* ⊕*www. thimothee.com* ⌑*12 rooms* ⌑*In-room: Wi-Fi. In-hotel: pool, parking (free)* ⊟*AE, D, MC, V.*

SPORTS & THE OUTDOORS

St-Raphaël's **beaches** form a snaking sliver of sand, starting just east of the port and finally petering out against the red cliffs of the Estérel. From that point on, you'll find tiny calanques and *criques* (coves and finger bays) for swimming and basking on the rocks.

The spectacularly sited 9-hole **Golf de Cap Estérel** (⊠ *RN 98, Saint-Agay* ☎ *04–94–82–55–00*) hovers directly over the sea behind Agay.

St-Raphaël is a serious **sailing and boating** center, with nautical complexes at four different sites along the coast: the Vieux Port, Santa Lucia (by Fréjus-Plage), Le Dramont (at the base of a dramatic little cape below the Estérel), and within Agay's quiet harbor. For information on boat rentals, training sessions, and diving lessons, contact the **Club Nautique St-Raphaël** (☎ *04–94–95–11–66* ⊕ *www.cnsr.fr*).

To explore the wilds of the Estérel on foot, consider a guided **hike** led by a qualified staffer from the tourist office. Mountain biking is now discouraged in the Estérel for environmental reasons.

THE CORNICHE DE L'ESTÉREL

Stay on N98 and you'll find yourself careening along a stunning coastal drive, the Corniche de l'Estérel, which whips past tiny calanques and sheer rock faces that plunge down to the sea. At the dramatic Pointe de Cap Roux, an overlook allows you to pull off the narrow two-lane highway (where high-season sightseers can cause bumper-to-bumper traffic) and contemplate the spectacular view up and down the coast. Train travelers have the good fortune to snake along this cliff side for constant panoramas. It's also a hiker's haven. Some 15 trails strike out from designated parking sites along the way, leading up into the jagged rock peaks for extraordinary sea views. (Don't leave valuables in the car, as the sites are littered with glass from break-ins.) For trail maps, ask at the St-Raphaël tourist office across from the train station. There is also a *sentier du littoral* (waterfront trail), leaving from the St-Raphaël port and following the rocky coast all the way to Agay; you'll see a mix of wild, rocky criques and glamorous villas.

THÉOULE-SUR-MER

21 km (13 mi) northeast of Agay, 2 km (1 mi) south of La Napoule.

Tucked into a tiny bay on the Golfe de Napoule, Théoule seems far removed from the major resorts around it. A sliver of beach, a few shops and villas, and magnificent views toward Cannes make it a pleasant home base for forays along the coast.

WHERE TO EAT

$ ✕ **Nino's.** At the far southeast tip of Théoule's miniature bay, this unpretentious pizzeria serves simple Italian specialties—but, oh, what a setting. A few tables line a wooden "boathouse" porch directly over the lapping water, and at night the whole glittering necklace of Cannes reflects its luxurious glow over the bay. Good wood-oven pizzas and pastas add superfluous pleasure. ⊠6 *chemin Débarcadère* ☎*04–92–97–61–11* ▭*MC, V* ⊘*Closed Oct.–Mar.*

MANDELIEU–LA NAPOULE

32 km (20 mi) northeast of St-Raphaël, 8 km (5 mi) southwest of Cannes.

GETTING HERE
From Terminal 1 or 2 at Nice airport, take the A8 exit No. 40 (about 30 mins) or the 30-minute airport bus (direction St-Raphaël, €11.60). The closest train stops in Cannes and you can either take a taxi (about €30 to the centre ville during the day) or catch the No. 20 bus from Cannes train station, departing every 90 minutes, for €1.

VISITOR INFORMATION
Mandelieu–La Napoule Tourist Office (⊠*340 av. Jean-Monnet, Mandelieu–La Napoule* ☎*04–92–97–99–27* ⊕*www.ot-mandelieu.fr*).

EXPLORING
La Napoule is the small, old-fashioned port village, Mandelieu the big-fish resort town that devoured it. You can visit Mandelieu for a golf-and-sailing retreat—the town is replete with many sporting facilities and hosts a bevy of sporting events, including sailing regattas, windsurfing contests, and golf championships (there are two major golf courses in Mandelieu right in the center of town by the sea). A yacht-crammed harbor sits under the shadow of some high-rise resort hotels. La Napoule, on the other hand, offers the requisite quaintness, ideal for a port-side stroll, casual meal, beach siesta, or visit to its peculiar castle. Unless you're here for the sun and surf, however, these twinned towns mostly serve as a home base for outings to Cannes, Antibes, and the Estérel. In fact, the easternmost beach in Mandelieu dovetails with the first, most democratic beaches of its glamorous neighbor, Cannes.

Fodor'sChoice ★ Set on Pointe des Pendus (Hanged Man's Point), the **Château de la Napoule,** looming over the sea and the port, is a bizarrely wonderful hybrid of Romanesque, Gothic, Moroccan, and Hollywood cooked up by the eccentric American sculptor Henry Clews (1876–1937). Working with his architect-wife, he transformed the 14th-century bastion into something that suited his personal expectations and then filled the place with his own fantastical sculptures. Fond of spouting Nietzsche to his titled dinner guests, surrounding himself with footmen, and dedicating his house to Don Quixote (its name is actually "Mancha"), Henry Clews may have had a dubious artisitic vision but he certainly enjoyed a vibrant sense of fantasy. The couple resides in their tombs in the tower crypt, its windows left slightly ajar to permit their souls to escape and allow them to "return at eventide as sprites and dance upon the windowsill." Today the château's stylish and well-funded foundation hosts visiting writers and artists, many of whom are American, who set to work surrounded by Clews's gargoyle-like sculptures. You may visit the gardens without the guided castle tour. ⊠*Av. Henry Clews* ☎*04–93–49–95–05* ⊕*www.chateau-lanapoule.com* ⊠€6; €3.50

(garden only) ⊗ *Feb. 7–Nov. 7, daily 10–6; guided visits at 11:30, 2:30, 3:30, 4:30; Nov. 8–Feb. 10, weekdays 2–5; guided visits at 2:30 and 3:30; weekends 10–5: guided visits 11:30, 2:30, and 3:30.*

WHERE TO EAT & STAY

$$$$ ✕**L'Oasis.** Long famed as a culinary landmark, this Gothic villa by the sea is now home to Stéphane Raimbault, a master of Provençal cuisine and a great connoisseur of Asian techniques and flavorings (thanks to a nine-year stint in Japan). Peer hungrily through the kitchen's glass walls and watch as they roll out unexpected collisions (not all entirely successful) like lobster chao-mian with teriyaki sauce in the "Oriental" menu. The "Traditional" menu dishes out crusted sea bass and breaded rack of lamb, all with a signature twist. It's expensive but the extras thrown in between courses will keep you purring. And few can quibble with the beauty of the famous garden terrace shadowed by gorgeous palm trees. ⊠*Rue Jean-Honoré-Carle* ☎*04–93–49–95–52* ⊕*www.oasis-raimbault.com* ▤*AE, MC, V* ⊗*Closed Sun. and Mon.; closed mid-Dec.–mid-Jan.*

$$$ ✕**Le Boucanier.** The drab, low-ceilinged dining room is upstaged by
★ wraparound plate-glass views of the marina and château at this waterfront favorite. Locals gather here for mountains of oysters and whole fish, simply grilled and impeccably filleted table-side. The seafood, market-fresh, speaks for itself. No one interferes beyond a drizzle of fruity olive oil, a pinch of rock salt, or a brief flambé in pastis. ⊠*Port La Napoule* ☎*04–93–49–80–51* ⊕*www.boucanier.fr* ▤*MC, V* ⊗*Closed Dec.*

$$$$ ▦**Royal Hôtel Casino.** As much a resort as a hotel, this modern waterfront complex has deluxe comforts on a grand scale, with a broad beach-terrace, outdoor pool, and vast conference facilities. Newly renovated guest rooms in light, softer hues have balconies and sea views from all sides and lounge chairs on the hotel's private sand beach will beckon you. At the loungy yet glamorous restaurant-grill you can dine decently while you gaze out over the floodlit swimming pool. **Pros:** 5 km (3 mi) to Cannes; lots of restaurants nearby. **Cons:** €5 for a can of soda; not close to any shops. ⊠*605 av. Général-de-Gaulle,* ☎*04–92–97–70–00* ⊕*www.accor.com* ⇆*213 rooms* ⊖*In-room: refrigerator, Wi-Fi. In-hotel: 2 restaurants, bar, tennis courts, pool, gym, some pets allowed* ▤*AE, DC, MC, V.*

¢ ▦**Villa Parisiana.** In the residential neighborhood of La Napoule, about 500 feet from the waterfront, this impeccably kept (nonsmoking) hotel offers simple comforts, chenille bedspreads, and a few updated bathrooms. The villa's big balcony-terrace overlooks a jungle of a garden but six of the rooms come with private terrace for only a few extra euros. **Pros:** great value, just a few hundred feet from Mandelieu–La Napoule train station. **Cons:** could be sticky in the summer months. ⊠*Rue de l'Argentière,* ☎*04–93–49–93–02* ⊕*www.villaparisiana.com* ⇆*13 rooms* ⊖*In-room: no a/c, Wi-Fi. In-hotel: some pets allowed, no-smoking rooms* ▤*AE, MC, V* ⊗ *Closed end Nov.–end Dec.*

SPORTS & THE OUTDOORS

★ The **Golf Club de Cannes-Mandelieu** (⊠*Rte. du Golf* ☎*04–92–97–32–00* ⊕*www.golfoldcourse.com*) is one of the most beautiful in the south of France, and is famous for its 100-year-old parasol pines that shade the greens. Posh and eccentric, it has a grand clubhouse in half-timber Normandy style and ferries golfers over the River Siagne—between holes. There are two courses—one 18 holes (par 71) and one 9 holes (par 33).

Classified as a *station voile* (sailing resort), Mandelieu–La Napoule is a major water-sports center. To rent a boat or charter a fully equipped yacht for one day or more, contact **Cayman Yachting** (☎*04–93–93–27–67*).

For windsurfing and small sailboats, contact **Centre Nautique** (☎*04–92–97–07–70*). Lessons and supplies for scuba diving are available from **Armand Ferrand Centre de Plongée** (⊠*Port de la Rague* ☎*04–93–49–74–33* ⊕*www.plongee-ferrand.com*).

There are two private beaches nestled in between the public beaches, the major difference between public and private being, as it always is, a question of comfort. You can spend the extra euros for a comfortable mattress, an access to shade, and the convenience of a nearby restaurant. On the public beach you have to supply your own comforts. If you have children with you and are on the public beach, keep your eye out for special clubs usually referred to as "Mickey Clubs," set up for young children with games, wading pools, and activities supervised by professionals. **La Voile d'Azur** (☎*04–93–49–20–44*) rents mattresses for €16, and has beach bar service and a restaurant that serves sandwiches and salads. **Le Sweet** (☎*04–93–49–87–33*) rents mattresses for €17, and has beach bar service and a restaurant that specializes in the catch of the day.

THE HAUT VAR & INTO HAUTE PROVENCE

The hills that back the Côte d'Azur are often called the *arrière-pays,* or backcountry, a catch-all term that applies to the hills and plateaus behind Nice as well. Yet this particular wedge of backcountry—north and west of Fréjus—has a character all its own. If the territory behind Nice has a strong Latin flavor, influenced for centuries by the Grimaldi dynasty and steeped in Italian culture, these westerly hills are deeply, unself-consciously Provençal: wild lavender and thyme sprout on dry, rocky hillsides; the earth under scrub oaks is snuffled by rooting boars; and hilltop villages are so isolated and quiet you can hear pebbles drop in their mossy fountains.

The rocky swells behind Cannes and Fréjus are known as the Haut Var, the highlands of the département called Var. The untamed, beautiful, and sometimes harsh landscape beyond these hills lies over the threshold of Haute Provence—itself loosely defined, more a climate and terrain than a region. The author Jean Giono, born in Manosque, evokes its landscape as windswept and often brutal, directly vulnerable to the mistral and the winds whistling down from the Alps. Its environs include southern bits of the département of Drôme and much of the Alpes-de-Haute-Provence.

It's possible to get a small taste of this backcountry on a day trip out of Fréjus or Cannes. On your way north you may choose to trace the steps of Napoléon himself, who followed what is now N85, today named for him, on his tentative comeback from Elba Island in 1815. But if you give yourself time to wind through the back roads, stop for the views, and linger in shady perched-village squares, you may be tempted to cancel your waterfront plans and settle in for an otherworldly experience.

FAYENCE

35.9 km (23 mi) north of Mandelieu–La Napoule, 27 km (17 mi) west of Grasse, 30 km (19 mi) northwest of Cannes.

GETTING HERE
There are no trains but three daily buses each from Cannes (1hr 35 mins; €3.50) and Grasse (1hr 10 min; €5.50). An hour's drive from Nice airport, take the No. 39 exit (FAYENCE/LES ADRETS) from the A8. Taxi to/from the airport will cost €95 (or €130 at night).

VISITOR INFORMATION
Fayence Tourist Office (⊠ *Pl. Léon-Roux, Fayence* ☎ *04–94–76–20–08* ⊕ *www. paysdefayence.com*).

EXPLORING
The most touristy of all the hill towns in the Haut Var backcountry, Fayence is easiest to reach from the coast and often filled with busloads of day-trippers. Nonetheless, it has a pretty Old Town at the top, magnificent wraparound views from its 18th-century church down to the Massif des Maures and the Estérel, and a plethora of artisans' galleries and boutiques. If the development—villa-fication, if you will, or perhaps California-fication—that spreads wider each year along its slopes seems off-putting compared to serene Seillans or Bargemon, locals point out that it's a living town, with year-round residents and an active community life that extends well beyond tourism.

WHERE TO EAT & STAY

$$ ✕ **Le Temps des Cerises.** Whether under the trellis at the gaily decked café tables or in the elegant, intimate beamed dining room, you'll find your *bonheur* (happiness) in this stylish, central restaurant. Owner/chef Louis Schroder maximizes on blending fresh Mediterranean produce with his Dutch origins. Sea bream and sweet and sour fennel, veal kidney in mustard sauce, and roasted duckling with sauerkraut and dates are served withsurprising chic for the middle of a tourist town. Too bad about the trucks and motorcycles roaring past. ⊠ *Pl. de la République* ☎ *04–94–76–01–19* ⊕ *www.descerises.com* ▤ *AE, MC, V* ⊗ *Closed Tues. and Dec.*

BEATING THE EURO

Check ahead to see where gas prices are cheapest en route at ⊕ *www.prix-carburants.gouv. fr.* This could save you some euros for that afternoon's village shopping.

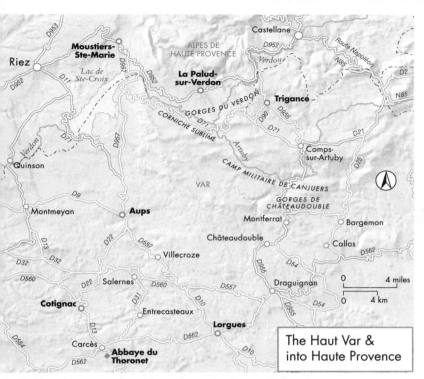

Riez

Moustiers-Ste-Marie

Lac de Ste-Croix

D11

D957

D952

D962

ALPES DE HAUTE PROVENCE

Castellane

D952

Verdon

La Palud-sur-Verdon

Route Napoléon

N85

D2

N85

D21

GORGES DU VERDON

D71

Trigancé

D90

D955

D71

CORNICHE SUBLIME

Artuby

D57

Verdon

D71

CAMP MILITAIRE DE CANJUERS

Comps-sur-Artuby

D25

Quinson

VAR

GORGES DE CHÂTEAUDOUBLE

D9

Montmeyan

Aups

Montferrat

Bargemon

D13

D22

D557

Châteaudouble

Callas

D562

D32

D22

D32

D560

D557

D54

D995

Villecroze

D560

D22

Salernes

Cotignac

D31

D10

Entrecasteaux

D13

D562

Lorgues

D995

Draguignan

D54

0   4 miles

0   4 km

Carcès

Abbaye du Thoronet

D562

D10

D564

The Haut Var & into Haute Provence

$$$$
Fodor'sChoice
★

Four Seasons Resort Provence at Terre Blanche. Keeping in mind this newish resort is larger than the Principality of Monaco, it's easy to see how it can be loaded with all the goodies: a 600-square-meter outdoor infinity pool, indoor ozone pool, 3,200-square-meter spa and fitness center, two golf courses, a kids' club plus four dining possibilities—including the Michelin-star Faventia—under chef Philippe Jourdin. You don't even have to walk: golf carts transport you to and from your villa or suite, elegantly contemporary in design and each with a separate living room and private terrace. This is the perfect spot for a spa-liday: to take day trips around the region and return for an end of day pampering at La Spa, the Cadillac of well-being, opened in 2007. And there's plenty of hiking and canyoning around, and this Four Seasons xanadu is only a half-hour drive from Cannes. Then again, strolling by the estate's fetching teakwood pavilions and stone dining loggias may be enough. Special rates can be found online. **Pros:** free tea/coffee in suites; orthopedic or hypo-allergenic pillows on request. **Cons:** need car to get here (and parking is €18/night); some services are expensive. ⊠*Domaine de Terre Blanche, Tourrettes (6 mi [10 km] east of Fayence)* ☎*04–94–93–90–00* ⊕*www.fourseasons.com/provence* ✑*114 suites* ♿*In-room: refrigerator, Internet. In-hotel: 3 restaurants, bar, tennis court, pools, gym, spa, Wi-Fi, some pets allowed* ☐*AE, D, MC, V* ⍟*BP.*

$$$
★

☷**Moulin de la Camandoule.** On 10 acres of stream-side greenery, this noble old olive mill has been turned into a lovely country inn, complete with beams, the original millwheel, and a *pressoir* (olive press) in the middle of the bar. Rooms are fresh and charming with quarry tiles, Persian rugs, and tiled baths. The restaurant serves elegant regional cooking changing menus monthly—crispy tart of red mullet, cod steak with spicy chorizo topping, or sea bass cooked to the bone. The relaxed, warm welcome of the Franco-British owners, whose faithful old dogs churn around their ankles, makes this feel like a weekend in a private country home. **Pros:** gorgeous viney grounds; minutes from village. **Cons:** no minibars in room; hard to find rates online. ⊠ *Rte. de Notre-Dame-des-Cyprés* ☏ *04–94–76–00–84* ⊕ *www.moulindela camandoule.com* ⇆ *9 rooms, 1 apartment* ⏃ *In-hotel: restaurant, bar, pool, Wi-Fi, parking, some pets allowed* ⊟ *AE, DC, MC, V.*

MONS

15 km (9 mi) north of Fayence, 46 km (28½ mi) west of Grasse, 44 km (27 mi) northwest of Cannes.

Prettier than Fayence but just that much harder to reach, this serene hilltop village stands neatly framed on the flat top of a high plateau. The breadth of its magnificent views contrasts vividly with its tidy, self-contained houses, turned inward on a warp and woof of tiny streets, dipping under arches and through arcades, and tucked into courts and up cobbled steps. It's easy to see how the plague overtook this intimate enclave more than once; and it's just as easy to see why, today, Mons (pronounced *mohnss*) is a popular summer-home retreat, not gentrified but quietly colonized. There are almost no shops and only one restaurant, but be sure to stop into the church to see its fabulous Baroque altarpieces, entirely covered in gold leaf.

SEILLANS

Fodor'sChoice
★

7 km (4½ mi) northwest of Fayence, 36 km (22 mi) northwest of Cannes.

Voted one of "France's most beautiful villages" with its ruined château and ramparts, fountains, flowers, and sunny maze of steeply raked cobblestone streets that suddenly break open over valley views, this is a charming old town that still smacks of yesteryear's Côte d'Azur. Its church—a Renaissance remake of an 11th-century structure—is the best spot from which to admire the panorama; it's worth a pause to take in the musty Latin atmosphere. There are old-style, competitive bakers here, and an active café life on a miniature scale. The French opera composer Gounod and the surrealist Max Ernst were regulars in Seillans; Ernst retired here. Year-round guided tours (€2) of the town are Thursdays at 10 and also Tuesday afternoons at 4 during the summer.

Just east of town on the Route de Fayence is the Romanesque chapel **Notre-Dame-de-l'Ormeau,** which contains a remarkable altarpiece dating from the 16th century. Sculpted portraits of the wise men and shepherds adoring the Christ child, strikingly real in emotion and gesture, contrast sharply with the simple ex-votos that pepper the walls. Guided visits (€2) take place through the year Thursdays at 11 and also Tuesdays at 5:15 during July and August. ⊠ *Rte. de Fayence*

WHERE TO EAT & STAY

¢ ✕ **Tilleuil Citron** Stop by this delightful salon du thé for a tarte salée of tomato, goat cheese, and basil or potato, onion, and bacon for only €8 (including salad!). Ditto price for vegetarian lasagna. Try one of their 30 teas with a yummy dessert while you take in the local art on display in this old cork maker's shop. This spot is open for breakfast (€6) and right through 7 at night, with terrace and interior seating available. ⊠ *La Bouchonnerie,* ☎ *04–94–50–47–64* ⚠ *Reservations recommended during summer* ⊟ *No credit cards* ⊘ *Closed Tues. Closed Jan.*

$$ ⊡ **Hôtel des Deux Rocs.** Picture a tiny square with a trickling fountain,
★ venerable plane trees, green valley views, and two massive rocks posing, sculpturelike, where they fell aeons ago. This is a magical place for a hotel. It's almost gilding the lily that the hotel should be small and personal to the point of eccentricity. From the fireplace in the salon to the bright, mixed fabrics in the rooms, to the dainty breakfast, this property exudes Provençal style. All bathrooms have been smartened up with fresh tile and updated fixtures. Ask for Room No. 10, which has corner views of the idyllic place. Chef David Carre whips up some real winners, including pasta gratin with truffles, sardine parcels on a bed of lettuce, and ham cooked in straw—for dessert, indulge in lavender-scented crème brûlée. You can dine in the romantic stone-and-beam restaurant or under the trees by the fountain. **Pros:** fab old stone house with modern decor; great food. **Cons:** little ventilation in rooms; damp in rainy weather. ⊠ *Pl. Font d'Amont* ☎ *04–94–76–87–32* ⊕ *www. hoteldeuxrocs.com* ⊷ *13 rooms* ⚠ *In-room: no a/c, no TV, Internet. In-hotel: restaurant, parking, some pets allowed* ⊟ *MC, V.*

TRIGANCE

32 km (21 mi) northwest of Seillansargemon, 90 km (56 mi) northwest of Cannes.

With a handful of gray-stone houses and a few artists' studios, this infinitesimal hill village between Comps-sur-Artuby and the Gorges du Verdon wouldn't merit more than a glance from the road but for the extraordinary medieval **Château de Trigance.** The castle was restored with a free hand and open purse by Jean-Claude Thomas, who bought it in 1971 and had it rebuilt stone by stone; it functions as a hotel-restaurant today.

WHERE TO EAT & STAY

$$$ ⊡ **Château de Trigance.** Here's a novelty for honeymooners and romantics: to stay in a restored medieval castle perched on a hilltop in the isolated countryside. Guest rooms are decked out in a sort of romantic medieval style, with *baldaquin* (four-poster) canopied beds and severe

oak furniture. For even more of a fairy-tale feeling, reserve the perfectly round tower room. Dine under a 10th-century stone barrel vault guarded by suits of armor and fleurs-de-lis, or on the broad terrace, wrapped by crenellated walls. The restaurant serves seasonal menus with a hefty classic cuisine of pigeon, and Provençal lamb. It's a Relais & Château property but not in its luxury class—after all, it's hard to find good serfs these days. **Pros:** fabulous views; warm service. **Cons:** dark interior; can feel too secluded. ✉ *Off D955,* ☎ *04–94–76–91–18* ⊕ *www.chateau-de-trigance.fr* ⤙ *8 rooms, 2 suites* ⟁ *In-room: no a/c. In-hotel: restaurant, bar, parking, some pets allowed* ▤ *AE, DC, MC, V* ⊘ *Closed Nov. 1–Apr. 1.*

LA PALUD-SUR-VERDON

14 km (9 mi) northwest of Trigance, 27 km (17 mi) southeast of Moustiers.

Though several towns bill themselves as *the* gateway to the Gorges du Verdon, this unassuming village stands in its center, on a plateau just north of the gorge's vertiginous drop (to gain the Gorges's southern flank, enter from the elegant village of Moustiers, *below*). It's a hikers' and climbers' town, and—as the Germans and Dutch are more *sportif* than the French—has an international feel. You'll see more beards and Volkswagen vans here than anywhere in France, and you'll probably share a café terrace with backpackers clad in boots and fleece easing off a load of ropes, picks, and cleats. The friendly grocery store sells flashlights and *camping gaz* (cooking propane), and the central intersection flaunts six public telephones, the better to call a taxi to carry you to your hiking departure point.

★ You are here for one reason only: to explore the extraordinary **Gorges du Verdon**, also known as—with only slight exaggeration over another, more famous version—the Grand Canyon. Through the aeons the jewel-green torrent of the Verdon River has chiseled away the limestone plateau and gouged a spectacular gorge lined with steep white cliffs and sloping rock falls carpeted with green forest. The jagged rock bluffs, roaring water, and dense wild boxwood create a savage world of genuinely awe-inspiring beauty, whether viewed from dozens of cliff-top overlooks or explored from the wilderness below. For an in-depth look ath the Gorges, see the Close-Up box, "The Gorges Challenge" in this chapter.

If you're driving from La Palud, follow the dramatic **Route des Crêtes** circuit (D23), a white-knuckle cliff-hanger not for the faint of heart. When you approach and leave La Palud, you'll do it via D952 between Castellane and Moustiers, with several breathtaking overlooks. The best of these is the **Point Sublime**, at the east end; leave your car by the hotel-restaurant and walk to the edge, holding tight to dogs and children—that's a 2,834-foot drop to the bottom.

If you want to hike, there are several trails that converge in this prime territory. The most spectacular is the branch of the GR4 that follows the bed of the canyon itself, along the **Sentier Martel.** This dramatic trail, beginning at the Chalet de la Maline and ending at the Point Sublime, was created in the 1930s by the Touring-Club de France and named for one of the gorge's first explorers. Easier circuits leave from the Point Sublime on *sentiers de découverte* (trails with commentary) into the gorge known as Couloir Samson.

WHERE TO EAT & STAY

$ ⭐ **Le Perroquet Vert.** In a restored 18th-century house on La Palud's only street, friendly *aventuriers* Michel and Sabine Jordan have created this lovely little sports store-cum-restaurant-cum-B&B complex. Next to their sports-equipment shop they have a cozy little restaurant that serves simple, fresh regional grillades—using local beef or fish brought in from coastal markets—along with special vinegar à la maison to top off fresh salads and even Pavés de Cofu Soya for vegetarian climbers. The couple also have rooms to rent of the simple, rustic variety: a room with a large double bed and a duplex with a double bed and three single beds. There is also a small house available for larger families or groups. Don't expect a TV, but rooms are furnished with a lot of good books and a CD player. To give you an idea of how healthy, natural, and good for you all this is, even the yogurt served for breakfast is homemade. **Pros:** fine bargain prices; breakfast is included. **Cons:** two rooms only; parking in village. ✉ *Rue Grande,* 🕾 *04–92–77–33–39* 🌐 *www.leperroquetvert.com* 📲 *1 room, 1 duplex* 🔧 *In-room: no a/c, refrigerator, no TV. In-hotel: restaurant* 🖃 *AE, MC, V* ☺ *Closed Nov. 1–Apr. 1* 🍴 *BP.*

MOUSTIERS-STE-MARIE

Fodor's Choice ★ *10 km (7 mi) northwest of La Palud-sur-Verdon.*

GETTING HERE

There is a bus from Manosque but it takes 90 minutes and costs €16— the bigger problem is that there is no shuttle up to the village so a car is your best bet. From the Côte d'Azur by car take the A8 highway, exit direction "Draguignan," then "Aups, Les Salles" to Moustiers, found just off D952 (1 hr 30 mins drive from Fréjus).

VISITOR INFORMATION

Moustiers Tourist Office (✉ *Place de l'Église, BP1, Moustiers* 🕾 *04–92–74–67–84* 🌐 *www.moustiers.fr*).

EXPLORING

At the edge of all this epic wilderness, it's a bit of a shock to find this picture-perfect village tucked into a spectacular cleft in vertical cliffs, its bluffs laced with bridges, draped with medieval stone houses, and crowned with church steeples. The Verdon gushes out of the rock at the village's heart, and between the two massive rocks that tower over the ensemble, a star swings suspended from a chain.

To most, the name *Moustiers* means faïence, the fine glazed earthenware that has been produced here since the 17th century, when a

The Gorges Challenge

To see the Gorges du Verdon up close and personal, instead of gawking over its precipices from the safety-railed overlooks, consider tackling the Sentier Martel. But make sure you're in shape before you test your mettle—it's no Sunday-after-lunch promenade. The famous 14 km (9 mi) stretch of the GR4 follows a steep, narrow path flanked on one side by rock wall and the other by nothingness, sometimes passing over loose rubble and sometimes over slick, mossy limestone at a 45-degree rake. And those are the easy parts. One of the trail's many engineered challenges: a series of wrought-iron ladder-stairs (240, count them if you dare) bolted deep into rock cliff and suspended over the chasm below. The grand finale: two womb-dark tunnels through shoe-deep water, one of them 2,198 feet long. Yet, if you're an experienced hiker, you'll be able to take your eyes off your feet and appreciate the magnificence of the setting, one of the grandest canyons in Europe.

Because the Verdon is regulated by two dams, you'll often be confronted with not-so-comforting signs showing a human stick figure running for his life before a tidal wave. This is to warn you to stick to the trail and not to linger on the low, beachlike riverbed when the water is low, as it could rise suddenly at any moment. If you choose to peel off your socks and boots and wade during a much-needed break, keep an escape route in mind. Wandering in to drape yourself over a rock for a quick nap is not recommended, as you may wake to find your retreat cut off by rising, roiling waters. The trail itself stays above the danger line at all times, sometimes so well above it that the risk of

drowning seems preferable to the risk of plunging 500 feet into the void.

The Sentier Martel takes anywhere from six to nine hours to complete. Wear good shoes with firm ankle support and textured soles. Carry plenty of water and a flashlight with good batteries; you won't be able to grope your way through the tunnels without it. Dogs and most children under six won't be able to handle the metal ladders. Follow the red-and-white GR marker, and don't leave the trail. You can arrange a taxi pickup at Point Sublime based on a rough estimate of your own abilities, or leave a car at the final destination and ask a taxi to carry you to your takeoff point. Most people depart from the Chalet de La Maline, striking out on the long descent and then working their way back up gradually to the Couloir du Samson and the Point Sublime.

The spelunker/explorer Edouard Martel (1859–1938) couldn't arrange a taxi, but first penetrated the Gorges in 1896 with a canvas canoe, an assistant, and two local trout fishermen. Despite repeated attempts, he didn't manage to negotiate the full canyon's length until 1905.

It was in the 1930s that the Touring Club blasted fire-escape-style ladders and catwalks along the precarious rock walls, and drilled two tunnels through solid stone. They added occasional rope railings and steps, and buttressed the trail with rock supports. But much of it crosses rubble slides that shift and change with the years, and steady maintenance can't keep natural erosion from changing the limestone profile over time. That's why it remains a challenge worthy of its intrepid namesake.

monk brought in the secret of enamel glazes from Faenza in Umbria. Its brilliant white finish caught the world's fancy, especially when the fashionable grotesques of Jean Berain, decorator to Louis XIV, were imitated and produced in exquisite detail. A colony of ceramists still creates Moustiers faïence today, from large commercial producers to independent artisans. Every two years (falling on even numbers) the village celebrates the Fete de la Cité de la Faïence over three days in late Spring with movies, dancing, walks, faïence demonstrations and, of course, food and apéros.

The small but excellent **Musée de la Faïence** has concise audiovisual explanations of the craft and displays a chronology of fine pieces. It is currently housed in a pretty 18th-century *hôtel particulier* (private mansion) with a lovely *salle de mariage* (wedding hall) lined in painted canvas. Entrance is free on Tuesdays in the summer. ⊠ *Pl. du Tricentenaire* ☎ *04–92–74–61–64* ✆ *€3* ⊘ *July and Aug., daily 10–12:30 and 2–7; Apr. 1–Oct. 31, daily 10–12:30 and 2–6. Closed Tues., Nov. 1–Mar. 31, and Jan.*

With all the faïence around, you may end up keeping your nose to the shop windows, where every form (and every quality) of the Moustiers product is for sale. But the walk through town is pretty, too, though it's little more than a double loop along the rushing stream, over a bridge or two, and a peek into the early Gothic church, with its sliver windows in pre-Raphaelite hues.

Moustiers was founded as a monastery in the 5th century, but it was in the Middle Ages that the **Chapelle Notre-Dame-de-Beauvoir** (first known as d'Entreroches, or "between rocks") became an important pilgrimage site. You can still climb the steep cobbled switchbacks, along with pilgrims, passing modern stations-of-the-cross panels in Moustiers faïence. From the porch of the 12th-century church, remodeled in the 16th century, you can look over the roofs of the village to the green valley, a patchwork of olive groves and red-tiled farmhouse roofs. The forefather of the star that swings in the wind over the village was first hung, it is said, by a crusader grateful for his release from Saracen prison. Remember, what goes up must come down—these worn stone steps yield little traction, so be careful.

★ Despite its civilized airs, Moustiers is another gateway to the Gorges du Verdon, providing the best access to the southern bank and the famous drive along D71 called the **Route de la Corniche Sublime.** (You may also approach from the southeast at Comps-sur-Artuby.) Breathtaking views over withering drop-offs punctuate this vertiginous road that's just wide enough for two cars if you all hold your breath. The best of the vistas is called the **Balcons de la Mescla,** with viewpoints built into the cliff face overlooking the torrential whirlpool where the Verdon and Artuby combine.

WHERE TO EAT & STAY

$$$$
Fodor's Choice
★
🔲 **La Bastide de Moustiers.** Gourmands from around the world flock to this lovely 17th-century *bastide* (country house) transformed by Alain Ducasse into a luxury country retreat surrounded by olive and chestnut

trees, cypress, lavender, and trellises filled with the blooms of creeping rose bushes. Individually decorated rooms with evocative names such as *Sunflower*, *Pumpkin*, and *Buttercup*—some with private terrace, some that lead directly into the park—are fresh and comfortable, an unpretentious mixture of antiques and country prints. Chef Wilfred Hocquet plans his multicourse Michelin-star menus daily according to nature's abundance, keeping in mind the ripeness of the produce in the vegetable garden and which fresh herbs in the herb garden marry best with the fowl just brought in that morning. It's hard to know which to admire more: the view over the hills from the restaurant terrace or the food itself, such as boned and stuffed rabbit, a cocotte (cast-iron pot) of spring vegetables, and roast pigeon with small artichokes, foie gras, and croutons. Cooking classes can be arranged, as can hot-air balloon rides over the region. Book well in advance, for here no season is low season. **Pros:** astronomical bliss; Raspberry room is wheelchair-friendly. **Cons:** not within easy walking distance to village; three rooms permit smoking. ⊠ *Chemin de Quinson*, ☎ 04–92–70–47–47 ⊕ *www. bastide-moustiers.com* ⇝ *6 rooms, 6 suites* ⌂ *In-room: refrigerator, Wi-Fi. In-hotel: restaurant, pool, parking, no-smoking rooms* ▤ *AE, DC, MC, V* ⊗ *Closed Jan.*

$$$ 🏨 **La Bouscatière.** Only the most discreet little sign indicates the presence
★ of this exceptional bed-and-breakfast, whose different levels are built down into the rock rather than upwards, offering views of the waterfall and unlikely little terraces (one is accessed through the bathroom). The divine stone garden even has a dart board should you feel the need to take a break from reading in one of the many cushioned chairs. Most of the furniture is 18th century to match the house, and the cooking is rustic and generous: summer grills over a wood oven and traditional family recipes in the winter season. **Pros:** romantic decadence in the heart of a village; you'll feel like part of the family. **Cons:** restaurant open for dinner only. ⊠ *Chemin Marcel Provence*, ☎ 04–92–74–67–67 ⊕ *www.labouscatiere.com* ⇝ *5 rooms* ⌂ *In-room: no a/c, no phone, no TV, Wi-Fi. In-hotel: restaurant, some pets allowed* ▤ *MC, V.*

$ 🏨 **Hôtel les Restanques.** Opened in spring 2008, this motelish-style building is only a five-minute walk from the village. Spacious and crispy clean, some ground-floor rooms open on to a terrace while others are carpeted. Our verdict: absolutely charming and affordable. **Pros:** beds in fab condition; friendly service. **Cons:** could be a few glitches as it's very new; few facilities. ⊠ *Rte des Gorges du Verdon*, ☎ 04–92–74–93–93 ⊕ *www.hotel-les-restanques.com* ⇝ *18 rooms, 2 suites* ⌂ *In-hotel: Wi-Fi, parking* ▤ *AE, MC, V* ⊗ *Closed Nov. 15–Mar. 15.*

SHOPPING

At **L'Atelier Soleil** (⊠ *Chemin de Quinson* ☎ 04–92–74–63–05 ⊕ *www. soleil-deux.fr*), next to the Bastide de Moustiers, second-generation potter Franck Scherer makes custom-made plates for Alain Ducasse's auberges—you can visit the workshop and buy pieces with tiny flaws at a reduced price. Stock up on local olive oils, soaps, fresh herbs, and tea at funky new **Le Souquet** (⊠ *Rue Marcel Provence* ☎ 06–77–96–24–30), run by two real oléicultureurs—maybe even join them for a game of backgammon. Hidden away off the main drag is **Saveurs et Nature**

(✉ *Rue Scipion* ☎04–92–74–64–48), where you can brace yourself for the hike up to the town cathedral with a freshly made juice or stock up on local beer, honey, and jam.

AUPS

23 km (14 mi) south of Moustiers.

Not perched, but rather nestled artfully in a valley of olive groves under imposing pine-covered hills, this village (pronounced *ohpss*) spills in a graceful delta of towers, campaniles, and tile-roofed cubes. Its Old Town, above the modern section, echoes with trickling fountains, and the square, under heavy plane trees, remains undisturbed by tourism. Many noble Old Town houses remain ungentrified, and the backstreets are lined with unpretentious cafés. It has ruins, too, of a 12th-century château-fort with traces of the medieval ramparts that once surrounded it. A terribly appealing town, Aups's claim to fame is the truffle, rooted up from the surrounding forests and sold in a Thursday morning market from November through February. But do keep an eye out for vendors selling fake truffles in the form of dog merde (they look similar) to the unknowing tourist.

5

COTIGNAC

11 km (7 mi) southwest of Aups, 66 km (41 mi) northwest of St-Raphaël.

The light changing on the stone bluff, revealing pockets of ancient stairs and dwellings tucked into shadowy hollows, gives this old mountain town, nestled at the foot of a dramatic rock cliff crowned by two medieval towers, a Turner-esque quality. Life in the Old Town below plays out in tones of tinted sepia, in the quiet Renaissance center and along the lazy, deep-shaded Cours Gambetta, where painted storefronts and cafés stand oblivious to time.

Though it's possible to make a running tour of hill villages, popping into churches, perusing the galleries, and drinking a quick one on the squares, Cotignac is a place to stop, stay, listen, and live—even briefly—the rhythm of a Provençal day. It is the place to drink a pastis slowly and practice your French with the couple at the neighboring table; they're likely to live here—and to welcome your attempts. The butcher is proud of his lamb, the bakers compete for your business, and the very few galleries maintain a low profile.

Take time to stroll through the Old Town, an inner sanctum within Baroque gates. On the Place de la Mairie, noble houses from the 16th and 17th centuries encircle a fountain and a lovely ironwork bell tower. Farther in, Rue Clastre is flanked by medieval houses with shutters painted in muted hues.

If you need a concrete goal, climb up the cliff face into one of the mysterious grottoes; these ancient hollows have served as refuges and lookouts for centuries. From this vantage point you can look down over the plane trees, elms, and red roofs of the otherworldly town.

OFF THE
BEATEN
PATH

Château D'Entrecasteaux. This long, lean château, on the pretty country roads outside Cotignac (D50 and D31), is a jewel of a sight that offers a change from the stocky medieval style in neighboring villages and deserves a side trip. Built into a forested rock wall, it was first constructed in the 9th century as a fortress, then expanded into its Italian Baroque style in the 16th century. There are vaulted galleries, a grand kitchen and cooks' apartments, a lavoir, and even a small classical garden designed by Le Nôtre (of Versailles fame; it's owned by the commune). The music room is a Baroque gem and in summer may host concerts. At press time, a complete restoration of the Oriental suites was in the works. The most recent owner, Alain Gayral, lives on-site and has been restoring and furnishing it in period-style piece by piece, including paintings, tapestries, and 17th-century furniture. Although the gardens are public, you'll need to take a tour to see the inside of the château and you must phone for a reservation. Nearby there's also a tiny Old Town with a fortified church. ☎04–94–04–43–95 ⌨*Château €7; garden free* ⊙*Easter–Oct.: garden, daily sunrise–sunset; château, guided tours only at 4; Aug., additional tour 11:30. Closed Sat.*

WHERE TO STAY

$ ★ ⊡**Marie et le Roy.** Tucked away in Cotignac's Old Town, this *maison d'hôtes* is surprisingly stylish, even hip (a word not often associated with Provençal villages). Dutch owner-painter Marcia Eecen greets guests with a friendly aperitif on their rooftop terrace before proudly showing the art displayed in the house. The individually decorated guest rooms, light and uncluttered—one unique with a hand-painted headboard and an antique bathtub, another made of cement—make this no ordinary B&B. Continental breakfast is served on the terrace. **Pros:** great village value; suite sleeps four. **Cons:** minimum two-night stay; must park in village. ⊠*7 rue Gabriel Philis,* ☎04–94–77–74–41 ⊕*www.marieetleroy.com* ➲*2 rooms, 1 suite* ⌂*In-room: no phone, no TV. In-hotel: Wi-Fi* ⊙*Closed Oct. 22–Apr. 25* ⦿*BP.*

ABBAYE DU THORONET

13 km (8 mi) southeast of Cotignac.

This 12th-century Cistercian abbey, an extraordinary example of Romanesque architecture, stands in an austere, isolated valley. The purity of the structure (or severity, if you will) was a reaction in its day to the luxurious extravagance of the abbey Cluny in Burgundy. Study the dense stonework and almost total absence of wooden support, and admire the near-perfect symmetry of the church's ground plan and its gentle forays into Gothic style. The cloister is stark and stolid compared to the delicate cloisters of Fréjus and Arles. ☎04–94–60–43–90 ⌨*€6.50* ⊙*Apr. 1–Sept. 30, daily 10–6:30; Oct. 1–Mar. 31, daily 10–1 and 2–5. Closed every Sun. 12–2.*

DRAGUIGNAN

30 km (19 mi) northwest of Fréjus, 56 km (35 mi) west of Grasse, 64 km (40 mi) northwest of Cannes.

Long the capital of the Var, this broad sprawl of a city suffers from intense modernization, starting with the rigid 19th-century reorganization by Baron Haussmann, who ironed out much of its charm. He spared the pretty Old Town, though, and it's in this charming neighborhood of shuttered houses, sculpted doors, and bubbling fountains that the animated market takes place (on Place du Marché) Wednesday and Saturday mornings.

At the heart of the Old Town, the imposing 17th-century **Tour de l'Horloge** *(Clock Tower)* rears up, flanked by scroll-like guard towers and topped with an elaborate campanile.

EN ROUTE If you're heading north from Draguignan toward Comps and the Gorges du Verdun, you'll pass through the **Gorges de Châteaudouble**, a deep, winding forest canyon that prepares you for the wilderness ahead.

En route you may choose to cut briefly north up to the tiny medieval hill town of **Châteaudouble**, where you can view the magnificent wooded gorge from above.

LORGUES

7 mi (12 km) northeast of Abbaye du Thoronet.

With a less-airbrushed look than some of its prettier neighbors, this 11th-century fortified village is underrated. Cheaper and a great pivot-point for discovering the region and nearby vineyards, Lorgues offers a lovely stop-and-slow-down alternative to travelers too intent on binge-visiting the region. There is actually tons of history to discover here: the numbered plaques throughout the old town shed some 12th-century religious light on a walking tour. Capping it all off is the church of St. Martin, one of the largest in the Var, with a signature tower that can be seen from far off in the distance. Tuesday is market day, and a farmers' market sets up shop on Friday. Village restaurants are nothing extraordinary but for something different, try the Deco shop-resto **Les Rêves d'Isabelle** (⊠*1 rue Église* ☎*04–94–73–96–28*) where for €13 you'll be served an assiette du jour, salad, and tart, or goat cheese, all homemade, in the courtyard. **Château de Berne** (⊠*Rte. de Salernes* ☎*04–94–60–43–53*) just north of town, has been making wine since 1750 and offers tours and wine tasting. Another historic goodie—take a few miles detour beforehand on the D50 towards Entrecasteaux—is the **Notre-Dame de Benva Chapel**, or the Bon Voyage Chapel, dating back to at least the 15th century.

WHERE TO EAT & STAY

$$$$ ✕**Restaurant Bruno.** For 25 years, Bruno has been serving 4 to 5 tonnes of truffles annually in his covered garden terrace just down the road from the village. Weekly set menus include five courses, and except for

LE TRANSHUMANCE

It happens throughout June for travelers in Haute Provence. Picture yourself sitting in a village café, hiking the arid hills, or perhaps driving around a tight switchback, when you suddenly hear the faint, ephemeral tonking and clonking of bells. Then come the sheep, in vast curving masses of fleece and a cacophony of bleets and baaahs. By the hundreds they flow, two-thousandfold. Solemn sheperds in safety orange trudge beside them, guiding the eddies and whorls of wool. Onlookers gape, children reach out tentative hands. Can this be the 21st century, or is it a wrinkle in time? It is the transhu-mance, the ancient, imperative spring ritual of guiding the herds from the dry lowlands to the juicy green meadows of the Alps. There they will gorge on mountain flowers until, fat and healthy, they descend again in autumn. Sheep raisers are reviving the tradition of transhumance, shunning trucks for the ways of old. To witness this primordial migration, station yourself at a Verdon-region crossroads—say, Comps-sur-Artuby or Castellane—in the early morning or late evening, when they walk to avoid the midday sun. Then watch for a wave from another world.

dessert, each plate is loaded with at least 15 grams of glorious *tuber aestivum* truffles. From an amuse-bouche of grilled bread soaked in truffle oil and layered with truffles to the signature *pomme de terrre de montagne cuite en robe de champs, crème de truffes et truffe* (potatoes drenched in a creamy truffle sauce sprinkled with fresh truffles), you can see where this meal is heading. Some of the main dishes may not live up to expectation but Bruno's remains an institution worth experiencing. Obviously, count on a couple of hours to truly savor this feast. ⊠*2435 rte. des Arcs* ☎*04–94–85–93–93* ⊕*www.restaurantbruno. com* ⌂*Reservations essential* ⊟*AE, D, MC, V.*

$$ **La Sarrazine.** Hilary Smith ditched the London high finance scene
★ for 3 acres in Provence, complete with 140 olive trees, shaded garden paths, and village views. Excellent value for your money, this nonsmoking chambre d'hôtes offers two double suites with private entrance off the garden, and a very large double room that could sleep three. All have en suite bathrooms, shared refrigerators, and are super clean and uncluttered. The lush grounds and the infinite hospitality of Hilary and her canine companion Freddy create a carefree home away from home, befitting of post day-tripping R&R. Dinners can be arranged. **Pros:** best breakfast terrace and hammock; 10-minute walk to town. **Cons:** credit cards not accepted. ⊠*375 chemin du Pendedi,* ☎*04–94–73–20–27* ⊕*www.lasarrazine.com* ⇆*3 rooms* ⌂*In-room: no a/c, no phone, no TV, Wi-Fi. In-hotel: pool, tennis court, parking, no kids under 12* ⊟*No credit cards* ⑩*BP.*

Nice & The Eastern Côte d'Azur

CANNES, ANTIBES, MONACO & THE HILL TOWNS

Casino, Monte-Carlo, Monaco

WORD OF MOUTH

"The fantastic thing about the Riviera is that everywhere is so easy to get to and, yet, one place can be completely different from the rest . . . ad infinitum. It doesn't matter where you stay if you hire a car—otherwise nearly anywhere else on the coast is only a few minutes away on the train or the bus (€1 to go anywhere!). The contrast between Nice as a busy, albeit charming, city and, say, Peillon, an 11th-century village 15 mins out of town, could not be more stark. It's all here—come and explore!"

—monacomike

WELCOME TO NICE & THE EASTERN CÔTE D'AZUR

Le Suquet, Cannes

TOP REASONS TO GO

★ **Monaco, toy kingdom:**
Yes, Virginia, you can afford to visit Monte-Carlo—that is, if you avoid its casinos and head instead for its magnificent tropical gardens.

★ **Picasso & Company:**
Because artists have long loved the Côte d'Azur, it is blessed with superb art museums, including the Fondation Maeght in St-Paul and the Musée Picasso in Antibes.

★ **Èze, island in the sky:**
The most perfectly perched of the coast's *villages perchés*, Èze has some of the most breathtaking views this side of a NASA space capsule.

★ **Nice, Queen of the Riviera:** With its bonbon-colored palaces, blue Baie des Anges, time-stained Old Town, and Musée Matisse, this is one of France's most colorful cities.

★ **Sunkissed Cap d'Antibes:**
Bordering well-hidden mansions and zillion-dollar hotels, the Sentier Tirepoil is a spectacular footpath along the sea.

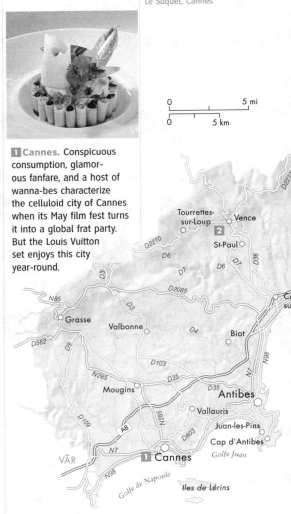

1 Cannes. Conspicuous consumption, glamorous fanfare, and a host of wanna-bes characterize the celluloid city of Cannes when its May film fest turns it into a global frat party. But the Louis Vuitton set enjoys this city year-round.

0 ____ 5 mi
0 ____ 5 km

2 St. Paul, Vence & Hill-towns. High in the hills overlooking Nice are the medieval walled villages of St-Paul and Vence, invaded by waves of artists in the 20th century. Today, you can hardly turn around without bumping into a Calder mobile, and top sights include the famous inn La Colombe d'Or and Matisse's sublime Chapelle du Rosaire.

3 Nice. Walking along the seaside Promenade des Anglais is one of the iconic Riviera experiences. Add in top-notch museums, a charming old quarter, scads of ethnic restaurants, and a raging nightlife, and Nice is a must-do.

 ALPES MARITIMES

ITALY

Menton

Peillon

Roquebrune-Cap-Martin

La Turbie

Èze

Monte-Carlo

Beaulieu

4 MONACO

3 Nice

Villefranche-sur-Mer

St-Jean-Cap-Ferrat

Golfe de St-Hospice

Mediterranean Sea

les Anges

St-Jean-Cap-Ferrat

Olive-oil tasting

4 Monaco and the Corniche Resorts. The 24-karat sun shines most brightly on the fabled glamour ports of **Villefranche-sur-Mer**, **Beaulieu**, and **St-Jean-Cap-Ferrat**. To the east of glittering Monaco lies **Menton**, an enchanting Italianate resort where winters are so mild that lemon trees bloom in January.

GETTING ORIENTED

Few places in the world have the same pull on the imagination as this stretch of France's fabled Riviera (the Côte d'Azur to the French). Little or no introduction is needed for the ooo-la-la opulence of St-Jean-Cap-Ferrat, the palm-tree-lined promenades of Nice, or the art villages of St-Paul and Vence. But as you get to know this region—which stretches from Cannes to the Italian border—you'll learn it is a land of contrasts and surprises.

6

NICE & THE EASTERN CÔTE D'AZUR PLANNER

Transportation Basics

As home to France's second-busiest airport, Nice is a natural starting point for seeing the area. The airport's location 15 minutes from the town center is particularly convenient, though beware the cost of taxis (the airport bus runs every quarter hour).

East and west of Nice, a train route connects all the main coastal towns—a magic carpet ride in terms of convenience for any travelers. Buses also spider out, but they can take a good two hours between Nice and Cannes (as opposed to 35 minutes on the train). It's a well-kept secret that the Biot train station is a five-minute walk from Marineland, a major attraction near Antibes. Trains also head up into the hills around Grasse.

Surely the biggest bargain in the south of France is the €1 bus ticket, valid anywhere between Cannes and Menton. The most scenic line is No. 100, running from Nice to Menton along the Moyenne Corniche. It runs every 15 minutes, but can get unpleasantly packed in high season. Buses connect Nice to Eze Village (20 minutes), St-Paul and Vence (about an hour); be sure to check the schedule, since they are not frequent.

Finding a Place to Stay

In this golden stretch you'll see the prices rise, even beyond those of the Estérel. The atmosphere changes, too. In the coastal resorts the majority of visitors seem to value proximity to the sea over cachet, and you'll often find yourself far from the land of Provençal cottons and cozy country inns. The decor here is a peculiar hybrid—vaguely Jazz Age, a little Hollywood—that falls into a loose category known as Côte d'Azur style. In Cannes the grand hotels are big on prestige (waterfront position, awe-inspiring lobbies, high-price sea views) and weak on swimming pools, which are usually just big enough to dip in; their private beaches are on the other side of the busy street, and you'll have to pay for access, just as nonguests do. Remember that July and August are the busiest months but plan ahead anytime between May and October. Hotel prices skyrocket during the Monaco Grand Prix and the Cannes Film Festival; off-season, there are great deals to be had. The glitziest hotels are in Cannes, Monaco, and the Cap d'Antibes; Nice provides a broader range of prices, while charming family-run hotels can be found around St-Paul and Vence. Renting a rural gîte (w *www.gites-de-france.com*) allows you to avoid overpriced breakfasts and make the most of the abundance at the markets.

Some Like It . . . Stony?

Despite its reputation as a beach paradise, the eastern Côte d'Azur waterfront is mainly surfaced by stretches of smooth, round rocks the size of your fist; from Cagnes-sur-Mer to Menton, you'll spread your beach blanket or towel over these hard lumps instead of nestling into sand. A thin foam mattress can make all the difference, as can a pair of slip-on rubber shoes for negotiating the stones. You might consider springing for a private plage (beach), where you can lie on a lounge chair or mattress. All along the coast there are patches of sand, and a few resorts have made an effort to haul in sand to cater to the expectations of swimmers. If you're lodging inland, leave early for the beach: traffic on N98, from which you'll access the waterfront throughout the length of the coast, often grinds to a halt.

Making the Most of Your Time

How you tackle this stretch of the Côte d'Azur will largely depend on the form of transport you have chosen. With a car, you can base yourself outside a major resort and combine day trips to Nice, Cannes, and Monaco with a taste of more leisurely Provençal life.

If you're dependent on public transport, you might stay in a larger center such as Nice and even find that you don't need to leave it very often, though buses and trains will easily take you along the coast and up to towns such as Eze and Grasse.

If sunbathing is a priority, you might prefer the sandy beaches of Cannes to the pebbles of Nice; in the height of summer, aim for the less populated beaches of St-Jean-Cap-Ferrat, Cap d'Ail, Eze, and the Iles de Lérins. Art is a major draw in this area, with must-see museums in Nice, St-Paul, Biot, and Antibes.

There is plenty for music fans, too: Nice and Juan-les-Pins hold major jazz festivals in the summer and Monaco's Printemps des Arts in March and April celebrates music, dance, cinema, and theater.

With so much to see it's tempting to pack too much into a visit to this area, so be sure to set aside some time for relaxing on café terraces—something that the locals have mastered.

Stroll through a colorful food market, perhaps the Marché Forville in Cannes or the Cours Saleya in Nice, to see how seriously this area takes its fresh produce, then visit a good local bistro to taste specialties such as pissaladière (caramelized onion tart), soupe de poissons (fish soup) and, of course, salade niçoise (which in Nice contains neither green beans nor potato).

DINING & LODGING PRICES IN EUROS

¢	$	$$	$$$	$$$$
Restaurants				
Under €13	€14–€19	€20–€24	€25–€31	Over €32
Hotels				
Under €55	€56–€85	€86–€135	€136–€200	Over €201

Restaurant prices are per person for a main course at dinner, including tax (19.6%) and service; note that if a restaurant offers only prix-fixe (set-price) meals, it has been given the price category that reflects the full prix-fixe price. Hotel prices are for a standard double room in high season, including tax (19.6%) and service charge.

When to Come

Southeast France is that magical corner of France where the sun always seems to shine. That's why it holds such a strong attraction for Parisians, who turn the beaches of Nice into one giant rocky bed in summer. If rain is almost unheard of in July and August, the region's short periods of intense rainfall, lasting half a day to a week, are otherwise hard to predict. The most likely periods are November and anytime from January to March, while late spring can also be surprisingly wet (locals swear that it always rains during the Cannes Film Festival). It's no secret that the coast is in its tropical prime July and August. But if you're anxious to enjoy the beaches, aim for June or September (or even April onward). Many hotels and restaurants close from November to Easter, though Nice and Monaco thrive year-round.

Cannes books early for the film festival in May, so unless you're determined to hover outside the Farfalla with an autograph book, aim for another month. But there are magical times all year on the coast. The eastern Côte d'Azur enjoys a gentle microclimate, protected by the Estérel from the mistral that razors through Fréjus to the west, and from northern winds by the Alps. If you're intent on strolling in shirtsleeves under the palms on a winter day, head for Menton, famous for having the mildest climate in France.

GETTING AROUND PLANNER

By Air

The Nice–Côte d'Azur Airport, the second-busiest in France, sits on a peninsula between Antibes and Nice. There are frequent flights between Paris and Nice on the low-cost airline easyJet and Air France, as well as direct flights on Delta Airlines from New York and Atlanta. In the off-season or if you book well in advance you can find a one-way trip from Paris to Nice for a spectacular €40; which definitely beats out both the SNCF and the cost of a rental car. The flight time between Paris and Nice is a little over one hour. A taxi from the airport into Nice proper—say, the train station or the Place Masséna—costs about €25.

Sunbus No. 98 from Nice makes the run to and from bus station every 20 minutes Monday–Saturday between 6 AM and 9 PM for a more reasonable €4 (which includes a one-day transit pass), and the No. 99 goes to and from the train station to the airport. In summer, the No. 98 goes beyond the bus station to the Port. Regular shuttle buses also serve Cannes, Antibes, Monte Carlo, and Menton.

Aéroport International Nice–Côte d'Azur (✉ 7 km [4½ mi] from Nice ☎ 08–20–42–33–33 ⊕ www.nice.aeroport.fr).

By Boat

The Côte d'Azur is one of the most beautiful coastlines in the world and there are several companies that allow you to drink it all in via boat and ferry service. Compagnie Maritime Cannoise offers routes between Cannes and Monaco and St-Tropez. Trans Côte d'Azur has routes including the Corniche de l'Estérel, Monaco, Porquerolles, and St-Tropez, plus specialty excursions that feature nighttime dining and glass-bottom boats. Trans Côte d'Azur has routes including the Corniche de l'Estérel, Monaco, Porquerolles, and St-Tropez. Note that some routes and destinations are only featured March to October.

Boat Travel Information **Horizon** (✉ Quai des Iles06400, Cannes ☎ 04–92–98–71–36 ⊕ www.cannes-horizon.com). **Trans Côte d'Azur** (✉ Quai Laubeuf, Cannes ☎ 04–92–98–71–30 ⊕ www.trans-cote-azur.com).

By Car

A8 flows briskly from Cannes to Antibes to Nice to the resorts on the Grand Corniche; N98 follows the coast more closely along the Corniche Infe'rieure. The Moyenne Corniche is highway N7. *For more info, see The Three Corniches Close-Up box in this chapter.* From Paris, the main southbound artery is A6/A7, known as the Autoroute du Soleil; it passes through Provence and joins the eastbound A8 at Aix-en-Provence. The best way to explore the secondary sights in this region, especially the deep backcountry, is by car. A car also allows you the freedom to zip along A8 between the coastal resorts and to enjoy the tremendous views from the three Corniches that trace the coast from Nice to the Italian border. A car is, of course, a liability in downtown Cannes and Nice, with parking garages expensive and curbside spots virtually nonexistent. Note: this is one of the most dangerous driving regions in Europe, and the speeds and aggressive Grand-Prix style of some drivers make it impossible to let your guard down. On the A8 toward Italy, tight curves, hills, tunnels, and construction keep things interesting. For English-language traffic reports (as well as BBC news) tune to 86.4 FM.

By Bus

If you want to penetrate deeper into backcountry spots not on the rail line, you can take a bus out of Cannes, Nice, Antibes, or Menton for a mere €1 per ticket. Pick up schedules at the train station, at tourist offices, and at the local *gare routière* (bus station). Note that the quickest way to get around is the great coastal train line between Cannes and Menton. In addition to town bus stations, hook up with buses heading everywhere using the bus station at the Nice airport (next to Terminal 1). Ligne d'Azur Bus No. 100 departs every 15 minutes (between 6 AM and 8 PM) and stops at all the villages between Nice and Menton along the Corniche Inférieure. For the villages set on the Moyenne Corniche, take Bus No. 112, which departs Nice six times a day (three on Sunday). Fewer villages are found on the Grande Corniche, the highest highway, but some, such as La Turbie are serviced by Ligne d'Azur No. 116. The No. 400 goes from Nice to St-Paul and Vence, stopping first in St-Paul (about 1 hr). In Cannes, Rapides Côtes d'Azur runs most routes from the station on Place Bernard Gentille, including Nice (€6, 1½ hrs), Mougins (€2, 20 mins), Grasse (€4, 45 mins), and Vallauris (€3, 30 mins). Within Cannes, use Bus Azur, with a ticket costing €1.30. In Nice, the new tram system is a great way to get from the train station to the Old Town; tickets cost €1. Monaco's buses help stitch together the principality's widely dispersed neighborhoods. Take a bus from Antibes bus station to Vallauris (€3, every 30 mins) or one running from the train station in Golfe-Juan. Antibes bus station is by Rue de la République, and buses connect with Nice (€5, every half hr), Cagnes-sur-Mer (€2.50, 20 mins), Biot (€1, 25 minutes), and Cannes (€2, 30 mins). Cagnes-sur-Mer is one of the coastal towns served by train, and then easily connect with adjacent St-Paul-de-Vence and Vence using Bus No. 400, with departures every 30 minutes from Cagnes Ville's bus station on Place de Général du Gaulle. Remember: bus drivers give change and hand you a ticket, which must be stamped (*composté*) in the ticket validator.

Cannes Gare Routière (Bus Station) (⊠ *Place Bernard Cornut Gentille* ☎ 04–93–38–01–41). **Nice Gare Routière** (⊠ *5 blvd. Jean-Jaurès* ☎ 04–93–85–61–81). **Phocéens Cars** (⊠ *2 pl. Masséna* ☎ 08–10–00–40–08). **Rapides Côte d'Azur** (☎ 08–20–48–11–11 ⊕ *www.rca.tm.fr*). **Société des Cars Alpes-Littoral** (☎ 04–92–51–06–05 ⊕ *www.scal-amv-voyages.com*). **Transports Alpes-Maritimes** (☎ 04–93–89–41–45).

By Train

Nice is the major rail crossroads for trains arriving from Paris and other northern cities and from Italy, too. To get from Paris to Nice (with stops in Cannes and other resorts along the coast), you can take the TGV, though it only maintains high speeds to Valence before returning to conventional rails and rates. Night trains arrive at Nice in the morning from Paris, Metz, and Strasbourg.

You can easily move along the coastal towns between Cannes, Nice, and Ventimiglia by train on the slick double-decker Côte d'Azur line, a highly tourist-pleasing branch of the SNCF lines, with more than two dozen trains running a day.

This line is called Marseille–Vintimille (Ventimiglia, in Italy) heading east to Italy and Vintimille–Marseille in the west direction. Some main stops on this line are: Antibes (€4, 30 mins), Cannes (€6, 40 mins), Menton (€4, 30 mins), and Monaco (€3, 25 mins); other stops include Villefranche-sur-Mer, Beaulieu, Cap Martin, St-Jean-Cap-Ferrat, and Èze-sur-Mer. No trains run to the hill villages, including St-Paul, Vence, and Peillon.

Gare Nice Ville (⊠ *Av. Thiers* ☎ 08–36–35–35–35). **Gare Cannes Ville** (⊠ *Rue Jean-Jaurès*). **SNCF** (☎ 08–36–35–35–35 ⊕ *www.ter-sncf.com/uk/paca*). **TGV** (☎ 877/284–8633 ⊕ *www.tgv.com, www.idtgv.com*). **www.beyond.fr** (⊕ *www.beyond.fr*).

Updated by
Rosa Jackson

WITH THE ALPS AND PRE-ALPS playing bodyguard against inland winds, and the sultry Mediterranean warming the sea breezes, the eastern slice of the Côte d'Azur is pampered by a nearly tropical climate that sets it apart from the rest of France's southern coast. This is where the real glamour begins: the dreamland of azure waters and indigo sky; white villas with balustrades edging the blue horizon; evening air perfumed with jasmine and mimosa; palm trees and parasol pines silhouetted against sunsets of apricot and gold. Ideal as a Jazz Age travel poster, this area lives up to the image of the Côte d'Azur, which seems to define happiness itself in the collective mind of the world.

Thus the dream confronts modern reality. On the hills that undulate along the cerulean waters, every cliff, cranny, gully, and plain bristles with hot-pink cement-cube "villas," their balconies skewed toward the sea. Like a rosy rash, they creep and spread, outnumbering the trees and blocking each other's views. Their owners and the renters who stream southward at every school vacation—Easter, Christmas, Carnaval, and All Saints'—choke the tiered highways, and on a hot day in high summer the traffic to the beach—slow going any day—coagulates and blisters in the sun.

There has been a constant march to this prime slice of the Côte d'Azur, going back to the ancient Greeks, who sailed eastward from Marseilles to market their goods to the indigenes. From the 18th-century English aristocrats, who claimed it as one vast treatment spa, to the 19th-century Russian nobles who transformed Nice into a tropical St. Petersburg, to the 20th-century American tycoons who cast themselves as sheikhs, the coast beckoned like a dreamscape, a blank slate for their whims. Like the modern vacationers who follow in their footsteps, all have left their mark: Moroccan palaces in Menton, a neo-Greek villa in Beaulieu, the Promenade des Anglais in Nice planted with tropical greenery, to suit English fancies—temples all to fantasy, inspired by the sensual pleasures of sun and sultry sea breezes.

The glamour of the coast, however, is merely skin deep—a veneer of luxury backed by a sharp ascent into relatively ascetic heights. True, the fantasy element spills slightly inland: day-trippers seeking contrast have transfigured the hills behind the Baie des Anges into something of a Provençal theme park, filled with historic towns and *villages perchés* (perched villages). Towns such as Mougins, where Picasso spent his last years, and Grasse, with its factories that make perfume from the region's abundant flowers, have transformed themselves to fulfill visitors' dreams of backcountry villages, and galleries, souvenir shops, and snack stands crowd the cobblestones of Old St-Paul, Vence, and Èze.

But let's recall that most of the earliest inhabitants of this region were fishermen, and peasants who grew wheat and olives, and grapes for wine. This was not one of those lush regions of France where the living was easy. There were no palaces or gracious châteaus, only small villages, with fortifications here and there for use when Celts, Vandals, Ostrogoths, Saracens, and pirates from Algeria's Barbary Coast were on the rampage. It was only in the middle of the 19th century that a troupe of kings and queens (including Victoria and dozens of her relatives), Russian grand dukes, princelings from obscure Balkan countries, English milords, and a rabble of nouveau riche camp followers began to make prolonged visits here. They had mansions and gardens built; luxury hotels sprung up in imitation of their palaces back home. The newcomers called the coastal strip the French Riviera. The French name for it is *la Côte d'Azur,* the blue—literally, sky-blue—coast. To the French, "Riviera" refers to the Italian coast farther east.

All these rich invaders withdrew to the cooler north for the summer months. No person of quality, and above all no lady of quality, would risk getting tanned like those laboring field hands. Until World War II, in fact, many hotels *closed* at the end of May, reopening in October. Up to that time, sea bathing was shunned by all, except as a drastic medical remedy. Then came the fun revolution. In the 1920s and 1930s people began to like it hot. The peasantry of the West were now pale factory and office workers, and their new badge of leisure and pleasure became the tan that their aristocratic predecessors had so assiduously avoided. Chanel, the famous couturier who made tans the chicest of fashion "accessories," decreed—from her first shop, set on Cannes's Croisette, at No. 5 (*mais naturellement*)—that suntans were chic in the 1920s.

More and more hotels, restaurants, and nightclubs were built. Fun became livelier and more informal. Toplessness, and even bottomlessness, arrived on the beaches. Today, for many travelers, the Côte remains a demi-paradise.

You could drive from Cannes to the Italian border in two hours and see much of the region, so small is this renowned stretch of Mediterranean coast; the swift A8 autoroute allows you to pick and choose your stopoffs. But like the artists and nobles who paved the way before you, you will likely be seduced to linger.

EXPLORING NICE & THE EASTERN CÔTE D'AZUR

Numbers in the text correspond to numbers in the margin and on the Eastern Côte d'Azur, Cannes, Nice, and Monaco maps.

It's easy to explore this part of the coast, and you can do it in depth without retracing your steps too often. There are parallel roads, especially along the three Corniches between Nice and Menton, that access different towns and reveal different points of view. A8, which runs parallel to the coast, makes zipping back to home base a breeze.

This region is the real heart of the Côte d'Azur. Its waterfront resorts—Cannes, Antibes, Villefranche, and Menton—draw energy from the thriving city of Nice, while jutting tropical peninsulas—Cap Ferrat, Cap Martin—frame the tiny principality of Monaco. Farther inland, medieval villages mushroom out of the nearby hills, offering refugees escaping from the coastal crowds a token taste of Old Provence. Deeper into the backcountry lies a scattering of wild, Latin-accented mountain towns, long cut off from the chic enclaves below. And backing it all,

The Three Corniches

The lay of the land east of Nice is nearly vertical, as the coastline is one great cliff, a corniche terraced by three parallel highways—the **Corniche Inférieure** (sometimes called the Basse Corniche and N98), the **Moyenne Corniche** (N7), and the **Grande Corniche** (D2564)—that snake along its graduated crests. The lowest (*inférieure*) is the slowest, following the coast and crawling through the main streets of resorts, including downtown Monte Carlo. Villefranche, Cap-Ferrat, and Beaulieu are some of the towns located along this 20-mi-long highway. The highest (*grande*) is the fastest, but its panoramic views are blocked by villas, and there are few safe overlooks (this is the highway Grace Kelly roared along in *To Catch a Thief*, and some 27 years later, crashed and died on). The middle (*moyenne*) offers views down over the shoreline and villages and passes through a few picturesque cliff-top towns, including Èze.

looming icy-white on a clear day, rise the Alps, telephoto-close behind the palm trees.

CANNES

GETTING HERE & AROUND

Cannes has one central train station, the *Gare SNCF* (✉ *Rue JeanJaurès* ⊕ *www.voyages-sncf.com*). All major trains pass through here—check out the SNCF Web site for times and prices—but many of the trains run the St-Raphaël–Ventimiglia route. You can also take the TGV directly from Paris (6½ hrs). Cannes's main bus station, which is on Place de l'Hôtel-de-Ville by the port, serves all coastal destinations. Rapides Côtes d'Azur runs most of the routes out of the central bus station on Place Bernard Gentille, including Nice (1½ hrs, €6), Mougins (20 mins, €2), Grasse (45 mins, €4), and Vallauris (30 mins, €3). Within Cannes, Bus Azur runs the routes, with a ticket costing €1.30 (a weekly ticket is available). The bus line RCA (☎ *04–93–85–64–44* ⊕ *www.rca.tm.fr*) goes to Nice along the coast road, stopping in all villages along the way, and to the Nice airport, every 30 minutes, Monday–Saturday, for a maximum ticket price of €13.70 round-trip. From the Gare SNCF, RCA goes to Grasse every 30 minutes Monday–Saturday and every hour Sunday, via Mougins. The other option is any of the Transport Alpes Maritimes (TAM) buses (☎ *08–10–06–10–06* ⊕ *www.lignedazur.com*), which service the same destinations and are now cheaper thanks to a government initiative toward communal transport and are a bargain-basement €1.30 to all destinations along the coast (but, be patient, you may not get a seat).

VISITOR INFORMATION

Cannes Tourist Office (✉ *Palais des Festivals, Esplanade G. Pompidou, B.P. 272, Cannes* ☎ *04–93–39–01–01* ⊕ *www.cannes.com*).

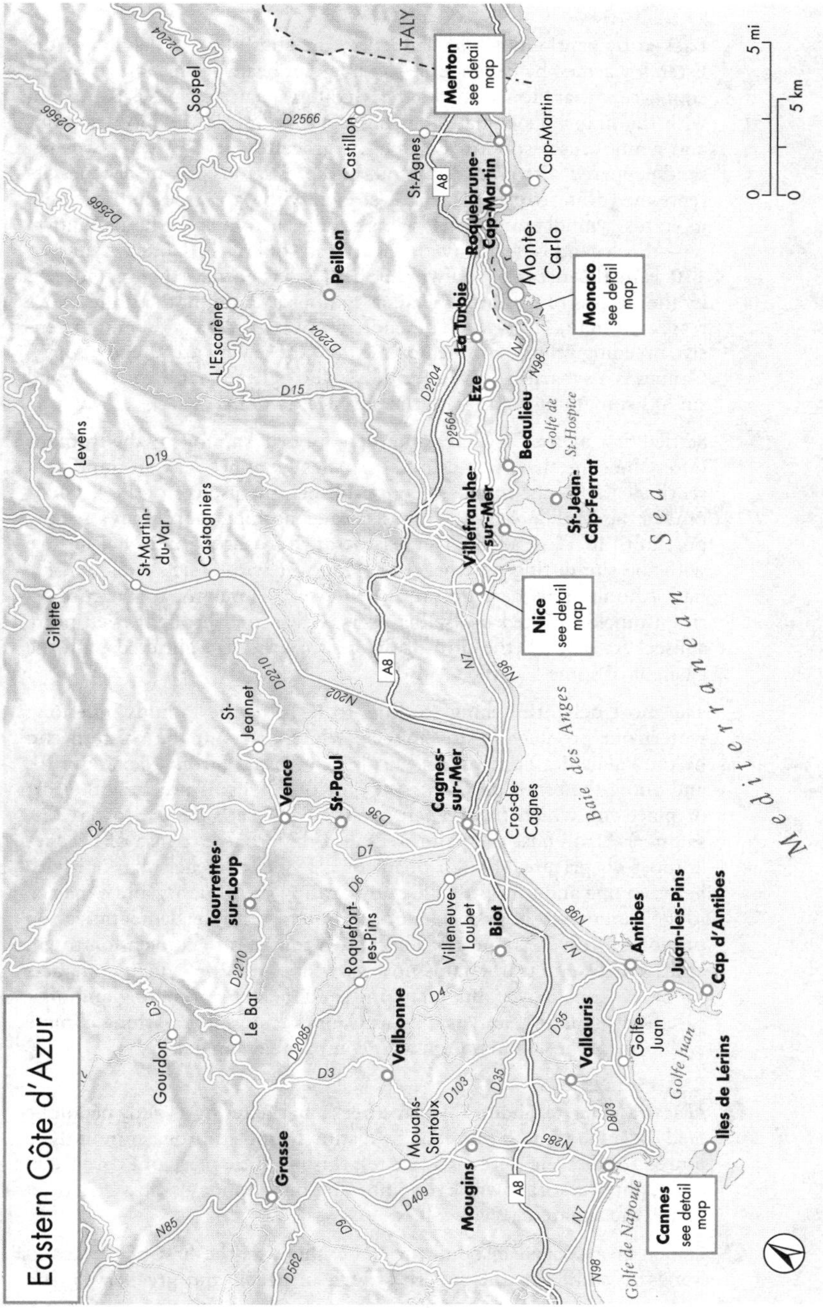

Eastern Côte d'Azur

6

EXPLORING

Backed by gentle hills and flanked to the south by the heights of the Esterel, warmed by dependable sun but kept bearable in summer by the cool breeze that blows in from the Mediterranean, Cannes is pampered with the luxurious climate that has made it one of the most popular and glamorous resorts in Europe. Its graceful curve of wave-washed sand peppered with chic restaurants and prestigious private beaches, its renowned waterfront promenade strewn with palm trees and poseurs, its status-symbol grand hotels vying for the custom of the Louis Vuitton set—this legend is, to many, the heart and soul of the Côte d'Azur. For 150 years the mecca of sun worshippers, it has been further glamorized by the success of its film festival, as famous as (and, in the trade, more respected than) Hollywood's Academy Awards. A tasteful and expensive breeding ground for the upscale (and those who are already "up"), Cannes is a sybaritic heaven for those who believe that life is short and sin has something to do with the absence of a tan.

Settled first by the Ligurians and then dubbed Cannoïs by the Romans (after the cane that waved in its marshes), Cannes was an important sentinel site for the monks who established themselves on Ile St-Honorat in the Middle Ages. Its bay served as nothing more than a fishing port until in 1834 an English aristocrat, Lord Brougham, fell in love with the site during an emergency stopover with a sick daughter. He had a home built here and returned every winter for a sun cure—a ritual quickly picked up by his peers. A railroad brought even more sunseekers, and by the turn of the century the bay glittered with the gaslight of some 50 hotels.

The most delightful thing to do is to head to the famous mile-long waterfront promenade, **La Croisette,** which starts at the western end by the Palais des Festivals and leads over to the Jardin Alexandre III, and allow the *esprit de Cannes* to take over. This is precisely the sort of place for which the French invented the verb *flâner* (to dawdle, saunter). Stroll past the palm trees and the broad expanse of beaches (almost all private, though open for a fee, each beach marked with between one and four little life buoys, rating their quality and expense) to the glamorous shops and luxurious hotels. With the democratization of modern travel, Cannes has become a tourist and convention town, and La Croisette traffic jams now slow up with 20 Twingo compacts for every Rolls-Royce. But glamour—and the perception of glamour—is self-perpetuating, and as long as Cannes enjoys its ravishing climate and location, it will maintain its incomparable panache.

SIGHTS TO SEE

❼ Allées de la Liberté. Shaded by plane trees and sheltering a sandy pétanque field (occupied round the clock by distinctly unglamorous grandfathers inured to the scene on La Croisette), this is a little piece of Provence in a big, glitzy resort town. Every morning but Monday a flower market paints the square in vivid colors.

❸ Carlton Inter-Continental. Built in 1912, this was the first of the grand hotels to stake out the superb stretch of beach and greenery on La

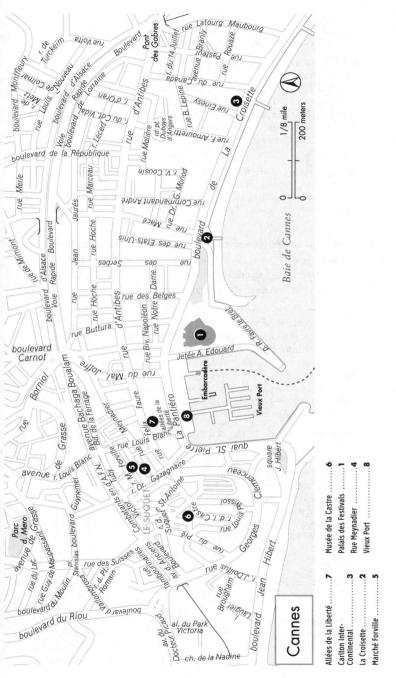

Cannes

6

Croisette, and thus is the best positioned. It is here that many of the film festival's grand banquets take place. ✉ *58 bd. de la Croisette* ☎ *04–93–06–40–06* ⊕ *www.intercontinental.com/cannes*

2 **La Croisette.** For many, this palm-studded promenade along the waterfront, backed by an imposing row of sumptuous apartment houses and hotels, epitomizes the Côte d'Azur. Stretching from the Palais des Festivals to the eastern point that juts into the bay, it's the perfect spot to park on a bench overlooking the Golfe de Napoule, the beach restaurants serving wind-screened meals at the water's edge, and the rows of deck chairs under umbrellas advertising the luxury hotels that own them.

If you need a culture fix, check out the modern art and photography exhibitions (varying admission prices) held at the **Malmaison,** a 19th-century mansion that was once part of the Grand Hotel. ✉ *47 La Croisette* ☎ *04–97–06–44–90* ☺ *Sept.–Apr., Tues.–Sun. 10–1 and 2–6; July and Aug., Tues.–Sun. 11–8, Fri. 11–10.*

NEED A BREAK?

Head down La Croisette and fight for a spot at Le 72 Croisette (✉ *72 La Croisette* ☎ *04–93–94–18–30*). The most feistily French of all La Croisette bars, it offers great ringside seats for watching the rich and famous enter the Martinez hotel next door. It's open 24 hours a day.

5 **Marché Forville** *(Forville market).* Under the permanent shelter that every morning (except Monday) draws the chefs, connoisseurs, and voyeurs of Cannes, you'll see showy displays of still-flipping fish from some 25 local fishing boats alongside glossy vegetables piled high, cheeses carried down from the mountains, and sausages, olives, and flower stands. Real farmers sell their fresh local produce down the central aisle—hand-mixed mesclun, fat asparagus, cherries picked yesterday, baby eggplants—but the whole scene gets hosed down by 1 PM, so don't linger too long over breakfast.

6 **Musée de la Castre.** In the château known as La Castre, built in the 11th century by the monks who inhabited the Iles de Lérins, this small museum is Cannes's token cultural attraction. The front half has been freshly renovated, drawing a large number of local visitors. In the vaulted Gothic chapel and a series of small castle rooms, the collection of 19th-century ethnological treasures—African drums, Asian flutes, and native clothing from America and Peru—seems out of place. But the handful of Impressionist paintings by Provençal artists shows landscapes you may recognize. ✉ *Pl. de la Castre* ☎ *04–93–38–55–26* ☞ *€3.20* ☺ *Sept.–June, Tues.–Sun. 10–1 and 2–6; July–Aug., Tues.–Sun. 10–7.*

1 **Palais des Festivals.** This is where it all happens: when the Cannes Film Festival is in town, jostling paparazzi crowd under the palm trees, popping flashbulbs at the glittering movie stars swanning up the broad, red-carpeted stairs to view a colleague's latest performance or creation, or, at last, to find out who has won the Palme d'Or (Golden Palm). Something of a shrine, these stairs are a popular spot for posing for souvenir snapshots. At the foot of the Palais and set into the surrounding pavement, the **Allée des Etoiles** (Stars' Alley) enshrines some 300 autographed imprints of film stars' hands—Gérard Depardieu, Meryl Streep, and Sharon Stone among others. ⊠*East of the tourist office on La Croisette.*

4 **Rue Meynadier.** You may not notice the pretty 18th-century houses that once formed the main street of Cannes, so distracting are the boutiques they now contain. Here inexpensive and trendy clothes alternate with rarified food and wine shops, and some of the best butchers in town. Don't miss the chic new patisserie, L'Atelier Jean-Luc Pelé, found at No. 36, whose delicate macarons come in flavors such as mint-anise, Menton lemon, and apricot-basil and whose ganache-filled chocolates are sublime. At one end of Rue Meynadier is **Rue d'Antibes,** Cannes's main high-end shopping street.

Fodor'sChoice ★ **Le Suquet.** On the site of the original Roman *castrum,* this ancient neighborhood seems to cling to the hill overlooking Cannes. Shops proffer crafts and Provençal goods, and the atmospheric theme restaurants give you a chance to catch your breath. Take time to lose yourself awhile on the tiny backstreets, ducking under arches and peeking into courtyards: the pretty pastel shutters, Gothic stonework, and narrow passageways are lovely distractions. At the top is **Place de la Castre**—from behind the square's 16th-century Église Notre-Dame-d'Esperance, take in magnificent views over Cannes and the Ile Ste-Marguerite. The hill is crowned by the 11th-century château, housing the **Musée de la Castre,** and the imposing four-sided **Tour du Suquet** (Suquet Tower), built in 1385 as a lookout against Saracen invasions.

8 **Vieux Port** (*Old Port*). Sparkling at the foot of Le Suquet, this narrow, well-protected port harbors a fascinating lineup of grand luxury yachts and slick little pleasure boats that creak and bob beside weathered-blue fishing barques. From the east corner, off La Pantiéro, you can catch a cruise to the Iles de Lérins.

WHERE TO EAT & STAY

$$$$ ✕**Mantel.** In a city where style often wins out over substance, food lovers treasure this Suquet address, run by former chef and maître d' Noël Mantel from Les Muscadins in Mougins and expanded in summer 2008. Find out for yourself with one of the seasonal prix-fixe menus drawing on the finest Mediterranean produce to deliver such simple yet eloquent dishes as pan-fried John Dory, asparagus risotto, and crêpes suzette. ⊠*22 rue St-Antoine* ☎*04–93–39–13–10* ⊕*www. restaurantmantel.fr* ⊟*MC, V* ⊗*No lunch Wed. or Thurs. Closed mid-July–mid-Aug.*

$$$$ ✕**Le Maschou.** If you're tired of choosing from complicated menus, visit this long-popular restaurant in Le Suquet, where the only thing you'll have to decide is what kind of meat you want off the grill. Every meal starts with a gigantic basket of whole raw vegetables, to be cut up and dipped in a selection of sauces. Then come the generous servings of beef, lamb, or chicken from the restaurant's charcoal grill. With a low, beamed ceiling and only a few tables Le Maschou is best visited in winter, but it's also a favorite during the Cannes film festival. ⊠*15*

rue St-Antoine, 06400 ☎*04–93–39–62–21* ✍*Reservations essential* ▤*AE, MC, V* ⊘*Closed Nov., Dec. and Sun. Sept.–June. No lunch.*

$$$ ✕**La Brouette de Grand'mère.** Monsieur Bruno's tiny, charming hole-in-the-wall, complete with lace curtains, painted-wood front, fireplace, and old posters, could be a set for one of the Festival's films. Yet it's a true-blue bistro, with a €33, three-course menu to choose from that includes both an aperitif and wine. There's quail roasted in cream, pot-au-feu with beef, pork, and chicken, andouillettes crisped in sweet muscadet, and sharp aged goat cheese. It's only open evenings, and feels especially right in winter. ✉*9 rue d'Oran* ☎*04–93–39–12–10* ▤*MC, V* ⊘*No lunch. Closed Sun.*

$$$ ✕**La Cave.** With walls strewn with Niçois memorabilia, this freshly renovated restaurant (established 1989) is where locals go to satisfy a craving for Provençal classics. Choosing from the affordable set menu, you might start with a plate of farcis (stuffed seasonal vegetables) before tasting an aïoli (cod with vegetables and garlic mayonnaise) or perhaps lamb stewed with artichokes. Desserts, such as crème brûlée or chocolate mousse, neither surprise nor disappoint. As the name suggests, wine plays a starring role here and you can choose from all the great French regions (including some worthy Provençal bottles). ✉*9 bd. de la République* ☎ *04–93–99–79–87* ⊕*www.restaurant-lacave.com* ▤*AE, MC, V* ⊘*Closed Sun. and last 2 wks in Aug. No lunch Sat.*

$$$ ✕**Ondine Beach Restaurant.** Ondine has long stood out among beach
★ restaurants in Cannes, and current owner Jean-Pierre Silva is keeping up that tradition. Each day he visits the market at 6:30 AM to select the perkiest ingredients for the restaurant's simply presented dishes, such as turbot with spring vegetables or lobster thermidor. A renowned chef in the region, he now works front-of-house with his wife, ensuring that each of the 250 customers served at noon is happy (there is no dinner except on Fridays and Saturdays in summer). He is passionate about wine, so this is the place to sip a fine Burgundy, Bordeaux, or champagne with sand between your toes. ✉*Bd. de la Croisette* ☎*04–93–94–23–15* ⊕*www.ondineplage.com* ▤*DC, MC, V* ⊘*Closed Wed., Sept.–June, late Nov.–late Dec. No dinner Sept.–June. No dinner Sun.–Thurs. in July and Aug.*

$$ ✕**La Mère Besson.** This long-standing favorite continues to please a largely foreign clientele with regional specialties such as sweet-and-sour sardines *à l'escabeche* (marinated in white wine and vinegar), monkfish Provençal (with tomatoes, fennel, and onion), and roast lamb with garlic puree. The formal interior, with damask linens and still-life paintings, is lightened up with clatter from the open kitchen. ✉*13 rue des Frères-Pradignac* ☎*04–93–39–59–24* ▤*DC, MC, V* ⊘*Closed Sun. No lunch except during festivals.*

$$ ✕**Pastis.** Just off La Croisette, Pastis looks like a spruced up New York diner but sticks mainly to tried-and-true French fare, though you will find chicken Caesar salad on the menu. The sidewalk terrace is the perfect spot to read the paper and sip a glass of—what else?—the anise-flavored pastis so beloved of southerners. The spot is a local favorite for the aperitif before moving on to Les Coulisses nearby. ✉*28 rue du*

Commandant André ☎04–92–98–95–40 ⊕*www.pastis-cannes.com* ⊟*MC, V* ⊘*No lunch Sun.*

$$$$ 🏨**Grand Hotel Cannes.** Eight blocks east of Cannes's super-charming
Fodor'sChoice Sucret old town, a short walk to the famous food market, and a stone's
★ throw from Chanel, this high-style hotel has an optimum location, which it flaunts by having the only hotel garden fronting La Croisette. Looming up in '70s-Miami Beach style——a retro look with a brand-new chic—— this ten-story, white brick-and-steel number is a fun and relaxing place to stay. The interior décor is mod mimimalist but done with eye-catching tubular chairs, super-sophisticated colors, and fine wood inlays; the size of most guest rooms is vast (as are the sea-view balconies). Service is excellent, partly because wings of the hotel are apartment residences. Downstairs, Le Cercle bar is very South Beach——giant rose photos pulse with colors——while Le Park 45 soars with glass windows and a nouvelle menu. Forget all those Michael Caine white-suited wannabees: this is today's Cannes——hip, young, and stylish. **Pros:** capacious room size; high-design furnishings; a good-to-be-alive vibe; friendly staff. **Cons:** guest rooms may be too modern for their own good——takes some doing to figure out all the buttons and controls. ⊠*45 bd. de la Croisette 06140* ☎*04–93–38–15–45* ⊕*www. grand-hotel-cannes.com* ⮑*70 rooms, six suites* ⭤*In-room: refrigerator, Ethernet, Wi-Fi. In-hotel: restaurant, bar, parking (fee)* ⊟*AE, DC, MC, V.*

$$$$ 🏨**Inter-Continental Carlton Cannes.** Used by Hitchcock as a suitably
★ glamorous frame for Grace Kelly in *To Catch a Thief,* this neoclassical landmark built in 1911 staked out the best position early on, with La Croisette seeming to radiate symmetrically from its figurehead waterfront site. No discreet setback here: the Carlton sits right on the sidewalk—the better for you to be seen on the popular brasserie's terrace, made even more noticeable by the gleaming, renovated facade. Seven sea-view suites are each named after a film star and decorated in Hollywood style. The main film festival banquets take place in its gilt-and-marble Grand Salon, as do, alas, year-round conferences. Seafront rooms have a retro Laura Ashley look; those in the back compensate with cheery Provençal prints. **Pros:** sense of history; great for star-spotting. **Cons:** some rooms are faded; outrageous cost of extras such as Internet and drinks. ⊠*58 bd. de la Croisette* ☎*04–93–06–40–06* ⊕*www.ichotelsgroup.com* ⮑*338 rooms, 35 suites* ⭤*In-room: refrigerator, Internet, Wi-Fi. In-hotel: 3 restaurants, bar, gym, spa, Internet terminal, Wi-Fi, parking (fee), some pets allowed* ⊟*AE, DC, MC.*

$$$$ 🏨**Martinez.** A Hollywood-style face-lift restored the Art Deco Martinez to a theatrical version of its original 1930s glamour. Renovated guest rooms have either a splashy neo-Deco or more sober look; avoid those on the interior overlooking the grim parking lot. The Palme d'Or restaurant overlooking La Croisette has a plush, extravagant burled-wood and ebony interior worthy of Napoléon (or Joan Collins). But despite all that, chef Christian Sinicropi draws lavish praise for his modern Mediterranean cuisine: red mullet fillets with squid salad and seaweed, pigeon with merguez sausage and Madeira sauce. This excellence carries over to the beach restaurant, considered to be the best of its kind

in Cannes. **Pros:** glamorous setting; generally excellent service; spacious bathrooms. **Cons:** be prepared to pay for extras such as a day on the hotel's private beach. ⊠*73 bd. de la Croisette,* ☎*04–92–98–73–00* ⊕*www.hotel-martinez.com* ⤴*369 rooms, 24 apartments* ⟁*In-room: refrigerator, Internet, Wi-Fi. In-hotel: 2 restaurants, bars, pool, spa, beachfront, Internet terminal, parking (paid), some pets allowed* ⊟*AE, DC, MC, V.*

$$$ ⬜**Splendid.** If you covet a waterfront position but can't afford the grand hotels on La Croisette, consider this traditional 1873 palace overlooking La Pantiéro and the Old Port. Maintained in simple comfort, it offers freshly decorated rooms and up-to-date bathrooms, particularly the recently modernized ones facing the sea. Small doubles take in spectacular seaside views; some first-floor rooms have terraces. It's family run and thus full of personal touches: flowers and fruit in rooms, robes and kitchenettes in those with sea views, and pretty Provençal furniture in the breakfast room. **Pros:** central location; balconies and terraces (some rooms). **Cons:** "Old Europe" feel (handheld showers, curtains that let in the light from the street). ⊠*Allées de la Liberté, entrance at 4–6 rue Félix-Faure,* ☎*04–97–06–22–22* ⊕*www. splendid-hotel-cannes.fr* ⤴*60 rooms* ⟁*In-room: kitchen, refrigerator, Internet. In-hotel: some pets allowed* ⊟*AE, DC, MC, V* ⊗*Closed 1st 2 wks in Jan.*

$$–$$$ ⬜**Molière.** Plush, intimate, and low-key, this hotel, set a couple of min-
★ utes' walk from the Croisette and near the city's main shopping street, has pretty tile baths and rooms in cool shades of peach with white-waxed oak. Nearly all overlook the vast, enclosed front garden, where palms and cypresses shade terrace tables, and breakfast is served in the garden most of the year. **Pros:** good breakfast; terraces overlooking garden. **Cons:** handheld showers. ⊠*5 rue Molière,* ☎*04–93–38–16–16* ⊕*www.hotel-moliere.com* ⤴*24 rooms* ⟁*In-hotel: bar, Wi-Fi, some pets allowed* ⊟*AE, MC, V* ⊗*Closed mid-Nov.–late Dec.* ⦿*BP.*

$$–$$$ ⬜**Renoir.** This graceful former mansion is on a quiet backstreet in a residential neighborhood only a few blocks back from the center and beach (some suites even have sea views), but it feels like another world. Highly charged sunflower prints (none of the ubiquitous pink Art Deco), the scent of lavender, and kitchenettes in every suite create a sense of Provence instead of the Côte d'Azur. Sea-view rooms overlook a busier street; for maximum quiet, ask for the backstreet side. **Pros:** spacious rooms; generous breakfast. **Cons:** sea-view rooms not worth the extra money; small elevator and steep steps at the entrance. ⊠*7 rue Edith Cavell,* ☎*04–92–99–62–62* ⊕*www.hotel-renoir-cannes. com* ⤴*10 rooms, 17 suites* ⟁*In-room: kitchen, refrigerator, Wi-Fi. In-hotel: bar, parking (paid), some pets allowed* ⊟*AE, DC, MC, V.*

$–$$ ⬜**La Villa Tosca.** Between the train station and the beach, this apparently modest little hotel run by smiley staff has more than its share of charm. Recent renovations have retained the marble fireplaces and original ceiling moldings while adding contemporary furnishings that contributes to the character of each room. Vintage framed postcards and black-and-white portraits line the bright breakfast room, which has a bar, long shared table, and lounge area. It's worth spending a little more on one of the superior rooms, which are much more spacious than the standards; some rooms have sunny balconies. **Pros:** helpful staff; charming breakfast room. **Cons:** standard rooms are small; reports of poor sound insulation between rooms. ⊠ *11 rue Hoche,* ☎*04–93–38–34–40* ⊕*www.villa-tosca.com* ⇆*22 rooms* ⌂*In-room: refrigerator, Wi-Fi* ⊟*AE, DC, MC, V.*

\$ ★ 🏨**Albert Ier.** In a quiet residential area above the Forville market—a 10-minute walk uphill from La Croisette and beaches—this neo-deco mansion has pretty pastel rooms (recently equipped with Wi-Fi) as well as tidy tile baths and an enclosed garden. You can have breakfast on the flowered, shady terrace or in the family-style salon. The hotel has had one owner since 1980, and it shows in the details. **Pros:** family-run feel; outdoor space; private parking. **Cons:** rather anonymous decor in the rooms. ⊠*68 av. de Grasse,* ☎*04–93–39–24–04* ⊕*www.hotel albert1ercannes.com* ⇆*11 rooms* ⌂*In-room: no a/c (some), refrigerator, Wi-Fi. In-hotel: Internet terminal, parking (free), some pets allowed* ⊟*MC, V.*

NIGHTLIFE & THE ARTS

As befits a glamorous seaside resort, Cannes has two casinos. The famous **Casino Croisette** (⊠*Palais des Festivals* ☎*04–92–98–78–00*), which traces its pedigree to 1907, draws more crowds to its slot machines than any other casino in France. The **Carlton Casino Club** (⊠*58 bd. de la Croisette* ☎*04–93–68–00–33*), a relative newcomer to the Cannes nightlife scene, encourages an exclusive feeling in its posh seventh-floor hideaway.

After sipping your aperitif at Pastis, take in the scene at the always-packed **Les Coulisses** (⊠*29 rue du Commandant André* ☎*04–92–99–17–17*). The place to shake your booty until dawn is incontestably the cavernous **Le Baoli** (⊠*Port Pierre Canto* ☎*04–93–43–03–43*), where the odd celebrity has been known to alight. **Le Loft** (⊠*13 rue du Dr Monod*), upstairs from the style-conscious Tantra, attracts a youthful, glamorous set.

During the **International Film Festival** the first two weeks in May, Cannes becomes virtually insane with more than 30,000 actors, producers, directors, and other accredited professionals of the seventh art, 3,500 journalists, and 200,000 tourists. It all adds up to crowds, hordes of police, barely suppressed chaos, and a certain manic pushiness from anyone who isn't Sharon Stone—who, incidentally, strolls up those celebrated red-carpeted steps of the Palais des Festivals (⊕*www.palaisdesfestivals.com*), shoes dangling off her fingers and a large, relaxed smile on her face. But likely you won't be able to catch a glimpse of her; it's impossible unless you're a linebacker, or just plain crazy enough to wait outside with the other hundred-thousand starstruck individuals.

SPORTS & THE OUTDOORS

Most of the **beaches** along La Croisette are owned by hotels and/or restaurants, though this doesn't necessarily mean the hotels or restaurants front the beach. It does mean they own a patch of beachfront bearing their name, from which they rent out chaises, mats, and umbrellas to the public and hotel guests (€15–€25 per day). One of the most fashionable is the Carlton Hotel's beach. Other beaches where you must pay a fee include the stretch belonging to the Martinez, which is the largest in Cannes, Long Beach, and Rado Plage. You can easily recognize public beaches by the crowds; they're interspersed between the color-coordinated private-beach umbrellas, and offer simple open showers and basic

> **STAR-GAZING?**
>
> Remember, the film screenings are *not* open to the public and the stars themselves no longer grace cafés, beaches, or the morning market; they hide in the privacy of the Hôtel du Cap–Eden Roc on the Cap d'Antibes. Your best bets are the red carpet events at the Palais des Festivals.

toilets. To be slightly removed from the city traffic and crowds, head west of town where the open stretches of sand run uninterrupted toward Mandelieu.

Sailboats can be rented—along with the staff and skipper to sail them—at **Locarama Rent a Boat** (⊠ *13 rue Latour Maubourg* ☎ *08–92–68–11–85* ⊕ *www.cannesboat.com*). A wide range of boats are available from **Le Club Nautique La Croisette** (⊠ *Plage Pointe Palm-Beach* ☎ *04–93–43–09–40*). The **Centre Nautique Municipal** (⊠ *9 rue Esprit-Violet* ☎ *04–93–47–40–55*) has a private windsurfing base off Ile Ste-Marguerite, and organizes diving sorties. The **Majestic Ski Club** (*Ponton du Majestic* ⊠ *At the Majestic private beach* ☎ *04–92–98–77–47*) can take you waterskiing, or pull you on a ski-board, an inflatable chair, or up over the water with a parachute.

Bicycles (⊠ *Pl. de la Gare*) can be rented from the train station for €20.

SHOPPING

Whether you're window-shopping or splurging on that little Galliano number in the Dior window, you'll find some of the best shopping outside Paris on the streets off La Croisette. For stores carrying designer names, try **Rond-point Duboys-d'Angers** off **Rue Amouretti**, **Rue des Serbes**, and **Rue des Belges**, all perpendicular to the waterfront. **Rue d'Antibes** is the town's main shopping drag, home base to every kind of clothing and shoe shop, as well as mouthwatering candy, fabric, and home-design stores. **Rue Meynadier** mixes trendy young clothes with high-end food specialties.

You can find almost any item, from moth-eaten uniforms to second-hand gravy boats, at the **brocante market** (⊠ *Allées de la Liberté*) that springs up every Saturday. The permanent **Marché Forville**, at the foot of Le Suquet, has every kind of fresh and regional food in its picturesque booths every morning but Monday, from 7 AM to 1 PM. On Mondays it fills up with flea-market wares and brocante from 8 to 6. On the first and third Saturday of each month, old books, posters, and postcards are sold at the **Marché du Livre Ancien et des Vieux Papiers** (*Antique Books and Paper Market* ⊠ *Pl. de la Justice*).

EATING WELL ON THE FRENCH RIVIERA

In these parts, particularly in the bigger cities, you can savor a *salade niçoise* or *soupe de poisson* (fish soup) on a sunny terrace at any time of day. The Niçois, in particular, celebrate snacking, and this city alone in France is famous for its street food. But don't bring high culinary expectations to the top people-watching venues, such as the Cours Saleya in Nice or the Vieux Port in Cannes, though it's a safe bet that the dry local rosé will be well chilled, and the food fresh, if not elaborate. As a rule, restaurants in the Old Towns of Nice, Cannes, or Antibes stick to traditional fare; the more inventive chefs tend to set up shop a little off the beaten path. You'll find these ambitious chefs in picture-perfect hill towns such as Mougins, while the smaller villages of the *arrière-pays* (backcountry) remain bastions of rustic traditional cooking. Here, you're unlikely to find a restaurant that will serve outside conventional mealtimes—entire towns indulge in the afternoon *sieste*.

This sunny, sea-warmed area mixes the best of Provençal specialties with fresh Mediterranean fish, including succulent fillets of *rouget* (mullet) and *loup* (sea bass), often served with pungent garlic sauce or grilled with a crunch of anise-perfumed fennel. Along the coast and into the hills, your plate will often be garnished with ratatouille, the garlicky

vegetable stew of sun-plumped eggplant, zucchini, and tomato. Zucchini flowers often appear on the table, too, stuffed and fried in batter. As a gateway port intimately allied with Genoa and Liguria and influenced by input from Corsica and North Africa, Nice developed a unique cuisine. In the Old Town off Place Garibaldi, in street stands and *traiteurs* (food shops), you can sample Niçois specialties such as *salade niçoise*, usually a confetti-bright mix of tomatoes, green beans, potatoes, eggs, anchovies or tuna (though true *salad niçoise* contains no cooked vegetables), and the signature tiny, shiny, black, violet, and green olives of Nice. Equally ubiquitous is the *pissaladière*, the father of modern pizza. It's a good picnic takeout, as is a hefty *pan bagnat*, a fat bun stuffed to bursting with tuna, hard-cooked eggs, tomatoes, peppers, and olives. Venture farther to find backstreet exotica: *socca*, a paste of ground chickpeas spread on a griddle and scraped up like a gritty pancake; *petits farcis*, a selection of red peppers, zucchini, and eggplant stuffed with spicy sausage paste and roasted; and sardine *beignets*, fresh, whole sardines fried in a thick puff of spicy batter, eaten crunchy bones and all. For a cook's tour of the region's great food, don't miss the special photo-feature, La Cuisine de Soleil, in Chapter 4.

SIDE TRIP FROM CANNES: ILES DE LÉRINS

15–20 minutes by ferry off the coast of Cannes.

GETTING HERE

Buy your tickets to Ile Ste-Marguerite island from one of the ferry companies at the booths on Cannes's Vieux Port; look for the **Horizon Company** (⊠ *Vieux Port, Quai des Iles, Larbeuf parking lot* ☎ *04–92–98–71–36*) or **Trans Côte d'Azur** (⊠ *Vieux Port, Quai des Iles, Lar-*

beuf parking lot ☎*04–92–98–71–30* ⊕*www.trans-cote-azur.com*). It's a 15-minute ride (€11 round-trip; daily approximate every hour on the hour from 9 AM to 5 PM, last boat back at 6 PM).

Boats to the Ile St-Honorat are run by the monks who inhabit the island and tickets must be purchased from their own company, **Planaria** (⊠*In front of the Sofitel at Quai St-Pierre* ☎*04–92–98–71–38*). Ile St-Honorat can be reached in 20 minutes (€11 round-trip) from in front of the Sofitel at Quai St-Pierre every hour from 8 to noon and at 2, 3, 4:30, and 5:30 (the last boat back is at 6 PM).

EXPLORING

When you're glutted on glamour and tired of dodging limos, skaters, and the leavings of dyed-to-match poodles, catch a boat from Cannes's Vieux Port to one of the two Iles de Lérins (Lérins Islands). On one of these two lovely getaways you can find car-free peace and lose yourself in a tropical landscape of palms, pines, and tidal pools. Ste-Marguerite Island has more in the way of attractions: a ruined prison-fortress, a museum, and a handful of restaurants. Smaller and wilder, St-Honorat Island is dominated by its active monastery and the ruins of its 10th-century original.

Allow at least a half day to enjoy either island; you can see both if you get an early start, but might regret the obligation to move on once you've arrived on the first one. Although Ste-Marguerite has some restaurants and snack shops, you would be wise to bring along a picnic and drinks; you'll have to do this if you spend the day on the noncommercial St-Honorat.

The larger of the two islands, Ile Ste-Marguerite, is covered with dense growths of palms, pines, and eucalyptus. On arriving, head left up the tiny main street lined with restaurants and snack shops, or cut uphill and left toward **Fort Royal,** built by Richelieu in the 18th century and improved by Vauban. The views over the ramparts to the rocky island coast and the open sea are as evocative as the prison buildings, one of which supposedly locked up the Man in the Iron Mask. Behind the prison buildings you'll find the **Musée de la Mer** (*Marine Museum* ☎*04–93–43–18–17*), with its Roman boat dating from the 1st century BC and its collection of amphorae and pottery recovered from ancient shipwrecks. The museum's hours are: October through March, Tuesday through Sunday 10:30–12:15 and 2:15–4:30; April through June, Tuesday through Sunday 10:30–12:15 and 2:15–5:30; and July and August, Tuesday through Sunday 10:30–12:15 and 2:15–6:30. Admission is €3. If you have time or prefer nature to history, head right from the port and follow the signs along the coast to the small **bird preserve,** populated by cormorants and talkative gulls, and the quiet beach beyond, a paradise of tidal pools which seethe with marine life at low tide.

Smaller and wilder than Ste-Marguerite, Ile St-Honorat is anchored by its active monastery, which traces its foundation here to the 4th century. That's when St-Honorat sought solitude on this island—and was swiftly followed by devotees also seeking solitude. The large 19th-century structure his heirs inhabit today encloses many older chapels and harbors a shop where the monks sell their herb liqueur, called Lerina. The majority of the island is covered with thick forests of pine and eucalyptus that belong to the monastery, punctuated by small chapels and crisscrossed by public paths. Wild and isolated rock-bound shores surround the island. On the island's southernmost point, just below its modern replacement, the remains of the 10th-century fortified **monastery** send thick walls plunging into the sea; the walls were built to protect the monks from marauding pirates. The monastery's medieval and magical complex of chapels, courtyards, and views from the crenellated rampart is worth the climb. ☎04–92–99–54–00 ⌧€2 July–Aug.; free Sept.–June ☉Sept.–June, Mon.–Sat. 9–4, Sun. 2–4; July–Aug., daily 10–noon and 2:30–4:30.

WHERE TO EAT

$$
Fodor'sChoice
★

✕**La Tonnelle.** It's hard to believe that this tranquil island is only 20 minutes from Cannes by boat, and even more so as you linger under the shade of the trellis at this classy restaurant run by Brother Marie-Pâques from the Ile St-Honorat monastery and chef Christian Nevière. The new owners have preserved the faded charm of this restaurant dating from the 19th century while giving it a St-Tropez feel, thanks to black-and-white pictures of 1950s movie stars who dined here and a private boat that whisks customers directly from their luxury hotels to the restaurant's pier. The menu focuses on the freshest grilled fish, with prices that seem aimed at modern-day celebrities, but you can also have a lighter (and cheaper) meal in the café. Take the opportunity to sample the wines, liqueurs, and eaux-de-vie that are produced by the island's busy monks. ⌧Abbaye Notre-Dame de Lérins, Ile Saint-Honorat ☎04–93–39–62–21 ⌲Reservations essential ▭AE, MC, V ☉No dinner.

INTO THE PAYS GRASSOIS

Just behind Cannes, the hills that block the mountain winds rise, sun-bleached and jungle-green. From the well-groomed Provençal village-cum-bedroom community of Mougins to the hill-city of Grasse, the hills are tiled with greenhouses that feed the region's perfume factories. Grasse itself supports modern industry and tourist industry with aplomb, offering a dense Italian-style Old Town as well. Beyond, you can head for the hills of the arrière-pays on the Route Napoléon.

MOUGINS

8 km (5 mi) north of Cannes, 11 km (7 mi) northwest of Antibes, 32 km (20 mi) southwest of Nice.

GETTING HERE

Getting to Mougins by public transport is time-consuming. Line No. 24 of the Sillages bus company goes to Mougins every 30 minutess 7 AM–7 PM (tickets €1) from in front of the SNCF train station in Cannes (Rue Jean-Jaurès) but the journey takes more than an hour, compared to 15 minutes by car from central Cannes. So if you don't have time to burn, opt for a taxi (around €20). From Nice, the train to Cannes costs €5.80 one way.

Passing through Mougins, a popular summer-house community convenient to Cannes and Nice, you may perceive little more than sleek, upscale suburban sprawl. But in 1961 Picasso found more to admire and settled into a *mas* (farmhouse) that became a mecca for artists and art lovers; he died there in 1973. Despite overbuilding today, Mougins claims extraordinary views over the coast and an Old Town (which is a *zone piétonne,* or pedestrian zone), on a hilltop above the fray, that has retained a pretty, ultragentrified charm. You'll see quite a few off-duty celebrities here and any number of wealthy Parisians who have chosen this for a Riviera pied-à-terre. Where they go, noted chefs follow, and Mougins is now a byword in gourmet circles.

VISITOR INFORMATION
Mougins Tourist Office (⊠ *15 av. Jean-Charles Mallet, Mougins* ☎*04–93–75–87–67* ⊕ *www.mougins-cotedazur.org*).

EXPLORING
You can find Picasso's final home and see why of all spots in the world he chose this one, by following D35 to the ancient ecclesiastical site of **Notre-Dame-de-Vie** (⊠ *Chemin de la Chapelle*). This was the hermitage, or monastic retreat, of the Abbey of Lérins, and its 13th-century bell tower and arcaded chapel form a pretty ensemble in a magnificent setting. Approached through an alley of ancient cypress, the house Picasso shared with his wife, Jacqueline, overlooks the broad bowl of the countryside (a bit blighted by modern construction). The estate has, alas, been enclosed in cane fencing by his heirs, who fight to preserve their privacy from art-loving pilgrims. The chapel is only open during Sunday Mass at 9 AM. Elsewhere in town are a small **Musée Municipal,** set in the 17th-century St-Bernardin Chapel, and a huge **Musée de l'Automobiliste,** with 100 vintage cars, in a modern structure on the Aire des Bréguières.

WHERE TO EAT & STAY

$$$$ ✕**Le Moulin de Mougins.** Housed in a 16th-century olive mill on a hill
★   above the coastal fray, this sophisticated inn houses one of the most famous restaurants in the region (€45–€150 prix fixe). Culinary wizard Roger Vergé sold it a few years ago to promising young chef Alain Llorca, and the loyal clientele watched in wary anticipation as the proud new owner initiated a radical face-lift for the much-loved institution in white, pink, and plum tones with remarkable silver and gold Baroque chandeliers. Sculptures by César, Arman, Folon, and guest artists stand beside the signatures of the restaurant's famous guests— Sharon Stone, Elizabeth Taylor—and the chairs are plush comfort. The menu got a full overhaul, too; the result is sun-drenched Mediterranean cooking that is excellent, if not quite as awe-inspiring as Vergé's cuisine. The menu is divided into classic, contemporary, and light dishes, with a €48 lunch menu that might include Basque ravioli (filled with vegetables and Espelette pepper), the tenderest breast of chicken with

lightly cooked summer vegetables, and a rose-flavored macaroon with sorbet. In summer dine outside under the awnings. The 11 adjoining guest rooms are elegant, if slightly lacking character; the four apartments small but deluxe. ⊠*Notre-Dame-de-Vie* ☎*04–93–75–78–24* ⊕*www.moulin-mougins.com* ↷ ⊟*AE, DC, MC, V.*

$$$ ✕**Le Bistrot de Mougins.** Set in an old 15th-century stable with high, curved brick ceilings and no terrace, this is a restaurant that plays up to its historical past. Rustic chairs and flowered tablecloths offer a real picnic-in-the-country feel. Simple, Provençal-style dishes from chef Jean-Pierre Larata are hard to beat: escargots in butter and herbs, steak with a green peppercorn sauce, or sea bass grilled with fennel are top choices. Wines are also well-selected: look for bottles from Bordeaux and Burgundy alongside the expected Provençal rosés. ⊠*Place du Village* ☎*04–93–75–78–34* ⊟*MC, V* ⊙*Closed Dec.; closed late Jan.–early Feb. and Juy.–Aug. No lunch Thurs.–Tues., Sept.–Jun. Thurs.–Mon.*

$$$$ ⛫**Le Mas Candille.** Nestled in a huge private park, this 18th-century mas has been cleverly transformed into an ultraluxurious hotel. Today, this secluded property with sweeping views over Cannes acts as a magnet for movie stars and politicians. Guest rooms—all cool colors and country chic—are very refined: a profusion of pillows, heated towels, and all the hidden electrical hookups you could possibly need. Antique wallpapers, vintage furniture, and many other high-gloss touches make this place *Elle Decor*–worthy, if not really authentic to the locale. The opulent, saffron-hue restaurant is the well-ordered domain of chef Serge Gouloumès, whose impressive résumé includes stints at Ma Maison in Beverly Hills and the Poisson d'Or in Saint Martin. His succulent menus have caused quite a stir in gastronomic circles; watch for items like wild bass in a rosemary tempura crust or foie gras tatin with Armagnac. **Pros:** spectacular location; beautiful swimming pool; excellent restaurant. **Cons:** children under 16 are banned from using some facilities, including the main swimming pool; expensive breakfast is nothing special; sleepy in the off-season. ⊠*Bd. Clément Rebuffel,* ☎*04–92–28–43–43* ⊕*www.lemascandille.com* ↷*40 rooms* ⌂*Inroom: refrigerator, Wi-Fi. In-hotel: restaurant, golf course, pools, gym, spa, parking, some pets allowed* ⊟*AE, DC, MC, V.*

$$$$ ⛫**Royal Mougins Golf Resort Hotel.** What it lacks in Provençal character, this plush hotel opened in 2008 makes up for in modern comforts: decorated in soothing tones of beige and gray, each suite is an independent apartment with a separate living room and kitchenette. Most of the suites have vast terraces overlooking this exclusive and challenging 18-hole golf course with eight lakes, which has 600 members worldwide but is also open to guests at the hotel at a preferential rate with a maximum handicap of 28 for men and 32 for women (translation: the hotel only wants guests who are experienced golfers). The spa is located in an 18th-century bastide a few steps from the green, and the restaurant La Terrasse du 18 serves Provençal cuisine with an ethereal modern touch. **Pros:** for experienced golfers, the advantages of sleeping across from one of the world's best golf courses are obvious. **Cons:** the resort feels so much like another world that it might be tempting

not to bother with sightseeing. ☒*424 av. du Roy,* ☎*04–92–92–49–69* ⊕*www.royalmougins.fr* ⇌*29 suites* ♿*In-room: refrigerator, Wi-Fi. In-hotel: restaurant, bar, golf course, pool, spa, parking* ▤*AE, D, MC, V* ⦿*BP.*

$$$–$$$$ ☷ **Le Manoir de l'Etang.** Once a country-style inn, this hilltop hotel with expansive valley views has gone upscale since changing hands a few years ago. The Provençal 19th-century manor house is perched over a lotus pond; inside, guest rooms are *vacance*-stylish, most with a light and airy feel, accented with some striking nouvelle-mod pieces. Il Lago, the superb (and pricey) restaurant specializes in elegant Italian food made with ingredients from Piemont: perhaps gnocchi stuffed with goat cheese and arugula and served with smoked tomato sauce and bacon. Views of the surrounding countryside are also beautiful, as is the spare decor, and the price is gentle considering the competition. **Pros:** breathtaking setting; exceptional Italian restaurant. **Cons:** stone steps difficult for those with mobility problems; some might find the decor too minimalist. ☒*Bois de Fond Merle, Rte. d'Antibes,* ☎*04–92–28–36–00* ⊕*www.manoir-de-letang.com* ⇌*20 rooms* ♿*In-room: refrigerator. In-hotel: restaurant, bar, pool, Wi-Fi, parking, some pets allowed* ▤*AE, DC, MC, V* ⊘*Closed Nov.–Mar.*

GRASSE

10 km (6 mi) northwest of Mougins, 17 km (10½ mi) northwest of Cannes, 22 km (14 mi) northwest of Antibes, 42 km (26 mi) southwest of Nice.

GETTING HERE
Trains run approximately once an hour from Nice and Cannes to Grasse on the Mandelieu-Ventimiglia line, taking about 70 minutes from Nice (€8.40 one way) and 25 minutes from Cannes (€3.70). Bus No. 500 runs from the central bus station in Nice (5 bd. Jean-Jaurès) to Grasse about every 40 mins (about 90 mins). From Cannes, lines Nos. 600 and 610 run from in front of the SNCF train station (Rue Jean-Jaurès) about every 20 mins (every hr on Sunday); the 600 is a little faster, reaching Grasse in 40 mins. All bus tickets in the region cost €1.

VISITOR INFORMATION
Grasse Tourist Office (☒*Palais des Congrés, 22 cours Honoré Cresp, Grasse* ☎*04–93–36–66–66* ⊕*www.grasse.fr*).

EXPLORING
High on a plateau over the coast, this busy, modern town is usually given wide berth by anyone who isn't interested in its prime tourist industry, the making of perfume. But its unusual art museum featuring works of the 18th-century artist Fragonard and the picturesque backstreets of its very Mediterranean Old Town round out a pleasant day trip from the coast.

It's the Côte d'Azur's hothouse climate, nurturing nearly year-round shows of tropical-hue flowers, that fosters Grasse's perfume industry. The heady, heavy scent of orange blossoms, pittosporum, roses, lavender, jasmine, and mimosa wraps around you like silk in gardens along the coast, especially on a sultry night, and since time immemorial people have tried to capture that seductive scent in a bottle. In the past, perfume makers laid blossoms facedown in a lard-smeared tray, then soaked the essence away in alcohol; nowadays the scents are condensed in vast copper stills. Only the essential oils are kept, and

> ### SCENTS AND SENSIBILITY
>
> It takes 10,000 flowers to produce 2.2 pounds of jasmine petals and nearly 1 ton of petals to distill 1½ quarts of essence; this helps justify the sky-high cost of perfumes, priced by the proportion of essence their final blend contains.

the water thrown away—except rose water and orange water, which find their way into delicately perfumed pastries.

In Paris and on the outskirts of Grasse, these scents are blended by a professional *nez,* or "nose," who must distinguish some 500 distinct scents and may be able to identify 3,000. The products carry the household names of couturiers like Chanel and Dior, perfume houses like Guerlain. The laboratories where these great blends are produced are off-limits to visitors, but to accommodate the crowds of inquisitive scent-seekers, Grasse has set up three factories that create simple blends and demonstrate some of the industry's production techniques. You pass through a boutique of house perfumes on the way back to the bus and … well, you get the idea.

Fragonard (✉ *20 bd. Fragonard* ☎ *04–93–36–44–65*) occupies a factory built in 1782; it displays a small collection of stills, perfume bottles, and "necessaries" for women's—and men's—toilettes. Guided visits are free, just reserve in advance for groups.

Galimard (✉ *73 rte. de Cannes* ☎ *04–93–09–20–00* ⊕ *www.galimard. com*) offers two-hour "studios des fragrances," during which the house "nose" will coach you in designing your own personally labeled scent (€35, by reservation only). ⊘ *Sept.–June, daily 9–12:30 and 2–6:30, July–Aug., daily 9–6:30 Sun.*

Molinard (✉ *60 bd. Victor-Hugo* ☎ *04–93–36–01–62*) offers 90-minute workshops where you can blend your own scent (€40 per person, reserve in advance).

Fodor'sChoice ★ The **Musée International de la Parfumerie** *(International Museum of Perfume),* not to be confused with the small museum in the Fragonard perfume factory that calls itself the Musée de la Parfumerie, reopened in October 2008 after a spectacular €11 million renovation. Now twice its original size, it traces the 4,000-year history of perfume, cosmetics, and soaps with a display of 50,000 objects. Architect Frédéric Jung created a transparent nave between the original museum and the two adjoining buildings and incorporated the 15th-century ramparts that surround the museum into his striking design. Inside is a room equipped with pot-bellied copper stills and old machines; labels guide you through the steps of production in different eras. It also has a series of displays of exquisite perfume bottles and toiletries. There's even Marie Antoinette's *nécessaire* (travel kit). ⊠*8 pl. du Cours* ☏*04–97–05–58–00.*

The **Musée Fragonard** isn't named for the perfume factory, rather, it's the other way around. The grand old Fragonard family of Grasse figured large in the town's 17th-century industry—that of making perfumed leather gloves. (The scents themselves eventually outstripped the gloves in popularity.) The family's most famous son, Jean-Honoré Fragonard (1732–1806), became one of the great French artists of the period, and during the Revolution lived in the family mansion that houses the museum today. The lovely villa, decorated with reproductions of the rococo panels he created (the originals are at the Frick Museum in New York), contains a collection of drawings, engravings, and paintings by the artist, including two graceful self-portraits. Other rooms in the mansion display works by Fragonard's son Alexandre-Evariste and his grandson Théophile. ⊠*23 bd. Fragonard* ☏*04–93–36–93–10* ☏*€3.50* ☉*June–Sept., daily 10–7; Oct.–May, Wed.–Sun. 10–12:30 and 2–5:30.*

The **Musée d'Art et d'Histoire de Provence** *(Museum of the Art and History of Provence),* just down from the Fragonard perfumery, has a large collection of faïence from the region, including works from Moustiers, Biot, and Vallauris. Also on display in this noble 18th-century mansion are *santons* (terra-cotta figurines), furniture, local paintings, and folk costumes. ⊠*2 rue Mirabeau* ☏*04–93–36–80–20* ☏*€4* ☉*June–Sept., daily 10–7; Oct.–May, Wed.–Sun. 10–12:30 and 2–5:30.*

To lose yourself in the dense labyrinth of the **Vieille Ville** *(Old Town),* follow Rue Ossola down into the steep, narrow streets, enclosed on each side by shuttered houses five and six stories tall. Several little bakeries offer *fougassette à la fleur d'oranger,* a Grasse specialty profiting from the orange water created in its factories; the sweet, briochelike pastry is heavy with orange-blossom perfume.

On a cliff-top overlook at the Old Town's edge, the Romanesque **Cathédrale Notre-Dame-du-Puy** (⊠*Pl. du Petit Puy*) contains no fewer than three paintings by Rubens, a triptych by the famed 15th-century Provençal painter Louis Bréa, and *Lavement des Pieds* (*The Washing of the Feet*), by the young Fragonard.

The picturesque **Place aux Aires,** below the central cluster of museums and perfumeries, is lined with 17th- and 18th-century houses and their arcades. Every morning a flower market covers the square in Technicolor hues.

WHERE TO EAT & STAY

✗ **Café Arnaud.** Just off Place aux Aires, this easygoing corner bistro serves up inventive home cooking under a vaulted ceiling trimmed with grapevine stencils and pretty Provençal prints. The emphasis here is on traditional cooking: two of the new chef-owner's signature dishes are tête de veau (various bits of the veal head, formed into a terrine and served cold) and Niçois ravioli (filled with beef and chard). At lunch there's an imaginative fixed-price regional menu, which might include tomato baked with herbed chèvre, veal with pasta, or *pieds et paquets* (pigs' feet and tripe). ✉*10 pl. de la Foux* ☎*04–93–36–44–88* ⊟*AE, DC, MC, V.*

$$$$
Fodor'sChoice
★

🏠**La Bastide Saint-Antoine.** The cicadas live better than most humans at this picture-perfect 18th-century estate overlooking the Estéva, once home of an industrialist who hosted Kennedys and Rolling Stones. Now the domain of celebrated chef Jacques Chibois, it welcomes you with old stone walls, shaded walkways, an enormous pool, and a mouthwatering ocher-hue and blue-shutter mansion draped with red trumpet-flower begonia and purple bougainvillea. The guest rooms glossily mix Louis XVI–style chairs, Provençal embroidered bedspreads, and high-tech delights (massaging showers). Although the restaurant is excellent (try the extraordinary truffle, cream, and foie gras soup) and expensive (lobster with a black-olive fondue and beet juice will run you €60), lunch here is a bargain at €53. ✉*48 av. Henri-Dunant,* ☎*04–93–70–94–94* ⊕*www.jacques-chibois.com* ⇆*16 rooms* ⌂*In-room: refrigerator, Wi-Fi. In-hotel: restaurant, pool, gym, parking, some pets allowed* ⊟*AE, DC, MC, V.*

ROUTE NAPOLÉON

6

Extends 176 km (109 mi) from Grasse to Sisteron.

One of the most famous and panoramic roads in France, this was the route followed by Napoléon Bonaparte in 1815 after his escape from imprisonment on the Mediterranean island of Elba. Napoléon landed at Golfe-Juan, near Cannes, on March 1 and forged northwest to Grasse, then through dramatic, hilly countryside to Castellane, Digne, and Sisteron. In Napoléon's day, most of this road (now N85) was little more than a winding dirt track. Commemorative plaques bearing the imperial eagle stud the route, inspired by Napoléon's remark, "The eagle will fly from steeple to steeple until it reaches the towers of Notre-Dame." That prediction came true. Napoléon covered the 176 km (109 mi) from the coast to Sisteron in just four days, romped north through Grenoble and Burgundy, and entered Paris in triumph on May 20.

Though the mighty warrior officially started his journey through this region from the coast, the route between Golfe-Juan and Grasse is mostly urban tangle, with the Route Napoléon generally considered to start north of Grasse, when it opens into scenic countryside. Except for the occasional inn with the name Napoléon, there are no historic buildings or monuments, except for the plaques. There are a few lavender-honey stands and souvenir shacks, but they're few and far between. It is the panoramic views as the road winds its way up into the Alps that make this route worth traveling.

Unless you are heading north to Grenoble, you can easily make a circular day trip along the Route Napoléon, starting from the coast at Grasse. Without stopping, you could reach **Sisteron** in 90 minutes, so take your time and stop for a picnic along the way. Sisteron, which is guarded by a medieval citadel perched 1,650 feet above the river, is the gateway between Provence and the Alpine region of Dauphine. It's also famous for its tender lamb, favored by Provençal chefs. If you forge all the way to Sisteron, pick up A51 down to Aix-en-Provence, and then join A6 to return to the Côte d'Azur.

You can make a beeline up the Route Napoléon to Castellane and west to the Gorges du Verdon, the main tourist goal in the region, or take your time winding through the hill towns to the west. The hill towns just east of Grasse—Vence and St-Paul—are much more developed and more frequented by tourists.

VALBONNE

18 km (11 mi) north of Cannes, 14 km (9 mi) northwest of Antibes.

A kind of little-England-on-the-Brague (the river that flows through town), this fiercely Provençal hill town has been adopted by the British, especially those working at the nearby high-tech complex Sophia-Antipolis. Thus it exudes a peculiar kind of mixed-country charm, *plus Provençal que les Provençaux,* with a plethora of tasteful restorations. Its principal cachet is the novel layout of the Old Town, designed in a grid system in the 16th century by the monks of Lérins. A checkerboard of ruler-straight *ruelles* (little streets) lies within a sturdy rampart of wraparound houses; at the center, a grand *place* is framed by Renaissance arcades and shady elms.

WHERE TO EAT

$$$ ✕**Lou Cigalon.** For a taste of the Côte d'Azur at its most creative, visit
★ this wave-making restaurant overseen by chef Alain Parodi, with Sébastien Broda in the kitchen. Fixed-price menus start at €29 at lunch and go up to €105 for the evening tasting menu. Expect the unpredictable, such as langoustines with curry and clementines, or duck foie gras with sesame caramel and saffron, followed by waffle with quince jelly or a prune-and-Armagnac soufflé. The two dining rooms have old-fashioned charm with stone walls, wooden beams, and pottery by the Niçois artist Emmanuel Bailet. Watch out for the pricey wines, though the list is undeniably well selected and expertly presented. ✉ *4 bd. Carnot* ☎ *04–93–12–27–07* ☐ *AE, MC, V* ☉ *Closed Sun. and Mon.*

BETWEEN CANNES & NICE

The coastline spanning the brief distance from Cannes to Antibes and Nice has a personality all its own, combining some of the most accessible and democratic waterfront resorts (Juan-les-Pins, Villeneuve, and Cagnes) with one of the most elite (Cap d'Antibes). This is vacationland, with a culture of commercial entertainment that smacks of the worst of Florida in the '60s. Hot, poky N98, which goes from Antibes to Cagnes, crawls past a jungle of amusement parks, beach discos, and even a horse-race track. The hill towns of Vallauris and Biot cater to souvenir hunters and lunch sorties. Juan-les-Pins is a party town, its cafés and brasseries thriving into the wee hours. And the glass high-rise monstrosities curving over the waterfront below Cagnes and Villeneuve glow unnaturally bright until dawn. Yet minutes away on a peninsula jutting into the sea, the Cap d'Antibes floats aloof, its mansions and manicured gardens turning their backs on the cheaper real estate on the "mainland."

Everyone visiting this little piece of the Côte d'Azur, whether staying in a villa or a concrete cube, is after the same experience: to sit on a balcony, to listen to the waves washing over the sand, and to watch the sun setting over the oil-painted backdrop of the Alpes de Provence. Wherever you base yourself, you are always just a 20-minute zip from Cannes or Nice, and you can easily wend your way into the hills to visit the ancient villages of St-Paul, Vence, and beyond.

VALLAURIS

6 km (4 mi) northeast of Cannes, 6 km (4 mi) west of Antibes.

GETTING HERE

The SNCF Golfe-Juan train station is in Place Pierre Sémard in the center of Vallauris-Golfe-Juan. Tickets cost €4.80 one-way from Nice and €1.70 from Cannes. Buses 8 and 20, part of the Envibus network, run between the Golfe-Juan train station and Vallauris about every 20 minutes (40 minutes on Sundays). From place Guynemer in Antibes, Envibus Line 5 goes to Vallauris with frequent departures. Line 200, connecting Nice and Cannes, stops in Golfe-Juan and runs about every 40 mins. Bus tickets cost €1.

EXPLORING

This ancient village in the low hills above the coast, dominated by a blocky Renaissance château, owes its four-square street plan to a form of medieval urban renewal. Ravaged and eventually wiped out by waves of the plague in the 14th century, the village was rebuilt by 70 Genovese families imported by the Abbaye de Lérins in the 16th century to repopulate the abandoned site. They brought with them a taste for Roman planning—hence the grid format in the Old Town—but more important, a knack for pottery making. Their skills and the fine clay of Vallauris were a perfect marriage, and the village thrived as a pottery center for hundreds of years. In the 1940s Picasso found inspiration in the malleable soil and settled here, giving the flagging industry new life. Nowadays, Vallauris has a split personality: the commercial, souvenir-shop tourist section vaunting bins of pottery below, the dense medieval gridwork of the Old Town looming barren and isolated above, with little to see but laundry and cats.

During his years here, sequestered in a simple stone house, Picasso created pottery art with a single-minded passion, sometimes dozens of works a day. But he was a painter first and foremost, and he returned to that medium in 1952 to create one of his masterworks in the château's barrel-vaulted Romanesque chapel, the vast multipanel composition called *La Guerre et la Paix* (*War and Peace*)—a difficult and forceful work, created in broad, ruthlessly simplistic strokes in the heat of post-war inspiration. Today the chapel is part of the **Musée National**

Picasso, where several of Picasso's ceramic pieces are displayed along with a collection of pre-Columbian works. ⊠ *Pl. de la Libération, 06220* ☎*04–93–64–71–83* ⊠*€3.25* ☉*June–Sept., Wed.–Mon. 10–12:15 and 2–6; Oct.–May, Wed.–Mon. 10–12:15 and 2–5.*

WHERE TO EAT

$ ✕**Café Llorca.** Following in the ★ footsteps of many of France's finest chefs, Alain Llorca has opened a laid-back bistro with modern furniture and a shady terrace to complement his high-class restaurant in Mougins. With starters costing €5 to €11 and main courses at around €14, this is the place to get a tantalizing taste of his precise style. The menu mainly sticks to southern classics such as cheese ravioli with basil sauce and sole meunière with potato purée, both served so generously (in pottery dishes from Vallauris) that it's hard to find room for the pastries by Alain's talented brother Jean-Michel. The café serves breakfast as well as afternoon tea, and you can also stop by to pick up pastries or other treats from the épicerie. ⊠*Place Paul Isnard, 06220* ☎*04–93–64–30–42* ⊕*www.cafellorca.com* ⊟*AE, DC, MC, V.*

> **BRING HOME A PICASSO**
>
> Along **Rue Hoche** and throughout the lower village are shops and galleries crammed with bright pottery and ceramic art. Look for the more elegant **Galerie Madoura** (⊠*Rue Suzanne et Georges Ramié, 06220* ☎*04–93–64–66–39*), owned by the ceramic house with which Picasso worked and still run by descendants of his friends Georges and Suzanne Ramié. You can buy good limited-edition reproductions of his ceramics here.

ANTIBES

11 km (7 mi) northeast of Cannes, 15 km (9 mi) southeast of Nice.

GETTING HERE

Antibes has one central train station, the **Gare SNCF** (⊠*Pl. Pierre-Semard* ⊕*www.voyages-sncf.com*), which is at the far end of town but still within walking distance of the Vieille Ville and only a block or so from the beach. Local trains are frequent, coming from Nice (20 mins, €4), Juan-les-Pins, Biot, Cannes (10 mins, €3), and almost all other coastal towns. There are also high-speed TGVs (Trains à Grand Vitesse) that depart from Antibes. Bus service, available at Antibes's **Gare Routière** (bus station) (⊠*1 pl. Guynemer*) is supplied by both the **RCA** lines (☎*04–93–85–64–44* ⊕*www.rca.tm.fr*) and the **TAM** lines (☎*04–93–85–61–81* ⊕*www.lignedazur.com*). One example is the No. 200 RCA bus between Cannes and Antibes, which runs every 20 minutes and costs €1.30. To get to Cannes, Nice, Cagnes-sur-Mer, Juan-les-Pins, or to catch local buses—including one that threads the big Cap d'Antibes peninsula—wait at the different posts on Place du Général-de-Gaulle; most lines run every 20 minutes.

VISITOR INFORMATION

Antibes/Juan-les-Pins Tourist Office (✉ *11 pl. de Gaulle, Antibes* ☎ *04-92-90-53-00* ⊕ *antibes-juanlespins.com*).

EXPLORING

With its broad stone ramparts scalloping in and out over the waves and backed by blunt medieval towers and a skew of tile roofs, Antibes (pronounced Awn-*teeb*) is one of the most relentlessly romantic old towns on the Mediterranean coast. Stroll Promenade Amiral-de-Grasse along the crest of Vauban's sea walls, watch the cormorants diving off jagged black rock and sleek yachts purring out to sea, and you'll understand why this place inspired Picasso to paint on a panoramic scale. Even more intoxicating, just off the waterfront, is the souklike maze of old streets, its market filled with fresh fish and goat cheese, wild herbs, and exotic spices. This is **Vieil Antibes,** and to our mind these Old Town streets have few peers for their pretty waywardness or achingly lovely charm. Their ambience is nearly Italianate, perhaps no great surprise considering that Antibes's great fort marked the border between Italy and France right up to the 19th century. So if you head to Antibes, be sure to set aside an afternoon to explore these atmospherey streets and, just adjacent to the south, the **Commune Libre du Safranier** (Free Commune of Safranier), a magical little 'hood with a character all its own. Here, not far off the seaside promenade and focused around the Place du Safranier, tiny houses hang heavy with flowers and vines and neighbors carry on conversations from window to window across the stone-stepped Rue du Bas-Castelet. It is said that Place du Safranier was once a tiny fishing port; now it's the scene of this sub-village's festivals.

Named Antipolis—meaning across from (*anti*) the city (*polis*)—by the Greeks who founded it in the 4th century BC, Antibes has always been the antithesis of Nice, gazing quietly across the harbor at its powerful and vital neighbor. Antibes flourished under the Romans' aristocratic rule, with an amphitheater, aqueducts, and baths. The early Christians established their bishopric here, the site of the region's cathedral until the 13th century. It was in the Middle Ages that the kings of France began fortifying this key port town, an effort that culminated in the recognizable star-shaped ramparts designed by Vauban. The young general Napoléon once headed this stronghold, living with his family in a humble house in the Old Town; his mother washed their clothes in a stream. There's still a *lavoir* (public laundry fountain) in the Old Town where locals, not unlike Signora Bonaparte, rinse their clothes and hang them like garlands over the narrow streets.

Antibes has its glamorous side, too. Whether you approach the waterfront from the train station or park along the Avenue de Verdun, you'll first confront the awesome expanse of luxury yachts in the **Port Vauban.** Some of them stretch as much as 500 feet and swan back and forth at will between Greece, Saudi Arabia, and other ports of call. They won't find a more dramatic spot to anchor, with the tableau of snowy Alps looming behind and the formidable medieval block towers of the **Fort Carré** (Square Fort) guarding entry to the port. This superbly symmetrical island fortress was completed in 1565 and restored in 1967, but can

Continued on page 306

STROKES OF

Matisse, Henri (1869-1954) Blue Nude II, 1952

GENIUS

A kind of artistic Garden of Eden exists in the mind of many painters, a magical place painted in the vivid colors of imagination—a promised land where they can bask in warm sunshine nearly every day of the year, swim in a placid sea of incredible blue, daub flowers so colorful they would challenge even the most riotous palette, and live life as sensually as they sketch it.

This is the dream would-be Adams sought in the late 19th century when, inspired by Impressionist *plein-air* (open-air) painting, artists abandoned the airless studios of Paris for the sunkissed towns of the South of France. By the 1920s, a virtual migration of painters and sculptors heeded the siren call of the Mediterranean muse and began to colonize the Côte d'Azur. Signac made St-Tropez the Riviera's first "Greenwich Village"; Cannes attracted Picasso and Van Dongen; Haut-de-Cagnes and St-Paul-de-Vence lured Renoir, Soutine, and Modigliani; and Matisse and Dufy settled in Nice. A veritable "museum without walls," these locales went on to

Ceramic Plate by Picasso, Galerie Madoura

nurture some of the biggest isms in 20th-century art. Creativity was unleashed, cares forgotten, and *le bonheur de vie* —the happiness of life—became a forceful leitmotiv. The result was an outpouring of art whose exuberance and energy led to the paradise that exists here today: a tightly packed 100-mile stretch of coastline crammed with the houses, gardens, and towns that inspired these artists. Be content to leave their masterpieces to museums scattered around the world, and get ready to savor instead a host of virtual Matisses, 3-D Renoirs, and pop-up Picassos. This rainbow curve of a coast will prove to be an unforgettable road trip through the history of modern art.

by Robert I.C. Fisher

IN FOCUS STROKES OF GENIUS

THE MODERN ART ROAD

MATISSE Stroll the stone ramparts of medieval **Vence**, then head out to its New Town to exult in the beauty of Matisse's famous Chapelle du Rosaire, created in 1947. Matisse's last testament is a jewel of stained glass and tiled drawings.

SIGNAC, MODIGLIANI, BONNARD Hilltop **St-Paul-de-Vence** was rediscovered in the 1920s when the artists Signac, Modigliani, and Bonnard met at La Colombe d'Or, an inn whose legendary charm remains intact.

RENOIR At the foot of **Haut-de Cagnes** is the Villa "Les Collettes," the last home of Auguste Renoir. He painted his final Impressionist paintings in the two glassed-in studios here, but you can best channel his spirit in the magical garden.

FERNAND LÉGER planned to create a sculpture garden in the medieval village of **Biot**. In 1960, his widow established instead the Musée National Fernand Léger, whose 350 artworks capture the sparkle of this master of Neo-Plasticism.

PICASSO lived or worked on the Riviera for five decades and his presence still resonates through the idyllic backstreets of Old **Antibes**, where he left a striking collection of work at the seaside Château Grimaldi. In **Vallauris**—the "town of a thousand potters"—Picasso's *Man with Sheep* statue anchors the Place du Marché, while nearby is the Musée National Picasso, his vast decorated chapel and "temple of peace" (which rivals *Guernica* for impact). Visit the Galerie Madoura to see the artist's witty ceramic artworks he created between 1947 and 1949.

Musée National Picasso, Vallauris

Peripheral Vision

Journey westward to discover three towns where 20th-century art was first incubated: **Arles**, Vincent van Gogh's promised land (see Chapter 1); **Aix-en-Provence**, Paul Cézanne's hometown (see Chapter 3); **St-Tropez**, where Matisse discovered abstract color (see Chapter 4).

Monte Carlo

MONACO

Beaulieu

Villefranche-
sur-Mer   St-Jean-Cap-Ferrat

Nice

*Mediterranean
Sea*

JEAN COCTEAU "The Prince of Poets" covered **Villefranche-sur-Mer**'s Chapelle Saint-Pierre in 1957 with his fanciful curlicues, angels, and eyes, while more of his work can be found up the coast in Menton in the seaside Musée Jean Cocteau and the pretty Marriage Hall of the town Hôtel de Ville.

A banquet of museums entices the art lover to **Nice**, including the Musée Matisse (below), the Musée National Message Biblique Marc Chagall, and the Musée d'Art Moderne, but don't forget to stroll to Matisse's favorite spots—the elegant Promenade des Anglais, Jardin Albert Premier, and enchanting Cours Saleya marketplace.

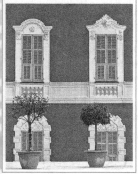

"The days follow each other here with a beauty which I would describe as insolent."
—Nietzsche,
writing from Èze, near Beaulieu, 1883

6

IN FOCUS STROKES OF GENIUS

Musée Fernand Léger, Biot

Chapelle du Rosaire, Vence

PICASSO & MATISSE: THE ODD COUPLE

PABLO PICASSO

Born: October 25, 1881, in Málaga, Spain.

Died: April 8, 1973, in Mougins, Côte d'Azur.

Personality Profile: Genius, philosopher-sage, egoist.

Claim to Fame: A one-man history of 20th-century art, Picasso changed styles as often as he did mistresses, but he is best known as the founder of Cubism.

Picasso Peeking: Cane-fencing has been erected around Picasso's last retreat of Notre-Dame-de-Vie in Mougins by his heirs and you are obliged to view his majestic Château de Vauvenargues (where he lies buried) through binoculars.

Picasso Peaking: the Musée Picasso in Antibes and his War and Peace Chapel in Vallauris are top spots to view his masterworks.

Best-Known Works: *Les Demoiselles d'Avignon, Guernica, Au Lapin Agile, Minotauomachy.*

Quote: "You see, I have to paint for the both of us now" (on hearing of Matisse's death).

The "North Pole and South Pole" of 20th century art (to use Picasso's phrase), the two heavyweights of modernism were polar opposites and had a famous push-pull friendship. No matter that Picasso was a structuralist and Matisse a sensualist, or that Picasso was as egocentric and capricious as Matisse was serene and self-effacing—the two masters engaged in a decades-long artistic "game of chess," often played out on the Côte d'Azur, where they were neighbors. It was Matisse's mesmerizingly beautiful paintings created in Nice in the 1930s that probably inspired Picasso's move to the South of France in 1946. He wound up painting in Antibes, sculpting in Vallauris, wooing in Golfe-Juan, and seducing in Mougins. But their ventriloquous dialogue began in 1906 when they first met in the Parisian salon of Gertrude Stein (who lost little time in baiting the artists against each other).

Matisse had already created a revolution in color; Picasso, 12 years younger, was about to create one in form with *Les Demoiselles d'Avignon*—the "first" 20th-century painting, whose cubistic structure was inspired by African sculpture—as it turns out, Matisse's African sculpture, since Picasso had studied his collection of Senegalese totems. When Picasso moves to the Midi in 1946, Matisse presents him with a dove, which inspired Picasso to create his famous poster in homage to France's newly-won peace.

The same year, Picasso is given the keys to Antibes' seaside Chateau Grimaldi, and then bestows on the castle the 30 paintings he created there. Sea-borne light floods canvas after canvas depicting mermaids and minotaurs, satyrs and centaurs, all prancing about in direct homage to Matisse's famously joyous paintings, *La Joie de Vie* and *La Danse.*

Jacqueline. 1960. Coll. Picasso, Mougins

HENRI MATISSE

Born: December 31, 1869, in Le Cateau, Northern France.

Died: November 3, 1954, in Nice, Côte d'Azur.

Personality Profile: Buddha, bon vivant, hedonist.

Claim to Fame: As father of the Fauves—the phrase "wild beast" described their expressive use of shade and hue—his works simplified design and exalted color.

Meeting Matisse: Musée Matisse in Nice, Rosary Chapel in Vence.

Matisse's muse: A decade before Sister Jacques-Marie inspired Matisse's Chapelle du Rosaire, she had been a nurse and model to him.

Best-Known Works: *Luxe, Calme, et Volupté, The Dance, Jazz, The Red Studio, Pink Nude.*

Be Matisse: Rent the Villa Le Rêve, the lovely Vence address he called home for five years. At 261 Avenue Henri Matisse, it is available for $490-$590 (04-93-58-82-68, www.villalerevence.com) rented by the week.

Quote: "Picasso sees everything."

What Tahiti was to Gauguin, Nice was to Matisse. Its flower marketplaces, palaces painted in bonbon pastels, and magnificent palm trees soothed and, together with the constantly changing show of light—so different from the relentless glare of St-Tropez (where, in 1904, he first committed chromatic mayhem with his Fauve "wild beast" masterpiece, *Luxe, Calme, et Volupté*)—inspired him.

By 1919, ailing with bronchitis, he had moved to Nice, where he started to paint images of unrivaled voluptuousness: Semi-nude odalisques skimpily clad in harem pantaloons and swathed in Moroccan fabrics. Their popular success allowed Matisse to relocate, in 1921, to a rooftop apartment at 1 Place Charles Félix, which magnificently overlooked the Cours Saleya flower market and the brilliantly Matissean Place de la Senat Ancien (it is painted a dazzling yellow). To view his art, head for the city's Cimiez suburb and its Musée Matisse—movingly set next to the Hôtel Regina belle-époque apartments, his last residence until his death—and the Monastère de Cimiez cemetery, where you'll find his grave.

But to sense his true spirit venture to nearby Vence, where he moved in 1943 when Nice was threatened by World War II. Here he created the sublime Chapelle du Rosaire, his masterpiece ("in spite of all its imperfections") of black-on-white tile drawings and exalted stained-glass windows of emerald, blue, and yellow—best seen, so the artist noted, at 11 o'clock on a winter's morning. The intensely competitive Picasso also saw it, of course, as a challenge. So, in 1952—53 he transformed an empty Romanesque chapel in nearby Vallauris into a "temple of peace" with scenes of *La Guerre* (war) and *La Paix* (peace). Unlike Matisse, however, he designed no liturgical gear, chasubles, or altar, since Picasso remained an avowed atheist.

Matisse's Chapel of the Rosary chasuble

IN LIVING COLOR: LA COLOMBE D'OR

Heading into the hills high above Nice, the road turns and slopes, allowing the full beauty of the rugged coast to be appreciated. A panorama of unexpected charm unfolds upon arriving at St-Paul-de-Vence, a little village perched high on the hills behind its medieval ramparts looking for all the world as if it was a 15th-century Brigadoon. As it turns out, this proved to be one of the cradles of 20th-century art. In the early 1920s, word got out that the owners of its beautiful Colombe d'Or inn would accept paintings and sketches in lieu of payment. Before you knew it, little-known artists were heading to dine and sleep here. The fact that those painters happened to turn out to be Picasso, Matisse, and Braque means that La Colombe d'Or is today one of France's most unique museums—a "museum" you can sleep and dine in. Frankly, if you don't stay or dine here, you simply haven't been to the French Riviera

A "museum" you can sleep and dine in.

If Those Paintings Could Talk

Set just outside the walls of St-Paul—a great location, for summer crowds can easily make you claustrophobic within them—this stone-and-beam auberge occupies a lovely, rose-stone Renaissance-era mansion. Walk into the dining room and you'll do a double take. Yes, those are real Mirós, Bonnards, and Légers on those rustic walls (and yes, they are now nailed down!), indeed given in payment by the artists in hungrier days when this inn was known as the "Café-Restaurant Robinson." It soon became the heart and soul of St-Paul's artistic revival, and the cream of 20th-century France lounged together under its fig trees—Picasso and Chagall, Maeterlinck and Kipling, Yves Montand and Simone Signoret (who met and married here). Off-duty celebs still flock here and it is one of the few places in the world where movie-stars are happy to be recognized.

The Garden Loggia

Choosing the cheese course

Under the Fig Trees

Today, the Colombe is now presided over by François and Danielle Roux, the fourth generation in charge, and the famille Roux's extraordinary sense of style would have delighted Pablo, Juan, and Henri. Give in to the green-shaded loveliness of the restaurant terrace and the creamy manners of the waitstaff. Set under timeless fig trees, a luncheon table here is lorded over by a ceramic Léger mural, while the pool is an idyllic garden bower, complete with a Calder stabile, and there's even a Braque by the fireplace in the bar. It is a lesson in self-denial to disregard the famous *"hors d'oeuvres de la Colombe"* (gigantic shrimp, hunks of charcuterie, and other goodies) on the menu. Segue on to the snail casserole, Sisteron lamb, or salmon quenelles, then enjoy the house's signature orange-flavored grappa with dessert while you tune into your neighbor's conversation (". . . the Picasso on my yacht dates from. . . ."). No matter the menu prices are as fabulous as the art collection—a meal here is a must.

Mind that Calder!

Head upstairs to your room—you'll have to dodge a Calder mobile (painted red with the artist's permission, to offset it from the white walls)—to be bewitched by Louis XIII armoires, medieval fourposters, wood beams, Provençal borders and painted murals; take a look out your window and you might find yourself staring at a roof of tiles painted every shade of the rainbow. While there are two annexes to the main house, all the guest rooms are flawless in taste (note you can enjoy a dinner or drink here without being a hotel guest). The pool is a dazzler, the bronzed bodies invariably Modigliani–sleek. Henri Matisse once called La Colombe d'Or "a small paradise"—and who are you to argue? Address: Place Général-de-Gaulle, 06570, St-Paul-de-Vence. Phone: 04-93-32-80-02. Web Site: www.la-colombe-dor.com. 15 rooms, 11 apartments. Restaurant, pool, in-room safes, cable TV, bar, some pets allowed. AE, DC, MC, V. Closed Oct. 26-Dec. 20.

Enjoying the pool

Dining under the fig trees

only be admired from afar. Across the Quai Rambaud, which juts into the harbor, a tiny crescent of soft sand beach called **La Gravette** offers swimmers one of the last soft spots on the coast before the famous Riviera pebble beaches begin.

To visit old Antibes, stroll the **Cours Masséna,** where an exotic little sheltered market sells lemons, olives, and hand-stuffed sausages, and the vendors take breaks in the shoebox cafés flanking one side. Find the cours by passing through the Porte Marine, an arched gateway in the rampart wall that leads from the port into the town, then follow Rue Aubernon.

> ## GUIDED TOURS
>
> The first Tuesday of each month, Antibes offers free guided tours of its Old Town leaving from L'Antiboulenc at 3 PM. The Antibes Tourist Office also organizes a day-long tour which traces the footsteps of Picasso from Antibes to Mougins. In the morning a private lecturer will accompany you to the museum in Antibes. The afternoon is spent at the photography museum in Mougins. These tours must be reserved in advance with the Tourist Office.

★ The **Église de l'Immaculée-Conception,** located between the Cours Masséna and the seafront, served as the region's cathedral until the bishopric was transferred to Grasse in 1244. Its stout medieval watchtower was built in the 11th century with stones "mined" from Roman structures—one reason the town has no amphitheater or ruins today. The church's 18th-century facade, a marvelously Latin mix of classical symmetry and fantasy, has been restored in shades of ocher and cream. Inside you'll find a Baroque altarpiece of the Virgin and Child draping a protective cloak and rosary over the people, humbly underscaled, below; this central composition and the 18 fascinating miniatures that surround it were painted by the Niçois artist Louis Bréa in 1515. A moving *gisant* (full-body death portrait) of Christ, carved in wood in 1447, stands to the altar's right. ⊠ *Pl. de la Cathédrale.*

Fodor'sChoice Looming over the Place de la Cathédrale, the famous **Musée Picasso** is ★ housed in the medieval **Château Grimaldi.** A grand structure, it rises on a Roman foundation, in turn constructed on a Greek base. Its square watchtower, along with the bell tower of the neighboring church, defines Antibes's silhouette. The bishops lived here in the church's heyday, and the Grimaldi family until the Revolution. But this fine old castle, high over the water, was little more than a monument until in 1946 its curator offered use of its vast chambers to Picasso, where he was to work with a singular passion against the inspiring backdrop of mountains, village, and sea. Here Picasso experimented with techniques, scale, and mediums, creating vast paintings on wood, canvas, paper, and walls. This extraordinary collection of works, alive with nymphs, fauns, and centaurs, as well as earthy fishermen, forms the core of the Musée Picasso, which reopened in summer 2008 after two years of renovations that made the museum wheelchair-accessible, reorganized the exhibits, and opened up more exhibition space. A rotating display on the second floor (third story) includes more than 300 works by the artist, as well as pieces by Miró, Calder, and Léger. On the first floor (second story) are the temporary exhibitions as well as a room dedicated to the works of Nicolas de Staël (1914–55), who spent the last winter of his life in Antibes creating more than 300 paintings before throwing himself from a window. These cool, lonely late works offer a marked contrast to Picasso's sunny joie de vivre. Overlooking the blue, blue sea is a beautiful sculpture terrace, fetchingly framed by flowers and exotic cacti. ✉ *Pl. du Château* ☎ *04–92–90–54–20* 💶 *€6* 🕙 *Mid-June–mid-Sept., Tues.–Sun. 10–6, Wed. and Fri. nights until 8 PM in July–Aug.; mid-Sept.–mid-June, Tues.–Sun. 10–noon and 2–6.*

The old **Portail de l'Orme** *(Gate of the Elm)*, built of quarried Roman stone and enlarged in the Middle Ages, leads you from the Cours Masséna and the market toward compelling seaside ramparts.

The Promenade Amiral de Grasse—a marvelous spot for pondering the mountains and tides—leads directly to the Bastion St-André, a squat Vauban fortress that now houses the **Musée Archéologique** *(Archaeology Museum)*. In its glory days this 17th-century stronghold sheltered a garrison; the bread oven is still visible in the vaulted central hall. The museum collection focuses on Antibes's classical history, displaying amphorae and sculptures found in local digs as well as in shipwrecks from the harbor. ✉ *Av. Général-Maizières* ☎ *04–92–90–56–87* 💶 *€3* 🕙 *Oct.–May, Tues.–Sun. 10–noon and 2–6; June–Sept., Tues.–Sun. 10–6 (open Wed. and Fri. until 8 PM in July and Aug.),*

From the Commune quarter it's easy to drift farther into the Old Town streets, exploring the mix of shops, galleries, restaurants, and bakeries. Aim to wind up on **Place Nationale,** the site of the Roman forum. It's a pleasant place for a drink under the broad plane trees.

WHERE TO EAT & STAY

$$$$

Fodor's Choice ★

✕ **Le Figuier de Saint-Esprit.** After a three-year absence from the restaurant world, acclaimed chef Christian Morrisset has opened what is already being described as the best restaurant in the Old Town of Antibes, on the site of what was formerly La Jarre. In a contemporary setting with dark wood tables and gorgeously shaded by a 40-year-old fig tree and a canopy of vines, the former chef of Juana is keeping his prices democratic at lunchtime, when a meal costs around €30; you can easily spend twice as much at dinner. Typical of his style, which focuses on local ingredients, is a saddle of lamb from the Alpilles cooked in a crust of Vallauris clay with wild mushroom polenta and thyme jus. Delicious, too, is the shady street—one of the most picturesque in town. ✉ *14 rue St-Esprit, 06600* ☎ *04–93–34–50–12* 🌐 *www.christianmorisset.fr* 🍴 *AE, D, MC, V* 🕙 *Closed Tues. No lunch Wed.*

$$$

✕ **Le Brûlot.** One street back from the thriving market, this bistro remains one of the busiest in Antibes. Burly chef Christian Blancheri hoists anything from pigs to apple pies in and out of his roaring wood oven, and it's all delicious. Watch for the sardines *à l'escabèche* (in a tangy sweet-and-sour marinade), sizzling lamb chops, or grilled fresh fish. The interior is rustic and chaotic and the seating so close it's almost unavoidable to become part of one large, unruly crowd. The next-door annex, Brûlot Pasta (2 rue Frédéric Isnard), serves homemade noodles and ravioli with a huge selection of sauces, as well as pizzas with thick or thin crust on request and a handful of meat dishes. ⊠*3 rue Frédéric Isnard, 06600* ☎*04–93–34–17–76* ⊕*www.brulot.com* ▤*AE, D, MC, V* ⊗*Closed Sun. No lunch Mon.–Wed.*

$$ ╳**Taverne le Safranier.** Part of a tiny Old Town enclave determined to resist the press of tourism, this casual tavern is headquarters for the Commune Libre du Safranier. A handful of tables scattered on the Place Safranier hold locals and visitors relishing spicy fish soup, thick hand-made ravioli, and whole *dorade,* a delicate Mediterranean fish that is unceremoniously split, fried, and garnished with lemon. A laid-back staff in shorts and rubber sandals shouts your order into the nautical-decor bar. Blackboard specials are cheap, homemade, and satisfying. ⊠*1 pl. Safranier, 06600* ☎*04–93–34–80–50* ▤*MC, V* ⊗*Closed Mon. Sept.–June and closed mid-Nov.–mid-Feb. No dinner Sun. Sept.– June; no lunch Mon. and Tues. in July and Aug.*

$$–$$$ ▦**Le Mas Djoliba.** Tucked into a residential neighborhood on the crest between Antibes and Juan-les-Pins, this cool, cozy inn feels like the private home it once was. Surrounded by greenery and well protected from traffic noise, the swimming pool is a haven if you're too relaxed to hike down to the beach. Rooms, decked in bright colors and floral prints and equipped with air-conditioning, have either views of the garden or the sea; from the family room on the top that sleeps four, there's a balcony overlooking the Cap d'Antibes. Half-board rates are available, with dinner served as well as breakfast. **Pros:** peaceful neighborhood; bed-and-breakfast atmosphere; delicious home cooking. **Cons:** some complaints about service following a change in management, but problems seem to have been resolved. ⊠*29 av. de Provence* ☎*04–93–34–02–48* ⊕*www.hotel-djoliba.com* ⇱*13 rooms* ⌂*In-room: refrigerator, Wi-Fi. In-hotel: pool, Internet, parking* ▤*AE, MC, V* ⊗*Closed Nov.–Jan.*

$–$$ ▦**L'Auberge Provençale.** Overlooking the largest square in Antibes's Old
★   Town, this onetime abbey now has six romantically named rooms complete with exposed beams, canopy beds, and lovely antique furniture. The dining room and the arbored garden are informed with the same impeccable taste; the menu tempts with classic bouillabaisse or grilled fish straight from the Mediterranean; you'll also find meatier choices such as duck breast with orange honey and ginger or grilled lamb. The restaurant is closed Monday and for Tuesday lunch. ⊠*61 pl. Nationale* ☎*04–93–34–13–24* ⊕*www.aubergeprovencale.com* ⇱*7 rooms* ⌂*In-hotel: restaurant, some pets allowed* ▤*MC, V.*

FESTIVALS & EVENTS

Consider coming to the **Antique Show of Old Antibes** (⊠*Old Port* ☎*04–93–34–65–65 for information*) held for two weeks each April. About 30,000 people from all over the world come to view the treasures and pick up a little something for back home; it's one of the largest events of its kind in France. The first week of June, check out the **Voiles d'Antibes** (⊠*Old Port* ☎*04–93–34–42–47 for information*), a major meeting of beautiful old teak and brass sailing vessels, metric classes, and maxi-cruisers more than 20 meters long. Don't miss the **Pyromelodic Festival** (☎*04–92–90–53–00 for information*) that takes place once a week in August. Three countries compete for first place in an amazing musical fireworks display that lights up both the water and the sky. Fireworks are set off from boats in Juan-les-Pins; there are great views from the beaches.

NIGHTLIFE

If you're ready to party all night, **La Siesta** (⊠*North on Rte. du Bord de Mer* ☎*04–93–33–31–31*) is the place; it's enormous, with open-air dance floors, a restaurant, bars, slot machines, and roulette. Laid-back describes the **Colonial Pub and Hop Store Irish Pub** (⊠*36 bd. d'Aiguillon* ☎*04–93–34–15–33*), the haunts of British expats and visitors.

THE OUTDOORS

Antibes and Juan-les-Pins together claim 25 km (15½ mi) of coastline and 48 **beaches** (including Cap d'Antibes). In Antibes you can choose between small sandy inlets, such as **La Gravette,** below the port; the central **Plage du Ponteil; Plage de la Salis** toward the Cap; rocky escarpments around the Old Town; or the vast stretch of sand above the Fort Carré. The Plage de la Salis may be one of the prettiest beach sites on the coast, with the dark pines of the cape on one side and the old stones of Antibes on the other, all against a backdrop of Alpine white. Juan-les-Pins is one big city beach, lined by a boulevard and promenade peppered with cafés and restaurants.

SHOPPING

At the **market** on Antibes's Cours Masséna, you can buy fruits, vegetables, and a tempting array of other regional products daily until 1 PM. An **antiques and flea market** takes place Thursday and Saturday from 7 to 6 on Place Nationale. You can also find plenty of eclectic little boutiques and gallery shops in the Old Town, especially along Rue Sade and Rue de la République.

CAP D'ANTIBES

2 km (1 mi) south of Antibes.

GETTING HERE

Cap d'Antibes doesn't have its own train station; the closest is the SNCF train station in Antibes (place Pierre Semard). SNCF trains run frequently between Nice and Cannes, stopping in Antibes about halfway (20 mins from Nice or Cannes). From the bus station at place Guynemer in Antibes, bus No. 2, operated by Envibus, wends its way around the Cap d'Antibes, leaving about every 40 minutes and taking 15 minutes to reach the other end of the Cap. Stops include Phare du Cap (lighthouse), Garoupe, and Eden Roc (the terminus). Tickets cost €1.

EXPLORING

For the most part extravagantly idyllic and protected from the concrete plague infecting the mainland coast, this fabled 4-mi-long peninsula has been carved up into luxurious estates perched high above the water and shaded by thick, tall pines. Since the 19th century its wild greenery and isolation have drawn a glittering assortment of aristocrats, artists, literati, and the merely fabulously wealthy. Among those claiming the prestigious Cap d'Antibes address over the years: Guy de Maupassant, Anatole France, Claude Monet, the Duke and Duchess of Windsor, the Greek shipping tycoon Stavros Niarchos, and the cream of the Lost Generation, including Ernest Hemingway, John Dos Passos, Dorothy Parker, Alice B. Toklas, Gertrude Stein, and Scott and Zelda Fitzgerald. Now the focal point is the famous Hotel Eden Roc, rendezvous and weekend getaway of film stars from Madonna and Robert De Niro to Clint Eastwood and Alain Delon.

★ To fully experience the Riviera's heady hothouse exoticism, head midway out on the Cap to visit the glorious **Jardin Thuret** *(Thuret Garden)*, established by botanist Gustave Thuret in 1856 as a testing ground for subtropical plants and trees. Thuret was responsible for the introduction of the palm tree, forever changing the profile of the Côte d'Azur. On his death the property was left to the Ministry of Agriculture, which continues to dabble in the introduction of exotic species. From the Port du Croûton head up Chemin de l'Aureto, then Chemin du Tamisier, and turn right on the Boulevard du Cap. ⊠*62 bd. du Cap* ☎*04–93–67–88–66* ⊕*jardin-thuret.antibes.inra.fr* ⊠*Free* ☉*Weekdays 8:30–5:30.*

At the southwest tip of the peninsula, an ancient battery is home to the **Musée Naval et Napoléonien** *(Naval and Napoleonic Museum)*, where you can peruse a collection of watercolors of Antibes, lead soldiers, and scale models of military ships. ⊠*Batterie du Grillon, Av. Kennedy* ☎*04–93–61–45–32* ⊕*www.antibes-juanlespins.com* ⊠*€3* ☉*Mid-Sept.–mid-June, Tues.–Sat.* 10–4:30; mid-June–mid-Sept., daily 10–6.

You can sample a little of what draws them to the site by walking up the Chemin de Calvaire from the Plage de la Salis in Antibes (about 1.2 km [¾ mi]), and taking in the extraordinary views from the hill that supports the old lighthouse, called the **Phare de la Garoupe** *(Garoupe Lighthouse)*.

Next to the Phare de la Garoupe, the 16th-century double chapel of **Notre-Dame-de-la-Garoupe** contains ex-votos and statues of the Virgin, all in the memory and for the protection of sailors. ⊠*Follow Bd. du Cap, then follow signs to Phare* ☎04–92–90–53–00 ☉*Easter–Sept., daily 10–noon and 2:30–7; Oct.–Easter, daily 10–noon and 2:30–5.*

Fodor'sChoice At the very tip of the Cap is the **Villa Eilenroc,** designed by Charles Gar-
★ nier, who created the Paris Opera—which should give you some idea of its style. The estate commands a vast acreage, threaded with paths and much of it given over to a grand and glamorous garden. Here, in the Roserie you can glimpse the even-grander Château de la Croë, whose shimmering white portico once sheltered the likes of Garbo and Onassis (it was bought in 2005 by a Russian syndicate, whose billionaires' club will now use it as a winter palace, conjuring up the days of the 1920s, when exiled White Russians first colonized the Riviera). You may tour Eilenroc's grounds freely, but during summer months the house remains closed. But from September to June on Wednesdays visitors are allowed to wander through the reception salons, which retain

the Louis Seize–Trianon feel of the noble facade. The Winter Salon still has its "1,001 Nights" wall mural painted by Jean Dunand, the famed Art Deco designer; display cases are filled with memorabilia donated by Caroline Groult-Flaubert (Antibes resident and goddaughter of the great author); while the boudoir has boiseries from the Marquis de Sévigné's Paris mansion. Bring a discreet bag luncheon to enjoy on the terrace chairs overlooking the Bay of Millionaires and give thanks to Mrs. L.D. Beaumont, whose legacy allows us to experience her regal estate and what the Cap was like in its gilded age. ⊠*Near peninsula's tip* ☎*04–93–67–74–33* ⊕*www.antibes-juanlespins.com* ✒*Free* ⊙*House: mid-Sept.–June, Wed. 9–noon and 1:30–5, closed July–Aug.; Gardens: mid-Sept.–June, Tues. and Wed. 9–5.*

Fodor's Choice ★ Bordering the Cap's zillion-dollar hotels and fabled estates is one of the most spectacular walks in the world: the **Sentier Tirepoil**, which runs about 1½ km (1 mi) along the outermost tip of the peninsula. It begins gently enough at the pretty Plage de la Garoupe (where Cole Porter, Picasso, and Gerard Murphy used to hang out), with a paved walkway and dazzling views over the Baie de la Garoupe and the faraway Alps. Round the far end of the cap, however, and the paved promenade soon gives way to a boulder-studded pathway that picks its way along 50-foot cliffs, dizzying switchbacks, and thundering breakers (*Attention Mort*— "Beware: Death"—read the signs, reminding you this path can be very dangerous in stormy weather). On sunny days, with exhilarating winds and spectacular breakers coming in from the sea, you'll have company (families, even), although for most stretches all signs of civilization completely disappear, except for a yacht or two. The walk is long, and takes about two hours to complete, but it may prove two of the more unforgettable hours of your life (especially if you tackle it at sunset).

WHERE TO EAT & STAY

$$$$ ✕**Les Pêcheurs.** In 1954 French resistance hero Camille Rayon built a
★ restaurant on the Cap d'Antibes between two stone fishing huts dating from the early 20th century. It wasn't long before La Maison des Pêcheurs became a fashionable address, though the site was abandoned in the 1990s before being transformed into a beach resort in 2003. A luxury hotel is scheduled to open here in May 2009, completing this rags-to-riches story. At that time Les Pêcheurs will move inside the hotel and sous-chef Hervé Busson will take over from Francis Chauveau, who has set a lofty standard with updated Provençal dishes that make the most of local ingredients. Fish play a starring role, backed up by vegetables and fruits from the nearby hills; don't miss the stunning desserts, which will give you an excuse to linger as the sun sets over the Iles de Lérins and the Esterel. ⊠*10 Bd. Maréchal Juin, 06160* ☎*04–92–93–13–30* ⊕*www. lespecheurs-lecap.com* ▤*AE, DC, MC, V* ⊙*Closed Tues. and Wed. Sept.– June; closed Tues. in July and Aug. No lunch in July and Aug.*

$$$$ ✕**Restaurant de Bacon.** Bacon (pronounce the "a" as in "baa") seems
★ a strange name for a restaurant known as *the* spot for seafood on the Côte d'Azur since 1948, a restaurant that prides itself on fish so fresh it's still twitching. The fish-loving Sordello brothers prowl the markets

when the boats come, then they simply choose the best. You have to decide whether to have it minced in lemon ceviche, floating in perfect bouillabaisse, or simply grilled with fennel, crisped with hillside herbs, or baked in parchment. Such purity doesn't come cheap, but the warm welcome, discreet service, sunny dining room, and dreamy terrace over the Baie des Anges, with views of the Antibes ramparts, justify extravagance. Fixed-price menus (€49 at lunch, €79 at lunch or dinner) can help keep the bill down. Meat lovers, don't worry; there's something on the menu for you, too, including a melt-in-your-mouth foie gras. ⊠ *Bd. de Bacon, 06160* ☎*04–93–61–50–02* ⊕*www.restaurantdebacon.com* ⚘*Reservations essential* ☐*AE, DC, MC, V* ☉*Closed Mon. and Nov 1–Feb. 28, no lunch Tues.*

\$\$\$\$
★ ⚏ **La Baie Dorée.** Clinging to the waterfront and skewed toward the open sea, this spiffy inn provides private sea-view terraces off every room. The exterior gleams with new paint, the rooms are plush and subdued, the ambience discreet to the point of self-effacing, and the reception area is as small as a coat check—yet even the standard doubles feel deluxe when you look out the window. The public grounds and terraces fall in tiers down to the water, from the shaded restaurant (open from late May to late September) and bar to the boat dock to the private beach on the Baie de la Garoupe. **Pros:** some rooms have balconies with spectacular sea views; beach offers water sports; small size gives it a homey feel. **Cons:** food is pricey (though delicious); furniture is modest; some rooms are small. ⊠*579 bd. de la Garoupe,* ☎*04–93–67–30–67* ⊕*www.baiedoree.com* ⚏*17 rooms* ⚬*In-room: safe, refrigerator, Wi-Fi. In-hotel: restaurant, bar, beachfront, pool, spa, parking, some pets allowed* ☐*AE, DC, MC, V* ⚏*FAP.*

\$\$\$\$
★ ⚏ **Hôtel du Cap–Eden Roc.** In demand by celebrities from De Niro to Madonna, this extravagantly expensive hotel has long catered to the world's fantasy of a subtropical idyll on the Côte d'Azur. First opened in 1879, the Villa Soleil, as this retreat for ailing artists was then called, joined forces and facilities with the neighboring Eden Roc tearoom in 1914, and expanded its luxuries to include a swimming pool blasted into seaside bedrock. After the Great War, two stylish American intellectuals, Sara and Gerald Murphy, rented the entire complex and invited all their friends, a stellar lot ranging from the Windsors to Rudolf Valentino and Marlene Dietrich. Their most frequent guests were Zelda and F. Scott Fitzgerald, who used it as the model for Hôtel des Etrangers in his *Tender is the Night.* Today its broad, sun-drenched rooms, thickly carpeted and furnished with antiques in the main Second Empire mansion, look out on 22 acres of immaculate tropical gardens bordered by rocky shoreline. Down by the water is the Pavillon Eden Roc wing, more modern but with sheer-horizon views. The pool seems to spill directly into the sea, and a sense of playful indulgence reigns, with trapeze rings suspended over the water, a pontoon swimming dock straight out of summer camp, and a diving board that invites you to jackknife into the indigo sea. Everyone dresses stylishly for dinner. Credit cards are not accepted; the hotel can arrange for a bank transfer. And if you're not a celebrity, tip big to keep the staff interested. **Pros:** spectacular grounds; superb restaurant; gorgeous

pool and clients. **Cons:** no minibars in rooms; sometimes snooty service; exorbitant cost of all extras. ✉ *Bd. Kennedy* ☎ *04–93–61–39–01* ⊕ *www.edenroc-hotel.fr* ➯ *120 rooms* ♿ *In-room: Ethernet. In-hotel: 2 restaurants, bar, tennis courts, pool, gym, spa, Wi-Fi, parking* ▤ *No credit cards* ⊘ *Closed mid-Oct.–Mar.*

$$ ⛺ **La Garoupe-Gardiole.** Cool, simple, and accessible to non–movie stars, this pair of partnered hotels offers a chance to sleep on the hallowed Cap peninsula and bike or walk to the pretty Garoupe beach. A sizable pool, framed by high walls and tall pines, offers cool-down time. Guest rooms are comfortably furnished in both buildings, with the Garoupe offering modern decor and the Gardiole with rustic Provençal design. **Pros:** location among million-dollar mansions; spacious rooms available for families. **Cons:** breakfast costs extra, and there are no cafés nearby; some rooms are small. ✉ *60–74 chemin de la Garoupe* ☎ *04–92–93–33–33* ⊕ *www.hotel-lagaroupe-gardiole.com* ➯ *40 rooms* ♿ *In-room: safe, refrigerator. In-hotel: bar, pool, Wi-Fi* ▤ *AE, MC, V* ⊘ *Closed mid-Oct.–early Apr.*

$–$$ ⛺ **Hôtel La Jabotte.** A few steps from a sandy beach, this adorable guest-★ house is built around a central courtyard, where guests relax over a breakfast (included in the room price) of croissants, baguette, fresh juice, and homemade jam. Guest rooms are tastefully decorated with motifs of birds, flowers or calligraphy, and the owners are as charming as the setting: each night between 6 and 8 they serve a different house cocktail so that guests can relax and mingle. Be warned that because of the very accessible prices and idyllic location, La Jabotte is booked up months in advance. **Pros:** the unique charm that comes from the owners' attention to detail; the high quality of the breakfast. **Cons:** rooms here are coveted, so book well ahead; room No. 3 has a separate toilet in the hall. ✉ *13 av. Max-Maurey,* ☎ *04–93–61–45–89* ⊕ *www. jabotte.com* ➯ *10 rooms* ♿ *In-room: no a/c, refrigerator, Wi-Fi. In-hotel: bar, parking* ▤ *MC, V* ⊙ *BP.*

JUAN-LES-PINS

5 km (3 mi) southwest of Antibes.

GETTING HERE

Regional trains connect the SNCF Juan-les-Pins train station to Nice (€4.20 one way), Cannes (€2.10) and other coastal towns. Antibes–Juan-les-Pins can also be reached by taking the No. 200 bus from the central bus station in Nice to place Guynemer (1 hour, €1). From here, there is a bus connection (No. 3 Envibus) to the Juan-les-Pins train station. Starting at that station, Bus No. 15 loops through Juan-les-Pins, stopping at the public beach. Buses cost €1.

VISITOR INFORMATION

Antibes/Juan-les-Pins Tourist Office (✉ *11 pl. de Gaulle, Antibes* ☎ *04–92–90–53–00* ⊕ *antibes-juanlespins.com*).

EXPLORING

From Old Antibes you can jump on a bus over the hill to Juan-les-Pins, the jazzy younger-sister resort town that, with Antibes, bracelets the wrist of the Cap d'Antibes. This stretch of beach was "discovered" by the Jazz Age jet set, who adopted it with a vengeance; F. Scott and Zelda Fitzgerald lived in a seaside villa here in the early 1920s, dividing their idylls between what is now the Hôtel Belle Rives and the mansions on the Cap d'Antibes. Here they experimented with the newfangled fad of waterskiing, still practiced from the docks of the Belle Rives today. Ladies with bobbed hair and beach pajamas exposed lily-white skin to the sun, browning themselves like peasants and flaunting bare, tanned arms. American industrialists had swimming pools introduced to the seaside, and the last of the leisure class, weary of stateside bathtub gin, wallowed in Europe's alcoholic delights. Nowadays, the scene along Juan's waterfront is something to behold, with thousands of international sunseekers flowing up and down the promenade or lying flank to flank on its endless stretch of sand. The **Plage de Juan-les-Pins** is made up of sand, not pebbles, and ranks among the Riviera's best (rent a beach chair from the nearby hotel concessions). Along with these white powder wonders, Juan is famous for the quality—some pundits say quantity—of its nightlife. There are numerous nightclubs where you can do everything but sleep, ranging from casinos to discos to strip clubs. If all this sounds too much hard work, wait for July's jazz festival—one of Europe's most prestigious—or simply repair to the Juana or Les Belles Rives; if you're lucky enough to be a guest at either hotel, you'll understand why F. Scott Fitzgerald set his *Tender Is the Night* in "Juantibes," as both places retain the golden glamour of the Riviera of yore. These hotels are surrounded by the last remnants of the pine forests that gave Juan its name. Elsewhere, however, Juan-les-Pins suffers from a plastic feel and you might get more out of Antibes.

WHERE TO EAT & STAY

$$$–$$$$
Fodor'sChoice
★

Les Belles Rives. If living well is the best revenge, then vacationers at this landmark hotel should know. Not far from the onetime villa of Gerald and Sara Murphy—those Roaring Twenties millionaires who devoted their life to proving this maxim—the Belles Rives became the home-away-from-home for literary giant F. Scott Fitzgerald and his wife Zelda (chums of the Murphys). Lovingly restored to 1930s glamour, this hotel pioneered the idea of an inn *pieds dans l'eau* (with its feet in the water), with terraces directly on the waterfront—something that disappointingly few hotels along the Côte d'Azur offer today. It was here that the newly invented sport of waterskiing caught on like wildfire, drawing jazz greats as well as royalty. Inside, the original Art Deco furniture remains, artfully preserved in an almost museum-like *neoclassique* milieu, though the grand glass doors lead to a vivid and lively waterfront scene. Rooms have fresh, updated fabrics, and sea views are poster-perfect. The restaurant La Passagère serves a sophisticated take on French Mediterranean food on the Belles Rives beach, as well as on the hotel's terrace and in the dining room. There is no pool, but happily the private beach—where the water-sport tradition continues—is just steps away. ⊠ *33 Bd. Edouard Baudoin* ☎ *04–93–61–02–79* ⊕ *www.*

bellesrives.com ⟿*43 rooms* ⟐*In-room: refrigerator, Wi-Fi. In-hotel: 3 restaurants, bar, beachfront, Internet terminal parking (free), some pets allowed* ⊟*AE, DC, MC, V.*

$$–$$$ ⬚**Hotel des Mimosas.** This hotel's fabulous setting—in an enclosed hilltop garden studded with tall palms, mimosa, and tropical greenery—makes up for the trafficky hike down to the beach, although most guests lounge around the pool anyway. Rooms are small and modestly decorated in Victorian florals. Ask for one with a functioning balcony: many overlook the garden and pool, which is bigger than most. The lobby and lounge are doily-cozy, with Oriental rugs and bric-a-brac, but you'll probably be drawn to the palm-shaded lawns to relax. **Pros:** aim for a room with a spacious terrace overlooking the pool and garden; rooms have old-fashioned charm. **Cons:** hillside setting and lack of elevator could be difficult for those with mobility problems; bathrooms are basic. ⊠*Rue Pauline,* ☎*04–93–61–04–16* ⊕*www.hotel-mimosas. fr* ⟿*34 rooms* ⟐*In-room: refrigerator. In-hotel: bar, pool, Wi-Fi, parking (free)* ⊟*AE, MC, V* ⊘*Closed Oct.–Apr.* ⦿*MAP.*

NIGHTLIFE & THE ARTS

Every July the **Festival International Jazz à Juan** (⊠*Antibes Tourist Office: 11 pl. du Général de Gaulle* ☎*04–97–23–11–11;* ⊠*Juan-les-Pins Tourist Office: 51 bd. Guillaumont* ☎*04–97–23–11–10*) challenges Montreux for its stellar lineup and romantic outdoor venue under ancient pines. Tickets may be purchased as early as May and range from €30–€60, depending on the popularity of the artist. There are also a host of exceptional freebies during the festival at various squares throughout town, and a daily marching band that weaves its way through the streets of Antibes. It's one of the oldest festivals in Europe and claims to have had the European debut performances of Miles Davis (pronounce that Meels Dah-*vees*) and Ray Charles. More recent jazz greats gracing the tropical nights include Keith Jarrett, Marcus Miller, and a bluesy Joe Cocker. Though it's a poor heir to the grand casino of Scott-and-Zelda days, the modern glassed-in complex of the **Eden Casino** (⊠*Bd. Baudoin* ☎*04–92–93–71–71*) houses restaurants, bars, dance clubs, and a casino, many with sea views. The cavernous **Le Village** (⊠*1 bd. de la Pinède* ☎*04–92–93–92–00*) sets the standard for cool in Juan-les-Pins with thumping music played by the best DJs in town.

THE OUTDOORS

Antibes and Juan-les-Pins together claim 25 km (15½ mi) of coastline and 48 **beaches** (including Cap d'Antibes). Juan-les-Pins is one big city beach, lined by a boulevard and promenade peppered with cafés and restaurants. To study underwater life while circling the cape, contact **Visiobulle** (⊠*Ponton Courbet—bd. Guillaumont* ☎*04–93–67–02–11* ⊕*www.visiobulle.com*), which organizes one-hour cruises (€12 for adults, €6 for children 2–11) in tiny, yellow glass-bottom boats. Boats leave from the Ponton Courbet in Juan-les-Pins three to seven times a day depending on the season; it's best to reserve ahead by phone in summer.

6

SHOPPING

Patounet (⊠*Promenade du Soleil* ☎04–93–61–16–10) is the place for the latest in swimwear from top designers. **Maud** (⊠*21 rue Dauthville* ☎04–93–67–11–04) has irresistible summery dresses and casual wear.

BIOT

Fodor'sChoice
★
6 km (4 mi) northeast of Antibes, 15 km (9 mi) northeast of Cannes, 18 km (11 mi) southwest of Nice.

VISITOR INFORMATION

Biot Tourist Office (⊠*46 rue St-Sébastien, Biot* ☎04–93–65–78–00 ⊕*www. biot-coteazur.com*).

EXPLORING

Rising above commercial-industrial quarter up the coast from Antibes, the spectacularly charming *village perché* of Biot (pronounced Bee-*otte*) sits neatly on a hilltop. For centuries home to a pottery industry, known for its fine yellow clay that stretched into massive, solid oil jars, it has in recent generations made a name for itself as a glass-art town. Nowadays its enchanting cobblestoned streets are lined with boutiques and galleries, their display windows flashing a staggering collection of goods in vividly colored glass.

Yet despite the commercialism, traces of old Provence remain, especially in the evening after the busloads of shoppers leave and the deep-shaded *placettes* (small squares) under the plane trees fall quiet. Then you can meander around the edges of the Old Town to find the stone arch gates known as the **Porte des Tines** and the **Porte des Migraniers;** they're the last of the 16th-century fortifications that once enclosed Biot. Step into the 15th-century **église,** which contains an early-16th-century altarpiece attributed to Louis Bréa and depicting the Virgin Mary shielding humanity under her cloak; the surrounding portraits are as warmly detailed as the faces and hands in the central panel. **Place des Arcades,** between the tourist office and the church, just behind Rue Barri, has an otherworldly grace, with its Gothic arcades and tall palm trees.

Long a regular on the Côte d'Azur, Fernand Léger fell under Biot's spell and bought a farmhouse here in 1955 to house an unwieldy collection of his sculptures. On his death his wife converted the house to a museum of his works, and in 1967 she donated it to France. The modernized
★ structure of the **Musée National Fernand-Léger** is striking, its facade itself a vast mosaic in his signature style of heavily outlined color fields. Within you can trace the evolution of Léger's technique, from his fascination with the industrial to freewheeling abstractions. The museum reopened in summer 2008 after a long period of renovations: architect Marc Barani has redesigned the entrance hall to let in light from the freshly landscaped garden, a temporary exhibition space has been added, and there is also a new reading room and boutique. The staff even have new outfits, designed by the Biot-based brand Chacok, that reflect the spirit of the museum. ⊠*Chemin du Val de Pomme* ☎04–

92–91–50–30 ⊕*www.musee-fernandleger.fr* ⊠€6,50 ⊗*June–Oct.,* *Wed.–Mon. 10–6; Nov.–Apr. 10–5.*

On the edge of town, follow the pink signs to **La Verrerie de Biot** *(Biot Glassworks)*, which has developed into something of a cult industry since its founding in the 1950s. Here you can observe the glassblowers at work, visit the extensive galleries of museum-quality art glass (which is of much better quality than the kitsch you find in the village shop windows), and start a collection of bubbled-glass goblets, cruets, or pitchers, just as Jackie Kennedy did when the rage first caught hold (she liked cobalt blue). The bubbles come from baking soda applied to the melted glass. Despite the extreme commercialism—there are a souvenir shop, a boutique of home items, audio tours of the glassworks, a bar, and a restaurant—it's a one-of-a-kind artisanal industry, and the product is made before your eyes. Should you wish to delve deeper into the world of glass, introductory workshops are offered all year round (five 1½-hour classes for €230). ⊠*5 chemin des Combes* ☎*04–93–65–03–00* ⊕*www.verreriebiot.com* ⊠*€3* ⊗*May–Sept., Mon.–Sat. 9:30–8, Sun. 10:30–1:30 and 2:30–7:30; Oct.–Apr., Mon.–Sat. 9:30–6, Sun. 10:30–1:30 and 2:30–6:30.*

☾ Marketed under the umbrella title of **Parc de la Mer** *(Sea Park)*, this extremely commercial amusement complex provides parents with bargaining leverage for a day of Picasso and pottery shopping. There's a small **Marineland,** with lively scripted dolphin shows, dancing killer whales, and a Plexiglass walk-through aquarium that allows sharks to swim over your head. Animal lovers may wish to avoid this circus and head instead to the surprisingly deep and fascinating collection of old sea paraphernalia in its museum. Next door is the **Ile Magique aux Oiseaux,** a collection of colorful birds. There's **Aquasplash,** with a wave pool and 12 slides, and beside that, **La Petite Ferme,** a petting zoo. It's only a short distance from Antibes and Biot; take N7 north, then head left at La Brague onto D4, toward Biot. ⊠*309 rue Mozart* ☎*04–93–33–49–49* ⊠*€9–€33 depending on the attraction and the season. Joint-ticket admission and two-day passport for all parks available on request* ⊗*July–Oct., daily 10* AM–*midnight for dolphin shows; 10–7 for other attractions. Hours variable in winter.*

WHERE TO EAT & STAY

$–$$
★ ⊞**Galerie des Arcades.** Tucked away behind the beauteous palm-lined Place des Arcades in the Old Town, this combination hotel-restaurant–art gallery draws a chic and loyal clientele. They come to browse in the gallery, enjoy a weekend in one of the extraordinary guest rooms, or dine on the serious, unpretentious, authentic Provençal food: rabbit sautéed in fresh herbs, stuffed sardines, or a Friday *aïoli* (fish and crudités served with garlic mayonnaise). Eat at the checked-cloth-covered tables, either under the arcades or under the cozy beams indoors. Then ask for one of the three *grandes chambres* (large rooms) and revel in antiquity: four-poster beds, stone sinks and fireplaces, beams, and a tapestry-rich color scheme. **Pros:** great decor, memorable cuisine, all for a nearly bargain price. **Cons:** smaller rooms are nothing to write home about. ⊠*16 pl. des Arcades,* ☎*04–93–65–01–04* ⊕*www.hotel-restaurant-les-arcades.*

com 🛏12 *rooms* 🚪*In-room: no a/c. In-hotel: restaurant, bar, Internet terminal, some pets allowed* 🗂*AE, DC, MC, V.*

HAUT-DE-CAGNES

Fodor'sChoice *14 km (9 mi) southwest of Nice, 10 km (6 mi) north of Antibes.*
★

VISITOR INFORMATION

Cagnes-sur-Mer Tourist Office (✉*6 bd. Maréchal Juin, B.P. 48, Cagnes-sur-Mer* ☎*04–93–20–61–64* ⊕ *www.cagnes-tourisme.com*).

EXPLORING

Although from N7 you may be tempted to give wide berth to Cagnes-sur-Mer—with its congested sprawl of freeway overpasses, tacky tourist-oriented stores, beachfront pizzerias, and train station—follow the brown signs inland touting BOURG MÉDIÉVAL and up into one of the most beautiful *villages perchés* (perched villages) along the Riviera: Haut-de-Cagnes. Alice of Wonderland fame would adore this steeply cobbled Old Town, honeycombed as it is with tiny piazzas, return-to-your-starting-point-twice alleys, and winding streets that abruptly change to stairways. You'll find it a total pleasure to wander its old byways, some with cobbled steps, others passing under vaulted arches draped with bougainvillea. Many of the pretty residences are dollhouse-sized (especially the hobbit houses on Rue Passebon) and most date from the 14th and 15th centuries. There is nary a shop, so the commercial horrors of Mougins or St-Paul-de-Vence are left far behind. It is little wonder the rich and literate—Soutine, Modigliani, and Simone de Beauvoir, among them—have long kept Haut-de-Cagnes a secret forgetaway. Or almost: enough cars now arrive that a garage (Parking du Planastel) has been excavated out of the hillside, while a free *navette* shuttlebus links Haut-de-Cagnes with the bus station of Cagnes-sur-Mer (about an eight-block walk from the town train station, which lies on the main coastal rail route).

★ Crowning Haut-de-Cagnes is the fat, crenellated **Château-Museé de Cagnes.** Built in 1310 by the Grimaldis and reinforced over the centuries, this imposing fortress lords over the coastline, banners flying from its square watchtower. You are welcomed inside by a grand balustraded stairway and triangular Renaissance courtyard with a triple row of classical arcades infinitely more graceful than the exterior. Filling nearly the entire courtyard is a mammoth, 200-year-old pepper tree—a spectacular sight. Beyond lie vaulted medieval chambers, a vast Renaissance fireplace, and a splendid 17th-century trompe-l'oeil fresco of the fall of Phaëthon from his sun chariot. The château also contains three highly specialized museums: the **Musée de l'Olivier** (Olive Tree Museum), an introduction to the history and cultivation of this Provençal mainstay; the obscure and eccentric **Collection Suzy-Solidor,** a group of portraits of the cabaret chanteuse painted by her artist friends, including Cocteau and Dufy; and the **Musée d'Art Moderne Méditerranéen** (Mediterranean Museum of Modern Art), which contains paintings by some of the 20th-century devotees of the Côte d'Azur, including Chagall, Cocteau, and Dufy. If you've climbed this far, continue to the **tower** and look over the coastline views in the same way that the guards once watched for Saracens. ⊠ *Pl. Grimaldi* ☎ *04–92–02–47–30* 🎟 *€3* ⊙ *Oct.–Apr., Wed.–Sun. 10–noon and 2–5; May–Sept., Wed.– Sun. 10–noon and 2–6.*

Nearly hidden in the hillside and entered by an obscure side door, the grand **Chapelle Notre-Dame-de-la-Protection,** with its Italianate bell tower, was first built in the 13th century after the fortress had been destroyed; as a hedge against further invasion, they placed this plea for Mary's protection at the village edge. In 1936 the *curé* (priest) discovered traces of fresco under the bubbling plaster; a full stripping revealed every inch of the apse to have been decorated in scenes of the life of the Virgin and Jesus, roughly executed late in the 16th century. From the chapel's porch are sweeping sea views. Be sure to note the trompe-l'oeil "shadows" delightfully painted on the bell tower portal. ⊠ *Rue Hippolyte Guis.*

The beloved Impressionist painter Auguste Renoir (1841–1919) was particularly fond of the Chapelle Notre-Dame-de-la-Protection, and of the whole town as well. After visiting his friend painter Ferdinand de Conchy and falling in love with "la vie Cagnoise," Renoir settled in a house in Les Collettes, an estate set in the town of Cagnes-sur-Mer, just below hilltop Haut-de-Cagnes (from Cagnes's main square, Place de Gaulle, take Avenue Auguste-Renoir right to La Gaude and then to the Chemin des Collettes; Bus 4 from Square Bourdet; or stop Béat– Les Collettes on the Antibes or Nice bus). Built by the painter in 1908,
★ Les Collettes is now the **Musée Renoir.** Here he passed the last 12 years of his life, painting the landscape around him, working in bronze, and rolling his wheelchair through the luxuriant garden of olive, lemon, and orange trees. You can view his home and studio as it was preserved by his children, including his bed, his wheelchair, and of course his paintbrushes and easel. You can also view 11 of his last Cagnes Period paintings and a bronze Venus in the garden bearing testimony to his successful ventures into sculpture; a former barn on the property is now a boutique. On Thursdays in July and August there are English-language guided tours. ⊠ *Chemin des Collettes* ☎ *04–93–20–61–07* 🎟 *€3* ⊙ *Oct.–Apr., Wed.–Mon. 10–12 and 2–5; May–Oct., Wed.– Mon. 10–12 and 2–6. Guided tours in English, Thurs. July and Aug.*

WHERE TO EAT & STAY

$ ✕ **Les Baux.** So where do the locals eat in this storybook village? Les Baux, whose little terrace lies just around the corner from the restaurant-lined main square, seems to be the answer: the owners greet most of the diners with kisses on both cheeks, and you'll hear little English spoken even in the height of summer. Expect unpretentious home cooking with few modern flourishes, perhaps steak au poivre with a baked potato, grilled sole, or spoon-tender sautéed veal with peaches cooked in red wine. The friendly owners also run a bed-and-breakfast (⊕ www.loustalounet.com) complete with swimming pool a short walk from here. ⊠ *2 pl. du Château, 06800* ☎ *04–93–73–14–00* ▭ *AE, MC, V* ⊙ *Closed Mon. No dinner Sun.*

$$$-$$$$ 🖼 **Hôtel Le Cagnard.** What better

Fodor'sChoice way to experience Old Haut-de-

★ Cagnes's grand castle views than to stay in a 13th-century manor perched on the ramparts of the Grimaldi fortress? Maintaining a discreet sense of medieval atmosphere—pastel-rubbed beams, restored murals and vaulting, a few four-poster beds—this enchantingly romantic inn offers regal comfort (bathrooms are ablaze with modern luxe) and storybook allure. Mostly set in adjoining town houses, many guest rooms look out over the Old Town and on toward the sea. The hub of Le Cagnard is its famous restaurant, where you'll want to enjoy both lunch and dinner. Luncheons are served in a seignorial

14th-century Salle des Gardes, whose vaulted walls were covered by "courtly" paintings by one of Haut-de-Cagnes bohemian residents at the beginning of the 20th century. Dinner is held in an adjacent salon whose remarkable ceiling, covered in Renaissance-style caissons, can be retracted to show off the night sky (cute: they only open it *after* the village birds have eaten and flown over the hill to nest). The lavish menu (no lunch Monday and Tuesday; closed Thursday and mid-November to mid-December; reservations essential) lives up to the surrounding splendor with dishes like foie gras cooked with figs, peaches, apricots, and rosemary; an indescribably delcious rouget served tempura-fashion with spring rolls; or the subtle black truffle lasagna. If you are arriving on the town square by the shuttle-bus, the hotel's *voiturier* will be sent to pick up your luggage. **Pros:** the talents of chef Yves Johany; magical restaurant decor. **Cons:** lots of steps; virtually no lobby. ⊠ *54 rue sous-Barri* 🕾 *04–93–20–73–21* ⊕ *www.le-cagnard.com* ⬩ *20 rooms* ⬩ *In-room: refrigerator. In-hotel: restaurant, bar, Wi-Fi, parking, some pets allowed* ☰ *AE, DC, MC, V.*

$$$ 🖼 **Grimaldi.** More of a bed-and-breakfast, this little hotel is smack in the middle of the Haut-de-Cagnes' liveliest square, complete with picture-perfect pétanque matches. Guest rooms are decorated in muted tones of beige and gray with a mix of contemporary and antique furniture, their windows looking onto the square and the hills beyond Cagnes. Set in a fetching weathered stone house, the Grimaldi also houses one of the upper town's best restaurants, where chef Patrick Remy turns out tried-and-true dishes such as pan-fried artichoke hearts with gambas and Simmental beef with an assortment of vegetable purées. This is not the place to hone your French; Swedish host Tomaz, who speaks perfect English, might give you a blank look. **Pros:** great views from the rooms; helpful English-speaking owners; near-flawless food. **Cons:** with only five rooms, the hotel fills up quickly. ⊠ *6 pl. du Château,*

06800 ☎04–93–20–60–24 ⊕*www.hotelgrimaldi.com* ⤶*5 rooms* ⚄*In-hotel: restaurant, Wi-Fi* ⊟*MC, V* ⑩|*BP.*

THE HILL TOWNS: ON THE TRAIL OF PICASSO & MATISSE

The hills that back the Côte d'Azur are often called the arrière-pays, or backcountry. This particular wedge of backcountry—behind the coast between Cannes and Antibes—has a character all its own: deeply, unself-consciously Provençal, with undulating fields of lavender watched over by villages perched on golden stone. Many of these villages look as if they do not belong to the last century—but they do, since they played the muse to some of modern art's most famous exemplars, notably Pablo Picasso and Henri Matisse. A highlight here is the Maeght Foundation, in St-Paul-de-Vence, one of France's leading museums of modern art. Its neighbor, Vence, has the Chapelle du Rosaire, entirely designed and decorated by Matisse. It's possible to get a small taste of this backcountry on a day trip out of Fréjus, Cannes, or Antibes; even if you're vacationing along the coast, you may want to settle in for a night or two.

High in the hills these villages loom, parallel to the sea, smelling fragrantly of wild herbs and medieval history ... and soap shops. So hungry have the hordes that flock to the Riviera become for a taste of Picasso-and-Peter-Mayle that many of the hill towns have been only too happy to oblige. Many of these old stone villages, which once hunkered down against the onslaught of Moors, now open their pale-blue shutters wide to surges of day-trippers from the beach. Stooped stone rowhouses are now galleries and boutiques offering everything from neo–Van Gogh sofa art to assembly-line lavender sachets, and everywhere you'll hear the gentle *breet-breet* of mechanical souvenir *cigales* (cicadas).

As the most conveniently accessible of the famous hill villages, St-Paul and to a slightly lesser degree Vence have become overwhelmingly commercialized, especially in high season. If you're allergic to souvenir shops, artsy-craftsy boutiques, and middle-brow art galleries, aim to visit off-season or after hours, when the stone-paved alleys, backstreets, placettes, and rampart overlooks empty of tourists, and when the scent of strawberry potpourri is washed away by the natural perfume of bougainvillea and jasmine wafting from terra-cotta jars.

LA COLLE SUR LOUP

17 km (10 mi) northwest of Nice.

This little town 3 km (1½ mi) southwest from St-Paul has been largely overlooked by tourists, and undeservedly so. What it lacks in sweeping views across the valley it makes up for in authentic Provençal charm, especially now that the whole village has been spruced up with careful restoration of its 17th-century buildings and new paving stones in the traditional style. There aren't many shops, but the town has more than its share of good places to eat, from crêperies to gourmet bistros. If you're a pottery fan, be sure to visit **Francine Le Coq** (⊠*21 rue Maréchal Foch* ☎*04–93–24–30–08* ⊙*Closed Sun.–Mon.*) who makes beautiful, almost Japanese-style bowls, vases, and cups glazed in white or red in her sunny open workshop. Located in a protected area, La Colle is surrounded by unspoiled hills: cutting through these are Les Gorges du Loup, a canyon whose narrow beaches serve as secret bathing spot for those who prefer to avoid the crowds and blazing sun of the coast.

WHERE TO EAT & STAY

$$$$ ✕**La Vie est Belle.** Of the surprising number of restaurants in La Colle's historic center, this bistro run by host Rémy Gélis and chef Michel Esposito is widely considered to be the best. The dining room—the original white tiles on the walls hint that this was once a butcher shop—has room for just 10 people but in summer most people aim for the traffic-free terrace. The food is a cut above standard Provençal fare: you'll find foie gras in various guises and fish dishes such as a millefeuille of seared tuna with grilled vegetables and balsamic cream on the €32 prix-fixe menu. The Japanese-style furniture in the dining room hints at the chef's passion for sushi—he even offers a separate sushi menu, all of it made on the premises. ⊠*1 rue George Clémenceau 06480* ☎*04–93–32–19–40* ⊕*www.restoviebelle.com* ⊟*MC, V* ⊙*No lunch Tues.–Sat. No dinner Sun. mid-Sept.–mid-June; no lunch Sun. mid-June–mid-Sept.*

$$ ▥**Un Ange Passe.** You could be in Kenya or southern India, so lush is the vegetation in the cascading garden of this thoughtfully decorated bed and breakfast expertly run by Martine Deloupy and her husband Bernard (he writes detective novels set in Nice). Wooden tables, lounge chairs, and hammocks are set in quiet corners and around the sparkling clean swimming pool—whose water comes from a natural source—inviting you to linger on the property all day, perhaps making use of the shared kitchen rather than joining the hordes of tourists in nearby St-Paul. From the garden there is barely a building to be seen, making it hard to believe you are 25 minutes from Nice. **Pros:** lush natural surroundings; the owners' sense of hospitality. **Cons:** steep staircases would be difficult for those with mobility problems. ⊠*419 Av. Leonardi,* ☎*04–93–32–60–39* ⊕*www.unangepasse.fr* ⤴*5 rooms* ⌂*In-room: no phone, refrigerator. In-hotel: pool, parking, some pets allowed* ⊟ *No credit cards* ⦿*BP.*

ST-PAUL

18 km (11 mi) northwest of Nice.

VISITOR INFORMATION
St-Paul Tourist Office (⊠*2 rue Grande, St-Paul* ☎*04–93–32–86–95*).

EXPLORING
The medieval village of St-Paul-de-Vence can be seen from afar, standing out like its companion, Vence, against the skyline. In the Middle Ages St-Paul was basically a city-state, and it controlled its own political destiny for centuries. But by the early 20th century St-Paul had

faded to oblivion, overshadowed by the growth of Vence and Cagnes—until it was rediscovered in the 1920s when a few penniless artists began paying for their drinks at the local auberge with paintings. Those artists turned out to be Signac, Modigliani, and Bonnard, who met at the **Auberge de la Colombe d'Or** (see the photo-feature, "Strokes of Genius" in this chapter), now a sumptuous inn, where the walls are still covered with their ink sketches and daubs. Nowadays art of a sort still dominates in the myriad tourist traps that take your eyes off the beauty of St-Paul's old stone houses and its rampart views. The most commercially developed of Provence's hilltop villages, St-Paul is none-theless a magical place when the tourist crowds thin. Artists are still drawn to its light, its pure air, its wraparound views, and its honey-color stone walls, soothingly cool on a hot Provençal afternoon. Even so, you have to work hard to find the timeless aura of St-Paul; get here early in the day to get a jump on the cars and tour buses, which can clog the main D36 highway here by noon, or plan on a stay-over. Either way, consider experiencing a luncheon or dinner beneath the Picassos at the Colombe d'Or, even if the menu prices seem almost as fabulous as the collection.

It won't take you long to "do" St-Paul; a pedestrian circuit leads you inevitably through its Rue-Grande to the *donjon* (fortress tower) and austere Gothic church. But break away and slip into a few mosaic-cobbled backstreets, little more than alleys; door after door, window after niche spill over with potted flowers and orange trees. The shuttered stone houses rear up over the streets, so close you could shake hands from window to window. And no matter which way you turn, you'll suddenly break into the open at the rampart walls; follow along the walkway to see the Tuscan-pretty landscape that quilts over the hills below, backed by an ivory sprawl of Alps. From St-Paul, there is a scenic hiking path to Vence (next to the Chapelle Ste-Claire); the walk takes an hour and 20 minutes.

On your way from the overpriced parking garages, you'll pass a Provençal scene played out with cinematic flair yet still authentic: the perpetual game of pétanque outside the **Café de la Place** (⊠ *Pl. de Gaulle* ☎ *04–93–32–80–03*). A sun-weathered pack of men (as for the lack of women playing this game anywhere, you're welcome to your own discussions of sexism) in caps, cardigans, and workers' blues—occasionally joined by a passing professional with tie and rolled-up sleeves—gathers under the massive plane trees and stands serene, silent, and intent to toss metal balls across the dusty square. Until his death, Yves Montand made regular appearances here, participating in this ultimate southern scenario.

Jean-Michel Folon had a deep affection for the town of St-Paul de Vence, where he befriended artists such as César, so it seems fitting that the decoration of its 17th-century **Chapelle des Pénitents Blanc** was one of the Belgian artist's last projects before his death in 2005. The overwhelming sensations as you enter the chapel are of peace and clarity: eight oil paintings in pastel colors by Folon collaborator Michel Lefebvre line the walls on either side and four stained-glass windows reinforce the themes of generosity and freedom. Sculptures take the place of the traditional altar and font, and the back wall is covered with a mosaic of the town made up of more than 1 million pieces. Demonstrating the versatility of this artist, the chapel reflects the town's ability to celebrate its past while keeping an eye on the future. ⊠ *Pl. de l'Eglise,* ☎ *04–93–32–86–95 (tourist office)* ⊕ *www.saint-pauldevence. com* ⊠ *€5* ♡ *Open 3–6.*

Fodor's Choice   One of the world's most famous small museums of modern art is a
★ big reason why many people come to St-Paul. Located a kilometer (½ mi) outside the village, **Fondation Maeght** is a temple of 20th-century art founded in 1964 by celebrated art dealer Aimé Maeght. Set on a wooded cliff top high above the medieval town, the museum is an extraordinary marriage of the arc-and-plane architecture of José Maria Sert; the looming sculptures of Miró and Moore; and its humbling setting of pines, vines, and flowing planes of water. On display is an intriguing and ever-varying collection of the work of modern masters, including the wise and funny late-life masterwork *La Vie (Life)* by Chagall. Giacometti's figures stride the courtyards, Miró's *Egg* emerges from the pool, while mobiles by Calder and Arp shift in the breeze. Inside, the multilevel, light-filled museum displays an ever-changing feast of works by Braque, Léger, Dubuffet, and other masters of 20th-century art. In addition, there are temporary exhibitions, artists' studios, a library, cinema, and auditorium (where concerts are held). You can get to the museum using the Nice–Vence bus. ⊠ *Colline des Gardettes, 06570* ☎ *04–93–32–81–63* ⊕ *www.fondation-maeght.com* ⊠ *€11* ♡ *July–Sept., daily 10–7; Oct.–June, daily 10–6.*

WHERE TO EAT & STAY

$ ✕ **Hostellerie de la Fontaine.** Not every meal in France has to be a spectacular chef's creation: sometimes a generously served tartine (open-faced sandwich) provides just the burst of energy you need for another few hours of sightseeing. Inside, this café in the center of the old village feels like a locals' wine bar, with wooden tables, modern paintings, and a few regulars hanging around the bar; there are also a few seats on the second-story terrace overlooking the street below. If the tartines such as tomato-mozzarella or chicken-avocado (served with lentils and beets on the side) don't grab you, there are also a few hot dishes such as gnocchi with pistou (pesto) and osso bucco. ⊠ *10 montée de la Castre* ☎ *04–93–32–80–29* ⊟ *AE, MC, V* ♡ *Closed Jan. and Tues. Oct.–May.*

¢–$ ✕ **Le Tilleul.** Before you plunge into the dense tangle of ruelles in old St-Paul, stop on the ramparts under the century-old lime tree for a light meal or snack at this atmospheric outdoor café-tearoom, whose breezy terrace looks onto the valley and the Alps. The kitchen makes more of an effort than you might expect, turning out colorful salads and pastas at lunch and more creative fare in the evening, perhaps a bouillabaisse-style fish stew or wok-sautéed scallops with Asian vegetables. Across the street, Le Tilleul sells freshly made sorbets and ice creams to go, with flavors like wild peach or almond milk with sour cherry. ⊠ *Pl. Tilleul* ☎ *04–93–32–80–36* ⊟ *No credit cards* ♡ *Closed Jan.*

$$$ ★ ⬚ **Le Hameau.** Less than a mile below tourist-packed St-Paul, with views of the valley and the village, this lovely little inn is a jumble of terraces, trellises, archways, orange trees, olives, and heavy-scented honeysuckle vines. The main hotel, built in 1920, has good-sized rooms and old Provençal furniture; you can also opt for the 18th-century farmhouse, with smaller, more modern rooms but wonderful views. Each room seems to skew toward a private world, several with individual terraces for *grasses matinées* (late, lazy breakfasts). The beautiful pool has hydromassage and the hotel added a small fitness area with a snack shop in 2005. **Pros:** relaxing setting; old-fashioned charm. **Cons:** short uphill walk to St-Paul with no sidewalk; handheld showers. ⊠ *528 rte. de La Colle* ☎ *04–93–32–80–24* ⊕ *www.le-hameau.com* ⬥ *17 rooms* ⬧ *In-room: refrigerator. In-hotel: bar, pool, spa, Wi-Fi, parking, some pets allowed* ▤ *AE, MC, V* ⊗ *Closed mid-Nov.–mid-Feb.*

¢–$ ★ ⬚ **Hostellerie les Remparts.** This utterly charming medieval inn is the place to stay in St-Paul if you're on a budget. You'll find antique Provençal furniture in the simple, freshly painted rooms, which are free of modern distractions such as television (though there is Internet access). The restaurant (open for lunch and dinner in summer and only on Friday and Saturday nights in winter) serves straightforward Provençal cooking—fish soup, spaghetti with pistou, rack of lamb with tapenade—and its enchanting terrace presides over the same sweeping view as those of far pricier places. **Pros:** old-fashioned charm, the views from the terrace. **Cons:** it's not a Relais & Châteaux but at this price it's hard to complain. ⊠ *72 rue Grande* ☎ *04–93–32–09–88* ⬥ *8 rooms* ⬧ *In-room: no a/c (some), refrigerator, no TV, Wi-Fi. In-hotel: 2 restaurants, Wi-Fi, some pets allowed* ▤ *D, MC, V* ⊗ *Closed 1 wk in Nov. and 1 wk in Jan.*

VENCE

4 km (2½ mi) north of St-Paul, 22 km (14 mi) north of Nice.

VISITOR INFORMATION
Vence Tourist Office (⊠ *Pl. du Grand Jardin, Vence* ☎ *04–93–58–06–38* ⊕ *www. vence.fr*).

EXPLORING
If you've visited St-Paul first, Vence will come as something of a relief. Just outside the Old Town, its morning food market, though not extensive, attracts genuine producers from the area (look for Tony and his exceptional socca, a pancake made with chickpea flour), and the cafés facing this square feel more down-to-earth than anything in St-Paul. Inside the stone walls of the Cité Historique (Historical City), the newly restored Place du Peyra invites you to linger with its restaurant terraces, relatively tasteful shops selling tablecloths or pottery, and pretty drinking fountain whose water comes directly from the Peyra source. Vence is slightly more conscious of its history than St-Paul—plaques guide you through its historic squares and *portes* (gates). Wander past the pretty Place du Peyra, with its fountains, and Place Clémenceau, with its ocher-color Hôtel-de-Ville (Town Hall), to Place du Frêne, with its

6

ancient ash tree planted in the 16th century, and don't miss the Rue du Marché's old-fashioned food shops, including a butcher, a baker, and a fishmonger.

On Place Godeau, in the Old Town center, the **Cathédrale de la Nativité de la Vierge** *(Cathedral of the Birth of the Virgin, on Place Godeau)* was built on the Roman's Champ de Mars (military drilling field) and traces bits and pieces to Carolingian and even Roman times. It's a hybrid of Romanesque and Baroque styles, expanded and altered over the centuries. The carved-wood choir stalls are worth studying (if access to the loft isn't blocked); they were sculpted between 1463 and 1467 by the Grasse cabinetmaker Jacques Bellot, and their detail and characterizations border on the risqué. In the baptistery is a ceramic mosaic of Moses in the bulrushes by Chagall.

FodorsChoice ★ On the outskirts of Vence "new town," toward St-Jeannet, it's easy to bypass a humble white chapel below the road, indistinguishable from a home except for its imposing cast-iron cross. But the **Chapelle du Rosaire** *(Chapel of the Rosary)*, decorated with beguiling simplicity and clarity by Matisse between 1947 and 1951, reflects the reductivist style of the era: the walls, floor, and ceiling are gleaming white, with color provided by the light streaming through the small stained-glass windows of green and blue. Stylized biblical characters are roughly sketched in thick black outline; in the annex behind the chapel you can see that earlier versions were more detailed. "Despite its imperfections I think it is my masterpiece ... the result of a lifetime devoted to the search for truth," wrote Matisse, who designed and dedicated the chapel when he was in his 80s and nearly blind. ⇨ *For more on Matisse, see "Strokes of Genius" in this chapter.* ✉ *Av. Henri-Matisse* ☎04–93–58–03–26 💶€2.50 ⏱ *Tues. and Thurs. 10–11:30 and 2–5:30; Fri. and Sat. 2–5:30; Mass, Sun. at 10.*

WHERE TO EAT & STAY

$$$$ ★ ✕ **Les Bacchanales.** After establishing himself as one of the region's best young chefs in Tourrettes-sur-Loup, Christophe Dufau has given himself and his cooking more breathing space in a rather grand villa on a country road just outside the center of Vence (it's on the left just after the bridge). A tireless globe-trotter who loves to pick up flavors from all over the world and once lived in Denmark, he has come back to his roots with cooking that finds most of its inspiration along the Mediterranean. The daily changing menu is a model of concision (two choices of main course at lunch, a handful at dinner), allowing him to use only the freshest ingredients in dishes such as caramelized melon with crumbled ricotta and a sauce made from spicy soubressade sausage, the sea bream with sauce vierge and wild mint, and a dessert that combines an intense chocolate sorbet, a vanilla "mayonnaise," and blackberries to dramatic effect. His loyal customers had already followed him from Tourrettes shortly after the restaurant's opening, and new fans are sure to join them. ✉ *247 av. de Provence* ☎04–93–24–19–19 ⌨ *Reservations essential* 🗐*AE, MC, V* ⏱ *Closed Tues., Wed. and 3 wks end of Nov.–early Dec.*

$ ✕**Le Pigeonnier.** The sight of a lone diner savoring a giant bowl of freshly picked broad beans in their pods sets the tone at this restaurant, which takes pride in its local ingredients. Foie gras terrine, smoked salmon, and fresh pasta are made on the premises, and the *souris d'agneau* (knuckle of lamb) is a specialty, as is an unlikely dish of beef Wellington under its puffy crust. The terrace stretches over a large part of Place du Peyra, and there are dining rooms on two levels indoors. ✉*3 pl. du Peyra* ☎*04–93–58–03–00* ⊕*le-pigeonnier.monsite.orange.fr* ▤*AE, MC, V* ☺*Closed Sun. and Mon. June–Sept.; Mon. from Oct.–May, and Jan.–mid-Feb.*

$$$$ ⌂**Château du Domaine St-Martin.** Exuding an expensive charm, this
★ famous domain occupies the ancient site of a fortress of the Knights Templars. Sitting on a hilltop perch and surrounded by acres of greenery designed by Jean Mus, the huge manor welcomes you with public salons that are light and airy—perhaps too much, as they seem to be overly renovated. All guest rooms are, in fact, junior suites, except for six *bastides* (two- and three-bedroom villas) accented with beautiful antiques. Le Saint-Martin restaurant is perhaps the best reason to come here, thanks to its stunning walls adorned with antique china, chef Yannick Franques' superb creations, and one of the most panoramic terraces around—the views over Old Vence to the Baie des Anges are eye-popping. **Pros:** polished and professional; beautiful pool and stunning grounds. **Cons:** service can feel a little too formal; public areas could be a little cozier. ✉*Av. des Templiers,* ☎*04–93–58–02–02* ⊕*www.chateau-st-martin.com* ⚲*34 junior suites, 6 villas* ⌂*In-room: refrigerator, Wi-Fi. In-hotel: 2 restaurants, bar, tennis courts, pool, spa, gym, Internet terminal, parking (free), some pets allowed* ▤*AE, MC, V* ☺*Closed mid-Dec.–mid-Feb.* ⍾*MAP.*

$$–$$$ ⌂**Villa Roseraie.** Although it doesn't have a rose garden, this 100-year-old house has a giant magnolia that spreads its venerable branches over the terrace. Inside, owners Monsieur and Madame Martefon have kept all the charming regional details: mix-and-match old furniture, fine local tiles and fabrics, even homemade bath salts and jams. You can enjoy the generous breakfast on the terrace and lounge by the pool much of the year, and it's a quick walk down to Old Vence. A nearby spa is open to hotel guests, if you prefer to indulge in some pampering. ✉*128 av. Henri-Giraud,* ☎*04–93–58–02–20* ⊕*www.villaroseraie. com* ⚲*12 rooms* ⌂*In-room: no a/c (some), refrigerator. In-hotel: bar, pool, Wi-Fi, parking (free)* ▤*AE, MC, V* ☺*Closed mid-Nov.–mid-Dec., and Jan.*

$$ ⌂**L'Auberge des Seigneurs et du Lion d'Or.** This extraordinary little inn
★ occupies a wing in an Old Town manor house overlooking the famous landmark ash tree reputedly planted by François I. Eccentrically decorated with antiques and modern art, it is personally managed by Madame Rodi and her daughter—the third generation. Guest rooms are spare but manorial, with dark antiques made cheery by Provençal fabrics. The restaurant is formal and a tad stuffy—though it has a summertime terrace—but the fireplace, spit-roasted rack of lamb, and chicken are legendary (prix-fixe menus cost €30 to €42). **Pros:** great value for location in center of Vence and spacious rooms; helpful own-

ers. **Cons:** best for those who prefer old-fashioned charm to modern amenities. ✉ *Pl. du Frêne,* ☎ *04–93–58–04–24* ⊕ *www.auberge-seigneurs.com* ⇆ *6 rooms* ⌂ *In-room: no a/c, no TV. In-hotel: restaurant, bar, Internet terminal, some pets allowed* ☐ *AE, MC, V* ⊘ *Closed 2 wks in Jan.*

NICE

GETTING HERE & AROUND

Nice is the main point of entry into the French Riviera region. It's home to the second-largest airport in France, which sits on a peninsula between Antibes and Nice, the **Aéroport Nice-Côte d'Azur** (☎ *08–20–42–33–33* ⊕ *www.nice.aeroport.fr*), which is 7 km (4 mi) south of the city. From the airport, you can take a bus to almost anywhere.

There are a few options: **RCA** (☎ *04–93–85–64–44* ⊕ *www.rca.tm.fr*), which is more comfortable and more expensive (⊠ *€6*) to Nice or the **Transport Alpes Maritimes** (TAM) buses (☎ *08–10–06–10–06* ⊕ *www. lignedazur.com*), which service the same destinations and are cheaper (⊠ *€1.30*). To go to the center of Nice, take the No. 98 bus from the airport (⊠ *€1.30*), which will take you to the main **Gare Routière**, or bus station (✉ *5 bd. Jean-Jaurès* ☎ *04–93–85–61–81*), and from here you can transfer on to any number of lines that spider the city.

If you plan on heading on via train, take the No. 99 bus from the airport (⊠ *€1.30*), which will take you to the main **Gare SNCF** train station (✉ *Av. Thiers* ☎ *04–92–14–80–80*). From here you can access all coastal major cities by train. For departure time and train prices to most destinations in this chapter, check out ☎ *08–36–35–35–35* ⊕ *www.voyages-sncf.com*. In Nice, the Sunbus is a convenient way to cut across town; a day pass costs €4, and a one-way ticket is €1.30. Get tickets at neighborhood tabacs (tobacconists) or at their ticket office at 10 avenue Félix Faure or their Station Centrale on Square Général Leclerc. Their main routes include No. 12, from train station to Promenade des Anglais, and No. 30, from train station to Vieux Nice. The Sunbus station is on Square Général Leclerc (☎ *08–10–06–10–06* ⊕ www.lignedazur.com.com).

VISITOR INFORMATION

Nice Tourist Office (✉ *5 promenade des Anglais, Nice* ☎ *08-92-70-74-07* ⊕ *www.nicetourism.com*).

EXPLORING

It's easy to become attached to Nice, whether you stay for a few days, a few weeks, or a few years. United with France only since 1860, the country's fifth largest city has its own history and atmosphere, exemplified by the stark contrast between the almost Florida-style Promenade des Anglais and narrow, ochre-tinted streets of the Old Town. Despite the inevitable urban sprawl north of the A8 autoroute No. 1, Nice remains an eminently manageable city, with the country's second-busiest international airport only 15 minutes from the center of town and the sleek new tramway whizzing down the main shopping thoroughfare avenue Jean Médecin. No wonder so many visitors come to Nice for a day or two on their way to somewhere else and fall head over heels for this city (though don't tell Parisians, who still think of this increasingly hip town as a dull retreat for retired people). Nice's waterfront, paralleled by the famous Promenade des Anglais and lined by grand hotels and mansions, is one of the noblest in France. It's capped by a dramatic promontory (called "the château") whose slopes plunge almost into the sea and at whose base unfolds a bewitching warren of ancient streets reminiscent of Italy, Greece, or old Sardinia. The city's first tramway line has been running without a hitch since late 2007 and new mayor Christian Estrosi is planning a second line along the Promenade des Anglais.

GUIDED TOURS

The city of Nice arranges individual guided tours on an à la carte basis, according to your needs. For information, contact the **Bureau d'Accueil** (*5 promenade des Anglais, 08-92-70-74-07*), and specify your dates and language preferences. A small tourist train (*04-93-92-45-59*) goes along the waterfront from the Jardin Albert Ier on the Promenade des Anglais. **Santa Azur** (*11 av. Jean-Médecin 04-97-03-60-00*) organizes bus excursions to sights near Nice, including Monaco and Cannes, leaving from the Promenade des Anglais. English-language tours are available with advance request.

It was on the now château-less Colline du Château and at what is now the Plage des Ponchettes, in front of the Old Town, that the Greeks established a market-port and named it Nikaia. Having already established Marseilles as early as the 4th century BC, they branched out along the coast soon afterward and founded the city that would become Marseilles's chief coastal rival. The Romans established themselves a little later on the hills of Cimiez (Cemenelum), already previously occupied by Ligurians and Celts, and quickly overshadowed the waterfront port. After falling to the Saracen invasions, Nice regained power as an independent state, developing into an important port in the early Middle Ages.

So cocksure did it become that in 1388, Nice, along with the hill towns behind, effectively seceded from the county of Provence, under Louis d'Anjou, and allied itself with Savoie. Thus began its intimate liaison with the House of Savoy, and through it with Piedmont and Sardinia, as the Comté de Nice (Nice County). It was a relationship that lasted some 500 years, tinting the culture, architecture, and dialect in rich Italian hues.

By the 19th century Nice was flourishing commercially, locked in rivalry with the neighboring shipping port of Genoa. Another source of income: the dawning of tourism, as first the English, then the Russian nobility discovered its extraordinary climate and superb waterfront position. A parade of fine stone mansions and hotels closed into a nearly solid wall of masonry, separated from the smooth-round rocks of the beach by the appropriately named Promenade des Anglais (promenade of the English).

Today Nice strikes an engaging balance between Old World grace, port-town exotica, urban energy, whimsy, and—in its extraordinary museums and thriving arts life—high culture (albeit tinged with a soupçon of corruption, a legacy of late mayor Jacques Médecin, who also authored a Niçois cookbook). Mayor Estrosi has promised many new improvements to the city, and since July 2008 admission to all museums has been free. Thanks to its two universities, there's a healthy dose of the young and hip, too. You could easily spend your vacation here and emerge days or weeks later subtly Latinized, sensually and aesthetically engaged, attuned to Nice's quirks, its rhythms, and its Mediterranean tides.

VIEUX NICE

Framed by the "château"—really a rocky promontory—and Cours Saleya, the Old Town of Nice is its strongest drawing point and, should you only be passing through, the best place to capture the city's historic feeling. Its grid of narrow streets, darkened by houses five and six stories high with bright splashes of laundry fluttering overhead and jewel-box Baroque churches on every other corner, creates a magic that seems utterly removed from the Côte d'Azur fast lane.

A GOOD WALK

Begin your exploration on **Cours Saleya**, preferably in the morning so you can experience the market in full swing. Its cafés, restaurants, and market stalls throng with the sounds, smells, and sights of Old Nice. At its center you'll find the florid Baroque **Chapelle de la Miséricorde**, worthy of a stop. Then make your way to the far end of the Cours. The tall yellow-stone building at its end, its top floor wrapped around with a balcony, was where Henri Matisse lived from 1921 to 1938; from the apartments on its top floors he took in magnificent views over the sea. Turn left up Rue de la Poissonerie to find the extravagant **Chapelle de l'Annonciation**. Continue up Poissonerie to Rue de la Place Vieille, then head right to Rue Droite. The **Eglise du Gésù** looms large and baroque in comparison with neighboring chapels. Turn left on Rue Rossetti and cross the square to the **Cathédrale Ste-Réparate**, its restored ocher facade an inspired balance of Italianate arcs and lines.

NEED A BREAK? For fresh, homemade gelato-style ice cream offered in a rainbow of flavors and colors, stop at **Glacier Fenocchio** (✉ *6 rue de la Poissonnerie* ☎ *04-93-62-88-80*). There's even a choice of locally grown citrus flavors, including orange, mandarin, and lemon.

Now take a break from the sacred, doubling back up Rue Rossetti and continuing left up narrow Rue Droite to the magnificent **Palais Lascaris**, whose broad classical facade squeezed onto this narrow street belies the Baroque extravagance within. Continue up Rue Droite to **Place St-François**, where a fish market holds forth every morning (though some of the fish have traveled a great distance to get here).

Head up Rue Pairolière, but take time to duck left and right up the tiny alleys and steep streets that plunge you into a concentration of popular

CLOSE UP

Flowers, Floats & Fatheads

If the word carnival means masked balls in Venice to most, or conjures images of feather-clad dancers writhing rhythmically through the streets of Rio, few people associate Nice with this pre-Lenten festival of excess and droll debauchery. Yet this most Latin of French cities is the capital of Carnaval in France, and transforms itself every February from a relatively sedate seaside metropolis into one vast party. The streets behind the waterfront and around Place Masséna explode in bright lights and color, and parades, masks, and impromptu street celebrations are everyday sights.

It's a tradition that dates back to pagan times, when the Romans fêted the end of winter and the dawning of spring. The festival translated easily into Christian terms, when the Church established the period of partial fasting before Easter. We call it Lent; the French call it Carême; but in Church Latin it was *carne levare* (crudely translated, "take out the meat"), and easily evolved into the word *carnaval*. Thus *mardi gras* (Fat Tuesday) was the last chance to indulge before Ash Wednesday and the deprivations of Lent. It wasn't long, however, before the pleasures of Carnaval outstripped those of Mardi Gras and shook free of their sacred meaning. The festival these days lasts a good two weeks and often takes place smack in the middle of Lent.

Nice's Carnaval is extremely user-friendly, with a published calendar of events and easy advance ticket sales for any seated events. There's the presentation of towering effigies of King and Queen Carnaval on Place Masséna, which is transformed into an electric fantasyland of music and blinking lights. There are parades of

magnificently crafted *grosses têtes* (literally, "fatheads"), enormous puppetlike personages that make Macy's balloons look like so much rubber. And there are the famous *batailles des fleurs* (flower battles), really full-scale parades complete with marching bands, clowns, and samba troupes. Elaborate floats heaped with Côte d'Azur flowers cruise down the Promenade des Anglais hauling a cargo of spectacularly costumed beauty queens who toss fresh flowers into the crowd. The crowds in the bleachers lining the Promenade des Anglais toss back confetti, wave branches of lemon-yellow mimosa, and cheer for their favorite floats. Weaving between the floats are stilt-walkers, jugglers, and street-theater troupes dressed in phantasmagoric excess who leer at onlookers and tease gawking children. Imagination reigns, and no image is too extreme, too bizarre, too extravagant.

The grand finale of Carnaval, which draws the days and nights of festivity to a close, takes on a solemn air. For the last time the towering dummy-king is paraded down Avenue Jean-Médecin and stands, still and lonely, on the dark pebble beach below the promenade. A parade of torchbearers in friars' robes cuts a glowing swath through the crowd and sets fire to the royal puppet. A silence falls over the crowd, then a cheer—really a primal roar—rises. The flames glow across the water as they engulf the king and, from a boat hovering offshore, fireworks burst in confetti colors over the waterfront. The party's over ... at least until next year.

6

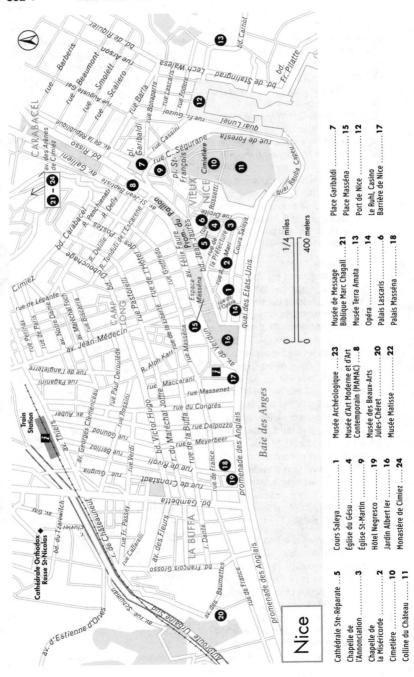

Nice

Cathédrale Ste-Réparate ...**5**	
Chapelle de l'Annonciation ...**3**	
Chapelle de la Miséricorde ...**2**	
Cimetière ...**10**	
Colline du Château ...**11**	
Cours Saleya ...**1**	
Église du Gésu ...**4**	
Église St-Martin ...**9**	
Hôtel Negresco ...**19**	
Jardin Albert Ier ...**16**	
Monastère de Cimiez ...**24**	

Musée Archéologique ...**23**	
Musée d'Art Moderne et d'Art Contemporain (MAMAC) ...**8**	
Musée des Beaux-Arts Jules-Chéret ...**20**	
Musée Matisse ...**22**	

Musée de Message Biblique Marc Chagall ...**21**	
Musée Terra Amata ...**13**	
Opéra ...**14**	
Palais Lascaris ...**6**	
Palais Masséna ...**18**	

Place Garibaldi ...**7**	
Place Masséna ...**15**	
Port de Nice ...**12**	
Le Ruhl, Casino ...**4**	
Barrière de Nice ...**17**	

1/4 miles

400 meters

Cathédrale Orthodox Russe St-Nicolas

cafés and restaurants, including the landmark (if overrated) street-food hangout called Chez René/Socca. You'll emerge on Boulevard Jean-Jaurès and empty onto the grand arcaded **Place Garibaldi**, which would be at home in Milan or Turin. One of its five street-spokes points straight to the **Musée d'Art Moderne et d'Art Contemporain**, a bold sculpture of a building anchoring a sleek plaza.

From Place Garibaldi and Boulevard Jean-Jaurès, follow Rue Neuve to the **Église St-Martin**, the oldest church. From here wind your way up Rue de la Providence and Rue Jouane Nicolas to the **Cimetière** and ultimately the ruins of the castle, now a park called the **Colline du Château**, with a wraparound panorama of Nice and the coast. From here you can either follow the switchback steps down or take the *ascenseur* (elevator) to the foot of the fat Tour Bellanda (Bellanda Tower), where the French composer Hector Berlioz once lived.

Next, you can cross Quai des États-Unis to the pebbled beach and rest your weary feet. Or, if you're still feeling energetic, swing left away from the Old Town and hike around the tidy rectangle of the **Port de Nice**, with its neat rows of pleasure boats, and from its end follow Boulevard Carnot to the **Musée Terra Amata**, marking the settlement where man first flourished some 400,000 years ago.

SIGHTS TO SEE

⑤ Cathédrale Ste-Réparate. Named for the 15-year-old Palestinian martyr whose body washed ashore at Nice to become the city's patron saint many centuries ago, this superb ensemble of columns, cupolas, and symmetrical ornaments dominates the Old Town, flanked by its own 18th-century bell tower and capped by a glossy ceramic-tile dome. The cathedral's interior, restored to a bright color palette of ocher golds and rusts, has elaborate plasterwork and decorative frescoes on every surface. Look for the **Chapelle du St-Sacrement** in the north transept, dating from 1707; its twisted marble columns and exuberant sculpture are worthy of Bernini and St. Peter's in Rome. ⊠ *Rue Ste-Réparate.*

③ Chapelle de l'Annonciation. Also known through typical Nice-lore obfuscation as St-Jaume, St-Giaume, or Ste-Rita, this 17th-century Carmelite chapel is a classic example of pure Niçois Baroque, from its sculpted door to its extravagant marble work and the florid symmetry of its arches and cupolas. The interior concentrates every form of colored faux-stonework, rich marble inlay, gilt, and frescoes—a lot of bombast squeezed into a finite space. Though it's officially dedicated to St. James the Apostle, the people of Nice lavish flowers and candles on the statue of Ste-Rita in the first chapel on the left; having suffered from a leprous sore and a lifetime of isolation in the 14th century, she has come to represent help for the terminally ill. ⊠ *Rue de la Poissonerie.*

② Chapelle de la Miséricorde. If you step inside only one Baroque chapel here, this superb 1740 structure on Cours Saleya should be it. A superbly balanced pièce-montée of half-domes and cupolas decorated within an inch of its life with frescoes, faux marble, gilt, and crystal chandeliers, it's the ultimate example of Nice Baroque at its most excessive and successful. A magnificent Bréa altarpiece crowns the ensemble. ⊠ *Cours Saleya.*

🔟 **Cimetière** *(Cemetery).* This solemn cluster of white tombs looms prominently over the city below, providing a serene or macabre detail of daily life, depending on your mood. Under Nice's blue skies, the gleaming white marble and Italian mix of melodrama and exuberance in the decorations, dedications, photo portraits, and sculptures are somehow oddly life-affirming. There are three sections, to this day segregating Catholics, Protestants, and Jews. ⊠ *Allée François-Aragon.*

> ### MATISSE'S MAGIC
>
> You don't need to visit the city's famous Musée Matisse to understand this great artist: Simply stand in the doorway of his former apartment (at 1 place Charles Félix) and study the Place de l'Ancien Senat 10 feet away—it's a golden Matisse pumped up to the nth power.

🔟 **Colline du Château** *(Château Hill).* Though nothing remains of this once-massive medieval stronghold but a few ruins left after its 1706 dismantling, the name château still applies to this high plateaulike park, from which you can take in extraordinary views of the Baie des Anges, the length of the Promenade des Anglais, and the red-ocher roofs of the Old Town. Children can let off steam at the playground, which has panoramic views and a bit of shade. ⊠ *At east end of Promenade des Anglais* ⊙ *Daily 7–7.*

❶ **Cours Saleya.** This long pedestrian thoroughfare, half street, half square, is the nerve center of Old Nice, the heart of the Vieille Ville and the stage-set for the daily dramas of marketplace and café life. Framed with 18th-century houses and shaded by plane trees, the long, narrow square bursts into a fireworks-show of color Tuesday through Sunday, when flower-market vendors roll armloads of mimosas, irises, roses, and orange blossoms into *cornets* (paper cones) and thrust them into the arms of shoppers (Tuesday–Saturday 6 AM–5:30 PM, Sunday 6–noon). Cafés and restaurants, all more or less touristy, fill outdoor tables with onlookers who bask in the sun. At the far-east end, antiques and *brocante* (collectibles) draw avid junk-hounds every Monday morning. Just beyond, Place Félix seems to lure the most fashionable crowd to see and be seen, perhaps because there are no market stands to get in the way of the most visible café tables, or because it provides clearest access to sun on cool winter days. ⊠ *2 blocks back from the Quai des États-Unis, in the center of the Old Town.*

Fodor's Choice ★

❼ **Eglise du Gésù.** If Nice's other chapels are jewel boxes, this is a barn. Broad, open, and ringing hollow after the intense concentration of sheer matter in the Miséricorde and Ste-Rita, it seems austere by comparison. That's only because the decoration is spread over a more expansive surface. If it's possible, this 17th-century Baroque chapel is even more theatrical and over-the-top than its peers. Angels throng in plaster and fresco, pillars spill over with extravagantly sculpted capitals, and from the pulpit (to the right, at the front), the crucifix is supported by a disembodied arm. ⊠ *Corner of Rue Droite and Rue du Jésus.*

⑨ Église St-Martin. Also known as St-Augustin, this serene Baroque structure at the foot of the château anchors the oldest church-parish in Nice. Built in 1405, it was here that Martin Luther preached in 1510 and Garibaldi was baptized in 1807. ✉ *Rue Sincaire.*

⑧ Musée d'Art Moderne. Moored by four marble-front towers, joined by the transparent arcs of pedestrian bridges, and dramatically framing a concourse decked with outdoor sculptures, this building is a bold and emphatic statement of Nice's presence in the modern world. The art collection inside focuses intently and thoroughly on contemporary art from the late 1950s onward, featuring works of the École de Nice (Nice School), the self-dubbed Nouveau Réalistes (New Realists) such as artists César, Bernar Venet, Ben, Yves Klein, Daniel Spoerri, Jean Tinguely, and Niki de Saint-Phalle. The collection includes international acquisitions, too, ranging from Jim Dine and Frank Stella to Miró and Giacometti. Be sure to climb along the rooftop sculpture terrace, a catwalk overlooking the whole of the city. ✉ *Promenade des Arts* ☏ *04–97–13–42–01* ⊕ *www.mamac-nice.org* ✉ *Free. Wed. €3 guided tour offered* ✆ *Tues.–Sun. 10–6.*

⑬ Musée Terra Amata. During the digging for the foundation of a building in 1966, the shovels revealed the remains of a temporary settlement once used by elephant hunters around 380,000 BC. They were perhaps the oldest known inhabitants of Europe. Now the site is a museum reconstructing the ancient beach-camp known as Terra Amata ("beloved land") as it was, lodgings and all—incorporating a real human footprint, calcified in the sand. There are recorded commentaries in English, and films explaining the lifestyle of these earliest Europeans. Don't expect a blockbuster anthropology expo; displays are small-scale and mainly limited to tiny models, even if the museum has been recently renovated. ✉ *25 bd. Carnot* ☏ *04–93–55–59–93* ⊕ *www.musee-terra-amata.org* ✉ *Free* ✆ *Tues.–Sun. 10–6.*

⑥ Palais Lascaris. ★ This aristocratic palace was built in 1648 for Jean-Baptiste Lascaris-Vintimille, marechal (marshal) to the duke of Savoy, in a manner grand enough to put the neighboring chapels to shame. The magnificent vaulted staircase with its massive stone balustrade and niches filled with classical gods is only surpassed in grandeur by the Flemish tapestries (after Rubens) and the extraordinary trompe-l'oeil fresco of the fall of Phaëthon. On the ground floor an 18th-century pharmacy has been imported from Besançon and reconstructed, complete with built-in wooden cabinets and a lovely collection of faïence jars. There's also a collection of cookware and tools from daily life at the other end of the income scale. Like much of Old Nice, this is a quirky, atmospheric museum, worth a stopover as you explore the backstreets. ✉ *15 rue Droite* ☏ *04–93–62–72–40* ⊕ *www.nice.fr* ✉ *Free; €3 guided tour, including the Vieille Ville* ✆ *Wed.–Mon. 10–6.*

⑦ Place Garibaldi. Encircled by grand vaulted arcades stuccoed in rich yellow, this broad pentagon of a square could have been airlifted out of Turin: it's looking especially majestic now that work on the tramway is finished. In the center the shrinelike fountain-sculpture of Garibaldi

6

surveys the passersby, who stroll under the arcades and lounge in its cafés. Garibaldi is held in high esteem here: the Italian general fought beside his own sons in the French ranks during the war of 1870.

⑫ Port de Nice. In 1750 the Duke of Savoy ordered a port to be dug into the waterfront to shelter the approach of the freight ships, fishing boats, and yachts that still sail into its safety today. Surrounded in rhythmic symmetry by the ocher facades of 19th-century houses, it makes for a pleasant walk far from the beach crowds.

ALONG THE PROMENADE DES ANGLAIS

Nice takes on a completely different character west of Cours Saleya, with broad city blocks, vast Neoclassical hotels and apartment houses, and a series of inviting parks dense with palm trees, greenery, and splashing fountains. From the Jardin Albert Ier, once the delta of the Paillon River, the famous Promenade des Anglais stretches the length of the city's waterfront.

The original promenade was the brainchild of Lewis Way, an English minister in the growing community of British refugees drawn to Nice's climate. They needed a proper walkway on which to take the sea air, and pooled resources to build a 6½-foot-wide road meandering through an alley of shade trees. Nowadays it's a wide, multilane boulevard thick with traffic—in fact, it's the last gasp of the coastal highway N98. Beside it runs its charming parallel, the wide, sun-washed pedestrian walkway with intermittent steps leading down to the smooth-rock beach; its foundation is a seawall that keeps all but the wildest storms from sloshing waves over the promenade. A daily parade of *promeneurs,* rollerbladers, joggers, and sun-baskers strolls its broad pavement, looking out over the hypnotic blue expanse of the sea. Only in the wee hours is it possible to enjoy the waterfront stroll as the cream of Nice's international society did, when there were nothing more than hoof beats to compete with the roar of the waves.

SIGHTS TO SEE

⑲ Hôtel Negresco. This vast neoclassical palace hotel dominates a full block of the promenade, and remains, for many, an enduring symbol of Côte d'Azur luxury. Its famous Salon Royal, a broad rotunda at the hotel's center, is classed as a historic monument, with its Gustav Eiffel leaded-glass dome and Baccarat chandelier commissioned by Czar Nicholas II. Like many grand hotels trying to make ends meet these days, it now caters to conferences and tour groups, but of all the hotels in town it remains the most quintessentially Niçois. ✉37 *promenade des Anglais* ☎04–93–16–64–00.

⑯ Jardin Albert Ier *(Albert I Garden).* Sandwiched between two busy streets, this garden of tropical greenery stands over the delta of the River Paillon, underground since 1882. Flowers and palm trees are thrown into exotic relief by nighttime illumination, and the wonderful old-fashioned merry-go-round provides a parents' dream photo opportunity.

㉔ Musée des Beaux-Arts Jules-Chéret *(Jules-Chéret Fine Arts Museum).* While the collection here is impressive, it is the 19th-century Italian-ate mansion that houses it that remains the showstopper. Originally built for a member of Nice's Old Russian community, the princess Kotschoubey, this was a Belle Époque wedding cake, replete with one of the grandest staircases on the coast, salons decorated with neo-Pompéienne frescoes, an English-style garden, and white columns and balustrades by the dozen. After the *richissime* American James Thompson took over and the last glittering ball was held here, the villa was bought by the municipality as a museum in the 1920s. Unfortunately, much of the period decor was sold but in its place now hang paintings by Degas, Boudin, Monet, Sisley, Dufy, and Jules Chéret, whose posters of winking *damselles* distill all the *joie* of the Belle Époque. ✉*33 av. des Baumettes* ☎*04–92–15–28–28* ⊕*www.musee-beaux-arts-nice.org* ▭*Free* ⊙*Tues.–Sun. 10–6.*

⑭ Opéra. Demolished by a devastating 1881 fire, the victims of which lie in the cemetery on the hillside of the château, this magnificent Italian-style opera house rose from the ashes in 1885. Charles Garnier, architect of the Paris Opéra, consulted on its design. It's home today to the Opéra de Nice, with a permanent chorus, orchestra, and ballet corps. ✉*4 rue St-François-de-Paul* ☎*04–92–17–40–00.*

⑱ Palais Masséna *(Masséna Palace).* This handsome Belle Époque villa,
★ which reopened in March 2008 after extensive renovations, was built by a grandson of Napoléon's, Marechal Masséna; his great-grandson donated it to Nice under the proviso that it house a museum of the city's history. The resulting **Musée d'Art et d'Histoire** (Museum of Art and History) is a fascinating hodgepodge of private collections reflecting every aspect of Nice's past, from Garibaldi's death sheet to Asian jewelry collected in imperial days to Empress Josephine's tiara, carved entirely in cameo. It also contains extraordinary notebook sketches of Napoléon by Neoclassical painter Jacques-Louis David, as vivid and natural as snapshots, as well as relief models of Nice in the 1930s and 1954—a desert-island wasteland compared to today's congested over-building. There's even a Bréa polyptych of St-Marguerite. It's a must if you love the offbeat, the obscure, and the treasure hunt. ✉*Entrance at 65 rue de France* ☎*04–93–91–19–10* ▭*Free.*

⑮ Place Masséna. As Cours Saleya is the heart of the Old Town, so this broad and noble square is the heart of the city as a whole. It's framed by an ensemble of Italian-style arcaded buildings first built in 1815, their facades stuccoed in rich red ocher. At its center is a heroic fountain in which thick-muscled bronze figures surge from the water; nearby, the new city tram sweeps though between modern sculptures on pedestals that light up at night. The central activities of the February Carnaval are traditionally held here, though they have been moved to the Promenade des Anglais during work on the tramway. Behind the Place and following the ancient riverbed, stretches the inviting **Escape Masséna,** a long public plaza with fountains, permanent performance spaces, grassy park grounds, and dozens of skateboarders at any given moment.

6

17 **Le Ruhl, Casino Barrière de Nice.** Renovated to the tune of €5 million by the Barrière group, which purchased this casino a few years ago, Le Ruhl now lures in the summer vacationers and the winter convention crowd with vivid colors and fiber-optic lighting. Some sign into the hushed gaming room for roulette and blackjack, others try their luck at one of the 300-some slot machines. ☒*1 promenade des Anglais* ☏*04–97–03–12–22* ☻*Sept.–July, Fri.–Sun. 10 AM–5 AM, Mon.–Thurs. 10 AM–4 AM, Aug., daily 10 AM–5 AM.*

OFF THE
BEATEN
PATH

Cathédrale Orthodoxe Russe St-Nicolas. From the Promenade, hop Bus 7 up Boulevard Gambetta and get off at either the Thiers-Gambetta or Parc Imperial stop, or walk west from the train station to visit this magnificent Russian Orthodox cathedral. Built in 1896 to accommodate the sizable population of Russian aristocrats who had adopted Nice as their winter home, this Byzantine fantasy is the largest of its kind outside the motherland. The church has no fewer than six gold-leaf onion domes, rich ceramic mosaics on its facade, and extraordinary icons framed in silver and jewels. The benefactor was Nicholas II himself, whose family attended the inauguration in 1912. ☒*Av. Nicolas II* ☏*04–93–96–88–02* ☻*Daily, May–Sept. 9–noon and 2:30–6, Oct. 9:15–noon and 2:30–5:30, Nov.–mid-Feb. 9:30–noon and 2:30–5, mid-Feb.–Apr. 9:15–noon and 2:30–5:30.*

CIMIEZ

Once the site of the powerful Roman settlement Cemenelum, the hilltop neighborhood of Cimiez—4 km (2½ mi) north of Cours Saleya—is Nice's most luxurious quarter. Villas seem in competition to outdo each other in opulence, and the combination of important art museums, Roman ruins, and a historic monastery make it worth a day's exploration. To visit Cimiez and nearby museums, you need to combine a bus pass or taxi fare with strong legs and comfortable shoes. If you brave the route by car, arm yourself with a map and a navigator. Bus 15 from Place Masséna or Avenue Jean-Médecin takes you to both the Chagall and Matisse museums; from the latter you can visit the ruins and monastery.

SIGHTS TO SEE

24 **Monastère de Cimiez.** High over Nice and its château-bearing hill, this fully functioning monastery, originally established in the 16th century, is worth the pilgrimage. There's a lovely **garden**, replanted following the original 16th-century lines. There's also the **Musée Franciscain** (Franciscan Museum), a didactic museum tracing the history of the Franciscan order, and a 15th-century **church**. The pretty, single-nave chapel contains three works of remarkable power and elegance by Bréa: the early *Pietà* (1475) flanked by portraits of High Renaissance grace; the *Crucifixion* (1512); and the *Deposition* (1520), with intense suppressed emotion. ☒*Pl. du Monastère* ☏*04–93–81–00–04* ☒*Free* ☻*Mon.–Sat. 10–noon and 3–6.*

23 **Musée Archéologique** *(Archaeology Museum).* This contemporary building houses a dense and intriguing collection of objects extracted from digs around the Roman city of Cemenelum, which flourished from the 1st to the 5th centuries and dwarfed its waterfront neighbor with a population of 20,000 in its prime. The examples of Greek and Italian treasures—ceramics, jewelry, and coins—attest to the cosmopolitan nature of coastal commerce. Behind the museum, you can wander through the **ruins** and digs, including the *thermes* (baths) and an early Christian baptistery. Just beyond, the Roman *arènes* (arena) seats 4,000 for the annual jazz festival. ✉ *160 av. des Arènes-de-Cimiez* ☎ *04–93–81–59–57* ⊕ *www.musee-archeologique-nice.org* 💲 *Free* ⊘ *Wed.–Mon. 10–6.*

㉒ **Musée Matisse.** In the '60s, the city of Nice bought this lovely, light-
FodorśChoice bathed 17th-century villa, surrounded by the ruins of Roman civili-
★ zation, and restored it to house a large collection of Henri Matisse's works. Matisse settled in Nice in 1917, seeking a sun cure after a bout with pneumonia, and remained here until his death in 1954. During his years on the Côte d'Azur, Matisse maintained intense friendships and artistic liaisons with Renoir, who lived in Cagnes, and with Picasso, who lived in Mougins and Antibes. Settling first along the waterfront, he eventually moved up to the rarified isolation of Cimiez and took an apartment in the Hotel Regina (now an apartment building), where he lived out the rest of his life. Matisse walked often in the parklands around the Roman remains and was buried in an olive grove outside the Cimiez Cemetery. The collection of artworks includes several pieces donated to the city by the artist himself before his death; the rest was donated by his family. In every medium and context—paintings, gouache cutouts, engravings, and book illustrations—it represents the evolution of his art, from Cézanne-like still lifes to exuberant dancing paper dolls. Even the furniture and decorations speak of Matisse, from the Chinese vases to the bold-printed fabrics with which he surrounded himself. A series of black-and-white photographs captures the artist at work, surrounded by personal—and telling—details. ✉ *164 av. des Arènes-de-Cimiez* ☎ *04–93–81–08–08* ⊕ *www.musee-matisse-nice.org* 💲 *Free* ⊘ *Wed.–Mon. 10–6.*

㉑ **Musée du Message Biblique Marc-Chagall** *(Marc Chagall Museum of Bibli-*
★ *cal Themes).* Superbly displayed in a modern structure bathed in light and surrounded by coastal greenery, this is one of the finest permanent collections of the artist's late works. Included here are 17 vast canvases on biblical themes, each in emphatic and joyous color schemes; they celebrate the stories of Adam and Eve, Noah, Abraham, and Moses, and the sensual, mystical Song of Solomon, dedicated to his wife. Preparatory sketches, sculptures, and ceramic pieces enhance the exhibit, as well as a tapestry and, outside, a mosaic. ✉ *Av. du Dr-Ménard (head up Av. Thiers, then take a left onto Av. Malausséna, cross the railway tracks, and take the first right up Av. de l'Olivetto)* ☎ *04–93–53–87–20* 💲 *Free* ⊘ *May–Oct., Wed.–Mon. 10–6; Nov.–Apr., Wed.–Mon. 10–5.*

6

WHERE TO EAT & STAY

$$$$ ✕**Chantecler.** Long a showplace for Riviera luxury, replete with Régence-
★   fashion salons decked out with 18th-century wood boiserie and Aubusson carpet, the Negresco's main dining room has been playing musical
chefs for the past few years. The newly named chef, Jean-Denis Rieu-
bland, worked in many of the French Riviera's top restaurants before
taking over the kitchen here. Though you'll find Mediterranean touches
in the cooking, he is not afraid to challenge local traditions with lusty
dishes inspired by his native southwest France: typical of his style are
veal sweetbreads studded with chorizo and served with wild mush-
rooms, pearl onions, and a sophisticated take on macaroni, or seared
foie gras with raspberries, rhubarb, and white balsamic glaze. Winner of the prestigious Meilleur Ouvrier de France award, he seems a
likely candidate to restore this restaurant to its former glory. If you're
watching your centimes, try the *menu plaisir* at lunch for €45. ✉*Hôtel
Negresco, 37 promenade des Anglais* ☎*04–93–16–64–00* ⊕*www.
hotel-negresco-nice.com* ⚑*Reservations essential* ▤*AE, DC, MC, V*
⊘*Closed Mon., Tues., and early Jan.–early Feb.*

$$$$ ✕**La Réserve de Nice.** Finnish-born, Alain Ducasse–trained chef Jouni
Tormanen has moved to a spectacular seaside dining room that befits
his talent. Downstairs in this Art Deco building jutting over the sea is
his casual-chic bistro, Le Bistrot de la Réserve, while upstairs, Jouni
l'Atelier du Goût is the place to pull out all the stops. Tormanen's style
is sometimes disarmingly straightforward, putting the focus firmly on
carefully sourced ingredients from along the French and Italian Riviera,
but he shows a more playful side in the bistro with dishes such as fish
and chips or pan-fried foie gras with lemon marmalade. His animated
partner Giuseppe Serena sets the tone in the dining room, where the
staff dress in striped sailor tops. La Réserve also houses one of the city's
most stylish bars. Be warned that even in the bistro it's easy to run up a
bill of more than €150 per couple. ✉*60 bd. Frank Pilatte, Mont Boron*
☎*04–97–08–29–98* ⊕*www.lareservedenice.com* ▤*AE, DC, MC, V*
⊘*Closed 3 wks Nov.–Dec.*

$$$ ✕**L'Aromate.** Mickäel Gracieux has joined the ranks of ambitious young
chefs in Nice with this chic modern bistro in green, black, and stone
near Notre Dame cathedral. Though the menu draws on seasonal
ingredients, you won't find any Provençal clichés here: instead, the
waiter might whisk off a cubic "cloche" to reveal a goldfish bowl con-
taining crab in ginger jelly with a tart cream sauce and a fennel emul-
sion (being from Brittany, the chef is not afraid to be generous with the
crème fraîche). Evening menus are pricey but worth it at €50 or €70,
while lunch is a simpler affair, often featuring variations on risotto.
✉*20 av. Maréchal Foch, New Town* ☎*04–93–62–98–24* ▤*MC, V*
⊘*Closed Sun. and Mon.*

$$$ ✕**La Merenda.** The back-to-bistro boom climaxed here when Domin-
★   ique Le Stanc retired his crown at the Negresco to take over this tiny,
unpretentious landmark of Provençal cuisine. Now he works in the
miniature open kitchen creating the ultimate versions of stuffed sardines, tagliatelle with pistou, slow-simmered daubes (beef stews), and
the quintessential stockfish (the local lutefisk), while his wife whisks

Cooking the Nicoise Way

Nowhere in France is the food more seductive than along the Côte d'Azur and Provence. No wonder southern French cooking holidays à la Patricia Wells are so popular—yet, except for the most dedicated cooks, a full week can be too big a time and money commitment. That's why longtime food writer and Cordon Bleu–trained cook Rosa Jackson created the home-based cooking school **Les Petits Farcis** (✉ *7 rue du Jésus, Nice* ☎ *06–81–67–41–22* ⊕ *www.petits-farcis.com*) in the Vieux Nice neighborhood, a minute's walk from the celebrated Cours Saleya food market. In the yellow-and-burgundy kitchen of her renovated 17th-century apartment, complete with wooden beams and a handmade chandelier of chili peppers and silver cutlery, Jackson teaches students the classics of Niçois cooking: *les petits farcis,* of course (a local stuffed vegetable dish), but also *pissaladière* (caramelized onion tart), *poulet à la niçoise* (chicken stewed with tomatoes, bell peppers, and eau de vie), *daube à la provençale* (beef stew with wine and herbs), local fish dishes, and fruit-based desserts. A class always begins with a trip to the market, where Jackson explains the origins of Niçois cooking—Nice was part of the Italian-ruled Kingdom of Savoy until 1860. After visiting a local wine cellar and choosing their cheeses at the local *fromagerie* (cheesemonger), students head back to the kitchen for an informal, hands-on class where they learn as much about local culture as cooking techniques. Following a four-course lunch, those who wish can continue with an olive oil tasting and food walk through the Old Town, ending at 6 PM with a glass of organic wine. Classes run from €200 to €290.

6

the dishes into the dining room. It's one man's private mission; stop by in person to reserve entry to the inner sanctum (there are two sittings at both lunch and dinner) as there's no phone. ✉ *4 rue de la Terrasse, Old Town/Port* ☎ *No phone* ▤ *No credit cards* ⊘ *Closed weekends, last wk July, and 1st 2 wks Aug.*

$$$ ✕ **Sapore.** Chef Anthony Riou has found a winning formula with his generous five-course, €28 tapas menu, which changes frequently to keep the locals coming back to this sleek red-and-gray-walled dining room with ancient wooden beams and an open kitchen. The key to his cooking is simple, bold flavors, as in a thick crab velouté, goat cheese, and very thin bacon slices on toast, deboned duck confit on potato purée, and chocolate cake with mango. Choose from Spanish and French wines to complete this Spanish-accented experience, which attracts a young and fashionable French crowd. ✉ *19 rue Bonaparte, Place du Pin, Old Town/Port* ☎ *04–92–04–22–09* ⊕ *www.restaurant-sapore. com* ▤ *No credit cards* ⊘ *Closed Sun. and Mon. and 3 wks in Aug. No lunch.*

$$$ ✕ **La Zucca Magica.** Tucked in a cozy, rustic shoebox along the port, this vegetarian-Italian bistro, The Magic Pumpkin, is all the rage, thanks to the imaginative cooking of Roman chef Marco Folicaldi. The eat-'til-you-drop five-course menu changes daily according to the season, and offers a taste of the rich flavors that the best local markets have

to offer: grilled fresh vegetables smothered in smoked cheese, minestrone, cannelloni, stuffed peppers, delicious pizzas, and the justly famous pumpkin-based recipes when autumn arrives. The chef's gruff friendliness, the noisy camaraderie of crowded diners, and the surreal pumpkin art in every form make for a real dining event. ✉ *4 bis quai Papacino, Old Town/Port* ☎ *04–93–56–25–27* 🚫 *No credit cards* 🕙 *Closed Sun. and Mon.*

$$ ✕ **Cave de l'Origine.** Once an industrial space where arms were produced, the Cave de l'Origine now has a more peaceful mission: to spread joy through good food and wine. At the front is an épicerie displaying carefully selected products from all over France, while lining the walls are bottles of wine from small producers, many of them organic. In two spacious rooms with red and gray walls, you can sip a glass of wine and perhaps nibble a plate of thinly sliced saucisson or smoked tuna, or come for a meal highlighting produce hand-selected from small farmers at the Cours Saleya market. Carlo and Isabelle are enthusiastic hosts and English speakers get a warm welcome. ✉ *3 rue Dalpozzo* ☎ *04–83–50–09–60* 🚫 *MC, V* 🕙 *Closed Sun.–Mon.*

$$ ✕ **Luc Salsedo.** Young chef Luc Salsedo, who trained at the Louis XV in Monaco, has a hit on his hands with this little ochre-walled bistro. His brief menu, which changes completely every three weeks, often involves modern twists on traditional Niçois dishes such as socca (a chickpea flour pancake) wrapped around stir-fried spring vegetables. Servings are generous—expect a generous appetizer plate and mignardises in addition to the three copious courses—and the dining room staff, led by Luc's wife, are adorable. ✉ *14 rue Maccarani* ☎ *04–93–82–24–12* ⊕ *www.restaurant-salsedo.com* 🚫 *MC, V* 🕙 *Closed Wed.; No lunch Thurs. and Sat.; July–Aug.: closed for lunch Mon.–Sat.; 3 wks in Jan.; last wk June.*

$$ ✕ **Le Safari.** The Cours Saleya's desirable terrace tables provide an excuse for many of the restaurants along this strip to get away with culinary murder. That's not the case at Le Safari, at No. 1, which pays more attention than most to ingredients and presentation (even if you shouldn't expect miracles). Choose from traditional Niçois dishes—the fish soup served with croutons, spicy mayonnaise, and cheese is particularly good—and Italian-inspired fare such as creamy risotto. Inside the colorful dining room is where the locals eat, and some even claim the food is a notch better there. ✉ *1 cours Saleya, Old Town/Port* ☎ *04–93–80–18–44* ⊕ *www.restaurantsafari.fr* 🚫 *AE, D, MC, V.*

$ ✕ **Pipo Socca.** There are plenty of places where you can sample socca in
Fodor's Choice   the Old Town, but if you want to understand why so much fuss is made
★   in Nice over this chickpea pancake, this out-of-the-way café behind the Port is the place to go. As always, a batter of chickpea flour, water, olive oil, and salt is baked in giant copper tins in a wood-fired oven, but here the cook expertly scrapes the surface of the nearly-cooked dough with a metal spatula so that it comes out extra-crispy. It's hard to explain why, but this is socca you can eat in large quantities even if you're not hungry: proof is the line on weekend nights, when people are willing to wait an hour or more for their petite or grande plates (the trick is to show up around 5:30, when Pipo first opens). ✉ *13 rue Bavastro, Old*

Town/Port ☎04–93–55–88–82 ▤No credit cards ⊘*Closed Mon. Sept.–June, Sat. in July and Aug. No lunch.*

¢ ✕**Le Bistrot d'Antoine.** Armand Crespo, who previously worked at Lou
★ Cigalon in Valbonne, has turned this former café into the bistro where locals go to eat well in the Old Town. Though there are always a couple of fish dishes available—the salmon gravlax with fennel and carrots sliced paper-thin is delicious—this restaurant caters best to carnivores with juicy steak and duck magret off the grill and Niçois specialties such as lentils with Perugina sausages. Crespo can often be seen buying from small producers at the Cours Saleya market and this attention to quality shows in every dish. There is always a lively bistro atmosphere, wines are well-chosen and affordable, and service is both friendly and professional. What more could anyone ask? ✉*27 rue de la Préfecture, Old Town/Port* ☎04–93–85–29–57 ▤*MC, V* ⌦*Reservations essential* ⊘*Closed Sun. and Aug.*

¢ ✕**La Part des Anges.** This wine shop with a few tables and chairs at the back is really about vins naturels—unfiltered, unsulfured, hand-harvested wines from small producers—but the often-simple food also happens to be excellent. Whether you choose a charcuterie or cheese plate or one of the handful of hot dishes such as spaghetti with razor clams or octopus daube (cooked with red wine), you can expect it to be generous and fresh. No corkage fee is charge for wines off the shelf, a rarity for a wine bar. Bilingual owner Olivier will be happy to explain that "here it's all about talking and sharing with the customers." Reservations are best for Friday and Saturday nights. ✉*17 rue Gubernatis, New Town* ☎04–93–62–69–80 ▤*AE, D, MC, V* ⊘*Closed Sun. and 1 wk in Aug.*

$$$$ ▦**Boscolo Hotel Exedra Nizza.** Certainly the most stylish hotel in Nice—
Fodor'sChoice if not the Riviera—this magnificent extravaganza raises the hotel bar
★ of southern France to brand new heights. Owned by the Boscolo family chain (whose eye-knocking Aleph and Exedra set Rome on its ear) and located seven blocks off the waterfront in a ritzy neighborhood, this is set in a wedding-cake, marble 1910 landmark building. But one step in the door and you've blasted off into the nether regions of the 21st century—think the white-on-white, rococo-ed rooms at the end of Kubrick's 2001: A Space Odyssey. Louis Quinze armchairs, minimal mod tables, soaring skylights (in this case, a re-do of one originally fashioned by Gustave Eiffel himself), plus acres of teakwood walls, 50's-kidney-shaped sofas, and some of the biggest black-and-white Murano chandeliers in the world. A supermodel of a hotel, this also has guest rooms to die for, replete with cascading diamond-like ceiling lights, sculpted rose door-handles, the very latest in push-button luxury, and a white-on-white color scheme. In the basement is one of the most striking spas around, the kind with plasma TVs in the saunas. A destination in itself, this is now the place to go in Nice. **Pros:** infinite chic, infinite taste. **Cons:** don't look for old-world Nice here; restaurant is a bit of a let-down, décor-wise. ✉*12 bd. Victor Hugo, New Town 06000* ☎04–93–16–75–70 ⊕*www.boscolohotels.com* ⇆*100 rooms, 8 suites* ♿*In-room: refrigerator, Ethernet, Wi-Fi. In-hotel: restaurant, 2 bars, pool, gym, spa, public Wi-Fi* ▤*AE, DC, MC, V.*

6

$$$$
Fodor's Choice
★

🏨 **Hôtel Negresco.** One of those names, like the Pierre or Claridges, that is synonymous with "Grand Hotel," the Negresco is a wedding-cake, white-stucco slice of old-fashioned Riviera extravagance. Still the icon of Nice and a living monument to the city's golden age of travel, it has hosted everyone from the Beatles to the Burtons, and you'll feel a bit like a V.I.P. just pulling up in front of the entrance as the doorman, in uniformed splendor (knee-breeches and ostrich-plumed tricorn), helps you with your luggage. No other hotel can boast today of quite so many pillars, busts, coffered and painted ceilings, or, indeed, so many acres of white paint and gilding. The place is, in short, the very epitome of La Belle Epoque, justly so since it was built by Henri Negresco in 1912. Yes, the main hall, now denuded of the world's largest Aubusson carpet, is a bit forlorn, but its Gustave Eiffel glass ceiling still awes, as does its *qualité du Louvre* collection of Old Master paintings. Upstairs, each floor is devoted to an era from French history; Napoléon III on the fifth, Louis XV on the third, with some jarring modern notes, like the plastic-glitter bathtubs, the Vasarely Op-art carpet, and the rotating Niki de Saint Phalle sculpture. Happily, each guest room is decorated differently and even the smallest have been done up with elegance and swank. Downstairs, Le Chantecler ranks among the very finest restaurants in France, while the Carrousel Room (complete with merry-go-round horses and Folies Bérgère chandelier) is an over-the-top setting for your breakfast buffet. **Pros:** the sometimes kitsch extravagance; a sense of being part of history. **Cons:** this grande dame could use a discreet face-lift. ✉ *37 promenade des Anglais, Promenade des Anglais,* ☎ *04–93–16–64–00* ⊕ *www.hotel-negresco-nice.com* ⇱ *145 rooms* ⌂ *In-room: Internet. In-hotel: 2 restaurants, bar, beachfront, Wi-Fi, parking (free), some pets allowed* ☰ *AE, DC, MC, V.*

$$$–$$$$
★

🏨 **La Pérouse.** Just past the Old Town, at the foot of the château, this anti-palace is a secret treasure cut into the cliff (an elevator takes you up to reception). Most rooms have breathtaking views of the Baie des Anges. Some of the best not only overlook the azure sea but also look down into an intimate garden with lemon trees and a cliff-side pool. A sundeck and sauna by the pool, as well as valet parking, add to the sense of private luxury. Most rooms are fairly large; some are decorated in somber plaids, others have painted Provençal furniture. The restaurant serves meals in the candlelit garden May through September. **Pros:** the location between the Old Town and the Parc du Chateau; the pool with its sweeping view of the sea. **Cons:** some rooms are surprisingly small; staff can be snooty. ✉ *11 quai Rauba-Capeau, Old Town/Port,* ☎ *04–93–62–34–63* ⊕ *www.hotel-la-perouse.com* ⇱ *63 rooms* ⌂ *In-room: refrigerator (some), Wi-Fi. In-hotel: restaurant, bar, pool, gym, Internet terminal, parking (paid), some pets allowed, no-smoking rooms AE, DC, MC, V.*

$$–$$$

🏨 **Nice Pebbles and Riviera Pebbles.** If you've ever fantasized about living on the French Riviera, renting a furnished apartment is the next best thing. Established a few years ago, the friendly agency Nice Pebbles has a wide variety of comfortable apartments to choose from, many of them in the Old Town and all less than 20 minutes' walk from the beach. Fully equipped kitchens allow you to make the most of the fabulous produce at the local markets, and a welcome pack of local delicacies comes with each rental. Riviera Pebbles has a further selection of apartments in Nice, as well as apartments and villas in other key locations along the Côte d'Azur. Note that there while all apartments have kitchens, some do not have swimming pools, elevators, telephones, air-conditioning, or Wi-Fi. ⊠*7 rue du Collet, Old Town* ☎*09–52–78–27–65* ⊕*www.nicepebbles.com,www.rivierapebbles.com* ⥂*69 apartments* ⊟*MC, V.*

$$–$$$ 🖼**Suisse.** Charging modest prices for a spectacular view from the top end of the seafront, where the promenade winds around to the port, the Hôtel Suisse far outclasses most other hotels in this price range. You'll pay a little extra for a balcony with a sea view, but it will be oh-so-worth-it for the sight of the turquoise water glittering below. Recently redecorated by architect J.P. Nuel, the rooms provide all the modern comforts with pleasing cream-and-brown or cream-and-burgundy color schemes, and the lobby/breakfast room has also had been given a hip new look. **Pros:** clean, modern rooms; balconies with breathtaking sea views; accessible prices in low season. **Cons:** lack of space in some rooms; pricey breakfast at €15. ⊠*15 quai Raubà Capéù, Old Town/ Port* ☎*04–92–17–39–00* ⊕ *www.hotels-ocre-azur.com* ⥂*42 rooms* ♿*In-room: Internet. In-hotel: bar, Wi-Fi* ⊟*AE, DC, MC, V.*

$$ 🖼**La Fontaine.** Downtown and a block from the waterfront, this immaculate, simply designed hotel on a bustling shopping street offers a friendly welcome from its house-proud owners. Rooms are small and comfortable, in cheery blues and yellows and with freshly tiled bathrooms. It even has a pretty little courtyard where breakfast is served. Nearby is Le Sporting Plage, one of the city's best private beaches. **Pros:** helpful staff; leafy courtyard; location near the Negresco. **Cons:** rooms overlooking the street can be noisy; breakfast overpriced. ⊠*49 rue de France, New Town* ☎*04–93–88–30–38* ⊕*www.hotel-fontaine. com* ⥂*29 rooms* ♿*In-room: safe, Internet, Wi-Fi. In-hotel: bar, room service some pets allowed* ⊟*AE, DC, MC, V.*

$$ 🖼**Villa les Cygnes.** The Baumettes neighborhood is an area not normally explored by tourists, but it's worth getting to know it for the sake of staying in this new hotel, which is really more like a luxury bed-and-breakfast. Each of the five rooms has its unique charms: on the main floor, one of the rooms opens directly onto the garden while the other has a terrace; upstairs, the rooms have balconies. You'll find the comforts of a top-notch hotel—air-conditioning, Wi-Fi, spacious bathrooms—along with feeling of staying in a family home. Meals are available if you request them the day before, and the hotel has a bar. Keep in mind that it's a bit of a hike (around 30 minutes) from here to the Old Town, where most of the action is. **Pros:** owners warm and welcoming; generous breakfast; thoughtfully decorated; big bathrooms. **Cons:** a little far from the tourist center of Nice. ⊠*6 av. du Château de la Tour, New Town* ☎*04–97–03–23–35* ⊕*www.villalescygnes.com* ⥂*5 rooms* ♿*In-room: Wi-Fi. In-hotel: bar, Wi-Fi* ⊟*MC, V.*

$$ 🖼**Windsor.** This is a memorably eccentric hotel with a vision: most of its white-on-white rooms either have frescoes of mythical themes or are works of contemporary artists' whimsy. There's also a "relaxation room" on the top floor, where you can exercise, meditate, or have a steam bath and massage. But the real draw of this otherworldly place is its astonishing city-center garden—a tropical delight of lemon, magnolia, and palm trees. Exotic finches flutter through the leaves, and a toucan caws beside the breakfast buffet; a small pool is screened by flowering shrubs. You can breakfast or dine here by candlelight (guests only). Book well ahead to immerse yourself in an exoticism that is particularly Niçois. **Pros:** funky rooms decorated by artists; tropical garden with small pool. **Cons:** rooms not decorated by artists seem comparatively drab; streetside rooms can be noisy. ⊠ *11 rue Dalpozzo, New Town* ☎ *04–93–88–59–35* ⊕ *www.hotelwindsor.com* ↩ *57 rooms* ⬠ *In-room: refrigerator, Wi-Fi. In-hotel: restaurant, bar, pool, gym, spa, Internet, some pets allowed* ⊟ *AE, DC, MC, V* ⧖ *MAP.*

$ **Nice Garden Hotel.** It's hard to believe that this freshly renovated little hotel, with its own courtyard garden, is smack in the middle of Nice, next to the pedestrian shopping streets and a few minutes' walk from the Old Town. Rooms, with original ceiling moldings and chandeliers, are done up in romantic style and all of them look onto the garden scented with Mediterranean flowers and citrus fruits. This find was a bit of a secret at the time of writing, but is unlikely to remain so for long. **Pros:** breakfast with homemade jam in the garden; extremely helpful owner. **Cons:** some rooms (and showers) are small, though still good value for money. ⊠ *11 rue du Congrès, New Town* ☎ *04–93–87–35–62* ⊕ *www.nicegardenhotel.com* ↩ *9 rooms* ⬠ *In-room: refrigerator, Wi-Fi* ⊟ *MC, V.*

¢–$ **Felix.** On popular, pedestrian Rue Masséna and a block from the beach, this tiny budget hotel is owned by a hard-working couple (both fluent in English) who make you feel welcome. Rooms are slightly tatty—vinyl wallpaper, saggy beds—but four have tiny balconies with ringside seats over the pedestrian thoroughfare. In-room picnics are encouraged with cups and plates, and there are even direct phone lines to each room and TV with CNN. ⊠ *41 rue Masséna, New Town* ☎ *04–93–88–67–73* ↩ *14 rooms* ⬠ *In-hotel: bar* ⊟ *AE, DC, MC, V.*

¢–$ **Solara.** One block from the beach and two from the Place Masséna, this tiny budget hotel perches on the fourth and fifth floors, high above the main shopping street. The new owner has brightened up the rooms, some of which have terraces looking onto the lively pedestrian street below; breakfast is served here on request. Don't be put off by the unsavory-seeming ground-floor entrance and tiny, apparently rickety elevator, which is common in French buildings. **Pros:** location near the beach; top-floor terraces overlooking pedestrian street. **Cons:** unpromising street entrance; small elevator. ⊠ *7 rue de France, New Town,* ☎ *04–93–88–09–96* ⊕ *www.hotel-solara.net* ↩ *14 rooms* ⬠ *In-room: refrigerator (some), Internet, Wi-Fi. In-hotel: room service, no-smoking rooms* ⊟ *MC, V.*

¢–$ **Villa Rivoli.** The owners of the popular budget hotel Villa La Tour in the Old Town recently opened this second establishment in the chic Quartier des Musiciens, a couple of streets back from the beach. With equally affordable prices, Belle Epoque architecture, and the owners' trademark sense of style-on-a-shoestring, it promises to be another hit. Aim for one of the rooms with a small balcony. **Pros:** Belle Epoque style; authentic French feel. **Cons:** still undergoing renovations at the time of writing. ✉*10 rue de Rivoli, New Town* ☎*04–93–88–80–25* ⊕*www.villa-rivoli.com* ⇥*24 rooms* ⌂*In-room: refrigerator. In-hotel: room service, bar, Wi-Fi, some pets allowed* ⊟*AE, MC, V.*

NIGHTLIFE & THE ARTS

Nice has the most active café society and nightlife on the coast. If you want to explore in-depth, pick up a copy of *Le Pitchoun*, a free, French-language guide to clubs, restaurants, and leisure activities. The year gets rolling in high style in late February when the Niçois let loose at their **Nice Carnival** (⊕*www.nicecarnaval.com*), two weeks of parades featuring satirical floats (often focusing on French political figures), dancers of varying levels of expertise and enthusiasm, and flowers galore. To mark the end of the festivities the gigantic "Carnival King" (made of paper) is set on fire and tossed off a boat into the sea. For the best view it's worth investing in tickets, though you can catch the parades for free at the corner of the Promenade des Anglais and the Avenue de Verdun or, even better, access the standing area for free if you're wearing a costume.

The glamorous **Le Ruhl, Casino Barrière de Nice** (✉*1 promenade des Anglais* ☎*04–97–03–12–22*), gleaming neon-bright and modern, is a sophisticated Riviera landmark that's open daily 10 AM to dawn. If you're all dressed up and have just won big, invest in a drink in the intimate walnut-and-velvet **Bar Le Relais** (✉*37 promenade des Anglais* ☎*04–93–16–64–00*) in the Hôtel Negresco.

L'Ascenseur (✉*18 bis rue Emmanuel Philibert* ☎*04–93–26–35–30*), two blocks east of Place Garibaldi, is the most popular gay and lesbian club in town. Young fans of Brit pop—especially Americans and English—drink and dance at **Wayne's** (✉*15 rue de la Préfecture* ☎*04–93–13–46–99*). **Iguane Café** (✉*5 quai Deux-Emmanuels* ☎*04–93–56–83–83*), along the port, pounds with Latin rhythms and techno until 4 AM. **L'Ambassade** (✉*18 rue du Congrès* ☎*04–93–88–88–87*) draws the crème-de-la-crème of the well-groomed, upscale Niçois young-and-restless. Dress well to get past the sharp-eyed screeners. At **Butterfly** (✉*67 quai des États-Unis* ☎*04–93–92–27–31*), in the Old Town, dance and drink to contemporary pop with a young, laid-back crowd. To stay in touch with friends and family back home, plug into the **Vieux Cyber** (✉*4 rue Rossetti* ☎*04–93–62–68–86*) in the Old Town, which is open 10–9, Sunday–Thursday, and 10–midnight, Friday and Saturday. An increasing number of cafés on and around the Cours Saleya have Wi-Fi access.

In late July, the **Nice Jazz Festival** (☎*04–92–17–77–77* ⊕*www.nicejazz-festival.fr*) draws international performers for outdoor concerts in the Parc de Cimiez north of the center, some in the Matisse museum and some in the Roman arena. During past festivals, big-name jazz artists have gathered in the Madisson Lounge of the **Hotel Radisson SAS** (✉*223 promenade des Anglais* ☎*04–93–37–17–17*) for impromptu jam sessions into the wee hours. The **Théâtre de Verdure** (⊠ *Jardin Albert Ier*) is another spot for jazz and pop. Large concerts relocate to the outdoor venue amongst ancient ruins, the **Arènes de Cimiez** (⊠ *Place du Monastère de Cimiez*) in summer. Classical music and ballet performances take place at Nice's convention center, the **Acropolis** (⊠ *Palais des Congrès, Esplanade John F. Kennedy* ☎ *04–93–92–83–00*).

The season at the **Opéra de Nice** (⊠ *4 rue St-François-de-Paul* ☎ *04–92–17–40–00* ⊕ *www.opera-nice.org*) runs from September to June. The **Théâtre Municipal Francis-Gag** (⊠ *4 rue St-Joseph* ☎ *04–93–62–00–03* ⊕ *www.theatre-francis-gag.org*) offers a wide and varied selection of independent theater productions. The **Théâtre National de Nice** (⊠ *Promenade des Arts* ☎ *04–93–13–90–90* ⊕ *www.tnn.fr*), headed by Daniel Benoin, plays host to productions from all over Europe as part of a new initiative to become a center for innovative European theater.

SPORTS & THE OUTDOORS

Nice's **beaches** extend all along the Baie des Anges, backed full-length by the Promenade des Anglais and a thriving and sophisticated downtown. This leads to the peculiar phenomenon of seeing power-suited executives and secretaries stripping down to a band of Lycra, tanning over the lunch hour, then suiting back up for the afternoon's work a block or two away. The absence of sand (there's nothing but those famous Riviera pebbles) helps maintain that dress-for-success look. The downside of the location: the otherwise stylish streets downtown tend to fill up with underdressed, sunburned tourists caked with salt during beach season.

Posh private beaches have full restaurants and bar service, color-coordinated mattresses and beach umbrellas, and ranks of tanners with phones glued to their ears. Several of the beaches lure clients with waterskiing, parasailing, windsurfing, and jet skiing; if you're looking for a particular sport, signs are posted at the entrance with the restaurant menus. In summer, lifeguards are posted near the Ruhl beach; check the flags to see if it's safe to swim on a windy day. Nice's largest private beach is the **Beau Rivage** (☎ *04–93–80–75–06*), across from the Cours Saleya, which has jet skiing and a popular restaurant seating 250 indoors, 150 on the terrace. Here €20 will rent you a cushy lounge chair, an umbrella, a towel and access to a changing room, hot showers, and bar service. At **Ruhl** (☎ *04–93–87–09–70*), across from the casino, waterskiing and parasailing boats run steadily all day. Opened in 2008, the **Hi Beach** (☎ *04–97–14–00–83*) is the funkiest of the private beaches, with design by Philippe Starck protégé Matali Crasset and a restaurant overseen by top chef Keisuke Matsushima (think burgers with a Japanese twist and sushi plates). Fees for private beaches average €12–€17 for a dressing room and mattress, €3–€4 for a parasol, and €4–€6 for a cabana to call your own. Private beaches alternate with open stretches of public frontage served by free toilets and open "showers" (a cold elevated faucet for rinsing off salt). Enterprising vendors cruise the waterfront, hawking ice cream, slabs of melon, coffee, ice-cold sodas, and beer.

Bicycles (✉ *17 av. Thiers*) can be rented at the train station. At Da Vinci parking lots (such as the one under the Cours Saleya) the lending of a bike is included in the cost of parking. The entire Promenade des Anglais is closed to traffic on the first Sunday of every month (except for July and August), making for a terrific 10-km (6-mi) ride along the waterfront.

SHOPPING

Nice's main shopping street, **Avenue Jean-Médecin,** runs inland from Place Masséna; all needs and most tastes are catered to in its big department stores (Galeries Lafayette, Monoprix, and the split-level Étoile mall). The new tramway, launched in late 2007, has made this mini Champs-Elysées all the more accessible, so expect crowds on Saturdays (shops are closed on Sundays). Luxury boutiques, such as Emporio Armani, Kenzo, Chanel, and Sonia Rykiel, line Rue du Paradis, while Rue de France and the Old Town have more accessible shops. The cooking school Les Petits Farcis leads guided half-day gourmet food walks through the Old Town (⊕*www.petitsfarcis.com*).You'll find the best selection of Provençal olive oils in town at **Oliviera** (✉*8 bis rue du Collet* ☎*04–93–13–06–45* ⊕*www.oliviera.com*), run by the passionate Nadim Beyrouti in the Old Town, who also serves Mediterranean dishes made with the finest local ingredients.

The venerable **Henri Auer** (✉*7 rue St-François-de-Paule* ☎*04–93–85–77–98*) has sold its beautiful selection of crystallized fruit, a Nice specialty once thought to promote fertility, since 1820. Another good, though more commercial, source for crystallized fruit is the **Confiserie du Vieux-Nice** (✉*14 quai Papacino* ☎*04–93–55–43–50*), on the west side of the port.

Seafood of all kinds is sold at the **fish market** on Place St-François every morning except Monday; not much of it comes from the local waters, however. At the **market** on Cours Saleya, you can find all kinds of plants, olives galore, and mounds of locally grown fruits and vegetables (Tuesday–Saturday 7 AM–noon [food] and 7 AM–5:30 PM [flowers] and Sunday 7–noon).

The **antiques and brocante market** (✉*Pl. Robilante*) by the Old Port is held Tuesday through Saturday. For brocante on Monday check out Cours Saleya.

MONACO & THE CORNICHES RESORTS

Purists and hard-core regional historians insist that this final sunny sliver of coast—from Cap Ferrat to the Italian border—is the one and only, true Côte d'Azur. It is certainly the most dramatically endowed, backed by forested mountains and crystalline Alps, with Mediterranean breezes relieving the summer heat and radiant light soothing midwinter days. Banana trees and date palms, cactus and figs luxuriate in the climate, and the hills, bristling with wind-twisted parasol pines, are paved with hothouses where roses and carnations profit from the year-round sun.

Terraced by three parallel, panoramic highways—the Basse Corniche, the Moyenne Corniche, and the Grande Corniche—that snake along its graduated crests, this stretch of the coast is studded with fabled resorts, their names as evocative of luxury and glamour as a haute-couture logo: Cap Ferrat, Beaulieu, and Monte Carlo.

Yet it must be said: these pockets of elegance have long since over-flowed, and it's a rare stretch of cliff side that hasn't sprouted a cluster of concrete cubes in cloying hues of pineapple, apricot, and Pepto-Bis-mol pink. The traffic along the corniche routes—especially the Cor-niche Inférieure that follows the coast—is appalling in peak season (so spare yourself and visit May–June or September–October, or even in the temperate winter, the fashionable season during the 19th century), exacerbated by the manic Italian driving style and self-absorbed luxury roadsters that turn the pavement into a bumper-car battle.

But there are moments. Wrench your car out of the flow, pull over at a rare overlook on the Haute Corniche, and walk to the extremity. Like the ancient Ligurians who first built their settlements here, you can hang over the infinite expanse of teal-blue sea and glittering waves and survey the resorts draped gracefully along the curves of the coast. It was from these cliffs that for 2,500 years castles and towers held watch over the waters, braced against the influx of new peoples—first the Greeks, then the Romans, the Saracens, trade ships from Genoa, battleships under Napoléon, Edwardian cruise ships on the Grand Tour, and the Allies in the Second World War. The influx continues today, of course, in the great waves of vacationers who storm the coast, spring to early fall.

VILLEFRANCHE-SUR-MER

★ *10 km (6 mi) east of Nice.*

VISITOR INFORMATION
Villefranche-sur-Mer Tourist Office (✉ *Jardin François-Binon, Villefranche-sur-Mer* ☎ *04-93-01-73-68* ⊕ *www.villefranche-sur-mer.com*).

EXPLORING
Nestled discreetly along the deep scoop of harbor between Nice and Cap Ferrat, this pretty watercolor of a fishing port seems sur-real, flanked as it is by the big city of Nice and the assertive wealth of Monaco. The town is a stage set of brightly colored houses—the sort of place where Pagnol's *Fanny* could have been filmed. Genuine fishermen skim up to the docks here in weathered-blue *barques,* and the streets of the Vieille Ville flow directly to the waterfront, much as they did in the 13th century. Some of the prettiest spots in town are around Place de la Paix, Rue du Poilu, and Place du Conseil, which looks out over the water. The deep harbor, in the caldera of a volcano, was once preferred by the likes of Onassis and Niarchos and the royals on their yachts. But the character of the place was subtly shaped by the artists and authors who gathered at the **Hôtel Welcome**—Diaghilev and Stravinsky, taking a break from the Ballet Russe in Monaco; Somerset Maugham and Evelyn Waugh; and, above all, Jean Cocteau, who came here to

recover from the excesses of Paris life. Nowadays, its population consists mainly of wealthy retired people, though families do head here to enjoy its sandy (well, gravelly) beach.

So enamored was Cocteau of this painterly fishing port that he decorated the 14th-century **Chapelle St-Pierre** with images from the life of St. Peter and dedicated it to the village's fishermen. Working in crayon and chalk fixed with paraffin, he covered the walls with earthy, simplistic drawings, heavily outlined and surprisingly—even disappointingly—realistic for this master of the surreal. ⊠*Pl. Pollanais* ☎*04–93–76–90–70* 🎫*€2* ☉*Tues.–Sun., 10–noon and 2–6.*

Villefranche's Old Town is made for wandering, with steeply stepped streets leading up into alleys and passageways arching over the cobbles. The extraordinary 13th-century **Rue Obscure** (literally, "dark street") is entirely covered by vaulted arcades; it sheltered the town's residents when the Germans fired their parting shots—an artillery bombardment—near World War II's end.

The modest Baroque **Église St-Michel** (⊠*Pl. Poullan*), just above Rue Obscure, contains a movingly realistic sculpture of Christ carved in fig wood by an anonymous 17th-century convict.

The stalwart 16th-century **Citadelle St-Elme,** restored to perfect condition, anchors the harbor with its broad, sloping stone walls. Beyond its drawbridge lie the city's offices and a group of minor gallery-museums. Whether or not you stop into these private collections of local art (all free of charge), you are welcome to stroll around the inner grounds and circle the imposing exterior.

WHERE TO EAT & STAY

$$$ ✕**Beluga.** This recently opened restaurant and lounge bar has become the hip place to be in not-so-hip Villefranche. The surprise is the quality of the food: if you look beyond the artistic drizzlings of sauce and dabs of spices on the plate, it's really simple fare made with fresh ingredients. Typical of the cooking are shrimp and crayfish salad with lime and ginger, duck breast with honey and goat cheese, and a mixed chocolate dessert plate. There is live music some nights and the terrace facing the sea offers a spectacular view of one of the world's most beautiful bays. A second Beluga was scheduled to open in nearby Beaulieu at the time of this writing. ⊠*3 Quai Ponchardier* ☎*04–93–80–28–34* ⊕*www. restaurant-beluga.com* 🖃*AE, DC, MC, V* ☉*Closed Mon. and Nov. 15–Dec. 25.*

$ ✕**Cosmo Bar.** Once you've discovered Cosmo, it's a place you're likely
★   to come back to again and again. Facing the Cocteau chapel with an enviable view of the sea from its terrace, this modern brasserie could easily get away with being merely mediocre. Instead, it serves fresh, colorful Mediterranean food that runs from an addictive anchoïade—crudités with anchovy dip—to Moroccan-inspired monkfish tagine. It's a favorite of English-speaking expats in Villefranche and it's easy to understand why, since it brings together all the ingredients that make for a casual yet memorable meal on the French Riviera. Call ahead to

6

be sure of securing a coveted terrace table. ⊠*11 pl. Amélie Pollonnais* ☎*04–93–01–84–05* ⌂*Reservations essential* ▭*AE, DC, MC, V.*

$ ✕**Le Serre.** It might look like just another pizzeria, but Le Serre is a family-run restaurant where everything from the pizzas to the local specialties is prepared with care. Daube, the Provençal beef-and-wine stew with herbs, is served all year round and the chef starts its preparation at midnight for the next day. The warm welcome ensures that the restaurant attracts plenty of locals who have learned to tread carefully around tourist traps. ⊠*16 rue de May* ☎*04–93–76–79–91* ▭*AE* ⊘*Closed Mon. and Tues from Sept.–June. No lunch in July and Aug.*

$$–$$$ ▦**Hôtel Welcome.** When Villefranche harbored a community of artists ★ and writers, this waterfront landmark was their adopted headquarters. Somerset Maugham holed up in one of the tiny crow's-nest rooms at the top, and Jean Cocteau moved into one of the corners, with windows opening onto two balconies. Alec and Evelyn Waugh (and later, Liz and Dick) used to tie one on in the bar, and film directors shooting action scenes in the bay sent the guests flowers when special-effects explosions disturbed their repose. The rooms are bright and comfortable—freshly renovated; some in soothing shades of talc-blue with bold striped accessories; some covered in pale flowers. Be sure to request a room with a balcony, it's definitely worth it; and have your aperitif or digestif on the veranda of the "wine pier" that specializes in *vin du terroir*, wine from local vineyards. **Pros:** watching the sunrise from the balcony; friendly, helpful staff; selection of wines at the bar. **Cons:** pricey breakfast; some rooms are very small; elevator stops short of top floor. ⊠*3 quai Amiral Courbet,* ☎*04–93–76–27–62* ⊕*www.welcomehotel. com* ⌖*36 rooms, 2 suites* ⌂*In-room: refrigerator. In-hotel: bar, Internet terminal, parking (paid), some pets allowed* ▭*AE, DC, MC, V* ⊘*Closed mid-Nov.–Christmas.*

$$ ▦**Hôtel Provençal.** Within walking distance of the port, this inexpensive hotel may not look like much from the outside but is friendly and accommodating. The rooms are large and humbly decorated with deep blue carpets, green velour chairs, and white bedspreads. About half of the rooms have a sea view; the other half look out over colorful rooftops. The Provençal-style restaurant serves up tasty items ranging from freshly grilled fish to hearty soups on a large terrace overflowing with flowers. **Pros:** balconies with sea view (ask for this when booking); high quality of the breakfast served on the terrace. **Cons:** room decor and bathrooms are modest. ⊠*4 av. Maréchal Joffre* ☎*04–93–76–53–53* ⊕*www.hotelprovencal.com* ⌖*45 rooms* ⌂*In-room: refrigerator, Wi-Fi. In-hotel: bar, tennis, pool, gym, spa, Internet terminal, Wi-Fi, some pets allowed* ▭*MC, V* ⊘*Closed 4–10 Nov. 26–Dec.*

BEAULIEU-SUR-MER

4 km (2½ mi) east of Villefranche, 14 km (9 mi) east of Nice.

With its back pressed hard against the cliffs of the corniche and sheltered between the peninsulas of Cap Ferrat and Cap Roux, this once-grand resort basks in a tropical microclimate that earned its central neighborhood the name "Petite Afrique." The town was the pet of

19th-century society, and its grand hotels welcomed Empress Eugénie, the Prince of Wales, and Russian nobles.

★ One manifestation of its Belle Époque excess is the extravagant **Villa Kerylos,** a mansion built in 1902 in the style of classical Greece. It was the dream house of the amateur archeologist Théodore Reinach, who commissioned an Italian architect to surround him with Grecian delights: cool Carrara marble, alabaster, rare fruitwoods, a mosaic-lined bath/pool worthy of a 1950s toga movie, and a dining room where guests draped themselves on the floor to eat *à la grecque.* ⊠ *Impasse Gustave-Eiffel* ☎*04–93–01–01–44* ⊕*www.villa-kerylos.com* ☎*€8.50, €13.50 to visit both Villa Kerylos and Villa Ephrussi de Rothschild in same wk* ⊙*Mid-Feb.–June and Sept.–Oct., daily 10–6; Nov.–mid-Feb., weekdays 2–6, weekends 10–6; July and Aug., daily 10–7.*

Today Beaulieu is usually spoken of in the past tense and has taken on a rather stuffy ambience, though its small beach attracts families with children. But on the **Promenade Maurice-Rouvier,** a paved pedestrian path which begins not far from the Villa Kerylos, you can stroll the waterfront, past grand villas and their tropical gardens, all the way to St-Jean-Cap-Ferrat. The 30-minute-walk winds seaside along the Baie des Fourmis (Bay of Ants), whose name alludes to the black rocks "crawling" up from the sea. The name doesn't quite fit, but the walk will give you great views of the sparkling Mediterranean and surrounding mountains.

WHERE TO EAT & STAY

$$$$ 🏨**La Réserve.** Supremely sumptuous, this Riviera xanada is gorgeous
FodorsChoice but perhaps too sleekly renovated for its own good. Since the 19th
★ century it has been the haunt of royalty and high society, from Queen Victoria to the notorious British journalist and playboy Gordon Bennet (the hotel has named a suite after him and the bar after him). Decorated in 19th-century French style, the guest rooms are designed for maximum comfort, right down to the "Accueil personnalisé," replete with flowers, champagne, and strawberries á la Chantilly; three of the double rooms are in the hotel's round tower, with panoramic views of the garden and the sea. Under chef Olivier Brulard, the Restaurant des Rois has maintained its reputation as one of the finest places to indulge your senses in the south of France; there is also a summer restaurant, Le Vent Debout, named after a boat that once linked Nice and Beaulieu. None of this comes cheap—and most people here are not counting their pennies—but if you're thinking of splashing out it's worth looking into the various off-season packages. **Pros:** rooms and grounds perfectly maintained; sense of discreet elegance. **Cons:** if money is not an object, it's hard to fault La Réserve for being anything other than too perfect. ⊠*5 bd. du Maréchal Leclerc06160* ☎*04–93–01–00–01* ⊕*www.reservebeaulieu.com* ⇒*37 rooms and 2 villas* ⌂*In-room: refrigerator, Wi-Fi. In-hotel: 2 restaurants, bar, pool, spa, parking (paid), some pets allowed* ⊟*AE, DC, MC, V* ⊙*Closed Oct. 19–Dec. 19.*

6

ST-JEAN-CAP-FERRAT

2 km (1 mi) south of Beaulieu on D25.

VISITOR INFORMATION
St-Jean-Cap-Ferrat Tourist Office (✉ *59 av. Denis Semeria, St-Jean–Cap-Ferrat* ☎ *04–93–76–08–90* ⊕ *www.saintjeancapferrat.fr*).

EXPLORING
The luxuriously sited pleasure port of St-Jean moors the peninsula of Cap Ferrat; from its port-side walkways and crescent of beach you can look over the sparkling blue harbor to the graceful green bulk of the corniches. Yachts purr in and out of port, and their passengers scuttle into cafés for take-out drinks to enjoy on their private decks.

★ Between the port and the mainland, the gaudily beautiful **Villa Ephrussi de Rothschild** stands as a testament to the wealth and worldly taste of the Baroness Ephrussi de Rothschild, who had it built (though she only stayed here a week or two per year). Constructed in 1905 and donated to the Academy of Beaux Arts in 1934, the house was created around the artworks, decorations, and furniture brought to Beatrice de Rothschild's door by eager dealers. Designed in neo-Venetian style (its flamingo-pink facade was thought not to be in the best of taste by the local gentry), the house was baptized "Ile-de-France" in homage to the Baroness Bétrice's favorite ocean liner (her staff used to wear sailing costumes and her ship travel kit is on view in her bedroom). Precious artworks, tapestries, and furniture adorn the salons—in typical Rothschildian fashion, each room is given over to a different ancièn regime "époque." On a guided tour of the upstairs, you can see things, things, and more things, including some fine little etchings by Fragonard, but allow yourself time to wander in the gardens. They are one of the few places on the coast where you'll be allowed to experience the lavish pleasures of the Belle Époque Côte d'Azur. There are no less than seven themed gardens (she liked to collect). The extraordinary ensemble reigns over a hilltop at the crest of the peninsula, taking in spectacular, symmetrical views of the coastline. Tea and light lunches are served on a glassed-in porch overlooking the grounds—you can enjoy a truly paradisical moment here. ✉*Av. Ephrussi* ☎*04–93–01–33–09* 🖱*Access to ground floor and gardens €10, €15 joint ticket for Villa Kerylos to be used in same wk, guided tour upstairs €3 extra* ⊙*Feb.– June and Sept.–Nov., daily 10–6; July and Aug., daily 10–7; Nov.–Jan., weekdays 2–6, weekends and holidays 10–6.*

The signs pointing to all the different walkways in St-Jean are confusing; if you're really at a loss, visit the tourist office at 59 avenue Denis-Séméria. Otherwise, just go south on the **Promenade Maurice Rouvier**, which runs along the eastern edge of the peninsula. You'll stumble upon reasonably priced cafés, pizzerias, and ice cream parlors on the promenade of the **Plage de St-Jean**. The best swimming is a bit farther south, past the port, at **Plage Paloma**. Keep trekking around the wooded area where a beautiful path (*sentier pédestre*) leads along the outermost edge of Cap-Ferrat. Other than the occasional yacht, all traces of civilization disappear, and the water is a dizzying blue.

The residents of Cap-Ferrat fiercely protect it from curious tourists; its grand old villas are hidden for the most part in the depths of tropical gardens. You can nonetheless try to catch peeks of them from the coastline promenade if you strike out from the port; from the restaurant Capitaine Cook, cut right up Avenue des Fossés, turn right on Avenue Vignon, and follow the Chemin de la Carrière. The 11-km (7-mi) walk passes through rich tropical flora and, on the west side, over white cliffs buffeted by waves. When you've traced the full outline of the peninsula, veer up the Chemin du Roy past the fabulous gardens of the **Villa des Cèdres,** once owned by King Leopold II of Belgium at the turn of the last century. The king owned several opulent estates along the Côte d'Azur, undoubtedly paid for by his enslavement of the Belgian Congo. His African plunder also stocked the private zoo on his villa grounds, today the town's **Parc Zoologique** (Bd. du Général-de-Gaulle). Past the gardens, you'll reach the **Plage de Passable,** from which you cut back across the peninsula's wrist.

A shorter loop takes you from town out to the **Pointe de St-Hospice,** much of the walk shaded by wind-twisted pines. From the port climb Avenue Jean Mermoz to Place Paloma and follow the path closest to the waterfront. At the point are an 18th-century prison tower, a 19th-century chapel, and unobstructed views of Cap Martin.

6

WHERE TO EAT & STAY

$$$ ✕**Le Sloop.** Among the touristy cafés and snack shops along the port, this sleek blue-and-white restaurant caters to the yachting crowd and sailors who cruise in to dock for lunch. The focus is fish, of course: *soupe de poisson* (fish soup), St-Pierre (John Dory) steamed with asparagus, or whole sea bass roasted with olives and pistou. Its outdoor tables surround a tiny "garden" of potted palms, and the view of the cliffs and bobbing boats is mesmerizing. ✉*Port de Plaisance* ☎*04–93–01–48–63* ⊕*www.restaurantsloop.com* ⊟*MC, V* ⊘*Closed Wed. mid-Sept.–mid-Apr. No lunch Tues. and Wed. mid-Apr.–mid-Sept.*

$$$$ ⊞**Royal Riviera.** Completely revamped by Parisian designer guru Grace
★ Leo Andrieu, this former *residence hôtelière* for British aristos now invites visitors on an intimate voyage into neo-Hellenic style, complete with an admiring wink at the nearby Villa Kerylos museum. Inside, shades of ocher, wrought-iron, and a judicious mix of contemporary and classic furniture make a striking statement. Rooms in the main building have views of the sea, garden, and/or mountains, while tropical vegetation surrounds L'Orangerie's recently added 16 rooms and suites, which face a vast swimming pool. The Royal Riviera makes a special effort for families: cribs and baby supplies are complimentary, the restaurants have children's menus, and kids' films can be shown on request in a room adjoining the restaurant. Only drawback: the hotel is sited a little too close to the main railway tracks—so request a room away from them. **Pros:** this is a luxury hotel with a sense of humor: have a look at the "staff training" video on the Web site; children are especially welcome. **Cons:** those railway tracks. ✉*3 av. Jean Monnet,* ☎*04–93–76–31–00* ⊕*www.royal-riviera.com* ↝*96 rooms, 3 suites* ⚲*In-room: refrigerator, Wi-Fi. In-hotel: restaurant, bar, pool, gym,*

spa, beachfront, parking (free), some pets allowed ⊟*AE, DC, MC, V* ⊙*Closed Dec.–mid-Jan.*

$$$
Fodor's Choice
★

Brise Marine. With a glowing Provençal-ocher facade, bright blue shutters, and balustraded sea terrace, this lovely 1878 villa fulfills most desires for that perfect, picturesque Cap Ferrat hotel. Though it overlooks one of the cape's many exclusive mansions, complete with vast garden and much-vaunted *chien très méchant* (very nasty dog), *this* little mansion remains unpretentious and accessible, with pretty little pastel guest rooms that feel like bedrooms in a private home—many offer window views of the gorgeous peninsula stunningly framed by statuesque palms. The terraces are shared, the aperitif is a social occasion, and the setting is first-class. There is also a private three-bedroom villa for rent, Le Parc du Soleil, with access to a swimming pool. **Pros:** location looking onto the sea and near the town's best beaches; family-run feel. **Cons:** rooms might seem underwhelming if you're expecting a luxury hotel; no elevator. ⊠*58 av. Jean Mermoz,* ☎*04–93–76–04–36* ⊕*www.hotel-brisemarine.com* ↻*16 rooms, 1 villa* △*In-room: refrigerator, Wi-Fi (some). In-hotel: parking (paid), some pets allowed* ⊟*AE, DC, MC, V* ⊙*Closed Nov.–Jan.*

$$–$$$

Clair Logis. With soft pastels, antique furniture, and large picture windows, this converted villa is perfectly framed by a sprawling garden park. The main house offers up subtle bourgeois elegance; for the budget-conscious there are simpler, airy rooms scattered over several small buildings. Most have charming balconies looking out over gently swaying palms. There's no pool, but breakfast on the cobblestone terrace is lovely, and it's a good way to gear up for the 15-minute walk down to the beach. **Pros:** location in a park with free parking. **Cons:** there have been complaints in the past about poor service and tired rooms, but a new owner took over in 2008. ⊠*12 av. du Prince Rainier III de Monaco, Point de St-Jean,* ☎*04–93–76–51–81* ⊕*www. hotel-clair-logis.fr* ↻*18 rooms* △*In-room: no a/c (some), refrigerator, Wi-Fi. In-hotel: parking (free), some pets allowed* ⊟*AE, MC, V* ⊙*Closed mid-Nov.–mid-Dec. and mid-Jan.–mid-Feb.*

ÈZE

Fodor's Choice
★

2 km (1 mi) east of Beaulieu, 12 km (7 mi) east of Nice, 7 km (4½ mi) west of Monte Carlo.

GETTING HERE

By car, you should arrive using the Moyenne Corniche, which deposits you near the gateway to Èze Village; buses (from Nice and Monaco) also use this highway. By train, you'll arrive at the station in Èze-sur-Mer, where (most months) a navette shuttle bus takes you up to hilltop Èze, a trip which, with its 1,001 switchbacks up the steep mountainside, takes a full 15 minutes (keep this in mind if you're hiring a taxi to "rush" you down to the train station).

VISITOR INFORMATION

St-Jean-Cap-Ferrat Tourist Office (⊠*Pl. de Gaulle, Èze* ☎*04–93–41–26–00* ⊕*www.eze-riviera.com*).

EXPLORING

Magical, medieval, and magnificent, towering like an eagle's nest above the coast and crowned with ramparts and the ruins of a medieval château, Èze (pronounced *ehz*) is unfortunately the most accessible of all the perched villages. So even during off-season its streets pour with a lava flow of tourists, some not-so-fresh from the beach, and it earns unique status as the only town to post pictorial warnings that say, in effect, "No Shoes, No Shirt, No Service." It is, nonetheless, the most spectacularly sited; if you can manage to shake the crowds and duck off to a quiet overlook, the village casts an extraordinary spell. Its streets are steep and, in places, only for the flamboyantly fit; its time-stained stone houses huddle together in storybook fashion, and its history is remarkable: Colonized milennia ago by the Romans (who may have built a temple here to the Egyptian goddess, Isis—hence the town name), this mountain peak aerie was much coveted by locals fleeing from pirating Saracens. By the 19th century, only peasants were left, but when the Riviera became fashionable, Èze's splendid views up and down the coast became one of the draws that lured fabled visitors—lots of crowned heads, Georges Sand, Friedrich Nietzsche, and Consuelo Vanderbilt, who, when she was tired of being Duchess of Marlborough, traded in Blenheim Palace for a custom-built house in Èze. Remember that if you choose to stay here, it gets very quiet at night, even in high season.

From the crest-top **Jardin Exotique** *(Tropical Garden)*, full of rare succulents, you can pan your videocam all the way around the hills and waterfront (and then, just a few feet from the entrance, take a time-out lunch at the Nid d'Aigle, an inexpensive eaterie featuring focaccias and salads, quaintly set on stone levels rising up around a tall tree). But if you want a prayer of a chance of enjoying the magnificence of the village's arched passages, stone alleyways, and ancient fountains, come at dawn or after sunset—or (if you have the means) stay the night— but spend the midday elsewhere. The church of **Notre-Dame**, consecrated in 1772, glitters inside with Baroque retables and altarpieces. Èze's tourist office, on Place du Général-de-Gaulle, can direct you to the numerous footpaths—the most famous being the **Sentier Friedrich Nietzsche**—that thread Èze with the coast's three corniche highways. Èze Village is the famous hilltop destination, but Èze extends down to the coastal beach and the township of Èze-sur-Mer; on either side a vast **Grande Corniche Parc** keeps things green and verdant.

WHERE TO EAT & STAY

$$$ ✕**Troubadour.** Amid the clutter and clatter of the perched village, this is a wonderful find: comfortably relaxed, this old family house proffers pleasant service and excellent dishes like roasted scallops with chicken broth and squab with citrus zest and beef broth. The chef hand-picks his produce in the region's outdoor markets each morning, coming back with such rarities as celtuce (an Asian green that resembles both lettuce and asparagus) and Italian white truffles. He also has a penchant for ingredients from southwest France, notably foie gras. Full-course menus range from €39 to €52. ✉*4 rue du Brec* ☎*04–93–41–19–03* ▭*MC, V* ✆*Closed Sun. and Mon., also mid-Nov.–mid-Dec., first wk Mar., first wk July.*

$$$$
FodorsChoice
★

⚏Château de la Chèvre d'Or. Giving substance to Riviera fairy tales, this extraordinary xanadu seems to sit just below cloud level in sky-high Èze. Like a Hilton penthouse, medieval-style, this magnificent conglomerate of weathered-stone houses lets you enjoy "the high life" while turning your back on the world and drinking in unsurpassed sea views. The "château of the Golden Goat" is actually an entire stretch of the village, streets and all, bordered by gardens that cling to the mountainside in nearly Babylonian style. Nearby are some of the fanciest rooms, little *cabanon* houses built into the cliff and exquisite in decor: stone boulder walls accented with Louis Seize torchières, peasant-luxe fireplaces with faux 15th-century panel paintings, chandeliered rock-grotto bathrooms. Nearly all rooms have exposed stone, arched windows, exposed beams, and brass touches, while even the cheapest (a pretty penny, nonetheless) are stylishly done up and have views over Èze's charming tile roofs. No fewer than five restaurants, ranging from the summertime Eden Terrasse serving world fusion cuisine to the *haute gastronomique* grand dining room with its panoramic view, regale some of the world's most pampered citizens. The swimming pool alone, clinging like a swallow's nest to the hillside, may justify the investment, as do the liveried footmen who greet you at the village entrance to wave you, VIP-style, past the cattle-drive of tourists. **Pros:** fairy-tale setting; extensive private grounds; choice of restaurants. **Cons:** many steps to climb, this being a medieval town; some rooms are small. ⊠*Rue du Barri,* ☎*04–92–10–66–66* ⊕*www.chevredor.com* ⤴*30 rooms, 4 suites* ⚭*In-room: refrigerator, Wi-Fi (some). In-hotel: 5 restaurants, bar, tennis court, pool, gym, spa, Internet terminal, some pets allowed* ☐*AE, DC, MC, V* ☯*Closed Dec.–Feb.*

$$$$
★

⚏Château Eza. Vertiginously perched on the edge of a cliff 3,000 feet above the crouching tiger of St-Jean-Cap-Ferrat, this former residence of Prince William of Sweden is one of the most dramatic, romantic, and expensive inns on the entire Mediterranean coast. Surprisingly, the public salons are cool, sleek, and modern, almost letting you think you're wandered into New York's Soho. But the guest rooms—there are only 10—are spread among a cluster of striking Romanesque 13th-century buildings on cobblestone streets too narrow for cars. Most have private entrances and all are luxed out to the max: canopy beds, costly objets d'art and antiques, exquisite carpets and tapestries, wood-burning fireplaces, and unbelievable views. If you're not staying the night, the views from the panoramic restaurant and outdoor terrace are just as good. The wine list is one of the best on the Côte, and chef Axel Wagner serves pared-down haute cuisine that puts the emphasis on the ingredients (prix-fixe menus start at €40 at lunch). The hotel is nearly at the top of the village's steep alleyways, so your luggage will need to be picked up by the hotel porters. **Pros:** the view, the view, the view (oh, and the view). **Cons:** limited services (no pool, no elevator) for luxury hotel. ⊠*Rue de la Pise,* ☎*04–93–41–12–24* ⊕*www.chateaueza. com* ⤴*10 rooms, 4 suites* ⚭*In-room: refrigerator. In-hotel: restaurant* ☐*AE, DC, MC, V* ☯*Closed Nov.–mid-Dec.*

PEILLON

★ *15 km (9 mi) northeast of Nice via D2204 and D53.*

Perhaps because it's difficult to reach and not on the way to or from anything else, Peillon—one of the most idyllic villages perchés in France—has maintained the magic of its medieval origins. You can hear the bell toll here, walk in silence up its weathered cobblestones, and smell the thyme crunching underfoot if you step past the settlement's minuscule boundaries onto the unspoiled hillsides. And its streets are utterly and completely commerce-free; the citizens have voted to vaccinate themselves against the plague of boutiques, galleries, and cafés that have infected its peers along the coast. There is not much to do here other than bask in the cool mountain air, soak up the views, and savor a sophisticated meal on a terrace—the downside of the lack of shops is the accompanying lack of almost any street life.

WHERE TO EAT & STAY

$$–$$$ **L'Auberge de la Madone.** This is what you call getting away from
★ it all. Owner Christian Millo and his partner/sister Marie-José come from a traditional farming family with a deep love for this region. Chef Millo and his sous-chef, son Thomas, who studied under Alain Ducasse, are interested in a fresh, organic cuisine using only local products: the cheese served at breakfast comes from a farm down the road; the honey from a local beekeeper; the vegetables are picked fresh from the garden out back; and, to give you an idea of the quality, the olive oil comes from the olives you see hanging on the trees. The cooking itself is a trifle fussy, but there's no disputing the passion that goes into this food. The inn has a tennis court on the slope above, and six little rooms in a village annex called Lou Pourtail, which offers shelter at bargain rates. It does have an unusual quirk, though: the hotel staff is off on Wednesday, meaning that guests are left to their own devices (with the key to the front door). **Pros:** quality of the restaurant; views at sunset. **Cons:** somewhat isolated setting; Wednesday closing of hotel and restaurant. ⊠*3 place Auguste Arnulf, 06440Peillon Village* ☎*04–93–79–91–17* ⊕*www.auberge-madone-peillon.com* ⇆*14 rooms, 3 suites* ⌂*In-room: no a/c, refrigerator, Wi-Fi. In-hotel: restaurant, tennis court, Wi-Fi, parking, some pets allowed* ▭*AE, MC, V* ⊗*Closed Wed.* ⏹*MAP.*

MONACO

7 km (4½ mi) east of Èze, 21 km (13 mi) east of Nice.

GETTING HERE & AROUND

From the Nice airport, there's a direct bus service from **Compagnie des Autobus de Monaco** (☎*377/97–70–22–22* ⊕*www.cam.mc*) to the Place du Casino (in front of the Monte Carlo casino); it takes 50 minutes and costs €12.50. This company also runs a bus line that threads the avenues of Monaco. Both buses and trains connect Nice with Monaco. **RCA** (☎*04–93–85–64–44* ⊕*www.rca.tm.fr*) has buses connecting with Nice's center-city bus station (⊠*Gare routière, 5 bd.*

Jean-Jaurès ☎04–93–85–61–81);
tickets cost €15.50. The 100TAM
bus (Transport Alpes Maritimes)
(☎08–10–06–10–06   ⊕*www.
lignedazur.com*) costs €1.30 and
leaves from the main bus station
in Nice, but be prepared as it takes
about two hours to get there. From
Nice's train station (⊠*Gare SNCF,
Av. Thiers* ☎04–92–14–80–80
⊕*www.voyages-sncf.com*),
Monaco is serviced by regular
trains along the Cannes–Ventimiglia line; Monaco's train station
is on Avenue Prince Pierre. From
Nice the journey costs €3.50 one-
way and takes 20 minutes. A taxi
(☎04–93–13–78–78) from Nice
will cost around €100, depending
on the season and the time of day.

GRACE'S KINGDOM

Thanks in part to the pervasive
odor of money-to-burn, Monaco
remains the playground of royalty,
wealthy playboys, and glamorous
film stars. One of the loveliest of
the latter, in fact, became Monaco's princess when Hollywood
darling Grace Kelly married Prince
Rainier in 1956; their wedding,
marriage, and her tragic death in
a car accident—eerily presaged in
scenes filmed in Alfred Hitchcock's
To Catch a Thief—have only added
to the mythology of this fairy-tale
mini-principality.

VISITOR INFORMATION
Monaco Tourist Office (⊠*2a bd. des Moulins, Monte Carlo, Monaco* ☎377/
92-16-61-66 ⊕*www.monaco-tourisme.com*).

EXPLORING
It's positively feudal, the idea that an ancient dynasty of aristocrats
could still hold fast to its patch of coastline, the last scrap of a once-vast
domain. But that's just what the Grimaldi family has done, clinging to
a few acres of glory and maintaining their own license plates, their own
telephone area code (377), and their own highly forgiving tax system.
Yet the Principality of Monaco covers just 473 acres and would fit
comfortably inside New York's Central Park or a family farm in Iowa.
And its 5,000 pampered citizens would fill only a small fraction of the
seats in Yankee Stadium.

The present ruler, Prince Albert II (following the death of Prince Rainier III in April 2005), traces his ancestry to Otto Canella, who was
born in 1070. The Grimaldi dynasty began with Otto's great-great-
great-grandson, Francesco Grimaldi, also known as Frank the Rogue.
Expelled from Genoa, Frank and his cronies disguised themselves as
monks and in 1297 seized the fortified medieval town known today
as Le Rocher (the Rock). Except for a short break under Napoléon,
the Grimaldis have been here ever since, which makes them the oldest
reigning family in Europe.

In the 1850s a Grimaldi named Charles III made a decision that turned
the Rock into a giant blue chip. Needing revenue but not wanting to
impose additional taxes on his subjects, he contracted with a company
to open a gambling facility. The first spin of the roulette wheel was on
December 14, 1856. There was no easy way to reach Monaco then—no
carriage roads or railroads—so no one came. Between March 15 and

March 20, 1857, one person entered the casino—and won two francs. In 1868, however, the railroad reached Monaco, and it was filled with Englishmen who came to escape the London fog. The effects were immediate. Profits were so great that Charles eventually abolished all direct taxes. Almost overnight, a threadbare principality became an elegant watering hole for European society. Dukes (and their mistresses) and duchesses (and their gigolos) danced and dined their way through a world of spinning roulette wheels and bubbling champagne—preening themselves for nights at the opera, where such artists as Vaslav Nijinsky, Sarah Bernhardt, and Enrico Caruso came to perform.

But it's the tax system, not the gambling, that's made Monaco one of the most sought-after addresses in the world—that and its sensational position on a broad, steep peninsula that bulges into the Mediterranean, its harbor sparkling with luxury cruisers, its posh mansions angling awnings toward the nearly perpetual sun. The latest French celebrity to declare himself "Monegasque," thus giving up his French passport, is superchef Alain Ducasse, who said that he made the choice out of affection for Monaco rather than tax reasons. The population explosion here has allowed Monaco to break another French code, that of construction restraints. Thus it bristles with gleaming glass-and-concrete corncob-towers 20 and 30 stories high and with vast apartment complexes, their terraces landscaped like miniature gardens.

The Monagesques themselves add to the sense of flossy, flashy self-contentment. Nearly everything is dyed-to-match here, even the lap dog in the Vuitton bag, and fur coats flourish from September through May. Doormen and policemen dress in ice-cream–colored uniforms worthy of an operetta, and along the port yacht clubs host exclusive birthday parties for little-rich-girls in couture party dresses. Pleasure boats vie with luxury cruisers in their brash beauty and Titanic scale, and teams of handsome young men—themselves dyed blond and tanned to match—scour and polish every gleaming surface. Prince Albert II, who has made the most of his extended bachelorhood, admitted the day after the three-month mourning period following his father's death that he had fathered a child with former air hostess Nicole Coste—his son Alexandre will never become prince as he is not the product of a Catholic marriage, but will inherit part of his €2 billion fortune.

Monaco's gleaming profile is due, for the most part, to an entertainment organization called SBM: the Societé des Bains de Mer. Founders in the 19th century of the original casino, they have burgeoned to reign over a mega-complex of 23 restaurants, four hotels, nightclubs, cabarets, and all the casinos in town.

In the 1990s they added **Les Thermes Marins de Monte-Carlo** (*Sea Baths of Monte-Carlo* ✉2 ave. de Monte-Carlo ☎377/98–06–69–00 ☉Daily 7–9), a seawater-therapy treatment center that stretches between the landmark Hôtel de Paris and its sister, the Hermitage. Within its sleek, multilevel complex you can pursue every creature comfort, from underwater massage to seaweed body wraps to light, elegant spa-style lunches—almost all with views over the port.

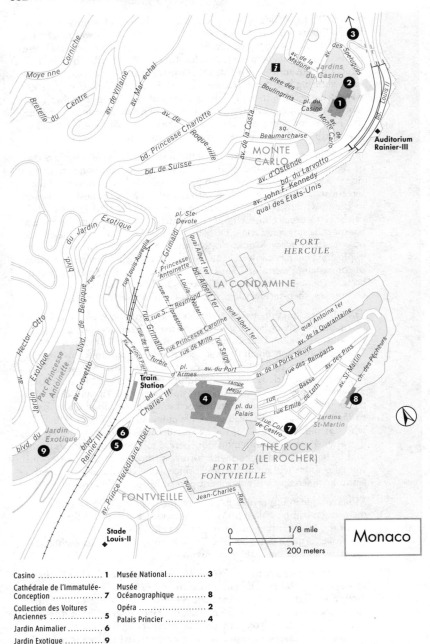

Monaco

0 ————— 1/8 mile
0 ————— 200 meters

You may well gather that Monaco can be intimidating for budget travelers. Eating is expensive, and even the most modest hotels cost more here than in nearby Nice or Menton. As for taxis, they don't even have meters so you are completely at the driver's mercy (expect to pay at least €12 for the shortest possible hop, with prices skyrocketing during events such as the Grand Prix). For the frugal, Monaco is the ultimate day trip, although parking is as coveted as a room with a view.

The harbor district, known as **La Condamine,** connects the new quarter, officially known as **Monte Carlo,** with the Vieille Ville, officially known as **Monaco-Ville** (or Le Rocher), the medieval town on the Rock, topped by the palace, the cathedral, and the Oceanography Museum. Have no fear that you'll need to climb countless steps to get to the Vieille Ville, as there are plenty of elevators and escalators climbing the steep cliffs. But shuttling between the lovely casino grounds of Monte Carlo and Old Monaco, separated by a vast port, is a daunting proposition for ordinary mortals without wings.

Before starting off, arm yourself with a map and a bus schedule or an excellent pair of walking shoes and start at the **tourist office** (⊠*2a bd. des Moulins* ☎*377/92–16–61–66* ⊕*www.monaco-tourisme.com*), just north of the casino gardens.

6

❶ Place du Casino is the center of Monte Carlo and the **Casino** is a must-
★ see, even if you don't bet a sou. Into the gold-leaf splendor of the Casino, where fortunes have been won, shirts lost, and any number of James Bond scenes filmed, the hopeful traipse from tour buses to tempt fate beneath the gilt-edged rococo ceiling.

❷ In the true spirit of the town, it seems that the **Opéra** (⊠*Pl. du Casino* ☎*377/98–06–28–28* ⊕*www.opera.mc* ⊙*Ticket office Tues.–Sat. 10–5:30*), with its 18-ton gilt-bronze chandelier and extravagant frescoes, is part of the casino complex. The designer, Charles Garnier, also built the Paris Opéra, so we are talking one fabulous jewel-box. On show are some of the coast's most significant performances of dance, opera, and orchestral music.

❸ From Place des Moulins there is an escalator down to the Larvotto Beach complex, artfully created with imported sand, and the **Musée National Automates et Poupées,** housed in a Garnier villa within a rose garden. There's a beguiling collection of 18th- and 19th-century dolls and mechanical automatons—more than 400 altogether. ⊠*17 av. Princesse Grace* ☎*377/98–98–91–26* ☜*€6* ⊙*Daily 10–6.*

It's a hike or a ride on bus No. 6 from Monte Carlo to the **port** along Boulevard Albert Ier, where pleasure boats of every shape flash white and blue. It's here that they erect the stands for fans of the Grand Prix. And it's from the far corner of the port that the Institut Océanographique launches research boats to study aquatic life in the Mediterranean, as its late director Jacques Cousteau did for some 30 years.

On the broad plateau known as Le Rocher, or **the Rock,** the majority of Monaco's touristic sights are concentrated with tidy, self-conscious charm. This is the medieval heart of Monaco, and where its cathedral, palace, and the Oceanography Museum can be found. You can either climb up a raked *rampe* from the Place d'Armes, behind the right corner of the port, or approach it by elevator from the seafront at the port's farthest end (past the Yacht Club).

At the center of the Rock's plateau, the broad Place du Palais knots up with crowds at 11:55, when the poker-faded guards—in black in winter, white in summer—change shifts, or, as the French say, relieve

4 themselves. They are protecting hallowed ground: the **Palais Princier,** where the royal family officially "resides" (they have plenty of other houses up and down the coast). You can tell they're home if the family banner flies from the mast above the main tower. A 40-minute guided tour (summer only) of this sumptuous chunk of history, first built in the 13th century and expanded and enhanced over the centuries, reveals an extravagance of 16th- and 17th-century frescoes, as well as tapestries, gilt furniture, and paintings on a grand scale. One wing of the palace, open throughout the year, is taken up by the **Musée Napoléon,** filled with Napoleonic souvenirs—including The Hat and a tricolor scarf—and genealogical charts. (The Grimaldis and the Bonapartes were related, you see.) There is an abundance of military paraphernalia, from uniforms to medals, etchings, and banners, all from the Prince's private collection. ⊠ *Pl. du Palais* ☎ 377/93–25–18–31 ☜€7; Musée Napoléon, €4 ☉ Jan.–Apr., daily 10:30–5; May–Sept., daily 10:30–5:30; Oct.-Dec., daily 10–5:30.

5 On the terrasses de Fontvieille are two remarkable sights (opened in
☾ 2003): the **Collection des Voitures Anciennes** *(Collection of Vintage Cars)* and the **Jardin Animalier** *(Animal Garden)*. The former is a collection of Prince Ranier's vintage cars from a De Dion Bouton to a Lambourghini Countach; the latter, a mini-zoo housing Prince Ranier's animal collection—an astonishing array of wild beasts including monkeys and exotic birds. ⊠ *Terrasses de Fontvielle* ☎ 377/92–05–28–56 or 377/93–25–18–31 ☜€6 *(Voitures)*; €4 *(Animalier)* ☉ Vintage Cars: daily 10–6; Animal Garden: June–Sept., 9–noon and 2–7; Oct.–Feb., 10–noon and 2–5; Mar.–May, 10–noon and 2–6.

7 Follow the flow of crowds down the last remaining streets of medieval Monaco to the **Cathédrale de l'Immaculée-Conception** (⊠ *Av. St-Martin* ☎ 377/93–30–87–70), an uninspired 19th-century version of Romanesque. It harbors nonetheless some wonderful artworks, including an **altarpiece** painted by Bréa in 1500. Now shielded behind glass at the north transept, it is, perhaps, his masterwork, depicting with tender detail the steady gaze of St-Nicolas; he is flanked by small panels portraying other saints, graceful, chastened, and demure. Despite the humility innate to the work, it's framed with unusual flamboyance in ornate gilt wood. Just beyond the Bréa polyptych, enter the curve of the apse to see the tombs of the Grimaldi clan. The first on entering the apse from the left is simply labeled *Gracia Patricain, Principis Rainerii*; Princess Grace's death date—1982—figures in Roman numerals. It's easy to identify her tomb without reading the inscription; even today it's heaped with fresh flowers.

❽
☽
★ At the prow of the Rock, the grand **Musée Océanographique** *(Oceanography Museum)* perches dramatically on a cliff, its many levels plunging dramatically to the sea. The splendid Edwardian structure was built under Prince Albert Ier to house specimens collected on amateur explorations, and evokes the grandeur of the days of imperialist discovery and the old National Geographic Society. Both the museum and its research organization, the Institut Océanographique (Oceanography Institute), were led by Jacques Cousteau (1910–97) from 1957 to 1988. Sumptuously decorated with mosaics of sea life, beveled-oak display cases, and gleaming brass, the museum contains a collection somewhat pared down from its heyday. The main floor displays skeletons and taxidermy of enormous sea creatures, including a 6½-foot-wide Japanese crab, and a magnificent life-scale model of a sperm whale, created from first-hand observation by the museum's conservateur/artist Maurizio Würtz. But the reason the throngs pour into this landmark is its famous **aquarium**, a vast complex of backlit tanks at eye level containing every imaginable genus of fish, crab, and eel. The wide-open piranha pond is a crowd pleaser. For a fine view and a restorative drink, take the elevator to the roof terrace. ✉ *Av. St-Martin* ☏ *377/93–15–36–00* ⊕ *www. oceano.mc* 🎟 *€12.50* ⊙ *Daily, Jan.–Mar., 10–6; Apr.–June, 9:30–7; July–Aug., 9:30–7:30; Sept., 9:30–7; Oct.–Dec., 10–6.*

❾
FodorśChoice
★ Six hundred varieties of cacti and succulents cling to a sheer rock face at the **Jardin Exotique** *(Tropical Garden)*, a brisk half-hour walk west from the palace. The garden traces its roots to days when Monaco's near-tropical climate nurtured unheard-of exotica, amazing visitors from the northlands as much as any zoo. The plants are of less interest today, especially to Americans familiar with southwestern flora. The views over the Rock and coastline, however, are spectacular. Also on the grounds, or actually under them, are the **Grottes de l'Observatoire**—spectacular grottoes and caves a-drip with stalagmites and spotlit with fairy lights. The largest cavern is called "La Grande Salle" and looks like a Romanesque rock cathedral. Traces of Cro-Magnon civilization have been found here so the grottoes now bear the official name the **Musée d'Anthropologie Préhistorique.** ✉ *Bd. du Jardin Exotique* ☏ *377/93–15–29–80* ⊕ *www.jardin-exotique.mc* 🎟 *€6.90* ⊙ *Daily, mid-May–mid-Sept., 9–7; mid-Sept.–mid-May, 9–6.*

WHERE TO EAT & STAY

$$$$
★ ✗ **BB & Co.** Formerly known as the Bar & Boeuf, Alain Ducasse's summer restaurant in the entertainment complex Le Sporting (an expensive cab ride from the center of town) is now looking beyond sea bass and beef to highlight other products, such as pedigreed lamb and Mediterranean sea bream. The dining room has had a makeover, too, with a dramatic black, white, and fuschia color scheme and designer chairs by Pierre Paulin. The two ingredients that originally inspired this restaurant still star, and each is presented in several forms: raw, spit-roasted, cooked à la plancha, skewered, or braised. Take the advice of the enthusiastic waiters and order the more adventurous dishes from the concise menu—sea bass tartare with a lime and pepper sorbet could prove as much of a revelation as the conversation at the next table ("I

have 52 million in my bank account"). ⊠*Le Sporting, Av. Princesse Grace, 98000* ☎*377/92–16–60–60* ♠*Reservations essential* ⊕*www.alain-ducasse.com* ⊟*AE, DC, MC, V* ⊙*Closed mid-Sept.–mid-May. No lunch.*

$$$$ ✕**Le Louis XV.** Louis Quinze to the initiated, this extravagantly showy
Fodor'sChoice restaurant stuns with neo-Baroque details, yet it manages to be upstaged
★ by its product: the superb cuisine of Alain Ducasse, one of Europe's most celebrated chefs. With too many tokens on his Monopoly board, Ducasse jets between his other, ever-growing interests leaving the Louis XV kitchen, for the most part, in the more-than-capable hands of chefs Franck Cerutti and Pascal Bardet. Cerutti grew up in the back country behind Nice, and by choosing the most perfect products at the Cours Saleya market in Nice and preparing them with extraordinary care he elevates peasant cooking to astonishing heights. A perfect example is his stockfish, a stew of salted fish and peppers that in his hands loses its rustic flavor to express the essence of the ingredients. There is probably little point in doing things halfway here: order one of the tasting menus (€190 or €250) and surrender yourself to the once-in-a-lifetime experience (or more if you happen to be one of the millionaires who frequent this restaurant). Resistance is futile when it comes to the glamorous iced lobster consommé with caviar or the risotto perfumed with Alba white truffles. The decor is magnificent—a surfeit of gilt, mirrors, and chandeliers—and the waitstaff seignorial as they proffer a footstool for madame's handbag. In Ducasse fashion, the Baroque clock on the wall is stopped just before 12. Cinderella should have no fears. ⊠*Hôtel de Paris, Pl. du Casino, 98000* ☎*377/92–16–30–01* ⊕*www.alain-ducasse.com* ⊟*AE, DC, MC, V* ⊙*Closed Dec. 1–30, late Feb.–mid-Mar., and Tues. and Wed. (except Wed. evenings mid-June–late Aug).*

$$$$ ✕**Maya Bay.** Soft-spoken Olivier Streiff is no ordinary chef, as his spiky black hair and heavy black eyeliner imply. In an East-meets-West setting replete with kimono wall hangings and Buddha statues, he serves globe-trotting Mediterranean cuisine such as "inverted sushi" of langoustine, melon, and tarragon or red mullet "spring roll" with olive chutney and tomato in sesame oil. Aim for the garden terrace at the back of the restaurant, where exotic birds in cages contribute to the tropical atmosphere. Because not everyone in Monte Carlo is a millionaire, the Maya Bay has a bargain €20 or €28 no-choice lunch menu that changes daily. The Maya Bar, a popular spot for a drink in Monaco, recently opened a sushi bar. ⊠*24 av. Princesse Grace* ☎*377/97–70–74–67* ⊕*www.mayabay.mc* ⊟*AE, DC, MC, V* ⊙*Closed Sun., Mon., and Nov.*

$$$ ✕**Café de Paris.** This landmark Belle Époque brasserie across from the casino offers classic dishes: shellfish, steak tartare, matchstick frites, and fish boned table-side. Supercilious, super-pro waiters fawn gracefully over Old World preeners, gentlemen, jet-setters, and tourists alike, serving good hot food until 2 AM. ⊠*Pl. du Casino, 98000* ☎*377/92–16–20–20* ⊕*www.sbm.mc* ⊟*AE, DC, MC, V.*

$$$ ✕**Quai des Artistes.** This warehouse-scale neo-Deco bistro on the port
★ is the chicest of the chic with Monagesque gentry, packing well-heeled diners shoulder-to-shoulder at banquettes lined up for maximum peo-

ple-watching. Rich brasserie classics (liver and onions, lentils with salt pork) are counterbalanced with high-flavor international experiments (mussels in a red-pepper ceviche, char-grilled salmon served sushi-rare). ⊠*4 quai Antoine Ier* ☎*377/97–97–97–77* ⊕*www.quaidesartistes.com* ⌦*Reservations essential* ⊟*AE, DC, MC, V.*

$$ ✕**Castelroc.** With its tempting pine-shaded terrace just across from the entrance to the Prince's Palace, you may take this for a tourist chaser, but this recently revamped restaurant is one of the more popular lunch spots in town with locals. The cuisine is a mix of classic and regional flavors, from *anchoïade* (anchovy paste) with olive oil to stuffed artichokes, and garlicky *stocafi* (stockfish) simmered with tomatoes and Provençal herbs. Don't miss the chance to try *barbajuans* (fried ravioli stuffed with Swiss chard or zucchini) if they are on the menu. ⊠*Pl. du Palais, 98000* ☎*377/93–30–36–68* ⊟*AE, D, MC, V* ⊘*Closed Sat., and Dec.–mid-June.*

$ ✕**Polpetta.** This popular little trattoria, a favorite with stars and politi-
★ cos since the 1970s, is close enough to the Italian border to pass for the real thing, and the exuberant Guasco brothers who greet you add to the authenticity. Enjoy a parade of antipasti, seafood risotto, osso buco perfumed with saffron, or the house specialty, *trofie* (skinny Ligurian-style gnocchi) with pesto and tomato sauce. There's a terrific list of Italian wines. ⊠*2 rue Paradis, 98000* ☎*377/93–50–67–84* ⊟*AE, MC, V* ⊘*Closed Tues. and 3 wks in June. No lunch Sat.*

$ ✕**Stars'n'Bars.** This American-style port-side bar/restaurant/entertainment center is such a phenomenal success with the Monagesque that it's worth a stop for the culture shock alone. Fat, juicy burgers, cookie sundaes, real ice tea in thick glasses, and (gasp!) pitchers of ice water draw homesick expats, burrito-starved backpackers—and mobs of locals wallowing in *la cuisine américaine.* Port-side tables are low-key; inside, soft rock, arcade games, and a friendly international bar scene mingle all ages and nationalities. ⊠*6 quai Antoine I, 98000er* ⊕*www. starsnbars.com* ⊟*AE, DC, MC, V* ⊘*Closed Mon. Nov.–May.*

$$$$ ☷**Hermitage.** They've all been here; the kings, the queens, Pavarotti in
★ jeans. A riot of frescoes and plaster flourishes embellished with gleaming brass, this landmark 1900 hotel nonetheless maintains a relatively low profile, set back a block from the casino scene. This is where the mink-and-Vuarnets set comes *not* to be seen. Even if you're not staying, walk through the lobby to admire the glass-dome Art Nouveau vestibule, designed by Gustav Eiffel. The best rooms face the sea or angle toward the port. At the formal, sophisticated restaurant Le Vistamar, chef Joël Garault buys his seafood from a local Monagesque fisherman. It's served in a tailored, modern room splashed with cobalt blue. Its broad, broad terrace offers one of the most glamorous dining settings in Monaco. **Pros:** spacious rooms, terraces overlooking Casino, outstanding service. **Cons:** public spaces not very lively; rooms on street side have some traffic noise; watch out for €32/day parking charge. ⊠*Sq. Beaumarchais,* ☎*377/92–16–40–00* ⊕*www.hotelhermitage montecarlo.com* ⛱*280 rooms, 20 suites* ⌂*In-room: refrigerator. In-hotel: restaurant, bar, pool, gym, spa, Internet terminal, parking (paid), some pets allowed* ⊟*AE, DC, MC, V.*

\$\$\$\$ ⬚ **Metropole.** This Belle Epoque hotel, set on land that once belonged ★ to Pope Leon XIII, has pulled out all the stops in its decoration— famed Paris designer Jacques Garcia has given the rooms his signature hyper-aristocratic look and the chef is none other than Joël Robuchon (though, since he can't be in Paris, Las Vegas, Tokyo, Monte Carlo, and on television at once, Christophe Cussac runs the open kitchen day-to-day). If you don't want a full-blown meal, lighter food is served all day in the bar and spa. The garden has also been transformed into an urban oasis, now harboring some 3,000 species of plants. Guests can choose from a number of chauffeur-driven half-day and a day trips, plus children's programs and—*mais, oui*—dogs' programs. **Pros:** warm service; great location; modern bathrooms. **Cons:** no Wi-Fi in rooms; the occasional service glitch. ⊠*4 av. de la Madone,* ☎*377/93–15–15–15* ⊕*www.metropole.com* ⥲*141 rooms and suites* ⚐*In-room: refrigerator. In-hotel: restaurant, bar, pool, gym, spa, Internet terminal, parking (paid), some pets allowed* ⊟*AE, DC, MC, V* ⦿*MAP.*

\$\$\$\$ ⬚ **Monte-Carlo Bay Hotel.** This massive luxury resort opened in 2005 immodestly bills itself as "a natural Eden reinvented." Perched on a 10-acre peninsula, it seeks to evoke the Côte d'Azur's 1920s heyday with its neoclassical columns and arches, exotic gardens, lagoon swimming pool, casino, and concert hall. It might all seem just a little over the top, but there is no denying the spaciousness and comfort of the rooms, nor the appeal of the sandy-bottomed lagoon stretching out towards the sea. If the helipad and yacht mooring seem superfluous, then you probably don't belong. There are four restaurants to choose from, the best of which is the Blue Bay, where chef Marcel Ravin serves world cuisine in a hip contemporary setting. **Pros:** ultra-luxurious, with so much to do that there is no need to leave the hotel; sofas on balconies. **Cons:** pool and poolside can become crowded. ⊠*40 av. Princesse Grace ,* ☎*377/98–06–25–25* ⊕*www.montecarlobay.com* ⥲*300 rooms, 40 suites* ⚐*In-room: refrigerator, Wi-Fi. In-hotel: 4 restaurants, bar, tennis courts, pool, gym, spa, parking (paid)* ⊟*AE, DC, MC, V.*

\$\$\$ ⬚ **Alexandra.** The friendly proprietress makes you feel right at home at this central, comfortable spot just north of the Casino. Though the color schemes clash and the bedrooms are spare, bathrooms are spacious and up to date, and insulated windows keep traffic noise out. Breakfast is included in the price. **Pros:** central location; affordable prices for Monaco. **Cons:** tired, old-fashioned decor; lack of Web site makes it hard to book. ⊠*35 bd. Princesse-Charlotte,* ☎*377/93–50–63–13* ⥲*56 rooms* ⚐*In-room: refrigerator, Wi-Fi. In-hotel: Internet terminal* ⊟*AE, DC, MC, V* ⦿*BP.*

NIGHTLIFE & THE ARTS

The **Living Room** (⊠*7 av. des Spélugues* ☎*377/93–50–80–31*) is a popular, crowded piano bar and discotheque open year-round. For a relatively low-key night, try **Sparco Café** (⊠*19 av. Charles-III* ☎*377/93–30–41–06*), a piano bar that often attracts good jazz singers.

Monte Carlo's **Printemps des Arts** (⊕*www.printempsdesarts.com*) takes place from early April to mid-May and includes the world's top ballet, operatic, symphonic, and chamber performers. For schedules and infor-

Want to Break the Bank?

There's no need to go to bed before dawn in Monte Carlo when you can go to the grand casinos. The casinos fix no closing times, but keep the doors open as long as the games are rolling.

The bastion and landmark of Monte Carlo gambling is, of course, the gorgeously ornate **Casino de Monte-Carlo**. The main gambling hall is the **Salle Européene** (European Room), where for an €8 entry fee you can play roulette, trente et quarante, or blackjack. The slot machines stand apart in the **Salle Blanche** (White Room) and the **Salon Rose** (Pink Salon), where unclad nymphs float about on the ceiling smoking cigarillos.

The **Salles Privées** (Private Rooms) are for high rollers; pay another €15 to play for a minimum stake of €80. Jacket and tie are required in the back rooms, which open at 3 PM. Bring your passport (under-21s not admitted). ⊠ *Pl. du Casino* ☎ *377/92–16–20–00* ⊙ *3 PM–noon.*

Once owned by the rival Loews Hotel (now the Monte Carlo Grand), the **Sun Casino** has been absorbed by SBM, though its long, low hall remains inside the Monte Carlo Grand hotel and just beside the waterfront convention center. There are no fewer than 435 slot machines here, as well as craps, blackjack, and *roulette américaine.* ⊠ *12 av. des Spélugues* ☎ *377/92–16–21–23* ⊙ *Tables open weekdays at 5 PM and weekends at 4 PM; slot machines open daily at 11 AM.*

Behind the dining room of the **Café de Paris** you'll find *les jeux américains:* row upon row of slot machines as well as American roulette, craps, and blackjack. ⊠ *Pl. du Casino* ☎ *377/92–16–21–24* ⊙ *Tables open daily at 5 PM; slot machines open daily at 10 AM.*

SBM's Le Sporting, a summer-only entertainment complex on the waterfront, has opened the **Salle des Palmiers** for the full panoply of European games, from English roulette to *chemin de fer.* Its games are open only at night. ⊠ *Le Sporting, Av. Princess Grace* ☎ *377/92–16–21–25* ⊙ *Late June–mid-Sept., tables open daily at 10 PM.*

mation contact the **Direction des Affaires Culturelles** (⊠ *4 bd. des Moulins* ☎ *377/93–15–85–15*). Year-round ballet and classical music can be enjoyed at the **Salle Garnier** (⊠ *Pl. du Casino* ☎ *377/92–16–22–99*), the main venue of the Opéra de Monte-Carlo and the Orchestre Philharmonique de Monte-Carlo, both worthy of the magnificent hall. The **Théâtre Princesse Grace** (⊠ *12 av. d'Ostende* ☎ *377/93–25–32–27*) stages a number of plays during the Spring Arts Festival; off-season there's usually a new show each week.

SPORTS & THE OUTDOORS

The **Monte Carlo Tennis Open** (☎ *377/04–93–41–30–15 for information* ⊕ *www.masters-series.com/montecarlo*) is held in late April in the Monte Carlo Country Club, which lies in the outskirts of Monaco in the French commune of Roquebrune–Cap-Martin.

The **Grand Prix de Monaco** (☎ *377/93–15–26–00 for information* ⊕ *www. grand-prix-monaco.com*) takes place in mid-May. Monaco goes a bit wacky during this car race around the principality in a way that only a city that prides itself on the outlandish amount of wealth it can display … well, outlandishly, can. During the Grand Prix the streets are roped off, the liquor is iced, and the brass is polished, and the enormously wealthy gracefully alight upon the city to lean over balconies—some rented for a mere €10,000 for the two-day stint. The cars fly through the city in a hot blur of Formula One super-speed. It's an exciting event if you can get close enough to the high-priced action.

Probably the best of the private beaches is **La Note Bleu** (⊠ *Plage du Larvotto* ☎ *377/93–50–05–02*) which has something for everyone with activities for kids, jazz concerts, and an excellent beach restaurant serving Mediterranean-Asian food. It's also a jellyfish-free zone, with nets that keep their tentacles at bay.

ROQUEBRUNE–CAP-MARTIN

5 km (3 mi) east of Monaco.

GETTING HERE
Regional trains (the Mandelieu–Ventimiglia line) run between Cannes, Nice, and Roquebrune-Cap Martin, taking about 30 minutes from Nice (€3.90). There is a second stop, Carnolès, closer to Menton. From the Roquebrune-Cap Martin train station, it's a one-hour hike up to the perched village or a €20 taxi ride. The Nice–Menton bus No.100, which runs from the bus station in Nice every 15 minutes (€1), also stops in the lower part of Roquebrune.

VISITOR INFORMATION
Roquebrune-Cap-Martin Tourist Office (⊠ *20 av. Paul Doumer, Roquebrune–Cap-Martin* ☎ *04–93–35–62–87* ⊕ *www.roquebrune-cap-martin.com*).

EXPLORING
In the midst of the frenzy of overbuilding that defines this last gasp of the coast before Italy, two twinned havens have survived, each in its own way: the perched Vieille Ville of Roquebrune, which gives its name to the greater area, and Cap-Martin—luxurious, isolated, exclusive, and the once favored retreat of the Empress Eugénie and Winston Churchill. With its lovely tumble of raked tile roofs and twisting streets, fountains, archways, and quiet squares, Roquebrune retains many of the charms of a hilltop village, although it has become heavily gentrified and commercialized. Rue Moncollet is lined with arcaded passageways and a number of medieval houses. Somerset Maugham—who once memorably described these environs as a "sunny place for shady people"—resided in the town's famous Villa Mauresque (still private) for many years.

Roquebrune's main attraction is the **Château Féodal** *(Feudal Castle)* at the top of the Old Town. Around the remains of a 10th-century tower, the Grimaldis erected an impregnable fortress that was state-of-the-art in the 16th century, with crenellation, watchtowers, and a broad moat. Nowadays this stronghold is besieged by tourists, who invade its restored halls and snap pictures from its wraparound walkway. Guided visits of the fort and village are held on Saturdays at 3 PM (€3.50, book ahead at the tourist office); wear hiking shoes and be prepared for some vigorous exercise. ☎04–93–35–07–22 ☜€3,70 ⊙ *Daily 10–12:30 and 2–6.*

In the **cemetery,** at the far eastern end of the Old Town, Swiss-French architect Le Corbusier lies buried with his wife in a tomb of his own design. He kept a humble *cabanot* (beach bungalow) on the rocky shores of the Cap-Martin, where he drowned while swimming in 1965.

★ You can visit Le Corbusier's stunningly idyllic "cabanon" bungalow and see the glorious flora of the cape by walking the **Promenade Le Corbusier.** It leads over chalk cliffs and through dense Mediterranean flora to his tiny retreat, a modular cube of tiny proportions (3.66 × 3.66 meters) which appealed to his rigorous sense of minimalism. Guided tours can be arranged on Tuesdays or Fridays for €8 through the tourist office. Park at the tip of the cape on Avenue Winston-Churchill and follow the signs.

WHERE TO EAT & STAY

$$ ▦ **Les Deux Frères.** Magnificently sited, eccentric, and oozing with
★ charm, this whitewashed 1854 schoolhouse has been transformed into an inn overlooking the sea. Every room is designed with a different theme—African safari, flower power, medieval castle, 1,001 nights— and tied-in videocassettes stand by to back up the mood. It's not as silly as it sounds, but is executed with modern, high-tech style and quality materials. The restaurant (closed Monday, no dinner Sunday, no lunch Tuesday) has set-price menus only (€28 for lunch including half a bottle of wine per person, €48 for dinner) and offers ambitious and generous French cooking, either indoors by the crackling fireplace or on the terrace *place* overlooking the whole of the Côte d'Azur. Homemade terrines, herbed lamb, and good cheeses and pastries draw a local clientele for picturesque culinary excursions. ⊠*1 place des Deux Frères (with GPS 1 av. Raymond Pointcarré),* ☎*04–93–28–99–00* ⊕*www. lesdeuxfreres.com* ⇩*10 rooms* ⚬*In-room: refrigerator. In-hotel: restaurant, bar, Wi-Fi parking, some pets allowed* ⊟*AE, MC, V* ⊙*Closed mid-Nov.–mid-Dec., 1 wk in Mar.*

MENTON

1 km (²/₃ mi) east of Roquebrune, 9 km (5½ mi) east of Monaco.

VISITOR INFORMATION
Menton Tourist Office (⊠*Palais de l'Europe, Av. Boyer, Menton* ☎*04–92–41–76–76* ⊕*www.menton.fr*).

EXPLORING
Menton, the most Mediterranean of the French resort towns, rubs shoulders with the Italian border and owes some of its balmy climate to the protective curve of the Ligurian shore. Its Cubist skew of terra-cotta roofs and yellow-ocher houses, Baroque arabesques capping the church

facades, and ceramic tiles glistening on their steeples, all evoke the villages of the Italian coast. Yet there's a whiff of influence from Spain, too, in its fantastical villas, exotic gardens, and whimsical patches of ceramic color, and a soupçon of Morocco, Corsica, and Greece. It is, in fact, the best of all Mediterranean worlds—and humble to boot: Menton is the least pretentious of the Côte d'Azur resorts, and all the more alluring for its modesty (though it can be quite a sleepy place compared to Nice, Antibes, or Cannes).

Its near-tropical climate nurtures orange and lemon trees that hang heavy with fruit in winter. There's another Florida parallel: the warmth attracts flocks of senior citizens who warm their bones far from northern fog and ice. Thus a large population of elderly visitors basks on its waterfront benches and browses its downtown shops. But Menton has a livelier, younger side, too, and the farther you penetrate toward the east, the more intriguing and colorful it becomes.

> ## GUIDED TOURS
>
> Menton acquaints you with its rich architectural heritage by offering regular *visites du patrimoine* (heritage tours) to its gardens, cemetery, museums, and villas. Details on each visit and points and times of departure are published in the city's free *Programme des manifestations* (events program), published bimonthly by the tourist office. For information, contact the **Maison du Patrimonie** (*24 rue St-Michel, 04-92-10-97-10*) or the Menton Tourist Office—ask about the *Passeport Menton Côté Charme* pass.

To get a feel for the territory, start your exploration at the far-east end of the Vieille Ville (Old Town) and walk out to the end of the **Quai Napoléon III**, jutting far out into the water. Above the masts of pleasure boats, all of Menton spreads over the hills, and the mountains of Italy loom behind.

Up a set of grand tiered stairs that lead from the Quai Bonaparte and the Jetée Emperatrice Eugénie the **Parvis St-Michel,** a broad plaza paved in round white and gray stones patterned in the coat of arms of the Grimaldi family. The plaza was created in the 17th century by Prince Honoré II; the letter H is mingled into the design as a kind of signature at the base of his great gift to the city.

❶ The majestic, Baroque **Basilique St-Michel,** on Parvis St-Michel, dominates the skyline of Menton with its bell tower. A humbler Renaissance church was destroyed by order of the prince to make way for something on a grander scale, and its towering belfry secured its conspicuousness in 1701. Beyond the beautifully proportioned facade—a 19th-century addition—the richly frescoed nave and chapels contain several works by Genovese artists and a splendid 17th-century organ. Visiting hours are daily from 10 to noon and 3 to 5 (afternoons only from Nov. 1–Dec. 15).

❷ Just above the Basilique St-Michel, the smaller **Chapelle de Pénitents Blancs** answers with its own pure Baroque beauty, dating from 1687. Between

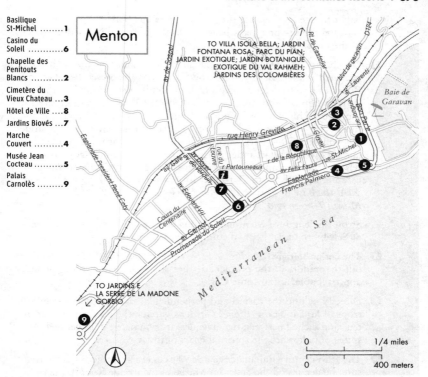

Menton

TO VILLA ISOLA BELLA; JARDIN FONTANA ROSA; PARC DU PIAN; JARDIN EXOTIQUE; JARDIN BOTANIQUE EXOTIQUE DU VAL RAHMEH; JARDINS DES COLOMBIÈRES

Baie de Garavan

Mediterranean Sea

TO JARDINS E LA SERRE DE LA MADONE GORBIO

0   1/4 miles

0   400 meters

3 and 5 PM you can slip in to see the graceful trompe l'oeil over the altar and the ornate gilt lanterns the penitents carried in processions.

❸ High above the Parvis St-Michel, the **Cimetière du Vieux-Château** *(Old Château Cemetery)* lies on the terraced plateau where once stood a medieval castle. The Victorian graves here are arranged by nationality, with an entire section of Russian royalty. The birth and death dates often attest to the ugly truth: even Menton's balmy climate couldn't reverse the ravages of tuberculosis.

Two blocks below the plaza, **Rue St-Michel** serves as the main commercial artery of the Vieille Ville, lined with shops, cafés, and orange trees.

❹ Between the lively pedestrian Rue St-Michel and the waterfront, the marvelous **Marché Couvert** *(Covered Market)* sums up Menton style with its Belle Époque facade decorated in jewel-tone ceramics. Inside, it's just as appealing, with merchants vaunting chewy bread, mountain cheeses, oils, fruit, and Italian delicacies in Caravaggesque disarray. Outside its walls, other merchants bargain away their garden vegetables and hand-wound bundles of herbs. The market is open daily from 7 AM to 1 PM.

Right by the market, the pretty little **Place aux Herbes** is a picturesque spot for a pause on a park bench, a drink, or a meal in the deep shade of the plane trees.

5 On the waterfront opposite the market, a squat medieval bastion crowned with four tiny watchtowers houses the **Musée Jean-Cocteau.** Built in 1636 to defend the port, the structure was spotted by the artist-poet-filmmaker Jean Cocteau (1889–1963) as the perfect site for a group of his works; he planned and supervised its reconstruction but never saw it finished. Outside its walls, a mosaic in round stone (an homage to the Parvis St-Michel) depicts a lizard; the inside floor answers with a salamander mosaic. There are bright, cartoonish pastels of fishermen and wenches in love, and a fantastical assortment of ceramic animals in the wrought-iron windows he designed himself. ✉ *At the base of Quai Napoléon* ☎ *04–93–57–72–30* 💳 *€3* ⊙ *Wed.–Mon. 10–noon and 2–6.*

Stroll the length of Menton's famous beachfront along the **Promenade du Soleil,** broad, white, and studded with palm trees.

6 The **Casino Barrière** (✉ *2 bis av. Félix-Faure* ☎ *04–93–10–16–16*) stakes out the middle of the promenade that shares its name; it's a modest, approachable, anti–Monte Carlo.

7 Directly behind the casino and perpendicular to the beach, the broad tropical **Jardins Biovès** *(Biovès Gardens)* stretch the breadth of the center, sandwiched between two avenues. Its symmetrical flower beds and spires of palms are the spiritual heart of town.

8 The 19th-century Italianate **Hôtel de Ville** conceals another Cocteau treasure: he decorated the **Salle des Mariages** (Marriage Room), the room in which civil marriages take place, with vibrant allegorical scenes. ✉ *17 av. de la République* ☎ *04–93–10–50–29* 💳 *€2* ⊙ *Weekdays 8:30–12:30 and 1:30–5.*

9 At the far west end of town, toward Roquebrune, stands the 18th-century **Palais Carnolès**, in vast gardens luxuriant with 400 citrus trees representing 50 different species. It was once the summer retreat of the princes of Monaco; today it contains a sizable collection of European paintings from the Renaissance to the present day. The halls of the palace themselves are as interesting as the artworks; the **Grand Salon d'Honneur** (Grand Salon of Honor) retains a rich ensemble of Neoclassical grotesques and bas-reliefs. ✉ *3 av. de la Madone* ☎ *04–93–35–49–71* 💳 *Free* ⊙ *Wed.–Mon. 10–noon and 2–6.*

WHERE TO EAT & STAY

$$$$ ✕ **Mirazur.** Avant-garde French cuisine by an Argentinian-Italian chef? ★ Why not if you're perched on the border of France and Italy, like this restaurant overlooking a cascading tropical garden and the sea on the outer edge of Menton. Mauro Colagreco learned his craft in Latin America before acquiring a solid French base with the likes of Bernard Loiseau in Burgundy, and both Alain Passard and Alain Ducasse in Paris. Today, he is a perfect example of the wave of young chefs whose style has been dubbed "la jeune cuisine": for him, the plate is a palette

Paradise Found: The Magnificent Gardens of Menton

The Côte d'Azur was famed for its panoply of grand villas and even grander gardens built by Victorian dukes, Spanish exiles, Belgian royals, and American blue bloods. Although its hothouse crescent blooms everywhere with palm and lemon trees and jungle flowers, nowhere else does it bloom so extravagantly than in Menton, famous for its temperate climes and 24-karat sun.

With a temperate microclimate created by its southeastern and sunny exposure (the Alps were a natural buffer against cold winds), Menton attracted a great share of wealthy hobbyists, including Major Lawrence Johnston, a gentleman gardener best known for his Cotswolds wonderland, Hidcote Manor.

Fair-haired and blue-eyed, this gentle American wound up buying a choice estate in the village of Gorbio—one of the loveliest of all perched seaside villages, set 10 km (6 mi) west of Menton—and spent the 1920s and 1930s making the **Serre de la Madone** one of the horticultural masterpieces of the coast.

He brought back exotica from his many trips to South Africa, Mexico, and China, and planted them in a series of terraces, accented by little pools, vistas, and stone steps. While most of his creeping plumbago, pink belladona, and night-flowering cacti are now gone, his garden has been reopened by the municipality. It is best to call for a reservation at the Serre de la Madone; car facilities are very limited but the garden can also be reached from Menton via bus No. 7 (get off at Mers et Monts stop).

Back in Menton, green-thumbers will also want to visit the town's Jardin Botanique, the Val Rahmeh Botanical Garden (Av. St-Jacques), planted by Maybud Campbell in the 1910s, much prized by connoisseurs, bursting with rare ornamentals and subtropical plants, and adorned with water-lily pools and fountains.

The tourist office can also give you directions to other gardens around Menton, including the Fontana Rosa, the Villa Maria Serena, and the Villa Les Colombièrs, as well as issue Heritage Passports for select garden visits; log onto www.menton.com. ⊠ *Serre de la Madone: 74 route de Gorbio* ☎ *04–93–57–73–90* ⊕ *www. serredelamadone.com* 🎫 *€8 for Serre, €4 for Val Rehmeh* ⊙ *Apr.–Oct., Tues.–Sun. 10–6; Dec.–Mar., Tues.–Sun. 10–5. Tours (in French) Tues.–Sun. 3* ᴘᴍ*; in English on request by calling 04–92–10–33–66.*

6

---

and each ingredient has its precise place and significance. His airy dining room overlooking the sea makes the perfect setting for this expressive cooking, which makes liberal use of those much-talked-about Spanish "techniques" such as spuma (foam). Set menus start at €35 at lunch and go up to €90. ⊠ *30 av. Aristide Briand* ☎*04–92–41–86–86* ⊕*www.mirazur.fr* ⟍*Reservations essential* 🖃*AE, MC, V* ⊙*Closed Mon., Tues., mid-Oct.–mid-Feb.*

$$–$$$
Fodor's Choice
★

🏨 **Aiglon.** Sweep down the curving stone stairs to the terrazzo mosaic lobby of this lovely 1880 garden villa for a drink or a meal by the pool (which is heated in winter), or settle onto your little balcony overlooking the grounds and a tiny wedge of sea. There's a room for every whim, all soft-edged, comfortable, and romantic, although you will be loath to leave the grand salon, a picture-perfect confection of 19th-century elegance that wouldn't shame some of the nobler houses in Paris. The poolside restaurant, Le Riaumont (€34–€48 prix-fixe menus), serves candlelit dinners of fresh, local fish lightly steamed and sauced with a Provençal accent; breakfast is served in a shady garden shelter. It's a three-minute walk from the beach. **Pros:** Belle Epoque style; heated pool; good restaurant. **Cons:** tired decor; traffic noise in street-facing rooms (ask for a room overlooking the garden). ⊠ *7 av. de la Madone,* ☎ *04–93–57–55–55* ⊕ *www.hotelaiglon.net* ⇗ *23 rooms, 5 suites* ♿ *In-room: refrigerator. In-hotel: restaurant, bar, pool, Wi-Fi, parking (paid), some pets allowed (fee)* ☰ *AE, DC, MC, V* ⍓ *MAP.*

$$–$$$
Fodor's Choice
★

⊡ **Napoléon.** Refurbished a few years ago, this elegantly modern hotel in Garavan—east of the town center towards Italy—is hard to beat when it comes to value for money. Attentive service, a swimming pool and fitness room, and contemporary furnishings make it feel more like a luxury hotel than the three-star it is; even the breakfast buffet shows unusual attention to detail, with delicious coffee. Each of the three suites is named after an artist who had an impact on Menton, such as Cocteau and Sutherland. Asked if the hotel takes pets, receptionist Mariella replied, "If they are well-behaved—and the same goes for their owners!" **Pros:** warm and efficient service; good breakfast buffet, sea and mountain views from rooms on upper floors. **Cons:** a bit of a walk from the town center; parking can be difficult in high season. ⊠ *29 porte de France,* ☎ *04–93–35–89–50* ⊕ *www.napoleon-menton. com* ⇗ *41 rooms, 3 suites* ♿ *In-room: refrigerator, Internet, Wi-Fi. In-hotel: restaurant, bar, pool, parking (free), some pets allowed* ☰ *AE, D, MC, V* ⍓ *FAP.*

NIGHTLIFE & THE ARTS

The **Casino Barrière** (⊠ *Promenade de Soleil* ☎ *04–92–10–16–16*) has the usual slot machines and roulette tables, as well as a disco and a cabaret in its Club 06. It's open daily 10 AM–3 AM.

★ In August the **Festival de Musique de Chambre** *(Chamber Music Festival)* takes place on the stone-paved plaza outside the St-Michel Church. The **Fête du Citron** *(Lemon Festival),* lasting two weeks at the end of February, celebrates the lemon with floats and sculptures, all made of real fruit.

FRENCH VOCABULARY

	ENGLISH	FRENCH	PRONUNCIATION
BASICS			
	Yes/no	Oui/non	wee/nohn
	Please	S'il vous plaît	seel voo play
	Thank you	Merci	mair-**see**
	You're welcome	De rien	deh ree-**ehn**
	Excuse me, sorry	Pardon	pahr-**don**
	Good morning/ afternoon	Bonjour	bohn-**zhoor**
	Good evening	Bonsoir	bohn-**swahr**
	Goodbye	Au revoir	o ruh-**vwahr**
	Mr. (Sir)	Monsieur	muh-**syuh**
	Mrs. (Ma'am)	Madame	ma-**dam**
	Miss	Mademoiselle	mad-mwa-**zel**
	Pleased to meet you	Enchanté(e)	ohn-shahn-**tay**
	How are you?	Comment allez-vous?	kuh-mahn- tahl-ay **voo**
	Very well, thanks	Très bien, merci	tray bee-ehn, mair-**see**
	And you?	Et vous?	ay voo?
NUMBERS			
	one	un	uhn
	two	deux	deuh
	three	trois	twah
	four	quatre	**kaht**-ruh
	five	cinq	sank
	six	six	seess
	seven	sept	set
	eight	huit	wheat
	nine	neuf	nuf
	ten	dix	deess
	eleven	onze	ohnz
	twelve	douze	dooz
	thirteen	treize	trehz

ENGLISH	FRENCH	PRONUNCIATION
fourteen	quatorze	kah-torz
fifteen	quinze	kanz
sixteen	seize	sez
seventeen	dix-sept	deez-**set**
eighteen	dix-huit	deez-**wheat**
nineteen	dix-neuf	deez-**nuf**
twenty	vingt	vehn
twenty-one	vingt-et-un	vehnt-ay-**uhn**
thirty	trente	trahnt
forty	quarante	ka-**rahnt**
fifty	cinquante	sang-**kahnt**
sixty	soixante	swa-**sahnt**
seventy	soixante-dix	swa-sahnt-**deess**
eighty	quatre-vingts	kaht-ruh-**vehn**
ninety	quatre-vingt-dix	kaht-ruh-vehn-**deess**
one hundred	cent	sahn
one thousand	mille	meel

COLORS

black	noir	nwahr
blue	bleu	bleuh
brown	brun/marron	bruhn/mar-**rohn**
green	vert	vair
orange	orange	o-**rahnj**
pink	rose	rose
red	rouge	rouge
violet	violette	vee-o-**let**
white	blanc	blahnk
yellow	jaune	zhone

DAYS OF THE WEEK

Sunday	dimanche	dee-**mahnsh**
Monday	lundi	luhn-**dee**

ENGLISH	FRENCH	PRONUNCIATION
Tuesday	mardi	mahr-**dee**
Wednesday	mercredi	mair-kruh-**dee**
Thursday	jeudi	zhuh-**dee**
Friday	vendredi	vawn-druh-**dee**
Saturday	samedi	sahm-**dee**

MONTHS

January	janvier	zhahn-vee-**ay**
February	février	feh-vree-**ay**
March	mars	marce
April	avril	a-**vreel**
May	mai	meh
June	juin	zhwehn
July	juillet	zhwee-**ay**
August	août	ah-**oo**
September	septembre	sep-**tahm**-bruh
October	octobre	awk-**to**-bruh
November	novembre	no-**vahm**-bruh
December	décembre	day-**sahm**-bruh

USEFUL PHRASES

Do you speak English?	Parlez-vous anglais?	par-lay **voo ahn**-glay
I don't speak . . .	Je ne parle pas . . .	zhuh nuh parl pah
French	français	frahn-**say**
I don't understand	Je ne comprends pas	zhuh nuh kohm-**prahn** pah
I understand	Je comprends	zhuh kohm-**prahn**
I don't know	Je ne sais pas	zhuh nuh say **pah**
I'm American/ British	Je suis américain/ anglais	a-may-ree-**kehn**/ ahn-**glay**
What's your name?	Comment vous ap pelez-vous?	ko-mahn voo za-pell-ay-**voo**
My name is . . .	Je m'appelle . . .	zhuh ma-**pell** . . .
What time is it?	Quelle heure est-il?	kel air eh-**teel**

ENGLISH	FRENCH	PRONUNCIATION
How?	Comment?	ko-**mahn**
When?	Quand?	kahn
Yesterday	Hier	yair
Today	Aujourd'hui	o-zhoor-**dwee**
Tomorrow	Demain	duh-**mehn**
Tonight	Ce soir	suh **swahr**
What?	Quoi?	kwah
What is it?	Qu'est-ce que c'est?	kess-kuh-**say**
Why?	Pourquoi?	**poor**-kwa
Who?	Qui?	kee
Where is . . .	Où est . . .	oo ay
the train station?	la gare?	la gar
the subway station?	la station de métro?	la sta-**syon** duh may-**tro**
the bus stop?	l'arrêt de bus?	la-**ray** duh **booss**
the post office?	la poste?	la post
the bank?	la banque?	la bahnk
the . . . hotel?	l'hôtel . . .?	lo-**tel**
the store?	le magasin?	luh ma-ga-**zehn**
the cashier?	la caisse?	la **kess**
the . . . museum?	le musée . . .?	luh mew-**zay**
the hospital?	l'hôpital?	lo-pee-**tahl**
the elevator?	l'ascenseur?	la-sahn-**seuhr**
the telephone?	le téléphone?	luh tay-lay-**phone**
Where are the restrooms?	Où sont les toilettes?	oo sohn lay twah-**let**
(men/women)	(hommes/femmes)	(**oh**-mm/**fah**-mm)
Here/there	Ici/là	ee-**see**/la
Left/right	A gauche/à droite	a goash/a draht
Straight ahead	Tout droit	too drwah
Is it near/far?	C'est près/loin?	say pray/lwehn
I'd like . . .	Je voudrais . . .	zhuh voo-**dray**

ENGLISH	FRENCH	PRONUNCIATION
a room	une chambre	ewn **shahm**-bruh
the key	la clé	la clay
a newspaper	un journal	uhn zhoor-**nahl**
a stamp	un timbre	uhn **tam**-bruh
I'd like to buy . . .	Je voudrais acheter . . .	zhuh voo-**dray ahsh**-tay
cigarettes	des cigarettes	day see-ga-**ret**
matches	des allumettes	days a-loo-**met**
soap	du savon	dew sah-**vohn**
city map	un plan de ville	uhn plahn de **veel**
road map	une carte routière	ewn cart roo-tee-**air**
magazine	une revue	ewn reh-**vu**
envelopes	des enveloppes	dayz ahn-veh-**lope**
writing paper	du papier à lettres	dew pa-pee-**ay** a **let**-ruh
postcard	une carte postale	ewn cart pos-**tal**
How much is it?	C'est combien?	say comb-bee-**ehn**
A little/a lot	Un peu/beaucoup	uhn peuh/bo-**koo**
More/less	Plus/moins	plu/mwehn
Enough/too (much)	Assez/trop	a-say/tro
I am ill/sick	Je suis malade	zhuh swee ma-**lahd**
Call a . . .	Appelez un . . .	a-play uhn
doctor	Docteur	dohk-**tehr**
Help!	Au secours!	o suh-**koor**
Stop!	Arrêtez!	a-reh-**tay**
Fire!	Au feu!	o fuh
Caution!/Look out!	Attention!	a-tahn-see-**ohn**

Travel Smart Provence & the French Riviera

GETTING HERE & AROUND

The entire Provence and the French Riviera region measures around 320 km (200 mi) from tip to tail, Montpellier to Monaco. Since many of its greatest attractions are tens of miles apart, carefully planning how you get around will save lots of time and money. Many trips begin by first contacting the French Government Tourist Organization offices: you'll find them listed under Visitor Information at the end of this chapter. Happy landings!

TRAVEL TIMES FROM NICE	BY AIR	BY TRAIN
To		
Avignon	1 hour to Marseille, then train or bus	1½ hours
Marseille	1 hour	1½ hours
Aix-en-Provence	1 hour to Marseille, then train/bus to Aix	3 hours
St-Tropez	Helicopter 20 minutes	1½ hours
Cannes	Helicopter 7–10 minutes	¾ hour
Monte Carlo	Helicopter 10–15 minutes	¾ hour

▌INTRODUCTION TO PUBLIC TRANSPORT

The "Getting Here" sections listed under many towns in the regional chapters of this book provide exact detailed information about bus and train routes; in many cases, prices, transport companies, and schedules to and from the towns are listed. As for an overview of the area's public transport, rest assured it is possible to have a very satisfying initiation to this broad region by train alone. There are sweeping, comprehensive connections all the way from Montpellier to Avignon to Marseille and on to the full length of the Italian coast. There are good regional bus networks, too, that connect out of train stations; they may not be the best thing for quick village-hopping and multi-stop sightseeing (their schedules rarely intersect with yours), but they can prove highly useful. When in doubt, just ask the tourist office or your hotel conciege—you'll be surprised how extensive the train and bus system of Provence and the French Riviera is.

Fares and Schedules Beyond (⊕www.beyond.fr). **SNCF** (⊕www.voyages-sncf.com).

Web Sites Eurail (⊕www.eurail.com). **Eurostar** (⊕www.eurostar.com). **SNCF** (☎08-36-35-35-35 ⊕www.voyages-sncf.com). **TGV** (☎877/284-8633 ⊕www.tgv.com). **www.beyond.fr** (⊕www.beyond.fr).

▌BY AIR

Flying time to Paris is an hour from London, 7½ hours from New York, 9 hours from Chicago, and 11 hours from Los Angeles. A direct flight from New York to Nice is 7 hours and 50 minutes. Scheduled flying time between Paris and Nice is approximately 1 hour and 35 minutes; between Paris and Marseille approximately 1 hour and 25 minutes.

It is wise, given the possibility of strikes in France, to call the day before your flight to reconfirm.

Airlines & Airports Airline and Airport Links.com (⊕www.airlineandairportlinks.com) has links to many of the world's airlines and airports.

Airline Security Issues Transportation Security Administration (⊕www.tsa.gov) has answers for almost every question that might come up.

AIRPORTS

The major gateways to France are Paris's Orly and Charles de Gaulle airports. Nice, Marseille, and Montpellier's airports are also served by frequent flights from Paris and London, and daily connections from Paris arrive at the smaller airports in Avignon and Nîmes.

Airport Information Avignon (☎04-90-81-51-51 ⊕www.avignon. aeroport.fr). **Paris Charles de Gaulle** (☎01-48-62-12-12 ⊕www.adp.fr). **Marseille–Provence** (☎04-42-14-14-14 ⊕www.marseille.aeroport.fr). **Montpellier–Meditérranée** (☎04-67-20-85-85, 04-67-20-85-00 for flight information ⊕www.montpellier.aeroport.fr). **Nice–Côte d'Azur** (☎04-89-88-98-28, 08-20-42-33-33 for flight information ⊕www.nice.aeroport.fr). **Nîmes–Arles–Camargue** (☎04-66-70-49-49). **Toulon Hyères** (☎08-25-01-83-87). **Paris Orly** (☎01-49-75-15-15 ⊕www.adp.fr).

FLIGHTS

Most major airlines fly to Paris and have connecting flights to the south of France on domestic airlines. The one exception is Delta, which flies nonstop to Nice from New York. From the United Kingdom, easyJet offers inexpensive nonstop service to Nice and Marseille; BMI British Midland and BMI Baby have direct flights to Nice; low-cost Ryanair flies to Nîmes and Montpellier.

Within France, Air France flies frequently from Paris to Avignon, Marseille, Nice, Montpellier, and Toulon. EasyJet has flights from both Paris airports to Nice.

Domestic Airlines Air France (☎800/992-3932 in the U.S., 00870/142-4343 in the U.K., 08-20-82-08-20 in France ⊕www.airfrance.com).

Major Airlines American Airlines (☎800/433-7300, 08-10-87-28-72 in France ⊕www.americanairlines.fr or www.aa.com). **Continental Airlines** (☎800/523-3273 for U.S. and Mexico reservations, 800/231-0856 for international reservations, 01-71-23-03-35 in France ⊕www.continental.com). **Delta Airlines** (☎800/221-1212 for U.S. reservations, 800/241-4141 for international reservations, 08-00-30-13-01 in France ⊕www.delta.com). **Northwest Airlines** (☎800/225-2525, 08-90-71-07-10 in France ⊕www.nwa.com). **United Airlines** (☎800/864-8331 for U.S. reservations, 800/538-2929 for international reservations, 08-10-72-72-72 in France ⊕www.united.com). **USAirways** (☎800/428-4322 for U.S. and Canada reservations, 800/622-1015 for international reservations, 08-10-63-22-22 in France ⊕www.usairways.com).

From the U.K. BMI British Midland (☎0870/607-0222 in the U.K., 01-55-69-83-06 in France ⊕www.flybmi.com). **British Airways** (☎0870/850-9850 in the U.K., 08-25-82-50-40 in France ⊕www.ba.com). **BMI Baby** (☎0870/264-2229 in the U.K., 08-90-71-00-81 in France ⊕www.bmibaby.com). **EasyJet** (☎0990/292-929 in the U.K., 08-25-08-25-08 in France ⊕www.easyjet.com or www.easyjet.fr). **Ryanair** (☎0870/156-9569 in the U.K., 08-92-55-56-66 in France ⊕www.ryanair.com).

TICKETS

Most domestic airline tickets are electronic; international tickets may be either electronic or paper. With an e-ticket the only thing you receive is an e-mailed receipt citing your itinerary and reservation and ticket numbers.

The greatest advantage of an e-ticket is that if you lose your receipt, you can simply print out another copy or ask the airline to do it for you at check-in. You usually pay a surcharge (up to $50) to get a paper ticket, if you can get one at all.

The sole advantage of a paper ticket is that it may be easier to endorse over to another airline if your flight is canceled and the airline with which you booked can't accommodate you on another flight.

■TIP→ Discount air passes that let you travel economically in a country or region must often be purchased before you leave home. In some cases you can only get them through a travel agent.

The least expensive airfares to France are often priced for round-trip travel and must usually be purchased in advance. Airlines generally allow you to change your return date for a fee; most low-fare tickets, however, are nonrefundable. If you plan on traveling to and from Paris aboard Air France, you can save on air travel within Europe. As part of their Euro Flyer program, you can buy three- to nine-flight coupons, valid on flights to more than 100 European cities, including many French cities. At $180 each (April–September) and $130 each (October–March), these coupons are a good deal, and the fine print still allows you plenty of freedom.

Europe by Air offers a similar program, which functions like Eurail. Their Flight-Passes are available for $99 per flight to non-European customers, and can be exchanged for one-way nonstop flights between any of 30-plus European cities. Their list includes Toulon, Nice, and Marseille, but the minimum purchase is three passes.

Air Pass Info **FlightPass** (EuropebyAir, ☎888/387-2479 ⊕www.europebyair. com). **SAS Air Passes** (Scandinavian Airlines, ☎800/221-2350, 0870/6072-7727 in the U.K., 1300/727-707 in Australia ⊕www.scandinavian.net).

▌ BY BUS

France's excellent train service means that long-distance buses are rare; regional buses are found mainly where train service is spotty. The weakest rail links in the south lie in the Luberon region of the Vaucluse, in the Alpilles, and in the backcountry of the Haut Var, Haute Provence, and the pre-Alpes behind Nice. To explore these lovely regions, you must work closely with a bus schedule (available at most train stations) and plan connections carefully.

Don't plan on too much multistop sight-seeing if you're limited to bus connections, as they rarely dovetail with your plans. To visit the popular hill towns just behind the Côte d'Azur—Grasse, St-Paul, Vence, and Biot—you can catch a regional bus or watch for commercial bus excursions advertised in the bigger coastal resorts. Tourist offices provide information on accompanied excursions. Excursions and bus holidays are organized by the SNCF and a plethora of private tour companies. Ask for a brochure at any major travel agent or contact France-Tourisme.

Buses from the U.K. generally depart from London, traveling via hovercraft or ferry from London to Paris. The most direct bus route to the south is from London to Avignon; Eurolines' weekly nonstop service takes 17½ hours and costs £89 round-trip.

If you're planning to travel extensively through Europe, you may wish to purchase a Eurolines Europass, valid for unlimited bus travel between 46 European cities (London, Paris, and Marseille included) for up to 60 days.

Bus Information For bus companies that service exact specific regions, see the Planner sections in each regional chapter.

From the U.K. **Eurolines/National Express** (✉52 Grosvenor Gardens, London ☎0870/580-8080 in the U.K., 08-92-89-90-91 in France ⊕www.eurolines. co.uk).

Within France **SNCF** (✉88 rue St-Lazare, Paris ☎08-20-87-94-79 ⊕www.voyages-sncf.com). **Le Pilote** (⊕www.lepilote.com).

Discount Passes **Eurolines/National Express** (✉52 Grosvenor Gardens, London ☎0870/580-8080 in the U.K., 08-92-89-90-91 in France ⊕www.eurolines. co.uk).

■ BY CAR

Your driver's license may not be recognized outside your home country. International driving permits (IDPs) are available from the American and Canadian automobile associations and, in the United Kingdom, from the Automobile Association and Royal Automobile Club. These international permits, valid only in conjunction with your regular driver's license, are universally recognized; having one may save you a problem with local authorities.

Car travel is the best way to see Provence, especially since the famous hilltop villages see a bus only once a day. However, a car may not be the fastest or most economical way to get to Provence: consider flying into Paris, connecting via a smaller airline to Nice or Marseille, and then renting your car in the south. Or purchase a rail-drive pass, available from the SNCF (French national rail company) or one of the larger car-rental companies. This will allow a few days' rail travel—say, from Paris to Nice—and a block of car-rental time. By using the train to cover the long distances, then exploring the region in depth by car, you can make the most of both modes of transit.

France's roads are classified into three types, numbered and prefixed A, N, or D. For the fastest roads between two points, look for roads marked A for *auto-routes*. A *péage* (toll) must be paid on most expressways: the rate varies but can be steep. Sample toll charges are €61.70 from Paris to Nice; €14.30 from Nice to Aix-en-Provence. At your first toll stop you will simply retrieve a ticket, and at the next toll you will pay. You may pay by credit card; Visa and American Express are accepted at most toll booths. The main toll roads through Provence are the A6 and A7, which connect Paris to Marseille via Lyon, Avignon, and Aix; and the east–west A8, which traverses the region from the Italian border to Aix via Nice.

The N (Route Nationale) roads, which are sometimes divided highways, are the route of choice for heavy freight trucks, and are often lined with industry and large chain stores. More scenic, though less trafficked than the Ns are the D (Route Départementale) roads, often also wide and fast.

Though routes are numbered, the French generally guide themselves from city to city and town to town by destination name. When reading a map, keep one eye on the next big city toward your destination as well as the next small town; most snap decisions will have to be based on town names, not road numbers.

Negotiating the back roads requires a careful mix of map and sign reading, often at high speeds around suburban *giratoires* (rotaries). But by the time you head out into the hills and the tiny roads—one of the best parts of Provence and the Côte d'Azur—give yourself over to road signs and pure faith: as is the case throughout France, directions are indicated by village name only, with route numbers given as a small-print afterthought. Of course, this means you have to recognize the names of minor villages en route.

To leave Paris by car, figure out which of the *portes* (gates) corresponds to the direction you are going. Major highways connect to Paris at these points, and directions are indicated by major cities. For instance, heading south out of the city, look for Porte d'Orléans (direction Lyons and Bordeaux); after Lyons, follow Avignon, and after Avignon follow Nice and/or Marseille. It's best to steer clear of rush hours (7–9:30 AM and 4:30–7:30 PM), although this is only a real concern between Aix and Marseille and around Nice.

GASOLINE

Gas is expensive, especially on expressways and in rural areas. When possible, buy gas before you get on the expressway and keep an eye on pump prices as you go.

These vary from €.90 to €1.30 per liter. The cheapest gas can be found at *hypermarchés* (very large supermarkets) but expect long lines. It is possible to go for many miles in the country without passing a gas station—don't let your tank get too low in rural areas. Many gas stations are closed on Sunday. If you are worried about your budget, ask for a diesel car; diesel fuel at gas pumps can be labeled as *diesel, gasoil,* or *gazole.* Unleaded gas will be labeled as *sans plomb* (SP95 for regular unleaded and SP98 for super unleaded). Be careful, as many gas stations still sell leaded gas, called *super.*

PARKING

Parking can be difficult in large towns; your best option (especially in a metropolis like Nice or Marseille) is to duck into the parking garage nearest the neighborhood you want to visit. Carry the ticket with you, and pay at the vending-machine-style ticket dispenser before you go back to your car. On the street, meters and ticket machines (pay and display) are common and work with parking cards (*cartes de stationnements*). Parking cards work like credit cards in the parking meters and come in three denominations: €10, €20, and €30. Parking cards are available at any café posting the red TABAC sign. Insert your card into the nearest meter, choose the approximate amount of time you expect to stay, and you'll receive a green receipt, which must be clearly visible to the meter patrol; place it on the dashboard on the inside of the front window on the passenger side. Be sure to check the signs before you park, as rules vary.

Be careful when parking your car overnight, especially in town and village squares; if your car is still there in the early morning on a market day, it will be towed. In smaller towns, parking may be permitted on one side of the street only—alternating every two weeks—so pay attention to signs.

The coastal area of Provence—especially the Camargue and the Calanques—as well as overlooks along the Côte d'Azur are extremely vulnerable to car break-ins, and the parking lots are often littered with broken windshield glass. It's important that you never leave valuables visible in the car, and think twice about leaving them in the trunk. Any theft should be reported formally to the police.

ROAD CONDITIONS

Road conditions in Provence are above average and potholes are rare, especially on highways. Check with the regional information center and the autoroutes hotline to find out whether there's anything you should know before setting off.

ROADSIDE EMERGENCIES

If your car breaks down on an expressway, go to a roadside emergency telephone (yellow boxes), which you'll find every two kilometers, and call for assistance. If you have a breakdown anywhere else, find the nearest garage or contact the police. If there is an injury, call the SAMU (ambulance service) or fire brigade.

Emergency Services Ambulance (SAMU) (☎15). **General Emergency Number from a Mobile Phone** (☎112). **Fire Department** (☎18). **Police** (☎17).

RULES OF THE ROAD

In France, you may use your own driver's license, but you must be able to prove you have third-party insurance. Drive on the right and yield to drivers coming from streets to the right. However, this rule does not necessarily apply at roundabouts, where you are obligated to yield to those already within (to your left)—but should watch out for just about everyone. You must wear your seat belt, and children under 10 may not travel in the front seat. Speed limits are 130 KPH (80 MPH) on expressways, 110 KPH (70 MPH) on divided highways, 90 KPH (55 MPH) on other roads, 50 KPH (30 MPH) in towns. French drivers break these limits and police dish out hefty on-the-spot fines with equal abandon.

Contacts Autoroute Information
(☎01-47-53-37-00 ⊕www.autoroutes.fr).

RENTAL CARS

When you reserve a car, ask about cancellation penalties, taxes, drop-off charges (if you're planning to pick up the car in one city and leave it in another), and surcharges (for being under or over a certain age, for additional drivers, or for driving across state or country borders or beyond a specific distance from your point of rental). All these things can add substantially to your costs. Request car seats and extras such as GPS when you book.

Rates are sometimes—but not always—better if you book in advance or reserve through a rental agency's Web site. There are other reasons to book ahead, though: for popular destinations, during busy times of the year, or to ensure that you get certain types of cars (vans, SUVs, exotic sports cars).

■TIP➡Make sure that a confirmed reservation guarantees you a car. Agencies sometimes overbook, particularly for busy weekends and holiday periods.

Though renting a car in France is expensive—up to twice as much as in the United States—as is gas (about €1.40 per liter at press time), it may pay off if you are traveling with two or more people. In addition, renting a car gives you the freedom to move around at your own pace that the train does not. Rates begin at about $50 a day and $265 per week for an economy car with a manual transmission (an automatic transmission will cost more). Mileage is extra, but there are often multiday packages or weekly rates including some number of kilometers. Be careful to check whether the price includes the 19.6% V.A.T. tax or, if you pick it up from the airport, the airport tax.

Also, price local car-rental companies—whose prices may be lower still, although their service and maintenance may not be as good as those of major rental agencies—and research rates on the Internet. ADA, a French-owned rental company, has offices in towns, train stations, and airports throughout Provence. The Renault Eurodrive program avoids usual car-rental taxes by offering short-term leases to customers. Offices are in Marseille, Montpellier, and Nice; cars must be rented for at least 20 days.

Remember to ask about required deposits, cancellation penalties, and drop-off charges if you're planning to pick up the car in one city and leave it in another. If you're traveling during a holiday period, also make sure that a confirmed reservation guarantees you a car.

In France your own driver's license is acceptable. You don't need an International Driver's Permit, unless you are planning on a long-term stay; you can get one from the American or Canadian automobile association, and, in the United Kingdom, from the Automobile Association or Royal Automobile Club.

Your driver's license may not be recognized outside your home country. You may not be able to rent a car without an International Driving Permit (IDP), which can be used only in conjunction with a valid driver's license and which translates your license into 10 languages. Check the AAA Web site for more info as well as for IDPs ($15) themselves.

Major Agencies Alamo (☎800/522-9696 ⊕www.alamo.com). **Avis** (☎800/331-1084 ⊕www.avis.com). **Budget** (☎800/472-3325 ⊕www.budget.com). **Hertz** (☎800/654-3001 ⊕www.hertz.com). **National Car Rental** (☎800/227-7368 ⊕www.nationalcar.com).

■ BY CRUISE SHIP

Many cruise lines offer trips that include a stop in the south of France—in Marseille, Cannes, or St-Tropez, for example—as part of a longer Mediterranean itinerary.

Cruise Lines **Celebrity Cruises** (☎800/647-2251 ⊕www.celebrity. com). **Costa Cruises** (☎954/266-5600 or 800/462-6782 ⊕www.costacruise. com). **Crystal Cruises** (☎310/785-9300 or 800/446-6620 ⊕www.crystalcruises. com). **Cunard Line** (☎661/753-1000 or 800/728-6273 ⊕www.cunard-france.com). **easyCruise** (⊕www.easycruise.com). **Holland America Line** (☎206/281-3535 or 877/932-4259 ⊕www.hollandamerica. com). **Mediterranean Shipping Cruises** (☎212/764-4800 or 800/666-9333 ⊕www. msccruises.com). **Norwegian Cruise Line** (☎305/436-4000 or 800/327-7030 ⊕www. ncl.com). **Oceania Cruises** (☎305/514-2300 or 800/531-5658 ⊕www.oceaniacruises. com). **Princess Cruises** (☎661/753-0000 or 800/774-6237 ⊕www.princess.com). **Radisson Seven Seas Cruises** (✉600 Corporate Dr., Suite 410, Fort Lauderdale, FL ☎954/776-6123 or 800/477-7500 ⊕www. rssc.com). **Regent Seven Seas Cruises** (☎954/776-6123 or 800/477-7500 ⊕www. rssc.com). **Royal Caribbean International** (☎305/539-6000 or 800/327-6700 ⊕www. royalcaribbean.com). **Seabourn Cruise Line** (☎305/463-3000 or 800/929-9391 ⊕www.seabourn.com). **SeaDream Yacht Club** (☎305/631-6110 or 800/707-4911 ⊕www.seadreamyachtclub.com). **Silversea Cruises** (☎954/522-4477 or 800/722-9955 ⊕www.silversea.com). **Star Clippers** (☎305/442-0550 or 800/442-0551 ⊕www.starclippers.com). **Windstar Cruises** (☎206/281-3535 or 800/258-7245 ⊕www. windstarcruises.com).

▌ BY TRAIN

RAIL PASSES

Before arriving in France, consider the following Rail Pass options that can give you breaks on ticket costs; note that they must be purchased before entering France. They are available through travel agents and a few authorized outlets.

For extensive train travel outside of Paris by train, consider purchasing a France Rail Pass, which allows four days of unlimited train travel (and a discount on Eurostar) in a one-month period. Prices begin at €125 each for two adults traveling together in second class and €189 second class for a solo traveler. First-class rates are €220 for two adults and €255 for a solo traveler. Additional days may be added for €30 a day in either class. Other options include the France Rail 'n Drive Pass (combining rail and rental car), France Rail 'n Fly Pass (rail travel and one air travel journey within France), and the France Fly Rail 'n Drive Pass (a rail, air, and rental car program all in one).

France is one of 17 countries in which you can use Eurail Passes, which provide unlimited first-class rail travel, in all of the participating countries, for the duration of the pass. If you plan to rack up the miles, get a standard pass. These are available for 15 days (€503), 21 days (€653), one month (€810), two months (€1,145), and three months (€1,413). If your plans call for only limited train travel, consider a three-country Eurorail Select pass which costs less money than a standard EurailPass. With the three-country pass you'll get five days of travel in three bordering countries (i.e., France, Spain, Italy) for €319. In addition to standard Eurail Passes, ask about special rail-pass plans. Among these are the Eurail Select pass Youth (for those under age 26) and the Eurail Select pass Saver (which gives a discount for two or more people traveling together).

TRAVELING BY TRAIN IN FRANCE

The SNCF is recognized as Europe's best national rail service: it's fast, punctual, comfortable, and comprehensive. You can get to Provence and the coast from all points west, north, and east, though lines out of Paris are by far the most direct. There are various options: local trains, overnight trains with sleeping accommodations, and the high-speed

TGV, the *Trains à Grande Vitesse* (high-speed trains).

France is rightly proud of its famed SNCF's TGV Méditerranée, the high-speed rail line connecting Paris to Avignon and Aix-en-Provence, which zooms along at 255 KPH (160 MPH). With the hassles of airport check-in and transfer, you may find train travel the most efficient way to get from Paris to Provence.

All trains to Provence leave from Paris's Gare de Lyon. Travel time from Paris is 2 hours and 40 minutes to Avignon; 3 hours to Nîmes, Marseille, and Aix-en-Provence; 3¼ hours to Montpellier; 4 hours to Toulon; and 5½ hours to Nice.

Certain models of the TGV, called a "train duplex," offer luxurious, state-of-the-art comfort, with double-decker seating and panoramic views. When one of these passes along the coast—especially from Nice to Menton—it makes for a dramatic sightseeing excursion, though it pokes along at a local-train snail's pace. Ask about duplex trains when you're connecting from one coastal city to another (Marseille–Toulon–Fréjus–Cannes–Nice–Menton).

Once you're in the south, though, choose your home base carefully. Places in hill country and the mountains—the Luberon, the Alpilles, and the backcountry hills behind Nice—are not accessible by train, and you'll have to get around by bus or rental car.

If you are traveling from Paris or any other terminus, get to the station half an hour before departure to ensure that you'll have a good seat.

Before boarding, you must punch your ticket (but not EurailPass) in one of the orange machines at the entrance to the platforms, or else the ticket collector will fine you €15 on the spot.

For overnight accommodations, you have the choice between high-priced *wag-ons-lits* (sleeping cars) and affordable *couchettes* (bunks, six to a compartment in second class, four to a compartment in first, with sheets and pillow provided, priced at €15–€18).

Traveling first class can cost about 50% more than second class, but, with the exception of wider seats, you won't get many more amenities. You'll still need to purchase food, although in first class you can order a hot meal, served on china, if you're willing to pay quite a high price for it.

Don't assume that your rail pass guarantees you a seat on the train you wish to ride. You need to book seats ahead even if you are using a rail pass; seat reservations are required on high-speed trains, and are a good idea on trains that may be crowded—particularly in summer on popular routes. You will also need a reservation for sleeping accommodations.

If you know what station you'll depart from, you can get a free train schedule there (while supplies last), or you can access the multilingual computerized schedule information network at any Paris station and at larger regional stations (Marseille and Nice). You can also make reservations and buy your ticket while at the computer.

SNCF offers a number of discount rail passes available only for purchase in France. When traveling together, two people can save money with the Prix Découverte à Deux. You'll get a 25% discount during "périodes bleus" (blue periods; weekdays and not on or near any holidays). Note that tickets are nontransferable; and you have to be with the person you said you would be traveling with.

You can get a reduced fare if you are over 60 with the SNCF's Carte Sénior, which costs €50 and entitles the bearer to deep discounts on rail and TGV travel for a year.

With the **Carte Enfant+** (⊕ *www.enfant-plus-sncf.com*), children under 12 can get 25%–50% off of a full year of travel for €70. There's a wonderful bonus, too: up to four accompanying passengers, whether blood relatives or not, get the discount, too.

If you purchase an individual ticket from SNCF in France and you're under 26, you will automatically get a 25% reduction (a valid ID, such as an ISIC card or your passport, is necessary). If you're going to be using the train quite a bit during your stay in France and if you're under 26, consider buying the **Carte 12–25** (€49 ⊕*www.12-25-sncf.com*), which offers unlimited 50% reductions for one year (provided that there's space available at that price, otherwise you'll just get the standard 25% discount).

If you don't benefit from any of these reductions and if you plan on traveling at least 1,000 km (620 mi) round-trip (including several stops), look into purchasing a Billet Séjour. This ticket gives you a 25% reduction if you stay over a Sunday and if you travel only during blue periods. It may be a major organizational feat, but you can save a lot of cash this way.

See the Planner sections in each regional chapter for information about local stations.

You must always make a seat reservation for the TGV—easily obtained at the ticket window or from an automatic machine. Seat reservations are reassuring but seldom necessary on other main-line French trains, except at busy holiday times.

Channel Tunnel Car Transport Eurotunnel (☎0870/535–3535 in the U.K., 070/223210 in Belgium, 03-21-00-61-00 in France ⊕www. eurotunnel.com). **French Motorail/Rail Europe** (☎0870/241–5415 ⊕www.raileurope.co.uk/frenchmotorail).

Channel Tunnel Passenger Service Eurostar (☎0870/518–6186, in the U.K. ⊕www. eurostar.co.uk). **Rail Europe** (☎888/382–7245 in the U.S., 0870/584–8848 in the U.K. inquiries and credit-card bookings ⊕www.raileurope. com).

Ticket Agents CIT Tours Corp (✉15 West 44th St., 10th floor, New York, NY ☎800/248–7245 for rail, 800/248–8687 for tours and hotels ⊕www.cit-tours.com). **DER Travel Services** (✉9501 W. Devon Ave., Rosemont, IL ☎800/782–2424 ⊕www.der. com). **Rail Europe** (✉226–230 Westchester Ave., White Plains, NY ☎800/438–7245 📠800/432–1329 ✉2087 Dundas E, Suite 105, Mississauga, Ontario ☎905/602–4195 ⊕www. raileurope.com).

ESSENTIALS

■ ACCOMMODATIONS

Provence and the Côte d'Azur may be the most accommodating region in France, with every kind of hotel, country inn, converted *mas* (Provençal farmhouse), luxury palace, bed-and-breakfast, and vacation rental imaginable. Consider the kind of vacation you want to spend—going native in a country *gîte* (rental house), being pampered in a luxury penthouse over the Mediterranean in Cannes, or getting to know the locals in a cozy B&B. Then check the Fodor's recommendations in each chapter, or contact the local tourist offices for more specific information.

The lodgings we list are the cream of the crop in each price category. We always list the facilities that are available, but we don't specify whether they cost extra; when pricing accommodations, always ask what's included and what costs extra. Properties are assigned price categories based on the range from their least-expensive standard double room at high season (excluding holidays) to the most expensive. For price charts, see the Planner section in each regional chapter.

■TIP→ Assume that hotels operate on the European Plan (EP, no meals) unless we specify that they use the Breakfast Plan (BP, with full breakfast), Continental Plan (CP, Continental breakfast), Full American Plan (FAP, all meals), Modified American Plan (MAP, breakfast and dinner) or are all-inclusive (AI, all meals and most activities).

APARTMENT & HOUSE RENTALS

The national rental network, the Fédération Nationale des Gîtes de France, rents rural homes with regional flavor, often restored farmhouses or village row houses in pretty country settings *(⇨ Close-Up: "The Gîte Way," in Chapter 3)*. In fact, the system grew out of a subsidized movement to salvage wonderful old houses falling to ruin. Gîtes-de-France are nearly always maintained by on-site owners, who greet you on your arrival and provide information on groceries, doctors, and nearby attractions.

A nationwide catalogue (€22) is available from the Fédération Nationale des Gîtes de France listing gîtes for rent. Called "Nouveaux Gîtes Ruraux," the catalogue only lists the newest additions to the network, because a comprehensive nationwide listing of all gîtes wouldn't fit between two covers. If you know you want to stay in Provence, you can order a regional catalogue (€4.57). Gîtes can also be searched and booked online. *See the Planner sections of each chapter on contact information for regional offices.*

Individual tourist offices often publish lists of *locations meublés* (furnished rentals); these are often inspected by the tourist office and rated by comfort standards. Usually they are booked directly through the individual owner, which generally requires some knowledge of French. Rentals that are not classified or rated by the tourist office should be undertaken with trepidation, and can fall well below your minimum standard of comfort.

Vacation rentals in France always book from Saturday to Saturday (with some offering weekend rates off-season). Most do not include bed linens and towels, but make them available for an additional fee. Always check on policies on pets and children, and specify if you need an enclosed garden for toddlers, a washing machine, a fireplace, etc. If you plan to have overnight guests during your stay, let the owner know; there may be additional charges. Insurance restrictions prohibit occupation beyond the specified capacity.

The French Government Tourist Office is another source for information about vacation rentals.

ONLINE BOOKING RESOURCES
At Home Abroad (☎212/421–9165 ⊕www. athomeabroadinc.com). **Barclay International Group** (☎516/364–0064 or 800/845–6636 ⊕www.barclayweb.com). **Drawbridge to Europe** (☎541/482–7778 or 888/268–1148 ⊕www.drawbridgetoeurope.com). **Forgetaway** (⊕www.forgetaway.weather.com). **Home Away** (☎512/493–0382 ⊕www.homeaway. com) **Homes Away** (☎416/920–1873 or 800/374–6637 ⊕www.homesaway.com). **Hometours International** (☎865/690–8484 ⊕thor.he.net/~hometour). **Interhome** (☎954/791–8282 or 800/882–6864 ⊕www. interhome.us). **Suzanne B. Cohen & Associates** (☎207/622–0743 ⊕www.villaeurope. com). **Vacation Home Rentals Worldwide** (☎201/767–9393 or 800/633–3284 ⊕www. vhrww.com). **Villanet** (☎206/417–3444 or 800/964–1891 ⊕www.rentavilla.com). **Villas & Apartments Abroad** (☎212/213–6435 or 800/433–3020 ⊕www.vaanyc.com). **Villas International** (☎415/499–9490 or 800/221–2260 ⊕www.villasintl.com). **Villas of Distinction** (☎707/778–1800 or 800/289–0900 ⊕www.villasofdistinction.com). **Wimco** (☎800/449–1553 ⊕www.wimco. com).

Local Agent **Gîtes de France** (✉59 rue St-Lazare, 75009 Paris Cedex 09 ☎01–49–70–75–75 ⊕www.gites-de-france. fr). **Anything Cannes** (☎0033/611–148–214 ⊕www.anythingcannes.com).

BED & BREAKFASTS

Bed-and-breakfasts, known in France as *chambres d'hôte*, are common in rural Provence, and less so along the Côte d'Azur. Check local tourist offices for details or contact Gîtes de France, the national vacation-lodging organization that lists B&Bs all over the country, from rustic to more luxurious. Often *table d'hôte* dinners (meals cooked by and eaten with the owners) can be arranged for an extra, fairly nominal fee. Note that in B&Bs, unlike hotels, it is more likely that the owners will only speak French. Staying in one may, however, give you

more of an opportunity to meet French people.

For B&B listings, Karen Brown's *France: Charming Bed & Breakfasts* and *Rivages Bed & Breakfasts of Character and Charm in France* are available in bookstores or from Fodor's Travel Publications.

Reservation Services **Bed & Breakfast. com** (☎512/322–2710 or 800/462–2632 ⊕www.bedandbreakfast.com) also sends out an online newsletter. **Bed & Breakfast Inns Online** (☎615/868–1946 or 800/215–7365 ⊕www.bbonline.com). **BnB Finder.com** (☎212/432–7693 or 888/547–8226 ⊕www. bnbfinder.com).

GÎTES (VACATION RENTALS)

Gîtes de France is a nationwide organization that rents vacation housing by the week, in the countryside, by the sea, or in the mountains. Houses and apartments are classified on a scale of one to five, according to comfort. Housing is strictly supervised, with an on-site welcome center from either a representative or the owners of the gîtes themselves. Some gîtes can be quite posh, with swimming pool and all the amenities—these go quickly, so be sure to reserve well in advance if this is the type of accomodation you want. Gîtes de France also has a list of regional bed-and-breakfast sites, and regional farms that open their doors and their dining rooms, where amazing dinners can be arranged. Just about everything served at these tables d'hôte comes from the farm itself; these dinners are growing in popularity and run from the simple to the gastronomique. Gîtes de France also organizes a variety of tours; hiking tours, canyoning with certified instructors, biking tours with all-terrain bikes, tours for the wine lover with a certified oenologue. Note that if you plan on traveling in July or August, you must do as the French do and organize well in advance. *(For more information about renting gîtes, see Close-Up: The Gîte Way in Chapter 2.)* Each town's tourist office usually publishes lists of independent rentals (*locations meublés*), many of them inspected and classified by the tourist office itself.

The region west of Nîmes, including some parts of the Camargue, lies in the département of Hérault. Gîtes de France offices for this department are based in Montpellier. Nîmes itself and environs are processed by the Gard office. Arles and the Alpilles gîtes are handled by the Bouches-du-Rhône departmental office. In Nice, you can rent a furnished Old Town apartment for a few days or up to several weeks from the English-speaking **Nice Time** (☎*06–81–67–41–22* ✉*landry. ph@free.fr*).

Gîtes Information—Chapter 2 **La Maison des Gîtes France et du Tourisme Vert** (Paris–head office ✉59 rue St-Lazare, Cedex 09, ☎01-49-70-75-75 🖷01-42-81-28-53 ✉info@gites-de-france.fr ⊕www. gites-de-france.com/gites/uk/rural_gites). **Montpellier** (✉B.P. 3070, Cedex 1, Montpellier ☎04-67-67-62-62). **Gard** (✉3 pl. des Arènes, B.P. 59, Cedex 4). **Nîmes** (☎04-66-27-94-94). **Bouches-du-Rhône** (✉Domaine du Vergon, B.P. 26). **Mallemort** (☎04-90-59-49-39).

Gîtes Information—Chapter 3 **Gîtes de France de Vacluse** (✉pl. Campana, by the Papal Palace in Avignon ✆B.P. 164, Cedex 1, 84008). **Avignon City** (☎04-90-85-88-49 ⊕www.gites-de-france-84.com).

Gîtes Information—Chapter 4 **Gîtes de France Bouches-du-Rhône** (✉Domaine du Vergon, Mallemort ☎04-90-59-49-39). **Gîtes de France du Var** (✉BP 215, Rond-Point du 04/12/1974 ☎04-94-50-93-93).

Gîtes Information—Chapter 5 **Gîtes de France du Var** (✉Rond-point du 3 Décembre 1974, B.P. 215, Draguignan Cedex ☎04-94-50-93-93 ⊕www.gites-de-france-var.fr). **Gîtes de France des Alpes-Maritimes** (✉55 promenade des Anglais, B.P. 1602, Cedex 01, Nice ☎04-92-15-21-30 ⊕www. gites-de-france-alpes-maritimes.com). **Gîtes de France des Alpes de Haute Provence** (✉B.P. 201, Dignes-les-Bains ☎04-92-31-52-39 ⊕www.gites-de-france-04.fr).

Gîtes Information—Chapter 6 **Gîtes de France des Alpes-Maritimes** (✉57 Promenade des Anglais, B.P. 1602, Cedex 01, Nice ☎04-92-15-21-30 ⊕www.gites-de-france-alpes-maritimes.com/index_en.php). **Gîtes de France du Var** (✉Rond-Point du 4 Décembre, B.P. 215. Draguignan Cédex ☎04-94-50-93-93 ⊕www.gites-de-france-var.fr).

HOTELS

Hotels are officially classified by the French government from one star to four-star deluxe. Prices must, by law, be posted at the hotel entrance and should include taxes and service. Rates are always by room, not per person. Remember that in France the first floor is one floor up (our second floor), and the higher up you go the quieter the street noise will be.

You should always check what bathroom facilities the price includes, if any. Because replumbing drains is often prohibitive, if not impossible, old hotels may have added bathrooms—often with *douches* (showers), not *baignoires* (tubs)—to the guest rooms, but not toilets. If you want a private bathroom, state your preference for shower or tub—the latter always costs more. Unless otherwise noted, lodging listings in this book include a private bathroom with a shower *or* tub.

When making your reservation, ask for a *grand lit* if you want a double bed. The quality of accommodations, particularly in older properties and even in luxury hotels, can vary greatly from room to room, as hotels are often renovated floor by floor; if you don't like the room you're given, ask to see another.

If you're counting on air-conditioning, you should make sure, in advance, that your hotel room is *climatisé* (air-conditioned). As the French generally haven't fallen in step with American tastes for cold air in a heat wave, air-conditioning is not a given, even at hotels in inland Provence, far from sea breezes. And when you throw open the windows, don't expect screens *(moustiquaires)*. Nowhere in Europe are they standard equipment, and the only exceptions are found occasionally in the Camargue marshlands, where mosquitoes are actually a problem.

Breakfast is not always included in the price, but you are sometimes expected to have it and are occasionally charged for it regardless. Make sure to inform the hotel if you are not going to be breakfasting there. In smaller rural hotels you may be expected to have your evening meal at the hotel, too.

Logis de France hotels are small and inexpensive and can be relied on for comfort, character, and regional cuisine. Look for its distinctive yellow and green sign. The Logis de France paperback guide is available from Logis de France (€4.88) or at the French Government Tourist Office. *See Visitor Information, below.*

Relais & Châteaux, Small Luxury Hotels of the World, and Leading Hotels of the World are three prestigious international groups with numerous converted châteaux and manor houses among their members. Not as luxurious, but strong on charm, is the Châteaux et Hôtels Independents group, which publishes its own catalog.

It's always a good idea to make hotel reservations as far in advance as possible, especially in late spring, summer, or fall. If you arrive without a reservation, however, the tourist office may be able to help.

Information Châteaux et Hôtels Independents (✉12 rue Auber, Paris ☎01-40-07-00-20 ⊕www.chateauxhotels. com). **Leading Hotels of the World** (✉99 Park Ave., New York, NY ☎212/515-5600 ⊕www.lhw.com/home.aspx?version=1). **Logis de France** (✉83 av. d'Italie, Paris ☎01-45-84-83-84 ⊕www.logis-de-france. fr). **Relais & Châteaux** (✉33 bd. Malesherbes, Paris ☎01-45-72-96-50 or 08-25-32-32-32 ✉11 E. 44th St., Suite 707, New York, NY ☎212/856-0115 or 800-735-2478 ⊕www.

relaischateaux.fr). **Small Luxury Hotels of the World** (✉14673 Midway Rd., Suite 201, Addison, TX ☎800/525-4800 for reservations, 972/866-8010 ✉James House, Bridge St., Leatherhead, Surrey, U.K. ☎44/01372-361873 ⊕www.slh.com).

∎ BEACHES

The beaches in Provence can vary from fine sand to small pebble to rocky, the latter being the least crowded but requiring mattresses for comfortable sunbathing.

If you're planning to devote a lot of time to beaches and haven't tackled the French coast before, get to **know the distinction between private and public.** All along the coast, the waterfront is carved up into private frontage, roped off and advertised by coordinated color awnings, parasols, and mattresses. These private beaches usually offer full restaurant and bar service, and rent mattresses, umbrellas, and lounge chairs by the day and half-day. Dressing rooms and showers are included; some even rent private cabanas. Prices can run from €10 to €20 or more a day. Private beaches compete with each other not only via fashionable cuisine and flashy colors, but by offering entertainment—children's wading pools, waterskiing, or parasailing.

But interspliced between these commercial beaches is plenty of public space, with open access and (usually) the necessary comforts of toilets and cold rinse "showers" for washing off the salt. At these you must provide your own mattress or mat (indispensable on the rocks) and you can profit from the democratic bar service provided by enterprising vendors who cruise the waterfront with drinks and snacks. Or better yet, have lunch at one of the many shaded snack bars that line the beach, serving fresh salads and sandwiches.

■ COMMUNICATIONS

INTERNET

If you use a major Internet provider, getting online in major cities in the south of France shouldn't be difficult. Most hotels have Wi-Fi access. Most laptops are dual-voltage, but you will need an adapter.

Think twice before packing your computer, though; it's easy to get online almost anywhere in France. Many hotels have Internet access in their lobbies or business centers, and Internet cafés are easy to find in any Provençal city. Ask at your hotel, or a computer store, for the nearest one.

Contacts **Cybercafes** (⊕ www.cybercafes. com) lists more than 4,000 Internet cafés worldwide.

PHONES

The good news is that you can now make a direct-dial telephone call from virtually any point on earth. The bad news? You can't always do so cheaply. Calling from a hotel is almost always the most expensive option; hotels usually add huge surcharges to all calls, particularly international ones. In some countries you can phone from call centers or even the post office. Calling cards usually keep costs to a minimum, but only if you purchase them locally. And then there are mobile phones (⇨ below), which are sometimes more prevalent—particularly in the developing world—than land lines; as expensive as mobile phone calls can be, they are still usually a much cheaper option than calling from your hotel.

The country code for France is 33. All phone numbers in France have a two-digit prefix determined by zone: Paris and the Ile-de-France, 01; the northwest, 02; the northeast, 03; the southeast, 04; and the southwest, 05. Numbers beginning with 08 are either toll-free or toll calls (with an additional charge on top of making the call). Numbers beginning with 06 are mobile phones.

Note that when dialing France from abroad, drop the initial 0 from the number. For instance, to call a telephone number in Paris from the United States, dial 011–33 plus the phone number minus the initial 0 (phone numbers in this book are listed with the full 10 digits, which you use to make local calls). To call France from the United Kingdom, dial 00–33, then dial the number in France minus the initial 0.

CALLING WITHIN FRANCE

To call anywhere in France while in France, dial the full 10-digit number, including the initial zero.

To find a number in France, dial 3912 for information. For international inquiries, dial 00–33–12 (–11 for the U.S., –44 for the U.K.).

Telephone booths can almost always be found at post offices, and often in cafés. A local call costs €.11 for every three minutes; half-price rates apply weekdays between 9:30 PM and 8 AM, from 1:30 PM Saturday, and all day Sunday.

CALLING OUTSIDE FRANCE

To call out of France, dial 00 and wait for the tone, then dial the country code (1 for the United States and Canada, 44 for the United Kingdom, 61 for Australia, 64 for New Zealand) and the area code (minus any initial 0) and number. Expect to be overcharged if you call from your hotel.

The country code for the United States is 1.

CALLING CARDS

Most French pay phones are operated by *télécartes* (phone cards), which you can buy from post offices, métro stations, and some tabacs (tobacco shops) for a cost of €10 for 50 units and €18 for 120. Coin-operated pay phones are scarce, found only in cafés (who can set their own rates) and post offices. Phone cards are accepted everywhere else. The easiest but most expensive way to phone is to use your own Visa card, which is accepted in all phone booths and works like a télécarte.

MOBILE PHONES

If you have a multiband phone (some countries use different frequencies than what's used in the United States) and your service provider uses the world-standard GSM network (as do T-Mobile, Cingular, and Verizon), you can probably use your phone abroad. Roaming fees can be steep, however: 99¢ a minute is considered reasonable. And overseas you normally pay the toll charges for incoming calls. It's almost always cheaper to send a text message than to make a call, since text messages have a very low set fee (often less than 5¢).

If you just want to make local calls, consider buying a new SIM card (note that your provider may have to unlock your phone for you to use a different SIM card) and a prepaid service plan in the destination. You'll then have a local number and can make local calls at local rates. If your trip is extensive, you could also simply buy a new cell phone in your destination, as the initial cost will be offset over time.

■TIP→ **If you travel internationally frequently, save one of your old mobile phones or buy a cheap one on the Internet; ask your cell phone company to unlock it for you, and take it with you as a travel phone, buying a new SIM card with pay-as-you-go service in each destination.**

Contacts **Cellular Abroad** (☎800/287–5072 ⊕www.cellularabroad.com) rents and sells GMS phones and sells SIM cards that work in many countries. **Mobal** (☎888/888–9162 ⊕www.mobalrental.com) rents mobiles and sells GSM phones (starting at $49) that will operate in 140 countries. Per-call rates vary throughout the world. **Planet Fone** (☎888/988–4777 ⊕www.planetfone.com) rents cell phones, but the per-minute rates are expensive.

▌CUSTOMS & DUTIES

You're always allowed to bring goods of a certain value back home without having to pay any duty or import tax. But there's a limit on the amount of tobacco and liquor you can bring back duty-free, and some countries have separate limits for perfumes; for exact figures, check with your customs department. The values of so-called "duty-free" goods are included in these amounts. When you shop abroad, save all your receipts, as customs inspectors may ask to see them as well as the items you purchased. If the total value of your goods is more than the duty-free limit, you'll have to pay a tax (most often a flat percentage) on the value of everything beyond that limit.

There is no restriction on goods brought in to France by EU nationals, as long as those goods are for personal use and not for resale. The duty-free allowance for non-EU residents visiting France is: 50 cigarettes or 25 cigarillos or 10 cigars or 50 grams of tobacco; 2 liters of table wine and (1) 1 liter of alcohol over 22% volume (most spirits) or (2) 1 liter of alcohol under 22% by volume (fortified or sparkling wine); 50 grams of perfume; 250 milliliters of toilet water; and other goods to the value of €175 (€90 for those under 15).

Information in Provence & the Côte d'Azur **Regional Customs and Excise Office— Provence** (⊠Hôtel des Douanes, Bd. du Château Double, Aix-en-Provence Cedex 02 ☎04-42-95-27-50 🖷04-42-59-46-58). **French Customs Office—U.S.** (⊠4104 Reservoir Rd. NW, Washington, D.C. ☎202/944-6375 🖷202/944-6517 ⊕www. ambafrance-us.org/spip.php?rubrique=2).

U.S. Information **U.S. Customs and Border Protection** (⊕www.cbp.gov).

▌ EATING OUT

The sooner you relax and go with the French flow, the more you'll enjoy your stay. Expect to spend at least two hours for lunch in a restaurant, savoring three courses and talking over the wine; dinner lasts even longer. If you keep one eye on your watch and the other on the waiter, you'll miss the point and spoil your own fun.

You may benefit from a few pointers on French dining etiquette. Diners in France don't negotiate their orders much, so don't expect serene smiles when you ask for sauce on the side. Order your coffee after dessert, not with it. When you're ready for the check, ask for it. No professional waiter would dare put a bill on your table while you're still enjoying the last sip of coffee. And don't ask for a doggy bag; it's just not done.

Also a word on the great mineral-water war: the French usually drink wine or mineral water—not soda or coffee—with their food. You may ask for a carafe of tap water, *une carafe d'eau,* but not always. In general, diners order mineral water if they don't order wine. It's not that the tap water is unsafe; it's usually fine—just not as tasty as Evian or slightly fizzy Badoit. To order flat mineral water ask for *eau naturelle;* fizzy is *eau gazeuse.*

Restaurants along the coast are generally more expensive than those inland; basic regional fixed-price menus average about €17 to €22, though the high end of this figure represents the usual cost of seafood so often featured on restaurant menus. In high summer reserve at popular restaurants, especially if you want a coveted outdoor table.

MEALS & MEALTIMES

If you're antsy to get to the next museum, or if you plan to spend the evening dining in grand style, consider lunching in a brasserie, where quick, one-plate lunches and full salads are available. Cafés often serve *casse croûtes* (snacks), including sandwiches, which are simply baguettes lightly filled with ham or cheese; or *croques monsieurs,* grilled ham and cheese open-face sandwiches with a rich layer of béchamel. Bakeries and *traiteurs* (delis) often sell savory items like quiches, tiny pizzas, or pastries filled with pâté. On the Côte d'Azur, you can profit from a wealth of street food, from the chickpea-based crepes called *socca* to *pissaladière* (onion-olive pizza) and *pan bagnat* (a tuna-and-egg-stuffed pita-style bun).

One of the wonderful aspects of breakfast in Provence and on the Côte d'Azur is eating outdoors, whether on the restaurant terrace or on your own tiny balcony. Breakfasts are light, consisting of croissants and bread, jam and butter, and wonderful coffee. Many hotels also serve yogurt, fruit juice, cereal, cheese, and even eggs upon request.

You'll notice here more than anywhere in France that the lunch hour begins after 1; some places don't even open before that. If you don't mind being a gauche foreigner, eating at noon is one way to get into those sought-after restaurants that do open at noon. If you want to really do as the Romans do, reserve for a lunch at 1 or 1:30.

Breakfast is usually served from 7:30 to 10:30; if you want it earlier, arrange a time the night before. Dinner is usually eaten after 8, and most restaurants do not open for the dinner service before 7:30.

Unless otherwise noted, the restaurants listed in this guide are open daily for lunch and dinner.

▌ ELECTRICITY

The electrical current in France is 220 volts, 50 cycles alternating current (AC). French electrical outlets have two round holes ("female") and a "male" ground; your appliances must either have a slender, two-prong plug that bypasses that ground, or a plug with two round prongs and a hole.

Consider making a small investment in a universal adapter, which has several types of plugs in one lightweight, compact unit. Most laptops and mobile phone chargers are dual voltage (i.e., they operate equally well on 110 and 220 volts), so require only an adapter. These days the same is true of small appliances such as hair dryers. Always check labels and manufacturer instructions to be sure. Don't use 110-volt outlets marked FOR SHAVERS ONLY for high-wattage appliances such as hair-dryers.

Contacts Steve Kropla's Help for World Traveler's (⊕www.kropla.com) has information on electrical and telephone plugs around the world. **Walkabout Travel Gear** (⊕www. walkabouttravelgear.com) has a good coverage of electricity under "adapters."

▌EMERGENCIES

France's emergency services are conveniently streamlined and universal, so no matter where you are in the country, you can dial the same phone numbers, listed below. Every town and village has a *médecin de garde* (on-duty doctor) for flus, sprains, tetanus shots, etc. To find out who's on any given evening, call any *généraliste* (general practitioner) and a recording will refer you. If you need an x-ray or emergency treatment, call the ambulance number and you'll be whisked to the hospital of your choice—or the nearest one. Note that outside of Paris it may be difficult to find English-speaking doctors.

In case of fire, hotels are required to post emergency exit maps inside every room door and multilingual instructions.

If you need assistance in an emergency, you can go to your country's embassy or consulate. Proof of identity and citizenship are generally required to enter. If your passport has been stolen, get a

police report then contact your embassy for assistance.

DOCTORS AND HOSPITALS

For information on doctors and hospitals throughout Provence and the Côte d'Azur, see the Planner section in each regional chapter.

OVER-THE-COUNTER REMEDIES

For a headache *(mal à la tête)* ask the pharmacist for *aspirine* (aspirin) or *dolip-rane* (Tylenol). For gas pains, ask for *smecta,* and for menstrual cramps you will be given *spasfon.* For car and boat sickness, *primperan.* For cuts, scrapes, and other minor "ouchies," which the French call "bobos," you will be given a disinfectant spray called *Bétadine. Gel d'Apis* treats mosquito bites (you may need this if you are traveling in the Carmargue). Sore throats are treated with lozenges called *pastilles,* and cough syrup is *sirop.* Diarrhea *(diarrhée)* is treated with *Immodium.*

FOREIGN EMBASSIES

United States U.S. Consulate Paris (⊠2 rue St-Florentin, 1er, Paris ☎01-43-12-22-22 in English, 01-43-12-23-47 in emergencies ⊕france.usembassy.gov ⓂConcorde ⊙Weekdays 9 AM–1 PM). **U.S. Consulates** (⊠12 bd. Paul Peytral, Marseille ☎04-91-54-92-00 ⊙Weekdays 9 AM–noon and 2–5 PM).

Australia Australian Embassy (⊠4 rue Jean-Rey, 15^e, Paris ☎01-40-59-33-00 ⊕www.france.embassy.gov.au ⓂBir Hakeim ⊙Weekdays 9:15–12:15 PM).

Canada Canadian Embassy (⊠35 av. Montaigne, 8e, Paris ☎01-44-43-29-02 ⊕www.amb-canada.fr ⓂFranklin-D.-Roosevelt ⊙Weekdays 8:30 AM–11 AM). **Canadian Consulate** (⊠10 rue Lamartine, Nice ☎04-93-92-93-22 ⊙Weekdays 8:30 AM–11 AM).

New Zealand New Zealand Embassy (⊠7 ter rue Léonardo da Vinci, 16e, Paris ☎01-45-01-43-43 ⊕www.nzembassy.com ⓂVictor Hugo ⊙Mon.–Thurs. 9 AM–1 PM and

2 PM–5.30 PM; Fri. 9 AM–1 PM and 2 PM–4 PM [early closing hours in July and Aug.]).

United Kingdom British Consulate Paris (✉18 bis rue d'Anjou, 8ᵉ, Paris ☎01–44–51–31–00 ⊕www.amb-grande bretagne.fr Ⓜ Madeleine ⊙Weekdays 9:30 AM–12:30 PM and 2:30 PM–5 PM). **British Consulate Marseille** (✉24 av. du Prado, Marseille ☎04–91–15–72–10 ⊙Weekdays 9 AM–noon and 2 PM–5 PM).

General Emergency Contacts General Emergency from a mobile phone (☎112). **Ambulance (SAMU)** (☎15). **Fire Department** (☎18). **Police** (☎17).

∎ GUIDED TOURS

Guided tours are a good option when you don't want to do it all yourself. You travel along with a group (sometimes large, sometimes small), stay in prebooked hotels, eat with your fellow travelers (the cost of meals sometimes included in the price of your tour, sometimes not), and follow a schedule.

But not all guided tours are an if-it's-Tuesday-this-must-be-Belgium experience. A knowledgeable guide can take you places that you might never discover on your own, and you may be pushed to see more than you would have otherwise. Tours aren't for everyone, but they can be just the thing for trips to places where making travel arrangements is difficult or time-consuming (particularly when you don't speak the language).

Whenever you book a guided tour, find out what's included and what isn't. A "land-only" tour includes all your travel (by bus, in most cases) in the destination, but not necessarily your flights to and from or even within it. Also, in most cases prices in tour brochures don't include fees and taxes. And remember that you'll be expected to tip your guide (in cash) at the end of the tour.

Maison de la France (⇨ *Visitor Information, below*) publishes many brochures on theme trips in France including "In the Footsteps of the Painters of Light in Provence" and "France for the Jewish Traveler."

GROUP TOURS

Among companies that sell tours to Provence and the Riviera, the following are nationally known, have a proven reputation, and offer plenty of options.

Super-Deluxe Abercrombie & Kent (✉1520 Kensington Rd., Oak Brook, IL ☎800/323–7308, 020/7559–4777 in the U.K. ⊕www.abercrombiekent.com). **Travcoa** (✉2350 S.E. Bristol St., Newport Beach, CA ☎800/992–2003, 61/2962–3366 in Australia, 416/927–9610 in Canada ⊕www.travcoa.com).

Deluxe Maupintour (✉10650 W. Charleston Blvd., Summerlin, NV ☎800/255–4266 ⊕www.maupintour.com). **Tauck Tours** (✉276 Post Rd. W, Westport, CT ☎203/226–6911, 800/788–7885 in the U.S., 1800/122–048 in Australia, 0800/961–834 in the U.K. ⊕www. tauck.com).

First-Class Caravan Tours (✉401 N. Michigan Ave., Chicago, IL ☎312/321–9800 or 888/227–2826 ⊕www.caravantours.com). **Collette Tours** (✉162 Middle St., Pawtucket, RI ☎401/728–3805 or 800/340–5158 ⊕www. collettetours.com).

Budget Tours of Provence (✉1700 Glen Bar Sq., Denver, CO ☎303/275–9899 ⊕www. toursofprovence.com).

Special-Interest Tours ⇨ *For a list of some of the top special-interest tours for art and antiques, biking, food and wine, hiking, and music, see the listings of Web sites under Online Resources, under Visitor Information, below.*

∎ HOURS OF OPERATION

Bank hours vary from branch to branch, but are generally weekdays 8:30 to 4. Most take a one-hour, or even a 90-minute, lunch break around noon. *See Mail & Shipping, below, for post-office hours.*

Gas stations on the autoroutes are generally open 24 hours. In towns, gas stations close at 8 PM, with the occasional station staying open until 10 PM. Outside the city centers, most stations are closed on Sunday.

Museum hours are somewhat lax in the south, with seasonal variations and a tendency to change slightly and often. Usual opening times are from 9:30 or 10 to 5 or 6, but many close for lunch (noon–2). To allow for long terrace lunches and an afternoon lag in business due to beach time, the lunch hour may be even longer in summer, with some later evening hours to compensate. Most museums are closed one day a week (generally Monday or Tuesday) and on national holidays: check museum hours before you go.

Large stores in big towns are open from 9 or 9:30 AM until 7 or 8 PM. Smaller shops often open earlier (8 AM) and close later (8 PM) but take a lengthy lunch break (1 to 4 or 4:30) in the south of France. Corner groceries frequently stay open until around 10 PM. Market days vary from town to town, but stalls generally close by about 1 PM.

HOLIDAYS

With 11 national *jours feriés* (holidays) and five weeks of paid vacation, the French have their share of repose. In May, there is a holiday nearly every week, so be prepared for stores, banks, and museums to shut their doors for days at a time. Be sure to call museums, restaurants, and hotels in advance to make sure they will be open.

Some holidays to keep in mind: January 1, New Year's Day; mid-April, Easter Monday; May 1, Labor Day; May 8, VE Day; mid- to late May, Ascension; late May to early June, Pentecost Monday; July 14, Bastille Day; August 15, Assumption; November 1, All Saints; November 11, Armistice; December 25, Christmas.

It's also useful to bear in mind France's school vacations, which tend to unleash hordes of families and *classes de mer* (school trips to the coast) on museums, castles, and family hotels. School vacations are divided by region and are spread out over about three weeks in late October–November, Christmas–New Year's, again in February, and finally in April. Provence and the Côte d'Azur are the most crowded during the summer holidays, usually the last week of July and all of August.

▌ MAIL

In this book, the postal code precedes the city or town in French mailing addresses, in keeping with the way envelopes are addressed in France.

Letters and postcards to the United States and Canada cost €.90 (about $1.05) for 20 grams. Letters and postcards within France and the rest of Europe (including the United Kingdom) cost €.55 (about 36 cents) for up to 20 grams. Stamps can be bought in post offices (*bureaux de poste*) and cafés displaying a red TABAC sign outside.

If you're uncertain where you'll be staying, have mail sent to the local post office, addressed as "poste restante," or to American Express, but remember that during peak seasons, American Express may refuse to accept mail. Bring your passport along to collect your mail.

▌ MONEY

The following prices are to give you an idea of costs. Note that it is less expensive to eat or drink standing at a café or bar counter than it is to sit at a table. Two prices are listed, *au comptoir* (at the counter) and *à salle* (at a table). Coffee in a bar: €1 to €1.50 (standing), €1.50 to €5 (seated); beer in a bar: €2 (standing), €3 to €6 (seated); Coca-Cola: €2 to €4 a can; ham sandwich: €3.50; one-mile taxi ride: €5.50; movie: €7.50 to €9.50 (sometimes less expensive for screenings before noon); foreign newspaper: €1.50 to €4; museum admission: €1.50 to €9.

Prices throughout this guide are given for adults. Substantially reduced fees are almost always available for children, students, and senior citizens.

■ TIP➔ **Banks never have every foreign currency on hand, and it may take as long as a week to order. If you're planning to exchange funds before leaving home, don't wait till the last minute.**

ATMS & BANKS

Your own bank will probably charge a fee for using ATMs abroad; the foreign bank you use may also charge a fee. Nevertheless, you'll usually get a better rate of exchange at an ATM than you will at a currency-exchange office or even when changing money in a bank. And extracting funds as you need them is a safer option than carrying around a large amount of cash.

■ TIP➔ **PIN numbers with more than four digits are not recognized at ATMs in many countries. If yours has five or more, remember to change it before you leave.**

ATMs (*distributeurs de billets*) are very common in major cities and larger towns and are one of the easiest ways to get cash; you'll find one in almost any but the very smallest towns. Banks usually offer excellent, wholesale exchange rates through ATMs.

To get cash at ATMs in France, your PIN must be four digits long. You may have more luck with ATMs if you are using a credit card or a debit card that is also a Visa or MasterCard, rather than just your bank card. Note, too, that you may be charged by your bank for using ATMs overseas; inquire at your bank about charges.

Using a debit card (with a Visa or Master-Card symbol on it) makes it easier to find ATMs that you can use.

Before you go, it's a good idea to get a list of ATM locations that you can use in France from your bank. Failing that, you can always ask a passerby on the street for the nearest *distributeur de billets*.

CREDIT CARDS

Throughout this guide, the following abbreviations are used: **AE**, American Express; **DC**, Diners Club; **MC**, Master-Card; and **V**, Visa.

It's a good idea to inform your credit-card company before you travel, especially if you're going abroad and don't travel internationally very often. Otherwise, the credit-card company might put a hold on your card owing to unusual activity—not a good thing halfway through your trip. Record all your credit-card numbers—as well as the phone numbers to call if your cards are lost or stolen—in a safe place, so you're prepared should something go wrong. Both MasterCard and Visa have general numbers you can call (collect if you're abroad) if your card is lost, but you're better off calling the number of your issuing bank, since MasterCard and Visa usually just transfer you to your bank; your bank's number is usually printed on your card.

If you plan to use your credit card for cash advances, you'll need to apply for a PIN at least two weeks before your trip. Although it's usually cheaper (and safer) to use a credit card abroad for large purchases (so you can cancel payments or be reimbursed if there's a problem), note that some credit-card companies *and* the banks that issue them add substantial percentages to all foreign transactions, whether they're in a foreign currency or not. Check on these fees before leaving home, so there won't be any surprises when you get the bill.

■ TIP➔ **Before you charge something, ask the merchant whether or not he or she plans to do a dynamic currency conversion (DCC). In such a transaction the credit-card *processor* (shop, restaurant, or hotel, not**

Visa or MasterCard) converts the currency and charges you in dollars. In most cases you'll pay the merchant a 3% fee for this service in addition to any credit-card company and issuing-bank foreign-transaction surcharges.

Dynamic currency conversion programs are becoming increasingly widespread. Merchants who participate in them are supposed to ask whether you want to be charged in dollars or the local currency, but they don't always do so. And even if they do offer you a choice, they may well avoid mentioning the additional surcharges. The good news is that you *do* have a choice. And if this practice really gets your goat, you can avoid it entirely thanks to American Express; with its cards, DCC simply isn't an option.

Many restaurants and stores take both credit and debit cards, though there is often a €10 or €15 minimum. Visa is more widely accepted than American Express, especially in smaller restaurants and hotels.

Reporting Lost Cards American Express (☎800/528–4800 in the U.S. or 336/393–1111 collect from abroad ⊕www.americanex press.com). **Diners Club** (☎800/234–6377 in the U.S. or 303/799–1504 collect from abroad ⊕www.dinersclub.com). **Master-Card** (☎800/627–8372 in the U.S. or 636/722–7111 collect from abroad ⊕www. mastercard.com). **Visa** (☎800/847–2911 in the U.S. or 410/581–9994 collect from abroad ⊕www.visa.com).

CURRENCY & EXCHANGE

France belongs to "Euroland" and uses the euro as its operating currency. Although prices in shops and on receipts are sometimes still displayed in both the old French francs and euros—and many older locals still refer to prices in francs—only euros are accepted as valid currency. Old franc notes can be exchanged at the central Banque de France until 2012, but the coins are now only good for souvenirs.

Under the euro system, there are seven notes: 5, 10, 20, 50, 100, 200, and 500 euros. Notes are the same for all countries. There are eight coins: 1 and 2 euros, plus 1, 2, 5, 10, 20, and 50 cents. On all coins, one side has the value of the euro on it and the other side has the national symbol of one of the countries participating in monetary union.

■TIP→ Even if a currency-exchange booth has a sign promising no commission, rest assured that there's some kind of huge, hidden fee. (Oh . . . that's right. The sign didn't say no *fee*.). And as for rates, you're almost always better off getting foreign currency at an ATM or exchanging money at a bank.

TRAVELER'S CHECKS

Some consider this the currency of the caveman, and it's true that fewer establishments accept traveler's checks these days. Nevertheless, they're a cheap and secure way to carry extra money, particularly on trips to urban areas. Both Citibank (under the Visa brand) and American Express issue traveler's checks in the United States, but Amex is better known and more widely accepted; you can also avoid hefty surcharges by cashing Amex checks at Amex offices. Whatever you do, keep track of all the serial numbers in case the checks are lost or stolen.

With the presence of banking machines in even the smallest Provençal towns, traveler's checks are obsolete. Store clerks are unwilling to deal with them, and even some banks now refuse to cash them. When you factor in that you will be given a better exchange rate at an ATM, this really underlines the fact that the era of traveler's checks may have finally come and gone.

Contacts American Express (☎888/412–6945 in the U.S., 801/945–9450 collect outside of the U.S. to add value or speak to customer service ⊕www.american express.com).

PACKING

Although you'll usually have no trouble finding a baggage cart at the airport, luggage restrictions on international flights are tight and baggage carts at railroad stations are not always available, so pack light. Even hotel staffs are becoming less and less tolerant of heavy suitcases and heaps of luggage worthy of a *Queen Mary* crossing. If you simply must have every item on your list, you can opt to send your luggage on ahead with a number of different companies, but be prepared to organize shipment at least two weeks in advance. Try **Luggage Concierge** (⊕*www.luggageconcierge.com*) or **Luggage Free** (⊕*www.luggagefree.com*).

Over the years, casual dress has become more acceptable, although the resorts along the Côte d'Azur and in the Luberon and Aix-en-Provence are still synonymous with smart dressers and fashion plates.

Jeans are very common, though they, too, are worn stylishly, with a nice button-down shirt, polo, or T-shirt without writing. Shorts, though longish per current trends, are a popular item for the younger crowd in most cities. More and more people are wearing sneakers, although you may still stand out as a tourist with them on, especially if you wear them when you go out at night.

There is no need to wear a tie and jacket at most restaurants (unless specified), even fancy ones, though you should still try to look nice. Most casinos and upscale nightclubs along the Côte d'Azur, however, require jackets and ties, and certainly no jeans allowed.

For beach resorts, take a decent cover-up; wearing your bathing suit on the street is frowned upon, even if topless when actually on the beach is commonly accepted.

Most of France is hot in the summer, cool in the winter. Since it rains all year round, bring a raincoat and umbrella. You'll need a sweater or warm jacket for the Mediterranean in winter, and you should also bring hats, scarves, and gloves.

If you are staying in budget hotels, take along soap. Many hotels either do not provide it or give you a very limited amount. You might also want to bring a washcloth.

Lighters, even empty ones, may also be confiscated at check-in.

▌PASSPORTS

All Australian, Canadian, New Zealand, U.K., and U.S. citizens, even infants, need only a valid passport to enter France for stays of up to 90 days. The cost to apply for a new passport is $100 for adults, $85 for children under 16; renewals are $75. Allow six weeks for processing, both for first-time passports and renewals. For an expediting fee of $60 you can reduce this time to about two weeks. If your trip is less than two weeks away, you can get a passport even more rapidly by going to a passport office with the necessary documentation. Private expediters can get things done in as little as 48 hours, but charge hefty fees for their services. Helpful note for safe-keeping purposes: Before your trip, make two copies of your passport's data page (one for someone at home and another for you to carry separately)—or scan the page and e-mail it to someone at home and/or yourself.

U.S. Passport Information U.S. Department of State (☎877/487–2778 ⊕travel.state.gov/passport).

▌SAFETY

Car break-ins have become part of daily life in the south, especially in the isolated parking lots where hikers set off to explore for the day. Be especially careful around the marshes of the Camargue, the departure point for the Iles d'Hyères ferries, the rocky Esterel between Fréjus and Cannes, and the coastal path around St-Tropez: take valuables with you and, if possible, leave your luggage at your hotel.

Also beware of petty theft—purse snatching and pickpocketing. Use common sense: avoid pulling out a lot of money in public, and wear a handbag with long straps that you can sling across your body, bandolier-style, with a zippered compartment for your money and passport. It's also a good idea to wear a money belt. Men should keep their wallets up front, as safely tucked away as possible.

Although cities in Provence are safe during the day, one should take caution at night, especially in port towns such as Marseille, Nice, and Toulon. Avignon also has a high crime rate, and tourists should be alert and walk purposefully through town at night.

■TIP→ **Distribute your cash, credit cards, IDs, and other valuables between a deep front pocket, an inside jacket or vest pocket, and a hidden money pouch. Don't reach for the money pouch once you're in public.**

▋TAXES

All taxes must be included in posted prices in France. The initials TTC (*toutes taxes comprises*—taxes included) sometimes appear on price lists but, strictly speaking, are superfluous. By law, restaurant and hotel prices must include 19.6% tax and hotels charge a daily habitation tax that usually runs between €1.20 to €2.30 per day (depending on the size of the room you are in).

A number of shops participating in the Tax-Free Shopping program (you'll see a sticker in the shop window) offer V.A.T. refunds to foreign shoppers. To qualify for the refund, you must be a national of a non-EU country, at least 15 years old at the time of purchase, and visiting France for less than six months. If you qualify, you are entitled to an Export Discount of 19.6%, depending on the item purchased, and only on purchases of at least €175 in a single store. Remember to ask for the refund, as some stores—especially larger ones—offer the service only upon request.

When making a purchase, ask for a V.A.T. refund form and find out whether the merchant gives refunds—not all stores do, nor are they required to. Have the form stamped like any customs form by customs officials when you leave the country or, if you're visiting several European Union countries, when you leave the EU. After you're through passport control, take the form to a refund-service counter for an on-the-spot refund (which is usually the quickest and easiest option), or mail it to the address on the form (or the envelope with it) after you arrive home. You receive the total refund stated on the form, but the processing time can be long, especially if you request a credit-card adjustment.

Global Refund is a Europe-wide service with 225,000 affiliated stores and more than 700 refund counters at major airports and border crossings. Its refund form, called a Tax Free Check, is the most common across the European continent. The service issues refunds in the form of cash, check, or credit-card adjustment.

V.A.T. Refunds Global Refund (☎800/566–9828 ⊕www.globalrefund.com).

▋TIME

The time difference between New York and France is 6 hours; when it's 1 PM in New York, it's 7 PM in France. France is 7 hours ahead of Chicago and 9 hours ahead of Los Angeles. France is 1 hour ahead of London. The time difference between France and Sydney is 8 to 9 hours, depending on when daylight saving time is or is not in effect.

▌ TIPPING

The French have a clear idea of when they should be tipped. Bills in bars and restaurants include 12.5% service fee, but it is customary to round out your bill with some small change unless you're dissatisfied. The amount of this varies: anywhere from €.10 if you've merely bought a beer, to €2 after a meal. Tip taxi drivers and hairdressers 10%–15%. In some theaters and hotels, coat check attendants may expect nothing (if there is a sign saying POURBOIRE INTERDIT—tips forbidden); otherwise give them €1. Same goes for washroom attendants, unless another sum is posted.

If you stay in a hotel for more than two or three days, it is customary to leave something for the chambermaid—about €1.50 per day. In expensive hotels you may well call on the services of a baggage porter (bell boy) and hotel porter and possibly the telephone receptionist. All expect a tip: plan on about €1.50 per item for the baggage boy, but the other tips will depend on how much you've used their services—common sense must guide you here. In hotels that provide room service, give €1 to the waiter (this does not apply to breakfast served in your room). If the chambermaid does some pressing or laundering for you, give her €1 on top of the charge made.

Gas-station attendants get nothing for gas or oil, but about €1 for checking tires. Train and airport porters get a fixed €1 to €1.50 per bag, but you're better off getting your own baggage cart if you can. Museum guides should give €1 to €1.50 after a guided tour, and it is standard practice to tip tour guides (and bus drivers) €1.50 to €3 after an excursion, depending on its length and your level of satisfaction.

TIPPING GUIDELINES FOR PROVENCE	
Bartender	$1 to $5 per round of drinks, depending on the number of drinks
Bellhop	$1 to $5 per bag, depending on the level of the hotel
Hotel Concierge	$5 or more, if he or she performs a service for you
Hotel Doorman	$1–$2 if he helps you get a cab
Hotel Maid	1$–$3 a day (either daily or at the end of your stay, in cash)
Hotel Room-Service Waiter	$1 to $2 per delivery, even if a service charge has been added
Porter at Airport or Train Station	$1 per bag
Skycap at Airport	$1 to $3 per bag checked
Taxi Driver	15%–20%, but round up the fare to the next dollar amount
Tour Guide	10% of the cost of the tour
Valet Parking Attendant	$1–$2, but only when you get your car
Waiter	15%–20%, with 20% being the norm at high-end restaurants; nothing additional if a service charge is added to the bill
Other	Restroom attendants in more expensive restaurants expect some small change or $1. Tip coat-check personnel at least $1–$2 per item checked unless there is a fee, then nothing.

▌ VISITOR INFORMATION

Local tourist offices are listed under towns in each regional chapter; central tourist offices for regions are listed in the Planner section of each regional chapter. The main French National Tourist Organization offices, as well as the main tourist office for the Provence-Cote d'Azur region, are listed directly below.

Contacts **French National Tourist Organization (tourist office directory worldwide)** (⊕www.franceguide.com). **France On-Call** (☎202/659–7779 ⊘Weekdays 9–9). **Chicago** (✉676 N. Michigan Ave., Chicago, IL ☎312/751–7800 🖷312/337–6339). **Los Angeles** (✉9454 Wilshire Blvd., Suite 715, Beverly Hills, CA ☎310/271–6665 🖷310/276–2835). **New York City** (✉444 Madison Ave., 16th floor, New York, NY ☎212/838–7500 🖷212/838–7855). **Australia** (✉Level 20, 25 Bligh St., Sydney, NSW ☎02/9231–5244 🖷02/9221–8682). **Canada** (✉1981 Ave. McGill College, Suite 490, Montréal, Québec ☎514/876–9881 🖷514/845–4868). **U.K.** (✉178 Piccadilly, London ☎09068/244–123 🖷020/7493–6594).

Regional Tourist Office **Comité Régional du Tourisme de Provence-Alpes-Côtes d'Azur** (PACA, Regional Committee on Tourism in Provence, the Alps, and the Côte d'Azur ✉12 pl. de la Joliette, Marseille ☎04–91–56–47–00 ⊕www.crt-paca.fr).

ONLINE RESOURCES

Do check out the World Wide Web when planning your trip. You'll find everything from weather forecasts to virtual tours of famous cities. We're really proud of our Web site: **Fodors.com** (⊕*www.fodors. com*) is a great place to begin any journey. It has travel information from A to Z about thousands of destinations. In addition, you can post your pressing questions in its Travel Talk forums.

All About Provence & the French Riviera **French Government Tourist Office/Maison de la France** (⊕www.francetourism.com or www.franceguide.com). **French Embassy in the U.S** (⊕www.info-france-usa.org). **Insurance Comparison Sites** (⊕www.insuremytrip. com ⊕www.squaremouth.com). **Provence Tourist Office** (⊕www.visitprovence.com). **Riviera Tourist Office** (⊕www.guide riviera.com).

Lodging Sites **French Youth Hostel Federation** (⊕www.fuaj.org). **French Bed and Breakfast Reservation Services** (⊕www. gitesdefrance.fr ⊕www.bedandbreakfast.com).

Newspapers **Nice-Matin** (⊕www.nicematin. com). **La Provence** (⊕www.laprovence.com). **Riviera Times** (⊕www.rivieratimes.com).

Special Interest Tours **Art & Antiques** (⊕www.europanache.com ⊕www.french paintbox.com ⊕www.sketching.com). **Biking** (⊕www.backroads.com ⊕www.trektravel.com). **Food & Wine** (⊕www.cookingwithfriends.com ⊕www.classicjourneys.com ⊕www.enchanted france.com). **Hiking** (⊕www.vangoghtours.com ⊕www.thewayfarers.com). **Music** (⊕www. musicetc.us).

Transportation Sites **Bus Information** (⊕www.lepilote.com ⊕www.beyond.fr). **Car Rental Agencies** (⊕www.autorent.fr ⊕www. easycar.com ⊕www.europecar.co.uk ⊕www. rentacar.fr ⊕www.locabest.fr). **Eurail** (⊕www. eurail.com). **Eurostar** (⊕www.eurostar.com). **SNCF** (⊕www.voyages-sncf.com).

INDEX

Photo Credits: 5, Chad Ehlers/age fotostock. **Chapter 1: Experience Provence & the French Riviera:** 7, Andreas G. Karelias/Shutterstock. 8 (top), FSG/age fotostock. 8 (bottom), Peter Bowater/age fotostock. 9 (top left), Bruno Morandi/age fotostock. 9 (top right), Walter Bibikow/viestiphoto.com. 9 (bottom), George Haling/age fotostock. 10 (top left), Alfio Ferlito/Shutterstock. 10 (top center), Jean-yves Courbon/Shutterstock. 10 (right), Claudio Giovanni Colombo/Shutterstock. 10 (bottom left), Carly Rose Hennigan/Shutterstock. 10 (bottom center), Elena Elisseeva/Shutterstock. 11 (top left), Sean Nel/ Shutterstock. 11 (top center), Franck Camhi/iStockphoto. 11 (top right), macumazahn/Shutterstock. 11 (bottom left), David Hughes/Shutterstock. 11 (bottom center), Astrida Valigorsky/iStockphoto. 11 (bottom right), Dubassy/Shutterstock. 14, George Haling/age fotostock. 15, Jon Arnold Images/age fotostock. 16, Walter Bibikow/age fotostock. 17 (left), Moulin des Mougins. 17 (center), Peres/Ask Images/ viestiphoto.com. 17 (right), Catherine Hensen/viestiphoto.com. 18, Kevin O'Hara/age footstock. 20, Roxane/viestiphoto.com. 22, Kevin O'Hara/age fotostock. **Chapter 2: The Alpilles, Arles & the Camargue:** 23, Walter Bibikow/age fotostock. 24 , Henry Ausloos/age fotostock. 25 (top) José Fuste Raga/ age fotostock. 25 (bottom left), Corbis. 25 (bottom right), Stanislaus Fautre/viestiphoto.com. 46, Henry Ausloos/age fotostock. 48, Roxane/viestiphoto.com. 49, Roxane/viestiphoto.com. 50 (top), Stanislaus Fautre/viestiphoto.com. 50 (bottom), Roxane/viestiphoto.com. 51, Mas de la Fouque. 58, Doug Scott/ age fotostock. 59, SuperStock/age fotostock. **Chapter 3: The Vaucluse:** 79, Doug Scott/age fotostock. 80 (top), Bruno Morandi/age fotostock. 80 (bottom), Bruno Morandi/age fotostock. 81, Johnny Stockshooter/age fotostock. 121 (top), Chad Ehlers/age fotostock. 121 (bottom), Renaud Visage/age fotostock. 122 (top), David Barnes/age fotostock. 122 (bottom left), David Buffington/age fotostock. 122 (bottom right), Craig Lovell/viestiphoto.com. 123 (left), Doug Scott/age fotostock. 123 (right), Bruno Morandi/age fotostock. 124 (top), Susan Jones/age fotostock. 124 (bottom), Plus Pix/age fotostock. 125 (top), Sergio Cozzi/Ask Images/viestiphoto.com. 125 (bottom), Plus Pix/age fotostock. 126, Sergio Cozzi/Ask Images/viestiphoto.com. 127 (top), P. Cherfils/Ask Images/viestiphoto.com. 127 (center), SGM/age fotostock. 127 (bottom), Doug Scott/age fotostock. 128, L'Occitane en Provence. **Chapter 4: Aix, Marseille & the Central Coast:** 147, Doug Scott/age fotostock. 148 (top), Walter Bibikow/ viestiphoto.com. 148 (bottom), Erich Lessing/Art Resource, NY. 149, Walter Bibikow/age fotostock. 162 (top and bottom), Robert Fisher. 163 (top), Erich Lessing/Art Resource, NY. 163 (bottom), Robert Fisher. 188, Owen Franken. 189 (top left), Enrico Bartolucci/Ask Images/viestiphoto.com. 189 (top right), Owen Franken. 189 (bottom), George Haling/age fotostock. 190, Owen Franken. 191, Owen Franken. 192 (top), Moulin de Mougins. 192 (bottom), Christian Etienne. 193 (top), Owen Franken. 193 (bottom), M. Cristofori/Ask Images/viestiphoto.com. **Chapter 5: The Western Côte d'Azur:** 219, Sylvain Grandadam/age fotostock. 220, Targa/age fotostock. 221 (top and bottom), Stanislaus Fautre/ viestiphoto.com. **Chapter 6: Nice & the Eastern Côte d'Azur:** 265, Sergio Pitamitz/age fotostock. 266 (top), Walter Bibikow/viestiphoto.com. 266 (bottom), Moulin de Mougins. 267 (left), Doug Scott/age fotostock. 267 (right), Walter Bibikow/viestiphoto.com. 298, Matisse, Henri (1869-1954) Blue Nude II, 1952. © 2006 Succession H. Matisse, Paris / Artists Rights Society (ARS), New York. Musee National d'Art Moderne, Centre Georges Pompidou, Paris, France. Photo Credit : CNAC/MNAM/Dist. Réunion des Musées Nationaux/Art Resource, NY. 299, © 2006 Estate of Pablo Picasso/Artists Rights Society (ARS), New York. Photo Credit: Galerie Madoura. 300, © 2006 Estate of Pablo Picasso/Artists Rights Society (ARS), New York. Photo Credit: Walter Bibikow/viestiphoto.com. 301 (top left), Walter Bibikow/viestiphoto.com. 301 (top right), © 2006 Artists Rights Society (ARS), New York/ADAGP, Paris. Photo Credit: SEF/Art Resource, NY. 301 (bottom left), © 2006 Artists Rights Society (ARS), New York/ADAGP, Paris. Photo Credit: Paul Cherfils/viestiphoto.com. 301 (bottom right), Matisse, Henri (1869-1954) Sanctuary with Altar and stained glass window showing the Tree of Life. Chapel of the Rosary, 1950-1951. © 2006 Succession H. Matisse, Paris / Artists Rights Society (ARS), New York. Photo: H. Del Olmo. Chapelle du Rosaire, Vence, France. Photo Credit : Réunion des Musées Nationaux/Art Resource, NY. 302 (top), Tramonto/age fotostock. 302 (bottom), © 2006 Estate of Pablo Picasso/Artists Rights Society (ARS), New York. Photo Credit: Scala/Art Resource. 303 (top), The Pierre Matisse Gallery Archives. The Pierpont Morgan Library/Art Resource, NY. 303 (bottom), Matisse, Henri (1869-1954) Maquette for red chasuble (front) designed for the Chapel of the Rosary of the Dominican Nuns of Vence (late 1950-52). © 2006 Succession H. Matisse, Paris/Artists Rights Society (ARS), New York. The Museum of Modern Art, New York, NY, U.S.A. Acquired through the Lillie P. Bliss Bequest. (176.1953.1). Photo Credit : Digital Image © The Museum of Modern Art/Licensed by SCALA / Art Resource, NY. 304-305 (all), Robert Fisher.

ABOUT OUR WRITERS

Sarah Fraser left the frozen Canadian tundra with the firm intention of finally finding warmth for her perpetually cold feet. Through a series of chance encounters, she ended up happily—and warmly—ensconced on the Mediterranean Coast and has not looked back since. Au contraire, she found a new home near resplendent Cannes. Further draws? An unmitigated passion for lavender-flavored crème brûlée; the sheer bliss of firewood crackling in a stone fireplace on a summer's night; and pure delight in 4-year-old Raphael and in the sweet smell of baby Ethan. Always in search of the perfect tapenade, Sarah happily tests restaurants and hotels for many travel publications, including Time Out and Fodor's. For this edition, she updated Chapters 2 and 4 plus our Travel Smart section, as well as writing our special photo features, "Don't Fence Me In: France's Wild West" and "Blue Gold: The Lavender Route."

Rosa Jackson lived in Paris for ten years before falling in love with a 17th-century apartment in the Vieux Nice, a few steps from the Cours Saleya market. She is now living her dream of teaching Niçois cooking in her home *(www.petitsfarcis. com)*, while seizing every opportunity to explore and write about Provence. For her, the ochre and pink tones of France's most Italian city provide the perfect complement to the more sober elegance of Paris, where she still spends a good part of the year writing about restaurants for Fodor's, Time Out, *Paris Notes,* and *Australian Gourmet Traveller,* while designing personalized food itineraries *(www. edible-paris.com).* Her six-year-old son Sam shows a similar penchant for the good life. For this edition, she updated Chapter 6 and wrote our special photo feature, "Cuisine of the Sun."

Nancy Wilson has been a travel writer and assistant editor of the English-language *Riviera Reporter* magazine *(www.rivierareporter.com)* since 2001 when she swapped Canada for the Côte d'Azur. Her beat in the South of France has had an international dimension for some time. She's been interviewed by the likes of CBS News and Associated Press; on other occasions she's taken the TGV with Tom Cruise to Marseille and sipped champagne with Paris Hilton in St-Tropez as part of her contributions to leading celeb glossies. A self-professed *fois gras* junkie, in her spare time Nancy can be found driving the unchartered roads of Provence in quest of the ultimate perched village vista or undiscovered *bonne table.* Bartering for antiques in Isle-sur-la-Sorgue, praying for the popes in Avignon, and floating in the Luberon's fields of lavender has only intensified her affection with her adopted country. For this edition, she updated Chapters 3 and 5.